FATHERS OF THE THIRD CENTURY:

GREGORY THAUMATURGUS, DIONYSIUS THE GREAT, JULIUS AFRICANUS, ANATOLIUS
AND MINOR WRITERS, METHODIUS, ARNOBIUS.

AMERICAN EDITION

CHRONOLOGICALLY ARRANGED, WITH BRIEF NOTES AND PREFACES,

BY

A. CLEVELAND COXE, D.D.

Τὰ ἀρχαῖα ἔθη κρατείτω.
THE NICENE COUNCIL.

INTRODUCTORY NOTICE

In this volume a mass of fragmentary material [1] has been reduced to method, and so harmonized as to present an integral result. The student has before him, therefore, (1) a view of the Christian Church emerging from the ten persecutions; (2) a survey of its condition on the eve of that great event, the (nominal) conversion of the empire; (3) an introduction to the era of Athanasius; and (4) a history of events that led to the calling of the first Catholic council at Nicæa.

The moral grandeur and predominance of the See of Alexandria are also here conspicuously illustrated. The mastery which its great school continued to exercise over Christian thought, its *hegemony* in the formation of Christian literature, its guardian influence in the development of doctrinal technology, and not less the Divine Providence that created it and built it up for the noble ends which it subserved in a Clement, an Origen, and an Athanasius, will all present themselves forcibly to every reflecting reader of this book. One half of this volume presents the Alexandrian school itself in its glorious succession of doctors and pupils, and the other half in the reflected light of its universal influence. Thus Methodius has no other distinction than that which he derives from his wholesome corrections of Origen, and yet the influence of Origen upon his own mind is betrayed even in his antagonisms. He objects to the excessive allegorizing of that great doctor, yet he himself allegorizes too much in the same spirit. Finally we come to Arnobius, who carries on the line of Latin Christianity in Northern Africa; but even here we find that Clement, and not Tertullian, is his model. He gives us, in a Latin dress, not a little directly borrowed from the great Alexandrian.

This volume further demonstrates — what I have so often touched upon — the historic fact that primitive Christianity was Greek in form and character, Greek from first to last, Greek in all its forms of dogma, worship, and polity. One idea only did it borrow from the West, and that not from the ecclesiastical, but the civil, Occident. It conformed itself to the imperial plan of exarchates, metropoles, and dioceses. Into this civil scheme it shaped itself, not by design, but by force of circumstances, just as the Anglo-American communion fell in with the national polity, and took shape in dioceses each originally conterminous with a State. Because it was the capital of the empire, therefore Rome was reckoned the *first*, but not the chief, of Sees, as the Council of Nicæa declared; and because Byzantium had become "New Rome," therefore it is made *second* on the list, but equal in dignity. Rome was the sole Apostolic See of the West, and, as such, reflected the honours of St. Paul, its founder, and of St. Peter, who also glorified it by martyrdom; but not a word of this is recognised at Nicæa as investing it even with a moral primacy. That was informally the endowment of Alexandria; unasserted because unquestioned, and unchallenged because as yet unholy ambition had not infected the Apostolic churches.

It is time, then, to disabuse the West of its narrow ideas concerning ecclesiastical history. Dean Stanley rebuked this spirit in his *Lectures on the Eastern Church*.[2] He complained that "Eastern Christendom is comparatively an untrodden field;" he quoted the German proverb,[3] "Behind the mountains there is yet a population;" he called on us to enlarge our petty Occidental horizon; and he added words of reproach which invite us to reform the entire scheme of

---

[1] See the Edinburgh series.　　　[2] See p. 3, ed. of 1861.　　　[3] "Hinter dem Berge sind auch Leute."

v

our ecclesiastical history by presenting the Eastern Apostolic churches as the main stem of Christendom, of which the church of Rome itself was for three hundred years a mere colony, unfelt in theology except by contributions to the Greek literature of Christians, and wholly unconscious of those pretensions with which, in a spirit akin to that of the romances about Arthur and the Round Table, the fabulous Decretals afterwards invested a succession of primitive bishops in Rome, wholly innocent of anything of the kind.

"The Greek Church," says Dean Stanley, "reminds us of the time when the tongue, not of Rome, but of Greece, was the sacred language of Christendom. It was a striking remark of the Emperor Napoleon, that the introduction of Christianity itself was, in a certain sense, the triumph of Greece over Rome; the last and most signal instance of the maxim of Horace, *Græcia capta ferum victorem cepit.* The early Roman church was but a colony of Greek Christians or Grecized Jews. The earliest Fathers of the Western Church wrote in Greek. The early *popes* were not Italians, but Greeks. The name of *pope* is not Latin, but Greek, the common and now despised name of every pastor in the Eastern Church. . . . *She is the mother*, and Rome the daughter. It is her privilege to claim a direct continuity of speech with the earliest times; to boast of reading the whole code of Scripture, Old as well as New, in the language in which it was read and spoken by the Apostles. The humblest peasant who reads his Septuagint or Greek Testament in his own mother-tongue on the hills of Bœotia may proudly feel that he has access to the original oracles of divine truth which pope and cardinal reach by a barbarous and imperfect translation; that he has a key of knowledge which in the West *is only to be found in the hands of the learned classes.*"

Before entering on the study of this volume, the student will do well to read the interesting work which I have quoted;[1] but the following extract merits a place just here, and I cannot deprive even the casual reader of the benefit of such a preface from the non-ecclesiastical and purely literary pen of the Dean. He says:[2] "The See of Alexandria was then the most important in the world.[3] . . . The Alexandrian church was the only great seat of Christian learning. Its episcopate was *the Evangelical* See, as founded by the chair of St. Mark. . . . Its occupant, as we have seen, was the only potentate of the time who bore the name of *pope.*[4] After the Council of Nicæa he became *the judge of the world*, from his decisions respecting the celebration of Easter; and the obedience paid to his judgment in all matters of learning, secular and sacred, almost equalled that paid in later days to the ecclesiastical authority of the popes of the West. 'The head of the Alexandrian church,' says Gregory Nazianzen, 'is the head of the world.'"

In the light of these all-important historic truths, these volumes of the Ante-Nicene Fathers have been elucidated by their American editor.[5] He begs to remind his countrymen that ecclesiastical history is yet to be written on these irrefragable positions, and the future student of history will be delivered from the most puzzling entanglement when once these *idols of the market* are removed from books designed for his instruction. Let American scholarship give us, at last, a Church history not written from a merely Western point of view, nor clogged with traditional phraseology perseveringly adhered to on the very pages which supply its refutation. It is the scandal of literature that the frauds of the pseudo-Decretals should be perpetuated by modern lists of "popes," beginning with St. Peter, in the very books which elaborately expose the empiricism of such a scheme, and quote the reluctant words by which this gigantic imposition has been consigned to infamy in the confessions of Jesuits and Ultramontanes themselves.

---

[1] Late editions are cheap in the market. It is filled with the author's idiosyncrasies, but it is brilliant and suggestive.

[2] Lect. vii. p. 268. On the verse of Horace (*Ep.*, i. book ii. 155), see Dacier's note, vol. ix. 389.

[3] He adds: "Alexandria, *till the rise of Constantinople*, was the most powerful city in the East. The prestige of its founder still clung to it."

[4] That is, of "*the* pope," as Wellington was called "*the* duke." But Cyprian was called *papa*, even by the Roman clergy.

[5] He owes his own introduction to a just view of these facts to a friend of his boyhood and youth, the late Rev. Dr. Hill of the American Mission in Athens. He was penetrated with love for Greek Christians.

THE

ANTE-NICENE FATHERS

TRANSLATIONS OF

The Writings of the Fathers down to A.D. 325

THE REV. ALEXANDER ROBERTS, D.D.,

AND

JAMES DONALDSON, LL.D.,

EDITORS

AMERICAN REPRINT OF THE EDINBURGH EDITION

REVISED AND CHRONOLOGICALLY ARRANGED, WITH BRIEF PREFACES AND
OCCASIONAL NOTES,

BY

A. CLEVELAND COXE, D.D.

VOLUME VI

GREGORY THAUMATURGUS, DIONYSIUS THE GREAT, JULIUS AFRICANUS, ANATOLIUS AND
MINOR WRITERS, METHODIUS, ARNOBIUS.

AUTHORIZED EDITION

T&T CLARK
EDINBURGH

WM. B. EERDMANS PUBLISHING COMPANY
GRAND RAPIDS, MICHIGAN

British Library Cataloguing in Publication Data

Ante-Nicene Fathers.
1. Fathers of the church
I. Robertson, Alexander II. Donaldson, James
230'.13   BR60.A62

T&T Clark ISBN 0 567 09379 4

Eerdmans ISBN 0-8028-8092-4

Reprinted, March 1993

CONTENTS OF VOLUME VI

GREGORY THAUMATURGUS

[TRANSLATED BY THE REV. S. D. F. SALMOND, M.A.]

INTRODUCTORY NOTE

TO

GREGORY THAUMATURGUS

[A.D. 205–240–265.] Alexandria continues to be the head of Christian learning.[1] It is delightful to trace the hand of God from generation to generation, as from father to son, interposing for the perpetuity of the faith. We have already observed the continuity of the great Alexandrian school: how it arose, and how Pantænus begat Clement, and Clement begat Origen. So Origen begat Gregory, and so the Lord has provided for the spiritual generation of the Church's teachers, age after age, from the beginning. Truly, the Lord gave to Origen a holy seed, better than natural sons and daughters; as if, for his comfort, Isaiah had written,[2] forbidding him to say, "I am a dry tree."

Our Gregory has given us not a little of his personal adventures in his panegyric upon his master, and for his further history the reader need only be referred to what follows. But I am anxious to supply the dates, which are too loosely left to conjecture. As he was ordained a bishop "very young," according to Eusebius, I suppose he must have been far enough under *fifty*, the age prescribed by the "Apostolic Canons" (so called), though probably not younger than *thirty*, the earliest canonical limit for the ordination of a presbyter. If we decide upon *five and thirty*, as a mean reckoning, we may with some confidence set his birth at A.D. 205, dating back from his episcopate, which began A.D. 240. He was a native of Neo-Cæsarea, the chief city of Pontus, — a fact that should modify what we have learned about Pontus from Tertullian.[3] He was born of heathen parentage, and lived like other Gentile boys until his fourteenth year (*circa* A.D. 218), with the disadvantage of being more than ordinarily imbued by a mistaken father in the polytheism of Greece. At this period his father died; but his mother, carrying out the wishes of her husband, seems to have been not less zealous in furthering his education according to her pagan ideas. He was, evidently, the inheritor of moderate wealth; and, with his brother Athenodorus, he was placed under an accomplished teacher of grammar and rhetoric, from whom also he acquired a considerable knowledge of the Latin tongue. He was persuaded by the same master to use this accomplishment in acquiring some knowledge of the Roman laws. This is a very important point in his biography, and it brings us to an epoch in Christian history too little noted by any writer. I shall return to it very soon. We find him next going to Alexandria to study the New Platonism. He speaks of himself as already prepossessed with Christian ideas, which came to him even in his boyhood, about the time when his father died. But it was not at Alexandria that he began his acquaintance with Christian learning. Next he seems to have travelled into Greece, and to have studied at Athens. But the great interest of his autobiography begins with the providential incidents, devoutly narrated by himself, which engaged him in a journey to Berytus just as Origen reached Cæsarea, A.D. 233, making it for a time his home and the seat of his school. His own good angel, as Gregory supposes, led him away from Berytus, where he purposed to prosecute his legal studies, and brought him to the feet of Origen, his Gamaliel; and "from the very first day of his receiving us," he says, "the true Sun began to rise upon me." This

---

[1] Vol. ii. pp. 165, 342.   [2] Isa. lvi. 3.   [3] Vol. iii. p. 271.

he accounts the beginning of his true life ; and, if we are right as to our dates, he was now about twenty-seven years of age.

If he tarried even a little while in Berytus, as seems probable, his knowledge of law was, doubtless, somewhat advanced. It was the seat of that school in which Roman law began its existence in the forms long afterward digested into the Pandects of Justinian. That emperor speaks of Berytus as "the mother and nurse" of the civil law. Caius, whose *Institutes* were discovered in 1820 by the sagacity of Niebuhr, seems to have been a Syrian. So were Papinian and Ulpian : and, heathen as they were, they lived under the illumination reflected from Antioch ; and, not less than the Antonines, they were examples of a philosophic regeneration which never could have existed until the Christian era had begun its triumphs. Of this sort of pagan philosophy Julian became afterwards the grand embodiment ; and in Julian's grudging confessions of what he had learned from Christianity we have a key to the secret convictions of others, such as I have named ; characters in whom, as in Plutarch and in many retrograde unbelievers of our day, we detect the operation of influences they are unwilling to acknowledge ; of which, possibly, they are blindly unconscious themselves. Roman law, I maintain, therefore, indirectly owes its origin, as it is directly indebted for its completion in the Pandects, to the new powers and processes of thought which came from " the Light of the World." It was light from Galilee and Golgotha, answering Pilate's question in the inward convictions of many a heathen sage.

It is most interesting, therefore, to find in our Gregory one who had come into contact with Berytus at this period. He describes it as already dignified by this school of law, and therefore Latinized in some degree by its influence. Most suggestive is what he says of this school : " I refer to those admirable laws *of our sages*, by which the affairs of all the subjects of the Roman Empire *are now* directed, and which are neither digested nor learnt without difficulty. They are wise and strict (if not *pious*) in themselves, they are manifold and admirable, and, in a word, *most thoroughly Grecian, although* expressed and delivered to us in the Roman tongue, which is a wonderful and magnificent sort of language, and one very aptly conformable to imperial authority, but still difficult to me." Nor is this the only noteworthy tribute of our author to Roman law while yet that sublime system was in its cradle. The rhetorician who introduced him to it and to the Latin tongue was its enthusiastic eulogist ; and Gregory says he learned the laws " in a *thorough way*, by his help. . . . And he said one thing to me which has proved to me the truest of all his sayings ; to wit, that *my education in the laws* would be my greatest *viaticum*, — my ἐφόδιον (for thus he phrased it) ; " i.e., for the journey of life. This man, one can hardly doubt, was a disciple of Caius (or Gaius) ; and there is little question that the *digested* system which Gregory eulogizes was " the Institutes " of that great father of the civil law, now recovered from a palimpsest, and made known to our own age, with no less benefit to jurisprudence than the discovery of the *Philosophumena* has conferred on theology.

Thus Gregory's *Panegyric* throws light on the origin of Roman law. He claims it for " our sages," meaning men of the East, whose vernacular was the Greek tongue. Caius was probably, like the Gaius of Scripture, an Oriental who had borrowed a Latin name, as did the Apostle of the Gentiles and many others. If he was a native of Berytus, as seems probable, that accounts for the rise of the school of laws at a place comparatively inconsiderable. Hadrian, in his journey to Palestine, would naturally discover and patronize such a jurist ; and that accounts for the appearance of Caius at Rome in his day. Papinian and Ulpian, both Orientals, were his pupils in all probability ; and these were the " sages " with whose works the youthful Gregory became acquainted, and by which his mind was prepared for the great influence he exerted in the East, where his name is a power to this day.

His credit with our times is rather impaired than heightened by the epithet *Thaumaturgus*, which clings to his name as a convenient specification, to distinguish him from the other [1] Grego-

---

[1] See Dean Stanley's *Eastern Church* and Neale's *Introduction.*

ries whose period was so nearly his own. But why make it his opprobrium? He is not responsible for the romances that sprung up after his death; which he never heard of nor imagined. Like the great Friar Bacon, who was considered a magician, or Faust, whose invention nearly cost him his life, the reputation of Gregory made him the subject of legendary lore long after he was gone. It is not impossible that God wrought marvels by his hand, but a single instance would give rise to many fables; and this very surname is of itself a monument of the fact that miracles were now of rare occurrence, and that one possessing the gift was a wonder to his contemporaries.

To like popular love of the marvellous I attribute the stupid story of a mock consecration by Phædimus. If a slight irregularity in Origen's ordination gave him such lifelong troubles, what would not have been the tumult such a sacrilege as this would have occasioned? Nothing is more probable than that Phædimus related such things as having occurred in a vision;[1] and this might have weighed with a mind like Gregory's to overcome his scruples, and to justify his acceptance of such a position at an early age.

We are already acquainted with the eloquent letter of Origen that decided him to choose the sacred calling after he left the school at Cæsarea. The *Panegyric*, which was his valedictory, doubtless called forth that letter. Origen had seen in him the makings of a κῆρυξ, and coveted such another Timothy for the Master's work. But the *Panegyric* itself abounds with faults, and greatly resembles similar college performances of our day. The custom of schools alone can excuse the expression of such enthusiastic praise in the presence of its subject; but Origen doubtless bore it as philosophically as others have done since, and its evident sincerity and heartfelt gratitude redeem it from the charge of fulsome adulation.

For the residue of the story I may refer my readers to the statements of the translator, as follows: —

TRANSLATOR'S NOTICE.

WE are in possession of a considerable body of testimonies from ancient literature bearing on the life and work of Gregory. From these, though they are largely mixed up with the marvellous, we gain a tolerably clear and satisfactory view of the main facts in his history, and the most patent features of his character.[2] From various witnesses we learn that he was also known by the name Theodorus, which may have been his original designation; that he was a native of Neo-Cæsareia, a considerable place of trade, and one of the most important towns of Pontus; that he belonged to a family of some wealth and standing; that he was born of heathen parents; that at the age of fourteen he lost his father; that he had a brother named Athenodorus; and that along with him he travelled about from city to city in the prosecution of studies that were to fit him for the profession of law, to which he had been destined. Among the various seats of learning which he thus visited we find Alexandria, Athens, Berytus, and the Palestinian Cæsareia mentioned. At this last place — to which, as he tells us, he was led by a happy accident in the providence of God — he was brought into connection with Origen. Under this great teacher he received lessons in logic, geometry, physics, ethics, philosophy, and ancient literature, and in due time also in biblical science and the verities of the Christian faith. Thus, having become Origen's pupil, he became also by the hand of God his convert. After a residence of some five years with the great Alexandrian, he returned to his native city. Soon, however, a letter followed him to Neo-Cæsareia, in which Origen urged him to dedicate himself to the ministry of the Church of Christ, and pressed strongly upon him his obligation to consecrate his gifts to the service of God, and in especial to devote his acquirements in heathen science and learning to the elucidation of the Scriptures. On receipt of this letter, so full of wise and faithful counsel and strong exhortation, from

---

[1] Recall Cyprian's narratives, vol. v., and this volume *infra*, Life of Dionysius of Alexandria.

[2] Thus we have accounts of him, more or less complete, in Eusebius (*Historia Eccles.*, vi. 30, vii. 14), Basil (*De Spiritu Sancto*, xxix. 74; *Epist.* 28, Num. 1 and 2; 204, Num. 2; 207, Num. 4; 210, Num. 3, 5, — Works, vol. iii. pp. 62, 107, 303, 311, etc., edit. Paris. BB. 1730), Jerome (*De viris illustr.*, ch. 65; in the *Comment. in Ecclesiasten*, ch. 4; and *Epist.* 70, Num. 4, — Works, vol. i. pp. 424 and 427, edit. Veron.), Rufinus (*Hist. Eccles.*, vii. 25), Socrates (*Hist. Eccles.*, iv. 27), Sozomen (*Hist. Eccles.*, vii. 27), Evagrius Scholasticus (*Hist. Eccles.*, iii. 31), Suidas in his *Lexicon*, and others of less moment.

the teacher whom he venerated and loved above all others, he withdrew into the wilderness, seeking opportunity for solemn thought and private prayer over its contents. At this time the bishop of Amasea, a city which held apparently a first place in the province, was one named Phædimus, who, discerning the promise of great things in the convert, sought to make him bishop of Neo-Cæsareia. For a considerable period, however, Gregory, who shrank from the responsibility of the episcopal office, kept himself beyond the bishop's reach, until Phædimus, unsuccessful in his search, had recourse to the stratagem of ordaining him in his absence, and declaring him, with all the solemnities of the usual ceremonial, bishop of his native city.[1] On receiving the report of this extraordinary step, Gregory yielded, and, coming forth from the place of his concealment, was consecrated to the bishopric with all the customary formalities ;[2] and so well did he discharge the duties of his office, that while there were said to be only seventeen Christians in the whole city when he first entered it as bishop, there were said to be only seventeen pagans in it at the time of his death. The date of his studies under Origen is fixed at about 234 A.D., and that of his ordination as bishop at about 240. About the year 250 his church was involved in the sufferings of the Decian persecution, on which occasion he fled into the wilderness, with the hope of preserving his life for his people, whom he also counselled to follow in that matter his example. His flock had much to endure, again, through the incursion of the northern barbarians about 260. He took part in the council that met at Antioch in 265 for the purpose of trying Paul of Samosata ; and soon after that he died, perhaps about 270, if we can adopt the conjectural reading which gives the name Aurelian instead of Julian in the account left us by Suidas.

The surname Thaumaturgus, or *Wonder-worker*, at once admonishes us of the *marvellous* that so largely connected itself with the *historical* in the ancient records of this man's life.[3] He was believed to have been gifted with a power of working miracles, which he was constantly exercising. But into these it is profitless to enter. When all the marvellous is dissociated from the historical in the records of this bishop's career, we have still the figure of a great, good, and gifted man, deeply versed in the heathen lore and science of his time, yet more deeply imbued with the genuine spirit of another wisdom, which, under God, he learned from the illustrious thinker of Alexandria, honouring with all love, gratitude, and veneration that teacher to whom he was indebted for his knowledge of the Gospel, and exercising an earnest, enlightened, and faithful ministry of many years in an office which he had not sought, but for which he had been sought. Such is, in brief, the picture that rises up before us from a perusal of his own writings, as well as from the comparison of ancient accounts of the man and his vocation. Of his well-accredited works we have the following: *A Declaration of Faith*, being a creed on the doctrine of the Trinity ; a *Metaphrase of the Book of Ecclesiastes;* a *Panegyric to Origen*, being an oration delivered on leaving the school of Origen, expressing eloquently, and with great tenderness of feeling, as well as polish of style, the sense of his obligations to that master ; and a *Canonical Epistle*, in which he gives a variety of directions with respect to the penances and discipline to be exacted by the Church from Christians who had fallen back into heathenism in times of suffering, and wished to be restored. Other works have been attributed to him, which are doubtful or spurious. His writings have been often edited, — by Gerard Voss in 1604, by the Paris editors in 1662, by Gallandi in 1788, and others, who need not be enumerated here.

---

[1] [See p. 5, *supra*. Cave pronounces it " without precedent," but seems to credit the story.]

[2] [So Gregory Nyssen says. It would have been impossible, otherwise, for him to rule his flock.]

[3] He could move the largest stones by a word; he could heal the sick; the demons were subject to him, and were exorcised by his fiat; he could give bounds to overflowing rivers; he could dry up mighty lakes; he could cast his cloak over a man, and cause his death; once, spending a night in a heathen temple, he banished its divinities by his simple presence, and by merely placing on the altar a piece of paper bearing the words, *Gregory to Satan — enter*, he could bring the presiding demons back to their shrine. One strange story told of him by Gregory of Nyssa is to the effect that, as Gregory was meditating on the great matter of the right way to worship the true God, suddenly two glorious personages made themselves manifest in his room, in the one of whom he recognised the Apostle John, in the other the Virgin. They had come, as the story goes, to solve the difficulties which were making him hesitate in accepting the bishopric. At Mary's request, the evangelist gave him then all the instruction in doctrine which he was seeking for; and the sum of these supernatural communications being written down by him after the vision vanished, formed the creed which is still preserved among his writings. Such were the wonders believed to signalize the life of Gregory.

PART I.—ACKNOWLEDGED WRITINGS.

A DECLARATION OF FAITH.[1]

THERE is one God, the Father of the living Word, *who is His* subsistent Wisdom and Power and Eternal Image:[2] perfect Begetter of the perfect *Begotten*, Father of the only-begotten Son. There is one Lord, Only of the Only,[3] God of God, Image and Likeness of Deity, Efficient Word,[4] Wisdom comprehensive[5] of the constitution of all things, and Power formative[6] of the whole creation, true Son of true Father, Invisible of Invisible, and Incorruptible of Incorruptible, and Immortal of Immortal, and Eternal of Eternal.[7] And there is One Holy Spirit, having His subsistence[8] from God, and being made manifest[9] by the Son, to wit to men:[10] Image[11] of the Son, Perfect *Image* of the Perfect;[12] Life, the Cause of the living; Holy Fount; Sanctity, the Supplier, *or Leader,*[13] of Sanctification; in whom is manifested God the Father, who is above all and in all, and God the Son, who is through all. There is a perfect Trinity, in glory and eternity and sovereignty, neither divided nor estranged.[14] Wherefore there is nothing either created or in servitude[15] in the Trinity;[16] nor anything superinduced,[17] as if at some former period it was non-existent, and at some later period it was introduced. And thus neither was the Son ever wanting to the Father, nor the Spirit to the Son;[18] but without variation and without change, the same Trinity *abideth* ever.[19]

---

[1] The title as it stands has this addition: "which he had by revelation from the blessed John the evangelist, by the mediation of the Virgin Mary, Parent of God." Gallandi, *Veterum Patrum Biblioth.*, Venice, 1766, p. 385. [Elucidation, p. 8, *infra.*]

[2] χαρακτῆρος ἀιδίου.

[3] μόνος ἐκ μόνου.

[4] λόγος ἐνεργός.

[5] περιεκτική.

[6] ποιητική.

[7] ἀίδιος ἀιδίου.

[8] ὕπαρξιν.

[9] πεφηνός.

[10] The words δηλαδὴ τοῖς ἀνθρώποις are suspected by some to be a gloss that has found its way into the text.

[11] εἰκών.

[12] So John of Damascus uses the phrase, εἰκὼν τοῦ Πατρὸς ὁ Υἱός, καὶ τοῦ Υἱοῦ, τὸ Πνεῦμα, the Son is the Image of the Father, and the Spirit is that of the Son, lib. i, *De fide orthod.*, ch. 13, vol. i. p. 151. See also Athanasius, *Epist.* i *ad Serap.*; Basil, lib. v. *contra Eunom.*; Cyril, *Dial.*, 7, etc.

[13] χορηγός.

[14] ἀπαλλοτριουμένη. See also Gregory Nazianz., *Orat.*, 37, p. 609.

[15] δοῦλον.

[16] Gregory Nazianz., *Orat.*, 40, p. 668, with reference apparently to our author, says: Οὐδὲν τῆς Τριάδος δοῦλον, οὐδὲ κτιστον, οὐδὲ ἐπείσακτον, ἤκουσα τῶν σοφῶν τινος λέγοντος — *In the Trinity there is nothing either in servitude or created, or superinduced, as I heard one of the learned say.*

[17] ἐπείσακτον.

[18] In one codex we find the following addition here: οὔτε αὔξεται μονὰς ‘εἰς δυάδα, οὐδὲ δυὰς εἰς τριάδα — *Neither again does the unity grow into duality, nor the duality into trinity;* or = *Neither does the condition of the one grow into the condition of the two, nor that of the two into the condition of the three.*

[19] [See valuable note and Greek text in Dr. Schaff's *History*, vol. ii. p. 799.]

ELUCIDATION.

THE story of the " Revelation " is of little consequence, though, if this were Gregory's genu-ine work, it would be easy to account for it as originating in a beautiful dream. But it is very doubtful whether it be a genuine work ; and, to my mind, it is most fairly treated by Lardner, to whose elaborate chapter concerning Gregory every scholar must refer.[1] Dr. Burton, in his edi-tion of Bishop Bull's works,[2] almost overrules that learned prelate's inclination to think it genu-ine, in the following words : " Hanc formulam minime esse Gregorii authenticam . . . multis *haud spernendis argumentis demonstrat* Lardner." Lardner thinks it a fabrication of the fourth century.

Cave's learned judgment is more favourable ; and he gives the text[3] from Gregory of Nyssa, which he translates as follows : " There is one God, the Father of the living Word and of the subsisting Wisdom and Power, and of Him who is His Eternal Image, the perfect begetter of Him that is perfect, the Father of the only-begotten Son. There is one Lord, the only *Son* of the only *Father*, God of God, the character and image of the Godhead, the powerful Word, the com-prehensive Wisdom, by which all things were made, and the Power that gave being to the whole creation, the true Son of the true Father, the Invisible of the Invisible, the Incorruptible of the Incorruptible, the Immortal of the Immortal, and the Eternal of Him that is Eternal. There is one Holy Ghost, having its subsistence of God, which appeared through the Son to mankind, the perfect Image of the perfect Son, the Life-giving Life, the holy Fountain, the Sanctity, and the Author of sanctification, by whom God the Father is made manifest, who is over all, and in all ; and God the Son, who is through all. A perfect Trinity, which neither in glory, eternity, or dominion is divided, or departed from itself."

---

[1] *Credibility*, vol. ii. p. 635.   [2] Vol. v. p. 423.   [3] Cave, *Lives of the Fathers*, vol. i. p. 402, ed. Oxford, 1840.

A METAPHRASE OF THE BOOK OF ECCLESIASTES.[1]

CHAP. I.[2]

THESE words speaketh Solomon, the son of David the king and prophet, to the whole Church of God, a prince most honoured, and a prophet most wise above all men. How vain and fruitless are the affairs of men, and all pursuits that occupy man! For there is not one who can tell of any profit attaching to those things which men who creep on earth strive by body and soul to attain to, in servitude all the while to what is transient, and undesirous of considering aught heavenly with the noble eye of the soul. And the life of men weareth away, as day by day, and in the periods of hours and years, and the determinate courses of the sun, some are ever coming, and others passing away. And the matter is like the transit of torrents as they fall into the measureless deep of the sea with a mighty noise. And all things that have been constituted by God for the sake of men abide the same: as, for instance, that man is born of earth, and departs to earth again; that the earth itself continues stable; that the sun accomplishes its circuit about it perfectly, and rolls round to the same mark again; and that the winds[3] in like manner, and the mighty rivers which flow into the sea, and the breezes that beat upon it, all act without forcing it to pass beyond its limits, and without themselves also violating their appointed laws. And these things, indeed, as bearing upon the good of this life of ours, are established thus fittingly. But those things which are of men's devising, whether words or deeds, have no measure. And there is a plenteous multitude of words, but there is no profit from random and foolish talking. But the race of men is naturally insatiate in its thirst both for speaking and for hearing what is spoken; and it is man's habit, too, to desire to look with idle eyes on all that happens. What can occur afterwards, or what can be wrought by men which has not been done already? What new thing is there worthy of mention, of which there has never yet been experience? For I think there is nothing which one may call new, or which, on considering it, one shall discover to be strange or unknown to those of old. But as former things are buried in oblivion, so also things that are now subsistent will in the course of time vanish utterly from the knowledge of those who shall come after us. And I speak not these things unadvisedly, as acting now the preacher.[4] But all these things were carefully pondered by me when entrusted with the kingdom of the Hebrews in Jerusalem. And I examined diligently, and considered discreetly, the nature of all that is on earth, and I perceived it to be most various;[5] and I saw that to man it is given to labour upon earth, ever carried about by all different occasions of toil, and with no result of his work. And all things here below are full of the spirit of strangeness and abomination, so that it is not possible for one to retrieve them now; nay, rather it is not possible for one at all to conceive what utter vanity[6] has taken possession of all human affairs. For once on a time I communed with myself, and thought that then I was wiser in this than all that were before me, and I was expert in understanding parables and the natures of things. But I learned that I gave myself to such pursuits to no purpose, and that if wisdom follows knowledge, so troubles attend on wisdom.

CHAP. II.

Judging, therefore, that it stood thus with this matter, I decided to turn to another manner of life, and to give myself to pleasure, and to take experience of various delights. And now I learned that all such things are vain; and I put a check on laughter, when it ran on carelessly; and restrained pleasure, according to the rule of moderation, and was bitterly wroth against it. And when I perceived that the soul is able to arrest the body in its disposition to intoxication and wine-bibbing, and that temperance makes lust its subject, I sought earnestly to observe what object of

[1] Gallandi, *Biblioth. Vet. Patr.*, iii. 387.
[2] [The wise benevolence of our author is more apparent than his critical skill. No book more likely to puzzle a pagan inquirer than this: so the metaphrase gives it meaning and consistency; but, over and over again, not Solomon's meaning, I am persuaded.]
[3] τὰ πνευματα, for which some propose ῥεύματα, streams, as the ἄνεμοι are mentioned in their own place immediately.

[4] νῦν ἐκκλησιάζων.
[5] ποικιλωτάτην.
[6] ἀτοπία.

9

true worth and of real excellence is set before men, which they shall attain to in this present life. For I passed through all those other objects which are deemed worthiest, such as the erecting of lofty houses and the planting of vines, and in addition, the laying out of pleasure-grounds, and the acquisition and culture of all manner of fruit-bearing trees ; and among them also large reservoirs for the reception of water were constructed, and distributed so as to secure the plentiful irrigation of the trees. And I surrounded myself also with many domestics, both man-servants and maid-servants ; and some of them I procured from abroad, and others I possessed and employed as born in my own house. And herds of four-footed creatures, as well of cattle as of sheep, more numerous than any of those of old acquired, were made my property. And treasures of gold and silver flowed in upon me ; and I made the kings of all nations my dependants and tributaries. And very many choirs of male and female singers were trained to yield me pleasure by the practice of all-harmonious song. And, I had banquetings ; and for the service of this part of my pleasure, I got me select cup-bearers of both sexes beyond my reckoning, — so far did I surpass in these things those who reigned before me in Jerusalem. And thus it happened that the interests of wisdom declined with me, while the claims of evil appetency increased. For when I yielded myself to every allurement of the eyes, and to the violent passions of the heart, that make their attack from all quarters, and surrendered myself to the hopes held out by pleasures, I also made my will the bond-slave of all miserable delights. For thus my judgment was brought to such a wretched pass, that I thought these things good, and that it was proper for me to engage in them. At length, awaking and recovering my sight, I perceived that the things I had in hand were altogether sinful and very evil, and the deeds of a spirit not good. For now none of all the objects of men's choice seems to me worthy of approval, or greatly to be desired by a just mind. Wherefore, having pondered at once the advantages of wisdom and the ills of folly, I should with reason admire that man greatly, who, being borne on in a thoughtless course, and afterwards arresting himself, should return to right and duty. For wisdom and folly are widely separated, and they are as different from each other as day is from night. He, therefore, who makes choice of virtue, is like one who sees all things plainly, and looks upward, and who holdeth his ways in the time of clearest light. But he, on the other hand, who has involved himself in wickedness, is like a man who wanders helplessly about in a moonless night, as one who is blind, and deprived of the sight of things by his dark-

ness.[1] And when I considered the end of each of these modes of life, I found there was no profit in the latter ;[2] and by setting myself to be the companion of the foolish, I saw that I should receive the wages of folly. For what advantage is there in those thoughts, or what profit is there in the multitude of words, where the streams of foolish speaking are flowing, as it were, from the fountain of folly? Moreover, there is nothing common to the wise man and to the fool, neither as regards the memory of men, nor as regards the recompense of God. And as to all the affairs of men, when they are yet apparently but beginning to be, the end at once surprises them. Yet the wise man is never partaker of the same end with the foolish. Then also did I hate all my life, that had been consumed in vanities, and which I had spent with a mind engrossed in earthly anxieties. For, to speak in brief, all my affairs have been wrought by me with labour and pain, as the efforts of thoughtless impulse ; and some other person, it may be a wise man or a fool, will succeed to them, I mean, the chill fruits of my toils. But when I cut myself off from these things, and cast them away, then did that real good which is set before man show itself to me, — namely, the knowledge of wisdom and the possession of manly virtue.[3] And if a man neglects these things, and is inflamed with the passion for other things, such a man makes choice of evil instead of good, and goes after what is bad instead of what is excellent, and after trouble instead of peace ; for he is distracted by every manner of disturbance, and is burdened with continual anxieties night and day, with oppressive labours of body as well as with ceaseless cares of mind, — his heart moving in constant agitation, by reason of the strange and senseless affairs that occupy him. For the perfect good does not consist in eating and drinking, although it is true that it is from God that their sustenance cometh to men ; for none of those things which are given for our maintenance subsist without His providence. But the good man who gets wisdom from God, gets also heavenly enjoyment ; while, on the other hand, the evil man, smitten with ills divinely inflicted, and afflicted with the disease of lust, toils to amass much, and is quick to put him to shame who is honoured by God in presence of the Lord of all, proffering useless gifts, and making things deceitful and vain the pursuits of his own miserable soul.

---

[1] The text is, τυφλός τε ὢν τὴν πρόσοψιν καὶ ὑπὸ τοῦ σκότους τῶν πραγματων ἀφηρημένος, for which it is proposed to read, τυφλός τε ὢν καὶ τὴν πρόσοψιν ὑπὸ τοῦ σκότους, etc.

[2] Or, as the Latin version puts it: And, in fine, when I considered the difference between these modes of life, I found nothing but that, by setting myself, etc.

[3] ἀνδρείας.

CHAP. III.

For this present time is filled with all things that are most contrary[1] to each other — births and deaths, the growth of plants and their uprooting, cures and killings, the building up and the pulling down of houses, weeping and laughing, mourning and dancing. At this moment a man gathers of earth's products, and at another casts them away; and at one time he ardently desireth *the beauty of* woman, and at another he hateth it. Now he seeketh something, and again he loseth it; and now he keepeth, and again he casteth away; at one time he slayeth, and at another he is slain; he speaketh, and again he is silent; he loveth, and again he hateth. For the affairs of men are at one time in a condition of war, and at another in a condition of peace; while their fortunes are so inconstant, that from bearing the semblance of good, they change quickly into acknowledged ills. Let us have done, therefore, with vain labours. For all these things, as appears to me, are set to madden men, as it were, with their poisoned stings. And the ungodly observer of the times and seasons is agape for this world,[2] exerting himself above measure to destroy the image[3] of God, as one who has chosen to contend against it[4] from the beginning onward to the end.[5] I am persuaded, therefore, that the greatest good for man is cheerfulness and well-doing, and that this shortlived enjoyment, which alone is possible to us, comes from God only, if righteousness direct our doings. But as to those everlasting and incorruptible things which God hath firmly established, it is not possible either to take aught from them or to add aught to them. And to men in general, those things, in sooth, are fearful and wonderful;[6] and those things indeed which have been, abide so; and those which are to be, have already been, as regards His foreknowledge. Moreover, the man who is injured has God as his helper. I saw in the lower parts the pit of punishment which receives the impious, but a different place allotted for the pious. And I thought with myself, that with God all things are judged and determined to be equal; that the righteous and the unrighteous, and objects with reason and without reason, are alike in His judgment. For that their time is measured out equally to all, and death impends over them, and *in this* the races of beasts and men are alike in the judgment of God, and differ from each other only in the matter of articulate speech; and all things else happen alike to them, and death receives all equally, not more so in the case of the other kinds of creatures than in that of men. For they have all the same breath *of life*, and men have nothing more; but all are, in one word, vain, deriving their present condition[7] from the same earth, and destined to perish, and return to the same earth again. For it is uncertain regarding the souls of men, whether they shall fly upwards; and regarding the others which the unreasoning creatures possess, whether they shall fall downward. And it seemed to me, that there is no other good save pleasure, and the enjoyment of things present. For I did not think it possible for a man, when once he has tasted death, to return again to the enjoyment of these things.[8]

CHAP. IV.

And leaving all these reflections, I considered and turned in aversion from all the forms of oppression[9] which are done among men; whence some receiving injury weep and lament, who are struck down by violence in utter default of those who protect them, or who should by all means comfort them in their trouble.[10] And the men who make might their right[11] are exalted to an eminence, from which, however, they shall also fall. Yea, of the unrighteous and audacious, those who are dead fare better than those who are still alive. And better than both these is he who, being destined to be like them, has not yet come into being, since he has not yet touched the wickedness which prevails among men. And it became clear to me also how great is the envy which follows a man from his neighbours, like the sting of a wicked spirit; and *I saw* that he who receives it, and takes it as it were into his breast, has nothing else but to eat his own heart, and tear it, and consume both soul and body, finding inconsolable vexation in the good fortune of others.[12] And a wise man would choose to have one of his hands full, if it were with ease and quietness, rather than both of them with travail and with the villany of a treacherous spirit. Moreover, there is yet another thing which I know to happen contrary to what is fit-

---

[1] The text reads ἐναντιωτήτων, for which Codex Anglicus has ἐναντιωτάτων.

[2] Or, age.

[3] πλάσμα.

[4] Or, *Him*.

[5] The Greek text is, καιροσκόπος δή τις πονηρὸς τὸν αἰῶνα τοῦτον περικεχηνεν, ἀφανίσαι ὑπερδιατεινόμενος τὸ τοῦ Θεοῦ πλάσμα, ἐξ ἀρχῆς αὐτῷ μεχρι τέλους πολεμεῖν ἡρημένος. It is well to notice how widely this differs from our version of iii. 11: "He hath made everything beautiful in his time," etc.

[6] The text is, ᾧ τινι οὖν, ἀλλ᾽ ἔστιν, ἐκεῖνα φοβερά τε ὁμοῦ καὶ θαυμαστά.

[7] σύστασιν.

[8] [The key to the interpretation of this book, as to much of the book of Job, is found in the brief expostulation of Jeremiah (chap. xii. 1), where he confesses his inability to comprehend the world and God's ways therein, yet utters a profession of unshaken confidence in His goodness. Here Solomon, in monologue, gives vent to similar misgivings; overruling all in the wonderful ode with which the book concludes. I say *Solomon*, not unadvisedly.]

[9] σικοφαντων.

[10] The text is, βίᾳ καταβεβλημένοι τῶν ἐπαμυνόντων ἢ ὅλως παραμυθησομένων αὐτοὺς πάσης πανταχόθεν κατεχούσης ἀπορίας. The sense is not clear. It may be: who are struck down in spite of those who protect them, and who should by all means comfort them when all manner of trouble presses them on all sides.

[11] χειροδικαι.

[12] Following the reading of Cod. Medic., which puts τιθέμενος for τιθεμενον. [See Cyprian, vol. v. p. 493, note 7, this series.]

ting, by reason of the evil will of man. He who is left entirely alone, having neither brother nor son, but prospered with large possessions, lives on in the spirit of insatiable avarice, and refuses to give himself in any way whatever to goodness. Gladly, therefore, would I ask such an one for what reason he labours thus, fleeing with headlong speed [1] from the doing of anything good, and distracted by the many various passions for making gain. [2] Far better than such are those who have taken up an order of life in common, [3] from which they may reap the best blessings. For when two men devote themselves in the right spirit to the same objects, though some mischance befalls the one, he has still at least no slight alleviation in having his companion by him. And the greatest of all calamities to a man in evil fortune is the want of a friend to help and cheer him. [4] And those who live together both double the good fortune that befalls them, and lessen the pressure of the storm of disagreeable events ; so that in the day they are distinguished for their frank confidence in each other, and in the night they appear notable for their cheerfulness. [5] But he who leads a solitary life passes a species of existence full of terror to himself ; not perceiving that if one should fall upon men welded closely together, he adopts a rash and perilous course, and that it is not easy to snap the threefold cord. [6] Moreover, I put a poor youth, if he be wise, before an aged prince devoid of wisdon, to whose thoughts it has never occured that it is possible that a man may be raised from the prison to the throne, and that the very man who has exercised his power unrighteously shall at a later period be righteously cast out. For it may happen that those who are subject to a youth, who is at the same time sensible, shall be free from trouble, — those, I mean, who are his elders. [7] Moreover, they who are born later cannot praise another, of whom they have had no experience, [8] and are led by an unreasoning judgment, and by the impulse of a contrary spirit. But in exercising the preacher's office, keep thou this before thine eyes, that thine own life be rightly directed, and that thou prayest in behalf of the foolish, that they may get understanding, and know how to shun the doings of the wicked.

---

[1] προτροπάδην.
[2] χρηματισασθαι.
[3] κοινωνίαν ἅμα βίου ἐστείλαντο.
[4] ἀνακτησομένου.
[5] The text is, καὶ νύκτωρ σεμνότητι σεμνύνεσθαι, for which certain codices read σεμνότητι φαιδρύνεσθαι, and others φαιδρότητι σεμνύνεσθαι.
[6] Jerome cites the passage in his Commentary on Ecclesiastes [iv. 12].
[7] Τοὺς ὅσοι προγενέστεροι. The sense is incomplete, and some words seem missing in the text. Jerome, in rendering this passage in his Commentary on Ecclesiastes, turns it thus: *ita autem ut sub sene rege versati sint ;* either having lighted on a better manuscript, or adding something of his own authority to make out the meaning.
[8] διὰ τὸ ἕτερον ἀπειράτως ἔχειν.

CHAP. V.

Moreover, it is a good thing to use the tongue sparingly, and to keep a calm and rightly balanced [9] heart in the exercise of speech. [10] For it is not right to give utterance in words to things that are foolish and absurd, or to all that occur to the mind ; but we ought to know and reflect, that though we are far separated from heaven, we speak in the hearing of God, and that it is good for us to speak without offence. For as dreams and visions of many kinds attend manifold cares of mind, so also silly talking is conjoined with folly. Moreover, see to it, that a promise made with a vow be made good in fact. This, too, is proper to fools, that they are unreliable. But be thou true to thy word, knowing that it is much better for thee not to vow or promise to do anything, than to vow and then fail of performance. And thou oughtest by all means to avoid the flood of base words, seeing that God will hear them. For the man who makes such things his study gets no more benefit by them than to see his doings brought to nought by God. For as the multitude of dreams is vain, so also the multitude of words. But the fear of God is man's salvation, though it is rarely found. Wherefore thou oughtest not to wonder though thou seest the poor oppressed, and the judges misinterpreting the law. But thou oughtest to avoid the appearance of surpassing those who are in power. For even should this prove to be the case, yet, from the terrible ills that shall befall thee, wickedness of itself will not deliver thee. But even as property acquired by violence is a most hurtful as well as impious possession, so the man who lusteth after money never finds satisfaction for his passion, nor good-will from his neighbours, even though he may have amassed the greatest possible wealth. For this also is vanity. But goodness greatly rejoiceth those who hold by it, and makes them strong, [11] imparting to them the capacity of seeing through [12] all things. And it is a great matter also not to be engrossed by such anxieties : for the poor man, even should he be a slave, and unable to fill his belly plentifully, enjoys at least the kind refreshment of sleep ; but the lust of riches is attended by sleepless nights and anxieties of mind. And what could there be then more absurd, than with much anxiety and trouble to amass wealth, and keep it with jealous care, if all the while one is but maintaining the occasion of countless evils to himself ? And this wealth, besides, must needs perish some time or other, and be lost, whether he who has acquired it has children or not ; [13] and the man himself, however unwillingly, is

---

[9] εὐσταθούσῃ.
[10] ἐν τῇ περὶ λόγους σπουδῇ.
[11] ἀνδρείους.
[12] καθορᾶν.
[13] Job xx. 20.

doomed to die, and return to earth in the self-same condition in which it was his lot once to come into being.[1] And the fact that he is destined thus to leave earth with empty hands, will make the evil all the sorer to him, as he fails to consider that an end is appointed for his life similar to its beginning, and that he toils to no profit, and labours rather for the wind, as it were, than for the advancement of his own real interest, wasting his whole life in most unholy lusts and irrational passions, and withal in troubles and pains. And, to speak shortly, his days are darkness to such a man, and his life is sorrow. Yet this is in itself good, and by no means to be despised. For it is the gift of God, that a man should be able to reap with gladness of mind the fruits of his labours, receiving thus possessions bestowed by God, and not acquired by force.[2] For neither is such a man afflicted with troubles, nor is he for the most part the slave of evil thoughts; but he measures out his life by good deeds, being of good heart[3] in all things, and rejoicing in the gift of God.

CHAP. VI.

Moreover, I shall exhibit in discourse the ill-fortune that most of all prevails among men. While God may supply a man with all that is according to his mind, and deprive him of no object which may in any manner appeal to his desires, whether it be wealth, or honour, or any other of those things for which men distract themselves; yet the man, while thus prospered in all things, as though the only ill inflicted on him from heaven were just the inability to enjoy them, may but husband them for his fellow, and fall without profit either to himself or to his neighbours. This I reckon to be a strong proof and clear sign of surpassing evil. The man who has borne without blame the name of father of very many children, and spent a long life, and has not had his soul filled with good for so long time, and has had no experience of death meanwhile,[4] — this man I should not envy either his numerous offspring or his length of days; nay, I should say that the untimely birth that falls from a woman's womb is better than he. For as that came in with vanity, so it also departeth secretly in oblivion, without having tasted the ills of life or looked on the sun. And this is a lighter evil than for the wicked man not to know what is good, even though he measure his life by thousands of years.[5] And the end of both is death. The fool is proved above all things by his finding no satisfaction in any lust. But the discreet man is not held captive by these passions. Yet, for the most part, righteousness of life leads a man to poverty. And the sight of curious eyes deranges[6] many, inflaming their mind, and drawing them on to vain pursuits by the empty desire of show.[7] Moreover, the things which are now are known already; and it becomes apparent that man is unable to contend with those that are above him. And, verily, inanities have their course among men, which only increase the folly of those who occupy themselves with them.

CHAP. VII.

For though a man should be by no means greatly advantaged by knowing all in this life that is destined to befall him according to his mind (let us suppose such a case), nevertheless with the officious activity of men he devises means for prying into and gaining an apparent acquaintance with the things that are to happen after a person's death. Moreover, a good name is more pleasant to the mind[8] than oil to the body; and the end of life is better than the birth, and to mourn is more desirable than to revel, and to be with the sorrowing is better than to be with the drunken. For this is the fact, that he who comes to the end of life has no further care about aught around him. And discreet anger is to be preferred to laughter; for by the severe disposition of countenance the soul is kept upright.[9] The souls of the wise, indeed, are sad and downcast, but those of fools are elated, and given loose to merriment. And yet it is far more desirable to receive blame from one wise man, than to become a hearer of a whole chorus of worthless and miserable men in their songs. For the laughter of fools is like the crackling of many thorns burning in a fierce fire. This, too, is misery, yea the greatest of evils, namely oppression;[10] for it intrigues against the souls of the wise, and attempts to ruin the noble way of life[11] which the good pursue. Moreover, it is right to commend not the man who begins, but the man who finishes a speech;[12] and what is moderate ought to approve itself to the mind, and not what is swollen and inflated. Again, one ought certainly to keep wrath in check, and not suffer himself to be carried rashly into anger, the slaves of which are fools. Moreover, they are in error who assert that a better

---

[1] Job i. 21; 1 Tim. vi. 7.
[2] ἁρπακτικα in the text, for which the Cod. Medic. has ἁρπακτα.
[3] ἐνθυμούμενος.
[4] θανατον πεῖραν οὐ λαβων, for which we must read probably θανάτου. etc.
[5] The text gives, ἤπερ τῷ πονηρῷ . . . ἀναμετρησαμενῳ ἀγαθοτητα μὴ ἐπιγνῳ, for which we may read either ἤπερ τῷ πονηρῷ . . . ἀναμετρησαμενος . . . ἐπιγνῷ, or better, . . . ἀναμετρησαμενῳ . . . ἐπιγνῶναι.

[6] ἐξίστησι.
[7] τοῦ ὀφθῆναι.
[8] Prov. xxii. 1.
[9] κατορθοῦται.
[10] Calumny, συκοφαντία.
[11] ἐνστασιν.
[12] λόγων δέ, etc. But Cod. Medic. reads, λόγον δέ, etc., = it is right to commend a speech not in its beginning, but in its end.

manner of life was given to those before us, and they fail to see that wisdom is widely different from mere abundance of possessions, and that it is as much more lustrous [1] than these, as silver shines more brightly than its shadow. For the life of man hath its excellence [2] not in the acquisition of perishable riches, but in wisdom. And who shall be able, tell me, to declare the providence of God, which is so great and so beneficent? or who shall be able to recall the things which seem to have been passed by of God? And in the former days of my vanity I considered all things, *and saw* a righteous man continuing in his righteousness, and ceasing not from it until death, but even suffering injury by reason thereof, and a wicked man perishing with his wickedness. Moreover, it is proper that the righteous man should not seem to be so overmuch, nor exceedingly and above measure wise, that he may not, as in making some slip, *seem to* sin many times over. And be not thou audacious and precipitate, lest an untimely death surprise thee. It is the greatest of all good to take hold of God, and by abiding in Him to sin in nothing. For to touch things undefiled with an impure hand is abomination. But he who in the fear of God submits himself,[3] escapes all that is contrary. Wisdom availeth more in the way of help than a band of the most powerful men in a city, and it often also pardons righteously those who fail in duty. For there is not one that stumbleth not.[4] Also it becomes thee in no way to attend upon the words of the impious, that thou mayest not become an ear-witness [5] of words spoken against thyself, such as the foolish talk of a wicked servant, and being thus stung in heart, have recourse afterwards thyself to cursing in turn in many actions. And all these things have I known, having received wisdom from God, which afterwards I lost, and was no longer able to be the same.[6] For wisdom fled from me to an infinite distance, and into a measureless deep, so that I could no longer get hold of it. Wherefore afterwards I abstained altogether from seeking it; and I no longer thought of considering the follies and the vain counsels of the impious, and their weary, distracted life. And being thus disposed, I was borne on to the things themselves; and being seized with a fatal passion, I knew woman — that she is like a snare or some such other object.[7] For her heart ensnares those who pass her; and if she but join hand to hand, she holds one as securely as though she dragged

him on bound with chains.[8] And from her you can secure your deliverance only by finding a propitious and watchful superintendent in God;[9] for he who is enslaved by sin cannot (otherwise) escape its grasp. Moreover, among all women I sought for the chastity [10] proper to them, and I found it in none. And verily a person may find one man chaste among a thousand, but a woman never.[11] And this above all things I observed, that men being made by God simple [12] in mind, contract [13] for themselves manifold reasonings and infinite questionings, and while professing to seek wisdom, waste their life in vain words.

CHAP. VIII.

Moreover, wisdom, when it is found in a man, shows itself also in its possessor's face, and makes his countenance to shine; as, on the other hand, effrontery convicts the man in whom it has taken up its abode, so soon as he is seen, as one worthy of hatred. And it is on every account right to give careful heed to the words of the king, and by all manner of means to avoid an oath, especially one taken in the name of God. It may be fit at the same time to notice an evil word, but then it is necessary to guard against any blasphemy against God. For it will not be possible to find fault with Him when He inflicts any penalty, nor to gainsay the decrees of the Only Lord and King. But it will be better and more profitable for a man to abide by the holy commandments, and to keep himself apart from the words of the wicked. For the wise man knows and discerneth beforehand the judgment, which shall come at the right time, and sees that it shall be just. For all things in the life of men await the retribution from above; but the wicked man does not seem to know verily [14] that as there is a mighty providence over him, nothing in the future shall be hid. He knoweth not indeed the things which shall be; for no man shall be able to announce any one of them to him duly: for no one shall be found so strong as to be able to prevent the angel who spoils him of his life;[15] neither shall any means be devised for cancelling in any way the appointed time of death. But even as the man who is captured in the midst of the battle can only see

---

1   φανερωτέρα, for which φανοτέρα is proposed.
2   περιγίγνεται.
3   ὑπείκων.
4   1 Kings viii. 46; 2 Chron. vi. 36; Prov. xx. 9; 1 John i. 8.
5   αὐτήκοος.
6   ὅμοιος.
7   The text is evidently corrupt: for τὴν γυναῖκα, γῆν τινά, etc., Cotelerius proposes, τὴν γυναῖκα, σαγήνην τινά, etc.; and Bengel, πάγην τινά, etc.

8   κατέχει ἢ εἰ. This use of ἢ εἰ is characteristic of Gregory Thaumaturgus. We find it again in his *Panegyr. ad Orig.*, ch. 6, ἢ εἰ καὶ παρὰ πάντας, etc. It may be added, therefore, to the proofs in support of a common authorship for these two writings.
9   ἐπόπτην.
10   σωφροσύνην.
11   [Our English version gives no such idea, nor does that of the LXX. The σωφροσύνη of our author is *discretion*, or perhaps *entire balance of mind*. Wordsworth gives us the thought better in his verse: "A perfect woman, nobly planned." It was not in Judaism to give woman her place: the *Magnificat* of the Virgin celebrated the restoration of her sex.]
12   Upright, ἁπλοῖ.
13   ἐπισπῶνται.
14   λίαν.
15   ψυχήν.

flight cut off on every side, so all the impiety of man perisheth utterly together. And I am astonished, as often as I contemplate what and how great things men have studied to do for the hurt of their neighbours. But this I know, that the impious are snatched prematurely from this life, and put out of the way because they have given themselves to vanity. For whereas the providential judgment [1] of God does not overtake all speedily, by reason of His great long-suffering, and the wicked is not punished immediately on the commission of his offences, — for this reason he thinks that he may sin the more, as though he were to get off with impunity, not understanding that the transgressor shall not escape the knowledge of God even after a long interval. This, moreover, is the chief good, to reverence God; for if once the impious man fall away from Him, he shall not be suffered long to misuse his own folly. But a most vicious and false opinion often prevails among men concerning both the righteous and the unrighteous. For they form a judgment contrary to truth regarding each of them; and the man who is really righteous does not get the credit of being so, while, on the other hand, the impious man is deemed prudent and upright. And this I judge to be among the most grievous of errors. Once, indeed, I thought that the chief good consisted in eating and drinking, and that he was most highly favoured of God who should enjoy these things to the utmost in his life; and I fancied that this kind of enjoyment was the only comfort in life. And, accordingly, I gave heed to nothing but to this conceit, so that neither by night nor by day did I withdraw myself from all those things which have ever been discovered to minister luxurious delights to men. And this much I learned thereby, that the man who mingles in these things shall by no means be able, however sorely he may labour with them, to find the real good.

CHAP. IX.

Now I thought at that time that all men were judged worthy of the same things. And if any wise man practised righteousness, and withdrew himself from unrighteousness, and as being sagacious avoided hatred with all (which, indeed, is a thing well pleasing to God), this man seemed to me to labour in vain. For there seemed to be one end for the righteous and for the impious, for the good and for the evil, for the pure and for the impure, for him that worshipped [2] God, and for him that worshipped not. For as the unrighteous man and the good, the man who sweareth a false oath, and the man who avoids swearing altogether, were suspected by me to be driving toward the same end, a certain sinister opinion stole secretly into my mind, that all men come to their end in a similar way. But now I know that these are the reflections of fools, and errors and deceits. And they assert largely, that he who is dead has perished utterly, and that the living is to be preferred to the dead, even though he may lie in darkness, and pass his life-journey after the fashion of a dog, *which is* better at least than a dead lion. For the living know this at any rate, that they are to die; but the dead know not anything, and there is no reward proposed to them after they have completed their necessary course. Also hatred and love with the dead have their end; for their envy has perished, and their life also is extinguished. And he has a portion in nothing who has once gone hence. Error harping still on such a string, gives also such counsel as this: What meanest thou, O man, that thou dost not enjoy thyself delicately, and gorge thyself with all manner of pleasant food, and fill thyself to the full with wine? Dost thou not perceive that these things are given us from God for our unrestrained enjoyment? Put on newly-washed attire, and anoint thy head with myrrh, and see this woman and that, and pass thy vain life vainly.[3] For nothing else remaineth for thee but this, neither here nor after death. But avail thou thyself of all that chanceth; for neither shall any one take account of thee for these things, nor are the things that are done by men known at all outside the circle of men. And Hades, whatever that may he, whereunto we are said to depart, has neither wisdom nor understanding. These are the things which men of vanity speak. But I know assuredly, that neither shall they who seem the swiftest accomplish that great race; nor shall those who are esteemed mighty and terrible in the judgment of men, overcome in that terrible battle. Neither, again, is prudence proved by abundance of bread, nor is understanding wont to consort with riches. Nor do I congratulate those who think that all shall find the same things befall them. But certainly those who indulge such thoughts seem to me to be asleep, and to fail to consider that, caught suddenly like fishes and birds, they will be consumed with woes, and meet speedily their proper retribution. Also I estimate wisdom at so high a price, that I should deem a small and poorly-peopled city, even though besieged also by a mighty king with his forces, to be indeed great and powerful, if it had but one wise man, however poor, among its citizens. For such a man would be able to deliver his city both from enemies and from entrenchments. And other men, it may be, do not recognise that wise man,

---

[1] πρόνοια.
[2] ἱλασκομένου.

[3] The text gives, κἀκείνην δὲ ματαίως, etc.

poor as he is; but for my part I greatly prefer the power that resides in wisdom, to this might of the mere multitude of the people. Here, however, wisdom, as it dwells with poverty, is held in dishonour. But hereafter it shall be heard speaking with more authoritative voice than princes and despots who seek after things evil. For wisdom is also stronger than iron; while the folly of one individual works danger for many, even though he be an object of contempt to many.[1]

CHAP. X.

Moreover, flies falling into myrrh, and suffocated therein, make both the appearance of that pleasant ointment and the anointing therewith an unseemly thing;[2] and to be mindful of wisdom and of folly together is in no way proper. The wise man, indeed, is his own leader to right actions; but the fool inclines to erring courses, and will never make his folly available as a guide to what is noble. Yea, his thoughts also are vain and full of folly. But if ever a hostile spirit fall upon thee, my friend, withstand it courageously, knowing that God is able to propitiate[3] even a mighty multitude of offences. These also are the deeds of the prince and father of all wickedness: that the fool is set on high, while the man richly gifted with wisdom is humbled; and that the slaves of sin are seen riding on horseback, while men dedicated to God walk on foot in dishonour, the wicked exulting the while. But if any one devises another's hurt, he forgets that he is preparing a snare for himself first and alone. And he who wrecks another's safety, shall fall by the bite of a serpent. But he who removeth stones, indeed shall undergo no light labour;[4] and he who cleaveth wood shall bear danger with him in his own weapon. And if it chance that the axe spring out of the handle,[5] he who engages in such work shall be put to trouble, gathering for no good[6] and having to put to more of his iniquitous and shortlived strength.[7] The bite of a serpent, again, is stealthy; and the charmers will not soothe the pain, for they are vain. But the good man doeth good works for himself and for his neighbours alike; while the fool shall sink into destruction through his folly. And when he has once opened his mouth, he begins foolishly and soon comes to an end, exhibiting his senselessness in all. Moreover, it is impossible for man to know anything, or to learn from man either what has been from the beginning, or what shall be in the future. For who shall be the declarer thereof? Besides, the man who knows not to go to the good city, sustains evil in the eyes and in the whole countenance. And I prophesy woes to that city the king of which is a youth, and its rulers gluttons. But I call the good land blessed, the king of which is the son of the free: there those who are entrusted with the power of ruling shall reap what is good in due season. But the sluggard and the idler become scoffers, and make the house decay; and misusing all things for the purposes of their own gluttony, like the ready slaves of money,[8] for a small price they are content to do all that is base and abject. It is also right to obey kings and rulers or potentates, and not to be bitter against them, nor to utter any offensive word against them. For there is ever the risk that what has been spoken in secret may somehow become public. For swift and winged messengers convey all things to Him who alone is King both rich and mighty, discharging therein a service which is at once spiritual and reasonable.

CHAP. XI.

Moreover, it is a righteous thing to give (to the needy) of thy bread, and of those things which are necessary for the support of man's life. For though thou seemest forthwith to waste it upon some persons, as if thou didst cast thy bread upon the water, yet in the progress of time thy kindness shall be seen to be not unprofitable for thee. Also give liberally, and give a portion of thy means to many; for thou knowest not what the coming day doeth. The clouds, again, do not keep back their plenteous rains, but discharge their showers upon the earth. Nor does a tree stand for ever; but even though men may spare it, it shall be overturned by the wind at any rate. But many desire also to know beforehand what is to come from the heavens; and there have been those who, scrutinizing the clouds and waiting for the wind, have had nought to do with reaping and winnowing, putting their trust in vanity, and being all incapable of knowing aught of what may come from God in the future; just as men cannot tell what the woman with child shall bring forth. But sow thou in season, and thus reap thy fruits whenever the time for that comes on. For it is not manifest what shall be better than those among all natural things.[9] Would, indeed, that all things turned out well! Truly, when a man considers with himself that the sun is good, and that this life is sweet, and that it is a pleasant thing to have many years wherein one can delight himself

---

[1] κἂν πολλοῖς καταφρόνητος ᾖ: so the Cod. Bodleian. and the Cod. Medic. read. But others read πολὺ = an object of great contempt. For καταφρόνητος the Cod. Medic. reads εὐκαταφρόνητος.
[2] The text gives χρίσιν, for which Cod. Medic. reads χρῆσιν, use.
[3] ἱλάσασθαι.
[4] Reading ἀλλὰ μήν for ἀλλὰ μή.
[5] στελεοῦ, for which others read στελέχους.
[6] οὐκ ἐπ᾿ ἀγαθῷ συγκομίζων.
[7] ἐπαύξων αὐτὸς τὴν ἑαυτοῦ ἄδικον καὶ ὠκύμορον δύναμιν.

[8] ἀργυρίῳ ἀγώγιμοι.
[9] ὁποῖα αὐτῶν ἔσται ἀμείνω τῶν φυέντων, perhaps = which of those natural productions shall be the better.

continually, and that death is a terror and an endless evil, and a thing that brings us to nought, he thinks that he ought to enjoy himself in all the present and apparent pleasures of life. And he gives this counsel also to the young, that they should use to the uttermost [1] the season of their youth, by giving up their minds to all manner of pleasure, and indulge their passions, and do all that seemeth good in their own eyes, and look upon that which delighteth, and avert themselves from that which is not so. But to such a man I shall say this much: Senseless art thou, my friend, in that thou dost not look for the judgment that shall come from God upon all these things. And profligacy and licentiousness are evil, and the filthy wantonness of our bodies carries death in it. For folly attends on youth, and folly leads to destruction.

CHAP. XII.

Moreover, it is right that thou shouldest fear God while thou art yet young, before thou givest thyself over to evil things, and before the great and terrible day of God cometh, when the sun shall no longer shine, neither the moon, nor the rest of the stars, but when in that storm and commotion of all things, the powers above shall be moved, that is, the angels who guard the world; so that the mighty men shall fail, and the women shall cease their labours, and shall flee into the dark places of their dwellings, and shall have all the doors shut. And a woman shall be restrained from grinding by fear, and shall speak with the weakest voice, like the tiniest bird; and all the impure women shall sink into the earth; and cities and their blood-stained governments shall wait for the vengeance that comes from above, while the most bitter and bloody of all times hangs over them like a blossoming almond, and continuous punishments impend like a multitude of flying locusts, and the transgressors are cast out of the way like a black and despicable caper-plant. And the good man shall depart with rejoicing to his own everlasting habitation; but the vile shall fill all their places with wailing, and neither silver laid up in store, nor proved gold, shall be of use any more. For a mighty stroke [2] shall fall upon all things, even to the pitcher that standeth by the well, and the wheel of the vessel which may chance to have been left in the hollow, when the course of time comes to its end [3] and the ablution-bearing period of a life that is like water has passed away.[4] And for men who lie on earth there is but one salvation, that their souls acknowledge and wing their way to Him by whom they have been made. I say, then, again what I have said already, that man's estate is altogether vain, and that nothing can exceed the utter vanity which attaches to the objects of man's inventions. And superfluous is my labour in preaching discreetly, inasmuch as I am attempting to instruct a people here, so indisposed to receive either teaching or healing. And truly the noble man is needed for the understanding of the words of wisdom. Moreover, I, though already aged, and having passed a long life, laboured to find out those things which are well-pleasing to God, by means of the mysteries of the truth. And I know that the mind is no less quickened and stimulated by the precepts of the wise, than the body is wont to be when the goad is applied, or a nail is fastened in it.[5] And some will render again those wise lessons which they have received from one good pastor and teacher, as if all with one mouth and in mutual concord set forth in larger detail the truths committed to them. But in many words there is no profit. Neither do I counsel thee, my friend, to write down vain things about what is fitting,[6] from which there is nothing to be gained but weary labour. But, in fine, I shall require to use some such conclusion as this: O men, behold, I charge you now expressly and shortly, that ye fear God, who is at once the Lord and the Overseer [7] of all, and that ye keep also His commandments; and that ye believe that all shall be judged severally in the future, and that every man shall receive the just recompense for his deeds, whether they be good or whether they be evil.[8]

---

1 καταχρῆσθαι.

2 καθέξει πληγή. Œcolampadius renders it, *magnus enim fons*, evidently reading πηγή.

3 The text is, ἐν τῷ κοιλώματι παυσαμένης χρόνον τε περιδρομῆς, for which we may read, ἐν τῷ κοιλώματι, παυσαμένης χρόνων τε περιδρομῆς. Others apparently propose for παυσαμένης, δεξαμενῆς = at the hollow of the cistern.

4 The text is, καὶ τῆς δι' ὕδατος ζωῆς παροδεύσαντος τοῦ λουτροφόρου αἰῶνος. Billius understands the age to be called λουτροφόρου, because, as long as we are in life, it is possible to obtain remission for any sin, or as referring to the rite of baptism.

5 ἠλῳ ἐμπεπορνηθέντα. The Septuagint reads, λόγοι σοφῶν ὡς τὰ βούκεντρα καὶ ὡς ἧλοι πεφυτευμένοι, like nails planted, etc. Others read πεπυρωμένοι, *igniti*. The Vulg. has, *quasi clavi in altum defixi*.

6 περὶ τὸ προσῆκον, for which some read, παρὰ τὸ προσῆκον, beyond or contrary to what is fitting.

7 ἐπόπτης.

8 [The incomparable beauty of our English version of this twelfth chapter of *Koheleth* is heightened not a little by comparison with this turgid metaphrase. It fails, in almost every instance, to extract the kernel of the successive στίχοι of this superlatively poetic and didactic threnode. It must have been a youthful work.]

CANONICAL EPISTLE.[1]

CANON I.

THE meats are no burden to us, most holy father,[2] if the captives ate things which their conquerors set before them, especially since there is one report from all, viz., that the barbarians who have made inroads into our parts have not sacrificed to idols. For the apostle says, "Meats for the belly, and the belly for meats: but God shall destroy both it and them."[3] But the Saviour also, who cleanseth all meats, says, "Not that which goeth into a man defileth the man, but that which cometh out."[4] And this meets the case of the captive women defiled by the barbarians, who outraged their bodies. But if the previous life of any such person convicted him of going, as it is written, after the eyes of fornicators, the habit of fornication evidently becomes an object of suspicion also in the time of captivity. And one ought not readily to have communion with such women in prayers. If any one, however, has lived in the utmost chastity, and has shown in time past a manner of life pure and free from all suspicion, and now falls into wantonness through force of necessity, we have an example for our guidance, — namely, the instance of the damsel in Deuteronomy, whom a man finds in the field, and forces her, and lies with her. "Unto the damsel," he says, "ye shall do nothing; there is in the damsel no sin worthy of death: for as when a man riseth against his neighbour, and slayeth him, even so is this matter: the damsel cried, and there was none to help her."[5]

CANON II.

Covetousness is a great evil; and it is not possible in a single letter to set forth those scriptures in which not robbery alone is declared to be a thing horrible and to be abhorred, but in general the grasping mind, and the disposition to meddle with what belongs to others, in order to satisfy the sordid love of gain. And all persons of that spirit are excommunicated from the Church of God. But that at the time of the irruption, in the midst of such woful sorrows and bitter lamentations, some should have been audacious enough to consider the crisis which brought destruction to all the very period for their own private aggrandizement, that is a thing which can be averred only of men who are impious and hated of God, and of unsurpassable iniquity. Wherefore it seemed good to excommunicate such persons, lest the wrath (of God) should come upon the whole people, and upon those first of all who are set over them in office, and yet fail to make inquiry. For I am afraid, as the Scripture says, lest the impious work the destruction of the righteous along with his own.[6] "For fornication," it says,[7] "and covetousness *are things* on account of which the wrath of God cometh upon the children of disobedience. Be not ye therefore partakers with them. For ye were sometimes darkness, but now are ye light in the Lord: walk as children of light (for the fruit of the light[8] is in all goodness, and righteousness, and truth), proving what is acceptable unto the Lord. And have no fellowship with the unfruitful works of darkness, but rather reprove them; for it is a shame even to speak of those things which are done of them in secret. But all things that are reproved are made manifest by the light." In this wise speaks the apostle. But if certain parties who pay the proper penalty for that former covetousness of theirs, which exhibited itself in the time of peace, now turn aside again to the indulgence of covetousness in the very time of trouble (i.e., in the troubles of the inroads by the barbarians), and make gain out of the blood and ruin of men who have been utterly despoiled, or taken captive, (or) put to death, what else ought to be expected, than that those who struggle so hotly for covetousness should heap up wrath both for themselves and for the whole people?

---

[1] Of the holy Gregory, archbishop of Neo-Cæsareia, surnamed Thaumaturgus, concerning those who, in the inroad of the barbarians, ate things sacrificed to idols, or offended in certain other matters. Gallandi, iii. p. 400. [Written A.D. 258 or 262.] There are scholia in Latin by Theodorus Balsamon and Joannes Zonaras on these canons. The note of the former on the last canon may be cited: — The present saint has defined shortly five several positions for the penitent; but he has not indicated either the times appointed for their exercise, or the sins for which discipline is determined. Basil the Great, again, has handed down to us an accurate account of these things in his canonical epistles. [Elucidation II.] Yet he, too, has referred to episcopal decision the matter of recovery through penalties [i.e., to the decision of his comprovincial bishops, as in Cyprian's example. See vol. v. p. 415, Elucidation XIII.; also Elucidation I. p. 20, *infra*.

[2] [Elucidation III. p. 20.]
[3] 1 Cor. vi. 13.
[4] Matt. xv. 11.
[5] Deut. xxii. 26, 27.

[6] Gen. xviii. 23, 25.
[7] Eph. v. 5-13.
[8] τοῦ φωτός for the received πνεύματος.

CANON III.

Behold, did not Achar[1] the son of Zara transgress in the accursed thing, and trouble then lighted on all the congregation of Israel? And this one man was alone in his sin; but he was not alone in the death that came by his sin. And by us, too, everything of a gainful kind at this time, which is ours not in our own rightful possession, but as property strictly belonging to others, ought to be reckoned a thing devoted. For that Achar indeed took of the spoil; and those men of the present time take also of the spoil. But he took what belonged to enemies; while these now take what belongs to brethren, and aggrandize themselves with fatal gains.

CANON IV.

Let no one deceive himself, nor put forward the pretext of having found such property. For it is not lawful, even for a man who has found anything, to aggrandize himself by it. For Deuteronomy says: "Thou shalt not see thy brother's ox or his sheep go astray in the way, and pay no heed to them; but thou shalt in any wise bring them again unto thy brother. And if thy brother come not nigh thee, or if thou know him not, then thou shalt bring them together, and they shall be with thee until thy brother seek after them, and thou shalt restore them to him again. And in like manner shalt thou do with his ass, and so shalt thou do with his raiment, and so shalt thou do with all lost things of thy brother's, which he hath lost, and thou mayest find."[2] Thus much in Deuteronomy. And in the book of Exodus it is said, with reference not only to the case of finding what is a friend's, but also of finding what is an enemy's: "Thou shalt surely bring them back to the house of their master again."[3] And if it is not lawful to aggrandize oneself at the expense of another, whether he be brother or enemy, even in the time of peace, when he is living at his ease and delicately, and without concern as to his property, how much more must it be the case when one is met by adversity, and is fleeing from his enemies, and has had to abandon his possessions by force of circumstances!

CANON V.

But others deceive themselves by fancying that they can retain the property of others which they may have found as an equivalent for their own property which they have lost. In this way verily, just as the Boradi and Goths brought the havoc of war on them, they make themselves Boradi and Goths to others. Accordingly we have sent to you our brother and comrade in old age, Euphrosynus, with this view, that he may deal with you in accordance with our model here, and teach you against whom you ought to admit accusations,[4] and whom you ought to exclude from your prayers.

CANON VI.[5]

Moreover, it has been reported to us that a thing has happened in your country which is surely incredible, and which, if done at all, is altogether the work of unbelievers, and impious men, and men who know not the very name of the Lord; to wit, that some have gone to such a pitch of cruelty and inhumanity, as to be detaining by force certain captives who have made their escape. Dispatch ye commissioners into the country, lest the thunderbolts of heaven fall all too surely upon those who perpetrate such deeds.

CANON VII.[6]

Now, as regards those who have been enrolled among the barbarians, and have accompanied them in their irruption in a state of captivity, and who, forgetting that they were from Pontus, and Christians, have become such thorough barbarians, as even to put those of their own race to death by the gibbet[7] or strangulation, and to show their roads or houses to the barbarians, who else would have been ignorant of them, it is necessary for you to debar such persons even from being auditors in the public congregations,[8] until some common decision about them is come to by the saints assembled in council, and by the Holy Spirit antecedently to them.

CANON VIII.[9]

Now those who have been so audacious as to invade the houses of others, if they have once been put on their trial and convicted, ought not to be deemed fit even to be hearers in the public congregation. But if they have declared themselves and made restitution, they should be placed in the rank of the repentant.[10]

CANON IX.[11]

Now, those who have found in the open field or in their own houses anything left behind them by the barbarians, if they have once been put on their trial and convicted, ought to fall under the same class of the repentant. But if they

---

[1] Josh. vii.
[2] Deut. xxii. 1–3.
[3] Ex. xxiii. 4.

[4] ὧν δεῖ τὰς κατηγορίας προσίεσθαι.
[5] Concerning those who forcibly detain captives escaped from the barbarians.
[6] Concerning those who have been enrolled among the barbarians, and who have dared to do certain monstrous things against those of the same race with themselves.
[7] ξύλῳ.
[8] ἀκροάσεως.
[9] Concerning those who have been so audacious as to invade the houses of others in the inroad of the barbarians.
[10] τῶν ὑποστρεφόντων.
[11] Concerning those who have found in the open field or in private houses property left behind them by the barbarians.

have declared themselves and made restitution, they ought to be deemed fit for the privilege of prayer.[1]

CANON X.

And they who keep the commandment ought to keep it without any sordid covetousness, demanding neither recompense,[2] nor reward,[3] nor fee,[4] nor anything else that bears the name of acknowledgment.

CANON XI.[5]

Weeping[6] takes place without the gate of the oratory; and the offender standing there ought

---

[1] [Partially elucidated below in (the spurious) Canon XI. See Marshall's *Penitential Discipline of the Primitive Church.*]
[2] μήνυτρα, the price of information.
[3] σώστρα, the reward for bringing back a runaway slave.
[4] εὕρετρα, the reward of discovery.
[5] [This canon is rejected as spurious. Lardner, *Credib.*, ii. p. 633.]
[6] πρόσκλαυσις, discipline.

to implore the faithful as they enter to offer up prayer on his behalf. Waiting on the word,[7] again, takes place within the gate in the porch,[8] where the offender ought to stand until the catechumens *depart*, and thereafter he should go forth. For let him hear the Scriptures and doctrine, it is said, and then be put forth, and reckoned unfit for the privilege of prayer. Submission,[9] again, is that one stand within the gate of the temple, and go forth along with the catechumens. Restoration [10] is that one be associated with the faithful, and go not forth with the catechumens; and last of all comes the participation in the holy ordinances.[11]

---

[7] ἀκρόασις.
[8] ἐν τῷ νάρθηκι.
[9] ὑπόπτωσις.
[10] σύστασις.
[11] ἁγιασμάτων.

ELUCIDATIONS.

I.

(The title, p. 18.)

THIS is a genuine epistle, all but the eleventh canon. It is addressed to an anonymous bishop; one of his suffragans, some think. I suppose, rather, he consults, as Cyprian did, the bishop of the nearest Apostolic See, and awaits his concurrence. It refers to the ravages of the Goths in the days of Gallienus (A.D. 259–267), and proves the care of the Church to maintain discipline, even in times most unfavourable to order and piety. The last canon is an explanatory addition made to elucidate the four degrees or classes of penitents. It is a very interesting document in this respect, and sheds light on the famous canonical epistles of St. Basil.

II.

(Basil the Great, p. 18, note.)

The "Canonical Epistles" of St. Basil are not private letters, but canons of the churches with which he was nearest related. When there was no art of printing, the chief bishops were obliged to communicate with suffragans, and with their brethren in the Apostolic See nearest to them. See them expounded at large in Dupin, *Ecclesiastical Writers of the Fourth Century, Works*, vol. i., London, 1693 (translated), p. 139, etc.

III.

(Most holy father, p. 18.)

This expression leads me to think that this epistle is addressed to the Bishop of Antioch or of some other Apostolic See. It must not be taken as a prescribed formula, however, as when we say "Most Reverend" in our days; e.g., addressing the Archbishop of Canterbury. Rather, it is an expression of personal reverence. As yet, titular distinctions, such as these, were not known. In the West existing usages seem to have been introduced with the Carlovingian system of dignities, expounded by Gibbon.

THE ORATION AND PANEGYRIC ADDRESSED TO ORIGEN.[1]

ARGUMENT I. — FOR EIGHT YEARS GREGORY HAS GIVEN UP THE PRACTICE OF ORATORY, BEING BUSIED WITH THE STUDY CHIEFLY OF ROMAN LAW AND THE LATIN LANGUAGE.

AN excellent[2] thing has silence proved itself in many another person on many an occasion, and at present it befits myself, too, most especially, who with or without purpose may keep the door of my lips, and feel constrained to be silent. For I am unpractised and unskilled[3] in those beautiful and elegant addresses which are spoken or composed in a regular and unbroken[4] train, in select and well-chosen phrases and words; and it may be that I am less apt by nature to cultivate successfully this graceful and truly Grecian art. Besides, it is now eight years since I chanced myself to utter or compose any speech, whether long or short; neither in that period have I heard any other compose or utter anything in private, or deliver in public any laudatory or controversial orations, with the exception of those admirable men who have embraced the noble study of philosophy, and who care less for beauty of language and elegance of expression. For, attaching only a secondary importance to the words, they aim, with all exactness, at investigating and making known the things themselves, precisely as they are severally constituted. Not indeed, in my opinion, that they do not desire, but rather that they do greatly desire, to clothe the noble and accurate results of their thinking in noble and comely[5] language. Yet it may be that they are not able so lightly to put forth this sacred and godlike power (faculty) in the exercise of its own proper conceptions, and at the same time to practise a mode of discourse eloquent in its terms, and thus to comprehend in one and the same mind — and that,

too, this little mind of man — two accomplishments, which are the gifts of two distinct persons, and which are, in truth, most contrary to each other. For silence is indeed the friend and helpmeet of thought and invention. But if one aims at readiness of speech and beauty of discourse, he will get at them by no other discipline than the study of words, and their constant practice. Moreover, another branch of learning occupies my mind completely, and the mouth binds the tongue if I should desire to make any speech, however brief, with the voice of the Greeks; I refer to those admirable laws of our sages[6] by which the affairs of all the subjects of the Roman Empire are now directed, and which are neither composed[7] nor learnt without difficulty. And these are wise and exact[8] in themselves, and manifold and admirable, and, in a word, most thoroughly Grecian; and they are expressed and committed to us in the Roman tongue, which is a wonderful and magnificent sort of language, and one very aptly conformable to royal authority,[9] but still difficult to me. Nor could it be otherwise with me, even though I might say that it was my desire that it should be.[10] And as our words are nothing else than a kind of imagery of the dispositions of our mind, we should allow those who have the gift of speech, like some good artists alike skilled to the utmost in their art and liberally furnished in the matter of colours, to possess the liberty of painting their word-pictures, not simply of a uniform complexion, but also of various descriptions and of richest beauty in the abundant mixture of flowers, without let or hindrance.

---

[1] Delivered by Gregory Thaumaturgus in the Palestinian Cæsareia, when about to leave for his own country, after many years' instruction under that teacher. [*Circa* A.D. 238.] Gallandi, *Opera*, p. 413.

[2] καλόν, for which Hœschelius has ἀγαθόν.

[3] ἄπειρος, for which Hœschelius has ἀνάσκητος.

[4] ἀκωλύτῳ, for which Bengel suggests ἀκολούθῳ.

[5] εὐειδεῖ, for which Ger. Vossius gives ἀψευδεῖ.

[6] [See my introductory note, *supra*. He refers to Caius, Papinian, Ulpian; all, probably, of Syrian origin, and using the Greek as their vernacular.]

[7] συγκείμενοι, which is rendered by some *conduntur*, by others *confectæ sunt*, and by others still *componantur*, harmonized, — the reference then being to the difficulty experienced in learning the laws, in the way of harmonizing those which apparently oppose each other.

[8] ἀκριβεῖς, for which Ger. Vossius gives εὐσεβεῖς, pious.

[9] [A noteworthy estimate of Latin by a Greek.]

[10] εἰ καὶ βουλητόν, etc., for which Hœschelius gives οὔτε βουλητόν, etc. The Latin version gives, *non enim aliter sentire aut posse aut velle me unquam dixerim.*

ARGUMENT II. — HE ESSAYS TO SPEAK OF THE
WELL-NIGH DIVINE ENDOWMENTS OF ORIGEN IN
HIS PRESENCE, INTO WHOSE HANDS HE AVOWS
HIMSELF TO HAVE BEEN LED IN A WAY BEYOND
ALL HIS EXPECTATION.

But we, like any of the poor, unfurnished
with these varied specifics [1] — whether as never
having been possessed of them, or, it may be,
as having lost them — are under the necessity
of using, as it were, only charcoal and tiles, that
is to say, those rude and common words and
phrases ; and by means of these, to the best of
our ability, we represent the native dispositions
of our mind, expressing them in such language
as is at our service, and endeavouring to exhibit
the impressions of the figures [2] of our mind, if
not clearly or ornately, yet at least with the faithfulness of a charcoal picture, welcoming gladly
any graceful and eloquent expression which may
present itself from any quarter, although we make
little of such.[3] But, furthermore,[4] there is a third
circumstance which hinders and dissuades me
from this attempt, and which holds me back
much more even than the others, and recom-
mends me to keep silence by all means, — I
allude to the subject itself, which made me indeed ambitious to speak of it, but which now
makes me draw back and delay. For it is my
purpose to speak of one who has indeed the
semblance and repute of being a man, but who
seems, to those who are able to contemplate the
greatness of his intellectual calibre,[5] to be endowed with powers nobler and well-nigh divine.[6]
And it is not his birth or bodily training that I
am about to praise, and that makes me now
delay and procrastinate with an excess of caution. Nor, again, is it his strength or beauty ;
for these form the eulogies of youths, of which
it matters little whether the utterance be worthy
or not.[7] For, to make an oration on matters of
a temporary and fugitive nature, which perish in
many various ways and quickly, and to discourse
of these with all the grandeur and dignity of
great affairs, and with such timorous delays,
would seem a vain and futile procedure.[8] And
certainly, if it had been proposed to me to speak
of any of those things which are useless and
unsubstantial, and such as I should never voluntarily have thought of speaking of, — if, I say, it

had been proposed to me to speak of anything
of that character, my speech would have had
none of this caution or fear, lest in any statement I might seem to come beneath the merit
of the subject. But now, my subject dealing
with that which is most godlike in the man, and
that in him which has most affinity with God,
that which is indeed confined within the limits
of this visible and mortal form, but which strains
nevertheless most ardently after the likeness of
God ; and my object being to make mention
of this, and to put my hand to weightier matters,
and therein also to express my thanksgivings to
the Godhead, in that it has been granted to me
to meet with such a man beyond the expectation of men, — the expectation, verily, not only
of others, but also of my own heart, for I neither
set such a privilege before me at any time, nor
hoped for it ; it being, I say, my object, insignificant and altogether without understanding as
I am, to put my hand to such subjects, it is not
without reason [9] that I shrink from the task, and
hesitate, and desire to keep silence. And, in
truth, to keep silence seems to me to be also the
safe course, lest, with the show of an expression
of thanksgiving, I may chance, in my rashness,
to discourse of noble and sacred subjects in
terms ignoble and paltry and utterly trite, and
thus not only miss attaining the truth, but even,
so far as it depends on me, do it some injury
with those who may believe that it stands in
such a category, when a discourse which is weak
is composed thereon, and is rather calculated to
excite ridicule than to prove itself commensurate in its vigour with the dignity of its themes.
But all that pertains to thee is beyond the touch
of injury and ridicule, O dear soul ; or, much
rather let me say, that the divine herein remains
ever as it is, unmoved and harmed in nothing
by our paltry and unworthy words. Yet I know
not how we shall escape the imputation of boldness and rashness in thus attempting in our folly,
and with little either of intelligence or of preparation, to handle matters which are weighty, and
probably beyond our capacity. And if, indeed,
elsewhere and with others, we had aspired to
make such youthful endeavours in matters like
these, we would surely have been bold and
daring ; nevertheless in such a case our rashness
might not have been ascribed to shamelessness,
in so far as we should not have been making the
bold effort with thee. But now we shall be filling out the whole measure of senselessness, or
rather indeed we have already filled it out, in
venturing with unwashed feet (as the saying
goes) to introduce ourselves to ears into which
the Divine Word Himself — not indeed with
covered feet, as is the case with the general mass

---

[1] φαρμάκων.
[2] χαρακτῆρας τῶν τῆς ψυχῆς τύπων.
[3] ἀσπασάμενοι ἡδέως, ἐπεὶ καὶ περιφρονήσαντες. The passage
is considered by some to be mutilated.
[4] The text is, ἀλλὰ γὰρ ἐκ τρίτων αὖθις ἄλλως κωλύει, etc. For
ἄλλως Hoeschelius gives ἀλλὰ δή. Bengel follows him, and renders
it, sed rursum, tertio loco, aliud est quod prohibet. Delarue
proposes, ἀλλὰ γὰρ ἐν τρίτον αὖθις ἄλλως κωλύει.
[5] τὸ δὲ πολὺ τῆς ἕξεως.
[6] This is the rendering according to the Latin version. The text
is, ἀπεσκευασμένου ἤδη μείζονι παρασκευῇ μεταναστάσεως τῆς πρὸς
τὸ θεῖον. Vossius reads, μετ' ἀναστάσεως.
[7] ὧν ἥττων φροντὶς κατ' ἀξίαν τε καὶ μὴ, λεγομένων.
[8] The text is, μὴ καὶ ψυχρὸν ἢ πέρπερον ᾖ, where, according to
Bengel, μὴ has the force of ut non dicam.

[9] But the text reads, οὐκ εὐλόγως.

of men, and, as it were, under the thick coverings of enigmatical and obscure [1] sayings, but with unsandalled feet (if one may so speak) — has made His way clearly and perspicuously, and in which He now sojourns ; while we, who have but refuse and mud to offer in these human words of ours, have been bold enough to pour them into ears which are practised in hearing only words that are divine and pure. It might indeed suffice us, therefore, to have transgressed thus far ; and now, at least, it might be but right to restrain ourselves, and to advance no further with our discourse. And verily I would stop here most gladly. Nevertheless, as I have once made the rash venture, it may be allowed me first of all to explain the reason under the force of which I have been led into this arduous enterprise, if indeed any pardon can be extended to me for my forwardness in this matter.

ARGUMENT III. — HE IS STIMULATED TO SPEAK OF HIM BY THE LONGING OF A GRATEFUL MIND. TO THE UTMOST OF HIS ABILITY HE THINKS HE OUGHT TO THANK HIM. FROM GOD ARE THE BEGINNINGS OF ALL BLESSINGS ; AND TO HIM ADEQUATE THANKS CANNOT BE RETURNED.

Ingratitude appears to me to be a dire evil ; a dire evil indeed, yea, the direst of evils. For when one has received some benefit, his failing to attempt to make any return by at least the oral expression of thanks, where aught else is beyond his power, marks him out either as an utterly irrational person, or as one devoid of the sense of obligations conferred, or as a man without any memory. And, again, though [2] one is possessed naturally and at once by the sense and the knowledge of benefits received, yet, unless he also carries the memory of these obligations to future days, and offers some evidence of gratitude to the author of the boons, such a person is a dull, and ungrateful, and impious fellow ; and he commits an offence which can be excused neither in the case of the great nor in that of the small : — if we suppose the case of a great and high-minded man not bearing constantly on his lips his great benefits with all gratitude and honour, or that of a small and contemptible man not praising and lauding with all his might one who has been his benefactor, not simply in great services, but also in smaller. Upon the great, therefore, and those who excel in powers of mind, it is incumbent, as out of their greater abundance and larger wealth, to render greater and worthier praise, according to their capacity, to their benefactors. But the humble also, and those in narrow circumstances, it beseems

neither to neglect those who do them service, nor to take their services carelessly, nor to flag in heart as if they could offer nothing worthy or perfect ; but as poor indeed, and yet as of good feeling, and as measuring not the capacity of him whom they honour, but only their own, they ought to pay him honour according to the present measure of their power, — a tribute which will probably be grateful and pleasant to him who is honoured, and in no less consideration with him than it would have been had it been some great and splendid offering, if it is only presented with decided earnestness, and with a sincere mind. Thus is it laid down in the sacred writings,[3] that a certain poor and lowly woman, who was with the rich and powerful that were contributing largely and richly out of their wealth, alone and by herself cast in a small, yea, the very smallest offering, which was, however, all the while her whole substance, and received the testimony of having presented the largest oblation. For, as I judge, the sacred word has not set up the large outward quantity of the substance given, but rather the mind and disposition of the giver, as the standard by which the worth and the magnificence of the offering are to be measured. Wherefore it is not meet even for us by any means to shrink from this duty, through the fear that our thanksgivings be not adequate to our obligations ; but, on the contrary, we ought to venture and attempt everything, so as to offer thanksgivings, if not adequate, at least such as we have it in our power to exhibit, as in due return. And would that our discourse, even though it comes short of the perfect measure, might at least reach the mark in some degree, and be saved from all appearance of ingratitude ! For a persistent silence, maintained under the plausible cover of an inability to say anything worthy of the subject, is a vain and evil thing ; but it is the mark of a good disposition always to make the attempt at a suitable return, even although the power of the person who offers the grateful acknowledgment be inferior to the desert of the subject. For my part, even although I am unable to speak as the matter merits, I shall not keep silence ; but when I have done all that I possibly can, then I may congratulate myself. Be this, then, the method of my eucharistic discourse. To God, indeed, the God of the universe, I shall not think of speaking in such terms : yet is it from Him that all the beginnings of our blessings come ; and with Him consequently is it that the beginning of our thanksgivings, or praises, or laudations, ought to be made. But, in truth, not even though I were to devote myself wholly to that duty, and that, too, not as I now am — to

---

[1] ἀσαφῶν. But Ger. Voss has ἀσφαλῶν, safe.
[2] Reading ὅτῳ, with Hœschelius, Bengel, and the Paris editor, while Voss. reads ὅτι.

[3] Luke xxi. 2.

wit, profane and impure, and mixed up with and stained by every unhallowed [1] and polluting evil — but sincere and as pure as pure may be, and most genuine, and most unsophisticated, and uncontaminated by anything vile ; — not even, I say, though I were thus to devote myself wholly, and with all the purity of the newly born, to this task, should I produce of myself any suitable gift in the way of honour and acknowledgment to the Ruler and Originator of all things, whom neither men separately and individually, nor yet all men in concert, acting with one spirit and one concordant impulse, as though all that is pure were made to meet in one, and all that is diverse from that were turned also to that service, could ever celebrate in a manner worthy of Him. For, in whatsoever measure any man is able to form right and adequate conceptions of His works, and (if such a thing were possible) to speak worthily regarding Him, then, so far as that very capacity is concerned, — a capacity with which he has not been gifted by any other one, but which he has received from Him alone, he cannot possibly find any greater matter of thanksgiving than what is implied in its possession.

ARGUMENT IV. — THE SON ALONE KNOWS HOW TO PRAISE THE FATHER WORTHILY. IN CHRIST AND BY CHRIST OUR THANKSGIVINGS OUGHT TO BE RENDERED TO THE FATHER. GREGORY ALSO GIVES THANKS TO HIS GUARDIAN ANGEL, BECAUSE HE WAS CONDUCTED BY HIM TO ORIGEN.

But let us commit the praises and hymns in honour of the King and Superintendent of all things, the perennial Fount of all blessings, to the hand of Him who, in this matter as in all others, is the Healer of our infirmity, and who alone is able to supply that which is lacking ; to the Champion and Saviour of our souls, His first-born Word, the Maker and Ruler of all things, with whom also alone it is possible, both for Himself and for all, whether privately and individually, or publicly and collectively, to send up to the Father uninterrupted and ceaseless thanksgivings. For as He is Himself the Truth, and the Wisdom, and the Power of the Father of the universe, and He is besides in Him, and is truly and entirely made one with Him, it cannot be that, either through forgetfulness or unwisdom, or any manner of infirmity, such as marks one dissociated from Him, He shall either fail in the power to praise Him, or, while having the power, shall willingly neglect (a supposition which it is not lawful, surely, to indulge) to praise the Father. For He alone is able most perfectly to fulfil the whole meed of honour which is proper to Him, inasmuch as the Father of all things has

made Him one with Himself, and through Him all but completes the circle of His own being objectively,[2] and honours Him with a power in all respects equal to His own, even as also He is honoured ; which position He first and alone of all creatures that exist has had assigned Him, this Only-begotten of the Father, who is in Him, and who is God the Word ; while all others of us are able to express our thanksgiving and our piety only if, in return for all the blessings which proceed to us from the Father, we bring our offerings in simple dependence on Him alone, and thus present the meet oblation of thanksgiving to Him who is the Author of all things, acknowledging also that the only way of piety is in this manner to offer our memorials through Him. Wherefore, in acknowledgment of that ceaseless providence which watches over all of us, alike in the greatest and in the smallest concerns, and which has been sustained even thus far, let this Word [3] be accepted as the worthy and perpetual expression for all thanksgivings and praises, — I mean the altogether perfect and living and verily animate Word of the First Mind Himself. But let this word of ours be taken primarily as an eucharistic address in honour of this sacred personage, who stands alone among all men ; [4] and if I may seek to discourse [5] of aught beyond this, and, in particular, of any of those beings who are not seen, but yet are more godlike, and who have a special care for men, it shall be addressed to that being who, by some momentous decision, had me allotted to him from my boyhood to rule, and rear, and train, — I mean that holy angel of God who fed me from my youth,[6] as says the saint dear to God, meaning thereby his own peculiar one. Though he, indeed, as being himself illustrious, did in these terms designate some angel exalted enough to befit his own dignity (and whether it was some other one, or whether it was perchance the Angel of the Mighty Counsel Himself, the Common Saviour of all, that he received as his own peculiar guardian through his perfection, I do not clearly know), — he, I say, did recognise and praise some superior angel as his own, whosoever that was. But we, in addition to the homage we offer to the Common Ruler of all men, acknowledge and praise that being, whosoever he is, who has been the wonderful guide of our childhood, who in all other matters has been in time past my beneficent tutor and guardian. For this office of tutor and guardian is one which evidently can suit [7] neither

---

[1] παναγεῖ, which in the lexicons is given as bearing only the good sense, *all-hallowed*, but which here evidently is taken in the opposite.

[2] ἐκπεριών in the text, for which Bengel gives ἐκπεριϊών, a word used frequently by this author. In Dorner it is explained as = *going out of Himself in order to embrace and encompass Himself.* See the *Doctrine of the Person of Christ*, A. II. p. 173 (Clark).
[3] λόγος.
[4] [The unformed theological mind of a youth is here betrayed.]
[5] The text gives μελληγορεῖν, for which others read μεγαλληγορεῖν.
[6] Gen. xlviii. 15. [Jacob refers to the Jehovah-Angel.]
[7] The text gives ἐμοί, etc., . . . συμφέρον εἶναι καταφαίνεται. Bengel's idea of the sense is followed in the translation.

me nor any of my friends and kindred; for we are all blind, and see nothing of what is before us, so as to be able to judge of what is right and fitting; but it can suit only him who sees beforehand all that is for the good of our soul: *that angel, I say,* who still at this present time sustains, and instructs, and conducts me; and who, in addition to all these other benefits, has brought me into connection with this man, which, in truth, is the most important of all the services done me. And this, too, he has effected for me, although between myself and that man of whom I discourse there was no kinship of race or blood, nor any other tie, nor any relationship in neighbourhood or country whatsoever; things which are made the ground of friendship and union among the majority of men. But to speak in brief, in the exercise of a truly divine and wise forethought he brought us together, who were unknown to each other, and strangers, and foreigners, separated as thoroughly from each other as intervening nations, and mountains, and rivers can divide man from man, and thus he made good this meeting which has been full of profit to me, having, as I judge, provided beforehand this blessing for me from above from my very birth and earliest upbringing. And in what manner this has been realized it would take long to recount fully, not merely if I were to enter minutely into the whole subject, and were to attempt to omit nothing, but even if, passing many things by, I should purpose simply to mention in a summary way a few of the most important points.

ARGUMENT V. — HERE GREGORY INTERWEAVES THE NARRATIVE OF HIS FORMER LIFE. HIS BIRTH OF HEATHEN PARENTS IS STATED. IN THE FOURTEENTH YEAR OF HIS AGE HE LOSES HIS FATHER. HE IS DEDICATED TO THE STUDY OF ELOQUENCE AND LAW. BY A WONDERFUL LEADING OF PROVIDENCE, HE IS BROUGHT TO ORIGEN.

For my earliest upbringing from the time of my birth onwards was under the hand of my parents; and the manner of life in my father's house was one of error,[1] and of a kind from which no one, I imagine, expected that we should be delivered; nor had I myself the hope, boy as I was, and without understanding, and under a superstitious father.[2] Then followed the loss of my father, and my orphanhood, which[3] perchance was also the beginning of the knowledge of the truth to me. For then it was that I was brought over first to the word of salvation and truth, in what manner I cannot tell, by constraint rather than by voluntary choice. For what power of decision had I then, who was but fourteen years of age? Yet from this very time this sacred Word began somehow to visit me, just at the period when the reason common to all men attained its full function in me; yea, then for the first time did it visit me. And though I thought but little of this in that olden time, yet now at least, as I ponder it, I consider that no small token of the holy and marvellous providence exercised over me is discernible in this concurrence, which was so distinctly marked in the matter of my years, and which provided that all those deeds of error which preceded that age might be ascribed to youth and want of understanding, and that the Holy Word might not be imparted vainly to a soul yet ungifted with the full power of reason; and which secured at the same time that when the soul now became endowed with that power, though not gifted with the divine and pure reason,[4] it might not be devoid at least of that fear which is accordant with this reason, but that the human and the divine reason[5] might begin to act in me at once and together, — the one giving help with a power to me at least inexplicable,[6] though proper to itself, and the other receiving help. And when I reflect on this, I am filled at once with gladness and with terror, while I rejoice indeed in the leading of providence, and yet am also awed by the fear lest, after being privileged with such blessings, I should still in any way fail of the end. But indeed I know not how my discourse has dwelt so long on this matter, desirous as I am to give an account of the wonderful arrangement (of God's providence) in the course that brought me to this man, and anxious as nevertheless I formerly was to pass with few words to the matters which follow in their order, not certainly imagining that I could render to him who thus dealt with me that 'tribute of praise, or gratitude, or piety which is due to him (for, were we to designate our discourse in such terms, while yet we said nothing worthy of the theme, we might seem chargeable with arrogance), but simply with the view of offering what may be called a plain narrative or confession, or whatever other humble title may be given it. It seemed good to the only one of my parents who survived to care for me — my mother, namely — that, being already under instruction in those other branches in which boys not ignobly born and nurtured are usually trained, I should attend also a teacher of public speaking, in the hope that I too should become a public speaker. And accordingly I did attend such a teacher; and those who could judge in that department then declared that I should in a short period be a public speaker. I for my own part know not how to pronounce on that, neither

---

[1] τὰ πάτρια ἔθη τὰ πεπλανημένα.
[2] [The force of the original is not opprobrious.]
[3] Reading ἢ δή. Others give ἢ δή: others, ἤδη; and the conjecture ἢ ἤβη, "or my youth," is also made.
[4] λόγου.
[5] Word.
[6] The text, however, gives ἀλέκτρῳ.

should I desire to do so ; for there was no apparent ground for that gift then, nor was there as yet any foundation for those forces [1] which were capable of bringing me to it. But that divine conductor and true curator, ever so watchful, when my friends were not thinking of such a step, and when I was not myself desirous of it, came and suggested (an extension of my studies) to one of my teachers under whose charge I had been put, with a view to instruction in the Roman tongue, not in the expectation that I was to reach the completest mastery of that tongue, but only that I might not be absolutely ignorant of it ; and this person happened also to be not altogether unversed in laws. Putting the idea, therefore, into this teacher's mind,[2] he set me to learn in a thorough way the laws of the Romans by his help. And that man took up this charge zealously with me ; and I, on my side, gave myself to it — more, however, to gratify the man, than as being myself an admirer of the study. And when he got me as his pupil, he began to teach me with all enthusiasm. And he said one thing, which has proved to me the truest of all his sayings, to wit, that my education in the laws would be my greatest *viaticum* [3] — for thus he phrased it — whether I aspired to be one of the public speakers who contend in the courts of justice, or preferred to belong to a different order. Thus did he express himself, intending his word to bear simply on things human ; but to me it seems that he was moved to that utterance by a diviner impulse than he himself supposed. For when, willingly or unwillingly, I was becoming well instructed in these laws, at once bonds, as it were, were cast upon my movements, and cause and occasion for my journeying to these parts arose from the city Berytus, which is a city not far distant [4] from this territory, somewhat Latinized,[5] and credited with being a school for these legal studies. And this revered man coming from Egypt, from the city of Alexandria, where previously he happened to have his home, was moved by other circumstances to change his residence to this place, as if with the express object of meeting us. And for my part, I cannot explain the reasons of these incidents, and I shall willingly pass them by. This however is certain, that as yet no necessary occasion for my coming to this place and meeting with this man was afforded by my purpose to learn our laws, since I had it in my power also to repair to the city of Rome itself.[6] How, then, was this effected?

The then governor of Palestine suddenly took possession of a friend of mine, namely my sister's husband, and separated him from his wife, and carried him off here against his will, in order to secure his help, and have him associated with him in the labours of the government of the country ; for he was a person skilled in law, and perhaps is still so *employed*. After he had gone with him, however, he had the good fortune in no long time to have his wife sent for, and to receive her again, from whom, against his will, and to his grievance, he had been separated. And thus he chanced also to draw us along with her to that same place. For when we were minded to travel, I know not where, but certainly to any other place rather than this, a soldier suddenly came upon the scene, bearing a letter of instructions for us to escort and protect our sister in her restoration to her husband, and to offer ourselves also as companion to her on the journey ; in which we had the opportunity of doing a favour to our relative, and most of all to our sister (so that she might not have to address herself to the journey either in any unbecoming manner, or with any great fear or hesitation), while at the same time our other friends and connections thought well of it, and made it out to promise no slight advantage, as we could thus visit the city of Berytus, and carry out there with all diligence [7] our studies in the laws. Thus all things moved me thither, — my sense of duty [8] to my sister, my own studies, and over and above these, the soldier (for it is right also to mention this), who had with him a larger supply of public vehicles than the case demanded, and more cheques [9] than could be required for our sister alone. These were the apparent reasons for our journey ; but the secret and yet truer reasons were these, — our opportunity of fellowship with this man, our instruction through that man's means [10] in the truth [11] concerning the Word, and the profit of our soul for its salvation. These were the real causes that brought us here, blind and ignorant, as we were, as to the way of securing our salvation. Wherefore it was not that soldier, but a certain divine companion and beneficent conductor and guardian, ever leading us in safety through the whole of this present life, as through a long journey, that carried us past other places, and Berytus in especial, which city at that time we seemed most bent on reaching,

---

[1] αἰτιῶν, causes.
[2] Reading τούτῳ ἐπὶ νοῦν βαλών.
[3] ἐφόδιον.
[4] The text is ἀποχέουσα. Hœschelius gives ἀπέχουσα.
[5] ῾Ρωμαικωτέρα πῶς.
[6] The text is, οὐδὲν οὕτως ἀναγκαῖον ἦν ὅσον ἐπὶ τοῖς νόμοις ἡμῶν, δυνατὸν ὄν καὶ ἐπὶ τὴν ῾Ρωμαίων ἀποδημῆσαι πόλιν. Bengel takes ὅσον as παρέλκον. Migne renders, *nullam ei fuisse necessitatem huc veniendi, discendi leges causa, siquidem Romam posset*

proficisci. Sirmondus makes it, *nulla causa adeo necessaria erat qua possem per leges nostras ad Romanorum civitatem proficisci.*
[7] The text gives ἐκπονήσαντες. Casaubon reads ἐκποιήσοντες.
[8] εὔλογον.
[9] σύμβολα.
[10] δι᾿ αὐτοῦ. Bengel understands this to refer to the *soldier*.
[11] The text is, τὴν ἀληθῆ δι᾿ αὐτοῦ περὶ τὰ τοῦ λόγου μαθήματα. Bengel takes this as an ellipsis, like τὴν ἑαυτοῦ, τὴν ἐμὴν μίαν, and similar phrases, γνώμην or ὁδόν, or some such word, being supplied. Casaubon conjectures καὶ ἀληθῆ, for which Bengel would prefer τὰ ἀληθῆ.

and brought us hither and settled us here, disposing and directing all things, until by any means he might bind us in a connection with this man who was to be the author of the greater part of our blessings. And he who came in such wise, that divine angel, gave over this charge[1] to him, and did, if I may so speak, perchance take his rest here, not indeed under the pressure of labour or exhaustion of any kind (for the generation of those divine ministers knows no weariness), but as having committed us to the hand of a man who would fully discharge the whole work of care and guardianship within his power.

ARGUMENT VI. — THE ARTS BY WHICH ORIGEN STUDIES TO KEEP GREGORY AND HIS BROTHER ATHENODORUS WITH HIM, ALTHOUGH IT WAS ALMOST AGAINST THEIR WILL ; AND THE LOVE BY WHICH BOTH ARE TAKEN CAPTIVE. OF PHILOSOPHY, THE FOUNDATION OF PIETY. WITH THE VIEW OF GIVING HIMSELF THEREFORE WHOLLY TO THAT STUDY, GREGORY IS WILLING TO GIVE UP FATHERLAND, PARENTS, THE PURSUIT OF LAW, AND EVERY OTHER DISCIPLINE. OF THE SOUL AS THE FREE PRINCIPLE. THE NOBLER PART DOES NOT DESIRE TO BE UNITED WITH THE INFERIOR, BUT THE INFERIOR WITH THE NOBLER.

And from the very first day of his receiving us (which day was, in truth, the first day to me, and the most precious of all days, if I may so speak, since then for the first time the true Sun began to rise upon me), while we, like some wild creatures of the fields, or like fish, or some sort of birds that had fallen into the toils or nets, and were endeavouring to slip out again and escape, were bent on leaving him, and making off for Berytus[2] or our native country, he studied by all means to associate us closely with him, contriving all kinds of arguments, and putting every rope in motion (as the proverb goes), and bringing all his powers to bear on that object. With that intent he lauded the lovers of philosophy with large laudations and many noble utterances, declaring that those only live a life truly worthy of reasonable creatures who aim at living an upright life, and who seek to know first of all themselves, what manner of persons they are, and then the things that are truly good, which man ought to strive after, and then the things that are really evil, from which man ought to flee. And then he reprehended ignorance and all the ignorant : and there are many such, who, like brute cattle,[3] are blind in mind, and have no understanding even of what they are, and are as far astray as though they were wholly

void of reason, and neither know themselves what is good and what is evil, nor care at all to learn it from others, but toil feverishly in quest of wealth, and glory, and such honours as belong to the crowd, and bodily comforts, and go distraught about things like these, as if they were the real good. And as though such objects were worth much, yea, worth all else, they prize the things themselves, and the arts by which they can acquire them, and the different lines of life which give scope for their attainment, — the military profession, to wit, and the juridical, and the study of the laws. And with earnest and sagacious words he told us that these are the objects that enervate us, when we despise that reason which ought to be the true master within us.[4] I cannot recount at present all the addresses of this kind which he delivered to us, with the view of persuading us to take up the pursuit of philosophy. Nor was it only for a single day that he thus dealt with us, but for many days; and, in fact, as often as we were in the habit of going to him at the outset ; and we were pierced by his argumentation as with an arrow from the very first occasion of our hearing him[5] (for he was possessed of a rare combination of a certain sweet grace and persuasiveness, along with a strange power of constraint), though we still wavered and debated the matter undecidedly with ourselves, holding so far by the pursuit of philosophy, without however being brought thoroughly over to it, while somehow or other we found ourselves quite unable to withdraw from it conclusively, and thus were always drawn towards him by the power of his reasonings, as by the force of some superior necessity. For he asserted further that there could be no genuine piety towards the Lord of all in the man who despised this gift of philosophy, — a gift which man alone of all the creatures of the earth has been deemed honourable and worthy enough to possess, and one which every man whatsoever, be he wise or be he ignorant, reasonably embraces, who has not utterly lost the power of thought by some mad distraction of mind. He asserted, then, as I have said, that it was not possible (to speak correctly) for any one to be truly pious who did not philosophize. And thus he continued to do with us, until, by pouring in upon us many such argumentations, one after the other, he at last carried us fairly off somehow or other by a kind of divine power, like people with his reasonings, and established us (in the practice of philosophy), and set us down without the power of movement, as it were, beside

---

[1] οἰκονομίαν.

[2] [I think Lardner's inclination to credit Gregory with some claim to be an *alumnus* of Berytus, is very fairly sustained.]

[3] θρεμμάτων.

[4] The text here is, ταῦθ' ἅπερ ἡμᾶς ἀνέσειε, μάλιστα λέγων καὶ μάλα τεχνικῶς, τοῦ κυριωτάτου, φησί, τῶν ἐν ἡμῖν λόγων, ἀμελήσαντας.

[5] The text gives ἐκ πρώτης ἡλικίας, which Bengel takes to be an error for the absolute ἐκ πρώτης, to which ἡμέρας would be supplied. Casaubon and Rhodomanus read ὁμιλίας for ἡλικίας.

himself by his arts. Moreover, the stimulus of friendship was also brought to bear upon us, — a stimulus, indeed, not easily withstood, but keen and most effective, — the argument of a kind and affectionate disposition, which showed itself benignantly in his words when he spoke to us and associated with us. For he did not aim merely at getting round us by any kind of reasoning ; but his desire was, with a benignant, and affectionate, and most benevolent mind, to save us, and make us partakers in the blessings that flow from philosophy, and most especially also in those other gifts which the Deity has bestowed on him above most men, or, as we may perhaps say, above all men of our own time. I mean the power that teaches us piety, the word of salvation, that comes to many, and subdues to itself all whom it visits : for there is nothing that shall resist it, inasmuch as it is and shall be itself the king of all ; although as yet it is hidden, and is not recognised, whether with ease or with difficulty, by the common crowd, in such wise that, when interrogated respecting it, they should be able to speak intelligently about it. And thus, like some spark lighting upon our inmost soul, love was kindled and burst into flame within us, — a love at once to the Holy Word, the most lovely object of all, who attracts all irresistibly toward Himself by His unutterable beauty, and to this man, His friend and advocate. And being most mightily smitten by this love, I was persuaded to give up all those objects or pursuits which seem to us befitting, and among others even my boasted jurisprudence, — yea, my very fatherland and friends, both those who were present with me then, and those from whom I had parted. And in my estimation there arose but one object dear and worth desire, — to wit, philosophy, and that master of philosophy, this inspired man. "And the soul of Jonathan was knit with David." [1] This word, indeed, I did not read till afterwards in the sacred Scriptures ; but I felt it before that time, not less clearly than it is written : for, in truth, it reached me then by the clearest of all revelations. For it was not simply Jonathan that was knit with David ; but those things were knit together which are the ruling powers in man — their souls, — those objects which, even though all the things which are apparent and ostensible in man are severed, cannot by any skill be forced to a severance when they themselves are unwilling. For the soul is free, and cannot be coerced by any means, not even though one should confine it and keep guard over it in some secret prison-house. For wherever the intelligence is, there it is also of its own nature and by the first reason. And if it seems to you to be in a kind of prison-house, it

is represented as there to you by a sort of second reason. But for all that, it is by no means precluded from subsisting anywhere according to its own determination ; nay, rather it is both able to be, and is reasonably believed to be, there alone and altogether, wheresoever and in connection with what things soever those actions which are proper only to it are in operation. Wherefore, what I experienced has been most clearly declared in this very short statement, that "the soul of Jonathan was knit with the soul of David ; " objects which, as I said, cannot by any means be forced to a separation against their will, and which of their own inclination certainly will not readily choose it. Nor is it, in my opinion, in the inferior subject, who is changeful and very prone to vary in purpose, and in whom singly there has been no capacity of union at first, that the power of loosing the sacred bonds of this affection rests, but rather in the nobler one, who is constant and not readily shaken, and through whom it has been possible to tie these bonds and to fasten this sacred knot. Therefore it is not the soul of David that was knit by the divine word with the soul of Jonathan ; but, on the contrary, the soul of the latter, who was the inferior, is said to be thus affected and knit with the soul of David. For the nobler object would not choose to be knit with one inferior, inasmuch as it is sufficient for itself ; but the inferior object, as standing in need of the help which the nobler can give, ought properly to be knit with the nobler, and fitted dependently to it : so that this latter, retaining still its sufficiency in itself, might sustain no loss by its connection with the inferior ; and that that which is of itself without order [2] being now united and fitted harmoniously with the nobler, might, without any detriment done, be perfectly subdued to the nobler by the constraints of such bonds. Wherefore, to apply the bonds is the part of the superior, and not of the inferior ; but to be knit to the other is the part of the inferior, and this too in such a manner that it shall possess no power of loosing itself from these bonds. And by a similar constraint, then, did this David of ours once gird us to himself ; and he holds us now, and has held us ever since that time, so that, even though we desired it, we could not loose ourselves from his bonds. And hence it follows that, even though we were to depart, he would not release this soul of mine, which, as the Holy Scripture puts it, he holds knit so closely with himself.

ARGUMENT VII. — THE WONDERFUL SKILL WITH WHICH ORIGEN PREPARES GREGORY AND ATHENODORUS FOR PHILOSOPHY. THE INTELLECT OF

---

[1] 1 Sam. xviii. 1.

[2] ἄτακτον.

EACH IS EXERCISED FIRST IN LOGIC, AND THE MERE ATTENTION TO WORDS IS CONTEMNED.

But after he had thus carried us captive at the very outset, and had shut us in, as it were, on all sides, and when what was best[1] had been accomplished by him, and when it seemed good to us to remain with him for a time, then he took us in hand, as a skilled husbandman may take in hand some field unwrought, and altogether unfertile, and sour, and burnt up, and hard as a rock, and rough, or, it may be, one not utterly barren or unproductive, but rather, perchance, by nature very productive, though then waste and neglected, and stiff and untractable with thorns and wild shrubs ; or as a gardener may take in hand some plant which is wild indeed, and which yields no cultivated fruits, though it may not be absolutely worthless, and on finding it thus, may, by his skill in gardening, bring some cultivated shoot and graft it in, by making a fissure in the middle, and then bringing the two together, and binding the one to the other, until the sap in each shall flow in one stream,[2] and they shall both grow with the same nurture : for one may often see a tree of a mixed and worthless[3] species thus rendered productive in spite of its past barrenness, and made to rear the fruits of the good olive on wild roots ; or one may see a wild plant saved from being altogether profitless by the skill of a careful gardener ; or, once more, one may see a plant which otherwise is one both of culture and of fruitfulness, but which, through the want of skilled attendance, has been left unpruned and unwatered and waste, and which is thus choked by the mass of superfluous shoots suffered to grow out of it at random,[4] yet brought to discharge its proper function in germination,[5] and made to bear the fruit whose production was formerly hindered by the superfluous growth.[6] In suchwise, then, and with such a disposition did he receive us at first; and surveying us, as it were, with a husbandman's skill, and gauging us thoroughly, and not confining his notice to those things only which are patent to the eye of all, and which are looked upon in open light, but penetrating into us more deeply, and probing what is most inward in us, he put us to the question, and made propositions to us, and listened to us in our replies ; and whenever he thereby detected anything in us not wholly fruitless and profitless and waste, he set about clearing the soil, and turning it up and irrigating it, and putting all things in movement, and brought his whole skill and care to bear on us, and wrought upon our mind. And thorns and thistles,[7] and every kind of wild herb or plant which our mind (so unregulated and precipitate in its own action) yielded and produced in its uncultured luxuriance and native wildness, he cut out and thoroughly removed by the processes of refutation and prohibition ; sometimes assailing us in the genuine Socratic fashion, and again upsetting us by his argumentation whenever he saw us getting restive under him, like so many unbroken steeds, and springing out of the course and galloping madly about at random, until with a strange kind of persuasiveness and constraint he reduced us to a state of quietude under him by his discourse, which acted like a bridle in our mouth. And that was at first an unpleasant position for us, and one not without pain, as he dealt with persons who were unused to it, and still all untrained to submit to reason, when he plied us with his argumentations ; and yet he purged us by them. And when he had made us adaptable, and had prepared us successfully for the reception of the words of truth, then, further, as though we were now a soil well wrought and soft, and ready to impart growth to the seeds cast into it, he dealt liberally with us, and sowed the good seed in season, and attended to all the other cares of the good husbandry, each in its own proper season. And whenever he perceived any element of infirmity or baseness in our mind (whether it was of that character by nature, or had become thus gross through the excessive nurture of the body), he pricked it with his discourses, and reduced it by those delicate words and turns of reasoning which, although at first the very simplest, are gradually evolved one after the other, and skilfully wrought out, until they advance to a sort of complexity which can scarce be mastered or unfolded, and which cause us to start up, as it were, out of sleep, and teach us the art of holding always by what is immediately before one, without ever making any slip by reason either of length or of subtlety. And if there was in us anything of an injudicious and precipitate tendency, whether in the way of assenting to all that came across us, of whatever character the objects might be, and even though they proved false, or in the way of often withstanding other things, even though they were spoken truthfully, — that, too, he brought under discipline in us by those delicate reasonings already mentioned, and by others of like kind (for this branch of philosophy is of varied form), and accustomed us not to throw in our testimony at one time, and again to refuse it, just at random, and as chance impelled, but to give it only after careful examination not only into things mani-

---

1 το πλεῖον.
2 The text gives συμβλύσαντα ὡς, for which Casaubon proposes συμφύσαντα εἰς ἕν, or ὡς ἕν. Bengel suggests συμβρύσαντα ὡς ἕν.
3 νόθον.
4 The text gives ἐκεῖ, for which Hœschelius and Bengel read εἰκῆ.
5 τελειοῦυθαι δὲ τῇ βλάστῃ.
6 ὑπ' ἀλλήλων.

7 τριβόλους.

fest, but also into those that are secret.[1] For many things which are in high repute of themselves, and honourable in appearance, have found entrance through fair words into our ears, as though they were true, while yet they were hollow and false, and have borne off and taken possession of the suffrage of truth at our hand, and then, no long time afterwards, they have been discovered to be corrupt and unworthy of credit, and deceitful borrowers of the garb of truth ; and have thus too easily exposed us as men who are ridiculously deluded, and who bear their witness inconsiderately to things which ought by no means to have won it. And, on the contrary, other things which are really honourable and the reverse of impositions, but which have not been expressed in plausible statements, and thus have the appearance of being paradoxical and most incredible, and which have been rejected as false on their own showing, and held up undeservedly to ridicule, have afterwards, on careful investigation and examination, been discovered to be the truest of all things, and wholly incontestable, though for a time spurned and reckoned false. Not simply, then, by dealing with things patent and prominent, which are sometimes delusive and sophistical, but also by teaching us to search into things within us, and to put them all individually to the test, lest any of them should give back a hollow sound, and by instructing us to make sure of these inward things first of all, he trained us to give our assent to outward things only then and thus, and to express our opinion on all these severally. In this way, that capacity of our mind which deals critically with words and reasonings, was educated in a rational manner ; not according to the judgments of illustrious rhetoricians — whatever Greek or foreign honour appertains to that title [2] — for theirs is a discipline of little value and no necessity : but in accordance with that which is most needful for all, whether Greek or outlandish, whether wise or illiterate, and, in fine, not to make a long statement by going over every profession and pursuit separately, in accordance with that which is most indispensable for all men, whatever manner of life they have chosen, if it is indeed the care and interest of all who have to converse on any subject whatever with each other, to be protected against deception.

ARGUMENT VIII. — THEN IN DUE SUCCESSION HE INSTRUCTS THEM IN PHYSICS, GEOMETRY, AND ASTRONOMY.

Nor did he confine his efforts merely to that form of the mind which it is the lot of the dialectics to regulate ; [3] but he also took in hand that humble capacity of mind, (which shows itself) in our amazement at the magnitude, and the wondrousness, and the magnificent and absolutely wise construction of the world, and in our marvelling in a reasonless way, and in our being overpowered with fear, and in our knowing not, like the irrational creatures, what conclusion to come to. That, too, he aroused and corrected by other studies in natural science, illustrating and distinguishing the various divisions of created objects, and with admirable clearness reducing them to their pristine elements, taking them all up perspicuously in his discourse, and going over the nature of the whole, and of each several section, and discussing the multiform revolution and mutation of things in the world, until he carried us fully along with him under his clear teaching ; and by those reasonings which he had partly learned from others, and partly found out for himself, he filled our minds with a rational instead of an irrational wonder at the sacred economy of the universe, and irreproveable constitution of all things. This is that sublime and heavenly study which is taught by natural philosophy — a science most attractive to all. And what need is there now to speak of the sacred mathematics, viz., geometry, so precious to all and above all controversy, and astronomy, whose course is on high? These different studies he imprinted on our understandings, training us in them, or calling them into our mind, or doing with us something else which I know not how to designate rightly. And the one he presented lucidly as the immutable groundwork and secure foundation of all, namely geometry ; and by the other, namely astronomy, he lifted us up to the things that are highest above us, while he made heaven passable to us by the help of each of these sciences, as though they were ladders reaching the skies.

ARGUMENT IX. — BUT HE IMBUES THEIR MINDS, ABOVE ALL, WITH ETHICAL SCIENCE ; AND HE DOES NOT CONFINE HIMSELF TO DISCOURSING ON THE VIRTUES IN WORD, BUT HE RATHER CONFIRMS HIS TEACHING BY HIS ACTS.

Moreover, as to those things which excel all in importance, and those for the sake of which, above all else, the whole [4] family of the philosophical labours, gathering them like good fruits produced by the varied growths of all the other studies, and of long practised philosophizing, — I mean the divine virtues that concern the moral nature, by which the impulses of the mind have their equable and stable subsistence, — through these, too, he aimed at making us truly proof

---

[1] The words ἀλλὰ κεκρυμμένα are omitted by Hœschelius and Bengel.
[2] εἰ τι Ἑλληνικὸν ἢ βάρβαρόν ἐστι τῇ φωνῇ.

[3] The text is, καὶ μὴ τοῦθ᾽ ὅπερ εἶδος διαλεκτικὴ κατορθοῦν μόνη εἴληχε.
[4] πᾶν τὸ φιλόσοφον. Hœschelius and Bengel read πῶς, etc.

against grief and disquietude under the pressure of all ills, and at imparting to us a well-disciplined and stedfast and religious spirit, so that we might be in all things veritably blessed. And this he toiled at effecting by pertinent discourses, of a wise and soothing tendency, and very often also by the most cogent addresses touching our moral dispositions, and our modes of life. Nor was it only by words, but also by deeds, that he regulated in some measure our inclinations, — to wit, by that very contemplation and observation of the impulses and affections of the mind, by the issue of which most especially the mind is wont to be reduced to a right estate from one of discord, and to be restored to a condition of judgment and order out of one of confusion. So that, beholding itself as in a mirror (and I may say specifically, viewing, on the one hand, the very beginnings and roots of evil in it, and all that is reasonless within it, from which spring up all absurd affections and passions; and, on the other hand, all that is truly excellent and reasonable within it, under the sway of which it remains proof against injury and perturbation in itself [1], and then scrutinizing carefully the things thus discovered to be in it), it might cast out all those which are the growth of the inferior part, and which waste our powers [2] through intemperance, or hinder and choke them through depression, — such things as pleasures and lusts, or pains and fears, and the whole array of ills that accompany these different species of evil. I say that thus it might cast them out and make away with them, by coping with them while yet in their beginnings and only just commencing their growth, and not leaving them to wax in strength even by a short delay, but destroying and rooting them out at once; while, at the same time, it might foster all those things which are really good, and which spring from the nobler part, and might preserve them by nursing them in their beginnings, and watching carefully over them until they should reach their maturity. For it is thus (he used to say) that the heavenly virtues will ripen in the soul: to wit, prudence, which first of all is able to judge of those very motions in the mind at once from the things themselves, and by the knowledge which accrues to it of things outside of us, whatever such there may be, both good and evil; and temperance, the power that makes the right selection among these things in their beginnings; and righteousness, which assigns what is just to each; and that virtue which is the conserver of them all — fortitude. And therefore he did not accustom us to a mere profession in words, as that prudence, for instance, is the knowledge [3] of good and evil, or of what ought

to be done, and what ought not: for that would be indeed a vain and profitless study, if there was simply the doctrine without the deed; and worthless would that prudence be, which, without doing the things that ought to be done, and without turning men away from those that ought not to be done, should be able merely to furnish the knowledge of these things to those who possessed her, — though many such persons come under our observation. Nor, again, did he content himself with the mere assertion that temperance is simply the knowledge of what ought to be chosen and what ought not; though the other schools of philosophers do not teach even so much as that, and especially the more recent, who are so forcible and vigorous in words (so that I have often been astonished at them, when they sought to demonstrate that there is the same virtue in God and in men, and that upon earth, in particular, the wise man is equal [4] to God), and yet are incapable of delivering the truth as to prudence, so that one shall do the things which are dictated by prudence, or the truth as to temperance, so that one shall choose the things he has learned by it; and the same holds good also of their treatment of righteousness and fortitude. Not thus, however, in mere words only did this teacher go over the truths concerning the virtues with us; but he incited us much more to the practice of virtue, and stimulated us by the deeds he did more than by the doctrines he taught.

ARGUMENT X. — HENCE THE MERE WORD-SAGES ARE CONFUTED, WHO SAY AND YET ACT NOT.

Now I beg of the philosophers of this present time, both those whom I have known personally myself, and those of whom I have heard by report from others, and I beg also of all other men, that they take in good part the statements I have just made. And let no one suppose that I have expressed myself thus, either through simple friendship toward that man, or through hatred toward the rest of the philosophers; for if there is any one inclined to be an admirer of them for their discourses, and wishful to speak well of them, and pleased at hearing the most honourable mention made of them by others, I myself am the man. Nevertheless, those facts (to which I have referred) are of such a nature as to bring upon the very name of philosophy the last degree of ridicule almost from the great mass of men; and I might almost say that I would choose to be altogether unversed in it, rather than learn any of the things which these men profess, with whom I thought it good no longer to associate myself in this life, — though in that, it may be, I formed an incorrect judgment. But I say that no one should suppose

---

[1] The text gives ὑφ᾽ ἑαυτῆς, for which Bengel reads ἐφ᾽ ἑαυτῆς.
[2] ἐκχέουσα ἡμᾶς.
[3] ἐπιστήμη, science.

[4] τὰ πρῶτα Θεῷ ἴσον εἶναι τὸν σοφὸν ἄνθρωπον.

that I make these statements at the mere prompt-
ing of a zealous regard for the praise of this
man, or under the stimulus of any existing ani-
mosity [1] towards other philosophers. But let all
be assured that I say even less than his deeds
merit, lest I should seem to be indulging in
adulation ; and that I do not seek out studied
words and phrases, and cunning means of laudation — I who could never of my own will, even
when I was a youth, and learning the popular
style of address under a professor of the art of
public speaking, bear to utter a word of praise,
or pass any encomium on any one which was not
genuine. Wherefore on the present occasion,
too, I do not think it right, in proposing to
myself the task simply of commending him, to
magnify him at the cost of the reprobation of
others. And, in good sooth,[2] I should speak
only to the man's injury, if, with the view of
having something grander to say of him, I should
compare his blessed life with the failings of
others. We are not, however, so senseless.[3]
But I shall testify simply to what has come within my own experience, apart from all ill-judged
comparisons and trickeries in words.

ARGUMENT XI. — ORIGEN IS THE FIRST AND THE
    ONLY ONE THAT EXHORTS GREGORY TO ADD TO
    HIS ACQUIREMENTS THE STUDY OF PHILOSOPHY,
    AND OFFERS HIM IN A CERTAIN MANNER AN
    EXAMPLE IN HIMSELF. OF JUSTICE, PRUDENCE,
    TEMPERANCE, AND FORTITUDE. THE MAXIM,
    KNOW THYSELF.

He was also the first and only man that urged
me to study the philosophy of the Greeks, and
persuaded me by his own moral example both
to hear and to hold by the doctrine of morals,
while as yet I had by no means been won over
to that, so far as other philosophers were concerned (I again acknowledge it), — not rightly
so, indeed, but unhappily, as I may say without
exaggeration, for me. I did not, however, associate with many at first, but only with some few
who professed to be teachers, though, in good
sooth, they all established their philosophy only
so far as words went.[4] This man, however, was
the first that induced me to philosophize by his
words, as he pointed the exhortation by deeds
before he gave it in words, and did not merely
recite well-studied sentences ; nay, he did not
deem it right to speak on the subject at all, but
with a sincere mind, and one bent on striving
ardently after the practical accomplishment of
the things expressed, and he endeavoured all the
while to show himself in character like the man

whom he describes in his discourses as the person who shall lead a noble life, and he ever exhibited (in himself), I would say, the pattern of
the wise man. But as our discourse at the outset proposed to deal with the truth, and not with
vain-glorious language,[5] I shall not speak of him
now as the exemplar of the wise man. And
yet, if I chose to speak thus of him, I should
not be far astray from the truth.[6] Nevertheless,
I pass that by at present. I shall not speak of
him as a perfect pattern, but as one who vehemently desires to imitate the perfect pattern,
and strives after it with zeal and earnestness,
even beyond the capacity of men, if I may so
express myself ; and who labours, moreover, also
to make us, who are so different,[7] of like character with himself, not mere masters and appre-
henders of the bald doctrines concerning the
impulses of the soul, but masters and appre-
henders of these impulses themselves. For he
pressed[8] us on both to deed and to doctrine,
and carried us along by that same view and
method,[9] not merely into a small section of each
virtue, but rather into the whole, if mayhap we
were able to take it in. And he constrained us
also, if I may so speak, to practise righteousness
on the ground of the personal action of the soul
itself,[10] which he persuaded us to study, drawing
us off from the officious anxieties of life, and
from the turbulence of the forum, and raising us
to the nobler vocation of looking into ourselves,
and dealing with the things that concern ourselves in truth. Now, that this is to practise
righteousness, and that this is the true righteousness, some also of our ancient philosophers have
asserted (expressing it as the *personal action*, I
think), and have affirmed that this is more profitable for blessedness, both to the men themselves
and to those who are with them,[11] if indeed it
belongs to this virtue to recompense according

---

[1] φιλοτιμία, for which φιλονεικία is read.
[2] The text is, ἢ κακῶν ἂν ἔλεγον, etc. The Greek ἢ and the
Latin *aut* are found sometimes thus with a force bordering on that
of *alioqui*.
[3] ἀφραίνομεν. The Paris editor would read ἀφραίνω μέν.
[4] ἀλλὰ γὰρ πᾶσι μέχρι ῥημάτων τὸ φιλοσοφεῖν στήσασιν.

[5] The text is, ἀλλ᾽ ἐπεὶ ἀλήθειαν ἡμῖν, οὐ κομψείαν ἐπηγγείλατο
ὁ λόγος ἄνωθεν. The Latin rendering is, *sed quia veritatem nobis,
non pompam et ornatum promisit oratio in exordio.*
[6] The text is, καίτοι γε εἰπεῖν ἐθέλων εἶναι τε ἀληθές. Bengel
takes the τε as pleonastic, or as an error for the article, τ᾽ ἀληθές. The
εἶναι in ἐθέλων εἶναι he takes to be the use of the infinitive which
occurs in such phrases as τὴν πρώτην εἶναι, *initio*, ἐκὼν εἶναι, *libenter*, τὸ δὲ νῦν εἶναι, *nunc vero*, etc.; and, giving ἐθέλων the sense
of μέλλων, makes the whole = And yet I shall speak thus.
[7] The text is, καὶ ἡμᾶς ἑτέρους. The phrase may be, as it is
given above, a delicate expression of difference, or it may perhaps
be an elegant redundancy, like the French *à nous autres*. Others
read, καὶ ἡμᾶς καὶ ἑτέρους.
[8] The reading in the text gives, οὐ λόγων ἐγκρατεῖς καὶ ἐπιστήμονας τῶν περὶ ὁρμῶν, τῶν δὲ ὁρμῶν αὐτῶν· ἐπὶ τὰ ἔργα καὶ λόγους
ἄγχων, etc. Others would arrange the whole passage differently,
thus: περὶ ὁρμῶν, τῶν δὲ ὁρμῶν αὐτῶν ἐπὶ τὰ ἔργα καὶ τοὺς λόγους
ἄγχων. Καί, etc. Hence Sirmondus renders it, *a motibus ipsis ad
opera etiam sermones*, reading also ἄγων apparently. Rhodomanus
gives, *impulsionum ipsarum et opera et verba ignavi et negli-
gentes*, reading evidently ἀργῶν. Bengel solves the difficulty by
taking the first clause as equivalent to οὐ λόγων ἐγκρατεῖς καὶ ἐπιο-
τήμονας . . . αὐτῶν τῶν ὁρμῶν ἐγκρατεῖς καὶ ἐπιστήμονας. We
have adopted this as the most evident sense. Thus ἄγχων is retained unchanged, and is taken as a parallel to the following participle ἐπιφέρων, and as bearing, therefore, a meaning something like
that of ἀναγκάζων. See Bengel's note in Migne.
[9] θεωρία.
[10] διὰ τὴν ἰδιοπραγίαν τῆς ψυχῆς, perhaps just "the private life."
[11] ἑαυτοῖς τε καὶ τοῖς προσιοῦσιν.

to desert, and to assign to each his own. For what else could be supposed to be so proper to the soul? Or what could be so worthy of it, as to exercise a care over itself, not gazing outwards, or busying itself with alien matters, or, to speak shortly, doing the worst injustice to itself, but turning its attention inwardly upon itself, rendering its own due to itself, and acting thereby righteously?[1] To practise righteousness after this fashion, therefore, he impressed upon us, if I may so speak, by a sort of force. And he educated us to prudence none the less, — teaching to be at home with ourselves, and to desire and endeavour to know ourselves, which indeed is the most excellent achievement of philosophy, the thing that is ascribed also to the most prophetic of spirits[2] as the highest argument of wisdom — the precept, *Know thyself*. And that this is the genuine function of prudence, and that such is the heavenly prudence, is affirmed well by the ancients; for in this there is one virtue common to God and to man; while the soul is exercised in beholding itself as in a mirror, and reflects the divine mind in itself, if it is worthy of such a relation, and traces out a certain inexpressible method for the attaining of a kind of apotheosis. And in correspondence with this come also the virtues of temperance and fortitude: temperance, indeed, in conserving this very prudence which must be in the soul that knows itself, if that is ever its lot (for this temperance, again, surely means just a sound prudence):[3] and fortitude, in keeping stedfastly by all the duties[4] which have been spoken of, without falling away from them, either voluntarily or under any force, and in keeping and holding by all that has been laid down. For he teaches that this virtue acts also as a kind of preserver, maintainer, and guardian.

ARGUMENT XII. — GREGORY DISALLOWS ANY ATTAIN-
MENT OF THE VIRTUES ON HIS PART. PIETY IS
BOTH THE BEGINNING AND THE END, AND THUS
IT IS THE PARENT OF ALL THE VIRTUES.

It is true, indeed, that in consequence of our dull and sluggish nature, he has not yet succeeded in making us righteous, and prudent, and temperate, or manly, although he has laboured zealously on us. For we are neither in real possession of any virtue whatsoever, either human or divine, nor have we ever made any near approach to it, but we are still far from it. And these are very great and lofty virtues, and none of them may be assumed by any common person,[5] but only by one whom God inspires with the power. We are also by no means so favourably constituted for them by nature, neither do we yet profess ourselves to be worthy of reaching them; for through our listlessness and feebleness we have not done all these things which ought to be done by those who aspire after what is noblest, and aim at what is perfect. We are not yet therefore either righteous or temperate, or endowed with any of the other virtues. But this admirable man, this friend and advocate of the virtues, has long ago done for us perhaps all that it lay in his power to do for us, in making us lovers of virtue, who should love it with the most ardent affection. And by his own virtue he created in us a love at once for the beauty of righteousness, the golden face of which in truth was shown to us by him; and for prudence, which is worthy of being sought by all; and for the true wisdom, which is most delectable; and for temperance, the heavenly virtue which forms the sound constitution of the soul, and brings peace to all who possess it; and for manliness, that most admirable grace; and for patience, that virtue peculiarly ours;[6] and, above all, for piety, which men rightly designate when they call it the mother of the virtues. For this is the beginning and the end of all the virtues. And beginning with this one, we shall find all the other virtues grow upon us most readily: if, while for ourselves we earnestly aspire after this grace, which every man, be he only not absolutely impious, or a mere pleasure-seeker, ought to acquire for himself, in order to his being a friend of God and a maintainer[7] of His truth, and while we diligently pursue this virtue, we also give heed to the other virtues, in order that we may not approach our God in unworthiness and impurity, but with all virtue and wisdom as our best conductors and most sagacious priests. And the end of all I consider to be nothing but this: By the pure mind make thyself like[8] to God, that thou mayest draw near to Him, and abide in Him.

ARGUMENT XIII. — THE METHOD WHICH ORIGEN
USED IN HIS THEOLOGICAL AND METAPHYSICAL
INSTRUCTIONS. HE COMMENDS THE STUDY OF
ALL WRITERS, THE ATHEISTIC ALONE EXCEPTED.
THE MARVELLOUS POWER OF PERSUASION IN
SPEECH. THE FACILITY OF THE MIND IN GIVING
ITS ASSENT.

And besides all his other patient and laborious efforts, how shall I in words give any account of

---

[1] The text is, τὸ πρὸς ἑαυτὴν εἶναι. Migne proposes either to read ἑαυτούς, or to supply τὴν ψυχήν.
[2] ὁ δὴ καὶ δαιμόνων τῷ μαντικωτάτῳ ἀνατίθεται.
[3] σωφροσύνην, σῶαν τινὰ φρόνησιν, an etymological play.
[4] ἐπιτηδεύσεσιν.
[5] The text is, οὐδὲ τῷ τυχεῖν. Migne suggests οὐδέ τῷ θέμις τυχεῖν = nor is it legitimate for any one to attain them.

[6] The text is, ὑπομονῆς ἡμῶν. Vossius and others omit the ἡμῶν. The Stuttgart editor gives this note: "It does not appear that this should be connected by apposition with ἀνδρείας (manliness). But Gregory, after the four virtues which philosophers define as *cardinal*, adds two which are properly *Christian*, viz., *patience*, and that which is the hinge of all — *piety*."
[7] The word is προήγορον. It may be, as the Latin version puts it, *familiaris*, one in fellowship with God.
[8] ἐξομοιωθῇτι προσελθεῖν. Others read ἐξομοιωθέντα προσελθεῖν.

what he did for us, in instructing us in theology and the devout character? and how shall I enter into the real disposition of the man, and show with what judiciousness and careful preparation he would have us familiarized with all discourse about the Divinity, guarding sedulously against our being in any peril with respect to what is the most needful thing of all, namely, the knowledge of the Cause of all things? For he deemed it right for us to study philosophy in such wise, that we should read with utmost diligence all that has been written, both by the philosophers and by the poets of old, rejecting nothing,[1] and repudiating nothing (for, indeed, we did not yet possess the power of critical discernment), except only the productions of the atheists, who, in their conceits, lapse from the general intelligence of man, and deny that there is either a God or a providence. From these he would have us abstain, because they are not worthy of being read, and because it might chance that the soul within us that is meant for piety might be defiled by listening to words that are contrary to the worship of God. For even those who frequent the temples of piety, as they think them to be, are careful not to touch anything that is profane.[2] He held, therefore, that the books of such men did not merit to be taken at all into the consideration of men who have assumed the practice of piety. He thought, however, that we should obtain and make ourselves familiar with all other writings, neither preferring nor repudiating any one kind, whether it be philosophical discourse or not, whether Greek or foreign, but hearing what all of them have to convey. And it was with great wisdom and sagacity that he acted on this principle, lest any single saying given by the one class or the other should be heard and valued above others as alone true, even though it might not be true, and lest it might thus enter our mind and deceive us, and, in being lodged there by itself alone, might make us its own, so that we should no more have the power to withdraw from it, or wash ourselves clear of it, as one washes out a little wool that has got some colour ingrained in it. For a mighty thing and an energetic is the discourse of man, and subtle with its sophisms, and quick to find its way into the ears, and mould the mind, and impress us with what it conveys; and when once it has taken possession of us, it can win us over to love it as truth; and it holds its place within us even though it be false and deceitful, overmastering us like some enchanter, and retaining as its champion the very man it has deluded. And, on the other hand, the mind of man is withal a thing easily deceived by speech, and very facile in yielding its assent; and, indeed, before it discriminates and inquires into matters in any proper way, it is easily won over, either through its own obtuseness and imbecility, or through the subtlety of the discourse, to give itself up, at random often, all weary of accurate examination, to crafty reasonings and judgments, which are erroneous themselves, and which lead into error those who receive them. And not only so; but if another mode of discourse aims at correcting it, it will neither give it admittance, nor suffer itself to be altered in opinion, because it is held fast by any notion which has previously got possession of it, as though some inexorable tyrant were lording over it.

ARGUMENT XIV. — WHENCE THE CONTENTIONS OF PHILOSOPHERS HAVE SPRUNG. AGAINST THOSE WHO CATCH AT EVERYTHING THAT MEETS THEM, AND GIVE IT CREDENCE, AND CLING TO IT. ORIGEN WAS IN THE HABIT OF CAREFULLY READING AND EXPLAINING THE BOOKS OF THE HEATHEN TO HIS DISCIPLES.

Is it not thus that contradictory and opposing tenets have been introduced, and all the contentions of philosophers, while one party withstands the opinions of another, and some hold by certain positions, and others by others, and one school attaches itself to one set of dogmas, and another to another? And all, indeed, aim at philosophizing, and profess to have been doing so ever since they were first roused to it, and declare that they desire it not less now when they are well versed in the discussions than when they began them: yea, rather they allege that they have even more love for philosophy now, after they have had, so to speak, a little taste of it, and have had the liberty of dwelling on its discussions, than when at first, and without any previous experience of it, they were urged by a sort of impulse to philosophize. That is what they say; and henceforth they give no heed to any words of those who hold opposite opinions. And accordingly, no one of the ancients has ever induced any one of the moderns, or those of the Peripatetic school, to turn to his way of thinking, and adopt his method of philosophizing; and, on the other hand, none of the moderns has imposed his notions upon those of the ancient school. Nor, in short, has any one done so with any other.[3] For it is not an easy thing to induce one to give up his own opinions, and accept those of others; although these might, perhaps, even be sentiments which, if he had been led to credit them before he began to philosophize, the man might at first have admired

---

[1] μηδὲν ἐκποιουμένους. Casaubon marks this as a phrase taken from law, and equivalent to, *nihil alienum a nobis ducentes*.
[2] The text is, ἧς οἴονται. We render with Bengel. The Latin interpreter makes it = Even those who frequent the temples do not deem it consistent with religion to touch anything at all profane.

[3] [The ultimate subjugation of Latin theology by Aristotelian philosophy, is a deplorable instance of what is here hinted at, and what Hippolytus has worked out. Compare Col. ii. 8.]

and accepted with all readiness: as, while the mind was not yet preoccupied, he might have directed his attention to that set of opinions, and given them his approval, and on their behalf opposed himself to those which he holds at present. Such, at least, has been the kind of philosophizing exhibited by our noble and most eloquent and critical Greeks: for whatever any one of these has lighted on at the outset, moved by some impulse or other, that alone he declares to be truth, and holds that all else which is maintained by other philosophers is simply delusion and folly, though he himself does not more satisfactorily establish his own positions by argument, than do all the others severally defend their peculiar tenets; the man's object being simply to be under no obligation to give up and alter his opinions, whether by constraint or by persuasion, while he has (if one may speak truth) nothing else but a kind of unreasoning impulse towards these dogmas on the side of philosophy, and possesses no other criterion of what he imagines to be true, than (let it not seem an incredible assertion) undistinguishing chance.[1] And as each one thus becomes attached to those positions with which he has first fallen in, and is, as it were, held in chains by them, he is no longer capable of giving attention to others, if he happens to have anything of his own to offer on every subject with the demonstration of truth, and if he has the aid of argument to show how false the tenets of his adversaries are; for, helplessly and thoughtlessly and as if he looked for some happy contingency, he yields himself to the reasonings that first take possession of him.[2] And such reasonings mislead those who accept them, not only in other matters, but above all, in what is of greatest and most essential consequence — in the knowledge of God and in piety. And yet men become bound by them in such a manner that no one can very easily release them. For they are like men caught in a swamp stretching over some wide impassable plain, which, when they have once fallen into it, allows them neither to retrace their steps nor to cross it and effect their safety, but keeps them down in its soil until they meet their end; or they may be compared to men in a deep, dense, and majestic forest, into which the wayfarer enters, with the idea, perchance, of finding his road out of it again forthwith, and of taking his course once

more on the open plain,[3] but is baffled in his purpose by the extent and thickness of the wood. And turning in a variety of directions, and lighting on various continuous paths within it, he pursues many a course, thinking that by some of them he will surely find his way out: but they only lead him farther in, and in no way open up an exit for him, inasmuch as they are all only paths within the forest itself; until at last the traveller, utterly worn out and exhausted, seeing that all the ways he had tried had proved only forest still, and despairing of finding any more his dwelling-place on earth, makes up his mind to abide there, and establish his hearth, and lay out for his use such free space as he can prepare in the wood itself. Or again, we might take the similitude of a labyrinth, which has but one apparent entrance, so that one suspects nothing artful from the outside, and goes within by the single door that shows itself; and then, after advancing to the farthest interior, and viewing the cunning spectacle, and examining the construction so skilfully contrived, and full of passages, and laid out with unending paths leading inwards or outwards, he decides to go out again, but finds himself unable, and sees his exit completely intercepted by that inner construction which appeared such a triumph of cleverness. But, after all, there is neither any labyrinth so inextricable and intricate, nor any forest so dense and devious, nor any plain or swamp so difficult for those to get out of, who have once got within it, as is discussion,[4] at least as one may meet with it in the case of certain of these philosophers.[5] Wherefore, to secure us against falling into the unhappy experience of most, he did not introduce us to any one exclusive school of philosophy; nor did he judge it proper for us to go away with any single class of philosophical opinions, but he introduced us to all, and determined that we should be ignorant of no kind of Grecian doctrine.[6] And he himself went on with us, preparing the way before us, and leading us by the hand, as on a journey, whenever anything tortuous and unsound and delusive came in our way. And he helped us like a skilled expert who has had long familiarity with such subjects, and is not strange or inexperienced in anything

---

[1] The text is, οὐκ ἄλλην τινὰ (εἰ δεῖ τ' ἀληθὲς εἰπεῖν) ἔχων ἢ τὴν πρὸς τῆς φιλοσοφίας ἐπὶ τάδε τὰ δόγματα ἄλογον ὁρμὴν· καὶ κρίσιν ὧν οἴεται ἀληθῶν (μὴ παράδοξον εἰπεῖν ᾖ) οὐκ ἄλλην ἢ τὴν ἄκριτον τύχην. Vossius would read, πρὸς τὴν φιλοσοφίαν καὶ ἐπὶ τάδε τὰ δόγματα. Migne makes it = nulla ei erat alia sententia (si verum est dicendum) nisi cæcus ille stimulus quo ante philosophiæ studium in ista actus erat placita: neque aliud judicium eorum quæ vera putaret (ne mirum sit dictu) nisi fortunæ temeritas. Bengel would read, πρὸ τῆς φιλοσοφίας.

[2] The text is, ἐπεὶ καὶ ἀβοήθητος, ἑαυτὸν χαρισάμενος καὶ ἐκδεχόμενος εἰκῇ ὥσπερ ἕρμαιον, τοῖς προκαταλαβοῦσιν αὐτὸν λόγοις. Bengel proposes ἐνδεχόμενον . . . ἕρμαιον, as = lucrum insperatum.

[3] καθαρῷ — ἕρκει. Sirmondus gives puro campo. Rhodomanus, reading ἀέσι, gives puro aëre. Bengel takes ἕρκος, septum, as derivatively = domus, fundus, regio septis munita.

[4] λόγος.

[5] The text is, εἰ τις εἴη κατ' αὐτῶν τῶνδέ τινων φιλοσόφων. Bengel suggests καταντῶν.

[6] [Beautiful testimony to the worth and character of Origen! After St. Bernard, who thought he was scriptural, but was blinded by the Decretals (no fault in him), Scripture and testimony (as defined to be the rule of faith by Tertullian and Vincent) ceased to govern in the West; and by syllogisms (see vol. v. p. 100) the Scholastic system was built up. This became the creed of a new church organization created at Trent, all the definitions of which are part of said creed. Thus the "Roman-Catholic Church" (so called when created) is a new creation (of A.D. 1564), in doctrine ever innovating, which has the least claim to antiquity of any Church pretending to Apostolic origin.]

of the kind, and who therefore may remain safe in his own altitude, while he stretches forth his hand to others, and effects their security too, as one drawing up the submerged. Thus did he deal with us, selecting and setting before us all that was useful and true in all the various philosophers, and putting aside all that was false. And this he did for us, both in other branches of man's knowledge, and most especially in all that concerns piety.

ARGUMENT XV. — THE CASE OF DIVINE MATTERS. ONLY GOD AND HIS PROPHETS ARE TO BE HEARD IN THESE. THE PROPHETS AND THEIR AUDITORS ARE ACTED ON BY THE SAME AFFLATUS. ORIGEN'S EXCELLENCE IN THE INTERPRETATION OF SCRIPTURE.

With respect to these human teachers, indeed, he counselled us to attach ourselves to none of them, not even though they were attested as most wise by all men, but to devote ourselves to God alone, and to the prophets. And he himself became the interpreter of the prophets[1] to us, and explained whatsoever was dark or enigmatical in them. For there are many things of that kind in the sacred words ; and whether it be that God is pleased to hold communication with men in such a way as that the divine word may not enter all naked and uncovered into an unworthy soul, such as many are, or whether it be, that while every divine oracle is in its own nature most clear and perspicuous, it seems obscure and dark to us, who have apostatized from God, and have lost the faculty of hearing through time and age, I cannot tell. But however the case may stand, if it be that there are some words really enigmatical, he explained all such, and set them in the light, as being himself a skilled and most discerning hearer of God ; or if it be that none of them are really obscure in their own nature, they were also not unintelligible to him, who alone of all men of the present time with whom I have myself been acquainted, or of whom I have heard by the report of others, has so deeply studied the clear and luminous oracles of God, as to be able at once to receive their meaning into his own mind, and to convey it to others. For that Leader of all men, who inspires[2] God's dear prophets, and suggests all their prophecies and their mystic and heavenly words, has honoured this man as He would a friend, and has constituted him an expositor of these same oracles ; and things of which He only gave a hint by others, He made matters of full instruction by this man's instrumentality ; and in things which He, who is worthy of all trust, either enjoined in regal fashion, or simply enunciated, He imparted to this man the gift of investigating and unfolding and explaining them : so that, if there chanced to be any one of obtuse and incredulous mind, or one again thirsting for instruction, he might learn from this man, and in some manner be constrained to understand and to decide for belief, and to follow God. These things, moreover, as I judge, he gives forth only and truly by participation in the Divine Spirit : for there is need of the same power for those who prophesy and for those who hear the prophets ; and no one can rightly hear a prophet, unless the same Spirit who prophesies bestows on him the capacity of apprehending His words. And this principle is expressed indeed in the Holy Scriptures themselves, when it is said that only He who shutteth openeth, and no other one whatever ;[3] and what is shut is opened when the word of inspiration explains mysteries. Now that greatest gift this man has received from God, and that noblest of all endowments he has had bestowed upon him from heaven, that he should be an interpreter of the oracles of God to men,[4] and that he might understand the words of God, even as if God spake them to him, and that he might recount them to men in such wise as that they may hear them with intelligence.[5] Therefore to us there was no forbidden subject of speech ;[6] for there was no matter of knowledge hidden or inaccessible to us, but we had it in our power to learn every kind of discourse, both foreign[7] and Greek, both spiritual and political, both divine and human ; and we were permitted with all freedom to go round the whole circle of knowledge, and investigate it, and satisfy ourselves with all kinds of doctrines, and enjoy the sweets of intellect. And whether it was some ancient system of truth, or whether it was something one might otherwise name that was before us, we had in him an apparatus and a power at once admirable and full of the most beautiful views. And to speak in brief, he was truly a paradise to us, after the similitude of the paradise of God, wherein we were not set indeed to till the soil beneath us, or to make ourselves gross with bodily nurture,[8] but only to increase the acquisitions of mind with all gladness and enjoyment, — planting, so to speak, some fair growths ourselves, or having them planted in us by the Author of all things.

ARGUMENT XVI. — GREGORY LAMENTS HIS DEPARTURE UNDER A THREEFOLD COMPARISON ; LIKENING IT TO ADAM'S DEPARTURE OUT OF PARADISE,

---

1 ὑποφητεύων.
2 ὑπηχῶν.

3 Isa. xxii. 22; Rev. iii. 7. [All these citations of the Scriptures should be noted, but specially those which prove the general reception of the Apocalypse in the East.]
4 [A noble sentence. Eph. iii. 8, 9.]
5 The text gives ὡς ἀκούσωσιν, with Voss. and Bengel. The Paris editor gives ἀκούουσιν.
6 ἄρρητον.
7 Barbarian.
8 σωματοτροφεῖν παχυνομένους.

TO THE PRODIGAL SON'S ABANDONMENT OF HIS
FATHER'S HOUSE, AND TO THE DEPORTATION OF
THE JEWS INTO BABYLON.

Here, truly, is the paradise of comfort; here
are true gladness and pleasure, as we have enjoyed them during this period which is now at
its end — no short space indeed in itself, and
yet all too short if this is really to be its conclusion, when we depart and leave this place behind
us. For I know not what has possessed me, or
what offence has been committed by me, that I
should now be going away — that I should now
be put away. I know not what I should say,
unless it be that I am like a second Adam and
have begun to talk, outside of paradise. How
excellent might my life be, were I but a listener
to the addresses of my teacher, and silent myself! Would that even now I could have learned
to be mute and speechless, rather than to present
this new spectacle of making the teacher the
hearer! For what concern had I with such a
harangue as this? and what obligation was there
upon me to make such an address, when it became me not to depart, but to cleave fast to the
place? But these things seem like the transgressions that sprung from the pristine deceit, and
the penalties of these primeval offences still await
me here. Do I not appear to myself to be disobedient[1] in daring thus to overpass the words
of God, when I ought to abide in them, and
hold by them? And in that I withdraw, I flee
from this blessed life, even as the primeval man
fled from the face of God, and I return to the
soil from which I was taken. Therefore shall I
have to eat of the soil all the days of my life
there, and I shall have to till the soil — the very
soil which produces thorns and thistles for me,
that is to say, pains and reproachful anxieties —
set loose as I shall be from cares that are good
and noble. And what I left behind me before,
to that I now return — to the soil, as it were,
from which I came, and to my common relation-
ships here below, and to my father's house —
leaving the good soil, where of old I knew not
that the good fatherland lay; leaving also the
relations in whom at a later period I began to
recognise the true kinsmen of my soul, and the
house, too, of him who is in truth our father, in
which the father abides, and is piously honoured
and revered by the genuine sons, whose desire
it also is to abide therein. But I, destitute alike
of all piety and worthiness, am going forth from
the number of these, and am turning back to
what is behind, and am retracing my steps. It
is recorded that a certain son, receiving from his
father the portion of goods that fell to him pro-
portionately with the other heir, his brother, departed, by his own determination, into a strange

country far distant from his father; and, living
there in riot, he scattered his ancestral substance, and utterly wasted it; and at last, under
the pressure of want, he hired himself as a swine-
herd; and being driven to extremity by hunger,
he longed to share the food given to the swine,
but could not touch it. Thus did he pay the
penalty of his dissolute life, when he had to exchange his father's table, which was a princely
one, for something he had not looked forward
to — the sustenance of swine and serfs. And we
also seem to have some such fortune before us,
now that we are departing, and that, too, without the full portion that falls to us. For though
we have not received all that we ought, we are
nevertheless going away, leaving behind us what
is noble and dear with you and beside you, and
taking in exchange only what is inferior. For
all things melancholy will now meet us in succession, — tumult and confusion instead of peace,
and an unregulated life instead of one of tranquillity and harmony, and a hard bondage, and
the slavery of market-places, and lawsuits, and
crowds, instead of this freedom; and neither
pleasure nor any sort of leisure shall remain to
us for the pursuit of nobler objects. Neither
shall we have to speak of the words of inspiration, but we shall have to speak of the works of
men, — a thing which has been deemed simply a
bane by the prophet,[2] — and in our case, indeed,
those of wicked men. And truly we shall have
night in place of day, and darkness in place of
the clear light, and grief instead of the festive
assembly; and in place of a fatherland, a hostile
country will receive us, in which I shall have no
liberty to sing my sacred song,[3] for how could
I sing it in a land strange to my soul, in which
the sojourners have no permission to approach
God? but only to weep and mourn, as I call
to mind the different state of things here, if indeed even that shall be in my power. We read[4]
that enemies once assailed a great and sacred
city, in which the worship of God was observed,
and dragged away its inhabitants, both singers
and prophets,[5] into their own country, which
was Babylon. And it is narrated that these captives, when they were detained in the land, refused, even when asked by their conquerors, to
sing the divine song, or to play in a profane
country, and hung their harps on the willow-trees,
and wept by the rivers of Babylon. Like one
of these I verily seem to myself to be, as I am
cast forth from this city, and from this sacred

[1] ἀπειθεῖν. Bengel and Hœschelius read ἀπελθεῖν, withdraw.

[2] ἁπλοῦς ἀρά τις εἶναι νενόμισται ἀνδρὶ προφήτῃ. Migne refers us to Ps. xvii.
[3] Ps. cxxxvii.
[4] 2 Kings xxiv., xxv.
[5] θεολόγους, used probably of the *prophets* here — namely of Ezekiel, Daniel, and others carried into exile with the people. On this
usage, see Suicer's *Thesaurus*, under the word θεολόγος, where from
the pseudo-Areopagite Dionysius he cites the sentence, των θεολόγων
εἷς, ὁ Ζαχαρίας, and again, ετερος των θεολόγων Ἰεζεκιήλ.

fatherland of mine, where both by day and by night the holy laws are declared, and hymns and songs and spiritual words are heard ; where also there is perpetual sunlight ; where by day in waking vision [1] we have access to the mysteries of God, and by night in dreams [2] we are still occupied with what the soul has seen and handled in the day ; and where, in short, the inspiration of divine things prevails over all continually. From this city, I say, I am cast forth, and borne captive to a strange land, where I shall have no power to pipe : [3] for, like these men of old, I shall have to hang my instrument on the willows, and the rivers shall be my place of sojourn, and I shall have to work in mud, and shall have no heart to sing hymns, even though I remember them ; yea, it may be that, through constant occupation with other subjects, I shall forget even them, like one spoiled of memory itself. And would that, in going away, I only went away against my will, as a captive is wont to do ; but I go away also of my own will, and not by constraint of another ; and by my own act I am dispossessed of this city, when it is in my option to remain in it. Perchance, too, in leaving this place, I may be going to prosecute no safe journey, as it sometimes fares with one who quits some safe and peaceful city ; and it is indeed but too likely that, in journeying, I may fall into the hands of robbers, and be taken prisoner, and be stripped and wounded with many strokes, and be cast forth to lie half-dead somewhere.

ARGUMENT XVII. — GREGORY CONSOLES HIMSELF.

But why should I utter such lamentations ? There lives still the Saviour of all men, even of the half-dead and the despoiled, the Protector and Physician for all, the Word, that sleepless Keeper of all. We have also seeds of truth which thou hast made us know as our possession, and all that we have received from thee, — those noble deposits of instruction, with which we take our course ; and though we weep, indeed, as those who go forth from home, we yet carry those seeds with us. It may be, then, that the Keeper who presides over us will bear us in safety through all that shall befall us ; and it may be that we shall come yet again to thee,

bringing with us the fruits and handfuls yielded by these seeds, far from perfect truly, for how could they be so ? but still such as a life spent in civil business [4] makes it possible for us to rear, though marred indeed by a kind of faculty that is either unapt to bear fruit altogether, or prone to bear bad fruit, but which, I trust, is one not destined to be further misused by us, if God grants us grace.[5]

ARGUMENT XVIII. — PERORATION, AND APOLOGY FOR THE ORATION.

Wherefore let me now have done with this address, which I have had the boldness to deliver in a presence wherein boldness least became me. Yet this address is one which, I think, has aimed heartily at signifying our thanks to the best of our ability, — for though we have had nothing to say worthy of the subject, we could not be altogether silent, — and one, too, which has given expression to our regrets, as those are wont to do who go abroad in separation from friends. And whether this speech of mine may not have contained things puerile *or* bordering on flattery, or things offending by excess of simplicity on the one hand, or of elaboration on the other, I know not. Of this, however, I am clearly conscious, that at least there is in it nothing unreal, but all that is true and genuine, in sincerity of opinion, and in purity and integrity of judgment.

ARGUMENT XIX. — APOSTROPHE TO ORIGEN, AND THEREWITH THE LEAVE-TAKING, AND THE URGENT UTTERANCE OF PRAYER.

But, O dear soul, arise thou and offer prayer, and now dismiss us ; and as by thy holy instructions thou hast been our rescuer when we enjoyed thy fellowship, so save us still by thy prayers in our separation. Commend us and set us constantly [6] before thee in prayer. Or rather commend us continually to that God who brought us to thee, giving thanks for all that has been granted us in the past, and imploring Him still to lead us by the hand in the future, and to stand ever by us, filling our mind with the understanding of His precepts, inspiring us with the godly fear of Himself, and vouchsafing us henceforward His choicest guidance.[7] For when we are gone from thee, we shall not have the same liberty for obeying Him as was ours when we were

---

[1] The text is, καὶ φῶς τὸ ἡλιακὸν καὶ τὸ διηνεκὲς, ἡμέρας ὑπερ ἡμῶν προσομιλούντων τοῖς θείος μυστηρίοις καὶ νυκτὸς ὢν ἐν ἡμέρα εἰδέ τε καὶ ἐπραξεν ἡ ψυχὴ ταῖς φαντασίαις κατεχομένων. Bengel proposes ὕπαρ for ὕπερ, so as to keep the antithesis between ἡμέρας ὕπαρ and νυκτὸς φαντασίαις ; and taking ἡμέρας and νυκτός as temporal genitives, he renders the whole thus : *cum interdiu, per visa, divinis aderamus sacramentis : et noctu earum rerum, quas viderat de die atque egerat anima, imaginibus detinebamur.*

[2] [" In dreams I still renew the rites," etc. — WILLIAM CROSWELL.]

[3] αὐλεῖν. The Jews had the harp, and so the word ψάλλειν is used of them in the preceding. But here, in speaking of himself, Gregory adopts the term οὔτε αὐλεῖν, *ne tibia quidem canere.* Bengel supposes that the verb is changed in order to convey the idea, that while the Jews only had to give up the use of instruments expressive of joyful feeling, Gregory feared he would himself be unable to play even on those of a *mournful* tone, — for in ancient times the pipe or flute was chiefly appropriated to strains of grief and sadness.

[4] [He was still proposing for himself a life of worldly occupation. Here turn to Origen's counsel, — a sort of reply to this Oration, — vol. iv. p. 393, and Cave's *Lives*, etc., vol. i. p. 400.]

[5] The text is, διεφθαρμένας μὲν τῇ δυναμει, ἢ ἀκάρπῳ ἢ κακοκάρπῳ τινί, μὴ καὶ προσδιαφθαρησομένη δὲ παρ' ἡμῶν, etc. Bengel reads μέν τοι for μὲν τῇ, and takes μὴ καὶ as = *utinam nc.*

[6] παραδίδου καὶ παρατίθεσο.

[7] ἐμβάλλοντα ἡμῖν τὸν θεῖον φόβον αὐτοῦ, παιδαγωγὸν ἄριστον ἐσόμενον. The Latin version makes the ἐσόμενον refer to the φόβον : *divinumque nobis timorem suum, optimum pædagogum immittens,* = and inspiring with the godly fear of Himself as our choicest guide.

with thee.[1]   Pray, therefore, that some encouragement may be conveyed to us from Him when we lose thy presence, and that He may send us a good conductor, some angel to be our comrade on the way.   And entreat Him also to turn our course, for that is the one thing which above all else will effectually comfort us, and bring us back to thee again.

[1] οὐ γὰρ ἐν τῇ μετὰ σοῦ ἐλευθερίᾳ καὶ ἀπελθόντες ὑπακούσομεν αὐτῷ.   Bengel paraphrases it thus: *hac libertate quæ tecum est carebo digressus; quare vereor ut Deo posthac paream, ni timore saltem munitus fuero.*   [He may probably have been only a *cate-chumen* at this period.   This peroration favours the suspicion.]

ELUCIDATION.

NEALE, in his valuable work,[1] does full justice to Dionysius, whose life is *twinned* with Gregory's ; but he seems to me most unaccountably to slight the truly great and commanding genius of Gregory.   I take opportunity, then, to direct attention to Neale's candid, and, on the whole, favourable view of Origen; but it grieves me whenever I see in critics a manifest inability to *put themselves back into the times* of which they write, as I think is the case, not infrequently, even with Dr. Neale.   The figure of this grand ornament of the mighty patriarchate and school of Alexandria is colossal.[2]   His genius is Titanic, and has left all Christendom profoundly his debtor to this day, by the variety of his work and the versatility of his speech and pen.   Doubtless the youthful Gregory's panegyric does contain, as he himself suggests, much that is " puerile or bordering on flattery ; " but, as he protests with transparent truthfulness, " there is nothing in it unreal."   It shines with " sincerity of thought and integrity of judgment."   And as such, what a portrait it presents us of the love and patient effort of this lifelong confessor !   Let me commend this example to professors of theology generally.   All can learn from it the power of sweetness and love, united with holiness of purpose, to stamp the minds and the characters of youth with the divine " image and superscription."

But, as to the sharpness of modern censures upon Origen's conspicuous faults, I must suggest three important considerations, which should be applied to all the Ante-Nicene doctors : (1) How could they who were working out the formulas of orthodoxy, be expected to use phrases with the skill and precision which became necessary only after the great Synodical period had embodied them in clear, dogmatic statements?   (2) How could the active intellect of an Origen have failed to make great mistakes in such an immensity of labours and such a variety of works?   (3) If, in our own day, we indulge speculative minds in large liberties so long as they never make shipwreck of the faith, how much more should we deem them excusable who were unable to consult libraries of well-digested thought, and to employ, as we do, the accumulated wealth of fifty generations of believers, whenever we are called to the solemn responsibility of impressing our convictions upon others?   The conclusion of Dr. Neale's review of Origen balances the praise and blame accorded to him by those nearest to his times ;[3] but let us reflect upon the painful conflicts of those times, and upon the pressure under which, to justify their own positions, they were often forced to object to any error glorified by even the apparent patronage of Origen.

---

[1] *The Patriarchate of Alexandria*, London, 1847.
[2] The ultimate influence of the school itself, Neale pronounces " an enigma " (vol. i. p. 38).   [3] Vol. i. p. 33.

PART II.—DUBIOUS OR SPURIOUS WRITINGS.

A SECTIONAL CONFESSION OF FAITH.[1]

I.

MOST hostile and alien to the Apostolic Confession are those who speak of the Son as assumed to Himself by the Father out of nothing, and from an emanational origin ;[2] and those who hold the same sentiments with respect to the Holy Spirit ; those who say that the Son is constituted divine by gift and grace, and that the Holy Spirit is made holy ; those who regard the name of the Son as one common to servants, and assert that thus He is the first-born of the creature, as becoming, like the creature, existent out of non-existence, and as being first made, and who refuse to admit that He is the only-begotten Son, — the only One that the Father has, and that He has given Himself to be reckoned in the number of mortals, and is thus reckoned first-born ; those who circumscribe the generation of the Son by the Father with a measured interval after the fashion of man, and refuse to acknowledge that the æon of the Begetter and that of the Begotten are without beginning ; those who introduce three separate and diverse systems of divine worship,[3] whereas there is but one form of legitimate service which we have received of old from the law and the prophets, and which has been confirmed by the Lord and preached by the apostles. Nor less alienated from the true confession are those who hold not the doctrine of the Trinity according to truth, as a relation consisting of three persons, but impiously conceive it as implying a triple being in a unity (Monad), formed in the way of synthesis,[4] and think that the Son is the wisdom in God, in the same manner as the human wisdom subsists in man whereby the man is wise, and represent the Word as being simply like the word which we utter or conceive, without any hypostasis whatever.

II.

But the Church's Confession, and the Creed that brings salvation to the world, is that which deals with the incarnation of the Word, and bears that He gave Himself over to the flesh of man which He acquired of Mary, while yet He conserved His own identity, and sustained no divine transposition or mutation, but was brought into conjunction with the flesh after the similitude of man ; so that the flesh was made one with the divinity, the divinity having assumed the capacity of receiving the flesh in the fulfilling of the mystery. And after the dissolution of death there remained to the holy flesh a perpetual impassibility and a changeless immortality, man's original glory being taken up into it again by the power of the divinity, and being ministered then to all men by the appropriation of faith.[5]

III.

If, then, there are any here, too, who falsify the holy faith, either by attributing to the divinity as its own what belongs to the humanity — progressions,[6] and passions, and a glory coming with accession [7] — or by separating from the divinity the progressive and passible body, as if subsisted of itself apart, — these persons also are

---

[1] Edited in Latin by Gerardus Vossius, *Opp. Greg. Thaum.*, Paris, 1662, in fol.; given in Greek from the Codex Vaticanus by Cardinal Mai, *Script. Vet.*, vii. p. 170. Vossius has the following argument: This is a second Confession of Faith, and one widely different from the former, which this great Gregory of ours received by revelation. This seems, however, to be designated an ἔκθεσις τῆς κατὰ μέρος πίστεως, either because it records and expounds the matters of the faith only *in part*, or because the Creed is explained in it *by parts*. The Jesuit theologian Franc. Torrensis (the interpreter and scholiast of this ἔκθεσις) has, however, rendered the phrase ἡ κατὰ μέρος πίστις, by the Latin *fides non universa sed in parte*. And here we have a *fides non universa sed in parte*, according to him, — a creed not of all the dogmas of the Church, but only of some, in opposition to the heretics who deny them. [The better view.]

[2] οἱ τὸν Υἱὸν ἐξ οὐκ ὄντων καὶ ἀποστελλομένης ἀρχῆς εἶναι ἐπίκτητον λέγοντες τῷ Πατρί. [Note, *Exucontians* = Arians.]

[3] ἀκοινωνήτους καὶ ξένας εἰσαγοντες λατρείας.

[4] ἐν μονάδι τὸ τριπλοῦν ἀσεβῶς κατὰ σύνθεσιν.

[5] ἐν τῇ τῆς πίστεως οἰκειώσει.

[6] προκοπάς.

[7] δόξαν τὴν ἐπιγινομένην.

outside the confession of the Church and of salvation. No one, therefore, can know God unless he apprehends the Son; for the Son is the wisdom by whose instrumentality all things have been created; and these created objects declare this wisdom, and God is recognised in the wisdom. But the wisdom of God is not anything similar to the wisdom which man possesses, but it is the perfect wisdom which proceeds from the perfect God, and abides for ever, not like the thought of man, which passes from him in the word that is spoken and (straightway) ceases to be. Wherefore it is not wisdom only, but also God; nor is it Word only, but also Son. And whether, then, one discerns God through creation, or is taught to know Him by the Holy Scriptures, it is impossible either to apprehend Him or to learn of Him apart from His wisdom. And he who calls upon God rightly, calls on Him through the Son; and he who approaches Him in a true fellowship, comes to Him through Christ. Moreover, the Son Himself cannot be approached apart from the Spirit. For the Spirit is both the life and the holy formation of all things; [1] and God sending forth this Spirit through the Son makes the creature [2] like Himself.

IV.

One therefore is God the Father, one the Word, one the Spirit, the life, the sanctification of all. And neither is there another God as Father,[3] nor is there another Son as Word of God, nor is there another Spirit as quickening and sanctifying. Further, although the saints are called both gods, and sons, and spirits, they are neither filled with the Spirit, nor are made like the Son and God. And if, then, any one makes this affirmation, that the Son is God, simply as being Himself filled with divinity, and not as being generated of divinity, he has belied the Word, he has belied the Wisdom, he has lost the knowledge of God; he has fallen away into the worship of the creature, he has taken up the impiety of the Greeks, to that he has gone back; and he has become a follower of the unbelief of the Jews, who, supposing the Word of God to be but a human son, have refused to accept Him as God, and have declined to acknowledge Him as the Son of God. But it is impious to think of the Word of God as merely human, and to think of the works which are done by Him as abiding, while He abides not Himself. And if any one says that the Christ works all things only as commanded by the Word, he will both make the Word of God

idle,[4] and will change the Lord's order into servitude. For the slave is one altogether under command, and the created is not competent to create; for to suppose that what is itself created may in like manner create other things, would imply that it has ceased to be like the creature.[5]

V.

Again, when one speaks of the Holy Spirit as an object made holy,[6] he will no longer be able to apprehend all things as being sanctified in (the) Spirit. For he who has sanctified one, sanctifies all things. That man, consequently, belies the fountain of sanctification, the Holy Spirit, who denudes Him of the power of sanctifying, and he will thus be precluded from numbering Him with the Father and the Son; he makes nought, too, of the holy (ordinance of) baptism, and will no more be able to acknowledge the holy and august Trinity.[7] For either we must apprehend the perfect Trinity [7] in its natural and genuine glory, or we shall be under the necessity of speaking no more of a Trinity, but only of a Unity;[8] or else, not numbering [9] created objects with the Creator, nor the creatures with the Lord of all, we must also not number what is sanctified with what sanctifies; even as no object that is made can be numbered with the Trinity, but in the name of the Holy Trinity baptism and invocation and worship are administered. For if there are three several glories, there must also be three several forms of cultus with those who impiously worship the creature; for if there is a distinction in the nature of the objects worshipped, there ought to be also with these men a distinction in the nature of the worship offered. What is recent [10] surely is not to be worshipped along with what is eternal; for the recent comprehends all that has had a beginning, while mighty and measureless is He who is before the ages. He, therefore, who supposes some beginning of times in the life of the Son and of the Holy Spirit, therewith also cuts off any possibility of numbering the Son and the Spirit with the Father. For as we acknowledge the glory to be one, so ought we also to acknowledge the substance in the Godhead to be one, and one also the eternity of the Trinity.

VI.

Moreover, the capital element of our salvation is the incarnation of the Word. We believe,

---

[1] μόρφωσις τῶν ὅλων.
[2] τὴν κτίσιν.
[3] οὔτε Θεὸς ἕτερος ὡς Πατήρ.

[4] ἀργόν.
[5] This seems the idea in the sentence, οὐ γὰρ ἐξισωσθήσεται τῷ κτίσματι αὐτὸ κατ᾽ οὐδένα τρόπον, ἵν᾽ ὡς ὑπ᾽ ἐκείνου ἔκτισται, οὕτω καὶ αὐτὸ κτίσῃ τὰ ἄλλα.
[6] ἡγιασμένον ποίημα.
[7] Trias. [See vol. ii. p. 101.]
[8] Monas.
[9] συναριθμεῖν.
[10] τὰ πρόσφατα.

therefore, that it was without any change in the Divinity that the incarnation of the Word took place with a view to the renewal of humanity. For there took place neither mutation nor transposition, nor any circumscription in will,[1] as regards the holy energy[2] of God; but while that remained in itself the same, it also effected the work of the incarnation with a view to the salvation of the world : and the Word of God, living[3] on earth after man's fashion, maintained likewise in all the divine presence, fulfilling all things, and being united[4] properly and individually with flesh; and while the sensibilities proper to the flesh were there, the *divine* energy maintained the impassibility proper to itself. Impious, therefore, is the man who introduces the passibility[5] into the energy. For the Lord of glory appeared in fashion as a man when He undertook the economy[6] upon the earth; and He fulfilled the law for men by His deeds, and by His sufferings He did away with man's sufferings, and by His death He abolished death, and by his resurrection He brought life to light; and now we look for His appearing from heaven in glory for the life and judgment of all, when the resurrection of the dead shall take place, to the end that recompense may be made to all according to their desert.

VII.

But some treat the Holy Trinity[7] in an awful manner, when they confidently assert that there are not three persons, and introduce (the idea of) a person devoid of subsistence.[8] Wherefore we clear ourselves of Sabellius, who says that the Father and the Son are the same. For he holds that the Father is He who speaks, and that the Son is the Word that abides in the Father, and becomes manifest at the time of the creation,[9] and thereafter reverts to God on the fulfilling of all things. The same affirmation he makes also of the Spirit. We forswear this, because we believe that three persons — namely, Father, Son, and Holy Spirit — are declared to possess the one Godhead : for the one divinity showing itself forth according to nature in the Trinity[10] establishes the oneness of the nature; and thus there is a (divinity that is the) property of the Father, according to the word, "There is one God the Father;"[11] and there is a divinity hereditary[12] in the Son, as it is written, "The Word

was God;"[13] and there is a divinity present according to nature in the Spirit — to wit, what subsists as the Spirit of God — according to Paul's statement, "Ye are the temple of God, and the Spirit of God dwelleth in you."[14]

VIII.

Now the person in each declares the independent being and subsistence.[15] But divinity is the property of the Father; and whenever the divinity of these three is spoken of as one, testimony is borne that the property[16] of the Father belongs also to the Son and the Spirit : wherefore, if the divinity may be spoken of as one in three persons, the trinity is established, and the unity is not dissevered; and the oneness which is naturally the Father's is also acknowledged to be the Son's and the Spirit's. If one, however, speaks of one person as he may speak of one divinity, it cannot be that the two in the one are as one.[17] For Paul addresses the Father as one in respect of divinity, and speaks of the Son as one in respect of lordship : "There is one God the Father, of whom are all things, and we for Him; and one Lord Jesus Christ, by whom are all things, and we by Him."[18] Wherefore if there is one God, and one Lord, and at the same time one person as one divinity in one lordship,[19] how can credit be given to (this distinction in) the words "of whom" and "by whom," as has been said before? We speak, accordingly, not as if we separated the lordship from the divinity, nor as estranging the one from the other, but as unifying them in the way warranted by actual fact and truth; and we call the Son God with the property of the Father,[20] as being His image and offspring; and we call the Father Lord, addressing Him by the name of the One Lord, as being His Origin and Begettor.

IX.

The same position we hold respecting the Spirit, who has that unity with the Son which the Son has with the Father. Wherefore let the hypostasis of the Father be discriminated by the appellation of God; but let not the Son be cut off from this appellation, for He is of God. Again, let the person of the Son also be discriminated by the appellation of Lord; only let not God be dissociated from that, for He is Lord as being the Father of the Lord. And as it is proper to the Son to exercise lordship, for He

---

[1] περικλεισμὸς ἐν νεύματι.
[2] δύναμιν.
[3] πολιτευσάμενος.
[4] συγκεκραμένος.
[5] τὸ πάθος.
[6] Meaning here the whole work and business of the incarnation, and the redemption through the flesh. — MIGNE.
[7] Trias.
[8] ἀνυπόστατον.
[9] δημιουργίας.
[10] φυσικῶς ἐν Τριάδι μαρτυρουμένη.
[11] I Cor. viii. 6.
[12] πατρῷον.

[13] John i. 1.
[14] I Cor. iii. 6.
[15] τὸ εἶναι αὐτὸ καὶ ὑφεστάναι δηλοῖ.
[16] By the ἰδιότητα τοῦ Πατρός is meant here the divinity belonging to the Father. — MIGNE.
[17] οὐκ ἔστιν ὡς ἐν τὰ δυο ἐν τῷ ἐνί.
[18] I Cor. viii. 6.
[19] καθ' ὃ θεότης μιᾶς κυριότητος.
[20] τῷ ἰδιώματι τοῦ Πατρός.

it is that made (all things) by Himself, and now rules the things that were made, while at the same time the Father has a prior possession of that property, inasmuch as He is the Father of Him who is Lord; so we speak of the Trinity as One God, and yet not as if we made the one by a synthesis of three: for the subsistence that is constituted by synthesis is something altogether partitive and imperfect.[1] But just as the designation Father is the expression of originality and generation, so the designation Son is the expression of the image and offspring of the Father. Hence, if one were to ask how there is but One God, if there is also a God of God, we would reply that that is a term proper to the idea of original causation,[2] so far as the Father is the one First Cause.[3] And if one were also to put the question, how there is but One Lord, if the Father also is Lord, we might answer that again by saying that He is so in so far as He is the Father of the Lord; and this difficulty shall meet us no longer.

X.

And again, if the impious say, How will there not be three Gods and three Persons, on the supposition that they have one and the same divinity? — we shall reply: Just because God is the Cause and Father of the Son; and this Son is the image and offspring of the Father, and not His brother; and the Spirit in like manner is the Spirit of God, as it is written, " God is a Spirit."[4] And in earlier times we have this declaration from the prophet David: " By the word of the Lord were the heavens stablished, and all the power of them by the breath (spirit) of His mouth."[5] And in the beginning of the book of the creation[6] it is written thus: " And the Spirit of God moved upon the face of the waters."[7] And Paul in his Epistle to the Romans says: " But ye are not in the flesh, but in the Spirit, if so be that the Spirit of God dwell in you."[8] And again he says: " But if the Spirit of Him that raised up Jesus from the dead dwell in you, He that raised up Christ from the dead shall also quicken your mortal bodies by His Spirit that dwelleth in you."[9] And again: " As many as are led by the Spirit of God, they are the sons of God. For ye have not received the spirit of bondage again to fear; but ye have received the Spirit of adoption, whereby we cry, Abba, Father."[10] And again: " I say the truth in Christ, I lie not, my conscience also bearing

me witness in the Holy Ghost."[11] And again: " Now the God of hope fill you with all joy and peace in believing, that ye may abound in hope, by the power of the Holy Ghost."[12]

XI.

And again, writing to those same Romans, he says: " But I have written the more boldly unto you in some sort, as putting you in mind, because of the grace that is given to me of God, that I should be the minister of Jesus Christ to the Gentiles, ministering the Gospel of God, that the offering up of the Gentiles might be acceptable, being sanctified by the Holy Ghost. I have therefore whereof I may glory through Jesus Christ in those things which pertain to God. For I dare not to speak of any of those things which Christ hath not wrought by me,[13] to make the Gentiles obedient, by word and deed, through mighty signs and wonders, by the power of the Holy Spirit."[14] And again: " Now I beseech you, brethren, for our Lord Jesus Christ's sake, and by the love of the Spirit."[15] And these things, indeed, are written in the Epistle to the Romans.[16]

XII.

Again, in the Epistle to the Corinthians he says: " For my speech and my preaching was not in the enticing words of man's wisdom, but in demonstration of the Spirit and of power; that your faith should not stand in the wisdom of men, but in the power of God."[17] And again he says: " As it is written, Eye hath not seen, nor ear heard, neither have entered into the heart of man, the things which God hath prepared for them that love Him. But God hath revealed them unto us by His Spirit: for the Spirit searcheth all things, yea, the deep things of God. For what man knoweth the things of a man, save the spirit of man which is in him? Even so the things of God knoweth no man, but the Spirit of God."[18] And again he says: " But the natural man receiveth not the things of the Spirit of God."[19]

XIII.

Seest thou that all through Scripture the Spirit is preached, and yet nowhere named a creature?

---

[1] μέρος γὰρ ἅπαν ἀτελὲς τὸ συνθέσεως ὑφιστάμενον.
[2] ἀρχῆς.
[3] ἀρχή.
[4] John iv. 24.
[5] Ps. xxxiii. 6.
[6] Κοσμοποιίας.
[7] Gen. i. 2.
[8] Rom. viii. 9.
[9] Rom. viii. 11.
[10] Rom. viii. 14, 15.

[11] Rom. ix. 1.
[12] Rom. xv. 13.
[13] [A reference to his *canon*, perhaps, recorded in 2 Cor. x. 13–16. Compare Rom. xv. 20. The canonists erect the discrimination between *Orders* and *Mission* upon these texts and (Acts xiii. 2, 3, etc.) Gal. ii. 8, 9. See vol. i. p. 495, note 3]
[14] Rom. xv. 15–19. [Concerning which remarkable passage, see vol. v. p. 409, Elucidation I.]
[15] Rom. xv. 30.
[16] [It is evident that St. Paul founded the Church at Rome. St. Peter (see note 13, *supra*) could only have come to Rome to look after the Jewish disciples there. Elucidation, p. 47, *infra*.]
[17] 1 Cor. ii. 4, 5.
[18] 1 Cor. ii. 9–11.
[19] 1 Cor. ii. 14.

And what can the impious have to say if the Lord sends forth His disciples to baptize in the name of the Father, and of the Son, and of the Holy Spirit?[1] Without contradiction, that implies a communion and unity between them, according to which there are neither three divinities nor (three) lordships; but, while there remain truly and certainly the three persons, the real unity of the three must be acknowledged. And in this way proper credit will be given to the *sending* and the *being sent*[2] (in the Godhead), according to which the Father hath sent forth the Son, and the Son in like manner sends forth the Spirit. For one of the persons surely could not (be said to) send Himself; and one could not speak of the Father as incarnate. For the articles of our faith will not concur with the vicious tenets of the heresies; and it is right that our conceptions should follow the inspired and apostolic doctrines, and not that our impotent fancies should coerce the articles of our divine faith.

XIV.

But if they say, How can there be three Persons, and how but one Divinity?— we shall make this reply: That there are indeed three persons, inasmuch as there is one person of God the Father, and one of the Lord the Son, and one of the Holy Spirit; and yet that there is but one divinity, inasmuch as the Son is the Image of God the Father, who is One, — that is, He is God of God; and in like manner the Spirit is called the Spirit of God, and that, too, of nature according to the very substance,[3] and not according to simple participation of God. And there is one substance[4] in the Trinity, which does not subsist also in the case of objects that are made; for there is not one substance in God and in the things that are made, because none of these is in substance God. Nor, indeed, is the Lord one of these according to substance, but there is one Lord the Son, and one Holy Spirit; and we speak also of one Divinity, and one Lordship, and one Sanctity in the Trinity; because the Father is the Cause[5] of the Lord, having begotten Him eternally, and the Lord is the Prototype[6] of the Spirit. For thus the Father is Lord, and the Son also is God; and of God it is said that "God is a Spirit."[7]

XV.

We therefore acknowledge one true God, the one First Cause, and one Son, very God of very God, possessing of nature the Father's divinity, — that is to say, being the same in substance with the Father;[8] and one Holy Spirit, who by nature and in truth sanctifies all, and makes divine, as being of the substance of God.[9] Those who speak either of the Son or of the Holy Spirit as a creature we anathematize. All other things we hold to be objects made, and in subjection,[10] created by God through the Son, (and) sanctified in the Holy Spirit. Further, we acknowledge that the Son of God was made a Son of man, having taken to Himself the flesh from the Virgin Mary, not in name, but in reality; and that He is both the perfect Son of God, and the (perfect) Son of man, — that the Person is but one, and that there is one worship[11] for the Word and the flesh that He assumed. And we anathematize those who constitute different worships, one for the divine and another for the human, and who worship the man born of Mary as though He were another than the God of God. For we know that "in the beginning was the Word, and the Word was with God, and the Word was God."[12] And we worship Him who was made man on account of our salvation, not indeed as made perfectly like in the like body,[13] but as the Lord who has taken to Himself the form of the servant. We acknowledge the passion of the Lord in the flesh, the resurrection in the power of His divinity, the ascension to heaven, and His glorious appearing when He comes for the judgment of the living and the dead, and for the eternal life of the saints.

XVI.

And since some have given us trouble by attempting to subvert our faith in our Lord Jesus Christ, and by affirming of Him that He was not God incarnated, but a man linked with God; for this reason we present our confession on the subject of the afore-mentioned matters of faith, and reject the faithless dogmas opposed thereto. For God, having been incarnated in the flesh of man, retains also His proper energy pure, possessing a mind unsubjected by the natural[14] and fleshly affections, and holding the flesh and the fleshly motions divinely and sinlessly, and not only unmastered by the power of death, but even destroying death. And it is the true God unincarnate that has appeared incarnate, the perfect One with the genuine and divine perfection; and in Him there are not two persons. Nor do

---

[1] Matt. xxviii. 19.
[2] The text is, ουτω γὰρ (τὸ ἀποστέλλον) καὶ τὸ ἀποστελλόμενον, οἰκείως ἀν πιστεύοιτο, καθ᾽ ὃ, etc.
[3] φυσικῶς κατ᾽ αὐτὴν τὴν οὐσίαν.
[4] οὐσία.
[5] ἀρχή.
[6] πρωτότυπος.
[7] John iv. 24.

[8] Note the phrase here, afterwards formulated, ὁμοούσιον τῷ Πατρί. [This phrase, with abundant other tokens, makes it apparent that the work is not Gregory's. It is further evident from section xviii. I should be glad to think otherwise.]
[9] καὶ θεοποιὸν ἐκ τῆς οὐσίας του Θεου ὑπάρχον.
[10] δοῦλα.
[11] προσκύνησιν.
[12] John i. 1.
[13] ἴσον ἐν ἴσῳ γενόμενον τῷ σώματί.
[14] ψυχικῶν.

we affirm that there are four to worship, viz., God and the Son of God, and man and the Holy Spirit. Wherefore we also anathematize those who show their impiety in this, and who thus give the *man* a place in the divine doxology. For we hold that the Word of God was made man on account of our salvation, in order that we might receive the likeness of the heavenly, and be made divine [1] after the likeness of Him who is the true Son of God by nature, and the Son of man according to the flesh, our Lord Jesus Christ.

XVII.

We believe therefore in one God, that is, in one First Cause, the God of the law and of the Gospel, the just and good ; and in one Lord Jesus Christ, true God, that is, Image of the true God, Maker of all things seen and unseen, Son of God and only-begotten Offspring, and Eternal Word, living and self-subsistent and active,[2] always being with the Father ; and in one Holy Spirit ; and in the glorious advent of the Son of God, who of the Virgin Mary took flesh, and endured sufferings and death in our stead, and came to resurrection on the third day, and was taken up to heaven ; and in His glorious appearing yet to come ; and in one holy Church, the forgiveness of sins, the resurrection of the flesh, and life eternal.

XVIII.

We acknowledge that the Son and the Spirit are consubstantial with the Father, and that the substance of the Trinity is one, — that is, that there is one divinity according to nature, the Father remaining unbegotten, and the Son being begotten of the Father in a true generation, and not in a formation by will,[3] and the Spirit being sent forth eternally from the substance of the Father through the Son, with power to sanctify the whole creation. And we further acknowledge that the Word was made flesh, and was manifested in the flesh-movement[4] received of a virgin, and did not simply energize in a man. And those who have fellowship with men that reject the *consubstantiality* as a doctrine foreign to the Scriptures, and speak of any of the persons in the Trinity as created, and separate that person from the one natural divinity, we hold as aliens, and have fellowship with none such.[5] There is one God the Father, and there is only one divinity. But the Son also is God, as being the true image of the one and only divinity, according to generation and the nature which He has from

the Father. There is one Lord the Son ; but in like manner there is the Spirit, who bears over[6] the Son's lordship to the creature that is sanctified. The Son sojourned in the world, having of the Virgin received flesh, which He filled with the Holy Spirit for the sanctification of us all ; and having given up the flesh to death, He destroyed death through the resurrection that had in view the resurrection of us all ; and He ascended to heaven, exalting and glorifying men in Himself ; and He comes the second time to bring us again eternal life.

XIX.

One is the Son, both before the incarnation and after the incarnation. The same (Son) is both man and God, both these together as though one ; and the God the Word is not one person, and the man Jesus another person, but the same who subsisted as Son before was made one with flesh by Mary, so constituting Himself a perfect, and holy, and sinless man, and using that economical position for the renewal of mankind and the salvation of all the world. God the Father, being Himself the perfect Person, has thus the perfect Word begotten of Him truly, not as a word that is spoken, nor yet again as a son by adoption, in the sense in which angels and men are called sons of God, but as a Son who is in nature God. And there is also the perfect Holy Spirit supplied[7] of God through the Son to the sons of adoption, living and life-giving, holy and imparting holiness to those who partake of Him, — not like an unsubstantial breath[8] breathed into them by man, but as the living Breath proceeding from God. Wherefore the Trinity is to be adored, to be glorified, to be honoured, and to be reverenced ; the Father being apprehended in the Son even as the Son is of Him, and the Son being glorified in the Father, inasmuch as He is of the Father, and being manifested in the Holy Spirit to the sanctified.

XX.

And that the holy Trinity is to be worshipped without either separation or alienation, is taught us by Paul, who says in his Second Epistle to the Corinthians : " The grace of our Lord Jesus Christ, and the love of God, and the communion of the Holy Ghost, be with you all." [9] And again, in that epistle he makes this explanation : " Now He which stablisheth us with you in Christ, and hath anointed us, is God, who hath also sealed us, and given the earnest of the Spirit in our hearts." [10] And still more clearly

---

[1] θεοποιηθῶμεν.
[2] ἐνεργόν.
[3] ποιήσει ἐκ βουλήσεως.
[4] κινήσει. [For the spiritual κίνησις, vol. iii. note 6, p. 622.]
[5] [Evidently after the Nicene Council; the *consubstantiality*, as a phrase and test of orthodoxy, belonging to the Nicene period.]

[6] διαπέμπων.
[7] χορηγούμενον.
[8] πνοήν.
[9] 2 Cor. xiii. 13.
[10] 2 Cor. i. 21, 22.

he writes thus in the same epistle : " When Moses is read, the veil is upon their heart. Nevertheless when it shall turn to the Lord, the veil shall be taken away. Now the Lord is that Spirit ; and where the Spirit of the Lord is, there is liberty. But we all with open face beholding as in a glass the glory of the Lord, are changed into the same image, from glory to glory, even as by the Spirit of the Lord." [1]

XXI.

And again Paul says : " That mortality might be swallowed up of life. Now He that hath wrought us for the selfsame thing is God, who also hath given unto us the earnest of the Spirit." [2] And again he says : " Approving ourselves as the ministers of God, in much patience, in afflictions, in necessities," [3] and so forth. Then he adds these words : " By kindness, by the Holy Ghost, by love unfeigned, by the word of truth, by the power of God." [4] Behold here again the saint has defined the holy Trinity, naming God, and the Word, and the Holy Ghost. And again he says : " Know ye not that ye are the temple of God, and that the Spirit of God dwelleth in you ? If any man defile the temple of God, him shall God destroy." [5] And again : " But ye are washed, but ye are justified in the name of our Lord Jesus, and by the Spirit of our God." [6] And again : " What ! know ye not that your bodies are the temple of the Holy Ghost which is in you, which ye have of God?" [7] " And I think also that I have the Spirit of God." [8]

XXII.

And again, speaking also of the children of Israel as baptized in the cloud and in the sea, he says : " And they all drank of the same spiritual drink : for they drank of that spiritual Rock that followed them, and that Rock was Christ." [9] And again he says : " Wherefore I give you to understand, that no man speaking by the Spirit of God calleth Jesus accursed : and that no man can say that Jesus is the Lord, but by the Holy Ghost. Now there are diversities of gifts, but the same Spirit. And there are differences of administrations, but the same Lord. And there are diversities of operations, but it is the same God which worketh all in all. But the manifestation of the Spirit is given to every man to profit withal. For to one is given by the Spirit

the word of wisdom ; to another the word of knowledge by the same Spirit ; to another faith by the same Spirit ; to another the gifts of healing by the same Spirit ; to another the working of miracles ; to another prophecy ; to another discerning of spirits ; to another divers kinds of tongues ; to another the interpretation of tongues : but all these worketh that one and the selfsame Spirit, dividing to every man severally as He will. For as the body is one, and hath many members, and all the members of that one body, being many, are one body ; so also is Christ. For by one Spirit are we all baptized into one body." [10] And again he says : " For if he who comes preaches another Christ whom we have not preached, or ye receive another spirit that ye have received not, or another gospel which ye have not obtained, ye will rightly be kept back." [11]

XXIII.

Seest thou that the Spirit is inseparable from the divinity ? And no one with pious apprehensions could fancy that He is a creature. Moreover, in the Epistle to the Hebrews he writes again thus : " How shall we escape, if we neglect so great salvation ; which at the first began to be spoken by the Lord, and was confirmed unto us by them that heard Him ; God also bearing them witness, both with signs and wonders, and with divers miracles, and gifts of the Holy Ghost?" [12] And again he says in the same epistle : " Wherefore, as the Holy Ghost saith, To-day, if ye will hear His voice, harden not your hearts, as in the provocation, in the day of temptation in the wilderness ; when your fathers tempted me, proved me, and saw my works forty years. Wherefore I was grieved with that generation, and said, They do always err in their heart ; for [13] they have not known my ways : as I sware in my wrath, that they should not enter into my rest." [14] And there, too, they ought to give ear to Paul, for he by no means separates the Holy Spirit from the divinity of the Father and the Son, but clearly sets forth the discourse of the Holy Ghost as one from the person of the Father, and thus as given expression to [15] by God, just as it has been represented in the before-mentioned sayings. Wherefore the holy Trinity is believed to be one God, in accordance with these testimonies of Holy Scripture ; albeit all through the inspired Scriptures numberless announcements are supplied us, all confirmatory of the apostolic and ecclesiastical faith.

[1] 2 Cor. iii. 15-18.
[2] 2 Cor. v. 4, 5.
[3] 2 Cor. vi. 4.
[4] 2 Cor. vi. 6, 7.
[5] 1 Cor. iii. 16, 17.
[6] 1 Cor. vi. 11.
[7] 1 Cor. vi. 19.
[8] 1 Cor. vii. 40.
[9] 1 Cor. x. 4.

[10] 1 Cor. xii. 3-13.
[11] καλῶς ἂν εἴχεσθε. Referring perhaps to Gal. i. 8, 9.
[12] Heb. ii. 3, 4.
[13] διότι.
[14] Heb. iii. 7-11.
[15] εἰρημένην.

A FRAGMENT OF THE SAME DECLARATION OF FAITH, ACCOMPANIED BY GLOSSES.[1]

FROM GREGORY THAUMATURGUS, AS THEY SAY, IN HIS SECTIONAL CONFESSION OF FAITH.

To maintain two natures[2] in the one Christ, makes a Tetrad of the Trinity, says he ; for he expressed himself thus : "And it is the true God, the unincarnate, that was manifested in the flesh, perfect with the true and divine perfection, not with two natures ; nor do we speak of worshipping four (persons), viz., God, and the Son of God, and man, and the Holy Spirit." First, however, this passage is misapprehended, and is of very doubtful import. Nevertheless it bears that we should not speak of two persons in Christ, lest, by thus acknowledging Him as God, and as in the perfect divinity, and yet speaking of two persons, we should make a Tetrad of the divine persons, counting that of God the Father as one, and that of the Son of God as one, and that of the man as one, and that of the Holy Spirit as one. But, again, it bears also against recognising two divine natures,[3] and rather for acknowledging Him to be perfect God in one natural divine perfection, and not in two ; for his object is to show that He became incarnate without change, and that He retains the divinity without duplication.[4] Accordingly he says shortly : "And while the affections of the flesh spring, the energy[5] retains the impassibility proper to it. He, therefore, who introduces the (idea of) passion into the energy is impious ; for it was the Lord of glory that appeared in human form, having taken to Himself the human economy."

[1] From the book against the Monophysites by Leontius of Jerusalem, in Mai, *Script. Vet.*, vol. vii. p. 147.
[2] φύσεις.
[3] φύσεις.
[4] ἀδιπλασιάστως.
[5] δύναμις.

ELUCIDATION.

(The minister . . . to the Gentiles, p. 43.)

If St. Peter had been at Rome, St. Paul would not have come there (2 Cor. x. 16). The two apostles had each his jurisdiction, and they kept to their own "line of things" respectively. How, then, came St. Peter to visit Rome? The answer is clear : unless he came involuntarily, as a prisoner, he came to look after the Church of the *Circumcision*,[1] which was " in his measure ;" and doubtless St. Paul urged him to this, the Hebrew Christians there being so large a proportion of the Church. St. Peter came "at the close of his life," doubtless attended by an apostolic companion, as St. Paul was, and Barnabas also (Acts xv. 39, 40). Linus probably laboured for St. Paul (in prison) among the Gentile Romans,[2] and Cletus for St. Peter among Jewish Christians. St. Peter *survived all his martyred associates*, and left Clement in charge of the whole Church. This most probable theory squares with all known facts, and reconciles all difficulties. Clement, then, was first bishop of Rome (A.D. 65) ; and so says Tertullian, vol iii. p. 258, note 9.

That compendious but superficial little work, Smith's *History of the First Ten Centuries*,[3] justly censures as " misleading " the usage, which it yet keeps up, of calling the early bishops of Rome " Popes." [4] The same author utterly misunderstands Cyprian's references to Rome as " *a* principal *cathedra*," " *a* root and *matrix*," etc. ; importing into the indefinite Latin *a definite article*. Cyprian applies a similar principle, after his master Tertullian (vol. iii. p. 260, this series), to all the Apostolic Sees, the *matrices* of Christian churches.

[1] Origen says so, expressly. See Cave, *Lives*, i. p. 230.   [2] 2 Tim. iv. 21.   [3] *The Student's Eccl. Hist.*, London, 1878.
[4] It accepts the statement that the earliest application of this term, by way of eminence, to the Bishop of Rome, is found in Evnodius of Pavia, *circa* A.D. 500. Robertson, vol. i. p. 560.

ON THE TRINITY.

FRAGMENT FROM THE DISCOURSE.[1]

GREGORY THAUMATURGUS, Bishop of Neo-Cæsareia in Pontus,[2] near successor of the apostles, in his discourse on the Trinity, speaks thus : —

I see in all three essentials — substance, genus, name. We speak of man, servant, curator (*curatorem*), — man, by reason of substance ; servant, by reason of genus or condition ; curator, by reason of denomination. We speak also of Father, Son, and Holy Spirit : these, however, are not names which have only supervened at some after period, but they are subsistences. Again, the denomination of *man* is not in actual fact a denomination, but a substance common to men, and is the denomination proper to all men. Moreover, names are such as these, — Adam, Abraham, Isaac, Jacob : these, I say, are names. But the Divine Persons are names indeed : and the names are still the persons ; and the persons then signify that which is and subsists, — which is the essence of God. The name also of the nature signifies subsistence ;[3] as if we should speak of the *man*. All (the persons) are one nature, one essence, one will, and are called the Holy Trinity ; and these also are names subsistent, one nature in three persons, and one genus. But the person of the Son is composite in its oneness (*unita est*), being one made up of two, that is, of divinity and humanity together, which two constitute one. Yet the divinity does not consequently receive any increment, but the Trinity remains as it was. Nor does anything new befall the persons even or the names, but these are eternal and without time. No one, however, was sufficient to know these until the Son being made flesh manifested them, saying : "Father, I have manifested Thy name to men ; glorify Thou me also, that they may know me as Thy Son."[4] And on the mount the Father spake, and said, "This is my beloved Son."[5] And the same sent His Holy Spirit at the Jordan. And thus it was declared to us that there is an Eternal Trinity in equal honour. Besides, the generation of the Son by the Father is incomprehensible and ineffable ; and because it is spiritual, its investigation becomes impracticable : for a spiritual object can neither be understood nor traced by a corporeal object, for that is far removed from human nature. We men know indeed the generation proper to us, as also that of other objects ; but a spiritual matter is above human condition, neither can it in any manner be understood by the minds of men. Spiritual substance can neither perish nor be dissolved ; ours, however, as is easy to understand, perishes and is dissolved. How, indeed, could it be possible for man, who is limited on six sides — by east, west, south, north, deep, and sky — understand a matter which is above the skies, which is beneath the deeps, which stretches beyond the north and south, and which is present in every place, and fills all vacuity ? But if, indeed, we are able to scrutinize spiritual substance, its excellence truly would be undone. Let us consider what is done in our body ; and, furthermore, let us see whether it is in our power to ascertain in what manner thoughts are born of the heart, and words of the tongue, and the like. Now, if we can by no means apprehend things that are done in ourselves, how could it ever be that we should understand the mystery of the uncreated Creator, which goes beyond every mind ? Assuredly, if this mystery were one that could be penetrated by man, the inspired John would by no means have affirmed this : "No man hath seen God at any time."[6] He, then, whom no man hath seen at any time, — whom can we reckon Him to resemble, so that thereby we should understand His generation ? And we, indeed, without ambiguity apprehend that our soul dwells in us in union with the body ; but still, who has ever seen his own soul ? who has been able to discern its conjunction with his body ? This one

---

[1] Mai, *Spicil. Rom.*, vol. iii. p. 696, from the Arabic Codex, 101.
[2] The Arabic Codex reads falsely, Cæsareæ Cappadociæ.
[3] Or, the name signifies the subsistence of the nature — *Nomen quoque naturæ significat subsistentiam.*
[4] John xvii. 6.
[5] Matt. iii. 17.
[6] John i. 18.

thing is all we know certainly, that there is a soul within us conjoined with the body. Thus, then, we reason and believe that the Word is begotten by the Father, albeit we neither possess nor know the clear *rationale* of the fact. The Word Himself is before every creature — eternal from the Eternal, like spring from spring, and light from light. The vocable *Word*, indeed, belongs to those three genera of words which are named in Scripture, and which are not substantial, — namely, the word *conceived*,[1] the word *uttered*,[2] and the word *articulated*.[3] The word *conceived*, certainly, is not substantial. The word *uttered*, again, is that voice which the prophets hear from God, or the prophetic speech itself; and even this is not substantial. And, lastly, the word *articulated* is the speech of man formed forth in air (*aëre efformatus*), composed of terms, which also is not substantial.[4] But the Word of God is substantial, endowed with an exalted and enduring nature, and is eternal with Himself, and is inseparable from Him, and

can never fall away, but shall remain in an everlasting union. This Word created heaven and earth, and in Him were all things made. He is the arm and the power of God, never to be separated from the Father, in virtue of an indivisible nature, and, together with the Father, He is without beginning. This Word took our substance of the Virgin Mary; and in so far as He is spiritual indeed, He is indivisibly equal with the Father; but in so far as He is corporeal, He is in like manner inseparably equal with us. And, again, in so far as He is spiritual, He supplies in the same equality (*æquiparat*) the Holy Spirit, inseparably and without limit. Neither were there two natures, but only one nature of the Holy Trinity before the incarnation of the Word, the Son; and the nature of the Trinity remained one also after the incarnation of the Son. But if any one, moreover, believes that any increment has been given to the Trinity by reason of the assumption of humanity by the Word, he is an alien from us, and from the ministry of the Catholic and Apostolic Church. This is the perfect, holy, Apostolic faith of the holy God. Praise to the Holy Trinity for ever through the ages of the ages. Amen.

---

[1] τὸ κατ᾽ ἔννοιαν.
[2] προφορικόν.
[3] ἀρθρικόν.
[4] On these terms, consult the Greek Fathers in Petavius, *de Trin.*, book vi. [See Elucidation below.]

ELUCIDATION.

PETAVIUS, to whom the translator refers his readers, may be trusted in points where he has no theory of his own to sustain, but must always be accepted with caution. The Greek Fathers in this very series, from Justin [1] onward, enable us to put the later terminology to the test of earlier exposition (see examples in the notes to the *Praxeas* of Tertullian, and consult Dr. Holmes' valuable note embodied in my elucidations).[2] We may go back to Theophilus for the distinction between the ἐνδιάθετος and the προφορικός, the immanent and the uttered Word.[3] Compare Tertullian, also, against Marcion.[4] Evidences, therefore, are abundant and *archaic*, indeed, to prove that the Ante-Nicene Fathers, with those of the Nicene and the Post-Nicene periods, were of one mind, and virtually of one voice.

---

[1] Vol. i. pp. 164, 166, 170, 178, 190–193, 263, 272; Irenæus, *Ibid.*, 468, 546, etc.
[2] Vol. iii. p. 628. Compare (same volume) notes 15, p. 602, and 1, p. 604.
[3] Vol. ii. p. 98, notes 1, 2; also p. 103, note 5. [4] Vol. iii. p. 299, note 19.

TWELVE TOPICS ON THE FAITH.

WHEREIN IS GIVEN ALSO THE FORMULA OF EXCOMMUNICATION, AND AN EXPLICATION IS SUBJOINED TO EACH.[1]

TOPIC I.

IF any one says that the body of Christ is uncreated, and refuses to acknowledge that He, being the uncreated Word (God) of God, took the flesh of created humanity and appeared incarnate, even as it is written, let him be anathema.

EXPLICATION.

How could the body be said to be uncreated? For the uncreated is the passionless, invulnerable, intangible. But Christ, on rising from the dead, showed His disciples the print of the nails and the wound made by the spear, and a body that could be handled, although He also had entered among them when the doors were shut, with the view of showing them at once the energy of the divinity and the reality of the body.

Yet, while being God, He was recognised as man in a natural manner; and while subsisting truly as man, He was also manifested as God by His works.[2]

TOPIC II.

If any one affirms that the flesh of Christ is consubstantial with the divinity, and refuses to acknowledge that He, subsisting Himself in the form of God as God before all ages, emptied Himself and took the form of a servant, even as it is written, let him be anathema.

EXPLICATION.

How could the flesh, which is conditioned by time, be said to be consubstantial[3] with the timeless divinity? For that is designated consubstantial which is the same in nature and in eternal duration without variableness.

TOPIC III.

If any one affirms that Christ, just like one of the prophets, assumed the perfect man, and refuses to acknowledge that, being begotten in the flesh of the Virgin,[4] He became man and was born in Bethlehem, and was brought up in Nazareth, and advanced in age, and on completing the set number of years (appeared in public and) was baptized in the Jordan, and received this testimony from the Father, "This is my beloved Son,"[5] even as it is written, let him be anathema.

EXPLICATION.

How could it be said that Christ (the Lord) assumed the perfect man just like one of the prophets, when He, being the Lord Himself, became man by the incarnation effected through the Virgin? Wherefore it is written, that "the first man was of the earth, earthy."[6] But whereas he that was formed of the earth returned to the earth, He that became the second man returned to heaven. And so we read of the "first Adam and the last Adam."[7] And as it is admitted that the second came by the first according to the flesh, for which reason also Christ is called man and the Son of man; so is the witness given that the second is the Saviour of the first, for whose sake He came down from heaven. And as the Word came down from heaven, and was made man, and ascended again to heaven, He is on that account said to be the second Adam from heaven.

TOPIC IV.

If any one affirms that Christ was born of the seed of man by the Virgin, in the same manner as all men are born, and refuses to acknowledge that He was made flesh by the Holy Spirit and the holy Virgin Mary, and became man of the seed of David, even as it is written, let him be anathema.

EXPLICATION.

How could one say that Christ was born of the seed of man by the Virgin, when the holy

---

[1] Works of Grester, vol. xv. p. 434, Ratisbon, 1741, in fol., from a manuscript codex.
[2] This paragraph is wanting in a very ancient copy.
[3] ομοουσιος.

[4] Reading ἐκ παρθένου for ἐκ παθόντος.
[5] Matt. iii. 17.
[6] 1 Cor. xv. 47.
[7] 1 Cor. xv. 45.

Gospel and the angel, in proclaiming the good tidings, testify of Mary the Virgin that she said, "How shall this be, seeing I know not a man?"[1] Wherefore he says, "The Holy Ghost shall come upon thee, and the power of the highest shall overshadow thee : therefore also that holy thing which shall be born of thee shall be called the Son of the Highest."[2] And to Joseph he says, "Fear not to take unto thee Mary thy wife : for that which is conceived in her is of the Holy Ghost. And she shall bring forth a son, and they shall call His name Jesus : for He shall save His people from their sins."[3]

TOPIC V.

If any one affirms that the Son of God who is before the ages is one, and He who has appeared in these last times is another, and refuses to acknowledge that He who is before the ages is the same with Him who appeared in these last times, even as it is written, let him be anathema.

EXPLICATION.

How could it be said that the Son of God who is before the ages, and He who has appeared in these last times, are different, when the Lord Himself says, "Before Abraham was, I am ;"[4] and, "I came forth from God, and I come, and again I go to my Father?"[5]

TOPIC VI.

If any one affirms that He who suffered is one, and that He who suffered not is another, and refuses to acknowledge that the Word, who is Himself the impassible and unchangeable God, suffered in the flesh which He had assumed really, yet without mutation, even as it is written, let him be anathema.

EXPLICATION.

How could it be said that He who suffered is one, and He who suffered not another, when the Lord Himself says, "The Son of man must suffer many things, and be killed, and be raised again the third day from the dead ;"[6] and again, "When ye see the Son of man sitting on the right hand of the Father ;"[7] and again, "When the Son of man cometh in the glory of His Father?"[8]

TOPIC VII.

If any one affirms that Christ is saved, and refuses to acknowledge that He is the Saviour of the world, and the Light of the world, even as it is written,[9] let him be anathema.

EXPLICATION.

How could one say that Christ is saved, when the Lord Himself says, "I am the life ;"[10] and, "I am come that they might have life ;"[11] and, "He that believeth on me shall not see death, but he shall behold the life eternal?"[12]

TOPIC VIII.

If any one affirms that Christ is perfect man and also God the Word in the way of separation,[13] and refuses to acknowledge the one Lord Jesus Christ, even as it is written, let him be anathema.

EXPLICATION.

How could one say that Christ is perfect man and also God the Word in the way of separation, when the Lord Himself says, "Why seek ye to kill me, a man that hath told you the truth, which I have heard of God?"[14] For God the Word did not give a man for us, but He gave Himself for us, having been made man for our sake. Wherefore He says : "Destroy this temple, and in three days I will raise it up. But He spake of the temple of His body."[15]

TOPIC IX.

If any one says that Christ suffers change or alteration, and refuses to acknowledge that He is unchangeable in the Spirit, though corruptible[16] in the flesh,[17] let him be anathema.

EXPLICATION.

How could one say that Christ suffers change or alteration, when the Lord Himself says, "I am, and I change not ;"[18] and again, "His soul shall not be left in Hades, neither shall His flesh see corruption?"[19]

TOPIC X.

If any one affirms that Christ assumed the man only in part, and refuses to acknowledge that He was made in all things like us, apart from sin, let him be anathema.

---

1 Luke i. 34.
2 Luke i. 35.
3 Matt. i. 20, 21.
4 John viii. 58.
5 John xiii. and xvi.
6 Matt. xvi. 21.
7 Matt. xxvi. 64; Mark xiv. 62.
8 Matt. xvi. 27.

9 Isa. ix.; Matt. iv.; John i., iii., viii., ix., xii.
10 John xi. 25, xiv. 6.
11 John x. 10.
12 John viii. 51.
13 διαιρετῶς.
14 John viii. 40.
15 Or, and incorruptible.
16 John ii. 20, 21.
17 [Christ's flesh being incorruptible, transubstantiation cannot be true: the holy food is digested in its material part.]
18 Mal. iii. 6.
19 Ps. xvi. 10; Acts ii. 31.

EXPLICATION.

How could one say that Christ assumed the man only in part, when the Lord Himself says, "I lay down my life, that I might take it again, for the sheep;"[1] and, "My flesh is meat indeed, and my blood is drink indeed;"[2] and, "He that eateth my flesh, and drinketh my blood, hath eternal life?"[3]

TOPIC XI.

If any one affirms that the body of Christ is void of soul and understanding,[4] and refuses to acknowledge that He is perfect man, one and the same in all things (with us), let him be anathema.

EXPLICATION.

How could one say that the body of the Lord (Christ) is void of soul and understanding? For perturbation, and grief, and distress, are not the properties either of a flesh void of soul, or of a soul void of understanding; nor are they the sign of the immutable Divinity, nor the index of a mere phantasm, nor do they mark the defect of human weakness; but the Word exhibited in Himself the exercise of the affections and susceptibilities proper to us, having endued Himself with our passibility, even as it is written, that "He hath borne our griefs, and carried our sorrows."[5] For perturbation, and grief, and distress, are disorders of soul; and toil, and sleep, and the body's liability to wounding, are infirmities of the flesh.

TOPIC XII.

If any one says that Christ was manifested in the world only in semblance, and refuses to acknowledge that He came actually in the flesh, let him be anathema.

EXPLICATION.

How could one say that Christ was manifested only in semblance in the world, born as He was in Bethlehem, and made to submit to the circumcising of the flesh, and lifted up by Simeon, and brought up on to His twelfth year (at home), and made subject to His parents, and baptized in Jordan, and nailed to the cross, and raised again from the dead?

Wherefore, when it is said that He was "troubled in spirit,"[6] that "He was sorrowful in soul,"[7] that "He was wounded in body,"[8] He places before us designations of susceptibilities proper to our constitution, in order to show that He was made man in the world, and had His conversation with men,[9] yet without sin. For He was born in Bethlehem according to the flesh, in a manner meet for Deity, the angels of heaven recognising Him as their Lord, and hymning as their God Him who was then wrapped in swaddling-clothes in a manger, and exclaiming, "Glory to God in the highest, and on earth peace, good-will among men."[10] He was brought up in Nazareth; but in divine fashion He sat among the doctors, and astonished them by a wisdom beyond His years, in respect of the capacities of His bodily life, as is recorded in the Gospel narrative. He was baptized in Jordan, not as receiving any sanctification for Himself, but as gifting a participation in sanctification to others. He was tempted in the wilderness, not as giving way, however, to temptation, but as putting our temptations before Himself on the challenge of the tempter, in order to show the powerlessness of the tempter.

Wherefore He says, "Be of good cheer, I have overcome the world."[11] And this He said, not as holding before us any contest proper only to a God, but as showing our own flesh in its capacity to overcome suffering, and death, and corruption, in order that, as sin entered into the world by flesh, and death came to reign by sin over all men, the sin in the flesh might also be condemned through the selfsame flesh in the likeness thereof;[12] and that that overseer of sin, the tempter, might be overcome, and death be cast down from its sovereignty, and the corruption in the burying of the body be done away, and the first-fruits of the resurrection be shown, and the principle of righteousness begin its course in the world through faith, and the kingdom of heaven be preached to men, and fellowship be established between God and men.

In behalf of this grace let us glorify the Father, who has given His only begotten Son for the life of the world. Let us glorify the Holy Spirit that worketh in us, and quickeneth us, and furnisheth the gifts meet for the fellowship of God; and let us not intermeddle with the word of the Gospel by lifeless disputations, scattering about endless questionings and logomachies, and making a hard thing of the gentle and simple word of faith; but rather let us work the work of faith, let us love peace, let us exhibit concord, let us preserve unity, let us cultivate love, with which God is well pleased.

As it is not for us to know the times or the seasons which the Father hath put in His own power,[13] but only to believe that there will come an end to time, and that there will be a manifes-

---

[1] John x. 17.
[2] John vi. 55.
[3] John vi. 56.
[4] ἄψυχον καὶ ἀνόητον.
[5] Isa. liii. 4.
[6] John xi. 33, xii. 27, xiii. 21.
[7] Matt. xxvi. 38.
[8] Isa. liii. 5.

[9] Baruch iii. 38.
[10] Luke ii. 14.
[11] John xvi. 33.
[12] Rom. v. 12, viii. 3.
[13] Acts i. 7.

tation of a future world, and a revelation of judgment, and an advent of the Son of God, and a recompense of works, and an inheritance in the kingdom of heaven, so it is not for us to know how the Son of God became man; for this is a great mystery, as it is written, " Who shall declare His generation? for His life is taken from the earth." [1] But it is for us to believe that the Son of God became man, according to the Scriptures; and that He was seen on the earth, and had His conversation with men, according to the Scriptures, in their likeness, yet without sin; and that He died for us, and rose again from the dead, as it is written; and that He was taken up to heaven, and sat down at the right hand of the Father, whence He shall come to judge the quick and the dead, as it is written; lest, while we war against each other with words, any should be led to blaspheme the word of faith, and that should come to pass which is written, " By reason of you is my name [2] continually blasphemed among the nations." [3]

[1] Isa. liii. 8.

[2] Or, the name of God.
[3] Isa. lii. 5.

ELUCIDATION.

THESE " twelve anathemas," as they are called, do evidently refute the Nestorians and later heretics. Evidently, therefore, we must assign this document to another author. And, as frequent references are made to such tests, I subjoin a list of Œcumenical or Catholic Councils, properly so called, as follows : —

1.	JERUSALEM,	against	*Judaism,*[1]		A.D. 50.
2.	NICÆA,	"	*Arianism*	(1),[2]	A.D. 325.
3.	CONSTANTINOPLE (I.),	"	*Semi-Arianism*	(2),	A.D. 381.
4.	EPHESUS,	"	*Nestorianism*	(3),	A.D. 431.
5.	CHALCEDON,	"	*Eutychianism*	(4),	A.D. 451.
6.	CONSTANTINOPLE (II.),	"	*Monophysitism*	(5),	A.D. 553.
7.	CONSTANTINOPLE (III.),	"	*Monothelitism*	(6),[3]	A.D. 680.[4]

These are all *the undisputed* councils. The *Seventh Council,* so called (A.D. 537), was not a free council, and was rejected by a free council of the West, convened at Frankfort A.D. 794. Its acceptance by the Roman pontiffs, subsequently, should have no logical force with the Easterns, who do not recognise their supremacy even over the councils of the West; and no free council has ever been held under pontifical authority. The above list, therefore, is a complete list of all the councils of the undivided Church as defined by Catholic canons. There has been no possibility of a *Catholic* council since the division of East and West. The Council of Frankfort is the pivot of subsequent history, and its fundamental importance has not been sufficiently insisted upon.

[1] As widely different from the other councils as the Apostles from their successors, and part of its decisions were local and temporary. For all that, it was the greatest of councils, and truly *General.*

[2] These numbers indicate the ordinary reckoning of writers, and is correct ecclesiastically. The Council of Jerusalem, however, is the base of Christian orthodoxy, and decided the great principles by which the " General Councils " were professedly ruled.

[3] Theological students are often puzzled to recall the councils in order, and not less to recall the rejected heresies. I have found two mnemonics useful, thus: (1) INCE *and* (CCC) *three hundred ;* (2) JAS. NEMM. *Dulce est desipere,* etc.

[4] A.D. 325 to 680 is the Synodical Period. Gregory I. (Rome) placed the *first four* councils next to the four Gospels.

ON THE SUBJECT OF THE SOUL.[1]

You have instructed us, most excellent Tatian,[2] to forward for your use a discourse upon the soul, laying it out in effective demonstrations. And this you have asked us to do without making use of the testimonies of Scripture, — a method which is opened to us, and which, to those who seek the pious mind, proves a manner of setting forth doctrine more convincing than any reasoning of man.[3] You have said, however, that you desire this, not with a view to your own full assurance, taught as you already have been to hold by the Holy Scriptures and traditions, and to avoid being shaken in your convictions by any subtleties of man's disputations, but with a view to the confuting of men who have different sentiments, and who do not admit that such credit is to be given to the Scriptures, and who endeavour, by a kind of cleverness of speech, to gain over those who are unversed in such discussions. Wherefore we were led to comply readily with this commission of yours, not shrinking from the task on account of inexperience in this method of disputation, but taking encouragement from the knowledge of your good-will toward us. For your kind and friendly disposition towards us will make you understand how to put forward publicly whatever you may approve of as rightly expressed by us, and to pass by and conceal whatever statement of ours you may judge to come short of what is proper. Knowing this, therefore, I have betaken myself with all confidence to the exposition. And in my discourse I shall use a certain order and consecution, such as those who are very expert in these matters employ towards those who desire to investigate any subject intelligently.

First of all, then, I shall propose to inquire by what criterion the soul can, according to its nature, be apprehended; then by what means it can be proved to exist; thereafter, whether it is a *substance* or an *accident*;[4] then consequently on these points, whether it is a body or is incorporeal; then, whether it is simple or compound; next, whether it is mortal or immortal; and finally, whether it is rational or irrational.

For these are the questions which are wont, above all, to be discussed, in any inquiry about the soul, as most important, and as best calculated to mark out its distinctive nature. And as demonstrations for the establishing of these matters of investigation, we shall employ those common modes of consideration[5] by which the credibility of matters under hand is naturally attested. But for the purpose of brevity and utility, we shall at present make use only of those modes of argumentation which are most cogently demonstrative on the subject of our inquiry, in order that clear and intelligible[6] notions may impart to us some readiness for meeting the gainsayers. With this, therefore, we shall commence our discussion.

I. WHEREIN IS THE CRITERION FOR THE APPREHENSION OF THE SOUL.

All things that exist are either known by sense[7] or apprehended by thought.[8] And what falls under sense has its adequate demonstration in sense itself; for at once, with the application, it creates in us the impression[9] of what underlies it. But what is apprehended by thought is known not by itself, but by its operations.[10] The soul, consequently, being unknown by itself, shall be known properly by its effects.

II. WHETHER THE SOUL EXISTS.

Our body, when it is put in action, is put in action either from without or from within. And that it is not put in action from without, is manifest from the circumstance that it is put in action neither by impulsion[11] nor by traction,[12] like soulless things. And again, if it is put in action from within, it is not put in action according to nature, like fire. For fire never loses its action as long

---

[1] A Topical Discourse by our holy father Gregory, surnamed Thaumaturgus, bishop of Neo-Cæsareia in Pontus, addressed to Tatian.
[2] [A person not known.]
[3] [True to the universal testimony of the primitive Fathers as to Holy Scripture.]
[4] [Aristotle, *Physica*. Elucidation I.]

[5] ἐννοίαις.
[6] εὐπαράδεκτα.
[7] αἰσθήσει.
[8] νοήσει.
[9] φαντασίαν.
[10] ἐνεργειῶν.
[11] ὠθούμενον.
[12] ἑλκόμενον.

as there is fire; whereas the body, when it has become dead, is a body void of action. Hence, if it is put in action neither from without, like soulless things, nor according to nature, after the fashion of fire, it is evident that it is put in action by the soul, which also furnishes life to it. If, then, the soul is shown to furnish the life to our body, the soul will also be known for itself by its operations.

III. WHETHER THE SOUL IS A SUBSTANCE.

That the soul is a substance,[1] is proved in the following manner. In the first place, because the definition given to the term substance suits it very well. And that definition is to the effect, that substance is that which, being ever identical, and ever one in point of numeration with itself, is yet capable of taking on contraries in succession.[2] And that this soul, without passing the limit of its own proper nature, takes on contraries in succession, is, I fancy, clear to everybody. For righteousness and unrighteousness, courage and cowardice, temperance and intemperance, are seen in it successively; and these are contraries. If, then, it is the property of a substance to be capable of taking on contraries in succession, and if the soul is shown to sustain the definition in these terms, it follows that the soul is a substance. And in the second place, because if the body is a substance, the soul must also be a substance. For it cannot be, that what only has life imparted should be a substance, and that what imparts the life should be no substance: unless one should assert that the non-existent is the cause of the existent; or unless, again, one were insane enough to allege that the dependent object is itself the cause of that very thing in which it has its being, and without which it could not subsist.[3]

IV. WHETHER THE SOUL IS INCORPOREAL.

That the soul is in our body, has been shown above. We ought now, therefore, to ascertain in what manner it is in the body. Now, if it is in juxtaposition with it, as one pebble with another, it follows that the soul will be a body, and also that the whole body will not be animated with soul,[4] inasmuch as with a certain part it will only be in juxtaposition. But if, again, it is mingled or fused with the body, the soul will become multiplex,[5] and not simple, and will thus be despoiled of the rationale proper to a soul. For what is multiplex is also divisible

and dissoluble; and what is dissoluble, on the other hand, is compound;[6] and what is compound is separable in a threefold manner. Moreover, body attached to body makes weight;[7] but the soul, subsisting in the body, does not make weight, but rather imparts life. The soul, therefore, cannot be a body, but is incorporeal.

Again, if the soul is a body, it is put in action either from without or from within. But it is not put in action from without; for it is moved neither by impulsion nor by traction, like soulless things. Nor is it put in action from within, like objects animated with soul; for it is absurd to talk of a soul of the soul: it cannot, therefore, be a body, but it is incorporeal.

And besides, if the soul is a body, it has sensible qualities, and is maintained by nurture. But it is not thus nurtured. For if it is nurtured, it is not nurtured corporeally, like the body, but incorporeally; for it is nurtured by reason. It has not, therefore, sensible qualities: for neither is righteousness, nor courage, nor any one of these things, something that is seen; yet these are the qualities of the soul. It cannot, therefore, be a body, but is incorporeal.

Still further, as all corporeal substance is divided into animate and inanimate, let those who hold that the soul is a body tell us whether we are to call it animate or inanimate.

Finally, if every body has colour, and quantity, and figure, and if there is not one of these qualities perceptible in the soul, it follows that the soul is not a body.[8]

V. WHETHER THE SOUL IS SIMPLE OR COMPOUND.

We prove, then, that the soul is simple, best of all, by those arguments by which its incorporeality has been demonstrated. For if it is not a body, while every body is compound, and what is composite is made up of parts, and is consequently multiplex, the soul, on the other hand, being incorporeal, is simple; since thus it is both uncompounded and indivisible into parts.

VI. WHETHER OUR SOUL IS IMMORTAL.

It follows, in my opinion, as a necessary consequence, that what is simple is immortal. And as to how that follows, hear my explanation: Nothing that exists is its own corrupter,[9] else it could never have had any thorough consistency, even from the beginning. For things that are subject to corruption are corrupted by contraries: wherefore everything that is corrupted is subject to dissolution; and what is subject to

---

[1] οὐσία.
[2] τῶν ἐναντίων παραμέρος εἶναι δεκτικόν. παραμέρος, here apparently = in turn, though usually = out of turn.
[3] The text has an apparent inversion: τὸ ἐν ᾧ τὴν ὕπαρξιν ἔχον καὶ οὗ ἄνευ εἶναι μὴ δυνάμενον, αἴτιον ἐκείνου εἶναι τοῦ ἐν ᾧ ἐστί. There is also a variety of reading: καὶ ὁ ἄνευ τοῦ εἶναι μὴ δυνάμενον.
[4] ἔμψυχον.
[5] πολυμερής.

[6] σύνθετον.
[7] ὄγκον.
[8] [These are Aristotle's accidents, of which, see Thomas Aquinas and the schoolmen passim.]
[9] φθαρτικὸν.

dissolution is compound ; and what is compound is of many parts ; and what is made up of parts manifestly is made up of diverse parts ; and the diverse is not the identical : consequently the soul, being simple, and not being made up of diverse parts, but being uncompound and indissoluble, must be, in virtue of that, incorruptible and immortal.

Besides, everything that is put in action by something else, and does not possess the principle of life in itself, but gets it from that which puts it in action, endures just so long as it is held by the power that operates in it ; and whenever the operative power ceases, that also comes to a stand which has its capacity of action from it. But the soul, being self-acting, has no cessation of its being. For it follows, that what is self-acting is ever-acting ; and what is ever-acting is unceasing ; and what is unceasing is without end ; and what is without end is incorruptible ; and what is incorruptible is immortal. Consequently, if the soul is self-acting, as has been shown above, it follows that it is incorruptible and immortal, in accordance with the mode of reasoning already expressed.

And further, everything that is not corrupted by the evil proper to itself, is incorruptible ; and the evil is opposed to the good, and is consequently its corrupter. For the evil of the body is nothing else than suffering, and disease, and death ; just as, on the other hand, its excellency is beauty, life, health, and vigour. If, therefore, the soul is not corrupted by the evil proper to itself, and the evil of the soul is cowardice, intemperance, envy, and the like, and all these things do not despoil it of its powers of life and action, it follows that it is immortal.

VII. WHETHER OUR SOUL IS RATIONAL.

That our soul is rational, one might demonstrate by many arguments. And first of all from the fact that it has discovered the arts that are for the service of our life. For no one could say that these arts were introduced casually and accidentally, as no one could prove them to be idle, and of no utility for our life. If, then, these arts contribute to what is profitable for our life, and if the profitable is commendable, and if the commendable is constituted by rea-

son, and if these things are the discovery of the soul, it follows that our soul is rational.

Again, that our soul is rational, is also proved by the fact that our senses are not sufficient for the apprehension of things. For we are not competent for the knowledge of things by the simple application of the faculty of sensation. But as we do not choose to rest in these without inquiry,[1] that proves that the senses, apart from reason, are felt to be incapable of discriminating between things which are identical in form and similar in colour, though quite distinct in their natures. If, therefore, the senses, apart from reason, give us a false conception of things, we have to consider whether things that are can be apprehended in reality or not. And if they can be apprehended, then the power which enables us to get at them is one different from, and superior to, the senses. And if they are not apprehended, it will not be possible for us at all to apprehend things which are different in their appearance from the reality. But that objects are apprehensible by us, is clear from the fact that we employ each in a way adaptable to utility, and again turn them to what we please. Consequently, if it has been shown that things which are can be apprehended by us, and if the senses, apart from reason, are an erroneous test of objects, it follows that the intellect[2] is what distinguishes all things in reason, and discerns things as they are in their actuality. But the intellect is just the rational portion of the soul, and consequently the soul is rational.

Finally, because we do nothing without having first marked it out for ourselves ; and as that is nothing else than just the high prerogative[3] of the soul, — for its knowlege of things does not come to it from without, but it rather sets out these things, as it were, with the adornment of its own thoughts, and thus first pictures forth the object in itself, and only thereafter carries it out to actual fact, — and because the high prerogative of the soul is nothing else than the doing of all things with reason, in which respect it also differs from the senses, the soul has thereby been demonstrated to be rational.

---

1 ἐπεὶ μηδὲ στῆναι περὶ αὐτὰ θέλομεν.
2 νοῦς.
3 ἀξίωμα. [Elucidation II.]

ELUCIDATIONS.

I.

(Substance or accident, p. 54.)

THIS essay is "rather the work of a philosopher than a bishop," says Dupin. He assigns it to an age when "Aristotle *began to be in some reputation*," — a most important concession as to the estimate of this philosopher among the early faithful. We need not wonder that such admissions, honourable to his candour and to his orthodoxy, brought on him the hatred and persecutions of the Jesuits. Even Bossuet thought he went too far, and wrote against him. But, the whole system of Roman dogma being grounded in Aristotle's *physics* as well as in his *metaphysics*, Dupin was not orthodox in the eyes of the society that framed Aristotle into a creed, and made it the creed of the "Roman-Catholic Church." Note, e.g., "transubstantiation," which is not true if Aristotle's theory of *accidents*, etc., is false.[1] It assumes an exploded science.

II.

(Prerogative of the soul, p. 56.)

If this "Discourse" be worthy of study, it may be profitably contrasted, step by step, with Tertullian's treatises on kindred subjects.[2] That the early Christians should reason concerning the Soul, the Mind, the immortal Spirit, was natural in itself. But it was also forced upon them by the "philosophers" and the heretics, with whom they daily came into conflict. This is apparent from the *Anti-Marcion*[3] of the great Carthaginian. The annotations upon that treatise, and those *On the Soul's Testimony* and *On the Soul*, may suffice as pointing out the best sources[4] of information on speculative points and their bearings on theology. Compare, however, Athenagoras[5] and the great Clement of Alexandria.[6]

---

[1] See Bacon's apophthegm, No. 275, p. 172, *Works*, London, 1730.
[2] Vol. iii. pp. 175-235, this series.
[3] Vol. iii. pp. 463, 474; also pp. 532, 537, 557, 570, and 587.
[4] Compare, also, Bishop Kaye's *Tertullian*, p. 199, etc.
[5] E.g., vol. ii. p. 157, etc.
[6] Vol. ii. pp. 440, 584 (Fragment), and what he says of free-will.

FOUR HOMILIES.[1]

ON THE ANNUNCIATION TO THE HOLY VIRGIN MARY.[2]

To-day are strains of praise sung joyfully by the choir of angels, and the light of the advent of Christ shines brightly upon the faithful. To-day is the glad spring-time to us, and Christ the Sun of righteousness has beamed with clear light around us, and has illumined the minds of the faithful. To-day is Adam made anew,[3] and moves in the choir of angels, having winged his way to heaven. To-day is the whole circle of the earth filled with joy, since the sojourn of the Holy Spirit has been realized to men. To-day the grace of God and the hope of the unseen shine through all wonders transcending imagination, and make the mystery that was kept hid from eternity plainly discernible to us. To-day are woven the chaplets of never-fading virtue. To-day, God, willing to crown the sacred heads of those whose pleasure is to hearken to Him, and who delight in His festivals, invites the lovers of unswerving faith as His called and His heirs; and the heavenly kingdom is urgent to summon those who mind celestial things to join the divine service of the incorporeal choirs. To-day is fulfilled the word of David, "Let the heavens rejoice, and let the earth be glad. The fields shall be joyful, and all the trees of the wood before the Lord, because He cometh."[4] David thus made mention of the trees;[5] and the Lord's forerunner also spoke of them as trees[6] "that should bring forth fruits meet for repentance,"[7]

or rather for the coming of the Lord. But our Lord Jesus Christ promises perpetual gladness to all those who believe on Him. For He says, "I will see you, and ye shall rejoice; and your joy no man taketh from you."[8] To-day is the illustrious and ineffable mystery of Christians, who have willingly[9] set their hope like a seal upon Christ, plainly declared to us. To-day did Gabriel, who stands by God, come to the pure virgin, bearing to her the glad annunciation, "Hail, thou that art highly favoured!"[10] And she cast in her mind what manner of salutation this might be. And the angel immediately proceeded to say, The Lord is with thee: fear not, Mary; for thou hast found favour with God. Behold,[11] thou shalt conceive in thy womb, and bring forth a son, and shalt call[12] His name Jesus. He shall be great, and shall be called the Son of the Highest; and the Lord God shall give unto Him the throne of His father David, and He shall reign over the house of Jacob for ever: and of His kingdom there shall be no end. Then said Mary unto the angel, How shall this be, seeing I know not a man?"[13] Shall I still remain a virgin? is the honour of virginity not then lost by me? And while she was yet in perplexity as to these things, the angel placed shortly before her the summary of his whole message, and said to the pure virgin, "The Holy Ghost shall come upon thee, and the power of the Highest shall overshadow thee; therefore also that holy thing which shall be born of thee shall be called the Son of God." For what it is, that also shall it be called by all means. Meekly, then, did grace make election of the pure Mary alone out of all generations. For she proved herself prudent truly in all things; neither has any woman been born like her in all generations. She was not like the primeval virgin Eve, who, keeping holiday[14] alone in paradise, with thoughtless mind, unguardedly hearkened to the word of the serpent, the author of all evil, and thus became

---

[1] [This very homily has been cited to prove the antiquity of the festival of the Annunciation, observed, in the West, March 25. But even Pellicia objects that this is a spurious work. The feast of the Nativity was introduced into the East by Chrysostom after the records at Rome had been inspected, and the time of the taxing at Bethlehem had been found. See his Sermon (A.D. 386), beautifully translated by Dr. Jarvis in his *Introduction*, etc., p. 541. Compare Tertullian, vol. iii. p. 164, and Justin, vol. i. p. 174, this series. Now, as the selection of the 25th of March is clearly based on this, we may say no more of that day. Possibly some Sunday was associated with the Annunciation. The four Sundays preceding Christmas are all observed by the Nestorians in commemoration of the Annunciation.]

[2] The secondary title is: The First Discourse of our holy father Gregory, surnamed Thaumaturgus, bishop of Neo-Cæsareia in Pontus, on the Annunciation to the most holy Virgin Mary, mother of God. Works of Gregory Thaumaturgus by Ger. Voss, p. 9.

[3] ἀνακεκαίνισται; others ἀνακέκληται, recovered.

[4] Ps. xcvi. 11-13.

[5] ξύλα.

[6] δένδρα.

[7] Matt. iii. 8.

[8] John xvi. 22.

[9] Others, ὁσίως, piously.

[10] Luke i. 28.

[11] Or, διό, wherefore.

[12] Or, καλέσουσι, they shall call.

[13] Luke i. 29, etc.

[14] χόρευσα.

depraved in the thoughts of her mind;[1] and through her that deceiver, discharging his poison and infusing death with it, brought it into the whole world; and in virtue of this has arisen all the trouble of the saints. But in the holy Virgin alone is the fall of that (first mother) repaired. Yet was not this holy one competent to receive the gift until she had first learned who it was that sent it, and what the gift was, and who it was that conveyed it. While the holy one pondered these things in perplexity with herself, she says to the angel, "Whence hast thou brought to us the blessing in such wise? Out of what treasure-stores is the pearl of the word despatched to us? Whence has the gift acquired its purpose[2] toward us? From heaven art thou come, yet thou walkest upon earth! Thou dost exhibit the form of man, and (yet) thou art glorious with dazzling light."[3] These things the holy one considered with herself, and the archangel solved the difficulty expressed in such reasonings by saying to her: "The Holy Ghost shall come upon thee, and the power of the Highest shall overshadow thee. Therefore also that holy thing which shall be born of thee shall be called the Son of God. And fear not, Mary; for I am not come to overpower thee with fear, but to repel the subject of fear. Fear not, Mary, for thou hast found favour with God. Question not grace by the standard of nature. For grace does not endure to pass under the laws of nature. Thou knowest, O Mary, things kept hid from the patriarchs and prophets. Thou hast learned, O virgin, things which were kept concealed till now from the angels. Thou hast heard, O purest one, things of which even the choir of inspired men[4] was never deemed worthy. Moses, and David, and Isaiah, and Daniel, and all the prophets, prophesied of Him; but the manner they knew not. Yet thou alone, O purest virgin, art now made the recipient of things of which all these were kept in ignorance, and thou dost learn[5] the origin of them. For where the Holy Spirit is, there are all things readily ordered. Where divine grace is present, all things are found possible with God. The Holy Ghost shall come upon thee, and the power of the Highest shall overshadow thee. Therefore also that holy thing which shall be born of thee shall be called the Son of God." And if He is the Son of God, then is He also God, of one form with the Father, and co-eternal; in Him the Father possesses all manifestation;[6] He is His image in the person, and through His reflection the (Father's) glory shines forth. And as from the ever-flowing

fountain the streams proceed, so also from this ever-flowing and ever-living fountain does the light of the world proceed, the perennial and the true, namely Christ our God. For it is of this that the prophets have preached: "The streams of the river make glad the city of God."[7] And not one city only, but all cities; for even as it makes glad one city, so does it also the whole world. Appropriately, therefore, did the angel[8] say to Mary the holy virgin first of all, "Hail, thou that art highly favoured, the Lord is with thee;" inasmuch as with her was laid up the full treasure of grace. For of all generations she alone has risen as a virgin pure in body and in spirit; and she alone bears Him who bears all things on His word. Nor is it only the beauty of this holy one in body that calls forth our admiration, but also the innate virtue of her soul. Wherefore also the angel[8] addressed her first with the salutation, "Hail, thou that art highly favoured,[9] the Lord is with thee, and no spouse of earth;" He Himself is with thee who is the Lord of sanctification, the Father of purity, the Author of incorruption, and the Bestower of liberty, the Curator of salvation, and the Steward and Provider of the true peace, who out of the virgin earth made man, and out of man's side formed Eve in addition. Even this Lord is with thee, and on the other hand also is of thee. Come, therefore, beloved brethren, and let us take up the angelic strain, and to the utmost of our ability return the due meed of praise, saying, "Hail,[10] thou that art highly favoured, the Lord is with thee!" For it is thine truly to rejoice, seeing that the grace of God, as he knows, has chosen to dwell with thee — the Lord of glory dwelling with the handmaiden; "He that is fairer than the children of men"[11] with the fair *virgin;* He who sanctifies all things with the undefiled. God is with thee, and with thee also is the perfect man in whom dwells the whole fulness of the Godhead. Hail, thou that art highly favoured, the fountain of the light that lightens all who believe upon Him! Hail, thou that art highly favoured, the rising of the rational Sun,[12] and the undefiled flower of life! Hail, thou that art highly favoured, the mead[13] of sweet savour! Hail, thou that art highly favoured, the ever-blooming vine, that makes glad the souls of those who honour thee? Hail, thou that art highly favoured! — the soil that, all untilled, bears bounteous fruit: for thou hast brought forth in accordance with the law of nature indeed, as it goes with us, and by the set

---

[1] Or, τῷ τῆς καρδίας φρονήματι, in the thoughts of her heart.
[2] ὑπόθεσιν; others ὑπόσχεσιν, the promise.
[3] καὶ λαμπάδα φωτὸς ἀπαστράπτεις.
[4] θεοφόρων.
[5] Or, ὑποδέχου καὶ μάνθανε, and receive thou and learn.
[6] φανέρωσιν.

[7] Ps. xlvi. 4.
[8] Or, archangel.
[9] Or, gifted with grace.
[10] Or, rejoice.
[11] Ps. xlv. 2.
[12] τοῦ νοητοῦ ἡλίου ἡ ἀνατολή; others, ἡλίου τῆς δικαιοσύνης, the rising of the Sun of righteousness.
[13] Λειμών.

time of practice,[1] and yet in a way beyond nature, or rather above nature, by reason that God the Word from above took His abode in thee, and formed the new Adam in thy holy womb, and inasmuch as the Holy Ghost gave the power of conception to the holy virgin; and the reality of His body was assumed from her body. And just as the pearl[2] comes of the two natures, namely lightning and water, the occult signs of the sea; so also our Lord Jesus Christ proceeds, without fusion and without mutation, from the pure, and chaste, and undefiled, and holy Virgin Mary; perfect in divinity and perfect in humanity, in all things equal to the Father, and in all things consubstantial with us, apart from sin.

Most of the holy fathers, and patriarchs, and prophets desired to see Him, and to be eye-witnesses of Him, but did not attaint hereto. And some of them by visions beheld Him in type, and darkly; others, again, were privileged to hear the divine voice through the medium of the cloud, and were favoured with sights of holy angels; but to Mary the pure virgin alone did the archangel Gabriel manifest himself luminously, bringing her the glad address, "Hail, thou that art highly favoured!" And thus she received the word, and in the due time of the fulfilment according to the body's course she brought forth the priceless pearl. Come, then, ye too, dearly beloved, and let us chant the melody which has been taught us by the inspired harp of David, and say, "Arise, O Lord, into Thy rest; Thou, and the ark of Thy sanctuary."[3] For the holy Virgin is in truth an ark, wrought with gold both within and without, that has received the whole treasury of the sanctuary. "Arise, O Lord, into Thy rest." Arise, O Lord, out of the bosom of the Father, in order that Thou mayest raise up the fallen race of the first-formed man. Setting these things forth,[4] David in prophecy said to the rod that was to spring from himself, and to sprout into the flower of that beauteous fruit, "Hearken, O daughter, and see, and incline thine ear, and forget thine own people and thy father's house; so shall the King greatly desire thy beauty: for He is the Lord thy God, and thou shalt worship Him."[5] Hearken, O daughter, to the things which were prophesied beforetime of thee, in order that thou mayest also behold the things themselves with the eyes of understanding. Hearken to me while I announce things beforehand to thee, and hearken to the archangel who declares expressly to thee the perfect mysteries. Come then, dearly beloved, and let us fall back on the

memory of what has gone before us; and let us glorify, and celebrate, and laud, and bless that rod that has sprung so marvellously from Jesse. For Luke, in the inspired Gospel narratives, delivers a testimony not to Joseph only, but also to Mary the mother of God, and gives this account with reference to the very family and house of David: "For Joseph went up," says he, "from Galilee, unto a city of Judea which is called Bethlehem, to be taxed with Mary his espoused wife, being great with child, because they were of the house and family of David. And so it was, that while they were there, the days were accomplished that she should be delivered; and she brought forth her son, the first-born of the whole creation,[6] and wrapped him in swaddling-clothes, and laid him in a manger, because there was no room for them in the inn."[7] She wrapped in swaddling-clothes Him who is covered with light as with a garment.[8] She wrapped in swaddling-clothes Him who made every creature. She laid in a manger Him who sits above the cherubim,[9] and is praised by myriads of angels. In the manger set apart for dumb brutes did the Word of God repose, in order that He might impart to men, who are really irrational by free choice, the perceptions of true reason. In the board from which cattle eat was laid the heavenly Bread,[10] in order that He might provide participation in spiritual sustenance for men who live like the beasts of the earth. Nor was there even room for Him in the inn. He found no place, who by His word established heaven and earth; "for though He was rich, for our sakes He became poor,"[11] and chose extreme humiliation on behalf of the salvation of our nature, in His inherent goodness toward us. He who fulfilled the whole administration[12] of unutterable mysteries of the economy[13] in heaven in the bosom of the Father, and in the cave in the arms of the mother, reposed in the manger. Angelic choirs encircled Him, singing of glory in heaven and of peace upon earth. In heaven He was seated at the right hand of the Father; and in the manger He rested, as it were, upon the cherubim. Even there was in truth His cherubic throne; there was His royal seat. Holy of the holy, and alone glorious upon the earth, and holier than the holy, was that wherein Christ our God rested. To Him be glory, honour, and power, together with the Father undefiled, and the altogether holy and quickening Spirit, now and ever, and unto the ages of the ages. Amen.

---

[1] ἀσκήσεως; better κυήσεως, conception.
[2] There is a similar passage in Ephræm's discourse, *De Margarita Pretiosa*, vol. iii.
[3] ἀγιάσματος. Ps. cxxxii. 8.
[4] πρεσβεύων.
[5] Or, and they shall worship Him. Ps. xlv. 10, 11.

[6] πρωτότοκον πασῆς τῆς κτίσεως. [Or, *the heir*, etc.]
[7] Luke ii. 4-7.
[8] Ps. civ. 2.
[9] Ps. lxxx. 1.
[10] Or, the Bread of life.
[11] 2 Cor. viii. 9.
[12] Or, righteousness.
[13] Or, the whole administration of the economy in an unutterable mystery.

THE SECOND HOMILY.

ON THE ANNUNCIATION TO THE HOLY VIRGIN MARY.[1]

DISCOURSE SECOND.

It is our duty to present to God, like sacrifices, all the festivals and hymnal celebrations; and first of all, the annunciation to the holy mother of God, to wit, the salutation made to her by the angel, "Hail, thou that art highly favoured!" For first of all wisdom[2] and saving doctrine in the New Testament was this salutation, "Hail, thou that art highly favoured!" conveyed to us from the Father of lights. And this address, "highly favoured,"[3] embraced the whole nature of men. "Hail, thou that art highly favoured"[3] in the holy conception and in the glorious pregnancy, "I bring you good tidings of great joy, which shall be to all people."[4] And again the Lord, who came for the purpose of accomplishing a saving passion, said, "I will see you, and ye shall rejoice; and your joy no man taketh from you."[5] And after His resurrection again, by the hand of the holy women, He gave us first of all the salutation "Hail!"[6] And again, the apostle made the announcement in similar terms, saying, "Rejoice evermore: pray without ceasing: in everything give thanks."[7] See, then, dearly beloved, how the Lord has conferred upon us everywhere, and indivisibly, the joy that is beyond conception, and perennial. For since the holy Virgin, in the life of the flesh, was in possession of the incorruptible citizenship, and walked as such in all manner of virtues, and lived a life more excellent than man's common standard; therefore the Word that cometh from God the Father thought it meet to assume the flesh, and endue the perfect man from her, in order that in the same flesh in which sin entered into the world, and death by sin, sin might be condemned in the flesh, and that the tempter of sin might be overcome in the burying[8] of the holy body, and that therewith also the beginning of the resurrection might be exhibited, and life eternal instituted in the world, and fellowship established for men with God the Father. And what shall we state, or what shall we pass by here? or who shall explain what is incomprehensible in the mystery? But for the present let us fall back upon our subject. Gabriel was sent to the holy virgin; the incorporeal was despatched to her who in the body pursued the incorruptible conversation, and lived in purity and in virtues. And when he came to her, he first addressed her with the salutation, "Hail, thou that art highly favoured! the Lord is with thee." Hail, thou that art highly favoured! for thou doest what is worthy of joy indeed, since thou hast put on the vesture of purity, and art girt with the cincture of prudence. Hail, thou that art highly favoured! for to thy lot it has fallen to be the vehicle of celestial joy. Hail, thou that art highly favoured! for through thee joy is decreed for the whole creation, and the human race receives again by thee its pristine dignity. Hail, thou that art highly favoured! for in thy arms the Creator of all things shall be carried. And she was perplexed by this word; for she was inexperienced in all the addresses of men, and welcomed quiet, as the mother of prudence and purity; (yet) being a pure, and immaculate, and stainless image[9] herself, she shrank not in terror from the angelic apparition, like most of the prophets, as indeed true virginity has a kind of affinity and equality with the angels. For the holy Virgin guarded carefully the torch of virginity, and gave diligent heed that it should not be extinguished or defiled. And as one who is clad in a brilliant robe deems it a matter of great moment that no impurity or filth be suffered to touch it anywhere, so did the holy Mary consider with herself, and said: Does this act of attention imply any deep design or seductive purpose? Shall this word "Hail" prove the cause of trouble to me, as of old the fair promise of being made like God, which was given her by the serpent-devil, proved to our first mother Eve? Has the devil, who is the author of all evil, become transformed again into an angel of light; and bearing a grudge against my espoused husband for his admirable temperance, and having assailed him with some fair-seeming address, and finding himself powerless to overcome a mind so firm, and to deceive the man, has he turned his attack upon me, as one endowed with a more susceptible mind; and is this word "Hail" (Grace be with thee) spoken as the sign of gracelessness hereafter? Is this benediction and salutation uttered in irony? Is there not some poison concealed in the honey? Is it not the address of one who brings good tidings, while the end of the same is to make me the designer's prey? And how is it that he can thus salute one whom he knows not? These things she pondered in perplexity with herself, and expressed in words. Then again the archangel addressed her with the announcement of a joy which all may believe in, and which shall not be taken away, and said to her, "Fear not, Mary, for thou hast found favour

---

[1] "The Encomium of the same holy Father Gregory, bishop of Neo-Cæsareia in Pontus, surnamed Thaumaturgus, on the Annunciation to the all-holy Mary, mother of God, and ever-virgin."
[2] Or, before all wisdom.
[3] Or, gifted with grace.
[4] Luke ii. 10.
[5] John xvi. 22.
[6] Matt. xxviii. 9.
[7] 1 Thess. v. 16-18.
[8] ἐν τῇ ταφῇ; others, ἐν τῇ ἀφῇ = in the touch or union of the holy body.
[9] ἄγαλμα.

with God." Shortly hast thou the proof of what has been said. For I not only give you to understand that there is nothing to fear, but I show you the very key to the absence of all cause for fear. For through me all the heavenly powers hail thee, the holy virgin : yea rather, He Himself, who is Lord of all the heavenly powers and of all creation, has selected thee as the holy one and the wholly fair ; and through thy holy, and chaste, and pure, and undefiled womb the enlightening Pearl comes forth for the salvation of all the world : since of all the race of man thou art by birth the holy one, and the more honourable, and the purer, and the more pious than any other ; and thou hast a mind whiter than the snow, and a body made purer than any gold, however fine, and a womb such as the object which Ezekiel saw, and which he has described in these terms : "And the likeness of the living creatures upon the head was as the firmament, and as the appearance of the terrible crystal, and the likeness of the throne above them was as the appearance of a sapphire-stone : and above the throne it was as the likeness of a man, and as the appearance of amber ; and within it there was, as it were, the likeness of fire round about." [1]   Clearly, then, did the prophet behold in type Him who was born of the holy virgin, whom thou, O holy virgin, wouldest have had no strength to bear, hadst thou not beamed forth for that time [2] with all that is glorious and virtuous.   And with what words of laudation, then, shall we describe her virgin-dignity ?   With what indications and proclamations of praise shall we celebrate her stainless figure ? With what spiritual song or word shall we honour her who is most glorious among the angels ?   She is planted in the house of God like a fruitful olive that the Holy Spirit overshadowed ; and by her means are we called sons and heirs of the kingdom of Christ.   She is the ever-blooming paradise of incorruptibility, wherein is planted the tree that giveth life, and that furnisheth to all the fruits of immortality.   She is the boast and glory of virgins, and the exultation of mothers.   She is the sure support of the believing, and the succourer [3] of the pious.   She is the vesture of light, and the domicile of virtue. [4] She is the ever-flowing fountain, wherein the water of life sprang and produced the Lord's incarnate manifestation.   She is the monument of righteousness ; and all who become lovers of her, and set their affections on virgin-like ingenuousness and purity, shall enjoy the grace of angels. All who keep themselves from wine and intoxication, and from the wanton enjoyments of strong

drink, shall be made glad with the products of the life-bearing plant.   All who have preserved the lamp of virginity unextinguished shall be privileged to receive the amaranthine crown of immortality.   All who have possessed themselves of the stainless robe of temperance shall be received into the mystical bride-chamber of righteousness.   All who have come nearer the angelic degree than others shall also enter into the more real enjoyment of their Lord's beatitude.   All who have possessed the illuminating oil of understanding, and the pure incense of conscience, shall inherit the promise of spiritual favour and the spiritual adoption.   All who worthily observe the festival of the Annunciation of the Virgin Mary, the mother of God, acquire as their meet recompense the fuller interest in the message, " Hail, thou that art highly favoured ! "   It is our duty, therefore, to keep this feast, seeing that it has filled the whole world with joy and gladness. And let us keep it with psalms, and hymns, and spiritual songs.   Of old did Israel also keep their festival, but then it was with unleavened bread and bitter herbs, of which the prophet says : " I will turn their feasts into afflictions and lamentation, and their joy into shame." [5] But our afflictions our Lord has assured us He will turn into joy by the fruits of penitence. [6] And again, the first covenant maintained the righteous requirements [7] of a divine service, as in the case of our forefather Abraham ; but these stood in the inflictions of pain in the flesh by circumcision, until the time of the fulfilment. " The law was given to them through Moses " for their discipline ; " but grace and truth " have been given to us by Jesus Christ. [8]   The beginning of all these blessings to us appeared in the annunciation to Mary, the highly-favoured, in the economy of the Saviour which is worthy of all praise, and in His divine and supramundane instruction.   Thence rise the rays of the light of understanding upon us.   Thence spring for us the fruits of wisdom and immortality, sending forth the clear pure streams of piety.   Thence come to us the brilliant splendours of the treasures of divine knowledge.   " For this is life eternal, that we may know the true God, and Jesus Christ whom He hath sent." [9]   And again, " Search the Scriptures, for in them ye think ye have eternal life." [10]   For on this account the treasure of the knowledge of God is revealed to them who search the divine oracles.   That treasure of the inspired Scriptures the Paraclete has unfolded to us this day.   And let the tongue of prophecy and the doctrine of apostles be the

---

[1] Ezek. i. 22, 26, 27.
[2] Or, by His throne.
[3] Or example, κατορθωμα.
[4] Or, truth.

[5] Amos viii. 10.
[6] Cf. Jer. xxxi.
[7] Or, justifying observances, δικαιώματα.
[8] Cf. John i.
[9] John xvii. 2.
[10] Or, ye will find eternal life. John v. 39.

treasure of wisdom to us; for without the law and the prophets, or the evangelists and the apostles, it is not possible to have the certain hope of salvation. For by the tongue of the holy prophets and apostles our Lord speaks, and God takes pleasure in the words of the saints; not that He requires the spoken address, but that He delights in the good disposition; not that He receives any profit from men, but that He finds a restful satisfaction in the rightly-affected soul of the righteous. For it is not that Christ is magnified by what we say; but as we receive benefits from Him, we proclaim with grateful mind His beneficence to us; not that we can attain to what is worthy therein, but that we give the meet return to the best of our ability. And when the Gospels or the Epistles, therefore, are read, let not your attention centre on the book or on the reader, but on the God who speaks to you from heaven. For the book is but that which is seen, while Christ is the divine subject spoken of. It brings us then the glad tidings of that economy of the Saviour which is worthy of all praise, to wit, that, though He was God, He became man through kindness toward man, and did not lay aside, indeed, the dignity which was His from all eternity, but assumed the economy that should work salvation. It brings us the glad tidings of that economy of the Saviour worthy of all praise, to wit, that He sojourned with us as a physician for the sick, who did not heal them with potions, but restored them by the inclination of His philanthropy. It brings us the glad tidings of this economy of the Saviour altogether to be praised, to wit, that to them who had wandered astray the way of salvation was shown, and that to the despairing the grace of salvation was made known, which blesses all in different modes; searching after the erring, enlightening the blinded, giving life to the dead, setting free the slaves, redeeming the captives, and becoming all things to all of us in order to be the true way of salvation to us: and all this He does, not by reason of our good-will toward Him, but in virtue of a benignity that is proper to our Benefactor Himself. For the Saviour did all, not in order that He might acquire virtue Himself, but that He might put us in possession of eternal life. He made man, indeed, after the image of God, and appointed him to live in a paradise of pleasure. But the man being deceived by the devil, and having become a transgressor of the divine commandment, was made subject to the doom of death. Whence, also, those born of him were involved in their father's liability in virtue of their succession, and had the reckoning of condemnation required of them. "For death reigned from Adam to Moses."[1] But the Lord, in His be-

nignity toward man, when He saw the creature He Himself had formed now held by the power of death, did not turn away finally from him whom He had made in His own image, but visited him in each generation, and forsook him not; and manifesting Himself first of all among the patriarchs, and then proclaiming Himself in the law, and presenting the likeness of Himself[2] in the prophets, He presignified the economy of salvation. When, moreover, the fulness of the times came for His glorious appearing, He sent beforehand the archangel Gabriel to bear the glad tidings to the Virgin Mary. And he came down from the ineffable powers above to the holy Virgin, and addressed her first of all with the salutation, "Hail, thou that art highly favoured." And when this word, "Hail, thou that art highly favoured," reached her, in the very moment of her hearing it, the Holy Spirit entered into the undefiled temple of the Virgin, and her mind and her members were sanctified together. And nature stood opposite, and natural intercourse at a distance, beholding with amazement the Lord of nature, in a manner contrary to nature, or rather above nature, doing a miraculous work in the body; and by the very weapons by which the devil strove against us, Christ also saved us, taking to Himself our passible body in order that He might impart the greater grace[3] to the being who was deficient in it. And "where sin abounded, grace did much more abound." And appropriately was grace sent to the holy Virgin. For this word also is contained in the oracle of the evangelic history: "And in the sixth month the angel Gabriel was sent to a virgin espoused to a man whose name was Joseph, of the house and lineage of David; and the virgin's name was Mary;"[4] and so forth. And this was the first month to the holy Virgin. Even as Scripture says in the book of the law: "This month shall be unto you the beginning of months: it shall be the first month among the months of the year to you."[5] "Keep ye the feast of the holy passover to the Lord in all your generations." It was also the sixth month to Zacharias. And rightly, then, did the holy Virgin prove to be of the family of David, and she had her home in Bethlehem, and was betrothed rightfully to Joseph, in accordance with the laws of relationship. And her espoused husband was her guardian, and possessor also of the untarnished incorruption which was hers. And the name given to the holy Virgin was one that became her exceedingly. For she was called Mary, and that, by interpretation, means *illumination*. And what shines more brightly that the light of

---

[1] Rom. v. 14.

[2] ὁμοιούμενος.
[3] Or, joy.
[4] Luke i. 26, 27. [*Marah* = bitterness, Exod. xv. 23.]
[5] Ex. xii. 2. [The name Mary is misinterpreted, *infra*.]

virginity? For this reason also the virtues are called virgins by those who strive rightly to get at their true nature. But if it is so great a blessing to have a virgin heart, how great a boon will it be to have the flesh that cherishes virginity along with the soul! Thus the holy Virgin, while still in the flesh, maintained the incorruptible life, and received in faith the things which were announced by the archangel. And thereafter she journeyed diligently to her relation Elisabeth in the hill-country. "And she entered into the house of Zacharias, and saluted Elisabeth," [1] in imitation of the angel. "And it came to pass, that, when Elisabeth heard the salutation of Mary, the babe leapt with joy in her womb; and Elisabeth was filled with the Holy Ghost." [1] Thus the voice of Mary wrought with power, and filled Elisabeth with the Holy Ghost. And by her tongue, as from an ever-flowing fountain, she sent forth a stream of gracious gifts in the way of prophecy to her relation; and while the feet of her child were bound in the womb,[2] she prepared to dance and leap. And that was the sign of a marvellous jubilation. For wherever she was who was highly favoured, there she filled all things with joy. "And Elisabeth spake out with a loud voice, and said, Blessed art thou among women, and blessed is the fruit of thy womb. And whence is this to me, that the mother of my Lord should come to me? Blessed art thou among women." [3] For thou hast become to women the beginning of the new creation.[4] Thou hast given to us boldness of access into paradise, and thou hast put to flight our ancient woe. For after thee the race of woman shall no more be made the subject of reproach. No more do the successors of Eve fear the ancient curse, or the pangs of childbirth. For Christ, the Redeemer of our race, the Saviour of all nature, the spiritual Adam who has healed the hurt of the creature of earth, cometh forth from thy holy womb. "Blessed art thou among women, and blessed is the fruit of thy womb." For He who bears all blessings for us is manifested as thy fruit. This we read in the clear words of her who was barren; but yet more clearly did the holy Virgin herself express this again when she presented to God the song replete with thanksgiving, and acceptance, and divine knowledge; announcing ancient things together with what was new; proclaiming along with things which were of old, things also which belong to the consummation of the ages; and summing up in a short discourse the mysteries of Christ. "And Mary said, My soul doth mag-

nify the Lord, and my spirit hath rejoiced in God my Saviour," and so forth. "He hath holpen His servant Israel in remembrance of His mercy, and of the covenant which He established with Abraham and with his seed for ever." [5] Thou seest how the holy Virgin has surpassed even the perfection of the patriarchs, and how she confirms the covenant which was made with Abraham by God, when He said, "This is the covenant which I shall establish between me and thee." [6] Wherefore He has come and confirmed the covenant with Abraham, having received mystically in Himself the sign of circumcision, and having proved Himself the fulfilment of the law and the prophets. This song of prophecy, therefore, did the holy mother of God render to God, saying, "My soul doth magnify the Lord, and my spirit hath rejoiced in God my Saviour: for He that is mighty hath done to me great things, and holy is His name." For having made me the mother of God, He has also preserved me a virgin; and by my womb the fulness of all generations is headed up together for sanctification. For He hath blessed every age, both men and women, both young men and youths, and old men. "He hath made strength with His arm," [7] on our behalf, against death and against the devil, having torn the handwriting of our sins. "He hath scattered the proud in the imagination of their hearts;" yea, He hath scattered the devil himself, and all the demons that serve under him. For he was overweeningly haughty in his heart, seeing that he dared to say, "I will set my throne above the clouds, and I will be like the Most High." [8] And now, how He scattered him the prophet has indicated in what follows, where he says, "Yet now thou shalt be brought down to hell," [9] and all thy hosts with thee. For He has overthrown everywhere his altars and the worship of vain gods, and He has prepared for Himself a peculiar people out of the heathen nations. "He hath put down the mighty from their seats, and exalted them of low degree." In these terms is intimated in brief the extrusion of the Jews and the admission of the Gentiles. For the elders of the Jews and the scribes in the law, and those who were richly privileged with other prerogatives, because they used their riches ill and their power lawlessly, were cast down by Him from every seat, whether of prophecy or of priesthood, whether of legislature or of doctrine, and were stripped of all their ancestral wealth, and of their sacrifices and multitudinous festivals, and of all the honourable privileges of the

---

[1] Luke i. 41.
[2] Or, and with the bound feet of her child in the womb.
[3] Luke i. 42, 43.
[4] Or, resurrection.

[5] Luke i. 46, etc.
[6] Gen. xvii. 11; Rom. iv. 11.
[7] Luke i. 51.
[8] Isa. xiv. 14.
[9] Isa. xiv. 15.

kingdom. Spoiled of all these boons, as naked fugitives they were cast out into captivity. And in their stead the humble were exalted, namely, the Gentile peoples who hungered after righteousness. For, discovering their own lowliness, and the hunger that pressed upon them for the knowledge of God, they pleaded for the divine word, though it were but for crumbs of the same, like the woman of Canaan;[1] and for this reason they were filled with the riches of the divine mysteries. For the Christ who was born of the Virgin, and who is our God, has given over the whole inheritance of divine blessings to the Gentiles. "He hath holpen His servant Israel."[2] Not any Israel in general, indeed, but His servant, who in very deed maintains the true nobility of Israel. And on this account also did the mother of God call Him servant (Son) and heir. For when He had found the same labouring painfully in the letter and the law, He called him by grace. It is such an Israel, therefore, that He called and hath holpen in remembrance of His mercy. "As He spake to our fathers, to Abraham and to his seed for ever." In these few words is comprehended the whole mystery of the economy. For, with the purpose of saving the race of men, and fulfilling the covenant that was made with our fathers, Christ has once "bowed the heavens and come down."[3] And thus He shows Himself to us as we are capable of receiving Him, in order that we might have power to see Him, and handle Him, and hear Him when He speaketh. And on this account did God the Word deem it meet to take to Himself the flesh and the perfect humanity by a woman, the holy Virgin; and He was born a man, in order that He might discharge our debt, and fulfil even in Himself[4] the ordinances of the covenant made with Abraham, in its rite of circumcision, and all the other legal appointments connected with it. And after she had spoken these words the holy Virgin went to Nazareth; and from that a decree of Cæsar led her to come again to Bethlehem; and so, as proceeding herself from the royal house, she was brought to the royal house of David along with Joseph her espoused husband. And there ensued there the mystery which transcends all wonders, — the Virgin brought forth and bore in her hand Him who bears the whole creation by His word. "And there was no room for them in the inn."[5] He found no room who founded the whole earth by His word. She nourished with her milk Him who imparts sustenance and life to everything that hath breath. She wrapped Him in swaddling-clothes who

binds the whole creation fast with His word. She laid Him in a manger who rides seated upon the cherubim.[6] A light from heaven shone round about Him who lighteneth the whole creation. The hosts of heaven attended Him with their doxologies who is glorified in heaven from before all ages. A star with its torch guided them who had come from the distant parts of earth toward Him who is the true Orient. From the East came those who brought gifts to Him who for our sakes became poor. And the holy mother of God kept these words, and pondered them in her heart, like one who was the receptacle of all the mysteries. Thy praise, O most holy Virgin, surpasses all laudation, by reason of the God who received the flesh and was born man of thee. To thee every creature, of things in heaven, and things on earth, and things under the earth, offers the meet offering of honour. For thou hast been indeed set forth as the true cherubic throne. Thou shinest as the very brightness of light in the high places of the kingdoms of intelligence;[7] where the Father, who is without beginning, and whose power thou hadst overshadowing thee, is glorified; where also the Son is worshipped, whom thou didst bear according to the flesh; and where the Holy Spirit is praised, who effected in thy womb the generation of the mighty King. Through thee, O thou that art highly favoured, is the holy and consubstantial Trinity known in the world. Together with thyself, deem us also worthy to be made partakers of thy perfect grace in Jesus Christ our Lord: with whom, and with the Holy Spirit, be glory to the Father, now and ever, and unto the ages of the ages. Amen.[8]

THE THIRD HOMILY.

ON THE ANNUNCIATION TO THE HOLY VIRGIN MARY.[9]

Again have we the glad tidings of joy, again the announcements of liberty, again the restoration, again the return, again the promise of gladness, again the release from slavery. An angel talks with the Virgin, in order that the serpent may no more have converse with the woman. In the sixth month, it is said, the angel Gabriel was sent from God to a virgin espoused to a man.[10] Gabriel was sent to declare the world-wide salvation; Gabriel was sent to bear to Adam the signature of his restoration; Gabriel was sent to a virgin, in order to transform the dishonour of the female sex into honour; Gabriel was sent to

---

[1] Matt. xv. 27.
[2] Luke i. 54.
[3] Ps. xviii. 9.
[4] μέχρις ἑαυτοῦ.
[5] Luke ii. 7.

[6] Ps. lxxx. 1.
[7] ἐν τοῖς ἄκροις τῶν νοητῶν βασιλειῶν. Others read νότου = in the high places of the kingdoms of the south.
[8] The close is otherwise given thus: To whom be the glory and the power unto the ages of the ages. Amen.
[9] "The Third Discourse by the same sainted Gregory, Bishop of Neo-Cæsarea, surnamed Thaumaturgus, on the Annunciation to the all-holy Virgin Mary, mother of God."
[10] Luke i. 26, 27.

prepare the worthy chamber for the pure spouse; Gabriel was sent to wed the creature with the Creator; Gabriel was sent to the animate palace of the King of the angels; Gabriel was sent to a virgin espoused to Joseph, but preserved for Jesus the Son of God. The incorporeal servant was sent to the virgin undefiled. One free from sin was sent to one that admitted no corruption. The light was sent that should announce the Sun of righteousness. The dawn was sent that should precede the light of the day. Gabriel was sent to proclaim Him who is in the bosom of the Father, and who yet was to be in the arms of the mother. Gabriel was sent to declare Him who is upon the throne, and yet also in the cavern. The subaltern was sent to utter aloud the mystery of the great King; the mystery, I mean, which is discerned by faith, and which cannot be searched out by officious curiosity; the mystery which is to be adored, not weighed; the mystery which is to be taken as a thing divine, and not measured. "In the sixth month Gabriel was sent to a virgin." What is meant by this sixth month? What? It is the sixth month from the time when Elisabeth received the glad tidings, from the time that she conceived John. And how is this made plain? The archangel himself gives us the interpretation, when he says to the virgin: "Behold, thy relation Elisabeth, she hath also conceived a son in her old age: and this is now the sixth month with her, who was called barren."[1] In the sixth month—that is evidently, therefore, the sixth month of the conception of John. For it was meet that the subaltern should go before; it was meet that the attendant should precede; it was meet that the herald of the Lord's coming should prepare the way for Him. In the sixth month the angel Gabriel was sent to a virgin espoused to a man; espoused, not united; espoused, yet kept intact. And for what purpose was she espoused? In order that the spoiler might not learn the mystery prematurely. For that the King was to come by a virgin, was a fact known to the wicked one. For he too heard these words of Isaiah: "Behold, a virgin shall conceive, and bear a son."[2] And on every occasion, consequently, he kept watch upon the virgin's words, in order that, whenever this mystery should be fulfilled, he might prepare her dishonour. Wherefore the Lord came by an espoused virgin, in order to elude the notice of the wicked one; for one who was espoused was pledged in fine to be her husband's. "In the sixth month the angel Gabriel was sent to a virgin espoused to a man whose name was Joseph." Hear what the prophet says about this man and the virgin: "This book that is sealed shall be delivered to a man that is learned."[3] What is meant by this sealed book, but just the virgin undefiled? From whom is this to be given? From the priests evidently. And to whom? To the artisan Joseph. As, then, the priests espoused Mary to Joseph as to a prudent husband, and committed her to his care in expectation of the time of marriage, and as it behoved him then on obtaining her to keep the virgin untouched, this was announced by the prophet long before, when he said: "This book that is sealed shall be delivered to a man that is learned." And that man will say, I cannot read it. But why canst thou not read it, O Joseph? I cannot read it, he says, because the book is sealed. For whom, then, is it preserved? It is preserved as a place of sojourn for the Maker of the universe. But let us return to our immediate subject. In the sixth month Gabriel was sent to a virgin—he who received, indeed, such injunctions as these: "Come hither now, archangel, and become the minister of a dread mystery which has been kept hid, and be thou the agent in the miracle. I am moved by my compassions to descend to earth in order to recover the lost Adam. Sin hath made him decay who was made in my image, and hath corrupted the work of my hands, and hath obscured the beauty which I formed. The wolf devours my nursling, the home of paradise is desolate, the tree of life is guarded by the flaming sword, the location of enjoyments is closed. My pity is evoked for the object of this enmity, and I desire to seize the enemy. Yet I wish to keep this mystery, which I confide to thee alone, still hid from all the powers of heaven. Go thou, therefore, to the Virgin Mary. Pass thou on to that animate city whereof the prophet spake in these words: 'Glorious things were spoken of thee, O city of God.'[4] Proceed, then, to my rational paradise; proceed to the gate of the east; proceed to the place of sojourn that is worthy of my word; proceed to that second heaven on earth; proceed to the light cloud, and announce to it the shower of my coming; proceed to the sanctuary prepared for me; proceed to the hall of the incarnation; proceed to the pure chamber of my generation after the flesh. Speak in the ears of my rational ark, so as to prepare for me the accesses of hearing. But neither disturb nor vex the soul of the virgin. Manifest thyself in a manner befitting that sanctuary, and hail her first with the voice of gladness. And address Mary with the salutation, 'Hail, thou that art highly favoured,' that I may show compassion for Eve in her depravation." The archangel heard these things, and considered them within himself, as was reason-

---

[1] Luke i. 36.
[2] Isa. vii. 14.

[3] Isa. xxix. 11.
[4] Ps. lxxxvii. 3.

able, and said: "Strange is this matter; passing comprehension is this thing that is spoken. He who is the object of dread to the cherubim, He who cannot be looked upon by the seraphim, He who is incomprehensible to all the heavenly [1] powers, does He give the assurance of His connection with a maiden? does He announce His own personal coming? yea more, does He hold out an access by hearing? and is He who condemned Eve, urgent to put such honour upon her daughter? For He says: 'So as to prepare for me the accesses of hearing.' But can the womb contain Him who cannot be contained in space? Truly this is a dread mystery." While the angel is indulging such reflections, the Lord says to Him: "Why art thou troubled and perplexed, O Gabriel? Hast thou not already been sent by me to Zacharias the priest? Hast thou not conveyed to him the glad tidings of the nativity of John? Didst thou not inflict upon the incredulous priest the penalty of speechlessness? Didst thou not punish the aged man with dumbness? Didst thou not make thy declaration, and I confirmed it? And has not the actual fact followed upon thy announcement of good? Did not the barren woman conceive? Did not the womb obey the word? Did not the malady of sterility depart? Did not the inert disposition of nature take to flight? Is not she now one that shows fruitfulness, who before was never pregnant? Can anything be impossible with me, the Creator of all? Wherefore, then, art thou tossed with doubt?" What is the angel's answer to this? "O Lord," he says, "to remedy the defects of nature, to do away with the blast of evils, to recall the dead members to the power of life, to enjoin on nature the potency of generation, to remove barrenness in the case of members that have passed the common limit,[2] to change the old and withered stalk into the appearance of verdant vigour, to set forth the fruitless soil suddenly as the producer of sheaves of corn, — to do all this is a work which, as it is ever the case, demands Thy power. And Sarah is a witness thereto, and along with her[3] also Rebecca, and again Anna, who all, though bound by the dread ill of barrenness, were afterwards gifted by Thee with deliverance from that malady. But that a virgin should bring forth, without knowledge of a man, is something that goes beyond all the laws of nature; and dost Thou yet announce Thy coming to the maiden? The bounds of heaven and earth do not contain Thee, and how shall the womb of a virgin contain Thee?" And the Lord says: "How did the tent of Abraham contain me?"[4] And the angel says: "As there were there the deeps of hospitality, O Lord, Thou didst show Thyself there to Abraham at the door of the tent, and didst pass quickly by it, as He who filleth all things. But how can Mary sustain the fire of the divinity? Thy throne blazes with the illumination of its splendour, and can the virgin receive Thee without being consumed?" Then the Lord says: "Yea surely, if the fire in the wilderness injured the bush, my coming will indeed also injure Mary; but if that fire which served as the adumbration of the advent of the fire of divinity from heaven fertilized the bush, and did not burn it, what wilt thou say of the Truth that descends not in a flame of fire, but in the form of rain?"[5] Thereupon the angel set himself to carry out the commission given him, and repaired to the Virgin, and addressed her with a loud voice, saying: "Hail, thou that are highly favoured! the Lord is with thee. No longer shalt the devil be against thee; for where of old that adversary inflicted the wound, there now first of all does the Physician apply the salve of deliverance. Where death came forth, there has life now prepared its entrance. By a woman came the flood of our ills, and by a woman also our blessings have their spring. Hail, thou that are highly favoured! Be not thou ashamed, as if thou wert the cause of our condemnation. For thou art made the mother of Him who is at once Judge and Redeemer. Hail, thou stainless mother of the Bridegroom[6] of a world bereft! Hail, thou that hast sunk in thy womb the death (that came) of the mother (Eve)! Hail, thou animate temple of God! Hail, thou equal[7] home of heaven and earth alike! Hail, thou amplest receptacle of the illimitable nature!" But as these things are so, through her has come for the sick the Physician; for them that sit in darkness, the Sun of righteousness; for all that are tossed and tempest-beaten, the Anchor and the Port undisturbed by storm. For the servants in irreconcilable enmity has been born the Lord; and One has sojourned with us to be the bond of peace and the Redeemer of those led captive, and to be the peace for those involved in hostility. For He is our peace;[8] and of that peace may it be granted that all we may receive the enjoyment, by the grace and kindness of our Lord Jesus Christ; to whom be the glory, honour, and power, now and ever, and unto all the ages of the ages. Amen.

---

[1] Or, angelic.
[2] ὑπερορίοις μέλεσιν.
[3] Or, and after her.

[4] Gen. xviii.
[5] Ps. lxxii. 6. [A sub-allusion, in bad taste, to Semele.]
[6] νυμφοτόκε. The Latin version gives it as = *sponsa, simul et mater*. [Apostrophe not worship.]
[7] ἰσόρροπον.
[8] Eph. ii. 14.

THE FOURTH HOMILY.

ON THE HOLY THEOPHANY, OR ON CHRIST'S BAPTISM.[1]

O ye who are the friends of Christ, and the friends of the stranger, and the friends of the brethren, receive in kindness my speech to-day, and open your ears like the doors of hearing, and admit within them my discourse, and accept from me this saving proclamation of the baptism[2] of Christ, which took place in the river Jordan, in order that your loving desires may be quickened after the Lord, who has done so much for us in the way of condescension. For even though the festival of the Epiphany of the Saviour is past, the grace of the same yet abides with us through all. Let us therefore enjoy it with insatiable minds; for insatiate desire is a good thing in the case of what pertains to salvation — yea, it is a good thing. Come therefore, all of us, from Galilee to Judea, and let us go forth with Christ; for blessed is he who journeys in such company on the way of life. Come, and with the feet of thought let us make for the Jordan, and see John the Baptist as he baptizes One who needs no baptism, and yet submits to the rite in order that He may bestow freely upon us the grace of baptism. Come, let us view the image of our regeneration, as it is emblematically presented in these waters. "Then cometh Jesus from Galilee to Jordan unto John, to be baptized of him."[3] O how vast is the humility of the Lord! O how vast His condescension! The King of the heavens hastened to John, His own forerunner, without setting in motion the camps[4] of His angels, without despatching beforehand the incorporeal powers as His precursors; but presenting Himself in utmost simplicity, in soldier-like form,[5] He comes up to His own subaltern. And He approached him as one of the multitude, and humbled Himself among the captives though He was the Redeemer, and ranged Himself with those under judgment though He was the Judge, and joined Himself with the lost sheep though He was the Good Shepherd who on account of the straying sheep came down from heaven, and yet did not forsake His heavens, and was mingled with the tares though He was that heavenly grain that springs unsown. And when the Baptist John then saw Him, recognising Him whom before in his mother's womb he had recognised and worshipped, and discerning clearly that this was He on whose account, in a manner surpassing the natural time, he had leaped in the womb of his mother, in violation of the limits of nature, he

drew his right hand within his double cloak, and bowing his head like a servant full of love to his master, addressed Him in these words: I have need to be baptized of Thee, and comest Thou to me?[6] What is this Thou doest, my Lord? Why dost Thou reverse the order of things? Why seekest Thou along with the servants, at the hand of Thy servant, the things that are proper to servants? Why dost Thou desire to receive what Thou requirest not? Why dost Thou burden me, Thy servitor, with Thy mighty condescension? I have need to be baptized of Thee, but Thou hast no need to be baptized of me. The less is blessed by the greater, and the greater is not blessed and sanctified by the less. The light is kindled by the sun, and the sun is not made to shine by the rush-lamp. The clay is wrought by the potter, and the potter is not moulded by the clay. The creature is made anew by the Creator, and the Creator is not restored by the creature. The infirm is healed by the physician, and the physician is not cured by the infirm. The poor man receives contributions from the rich, and the rich borrow not from the poor. I have need to be baptized of Thee, and comest Thou to me? Can I be ignorant who Thou art, and from what source Thou hast Thy light, and whence Thou art come? Or, because Thou hast been born even as I have been,[7] am I, then, to deny the greatness of Thy divinity? Or, because Thou hast condescended so far to me as to have approached my body, and dost bear me wholly in Thyself in order to effect the salvation of the whole man, am I, on account of that body of Thine which is seen, to overlook that divinity of Thine which is only apprehended? Or, because on behalf of my salvation Thou hast taken to Thyself the offering of my first-fruits, am I to ignore the fact that Thou "coverest Thyself with light as with a garment?"[8] Or, because Thou wearest the flesh that is related to me, and dost show Thyself to men as they are able to see Thee, am I to forget the brightness of Thy glorious divinity? Or, because I see my own form in Thee, am I to reason against Thy divine substance, which is invisible and incomprehensible? I know Thee, O Lord; I know Thee clearly. I know Thee, since I have been taught by Thee; for no one can recognise Thee, unless He enjoys Thine illumination. I know Thee, O Lord, clearly; for I saw Thee spiritually before I beheld this light. When Thou wert altogether in the incorporeal bosom of the heavenly Father, Thou wert also altogether in the womb of Thy handmaid and mother; and I, though held in the womb of Elisabeth by nature as in a prison, and bound with the indis-

---

[1] "A Discourse by our sainted Father Gregory, Bishop of Neo-Cæsareia, surnamed Thaumaturgus, on the Holy Theophany, or, as the title is also given, on the Holy Lights."
[2] καταδύσεως.
[3] Matt. iii. 13.
[4] Or, armies.
[5] Or subaltern, ἐν τῇ στρατιωτικῇ μορφῇ.

[6] Matt. iii. 14.
[7] Or, because for my sake Thou hast been born as I have been.
[8] Ps. civ. 2.

soluble bonds of the children unborn, leaped and celebrated Thy birth with anticipative rejoicings. Shall I then, who gave intimation of Thy sojourn on earth before Thy birth, fail to apprehend Thy coming after Thy birth? Shall I, who in the womb was a teacher of Thy coming, be now a child in understanding in view of perfect knowledge? But I cannot but worship Thee, who art adored by the whole creation; I cannot but proclaim Thee, of whom heaven gave the indication by the star, and for whom earth offered a kind reception by the wise men, while the choirs of angels also praised Thee in joy over Thy condescension to us, and the shepherds who kept watch by night hymned Thee as the Chief Shepherd of the rational sheep. I cannot keep silence while Thou art present, for I am a voice; yea, I am the voice, as it is said, of one crying in the wilderness, Prepare ye the way of the Lord.[1] I have need to be baptized of Thee, and comest Thou to me? I was born, and thereby removed the barrenness of the mother that bore me; and while still a babe I became the healer of my father's speechlessness, having received of Thee from my childhood the gift of the miraculous. But Thou, being born of the Virgin Mary, as Thou didst will, and as Thou alone dost know, didst not do away with her virginity; but Thou didst keep it, and didst simply gift her with the name of mother: and neither did her virginity preclude Thy birth, nor did Thy birth injure her virginity. But these two things, so utterly opposite — bearing and virginity — harmonized with one intent; for such a thing abides possible with Thee, the Framer of nature. I am but a man, and am a partaker of the divine grace; but Thou art God, and also man to the same effect: for Thou art by nature man's friend. I have need to be baptized of Thee, and comest Thou to me? Thou who wast in the beginning, and wast with God, and wast God;[2] Thou who art the brightness of the Father's glory;[3] Thou who art the perfect image of the perfect Father;[4] Thou who art the true light that lighteneth every man that cometh into the world;[5] Thou who wast in the world, and didst come where Thou wast; Thou who wast made flesh, and yet wast not changed into the flesh; Thou who didst dwell among us, and didst manifest Thyself to Thy servants in the form of a servant; Thou who didst bridge earth and heaven together by Thy holy name, — comest Thou to me? One so great to such a one as I am? The King to the forerunner? The Lord to the servant? But though Thou wast not ashamed to be born in the lowly measures of humanity, yet I have no ability to pass the measures of nature. I know how great is the measure of difference between earth and the Creator. I know how great is the distinction between the clay and the potter. I know how vast is the superiority possessed by Thee, who art the Sun of righteousness, over me who am but the torch of Thy grace. Even though Thou art compassed with the pure cloud of the body, I can still recognise Thy lordship. I acknowledge my own servitude, I proclaim Thy glorious greatness, I recognise Thy perfect lordship, I recognise my own perfect insignificance, I am not worthy to unloose the latchets of Thy shoes;[6] and how shall I dare to touch Thy stainless head? How can I stretch out the right hand upon Thee, who didst stretch out the heavens like a curtain,[7] and didst set the earth above the waters?[8] How shall I spread those menial hands of mine upon Thy head? How shall I wash Thee, who art undefiled and sinless? How shall I enlighten the light? What manner of prayer shall I offer up over Thee, who dost receive the prayers even of those who are ignorant of Thee?

When I baptize others, I baptize into Thy name, in order that they may believe on Thee, who comest with glory; but when I baptize Thee, of whom shall I make mention? and into whose name shall I baptize Thee? Into that of the Father? But Thou hast the Father altogether in Thyself, and Thou art altogether in the Father. Or into that of the Son? But beside Thee there is no other Son of God by nature. Or into that of the Holy Spirit? But He is ever together with Thee, as being of one substance, and of one will, and of one judgment, and of one power, and of one honour with Thee; and He receives, along with Thee, the same adoration from all. Wherefore, O Lord, baptize Thou me, if Thou pleasest; baptize me, the Baptist. Regenerate one whom Thou didst cause to be generated. Extend Thy dread right hand, which Thou hast prepared for Thyself, and crown my head by Thy touch, in order that I may run the course before Thy kingdom, crowned like a forerunner, and diligently announce the good tidings to the sinners, addressing them with this earnest call: "Behold the Lamb of God, that taketh away the sin of the world!"[9] O river Jordan, accompany me in the joyous choir, and leap with me, and stir thy waters rhythmically, as in the movements of the dance; for thy Maker stands by thee in the body. Once of old didst thou see Israel pass through thee, and thou didst divide thy floods, and didst wait in expectation of the passage of the people; but now divide thyself more

---

[1] Matt. iii. 3; Mark i. 3; Luke iii. 4; John i. 23.
[2] John i. 1.
[3] Heb. i. 3.
[4] Or, of the perfect Light; to wit, the Father.
[5] John i. 9.

[6] Luke iii. 16; John i. 27.
[7] Ps. civ. 2.
[8] Ps. cxxxvi. 6.
[9] John i. 29.

decidedly, and flow more easily, and embrace the stainless limbs of Him who at that ancient time did convey the Jews [1] through thee. Ye mountains and hills, ye valleys and torrents, ye seas and rivers, bless the Lord, who has come upon the river Jordan; for through these streams He transmits sanctification to all streams. And Jesus answered and said to him: Suffer it to be so now, for thus it becometh us to fulfil all righteousness.[2] Suffer it to be so now; grant the favour of silence, O Baptist, to the season of my economy. Learn to will whatever is my will. Learn to minister to me in those things on which I am bent, and do not pry curiously into all that I wish to do. Suffer it to be so now: do not yet proclaim my divinity; do not yet herald my kingdom with thy lips, in order that the tyrant may not learn the fact and give up the counsel he has formed with respect to me. Permit the devil to come upon me, and enter the conflict with me as though I were but a common man, and receive thus his mortal wound. Permit me to fulfil the object for which I have come to earth. It is a mystery that is being gone through this day in the Jordan. My mysteries are for myself and my own. There is a mystery here, not for the fulfilling of my own need, but for the designing of a remedy for those who have been wounded. There is a mystery, which gives in these waters the representation of the heavenly streams of the regeneration of men. Suffer it to be so now: when thou seest me doing what seemeth to me good among the works of my hands, in a manner befitting divinity, then attune thy praises to the acts accomplished. When thou seest me cleansing the lepers, then proclaim me as the framer of nature. When thou seest me make the lame ready runners, then with quickened pace do thou also prepare thy tongue to praise me. When thou seest me cast out demons, then hail my kingdom with adoration. When thou seest me raise the dead from their graves by my word, then, in concert with those thus raised, glorify me as the Prince of Life. When thou seest me on the Father's right hand, then acknowledge me to be divine, as the equal of the Father and the Holy Spirit, on the throne, and in eternity, and in honour. Suffer it to be so now; for thus it becometh us to fulfil all righteousness. I am the Lawgiver, and the Son of the Lawgiver; and it becometh me first to pass through all that is established, and then to set forth everywhere the intimations of my free gift. It becometh me to fulfil the law, and then to bestow grace. It becometh me to adduce the shadow, and then the reality. It becometh me to finish the old covenant, and then to dictate the new, and to write

it on the hearts of men, and to subscribe it with my blood,[3] and to seal it with my Spirit. It becometh me to ascend the cross, and to be pierced with its nails, and to suffer after the manner of that nature which is capable of suffering, and to heal sufferings by my suffering, and by the tree to cure the wound that was inflicted upon men by the medium of a tree. It becometh me to descend even into the very depths of the grave, on behalf of the dead who are detained there. It becometh me, by my three days' dissolution in the flesh, to destroy the power of the ancient enemy, death. It becometh me to kindle the torch of my body for those who sit in darkness and in the shadow of death. It becometh me to ascend in the flesh to that place where I am in my divinity. It becometh me to introduce to the Father the Adam reigning in me. It becometh me to accomplish these things, for on account of these things I have taken my position with the works of my hands. It becometh me to be baptized with this baptism for the present, and afterwards to bestow the baptism of the consubstantial Trinity upon all men. Lend me, therefore, O Baptist, thy right hand for the present economy, even as Mary lent her womb for my birth. Immerse me in the streams of Jordan, even as she who bore me wrapped me in children's swaddling-clothes. Grant me thy baptism even as the Virgin granted me her milk. Lay hold of this head of mine, which the seraphim revere. With thy right hand lay hold of this head, that is related to thyself in kinship. Lay hold of this head, which nature has made to be touched. Lay hold of this head, which for this very purpose has been formed by myself and my Father. Lay hold of this head of mine, which, if one does lay hold of it in piety, will save him from ever suffering shipwreck. Baptize me, who am destined to baptize those who believe on me with water, and with the Spirit, and with fire: with water, capable of washing away the defilement of sins; with the Spirit, capable of making the earthly spiritual; with fire, naturally fitted to consume the thorns of transgressions. On hearing these words, the Baptist directed his mind to the object of the salvation,[4] and comprehended the mystery which he had received, and discharged the divine command; for he was at once pious and ready to obey. And stretching forth slowly his right hand, which seemed both to tremble and to rejoice, he baptized the Lord. Then the Jews who were present, with those in the vicinity and those from a distance, reasoned together, and spake thus with themselves and with each other: Was it, then, without cause that we imagined John to be superior to Jesus? Was it without

---

cause that we considered the former to be greater than the latter? Does not this very baptism attest the Baptist's pre-eminence? Is not he who baptizeth presented as the superior, and he who is baptized as the inferior? But while they, in their ignorance of the mystery of the economy, babbled in such wise with each other, He who alone is Lord, and by nature the Father of the Only-begotten, He who alone knoweth perfectly Him whom He alone in passionless fashion begat, to correct the erroneous imaginations of the Jews, opened the gates of the heavens, and sent down the Holy Spirit in the form of a dove, lighting upon the head of Jesus, pointing out thereby the new Noah, yea the maker of Noah, and the good pilot of the nature which is in shipwreck. And He Himself calls with clear voice out of heaven, and says: "This is my beloved Son,"[1] — the Jesus there, namely, and not the John; the one baptized, and not the one baptizing; He who was begotten of me before all periods of time, and not he who was begotten of Zacharias; He who was born of Mary after the flesh, and not he who was brought forth by Elisabeth beyond all expectation; He who was the fruit of the virginity yet preserved intact, and not he who was the shoot from a sterility removed; He who has had His conversation with you, and not he who was brought up in the wilderness. This is my beloved Son, in whom I am well pleased: my Son, of the same substance with myself, and not

of a different; of one substance with me according to what is unseen, and of one substance with you according to what is seen, yet without sin. This is He who along with me made man. This is my beloved Son, in whom I am well pleased. This Son of mine and this son of Mary are not two distinct persons; but this is my beloved Son, — this one who is both seen with the eye and apprehended with the mind. This is my beloved Son, in whom I am well pleased; hear Him. If He shall say, I and my Father are one,[2] hear Him. If He shall say, He that hath seen me hath seen the Father,[3] hear Him. If He shall say, He that hath sent me is greater than I,[4] adapt the voice to the economy. If He shall say, Whom do men say that I the Son of man am?[5] answer ye Him thus: Thou art the Christ, the Son of the living God.[6] By these words, as they were sent from the Father out of heaven in thunder-form, the race of men was enlightened: they apprehended the difference between the Creator and the creature, between the King and the soldier (subject), between the Worker and the work; and being strengthened in faith, they drew near through the baptism of John to Christ, our true God, who baptizeth with the Spirit and with fire. To Him be glory, and to the Father, and to the most holy and quickening Spirit, now and ever, and unto the ages of the ages. Amen.

---

[1] Matt. iii. 17, xvii. 5; Mark i. 11; Luke ix. 35.

[2] John x. 30.
[3] John xiv. 9.
[4] John xiv. 28.
[5] Matt. xvi. 13.
[6] Matt. xvi. 16.

ELUCIDATION.

I CAN do no better than follow Dupin as to the authorship of these Homilies. He thinks the style of Proclus (of Constantinople) may be detected in them, though the fourth is beyond him for eloquence, and has even been thought worthy of St. Chrysostom. It was produced after Nicæa, and probably after Ephesus, its somewhat exaggerated praises of the θεοτόκος being unusual at an earlier period. The titles of these Homilies are the work of much later editors; and interpolations probably occur frequently, by the same hands.

ON ALL THE SAINTS.[1]

GRANT thy blessing, Lord.

It was my desire to be silent, and not to make a public[2] display of the rustic rudeness of my tongue. For silence is a matter of great consequence when one's speech is mean.[3] And to refrain from utterance is indeed an admirable thing, where there is lack of training; and verily he is the highest philosopher who knows how to cover his ignorance by abstinence from public address. Knowing, therefore, the feebleness of tongue proper to me, I should have preferred such a course. Nevertheless the spectacle of the onlookers impels me to speak. Since, then, this solemnity is a glorious one among our festivals, and the spectators form a crowded gathering, and our assembly is one of elevated fervour in the faith, I shall face the task of commencing an address with confidence.[4] And this I may attempt all the more boldly, since the Father[5] requests me, and the Church is with me, and the sainted martyrs with this object strengthen what is weak in me. For these have inspired aged men to accomplish with much love a long course, and constrained them to support their failing steps by the staff of the word;[6] and they have stimulated women to finish their course like the young men, and have brought to this, too, those of tender years, yea, even creeping children. In this wise have the martyrs shown their power, leaping with joy in the presence of death, laughing at the sword, making sport of the wrath of princes, grasping at death as the producer of deathlessness, making victory their own by their fall, through the body taking their leap to heaven, suffering their members to be scattered abroad in order that they might hold[7] their souls, and, bursting the bars of life, that they might open the gates[8] of heaven. And if any one believes not that death is abolished, that Hades is trodden under foot, that the chains thereof are broken, that the tyrant is bound, let him look on the martyrs disporting themselves[9] in the presence of death, and taking up the jubilant strain of the victory of Christ. O the marvel! Since the hour when Christ despoiled Hades, men have danced in triumph over death. "O death, where is thy sting! O grave, where is thy victory?"[10] Hades and the devil have been despoiled, and stripped of their ancient armour, and cast out of their peculiar power. And even as Goliath had his head cut off with his own sword, so also is the devil, who has been the father of death, put to rout through death; and he finds that the selfsame thing which he was wont to use as the ready weapon of his deceit, has become the mighty instrument of his own destruction. Yea, if we may so speak, casting his hook at the Godhead, and seizing the wonted enjoyment of the baited pleasure, he is himself manifestly caught while he deems himself the captor, and discovers that in place of the man he has touched the God. By reason thereof do the martyrs leap upon the head of the dragon, and despise every species of torment. For since the second Adam has brought up the first Adam out of the deeps of Hades, as Jonah was delivered out of the whale, and has set forth him who was deceived as a citizen of heaven to the shame of the deceiver, the gates of Hades have been shut, and the gates of heaven have been opened, so as to offer an unimpeded entrance to those who rise thither in faith. In olden time Jacob beheld a ladder erected reaching to heaven, and the angels of God ascending and descending upon it. But now, having been made man for man's sake, He who is the Friend of man has crushed with the foot of His divinity him who is the enemy of man, and has borne up the man with the hand of His Christhood,[11] and has made the trackless ether to be trodden by the feet of man. Then the angels were

---

[1] A discourse of Gregory Thaumaturgus published by Joannes Aloysius Mingarelli, Bologna, 1770.
[2] The codex gives δημοσιεύουσαν, for which we read δημοσιεύειν.
[3] The codex gives ἀτελής, for which εὐτελής is read by the editor.
[4] Reading θαρρούντως for θαρροῦντος.
[5] This is supposed by the Latin annotator to refer to the bishop, and perhaps to Phædimus of Amasea, as in those times no one was at liberty to make an address in the church when the bishop was present, except by his request or with his permission.
[6] Or, the Word.
[7] σφίγξωσι.
[8] Or, keys.

[9] κυβιστῶντες.
[10] 1 Cor. xv. 55.
[11] Χριστότητος, for which, however, χρηστότητος, benignity, is suggested. [Sometimes are intended ambiguity.]

ascending and descending; but now the Angel of the great counsel neither ascendeth nor descendeth: for whence or where shall He change His position, who is present everywhere, and filleth all things, and holds in His hand the ends of the world? Once, indeed, He descended, and once He ascended, — not, however, through any change[1] of nature, but only in the condescension[2] of His philanthropic Christhood;[3] and He is seated as the Word with the Father, and as the Word He dwells in the womb, and as the Word He is found everywhere, and is never separated from the God of the universe. Aforetime did the devil deride the nature of man with great laughter, and he has had his joy over the times of our calamity as his festal-days. But the laughter is only a three days' pleasure, while the wailing is eternal; and his great laughter has prepared for him a greater wailing and ceaseless tears, and inconsolable weeping, and a sword in his heart. This sword did our Leader forge against the enemy with fire in the virgin furnace, in such wise and after such fashion as He willed, and gave it its point by the energy of His invincible divinity, and dipped it in the water of an undefiled baptism, and sharpened it by sufferings without passion in them, and made it bright by the mystical resurrection; and herewith by Himself He put to death the vengeful adversary, together with his whole host. What manner of word, therefore, will express our joy or his misery? For he who was once an archangel is now a devil; he who once lived in heaven has now seen crawling like a serpent upon earth; he who once was jubilant with the cherubim, is now shut up in pain in the guard-house of swine; and him, too, in fine, shall we put to rout if we mind those things which are contrary to his choice, by the grace and kindness of our Lord Jesus Christ, to whom be the glory and the power unto the ages of the ages. Amen.

---

[1] μεταβάσει.
[2] συγκαταβάσει.
[3] Or, benignity.

ELUCIDATION.

THE feast of *All Saints* is very ancient in the Oriental churches, and is assigned to the *Octave of Pentecost*, the Anglican Trinity Sunday. See Neale, *Eastern Church*, vol. ii. pp. 734, 753. In the West it was instituted when Boniface III. (who accepted from the Emperor Phocas the title of "Universal Bishop," A.D. 607) turned the Pantheon into a church, and with a sort of practical epigram called it the church of "All the Saints." It was a local festival until the ninth century, when the Emperor Louis the Pious introduced it into France and Germany. Thence it came to England. It falls on the 1st of November.

The gates of the church at Rome are the same which once opened for the worship of "all the gods." They are of massive bronze, and are among the most interesting of the antiquities of the city.

The modern gates of St. Peter's, at Rome, are offensive copies of heathen mythology; and among the subjects there represented, is the shameful tale of Leda, — a symbol of the taste of Leo X.

ON THE GOSPEL ACCORDING TO MATTHEW.[1]

" The light of the body is the eye: if therefore thine eye be single, thy whole body shall be full of light. But if thine eye be evil, thy whole body shall be full of darkness. If therefore the light that is in thee be darkness, how great is that darkness!"

THE single eye is the love unfeigned ; for when the body is enlightened by it, it sets forth through the medium of the outer members only things which are perfectly correspondent with the inner thoughts. But the evil eye is the pretended love, which is also called hypocrisy, by which the whole body of the man is made darkness. We have to consider that deeds meet only for darkness may be within the man, while through the outer members he may produce words that seem to be of the light :[2] for there are those who are in reality wolves, though they may be covered with sheep's clothing. Such are they who wash only the outside of the cup and platter, and do not understand that, unless the inside of these things is cleansed, the outside itself cannot be made pure. Wherefore, in manifest confutation of such persons, the Saviour says : " If the light that is in thee be darkness, how great is that darkness ! " That is to say, if the love which seems to thee to be light is really a work meet for darkness, by reason of some hypocrisy concealed in thee, what must be thy patent transgressions !

---

[1] A fragment. (Gallandi, *Vet. Patr. Biblioth.*, xiv. p. 119; from a Catena on Matthew, Cod. MS. 168, Mitarelli.)

[2] The text is apparently corrupt here: ἄξια μὲν σκότους πράγματα ἐννοούμενον ἔσωθεν· διὰ δὲ τῶν ἔξωθεν μερῶν φωτὸς εἶναι δοκοῦντα προφερον ῥήματα. Migne suggests ἐννοοῦμεν τόν and προφέροντα.

DIONYSIUS

[TRANSLATED BY THE REV. S. D. F. SALMOND, M.A.]

INTRODUCTORY NOTICE

TO

DIONYSIUS, BISHOP OF ALEXANDRIA.

[A.D. 200–265.] The great Origen had twin children in Gregory and Dionysius. Their lives ran in parallel lines, and are said to have ended on the same day ; and nobly did they sustain the dignity and orthodoxy of the pre-eminent school which was soon to see its bright peculiar star in Athanasius. Dionysius is supposed to have been a native of Alexandria, of heathen parentage, and of a family possessed of wealth and honourable rank. Early in life he seems to have been brought under the influence of certain presbyters ; and a voice seemed to speak to him in a vision [1] encouraging him to " prove all things, and hold fast that which is good." We find him at the feet of Origen a diligent pupil, and afterwards, as a presbyter, succeeding Heraclas (A.D. 232) as the head of the school, sitting in Origen's seat. For about fifteen years he further illuminated this illustrious chair ; and then, in ripe years, about A.D. 246, he succeeded Heraclas again as bishop of Alexandria, at that time, beyond all comparison, the greatest and the most powerful See of Christendom.

For a year or two he fed his flock in peace ; but then troubles broke in upon his people, even under the kindly reign of Philip. Things grew worse, till under Decius the eighth persecution was let loose throughout the empire. Like Cyprian, Dionysius retired for a season, upon like considerations, but not until he had been arrested and providentially delivered from death in a singular manner. On returning to his work, he found the Church greatly disturbed by the questions concerning the lapsed, with which Cyprian's history has made us acquainted. In the letter to Fabius will be found details of the earlier persecution, and in that against Germanus are interesting facts of his own experience. The Epistle to the Alexandrians contains very full particulars of the pestilence which succeeded these calamities ; and it is especially noteworthy as contrasting the humanity and benevolence of Christians with the cruel and cowardly indifference of the pagans towards the dying and the dead. Seditions and tumults followed, on which we have our author's reflections in the Epistle to Hierax, with not a few animated touches of description concerning the condition of Alexandria after such desolations. In the affair of Cyprian with Stephen he stood by the great Carthaginian doctor, and maintained the positions expressed in the letter of Firmilian.[2] Wars, pestilences, and the irruptions of barbarians, make up the history of the residue of the period, through which Dionysius was found a " burning and a shining light " to the Church ; his great influence extending throughout the East, and to the West also. I may leave the residue of his story to the introductory remarks of the translator, and to his valuable annotations, to which it will not be necessary for me to add many of my own. But I must find room to express my admiration for his character, which was never found wanting amid many terrible trials of character and of faith itself. His pen was never idle ; his learning and knowledge of the Scriptures are apparent, even in the fragments that have come down to us ; his fidelity to the traditions received from Origen and Heraclas are not less conspicuous ; and in all his dealings with his brethren of the East and West there reigns over his conduct that pure spirit of the Gospel which proves that

---

[1] Epistle to Philemon, *infra.*   [2] Vol. v. p. 390, this series.

the virgin-age of the Church was not yet of the past. A beautiful moderation and breadth of sympathy distinguish his episcopal utterances; and, great as was his diocese, he seems equally devoid of prelatic pride and of that wicked ambition which too soon after the martyr-ages proved the bane of the Church's existence. The following is the

TRANSLATOR'S INTRODUCTORY NOTICE.

FOR our knowledge of the career of this illustrious disciple of Origen we are indebted chiefly to Eusebius, in the sixth and seventh books of his *Historia Ecclesiastica*, and in the fourteenth book of his *Præparatio Evangelica*.[1] He appears to have been the son of pagan parents; but after studying the doctrines of various of the schools of philosophy, and coming under the influence of Origen, to whom he had attached himself as a pupil, he was led to embrace the Christian faith. This step was taken at an early period, and, as he informs us, only after free examination and careful inquiry into the great systems of heathen belief. He was made a presbyter in Alexandria after this decision; and on the elevation of Heraclas to the bishopric of that city, Dionysius succeeded him in the presidency of the catechetical school there about A.D. 232. After holding that position for some fifteen years Heraclas died, and Dionysius was again chosen to be his successor; and ascending the episcopal throne of Alexandria about A.D. 247 or 248, he retained that See till his death in the year 265. The period of his activity as bishop was a time of great suffering and continuous anxiety; and between the terrors of persecution on the one hand, and the cares of controversy on the other, he found little repose in his office. During the Decian persecution he was arrested and hurried off by the soldiers to a small town named Taposiris, lying between Alexandria and Canopus. But he was rescued from the peril of that seizure in a remarkably providential manner, by a sudden rising of the people of the rural district through which he was carried. Again, however, he was called to suffer, and that more severely, when the persecution under Valerian broke out in the year 257. On making open confession of his faith on this occasion he was banished, at a time when he was seriously ill, to Cephro, a wild and barren district in Libya; and not until he had spent two or three years in exile there was he enabled to return to Alexandria, in virtue of the edict of Gallienus. At various times he had to cope, too, with the miseries of pestilence and famine and civil conflicts in the seat of his bishopric. In the many ecclesiastical difficulties of his age he was also led to take a prominent part. When the keen contest was waged on the subject of the rebaptism of recovered heretics about the year 256, the matter in dispute was referred by both parties to his judgment, and he composed several valuable writings on the question. Then he was induced to enter the lists with the Sabellians, and in the course of a lengthened controversy did much good service against their tenets. The uncompromising energy of his opposition to that sect carried him, however, beyond the bounds of prudence, so that he himself gave expression to opinions not easily reconcilable with the common orthodox doctrine. For these he was called to account by Dionysius bishop of Rome;[2] and when a synod had been summoned to consider the case, he promptly and humbly acknowledged the error into which his precipitate zeal had drawn him. Once more, he was urged to give his help in the difficulty with Paul of Samosata. But as the burden of years and infirmities made it impossible for him to attend the synod convened at Antioch in 265 to deal with that troublesome heresiarch, he sent his opinion on the subject of discussion in a letter to the council, and died soon after, towards the close of the same year. The responsible duties

---

[1] There are also passages, of larger or smaller extent, bearing upon his life and his literary activity, in Jerome (*De viris illustr.*, ch. 69: and *Præfatio ad Lib.*, xviii., *Comment. in Esaiam*), Athanasius (*De Sententia Dionysii*, and *De Synodi Nicænæ Decretis*), Basil (*De Spiritu Sancto*, ch. 29: *Epist. ad Amphiloch.*, and *Epist. ad Maximum*). Among modern authorities, we may refer specially to the Dissertation on his life and writings by S. de Magistris, in the folio edition issued under his care in Greek and Latin at Rome in 1796; to the account given by Basnage in the *Histoire de l'Eglise*, tome i. livre ii. ch. v. p. 68; to the complete collection of his extant works in Gallandi's *Bibliotheca Patrum*, iii. p. 481, etc.; as well as to the accounts in Cave's *Hist. Lit.*, i. p. 95, and elsewhere.

[2] [Not, however, as an inferior, but as one bishop in those days remonstrated with another, and as he himself remonstrated with Stephen. See *infra*.]

of his bishopric had been discharged with singular faithfulness and patience throughout the seventeen eventful years during which he occupied the office. Among the ancients he was held in the highest esteem both for personal worth and for literary usefulness; and it is related that there was a church dedicated to him in Alexandria. One feature that appears very prominently in his character, is the spirit of independent investigation which possessed him. It was only after candid examination of the current philosophies that he was induced to become a Christian; and after his adoption of the faith, he kept himself abreast of all the controversies of the time, and perused with an impartial mind the works of the great heretics. He acted on this principle through his whole course as a teacher, pronouncing against such writings only when he had made himself familiar with their contents, and saw how to refute them. And we are told in Eusebius,[1] that when a certain presbyter once remonstrated with him on this subject, and warned him of the injury he might do to his own soul by habituating himself to the perusal of these heterodox productions, Dionysius was confirmed in his purpose by a vision and a voice which were sent him, as he thought, from heaven to relieve him of all such fear, and to encourage him to read and prove all that might come into his hand, because that method had been from the very first the cause of faith to him. The moderation of his character, again, is not less worthy of notice. In the case of the Novatian schism, while he was from the first decidedly opposed to the principles of the party, he strove by patient and affectionate argumentation to persuade the leader to submit. So, too, in the disputes on baptism we find him urgently entreating the Roman bishop Stephen not to press matters to extremity with the Eastern Church, nor destroy the peace she had only lately begun to enjoy. Again, in the chiliastic difficulties excited by Nepos, and kept up by Coracion, we see him assembling all the parochial clergy who held these opinions, and inviting all the laymen of the diocese also to attend the conference, and discussing the question for three whole days with all these ministers, considering their arguments, and meeting all their objections patiently by Scripture testimony, until he persuades Coracion himself to retract, and receives the thanks of the pastors, and restores unity of faith in his bishopric. On these occasions his mildness, and benignity, and moderation stand out in bold relief; and on others we trace similar evidences of his broad sympathies and his large and liberal spirit. He was possessed also of a remarkably fertile pen; and the number of his theological writings, both formal treatises and more familiar epistles, was very considerable. All these, however, have perished, with the exception of what Eusebius and other early authors already referred to have preserved. The most important of these compositions are the following: 1. *A Treatise on the Promises*, in two books, which was written against Nepos, and of which Eusebius has introduced two pretty large extracts into the third and seventh books of his *History*. 2. *A Book on Nature*, addressed to Timotheus, in opposition to the Epicureans, of which we have some sections in the *Præpar. Evangel.* of Eusebius. 3. *A Work against the Sabellians*, addressed to Dionysius bishop of Rome, in four books or letters, in which he deals with his own unguarded statements in the controversy with Sabellius, and of which certain portions have come down to us in Athanasius and Basil. In addition to these, we possess a number of his epistles in whole or part, and a few exegetical fragments. There is a Scholium in the Codex Amerbachianus which may be given here: — It should be known that this sainted Dionysius became a hearer of Origen in the fourth year of the reign of Philip, who succeeded Gordian in the empire. On the death of Heraclas, the thirteenth bishop of the church of Alexandria, he was put in possession of the headship of that church; and after a period of seventeen years, embracing the last three years of the reign of Philip, and the one year of that of Decius, and the one year of Gallus and Volusianus the son of Decius, and twelve years of the reigns of Valerian and his son Gallus (Gallienus), he departed to the Lord. And Basilides was bishop of the parishes in the Pentapolis of Libya, as Eusebius informs us in the sixth and seventh books of his *Ecclesiastical History*.

---

[1] *Hist. Eccles.*, viii. 7.

THE WORKS OF DIONYSIUS.

EXTANT FRAGMENTS.

PART I.—CONTAINING VARIOUS SECTIONS OF THE WORKS.

I. — FROM THE TWO BOOKS ON THE PROMISES.[1]

1. BUT as they produce a certain composition by Nepos,[2] on which they insist very strongly, as if it demonstrated incontestably that there will be a (temporal) reign of Christ upon the earth, I have to say, that in many other respects I accept the opinion of Nepos, and love him at once for his faith, and his laboriousness, and his patient study in the Scriptures, as also for his great efforts in psalmody,[3] by which even now many of the brethren are delighted. I hold the man, too, in deep respect still more, inasmuch as[4] he has gone to his rest before us. Nevertheless the truth is to be prized and reverenced above all things else. And while it is indeed proper to praise and approve ungrudgingly anything that is said aright, it is no less proper to examine and correct anything which may appear to have been written unsoundly. If he had been present then himself, and had been stating his opinions orally, it would have been sufficient to discuss the question together without the use of writing, and to endeavour to convince the opponents, and carry them along by interrogation and reply. But the work is published, and is, as it seems to some, of a very persuasive character; and there are unquestionably some teachers, who hold that the law and the prophets are of no importance, and who decline to follow the Gospels, and who depreciate the epistles of the apostles, and who have also made large promises[5] regarding the doctrine of this composition, as though it were some great and hidden mystery, and who, at the same time, do not allow that our simpler brethren have any sublime and elevated conceptions either of our Lord's appearing in His glory and His true divinity, or of our own resurrection from the dead, and of our being gathered together to Him, and assimilated to Him, but, on the contrary, endeavour to lead them to hope[6] for things which are trivial and corruptible, and only such as what we find at present in the kingdom of God. And since this is the case, it becomes necessary for us to discuss this subject with our brother Nepos just as if he were present.

2. *After certain other matters, he adds the following statement:* — Being then in the Arsinoitic[7] prefecture — where, as you are aware, this

---

[1] In opposition to Noëtus, a bishop in Egypt. Eusebius, *Hist. Eccl.*, vii 24 and 25. Eusebius introduces this extract in the following terms: " There are also two books of his on the subject of the promises. The occasion of writing these was furnished him by a certain Nepos, a bishop in Egypt, who taught that the promises which were given to holy men in the sacred Scriptures were to be understood according to the Jewish sense of the same: and affirmed that there would be some kind of a millennial period, plenished with corporeal delights, upon this earth. And as he thought that he could establish this opinion of his by the Revelation of John, he had composed a book on this question, entitled *Refutation of the Allegorists*. This, therefore, is sharply attacked by Dionysius in his books on the Promises. And in the first of these books he states his own opinion on the subject; while in the second he gives us a discussion on the Revelation of John, in the introduction to which he makes mention of Nepos." [Of this Noëtus, see the *Philosophumena*, vol. v., this series.]

[2] As it is clear from this passage that this work by Dionysius was written against Nepos, it is strange that, in his preface to the eighteenth book of his Commentaries on Isaiah, Jerome should affirm it to have been composed against Irenæus of Lyons. Irenæus was certainly of the number of those who held millennial views, and who had been persuaded to embrace such by Papias, as Jerome himself tells us in the *Catalogue* and as Eusebius explains towards the close of the third book of his *History*. But that this book by Dionysius was written not against Irenæus, but against Nepos, is evident, not only from this passage in Eusebius, but also from Jerome himself, in his work *On Ecclesiastical Writers*, where he speaks of Dionysius. — VALES. [Compare (this series, *infra*) the comments of Victorinus of Petau for a Western view of the millennial subject.]

[3] τῆς πολλῆς ψαλμῳδίας. Christophorsonus interprets this of psalms and hymns composed by Nepos. It was certainly the practice among the ancient Christians to compose psalms and hymns in honour of Christ. Eusebius bears witness to this in the end of the fifth book of his *History*. Mention is made of these psalms in the Epistle of the Council of Antioch against Paul of Samosata, and in the penultimate canon of the Council of Laodicea, where there is a clear prohibition of the use of ψαλμοὶ ἰδιωτικοί in the church, i.e., of psalms composed by private individuals. For this custom had obtained great prevalence, so that many persons composed psalms in honour of Christ, and got them sung in the church. It is psalms of this kind, consequently, that the Fathers of the Council of Laodicea forbid to be sung thereafter in the church, designating them ἰδιωτικοι, i.e., composed by unskilled men, and not dictated by the Holy Spirit. Thus is the matter explained by Agobardus in his book *De ritu canendi psalmos in Ecclesia*. [See vol. v., quotation from Pliny.]

[4] ταυτῇ μᾶλλον ἢ προανεπαύσατο: it may mean, perhaps, *for the way in which he has gone to his rest before us.*

[5] κατεπαγγελλομένων, i.e., *diu ante promittunt quam tradunt.* The metaphor is taken from the mysteries of the Greeks, who were wont to promise great and marvellous discoveries to the initiated, and then kept them on the rack by daily expectation, in order to confirm their judgment and reverence by such suspense in the conveyance of knowledge, as Tertullian says in his book *Against the Valentinians.* — VALES. [Vol. iii. p. 503.]

[6] Reading ἐλπίζειν ἀναπειθόντων for ἐλπιζόμενα πειθόντων, with the Codex Mazarin.

[7] ἐν μὲν οὖν τῷ Ἀρσενοείτῃ. In the three codices here, as well as in Nicephorus and Ptolemy, we find this scription, although it is evident that the word should be written Αρσινοειτῃ, as the district took its name from Queen Arsinoe. — VALES.

doctrine was current long ago, and caused such division, that schisms and apostasies took place in whole churches — I called together the presbyters and the teachers among the brethren in the villages, and those of the brethren also who wished to attend were present. I exhorted them to make an investigation into that dogma in public. Accordingly, when they had brought this book before us, as though it were a kind of weapon or impregnable battlement, I sat with them for three days in succession, from morning till evening, and attempted to set them right on the subjects propounded in the composition. Then, too, I was greatly gratified by observing the constancy of the brethren, and their love of the truth, and their docility and intelligence, as we proceeded, in an orderly method, and in a spirit of moderation, to deal with questions, and difficulties, and concessions. For we took care not to press, in every way and with jealous urgency, opinions which had once been adopted, even although they might appear to be correct.[1] Neither did we evade objections alleged by others; but we endeavoured as far as possible to keep by the subject in hand, and to establish the positions pertinent to it. Nor, again, were we ashamed to change our opinions, if reason convinced us, and to acknowledge the fact; but rather with a good conscience, and in all sincerity, and with open hearts[2] before God, we accepted all that could be established by the demonstrations and teachings of the Holy Scriptures. And at last the author and introducer of this doctrine, whose name was Coracion, in the hearing of all the brethren present, made acknowledgment of his position, and engaged to us that he would no longer hold by his opinion, nor discuss it, nor mention it, nor teach it, as he had been completely convinced by the arguments of those opposed to it. The rest of the brethren, also, who were present, were delighted with the conference, and with the conciliatory spirit and the harmony exhibited by all.

3. *Then, a little further on, he speaks of the Revelation of John as follows:* — Now some before our time have set aside this book, and repudiated it entirely, criticising it chapter by chapter, and endeavouring to show it to be without either sense or reason. They have alleged also that its title is false; for they deny that

John is the author. Nay, further, they hold that it can be no sort of revelation, because it is covered with so gross and dense a veil of ignorance. They affirm, therefore, that none of the apostles, nor indeed any of the saints, nor any person belonging to the Church, could be its author; but that Cerinthus,[3] and the heretical sect founded by him, and named after him the Cerinthian sect, being desirous of attaching the authority of a great name to the fiction propounded by him, prefixed that title to the book. For the doctrine inculcated by Cerinthus is this: that there will be an earthly reign of Christ; and as he was himself a man devoted to the pleasures of the body, and altogether carnal in his dispositions, he fancied[4] that that kingdom would consist in those kinds of gratifications on which his own heart was set, — to wit, in the delights of the belly, and what comes beneath the belly, that is to say, in eating and drinking, and marrying, and in other things under the guise of which he thought he could indulge his appetites with a better grace,[5] such as festivals, and sacrifices, and the slaying of victims. But I, for my part, could not venture to set this book aside, for there are many brethren who value it highly. Yet, having formed an idea of it as a composition exceeding my capacity of understanding, I regard it as containing a kind of hidden and wonderful intelligence on the several subjects which come under it. For though I cannot comprehend it, I still suspect that there is some deeper sense underlying the words. And I do not measure and judge its expressions by the standard of my own reason, but, making more allowance for faith, I have simply regarded them as too lofty for my comprehension; and I do not forthwith reject what I do not understand, but I am only the more filled with wonder at it, in that I have not been able to discern its import.[6]

4. *After this, he examines the whole book of the Revelation; and having proved that it cannot possibly be understood according to the bald, literal sense, he proceeds thus:* — When the prophet now has completed, so to speak, the whole prophecy, he pronounces those blessed who should observe it, and names himself, too, in the number of the same: " For blessed," says

---

[1] εἰ καὶ φαίνοιντο. There is another reading, εἰ καὶ μὴ φαίνοιντο, *although they might not appear to be correct.* Christophorsonus renders it: ne illis quæ fuerant ante ab ipsis decreta, si quidquam in eis veritati repugnare videretur, mordicus adhærerent præcavebant.

[2] ἡπλωμέναις ταῖς καρδίαις. Christophorsonus renders it, *puris erga Deum ac simplicibus animis;* Musculus gives, *cordibus ad Deum expansis;* and Rufinus, *patefactis cordibus.* [The picture here given of a primitive synod searching the Scriptures under such a presidency, and exhibiting such tokens of brotherly love, mutual subordination (1 Pet. v. 5), and a prevailing love of the truth, is to me one of the most fascinating of patristic sketches. One cannot but reflect upon the contrast presented in every respect by the late Council of the Vatican.]

[3] This passage is given substantially by Eusebius also in book iii. c. 28.
[4] The text gives ὀνειροπολεῖν, for which ὀνειροπολεῖ or ὠνειροπόλει is to be read.
[5] δι᾽ ὧν εὐφημότερον ταῦτα ᾠήθη πορεύεσθαι. The old reading was εὐθυμότερον; but the present reading is given in the MSS., Cod. Maz., and Med., as also in Eusebius, iii. 28, and in Nicephorus, iii. 14. So Rufinus renders it: *et ut aliquid sacratius dicere videretur, legales aiebat festivitates rursum celebrandas.* [These gross views of millennial perfection entailed upon subsequent ages a reactionary neglect of the study of the Second Advent. A Papal aphorism, preserved by Roscoe, embodies all this: "Sub umbilico nulla religio." It was fully exemplified, even under Leo X.]
[6] [The humility which moderates and subdues our author's pride of intellect in this passage is, to me, most instructive as to the limits prescribed to argument in what Coleridge calls "the faith of reason."]

he, "is he that keepeth the words of the prophecy of this book; and I John *who* saw and heard these things."[1] That this person was called John, therefore, and that this was the writing of a John, I do not deny. And I admit further, that it was also the work of some holy and inspired man. But I could not so easily admit that this was the apostle, the son of Zebedee, the brother of James, and the same person with him who wrote the Gospel which bears the title *according to John*, and the catholic epistle. But from the character of both, and the forms of expression, and the whole disposition and execution[2] of the book, I draw the conclusion that the authorship is not his. For the evangelist nowhere else subjoins his name, and he never proclaims himself either in the Gospel or in the epistle.

And a little further on he adds: — John, moreover, nowhere gives us the name, whether as of himself directly (in the first person), or as of another (in the third person). But the writer of the Revelation puts himself forward at once in the very beginning, for he says: "The Revelation of Jesus Christ, which He gave to him to show to His servants quickly; and He sent and signified it by His angel to His servant John, who bare record of the Word of God, and of his testimony, and of all things that he saw."[3] And then he writes also an epistle, in which he says: "John to the seven churches which are in Asia, grace be unto you, and peace." The evangelist, on the other hand, has not prefixed his name even to the catholic epistle; but without any circumlocution, he has commenced at once with the mystery of the divine revelation itself in these terms: "That which was from the beginning, which we have heard, which we have seen with our eyes."[4] And on the ground of such a revelation as that the Lord pronounced Peter blessed, when He said: "Blessed art thou, Simon Bar-jona; for flesh and blood hath not revealed it unto thee, but my Father which is in heaven."[5] And again in the second epistle, which is ascribed to John, the apostle, and in the third, though they are indeed brief, John is not set before us by name; but we find simply the anonymous writing, "The elder." This other author, on the contrary, did not even deem it sufficient to name himself once, and then to proceed with his narrative; but he takes up his name again, and says: "I John, who also am your brother and companion in tribulation, and in the kingdom and patience of Jesus Christ,

was in the isle that is called Patmos for the Word of God, and for the testimony of Jesus Christ."[6] And likewise toward the end he speaks thus: "Blessed is he that keepeth the sayings of the prophecy of this book; and I John *who* saw these things and heard them."[1] That it is a John, then, that writes these things we must believe, for he himself tells us.

5. What John this is, however, is uncertain. For he has not said, as he often does in the Gospel, that he is the disciple beloved by the Lord, or the one that leaned on His bosom, or the brother of James, or one that was privileged to see and hear the Lord. And surely he would have given us some of these indications if it had been his purpose to make himself clearly known. But of all this he offers us nothing; and he only calls himself our brother and companion, and the witness of Jesus, and one blessed with the seeing and hearing of these revelations. I am also of opinion that there were many persons of the same name with John the apostle, who by their love for him, and their admiration and emulation of him, and their desire to be loved by the Lord as he was loved, were induced to embrace also the same designation, just as we find many of the children of the faithful called by the names of Paul and Peter.[7] There is, besides, another John mentioned in the Acts of the Apostles, with the surname Mark, whom Barnabas and Paul attached to themselves as companion, and of whom again it is said: "And they had also John to their minister."[8] But whether this is the one who wrote the Revelation, I could not say. For it is not written that he came with them into Asia. But the writer says: "Now when Paul and his company loosed from Paphos, they came to Perga in Pamphylia: and John, departing from them, returned to Jerusalem."[9] I think, therefore, that it was some other one of those who were in Asia. For it is said that there were two monuments in Ephesus, and that each of these bears the name of John.

6. And from the ideas, and the expressions, and the collocation of the same, it may be very reasonably conjectured that this one is distinct

[1] Rev. xxii. 7, 8.
[2] διεξαγωγῆς λεγομένης Musculus renders it *tractatum libri;* Christophorsonus gives *discursum;* and Valesius takes it as equivalent to οικονομιαν, as διεξαγαγεῖν is the same as διοικεῖν.
[3] Rev. i. 1, 2.
[4] 1 John i. 1.
[5] Matt. xvi. 17.

[6] Rev. i. 9.
[7] It is worth while to note this passage of Dionysius on the ancient practice of the Christians, in giving their children the names of Peter and Paul, which they did both in order to express the honour and affection in which they held these saints, and to secure that their children might be dear and acceptable to God, just as those saints were. Hence it is that Chrysostom in his first volume, in his oration on St. Meletius, says that the people of Antioch had such love and esteem for Meletius, that the parents called their children by his name, in order that they might have their homes adorned by his presence. And the same Chrysostom, in his twenty-first homily on Genesis, exhorts his hearers not to call their children carelessly by the names of their grandfathers, or great-grandfathers, or men of fame; but rather by the names of saintly men, who have been shining patterns of virtue, in order that the children might be fired with the desire of virtue by their example. — VALES. [A chapter in the history of civilization might here be given on the origin of Christian names and on the motives which should influence Christians in the bestowal of names. The subject is treated, after Plato, by De Maistre.]
[8] Acts xiii. 5.
[9] Acts xiii. 13.

from that.[1] For the Gospel and the Epistle agree with each other, and both commence in the same way. For the one opens thus, " In the beginning was the Word ; " while the other opens thus, " That which was from the beginning." The one says : " And the Word was made flesh, and dwelt among us ; and we beheld His glory, the glory as of the Only-begotten of the Father."[2] The other says the same things, with a slight alteration : " That which we have heard, which we have seen with our eyes, which we have looked upon, and our hands have handled, of the Word of life : and the life was manifested."[3] For these things are introduced by way of prelude, and in opposition, as he has shown in the subsequent parts, to those who deny that the Lord is come in the flesh. For which reason he has also been careful to add these words : " And that which we have seen we testify, and show unto you that eternal life which was with the Father, and was manifested unto us : that which we have seen and heard declare we unto you."[4] Thus he keeps to himself, and does not diverge inconsistently from his subjects, but goes through them all under the same heads and in the same phraseologies, some of which we shall briefly mention. Thus the attentive reader will find the phrases, " the life," " the light," occurring often in both ; and also such expressions as *fleeing from darkness, holding the truth, grace, joy, the flesh and the blood of the Lord, the judgment, the remission of sins, the love of God toward us, the commandment of love on our side toward each other;* as also, *that we ought to keep all the commandments, the conviction of the world, of the devil, of Antichrist, the promise of the Holy Spirit, the adoption of God, the faith* required of us in all things, *the Father and the Son,* named as such everywhere. And altogether, through their whole course, it will be evident that the Gospel and the Epistle are distinguished by one and the same character of writing. But the Revelation is totally different, and altogether distinct from this ; and I might almost say that it does not even come near it, or border upon it. Neither does it contain a syllable in common with these other books. Nay more, the Epistle — for I say nothing of the Gospel — does not make any men-

tion or evince any notion of the Revelation ; and the Revelation, in like manner, gives no note of the Epistle. Whereas Paul gives some indication of his revelations in his epistles ; which revelations, however, he has not recorded in writing by themselves.

7. And furthermore, on the ground of difference in diction, it is possible to prove a distinction between the Gospel and the Epistle on the one hand, and the Revelation on the other. For the former are written not only without actual error as regards the Greek language, but also with the greatest elegance, both in their expressions and in their reasonings, and in the whole structure of their style. They are very far indeed from betraying any barbarism or solecism, or any sort of vulgarism, in their diction. For, as might be presumed, the writer possessed the gift of both kinds of discourse,[5] the Lord having bestowed both these capacities upon him, viz., that of knowledge and that of expression. That the author of the latter, however, saw a revelation, and received knowledge and prophecy, I do not deny. Only I perceive that his dialect and language are not of the exact Greek type, and that he employs barbarous idioms, and in some places also solecisms. These, however, we are under no necessity of seeking out at present. And I would not have any one suppose that I have said these things in the spirit of ridicule ; for I have done so only with the purpose of setting right this matter of the dissimilarity subsisting between these writings.[6]

II. — FROM THE BOOKS ON NATURE.[7]

I. IN OPPOSITION TO THOSE OF THE SCHOOL OF EPICURUS WHO DENY THE EXISTENCE OF A PROVIDENCE, AND REFER THE CONSTITUTION OF THE UNIVERSE TO ATOMIC BODIES.

Is the universe one coherent whole, as it seems to be in our own judgment, as well as in that of the wisest of the Greek philosophers, such as Plato and Pythagoras, and the Stoics and Heraclitus ? or is it a duality, as some may possibly

---

[1] This is the second argument by which Dionysius reasoned that the Revelation and the Gospel of John are not by one author. For the first argument which he used in proof of this is drawn from the character and usage of the two writers ; and this argument Dionysius has prosecuted up to this point. Now, however, he adduces a second argument, drawn from the words and ideas of the two writers, and from the collocation of the expressions. For, with Cicero, I thus interpret the word σύνταξιν. See the very elegant book of Dionysius Hal. entitled Περὶ συντάξεως ὀνομάτων — On the Collocation of Names, although in this passage σύνταξις appears to comprehend the disposition of sentences as well as words. Further, from this passage we can see what experience Dionysius had in criticism; for it is the critic's part to examine the writings of the ancients, and distinguish what is genuine and authentic from what is spurious and counterfeit. — VALES.

[2] John i. 14.
[3] 1 Joh. i. 2.
[4] 1 Jo.. . , 3.

[5] The old reading was, τον λόγον, τὴν γνῶσιν. Valesius expunges the την γνῶσιν, as disturbing the sense, and as absent in various codices. Instead also of the reading, τόν τε τῆς σοφίας, τόν τε τῆς γνώσεως, the same editor adopts τον τε τῆς γνώσεως, τόν τε τῆς φράσεως, which is the reading of various manuscripts, and is accepted in the translation. Valesius understands that by the ἑκατερον λόγον Dionysius means the λόγος ἐνδιάθετος and the λόγος προφορικός, that is, the subjective discourse, or reason in the mind, and the objective discourse, or utterance of the same.

[6] [The jealousy with which, while the canon of New Testament Scripture was forming, every claim was sifted, is well illustrated in this remarkable essay. Observe its critical skill and the fidelity with which he exposes the objections based on the style and classicality of the Evangelist. The Alexandrian school was one of bold and original investigation, always subject in spirit, however, to the great canon of Prescription.]

[7] Against the Epicureans. In Eusebius, *Præpar. Evangel.*, book xiv. ch. 23-27. Eusebius introduces this extract in terms to the following effect: It may be well now to subjoin some few arguments out of the many which are employed in his disputation against the Epicureans by the bishop Dionysius, a man who professed a Christian philosophy, as they are found in the work which he composed on Nature. But peruse thou the writer's statements in his own terms.

have conjectured? or is it indeed something manifold and infinite, as has been the opinion of certain others who, with a variety of mad speculations and fanciful usages of terms, have sought to divide and resolve the essential matter [1] of the universe, and lay down the position that it is infinite and unoriginated, and without the sway of Providence? [2] For there are those who, giving the name of atoms to certain imperishable and most minute bodies which are supposed to be infinite in number, and positing also the existence of a certain vacant space of an unlimited vastness, allege that these atoms, as they are borne along casually in the void, and clash all fortuitously against each other in an unregulated whirl, and become commingled one with another in a multitude of forms, enter into combination with each other, and thus gradually form this world and all objects in it; yea, more, that they construct infinite worlds. This was the opinion of Epicurus and Democritus; only they differed in one point, in so far as the former supposed these atoms to be all most minute and consequently imperceptible, while Democritus held that there were also some among them of a very large size. But they both hold that such atoms do exist, and that they are so called on account of their indissoluble consistency. There are some, again, who give the name of atoms to certain bodies which are indivisible into parts, while they are themselves parts of the universe, out of which in their undivided state all things are made up, and into which they are dissolved again. And the allegation is, that Diodorus was the person who gave them their names as bodies indivisible into parts.[3] But it is also said that Heraclides attached another name to them, and called them "weights;"[4] and from him the physician Asclepiades also derived that name.[5]

II. A REFUTATION OF THIS DOGMA ON THE GROUND OF FAMILIAR HUMAN ANALOGIES.

How shall we bear with these men who assert that all those wise, and consequently also noble, constructions (in the universe) are only the works of common chance? those objects, I mean, of which each taken by itself as it is made, and the whole system collectively, were seen to be good by Him by whose command they came into existence. For, as it is said, "God saw everything that He had made, and, behold, it was very good." [6] But truly these men do not reflect on [7]

the analogies even of small familiar things which might come under their observation at any time, and from which they might learn that no object of any utility, and fitted to be serviceable, is made without design or by mere chance, but is wrought by skill of hand, and is contrived so as to meet its proper use. And when the object falls out of service and becomes useless, then it also begins to break up indeterminately, and to decompose and dissipate its materials in every casual and unregulated way, just as the wisdom by which it was skilfully constructed at first no longer controls and maintains it. For a cloak, for example, cannot be made without the weaver, as if the warp could be set aright and the woof could be entwined with it by their own spontaneous action; while, on the other hand, if it is once worn out, its tattered rags are flung aside. Again, when a house or a city is built, it does not take on its stones, as if some of them placed themselves spontaneously upon the foundations, and others lifted themselves up on the several layers, but the builder carefully disposes the skilfully prepared stones in their proper positions; while if the structure happens once to give way, the stones are separated and cast down and scattered about. And so, too, when a ship is built, the keel does not lay itself, neither does the mast erect itself in the centre, nor do all the other timbers take up their positions casually and by their own motion. Nor, again, do the so-called hundred beams in the wain fit themselves spontaneously to the vacant spaces they severally light on. But the carpenter in both cases puts the materials together in the right way and at the right time.[8] And if the ship goes to sea and is wrecked, or if the wain drives along on land and is shattered, their timbers are broken up and cast abroad anywhere, — those of the former by the waves, and those of the latter by the violence of the impetus. In like manner, then, we might with all propriety say also to these men, that those atoms of theirs, which remain idle and unmanipulated and useless, are introduced vainly. Let them, accordingly, seek for themselves to see into what is beyond the reach of sight, and conceive what is beyond the range of conception; [9] unlike him who in these terms confesses to God that things like these had been shown him only by God Himself: "Mine

---

[1] οὐσίαν.

[2] ἀπρονόητον.

[3] τῶν ἀμερῶν.

[4] ὄγκους.

[5] ἐκληρονόμησε τὸ ὄνομα. Eusebius subjoins this remark: ταῦτ' εἰπών, ἑξῆς ἀνασκευάζει τὸ δόγμα διὰ πολλῶν, ἀτὰρ δὲ διὰ τούτων, = having said thus much, he (Dionysius) proceeds to demolish this doctrine by many arguments, and among others by what follows. — GALL.

[6] Gen. i. 31.

[7] The text is, ἀλλ' οὐδὲ ἀπὸ τῶν μικρῶν τῶν συνήθων καὶ παρὰ πόδας νουθετούντων, etc. We adopt Viger's suggestion, and read νουθετοῦνται.

[8] The text is, ἑκατέρας συνεκόμισε καιριον, for which Viger proposes εἰς τὸν ἑκατέρας, etc.

[9] The text gives, ὁράτωσαν γὰρ τὰς ἀθεάτους ἐκεῖνοι, καὶ τὰς ἀνοήτους νοείτωσαν, οὐχ ὁμοίως ἐκείνω, etc. The passage seems corrupt. Some supply φύσεις as the subject intended in the ἀθεάτους and ἀνοήτους; but that leaves the connection still obscure. Viger would read, with one MS., ἀθέτους instead of ἀθαέτους, and makes this then the sense: that those Epicureans are bidden study more closely these unregulated and stolid (ἀνοήτους) atoms, not looking at them with a merely cursory and careless glance, as David acknowledges was the case with him in the thoughts of his own imperfect nature, in order that they may the more readily understand how out of such confusion as that in which they are involved nothing orderly and finished could possibly have originated. [P. 86, note 2, infra.]

eyes did see Thy work, being till then imperfect."[1] But when they assert now that all those things of grace and beauty, which they declare to be textures finely wrought out of atoms, are fabricated spontaneously by these bodies without either wisdom or perception in them, who can endure to hear[2] them talk in such terms of those unregulated[3] atoms, than which even the spider, that plies its proper craft of itself, is gifted with more sagacity?

III. A REFUTATION ON THE GROUND OF THE CONSTITUTION OF THE UNIVERSE.

Or who can bear to hear it maintained, that this mighty habitation, which is constituted of heaven and earth, and which is called "Cosmos" on account of the magnitude and the plenitude of the wisdom which has been brought to bear upon it, has been established in all its order and beauty by those atoms which hold their course devoid of order and beauty, and that that same state of disorder has grown into this true Cosmos, Order? Or who can believe that those regular movements and courses are the products of a certain unregulated impetus? Or who can allow that the perfect concord subsisting among the celestial bodies derives its harmony from instruments destitute both of concord and harmony? Or, again, if there is but one and the same substance[4] in all things, and if there is the same incorruptible nature[5] in all, — the only elements of difference being, as they aver, size and figure, — how comes it that there are some bodies divine and perfect,[6] and eternal,[7] as they would phrase it, or lasting,[8] as some one may prefer to express it; and among these some that are visible and others that are invisible, — the visible including such as sun, and moon, and stars, and earth, and water; and the invisible including gods, and demons, and spirits? For the existence of such they cannot possibly deny however desirous to do so. And again, there are other objects that are long-lived, both animals and plants. As to animals, there are, for example, among birds, as they say, the eagle, the

raven, and the phœnix; and among creatures living on land, there are the stag, and the elephant, and the dragon; and among aquatic creatures there are the whales, and such like monsters of the deep. And as to trees, there are the palm, and the oak, and the persea;[9] and among trees, too, there are some that are evergreens, of which kind fourteen have been reckoned up by some one; and there are others that only bloom for a certain season, and then shed their leaves. And there are other objects, again — which indeed constitute the vast mass of all which either grow or are begotten — that have an early death and a brief life. And among these is man himself, as a certain holy scripture says of him: "Man that is born of woman is of few days."[10] Well, but I suppose they will reply that the varying conjunctions of the atoms account fully for differences[11] so great in the matter of duration. For it is maintained that there are some things that are compressed together by them, and firmly interlaced, so that they become closely compacted bodies, and consequently exceedingly hard to break up; while there are others in which more or less the conjunction of the atoms is of a looser and weaker nature, so that they either quickly or after some time they separate themselves from their orderly constitution. And, again, there are some bodies made up of atoms of a definite kind and a certain common figure, while there are others made up of diverse atoms diversely disposed. But who, then, is the sagacious discriminator,[12] that brings certain atoms into collocation, and separates others; and marshals some in such wise as to form the sun, and others in such a way as to originate the moon, and adapts all in natural fitness, and in accordance with the proper constitution of each star? For surely neither would those solar atoms, with their peculiar size and kind, and with their special mode of collocation, ever have reduced themselves so as to effect the production of a moon; nor, on the other hand, would the conjunctions of these lunar atoms ever have developed into a sun. And as certainly neither would Arcturus, resplendent as he is, ever boast his having the atoms possessed by Lucifer, nor would the Pleiades glory in being constituted of those of Orion. For well has Paul expressed the distinction when he says: "There is one glory of the sun, and another glory of the moon, and another glory of the stars: for one star differeth from another star in glory."[13] And if the coalition effected among them has been an unintelligent one, as is the case with soulless[14] objects,

---

[1] Ps. cxxxix. 16. The text gives, τὸ ἀκατέργαστόν σου ἴδωσαν οἱ ὀφθαλμοί μου. This strange reading, instead of the usual τὸ ἀκατέργαστόν μου εἶδον (or ἴδον) οἱ ὀφθαλμοί σου, is found also in the Alexandrine exemplar of the Septuagint, which gives, τὸ ἀκατέργαστόν σου εἴδοσαν οἱ ὀφθαλμοί μου, and in the Psalter of S. Germanus in Calmet, which has, imperfectum tuum viderunt oculi mei. Viger renders it thus: quod ex tuis operibus imperfectum adhuc et impolitum videbatur, oculi tandem mei perviderunt; i.e., Thy works, which till now seemed imperfect and unfinished, my eyes have at length discerned clearly: to wit, because being now penetrated by greater light from Thee, they have ceased to be dimsighted. See Viger's note in Migne.

[2] [The reproduction of all this outworn nonsense in our age claims for itself the credit of progressive science. It has had its day, and its destiny is to be speedily wiped out by the next school of thinkers. Meanwhile let the believer's answer be found in Isa. xxxvii. 22, 23.]

[3] ἀρρυθμους.
[4] οὐσίας.
[5] φύσεως.
[6] ἀκήρατα.
[7] αἰώνια.
[8] μακραίωνα.

[9] περσέα, a sacred tree of Egypt and Persia, the fruit of which grew from the stem.
[10] Job xiv. 1.
[11] The text gives διαφθορᾶς, for which Viger suggests διαφορᾶς.
[12] φιλοκρινῶν.
[13] 1 Cor. xv. 41.
[14] ἀψύχων.

then they must needs have had some sagacious artificer ; and if their union has been one without the determination of will, and only of necessity, as is the case with irrational objects, then some skilful leader [1] must have brought them together and taken them under his charge. And if they have linked themselves together spontaneously, for a spontaneous work, then some admirable architect must have apportioned their work for them, and assumed the superintendence among them ; or there must have been one to do with them as the general does who loves order and discipline, and who does not leave his army in an irregular condition, or suffer all things to go on confusedly, but marshals the cavalry in their proper succession, and disposes the heavy-armed infantry in their due array, and the javelin-men by themselves, and the archers separately, and the slingers in like manner, and sets each force in its appropriate position, in order that all those equipped in the same way may engage together. But if these teachers think that this illustration is but a joke, because I institute a comparison between very large bodies and very small, we may pass to the very smallest.

Then we have what follows : — But if neither the word, nor the choice, nor the order of a ruler is laid upon them, and if by their own act they keep themselves right in the vast commotion of the stream in which they move, and convey themselves safely through the mighty uproar of the collisions, and if like atoms meet and group themselves with like, not as being brought together by God, according to the poet's fancy, but rather as naturally recognising the affinities subsisting between each other, then truly we have here a most marvellous democracy of atoms, wherein friends welcome and embrace friends, and all are eager to sojourn together in one domicile ; while some by their own determination have rounded themselves off into that mighty luminary the sun, so as to make day ; and others have formed themselves into many pyramids of blazing stars, it may be, so as to crown also the whole heavens ; and others have reduced themselves into the circular figure, so as to impart a certain solidity to the ether, and arch it over, and constitute it a vast graduated ascent of luminaries, with this object also, that the various conventions of the commoner atoms may select settlements for themselves, and portion out the sky among them for their habitations and stations.

Then, after certain other matters, the discourse proceeds thus : — But inconsiderate men do not see even things that are apparent, and certainly they are far from being cognisant of things that are unapparent. For they do not seem even to have any notion of those regulated risings and settings of the heavenly bodies, — those of the sun, with all their wondrous glory, no less than those of the others ; nor do they appear to make due application of the aids furnished through these to men, such as the day that rises clear for man's work, and the night that overshadows earth for man's rest. " For man," it is said, " goeth forth unto his work, and to his labour, until the evening." [2] Neither do they consider that other revolution, by which the sun makes out for us determinate times, and convenient seasons, and regular successions, directed by those atoms of which it consists. But even though men like these — and miserable men they are, however they may believe themselves to be righteous — may choose not to admit it, there is a mighty Lord that made the sun, and gave it the impetus [3] for its course by His words. O ye blind ones, do these atoms of yours bring you the winter season and the rains, in order that the earth may yield food for you, and for all creatures living on it ? Do they introduce summer-time, too, in order that ye may gather their fruits from the trees for your enjoyment ? And why, then, do ye not worship these atoms, and offer sacrifices to them as the guardians of earth's fruits ? [4] Thankless surely are ye, in not setting solemnly apart for them even the most scanty first-fruits of that abundant bounty which ye receive from them.

After a short break he proceeds thus : — Moreover, those stars which form a community so multitudinous and various, which these erratic and ever self-dispersing atoms have constituted, have marked off by a kind of covenant the tracts for their several possessions, portioning these out like colonies and governments, but without the presidency of any founder or housemaster ; and with pledged fealty and in peace they respect the laws of vicinity with their neighbours, and abstain from passing beyond the boundaries which they received at the outset, just as if they enjoyed the legislative administration of true princes in the atoms. Nevertheless these atoms exercise no rule. For how could these, that are themselves nothing, do that ? But listen to the divine oracles : " The works of the Lord are in judgment ; from the beginning, and from His making of them, He disposed the parts thereof. He garnished His works for ever, and their principles [5] unto their generations." [6]

Again, after a little, he proceeds thus : — Or what phalanx ever traversed the plain in such perfect order, no trooper outmarching the others, or falling out of rank, or obstructing the course,

---

[2] Ps. civ. 23.
[3] [Our author touches with sagacity this *crux* of theory : whence comes *force*, the origin and the perpetuation of *impetus* ? Christianity has thus anticipated the defects of " modern science."]
[4] ταῖς ἐπικάρποις.
[5] λόχας.
[6] Ecclus. xvi. 26, 27.

or suffering himself to be distanced by his comrades in the array, as is the case with that steady advance in regular file, as it were, and with close-set shields, which is presented by this serried and unbroken and undisturbed and unobstructed progress of the hosts of the stars? Albeit by side inclinations and flank movements certain of their revolutions become less clear. Yet, however that may be, they assuredly always keep their appointed periods, and again bear onward determinately to the positions from which they have severally risen, as if they made that their deliberate study. Wherefore let these notable anatomizers of atoms,[1] these dividers of the indivisible, these compounders of the uncompoundable, these adepts in the apprehension of the infinite, tell us whence comes this circular march and course of the heavenly bodies, in which it is not any single combination of atoms that merely chances all unexpectedly to swing itself round in this way;[2] but it is one vast circular choir that moves thus, ever equally and concordantly, and whirls in these orbits. And whence comes it that this mighty multitude of fellow-travellers, all unmarshalled by any captain, all ungifted with any determination of will, and all unendowed with any knowledge of each other, have nevertheless held their course in perfect harmony? Surely, well has the prophet ranked this matter among things which are impossible and undemonstrable, — namely, that two strangers should walk together. For he says, "Shall two come to the same lodging unless they know each other?"[3]

IV. A REFUTATION OF THE SAME ON THE GROUNDS OF THE HUMAN CONSTITUTION.

Further, these men understand neither themselves nor what is proper to themselves. For if any of the leaders in this impious doctrine only considered what manner of person he is himself, and whence he comes, he would surely be led to a wise decision, like one who has obtained understanding of himself, and would say, not to these atoms, but to his Father and Maker, "Thy hands have made me and fashioned me."[4] And he would take up, too, this wonderful account of his formation as it has been given by one of old: "Hast Thou not poured me out as milk, and curdled me as cheese? Thou hast clothed me with skin and flesh, and hast fenced me with bones and sinews. Thou hast granted me life and favour, and Thy visitation hath preserved my spirit."[5] For of what quantity and

of what origin were the atoms which the father of Epicurus gave forth from himself when he begat Epicurus? And how, when they were received within his mother's womb, did they coalesce, and take form and figure? and how were they put in motion and made to increase? And how did that little seed of generation draw together the many atoms that were to constitute Epicurus, and change some of them into skin and flesh for a covering, and make bone of others for erectness and strength, and form sinews of others for compact contexture? And how did it frame and adapt the many other members and parts — heart and bowels, and organs of sense, some within and some without — by which the body is made a thing of life? For of all these things there is not one either idle or useless: not even the meanest of them — the hair, or the nails, or such like — is so; but all have their service to do, and all their contribution to make, some of them to the soundness of bodily constitution, and others of them to beauty of appearance. For Providence cares not only for the useful, but also for the seasonable and beautiful.[6] Thus the hair is a kind of protection and covering for the whole head, and the beard is a seemly ornament for the philosopher. It was Providence, then, that formed the constitution of the whole body of man, in all its necessary parts, and imposed on all its members their due connection with each other, and measured out for them their liberal supplies from the universal resources. And the most prominent of these show clearly, even to the uninstructed, by the proof of personal experience, the value and service attaching to them: the head, for example, in the position of supremacy, and the senses set like a guard about the brain, as the ruler in the citadel; and the advancing eyes, and the reporting ears; and the taste which, as it were, is the tribute-gatherer;[7] and the smell, which tracks and searches out its objects; and the touch, which manipulates all put under it.

Hence we shall only run over in a summary way, at present, some few of the works of an all-wise Providence; and after a little we shall, if God grant it, go over them more minutely, when we direct our discourse toward one who has the repute of greater learning. So, then, we have the ministry of the hands, by which all kinds of works are wrought, and all skilful professions practised, and which have all their various faculties furnished them, with a view to the discharge of one common function; and we have the shoulders, with their capacity for bearing burdens; and the fingers, with their power

---

1 τῶν ἀτόμων τομεῖς.
2 οὕτω σφενδονισθέντος.
3 This sentence, which is quoted as from the Scriptures, is found nowhere there, at least *verbatim et ad litteram*. [Amos iii. 3.]
4 Ps. cxix. 73.
5 Job x. 10–12. [The milky element (*sperma*) marvellously changed into flesh, and the *embroidery* of the human anatomy, are here admirably brought out. Compare Ps. cxxxix. 12–16; also p. 86, note 1, *supra*.]

6 [Eccles. iii. 11. Note the force of the word *Cosmos*. Coleridge's *Aids to Reflection*, p. 251, ed. New York, 1840. Also, Coleridge's fancy about the τὸ καλόν *quasi* καλοῦν.]
7 ἐδωδὴ ὥσπερ φορολογοῦσα.

of grasping; and the elbows, with their faculty of bending, by which they can turn inwardly upon the body, or take an outward inclination, so as to be able either to draw objects toward the body, or to thrust them away from it. We have also the service of the feet, by which the whole terrestrial creation is made to come under our power, the earth itself is traversed thereby, the sea is made navigable, the rivers are crossed, and intercourse is established for all with all things. The belly, too, is the storehouse of meats, with all its parts arranged in their proper collocations, so that it apportions for itself the right measure of aliment, and ejects what is over and above that. And so is it with all the other things by which manifestly the due administration of the constitution of man is wisely secured.[1] Of all these, the intelligent and the unintelligent alike enjoy the same use; but they have not the same comprehension of them.[2] For there are some who refer this whole economy to a power which they conceive to be a true divinity,[3] and which they apprehend as at once the highest intelligence in all things, and the best benefactor to themselves, believing that this economy is all the work of a wisdom and a might which are superior to every other, and in themselves truly divine. And there are others who aimlessly attribute this whole structure of most marvellous beauty to chance and fortuitous coincidence. And in addition to these, there are also certain physicians, who, having made a more effective examination into all these things, and having investigated with utmost accuracy the disposition of the inward parts in especial, have been struck with astonishment at the results of their inquiry, and have been led to deify nature itself. The notions of these men we shall review afterwards, as far as we may be able, though we may only touch the surface of the subject.[4] Meantime, to deal with this matter generally and summarily, let me ask who constructed this whole tabernacle of ours, so lofty, erect, graceful, sensitive, mobile, active, and apt for all things? Was it, as they say, the irrational multitude of atoms? Nay, these, by their conjunctions, could not

mould even an image of clay, neither could they hew and polish a statue of stone; nor could they cast and finish an idol of silver or gold; but arts and handicrafts calculated for such operations have been discovered by men who fabricate these objects.[5] And if, even in these, representations and models cannot be made without the aid of wisdom, how can the genuine and original patterns of these copies have come into existence spontaneously? And whence have come the soul, and the intelligence, and the reason, which are born with the philosopher? Has he gathered these from those atoms which are destitute alike of soul, and intelligence, and reason? and has each of these atoms inspired him with some appropriate conception and notion? And are we to suppose that the wisdom of man was made up by these atoms, as the myth of Hesiod tells us that Pandora was fashioned by the gods? Then shall the Greeks have to give up speaking of the various species of poetry, and music, and astronomy, and geometry, and all the other arts and sciences, as the inventions and instructions of the gods, and shall have to allow that these atoms are the only muses with skill and wisdom for all subjects. For this theogony, constructed of atoms by Epicurus, is indeed something extraneous to the infinite worlds of order,[6] and finds its refuge in the infinite disorder.[7]

V. THAT TO WORK IS NOT A MATTER OF PAIN AND WEARINESS TO GOD.

Now to work, and administer, and do good, and exercise care, and such like actions, may perhaps be hard tasks for the idle, and silly, and weak, and wicked; in whose number truly Epicurus reckons himself, when he propounds such notions about the gods. But to the earnest, and powerful, and intelligent, and prudent, such as philosophers ought to be — and how much more so, therefore, the gods! — these things are not only not disagreeable and irksome, but ever the most delightful, and by far the most welcome of all. To persons of this character, negligence and procrastination in the doing of what is good are a reproach, as the poet admonishes them in these words of counsel: —

"Delay not aught till the morrow."[8]

And then he adds this further sentence of threatening: —

"The lazy procrastinator is ever wrestling with miseries."[9]

---

[1] The text is, καὶ τὰ ἄλλα δι’ ὅσων ἐμφανῶς ἡ διοίκησις τῆς ἀνθρωπείου μεμηχάνηται διανομῆς. Viger proposes διαμονῆς for διανομῆς, and renders the whole thus: "ac cætera quorum vi humanæ firmitatis et conservationis ratio continetur."

[2] The text is, ὧν ὁμοίως τοῖς ἄφροσιν ἔχοντες οἱ σοφοὶ τὴν κρίσιν, οὐκ ἴσχουσι τὴν γνῶσιν. We adopt Viger's suggestion, and read χρῆσιν for κρίσιν.

[3] We read, with Viger, θεότητα for ἀθεότητα. The text gives οἱ μὲν γὰρ εἰς ἣν ἂν οἰηθῶσιν ἀθεότητα, etc., which might possibly mean something like this: There are some who refer the whole economy to a power which (others) may deem to be no divinity, (but which is) the highest intelligence in all things, and the best benefactor, etc. Or the sense might be = There are some who refer this most intelligent and beneficent economy to a power which they deem to be no divinity, though they believe the same economy to be the work of a wisdom, etc.

[4] The text is, ἡμεῖς δὲ ὕστερον ὡς ἂν οἷοί τε γενώμεθα, κἂν ἐπιπολῆς, ἀναθεωρήσομεν. Viger renders it thus: "Nos eam postea, jejune fortassis et exiliter, ut pro facultate nostra, prosequemur." He proposes, however, to read ἐπὶ πολλοῖς (sc. ῥήμασι or λόγοις) for ἐπιπολῆς.

[5] The text is, χειρουργίαι τούτων ὑπ’ ἀνθρώπων εὕρηνται σωματουργῶν. Viger proposes σωματουργοί, "handicrafts for the construction of such bodies have been discovered by men."

[6] κόσμων. [See note 6, p. 88, supra.]

[7] ἀκοσμίαν.

[8] Hesiod's Works and Days, v. 408.

[9] Ibid., v. 411.

And the prophet teaches us the same lesson in a more solemn fashion, and declares that deeds done according to the standard of virtue are truly worthy of God,[1] and that the man who gives no heed to these is accursed : " For cursed be he that doeth the works of the Lord carelessly." [2] Moreover, those who are unversed in any art, and unable to prosecute it perfectly, feel it to be wearisome when they make their first attempts in it, just by reason of the novelty [3] of their experience, and their want of practice in the works. But those, on the other hand, who have made some advance, and much more those who are perfectly trained in the art, accomplish easily and successfully the objects of their labours, and have great pleasure in the work, and would choose rather thus, in the discharge of the pursuits to which they are accustomed, to finish and carry perfectly out what their efforts aim at, than to be made masters of all those things which are reckoned advantageous among men. Yea, Democritus himself, as it is reported, averred that he would prefer the discovery of one true cause to being put in possession of the kingdom of Persia. And that was the declaration of a man who had only a vain and groundless conception of the causes of things,[4] inasmuch as he started with an unfounded principle, and an erroneous hypothesis, and did not discern the real root and the common *law of* necessity in the constitution of natural things, and held as the greatest wisdom the apprehension of things that come about simply in an unintelligent and random way, and set up chance [5] as the mistress and queen of things universal, and even things divine, and endeavoured to demonstrate that all things happen by the determination of the same, although at the same time he kept it outside the sphere of the life of men, and convicted those of senselessness who worshipped it. At any rate, at the very beginning of his *Precepts* [6] he speaks thus : " Men have made an image [7] of chance, as a cover [8] for their own lack of knowledge. For intellect and chance are in their very nature antagonistic to each other.[9] And men have maintained that this greatest adversary to intelligence is its sovereign. Yea, rather, they completely subvert and do away with the one, while they establish the other in its place. For they do not celebrate intelligence as the fortunate,[10] but

they laud chance [11] as the most intelligent." [12] Moreover, those who attend to things conducing to the good of life, take special pleasure in what serves the interests of those of the same race with themselves, and seek the recompense of praise and glory in return for labours undertaken in behalf of the general good ; while some exert themselves as purveyors of ways and means,[13] others as magistrates, others as physicians, others as statesmen ; and even philosophers pride themselves greatly in their efforts after the education of men. Will, then, Epicurus or Democritus be bold enough to assert that in the exertion of philosophizing they only cause distress to themselves? Nay, rather they will reckon this a pleasure of mind second to none. For even though they maintain the opinion that the good is pleasure, they will be ashamed to deny that philosophizing is the greater pleasure to them.[14] But as to the gods, of whom the poets among them sing that they are the " bestowers of good gifts," [15] these philosophers scoffingly celebrate them in strains like these : " The gods are neither the bestowers nor the sharers in any good thing." And in what manner, forsooth, can they demonstrate that there are gods at all, when they neither perceive their presence, nor discern them as the doers of aught, wherein, indeed, they resemble those who, in their admiration and wonder at the sun and the moon and the stars, have held these to have been named *gods*,[16] from their *running* [17] such courses : when, further, they do not attribute to them any function or power of operation,[18] so as to hold them gods [19] from their *constituting*,[20] that is, from their *making* objects,[21] for thereby in all truth the one maker and operator of all things must be God : and when, in fine, they do not set forth any administration, or judgment, or beneficence of theirs in relation to men, so that we might be bound either by fear or by reverence to worship them? Has Epicurus then been able, forsooth, to see beyond this world, and to overpass the precincts of heaven? or has he gone forth by some secret gates known to himself alone, and thus obtained sight of the gods in the void? [22] and, deeming them blessed in their full felicity, and then becoming himself a passionate aspirant after such pleasure, and an ardent scholar in that life which they pursue in the void, does he now

---

1 θεοπρεπῆ.
2 ἀμελῶς. Jer. xlviii. 10.
3 The text gives, διὰ τὸ τῆς πείρας ἀληθές. We adopt Viger's emendation, ἀηθές.
4 [" Felix qui potuit rerum cognoscere causas." But see *Hippolytus* (vol. v.), and compare Clement, vol. ii. pp. 565–567, this series.]
5 τύχην.
6 ὑποθηκῶν.
7 εἴδωλον.
8 πρόφασιν.
9 φύσει γὰρ γνώμῃ τυχῇ μάχεται. Viger refers to the parallel in Tullius, *pro Marcello*, sec. 7: " Nunquam temeritas cum sapientia commiscetur, nec ad consilium casus admittitur."
10 εὐτυχῆ.

11 Fortune, τύχην.
12 ἐμφρονεστάτην.
13 τρέφοντες.
14 The text gives, ἡδὺ ὂν αὐτοῖς εἶναι τὸ φιλοσοφεῖν. Viger suggests ἡδίον for ἡδὺ ὄν.
15 δωτῆρας ἐάων. See Homer, *Odyssey*, viii. 325 and 335.
16 θεούς.
17 διὰ τὸ θέειν.
18 δημιουργίαν αὐτοῖς ἢ κατασκευήν.
19 θεοποιήσωσιν.
20 ἐκ τοῦ θεῖναι.
21 ποιῆσαι.
22 The text gives, οὓς ἐν τῷ κενῷ κατεῖδε θεούς. Viger proposes τοὺς for οὓς.

call upon all to participate in this felicity, and urge them thus to make themselves like the gods, preparing[1] as their true *symposium* of blessedness neither heaven nor Olympus, as the poets feign, but the sheer void, and setting before them the ambrosia of atoms,[2] and pledging them in[3] nectar made of the same? However, in matters which have no relation to us, he introduces into his books a myriad oaths and solemn asseverations, swearing constantly both negatively and affirmatively by Jove, and making those whom he meets, and with whom he discusses his doctrines, swear also by the gods, not certainly that he fears them himself, or has any dread of perjury, but that he pronounces all this to be vain, and false, and idle, and unintelligible, and uses it simply as a kind of accompaniment to his words, just as he might also clear his throat, or spit, or twist his face, or move his hand. So completely senseless and empty a pretence was this whole matter of the naming of the gods, in his estimation. But this is also a very patent fact, that, being in fear of the Athenians after (the warning of) the death of Socrates, and being desirous of preventing his being taken for what he really was — an atheist — the subtle charlatan invented for them certain empty shadows of unsubstantial gods. But never surely did he look up to heaven with eyes of true intelligence, so as to hear the clear voice from above, which another attentive spectator did hear, and of which he testified when he said, "The heavens declare the glory of God, and the firmament showeth His handiwork."[4] And never surely did he look down upon the world's surface with due reflection; for then would he have learned that "the earth is full of the goodness of the Lord,"[5] and that "the earth is the Lord's, and the fulness thereof;"[6] and that, as we also read, "After this the Lord looked upon the earth, and filled it with His blessings. With all manner of living things hath He covered the face thereof."[7] And if these men are not hopelessly blinded, let them but survey the vast wealth and variety of living creatures, land animals, and winged creatures, and aquatic; and let them understand then that the declaration made by the Lord on the occasion of His judgment of all things[8] is true: "And all things, in accordance with His command, appeared good."[9]

III. — FROM THE BOOKS AGAINST SABELLIUS.[10]

ON THE NOTION THAT MATTER IS UNGENERATED.[11]

These certainly are not to be deemed pious who hold that matter is ungenerated, while they allow, indeed, that it is brought under the hand of God so far as its arrangement and regulation are concerned; for they do admit that, being naturally passive[12] and pliable, it yields readily to the alterations impressed upon it by God. It is for them, however, to show us plainly how it can possibly be that the like and the unlike should be predicated as subsisting together in God and matter. For it becomes necessary thus to think of one as a superior to either, and that is a thought which cannot legitimately be entertained with regard to God. For if there is this defect of generation which is said to be the thing like in both, and if there is this point of difference which is conceived of besides in the two, whence has this arisen in them? If, indeed, God is the ungenerated, and if this defect of generation is, as we may say, His very essence, then matter cannot be ungenerated; for God and matter are not one and the same. But if each subsists properly and independently — namely, God and matter — and if the defect of generation also belongs to both, then it is evident that there is something different from each, and older and higher than both. But the difference of their contrasted constitutions is completely subversive of the idea that these can subsist on an equality together, and more, that this one of the two — namely, matter — can subsist of itself. For then they will have to furnish an explanation of the fact that, though both are supposed to be ungenerated, God is nevertheless impassible, immutable, imperturbable, energetic; while matter is the opposite, impressible, mutable, variable, alterable. And now, how can these properties harmoniously co-exist and unite? Is it that God has adapted Himself to the nature of the matter, and thus has skilfully wrought it? But it would be absurd to suppose that God works in gold, as men are wont to do, or hews or polishes stone, or puts His hand to any of the other arts by which different kinds of matter are made capable of receiving form and figure. But if, on the other hand, He has fashioned matter according to His own will, and after the dictates of His own wisdom, impressing upon it the rich and manifold forms produced by His own operation, then is this account of ours one both good and true, and still further

---

[1] συγκροτῶν.
[2] For ἀτόμων Viger suggests ἀτμῶν, " of vapours."
[3] Or, giving them to drink.
[4] Ps. xix. 1.
[5] Ps. xxxiii. 5.
[6] Ps. xxiv. 1.
[7] Ecclus. xvi. 29, 30.
[8] The text is, ἐπὶ τῇ πάντων κρίσει. Viger suggests κτίσει, "at the creation of all things."
[9] The quotation runs thus: καὶ πάντα κατὰ τὴν αὐτοῦ πρόσταξιν πέφηνε καλά. Eusebius adds the remark here: "These passages have been culled by me out of a very large number composed against Epicurus by Dionysius, a bishop of our own time." [Among the many excellent works which have appeared against the " hopelessly

blinded" Epicureans of this age, let me note *Darwinism tested by Language*, by E. Bateman, M.D. London, Rivingtons, 1877.]
[10] In Eusebius, *Præpar. Evangel.*, book vii. ch. 19.
[11] Eusebius introduces this extract thus: "And I shall adduce the words of those who have most thoroughly examined the dogma before us, and first of all Dionysius indeed, who, in the first book of his *Exercitations against Sabellius*, writes in these terms on the subject in hand." [Note the *primary* position of our author in the refutation of Sabellianism, and see (vol. v.) the story of Callistus.]
[12] παθητήν.

one that establishes the position that the ungenerated God is the hypostasis (the life and foundation) of all things in the universe. For with this fact of the defect of generation it conjoins the proper mode of His being. Much, indeed, might be said in confutation of these teachers, but that is not what is before us at present. And if they are put alongside the most impious polytheists,[1] these will seem the more pious in their speech.

IV. — EPISTLE TO DIONYSIUS BISHOP OF ROME.[2]

FROM THE FIRST BOOK.

1. There certainly was not a time when God was not the Father.[3]

2. Neither, indeed, as though He had not brought forth these things, did God afterwards beget the Son, but because the Son has existence not from Himself, but from the Father.

And after a few words he says of the Son Himself : —

3. Being the brightness of the eternal Light, He Himself also is absolutely eternal. For since light is always in existence, it is manifest that its brightness also exists, because light is perceived to exist from the fact that it shines, and it is impossible that light should not shine. And let us once more come to illustrations. If the sun exists, there is also day ; if nothing of this be manifest, it is impossible that the sun should be there. If then the sun were eternal, the day would never end ; but now, for such is not really the state of the case, the day begins with the beginning of the sun, and ends with its ending. But God is the eternal Light, which has neither had a beginning, nor shall ever fail. Therefore the eternal brightness shines forth before Him, and co-exists with Him, in that, existing without a beginning, and always begotten, He always shines before Him ; and He is that Wisdom which says, "I was that wherein He delighted, and I was daily His delight before His face at all times."[4]

And a little after he thus pursues his discourse from the same point : —

4. Since, therefore, the Father is eternal, the Son also is eternal, Light of Light. For where there is the begetter, there is also the offspring. And if there is no offspring, how and of what can He be the begetter? But both are, and always are. Since, then, God is the Light, Christ is the Brightness. And since He is a Spirit — for says He, "God is a Spirit"[5] — fittingly again

is Christ called Breath ; for "He,"[6] saith He, "is the breath of God's power."[7]

And again he says : —

5. Moreover, the Son alone, always co-existing with the Father, and filled with Him who *is*, Himself also *is*, since He is of the Father.

FROM THE SAME FIRST BOOK.

6. But when I spoke of things created, and certain works to be considered, I hastily put forward illustrations of such things, as it were little appropriate, when I said neither is the plant the same as the husbandman, nor the boat the same as the boatbuilder.[8] But then I lingered rather upon things suitable and more adapted to the nature of the thing, and I unfolded in many words, by various carefully considered arguments, what things were more true ; which things, moreover, I have set forth to you in another letter. And in these things I have also proved the falsehood of the charge which they bring against me — to wit, that I do not maintain that Christ is consubstantial with God. For although I say that I have never either found or read this word in the sacred Scriptures, yet other reasonings, which I immediately subjoined, are in no wise discrepant from this view, because I brought forward as an illustration human offspring, which assuredly is of the same kind as the begetter ; and I said that parents are absolutely distinguished from their children by the fact alone that they themselves are not their children, or that it would assuredly be a matter of necessity that there would neither be parents nor children. But, as I said before, I have not the letter in my possession, on account of the present condition of affairs ; otherwise I would have sent you the very words that I then wrote, yea, and a copy of the whole letter, and I will send it if at any time I shall have the opportunity. I remember, further, that I added many similitudes from things kindred to one another. For I said that the plant, whether it grows up from seed or from a root, is different from that whence it sprouted, although it is absolutely of the same nature ; and similarly, that a river flowing from a spring takes another form and name : for that neither is the spring called the river, nor the river the spring, but that these are two things, and that the spring indeed is, as it were, the father, while the river is the water from the spring. But they feign that they do not see these things and the like to them which are written, as if they were blind ; but they endeavour to assail me from a distance with expressions too carelessly used, as if they were stones, not observing that on things of which

---

[1] πρὸς τοὺς ἀθεωτάτους πολυθέους.

[2] Fragments of a second epistle of Dionysius, Bishop of Alexandria, or of the treatise which was inscribed the "Elenchus et Apologia." [A former epistle was written when Dionysius (of Rome) was a presbyter]

[3] And in what follows (says Athanasius) he professes that Christ *is* always, as being the Word, and the Wisdom, and the Power.

[4] Prov. viii. 30.

[5] John iv. 24.

[6] *Scil.* Wisdom.

[7] Wisd. vii. 25.

[8] From Athan., *Ep. de decret. Nic. Syn.*, 4. 18. [See remarks on *inevitable* discrepancies of language and figurative illustrations at this formative period, vol. iv. p. 223.]

they are ignorant, and which require interpretation to be understood, illustrations that are not only remote, but even contrary, will often throw light.

FROM THE SAME FIRST BOOK.

7. It was said above that God is the spring of all good things, but the Son was called the river flowing from Him ; because the word is an emanation of the mind, and — to speak after human fashion — is emitted from the heart by the mouth. But the mind which springs forth by the tongue is different from the word which exists in the heart. For this latter, after it has emitted the former, remains and is what it was before ; but the mind sent forth flies away, and is carried everywhere around, and thus each is in each although one is from the other, and they are one although they are two. And it is thus that the Father and the Son are said to be one, and to be in one another.

FROM THE SECOND BOOK.

8. The individual names uttered by me can neither be separated from one another, nor parted.[1] I spoke of the Father, and before I made mention of the Son I already signified Him in the Father. I added the Son ; and the Father, even although I had not previously named Him, had already been absolutely comprehended in the Son. I added the Holy Spirit ; but, at the same time, I conveyed under the name whence and by whom He proceeded. But they are ignorant that neither the Father, in that He is *Father*, can be separated from the Son, for that name is the evident ground of coherence and conjunction ; nor can the Son be separated from the Father, for this word *Father* indicates association *between* them. And there is, moreover, evident a Spirit who can neither be disjoined from Him who sends, nor from Him who brings Him. How, then, should I who use such names think that these are absolutely divided and separated the one from the other?

After a few words he adds : —

9. Thus, indeed, we expand the indivisible Unity into a Trinity ; and again we contract the Trinity, which cannot be diminished, into a Unity.

FROM THE SAME SECOND BOOK.

10. But if any quibbler, from the fact that I said that God is the Maker and Creator of all things, thinks that I said that He is also Creator of Christ, let him observe that I first called Him Father, in which word the Son also is at the same time expressed.[2] For after I called the Father the Creator, I added, Neither is He the Father of those things whereof He is Crea-

tor, if He who begot is properly understood to be a Father (for we will consider the latitude of this word *Father* in what follows). Nor is a maker a father, if it is only a framer who is called a maker. For among the Greeks, they who are wise are said to be makers of their books. The apostle also says, " a doer (*scil.* maker) of the law." [3] Moreover, of matters of the heart, of which kind are virtue and vice, men are called doers (*scil.* makers) ; after which manner God said, " I expected that it should make judgment, but it made iniquity." [4]

11. That neither must this saying be thus blamed ; [5] for he says that he used the name of Maker on account of the flesh which the Word had assumed, and which certainly was made. But if any one should suspect that that had been said of the Word, even this also was to be heard without contentiousness. For as I do not think that the Word was a thing made, so I do not say that God was its Maker, but its Father. Yet still, if at any time, discoursing of the Son, I may have casually said that God was His Maker, even this mode of speaking would not be without defence. For the wise men among the Greeks call themselves the makers of their books, although the same are fathers of their books. Moreover, divine Scripture calls us makers of those motions which proceed from the heart, when it calls us doers of the law of judgment and of justice.

FROM THE SAME SECOND BOOK.

12. *In the beginning was the Word.*[6] But that was not the Word which produced the Word.[7] For " the Word was with God." [6] The Lord is Wisdom ; it was not therefore Wisdom that produced Wisdom ; for " I was that," says He, " wherein He delighted." [8] Christ is truth ; but "blessed," says He, " is the God of truth."

FROM THE THIRD BOOK.

13. Life is begotten of life in the same way as the river has flowed forth from the spring, and the brilliant light is ignited from the inextinguishable light.[9]

FROM THE FOURTH BOOK.

14. Even as our mind emits from itself a word,[7] — as says the prophet, " My heart hath uttered forth a good word," [10] — and each of the two is distinct the one from the other, and maintaining a peculiar place, and one that is distin-

3 Rom. ii. 13; Jas. iv. 12. The Greek word ποιητης meaning either *maker* or *doer*, causes the ambiguity here and below.
4 Isa. v. 7.
5 Athanasius adds (*ut supra*, 4. 21), that Dionysius gave various replies to those that blamed him for saying that God is the Maker of Christ, whereby he cleared himself.
6 John i. 1. [For ῥημα, see vol. ii. p. 15, this series.]
7 Ex Athan., *Ep. de decret. Nic. Syn.*, 4. 25. [P. 94, notes 1, 2 *infra*.]
8 Prov. viii. 30.
9 Ex Athan., *Ep. de decret. Nic. Syn.*, 4. 18.
10 Ps. xlv. 1.

1 Ex Athan., *Ep. de decret. Nic. Syn.*, 4. 17.
2 *Ibid.*, 4. 20.

guished from the other ; since the former indeed abides and is stirred in the heart, while the latter has its place in the tongue and in the mouth. And yet they are not apart from one another, nor deprived of one another ; neither is the mind without the word, nor is the word without the mind ; but the mind makes the word and appears in the word, and the word exhibits the mind wherein it was made. And the mind indeed is, as it were, the word immanent, while the word is the mind breaking forth.[1] The mind passes into the word, and the word transmits the mind to the surrounding hearers ; and thus the mind by means of the word takes its place in the souls of the hearers, entering in at the same time as the word. And indeed the mind is, as it were, the father of the word, existing in itself ; but the word is as the son of the mind, and cannot be made before it nor without it, but exists with it, whence it has taken its seed and origin. In the same manner, also, the Almighty Father and Universal Mind has before all things the Son, the Word, and the discourse,[2] as the interpreter and messenger of Himself.

ABOUT THE MIDDLE OF THE TREATISE.

15. If, from the fact that there are three hypostases, they say that they are divided, there are three whether they like it or no, or else let them get rid of the divine Trinity altogether.[3]

AND AGAIN :

For on this account after the Unity there is also the most divine Trinity.[4]

THE CONCLUSION OF THE ENTIRE TREATISE.

16. In accordance with all these things, the form, moreover, and rule being received from the elders who have lived before us, we also, with a voice in accordance with them, will both acquit ourselves of thanks to you, and of the letter which we are now writing. And to God the Father, and His Son our Lord Jesus Christ, with the Holy Spirit, be glory and dominion for ever and ever. Amen.[5]

V. — THE EPISTLE TO BISHOP BASILIDES.[6]

CANON I.

Dionysius to Basilides, my beloved son, and my brother, a fellow-minister with me in holy

things, and an obedient servant of God, in the Lord greeting.

You have sent to me, most faithful and accomplished son, in order to inquire what is the proper hour for bringing the fast to a close[7] on the day of Pentecost.[8] For you say that there are some of the brethren who hold that that should be done at cockcrow, and others who hold that it should be at nightfall.[9] For the brethren in Rome, as they say, wait for the cock ; whereas, regarding those here, you told us that they would have it earlier.[10] And it is your anxious desire, accordingly, to have the hour presented accurately, and determined with perfect exactness,[11] which indeed is a matter of difficulty and uncertainty. However, it will be acknowledged cordially by all, that from the date of the resurrection of our Lord, those who up to that time have been humbling their souls with fastings, ought at once to begin their festal joy and gladness. But in what you have written to me you have made out very clearly, and with an intelligent understanding of the Holy Scriptures, that no very exact account seems to be offered in them of the hour at which He rose. For the evangelists have given different descriptions of the parties who came to the sepulchre one after another,[12] and all have declared that they found the Lord risen already. It was "in the end of the Sabbath," as Matthew has said ;[13] it was "early, when it was yet dark," as John writes ;[14] it was "very early in the morning," as Luke puts it ; and it was "very early in the morning, at the rising of the sun," as Mark tells us. Thus no one has shown us clearly the exact time when He rose. It is admitted, however, that those who came to the sepulchre in the end of the Sabbath, as it began to dawn toward the first day of the week,[15] found Him no longer lying in it. And let us not suppose that the evangelists disagree or contradict each other. But even although there may

---

[1] *Emanant.* [P. 49, *supra*, and vol. iii. p. 299, this series.]
[2] Sermonem [So Tertullian, *Sermo*, vol. iii. p. 299, note 19.]
[3] Ex Basilio, *lib. de Spir. Sancto*, chap. 29.
[4] *Ibid. cap. penult.*, p. 61.
[5] Of the work itself Athanasius thus speaks: Finally, Dionysius complains that his accusers do not quote his opinions in their integrity, but mutilated, and that they do not speak out of a good conscience, but for evil inclination; and he says that they are like those who cavilled at the epistles of the blessed apostle. Certainly he meets the individual words of his accusers, and gives a solution to all their arguments; and as in those earlier writings of his he confuted Sabellius most evidently, so in these later ones he entirely declares his own pious faith. [Conf. *Hermas*, vol. iii. p. 15, note 7, with note 2, *supra*.]
[6] Containing explanations which are answers to questions proposed by that bishop on various topics, and which have been received as canons. [The *Scholium*, p. 79, is transposed from here.]

[7] ἀπονηστίζεσθαι δεῖ. Gentianus Hervetus renders this by *jejunandus sit dies Paschæ*; and thus he translates the word by *jejunare*, "to fast," wherever it occurs, whereas it rather means always, *jejunium solvere*, "to have done fasting." In this sense the word is used in the *Apostolic Constitutions* repeatedly: see book v. chap. 12, 18, etc. It occurs in the same sense in the 89th Canon of the Concilium Trullanum. The usage must evidently be the same here: so that it does not mean, What is the proper hour for fasting on the day of Pentecost? but, What is the hour at which the antepaschal fast ought to be terminated — whether on the evening preceding the paschal festival itself, or at cockcrowing, or at another time? — GALL. See also the very full article in Suicer, *s.v.*
[8] I give the beginning of this epistle of Dionysius of Alexandria also as it is found in not a few manuscripts, viz., ἐπεστειλάς μοι . . . τῇ τοῦ πάσχα περιλυσει, — the common reading being, τὴν τοῦ πάσχα ἡμέραν. And the περιλυσις τοῦ πάσχα denotes the close of the paschal fast, as Eusebius (*Hist. Eccles.*, v. 23) uses the phrase τὰς τῶν ἀσιτιῶν ἐπιλυσεις, — the verbs περιλυειν, ἀπολυειν, ἐπιλυειν, καταλυειν, being often used in this sense. — COTELERIUS on the *Apostolic Constitutions*, v. 15.
[9] ἀφ' ἑσπερας.
[10] [Note this, and the Nicene decision which made the Alexandrian bishop the authority concerning the paschal annually, vol. ii. Elucidation II. p. 343.]
[11] πάνυ μεμετρημένην.
[12] κατὰ καιροὺς ἐνηλλαγμένους.
[13] Matt. xxviii. 1.
[14] John xx. 1.
[15] τῇ ἐπιφωσκούσῃ μιᾷ Σαββάτων.

seem to be some small difficulty as to the subject of our inquiry, if they all agree that the light of the world, our Lord, rose on that one night, while they differ with respect to the hour, we may well seek with wise and faithful mind to harmonize their statements. The narrative by Matthew, then, runs thus: "In the end of the Sabbath, as it began to dawn toward the first day of the week,[1] came Mary Magdalene, and the other Mary, to see the sepulchre. And, behold, there was a great earthquake: for the angel of the Lord descended from heaven, and came and rolled back the stone, and sat upon it. And his countenance was like lightning, and his raiment white as snow: and for fear of him the keepers did shake, and became as dead men. And the angel answered and said unto the women, Fear not ye: for I know that ye seek Jesus, which was crucified. He is not here; for He is risen, as He said."[2] Now this phrase "in the end" will be thought by some to signify, according to the common use[3] of the word, the *evening* of the Sabbath; while others, with a better perception of the fact, will say that it does not indicate that, but *a late hour in the night*,[4] as the phrase "in the end"[5] denotes slowness and length of time. Also because he speaks of *night*, and not of *evening*, he has added the words, "as it began to dawn toward the first day of the week." And the parties here did not come yet, as the others say, "bearing spices," but "to see the sepulchre;" and they discovered the occurrence of the earthquake, and the angel sitting upon the stone, and heard from him the declaration, "He is not here, He is risen." And to the same effect is the testimony of John. "The first day of the week," says he, "came Mary Magdalene early, when it was yet dark, unto the sepulchre, and seeth the stone taken away from the sepulchre."[6] Only, according to this "when it was yet dark," she had come in advance.[7] And Luke says: "They rested the Sabbath-day, according to the commandment. Now, upon the first day of the week, very early in the morning, they came unto the sepulchre, bringing the spices which they had prepared; and they found the stone rolled away from the sepulchre."[8] This phrase "very early in the morning"[9] probably indicates the early dawn[10] of the first day of the week; and thus, when the Sabbath itself was wholly past, and also the whole night succeeding it, and when another day had begun, they came, bringing spices and myrrh, and then it became apparent that He had

already risen long before. And Mark follows this, and says: "They had bought sweet spices, in order that they might come and anoint Him. And very early (in the morning), the first day of the week, they come unto the sepulchre at the rising of the sun."[11] For this evangelist also has used the term "very early," which is just the same as the "very early in the morning" employed by the former; and he has added, "at the rising of the sun." Thus they set out, and took their way first when it was "very early in the morning," or (as Mark says) when it was "very early;" but on the road, and by their stay at the sepulchre, they spent the time till it was sunrise. And then the young man clad in white said to them, "He is risen, He is not here." As the case stands thus, we make the following statement and explanation to those who seek an exact account of the specific hour, or half-hour, or quarter of an hour, at which it is proper to begin their rejoicing over our Lord's rising from the dead. Those who are too hasty, and give up even before midnight,[12] we reprehend as remiss and intemperate, and as almost breaking off from their course in their precipitation,[13] for it is a wise man's word, "That is not little in life which is within a little." And those who hold out and continue for a very long time, and persevere even on to the fourth watch, which is also the time at which our Saviour manifested Himself walking upon the sea to those who were then on the deep, we receive as noble and laborious disciples. On those, again, who pause and refresh themselves in the course as they are moved or as they are able, let us not press very hard:[14] for all do not carry out the six days of fasting[15] either equally or alike; but some pass even all the days as a fast, remaining without food through the whole; while others take but two, and others three, and others four, and others not even one. And to those who have laboured painfully through these protracted fasts, and have thereafter become exhausted and well-nigh undone, pardon ought to be extended if they are somewhat precipitate in taking food. But if there are any who not only decline such protracted fasting, but refuse at the first to fast at all, and rather indulge themselves luxuriously during the first four days, and then when they reach the last two days — viz., the preparation and the Sabbath — fast with due rigour during these, and these alone, and think that they do something grand and brilliant if they hold out till the morning, I cannot think that they have gone through the time on equal

---

[1] τῇ ἐπιφωσκούσῃ εἰς μίαν Σαββάτων.
[2] Matt. xxviii. 1–6.
[3] κοινότητα.
[4] νύκτα βαθείαν.
[5] ὀψέ, late.
[6] John xx. 1.
[7] παρὰ τοῦτο . . . προεληλύθει.
[8] Luke xxiii. 56, xxiv. 1, 2.
[9] ὄρθρου βαθέος.
[10] προϋποφαινομένην αὐτὴν ἑωθινὴν ἐμφανίζει.

[11] Mark xvi. 1, 2.
[12] πρὸ νυκτὸς ἐγγὺς ἤδη μεσούσης ἀνιέντας.
[13] ὡς παρ᾽ ὀλίγον προκαταλύοντας τὸν δρόμον.
[14] [1 Tim. iv. 8. Mark the moderation of our author in contrast with superstition. But in our days the peril is one of an opposite kind. Contrast St. Paul, 2 Cor. xi. 27.]
[15] That is, as Balsamon explains, the six days of the week of our Lord's passion.

terms with those who have been practising the same during several days before. This is the counsel which, in accordance with my apprehension of the question, I have offered you in writing on these matters.[1]

CANON II.

The question touching women in the time of their separation, whether it is proper for them when in such a condition either to enter the house of God, I consider a superfluous inquiry. For I do not think that, if they are believing and pious women, they will themselves be rash enough in such a condition either to approach the holy table or to touch the body and blood of the Lord. Certainly the woman who had the issue of blood of twelve years' standing did not touch *the Lord* Himself, but only the hem of His garment, with a view to her cure.[2] For to pray, however a person may be situated, and to remember the Lord, in whatever condition a person may be, and to offer up petitions for the obtaining of help, are exercises altogether blameless. But the individual who is not perfectly pure both in soul and in body, shall be interdicted from approaching the holy of holies.

CANON III.

Moreover, those who are competent, and who are advanced in years, ought to be judges of themselves in these matters. For that it is proper to abstain from each other by consent, in order that they may be free for a season to give themselves to prayer, and then come together again, they have heard from Paul in his epistle.[3]

CANON IV.

As to those who are overtaken by an involuntary flux in the night-time, let such follow the testimony of their own conscience, and consider themselves as to whether they are doubtfully minded[4] in this matter or not. And he that doubteth in the matter of meats, the apostle tells us, "is damned if he eat."[5] In these things, therefore, let every one who approaches God be of a good conscience, and of a proper confidence, so far as his own judgment is concerned. And, indeed, it is in order to show your regard for us (for you are not ignorant, beloved,) that you have proposed these questions to us, making us of one mind, as indeed we are, and of one spirit with yourself. And I, for my part, have thus set forth my opinions in public, not as a teacher, but only as it becomes us with all simplicity to confer with each other. And when you have examined this opinion of mine, my most intelligent son, you will write back to me your notion of these matters, and let me know whatever may seem to you to be just and preferable, and whether you approve of my judgment in these things.[6] That it may fare well with you, my beloved son, as you minister to the Lord in peace, is my prayer.

---

[1] To these canons are appended the comments of Balsamon and Zonaras, which it is not necessary to give here.
[2] Matt. ix. 20; Luke viii. 43.

[3] Referring to the relations of marriage, dealt with in 1 Cor. vii. 5, etc.
[4] διακρίνονται.
[5] Rom. xiv. 23. [Gr. κατακέκριται = is condemned = self-condemned. Wordsworth cites Cicero, *De Officiis*, i. 30.]
[6] [The entire absence of despotic authority in these episcopal teachings is to be noted. 2 Cor. i. 24.]

PART II.—CONTAINING EPISTLES, OR FRAGMENTS OF EPISTLES.

EPISTLE I.—TO DOMITIUS AND DIDYMUS.[1]

1. But it would be a superfluous task for me to mention by name our (martyr) friends, who are numerous and at the same time unknown to you. Only understand that they include men and women, both young men and old, both maidens and aged matrons, both soldiers and private citizens, — every class and every age, of whom some have suffered by stripes and fire, and some by the sword, and have won the victory and received their crowns. In the case of others, however, even a very long lifetime has not proved sufficient to secure their appearance as men acceptable to the Lord; as indeed in my own case too, that sufficient time has not shown itself up to the present. Wherefore He has preserved me for another convenient season, of which He knows Himself, as He says: "In an acceptable time have I heard thee, and in a day of salvation have I helped thee."[2]

2. Since, however, you have been inquiring[3] about what has befallen us, and wish to be informed as to how we have fared, you have got a full report of our fortunes; how when we — that is to say, Gaius, and myself, and Faustus, and Peter, and Paul — were led off as prisoners by the centurion and the magistrates,[4] and the sol-

---

[1] Eusebius, *Hist. Eccles.*, vii. 11.

[2] Isa. xlix. 8.
[3] Reading ἐπειδὴ πυνθάνεσθε, for which some codices give ἐπεὶ πυνθάνεσθαι.
[4] στρατηγῶν. Christophorsonus would read στρατηγοῦ, in the sense of *commander*. But the word is used here of the *duumviri*, or magistrates of Alexandria. And that the word στρατηγος was used

diers and other attendants accompanying them, there came upon us certain parties from Mareotis, who dragged us with them against our will, and though we were disinclined to follow them, and carried us away by force ;[1] and how Gaius and Peter and myself have been separated from our other brethren, and shut up alone in a desert and sterile place in Libya, at a distance of three days' journey from Praetonium.

3. *And a little further on, he proceeds thus :* — And they concealed themselves in the city, and secretly visited the brethren. I refer to the presbyters Maximus, Dioscorus, Demetrius, and Lucius. For Faustinus and Aquila, who are persons of greater prominence in the world, are wandering about in Egypt. I specify also the deacons who survived those who died in the sickness,[2] viz., Faustus, Eusebius, and Chæremon. And of Eusebius I speak as one whom the Lord strengthened from the beginning, and qualified for the task of discharging energetically the services due to the confessors who are in prison, and of executing the perilous office of dressing out and burying[3] the bodies of those perfected and blessed martyrs. For even up to the present day the governor does not cease to put to death, in a cruel manner, as I have already said, some of those who are brought before him ; while he wears others out by torture, and wastes others away with imprisonment and bonds, commanding also that no one shall approach them,

and making strict scrutiny lest any one should be seen to do so. And nevertheless God imparts relief to the oppressed by the tender kindness and earnestness of the brethren.

EPISTLE II. — TO NOVATUS.[4]

Dionysius to Novatus[5] his brother, greeting.

If you were carried on against your will, as you say, you will show that such has been the case by your voluntary retirement. For it would have been but dutiful to have suffered any kind of ill, so as to avoid rending the Church of God. And a martyrdom borne for the sake of preventing a division of the Church, would not have been more inglorious than one endured for refusing to worship idols ;[6] nay, in my opinion at least, the former would have been a nobler thing than the latter. For in the one case a person gives such a testimony simply for his own individual soul, whereas in the other case he is a witness for the whole Church. And now, if you can persuade or constrain the brethren to come to be of one mind again, your uprightness will be superior to your error ; and the latter will not be charged against you, while the former will be commended in you. But if you cannot prevail so far with your recusant brethren, see to it that you save your own soul. My wish is, that in the Lord you may fare well as you study peace.

EPISTLE III. — TO FABIUS[7] BISHOP OF ANTIOCH.

1. The persecution with us did not commence with the imperial edict, but preceded it by a whole year. And a certain prophet and poet, an enemy to this city,[8] whatever else he was, had previously roused and exasperated against us the masses of the heathen, inflaming them anew with the fires of their native superstition. Excited by him, and finding full liberty for the perpetration of wickedness, they reckoned this the only

---

in this *civil* acceptation, as well as in the common *military* application, we see by many examples in Athanasius, Ammianus Marcellinus, and others. Thus, as Valesius remarks, the *soldiers* (στρατιωτῶν) here will be the band with the centurion, and the attendants (ὑπηρετῶν) will be the civil followers of the magistrates.

[1] This happened in the first persecution under Decius, when Dionysius was carried off by the decision of the prefect Sabinus to Taposiris, as he informs us in his epistle to Germanus. Certainly any one who compares that epistle of Dionysius to Germanus with this one to Domitius, will have no doubt that he speaks of one and the same event in both. Hence Eusebius is in error in thinking that in this epistle of Dionysius to Domitius we have a narrative of the events relating to the persecution of Valerian, — a position which may easily be refuted from Dionysius himself. For in the persecution under Valerian, Dionysius was not carried off into exile under military custody, nor were there any men from Mareotis, who came and drove off the soldiers, and bore him away unwillingly, and set him at liberty again : nor had Dionysius on that occasion the presbyters Gaius and Faustus, and Peter and Paul, with him. All these things happened to Dionysius in that persecution which began a little before Decius obtained the empire, as he testifies himself in his epistle to Germanus. But in the persecution under Valerian, Dionysius was accompanied in exile by the presbyter Maximus, and the deacons Faustus, and Eusebius, and Chæremon, and a certain Roman cleric, as he tells us in the epistle to Germanus. — VALESIUS.

[2] ἐν τῇ νόσῳ. Rufinus reads νήσῳ, and renders it, " But of the deacons, some died in the island after the pains of confession." But Dionysius refers to the pestilence which traversed the whole Roman world in the times of Gallus and Volusianus, as Eusebius in his *Chronicon* and others record. See Aurelius Victor. Dionysius makes mention of this sickness again in the paschal epistle to the Alexandrians, where he also speaks of the deacons who were cut off by that plague. — VALES.

[3] περιστολὰς ἐκτελεῖν. Christophorsonus renders it: " to prepare the linen cloths in which the bodies of the blessed martyrs who departed this life might be wrapped." In this Valesius thinks he errs by looking at the modern method of burial, whereas among the ancient Christians the custom was somewhat different, the bodies being dressed out in full attire, and that often at great cost, as Eusebius shows us in the case of Astyrius, in the *Hist. Eccles.*, vii. 16. Yet Athanasius, in his *Life of Antonius*, has this sentence: " The Egyptians are accustomed to attend piously to the funerals of the bodies of the dead, and especially those of the holy martyrs, and to wrap them in linen cloths : they are not wont, however, to consign them to the earth, but to place them on couches, and keep them in private apartments."

---

[4] Eusebius, *Hist. Eccles.*, vi. 45.

[5] Jerome, in his *Catalogus*, where he adduces the beginning of this epistle, gives Novatianus for Novatus. So in the *Chronicon* of Georgius Syncellus we have Διονύσιος Ναυατιανῷ. Rufinus' account appears to be that there were two such epistles, — one to Novatus, and another to Novatianus. The confounding of these two forms seems, however, to have been frequent among the Greeks. [See Lardner, *Credib., sub voce Novat.* Wordsworth thinks the Greeks shortened the name, on the grounds which Horace notes *ad vocem* " Equotuticum." *Satires,* I. v, 87.]

[6] We read, with Gallandi, καὶ ἦν οὐκ ἀδοξυτέρα τῆς ἕνεκεν τοῦ μὴ ἰδωλολατρεῦσαι (sic) γινομένης, ἢ ἕνεκεν τοῦ μὴ σχίσαι μαρτυρία. This is substantially the reading of three Venetian codices, as also of Sophronius on Jerome's *De vir. illustr.*, ch. 69, and Georgius Syncellus in the *Chronogr.*, p.,374, and Nicephorus Callist., *Hist. Eccles.*, vi. 4. Pearson, in the *Annales Cyprian.*, Num. x. p. 31, proposes θῦσαι for σχίσαι. Rufinus renders it: " et erat non inferior gloria sustinere martyrium ne scindatur ecclesia quam est illa ne idolis immoletur."

[7] Eusebius, *Hist. Eccles.*, vi. 41, 42, 44. Certain codices read Fabianus for Fabius, and that form is adopted also by Rufinus. Eusebius introduces this epistle thus: " The same author, in an epistle written to Fabius bishop of Antioch, gives the following account of the conflicts of those who suffered martyrdom at Alexandria."

[8] καὶ φθάσας ὁ κακῶν, etc. Pearson, *Annales Cyprian. ad ann.*, 249, § 1, renders it rather thus : " et praevertens malorum huic urbi vates et auctor, quisquis ille fuit, commovit," etc.

piety *and* service to their demons,[1] namely, our slaughter.

2. First, then, they seized an old man of the name of Metras, and commanded him to utter words of impiety; and as he refused, they beat his body with clubs, and lacerated his face and eyes with sharp reeds, and then dragged him off to the suburbs and stoned him there. Next they carried off a woman named Quinta, who was a believer, to an idol temple, and compelled her to worship the idol; and when she turned away from it, and showed how she detested it, they bound her feet and dragged her through the whole city along the rough stone-paved streets, knocking her at the same time against the millstones, and scourging her, until they brought her to the same place, and stoned her also there. Then with one impulse they all rushed upon the houses of the God-fearing, and whatever pious persons any of them knew individually as neighbours, after these they hurried and bore them with them, and robbed and plundered them, setting aside the more valuable portions of their property for themselves, and scattering about the commoner articles, and such as were made of wood, and burning them on the roads, so that they made these parts present the spectacle of a city taken by the enemy. The brethren, however, simply gave way and withdrew, and, like those to whom Paul bears witness,[2] they took the spoiling of their goods with joy. And I know not that any of them — except possibly some solitary individual who may have chanced to fall into their hands — thus far has denied the Lord.

3. But they also seized that most admirable virgin Apollonia, then in advanced life, and knocked out all her teeth,[3] and cut her jaws; and then kindling a fire before the city, they threatened to burn her alive unless she would repeat along with them their expressions of impiety.[4] And although she seemed to deprecate[5] her fate for a little, on being let go, she leaped eagerly into the fire and was consumed. They also laid hold of a certain Serapion in his own house;[6] and after torturing him with severe cruelties, and breaking all his limbs, they dashed him headlong from an upper storey to the ground. And there was no road, no thoroughfare, no lane

even, where we could walk, whether by night or by day; for at all times and in every place they all kept crying out, that if any one should refuse to repeat their blasphemous expressions, he must be at once dragged off and burnt. These inflictions were carried rigorously on for a considerable time[7] in this manner. But when the insurrection and the civil war in due time overtook these wretched people,[8] that diverted their savage cruelty from us, and turned it against themselves. And we enjoyed a little breathing time, as long as leisure failed them for exercising their fury against us.[9]

4. But speedily was the change from that more kindly reign[10] announced to us; and great was the terror of threatening that was now made to reach us. Already, indeed, the edict had arrived; and it was of such a tenor as almost perfectly to correspond with what was intimated to us beforetime by our Lord, setting before us the most dreadful horrors, so as, if that were possible, to cause the very elect to stumble.[11] All verily were greatly alarmed, and of the more notable there were some, and these a large number, who speedily accommodated themselves to the decree in fear;[12] others, who were engaged in the public service, were drawn into compliance by the very necessities of their official duties;[13] others were dragged on to it by their friends, and on being called by name approached

[1] εὐσέβειαν τὴν θρησκείαν δαιμόνων. Valesius thinks the last three words in the text (= service to their demons) an interpolation by some scholiast. [Note θρησκείαν = *cultus*, Jas. i. 27.]

[2] Heb. x. 30.

[3] [To this day St. Apollonia is invoked all over Europe; and votive offerings are to be seen hung up at her shrines, in the form of teeth, by those afflicted with toothache.]

[4] τὰ τῆς ἀσεβείας κηρύγματα. What these precisely were, it is not easy to say. Dionysius speaks of them also as δύσφημα ῥήματα in this epistle, and as ἄθεοι φωναί in that to Germanus. Gallandi thinks the reference is to the practice, of which we read also in the Acts of Polycarp, ch. 9, where the proconsul addresses the martyr with the order: λοιδόρησον τὸν Χριστόν — Revile Christ. And that the test usually put to reputed Christians by the early persecutors was this cursing of Christ, we learn from Pliny, book x. epist. 97. [Vol. i. p. 41.]

[5] Or, shrink from.

[6] ἐφέστιον, for which Nicephorus reads badly, Ἐφέσιον.

[7] ἐπιπολύ.

[8] ἀθλίους. But Pearson suggests ἄθλους, = "when insurrection and civil war took the place of these persecutions." This would agree better with the common usage of διαδεχομαι.

[9] ἀσχολίαν τοῦ πρὸς ἡμᾶς θυμοῦ λαβόντων. The Latin version gives, "dum illorum cessaret furor." W. Lowth renders, "dum non vacaret ipsis furorem suum in nos exercere."

[10] This refers to the death of the Emperor Philip, who showed a very righteous and kindly disposition toward the Christians. Accordingly the matters here recounted by Dionysius took place in the last year of the Emperor Philip. This is also indicated by Dionysius in the beginning of this epistle, where he says that the persecution began at Alexandria a whole year before the edict of the Emperor Decius. But Christophorsonus, not observing this, interprets the μεταβολὴν τῆς βασιλείας as signifying a change in *the emperor's mind* toward the Christians, in which error he is followed by Baronius, ch. 102. — VALES.

[11] In this sentence the Codex Regius reads, τὸ προρρηθὲν ὑπὸ τοῦ Κυρίου ἡμῶν παραβραχὺ τὸ φοβερώτατον, etc., = "the one intimated beforetime by our Lord, *very nearly* the most terrible one." In Georgius Syncellus it is given as ἡ παρὰ βραχύ. But the reading in the text, ἀποφαίνον, "setting forth," is found in the Codices Maz., Med., Fuk., and Savilii; and it seems the best, the idea being that this edict of Decius was so terrible as in a certain measure to represent the most fearful of all times, viz., those of Antichrist. — VALES.

[12] ἀπήντων δεδιότες.

[13] οἱ δὲ δημοσιεύοντες ὑπὸ τῶν πράξεων ἤγοντο. This is rendered by Christophorsonus, "alii ex privatis ædibus in publicum raptati ad dilatea ducuntur a magistratibus." But δημοσιεύοντες is the same as τὰ δημόσια πράττοντες, i.e., decurions and magistrates. For when the edict of Decius was conveyed to them, commanding all to sacrifice to the immortal gods, these officials had to convene themselves in the court-house as usual, and stand and listen while the decree was there publicly recited. Thus they were in a position officially which led them to be the first to sacrifice. The word πράξεις occurs often in the sense of the acts and administration of magistrates: thus, in Eusebius, viii. 11; in Aristides, in the funeral oration on Alexander, τὰ δ' εἰς πράξεις τε καὶ πολιτείας, etc. There are similar passages also in Plutarch's Πολιτικὰ παραγγέλματα, and in Severianus's sixth oration on the Hexameron. So Chrysostom, in his eighty-third homily on Matthew, calls the decurions τοὺς τὰ πολιτικὰ πράττοντας. The word δημοσιεύοντες, however, may also be explained of those employed in the departments of law or finance; so that the clause might be rendered, with Valesius: "alii, qui in publico versabantur, rebus ipsis et reliquorum exemplo, ad sacrificandum ducebantur." See the note in Migne.

the impure and unholy sacrifices; others yielded pale and trembling, as if they were not to offer sacrifice, but to be themselves the sacrifices and victims for the idols, so that they were jeered by the large multitude surrounding the scene, and made it plain to all that they were too cowardly either to face death or to offer the sacrifices. But there were others who hurried up to the altars with greater alacrity, stoutly asserting[1] that they had never been Christians at all before; of whom our Lord's prophetic declaration holds most true, that it will be hard for such to be saved. Of the rest, some followed one or other of these parties *already mentioned;* and some fled, and some were seized. And of these, some went as far *in keeping their faith* as bonds and imprisonment; and certain persons among them endured imprisonment even for several days, and then after all abjured the faith before coming into the court of justice; while others, after holding out against the torture for a time, sank before the prospect of further sufferings.[2]

5. But there were also others, stedfast and blessed pillars of the Lord, who, receiving strength from Himself, and obtaining power and vigour worthy of and commensurate with the force of the faith that was in themselves, have proved admirable witnesses for His kingdom. And of these the first was Julianus, a man suffering from gout, and able neither to stand nor to walk, who was arranged along with two other men who carried him. Of these two persons, the one immediately denied *Christ;* but the other, a person named Cronion, and surnamed Eunus, and together with him the aged Julianus himself, confessed the Lord, and were carried on camels through the whole city, which is, as you know, a very large one, and were scourged in that elevated position, and finally were consumed in a tremendous fire, while the whole populace surrounded them. And a certain soldier who stood by them when they were led away to execution, and who opposed the wanton insolence of the people, was pursued by the outcries they raised against him; and this most courageous soldier of God, Besas by name, was arranged; and after bearing himself most nobly in that mighty conflict on behalf of piety, he was beheaded. And another individual, who was by birth a Libyan, and who at once in name and in real blessedness was also a true Macar,[3] although much was tried by the judge to persuade him to make a denial, did not yield, and was consequently burned alive. And these were succeeded by Epimachus and Alexander, who, after a long time[4] spent in chains, and after suf-

fering countless agonies and inflictions of the scraper[5] and the scourge, were also burnt to ashes in an immense fire.

6. And along with these there were four women. Among them was Ammonarium, a pious virgin, who was tortured for a very long time by the judge in a most relentless manner, because she declared plainly from the first that she would utter none of the things which he commanded her to repeat; and after she had made good her profession she was led off to execution. The others were the most venerable and aged Mercuria, and Dionysia, who had been the mother of many children, and yet did not love her offspring better than her Lord.[6] These, when the governor was ashamed to subject them any further to profitless torments, and thus to see himself beaten by women, died by the sword, without more experience of tortures. For truly their champion Ammonarium had received tortures for them all.

7. Heron also, and Ater,[7] and Isidorus,[8] who were Egyptians, and along with them Dioscorus, a boy of about fifteen years of age, were delivered up. And though at first he, *the judge,* tried to deceive the youth with fair speeches, thinking he could easily seduce him, and then attempted also to compel him by force of tortures, fancying he might be made to yield without much difficulty in that way, Dioscorus neither submitted to his persuasions nor gave way to his terrors. And the rest, after their bodies had been lacerated in a most savage manner, and their stedfastness had nevertheless been maintained, he consigned also to the flames. But Dioscorus he dismissed, wondering at the distinguished appearance he had made in public, and at the extreme wisdom of the answers he gave to his interrogations, and declaring that, on account of his age, he granted him further time for repentance. And this most godly Dioscorus is with us at present, tarrying for a greater conflict and a more lengthened contest. A certain person of the name of Nemesion, too, who was also an Egyptian, was falsely accused of being a companion of robbers; and after he had cleared himself of this charge before the centurion, and proved it to be a most unnatural calumny, he was informed against as a Christian, and had to come as a prisoner before the governor. And that most unrighteous magistrate inflicted on him a punishment twice as

---

[1] ἰσχυριζόμενοι here for διϊσχυριζόμενοι. — VALES.
[2] πρὸς τὸ ἑξῆς ἀπεῖπον. It may also mean, "renounced the faith in the prospect of what was before them."
[3] A blessed one. Alluding to Matt. v. 10, 12.
[4] μετὰ πολύν. But Codices Med., Maz., Fuk., and Savilii, as well as Georgius Syncellus, read μετ' οὐ πολύν, "after a short time."

[5] ξυστῆρας.
[6] Here Valesius adds from Rufinus the words καὶ Ἀμμωνάριον ἑτέρα, "and a second Ammonarium," as there are four women mentioned.
[7] In Georgius Syncellus and Nicephorus it is given as *Aster.* Rufinus makes the name Arsinus. And in the old Roman martyrology, taken largely from Rufinus, we find the form Arsenius. — VALES.
[8] In his *Bibliotheca,* cod. cxix., Photius states that Isidorus was full brother to Pierius, the celebrated head of the Alexandrian school, and his colleague in martyrdom. He also intimates, however, that although some have reported that Pierius ended his career by martyrdom, others say that he spent the closing period of his life in Rome after the persecution abated. — RUINART.

severe as that to which the robbers were subjected, making him suffer both tortures and scourgings, and then consigning him to the fire between the robbers. Thus the blessed martyr was honoured after the pattern of Christ.

8. There was also a body of soldiers,[1] including Ammon, and Zeno, and Ptolemy, and Ingenuus, and along with them an old man, Theophilus, who had taken up their position in a mass in front of the tribunal ; and when a certain person was standing his trial as a Christian, and was already inclining to make a denial, these stood round about and ground their teeth, and made signs with their faces, and stretched out their hands, and made all manner of gestures with their bodies. And while the attention of all was directed to them, before any could lay hold of them, they ran quickly up to the bench of judgment[2] and declared themselves to be Christians, and made such an impression that the governor and his associates were filled with fear ; and those who were under trial seemed to be most courageous in the prospect of what they were to suffer, while the judges themselves trembled. These, then, went with a high spirit from the tribunals, and exulted in their testimony, God Himself causing them to triumph gloriously.[3]

9. Moreover, others in large numbers were torn asunder by the heathen throughout the cities and villages. Of one of these I shall give some account, as an example. Ischyrion served one of the rulers in the capacity of steward for stated wages. His employer ordered this man to offer sacrifice ; and on his refusal to do so, he abused him. When he persisted in his non-compliance, his master treated him with contumely ; and when he still held out, he took a huge stick and thrust it through his bowels and heart, and slew him. Why should I mention the multitudes of those who had to wander about in desert places and upon the mountains, and who were cut off by hunger, and thirst, and cold, and sickness, and robbers, and wild beasts ? The survivors of such are the witnesses of their election and their victory. One circumstance, however, I shall subjoin as an illustration of these things. There was a certain very aged person of the name of Chæremon, bishop of the place called the city of the Nile.[4] He fled along with his partner to the Arabian mountain,[5] and never returned. The brethren, too, were unable to discover anything of them, although they made frequent search ; and they never could find either the men themselves, or their bodies. Many were also carried off as slaves by the barbarous Saracens[6] to that same Arabian mount. Some of these were ransomed with difficulty, and only by paying a great sum of money ; others of them have not been ransomed to this day. And these facts I have related, brother, not without a purpose, but in order that you may know how many and how terrible are the ills that have befallen us ; which troubles also will be best understood by those who have had most experience of them.

10. Those sainted martyrs, accordingly, who were once with us, and who now are seated with Christ,[7] and are sharers in His kingdom, and partakers with Him in His judgment,[8] and who act as His judicial assessors,[9] received there certain of the brethren who had fallen away, and who had become chargeable with sacrificing to the idols. And as they saw that the conversion and repentance of such might be acceptable to Him who desires not at all the death of the sinner,[10] but rather his repentance, they proved their sincerity, and received them, and brought them together again, and assembled with them, and had fellowship with them in their prayers and at their festivals.[11] What advice then, brethren, do you give us as regards these ? What should we do ? Are we to stand forth and act with the decision and judgment which these (martyrs) formed, and to observe the same graciousness with them, and to deal so kindly with those toward whom they showed such compassion ? or are we to treat their decision as an unrighteous one,[12] and to constitute ourselves judges of their

---

[1] σύνταγμα στρατιωτικόν. Rufinus and Christophorsonus make it *turmam militum*. Valesius prefers *manipulum* or *contubernium*. These may have been the apparitors or officers of the *præfectus Augustalis*. Valesius thinks rather that they were legionaries, from the legion which had to guard the city of Alexandria, and which was under the authority of the *præfectus Augustalis*. For at that time the *præfectus Augustalis* had charge of military affairs as well as civil.

[2] βάθρον. Valesius supposes that what is intended is the seat on which the accused sat when under interrogation by the judge.

[3] θριαμβεύοντος αὐτούς. Rufinus makes it, "God thus triumphing in them ;" from which it would seem that he had read δι' αὐτούς. But θριαμβεύειν is probably put here for θριαμβεύειν ποιεῖν, as βασιλεύειν is also used by Gregory Nazianzenus.

[4] That is, Nilopolis or Niloupolis. Eusebius, bishop of the same seat, subscribed the Council of Ephesus. — READING.

[5] τὸ Ἀράβιον ὄρος. There is a *Mons Arabicus* mentioned by Herodotus (ii. 8), which Ptolemy and others call Mons Troïcus. — VALES.

[6] This passage is notable from the fact that it makes mention of the Saracens. For of the writers whose works have come down to us there is none more ancient than Dionysius of Alexandria that has named the Saracens. Ammianus Marcellinus, however, writes in his fourteenth book that he has made mention of the Saracens in the Acts of Marcus Spartianus also mentions the Saracens in his *Niger*, and says that the Roman soldiers were beaten by them. — VALES. [" The barbarous Saracens :" what a *nominis umbra* projected by " coming events," in this blissfully ignorant reference of our author! Compare Robertson, *Researches*, on the conquest of Jerusalem.]

[7] As to the martyrs' immediate departure to the Lord, and their abode with Him, see Tertullian, *On the Resurrection of the Flesh*, ch. xliii., and *On the Soul*, v. 55. [Vol. iii. p. 576; *Ib.*, p. 231.]

[8] That the martyrs were to be Christ's assessors, judging the world with Him, was a common opinion among the fathers. So, after Dionysius, Eulogius, bishop of Alexandria, in his fifth book, *Against the Novatians*. Photius, in his *Bibliotheca*, following Chrysostom, objects to this, and explains Paul's words in 1 Cor. vi. 2 as having the same intention as Christ's words touching the men of Nineveh and the queen of the south who should rise up in the judgment and condemn that generation.

[9] συνδικάζοντες. See a noble passage in Bossuet, *Préface sur l'Apocal.*, § 28.

[10] Ezek. xxxiii. 11.

[11] Dionysius is dealing here not with public communion, such as was the bishop's prerogative to confer anew on the penitent, but with private fellowship among Christian people. — VALES.

[12] ἄδικον ποιησώμεθα is the reading of Codices Maz., Med., Fuk., and Savil., and also of Georgius Syncellus. Others read ἄδεκτον ποιησόμεθα, "we shall treat it as inadmissible."

opinion on such subjects, and to throw clemency into tears, and to overturn the established order?[1]

11. But I shall give a more particular account of one case here which occurred among us:[2] There was with us a certain Serapion, an aged believer. He had spent his long life blamelessly, but had fallen in the time of trial (the persecution). Often did this man pray (for absolution), and no one gave heed to him;[3] for he had sacrificed to the idols. Falling sick, he continued three successive days dumb and senseless. Recovering a little on the fourth day, he called to him his grandchild, and said, " My son, how long do you detain me? Hasten, I entreat you, and absolve me quickly. Summon one of the presbyters to me." And when he had said this, he became speechless again. The boy ran for the presbyter; but it was night, and the man was sick, and was consequently unable to come. But as an injunction had been issued by me,[4] that persons at the point of death, if they requested it then, and especially if they had earnestly sought it before, should be absolved,[5] in order that they might depart this life in cheerful hope, he gave the boy a small portion of the Eucharist,[6] telling him to steep it in water,[7] and drop it into the old man's mouth. The boy returned bearing the portion; and as he came near, and before he had yet entered, Serapion again recovered, and said, " You have come, my child, and the presbyter was unable to come;

but do quickly what you were instructed to do, and so let me depart." The boy steeped the morsel in water, and at once dropped it into the (old man's) mouth; and after he had swallowed a little of it, he forthwith gave up the ghost. Was he not then manifestly preserved? and did he not continue in life just until he could be absolved, and until through the wiping away of his sins he could be acknowledged[8] for the many good acts he had done?

EPISTLE IV. — TO CORNELIUS THE ROMAN BISHOP.[9]

In addition to all these, he writes likewise to Cornelius at Rome, after receiving his Epistle against Novatus. And in that letter he also shows that he had been invited by Helenus, bishop in Tarsus of Cilicia, and by the others who were with him — namely, Firmilian, bishop in Cappadocia, and Theoctistus in Palestine — to meet them at the Council of Antioch, where certain persons were attempting to establish the schism of Novatus. In addition to this, he writes that it was reported to him that Fabius was dead, and that Demetrianus was appointed his successor in the bishopric of the church at Antioch. He writes also respecting the bishop in Jerusalem, expressing himself in these very words: " And the blessed Alexander, having been cast into prison, went to his rest in blessedness."

EPISTLE V., WHICH IS THE FIRST ON THE SUBJECT OF BAPTISM ADDRESSED TO STEPHEN, BISHOP OF ROME.[10]

Understand, however, my brother,[11] that all the churches located in the east, and also in remoter districts,[12] that were formerly in a state of division, are now made one again;[13] and all those at the head of the churches everywhere are of one mind, and rejoice exceedingly at the peace which has been restored beyond all expectation. I may

---

[1] The words καὶ τὸν Θεὸν παροξύνομεν, " and provoke God," are sometimes added here; but they are wanting in Codices Maz., Med., Fuk., Savil., and in Georgius Syncellus.

[2] Eusebius introduces this in words to the following effect: " Writing to this same Fabius, who seemed to incline somewhat to this schism, Dionysius of Alexandria, after setting forth in his letter many other matters which bore on repentance, and after describing the conflicts of the martyrs who had recently suffered in Alexandria, relates among other things one specially wonderful fact, which I have deemed proper for insertion in this history, and which is as follows."

[3] That is, none either of the clergy or of the people were moved by his prayers to consider him a proper subject for absolution; for the people's suffrages were also necessary for the reception into the Church of any who had lapsed, and been on that account cut off from it. And sometimes the bishop himself asked the people to allow absolution to be given to the suppliant, as we see in Cyprian's Epistle 53, to Cornelius [vol. v. p. 336, this series], and in Tertullian, On Modesty, ch. xiii. [vol. iv. p. 86, this series]. Oftener, however, the people themselves made intercession with the bishop for the admission of penitents; of which we have a notable instance in the Epistle of Cornelius to Fabius of Antioch about that bishop who had ordained Novatianus. See also Cyprian, Epistle 59 [vol. v. p. 355]. — VALES.

[4] In the African Synod, which met about the time that Dionysius wrote, it was decreed that absolution should be granted to lapsed persons who were near their end, provided that they had sought it earnestly before their illness. See Cyprian in the Epistle to Antonianus [vol. v. p. 327, this series]. — VALES.

[5] There is a longer reading in Codices Fuk. and Savil., viz.: τῶν θείων δώρων τῆς μεταδόσεως ἀξιοῦσθαι καὶ οὕτως ἀφίεσθαι, " be deemed worthy of the imparting of the divine gifts, and thus be absolved."

[6] Valesius thinks that this custom prevailed for a long time, and cites a synodical letter of Ratherius, bishop of Verona (which has also been ascribed to Udalricus by Gretserus, who has published it along with his Life of Gregory VII.), in which the practice is expressly forbidden in these terms: " And let no one presume to give the communion to a laic or a woman, for the purpose of conveying it to an infirm person."

[7] ἀποβρέξαι. Rufinus renders it by infundere. References to this custom are found in Adamanus, in the second book of the Miracles of St Columba, ch. 6; in Bede, Life of St. Cuthbert, ch. 31, and in the poem on the life of the same; in Theodorus Campidunensis, Life of St. Magnus, ch. 22; in Paulus Bernriedensis, Life of Gregory VII., p. 113.

[8] ὁμολογηθῆναι. Langus, Wolfius, and Musculus render it confiteri, " confess." Christophorsonus makes it in numerum confessorum referri, " reckoned in the number of confessors:" which may be allowed, if it is understood to be a reckoning by Christ. For Dionysius alludes to those words of Christ in the Gospel: " Whosoever shall confess me before men, him will I confess also before my Father." — VALES.

[9] Eusebius, Hist. Eccles., vi. 46.

[10] In the second chapter of the seventh book of his Ecclesiastical History, Eusebius says: " To this Stephen, Eusebius wrote the first of his epistles on the matter of baptism." And he calls this the first, because Dionysius also wrote other four epistles to Xystus and Dionysius, two of the successors of Stephen, and to Philemon, on the same subject of the baptizing of heretics. — GALLANDI.

[11] Eusebius introduces the letter thus: " When he had addressed many reasonings on this subject to him (Stephen) by letter, Dionysius at last showed him that, as the persecution had abated, the churches in all parts opposed to the innovations of Novatus were at peace among themselves." [See vol. v. p. 275.]

[12] καὶ ἔτι προσωτέρω. These words are omitted in Codices Fulk. and Savil., as also by Christophorsonus; but are given in Codices Reg., Maz., and Med., and by Syncellus and Nicephorus.

[13] Baronius infers from this epistle that at this date, about 259 A.D., the Oriental bishops had given up their "error," and fallen in with Stephen's opinion, that heretics did not require to be rebaptized, — an inference, however, which Valesius deems false. [Undoubtedly so.]

mention Demetrianus in Antioch; Theoctistus in Cæsareia; Mazabanes in Ælia,[1] the successor of the deceased Alexander;[2] Marinus in Tyre; Heliodorus in Laodicea, the successor of the deceased Thelymidres; Helenus in Tarsus, and with him all the churches of Cilicia; and Firmilian and all Cappadocia. For I have named only the more illustrious of the bishops, so as neither to make my epistle too long, nor to render my discourse too heavy for you. All the districts of Syria, however, and of Arabia, to the brethren in which you from time to time have been forwarding supplies[3] and at present have sent letters, and Mesopotamia too, and Pontus, and Syria, and, to speak in brief, all parties, are everywhere rejoicing at the unanimity and brotherly love now established, and are glorifying God for the same.

THE SAME, OTHERWISE RENDERED.[4]

But know, my brother, that all the churches throughout the East, and those that are placed beyond, which formerly were separated, are now at length returned to unity; and all the presidents[5] *of the churches* everywhere think one and the same thing, and rejoice with incredible joy on account of the unlooked-for return of peace: to wit, Demetrianus in Antioch; Theoctistus in Cæsarea; Mazabenes in Ælia, after the death of Alexander; Marinus in Tyre; Heliodorus in Laodicea, after the death of Thelymidres; Helenus in Tarsus, and all the churches of Cilicia; Firmilianus, with all Cappadocia. And I have named only the more illustrious bishops, lest by chance my letter should be made too prolix, and my address too wearisome. The whole of the Syrias, indeed, and Arabia, to which you now and then send help, and to which you have now written letters; Mesopotamia also, and Pontus, and Bithynia; and, to comprise all in one word, all the lands everywhere, are rejoicing, praising God on account of this concord and brotherly charity.

[1] The name assigned by the pagans to Jerusalem was Ælia. It was so called even in Constantine's time, as we see in the *Tabula Peutingerorum* and the *Itinerarium Antonini*, written after Constantine's reign. In the seventh canon of the Nicene Council we also find the name Ælia. [Given by Hadrian A.D. 135.]

[2] The words κοιμηθεντος Ἀλεξάνδρου are given in the text in connection with the clause Μαρῖνος ἐν Τύρῳ. They must be transposed, however, as in the translation: for Mazabanes had succeeded Alexander the bishop of Ælia, as Dionysius informs us in his Epistle to Cornelius. So Rufinus puts it also in his Latin version. — VALES.

[3] Alluding to the generous practice of the church at Rome in old times in relieving the wants of the other churches, and in sending money and clothes to the brethren who were in captivity, and to those who toiled in the mines. To this effect we have the statement of Dionysius, bishop of Corinth, in his Epistle to Soter, which Eusebius cites in his fourth book. In the same passage, Eusebius also remarks that this commendable custom had been continued in the Roman church up to his own time; and with that object collections were made there, of which Leo Magnus writes in his *Sermones.* — VALES. [Note this to the eternal honour of this See in its early purity.]

[4] [In vol. v., to illustrate the history of Cyprian, reference is made to this letter; and in the Clark edition another rendering is there given (a preferable one, I think) of this same letter, which I have thought better to reserve for this place. It belongs here, and I have there noted its appearance in this volume.]

[5] [προεστῶτες. See Euseb., *Hist. Eccles.*, book viii. capp. 2, 3, and 4; also vol. v., this series, as above mentioned.]

EPISTLE VI. — TO SIXTUS, BISHOP.[6]

1. Previously, indeed, (Stephen) had written letters about Helanus and Firmilianus, and about all who were established throughout Cilicia and Cappadocia, and all the neighbouring provinces, giving them to understand that for that same reason he would depart from their communion, because they rebaptized heretics. And consider the seriousness of the matter. For, indeed, in the most considerable councils of the bishops, as I hear, it has been decreed that they who come from heresy should first be trained in *Catholic* doctrine, and then should be cleansed by baptism from the filth of the old and impure leaven. Asking and calling him to witness on all these matters, I sent letters.

And a little after Dionysius proceeds: —

2. And, moreover, to our beloved co-presbyters Dionysius and Philemon, who before agreed with Stephen, and had written to me about the same matters, I wrote previously in few words, but now I have written again more at length.

In the same letter, says Eusebius,[7] he informs Xystus[8] of the Sabellian heretics, that they were gaining ground at that time, in these words: —

3. For since of the doctrine, which lately has been set on foot at Ptolemais, a city of Pentapolis, impious and full of blasphemy against Almighty God and the Father of our Lord Jesus Christ; full of unbelief and perfidy towards His only begotten Son and the first-born of every creature, the Word made man, and which takes away the perception of the Holy Spirit, — on either side both letters were brought to me, and brethren had come to discuss it, setting forth more plainly as much as by God's gift I was able, — I wrote certain letters, copies of which I have sent to thee.

EPISTLE VII. — TO PHILEMON, A PRESBYTER.[9]

I indeed gave attention to reading the books and carefully studying the traditions of heretics, to the extent indeed of corrupting my soul with their execrable opinions; yet receiving from them this advantage, that I could refute them in my own mind, and detested them more heartily than ever. And when a certain brother of the order of presbyters sought to deter me, and feared lest I should be involved in the same wicked filthiness, because he said that my mind would be contaminated, and indeed with truth, as I myself perceived, I was strengthened by a vision that was sent me from God. And a word

[6] Dionysius mentions letters that had been written by him as well to the Presbyters Dionysius and Philemon as to Stephen, on the baptism of heretics and on the Sabellian heresy.

[7] Lib. vii. ch. 6.

[8] [i.e., Sixtus II.]

[9] Of Sixtus, bishop of Rome. [A.D. 257].

spoken to me, expressly commanded me, saying, Read everything which shall come into thy hands, for thou art fit to do so, who correctest and provest each one ; and from them to thee first of all has appeared the cause and the occasion of believing. I received this vision as being what was in accordance with the apostolic word, which thus urges all who are endowed with greater virtue, " Be ye skilful money-changers." [1]

Then, says Eusebius, he subjoins some things parenthetically about all heresies : —

This rule and form I have received from our blessed Father Heraclus : For thou, who came from heresies, even if they had fallen away from the Church, much rather if they had not fallen away, but when they were seen to frequent the assemblies of the faithful, were charged with going to hear the teachers of perverse doctrine, and ejected from the Church, he did not admit after many prayers, before they had openly and publicly narrated whatever things they had heard from their adversaries. Then he received them at length to the assemblies of the faithful, by no means asking of them to receive baptism anew. Because they had already previously received the Holy Spirit from that very baptism.

Once more, this question being thoroughly ventilated, he adds : —

I learned this besides, that this custom is not now first of all imported among the Africans [2] alone ; but moreover, long before, in the times of former bishops, among most populous churches, and that when synods of the brethren of Iconium and Synades were held, it also pleased as many as possible, I should be unwilling, by overturning their judgments, to throw them into strifes and contentions. For it is written, " Thou shalt not remove thy neighbour's landmark, which thy fathers have placed." [3]

EPISTLE VIII. — TO DIONYSIUS. [4]

For we rightly repulse Novatian, who has rent the Church, and has drawn away some of the brethren to impiety and blasphemies ; who has brought into the world a most impious doctrine concerning God, and calumniates our most merciful Lord Jesus Christ as if He were unmerciful : and besides all these things, holds the sacred laver as of no effect, and rejects it, and overturns faith and confession, which are put before

baptism, and utterly drives away the Holy Spirit from them, even if any hope subsists either that He would abide in them, or that He should return to them.

EPISTLE IX. — TO SIXTUS II. [5]

For truly, brother, I have need of advice, and I crave your judgment, lest perchance I should be mistaken upon the matters which in such wise happen to me. One of the brethren who come together to the church, who for some time has been esteemed as a believer, and who before my ordination, and, if I am not deceived, before even the episcopate of Heraclas himself, had been a partaker of the assembly of the faithful, when he had been concerned in the baptism of those who were lately baptized, and had heard the interrogatories and their answers, came to me in tears, and bewailing his lot. And throwing himself at my feet, he began to confess and to protest that this baptism by which he had been initiated among heretics was not of this kind, nor had it anything whatever in common with this of ours, because that it was full of blasphemy and impiety. And he said that his soul was pierced with a very bitter sense of sorrow, and that he did not dare even to lift up his eyes to God, because he had been initiated by those wicked words and things. Wherefore he besought that, by this purest laver, he might be endowed with adoption and grace. And I, indeed, have not dared to do this ; but I have said that the long course of communion had been sufficient for this. For I should not dare to renew afresh, after all, one who had heard the giving of thanks, and who had answered with others Amen ; who had stood at the holy table, and had stretched forth his hands [6] to receive the blessed food, and had received it, and for a very long time had been a partaker of the body and blood of our Lord Jesus Christ. Henceforth I bade him be of good courage, and approach to the sacred *elements* with a firm faith and a good conscience, and become a partaker of them. But he makes no end of his wailing, and shrinks from approaching to the table ; and scarcely, when entreated, can he bear to be present at the prayers.

EPISTLE X. — AGAINST BISHOP GERMANUS. [7]

1. Now I speak also before God, and He knoweth that I lie not : it was not by my own choice,[8] neither was it without divine instruction,

---

[1] 1 Thess. v. 21. [Euseb., vi. 7. The apostle is supposed to refer to one of the *reputed* sayings of our Lord, γίνεσθε δόκιμοι τραπεζίται = *examinatores*, i.e , of coins, rejecting the base, and laying up in store the precious. Compare Jer. xv. 19.]

[2] [I find that it is necessary to say that the " Africans " of Egypt and Carthage were no more negroes than we " Americans " are redmen. The Carthaginians were Canaanites, and the Alexandrians Greeks. I have seen Cyprian's portrait representing him as a Moor.]

[3] Deut xix. 14.

[4] At that time presbyter of Xystus, and afterwards his successor. He teaches that Novatian is deservedly to be opposed on account of his schism, on account of his impious doctrine, on account of the repetition of baptism to those who came to him.

[5] Of a man who sought to be introduced to the Church by baptism, although he said that he had received baptism, with other words and matters among the heretics.

[6] [Vol. v. See a reference to Cyril's *Catechetical Lectures.*]

[7] Eusebius, *Hist. Eccles.*, vi. 40, vii. 11.

[8] οὐδεμίαν ἐπ᾽ ἐμαυτοῦ βαλλόμενος. In Codex Fuk. and in the *Chronicon* of Syncellus it is ἐπ᾽ ἐμαυτῷ. In Codices Maz. and Med. it is ἐπ᾽ ἐμαυτοῦ. Herodotus employs the phrase in the genitive form — βαλλόμενος ἐφ᾽ ἑαυτοῦ πέπρηχε, i.e., *seipsum in consilium adhibens, sua sponte et proprio motu fecit.*

that I took to flight. But at an earlier period,[1] indeed, when the *edict for the* persecution under Decius was determined upon, Sabinus at that very hour sent a certain Frumentarius[2] to make search for me. And I remained in the house for four days, expecting the arrival of this Frumentarius. But he went about examining all other places, the roads, the rivers, the fields, where he suspected that I should either conceal myself or travel. And he was smitten with a kind of blindness, and never lighted on the house; for he never supposed that I should tarry at home when under pursuit. Then, barely after the lapse of four days, God giving me instruction to remove, and opening the way for me in a manner beyond all expectation, my domestics[3] and I, and a considerable number of the brethren, effected an exit together. And that this was brought about by the providence of God, was made plain by what followed: in which also we have been perhaps of some service to certain parties.

2. *Then, after a certain break, he narrates the events which befell him after his flight, subjoining the following statement:* — Now about sunset I was seized, along with those who were with me, by the soldiers, and was carried off to Taposiris. But by the providence of God, it happened that Timotheus was not present with me then, nor indeed had he been apprehended at all. Reaching the place later, he found the house deserted, and officials keeping guard over it, and ourselves borne into slavery.

3. *And after some other matters, he proceeds thus:* — And what was the method of this marvellous disposition of Providence in his case? For the real facts shall be related. When Timotheus was fleeing in great perturbation, he was met[4] by a man from the country.[5] This person asked the reason for his haste, and he told him the truth plainly. Then the man (he was on his way at the time to take part in certain marriage festivities; for it is their custom to spend the whole night in such gatherings), on hearing the fact, held on his course to the scene of the re-

joicings, and went in and narrated the circumstances to those who were seated at the feast; and with a single impulse, as if it had been at a given watchword, they all started up, and came on all in a rush, and with the utmost speed. Hurrying up to us, they raised a shout; and as the soldiers who were guarding us took at once to flight, they came upon us, stretched as we were upon the bare couches.[6] For my part, as God knows, I took them at first to be robbers who had come to plunder and pillage us; and remaining on the bedstead on which I was lying naked, save only that I had on my linen under-clothing, I offered them the rest of my dress as it lay beside me. But they bade me get up and take my departure as quickly as I could. Then I understood the purpose of their coming, and cried, entreated, and implored them to go away and leave us alone; and I begged that, if they wished to do us any good, they might anticipate those who led me captive, and strike off my head. And while I was uttering such vociferations, as those who were my comrades and partners in all these things know, they began to lift me up by force. And I threw myself down on my back upon the ground; but they seized me by the hands and feet, and dragged me away, and bore me forth. And those who were witnesses of all these things followed me, — namely, Caius, Faustus, Peter, and Paul. These men also took me up, and hurried me off[7] out of the little town, and set me on an ass without saddle, and in that fashion carried me away.

4. I fear that I run the risk of being charged with great folly and senselessness, placed as I am under the necessity of giving a narrative of the wonderful dispensation of God's providence in our case. Since, however, as one says, it is good to keep close the secret of a king, but it is honourable to reveal the works of God,[8] I shall come to close quarters with the violence of Germanus. I came to Æmilianus not alone; for there accompanied me also my co-presbyter Maximus, and the deacons Faustus and Eusebius and Chæremon; and one of the brethren who had come from Rome went also with us. Æmilianus, then, did not lead off by saying to me, "Hold no assemblies." That was indeed a thing superfluous for him to do, and the last thing which one would do who meant to go back to what was first and of prime importance:[9] for his concern was not about our gathering others together in assembly, but about our not being Christians ourselves. From this, therefore, he commanded

---

[1] ἀλλὰ καὶ πρότερον. Christophorsonus and others join the πρότερον with the διωγμοῦ, making it mean, "before the persecution." This is contrary to pure Greek idiom, and is also inconsistent with what follows; for by the αὐτῆς ὥρας is meant the very hour at which the edict was decreed, διωγμός here having much the sense of "edict for the persecution." — VALES.

[2] There was a body of men called *frumentarii milites*, employed under the emperors as secret spies, and sent through the provinces to look after accused persons, and collect floating rumours. They were abolished at length by Constantine, as Aurelius Victor writes. They were subordinate to the judges or governors of the provinces. Thus this Frumentarius mentioned here by Dionysius was deputed in obedience to Sabinus, the *præfectus Augustalis.* — VALES.

[3] οἱ παῖδες. Musculus and Christophorsonus make it "children." Valesius prefers "domestics."

[4] ἀπήντετο τις τῶν χωριτῶν. In Codices Maz., Med., Fuk., and Savil., ἀπήντα is written; in Georgius Syncellus it is ἀπηντάτο.

[5] χωριτῶν is rendered *indigenarum* by Chrystophorsonus, and *incolarum*, "inhabitants," by the interpreter of Syncellus; but it means rather "rustics." Thus in the Greek Councils the τῶν χωρῶν πρεσβύτεροι, *presbyteri pagorum*, are named. Instead of χωριτῶν, Codices Maz., Med., and Fuk. read χωρικῶν; for thus the Alexandrians named the country people, as we see in the tractate of Sophronius against Dioscorus, and the *Chronicon* of Theophanes, p. 139.

[6] ἀστρώτων σκιμπόδων.

[7] φοράδην ἐξήγαγον. The φοράδην may mean, as Valesius puts it, *in sella*, "on a stool or litter."

[8] Tobit xii. 7.

[9] τὸ τελευταῖον ἐπὶ τὸ πρῶτον ἀνατρέχοντι, i.e., to begin by interdicting him from holding Christian assemblies, while the great question was whether he was a Christian at all, would have been to place first what was last in order and consequence.

me to desist, thinking, doubtless, that if I myself should recant, the others would also follow me in that. But I answered him neither unreasonably nor in many words, "We must obey God rather than men." [1] Moreover, I testified openly that I worshipped the only true God and none other, and that I could neither alter that position nor ever cease to be a Christian. Thereupon he ordered us to go away to a village near the desert, called Cephro.

5. Hear also the words which were uttered by both of us as they have been put on record.[2] When Dionysius, and Faustus, and Maximus, and Marcellus, and Chæremon had been placed at the bar, Æmilianus, as prefect, said : "I have reasoned with you verily in free speech,[3] on the clemency of our sovereigns, as they have suffered you to experience it ; for they have given you power to save yourselves, if you are disposed to turn to what is accordant with nature, and to worship the gods who also maintain them in their kingdom, and to forget those things which are repugnant to nature. What say ye then to these things? for I by no means expect that you will be ungrateful to them for their clemency, since indeed what they aim at is to bring you over to better courses." Dionysius made reply thus : "All men do not worship all the gods, but different men worship different objects that they suppose to be true gods. Now we worship the one God, who is the Creator of all things, and the very Deity who has committed the sovereignty to the hands of their most sacred majesties Valerian and Gallienus. Him we both reverence and worship ; and to Him we pray continually on behalf of the sovereignty of these princes, that it may abide unshaken." Æmilianus, as prefect, said to them : "But who hinders you from worshipping this god too, if indeed he is a god, along with those who are gods by nature? for you have been commanded to worship the gods, and those gods whom all know as such." Dionysius replied : "We worship no other one." Æmilianus, as prefect, said to them : "I perceive that you are at once ungrateful to and insensible of the clemency of our princes. Wherefore you shall not remain in this city ; but you shall be despatched to the parts of Libya, and settled in a place called Cephro : for of this place I have made choice in accordance with the command of our princes. It shall not in any wise be lawful for you or for any others, either to hold assemblies or to enter those places which are called cemeteries. And if any one is seen not to have betaken himself to this place whither I have ordered him to repair, or if he be discovered in any assembly, he will prepare peril

for himself ; for the requisite punishment will not fail. Be off, therefore, to the place whither you have been commanded to go." So he forced me away, sick as I was ; nor did he grant me the delay even of a single day. What opportunity, then, had I to think either of holding assemblies, or of not holding them? [4]

6. *Then after some other matters he says :* — Moreover, we did not withdraw from the visible assembling of ourselves together, with the Lord's presence.[5] But those in the city I tried to gather together with all the greater zeal, as if I were present with them ; for I was absent indeed in the body, as I said,[6] but present in the spirit. And in Cephro indeed a considerable church sojourned with us, composed partly of the brethren who followed us from the city, and partly of those who joined us from Egypt. There, too, did God open to us a door[7] for the word. And at first we were persecuted, we were stoned ; but after a period some few of the heathen forsook their idols, and turned to God. For by our means the word was then sown among them for the first time, and before that they had never received it. And as if to show that this had been the very purpose of God in conducting us to them, when we had fulfilled this ministry, He led us away again. For Æmilianus was minded to remove us to rougher parts, as it seemed, and to more Libyan-like districts ; and he gave orders to draw all in every direction into the Mareotic territory, and assigned villages to each party throughout the country. But he issued instructions that we should be located specially by the public way, so that we might also be the first to be apprehended ; [8] for he evidently made his arrangements and plans with a view to an easy seizure of all of us whenever he should make up his mind to lay hold of us.

7. Now when I received the command to depart to Cephro, I had no idea of the situation of the place, and had scarcely even heard its name before ; yet for all that, I went away courageously and calmly. But when word was brought me that I had to remove to the parts of Colluthion,[9] those present know how I was affected ; for here I shall be my own accuser.

---

[1] Acts v. 29.
[2] ὑπεμνηματίσθη.
[3] ἀγράφως.

[4] Germanus had accused Dionysius of neglecting to hold the assemblies of the brethren before the persecution broke out, and of rather providing for his own safety by flight. For when persecution burst on them, the bishops were wont first to convene the people, in order to exhort them to hold fast the faith of Christ ; then infants and catechumens were baptized, to provide against their departing this life without baptism, and the Eucharist was given to the faithful. — VALES.
[5] αἰσθητῆς μετὰ τοῦ Κυρίου συναγωγῆς.
[6] ὡς εἶπον. Codices Maz. and Med. give εἰπεῖν, "so to speak :" Fuk. and Savil. give ὡς εἶπεν ὁ ἀπόστολος, "as the apostle said."
[7] [Acts xiv. 27 ; Rev. iii. 8. If the author here quotes the Apocalypse, it is noteworthy. Elucidation, p. 110.]
[8] ἡμας δὲ μαλλον ἐν ὁδῷ καὶ πρωτους καταληφθησομενους ἔταξεν.
[9] τὰ Κολλουθίωνος, supplying μέρη, as Dionysius has already used the phrase τὰ μέρη τῆς Λιβύης. This was a district in the Mareotic prefecture. Thus we have mention made also of τὰ Βουκόλου, a certain tract in Egypt, deriving its name from the old masters of the soil. Nicephorus writes Κολουθιον, which is probably more correct ; for Κολλουθιων is a derivative from Colutho, which was a com-

At first, indeed, I was greatly vexed, and took it very ill; for though these places happened to be better known and more familiar to us, yet people declared that the region was one destitute of brethren, and even of men of character, and one exposed to the annoyances of travellers and to the raids of robbers. I found comfort, however, when the brethren reminded me that it was nearer the city; and while Cephro brought us large intercourse with brethren of all sorts who came from Egypt, so that we were able to hold our sacred assemblies on a more extensive scale, yet there, on the other hand, as the city was in the nearer vicinity, we could enjoy more frequently the sight of those who were the really beloved, and in closest relationship with us, and dearest to us: for these would come and take their rest among us, and, as in the more remote suburbs, there would be distinct and special meetings.[1] And thus it turned out.

8. *Then, after some other matters, he gives again the following account of what befell him:* — Germanus, indeed, boasts himself of many professions *of faith*. He, forsooth, is able to speak of many adverse things which have happened to him! Can he then reckon up in his own case as many condemnatory sentences[2] as we can number in ours, and confiscations too, and proscriptions, and spoilings of goods, and losses of dignities,[3] and despisings of worldly honour, and contemnings of the laudations of governors and councillors, and patient subjections to the threatenings of the adversaries,[4] and to outcries, and perils, and persecutions, and a wandering life, and the pressure of difficulties, and all kinds of trouble, such as befell me in the time of Decius and Sabinus,[5] and such also as I

have been suffering under the present severities of Æmilianus? But where in the world did Germanus make his appearance? And what mention is made of him? But I retire from this huge act of folly into which I am suffering myself to fall on account of Germanus; and accordingly I forbear giving to the brethren, who already have full knowledge of these things, a particular and detailed narrative of all that happened.

EPISTLE XI. — TO HERMAMMON.[6]

1. But Gallus did not understand the wickedness of Decius, nor did he note beforehand what it was that wrought his ruin. But he stumbled at the very stone which was lying before his eyes; for when his sovereignty was in a prosperous position, and when affairs were turning out according to his wish,[7] he oppressed those holy men who interceded with God on behalf of his peace and his welfare. And consequently, persecuting them, he persecuted also the prayers offered in his own behalf.

2. And to John a revelation is made in like manner:[8] "And there was given unto him," he says, "a mouth speaking great things, and blasphemy; and power was given unto him, and forty and two months."[9] And one finds both things to wonder at in Valerian's case; and most especially has one to consider how different it was with him before these events,[10] — how mild and well-disposed he was towards the men of God. For among the emperors who preceded him, there was not one who exhibited so kindly and favourable a disposition toward them as he did; yea, even those who were said to have become Christians openly[11] did not receive them with that extreme friendliness and graciousness with which he received them at the beginning

---

mon name in Egypt. Thus a certain poet of note in the times of Anastasius, belonging to the Thebaid, was so named, as Suidas informs us. There was also a Coluthus, a certain schismatic, in Egypt, in the times of Athanasius, who is mentioned often in the *Apologia;* and Gregory of Nyssa names him Acoluthus in his *Contra Eunomium,* book ii. — VALES.

[1] κατὰ μέρος συναγωγαί. When the suburbs were somewhat distant from the city, the brethren resident in them were not compelled to attend the meetings of the larger church, but had meetings of their own in a basilica, or some building suitable for the purpose. The Greeks, too, gave the name προαστειον to places at some considerable distance from the city, as well as to suburbs immediately connected with it. Thus Athanasius calls Canopus a προαστειον; and so Daphne is spoken of as the προαστειον of Antioch, Achyrona as that of Nicomedia, and Septimum as that of Constantinople, though these places were distant some miles from the cities. From this place it is also inferred that in the days of Dionysius there was still but one church in Alexandria, where all the brethren met for devotions But in the time of Athanasius, when several churches had been built by the various bishops, the Alexandrians met in different places, κατα μέρος και διηρημένως, as Athanasius says in his first Apology to Constantius; only that on the great festivals, as at the paschal season and at Pentecost, the brethren did not meet separately, but all in the larger church, as Athanasius also shows us. — VALES.

[2] ἀποφάσεις.

[3] Maximus, in the scholia to the book of Dionysius the Areopagite, *De cælesti hierarchia,* ch. 5, states that Dionysius was by profession a *rhetor* before his conversion: ὁ γοῦν μέγας Διονύσιος ὁ Ἀλεξανδρέων ἐπίσκοπος, ὁ ἀπὸ ῥητόρων, etc. — VALES.

[4] τῶν ἐναντίων ἀπειλῶν.

[5] This Sabinus had been prefect of Egypt in the time of Decius; it is of him that Dionysius writes in his Epistle to Fabius, which is given above. The Æmilianus, prefect of Egypt, who is mentioned here, afterwards seized the imperial power, as Pollio writes in his *Thirty Tyrants,* who, however, calls him general (*ducem*), and not prefect of Egypt. — VALES.

[6] Eusebius, *Hist. Eccles.,* vii. 1, 10, 23. Eusebius introduces this extract thus: "In an epistle to Hermammon, Dionysius makes the following remarks upon Gallus" the Emperor.

[7] κατὰ νοῦν is the reading in the Codices Maz., Med., Fuk., and Savil., and adopted by Rufinus and others. But Robertus Stephanus, from the Codex Regius, gives κατὰ ῥοῦν, "according to the stream," i.e , favourably.

[8] Eusebius prefaces this extract thus: "Gallus had not held the government two full years when he was removed, and Valerian, together with his son Gallienus, succeeded him. And what Dionysius has said of him may be learned from his Epistle to Hermammon, in which he makes the following statement."

[9] ἐξο σια και μῆνες τεσσαρακονταδύο. Rev. xiii. 5. Baronius expounds the numbers as referring to the period during which the persecution under Valerian continued: see him, under the year 257 A.D., ch. 7 [See Introductory Note, p. 78, *supra.* Here is a quotation from the Apocalypse, to be noted in view of our author's questionings, part i., i. 5, p. 83, *supra.*]

[10] The text is, και τούτων μάλιστα τὰ πρὸ αὐτοῦ ὡς οὕτως ἔσχε συννοείν· ἕως ἤπιος, etc. Gallandi emends the sentence thus: και αὐτοῦ τὰ μάλιστα πρὸ τούτων, ὡς οὐχ οὕτως ἔσχε, συννοείν, ἕως ἤπιος, etc. Codex Regius gives ὡς μὲν ἤπιος. But Codices Maz. and Med. give ἕως ἤπιος, while Fuk. and Savil. give ἕως γαρ ἤπιος.

[11] He means the Emperor Philip, who, as many of the ancients have recorded, was the first of the Roman emperors to profess the Christian religion. But as Dionysius speaks in the plural number, to Philip may be added Alexander Severus, who had an image of Christ in the chapel of his Lares, as Lampridius testifies, and who favoured and sustained the Christians during the whole period of his empire. It is to be noted further, that Dionysius says of these emperors only that *they were said* and thought to be Christians, not that they were so in reality. — GALLANDI.

of his reign ; and his whole house was filled then with the pious, and it was itself a very church of God. But the master and president[1] of the Magi of Egypt[2] prevailed on him to abandon that course, urging him to slay and persecute those pure and holy men as adversaries and obstacles to their accursed and abominable incantations. For there are, indeed, and there were men who, by their simple presence, and by merely showing themselves, and by simply breathing and uttering some words, have been able to dissipate the artifices of wicked demons. But he put it into his mind to practise the impure rites of initiation, and detestable juggleries, and execrable sacrifices, and to slay miserable children, and to make oblations of the offspring of unhappy fathers, and to divide the bowels of the newly-born, and to mutilate and cut up the creatures made by God, as if by such means they[3] would attain to blessedness.

3. *Afterwards he subjoins the following:* — Splendid surely were the thank-offerings, then, which Macrianus brought them[4] for that empire which was the object of his hopes ; who, while formerly reputed as the sovereign's faithful public treasurer,[5] had yet no mind for anything which was either reasonable in itself or conducive to the public good,[6] but subjected himself to that curse of prophecy which says, "Woe unto those who prophesy from their own heart, and see not the public good!"[7] For he did not discern that providence which regulates all things ; nor did he think of the judgment of Him who is before all, and through all, and over all. Wherefore he also became an enemy to His Catholic Church ; and besides that, he alienated and estranged himself from the mercy of God, and fled to the utmost possible distance from His salvation.[8] And in this indeed he demonstrated the reality of the peculiar significance of his name.[9]

4. *And again, after some other matters, he proceeds thus :* — For Valerian was instigated to these acts by this man, and was thereby exposed to contumely and reproach, according to the word spoken *by the Lord* to Isaiah : "Yea, they have chosen their own ways, and their own abominations in which their souls delighted ; I also will choose their mockeries,[10] and will recompense their sin."[11] But this man[12] (Macrianus), being maddened with his passion for the empire, all unworthy of it as he was, and at the same time having no capacity for assuming the insignia of imperial government,[13] by reason of his crippled[14] body,[15] put forward his two sons as the bearers, so to speak, of their father's offences. For unmistakeably apparent in their case was the truth of that declaration made by God, when He said, "Visiting the iniquities of the fathers upon the children, unto the third and fourth generation of them that hate me." For he heaped his own wicked passions, for which he had failed in securing satisfaction,[16] upon the heads of his sons, and thus wiped off[17] upon them his own wickedness, and transferred to them, too, the hatred he himself had shown toward God.

5.[18] That man,[19] then, after he had betrayed the one and made war upon the other of the emperors preceding him, speedily perished, with his whole family, root and branch. And Gallienus was proclaimed, and acknowledged by all. And he was at once an old emperor and a new ; for he was prior to those, and he also survived them. To this effect indeed is the word spoken *by the Lord* to Isaiah : "Behold, the things which were from the beginning have come to pass ; and there are new things which shall now arise."[20] For as a cloud which intercepts the sun's rays, and overshadows it for a little, obscures it, and appears itself in its place, but again, when the cloud has passed by or melted away, the sun, which had risen before, comes forth again and shows itself : so did this Macrianus put himself forward,[21] and achieve access[22] for himself even to the very

---

1 ἀρχισυνάγωγος.

2 Baronius thinks that this was that *Magus* who, a little while before the empire of Decius, had incited the Alexandrians to persecute the Christians, and of whom Dionysius speaks in his Epistle to Fabius. What follows here, however, shows that Macrianus is probably the person alluded to.

3 εὐδαιμονήσοντας. So Codices Maz., Med., Fuk., and Savil. read ; others give εὐδαιμονήσαντας. It would seem to require εὐδαιμονήσοντα, "as if he would attain;" for the reference is evidently to Valerian himself.

4 By the αὐτοῖς some understand τοῖς βασιλεῦσι; others better, τοῖς δαίμοσι. According to Valesius, the sense is this: that Macrianus having, by the help and presages of the demons, attained his hope of empire, made a due return to them, by setting Valerian in arms against the Christians.

5 ἐπὶ τῶν καθόλου λόγων. The Greeks gave this name to those officials whom the Latins called *rationales*, or *procuratores summæ rei*. Under what emperor Macrianus was procurator, is left uncertain here.

6 οὐδὲν εὔλογον οὐδὲ καθολικὸν ἐφρόνησεν. There is a play here on the two senses of the word καθολικός, as seen in the official title ἐπὶ τῶν καθόλου λόγων, and in the note of character in οὐδὲ καθολικόν. But it can scarcely be reproduced in the English.

7 οὐαὶ τοῖς προφητεύουσιν ἀπὸ καρδίας αὐτῶν καὶ τὸ καθόλου μὴ βλέπουσιν. The quotation is probably from Ezek. xiii. 3, of which Jerome gives this interpretation: *Vae his qui prophetant ex corde suo et omnino non vident.*

8 Robertus Stephanus edits τῆς ἑαυτοῦ ἐκκλησίας, "from his Church," following the Codex Medicæus. But the best manuscripts give σωτηρίας.

9 A play upon the name *Macrianus*, as connected with μακράν, "at a distance." [This playfulness runs through the section.]

10 ἐμπαίγματα.

11 Isa. lxvi. 3, 4.

12 Christophorsonus refers this to Valerian. But evidently the οὗτος δὲ introduces a different subject in Macrianus; and besides, Valerian could not be said to have been originally unworthy of the power which he aspired to.

13 τὸν βασίλειον ὑποδῦναι κόσμον.

14 ἀναπήρῳ.

15 Joannes Zonaras, in his *Annals*, states that Macrianus was lame.

16 ὧν ἠτύχει. So Codex Regius reads. But Codices Maz., Med., and Fuk. give ηὐτύχει, "in which he succeeded."

17 ἐξωμόρξατο.

18 Eusebius introduces the extract thus: He (Dionysius) addressed also an epistle to Hermammon and the brethren in Egypt; and after giving an account of the wickedness of Decius and his successors, he states many other circumstances, and also mentions the peace of Gallienus. And it is best to hear his own relation as follows.

19 This is rightly understood of Macrianus, by whose treachery Valerian came under the power of the Persians. Aurelius Victor, Syncellus, and others, testify that Valerian was overtaken by that calamity through the treachery of his generals.

20 Isa. xlii. 9.

21 προστάς. But Valesius would read προσστάς, *adstans.*

22 προσπελάσας is the reading of three of the codices and of Nicephorus; others give προπελάσας.

empire of Gallienus now established ; but now he is *that* no more, because indeed he never was it, while this other, *i.e.*, *Gallienus*, is just as he was. And his empire, as if it had cast off old age, and had purged itself of the wickedness formerly attaching to it, is at present in a more vigorous and flourishing condition, and is now seen and heard of at greater distances, and stretches abroad in every direction.

6. *Then he further indicates the exact time at which he wrote this account, as follows :* — And it occurs to me again to review the days of the imperial years. For I see that those most impious men, whose names may have been once so famous, have in a short space become nameless. But our more pious and godly prince [1] has passed his septennium, and is now in his ninth year, in which we are to celebrate the festival.[2]

EPISTLE XII. — TO THE ALEXANDRIANS.[3]

1. To other men, indeed, the present state of matters would not appear to offer a fit season for a festival : and this certainly is no festal time to them ; nor, in sooth, is any other that to them. And I say this, not only of occasions manifestly sorrowful,[4] but even of all occasions whatsoever which people might consider to be most joyous.[5] And now certainly all things are turned to mourning, and all men are in grief, and lamentations resound through the city, by reason of the multitude of the dead and of those who are dying

day by day. For as it is written in the case of the first-born of the Egyptians, so now too a great cry has arisen. " For there is not a house in which there is not one dead." [6] And would that even this were all !

2. Many terrible calamities, it is true, have also befallen us before this. For first they drove us away ; and though we were quite alone, and pursued by all, and in the way of being slain, we kept our festival, even at such a time. And every place that had been the scene of some of the successive sufferings which befell any of us, became a seat for our solemn assemblies, — the field, the desert, the ship, the inn, the prison, — all alike. The most gladsome festival of all, however, has been celebrated by those perfect martyrs who have sat down at the feast in heaven. And after these things war and famine surprised us. These were calamities which we shared, indeed, with the heathen. But we had also to bear by ourselves alone those ills with which they outraged us, and we had at the same time to sustain our part in those things which they either did to each other or suffered at each other's hands ; while again we rejoiced deeply in that peace of Christ which He imparted to us alone.

3. And after we and they together had enjoyed a very brief season of rest, this pestilence next assailed us, — a calamity truly more dreadful to them than all other objects of dread, and more intolerable than any other kind of trouble whatsoever ; [7] and a misfortune which, as a certain writer of their own declares, alone prevails over all hope. To us, however, it was not so ; but in no less measure than other ills it proved an instrument for our training and probation. For it by no means kept aloof from us, although it spread with greatest violence among the heathen.

4. *To these statements he in due succession makes this addition :* — Certainly very many of our brethren, while, in their exceeding love and brotherly-kindness, they did not spare themselves, but kept by each other, and visited the sick without thought of their own peril, and ministered to them assiduously, and treated them for their healing in Christ, died from time to time most joyfully along with them, lading themselves with pains derived from others, and drawing upon themselves their neighbours' diseases, and willingly taking over to their own persons the burden of the sufferings of those around them.[8] And many who

---

[1] [Rom. xiii. 4, 6. St. Paul's strong expressions in this place must explain these expressions. A prince was, *quoad hoc*, comparatively speaking, godly and pious, as he " attended continually to this very thing." So, " most religious," in the Anglican Liturgy.]

[2] Who ever expressed himself thus, — that one after his seven years was passing his ninth year? This septennium (ἐπταετηρίς) must designate something peculiar, and different from the time following it. It is therefore the septennium of imperial power which he had held along with his father. In the eighth year of that empire, Macrianus possessed himself of the imperial honour specially in Egypt. After his assumption of the purple, however, Gallienus had still much authority in Egypt. At length, in the ninth year of Gallienus, that is, in 261, Macrianus the father and the two sons being slain, the sovereignty of Gallienus was recognised also among the Egyptians. And then Gallienus gave a rescript to Dionysius, Pinna, and Demetrius, bishops of Egypt, to re-establish the sacred places, — a boon which he had granted in the former year. The ninth year of Gallienus, moreover, began about the midsummer of this year: and the time at which this letter was written by Dionysius, as Eusebius observes, may be gathered from that, and falls consequently before the Paschal season of 262 A.D. — PEARSON, p. 72. GALL.

[3] Eusebius, *Hist. Eccles.*, vii. 22. Eusebius prefaces the 21st chapter of his seventh book thus: " When peace had scarcely yet been established, he (Dionysius) returned to Alexandria. But when sedition and war again broke out, and made it impossible for him to have access to all the brethren in that city, divided as they then were into different parties, he addressed them again by an epistle at the passover, as if he were still an exile from Alexandria." Then he inserts the epistle to Hierax; and thereafter, in ch. xxii., introduces the present excerpt thus: " After these events, the pestilence succeeding the war, and the festival being now at hand, he again addressed the brethren by letters, in which he gave the following description of the great troubles connected with that calamity."

[4] οὐχ ὅπως τῶν ἐπιλύπων is the reading of Codices Maz., Med., and Savil.; others give, less correctly, ἐπιλοίπων.

[5] The text gives, ἀλλ᾿ οὐδ᾿ εἰ τις περιχαρῆς ὃν οἰηθείεν μάλιστα, which is put probably for the mere regular construction, ὃν οἴοιντο ἂν μάλιστα περιχαρῆ. Nicephorus reads, εἰ τις περιχαρῆς ὧν οἰηθείη. The idea is, that the heathen could have no real festal time. All seasons, those apparently most joyous, no less than those evidently sorrowful, must be times void of all real rejoicing to them, until they learn the grace of God.

---

[6] Ex. xii. 30.

[7] Dionysius is giving a sort of summary of all the calamities which befell the Alexandrian church from the commencement of his episcopal rule: namely, first, persecution, referring to that which began in the last year of the reign of Philip: then war, meaning the civil war of which he speaks in his Epistle to Fabius: then pestilence, alluding to the sickness which began in the time of Decius, and traversed the land under Gallus and Volusianus. — VALES.

[8] ἀναμασσόμενοι τὰς ἀλγηδόνας. Some make this equivalent to *mitigantes*. It means properly to " wipe off," and so to become " responsible " for. Here it is used apparently to express much the same idea as the two preceding clauses.

had thus cured others of their sicknesses, and restored them to strength, died themselves, having transferred to their own bodies the death that lay upon these. And that common saying, which else seemed always to be only a polite form of address,[1] they expressed in actual fact then, as they departed this life, like the "*offscourings of all*.[2] Yea, the very best of our brethren have departed this life in this manner, including some presbyters and some deacons, and among the people those who were in highest reputation: so that this very form of death, in virtue of the distinguished piety and the stedfast faith which were exhibited in it, appeared to come in nothing beneath martyrdom itself.

5. And they took the bodies of the saints on their upturned hands,[3] and on their bosoms, and closed[4] their eyes, and shut their mouths. And carrying them in company,[5] and laying them out decently, they clung to them, and embraced them, and prepared them duly with washing and with attire. And then in a little while after they had the same services done for themselves, as those who survived were ever following those who departed before them. But among the heathen all was the very reverse. For they thrust aside any who began to be sick, and kept aloof even from their dearest friends, and cast the sufferers out upon the public roads half dead, and left them unburied, and treated them with utter contempt when they died, steadily avoiding any kind of communication and intercourse with death; which, however, it was not easy for them altogether to escape, in spite of the many precautions they employed.[6]

EPISTLE XIII. — TO HIERAX, A BISHOP IN EGYPT.[7]

1. But what wonder should there be if I find it difficult to communicate by letter with those who are settled in remote districts, when it seems beyond my power even to reason with myself, and to take counsel with[8] my own soul? For surely epistolary communications are very requisite for me with those who are, as it were, my own bowels, my closest associates, and my brethren — one in soul with myself, and members, too, of the same Church. And yet no way

opens up by which I can transmit such addresses. Easier, indeed, would it be for one, I do not say merely to pass beyond the limits of the province, but to cross from east to west, than to travel from this same Alexandria to Alexandria. For the most central pathway in this city[9] is vaster[10] and more impassable even than that extensive and untrodden desert which Israel only traversed in two generations; and our smooth and waveless harbours have become an image of that sea through which the people drove, at the time when it divided itself and stood up like walls on either side, and in whose thoroughfare the Egyptians were drowned. For often they have appeared like the Red Sea, in consequence of the slaughter perpetrated in them. The river, too, which flows by the city, has sometimes appeared drier than the waterless desert, and more parched than that wilderness in which Israel was so overcome with thirst on their journey, that they kept crying out against Moses, and the water was made to stream for them from the precipitous[11] rock by the power of Him who alone doeth wondrous things. And sometimes, again, it has risen in such flood-tide, that it has overflowed all the country round about, and the roads, and the fields, as if it threatened to bring upon us once more that deluge of waters which occurred in the days of Noah.

2. But now it always flows onward, polluted with blood and slaughters and the drowning struggles of men, just as it did of old, when on Pharaoh's account it was changed by Moses into blood, and made putrid. And what other liquid could cleanse water, which itself cleanses all things? How could that ocean, so vast and impassable for men, though poured out on it, ever purge this bitter sea? Or how could even that great river which streams forth from Eden,[12] though it were to discharge the four heads into which it is divided into the one channel of the Gihon,[13] wash away these pollutions? Or when will this air, befouled as it is by noxious exhalations which rise in every direction, become pure again? For there are such vapours sent forth from the earth, and such blasts from the sea, and breezes from the rivers, and reeking mists from the harbours, that for dew we might suppose ourselves to have the impure fluids[14] of the corpses which are rotting in all the underlying elements. And yet, after all this, men are amazed, and are at a loss to understand whence

---

[1] μόνης φιλοφροσύνης ἔχεσθαι.

[2] The phrase περίψημα πάντων refers to 1 Cor. iv. 13. Valesius supposes that among the Alexandrians it may have been a humble and complimentary form of salutation, ἐγώ εἰμι περίψημά σου; or that the expression περίψημα πάντων had come to be habitually applied to the Christians by the heathen.

[3] ὑπτίαις χερσί. [See Introductory Note, p. 77.]

[4] καθαιροῦντες.

[5] ὁμοφοροῦντες.

[6] [Compare Defoe, *Plague in London*.]

[7] Eusebius, *Hist. Eccles.*, vii. 21. The preface to this extract in Eusebius is as follows: "After this he (Dionysius) wrote also another Paschal epistle to Hierax, a bishop in Egypt, in which he makes the following statement about the sedition then prevailing at Alexandria."

[8] Or, for.

[9] μεσαιτάτη τῆς πόλεως. Codex Regius gives τῶν πόλεων. The sedition referred to as thus dividing Alexandria is probably that which broke out when Æmilianus seized the sovereignty in Alexandria. See Pollio's *Thirty Tyrants*.

[10] ἄπειρος. But Codices Fuk. and Savil. give ἄπορος, "impracticable."

[11] ἀκροτόμου. It may perhaps mean "smitten" here.

[12] Ἐδέμ.

[13] Written Γηών in Codex Alexandrinus, but Γεών in Codex Vaticanus.

[14] ἰχῶρας.

come these constant pestilences, whence these terrible diseases, whence these many kinds of fatal inflictions, whence all that large and multiform destruction of human life, and what reason there is why this mighty city no longer contains within it as great a number of inhabitants, taking all parties into account, from tender children up to those far advanced in old age, as once it maintained of those alone whom it called hale old men.[1] But those from forty years of age up to seventy were so much more numerous then, that their number cannot be made up now even when those from fourteen to eighty years of age have been added to the roll and register of persons who are recipients of the public allowances of grain. And those who are youngest in appearance have now become, as it were, equals in age with those who of old were the most aged. And yet, although they thus see the human race constantly diminishing and wasting away upon the earth, they have no trepidation in the midst of this increasing and advancing consumption and annihilation of their own number.

[1] ὡμογέροντας.

EPISTLE XIV. — FROM HIS FOURTH FESTIVAL EPISTLE.[2]

Love is altogether and for ever on the alert, and casts about to do some good even to one who is unwilling to receive it. And many a time the man who shrinks from it under a feeling of shame, and who declines to accept services of kindness on the ground of unwillingness to become troublesome to others, and who chooses rather to bear the burden of his own grievances than cause annoyance and anxiety to any one, is importuned by the man who is full of love to bear with his aids, and to suffer himself to be helped by another, though it might be as one sustaining a wrong, and thus to do a very great service, not to himself, but to another, in permitting that other to be the agent in putting an end to the ill in which he has been involved.

[2] ἐκ τῆς δ' ἑορταστικῆς ἐπιστολῆς. From the *Sacred Parallels* of *John of Damascus*, Works, ii. p. 753 C, edit. Paris, 1712. In his *Ecclesiastical History*, book vii. ch. 20, Eusebius says : " In addition to these epistles, the same Dionysius also composed others about this time, designated his *Festival Epistles*, and in these he says much in commendation of the Paschal feast. One of these he addressed to Flavius, and another to Domitius and Didymus, in which he gives the canon for eight years, and shows that the Paschal feast ought not to be kept until the passing of the vernal equinox. And besides these, he wrote another epistle to his co-presbyters at Alexandria."

ELUCIDATION.

(Apocalypse, note 7, p. 105, and note 9, p. 106.)

THE moderation of Dionysius is hardly less conspicuous than his fearlessness of inquiry in the questions he raises about the Apocalypse.[1] He utterly refuses to reject it.[2] He testifies to the value set upon it by his fellow-Christians. Only, he doubts as to (*the* John) the "inspired person" who was its author, and with critical skill exposes the inferiority of the Greek of the Apocalypse to that of the Gospel and Epistles of St. John. Obviously he accepts it as part of the canon, only doubting as to the author. Modestly he owns that it passes his understanding. So Calvin forbore to comment upon it, and owned to "headache" when he came to it.

[1] P. 84, note 6. [2] P. 82, note 6.

THE WORKS OF DIONYSIUS.

EXEGETICAL FRAGMENTS.[1]

I.—A COMMENTARY ON THE BEGINNING OF ECCLESIASTES.[2]

CHAP. I.

VER. 1. "*The words* of the son of David, king of Israel in Jerusalem."

In like manner also Matthew calls the Lord the son of David.[3]

3. "What profit hath a man of all his labour which he taketh under the sun?"

For what man is there who, although he may have become rich by toiling after the objects of this earth, has been able to make himself three cubits in stature, if he is naturally only of two cubits in stature? Or who, if blind, has by these means recovered his sight? Therefore we ought to direct our toils to a goal beyond the sun: for thither, too, do the exertions of the virtues reach.

4. "One generation passeth away, and another generation cometh: but the earth abideth for ever" (unto the age).

Yes, unto the age,[4] but not unto the ages.[5]

16. "I communed with mine own heart, saying, Lo, I am come to great estate, and have gotten more wisdom than all they that have been before me in Jerusalem; yea, my heart had great experience of wisdom and knowledge.

17. I knew parables and science: that this indeed is also the spirit's choice.[6]

18. For in multitude of wisdom is multitude of knowledge: and he that increaseth knowledge increaseth grief."

I was vainly puffed up, and increased wisdom; not the wisdom which God has given, but that wisdom of which Paul says, "The wisdom of this world is foolishness with God."[7] For in this Solomon had also an experience surpassing prudence, and above the measure of all the ancients. Consequently he shows the vanity of it, as what follows in like manner demonstrates: "And my heart uttered[8] many things: I knew wisdom, and knowledge, and parables, and sciences." But this was not the genuine wisdom or knowledge, but that which, as Paul says, puffeth up. He spake, moreover, as it is written,[9] three thousand parables. But these were not parables of a spiritual kind, but only such as fit the common polity of men; as, for instance, utterances about animals or medicines. For which reason he has added in a tone of raillery, "I knew that this also is the spirit's choice." He speaks also of the multitude of knowledge, not the knowledge of the Holy Spirit, but that which the prince of this world works, and which he conveys to men in order to overreach their souls, with officious questions as to the measures of heaven, the position of earth, the bounds of the sea. But he says also, "He that increaseth knowledge increaseth sorrow." For they search even into things deeper than these, — inquiring, for example, what necessity there is for fire to go upward, and for water to go downward; and when they have learned that it is because the one is light and the other heavy, they do but increase sorrow: for the question still remains, Why might it not be the very reverse?

CHAP. II.

Ver. 1. "I said in mine heart, Go to now, make trial as in mirth, and behold in good. And this, too, is vanity."

For it was for the sake of trial, and in accordance with what comes by the loftier and the severe life, that he entered into pleasure. And he makes mention of the mirth, which men call so. And he says, "in good," referring to what men call good things, which are not capable of giving life to their possessor, and which make

---

[1] See, in the *Bibliotheca Veterum Patrum* of Gallandi, the Appendix to vol. xiv., added from the manuscripts, after the editor's death, by an anonymous scholar.

[2] [Compare the *Metaphrase*, p. 9, *supra*. *Query*, are not these twin specimens of exegetical exercises in the school at Alexandria?]

[3] Matt i. 1.

[4] εἰς τὸν αἰῶνα.

[5] εἰς τοὺς αἰῶνας.

[6] προαίρεσις.

[7] 1 Cor. iii. 19.

[8] εἶπε, for which εἶδε, "discerned," is suggested.

[9] 1 Kings iv. 32.

the man who engages in them vain like themselves.

2. "I said of laughter, It is mad;[1] and of mirth, What doest thou?"

Laughter has a twofold madness; because madness begets laughter, and does not allow the sorrowing for sins; and also because a man of that sort is possessed with madness,[2] in the confusing of seasons, and places, and persons. For he flees from those who sorrow. "And to mirth, What doest thou?" Why dost thou repair to those who are not at liberty to be merry? Why to the drunken, and the avaricious, and the rapacious? And why this phrase, "as wine?"[3] Because wine makes the heart merry; and it acts upon the poor in spirit. The flesh, however, also makes the heart merry, when it acts in a regular and moderate fashion.

3. "And my heart directed me in wisdom, and to overcome in mirth, until I should know what is that good thing to the sons of men which they shall do under the sun for the number of the days of their life."

Being directed, he says, by wisdom, I overcame pleasures in mirth. Moreover, for me the aim of knowledge was to occupy myself with nothing vain, but to find the good; for if a person finds that, he does not miss the discernment also of the profitable. The sufficient is also the opportune,[4] and is commensurate with the length of life.

4. "I made me great works; I builded me houses; I planted me vineyards.

5. I made me gardens and orchards.

6. I made me pools of water, that by these I might rear woods producing trees.

7. I got me servants and maidens, and had servants born in my house; also I had large possessions of great and small cattle above all that were in Jerusalem before me.

8. I gathered me also silver and gold, and the peculiar treasure of kings and of the provinces. I gat me men-singers and women-singers, and the delights of the sons of men, as cups and the cupbearer.

9. And I was great, and increased more than all that were before me in Jerusalem: also my wisdom remained with me.

10. And whatsoever mine eyes desired, I kept not from them; I withheld not my heart from any pleasure."

You see how he reckons up a multitude of houses and fields, and the other things which he mentions, and then finds nothing profitable in them. For neither was he any better in soul by reason of these things, nor by their means did he gain friendship with God. Necessarily he is led to speak also of the true riches and the abiding property. Being minded, therefore, to show what kinds of possessions remain with the possessor, and continue steadily and maintain themselves for him, he adds: "Also my wisdom remained with me." For this alone remains, and all these other things, which he has already reckoned up, flee away and depart. Wisdom, therefore, remained with me, and I remained in virtue of it. For those other things fall, and also cause the fall of the very persons who run after them. But, with the intention of instituting a comparison between wisdom and those things which are held to be good among men, he adds these words, "And whatsoever mine eyes desired, I kept not from them," and so forth; whereby he describes as evil, not only those toils which they endure who toil in gratifying themselves with pleasures, but those, too, which by necessity and constraint men have to sustain for their maintenance day by day, labouring at their different occupations in the sweat of their faces. For the labour, he says, is great; but the art[5] by the labour is temporary, adding[6] nothing serviceable among things that please. Wherefore there is no profit. For where there is no excellence there is no profit. With reason, therefore, are the objects of such solicitude but vanity, and the spirit's choice. Now this name of "spirit" he gives to the "soul." For choice is a quality, not a motion.[7] And David says: "Into Thy hands I commit my spirit."[8] And in good truth "did my wisdom remain with me," for it made me know and understand, so as to enable me to speak of all that is not advantageous[9] under the sun. If, therefore, we desire the righteously profitable, if we seek the truly advantageous, if it is our aim to be incorruptible, let us engage in those labours which reach beyond the sun. For in these there is no vanity, and there is not the choice of a spirit at once inane and hurried hither and thither to no purpose.

12. "And I turned myself to behold wisdom, and madness, and folly: for what man is there that shall come after counsel in all those things which it has done?"[10]

He means the wisdom which comes from God, and which also remained with him. And by madness and folly he designates all the labours of men, and the vain and silly pleasure they have in them. Distinguishing these, therefore, and their measure, and blessing the true wisdom, he has added: "For what man is there that shall

---

[1] περιφοράν.
[2] περιφέρεται.
[3] ὡς οἶνον.
[4] Or, temporary.

[5] τέχνη.
[6] Reading προστιθεῖσα for προτιθεῖσα.
[7] ποιὸν οὐ κίνησις.
[8] Ps. xxxi. 5.
[9] περισσεία.
[10] ὃς ἐλεύσεται ὀπίσω τῆς βουλῆς σύμπαντα ὅσα ἐποίησεν αὕτη;

come after counsel?" For this counsel instructs us in the wisdom that is such indeed, and gifts us with deliverance from madness and folly.

13. "Then I saw that wisdom excelleth folly, as much as light excelleth darkness."

He does not say this in the way of comparison. For things which are contrary to each other, and mutually destructive, cannot be compared. But his decision was, that the one is to be chosen, and the other avoided. To like effect is the saying, "Men loved darkness rather than light."[1] For the term "rather" in that passage expresses the choice of the person loving, and not the comparison of the objects themselves.

14. "The wise man's eyes are in his head, but the fool walketh in darkness."

That man always inclines earthward, he means, and has the ruling faculty[2] darkened. It is true, indeed, that we men have all of us our eyes in our head, if we speak of the mere disposition of the body. But he speaks here of the eyes of the mind. For as the eyes of the swine do not turn naturally up towards heaven, just because it is made by nature to have an inclination toward the belly; so the mind of the man who has once been enervated by pleasures is not easily diverted from the tendency thus assumed, because he has not "respect unto all the commandments of the Lord."[3] Again: "Christ is the head of the Church."[4] And they, therefore, are the wise who walk in His way; for He Himself has said, "I am the way."[5] On this account, then, it becomes the wise man always to keep the eyes of his mind directed toward Christ Himself, in order that he may do nothing out of measure, neither being lifted up in heart in the time of prosperity, nor becoming negligent in the day of adversity: "for His judgments are a great deep,"[6] as you will learn more exactly from what is to follow.

14. "And I perceived myself also that one event happeneth to them all."

15. Then said I in my heart, As it happeneth to the fool, so it happeneth even to me; and why was I then more wise?"

The run of the discourse in what follows deals with those who are of a mean spirit as regards this present life, and in whose judgment the article of death and all the anomalous pains of the body are a kind of dreaded evil, and who on this account hold that there is no profit in a life of virtue, because there is no difference made in ills like these between the wise man and the fool. He speaks consequently of these as the words of a madness inclining to utter senselessness; whence he also adds this sentence, "For

the fool talks over-much;"[7] and by the "fool" here he means himself, and every one who reasons in that way. Accordingly he condemns this absurd way of thinking. And for the same reason he has given utterance to such sentiments in the fears of his heart; and dreading the righteous condemnation of those who are to be heard, he solves the difficulty in its pressure by his own reflections. For this word, "Why was I then wise?" was the word of a man in doubt and difficulty whether what is expended on wisdom is done well or to no purpose; and whether there is no difference between the wise man and the fool in point of advantage, seeing that the former is involved equally with the latter in the same sufferings which happen in this present world. And for this reason he says, "I spake over-largely[8] in my heart," in thinking that there is no difference between the wise man and the fool.

16. "For there is no remembrance of the wise equally with the fool for ever."

For the events that happen in this life are all transitory, be they even the painful incidents, of which he says, "As all things now are consigned to oblivion."[9] For after a short space has passed by, all the things that befall men in this life perish in forgetfulness. Yea, the very persons to whom these things have happened are not remembered all in like manner, even although they may have gone through like chances in life. For they are not remembered for these, but only for what they may have evinced of wisdom or folly, virtue or vice. The memories of such are not extinguished (equally) among men in consequence of the changes of lot befalling them. Wherefore he has added this: "And how shall the wise man die along with the fool? The death of sinners, indeed, is evil: yet the memory of the just is blessed, but the name of the wicked is extinguished."[10]

22. "For that falls to man in all his labour."

In truth, to those who occupy their minds with the distractions of life, life becomes a painful thing, which, as it were, wounds the heart with its goads, that is, with the lustful desires of increase. And sorrowful also is the solicitude connected with covetousness: it does not so much gratify those who are successful in it, as it pains those who are unsuccessful; while the day is spent in laborious anxieties, and the night puts sleep to flight from the eyes, with the cares of making gain. Vain, therefore, is the zeal of the man who looks to these things.

24. "And there is nothing good for a man, but what he eats and drinks, and what

---

[1] John iii. 19.
[2] τὸ ἡγεμονικόν.
[3] Ps. cxix. 6.
[4] Eph. v. 23.
[5] John xiv. 6.
[6] Ps. xxxvi. 6.

[7] ἐκ περισσεύματος.
[8] περισσόν.
[9] καθότι ἤδη τὰ πάντα ἐπελήσθη.
[10] Prov. x. 7.

will show to his soul good in his labour. This also I saw, that it is from the hand of God.

25. For who eats and drinks from his own resources?"[1]

That the discourse does not deal now with material meats, he will show by what follows; namely, "It is better to go to the house of mourning than to go to the house of feasting."[2] And so in the present passage he proceeds to add : "And (what) will show to his soul good in its labour." And surely mere material meats and drinks are not the soul's good. For the flesh, when luxuriously nurtured, wars against the soul, and rises in revolt against the spirit. And how should not intemperate eatings and drinkings also be contrary to God?[3] He speaks, therefore, of things mystical. For no one shall partake of the spiritual table, but one who is called by Him, and who has listened to the wisdom which says, "Take and eat."[4]

CHAP. III.

Ver. 3. "There is a time to kill, and a time to heal."

To "kill," in the case of him who perpetrates unpardonable transgression ; and to "heal," in the case of him who can show a wound that will bear remedy.

4. "A time to weep, and a time to laugh."

A time to weep, when it is the time of suffering ; as when the Lord also says, "Verily I say unto you, that ye shall weep and lament."[5] But to laugh, as concerns the resurrection : "For your sorrow," He says, "shall be turned into joy."[6]

4. "A time to mourn, and a time to dance."

When one thinks of the death which the transgression of Adam brought on us, it is a time to mourn ; but it is a time to hold festal gatherings when we call to mind the resurrection from the dead which we expect through the new Adam.[7]

6. "A time to keep, and a time to cast away."

A time to keep the Scripture against the unworthy, and a time to put it forth for the worthy. Or, again : Before the incarnation it was a time to keep the letter of the law ; but it was a time to cast it away when the truth came in its flower.

7. "A time to keep silence, and a time to speak."

A time to speak, when there are hearers who receive the word ; but a time to keep silence, when the hearers pervert the word ; as Paul

says : "A man that is an heretic, after the first and second admonition, reject."[8]

10. "I have seen, then, the travail which God hath given to the sons of men to be exercised in it.

11. Everything that He hath made is beautiful in its time : and He hath set the whole world in their heart ; so that no man can find out the work that God maketh from the beginning and to the end."

And this is true. For no one is able to comprehend the works of God altogether. Moreover, the world is the work of God. No one, then, can find out as to this world what is its space from the beginning and unto the end, that is to say, the period appointed for it, and the limits before determined unto it ; forasmuch as God has set the whole world as *a realm of* ignorance in our hearts. And thus one says : "Declare to me the shortness of my days."[9] In this manner, and for our profit, the end of this world (age) — that is to say, this present life — is a thing of which we are ignorant.

II. — THE GOSPEL ACCORDING TO LUKE.

AN INTERPRETATION. — CHAP. XXII. 42-48.

Ver. 42. "Father, if Thou be willing to remove[10] this cup from me : nevertheless not my will, but Thine, be done."

But let these things be enough to say on the subject of the will. This word, however, "Let the cup pass," does not mean, Let it not come near me, or approach me.[11] For what can "pass from Him," certainly must first come nigh Him ; and what does pass thus from Him, must be by Him. For if it does not reach Him, it cannot pass from Him. For He takes to Himself the person of man, as having been made man. Wherefore also on this occasion He deprecates the doing of the inferior, which is His own, and begs that the superior should be done, which is His Father's, to wit, the divine will ; which again, however, in respect of the divinity, is one and the same will in Himself and in the Father. For it was the Father's will that He should pass through every trial (temptation) ; and the Father Himself in a marvellous manner brought Him on this course, not indeed with the trial itself as His goal, nor in order simply that He might enter into that, but in order that He might prove Himself to be above the trial, and also beyond it.[12] And surely it is the fact, that the Saviour asks neither what is impossible, nor what

---

[1] παρ' αὐτοῦ.
[2] Eccles. vii. 2.
[3] The text gives, πῶς δὲ καὶ οὐκ παρὲκ Θεοῦ ἀσώτων βρωμάτων καὶ μέθη.
[4] Prov. ix. 5.
[5] Luke vi. 25; John xvi. 20.
[6] John xvi. 20.
[7] [The fast of the Paschal week, and the feast that follows, are here referred to. Of course the religious *saltation* of the Hebrews (2 Sam. vi. 14) is the thought of *Koheleth*, and figuratively it is here adopted for holy mirth.]

[8] Tit. iii. 10.
[9] Ps. cii. 24, τὴν ὀλιγότητα τῶν ἡμερῶν μου ἀνάγγειλόν μοι.
[10] παρενεγκεῖν.
[11] οὐκ ἐστι. Migne suggests οὐκέτι: "Let it no more come near me."
[12] μετ' αὐτόν. May it be, "and next to Himself" (the Father)?

is impracticable, nor what is contrary to the will of the Father. It is something possible; for Mark makes mention of His saying, "Abba, Father, all things are possible unto Thee." [1] And they are possible if He wills them; for Luke tells us that He said, "Father, if Thou be willing, remove [2] this cup from me." The Holy Spirit, therefore, apportioned among the evangelists, makes up the full account of our Saviour's whole disposition by the expressions of these several narrators together. He does not, then, ask of the Father what the Father wills not. For the words, "If Thou be willing," were demonstrative of subjection and docility, [3] not of ignorance or hesitancy. For this reason, the other scripture says, "All things are possible unto Thee." And Matthew again admirably describes the submission and humility [4] when he says, "If it be possible." For unless I adapt the sense in this way, [5] some will perhaps assign an impious signification to this expression, " If it be possible ; " as if there were anything impossible for God to do, except that only which He does not will to do. But . . . being straightway strengthened in His humanity by His ancestral [6] divinity, he urges the safer petition, and desires no longer that that should be the case, but that it might be accomplished in accordance with the Father's good pleasure, in glory, in constancy, and in fulness. For John, who has given us the record of the sublimest and divinest of the Saviour's words and deeds, heard Him speak thus: "And the cup which my Father hath given me, shall I not drink it?" [7] Now, to drink the cup was to discharge the ministry and the whole economy of trial with fortitude, to follow and fulfil the Father's determination, and to surmount all apprehensions. And the exclamation, " Why hast Thou forsaken me?" was in due accordance with the requests He had previously made: Why is it that death has been in conjunction with me all along up till now, and that I bear not yet the cup? This I judge to have been the Saviour's meaning in this concise utterance.

And He certainly spake truth then. Nevertheless He was not forsaken. But He drank out the cup at once, as His plea had implied, and then passed away. [8] And the vinegar which was handed to Him seems to me to have been a symbolical thing. For the turned wine [9] indicated very well the quick turning [10] and change

which He sustained, when He passed from His passion to impassibility, and from death to deathlessness, and from the position of one judged to that of one judging, and from subjection under the despot's power to the exercise of kingly dominion. And the sponge, as I think, signified the complete transfusion [11] of the Holy Spirit that was realized in Him. And the reed symbolized the royal sceptre and the divine law. And the hyssop expressed that quickening and saving resurrection of His, by which He has also brought health to us. [12]

43. " And there appeared an angel unto Him from heaven, strengthening Him.

44. And being in an agony, He prayed more earnestly ; and His sweat was as it were great drops of blood falling down to the ground."

The phrase, " a sweat of blood," is a current parabolic expression used of persons in intense pain and distress ; as also of one in bitter grief people say that the man " weeps tears of blood." For in using the expression, " as it were great drops of blood," he does not declare the drops of sweat to have been actually drops of blood. [13] For he would not then have said that these drops of sweat were like blood. For such is the force of the expression, " as it were great drops." But rather with the object of making it plain that the Lord's body was not bedewed with any kind of subtle moisture which had only the show and appearance of actuality, but that it was really suffused all over with sweat in the shape of large thick drops, he has taken the great drops of blood as an illustration of what was the case with Him. And accordingly, as by the intensity of the supplication and the severe agony, so also by the dense and excessive sweat, he made the facts patent, that the Saviour was man by nature and in reality, and not in mere semblance and appearance, and that He was subject to all the innocent sensibilities natural to men. Nevertheless the words, " I have power to lay down my life, and I have power to take it again," [14] show that His passion was a voluntary thing ; and besides that, they indicate that the life which is laid down and taken again is one thing, and the divinity which lays that down and takes it again is another.

He says, " one thing and another," not as making a partition into two persons, but as showing the distinction between the two natures. [15]

And as, by voluntarily enduring the death in the flesh, He implanted incorruptibility in it ; so

[1] Mark xiv. 36.
[2] παρενεγκε.
[3] ἐπιεικείας.
[4] The text gives κἂν τοῦτο πάλιν τὸ εἰκτικόν, etc. Migne proposes, κἂν τουτῳ πάλιν τὸ εὐκτικόν = and Matthew again describes the supplicatory and docile in Him.
[5] Reading οὕτως for οὔτε.
[6] πατρικῆς.
[7] John xviii. 11.
[8] παρελήλυθε.
[9] ἐκτροπίας οἶνος.
[10] τροπήν.

[11] ἀνάκρασιν.
[12] The text is, ἡμᾶς ὕγια ἔδειξεν. Migne proposes ὑγίασεν.
[13] [Note this somewhat *modern* " explaining away." It proves the freedom of our author from any predisposition to exegetical exaggeration, if nothing more.]
[14] John x. 18.
[15] This sentence is supposed to be an interpolation by the constructor of the *Catena*.

also, by taking to Himself of His own free-will the passion of our servitude,[1] He set in it the seeds of constancy and courage, whereby He has nerved those who believe on Him for the mighty conflicts belonging to their witness-bearing. Thus, also, those drops of sweat flowed from Him in a marvellous way like great drops of blood, in order that He might, as it were, drain off[2] and empty the fountain of the fear which is proper to our nature. For unless this had been done with a mystical import, He certainly would not, even had He been[3] the most timorous and ignoble of men, have been bedewed in this unnatural way with drops of sweat like drops of blood under the mere force of His agony.

Of like import is also the sentence in the narrative which tells us that an angel stood by the Saviour and strengthened Him. For this, too, bore also on the economy entered into on our behalf. For those who are appointed to engage in the sacred exertions of conflicts on account of piety, have the angels from heaven to assist them. And the prayer, "Father, remove the cup," He uttered probably not as if He feared the death itself, but with the view of challenging the devil by these words to erect the cross for Him. With words of deceit that personality deluded Adam; with the words of divinity, then, let the deceiver himself now be deluded. Howbeit assuredly the will of the Son is not one thing, and the will of the Father another.[4] For He who wills what the Father wills, is found to have the Father's will. It is in a figure, therefore, that He says, "not my will, but Thine." For it is not that He wishes the cup to be removed, but that He refers to the Father's will the right issue of His passion, and honours thereby the Father as the First.[5] For if the fathers[6] style one's disposition *gnomè*,[7] and if such disposition relates also to what is in consideration hidden as if by settled purpose, how say some that the Lord, who is above all these things, bears a gnomic will?[8] Manifestly that can be only by defect of reason.

45. "And when He rose from prayer, and was come to His disciples, He found them sleeping for sorrow;

46. And said unto them, Why sleep ye? Rise and pray, lest ye enter into temptation."

For in the most general sense it holds good that it is apparently not possible for any man[9] to remain altogether without experience of ill. For, as one says, "the whole world lieth in wickedness;"[10] and again, "The most of the days of man are labour and trouble."[11] But you will perhaps say, What difference is there between being tempted, and falling or entering into temptation? Well, if one is overcome of evil — and he will be overcome unless he struggles against it himself, and unless God protects him with His shield — that man has entered into temptation, and is in it, and is brought under it like one that is led captive. But if one withstands and endures, that man is indeed tempted; but he has not entered into temptation, or fallen into it. Thus Jesus was led up of the Spirit, not indeed to enter into temptation, but to be tempted of the devil.[12] And Abraham, again, did not enter into temptation, neither did God lead him into temptation, but He tempted (tried) him; yet He did not drive him into temptation. The Lord Himself, moreover, tempted (tried) the disciples. Thus the wicked one, when he tempts us, draws us into the temptations, as dealing himself with the temptations of evil. But God, when He tempts (tries), adduces the temptations (trials) as one untempted of evil. For God, it is said, "cannot be tempted of evil."[13] The devil, therefore, drives us on by violence, drawing us to destruction; but God leads us by the hand, training us for our salvation.

47. "And while He yet spake, behold a multitude, and he that was called Judas, one of the twelve, went before them, and drew near unto Jesus, and kissed Him.

48. But Jesus said unto him, Judas, betrayest thou the Son of man with a kiss?"

How wonderful this endurance of evil by the Lord, who even kissed the traitor, and spake words softer even than the kiss! For He did not say, O thou abominable, yea, utterly abominable traitor, is this the return you make to us for so great kindness? But, somehow, He says simply "Judas," using the proper name, which was the address that would be used by one who commiserated a person, or who wished to call him back, rather than of one in anger. And He did not say, "thy Master, the Lord, thy benefactor;" but He said simply, "the Son of man," that is, the tender and meek one: as if He meant to say, Even supposing that I was not your Master, or Lord, or benefactor, dost thou still betray one so guilelessly and so tenderly affected towards thee, as even to kiss thee in the hour of thy treachery, and that, too, when

---

[1] The text is, τῆς δουλείας. Migne suggests, τῆς δειλίας = " the feeling of our fear."
[2] ἀναξηράνῃ.
[3] The text is, οὐδὲ ἡ σφόδρα δειλότατος, etc. We read, with Migne, εἰ instead of ἡ.
[4] [Note the following sentence, without which, as explanatory, this might be quoted as a *Monothelite* statement. Garbling is a convenient resource for those who claim the Fathers for other false systems.]
[5] ἀρχήν.
[6] [This seems to be a quotation from the Alexandrian Fathers showing how early such questions began to be agitated. Settled in the Sixth Council, A.D. 681, the *last* " General Council."]
[7] γνώμη, gnomè.
[8] θέλημα γνωμικόν.

[9] μάλιστα ἴσως παντι ἀνθρώπῳ.
[10] 1 John v. 19.
[11] Ps. xc. 10.
[12] Matt. iv. 1
[13] Jas. i. 13.

the kiss was the signal for thy treachery? Blessed art Thou, O Lord! How great is this example of the endurance of evil that Thou hast shown us in Thine own person! how great, too, the pattern of lowliness! Howbeit, the Lord has given us this example, to show us that we ought not to give up offering our good counsel to our brethren, even should nothing remarkable be effected by our words.

For as incurable wounds are wounds which cannot be remedied either by severe applications, or by those which may act more pleasantly upon them;[1] so[2] the soul, when it is once carried captive, and gives itself up to any kind of[3] wickedness, and refuses to consider what is really profitable for it, although a myriad counsels should echo into it, takes no good to itself. But just as if the sense of hearing were dead within it, it receives no benefit from exhortations addressed to it; not because it cannot, but only because it will not. This was what happened in the case of Judas. And yet Christ, although He knew all these things beforehand, did not at any time, from the beginning on to the end, omit to do all in the way of counsel that depended on Him. And inasmuch as we know that such was His practice, we ought also unceasingly to endeavour to set those right[4] who prove careless, even although no actual good may seem to be effected by that counsel.

III. — ON LUKE XXII. 42, ETC.[5]

But let these things be enough to say on the subject of the will. This word, however, "Let the cup pass," does not mean, Let it not come near me, or approach me. For what can pass from Him must certainly first come nigh Him, and what does thus pass from Him must be by Him. For if it does not reach Him, it cannot pass from Him. Accordingly, as if He now felt it to be present, He began to be in pain, and to be troubled, and to be sore amazed, and to be in an agony. And as if it was at hand and placed before Him, He does not merely say "the cup," but He indicates it by the word "this." Therefore, as what passes from one is something which neither has no approach nor is permanently settled with one, so the Saviour's first request is that the temptation which has come softly and plainly upon Him, and associated itself lightly with Him, may be turned aside. And this is the first form of that freedom from falling into

temptation, which He also counsels the weaker disciples to make the subject of their prayers; that, namely, which concerns the approach of temptation: for it must needs be that offences come, but yet those to whom they come ought not to fall into the temptation. But the most perfect mode in which this freedom from entering into temptation is exhibited, is what He expresses in His second request, when He says not merely, "Not as I will," but also, "but as Thou wilt." For with God there is no temptation in evil; but He wills to give us good exceeding abundantly above what we ask or think. That His will, therefore, is the perfect will, the Beloved Himself knew; and often does He say that He has come to do that will, and not His own will, — that is to say, the will of men. For He takes to Himself the person of men, as having been made man. Wherefore also on this occasion He deprecates the doing of the inferior, which is His own, and begs that the superior should be done, which is His Father's, to wit, the divine will, which again, however, in respect of the divinity, is one and the same will in Himself and in His Father. For it was the Father's will that He should pass through every trial (temptation), and the Father Himself in a marvellous manner brought Him on this course; not, indeed, with the trial itself as His goal, nor in order simply that He might enter into that, but in order that He might prove Himself to be above the trial, and also beyond it. And surely it is the fact that the Saviour asks neither what is impossible, nor what is impracticable, nor what is contrary to the will of the Father. It is something possible, for Mark makes mention of His saying, "Abba, Father, all things are possible unto Thee;" and they are possible if He wills them, for Luke tells us that He said, "Father, if Thou be willing, remove this cup from me." The Holy Spirit therefore, apportioned among the evangelists, makes up the full account of our Saviour's whole disposition by the expressions of these several narrators together. He does not then ask of the Father what the Father wills not. For the words, "if Thou be willing," were demonstrative of subjection and docility, not of ignorance or hesitancy. And just as when we make any request that may be accordant with his judgment, at the hand of father or ruler or any one of those whom we respect, we are accustomed to use the address, though not certainly as if we were in doubt about it, "if you please;" so the Saviour also said, "if Thou be willing:" not that He thought that He willed something different, and thereafter learned the fact, but that He understood exactly God's willingness to remove the cup from Him, and as doing so also apprehended justly that what He wills is also possible unto Him. For this reason the other

---

[1] Some such clause as ιαθῆναι δύναται requires to be supplied here.
[2] Reading οὔτω for οὔτε.
[3] Reading ᾧτινιοῦν for ὁτιοῦν.
[4] ῥυθμίζειν.
[5] Another fragment from the Vatican Codex, 1611, fol. 291. See also Mai, *Bibliotheca Nova*, vi. 1. 165. This is given here in a longer and fuller form than in the Greek of Gallandi in his *Bibliotheca*, xiv., Appendix, p. 115, as we have had it presented above, and than in the Latin of Corderius in his *Catena* on Luke xxii. 42, etc. This text is taken from a complete codex.

scripture says, " All things are possible unto Thee." And Matthew again admirably describes the submission and the humility, when he says, " if it be possible." For unless we adapt the sense in this way, some will perhaps assign an impious signification to this expression " if it be possible," as if there were anything impossible for God to do, except that only which He does not will to do. Therefore the request which He made was nothing independent, nor one which pleased Himself only, or opposed His Father's will, but one also in conformity with the mind of God. And yet some one may say that He is overborne and changes His mind, and asks presently something different from what He asked before, and holds no longer by His own will, but introduces His Father's will. Well, such truly is the case. Nevertheless He does not by any means make any change from one side to another ; but He embraces another way, and a different method of carrying out one and the same transaction, which is also a thing agreeable to both ; choosing, to wit, in place of the mode which is the inferior, and which appears unsatisfying also to Himself, the superior and more admirable mode marked out by the Father. For no doubt He did pray that the cup might pass from Him ; but He says also, " Nevertheless, not as I will, but as Thou wilt." He longs painfully, on the one hand, for its passing from Him, but (He knows that) it is better as the Father wills. For He does not utter a petition for its not passing away now, instead of one for its removal ; but when its withdrawal is now before His view, He chooses rather that this should be ordered as the Father wills. For there is a twofold kind [1] of withdrawal : there is one in the instance of an object that has shown itself and reached another, and is gone at once on being followed by it or on outrunning it, as is the case with racers when they graze each other in passing ; and there is another in the instance of an object that has sojourned and tarried with another, and sat down by it, as in the case of a marauding band or a camp, and that after a time withdraws on being conquered, and on gaining the opposite of a success. For if they prevail they do not retire, but carry off with them those whom they have reduced ; but if they prove unable to win the mastery, they withdraw themselves in disgrace. Now it was after the former similitude that He wished that the cup might come into His hands, and promptly pass from Him again very readily and quickly ; but as soon as He spake thus, being at once strengthened in His humanity by the Father's divinity, He urges the safer petition, and desires no longer that that should be the case, but that it might be accomplished in accordance with the Father's good

pleasure, in glory, in constancy, and in fulness. For John, who has given us the record of the sublimest and divinest of the Saviour's words and deeds, heard Him speak thus : " And the cup which my Father hath given me, shall I not drink it ? " Now, to drink the cup was to discharge the ministry and the whole economy of trial with fortitude, to follow and fulfil the Father's determination, and to surmount all apprehensions ; and, indeed, in the very prayer which He uttered He showed that He was leaving these (apprehensions) behind Him. For of two objects, either may be said to be removed from the other : the object that remains may be said to be removed from the one that goes away, and the one that goes away may be said to be removed from the one that remains. Besides, Matthew has indicated most clearly that He did indeed pray that the cup might pass from Him, but yet that His request was that this should take place not as He willed, but as the Father willed it. The words given by Mark and Luke, again, ought to be introduced in their proper connection. For Mark says, " Nevertheless not what I will, but what Thou wilt ; " and Luke says, " Nevertheless not my will, but Thine be done." He did then express Himself to that effect, and He did desire that His passion might abate and reach its end speedily. But it was the Father's will at the same time that He should carry out His conflict in a manner demanding sustained effort,[2] and in sufficient measure. Accordingly He (the Father) adduced all that assailed Him. But of the missiles that were hurled against Him, some were shivered in pieces, and others were dashed back as with invulnerable arms of steel, or rather as from the stern and immoveable rock. Blows, spittings, scourgings, death, and the lifting up in that death,[3] all came upon Him ; and when all these were gone through, He became silent and endured in patience unto the end, as if He suffered nothing, or was already dead. But when His death was being prolonged, and when it was now overmastering Him, if we may so speak, beyond His utmost strength, He cried out to His Father, " Why hast Thou forsaken me ? " And this exclamation was in due accordance with the requests He had previously made : Why is it that death has been in such close conjunction with me all along up till now, and Thou dost not yet bear the cup past me ?[4] Have I not drunk it already, and drained it ? But if not, my dread is that I may be utterly consumed by its continuous pressure ;[5] and that is what would befall me, wert Thou to forsake me : then would the fulfilment abide, but I would pass away, and

---

[1] δύναμις.

[2] λιπαρῶς.
[3] τοῦ θανάτου τὸ ὕψωμα.
[4] παραφέρεις.
[5] ει δε οὐκ ἔπιον αὐτὸ ἤδη καὶ ἀνήλωσα· ἀλλὰ δέος μὴ ὑπ' αὐτοῦ πλήρης ἐπικειμένου καταποθείην.

be made of none effect.[1]   Now, then, I entreat Thee, let my baptism be finished, for indeed I have been straitened greatly until it should be accomplished. — This I judge to have been the Saviour's meaning in this concise utterance.   And He certainly spake truth then.   Nevertheless He was not forsaken.   Albeit He drank out the cup at once, as His plea had implied, and then passed away.   And the vinegar which was handed to Him seems to me to have been a symbolical thing.   For the turned wine indicated very well the quick turning and change which He sustained when He passed from His passion to impassibility, and from death to deathlessness, and from the position of one judged to that of one judging, and from subjection under the despot's power to the exercise of kingly dominion.   And the sponge, as I think, signified the complete transfusion of the Holy Spirit that was realized in Him.   And the reed symbolized the royal sceptre and the divine law.   And the hyssop expressed that quickening and saving resurrection of His by which He has also brought health to us.[2]   But we have gone through these matters in sufficient detail on Matthew and John.   With the permission of God, we shall speak also of the account given by Mark.   But at present we shall keep to what follows in our passage.

IV. — AN EXPOSITION OF LUKE XXII. 46, ETC.[3]

This prayer He also offered up Himself, falling repeatedly on His face ; and on both occasions He urged His request for not entering into temptation : both when He prayed, "If it be possible, let this cup pass from me ; " and when He said, " Nevertheless not as I will, but as Thou wilt."   For He spoke of not entering into temptation, and He made that His prayer ; but He did not ask that He should have no trial whatsoever in these circumstances, or [4] that no manner of hardship should ever befall Him. For in the most general application it holds good, that it does not appear to be possible for any man to remain altogether without experience of ill : for, as one says, " The whole world lieth in wickedness ; " [5] and again, " The most of the days of man are labour and trouble," [6] as men themselves also admit.   Short is our life, and full of sorrow.   Howbeit it was not meet that He should bid them pray directly that that curse might not be fulfilled, which is expressed thus : " Cursed is the ground in thy works : in sorrow shalt thou eat of it all the days of thy life ; " [7]

or thus, " Earth thou art, and unto earth shalt thou return." [8]   For which reason the Holy Scriptures, that indicate in many various ways the dire distressfulness of life, designate it as a valley of weeping.   And most of all indeed is this world a scene of pain to the saints, to whom He addresses this word, and He cannot lie in uttering it : " In the world ye shall have tribulation." [9] And to the same effect also He says by the prophet, " Many are the afflictions of the righteous." [10]   But I suppose that He refers to this entering not into temptation, when He speaks in the prophet's words of being delivered out of the afflictions.   For He adds, " The Lord will deliver him out of them all."   And this is just in accordance with the Saviour's word, whereby He promises that they will overcome their afflictions, and that they will participate in that victory which He has won for them.   For after saying, " In the world ye shall have tribulation," He added, " But be of good cheer, I have overcome the world."   And again, He taught them to pray that they might not fall into temptation, when He said, " And lead us not into temptation ; " which means, " Suffer us not to fall into temptation." And to show that this did not imply they should not be tempted, but really that they should be delivered from the evil, He added, " But deliver us from evil."   But perhaps you will say, What difference is there between being tempted, and falling or entering into temptation ?   Well, if one is overcome of evil — and he will be overcome unless he struggles against it himself, and unless God protects him with His shield — that man has entered into temptation, and is in it, and is brought under it like one that is led captive. But if one withstands and endures, that man is indeed tempted ; but he has not entered into temptation, or fallen under it.   Thus Jesus was led up of the Spirit, not indeed to enter into temptation, but " to be tempted of the devil." [11] And Abraham, again, did not enter into temptation, neither did God lead him into temptation, but He tempted (tried) him ; yet He did not drive him into temptation.   The Lord Himself, moreover, tempted (tried) the disciples.   And thus the wicked one, when he tempts us, draws us into the temptations, as dealing himself with the temptations of evil ; but God, when He tempts (tries), adduces the temptations as one untempted of evil.   For God, it is said, " cannot be tempted of evil." [12]   The devil, therefore, drives us on by violence, drawing us to destruction ; but God leads us by the hand, training us for our salvation.

---

1 κεκενωμένος.
2 [In these allegorical interpretations we see the pupil of Origen.]
3 Another fragment, connected with the preceding on Christ's prayer in Gethsemane.   Edited in a mutilated form, as given by Gallandi, in his *Bibliotheca*, xiv. p. 117, and here presented in its completeness, as found in the Vatican Codex 1611, f. 292, *b*.
4 Reading ἤ for ἡ.
5 1 John v. 19.
6 Ps. xc. 10.
7 Gen. iii. 17.

8 Gen. iii. 19.
9 John xvi. 33.
10 Ps. xxxiv. 19.
11 Matt. iv. 1.
12 Jas. i. 13.

V. — ON JOHN VIII. 12.[1]

Now this word "I am" expresses His eternal subsistence. For if He is the reflection of the eternal light, He must also be eternal Himself. For if the light subsists for ever, it is evident that the reflection also subsists for ever. And that this light subsists, is known only by its shining; neither can there be a light that does not give light. We come back, therefore, to our illustrations. If there is day, there is light; and if there is no such thing, the sun certainly cannot be present.[2] If, therefore, the sun had been eternal, there would also have been endless day. Now, however, as it is not so, the day begins when the sun rises, and it ends when the sun sets. But God is eternal light, having neither beginning nor end. And along with Him there is the reflection, also without beginning, and everlasting. The Father, then, being eternal, the Son is also eternal, being light of light; and if God is the light, Christ is the reflection; and if God is also a Spirit, as it is written, "God is a Spirit," Christ, again, is called analogously Spirit.[3]

VI. — OF THE ONE SUBSTANCE.[4]

The plant that springs from the root is something distinct from that whence it grows up; and yet it is of one nature with it. And the river which flows from the fountain is something distinct from the fountain. For we cannot call either the river a fountain, or the fountain a river. Nevertheless we allow that they are both one according to nature, and also one in substance; and we admit that the fountain may be

---

[1] A fragment. Edited from the Vatican Codex 1996, f. 78, belonging to a date somewhere about the tenth century.
[2] Reading πολλοῦ γε δεῖ. The text gives πόλυ γε δεῖ.
[3] ἀτμίς. If this strange reading ἀτμίς is correct, there is apparently a play intended on the two words πνεῦμα and ἀτμίς, = if God is a πνεῦμα, which word literally signifies Wind or Air, Christ, on that analogy, may be called ἀτμίς, that is to say, the Vapour or Breath of that Wind.
[4] That the Son is not different from the Father in nature, but connatural and consubstantial with Him. From the *Panoplia* of Euthymius Zigabenus in the Cod. xix. *Nanianæ Biblioth.*

conceived of as father, and that the river is what is begotten of the fountain.[5]

VII. — ON THE RECEPTION OF THE LAPSED TO PENITENCE.[6]

But now we are doing the opposite. For whereas Christ, who is the good *Shepherd*, goes in quest of one who wanders, lost among the mountains, and calls him back when he flees from Him, and is at pains to take him up on His shoulders when He has found him, we, on the contrary, harshly spurn such a one even when He approaches us. Yet let us not consult so miserably for ourselves, and let us not in this way be driving the sword against ourselves. For when people set themselves either to do evil or to do good to others, what they do is certainly not confined to the carrying out of their will on those others; but just as they attach themselves to iniquity or to goodness, they will themselves become possessed either by divine virtues or by unbridled passions. And the former will become the followers and comrades of the good angels; and both in this world and in the other, with the enjoyment of perfect peace and immunity from all ills, they will fulfil the most blessed destinies unto all eternity, and in God's fellowship they will be for ever (in possession of) the supremest good. But these latter will fall away at once from the peace of God and from peace with themselves, and both in this world and after death they will abide with the spirits of blood-guiltiness.[7] Wherefore let us not thrust from us those who seek a penitent return; but let us receive them gladly, and number them once more with the stedfast, and make up again what is defective in them.

---

[5] [See his explanations in the epistle to Dionysius, p. 92, *supra*.]
[6] A fragment, probably by the Alexandrian Dionysius. This seems to be an excerpt from his works *On Penitence*, three of which are mentioned by Jerome in his *De Script. Eccl.*, ch. 69. See Mai, *Classici Auctores*, x. 484. It is edited here from the Vatican Codex.
[7] τοῖς παλαμναίοις δαίμοσι. Or, with the demons of vengeance.

NOTE BY THE AMERICAN EDITOR.

FREQUENT references to *Gallandi*, whose collection I have been unable to inspect, the cost of the best edition being about two hundred dollars, makes it worth while to insert here, from a London book-catalogue, the following useful memoranda: " *Gallandii, Cong. Orat.* (Andr.) Bibliotheca Veterum Patrum Antiquorumque Scriptorum Ecclesiasticorum Græco-Latina; Opera silicet eorundum minora ac rariora usque ad xiii. Sæculum complexa, quorum clxxx. et amplius nec in Veteri Parisiensi, neque in postrema Lugdunensi edita sunt. Venet., 1765.

"The contents are given in Darling, col. 298–306. Of the three hundred and eighty-nine writers enumerated, it appears that nearly two hundred are not in the earlier collections.

"The contents of these great collections are, not the works of the Great Fathers, of whose writings separate editions have been published, but the works, often extensive and important, of those numerous Ecclesiastical writers whose works go, with the Greater Fathers referred to, to make up the sum of Church Patristic literature."

JULIUS AFRICANUS

INTRODUCTORY NOTICE

TO

JULIUS AFRICANUS.

[A.D. 200–232–245.] In a former volume, strengthened by a word from Archbishop Usher,[1] I have not hesitated to claim for Theophilus of Antioch a primary place among Christian chronologists. It is no detraction from the fame of our author to admit this, and truth requires it. But the great Alexandrian school must again come into view when we speak of any considerable achievements, among early Christian writers, in this important element of all biblical, in fact, all historical, science. Africanus was a pupil of Heraclas, and we must therefore date his pupilage in Alexandria before A.D. 232, when Dionysius succeeded Heraclas in the presidency of that school. It appears that in A.D. 226 he was performing some duty in behalf of Emmaus (Nicopolis) in Palestine; but Heraclas, who had acted subordinately as Origen's assistant as early as A.D. 218, could not have become the head of the school, even provisionally, till after Origen's unhappy ordination.[2] Let us assume the period of our author's attending the school under Heraclas to be between A.D. 228 and A.D. 232, however. We may then venture to reckon his birth as *circa* A.D. 200. And, if he became "bishop of Emmaus," it could hardly have been before the year 240, when he was of ripe age and experience. He adds additional lustre to the age of Gregory Thaumaturgus and Dionysius, as well as to that of their common mother in letters and theology, the already ancient academy of Pantænus and of Clement. His reviving credit in modern times has been largely due to the learned criticism of Dr. Routh, to whose edition of these Fragments the student must necessarily apply. Their chief interest arises from the important specimen which treats of the difficult question of the genealogies of our Lord cont......d in the evangelists. For a succinct statement of the points involved, and for a candid concession that they were not preserved to meet what modern curiosity would prefer to see established, I know of nothing more satisfactory than the commentary of Wordsworth,[3] from which I have borrowed almost wholly one of my elucidations.

The reader will remember the specimen of our author's critical judgment which is given with the works of Origen.[4] He differed with that great author, and the Church Catholic has sustained his judgment as just. I regret that the Edinburgh editors thought it necessary to make the *Letter to Origen concerning the Apocryphal Book of Susannah* a mere preface to Origen's answer. It might have been quoted there as a preface; but it is too important not to be included here, with the other fragments of his noble contributions to primitive Christian literature.

It does not clearly appear, from the Edinburgh edition, who the translator is; but here follows the

TRANSLATOR'S INTRODUCTORY NOTICE.

THE principal facts known to us in the life of Africanus are derived from himself and the *Chronicon* of Eusebius. He says of himself that he went to Alexandria on account of the fame

---

[1] Vol. ii. p. 87, this series.   [2] Vol. iv. p. 227.   [3] On St. Matt. i. 1–17.   [4] Vol. iv. p. 385.

of Heraclas. In the *Chronicon*, under the year 226, it is stated that "Nicopolis in Palestine, which formerly bore the name of Emmaus, was built, Africanus, the author of the *Chronology*, acting as ambassador on behalf of it, and having the charge of it." Dionysius Bar-Salibi speaks of Africanus as bishop of Emmaus.

Eusebius describes Africanus as being the author of a work called κεστοί.[1] Suidas says that this book detailed various kinds of cures, consisting of charms and written forms, and such like. Some have supposed that such a work is not likely to have been written by a Christian writer : they appeal also to the fact that no notice is taken of the κεστοί by Jerome in his notice of Africanus, nor by Rufinus in his translation of Eusebius. They therefore deem the clause in Eusebius an interpolation, and they suppose that two bore the name of Africanus, — one the author of the κεστοί, the other the Christian writer. Suidas identifies them, says that he was surnamed Sextus, and that he was a Libyan philosopher.

The works ascribed to Africanus, beside the *Cesti*, are the following : —

1. *Five Books of Chronology.* Photius[2] says of this work, that it was concise, but omitted nothing of importance. It began with the cosmogony of Moses, and went down to the advent of Christ. It summarized also the events from the time of Christ to the reign of the Emperor Macrinus.

2. A very famous letter to Aristides, in which he endeavoured to reconcile the apparent discrepancies in the genealogies of Christ given by Matthew and Luke.

3. A letter to Origen, in which he endeavoured to prove that the story of Susanna in Daniel was a forgery. A translation of this letter has been given with the *Works of Origen.*

The Acts of Symphorosa and her Seven Sons are attributed in the MSS. to Africanus ; but no ancient writer speaks of him as the author of this work.

---

[1] *Hist. Eccl.*, vi. 31.   [2] Cod. 34.

THE EXTANT WRITINGS OF JULIUS AFRICANUS.

I. — THE EPISTLE TO ARISTIDES.

I.

[AFRICANUS ON THE GENEALOGY IN THE HOLY GOSPELS.[1] — Some indeed incorrectly allege that this discrepant enumeration and mixing of the names both of priestly men, as they think, and royal, was made properly,[2] in order that Christ might be shown rightfully to be both Priest and King; as if any one disbelieved this, or had any other hope than this, that Christ is the High Priest of His Father, who presents our prayers to Him, and a supramundane King, who rules by the Spirit those whom He has delivered, a co-operator in the government of all things. And this is announced to us not by the catalogue of the tribes, nor by the mixing of the registered generations, but by the patriarchs and prophets. Let us not therefore descend to such religious trifling as to establish the kingship and priesthood of Christ by the interchanges of the names. For the priestly tribe of Levi, too, was allied with the kingly tribe of Juda, through the circumstance that Aaron married Elizabeth the sister of Naasson,[3] and that Eleazar again married the daughter of Phatiel,[4] and begat children. The evangelists, therefore, would thus have spoken falsely, affirming what was not truth, but a fictitious commendation. And for this reason the one traced the pedigree of Jacob the father of Joseph from David through Solomon; the other traced that of Heli also, though in a different way, the father of Joseph, from Nathan the son of David. And they ought not indeed to have been ignorant that both orders of the ancestors enumerated are the generation of David, the royal tribe of Juda.[5] For if Nathan was a prophet, so also was Solomon, and so too the father of both of them; and there were prophets belonging to many of the tribes, but priests belonging to none of the tribes, save the Levites only. To no purpose, then, is this fabrication of theirs. Nor shall an assertion of this kind prevail in the Church of Christ against the exact truth, so as that a lie should be con-trived for the praise and glory of Christ. For who does not know that most holy word of the apostle also, who, when he was preaching and proclaiming the resurrection of our Saviour, and confidently affirming the truth, said with great fear, " If any say that Christ is not risen, and we assert and have believed this, and both hope for and preach that very thing, we are false witnesses of God, in alleging that He raised up Christ, whom He raised not up?"[6] And if he who glorifies God the Father is thus afraid lest he should seem a false witness in narrating a mar-vellous fact, how should not he be justly afraid, who tries to establish the truth by a false state-ment, preparing an untrue opinion? For if the generations are different, and trace down no genuine seed to Joseph, and if all has been stated only with the view of establishing the position of Him who was to be born — to con-firm the truth, namely, that He who was to be would be king and priest, there being at the same time no proof given, but the dignity of the words being brought down to a feeble hymn, — it is evident that no praise accrues to God from that, since it is a falsehood, but rather judgment returns on him who asserts it, because he vaunts an unreality as though it were reality. Therefore, that we may expose the ignorance also of him who speaks thus, and prevent any one from stumbling at this folly, I shall set forth the true history of these matters.]

II.

For[7] whereas in Israel the names of their gen-erations were enumerated either according to nature or according to law, — according to nature,

---

[1] This letter, as given by Eusebius, is acephalous. A large por-tion of it is supplied by Cardinal Angelo Mai in the *Bibliotheca nova Patrum*, vol. iv. pp. 231 and 273. We enclose in brackets the parts wanting in Gallandi, who copied Eusebius (*Hist. Eccl.*, i. 7). On this celebrated letter of Africanus to Aristides, consult especially Eusebius (*Hist. Eccl.*, i. 7); also Jerome, comm. on Matt. i. 16; Augustine, *Retract.*, ii. 7; Photius, cod. xxxiv. p. 22; and in addi-tion to these, Zacharias Chrysopol. in *Bibl. P. P. Lugd.*, vol. xix. p. 751.
[2] δικαίως.
[3] Ex. vi. 23.
[4] Ex. vi. 25.
[5] [Heb. vii. 14.]
[6] 1 Cor. xv. 12, etc.
[7] Here what is given in Eusebius begins.

indeed, by the succession of legitimate offspring, and according to law whenever another raised up children to the name of a brother dying childless ; for because no clear hope of resurrection was yet given them, they had a representation of the future promise in a kind of mortal resurrection, with the view of perpetuating the name of one deceased ; — whereas, then, of those entered in this genealogy, some succeeded by legitimate descent as son to father, while others begotten in one family were introduced to another in name, mention is therefore made of both — of those who were progenitors in fact, and of those who were so only in name. Thus neither of the evangelists is in error, as the one reckons by nature and the other by law. For the several generations, viz., those descending from Solomon and those from Nathan, were so intermingled [1] by the raising up of children to the childless,[2] and by second marriages, and the raising up of seed, that the same persons are quite justly reckoned to belong at one time to the one, and at another to the other, i.e., to their reputed or to their actual fathers. And hence it is that both these accounts are true, and come down to Joseph, with considerable intricacy indeed, but yet quite accurately.

III.

But in order that what I have said may be made evident, I shall explain the interchange [3] of the generations. If we reckon the generations from David through Solomon, Matthan is found to be the third from the end, who begat Jacob the father of Joseph. But if, with Luke, we reckon them from Nathan the son of David, in like manner the third from the end is Melchi, whose son was Heli the father of Joseph. For Joseph was the son of Heli, the son of Melchi.[4] As Joseph, therefore, is the object proposed to us, we have to show how it is that each is represented as his father, both Jacob as descending from Solomon, and Heli as descending from Nathan : first, how these two, Jacob and Heli, were brothers ; and then also how the fathers of these, Matthan and Melchi, being of different families, are shown to be the grandfathers of Joseph. Well, then, Matthan and Melchi, having taken the same woman to wife in succession, begat children who were uterine brothers, as the law did not prevent a widow,[5] whether such by divorce or by the death

of her husband, from marrying another. By Estha, then — for such is her name according to tradition — Matthan first, the descendant of Solomon, begets Jacob ; and on Matthan's death, Melchi, who traces his descent back to Nathan, being of the same tribe but of another family, having married her, as has been already said, had a son Heli. Thus, then, we shall find Jacob and Heli uterine brothers, though of different families. And of these, the one Jacob having taken the wife of his brother Heli, who died childless, begat by her the third, Joseph — his son by nature and by account.[6] Whence also it is written, " And Jacob begat Joseph." But according to law he was the son of Heli, for Jacob his brother raised up seed to him. Wherefore also the genealogy deduced through him will not be made void, which the Evangelist Matthew in his enumeration gives thus : " And Jacob begat Joseph." But Luke, on the other hand, says, " Who was the son, as was supposed [7] (for this, too, he adds), of Joseph, the son of Heli, the son of Melchi." For it was not possible more distinctly to state the generation according to law ; and thus in this mode of generation he has entirely omitted the word " begat " to the very end, carrying back the genealogy by way of conclusion to Adam and to God.[8]

IV.

Nor indeed is this incapable of proof, neither is it a rash conjecture. For the kinsmen of the Saviour after the flesh, whether to magnify their own origin or simply to state the fact, but at all events speaking truth, have also handed down the following account : Some Idumean robbers attacking Ascalon, a city of Palestine, besides other spoils which they took from a temple of Apollo, which was built near the walls, carried off captive one Antipater, son of a certain Herod, a servant of the temple. And as the priest [9] was not able to pay the ransom for his son, Antipater was brought up in the customs of the Idumeans, and afterwards enjoyed the friendship of Hyrcanus, the high priest of Judea. And being sent on an embassy to Pompey on behalf of Hyrcanus, and having restored to him the kingdom which was being wasted by Aristobulus his brother, he was so fortunate as to obtain the title of pro-

---

[1] Reading συνεπεπλάκη. Migne would make it equivalent to " superimplexum est." Rufinus renders it, " Reconjunctum namque est sibi invicem genus, et illud per Salomonem et illud quod per Nathan deducitur," etc.

[2] ἀναστάσεσιν ἀτέκνων. Rufinus and Damascenus omit these words in their versions of the passage.

[3] The reading of the Codex Regius is ἀκολουθίαν, i.e., succession; the other leading MSS. give ἐπαλλαγήν, i.e., interchange or confusion.

[4] But in our text in Luke iii. 23, 24, and so, too, in the Vulgate, Matthat and Levi are inserted between Heli and Melchi. It may be that these two names were not found in the copy used by Africanus.

[5] Here Africanus applies the term " widow " (χηρεύουσαν) to one divorced as well as to one bereaved.

[6] κατὰ λόγον.

[7] Two things may be remarked here: first, that Africanus refers the phrase " as was supposed " not only to the words " son of Joseph," but also to those that follow, " the son of Heli ; " so that Christ would be the son of Joseph by legal adoption, just in the same way as Joseph was the son of Heli, which would lead to the absurd and impious conclusion that Christ was the son of Mary and a brother of Joseph married by her after the death of the latter. And second, that in the genealogy here assigned to Luke, Melchi holds the *third* place; whence it would seem either that Africanus's memory had failed him, or that as Bede conjectures in his copy of the Gospel Melchi stood in place of Matthat (Migne). [A probable solution.]

[8] Other MSS. read, " Adam the son of God."

[9] The word " priest " is used here perhaps improperly for " servant of the temple," i.e., ἱερεύς for ἱερόδουλος.

curator of Palestine.[1] And when Antipater was treacherously slain through envy of his great good fortune, his son Herod succeeded him, who was afterwards appointed king of Judea under Antony and Augustus by a decree of the senate. His sons were Herod and the other tetrarchs. These accounts are given also in the histories of the Greeks.[2]

V.

But as up to that time the genealogies of the Hebrews had been registered in the public archives, and those, too, which were traced back to the proselytes[3] — as, for example, to Achior the Ammanite, and Ruth the Moabitess, and those who left Egypt along with the Israelites, and intermarried with them — Herod, knowing that the lineage of the Israelites contributed nothing to him, and goaded by the consciousness of his ignoble birth, burned the registers of their families. This he did, thinking that he would appear to be of noble birth, if no one else could trace back his descent by the public register to the patriarchs or proselytes, and to that mixed race called *georæ*.[4] A few, however, of the studious, having private records of their own, either by remembering the names or by getting at them

in some other way from the archives, pride themselves in preserving the memory of their noble descent ; and among these happen to be those already mentioned, called *desposyni*,[5] on account of their connection with the family of the Saviour. And these coming from Nazara and Cochaba, Judean villages, to other parts of the country, set forth the above-named genealogy[6] as accurately as possible from the Book of Days.[7] Whether, then, the case stand thus or not, no one could discover a more obvious explanation, according to my own opinion and that of any sound judge. And let this suffice us for the matter, although it is not supported by testimony, because we have nothing more satisfactory or true to allege upon it. The Gospel, however, in any case states the truth.

VI.

Matthan, descended from Solomon, begat Jacob. Matthan dying, Melchi, descended from Nathan, begat Heli by the same wife. Therefore Heli and Jacob are uterine brothers. Heli dying childless, Jacob raised up seed to him and begat Joseph, his own son by nature, but the son of Heli by law. Thus Joseph was the son of both.[8]

---

[1] So Josephus styles him " procurator of Judea, and viceroy " (ἐπιμελητὴς τῆς Ἰουδαίας, and ἐπίτροπος).
[2] This whole story about Antipater is fictitious. Antipater's father was not Herod, a servant in the temple of Apollo, but Antipater an Idumean, as we learn from Josephus (xiv. 2). This Antipater was made prefect of Idumea by Alexander king of the Jews, and laid the foundation of the power to which his descendants rose. He acquired great wealth, and was on terms of friendship with Ascalon, Gaza, and the Arabians.
[3] Several MSS. read ἀρχιπροσηλύτων for ἄχρι προσηλύτων, whence some conjecture that the correct reading should be ἄχρι τῶν ἀρχιπροσηλύτων, i.e., back to the " chief proselytes," — these being, as it were, patriarchs among the proselytes, like Achior, and those who joined the Israelites on their flight from Egypt.
[4] This word occurs in the Septuagint version of Ex. xii. 19, and refers to the *strangers* who left Egypt along with the Israelites. For Israel was accompanied by a mixed body, consisting on the one hand of native Egyptians, who are named αὐτόχθονες in that passage of Exodus, and by the resident aliens, who are called γειῶραι. Justin Martyr has the form γηόραν in *Dialogue with Trypho*, ch. cxxii. The root of the term is evidently the Hebrew גֵּר, " stranger."

[5] The word δεσπόσυνοι was employed to indicate the Lord's relatives, as being His according to the flesh. The term means literally, " those who belong to a master," and thence it was used also to signify " one's heirs."
[6] προειρημένην. Nicephorus reads προκειμένην.
[7] ἐκ τε τῆς βίβλου τῶν ἡμερῶν. By this " Book of Days " Africanus understands those " day-books " which he has named, a little before this, ἰδιωτικὰς ἀπογραφάς. For among the Jews, most persons setting a high value on their lineage were in the habit of keeping by them private records of their descent copied from the public archives, as we see it done also by nobles among ourselves. Besides, by the insertion of the particle τε, which is found in all our codices, and also in Nicephorus, it appears that something is wanting in this passage. Wherefore it seems necessary to supply these words, καὶ ἀπὸ μνήμης ἐς ὅσον ἐξικνοῦντο, " and from memory," etc. Thus at least Rufinus seems to have read the passage, for he renders it: Ordinem supradictæ generationis partim memoriter, partim etiam ex dierum libris, in quantum erat possibile, perdocebant (Migne).
[8] [Elucidation I.]

II. — NARRATIVE OF EVENTS HAPPENING IN PERSIA ON THE BIRTH OF CHRIST.[1]

The best introduction to this production will be the following preface, as given in Migne : — Many men of learning thus far have been of opinion that the narrative by Africanus of events happening in Persia on Christ's birth,[2] is a fragment of that famous work which Sextus Julius Africanus, a Christian author of the third century after Christ, composed on the history of the world in the chronological order of events up to the reign of Macrinus, and presented in five books to Alexander, son of Mammæa, with the view of obtaining the restoration of his native town Emmaus. With the same expectation which I see incited Lambecius and his compendiator Nesselius, I, too, set myself with the greatest eagerness to go over the codices of our Electoral Library. . . . But, as the common proverb goes, I found coals instead of treasure. This narrative, so far from its being to be ascribed to a writer well reputed by the common voice of

---

[1] Edited from two Munich codices by J. Chr. von Aretin, in his *Beiträge zur Geschichte und Literatur*, anno 1804, p. ii. p. 49. [I place this apocryphal fragment here as a mere appendix to the Genealogical Argument. An absurd appendix, indeed.]
[2] Which is extant in two MSS. in the Electoral Library of Munich, and in one belonging to the Imperial Library of Vienna.

antiquity, does not contain anything worthy of the genius of the chronographer Africanus. Wherefore, since by the unanimous testimony of the ancients he was a man of consummate learning and sharpest judgment, while the author of the *Cesti*, which also puts forward the name of Africanus, has been long marked by critics with the character either of anile credulity, or of a marvellous propensity to superstitious fancies, I can readily fall in with the opinion of those who think that he is a different person from the chronographer, and would ascribe this wretched production also to him. But, dear reader, on perusing these pages, if your indignation is not stirred against the man's rashness, you will at least join with me in laughing at his prodigious follies, and will learn, at the same time, that the testimonies of men most distinguished for learning are not to be rated so highly as to supersede personal examination when opportunity permits.

EVENTS IN PERSIA:

ON THE INCARNATION OF OUR LORD AND GOD AND SAVIOUR JESUS CHRIST.

Christ first of all became known from Persia. For nothing escapes the learned jurists of that country, who investigate all things with the utmost care. The facts,[1] therefore, which are inscribed upon the golden plates,[2] and laid up in the royal temples, I shall record; for it is from the temples there, and the priests connected with them, that the name of Christ has been heard of. Now there is a temple there to Juno, surpassing even the royal palace, which temple Cyrus, that prince instructed in all piety, built, and in which he dedicated in honour of the gods golden and silver statues, and adorned them with precious stones, — that I may not waste words in a profuse description of that ornamentation. Now about that time (as the records on the plates testify), the king having entered the temple, with the view of getting an interpretation of certain dreams, was addressed by the priest Prupupius thus: I congratulate thee, master: Juno has conceived. And the king, smiling, said to him, Has she who is dead conceived? And he said, Yes, she who was dead has come to life again, and begets life. And the king said, What is this? explain it to me. And he replied, In truth, master, the time for these things is at hand. For during the whole night the images, both of gods and goddesses, continued beating the-ground, saying to each other, Come, let us congratulate Juno. And they say to me, Prophet, come forward; congratulate Juno, for she has been embraced. And I said, How can she be embraced who no longer exists? To which they reply, She has come to life again, and is no longer called Juno,[3] but Urania. For the mighty Sol has embraced her. Then the goddesses say to the gods, mak-

ing the matter plainer, *Pege*[4] is she who is embraced; for did not Juno espouse an artificer? And the gods say, That she is rightly called *Pege*, we admit. Her name, moreover, is *Myria;* for she bears in her womb, as in the deep, a vessel of a myriad talents' burden. And as to this title Pege, let it be understood thus : This stream of water sends forth the perennial stream of spirit, — a stream containing but a single fish,[5] taken with the hook of Divinity, and sustaining the whole world with its flesh as though it were in the sea. You have well said, She has an artificer [in espousal] ; but by that espousal she does not bear an artificer on an equality with herself. For this artificer who is born, the son of the chief artificer, framed by his excellent skill the roof of the third heavens, and established by his word this lower world, with its threefold sphere[6] of habitation.

Thus, then, the statues disputed with each other concerning Juno and Pege, and [at length] with one voice they said : When the day is finished, we all, gods and goddesses, shall know the matter clearly. Now, therefore, master, tarry for the rest of the day. For the matter shall certainly come to pass. For that which emerges is no common affair.

And when the king abode there and watched the statues, the harpers of their own accord began to strike their harps, and the muses to sing ; and whatsoever creatures were within, whether quadruped or fowl, in silver and gold, uttered their several voices. And as the king shuddered, and was filled with great fear, he was about to retire. For he could not endure the spontaneous tumult. The priest therefore said to him, Remain, O king, for the full revelation is at hand which the God of gods has chosen to declare to us.

And when these things were said, the roof was opened, and a bright star descended and

---

[1] The MSS. read γάρ, for.
[2] The term in the original (ἀλκλαρίαις) is one altogether foreign to Greek, and seems to be of Arabic origin. The sense, however, is evident from the use of synonymous terms in the context.
[3] There is a play upon the words, perhaps, in the original. The Greek term for Juno (Ἥρα) may be derived from ἔρα, *terra*, so that the antithesis intended is, "She is no longer called *Earthly*, but *Heavenly*."

[4] i.e., Fountain, Spring, or Stream.
[5] The initial letters of the Greek Ἰησοῦς Χριστὸς Θεοῦ Υἱὸς Σωτήρ, i.e., " Jesus Christ the Son of God the Saviour," when joined together, make the word ιχθυς, i.e., fish; and the fathers used the word, therefore, as a mystic symbol of Christ, who could live in the depth of our mortality as in the abyss of the sea. [Vol. ii. p. 297.]
[6] i.e., as sea, land, and sky.

stood above the pillar of Pege, and a voice was heard to this effect: Sovereign Pege, the mighty Son has sent me to make the announcement to you, and at the same time to do you service in parturition, designing blameless nuptials with you, O mother of the chief of all ranks of being, bride of the triune Deity. And the child begotten by extraordinary generation is called the *Beginning* and the *End*, — the beginning of salvation, and the end of perdition.

And when this word was spoken, all the statues fell upon their faces, that of Pege alone standing, on which also a royal diadem was found placed, having on its upper side a star set in a carbuncle and an emerald. And on its lower side the star rested.

And the king forthwith gave orders to bring in all the interpreters of prodigies, and the sages who were under his dominion. And when all the heralds sped with their proclamations, all these assembled in the temple. And when they saw the star above Pege, and the diadem with the star and the stone, and the statues lying on the floor, they said: O king, a root (offspring) divine and princely has risen, bearing the image of the King of heaven and earth. For Pege-Myria is the daughter of the Bethlehemite Pege. And the diadem is the mark of a king, and the star is a celestial announcement of portents to fall on the earth. Out of Judah has arisen a kingdom which shall subvert all the memorials of the Jews. And the prostration of the gods upon the floor prefigured the end of their honour. For he who comes, being of more ancient dignity, shall displace all the recent. Now therefore, O king, send to Jerusalem. For you will find the Christ of the Omnipotent God borne in bodily form in the bodily arms of a woman. And the star remained above the statue of Pege, called the Celestial, until the wise men came forth, and then it went with them.

And then, in the depth of evening, Dionysus appeared in the temple, unaccompanied by the Satyrs, and said to the images: Pege is not one of us, but stands far above us, in that she gives birth to a man whose conception is in divine fashion.[1] O priest Prupupius! what dost thou tarrying here? An action, indicated in writings of old,[2] has come upon us, and we shall be convicted as false by a person of power and energy.[3] Wherein we have been deceivers, we have been deceivers; and wherein we have ruled, we have ruled. No longer give we oracular responses. Gone from us is our honour. Without glory and reward are we become. There is One, and One only, who receives again at the hands of all His proper honour. For the rest,

be not disturbed.[4] No longer shall the Persians exact tribute of earth and sky. For He who established these things is at hand, to bring practical tribute[5] to Him who sent Him, to renew the ancient image, and to put image with image, and bring the dissimilar to similarity. Heaven rejoices with earth, and earth itself exults at receiving matter of exultation from heaven. Things which have not happened above, have happened on earth beneath. He whom the order of the blessed has not seen, is seen by the order of the miserable. Flame threatens those; dew attends these. To Myria is given the blessed lot of bearing Pege in Bethlehem, and of conceiving grace of grace. Judæa has seen its bloom, and this country is fading. To Gentiles and aliens, salvation is come; to the wretched, relief is ministered abundantly. With right do women dance, and say, Lady Pege, Spring-bearer, thou mother of the heavenly constellation. Thou cloud that bringest us dew after heat, remember thy dependants, O mistress.

The king then, without delay, sent some of the Magi under his dominion with gifts, the star showing them the way. And when they returned, they narrated to the men of that time those same things which were also written on the plates of gold, and which were to the following effect: —

When we came to Jerusalem, the sign, together with our arrival, roused all the people. How is this, say they, that wise men of the Persians are here, and that along with them there is this strange stellar phenomenon? And the chief of the Jews interrogated us in this way: What is this that attends you,[6] and with what purpose are you here? And we said: He whom ye call Messias is born. And they were confounded, and dared not withstand us. But they said to us, By the justice of Heaven, tell us what ye know of this matter. And we made answer to them: Ye labour under unbelief; and neither without an oath nor with an oath do ye believe us, but ye follow your own heedless counsel. For the Christ, the Son of the Most High, is born, and He is the subverter of your law and synagogues. And therefore is it that, struck with this most excellent response as with a dart,[7] ye hear in bitterness this name which has come upon you suddenly. And they then, taking counsel together, urged us to accept their gifts, and tell to none that such an event had taken place in that land of theirs, lest, as they say, *a revolt rise against us*. But we replied: We have brought gifts in His honour, with the view of proclaiming those mighty things which we know to have happened in our country on occasion of His birth; and do ye bid us take your bribes, and conceal

---

[1] θείας τύχης σύλλημμα.
[2] ἔγγραφος.
[3] ἐμπράκτου.

[4] The text gives θροβαδεῖ, for which Migne proposes θορύβηθι.
[5] πρακτικοὺς φόρους.
[6] τί τὸ ἐπόμενον, perhaps meant for, What business brings you?
[7] ὑπὲρ μαντείας ἀρίστης ὥσπερ κατατοξευόμενοι.

the things which have been communicated to us by the Divinity who is above the heavens, and neglect the commandments of our proper King? And after urging many considerations on us, they gave the matter up. And when the king of Judæa sent for us and had some converse with us, and put to us certain questions as to the statements we made to him, we acted in the same manner, until he was thoroughly enraged at our replies. We left him accordingly, without giving any greater heed to him than to any common person.

And we came to that place then to which we were sent, and saw the mother and the child, the star indicating to us the royal babe. And we said to the mother: What art thou named, O renowned mother? And she says: Mary, masters. And we said to her: Whence art thou sprung?[1] And she replies: From this district of the Bethlehemites.[2] Then said we: Hast thou not had a husband? And she answers: I was only betrothed with a view to the marriage covenant, my thoughts being far removed from this. For I had no mind to come to this. And while I was giving very little concern to it, when a certain Sabbath dawned, and straightway at the rising of the sun, an angel appeared to me bringing me suddenly the glad tidings of a son. And in trouble I cried out, Be it not so to me, Lord, for I have not a husband. And he persuaded me to believe, that by the will of God I should have this son.

Then said we to her: Mother, mother, all the gods of the Persians have called thee blessed. Thy glory is great; for thou art exalted above all women of renown, and thou art shown to be more queenly than all queens.

The child, moreover, was seated on the ground, being, as she said, in His second year, and having in part the likeness of His mother. And she had long hands,[3] and a body somewhat delicate; and her colour was like that of ripe wheat;[4] and she was of a round face, and had her hair bound up. And as we had along with us a servant skilled in painting from the life, we brought with us to our country a likeness of them both; and it was placed by our hand in the sacred[5] temple, with this inscription on it: To Jove the Sun, the mighty God, the King of Jesus, the power of Persia dedicated this.

And taking the child up, each of us in turn, and bearing Him in our arms, we saluted Him and worshipped Him, and presented to Him gold, and myrrh, and frankincense, addressing Him thus: We gift Thee with Thine own, O Jesus, Ruler of heaven. Ill would things unordered be ordered, wert Thou not at hand. In no other way could things heavenly be brought into conjunction with things earthly, but by Thy descent. Such service cannot be discharged, if only the servant is sent us, as when the Master Himself is present; neither can so much be achieved when the king sends only his satraps to war, as when the king is there himself. It became the wisdom of Thy system, that Thou shouldst deal in this manner with men.[6]

And the child leaped and laughed at our caresses and words. And when we had bidden the mother farewell,[7] and when she had shown us honour, and we had testified to her the reverence which became us, we came again to the place in which we lodged. And at eventide there appeared to us one of a terrible and fearful countenance, saying: Get ye out quickly, lest ye be taken in a snare. And we in terror said: And who is he, O divine leader, that plotteth against so august an embassage? And he replied: Herod; but get you up straightway and depart in safety and peace.

And we made speed to depart thence in all earnestness; and we reported in Jerusalem all that we had seen. Behold, then, the great things that we have told you regarding Christ; and we saw Christ our Saviour, who was made known as both God and man. To Him be the glory and the power unto the ages of the ages. Amen.

---

1 ὁρμωμένη.
2 Βηθλεωτῶν.
3 μακρὰς τὰς χεῖρας according to Migne, instead of the reading of the manuscript, μακρὶν τὴν κῆραν ἐχουσα.
4 σιτόχροος.

5 διοπετεῖ.
6 The manuscripts give ἀντάρτας, for which Migne proposes ἀνθρώπους or αντεργάτας. [Unworthy, wholly so, of our author. This curious specimen of the *romances* of antiquity might better have found its place with other *Protevangelia* in vol. viii., this series.]
7 συνταξάμενοι.

III. — THE EXTANT FRAGMENTS OF THE FIVE BOOKS OF THE CHRONOGRAPHY OF JULIUS AFRICANUS.

I.[1]

On the Mythical Chronology of the Egyptians and Chaldeans.

The Egyptians, indeed, with their boastful notions of their own antiquity, have put forth a sort of account of it by the hand of their astrologers in cycles and myriads of years; which some of those who have had the repute of studying such subjects profoundly have in a summary way called lunar years; and inclining no less than others to the mythical, *they think they* fall in with the eight or nine thousands of years which the Egyptian priests in Plato falsely reckon up to Solon.[2]

---

1 In Georgius Syncellus, *Chron.*, p. 17, ed. Paris, 14 Venet.

2 The text is: . . . συμπίπτουσι ταῖς ὀκτὼ καὶ ἐννέα χιλιάσιν ἐτῶν, ἃς Αἰγυπτίων οἱ παρὰ Πλάτωνι ἱερεῖς εἰς Σόλωνα καταριθμοῦντες οὐκ ἀληθεύουσι.

(And after some other matter:)

For why should I speak of the three myriad years of the Phœnicians, or of the follies of the Chaldeans, their forty-eight myriads? For the Jews, deriving their origin from them as descendants of Abraham, having been taught a modest mind, and one such as becomes men, together with the truth by the spirit of Moses, have handed down to us, by their extant Hebrew histories, the number of 5500 years as the period up to the advent of the Word of salvation, that was announced to the world in the time of the sway of the Cæsars.

II.[1]

When men multiplied on the earth, the angels of heaven came together with the daughters of men. In some copies I found "the sons of God." What is meant by the Spirit, in my opinion, is that the descendants of Seth are called the sons of God on account of the righteous men and patriarchs who have sprung from him, even down to the Saviour Himself; but that the descendants of Cain are named the seed of men, as having nothing divine in them, on account of the wickedness of their race and the inequality of their nature, being a mixed people, and having stirred the indignation of God.[2] But if it is thought that these refer to angels, we must take them to be those who deal with magic and jugglery, who taught the women the motions of the stars and the knowledge of things celestial, by whose power they conceived the giants as their children, by whom wickedness came to its height on the earth, until God decreed that the whole race of the living should perish in their impiety by the deluge.

III.[3]

Adam, when 230 years old, begets Seth; and after living other 700 years he died, that is, a second death.

Seth, when 205 years old, begat Enos; from Adam therefore to the birth of Enos there are 435 years in all.

Enos, when 190 years old, begets Cainan.

Cainan again, when 170 years old, begets Malaleel;

And Malaleel, when 165 years old; begets Jared;

And Jared, when 162 years old, begets Enoch;

And Enoch, when 165 years old, begets Mathusala; and having pleased God, after a life of other 200 years, he was not found.

Mathusala, when 187 years old, begat Lamech.

Lamech, when 188 years old, begets Noe.

IV.[4]

On the Deluge.

God decreed to destroy the whole race of the living by a flood, having threatened that men should not survive beyond 120 years. Nor let it be deemed a matter of difficulty, because some lived afterwards a longer period than that. For the space of time meant was 100 years up to the flood in the case of the sinners of that time; for they were 20 years old. God instructed Noe, who pleased him on account of his righteous-ness, to prepare an ark; and when it was finished, there entered it Noe himself and his sons, his wife and his daughters-in-law, and firstlings of every living creature, with a view to the duration of the race. And Noe was 600 years old when the flood came on. And when the water abated, the ark settled on the mountains of Ararat, which we know to be in Parthia;[5] but some say that they are at Celænæ[6] of Phrygia, and I have seen both places. And the flood prevailed for a year, and then the earth became dry. And they came out of the ark in pairs, as may be found, and not in the manner in which they had entered, viz., distinguished according to their species, and were blessed by God. And each of these things indicates something useful to us.

V.[7]

Noe was 600 years old when the flood came on. From Adam, therefore, to Noe and the flood, are 2262 years.

VI.[8]

And after the flood, Sem begat Arphaxad.

Arphaxad, when 135 years old, begets Sala in the year 2397.

Sala, when 130 years old, begets Heber in the year 2527.

Heber, when 134 years old, begets Phalec in the year 2661, so called because the earth was divided in his days.

Phalec, when 130 years old, begat Ragan, and after living other 209 years died.

VII.[9]

In the year of the world 3277, Abraham entered the promised land of Canaan.

VIII.[10]

Of Abraham.

From this rises the appellation of the *Hebrews*. For the word *Hebrews* is interpreted to mean

---

[1] In Georgius Syncellus, *Chron.*, p. 19, al. 15.
[2] The text here is manifestly corrupt: ἐπιμιχθέντων αὐτῶν, τὴν ἀγανάκτησιν ποιήσασθαι τὸν Θεόν.
[3] In Georgius Syncellus, *Chron.*, p. 81, al. 65.
[4] In Georgius Syncellus, *Chron.*, p. 21, al. 17.
[5] That is, in Armenia.
[6] For there was a hill Ararat in Phrygia, from which the Marsyas issued, and the ark was declared to have rested there by the Sibylline oracles. [But see vol. v. p. 149.]
[7] In Georgius Syncellus, *Chron.*, p. 83, al. 67.
[8] In the same, p. 86, al. 68.
[9] In the same, p. 93, al. 74. [Compare vol. v. p. 148.]
[10] In the same, p. 99, al. 79. [עָבַר is the verb.]

those who migrate across, viz., who crossed the Euphrates with Abraham ; and it is not derived, as some think, from the fore-mentioned Heber. From the flood and Noe, therefore, to Abraham's entrance into the promised land, there are in all 1015 years ; and from Adam, in 20 generations, 3277 years.

IX.[1]

Of Abraham and Lot.

When a famine pressed the land of Canaan, Abraham came down to Egypt ; and fearing lest he should be put out of the way on account of the beauty of his wife, he pretended that he was her brother. But Pharaoh took her to himself when she was commended to him ; for this is the name the Egyptians give their kings. And he was punished by God ; and Abraham, along with all pertaining to him, was dismissed enriched. In Canaan, Abraham's shepherds and Lot's contended with each other ; and with mutual consent they separated, Lot choosing to dwell in Sodom on account of the fertility and beauty of the land, which had five cities, Sodom, Gomorrah, Adama, Seboim, Segor, and as many kings. On these their neighbours the four Syrian kings made war, whose leader was Chodollogomo king of Ælam. And they met by the Salt Sea, which is now called the Dead Sea. In it I have seen very many wonderful things. For that water sustains no living thing, and dead bodies are carried beneath its depths, while the living do not readily even dip under it. Lighted torches are borne upon it, but when extinguished they sink. And there are the springs of bitumen ; and it yields alum and salt a little different from the common kinds, for they are pungent and transparent. And wherever fruit is found about it, it is found full of a thick, foul smoke. And the water acts as a cure to those who use it, and it is drained in a manner contrary to any other water.[2] And if it had not the river Jordan feeding it like a shell,[3] and to a great extent withstanding its tendency, it would have failed more rapidly than appears. There is also by it a great quantity of the balsam plant ; but it is supposed to have been destroyed by God on account of the impiety of the neighbouring people.

X.[4]

Of the Patriarch Jacob.

1. The shepherd's tent belonging to Jacob, which was preserved at Edessa to the time of Antonine Emperor of the Romans, was destroyed by a thunderbolt.[5]

2. Jacob, being displeased at what had been done by Symeon and Levi at Shecem against the people of the country, on account of the violation of their sister, buried at Shecem the gods which he had with him near a rock under the wonderful terebinth,[6] which up to this day is reverenced by the neighbouring people in honour of the patriarchs, and removed thence to Bethel. By the trunk of this terebinth there was an altar on which the inhabitants of the country offered *ectenæ*[7] in their general assemblies ; and though it seemed to be burned, it was not consumed. Near it is the tomb of Abraham and Isaac. And some say that the staff of one of the angels who were entertained by Abraham was planted there.

XI.[8]

From Adam, therefore, to the death of Joseph, according to this book, are 23 generations, and 3563 years.

XII.[9]

From this record,[10] therefore, we affirm that Ogygus,[11] from whom the first flood (in Attica) derived its name,[12] and who was saved when many perished, lived at the time of the exodus of the people from Egypt along with Moses.[13] (*After a break*) : And after Ogygus, on account of the vast destruction caused by the flood, the present land of Attica remained without a king till the time of Cecrops, 189 years.[14] Philochorus, however, affirms that Ogygus, Actæus, or whatever other fictitious name is adduced, never existed. (*After another break*) : From Ogygus to Cyrus, as from Moses to his time, are 1235 years.

XIII.[15]

1. Up to the time of the Olympiads there is no certain history among the Greeks, all things before that date being confused, and in no way consistent with each other. But these *Olympiads*

---

6 On this terebinth, see Scaliger (*ad Græca Euseb.*, p. 414); Franciscus Quaresimus, in *Elucid. terræ sanctæ ;* Eugenius Rogerius, etc.; and also Valesius, *ad Euseb. De Vit. Constant.,* iii. 53, notes 3 and 5.
7 Scaliger acknowledges himself ignorant of this word ἐκτενάς. In the Eastern Church it is used to denote protracted prayers (*preces protensiores*) offered by the deacon on behalf of all classes of men, and the various necessities of human life. See Suicer, *sub voce.* Allatius thinks the text corrupt, and would read, ἐφ᾽ ὃν τά τε ὁλοκαυτώματα καὶ τὰς ἑκατόμβας ἀνεφερον = on which they offered both holocausts and hecatombs. [Littledale, *Eastern Offices,* p. 253.]
8 In Georgius Syncellus, *Chron.,* p. 106, al. 85
9 In the same, p. 148, al. 118, from the Third Book of the *Chron.* of Africanus.
10 συντάγματος.
11 Others write Ogyges. Josephus (*in Apionem*), Euseb. (*de Præpar.*). Tatian [vol. ii. p. 81], Clemens [not so, vol. ii. p. 324], and others, write Ogygus.
12 The text is, ὃς τοῦ πρώτου κατακλυσμοῦ γεγονεν ἐπώνυμος. The word ἐπώνυμος is susceptible of two meanings, either "taking the name from" or "giving the name to." Ὠγυγια κακα was a proverbial expression for primeval ills.
13 The text is here, κατὰ τὴν Αἴγυπτον τοῦ λαοῦ μετὰ Μωυσέως ἐξϊδον γενεσθαι, for which we may read κατὰ τὴν ἐξ Αἴγυπτον, etc.
14 Ὠγυγον Ἀκταίον ἤ τὰ πλασσόμενα τῶν ὀνομάτων. Compare xiii. 6, where we have τὸν γὰρ μετὰ Ὠγυγον Ἀκταίον, etc.
15 From Georgius Syncellus, *Chron.,* Third Book. In Euseb., *Præpar.,* x. 40. [Compare vol. ii. pp. 324-334.]

---

1 In Georgius Syncellus, *Chron.,* p. 100, al. 80.
2 ληγει τε παντὶ ὕδατι πάσχων ταἐναντια.
3 ὡς πορθήσαν.
4 In Georgius Syncellus, *Chron.,* p. 107, al. 86.
5 Heliogabalus is probably intended, in whose time Africanus flourished. At least so thinks Syncellus.

were thoroughly investigated[1] by many, as the Greeks made up the records of their history not according to long spaces, but in periods of four years. For which reason I shall select the most remarkable of the mythical narratives before the time of the first Olympiad, and rapidly run over them. But those after that period, at least those that are notable, I shall take together, Hebrew events in connection with Greek, according to their dates, examining carefully the affairs of the Hebrews, and touching more cursorily on those of the Greeks; and my plan will be as follows: Taking up some single event in Hebrew history synchronous with another in Greek history, and keeping by it as the main subject, subtracting or adding as may seem needful in the narrative, I shall note what Greek or Persian of note, or remarkable personage of any other nationality, flourished at the date of that event in Hebrew history; and thus I may perhaps attain the object which I propose to myself.

2. The most famous exile that befell the Hebrews, then — to wit, when they were led captive by Nabuchodonosor king of Babylon — lasted 70 years, as Jeremias had prophesied. Berosus the Babylonian, moreover, makes mention of Nabuchodonosor. And after the 70 years of captivity, Cyrus became king of the Persians at the time of the 55th Olympiad, as may be ascertained from the *Bibliothecæ* of Diodorus and the histories of Thallus and Castor, and also from Polybius and Phlegon, and others besides these, who have made the Olympiads a subject of study. For the date is a matter of agreement among them all. And Cyrus then, in the first year of his reign, which was the first year of the 55th Olympiad, effected the first partial restoration of the people by the hand of Zorobabel, with whom also was Jesus the son of Josedec, since the period of 70 years was now fulfilled, as is narrated in Esdra the Hebrew historian. The narratives of the beginning of the sovereignty of Cyrus and the end of the captivity accordingly coincide. And thus, according to the reckoning of the Olympiads, there will be found a like harmony of events even to our time. And by following this, we shall also make the other narratives fit in with each other in the same manner.

3. But if the Attic time-reckoning is taken as the standard for affairs prior to these, then from Ogygus, who was believed by them to be an autochthon, in whose time also the first great flood took place in Attica, while Phoroneus reigned over the Argives, as Acusilaus relates, up to the date of the first Olympiad, from which period the Greeks thought they could fix dates accurately, there are altogether 1020 years; which number

both coincides with the above-mentioned, and will be established by what follows. For these things are also recorded by the Athenian[2] historians Hellanicus and Philochorus, who record Attic affairs; and by Castor and Thallus, who record Syrian affairs; and by Diodorus, who writes a universal history in his *Bibliothecæ*; and by Alexander Polyhistor, and by some of our own time, yet more carefully, and[3] by all the Attic writers. Whatever narrative of note, therefore, meets us in these 1020 years, shall be given in its proper place.

4. In accordance with this writing, therefore, we affirm that Ogygus, who gave his name to the first flood, and was saved when many perished, lived at the time of the exodus of the people from Egypt along with Moses.[4] And this we make out in the following manner. From Ogygus up to the first Olympiad already mentioned, it will be shown that there are 1020 years; and from the first Olympiad to the first year of the 55th, that is the first year of King Cyrus, which was also the end of the captivity, are 217 years. From Ogygus, therefore, to Cyrus are 1237. And if one carries the calculation backwards from the end of the captivity, there are 1237 years. Thus, by analysis, the same period is found to the first year of the exodus of Israel under Moses from Egypt, as from the 55th Olympiad to Ogygus, who founded Eleusis. And from this point we get a more notable beginning for Attic chronography.

5. So much, then, for the period prior to Ogygus. And at his time Moses left Egypt. And we demonstrate in the following manner how reliable is the statement that this happened at that date. From the exodus of Moses up to Cyrus, who reigned after the captivity, are 1237 years. For the remaining years of Moses are 40. The years of Jesus, who led the people after him, are 25; those of the elders, who were judges after Jesus, are 30; those of the judges, whose history is given in the book of Judges, are 490; those of the priests Eli and Samuel are 90; those of the successive kings of the Hebrews are 490. *Then come the 70 years of the captivity,*[5] the last year of which was the first year of the reign of Cyrus, as we have already said.

6. And from Moses, then, to the first Olympiad there are 1020 years, as to the first year of the 55th Olympiad from the same are 1237, in which enumeration the reckoning of the Greeks coincides with us. And after Ogygus, by reason

---

[2] There is a difficulty in the text: Viger omits "Athenian."
[3] The Latin translator expunges the "and" (καὶ), and makes it = more careful *than* all the Attic writers.
[4] The original here, as in the same passage above, is corrupt. It gives κατὰ τὴν Αἰγύπτον, which Migne would either omit entirely or replace by ἀπ' Αἰγύπτου.
[5] These words are inserted according to Viger's proposal, as there is a manifest omission in the text.

of the vast destruction caused by the flood, the present land of Attica remained without a king up to Cecrops, a period of 189 years. For Philochorus asserts that the Actæus who is said to have succeeded Ogygus, or whatever other fictitious names are adduced, never existed. *And again :* From Ogygus, therefore, to Cyrus, *says he*, the same period is reckoned as from Moses to the same date, viz., 1237 years ; and some of the Greeks also record that Moses lived at that same time. Polemo, for instance, in the first book of his *Greek History*, says : In the time of Apis, son of Phoroneus, a division of the army of the Egyptians left Egypt, and settled in the Palestine called Syrian, not far from Arabia : these are evidently those who were with Moses. And Apion the son of Poseidonius, the most laborious of grammarians, in his book *Against the Jews*, and in the fourth book of his *History*, says that in the time of Inachus king of Argos, when Amosis reigned over Egypt, the Jews revolted under the leadership of Moses. And Herodotus also makes mention of this revolt, and of Amosis, in his second book, and in a certain way also of the Jews themselves, reckoning them among the circumcised, and calling them the Assyrians of Palestine, perhaps through Abraham. And Ptolemy the Mendesian, who narrates the history of the Egyptians from the earliest times, gives the same account of all these things ; so that among them in general there is no difference worth notice in the chronology.

7. It should be observed, further, that all the legendary accounts which are deemed specially remarkable by the Greeks by reason of their antiquity, are found to belong to a period posterior to Moses ; such as their floods and conflagrations, Prometheus, Io, Europa, the Sparti, the abduction of Proserpine, their mysteries, their legislations, the deeds of Dionysus, Perseus, the Argonauts, the Centaurs, the Minotaur, the affairs of Troy, the labours of Hercules, the return of the Heraclidæ, the Ionian migration and the Olympiads. And it seemed good to me to give an account especially of the before-noted period of the Attic sovereignty, as I intend to narrate the history of the Greeks side by side with that of the Hebrews. For any one will be able, if he only start from my position, to make out the reckoning equally well with me. Now, in the first year of that period of 1020 years, stretching from Moses and Ogygus to the first Olympiad, the passover and the exodus of the Hebrews from Egypt took place, and also in Attica the flood of Ogygus. And that is according to reason. For when the Egyptians were being smitten in the anger of God with hail and storms, it was only to be expected that certain parts of the earth should suffer with them ; and, in especial, it was but to be expected that the Athenians should

participate in such calamity with the Egyptians, since they were supposed to be a colony from them, as Theopompus alleges in his *Tricarenus*, and others besides him. The intervening period has been passed by, as no remarkable event is recorded during it among the Greeks. But after 94 years Prometheus arose, according to some, who was fabulously reported to have formed men ; for being a wise man, he transformed them from the state of extreme rudeness to culture.

<h3 style="text-align:center">XIV.[1]</h3>

Æschylus, the son of Agamestor, ruled the Athenians twenty-three years, in whose time Joatham reigned in Jerusalem.

And our canon brings Joatham king of Juda within the first Olympiad.

<h3 style="text-align:center">XV.[2]</h3>

And Africanus, in the third book of his History, writes: Now the first Olympiad recorded — which, however, was really the fourteenth — was the period when Corœbus was victor ;[3] at that time Ahaz was in the first year of his reign in Jerusalem. *Then in the fourth book he says:* It is therefore with the first year of the reign of Ahaz that we have shown the first Olympiad to fall in.

<h3 style="text-align:center">XVI.[4]</h3>

On the Seventy Weeks of Daniel.

1. This passage, therefore, as it stands thus, touches on many marvellous things. At present, however, I shall speak only of those things in it which bear upon chronology, and matters connected therewith. That the passage speaks then of the advent of Christ, who was to manifest Himself after seventy weeks, is evident. For in the Saviour's time, or from Him, are transgressions abrogated, and sins brought to an end. And through remission, moreover, are iniquities, along with offences, blotted out by expiation ; and an everlasting righteousness is preached, different from that which is by the law, and visions and prophecies (are) until John, and the Most Holy is anointed. For before the advent of the Saviour these things were not yet, and were therefore only looked for. And the beginning of the numbers, that is, of the seventy weeks which make up 490 years, the angel instructs us to take from the going forth of the commandment to answer and to build Jerusalem. And

---

[1] From Georgius Syncellus, Third Book. In the *Chron. Paschal.*, p. 104, ed. Paris, 84 Venet.
[2] From the same, Book III., and from Book IV. In Syncellus p. 197, al. 158.
[3] The text is, ἀναγραφῆναι δὲ πρώτην τὴν τεσσαρεσκαιδεκάτην, etc.
[4] From Book v. In Eusebius, *Demonst. Evang.*, Book VIII ch. ii. p. 389, etc. The Latin version of this section is by Bernardinus Donatus of Verona. There is also a version by Jerome given in his commentary on Dan ix. 24.

this happened in the twentieth year of the reign of Artaxerxes king of Persia. For Nehemiah his cup-bearer besought him, and received the answer that Jerusalem should be built. And the word went forth commanding these things; for up to that time the city was desolate. For when Cyrus, after the seventy years' captivity, gave free permission to all to return who desired it, some of them under the leadership of Jesus the high priest and Zorobabel, and others after these under the leadership of Esdra, returned, but were prevented at first from building the temple, and from surrounding the city with a wall, on the plea that that had not been commanded.

2. It remained in this position, accordingly, until Nehemiah and the reign of Artaxerxes, and the 115th year of the sovereignty of the Persians. And from the capture of Jerusalem that makes 185 years. And at that time King Artaxerxes gave order that the city should be built; and Nehemiah being despatched, superintended the work, and the street and the surrounding wall were built, as had been prophesied. And reckoning from that point, we make up seventy weeks to the time of Christ. For if we begin to reckon from any other point, and not from this, the periods will not correspond, and very many odd results will meet us. For if we begin the calculation of the seventy weeks from Cyrus and the first restoration, there will be upwards of one hundred years too many, and there will be a larger number if we begin from the day on which the angel gave the prophecy to Daniel, and a much larger number still if we begin from the commencement of the captivity. For we find the sovereignty of the Persians comprising a period of 230 years, and that of the Macedonians extending over 370 years, and from that to the 16th [1] year of Tiberius Cæsar is a period of about 60 years.

3. It is by calculating from Artaxerxes, therefore, up to the time of Christ that the seventy weeks are made up, according to the numeration of the Jews. For from Nehemiah, who was despatched by Artaxerxes to build Jerusalem in the 115th year of the Persian empire, and the 4th year of the 83d Olympiad, and the 20th year of the reign of Artaxerxes himself, up to this date, which was the second year of the 202d Olympiad, and the 16th year of the reign of Tiberius Cæsar, there are reckoned 475 years, which make 490 according to the Hebrew numeration, as they measure the years by the course of the moon; so that, as is easy to show, their year consists of 354 days, while the solar year has 365¼ days. For the latter exceeds the period of twelve months, according to the moon's course, by 11¼ days. Hence the Greeks and the Jews insert three intercalary months every 8 years. For 8 times 11¼ days makes up 3 months. Therefore 475 years make 59 periods of 8 years each, and 3 months besides. But since thus there are 3 intercalary months every 8 years, we get thus 15 years *minus* a few days; and these being added to the 475 years, make up in all the 70 weeks.

XVII.[2]

On the Fortunes of Hyrcanus and Antigonus, and on Herod, Augustus, Antony, and Cleopatra, in abstract.

1. Octavius Sebastus, or, as the Romans call him, Augustus, the adopted son of Caius, on returning to Rome from Apollonias in Epirus, where he was educated, possessed himself of the first place in the government. And Antony afterwards obtained the rule of Asia and the districts beyond. In his time the Jews accused Herod; but he put the deputies to death, and restored Herod to his government. Afterwards, however, along with Hyrcanus and Phasælus his brother, he was driven out, and betook himself in flight to Antony. And as the Jews would not receive him, an obstinate battle took place; and in a short time after, as he had conquered in battle, he also drove out Antigonus, who had returned. And Antigonus fled to Herod the Parthian king, and was restored by the help of his son Pacorus, which help was given on his promising to pay 1000 talents of gold. And Herod then in his turn had to flee, while Phasælus was slain in battle, and Hyrcanus was surrendered alive to Antigonus. And after cutting off his ears, that he might be disqualified for the priesthood, he gave him to the Parthians to lead into captivity; for he scrupled to put him to death, as he was a relation of his own. And Herod, on his expulsion, betook himself first to Malichus king of the Arabians; and when he did not receive him, through fear of the Parthians, he went away to Alexandria to Cleopatra. That was the 185th Olympiad. Cleopatra having put to death her brother, who was her consort in the government, and being then summoned by Antony to Cilicia to make her defence, committed the care of the sovereignty to Herod; and as he requested that he should not be entrusted with anything until he was restored to his own government,[3] she took him with her and went to Antony. And as he was smitten with love for the princess, they despatched Herod to Rome to Octavius Augustus, who, on behalf of Antipater, Herod's father, and on behalf of Herod himself, and also because Antigonus was established as king by the help of the Par-

---

1 Jerome in his version gives the 15th (*quintum decimum*).

2 In Syncellus, p. 307, al. 244.
3 The sense is doubtful here: καὶ ὡς οὐδὲν ἠξίου πιστεύεσθαι ἐστ᾽ ἂν καταχθῇ εἰς τὴν ἑαυτοῦ ἀρχήν, etc.

thians, gave a commission to the generals in Palestine and Syria to restore him to his government. And in concert with Sosius he waged war against Antigonus for a long time, and in manifold engagements. At that time also, Josephus, Herod's brother, died in his command. And Herod coming to Antony [1] . . .

2. For three years they besieged Antigonus, and then brought him alive to Antony. And Antony himself also proclaimed Herod as king, and gave him, in addition, the cities Hippus, Gadara, Gaza, Joppa, Anthedon, and a part of Arabia, Trachonitis, and Auranitis, and Sacia, and Gaulanitis; [2] and besides these, also the procuratorship of Syria. Herod was declared king of the Jews by the senate and Octavius Augustus, and reigned 34 years. Antony, when about to go on an expedition against the Parthians, slew Antigonus the king of the Jews, and gave Arabia to Cleopatra; and passing over into the territory of the Parthians, sustained a severe defeat, losing the greater part of his army. That was in the 186th Olympiad. Octavius Augustus led the forces of Italy and all the West against Antony, who refused to return to Rome through fear, on account of his failure in Parthia, and through his love for Cleopatra. And Antony met him with the forces of Asia. Herod, however, like a shrewd fellow, and one who waits upon the powerful, sent a double set of letters, and despatched his army to sea, charging his generals to watch the issue of events. And when the victory was decided, and when Antony, after sustaining two naval defeats, had fled to Egypt along with Cleopatra, they who bore the letters delivered to Augustus those which they had been keeping secretly for Antony. And on Herod falls [3] . . .

3. Cleopatra shut herself up in a mausoleum, [4] and made away with herself, employing the wild asp as the instrument of death. At that time Augustus captured Cleopatra's sons, Helios and Selene, [5] on their flight to the Thebaid. Nicopolis was founded opposite Actium, and the games called Actia were instituted. On the capture of Alexandria, Cornelius Gallus was sent as first governor of Egypt, and he destroyed the cities of the Egyptians that refused obedience. Up to this time the Lagidæ ruled; and the whole duration of the Macedonian empire after the subversion of the Persian power was 298 years. Thus is made up the whole period from the foundation of the Macedonian empire to its subversion in the time of the Ptolemies, and under Cleopatra, the last of these, the date of

which event is the 11th year of the monarchy and empire of the Romans, and the 4th year of the 187th Olympiad. Altogether, from Adam 5472 years are reckoned.

4. After the taking of Alexandria the 188th Olympiad began. Herod founded anew the city of the Gabinii, [6] the ancient Samaria, and called it Sebaste; and having erected its seaport, the tower of Strato, into a city, he named it Cæsarea after the same, and raised in each a temple in honour of Octavius. And afterwards he founded Antipatris in the Lydian plain, so naming it after his father, and settled in it the people about Sebaste, whom he had dispossessed of their land. He founded also other cities; and to the Jews he was severe, but to other nations most urbane.

It was now the 189th Olympiad, which (Olympiad) in the year that had the bissextile day, the 6th day before the Calends of March, — i.e., the 24th of February, — corresponded with the 24th year of the era of Antioch, whereby the year was determined in its proper limits. [7]

XVIII. [8]

On the Circumstances connected with our Saviour's Passion and His Life-giving Resurrection.

1. As to His works severally, and His cures effected upon body and soul, and the mysteries of His doctrine, and the resurrection from the dead, these have been most authoritatively set forth by His disciples and apostles before us. On the whole world there pressed a most fearful darkness; and the rocks were rent by an earthquake, and many places in Judea and other districts were thrown down. This darkness Thallus, in the third book of his *History*, calls, as appears to me without reason, an eclipse of the sun. For the Hebrews celebrate the passover on the 14th day according to the moon, and the passion of our Saviour falls on the day before the passover; but an eclipse of the sun takes place only when the moon comes under the sun. And it cannot happen at any other time but in the interval between the first day of the new moon and the last of the old, that is, at their junction: how then should an eclipse be supposed to happen when the moon is almost diametrically opposite the sun? Let that opinion pass however; let it carry the majority with it; and let this por-

---

[1] There is a break here in the original.
[2] This is according to the rendering of the Latin version.
[3] Here again there is a blank in the original.
[4] The text is corrupt here. It gives, ἐν τῷ μεσαιολίῳ, a word unknown in Greek. Scaliger reads Μαισαιόλιον. Goarus proposes Μαυσωλαιον, which we adopt in the translation.
[5] i.e., *sun* and *moon*.

[6] Samaria was so named in reference to its restoration by Gabinius, the proconsul of Syria. See Josephus (*Antiq.*, book xiv. ch. x.), who states that Gabinius traversed Judea, and gave orders for the rebuilding of such towns as he found destroyed; and that in this way Samaria, Azotus, Scythopolis, Antedon, Raphia, Dora, Marissa, and not a few others, were restored.
[7] The text is: ἦν Ὀλυμπιὰς ρπθ′, ἥτις πρὸ ϛ′ καλανδῶν Μαρτίων κατὰ Ἀντιοχεῖς κδ′ ἔτει ἤχθη, δι′ ἧς ἐπὶ τῶν ἰδίων ὁρίων ἔστη ὁ ἐνιαυτός. In every fourth year the 24th day of February (= vi. Cal. Mart.) was reckoned twice. There were three different eras of Antioch, of which the one most commonly used began in November 49 B.C. Migne refers the reader to the notes of Goarus on the passage, which we have not seen. The sense of this obscure passage seems to be, that that period formed another fixed point in chronology.
[8] In Georgius Syncellus, *Chron.*, p. 322 or 256.

tent of the world be deemed an eclipse of the sun, like others a portent only to the eye.[1] Phlegon records that, in the time of Tiberius Cæsar, at full moon, there was a full eclipse of the sun from the sixth hour to the ninth — manifestly that one of which we speak. But what has an eclipse in common with an earthquake, the rending rocks, and the resurrection of the dead, and so great a perturbation throughout the universe? Surely no such event as this is recorded for a long period. But it was a darkness induced by God, because the Lord happened then to suffer. And calculation makes out that the period of 70 weeks, as noted in Daniel, is completed at this time.

2. From Artaxerxes, moreover, 70 weeks are reckoned up to the time of Christ, according to the numeration of the Jews. For from Nehemiah, who was sent by Artaxerxes to people Jerusalem, about the 120th year of the Persian empire, and in the 20th year of Artaxerxes himself, and the 4th year of the 83d Olympiad, up to this time, which was the 2d year of the 102d Olympiad, and the 16th year of the reign of Tiberius Cæsar, there are given 475 years, which make 490 Hebrew years, since they measure the years by the lunar month of $29\frac{1}{2}$ days, as may easily be explained, the annual period according to the sun consisting of $365\frac{1}{4}$ days, while the lunar period of 12 months has $11\frac{1}{4}$ days less. For which reason the Greeks and the Jews insert three intercalary months every eight years. For 8 times $11\frac{1}{4}$ days make 3 months. The 475 years, therefore, contain 59 periods of 8 years and three months over: thus, the three intercalary months for every 8 years being added, we get 15 years, and these together with the 475 years make 70 weeks. Let no one now think us unskilled in the calculations of astronomy, when we fix without further ado the number of days at $365\frac{1}{4}$. For it is not in ignorance of the truth, but rather by reason of exact study,[2] that we have stated our opinion so shortly. But let what follows also be presented as in outline [3] to those who endeavour to inquire minutely into all things.

3. Each year in the general consists of 365 days; and the space of a day and night being divided into nineteen parts, we have also five of these. And in saying that the year consists of $365\frac{1}{4}$ days, and there being the five nineteenth parts . . . to the 475 there are $6\frac{1}{4}$ days. Furthermore, we find, according to exact computation, that the lunar month has $29\frac{1}{2}$ days. . . . [4]

And these come to [5] a little time. Now it happens that from the 20th year of the reign of Artaxerxes (as it is given in Ezra among the Hebrews), which, according to the Greeks, was the 4th year of the 80th Olympiad, to the 16th year of Tiberius Cæsar, which was the second year of the 102d Olympiad, there are in all the 475 years already noted, which in the Hebrew system make 490 years, as has been previously stated, that is, 70 weeks, by which period the time of Christ's advent was measured in the announcement made to Daniel by Gabriel. And if any one thinks that the 15 Hebrew years added to the others involve us in an error of 10, nothing at least which cannot be accounted for has been introduced. And the $1\frac{1}{2}$ week which we suppose must be added to make the whole number, meets the question about the 15 years, and removes the difficulty about the time; and that the prophecies are usually put forth in a somewhat symbolic form, is quite evident.

4. As far, then, as is in our power, we have taken the Scripture, I think, correctly; especially seeing that the preceding section about the vision seems to state the whole matter shortly, its first words being, "In the third year of the reign of Belshazzar,"[6] where he prophesies of the subversion of the Persian power by the Greeks, which empires are symbolized in the prophecy under the figures of the ram and the goat respectively.[7] "The sacrifice," he says, "shall be abolished, and the holy places shall be made desolate, so as to be trodden under foot; which things shall be determined within 2300 days."[7] For if we take the day as a month, just as elsewhere in prophecy days are taken as years, and in different places are used in different ways, reducing the period in the same way as has been done above to Hebrew months, we shall find the period fully made out to the 20th year of the reign of Artaxerxes, from the capture of Jerusalem. For there are given thus 185 years, and one year falls to be added to these — the year in which Nehemiah built the wall of the city. In 186 years, therefore, we find 2300 Hebrew months, as 8 years have in addition 3 intercalary months. From Artaxerxes, again, in whose time the command went forth that Jerusalem should be built, there are 70 weeks. These matters, however, we have discussed by themselves, and with greater exactness, in our book *On the Weeks and this Prophecy.* But I am amazed that the Jews deny that the Lord has yet come, and that the followers of Marcion refuse to admit that His coming was predicted in the prophecies when the Scriptures display the matter so openly to our

---

[1] ἐν τι κατὰ τὴν ὄψιν. [Vol. iii. p. 58, Elucid. V., this series.]
[2] διὰ τὴν λεπτολογίαν.
[3] Or, on a table; ὡς ἐν γραφῇ.
[4] The text in the beginning of this section is hopelessly corrupt. Scaliger declares that neither could he follow these things, nor did the man that dreamt them understand them. We may subjoin the Greek text as it stands in Migne: Μεταξὺ δὲ τοῦ λέγειν τὸν ἐνιαυτὸν ἡμερῶν τξε, καὶ τετραμορίου, καὶ τῶν ἀπὸ ιθ΄ τῆς νυχθημέρου, μερῶν ε . . . εἰς τὰ νοε, ἡμέραι τὸ παραλληλον εἰσὶ ς΄, καὶ τετραμόριον. Ἔτι γε μὴν τὸν τῆς σελήνης μῆνα κατὰ τὴν ἀκριβῆ λεπτο-

λογίαν εὑρίσκομεν κθ΄, καὶ ἡμισείας ἡμέρας καὶ νυκτὸς διαιρεθείσης εἰς μέρη σέ, τούτων τὰ ο, καὶ ἥμισυ . . . ἃ γίνεται ἐννενηκοστοτε- ταρτα τρία.
[5] καταγίνεται.
[6] Dan. viii. 1.
[7] Dan. viii. 13, 14.

view. *And after something else:* The period, then, to the advent of the Lord from Adam and the creation is 5531 years, from which epoch to the 250th Olympiad there are 192 years, as has been shown above.

XIX.[1]

For we who both know the measure of those

words,[2] and are not ignorant of the grace of faith, give thanks to the Father,[3] who has bestowed on us His creatures Jesus Christ the Saviour of all, and our Lord;[4] to whom be glory and majesty, with the Holy Spirit, for ever.

[1] In Basil, *De Spiritu Sancto,* ch. xxix. § 73; *Works,* vol. iii. p. 61, edit. Paris. [Elucidation II.]

[2] For ῥηματων, words, three MSS. give ῥητῶν, sayings.
[3] For ἡμίν Πατρι there is another reading, ἡμων πατράσι = to Him who gave to our fathers.
[4] These words, "and our Lord," are wanting in three MSS.

IV. — THE PASSION OF ST. SYMPHOROSA AND HER SEVEN SONS.[1]

THE text is given from the edition of Ruinart. His preface, which Migne also cites, is as follows: "The narrative of the martyrdom of St. Symphorosa and her seven sons, which we here publish, is ascribed in the MSS. to Julius Africanus, a writer of the highest repute. And it may perhaps have been inserted in his books on *Chronography,* — a work which Eusebius (*Hist. Eccles.,* vi. 31) testifies to have been written with the greatest care, since in these he detailed the chief events in history from the foundation of the world to the times of the Emperor Heliogabalus. As that work, however, is lost, that this narrative is really to be ascribed to Africanus, I would not venture positively to assert, although at the same time there seems no ground for doubting its genuineness. We print it, moreover, from the editions of Mombritius, Surius, and Cardulus, collated with two Colbert MSS. and one in the library of the Sorbonne. The occasion for the death of these saints was found in the vicinity of that most famous palace which was built by Adrian at his country seat at Tiber, according to Spartianus. For when the emperor gave orders that this palace, which he had built for his pleasure, should be purified by some piacular ceremonies, the priests seized this opportunity for accusing Symphorosa, alleging that the gods would not be satisfied until Symphorosa should either sacrifice to them or be herself sacrificed; which last thing was done by Hadrian, whom, from many others of his deeds, we know to have been exceedingly superstitious, about the year of Christ 120, that is, about the beginning of his reign, at which period indeed, as Dio Cassius observes, that emperor put a great number to death. The memory of these martyrs, moreover, is celebrated in all the most ancient martyrologies, although they assign different days for it. The Roman, along with Notker, fixes their festival for the 18th July, Rabanus for the 21st of the same month, Usuardus and Ado for the 21st June. In the Tiburtine road there still exists the rubbish of an old church, as Aringhi states (*Rom. Subter.,* iv. 17), which was consecrated to God under their name, and which still retains the title, *To the Seven Brothers.* I have no doubt that it was built in that place to which the pontiffs in the *Acta,* sec. iv., gave the name, *To the Seven Biothanati,* i.e., those cut off by a violent death, as Baronius remarks, at the year 138." So far Ruinart: see also Tillemont, *Mém. Eccles.,* ii. pp. 241 and 595; and the Bollandists, *Act. S.S. Junii,* vol. iv. p. 350.

1. When Adrian had built a palace, and wished to dedicate it by that wicked ceremonial, and began to seek responses by sacrifices to idols, and to the demons that dwell in idols, they replied,[2] and said: "The widow Symphorosa, with her seven sons, wounds us day by day in invoking her God. If she therefore, together with her sons, shall offer sacrifice, we promise to make good all that you ask." Then Adrian ordered her to be seized, along with her sons, and advised them in courteous terms to consent to offer sacrifice to the idols. To him, however, the blessed Symphorosa answered: "My husband Getulius,[3] together with his brother Amantius, when they were tribunes in thy service, suffered different punishments for the name of Christ, rather than consent to sacrifice to idols, and, like good athletes, they overcame thy demons in death. For, rather than be prevailed on, they chose to be beheaded, and suffered death; which death, being endured for the name of Christ, gained them temporal ignominy indeed

[1] Gallandi, *Bibl. Patrum,* vol. i. Proleg. p. lxxi. and p. 329.
[2] See Eusebius, *Life of Constantine,* ii. 50.

[3] The Martyrologies celebrate their memory on the 10th June; one of the Colbert MSS. gives *Zoticus* for *Getulius.*

among men of this earth, but everlasting honour and glory among the angels; and moving now among them, and exhibiting[1] trophies of their sufferings, they enjoy eternal life with the King eternal in the heavens."

2. The Emperor Adrian said to the holy Symphorosa: "Either sacrifice thou along with thy sons to the omnipotent gods, or else I shall cause thee to be sacrificed thyself, together with thy sons." The blessed Symphorosa answered: "And whence is this great good to me, that I should be deemed worthy along with my sons to be offered as an oblation to God?"[2] The Emperor Adrian said: "I shall cause thee to be sacrificed to my gods." The blessed Symphorosa replied: "Thy gods cannot take me in sacrifice; but if I am burned for the name of Christ, my God, I shall rather consume those demons of thine." The Emperor Adrian said: "Choose thou one of these alternatives: either sacrifice to my gods, or perish by an evil death." The blessed Symphorosa replied: "Thou thinkest that my mind can be altered by some kind of terror; whereas I long to rest with my husband Getulius,[3] whom thou didst put to death for Christ's name." Then the Emperor Adrian ordered her to be led away to the temple of Hercules, and there first to be beaten with blows on the cheek, and afterwards to be suspended by the hair. But when by no argument and by no terror could he divert her from her good resolution, he ordered her to be thrown into the river with a large stone fastened to her neck. And her brother Eugenius, principal of the district of Tiber, picked up her body, and buried it in a suburb of the same city.

3. Then, on another day, the Emperor Adrian ordered all her seven sons to be brought before him in company; and when he had challenged them to sacrifice to idols, and perceived that they yielded by no means to his threats and terrors, he ordered seven stakes to be fixed around the temple of Hercules, and commanded them to be stretched on the blocks there. And he ordered Crescens, the first, to be transfixed in the throat; and Julian, the second, to be stabbed in the breast; and Nemesius, the third, to be struck through the heart; and Primitivus, the fourth, to be wounded in the navel; and Justin, the fifth, to be struck through in the back with a sword; and Stracteus,[4] the sixth, to be wounded in the side; and Eugenius, the seventh, to be cleft in twain from the head downwards.

4. The next day again the Emperor Adrian came to the temple of Hercules, and ordered their bodies to be carried off together, and cast into a deep pit; and the pontiffs gave to that place the name, *To the Seven Biothanati.*[5] After these things the persecution ceased for a year and a half, in which period the holy bodies of all the martyrs were honoured, and consigned with all care to tumuli erected for that purpose, and their names are written in the book of life. The natal day, moreover, of the holy martyrs of Christ, the blessed Symphorosa and her seven sons, Crescens, Julian, Nemesius, Primitivus, Justin, Stracteus, and Eugenius, is held on the 18th July. Their bodies rest on the Tiburtine road, at the eighth mile-stone from the city, under the kingship of our Lord Jesus Christ, to whom is honour and glory for ever and ever. Amen.

---

[1] A Colbert MS. gives "laudantes" = praising.
[2] This response, along with the next interrogation, is wanting in the Colbert manuscript.
[3] Sur., Card., and the Colbert Codex give "Zoticus."

[4] The Colbert Codex reads "Extacteus;" Cardulus gives "Stacteus," by which name he is designated beneath by them all.
[5] In one of the Colbert codices, and in another from the Sorbonne, there is a passage inserted here about the death of Adrian, which is said to have happened a little after that of these martyrs.

ELUCIDATIONS.

I.

(Joseph the son of both, p. 127.)

THE opinion that Luke's genealogy is that of *Mary* was unknown to Christian antiquity. In the fifteenth century it was first propounded by Latin divines to do honour (as they supposed) to the Blessed Virgin. It was first broached by Annius of Viterbo, A.D. 1502. Christian antiquity is agreed that:—

1. Both genealogies are those of Joseph.

2. That Joseph was the son of Jacob or of Heli, either by adoption, or because Jacob and Heli were either own brothers or half-brothers; so that,—

3. On the death of one of the brothers, without issue, the surviving brother married his

widow, who became the mother of Joseph by this marriage ; so that Joseph was reckoned the son of Jacob and the son of Heli.[1]

4. Joseph and Mary were of the same lineage, but the Hebrews did not reckon descent from the side of the woman. *For them* St. Luke's genealogy is the sufficient register of Christ's royal descent and official claim. St. Luke gives his *personal* pedigree, ascending to Adam, and identifying Him with the whole human race.

II.

(Conclusion, cap. xix. p. 138.)

On Jewish genealogies, note Dean Prideaux,[2] vol. i. p. 296, and compare Lardner, vol. ii. 129, *et alibi*. Stillingfleet[3] should not be overlooked in what he says of the *uncertainties* of heathen chronology.

Lardner repeatedly calls our author a "great man;" and his most valuable account,[4] digested from divers ancient and modern writers, must be consulted by the student. Let us observe the books of Scripture which his citations attest, and the great value of his attestation of the two genealogies of our Lord. Lardner dates the Letter to Origen[5] A.D. 228 or 240, according to divers conjectures of the learned. He concludes with this beautiful tribute: "We may glory in Africanus as a Christian" among those "whose shining abilities rendered them the ornament of the age in which they lived, — men of unspotted characters, giving evident proofs of honesty and integrity."

NOTE.

THE valuable works of Africanus are found in vol. ix. of the Edinburgh edition, mixed up with the spurious *Decretals* and remnants of preceding volumes. I am unable to make out very clearly who is the translator, but infer that Drs. Roberts and Donaldson should be credited with this work.

---

[1] Routh, *Reliqu. Sacræ*, vol. ii. pp. 233, 339, 341, 355. Compare also vol. ii. 334 and 346, this series.

[2] Also on the *Seventy Weeks* (p. 134, *supra*), vol i. pp. 227-240 and 322.

[3] *Origines Sacræ*, vol. i. pp. 64-120.

[4] *Works*, vol. ii. pp. 457-468.

[5] See Introductory Notice, p. 123, note 4, *supra*.

ANATOLIUS AND MINOR WRITERS.

[TRANSLATED BY THE REV. S. D. SALMOND, M.A.]

INTRODUCTORY NOTICE

TO

ANATOLIUS AND MINOR WRITERS.

INSTEAD of reprinting a disjointed mass of " Fragments," I have thought it desirable to present them in a group, illustrative of the Alexandrian school. I give to Anatolius the deserved place of prominence, marking him as the meet successor of Africanus in ability if not in the nature of his pursuits. His writings and the testimony of Eusebius prove him to have been a star of no inferior magnitude, even in the brilliant constellation of faith and genius of which he is part.

These minor writers I have arranged, not with exclusive reference to minute chronology, but with some respect to their material, as follows : —

I.	Anatolius,	A.D. 270.
II.	Alexander of Cappadocia,	A.D. 250.
III.	Theognostus,	A.D. 265.
IV.	Pierius,	A.D. 300.
V.	Theonas,	A.D. 300.
VI.	Phileas,	A.D. 307.
VII.	Pamphilus,	A.D. 309.

ANATOLIUS AND MINOR WRITERS.

ANATOLIUS OF ALEXANDRIA.

TRANSLATOR'S BIOGRAPHICAL NOTICE.

[A.D. 230–270–280.]   From Jerome [1] we learn that Anatolius flourished in the reign of Prob and Carus, that he was a native of Alexandria, and that he became bishop of Laodicea.   Euse bius gives a somewhat lengthened account of him,[2] and speaks of him in terms of the strongest laudation, as one surpassing all the men of his time in learning and science.   He tells us that he attained the highest eminence in arithmetic, geometry, and astronomy, besides being a great proficient also in dialectics, physics, and rhetoric.   His reputation was so great among the Alex andrians that they are said to have requested him to open a school for teaching the Aristotelian philosophy in their city.[3]   He did great service to his fellow-citizens in Alexandria on their being besieged by the Romans in A.D. 262, and was the means of saving the lives of numbers of them. After this he is said to have passed into Syria, where Theotecnus, the bishop of Cæsareia, ordained him, destining him to be his own successor in the bishopric.   After this, however, having occasion to travel to Antioch to attend the synod convened to deal with the case of Paul of Samosata, as he passed through the city of Laodicea, he was detained by the people and made bishop of the place, in succession to Eusebius.[4]   This must have been about the year 270 A.D.   How long he held that dignity, however, we do not know.   Eusebius tells us that he did not write many books, but yet enough to show us at once his eloquence and his erudition.   Among these was a treatise on the *Chronology of Easter*, of which a considerable extract is preserved in Eusebius.   The book itself exists now only in a Latin version, which is generally ascribed to Rufinus, and which was published by Ægidius Bucherius in his *Doctrina Temporum*, which was issued at Antwerp in 1634.   Another work of his was the *Institutes of Arithmetic*, of which we have some fragments in the θεολογούμενα τῆς ἀριθμητικῆς, which was published in Paris in 1543.   Some small fragments of his mathematical works, which have also come down to us, were published by Fabricius in his *Bibliotheca Græca*, iii. p. 462.

---

[1] *De illustr. viris.*, ch. 73.   [The dates which are known suggest conjectural dates of our author's birth and death.]

[2] In the 32d chapter of the seventh book of his *Ecclesiastical History*.

[3] ["There were giants in those days." How gloriously, even in the poverty and distress of the martyr-ages, the cultivation of learn ing was established by Christianity!]

[4] [This Eusebius was a learned man, born at Alexandria.]

THE PASCHAL CANON OF ANATOLIUS OF ALEXANDRIA.[1]

I.

As we are about to speak on the subject of the order of the times and alternations of the world, we shall first dispose of the positions of diverse calculators ; who, by reckoning only by the course of the moon, and leaving out of account the ascent and descent of the sun, with the addition of certain problems, have constructed diverse periods,[2] self-contradictory, and such as are never found in the reckoning of a true computation ; since it is certain that no mode of computation is to be approved, in which these two measures are not found together. For even in the ancient exemplars, that is, in the books of the Hebrews and Greeks, we find not only the course of the moon, but also that of the sun, and, indeed, not simply its course in the general,[3] but even the separate and minutest moments of its hours all calculated, as we shall show at the proper time, when the matter in hand demands it. Of these Hippolytus made up a period of sixteen years with certain unknown courses of the moon. Others have reckoned by a period of twenty-five years, others by thirty, and some by eighty-four years, without, however, teaching thereby an exact method of calculating Easter. But our predecessors, men most learned in the books of the Hebrews and Greeks, — I mean Isidore and Jerome and Clement, — although they have noted similar beginnings for the months, just as they differ also in language, have, nevertheless, come harmoniously to one and the same most exact reckoning of Easter, day and month and season meeting in accord with the highest honour for the Lord's resurrection.[4] But Origen also, the most erudite of all, and the acutest in making calculations, — a man, too, to whom the epithet χαλκευτής[5] is given, — has published in a very elegant manner a little book on Easter. And in this book, while declaring, with respect to the day of Easter, that attention must be given not only to the course of the moon and the transit of the equinox, but also to the passage (transcensum) of the sun, which removes every foul ambush and offence of all darkness, and brings on the advent of light and the power and inspiration of the elements of the whole world, he speaks thus : In the (matter of the) day of Easter, he remarks, I do not say that it is to be observed that the Lord's day should be found, and the seven[6] days of the moon which are to elapse, but that the sun should pass that division, to wit, between light and darkness, constituted in an equality by the dispensation of the Lord at the beginning of the world ; and that, from one hour to two hours, from two to three, from three to four, from four to five, from five to six hours, while the light is increasing in the ascent of the sun, the darkness should decrease.[7]

. . . and the addition of the twentieth number being completed, twelve parts should be supplied in one and the same day. But if I should have attempted to add any little drop of mine[8] after the exuberant streams of the eloquence and science of some, what else should there be to believe but that it should be ascribed by all to ostentation, and, to speak more truly, to madness, did not the assistance of your promised prayers animate us for a little? For we believe that nothing is impossible to your power of prayer, and to your faith. Strengthened, therefore, by this confidence, we shall set bashfulness aside, and shall enter this most deep and unforeseen sea of the obscurest calculation, in which swelling questions and problems surge around us on all sides.

II.

There is, then, in the first year, the new moon of the first month, which is the beginning of every cycle of nineteen years, on the six and twentieth day of the month called by the Egyptians Phamenoth.[9] But, according to the months of the Macedonians, it is on the two-and-twentieth day of Dystrus. And, as the Romans would say, it is on the eleventh day before the Kalends of April. Now the sun is found on the said six-and-twentieth day of Phamenoth, not only as having mounted to the first segment, but as already passing the fourth day in it. And this segment they are accustomed to call the first dodecatemorion (twelfth part), and the equinox, and the beginning of months, and the head of

---

[1] First edited from an ancient manuscript by Ægidius Bucherius, of the Society of Jesus.
[2] *Circulos.* [Note the reference to Hippolytus.]
[3] *Gressus*, Vol. v. p. 3; also Bunsen, i. pp. 13, 281.]
[4] [It seems probable that the *hegemony* which Alexandria had established in all matters of learning led to that full recognition of it, by the Council of Nicæa, which made its bishop the dictator to the whole Church in the annual calculation of Easter. Vol. ii. 343.]
[5] i.e., "smith" or "brasier," probably from his *assiduity*.

[6] Lunae vii. Perhaps, as Bucher conjectures, Lunae xiv., fourteen days, &c.
[7] The text is doubtful and corrupt here.
[8] *Aliquid stilicidii.*
[9] [The Church's Easter-calculations created modern astronomy, which passed to the Arabians from the Church. (See Whewell's *Inductive Sciences.*) They preserved it, but did not improve it, in Spain. Christianity re-adopted it, and the presbyter Copernicus new-created it. The court of Rome (not the Church Catholic) persecuted Galileo; but it did so under the lead of professional "Science," which had darkened the human mind, from the days of Pythagoras, respecting *his* more enlightened system.]

the cycle, and the starting-point[1] of the course of the planets. And the segment before this they call the last of the months, and the twelfth segment, and the last dodecatemorion, and the end of the circuit[2] of the planets. And for this reason, also, we maintain that those who place the first month in it, and who determine the fourteenth day of the Paschal season by it, make no trivial or common blunder.

III.

Nor is this an opinion confined to ourselves alone. For it was also known to the Jews of old and before Christ, and it was most carefully observed by them.[3] And this may be learned from what Philo, and Josephus, and Musæus have written ; and not only from these, but indeed from others still more ancient, namely, the two Agathobuli,[4] who were surnamed the Masters, and the eminent Aristobulus,[5] who was one of the Seventy who translated the sacred and holy Scriptures of the Hebrews for Ptolemy Philadelphus and his father, and dedicated his exegetical books on the law of Moses to the same kings. These writers, in solving some questions which are raised with respect to Exodus, say that all alike ought to sacrifice the Passover[6] after the vernal equinox in the middle of the first month. And that is found to be when the sun passes through the first segment of the solar, or, as some among them have named it, the zodiacal circle.

IV.

But this Aristobulus also adds, that for the feast of the Passover it was necessary not only that the sun should pass the equinoctial segment, but the moon also. For as there are two equinoctial segments, the vernal and the autumnal, and these diametrically opposite to each other, and since the day of the Passover is fixed for the fourteenth day of the month, in the evening, the moon will have the position diametrically opposite the sun ; as is to be seen in full moons. And the sun will thus be in the segment of the vernal equinox, and the moon necessarily will be at the autumnal equinox.

V.

I am aware that very many other matters were discussed by them, some of them with considerable probability, and others of them as matters of the clearest demonstration,[7] by which they endeavour to prove that the festival of the Passover and unleavened bread ought by all means to be kept after the equinox. But I shall pass on without demanding such copious demonstrations (on subjects[8]) from which the veil of the Mosaic law has been removed ; for now it remains for us with unveiled face to behold ever as in a glass Christ Himself and the doctrines and sufferings of Christ. But that the first month among the Hebrews is about the equinox, is clearly shown also by what is taught in the book of Enoch.[9]

VI.

And, therefore, in this concurrence of the sun and moon, the Paschal festival is not to be celebrated, because as long as they are found in this course the power of darkness is not overcome ; and as long as equality between light and darkness endures, and is not diminished by the light, it is shown that the Paschal festival is not to be celebrated. Accordingly, it is enjoined that that festival be kept after the equinox, because the moon of the fourteenth,[10] if before the equinox or at the equinox, does not fill the whole night. But after the equinox, the moon of the fourteenth, with one day being added because of the passing of the equinox, although it does not extend to the true light, that is, the rising of the sun and the beginning of day, will nevertheless leave no darkness behind it. And, in accordance with this, Moses is charged by the Lord to keep seven days of unleavened bread for the celebration of the Passover, that in them no power of darkness should be found to surpass the light. And although the outset of four nights begins to be dark, that is, the 17th and 18th and 19th and 20th, yet the moon of the 20th, which

---

[1] The word is ἄφεσις, which Valesius makes equivalent to ἀφετηρια, the rope or post from which the chariots started in the race, and so = starting-point. — TR.

[2] περιόδου.

[3] πρὸς αυτῶν — others read πρό, before them.

[4] Anatolius writes that there were two Agathobuli with the surname Masters: but I fear that he is wrong in his opinion that they were more ancient than Philo and Josephus. For Agathobulus, the philosopher. flourished in the times of Adrian, as Eusebius writes in his *Chronicon*, and after him Georgius Syncellus. — VALES.

[5] Ἀριστοβούλου τοῦ πάνυ — Rufinus erroneously renders it *Aristobulum ex Paneade*, Aristobulus of Paneas. Scaliger also, in his *Animadversiones Eusebianæ*, p. 130, strangely thinks that the text should be corrected from the version of Rufinus. And Bede, in his *De Ratione Computi*, also follows the faulty rendering of Rufinus, and writes *Aristobulus et Paniada*, as though the latter word were the proper name of a Jewish writer, finding probably in the *Codex* of Rufinus, which he possessed, the reading *Aristobulus et Paneada*, which indeed is found in a very ancient Paris manuscript, and also in the *Codex Corbeiensis*. But that that Aristobulus was not one of the seventy translators, is proved by Scaliger from the work cited above. This Aristobulus was also surnamed διδάσκαλος, or *Master*, as we see from the Maccabees, ii. 1. For I do not agree with Scaliger in distinguishing this Aristobulus, of whom mention is made in the Maccabees, from the Peripatetic philosopher who dedicated his *Commentaries on the Law of Moses* to Ptolemy Philometor. — VALES. [See vol. ii. p. 487, and Elucidation II. p. 520, same volume, this series.]

[6] τα διαβητηρια θύειν.

[7] κυριακὰς ἀποδείξεις — Christophorsonus renders it *ratas;* Rufinus gives *validissimas assertiones.* The Greeks use κύριος in this sense, κυριαι δικαι, δοξαι, &c., *decisive, valid*, judgments, opinions, &c.

[8] The text gives ἀπαιτῶν ὧν περιήρηται, &c.; various codices read ἀπ' αὐτῶν, &c. Valesius now proposes ὑλας ἀπαιτῶν · ᾧ περιήρηται, *I shall pass on without . . . for the veil is removed from me.*

[9] An apocryphal book of some antiquity, which professes to proceed from the patriarch of that name, but of whose existence prior to the Christian era there is no real evidence. The first author who clearly refers to it by name is Tertullian. [Vol. iii. p. 62, and iv. 380.]

[10] xiv. luna. The Romans used the phrase *luna prima, secunda,* &c., as meaning, the first, second day, &c., after new moon. — TR.

rises before that, does not permit the darkness to extend on even to midnight.

VII.

To us, however, with whom it is impossible for all these things to come aptly at one and the same time, namely, the moon's fourteenth, and the Lord's day, and the passing of the equinox, and whom the obligation of the Lord's resurrection binds to keep the Paschal festival on the Lord's day, it is granted that we may extend the beginning of our celebration even to the moon's twentieth. For although the moon of the 20th does not fill the whole night, yet, rising as it does in the second watch, it illumines the greater part of the night. Certainly if the rising of the moon should be delayed on to the end of two watches, that is to say, to midnight, the light would not then exceed the darkness, but the darkness the light. But it is clear that in the Paschal feast it is not possible that any part of the darkness should surpass the light; for the festival of the Lord's resurrection is *one of* light, and there is no fellowship between light and darkness. And if the moon should rise in the third watch, it is clear that the 22d or 23d of the moon would then be reached, in which it is not possible that there can be a true celebration of Easter. For those who determine that the festival may be kept at this age of the moon, are not only unable to make that good by the authority of Scripture, but turn also into the crime of sacrilege and contumacy, and incur the peril of their souls; inasmuch as they affirm that the true light may be celebrated along with something of that power of darkness which dominates all.

VIII.

Accordingly, it is not the case, as certain calculators of Gaul allege, that this assertion is opposed by that passage in Exodus,[1] where we read: "In the first month, on the fourteenth day of the first month, at even, ye shall eat unleavened bread until the one-and-twentieth day of the month at even. Seven days shall there be no leaven found in your houses." From this they maintain that it is quite permissible to celebrate the Passover on the twenty-first day of the moon; understanding that if the twenty-second day were added, there would be found eight days of unleavened bread. A thing which cannot be found with any probability, indeed, in the Old Testament, as the Lord, through Moses, gives this charge: "Seven days ye shall eat unleavened bread."[2] Unless perchance the fourteenth day is not reckoned by them among the days of unleavened bread with the celebration

of the feast; which, however, is contrary to the Word of the Gospel which says: "Moreover, on the first day of unleavened bread, the disciples came to Jesus."[3] And there is no doubt as to its being the fourteenth day on which the disciples asked the Lord, in accordance with the custom established for them of old, "Where wilt Thou that we prepare for Thee to eat the Passover?" But they who are deceived with this error maintain this addition, because they do not know that the 13th and 14th, the 14th and 15th, the 15th and 16th, the 16th and 17th, the 17th and 18th, the 18th and 19th, the 19th and 20th, the 20th and 21st days of the moon are each found, as may be most surely proved, within a single day. For every day in the reckoning of the moon does not end in the evening as the same day in respect of number, as it is at its beginning in the morning. For the day which in the morning, that is up to the sixth hour and half, is numbered the 13th day of the month, is found at even to be the 14th. Wherefore, also, the Passover is enjoined to be extended on to the 21st day at even; which day, without doubt, in the morning, that is, up to that term of hours which we have mentioned, was reckoned the 20th. Calculate, then, from the end of the 13th[4] day of the moon, which marks the beginning of the 14th, on to the end of the 20th, at which the 21st day also begins, and you will have only seven days of unleavened bread, in which, by the guidance of the Lord, it has been determined before that the most true feast of the Passover ought to be celebrated.

IX.

But what wonder is it that they should have erred in the matter of the 21st day of the moon who have added three days before the equinox, in which they hold that the Passover may be celebrated? An assertion which certainly must be considered altogether absurd, since, by the best-known historiographers of the Jews, and by the Seventy Elders, it has been clearly determined that the Paschal festival cannot be celebrated at the equinox.

X.

But nothing was difficult to them with whom it was lawful to celebrate the Passover on any day when the fourteenth of the moon happened after the equinox. Following their example up to the present time all the bishops of Asia — as themselves also receiving the rule from an unimpeachable authority, to wit, the evangelist John, who leant on the Lord's breast, and drank in instructions spiritual without doubt — were in

---

[1] Exod. xii. 18, 19.
[2] Exod. xii. 15; Levit. xxiii. 6.

[3] Matt. xxvi. 17; Mark xiv. 12; Luke xxii. 7.
[4] But the text gives 12th.

the way of celebrating the Paschal feast, without question, every year, whenever the fourteenth day of the moon had come, and the lamb was sacrificed by the Jews after the equinox was past; not acquiescing, so far as regards this matter, with the authority of some, namely, the successors of Peter and Paul, who have taught all the churches in which they sowed the spiritual seeds of the Gospel, that the solemn festival of the resurrection of the Lord can be celebrated only on the Lord's day. Whence, also, a certain contention broke out between the successors of these, namely, Victor, at that time bishop of the city of Rome, and Polycrates, who then appeared to hold the primacy among the bishops of Asia. And this contention was adjusted most rightfully by Irenæus,[1] at that time president of a part of Gaul, so that both parties kept by their own order, and did not decline from the original custom of antiquity. The one party, indeed, kept the Paschal day on the fourteenth day of the first month, according to the Gospel, as they thought, adding nothing of an extraneous kind, but keeping through all things the rule of faith. And the other party, passing the day of the Lord's Passion as one replete with sadness and grief, hold that it should not be lawful to celebrate the Lord's mystery of the Passover at any other time but on the Lord's day, on which the resurrection of the Lord from death took place, and on which rose also for us the cause of everlasting joy. For it is one thing to act in accordance with the precept given by the apostle, yea, by the Lord Himself, and be sad with the sad, and suffer with him that suffers by the cross, His own word being : "My soul is exceeding sorrowful, even unto death;"[2] and it is another thing to rejoice with the victor as he triumphs over an ancient enemy, and exults with the highest triumph over a conquered adversary, as He Himself also says : "Rejoice with Me; for I have found the sheep which I had lost."[3]

XI.

Moreover, the allegation which they sometimes make against us, that if we pass the moon's fourteenth we cannot celebrate the beginning of the Paschal feast in light,[4] neither moves nor disturbs us. For, although they lay it down as a thing unlawful, that the beginning of the Paschal festival should be extended so far as to the moon's twentieth; yet they cannot deny that it ought to be extended to the sixteenth and seventeenth, which coincide with the day on which the Lord rose from the dead. But we

decide that it is better that it should be extended even on to the twentieth day, on account of the Lord's day, than that we should anticipate the Lord's day on account of the fourteenth day; for on the Lord's day was it that light was shown to us in the beginning, and now also in the end, the comforts of all present and the tokens of all future blessings. For the Lord ascribes no less praise to the twentieth day than to the fourteenth. For in the book of Leviticus[5] the injunction is expressed thus : "In the first month, on the fourteenth day of this month, at even, is the Lord's Passover. And on the fifteenth day of this month is the feast of unleavened bread unto the Lord. Seven days ye shall eat unleavened bread. The first day shall be to you one most diligently attended[6] and holy. Ye shall do no servile work thereon. And the seventh day shall be to you more diligently attended[7] and holier; ye shall do no servile work thereon." And hence we maintain that those have contracted no guilt[8] before the tribunal of Christ, who have held that the beginning of the Paschal festival ought to be extended to this day. And this, too, the most especially, as we are pressed by three difficulties, namely, that we should keep the solemn festival of the Passover on the Lord's day, and after the equinox, and yet not beyond the limit of the moon's twentieth day.

XII.

But this again is held by other wise and most acute men to be an impossibility, because within that narrow and most contracted limit of a cycle of nineteen years, a thoroughly genuine Paschal time, that is to say, one held on the Lord's day and yet after the equinox, cannot occur. But, in order that we may set in a clearer light the difficulty which causes their incredulity, we shall set down, along with the courses of the moon, that cycle of years which we have mentioned; the days being computed before in which the year rolls on in its alternating courses, by Kalends and Ides and Nones, and by the sun's ascent and descent.

XIII.

The moon's age set forth in the Julian Calendar.

January, on the Kalends, one day, the moon's first (day); on the Nones, the 5th day, the moon's 5th; on the Ides, the 13th day, the moon's 13th. On the day before the Kalends of February, the 31st day, the moon's 1st; on the Kalends of February, the 32d day, the moon's

---

[1] [Vol. iii. p. 630. The *convenire ad* of Irenæus is thus shown to be geographical, not ecclesiastical. Vol. i. pp. 415, 569.]
[2] Matt xxvi. 38.
[3] Luke xv. 6.
[4] *Lucidum.*

[5] Levit. xxiii. 5-7.
[6] *Celeberrimus*, honoured, solemn.
[7] Solemn.
[8] [The *sanctification* of the Lord's Day is thus shown to be a Christian principle The feast of Easter was the Great Lord's Day, but the rule was common to the weekly Easter.]

2d ; on the Nones, the 36th day, the moon's 6th ; on the Ides, the 44th day, the moon's 14th. On the day before the Kalends of March, the 59th day, the moon's 29th ; on the Kalends of March, the 60th day, the moon's 1st ; on the Nones, the 66th day, the moon's 7th ; on the Ides, the 74th day, the moon's 15th. On the day before the Kalends of April, the 90th day, the moon's 2d ; on the Kalends of April, the 91st day, the moon's 3d ; on the Nones, the 95th day, the moon's 7th ; on the Ides, the 103d day, the moon's 15th. On the day before the Kalends of May, the 120th day, the moon's 3d ; on the Kalends of May, the 121st day, the moon's 4th ; on the Nones, the 127th day, the moon's 10th ; on the Ides, the 135th day, the moon's 18th. On the day before the Kalends of June, the 151st day, the moon's 3d ; on the Kalends of June, the 152d day, the moon's 5th ; on the Nones, the 153d day, the moon's 9th ; on the Ides, the 164th day, the moon's 17th. On the day before the Kalends of July, the 181st day, the moon's 5th ; on the Kalends of July, the 182d day, the moon's 6th ; on the Nones, the 188th day, the moon's 12th ; on the Ides, the 196th day, the moon's 20th. On the day before the Kalends of August, the 212th day, the moon's 5th ; on the Kalends of August, the 213th day, the moon's 7th ; on the Nones, the 217th day, the moon's 12th ; on the Ides, the 225th day, the moon's 19th. On the day before the Kalends of September, the 243d day, the moon's 7th ; on the Kalends of September, the 244th day, the moon's 8th ; on the Nones, the 248th day, the moon's 12th ; on the Ides, the 256th day, the moon's 20th. On the day before the Kalends of October, the 273d day, the moon's 8th ; on the Kalends of October, the 247th day, the moon's 9th ; on the Nones, the 280th day, the moon's 15th ; on the Ides, the 288th day, the moon's 23d. On the day before the Kalends of November, the 304th day, the moon's 9th ; on the Kalends of November, the 305th day, the moon's 10th ; on the Nones, the 309th day, the moon's 14th ; on the Ides, the 317th day, the moon's 22d. On the day before the Kalends of December, the 334th day, the moon's 10th ; on the Kalends of December, the 335th day, the moon's 11th ; on the Nones, the 339th day, the moon's 15th ; on the Ides, the 347th day, the moon's 23d. On the day before the Kalends of January, the 365th day, the moon's 11th ; on the Kalends of January, the 366th day, the moon's 12th.

XIV.

The Paschal or Easter Table of Anatolius.

Now, then, after the reckoning of the days and the exposition of the course of the moon, whereon the whole revolves on to its end, the cycle of the years may be set forth from the commencement.[1] This makes the Passover (Easter season) circulate between the 6th day before the Kalends of April and the 9th before the Kalends of May, according to the following table : —

EQUINOX.	MOON.	EASTER.	MOON.
1. SABBATH . .	XXVI.	XVth before the Kalends of May, i.e., 17th April . .	XVIII.
2. LORD'S DAY .	VII.	Kalends of April, i.e., 1st April	XIV.
3. IId DAY (FE-RIAL) . .	XVIII.	XIth before the Kalends of May, i.e., 21st April . .	XVI.
4. IIId DAY . .	XXIX.	Ides of April, i.e., 13th April	XIX.
5. IVth DAY .	X.	IVth before the Kalends of April, i.e., 29th March .	XIV.
6. Vth DAY . .	XXI.	XIVth before the Kalends of May, i.e., 18th April .	XVI.
7. SABBATH[2] .	II.	VIth before the Kalends of April, i.e., 27th March .	XVII.
8. LORD'S DAY .	XIII.	Kalends of April, i.e., 1st April	XX.
9. IId DAY . .	XXIV.	XVIIIth before the Kalends of May, i.e., 14th March,	XV.
10. IIId DAY . .	V.	VIIIth before the Ides of April, i.e., 6th April . .	XV.
11. IVth DAY .	XVI.	IVth before the Kalends of April, i.e., 29th March .	XX.
12. Vth DAY . .	XXVII.	IIId before the Ides of April, i.e., 11th April .	XV.
13. VIth DAY .	VIII.	IIId before the Nones of April, i.e., 3d April . .	XVII.
14. SABBATH . .	XX.	IXth before the Kalends of May, i.e., 23d April . .	XX.
15. LORD'S DAY .	I.	VIth before the Ides of April, i.e., 8th April . .	XV.
16. IId DAY . .	XII.	IId before the Kalends of April, i.e., 31st March .	XVIII.
17. IVth DAY[2] .	XXIII.	XIVth before the Kalends of May, i.e., 18th April .	XIX.
18. Vth DAY . .	IV.	IId before the Nones of April, i.e., 4th April . .	XIV.
19. VIth DAY .	XV.	VIth before the Kalends of April, i.e., 27th March .	XVII.

XV.

This cycle of nineteen years is not approved of by certain African investigators who have drawn up larger cycles, because it seems to be somewhat opposed to their surmises and opinions. For these make up the best proved accounts according to their calculation, and determine a certain beginning or certain end for the Easter season, so as that the Paschal festival shall not be celebrated before the eleventh day before the Kalends of April, i.e., 24th March, nor after the

---

[1] *Annorum circuli principium inchoandum est.*
[2] Bissextile reckoning. [Compare note 2, p. 110, *supra.*]

moon's twenty-first, and the eleventh day before the Kalends of May, i.e., 21st April. But we hold that these are limits not only not to be followed, but to be detested and overturned. For even in the ancient law it is laid down that this is to be seen to, viz., that the Passover be not celebrated before the transit of the vernal equinox, at which the last of the autumnal *term* is overtaken,[1] on the fourteenth day of the first month, which is one calculated not by the beginnings of the day, but by those of the moon.[2] And as this has been sanctioned by the charge of the Lord, and is in all things accordant with the Catholic faith, it cannot be doubtful to any wise man that to anticipate it must be a thing unlawful and perilous. And, accordingly, this only is it sufficient for all the saints and Catholics to observe, namely, that giving no heed to the diverse opinions of very many, they should keep the solemn festival of the Lord's resurrection within the limits which we have set forth.

XVI.

Furthermore, as to the proposal subjoined to your epistle, that I should attempt to introduce into this little book some notice of the ascent and descent of the sun, which is made out in the distribution of days and nights. The matter proceeds thus : In fifteen days and half an hour, the sun ascending by so many minutes, that is, by four in one day, from the eighth day before the Kalends of January, i.e., 25th December, to the eighth before the Kalends of April, i.e., 25th March, an hour is taken up ;[3] at which date there are twelve hours and a twelfth. On this day, towards evening, if it happen also to be the moon's fourteenth, the lamb was sacrificed among the Jews. But if the number went beyond that, so that it was the moon's fifteenth or sixteenth on the evening of the same day, on the fourteenth day of the second moon, in the same month, the Passover was celebrated ; and the people ate unleavened bread for seven days, up to the twenty-first day at evening. Hence, if it happens in like manner to us, that the seventh day before the Kalends of April, 26th March, proves to be both the Lord's day and the moon's fourteenth, Easter is to be celebrated on the fourteenth. But if it proves to be the moon's fifteenth or sixteenth, or any day up to the twentieth, then our regard for the Lord's resurrection, which took place on the Lord's day, will lead us to celebrate it on the same principle ; yet this should be done so as that the beginning of Easter may not pass beyond the

close of their festival, that is to say, the moon's twentieth. And therefore we have said that those parties have committed no trivial offence who have ventured either on anticipating or on going beyond this number, which is given us in the divine Scriptures themselves. And from the eighth day before the Kalends of April, 25th March, to the eighth before the Kalends of July, 24th June, in fifteen days an hour is taken up : the sun ascending every day by two minutes and a half, and the sixth part of a minute. And from the eighth day before the Kalends of July, 24th June, to the eighth before the Kalends of October, 24th September, in like manner, in fifteen days and four hours, an hour is taken up : the sun descending every day by the same number of minutes. And the space remaining on to the eighth day before the Kalends of January, 25th December, is determined in a similar number of hours and minutes. So that thus on the eighth day before the Kalends of January, for the hour there is the hour and half. For up to that day and night are distributed. And the twelve hours which were established at the vernal equinox in the beginning by the Lord's dispensation, being distributed over the night on the eighth before the Kalends of July, the sun ascending through those eighteen several degrees which we have noted, shall be found conjoined with the longer space in the twelfth. And, again, the twelve hours which should be fulfilled at the autumnal equinox in the sun's descent, should be found disjoined on the sixth before the Kalends of January as six hours divided into twelve, the night holding eighteen divided into twelve. And on the eighth before the Kalends of July, in like manner, it held six divided into twelve.

XVII.

Be not ignorant of this, however, that those four determining periods,[4] which we have mentioned, although they are approximated to the Kalends of the following months, yet hold each the middle of a season, viz., of spring and summer, and autumn and winter. And the beginnings of the seasons are not to be fixed at that point at which the Kalends of the month begin. But each season is to be begun in such way that the equinox divides the season of spring from its first day ; and the season of summer is divided by the eighth day before the Kalends of July, and that of autumn by the eighth before the Kalends of October, and that of winter by the eighth before the Kalends of January in like manner.[5]

---

[1] *In quo autumnalis novissima pars vincitur.*
[2] *Lunæ orsibus.*
[3] *Diminuitur.* [This year (1886) we have the lowest possible Easter.]

[4] *Temporum confinia.*
[5] [Compare what is said of Hippolytus, vol. v. p. 3, this series. See the valuable work of Professor Seabury on the Calendar, ed. 1872.]

FRAGMENTS OF THE BOOKS ON ARITHMETIC.[1]

What is mathematics?

Aristotle thinks that all philosophy consisted of theory and practice,[2] and divides the practical into ethical and political, and the theoretic again into the theological, the physical, and the mathematical. And thus very clearly and skilfully he shows that mathematics is (a branch of) philosophy.

The Chaldæans were the originators of astronomy, and the Egyptians of geometry and arithmetic. . . .

And whence did mathematics derive its name?

Those of the Peripatetic school affirmed that in rhetoric and poetry, and in the popular music, any one may be an adept though he has gone through no process of study ; but that in those pursuits properly called studies,[3] none can have any real knowledge unless he has first become a student of them. Hence they supposed that the theory of these things was called *Mathematics*, from μάθημα, study, science. And the followers of Pythagoras are said to have given this more distinctive name of mathematics to geometry and arithmetic alone. For of old these had each its own separate name ; and they had up till then no name common to both. And he (Archytas) gave them this name, because he found science[4] in them, and that in a manner suitable to man's study.[5] For they (the Pythagoreans) perceived that these studies dealt with things eternal and immutable and perfect,[6] in which things alone they considered that science consisted. But the more recent philosophers have given a more extensive application to this name, so that, in their opinion, the mathematician deals not only with substances[7] incorporeal, and falling simply within the province of the understanding,[8] but also with that which touches upon corporeal and sensible matter. For he ought to be cognisant of[9] the course of the stars, and their velocity, and their magnitudes, and forms, and distances. And, besides, he ought to investigate their dispositions to vision, examining into the causes, why they are not seen as of the same form and of the same size from every distance, retaining, indeed, as we know them to do, their dispositions relative to each other,[10] but producing, at the same time, deceptive appearances, both in respect of order and position. And these are so, either as determined by the state of the heavens and the air, or as seen in reflecting and all polished surfaces and in transparent bodies, and in all similar kinds. In addition to this, they thought that the man ought to be versed in mechanics and geometry and dialectics. And still further, that he should engage himself with the causes of the harmonious combination of sounds, and with the composition of music ; which things are bodies,[11] or at least are to be ultimately referred to sensible matter.

What is mathematics?

Mathematics is a theoretic science[12] of things apprehensible by perception and sensation for communication to others.[13] And before this a certain person indulging in a joke, while hitting his mark, said that mathematics is that science to which Homer's description of Discord may be applied : —

" Small at her birth, but rising every hour,
   While scarce the skies her horrid (mighty) head can bound,
 She stalks on earth and shakes the world around." [14]

For it begins with a point and a line,[15] and forthwith it takes heaven itself and all things within its compass.

How many divisions are there of mathematics?

Of the more notable and the earliest mathematics there are two principal divisions, viz., arithmetic and geometry. And of the mathematics which deals with things sensible there are six divisions, viz., computation (practical arithmetic), geodesy, optics, theoretical music, mechanics, and astronomy. But that neither the so-called tactics nor architecture,[16] nor the popular music, nor physics, nor the art which is called equivocally the mechanical, constitutes, as some think, a branch of mathematics, we shall prove, as the discourse proceeds, clearly and systematically.

As to the circle having eight solids and six superficies and four angles. . . . What branches of arithmetic have closest affinity with each other? Computation and theoretical music have a closer

---

[1] Fabricius, *Biblioth. Græca*, ed. Harles, vol. iii. p. 462. Hamburg, 1793.
[2] θεωρίας καὶ πράξεως.
[3] μαθήματα.
[4] τὸ ἐπιστημονικόν.
[5] μάθησιν.
[6] εἰλικρινῆ, absolute.
[7] ὕλην.
[8] νοητήν.
[9] θεωρητικός.
[10] τοὺς πρὸς ἄλληλα λόγους.
[11] σώματα, substances.
[12] ἐπιστήμη θεωρητική.
[13] πρὸς τὴν τῶν ὑποπιπτόντων δόσιν.
[14] *Iliad*, iv. 442-443 (Pope).
[15] σημείου καὶ γραμμῆς.
[16] τὸ ἀρχιτεκτονικόν.

affinity than others with arithmetic ; for this.department, being one also of quantity and ratio, approaches it in number and proportion.[1] Optics and geodesy, again, are more in affinity with geometry. And mechanics and astrology are in general affinity with both.

As to mathematics having its principles[2] in hypothesis and about hypothesis. Now, the term hypothesis is used in three ways, or indeed in many ways. For according to one usage of the term we have the dramatic revolution ;[3] and in this sense there are said to be hypotheses in the dramas of Euripides. According to a second meaning, we have the investigation of matters in the special in rhetoric ; and in this sense the Sophists say that a hypothesis must be proposed. And, according to a third signification, the beginning of a proof is called a hypothesis, as being the begging of certain matters with a view to the establishment of another in question. Thus it is said that Democritus[4] used a hypothesis, namely, that of atoms and a vacuum ; and Asclepiades[5] that of atoms[6] and pores. Now, when applied to mathematics, the term hypothesis is to be taken in the third sense.

That Pythagoras was not the only one who duly honoured arithmetic, but that his best known disciples did so too, being wont to say that " all things fit number." [7]

That arithmetic has as its immediate end chiefly the theory of science,[8] than which there is no end either greater or nobler. And its second end is to bring together in one all that is found in determinate substance.[9]

Who among the mathematicians has made any discovery ?

Eudemus[10] relates in his *Astrologies* that Œnopides[11] found out the circle of the zodiac and the cycle[12] of the great year. And Thales[13] discovered the eclipse of the sun and its period in the tropics in its constant inequality. And Anaximander[14] discovered that the earth is poised in space,[15] and moves round the axis of the universe. And Anaximenes[16] discovered that the moon has her light from the sun, and found out also the way in which she suffers eclipse. And the rest of the mathematicians have also made additions to these discoveries. We may instance the facts — that the fixed stars move round the axis passing through the poles, while the planets remove from each other[17] round the perpendicular axis of the zodiac ; and that the axis of the fixed stars and the planets is the side of a pentedecagon with four-and-twenty parts.

---

[1] ἀναλογίας.
[2] ἀρχάς, beginnings.
[3] περιπέτεια, reversal of circumstances on which the plot of a tragedy hinges.
[4] A native of Abdera, in Thrace, born about 460 B.C., and, along with Leucippus, the founder of the philosophical theory of atoms, according to which the creation of all things was explained as being due to the fortuitous combination of an infinite number of atoms floating in infinite space.
[5] A famous physician, a native of Bithynia, but long resident in great repute at Rome in the middle of the first century B.C. He adopted the Epicurean doctrine of atoms and pores, and tried to form a new theory of disease, on the principle that it might be in all cases reduced to obstruction of the pores and irregular distribution of the atoms.
[6] ὄγκοις.

[7] [Wisd. xi. 20; Ecclus. xxxviii. 29 and xlii. 7.]
[8] τὴν ἐπιστημονικὴν θεωρίαν.
[9] συλλήβδην καταλαβεῖν πόσα τῇ ὡρισμένῃ οὐσίᾳ συμβέβηκεν.
[10] A native of Rhodes, a disciple of Aristotle, and editor of his works.
[11] A native of Chios, mentioned by Plato in connection with Anaxagoras, and therefore supposed by some to have been a contemporary of the latter sage.
[12] περίστασιν, revolution.
[13] Of Miletus, one of the sages, and founder of the Ionic school.
[14] Of Miletus, born 610 B.C., the immediate successor of Thales in the Ionic school of philosophy.'
[15] μετεώρος.
[16] Of Miletus, the third in the series of Ionic philosophers.
[17] ἀπεχουσιν αλλήλων.

ALEXANDER OF CAPPADOCIA.

TRANSLATOR'S BIOGRAPHICAL NOTICE.

[A.D. 170–233–251.] Alexander was at first bishop of a church in Cappadocia, but on his visiting Jerusalem he was appointed to the bishopric of the church there, while the previous bishop Narcissus was alive, in consequence of a vision which was believed to be divine.[1] During the Decian persecution he was thrown into prison at Cæsarea, and died there,[2] A.D. 251. The only writtings of his which we know are those from which the extracts are made.[3]

---

[1] Euseb., *Hist. Eccles.*, vi. 11. [Narcissus must have been born about A.D. 121. Might have known Polycarp.]
[2] *Ibid.*, vi. 46. [Narcissus lived till A.D. 237, and died a martyr, aged 116.]
[3] [He was a pupil of Pantænus, continued under Clement, and defended Origen against the severity of Demetrius. Two dates which are conjectural are adjusted to these facts. I find it difficult to reconcile them with those *implied* by Eusebius.]

FROM THE EPISTLES OF ALEXANDER.

I. AN EPISTLE TO THE PEOPLE OF ANTIOCH.[1]

Alexander, a servant and prisoner of Jesus Christ, sends greeting in the Lord to the blessed church of Antioch. Easy and light has the Lord made my bonds to me during the time of my imprisonment, since I have learned that in the providence of God, Asclepiades — who, in regard to the right faith, is most eminently qualified for the office — has undertaken the episcopate of your holy church of Antioch. And this epistle, my brethren and masters, I have sent by the hand of the blessed presbyter Clement,[2] a man virtuous and well tried, whom ye know already, and will know yet better; who also, coming here by the providence and supervision of the Master, has strengthened and increased the Church of the Lord.

II. FROM AN EPISTLE TO THE ANTINOITES.[3]

Narcissus salutes you, who held the episcopate in this district before me, who is now also my colleague and competitor in prayer for you,[4] and who, having now attained to [5] his hundred and tenth year, unites with me in exhorting you to be of one mind.[6]

III. FROM AN EPISTLE TO ORIGEN.[7]

For this, as thou knowest, was the will of God, that the friendship subsisting between us from our forefathers should be maintained unbroken, yea rather, that it should increase in fervency and strength. For we are well acquainted with those blessed fathers who have trodden the course before us, and to whom we too shall soon go: Pantænus, namely, that man verily blessed, my master; and also the holy Clement, who was once my master and my benefactor; and all the rest who may be like them, by whose means also I have come to know thee, my lord and brother, who excellest all.[8]

IV. FROM AN EPISTLE TO DEMETRIUS, BISHOP OF ALEXANDRIA.[9]

And he [10] — i.e., *Demetrius* — has added to his letter that this is a matter that was never heard of before, and has never been done now, — namely, that laymen should take part *in public speaking*,[11] when there are bishops present. But in this assertion he has departed evidently far from the truth by some means. For, indeed, wherever there are found persons capable of profiting the brethren, such persons are exhorted by the holy bishops to address the people. Such was the case at Laranda, where Evelpis was thus exhorted by Neon; and at Iconium, Paulinus was thus exhorted by Celsus; and at Synada, Theodorus also by Atticus, our blessed brethren. And it is probable that this is done in other places also, although we know not the fact.[12]

---

[1] A fragment. In Eusebius, *Hist. Eccles.*, book vi. ch. xi.

[2] It was the opinion of Jerome in his *Catalogus* that the Clement spoken of by Alexander was Clement of Alexandria. This Clement, at any rate, did live up to the time of the Emperor Severus, and sojourned in these parts, as he tells us himself in the first book of his *Stromateis*. And he was also the friend of bishop Alexander, to whom he dedicated his book *On the Ecclesiastical Canon, or Against the Jews*, as Eusebius states in his *Eccles. Hist.*, book vi. ch. xiii. (Migne). [But from the third of these epistles one would certainly draw another inference. How could he, a pupil of Clement, describe and introduce his *master* in such terms as he uses here?]

[3] In Euseb., *Hist. Eccles.*, book vi. ch. xi.

[4] συνεξεταζόμενός μοι διὰ τῶν εὐχῶν. Jerome renders it: Salutat vos Narcissus, qui ante me hic tenuit episcopalem locum et nunc mecum eundem orationibus regit.

[5] ἠνυκώς.

[6] The text gives ὁμοίως ἐμοὶ φρονῆσαι. Several of the codices and also Nicephorus give the better reading, ὁμοίως ἐμοὶ ὁμοφρονῆσαι, which is confirmed by the interpretations of Rufinus and Jerome.

[7] In Euseb., *Hist. Eccles.*, ch xiv.

[8] [This contemporary tribute confirms the enthusiastic eulogy of the youthful Gregory. See p. 38, *supra*.]

[9] In Euseb., *Hist. Eccles.*, ch. xix.

[10] Demetrius is, for honour's sake, addressed in the third person. Perhaps ἡ σὴ ἁγιότης or some such form preceded.

[11] ὁμιλεῖν.

[12] [This precise and definite testimony is not to be controverted. It follows the traditions of the Synagogue (Acts xiii. 15), and agrees with the Pauline prescription as to the use of the *charismata* in 1 Cor. xiv. The chiefs of the Synagogue retained the power of giving this liberty, and this passed to the Christian authorities.]

NOTE BY THE AMERICAN EDITOR.

If Alexander died in the Decian persecution, it is noteworthy how far the sub-apostolic age extended. This contemporary of Cyprian was coadjutor to Narcissus, who may have seen those who knew St. John. See vol. i. p. 416, note 1, this series; also vol i. p. 568, Fragment ii.

THEOGNOSTUS OF ALEXANDRIA.

TRANSLATOR'S BIOGRAPHICAL NOTICE.

[A.D. 260. I can add nothing but conjectures to the following:] Of this Theognostus we have no account by either Eusebius or Jerome. Athanasius, however, mentions him more than once with honour. Thus he speaks of him as ἀνὴρ λόγιος, an *eloquent* or learned man.[1] And again as Θεόγνωστος ὁ θαυμάσιος καὶ σπουδαῖος, the admirable and zealous Theognostus.[2] He seems to have belonged to the Catechetical school of Alexandria, and to have flourished there in the latter half of the third century, probably about A.D. 260. That he was a disciple of Origen, or at least a devoted student of his works, is clear from Photius.[3] He wrote a work in seven books, the title of which is thus given by Photius:[4] *The Outlines of the blessed Theognostus, the exegete of Alexandria.* Dodwell and others are of opinion that by this term *exegete,*[5] is meant the presidency of the Catechetical school and the privilege of public teaching; and that the title, *Outlines,*[6] was taken from Clement, his predecessor in office. According to Photius, the work was on this plan. The first book treated of God the Father, as the maker of the universe; the second, of the necessary existence of the Son; the third, of the Holy Spirit; the fourth, of angels and demons; the fifth and sixth, of the incarnation of God; while the seventh bore the title, *On God's Creation.*[7] Photius has much to say in condemnation of Thegnostus, who, however, has been vindicated by Bull[8] and Prudentius Maranus.[9] Gregory of Nyssa has also charged him with holding the same error as Eunomius on the subject of the Son's relation to the work of creation.[10] He is adduced, however, by Athanasius as a defender of the Homoüsian doctrine.

FROM HIS SEVEN BOOKS OF HYPOTYPOSES OR OUTLINES.

I.[11]

The substance[12] of the Son is not a substance devised extraneously,[13] nor is it one introduced out of nothing;[14] but it was born of the substance of the Father, as the reflection of light or as the steam of water. For the reflection is not the sun itself, and the steam is not the water itself, nor yet again is it anything alien; *neither is He Himself the Father, nor is He alien, but He is*[15] an emanation[16] from the substance of the Father, this substance of the Father suffering the while no partition. For as the sun remains the same and suffers no diminution from the rays that are poured out by it, so neither did the substance of the Father undergo any change in having the Son as an image of itself.

II.[17]

Theognostus, moreover, himself adds words to this effect: He who has offended against the first term[18] and the second, may be judged to deserve smaller punishment; but he who has also despised the third, can no longer find pardon.

---

1 *De Decret. Nic. Syn.*, 25, Works, vol. i. part i. p. 230.
2 *Epist.* 4, to Serapion, sec. 9, vol. i. part ii. p. 702.
3 *Bibl.*, cod. 106.
4 τοῦ μακαρίου Θεογνώστου Ἀλεξανδρέως καὶ ἐξηγητοῦ ὑποτυπώσες.
5 ἐξηγητοῦ.
6 ὑποτυπώσεις.
7 *De Dei Creatione.*
8 *Defens. fid. Nic.*, sec. ii. chap. 10. [Bull always *vindicates* where he can do so, on the principle of justice, for which I have contended on p. v. (prefatory) of vol. iv.]
9 *Divinit I. C.*, iv. 24.
10 Book iii., *against Eunomius.*
11 From book ii. In Athanasius, *On the Decrees of the Nicene Council*, sec. xxv. From the edition BB., Paris, 1608, vol. i. part i. p. 230. Athanasius introduces this fragment in the following terms: — Learn then, ye Christ-opposing Arians, that Theognostus, a man of learning, did not decline to use the expression " *of the substance*" (ἐκ τῆς οὐσίας). For, writing of the Son in the second book of his *Outlines*, he has spoken thus: *The substance of the Son.* — Tr.
12 οὐσία.
13 ἔξωθεν ἐφευρεθεῖσα.
14 ἐκ μὴ ὄντων ἐπεισηχθη.

15 The words in italics were inserted by Routh from a Catena on the Epistle to the Hebrews, where they are ascribed to Theognostus: " He Himself" is the Son.
16 ἀπόρροια.
17 In Athanasius, *Epist.* 4, to Serapion, sec. 11, vol. i. part ii. p. 703.
18 ὅρον.

For by the first term and the second, he says, is meant the teaching concerning the Father and the Son ; but by the third is meant the doctrine committed to us with respect to the perfection[1] and the partaking of the Spirit. And with the view of confirming this, he adduces the word spoken by the Saviour to the disciples : " I have yet many things to say unto you, but ye cannot bear them now. But when the Holy Spirit is come, He will teach you."[2]

III.[3]

Then he says again : As the Saviour converses with those not yet able to receive what is per-fect,[4] condescending to their littleness, while the Holy Spirit communes with the perfected, and yet we could never say on that account that the teaching of the Spirit is superior to the teaching of the Son, but only that the Son condescends to the imperfect, while the Spirit is the seal of the perfected ; even so it is not on account of the superiority of the Spirit over the Son that the blasphemy against the Spirit is a sin excluding impunity and pardon, but because for the imperfect there is pardon, while for those who have tasted the heavenly gift,[5] and been made perfect, there remains no plea or prayer for pardon.

---

[1] τελειώσει. [i.e., making the disciples τέλειοι. Jas. i. 4.]
[2] Jno. xvi. 12, 13.
[3] From Athanasius, as above, p. 155.

[4] τὰ τέλεια.
[5] Heb. vi. 4. [Compare Matt. xii. 31.]

PIERIUS OF ALEXANDRIA.[1]

TRANSLATOR'S BIOGRAPHICAL NOTICE.

[A.D. 275.] Among the very eminent men who flourished near his own time, Eusebius mentions Pierius, a presbyter of Alexandria, and speaks of him as greatly renowned for his voluntary poverty, his philosophical erudition and his skill in the exposition of Scripture and in discoursing to the public assemblies of the Church.[2] He lived in the latter part of the third century, and seems to have been for a considerable period president of the Catechetical school at Alexandria. Jerome says that he was called *Origenes, junior ;* and according to Photius, he shared in some of the errors of Origen, on such subjects especially as the doctrine of the Holy Ghost and the pre-existence of souls.[3] In his manner of life he was an ascetic. After the persecution under Galerius or Maximus he lived at Rome. He appears to have devoted himself largely to sacred criticism and the study of the text of Scripture ; and among several treatises written by him, and extant in the time of Photius, we find mention made of one on the prophet Hosea. And, in addition to the *Commentary on the First Epistle to the Corinthians,*[4] Photius notices twelve books of his, and praises both their composition and their matter.[5]

---

[1] [See Introductory Note, p. 143, *supra ;* also p. 99, note 8, *supra.*]

[2] *Hist. Eccl.,* vii. 32.

[3] [Perhaps only speculatively (see Frag. II. *infra*), not dogmatically. Compare Wordsworth's Platonic *Ode on Immortality.*]

[4] Lardner (part ii. book i. chap. xxiv.) does not think that there was a commentary written by Pierius on this epistle, but only that the word of Paul, mentioned below, was expounded at length in some work or other by Pierius. Fabricius holds the opposite opinion. — Tr.

[5] See Eusebius as above, Jerome in the preface to Hosea, *Photius,* cod. 118, 119; *Epiphanius,* 69, 2; *Lardner,* part ii. book i. chap. 24; &c.

I. — A FRAGMENT OF A WORK OF PIERIUS ON THE FIRST EPISTLE OF PAUL TO THE CORINTHIANS.[1]

Origen, Dionysius, Pierius, Eusebius of Cæsareia, Didymus, and Apollinaris, have interpreted this epistle most copiously;[2] of whom Pierius, when he was expounding and unfolding the meaning of the apostle, and purposed to explain the words, *For I would that all men were even as I myself*,[3] added this remark: In saying this, Paul, without disguise, preaches celibacy.[4]

---

[1] This very brief quotation is preserved in Jerome's Second Epistle to Pammachius.
[2] *Latissime.*

[3] 1 Cor. vii. 7.
[4] Vol. iv. p. 243, edit. Benedictin. [No doubt he does, as did his Master, Christ, before him, and under the same limitations. Matt. xix. 12.]

II. — A SECTION ON THE WRITINGS OF PIERIUS.[1]

DIFFERENT DISCOURSES OF THE PRESBYTER PIERIUS.

There was read a book by Pierius the presbyter, who, they say, endured the conflict[2] for Christ, along with his brother Isidorus. And he is reputed to have been the teacher of the martyr Pamphilus in ecclesiastical studies, and to have been president of the school at Alexandria. The work contained twelve books.[3] And in style he is perspicuous and clear, with the easy flow, as it were, of a spoken address, displaying no signs of laboured art,[4] but bearing us quietly along, smoothly and gently, like off-hand speaking. And in argument he is most fertile, if any one is so. And he expresses his opinion on many things outside what is now established in the Church, perhaps in an antique manner;[5] but with respect to the Father and the Son, he sets forth his sentiments piously, except that he speaks of two substances and two natures; using, however, the terms substance and nature, as is apparent from what follows, and from what precedes this passage, in the sense of person[6] and not in the sense put on it by the adherents of Arius. With respect to the Spirit, however, he lays down his opinion in a very dangerous and far from pious manner. For he affirms that He is inferior to the Father and the Son in glory.[7] He has a passage also in the book[8] entitled, *On the Gospel according to Luke*, from which it is possible to show that the honour or dishonour of the image is also the honour or dishonour of the original. And, again, he indulges in some obscure speculations, after the manner of the nonsense of Origen, on the subject of the " pre-existence of souls." And also in the book on the Passover (Easter) and on Hosea, he treats both of the cherubim made by Moses, and of the pillar of Jacob, in which passages he admits the actual construction of those things, but propounds the foolish theory that they were given economically, and that they were in no respect like other things which are made; inasmuch as they bore the likeness of no other form, but had only, as he foolishly says, the appearance of wings.[9]

---

[1] From the *Bibliotheca* of Photius, cod. 119, p. 300, ed. Hoeschel.
[2] Of martyrdom.
[3] λόγους.
[4] ἐπιμελὲς ἐνδεικνύμενος.
[5] [e.g., his Platonic ideas, as explained in note 3, p. 156, *supra*.]
[6] ὑπόστασις. [See my remarks, vol. iv. p. v., introductory.]

[7] [Photius must often be received with a grain of salt.]
[8] εἰς τὸν λόγον. [On images, etc., Photius is no authority.]
[9] The text here is evidently corrupt. It runs thus: οἰκονομίας δὲ λόγῳ συγχωρηθῆναι ματαιολογεῖ ὡς οὐδὲν ἦσαν ὡς ἕτερα τὰ γεγενημένα, ὡς οὐδὲ τύπον ἄλλον ἔφερε μορφῆς, ἀλλὰ μόνον πτερύγων κενολογεῖ φέρειν αὐτὰ σχῆμα. Hoeschelius proposes ὡς οὐδὲν ἦσαν, ὡς ἕτερον ἦσαν, ὡς ἕτερα, &c., and he rejects the ὡς in ὡς οὐδὲν τύπον on the authority of four codices. — Tr.

THEONAS OF ALEXANDRIA.

TRANSLATOR'S BIOGRAPHICAL NOTICE.

[A.D. 300.] Of this Theonas we know extremely little. Eusebius[1] tells us that Maximus, who had held the episcopal office at Alexandria for eighteen years after the death of Dionysius, was succeeded by Theonas. That bishopric, we also learn, he held for nineteen years. His date is fixed as from about 282 to 300 A.D. The only thing of his that has come down to our time is his letter to Lucianus, the chief chamberlain,[2] and a person in high favour with the emperor. This epistle, which is a letter of advice to that individual on the duties of his office, was first published in the *Spicilegium* of Dacherius, and again in Gallandi's *Bibliotheca*. The name of the emperor is not given, neither does the letter itself tell us who the Bishop Theonas was who wrote it. Hence some have, without much reason, supposed another Theonas, bishop of Cyzicus, as the author. And some, such as Cave, have thought the emperor in question was Constantius Chlorus. But the whole circumstances suit Diocletian best.[3] Some infer from the diction of the epistle, as we have it, that it is a translation from a Greek original.

THE EPISTLE OF THEONAS, BISHOP OF ALEXANDRIA, TO LUCIANUS, THE CHIEF CHAMBERLAIN.[4]

BISHOP THEONAS TO LUCIANUS, THE CHIEF CHAMBERLAIN OF OUR MOST INVINCIBLE EMPEROR.

I.

I give thanks to Almighty God and our Lord Jesus Christ, who has not given over the manifesting of His faith throughout the whole world, as the sole specific for our salvation,[5] and the extending of it even in the course of the persecutions of despots. Yea, like gold reduced in the furnace, it has only been made to shine the more under the storms of persecution, and its truth and grandeur have only become always the more and more illustrious, so that now, peace being granted to the churches by our gracious prince, the works of Christians are shining even in sight of the unbelieving, and God your Father, who is in heaven, is glorified thereby ;[6] a thing which, if we desire to be Christians in deed rather than in word, we ought to seek and aspire after as our first object on account of our salva-tion. For if we seek our own glory, we set our desire upon a vain and perishing object, and one which leads ourselves on to death. But the glory of the Father and of the Son, who for our salvation was nailed to the cross, makes us safe for the everlasting redemption ; and that is the greatest hope of Christians.

Wherefore, my Lucianus, I neither suppose nor desire that you should make it a matter of boasting, that by your means many persons belonging to the palace of the emperor have been brought to the knowlege of the truth ; but rather does it become us to give the thanks to our God who has made thee a good instrument for a good work, and has raised thee to great honour with the emperor, that you might diffuse the sweet savour of the Christian name to His own glory and to the salvation of many. For just the more completely that the emperor himself, though not yet attached[7] to the Christian religion, has entrusted the care of his life and person to these same Christians as his more faithful servants, so much the more careful ought ye to be, and the more diligent and watchful in seeing to his safety and in attending upon him, so that the name of Christ may be greatly glorified thereby, and His

---

[1] *Hist. Eccl.*, vii. 32.
[2] *Præpositus cubiculariorum.*
[3] See Neander's *Church History*, vol. i. p. 197 (Bohn). [Christians began to be preferred for their probity. Diocletian's reign at first gave the Church a long peace (see vol. iv. p. 126) of well-nigh ten years.]
[4] In *Dacherii Spicilegium*, iii pp. 297-299
[5] *In salutis nostræ unicum remedium.*
[6] Matt. v. 16.

[7] *Ascriptus.*

faith extended daily through you who wait upon the emperor. For in old times some former princes thought us malevolent and filled with all manner of crime; but now, seeing your good works, they should not be able to avoid glorifying Christ Himself.[1]

II.

Therefore you ought to strive to the utmost of your power not to fall into a base or dishonourable, not to say an absolutely flagitious way of thinking, lest the name of Christ be thus blasphemed even by you. Be it far from you that you should sell the privilege of access to the emperor to any one for money, or that you should by any means place a dishonest account of any affair before your prince, won over either by prayers or by bribes. Let all the lust of avarice be put from you, which serves the cause of idolatry rather than the religion of Christ.[2] No filthy lucre, no duplicity, can befit the Christian who embraces the simple and unadorned[3] Christ. Let no scurrilous or base talk have place among you. Let all things be done with modesty, courteousness, affability, and uprightness, so that the name of our God and Lord Jesus Christ may be glorified in all.

Discharge the official duties to which you are severally appointed with the utmost fear of God and affection to your prince, and perfect carefulness. Consider that every command of the emperor which does not offend God has proceeded from God Himself;[4] and execute it in love as well as in fear, and with all cheerfulness. For there is nothing which so well refreshes a man who is wearied out with weighty cares as the seasonable cheerfulness and benign patience of an intimate servant; nor, again, on the other hand, does anything so much annoy and vex him as the moroseness and impatience and grumbling of his servant. Be such things far from you Christians, whose walk is in zeal for the faith.[5] But in order that God may be honoured[6] in yourselves, suppress ye and tread down all your vices of mind and body. Be clothed with patience and courtesy; be replenished with the virtues and the hope of Christ. Bear all things for the sake of your Creator Himself; endure all things; overcome and get above all things, that ye may win Christ the Lord. Great are these duties, and full of painstaking. But he that striveth for the mastery[7] is temperate in all things; and they do it to obtain a corruptible crown, but we an incorruptible.

III.

But because, as I apprehend it, ye are assigned to different offices, and you, Lucianus, are styled the head of them all, whom, also, by the grace of Christ given you, you are able to direct and dispose in their different spheres, I am certain that it will not displease you if I also bring before your notice, in a particular and summary manner, some of my sentiments on the subject of these offices. For I hear that one of you keeps the private moneys of the emperor; another the imperial robes and ornaments; another the precious vessels; another the books, who, I understand, does not as yet belong to the believers; and others the different parts of the household goods. And in what manner, therefore, these charges ought, in my judgment, to be executed, I shall indicate in a few words.

IV.

He who has charge of the private moneys of the emperor ought to keep every thing in an exact reckoning. He should be ready at any time to give an accurate account of all things. He should note down every thing in writing, if it is at all possible, before giving money to another. He should never trust such things to his memory, which, being drawn off day by day to other matters, readily fails us, so that, without writing, we sometimes honestly certify things which have never existed; neither should this kind of writing be of a commonplace order, but such as easily and clearly unfolds all things, and leaves the mind of the inquirer without any scruple or doubt on the subject; a thing which will easily be effected if a distinct and separate account is kept in writing of all receipts, and of the time when, and the person by whom, and the place at which they were made.[8] And, in like manner, all that is paid out to others, or expended by order of the emperor, should be entered in its own place by itself in the reckoning; and that servant should be faithful and prudent, so that his lord may rejoice that he has set him over his goods,[9] and may glorify Christ in him.

V.

Nor will the diligence and care of that servant be less who has the custody of the robes and imperial ornaments. All these he should enter in a most exact catalogue, and he should keep a note of what they are and of what sort, and in what places stored, and when he received them, and from whom, and whether they are soiled or unsoiled. All these things he should keep in his diligence; he should often review again, and he

---

1 [A beautiful concern of our author for the honour of the Master seems to have dictated this noble letter. Matt. v. 16.]
2 Eph. v. 4, 5.
3 *Nudum.*
4 [See note 1, p. 108, *supra.*]
5 *Qui zelo fidei inceditis.*
6 1 Peter iv. 11.
7 1 Cor. ix. 25.

8 [A most important hint to the clergy in their accounts with the Church.]
9 Matt. xxiv. 45, 47.

should often go over them that they may be the more readily known again. All these he should have at hand, and all in readiness ; and he should always give the clearest information on every matter on which it is sought, to his prince or his superior, whenever they ask about any thing ; and all this at the same time in such wise that every thing may be done in humility and cheerful patience, and that the name of Christ may be praised even in a small matter.

VI.

In a similar manner should he conduct himself to whose fidelity are entrusted the vessels of silver and gold, and crystal or murrha,[1] for eating or for drinking. All these he should arrange suitably, of them all he should keep an account, and with all diligence he should make an inventory of how many and which sort of precious stones are in them. He should examine them all with great prudence ; he should produce them in their proper places and on their proper occasions. And he should observe most carefully to whom he gives them, and at what time, and from whom he receives them again, lest there should occur any mistake or injurious suspicion, or perhaps some considerable loss in things of value.

VII.

The most responsible person, however, among you, and also the most careful, will be he who may be entrusted by the emperor with the custody of his library. He will himself select for this office a person of proved knowledge, a man grave and adapted to great affairs, and ready to reply to all applications for information, such a one as Philadelphus chose for this charge, and appointed to the superintendence of his most noble library — I mean Aristeus, his confidential chamberlain, whom he sent also as his legate to Eleazar, with most magnificent gifts, in recognition of the translation of the Sacred Scriptures ; and this person also wrote the full history of the Seventy Interpreters. If, therefore, it should happen that a believer in Christ is called to this same office, he should not despise that secular literature and those Gentile intellects which please the emperor.[2] To be praised are the poets for the greatness of their genius, the acuteness of their inventions, the aptness and lofty eloquence of their style. To be praised are the orators ; to be praised also are the philosophers in their own class. To be praised, too, are the historians, who unfold to us the order of exploits, and the manners and institutions of our ancestors, and show us the rule of life from the proceedings of the ancients. On occasion also he will endeavour to laud the divine Scriptures, which, with marvellous care and most liberal expenditure, Ptolemy Philadelphus caused to be translated into our language ;[3] and sometimes, too, the Gospel and the Apostle will be lauded for their divine oracles ; and there will be an opportunity for introducing the mention of Christ ; and, little by little, His exclusive divinity will be explained ; and all these things may happily come to pass by the help of Christ.

He ought, therefore, to know all the books which the emperor possesses ; he should often turn them over, and arrange them neatly in their proper order by catalogue ; if, however, he shall have to get new books, or old ones transcribed, he should be careful to obtain the most accurate copyists ; and if that cannot be done, he should appoint learned men to the work of correction, and recompense them justly for their labours. He should also cause all manuscripts to be restored according to their need, and should embellish them, not so much with mere superstitious extravagance, as with useful adornment ; and therefore he should not aim at having the whole manuscripts written on purple skins and in letters of gold, unless the emperor has specially required that. With the utmost submission, however, he should do every thing that is agreeable to Cæsar. As he is able, he should, with all modesty, suggest to the emperor that he should read, or hear read, those books which suit his rank and honour, and minister to good use rather than to mere pleasure. He should himself first be thoroughly familiar with those books, and he should often commend them in presence of the emperor, and set forth, in an appropriate fashion, the testimony and the weight of those who approve them, that he may not seem to lean to his own understanding only.

VIII.

Those, moreover, who have the care of the emperor's person should be in all things as prompt as possible ; always, as we have said, cheerful in countenance, sometimes merry, but ever with such perfect modesty as that he may commend it above all else in you all, and perceive that it is the true product of the religion of Christ. You should also all be elegant and tidy in person and attire, yet, at the same time, not in such wise as to attract notice by extravagance or affectation, lest Christian modesty be scandalised.[4] Let every thing be ready at its

---

[1] Murrhine vessels were first introduced into Rome by Pompey. They were valued chiefly for their variegated colours, and were extremely costly　Some think they were made of onyx stone, others of variegated glass: but most modern writers suppose that what is meant was some sort of porcelain.

[2] [A lofty spirit of liberal love for literature is here exemplified.]

[3] It is from these words that the inference is drawn that this epistle was written by a Greek.

[4] [The teachings of Clement had formed the minor morals of Christians. See vol. ii. book ii. pp. 237, 284.]

proper time, and disposed as well as possible in its own order. There should also be due arrangement among you, and carefulness that no confusion appear in your work, nor any loss of property in any way ; and appropriate places should be settled and suitably prepared, in accordance with the capacity (*captu*) and importance of the places.

Besides this, your servants should be the most thoroughly honest, and circumspect, and modest, and as serviceable to you as possible. And see that you instruct and teach them in true doctrine with all the patience and charity of Christ ; but if they despise and lightly esteem your instructions, then dismiss them, lest their wickedness by any hap recoil upon yourselves. For sometimes we have seen, and often we have heard, how masters have been held in ill-repute in consequence of the wickedness of their servants.

If the emperor visits her imperial majesty, or she him, then should ye also be most circumspect in eye and demeanour, and in all your words. Let her mark your mastery of yourselves and your modesty ;[1] and let her followers and attendants mark *your demeanour ;* let them mark it and admire it, and by reason thereof praise Jesus Christ our Lord in you. Let your conversation always be temperate and modest, and seasoned with religion as with salt.[2] And, further, let there be no jealousy among you or contentiousness, which might bring you into all manner of confusion and division, and thus also make you objects of aversion to Christ and to the emperor, and lead you into the deepest abomina-

tion, so that not one stone of your building could stand upon another.

IX.

And do thou, my dearest Lucianus, since thou art wise, bear with good-will the unwise ;[3] and they too may perchance become wise. Do no one an injury at any time, and provoke no one to anger. If an injury is done to you, look to Jesus Christ ; and even as ye desire that He may remit your transgressions, do ye also forgive them theirs ;[4] and then also shall ye do away with all ill-will, and bruise the head of that ancient serpent,[5] who is ever on the watch with all subtlety to undo your good works and your prosperous attainments. Let no day pass by without reading some portion of the Sacred Scriptures, at such convenient hour as offers, and giving some space to meditation.[6] And never cast off the habit of reading in the Holy Scriptures ; for nothing feeds the soul and enriches the mind so well as those sacred studies do. But look to this as the chief gain you are to make by them, that, in all due patience, ye may discharge the duties of your office religiously and piously — that is, in the love of Christ — and despise all transitory objects for the sake of His eternal promises, which in truth surpass all human comprehension and understanding,[7] and shall conduct you into everlasting felicity.

A happy adieu to you in Christ, my Lord Lucianus.

---

[1] [Thus is reflected the teaching of St. Paul, 1 Tim. v. 2. All women to be *honoured*, and " all purity " to characterize society with them.]
[2] Col. iv. 6.

[3] 2 Cor. xi. 19.
[4] Mark xi. 25.
[5] Rom. xvi. 20.
[6] [Blessed spirit of primitive piety! Is not this rule too much relaxed in our own Laodicean age?]
[7] Phil. iv. 7. [How much there is in this letter which ought to prick the consciences of wealthy and " fashionable " Christians of our day !]

PHILEAS.

TRANSLATOR'S BIOGRAPHICAL NOTICE.

[A.D. 307.] From Jerome[1] we learn that this Phileas belonged to Thmuis, a town of Lower Egypt, the modern *Tmai*, which was situated between the Tanite and Mendesian branches of the Nile, an episcopal seat, and in the time of Valentinian and Theodosius the Great a place of considerable consequence, enjoying a separate government of its own. Eusebius[2] speaks of him as a man not less distinguished for his services to his country than for his eminence in philosophical studies and his proficiency in foreign literature and science. He tells us further, that, along with another person of considerable importance, by name Philoromus, being brought to trial for his

---

[1] *De vir. illustr.*, chap. 78.
[2] *Hist. Eccles.*, viii. 9 and 10.

faith, he withstood the threats and insults of the judge, and all the entreaties of relatives and friends, to compromise his Christian belief, and was condemned to lose his head. Jerome also, in the passage already referred to, names him a *true philosopher, and, at the same time, a godly martyr;* and states, that *on assuming the bishopric of his native district, he wrote a very elegant book in praise of the martyrs.* Of this book certain fragments are preserved for us in Eusebius. In addition to these we have also an epistle which the same Phileas seems to have written in the name of three other bishops, as well as himself, to Meletius, the bishop of Lycopolis, and founder of the Meletian schism. This epistle appears to have been written in Greek; but we possess only a Latin version, which, however, from its abrupt style, is believed to be very ancient. The four bishops whose names stand at the head of the Epistle — viz., Hesychius, Pachomius, Theodorus, and Phileas, are also mentioned by Eusebius (*Hist. Eccl.,* viii. 13) as distinguished martyrs. This epistle was written evidently when those bishops were in prison, and its date is determined by the mention of Peter as the then bishop of Alexandria. The martyrdom of Phileas is fixed with much probability as happening at Alexandria, under Maximus, about the year 307 A.D.[1] [But see Neale, *Patriarchate of Alex.,* i. pp. 97–101, for his view of two bearing this name.]

FRAGMENTS OF THE EPISTLE OF PHILEAS TO THE PEOPLE OF THMUIS.[2]

I.

Having before them all these examples and signs and illustrious tokens which are given us in the divine and holy Scriptures, the blessed martyrs who lived with us did not hesitate, but, directing the eye of their soul in sincerity to that God who is over all, and embracing with willing mind the death which their piety cost them, they adhered steadfastly to their vocation. For they learned that our Lord Jesus Christ endured man's estate on our behalf, that He might destroy all sin, and furnish us with the provision needful for our entrance into eternal life. "For He thought it not robbery to be equal with God: but made Himself of no reputation, taking upon Him the form of a servant: and being found in fashion as a man, He humbled Himself unto death, even the death of the cross."[3] For which reason also these Christ-bearing[4] martyrs sought zealously the greater gifts, and endured, some of them, every kind of pain and all the varied contrivances of torture not merely once, but once and again; and though the guards showed their fury against them not only by threatenings in word, but also by deeds of violence, they did not swerve from their resolution, because *perfect love casteth out fear.*[5]

II.

And to narrate their virtue and their manly endurance under every torment, what language would suffice? For as every one who chose was at liberty to abuse them, some beat them with wooden clubs,[6] and others with rods, and others with scourges, and others again with thongs, and others with ropes. And the spectacle of these modes of torture had great variety in it, and exhibited vast malignity. For some had their hands bound behind them, and were suspended on the rack and had every limb in their body stretched with a certain kind of pulleys.[7] Then after all this the torturers, according to their orders, lacerated with the sharp iron claws[8] the whole body, not merely, as in the case of murderers, the sides only, but also the stomach and the knees and the cheeks. And others were hung up in mid-air, suspended by one hand from the portico, and their sufferings were fiercer than any other kind of agony by reason of the distention of their joints and limbs. And others were bound to pillars, face to face, not touching the ground with their feet, but hanging with all the weight of the body, so that their chains were drawn all the more tightly by reason of the tension. And this they endured not simply as long as the governor[9] spoke with them, or had leisure to hear them, but well-nigh through the whole day. For when he passed on to others he left some of those under his authority to keep watch over these former, and to observe whether any of them, being overcome by the torture, seemed

---

[1] [His diocese belonged to the region over which Alexandria had the primacy by the "ancient usages."]

[2] In Eusebius, *Hist. Eccles.,* viii. 10.

[3] Phil. ii. 6–8.

[4] χριστοφόροι. So Ignatius of Antioch was called θεοφόρος, God-bearer. [Vol. i. pp. 45, 49, this series.]

[5] 1 John iv. 18.

[6] ξύλοις. What is meant, however, may be the instrument called by the Romans *equuleus,* a kind of rack in the shape of a horse, commonly used in taking the evidence of slaves.

[7] μαγγάνοις τισί.

[8] The text gives ἀμυντηρίοις ἐκόλαζον, for which Nicephorus reads ἀμυντηρίοις τὰς κολάσεις. The ἀμυντηρια were probably the Latin *ungulæ,* an instrument of torture like claws. So Rufinus understands the phrase.

[9] ἡγεμών. That is probably the Roman Præfectus Augustalis.

likely to yield. But he gave them orders at the same time to cast them into chains without sparing, and thereafter, when they were expiring, to throw them on the ground and drag them along. For they said that they would not give themselves the slightest concern about us, but would look upon us and deal with us as if we were nothing at all. This second mode of torture our enemies devised then over and above the scourging.

III.

And there were also some who, after the tortures, were placed upon the stocks and had both their feet stretched through all the four holes, so that they were compelled to lie on their back on the stocks, as they were unable (to stand) in consequence of the fresh wounds they had over the whole body from the scourging. And others being thrown upon the ground lay prostrated there by the excessively frequent application of the tortures; in which condition they exhibited to the onlookers a still more dreadful spectacle than they did when actually undergoing their torments, bearing, as they did, on their bodies the varied and manifold tokens of the cruel ingenuity of their tortures. While this state of matters went on, some died under their tortures, putting the adversary to shame by their constancy. And others were thrust half-dead into the prison, where in a few days, worn out with their agonies, they met their end. But the rest, getting sure recovery under the application of remedies, through time and their lengthened detention in prison, became more confident. And thus then, when they were commanded to make their choice between these alternatives, namely, either to put their hand to the unholy sacrifice and thus secure exemption from further trouble, and obtain from them their abominable sentence of absolution and liberation,[1] or else to refuse to sacrifice, and thus expect the judgment of death to be executed on them, they never hesitated, but went cheerfully to death.[2] For they knew the sentence declared for us of old by the Holy Scriptures: "He that sacrificeth to other gods," it is said, "shall be utterly destroyed."[3] And again,[4] "Thou shalt have no other gods before Me."[5]

---

1 τῆς ἐπαράτου ἐλευθερίας.
2 [It is impossible to accept modern theories of the *inconsiderable* number of the primitive martyrs, in view of the abounding evidences of a chronic and continuous persecution always evidenced by even these fragments of authentic history. See vol. iv. p. 125.]
3 Exod. xxii. 20.
4 Exod. xx. 3.
5 Eusebius, after quoting these passages, adds: — "These are the words of a true philosopher, and one who was no less a lover of God than of wisdom, which, before the final sentence of his judge, and while he lay yet in prison, he addressed to the brethren in his church, at once to represent to them in what condition he was himself, and to exhort them to maintain steadfastly, even after his speedy death, their piety towards Christ." — Tr.

THE EPISTLE OF THE SAME PHILEAS OF THMUIS TO MELETIUS, BISHOP OF LYCOPOLIS.

THE BEGINNING OF THE EPISTLE OF THE BISHOPS.[1]

Hesychius, Pachomius, Theodorus, and Phileas, to Meletius, our friend and fellow-minister in the Lord, greeting. Some reports having reached us concerning thee, which, on the testimony of certain individuals who came to us, spake of certain things foreign to divine order and ecclesiastical rule which are being attempted, yea, rather which are being done by thee, we, in an ingenuous manner held them to be untrustworthy, regarding them to be such as we would not willingly credit, when we thought of the audacity implied in their magnitude and their uncertain attempts. But since many who are visiting us at the present time have lent some credibility to these reports, and have not hesitated to attest them as facts, we, to our exceeding surprise, have been compelled to indite this letter to thee. And what agitation and sadness have been caused to us all in common and to each of us individually by (the report of) the ordination carried through by thee in parishes having no manner of connection with thee, we are unable sufficiently to express. We have not delayed, however, by a short statement to prove your practice wrong. There is the law of our fathers and forefathers, of which neither art thou thyself ignorant, established according to divine and ecclesiastical order; for it is all for the good pleasure of God and the zealous regard of better things.[2] By them it has been established and settled that it is not lawful for any bishop to celebrate ordinations in other parishes[3] than his own; a law which is exceedingly important[4] and wisely devised. For, in the first place, it is but right that the conversation and life of those who are ordained should be examined with great care; and in the second place, that all confusion and turbulence should be done away with. For every one shall have enough to do in managing his own parish, and in finding with great care and many anxieties

---

1 This epistle was first edited by Scipio Maffeius from an ancient Verona manuscript in the *Osserv. Letter*, vol. iii. pp. 11-17, where is given the *Fragment of a History of the Meletian Schism*. See Neander's important remarks on this whole document, *Church History*, iii. p. 310 (Bohn). — Tr.

2 *Zelo meliorum*.
3 [*Parishes* = dioceses (so called now); but they were very small territorially, and every city had its "bishop." See Bingham, book ix. cap. 2, and Euseb., book v. cap. 23. Comp. note 1, p. 106, *supra*.]
4 *Bene nimis magna*.

suitable subordinates *among these* with whom he has passed his whole life, and who have been trained under his hands. But thou, neither making any account of these things, nor regarding the future, nor considering the law of our sainted fathers and those who have been taken to Christ time after time, nor the honour of our great bishop and father,[1] Peter,[2] on whom we all depend in the hope which we have in the Lord Jesus Christ, nor softened by our imprisonments and trials, and daily and multiplied reproach, hast ventured on subverting all things at once. And what means will be left thee for justifying thyself with respect to these things? But perhaps thou wilt say: I did this to prevent many being drawn away with the unbelief of many, because the flocks were in need and forsaken, there being no pastor with them. Well, but it is most certain that they are not in such destitution: in the first place, because there are many going about them and in a position to act as visitors; and in the second place, even if there was some measure of neglect on their side, then the proper way would have been for the representation to be made promptly by the people, and for us to take account of them according to their desert.[3] But they knew that they were in no want of ministers, and therefore they did not come to seek them. They knew that we were wont to discharge them with an admonition from such inquisition for matter of complaint, or that everything was done with all carefulness which seemed to be for their profit; for all was done under correction,[4] and all was considered with well-approved honesty. Thou, however, giving such strenuous attention to the deceits of certain parties and their vain words, hast made a stealthy leap to the celebrating of ordinations. For if, indeed, those with thee were constraining thee to this, and in their ignorance were doing violence to ecclesiastical order, thou oughtest to have followed the common rule and have informed us by letter; and in that way what seemed expedient would have been done. And if perchance some persuaded you to credit their story that it was all over with us, — a thing of which thou couldest not have been ignorant, because there were many passing and repassing by us who might visit you, — even although, I say, this had been the case, yet thou oughtest to have waited for the judgment of the superior father and for his allowance of this practice. But without giving any heed to these matters, but indulging a different expectation, yea rather, indeed, denying all respect to us, thou hast pro-

vided certain rulers for the people. For now we have learned, too, that there were also divisions,[5] because thy unwarrantable exercise of the right of ordination displeased many. And thou wert not persuaded to delay such procedure or restrain thy purpose readily even by the word of the Apostle Paul, the most blessed seer,[6] and the man who put on Christ, who is the Christ of all of us no less; for he, in writing to his dearly-beloved son Timothy, says: "Lay hands suddenly on nò man, neither be partaker of other men's sins."[7] And thus he at once shows his own anxious consideration for him,[8] and gives him his example and exhibits the law according to which, with all carefulness and caution, parties are to be chosen for the honour of ordination.[9] We make this declaration to thee, that in future thou mayest study[10] to keep within the safe and salutary limits of the law.

THE CONCLUSION OF THE EPISTLE OF THE BISHOPS.

After receiving and perusing this epistle, he neither wrote any reply nor repaired to them in the prison, nor went to the blessed Peter. But when all these bishops and presbyters and deacons had suffered martyrdom in the prison at Alexandria, he at once entered Alexandria. Now in that city there was a certain person, by name Isidorus, turbulent in character, and possessed with the ambition of being a teacher. And there was also a certain Arius, who wore the habit of piety, and was in like manner possessed with the ambition to be a teacher. And when they discovered the object of Meletius's passion[11] and what it was that he sought, hastening to him, and looking with an evil eye on the episcopal authority of the blessed Peter, that the aim and desire of Meletius might be made patent,[12] they discovered to Meletius certain presbyters, then in hiding, to whom the blessed Peter had given power to act as parish-visitors. And Meletius recommending them to improve the opportunity given them for rectifying their error, suspended them for the time, and by his own authority ordained two persons in their place,[13] namely, one in prison and another in the mines. On learning these things the blessed Peter, with much endurance, wrote to the people of Alexandria an epistle in the following terms.[14]

---

1 [The bishops of Alexandria are called *popes* to this day, and were so from the beginning. See vol. v. p 154.]
2 [Peter succeeded Theonas as sixteenth bishop and primate of Alexandria. See vol. iv. p. 384; also Neale, *Pat. of Alex.*, i. p. 90.]
3 *Oportuerat ex populo properare ac nos exigere pro merito.*
4 *Sub arguente.*

5 The manuscript reads *chrismata*, for which *schismata* is proposed.
6 *Provisoris* — perhaps rather, THE PROVIDER — *the saint who with careful forethought has mapped out our proper course in such matters.*
7 1 Tim. v. 22.
8 *Erga illum providentiam.*
9 The manuscript gives *ordinando adnuntias*, for which is proposed *ordinandi. Adnuntiamus.*
10 Reading *studeas* for *studetur.*
11 *Cupiditatem.*
12 *Ut cognoscatur concupiscentia Meletii.*
13 The text is — *Commendans ei occasionem Meletius, separavit eos*, &c.: on which see especially Neander, iii. p. 311 (Bohn).
14 This epistle is given elsewhere. [This volume, *infra.*]

PAMPHILUS.

TRANSLATOR'S BIOGRAPHICAL NOTICE.

[A.D. 309.] According to the common account Pamphilus was a native of Berytus, the modern Beirût, and a member of a distinguished Phœnician family. Leaving Berytus, however, at an early period, he repaired to Alexandria and studied under Pierius, the well-known head of the Catechetical school there. At a subsequent period he went to the Palestinian Cæsareia, and was made a presbyter of the Church there under Bishop Agapius. In course of the persecutions of Diocletian he was thrown into prison by Urbanus, the governor of Palestine. This took place towards the end of the year 307 A.D., and his confinement lasted till the beginning of the year 309, when he suffered martyrdom by order of Firmilianus, who had succeeded Urbanus in the governorship of the country. During his imprisonment he enjoyed the affectionate attendance of Eusebius, the Church historian, and the tender friendship which subsisted long between the two is well known. It was as a memorial of that intimacy that Eusebius took the surname of Pamphili. Pamphilus appears to have given himself up with great enthusiasm to the promotion of Biblical studies, and is spoken of as the founder of a theological school in which special importance was attached to exposition. He busied himself also with the transcription and dissemination of the Scriptures and other writings, such as those of Origen, of whom he was a devoted follower. At Cæsareia he established a great public library,[1] consisting mainly of ecclesiastical writers ; and among the treasures of that library are mentioned the *Tetrapla* and *Hexapla* of Origen, from which, with the help of Eusebius, he produced a new and revised edition of the Septuagint. There is a statement in Jerome[2] to the effect that, though he was so great a student of the writings of others, Pamphilus, through an excess of modesty, wrote no work of his own, with exception of some letters to his friends.[3] But there is a work bearing the title of *An Exposition of the Chapters of the Acts of the Apostles*, which is attributed by many to him, although others ascribe it to Euthalius, bishop of Sulce. And besides this there is also the *Apology for Origen*, of which, according to the statement of Photius,[4] the first five books were compiled by Pamphilus, in conjunction with Eusebius, during the period of his imprisonment, the sixth book being added by Eusebius after his friend's martyrdom. Of this *Apology* we possess now only the first book, and that, too, only in the faulty Latin version of Rufinus. There are repeated and warmly eulogistic references to Pamphilus in the *Ecclesiastical History* of Eusebius. Thus he speaks of him as *that holy martyr of our day ;*[5] and as *that most eloquent man, and that philosopher truly such in his life ;*[6] and again, as *that most admirable man of our times, that glory of the church of Cæsareia.*[7] He devotes the eleventh chapter of the eighth book also to a notice of Pamphilus and other martyrs. And besides all this he wrote a separate life of his friend, in three books, of which, however, all has perished, with exception of a few disputed fragments.[8]

---

[1] [Another glorious product of the school of Alexandria.]

[2] *Apol. contr. Ruf.*, book i. num. 9, Works, ii. p. 465.

[3] *Proprii operis nihil omnino scripsit, exceptis epistolis quas ad amicos forte mittebat ; in tantum se humilitate dejecerat.*

[4] *Bibl. Cod.*, cxviii. p. 295.

[5] *Ibid.*, vi. 32.

[6] *Ibid.*, vii. 32.

[7] *Ibid.*, viii. 13.

[8] [Evidently he impressed Eusebius as an extraordinary man in an age of colossal minds, and we must lament the loss of his writings.]

AN EXPOSITION OF THE CHAPTERS OF THE ACTS OF THE APOSTLES.[1]

Having had ourselves the advantage of the method and model received from our fathers and teachers, we attempt, in a modest way, to give these in this exposition of the chapters, entreating your forgiveness for the rashness of such an endeavour in us who are young in point both of years and of study,[2] and looking to have the indulgence[3] of every one who reads this writing in prayer on our behalf. We make this exposition, therefore, after the history of Luke, the evangelist and historian. And, accordingly, we have indicated whole chapters by the letters of the alphabet,[4] and their subdivisions into parts we have noted by means of the asterisk.[5]

A. Of Christ's teaching after His resurrection, and of His appearing to the disciples, and of the promise of the gift of the Holy Ghost, and of the spectacle and manner of Christ's assumption.[6]

B. Peter's discourse to those who were made disciples, on the subject of the death and reprobation[7] of Judas;[8] * in this chapter we have also the section on the substitution of Matthias, who was elected by lot through the grace of God with prayer.

C. Of the divine descent[9] of the Holy Ghost on the day of Pentecost which lighted on them who believed. In this we have also * the instruction delivered by Peter, and * passages from the prophets on the subject, and * on the passion and resurrection and assumption of Christ, and the gift of the Holy Ghost; also * of the faith of those present, and their salvation by baptism; and, further,* of the unity of spirit pervading the believers and promoting the common good, and of the addition made to their number.

D. Of the healing in (the name of) Christ of the man lame from his birth; and of the discourse[10] of Peter, in which he reasons and sympathizes and counsels with respect to his[11] salvation. And here we have * the interposition[12] of the chief priests through jealousy of what had taken place, and their judgment on the miracle, and Peter's confession[13] of the power and grace of Christ. Also the section on * the unbelieving chief priests, commanding that they should not speak boldly in the name of Christ,[14] and of the dismissal[15] of the apostles. Then * the thanksgivings offered up by the Church for the faithful constancy of the apostles.

E. Of the harmonious and universal fellowship of the believers; and also * of Ananias and Sapphira and their miserable end.

F. Of the apostles being cast into prison, and led out of it by night by the angel of the Lord, who enjoined them to preach Jesus without restraint; and * of the fact that, on the following day, the chief priests apprehended them again, and, after scourging them, sent them away with the charge not to teach any longer. Then * the trusty opinion of Gamaliel touching the apostles, together with certain examples and proofs.

G. Of the election of the seven deacons.

H. The rising and slanderous information of the Jews against Stephen, and his address concerning the covenant of God with Abraham, and concerning the twelve patriarchs. Also the account of the famine and the buying of corn, and the mutual recognition of the sons of Jacob, and of the birth of Moses and the appearance of God[16] to Moses, which took place at Mount Sinai. * Also of the exodus and and calf-making of Israel (and other matters), up to the times of Solomon and the building of the temple. * Then the acknowledgment of the supercelestial glory of Jesus Christ which was revealed to Stephen himself, on account of which Stephen was himself stoned, and fell asleep piously.

I. Of the persecution of the Church and the burial of Stephen; also * of the healing of many in Samaria by Philip the apostle.

---

[1] This ἔκθεσις was edited, under the name of *Euthalius, Bishop of Sulce*, towards the end of the preceding century, by Laurentius Zacagnius, in the collection of *Monumenta Vetera*, p. 428, published at Rome. Fabricius also compared the edition of Montfaucon with the Roman. This collation is added here. — MIGNE.

[2] The text is νέοι χρόνῳ τε καὶ μαθημάτων, ἑκάστου, &c.; for which Euthal., χρόνων τε καὶ μαθημάτων παρ' ὑμῶν ἑκάστου.

[3] συμπεριφορὰν κομιζόμενοι.

[4] But Euthal., διὰ μὲν τοῦ μέλανος . . . διὰ δὲ τοῦ κινναβάρεως, i.e., by the different colours of black and vermilion.

[5] These marks are wholly wanting in the Coislin Codex, from which Montfaucon edited the piece. But they are found in the Vatican Codex. — TR.

[6] Euthal. adds, καὶ περὶ τῆς ἐνδόξου καὶ δευτέρας αὐτοῦ παρουσίας, i.e, and of His glorious and second coming.

[7] ἀποβολῆς.

[8] But Euthal. ἀποστολῆς, *apostleship.*

[9] ἐπιφοιτήσεως.

[10] κατηχήσεως.

[11] But Euthal., αὐτῶν, *their.*

[12] ἐπίστασια.

[13] Euthal. inserts περὶ ἀπειλῆς, *and of the threatening of the chief priests.*

[14] ἐπὶ τῷ ὀνόματι; but Euthal., ἐπὶ τὸ ὄνομα.

[15] Reading ἀνέσεως with Euthal., instead of ἀνανεώσεως.

[16] θεοφανεία.

J. Of Simon Magus, who believed and was baptized with many others ; also * of the sending of Peter and John to them, and their praying for the descent of the Holy Ghost upon the baptized.

K. That the participation of the Holy Ghost was not given [1] for money,[2] nor to hypocrites, but to saints by faith ; also * of the hypocrisy and the reproof of Simon.

L. That the Lord helps the good and the believing on the way to salvation, as is shown from the instance of the eunuch.

M. Of the divine call that came from heaven for Paul to the apostleship of Christ ; also * of the healing and the baptism of Paul by the hand of Ananias, in accordance with the revelation from God, and of his boldness of speech and his association with the apostles by the instrumentality of Barnabas.[3]

N. Of the paralytic Æneas who was cured by Peter at Lydda. Also * the account of Tabitha, the friend of widows, whom Peter raised from the dead by means of prayer in Joppa.

O. Of Cornelius, and what the angel said to him. Also what was spoken [4] to Peter from heaven with respect to the calling of the Gentiles. Then * that Peter, on being summoned, came to Cornelius. * The repetition by Cornelius of the things which the angel said [5] to Cornelius himself.* Peter's instruction of them in Christ, and the gift of the Holy Ghost upon those who heard him, and how those who believed from among the Gentiles were baptized there.

P. That Peter recounts to the apostles who contended with him [6] all the things that had happened in order and separately. * Then the sending of Barnabas to the brethren in Antioch.

Q. The prophecy of Agabus respecting the famine in the world,[7] and the liberal relief sent to the brethren in Jerusalem.

R. The slaying of the Apostle James. * Also the apprehension of Peter by Herod, and the account of the manner in which the angel by divine command delivered him from his bonds, and how Peter, after showing himself to the disciples by night, quietly withdrew. Also of the punishment of the keepers, and then of the

miserable and fatal overthrow [8] of the impious Herod.

S. The sending of Barnabas and Paul by the Holy Ghost to Cyprus. * The things which he did [9] there in the name of Christ on Elymas the sorcerer.

T. Paul's admirable [10] exposition of the truth concerning Christ, both from the law and from the prophets in their order, both historical and evangelical ; * his use both of the confuting and the argumentative mode of discourse on the subject of the transference of the word of preaching to the Gentiles, and of their persecution and their arrival at Iconium.

U. How, when they had preached Christ in Iconium, and many had believed, the apostles were persecuted.

V. Of the man lame from his birth in Lystra who was healed by the apostles ; on account of which they were taken by the people of the place for gods who had appeared on earth. After that, however, Paul is stoned there by the neighbouring people.

W. That according to the decree and judgment of the apostles, the Gentiles who believe ought not to be circumcised. Here, also, is the epistle of the apostles themselves to those from among the Gentiles, on the subject of the things from which they should keep themselves.[11] * The dissension of Paul with Barnabas on account of Mark.

X. Of the teaching of Timothy, and of the coming of Paul into Macedonia according to revelation. * Of the faith and salvation of a certain woman Lydia, and * of the cure of the damsel having a spirit of divination, on account of which the masters of the damsel cast Paul into prison ; and * of the earthquake and miracle which happened there ; and how the jailer believed and was baptized forthwith that same night with all his house.[12] * That the apostles on being besought went out from the prison.

Y. Of the tumult that arose in Thessalonica on account of their preaching, and of the flight of Paul to Berea, and thence to Athens.

Z. Of the inscription on the altar at Athens, and of the philosophic preaching and piety of Paul.

---

[1] ἐδίδοτο; Euthal., δίδοται is given.
[2] ὅτι οὐκ ἀργυρίου; Euthal., οὐ δι' ἀργυρίου.
[3] Euthal., διὰ Βαρνάβαν, on Barnabas's account.
[4] Euthal. inserts πάλιν, again.
[5] The text is ὧν εἶπεν ὁ ἄγγελος, &c. But Euthal., ὧν ὁ ἄγγελος ἐπεμαρτύρησε καὶ ὑφηγήσατο, which the angel testified and showed.
[6] διακριθεῖσι πρὸς αὐτόν.
[7] The text gives οἰκουμενικῆς; Euthal., οἰκουμένης.

[8] The text gives κατασφαγῆς; Euthal., καταστροφῆς.
[9] Euthal., ειργασαντο, they did.
[10] εὐθαλῆς.
[11] Reading φυλακτέων with Euthal., instead of φυλακέων.
[12] The text gives πανευτιος; Euthal., πανεστιος. Montfaucon reads πανοικί.

AA. Of Aquila and Priscilla, and the unbelief of the Corinthians, and of the good-will of God towards them according to fore-knowledge revealed to Paul. Also * of Priscus,[1] the chief ruler of the synagogue, who believed with certain others and was baptized. And * that a tumult being stirred up in Corinth, Paul departed; and coming to Ephesus, and having dis-coursed there, he left it. * And con-cerning Apollos, an eloquent man and a believer.

BB. Of baptism and the gift of the Holy Ghost conferred by means of the prayer of Paul on those who believed in Ephesus, and of the healing of the people. * Of the sons of Sceva, and as to its not being meet to approach[2] those who have be-come unbelieving and unworthy of the faith; and of the confession of those who believed; * and of the tumult that was stirred up in Ephesus by Demetrius, the silversmith, against the apostles.

CC. Of the circuit of Paul, in which also we have the account of the death of Euty-chus and his restoration by prayer in Troas; also Paul's own pastoral exhorta-tions[3] to the presbyters at Ephesus; also Paul's voyage from Ephesus to Cæsareia in Palestine.

DD. The prophecy of Agabus as to what should befall Paul in Jerusalem.

EE. The address of James to Paul touching the matter that he should not offer to keep the Hebrews back from the prac-tice of circumcision.

FF. Of the tumult that was excited against Paul in Jerusalem, and how the chief-cap-tain rescues him from the mob. * Also Paul's speech[4] concerning himself and his

vocation to be an apostle; * and of what Ananias said to Paul in Damascus, and of the vision and the voice of God that befell him once in the temple. * And that when Paul was about to be beaten for these words, on declaring that he was a Roman, he was let go.

GG. What Paul endured, and what he said, and what he did exactly[5] when he came down into the council.

HH. Of the ambush planned by the Jews against Paul, and its discovery to Lysias; * and that Paul was sent to Cæsareia to the governor with soldiers and with a letter.

II. Of the accusation laid by Tertullus in Paul's case, and of his defence of himself be-fore the governor.

JJ. Of the removal of Felix and the arrival of Festus as his successor, and of Paul's pleading before them,[6] and his dismissal.

KK. The coming of Agrippa and Bernice, and their inquiry into the case of Paul.[7] * Paul's defence of himself before Agrippa and Bernice, respecting his nurture in the law, and his vocation to the Gospel. That Paul does no wrong to the Jews, Agrippa said to Festus.

LL. Paul's voyage to Rome, abounding in very many and very great perils. * Paul's ex-hortation to those with him as to his hope of deliverance. The shipwreck of Paul, and how they effected their safety on the island of Melita, and what mar-vellous things he did on it.

MM. How Paul reached Rome from Melita.

NN. Of Paul's discourse with the Jews in Rome.

There are in all forty chapters; and the sec-tions following these, and marked with the aster-isk,[8] are forty-eight.

---

[1] But Euthal., Κρίσπου, Crispus.
[2] προσχωρεῖν; Euthal., ἐγχειρεῖν.
[3] Euthal., παραίνεσις ποιμαντική, pastoral exhortation.
[4] κατάστασις.

[5] εὐθυβόλως, perhaps here, as Montfaucon makes it, sagaciously.
[6] Euthal., ἐπ᾽ αὐτοῦ, before him.
[7] Euthal., κατὰ Παῦλον, against Paul.
[8] Euthal., διὰ κινναβάρεως, with the vermilion.

MALCHION.

TRANSLATOR'S BIOGRAPHICAL NOTICE.

[A.D. 270.] Eusebius[1] speaks of Malchion as a man accomplished in other branches of learn-ing[2] and well-versed in Greek letters in particular, and as holding the presidency of the Sophists' school at Antioch. Jerome[3] says that he taught rhetoric most successfully in the same city.

---

[1] Hist. Eccl., vii. 29.   [2] ἀνὴρ τά τε ἄλλα λόγιος.   [3] De viris illustr., ch. 71.

Nor was it only that he excelled in secular erudition ; but for the earnest sincerity of his Christian faith he obtained the dignity of presbyter in the church of that place, as Eusebius also tells us. He took part in the Synod of Antioch, which Eusebius calls the final council, and which Gallandi and others call the *second*, in opposition to Pearson, who holds that there was but one council at Antioch. This synod met apparently about A.D. 269, and dealt with Paul of Samosata, who had introduced the heresy of Artemon into the church of Antioch ; and Eusebius says that Malchion was the only one who, in the discussion which took place there with the arch-heretic, and which was taken down by stenographers who were present, was able to detect the subtle and crafty sentiments of the man. Paul's real opinions being thus unveiled, after he had baffled the acuteness of his ecclesiastical judges for some time, he was at length convicted ; and the discussion was published, and a synodical epistle was sent on the subject to Dionysius, bishop of Rome, and to Maximus of Alexandria, and to all the provinces, which, according to Jerome (*De vir. illustr.*, ch. 71), was written by Malchion, and of which we have extracts in Eusebius.[1]

I. — THE EPISTLE WRITTEN BY MALCHION, IN NAME OF THE SYNOD OF ANTIOCH, AGAINST PAUL OF SAMOSATA.[1]

To Dionysius and Maximus, and to all our fellows in the ministry throughout the world, both bishops and presbyters and deacons, and to the whole Catholic Church under heaven, Helenus and Hymenæus and Theophilus and Theotecnus and Maximus, Proclus, Nicomas, and Aelianus, and Paul and Bolanus and Protogenes and Hierax and Eutychius and Theodorus and Malchion and Lucius, and all the others who are with us, dwelling in the neighbouring cities and nations, both bishops and presbyters and deacons, together with the churches of God, send greeting to our brethren beloved in the Lord.

1. After some few introductory words, they proceed thus : — We wrote to many of the bishops, even those who live at a distance, and exhorted them to give their help in relieving us from this deadly doctrine ; among these, we addressed, for instance, Dionysius, the bishop of Alexandria, and Firmilian of Cappadocia, those men of blessed name. Of these, the one wrote to Antioch without even deigning to honour the leader in this error by addressing him ; nor did he write to him in his own name, but to the whole district,[2] of which letter we have also subjoined a copy. And Firmilian, who came twice in person, condemned the innovations in doctrine, as we who were present know and bear witness, and as many others know as well as we. But when he (Paul) promised to give up these opinions, he believed him ; and hoping that, without any reproach to the Word, the matter would be rightly settled, he postponed his decision ; in which action, however, he was deceived by that denier of his God and Lord, and betrayer of the faith

which he formerly held. And now Firmilian was minded to cross to Antioch ; and he came as far as Tarsus, as having already made trial of the man's infidel[3] iniquity. But when we had just assembled, and were calling for him and waiting for his arrival, his end came upon him.

2. After other matters again, they tell us in the following terms of what manner of life he was : — But there is no need of judging his actions when he was outside (the Church), when he revolted from the faith and turned aside to spurious and illegitimate doctrines. Nor need we say any thing of such matters as this, that, whereas he was formerly poor and beggarly, having neither inherited a single possession from his fathers, nor acquired any property by art or by any trade, he has now come to have excessive wealth by his deeds of iniquity and sacrilege, and by those means by which he despoils and concusses the brethren, casting the injured unfairly in their suit,[4] and promising to help them for a price, yet deceiving them all the while and to their loss, taking advantage of the readiness of those in difficulties to give in order to get deliverance from what troubled them, and thus supposing that gain is godliness.[5] Neither need I say any thing about his pride and the haughtiness with which he assumed worldly dignities, and his wishing to be styled procurator[6] rather than bishop, and his strutting through the market-places, and reading letters and reciting them[7] as he walked in public, and his being escorted by multitudes of

---

[1] In Eusebius, vii. 30. [Elucidation I., p. 172.]
[2] παροικίᾳ [= jurisdiction. See p. 163, note 3, *supra*.]

[3] ἀρνησιθέου.
[4] καταβραβεύων, perhaps = receiving bribes from.
[5] 1 Tim. vi. 5.
[6] δουκηνάριος, the name given under the Emperors to those procurators who received 200 sestertia of annual salary.
[7] ὑπαγορεύων. [Letters, e.g., from Zenobia.]

people going before him and following him ; so that he brought ill-will and hatred on the faith by his haughty demeanour and by the arrogance of his heart. Nor shall I say any thing of the quackery which he practises in the ecclesiastical assemblies, in the way of courting popularity and making a great parade, and astounding by such arts the minds of the less sophisticated ; nor of his setting up for himself a lofty tribunal and throne, so unlike a disciple of Christ ; nor of his having a secretum [1] and calling it by that name, after the manner of the rulers of this world ; nor of his striking his thigh with his hand and beating the tribunal with his feet ; nor of his censuring and insulting those who did not applaud him nor shake their handkerchiefs,[2] as is done in the theatres, nor bawl out and leap about after the manner of his partisans, both male and female, who were such disorderly listeners to him, but chose to hear reverently and modestly as in the house of God ; nor of his unseemly and violent attacks in the congregation upon the expounders of the Word who have already departed this life, and his magnifying of himself, not like a bishop, but like a sophist and juggler ; nor of his putting a stop to the psalms sung in honour of our Lord Jesus Christ, as the recent compositions of recent men, and preparing women to sing psalms in honour of himself in the midst of the Church, in the great day of the Paschal festival, which choristers one might shudder to hear. And besides, he acted on those bishops and presbyters, who fawned upon him in the neighbouring districts and cities, to advance the like opinions in their discourses to their people.

3. For we may say, to anticipate a little what we intend to write below, that he does not wish to acknowledge that the Son of God came down from heaven. And this is a statement which shall not be made to depend on simple assertion ; for it is proved abundantly by those memoranda which we sent you, and not least by that passage in which he says that Jesus Christ is from below. And they who sing his praise and eulogise him among the people, declare that their impious teacher has come down as an angel from heaven. And such utterances the haughty man does not check, but is present even when they are made. And then again there are these women — these adopted sisters,[3] as the people of Antioch call them — who are kept by him

and by the presbyters and deacons with him, whose incurable sins in this and other matters, though he is cognisant of them, and has convicted them, he connives at concealing, with the view of keeping the men subservient to himself, and preventing them, by fear for their own position, from daring to accuse him in the matter of his impious words and deeds. Besides this, he has made his followers rich, and for that he is loved and admired by those who set their hearts on these things. But why should we write of these things? For, beloved, we know that the bishop and all the clergy [4] ought to be an example in all good works to the people. Nor are we ignorant of the fact that many have fallen away through introducing these women into their houses, while others have fallen under suspicion. So that, even although one should admit that he has been doing nothing disgraceful in this matter, yet he ought at least to have avoided the suspicion that springs out of such a course of conduct, lest perchance some might be offended, or find inducement to imitate him. For how, then, should any one censure another, or warn him to beware of yielding to greater familiarity with a woman, lest perchance he might slip, as it is written : [5] if, although he has dismissed one, he has still retained two with him, and these in the bloom of their youth, and of fair countenance ; and if when he goes away he takes them with him ; and all this, too, while he indulges in luxury and surfeiting?

4. And on account of these things all are groaning and lamenting with themselves ; yet they have such a dread of his tyranny and power that they cannot venture on accusing him. And of these things, as we have said already, one might take account in the case of a man who held Catholic sentiments and belonged to our own number ; but as to one who has betrayed [6] the mystery (of the faith), and who swaggers [7] with the abominable heresy of Artemas, — for why should we hesitate to disclose his father? — we consider it unnecessary to exact of him an account for these things.

5. *Then at the close of the epistle they add the following words :* — We have been compelled, therefore, to excommunicate this man, who thus opposeth God Himself, and refuses submission, and to appoint in his place another bishop for the Church Catholic, and that, as we trust, by the providence of God — namely, the son of Demetrianus, a man of blessed memory, and one who presided over the same Church with distinction in former times, Domnus by name, a man endowed with all the noble qualities which

---

[1] σήκρητον (from the Latin *secerno*, to separate) was the name given to the elevated place, railed in and curtained, where the magistrate sat to decide cases.
[2] κατασειουσι ταις ὀθόναις, alluding to the custom of shaking the *oraria* or linen handkerchiefs as a token of applause. [Elucid. II.]
[3] συνεισάκτους γυναικας, priests'-housekeepers. See Lange on Nicephorus, vi. 30, and B. Rhenanus on Rufinus, vii. The third canon of the Nicene Council in the Codex Corbeiensis has this title, *De subintroductis id est adoptivis sororibus, Of the subintroduced, that is, the adopted sisters.* See also on the abuse, Jerome, in the *Epistle to Eustochius.* They appear also to have been called *commanentes* and *agapetæ.* See the note of Valesius in Migne. [Vol. ii. p. 47, and (same vol.) Elucidation II. p. 57.]

[4] ἱερατεῖον.
[5] Referring either to Proverbs vi. or to Ecclesiasticus xxv.
[6] ἐξορχησάμενον, danced away.
[7] ἐμπομπευοντα.

become a bishop. And this fact we have communicated to you in order that ye may write him, and receive letters of communion[1] from him. And that other may write to Artemas, if it please him ; and those who think with Artemas may hold communion with him, if they are so minded.

II. — FRAGMENTS APPARENTLY OF THE SAME EPISTLE OF THE SYNOD OF ANTIOCH ; TO WIT, OF THAT PART OF IT WHICH IT IS AGREED THAT EUSEBIUS LEFT UNNOTICED.[1]

He says, therefore, in the commentaries (they speak of Paul), that he maintains the dignity of wisdom.

And thereafter :

If, however, he had been united[2] according to formation and generation, this is what befalls the man. *And again :* For that wisdom, as we believe, was not congenerate[3] with humanity substantially, but qualitatively.[4]

And thereafter :

In what respect, moreover, does he mean to allege that the formation[5] of Christ is different and diverse from ours, when we hold that, in this one thing of prime consequence, His constitution differs from ours, to wit, that what in us is the interior man, is in Him the Word.[6]

And thereafter :

If he means to allege that Wisdom dwells in Him as in no other, this expresses indeed the same mode of inhabitation, though it makes it excel in respect of measure and multitude ; He being supposed to derive a superior knowledge from the Wisdom, say for example, twice as large as others, or any other number of times as large ; or, again, it may be less than twice as large a knowledge as others have. This, however, the catholic and ecclesiastical canons disallow, and hold rather that other men indeed received of Wisdom as an inspiration from without, which, though with them, is distinct from them ;[7] but that Wisdom in verity came of itself substantially into His body by Mary.

And after other matters :

And they hold that there are not two Sons. But if Jesus Christ is the Son of God, and if Wisdom also is the Son of God ; and if the Wisdom is one thing and Jesus Christ another, there are two Sons.

And thereafter :

Moreover understand (Paul would say) the union with Wisdom in a different sense, namely as being one according to instruction and participation ;[8] but not as if it were formed according to the substance in the body.

And after other matters :

Neither was the God who bore the human body and had assumed it, without knowledge[9] of human affections[10] in the first instance ;[11] nor was the human body without knowledge, in the first instance, of divine operations in him in whom He (the God) was, and by whom He wrought these operations. He was formed, in the first instance, as man in the womb ; and, in the second instance,[12] the God also was in the womb, united essentially with the human,[13] that is to say, His substance being wedded with the man.

---

[1] In *Leontius of Byzantium, contra Nestor.*, book iii., towards the end.
[2] *Copulatus erat.*
[3] *Congeneratam.*
[4] *Secundum qualitatem.*
[5] *Formationem.*
[6] We say, that as the exterior and the interior man are one person, so God the Word and humanity have been assumed as one person, a thing which Paul denies. — CAN.

[7] *Alia est apud ipsos.*
[8] *Secundum disciplinam et participationem.* Paul of Samosata used to say that the humanity was united with the Wisdom as instruction (*disciplina*) is united with the learner by participation. — CAN. [See Hooker, book v. cap. 52, sec. 4.]
[9] *Expers.*
[10] *Passionum*, sufferings.
[11] *Principaliter.*
[12] *Secundario*, i.e., κατὰ δεύτερον λόγον. — TURRIAN.
[13] συνουσιωμένος τῷ ἀνθρωπίνῳ.

III.—FROM THE ACTS OF THE DISPUTATION CONDUCTED BY MALCHION AGAINST PAUL OF SAMOSATA.[1]

The compound is surely made up of the simple elements,[2] even as in the instance of Jesus Christ, who was made one (person), constituted by God the Word, and a human body which is of the seed of David, and who subsists without having any manner of division between the two, but in unity. You, however, appear to me to decline to admit a constitution[3] after this fashion: to the effect that there is not in this person, the Son of God according to substance, but only the Wisdom according to participation. For you made this assertion, that the Wisdom bears dispensing, and therefore cannot be compounded;[4] and you do not consider that the divine Wisdom remained undiminished, even as it was before it evacuated itself;[5] and thus in this self-evacuation, which it took upon itself in compassion (for us), it continued undiminished and unchangeable. And this assertion you also make, that the Wisdom dwelt in Him, just as we also dwell in houses, the one in the other,[6] and yet not as if we formed a part of the house, or the house a part of us.

---

[1] In Petrus Diaconus, *De Incarnat. ad Fulgentium*, ch. 6. Among the works of Fulgentius, Epistle 16.
[2] *Ex simplicibus fit certe compositum.*
[3] *Compositionem.*

[4] *Quia sapientia dispendium patiatur et ideo composita esse non possit* — the sense intended being perhaps just that Paul alleged that the divine Wisdom admitted of being dispensed or imparted to another, but not of being substantially united with him. — Tr.
[5] *Exinanisset.*
[6] Some read *alter in altero*, others *alter in altera*.

IV.—A POINT IN THE SAME DISPUTATION.[1]

Did I not say before that you do not admit that the only-begotten Son, who is from all eternity before every creature, was made substantially existent[2] in the whole person of the Saviour;[3] that is to say, was united *with Him* according to substance?

---

[1] From the same *Acts* in Leontius, as above.

[2] οὐσιῶσθαι.
[3] *In toto Salvatore.*

ELUCIDATIONS.

I.

(The epistle written by Malchion, p. 169.)

MALCHION, though a presbyter of Antioch, reflects the teaching of Alexandria, and illustrates its far-reaching influence. Firmilian, presiding at the Council of Antioch, was a pupil of Origen; and Dionysius was felt in the council, though unable to be present. Malchion and Firmilian, therefore, vindicate the real mind of Origen, though speaking in language matured and guarded. This council was, providentially, a rehearsal for Nicæa.

II.

(Putting a stop to psalms, etc., p. 170.)

Coleridge notes this, with an amusing comment on *Paulus Samosatenus*,[1] and refers to Pliny's letter, of which see vol. v. p. 604, this series. Jeremy Taylor, from whom Coleridge quotes, gives the passage of our author as follows: "Psalmos et cantus qui ad Dom. nostri J. C. honorem decantari solent, tanquam recentiores et a viris recentioris memoriæ editos, exploserit" (*Works*, ii. p. 281, ed. Bohn, 1844). Observe what Coleridge says elsewhere[2] on errors attributed to Origen: "Never was a great man so misunderstood as Origen." He adds: "The *caro noumenon* was what Origen meant by Christ's 'flesh consubstantial with His Godhead.'"

---

[1] *Notes on English Divines*, vol. i. p. 199.   *Ibid.*, p. 313.

ARCHELAUS

[TRANSLATED BY THE REV. S. D. F. SALMOND, M.A.]

INTRODUCTORY NOTICE

TO

ARCHELAUS.

[A.D. 277.] The Manichæan heresy, which was destined to operate so terribly against the Church and the purity of the Gospel, encountered its earliest successful antagonism in the *Thebaid;* and I have not doubted the wisdom of prefixing this *Disputation* to the veritable name and work of Alexander of Lycopolis, as important to the complete history of the great Alexandrian school. The Edinburgh translator of this work regards it as an "authentic relic of antiquity," in spite of Beausobre, who treats it as a romance. I have forced myself, in this republication, to reject no theory of the Edinburgh collaborators to which I have not been able to give as much critical attention, at least, as they have evidently bestowed upon their work. It seems to me a well-sustained presumption that the work is fundamentally real, and Dr. Neander admits its base of fact. It is useful, at any rate, in its form and place, as here presented, and so much may be inferred from the following : —

TRANSLATOR'S INTRODUCTORY NOTICE.

A CERTAIN memorable Disputation, which was conducted by a bishop of the name of Archelaus with the heretic Manes, is mentioned by various writers of an early date.[1] What professes to be an account of that Disputation has come down to us in a form mainly Latin, but with parts in Greek. A considerable portion of this Latin version was published by Valesius in his edition of Socrates and Sozomen, and subsequently by others in greater completeness, and with the addition of the Greek fragments.[2] There seems to be a difference among the ancient authorities cited above as to the person who committed these *Acts* to writing. Epiphanius and Jerome take it to have been Archelaus himself, while Heraclianus, bishop of Chalcedon, represents it to have been a certain person named Hegemonius. In Photius[3] there is a statement to the effect that this Heraclianus, in confuting the errors of the Manichæans, made use of certain Acts of the Disputation of Bishop Archelaus with Manes which were written by Hegemonius. And there are various passages in the *Acts* themselves which appear to confirm the opinion of Heraclianus.[4] Zacagnius, however, thinks that this is but an apparent discrepancy, which is easily reconciled on

---

[1] Thus Cyril of Jerusalem, in the sixth book of his *Catecheses*, §§ 27 and 30, tells us how Manes fled into Mesopotamia, and was met there by that shield of righteousness (ὅπλον δικαιοσύνης) Bishop Archelaus, and was refuted by him in the presence of a number of Greek philosophers, who had been brought together as judges of the discussion. Epiphanius, in his *Heresies*, lxvi., and again in his work *De Mensuris et Poderibus*, § 20, makes reference to the same occasion, and gives some excerpts from the *Acts of the Disputation*. And there are also passages of greater or less importance in Jerome (*De vir. illustr.*, ch 72), Socrates (*Hist. Eccles.*, i. 22), Heraclianus bishop of Chalcedon (as found in Photius, *Bibliotheca*, Cod. xcv.), Petrus Siculus (*Historia Manichæorum*, pp. 25, 35, 37), Photius (*Adversus Manichæos*, book i., edited in the *Biblioth. Coislin.*, Montfaucon, pp. 356, 358), and the anonymous authors of the *Libellus Synodicus*, ch. 27, and the *Historia Hæreseos Manichæorum* in the Codex Regius of Turin. [See Cyril's text in Routh, *R. S.*, vol. v. pp. 198-205.]

[2] As by Zacagnius at Rome, in 1698, in his *Collectanea Monumentorum Veterum Ecclesiæ Græcæ ac Latinæ;* by Fabricius, in the *Spicilegium Sanctorum Patrum Sæculi*, iii., in his edition of Hippolytus, etc.

[3] *Biblioth.*, Cod. lxxxv. [Coleridge thinks "Manes" himself a myth, "a doubtful *Ens*."]

[4] See especially ch. 39 and 55. [Note reference to John de Soyres, vol. v. p. 604, this series.]

the supposition that the book was first composed by Archelaus himself in Syriac, and afterwards edited, with certain amendments and additions, by Hegemonius. That the work was written originally in Syriac is clear, not only from the express testimony of Jerome,[1] but also from internal evidence, and specially from the explanations offered now and again of the use of Greek equivalents. It is uncertain who was the author of the Greek version; and we can only conjecture that Hegemonius, in publishing a new edition, may also have undertaken a translation into the tongue which would secure a much larger audience than the original Syriac. But that this Greek version, by whomsoever accomplished, dates from the very earliest period, is proved by the excerpts given in Epiphanius. As to the Latin interpretation itself, all that we can allege is, that it must in all probability have been published after Jerome's time, who might reasonably be expected to have made some allusion to it if it was extant in his day; and before the seventh century, because, in quoting the Scriptures, it does not follow the Vulgate edition, which was received generally throughout the West by that period. That the Latin translator must have had before him, not the Syriac, but the Greek copy, is also manifest, not only from the general idiomatic character of the rendering, but also from many nicer indications.[2]

The precise designation of the seat of the bishopric of Archelaus has been the subject of considerable diversity of opinion. Socrates[3] and Epiphanius[4] record that Archelaus was bishop *of Caschar*, or *Caschara*.[5] Epiphanius, however, does not keep consistently by that scription.[6] In the opening sentence of the *Acts* themselves it appears as Carchar.[7] Now we know that there were at least two towns of the name of Carcha: for the anonymous Ravenna geographer[8] tells us that there was a place of that name in Arabia Felix; and Ammianus Marcellinus[9] mentions another beyond the Tigris, within the Persian dominion. The clear statements, however, to the effect that the locality of the bishopric of Archelaus was in Mesopotamia, make it impossible that either of these two towns could have been the seat of his rule. Besides this, in the third chapter of the *Acts* themselves we find the name *Charra* occurring; and hence Zacagnius and others have concluded that the place actually intended is the scriptural *Charran*, or Haran, in Mesopotamia, which is also written *Charra* in Paulus Diaconus,[10] and that the form Carchar or Carchara was either a mere error of the transcribers, or the vulgar provincial designation. It must be added, however, that Neander[11] allows this to be only a very uncertain conjecture, while others hold that *Caschar* is the most probable scription, and that the town is one altogether different from the ancient Haran.

The date of the Disputation itself admits of tolerably exact settlement. Epiphanius, indeed,[12] says that Manes fled into Mesopotamia in the ninth year of the reign of Valerianus and Gallienus, and that the discussion with Archelaus took place about the same time. This would carry the date back to about 262 A.D. But this statement, although he is followed in it by Petrus Siculus and Photius, is inconsistent with the specification of times which he makes in dealing with the error of the Manichæans in his book *On the Heresies*. From the 37th chapter of the *Acts*, however, we find that the Disputation took place, not when Gallienus, but when Probus held the

---

[1] *De vir. illustr.*, ch. 72.

[2] Such as the apparent confusion between ἀήρ and ἀνήρ in ch. 8, and again between λοιμός and λιμός in the same chapter, and between πήσσει and πλήσσει in ch. 9, and the retention of certain Greek words, sometimes absolutely, and at other times with an explanation, as *cybi, apocrusis*, etc.

[3] *Hist. Eccles.*, i. 22.

[4] *Hæres.*, lxvi. ch. 5 and 7, and *De Mens. et Pond.*, ch. 20.

[5] Κασχάρων.

[6] For elsewhere (*Hæres.*, lxvi. 11) he writes Κασχάρην, or, according to another reading, which is held by Zacagnius to be corrupt Καλχάρων.

[7] And that form is followed by Petrus Siculus (*Hist. Manich.*, p. 37) and Photius (lib. i., *Adv. Manich.*), who, in epitomizing the statements of Epiphanius, write neither Κασχάρων nor Καλχάρων, but Καρχάρων.

[8] *Geogr.*, book ii. ch. 7.

[9] Book xviii. 23, and xxv. 20, 21.

[10] *Hist. Misc.*, xxii. 20.

[11] *Church History*, ii. p. 165, ed. Bohn.

[12] *De Mensur. et Pond.*, ch. 20.

empire, and that is confirmed by Cyril of Jerusalem.[1] The exact year becomes also clearer from Eusebius, who[2] seems to indicate the second year of the reign of Probus as the time when the Manichæan heresy attained general publicity — *Secundo anno Probi . . . insana Manichæorum hæresis in commune humani generis malum exorta ;* and from Leo Magnus, who in his second *Discourse on Pentecost* also avers that Manichæus became notorious in the consulship of Probus and Paulinus. And as this consulship embraced part of the first and part of the second years of the empire of Probus, the Disputation itself would thus be fixed as occurring in the end of A.D. 277 or the beginning of 278, or, according to the precise calculation of Zacagnius, between July and December of the year 277.

That the *Acts* of this Disputation constitute an authentic relic of antiquity, seems well established by a variety of considerations. Epiphanius, for instance, writing about the year A.D. 376, makes certain excerpts from them which correspond satisfactorily with the extant Latin version. Socrates, again, whose *Ecclesiastical History* dates about 439, mentions these *Acts*, and acknowledges that he drew the materials for his account of the Manichæan heresy from them. The book itself, too, offers not a few evidences of its own antiquity and authenticity. The enumeration given of the various heretics who had appeared up to the time of Archelaus, the mention of his presence at the siege of the city,[3] and the allusions to various customs, have all been pressed into that service, as may be seen in detail in the elaborate dissertation prefixed by Zacagnius in his *Collectanea Monumentorum Ecclesiæ Græcæ.* At the same time, it is very evident that the work has come down to us in a decidedly imperfect form. There are, for example, arguments by Manes and answers by Archelaus recorded in Cyril[4] which are not contained in our Latin version at all. And there are not a few notes of discrepancy and broken connections in the composition itself,[5] which show that the manuscripts must have been defective, or that the Latin translator took great liberties with the Greek text, or that the Greek version itself did not faithfully reproduce the original Syriac. On the historical character of the work Neander[6] expresses himself thus :[7] " These *Acts* manifestly contain an ill-connected narrative, savouring in no small degree of the romantic. Although there is some truth at the bottom of it — as, for instance, in the statement of doctrine there is much that wears the appearance of truth, and is confirmed also by its agreement with other representations : still the Greek author seems, from ignorance of Eastern languages and customs, to have introduced a good deal that is untrue, by bringing in and confounding together discordant stories through an uncritical judgment and exaggeration."

---

[1] *Cateches.*, vi. p. 140.
[2] *Chronicon, lib. post.*, p. 177.
[3] In ch. 24.
[4] *Catech.*, vi. p. m. 147.
[5] As in the 12th, 25th, and 28th chapters.
[6] [Compare Routh, *Reliquiæ Sacræ*, vol. v. pp. 4–206, and his everywhere learned notes.]
[7] *Church History*, ii. pp. 165, 166, ed. Bohn. [Compare Robertson, vol. i. pp. 136–144.]

THE ACTS OF THE DISPUTATION [1]
WITH THE HERESIARCH MANES.

1. THE true THESAURUS; [2] to wit, the Disputation conducted in Carchar, a city of Mesopotamia, before Manippus [3] and Ægialeus and Claudius and Cleobolus, who acted as judges. In this city of Mesopotamia there was a certain man, Marcellus by name, who was esteemed as a person worthy of the highest honour for his manner of life, his pursuits, and his lineage, and not less so for his discretion and his nobility of character: he was possessed also of abundant means; and, what is most important of all, he feared God with the deepest piety, and gave ear always with due reverence to the things which were spoken of Christ. In short, there was no good quality lacking in that man, and hence it came to pass that he was held in the greatest regard by the whole city; while, on the other hand, he also made an ample return for the good-will of his city by his munificent and oft-repeated acts of liberality in bestowing on the poor, relieving the afflicted, and giving help to the distressed. But let it suffice us to have said thus much, lest by the weakness of our words we rather take from the man's virtues than adduce what is worthy of their splendour. I shall come, therefore, to the task which forms my subject. On a certain occasion, when a large body of captives were offered to the bishop Archelaus by the soldiers who held the camp in that place, their numbers being some seven thousand seven hundred, he was harassed with the keenest anxiety on account of the large sum of money which was demanded by the soldiers as the price of the prisoners' deliverance. And as he could not conceal his solicitude, all aflame for the religion and the fear of God, he at length hastened to Marcellus, and explained to him the importance and difficulty of the case. And when that pattern of piety, Marcellus, heard his narration, without the least delay he went into his house, and provided the price demanded for the prisoners, according to the value set upon them by those who had led them captive; and unlocking the treasures of his goods, he at once distributed the gifts of piety [4] among the soldiers, without any severe consideration of number or distinction, [5] so that they seemed to be presents rather than purchase-moneys. And those soldiers were filled with wonder and admiration at the grandeur of the man's piety and munificence, and were struck with amazement, and felt the force [6] of this example of pity; so that very many of them were added to the faith of our Lord Jesus Christ, and threw off the belt of military service, [7] while others withdrew to their camp, taking scarcely a fourth part of the ransom, and the rest made their departure without receiving even so much as would defray the expenses of the way.

2. Marcellus, as might well be expected, was exceedingly gratified by these incidents; and summoning one of the prisoners, by name Cortynius, he inquired of him the cause of the war, and by what chance it was that they were overcome and bound with the chains of captivity. And the person addressed, on obtaining liberty to speak, began to express himself in these terms: "My lord Marcellus, we believe in the living God alone. And we have a custom of such a nature as I shall now describe, which has descended to us by the tradition of our brethren *in the faith*, and has been regularly observed by us up to the present day. The practice is, that every year we go out beyond the bounds of the city, in company with our wives and children, and offer up supplications to the only and invisible God, praying Him to send us rains for our fields and crops. [8] Now, when we were celebrating this observance at the usual time and in the wonted manner, evening surprised us as we lingered there, and were still fasting. Thus we

---

[1] Of Archelaus, bishop of Caschar in Mesopotamia.
[2] *Treasury.*
[3] In Epiphanius, *Hæres.*, lxvi. 10, it is Marsipus.

[4] *Pietatis pretia.*
[5] Nec numero aliquo nec discretione ulla distinguit. For *distinguit*, some propose *distribuit.*
[6] Reading *commonentur*, as in the text. *Commoventur* is also suggested, = "were deeply moved."
[7] On the attitude of the Christians of the primitive Church towards warfare, see Tertullian's *De Corona Militis*, ch. 11, and the twelfth canon of the Nicene Council.
[8] [The similar institution of the Rogation fasts in the West is referred to the fifth century. Pellicia, p. 372; Hooker, book v. cap. xli. 2.]

were feeling the pressure of two of the most try-ing things men have to endure, — namely, fast-ing and want of sleep. But about midnight sleep enviously and inopportunely crept upon us, and with necks drooping and unstrung, and heads hanging down, it made our faces strike against our knees.[1] Now this took place because the time was at hand when by the judgment of God we were to pay the penalty proper to our deserts, whether it might be that we were offenders in ignorance, or whether it might be that with the consciousness of wrong we nevertheless had not given up our sin. Accordingly at that hour a multitude of soldiers suddenly surrounded us, supposing us, as I judge, to have lodged our-selves in ambush there, and to be persons with full experience and skill in fighting battles; and without making any exact inquiry into the cause of our gathering there, they threatened us with war, not in word, but at once by the sword. And though we were men who had never learned to do injury to any one, they wounded us pitilessly with their missiles, and thrust us through with their spears, and cut our throats with their swords. Thus they slew, indeed, about one thousand and three hundred men of our num-ber, and wounded other five hundred. And when the day broke clearly, they carried off the survivors amongst us as prisoners here, and that, too, in a way showing their utter want of pity for us. For they drove us before their horses, spur-ring us on by blows from their spears, and im-pelling us forward by making the horses' heads press upon us. And those who had sufficient powers of endurance did indeed hold out; but very many fell down before the face of their cruel masters, and breathed out their life there; and mothers, with arms wearied, and utterly powerless with their burdens, and distracted by the threats of those behind them, suffered the little ones that were hanging on their breasts to fall to the ground; while all those on whom old age had come were sinking, one after the other, to the earth, overcome with their toils, and ex-hausted by want of food. The proud soldiers nevertheless enjoyed this bloody spectacle of men continually perishing, as if it had been a kind of entertainment, while they saw some stretched on the soil in hopeless prostration, and beheld others, worn out by the fierce fires of thirst and with the bands of their tongues utterly parched, lose the power of speech, and beheld others with eyes ever glancing backwards, groaning over the fate of their dying little ones, while these, again, were constantly appealing to their most unhappy mothers with their cries, and the mothers themselves, driven frantic by the severities of the robbers, responded with their

lamentations, which indeed was the only thing they could do freely. And those of them whose hearts were most tenderly bound up with their offspring chose voluntarily to meet the same pre-mature fate of death with their children; while those, on the other hand, who had some capacity of endurance were carried off prisoners here with us. Thus, after the lapse of three days, during which time we had never been allowed to take any rest, even in the night, we were conveyed to this place, in which what has now taken place after these occurrences is better known to yourself."

3. When Marcellus, the man of consummate piety, had heard this recital, he burst into a flood of tears, touched with pity for misfortunes so great and so various. But making no delay, he at once prepared victuals for the sufferers, and did service with his own hand for the wearied; in this imitating our father Abraham the patriarch, who, when he entertained the angels hospitably on a certain occasion, did not content himself with merely giving the order to his slaves to bring a calf from the herd, but did himself, though advanced in years, go and place it on his shoulders and fetch it in, and did with his own hand prepare food, and set it before the angels. So Marcellus, in discharge of a sim-ilar office, directed them to be seated as his guests in companies of ten; and when the seven hundred tables were all provided, he refreshed the whole body of the captives with great de-light, so that those who had had strength to sur-vive what they had been called to endure, forgot their toils, and became oblivious of all their ills. When, however, they had reached the fifteenth day, and while Marcellus was still liberally sup-plying all things needful for the prisoners, it seemed good to him that they should all be put in possession of the means of returning to their own parts, with the exception of those who were detained by the attention which their wounds demanded; and providing the proper remedies for these, he instructed the rest to depart to their own country and friends. And even to all these charities Marcellus added yet larger deeds of piety. For with a numerous band of his own dependants he went to look after the burying of the bodies of those who had perished on the march; and for as many of these as he could discover, of whatsoever condition, he secured the sepulture which was meet for them. And when this service was completed he returned to Charra, and gave permission to the wounded to return thence to their native country when their health was sufficiently restored, providing also most liberal supplies for their use on their jour-ney. And truly the estimate of this deed made a magnificent addition to *the repute of* the other noble actions of Marcellus; for through that whole territory the fame of the piety of Marcellus

---

[1] Reading *cervicibus degravatis et laxis, demisso capite, frontem genibus elidit.* The text gives *demerso.*

spread so grandly, that large numbers of men belonging to various cities were inflamed with the intensest desire to see and become acquainted with the man, and most especially those persons who had not had occasion to bear penury before, — to all of whom this remarkable man, following the example of a Marcellus of old, furnished aid most indulgently, so that they all declared that there was no one of more illustrious piety than this man. Yea, all the widows, too, who were believers in the Lord had recourse to him, while the imbecile also could reckon on obtaining at his hand most certain help to meet their circumstances ; and the orphaned, in like manner, were all supported by him, so that his house was declared to be the hospice for the stranger and the indigent. And above all this, he retained in a remarkable and singular measure his devotion to the faith, building up his own heart upon the rock that shall not be moved.

4. Accordingly,[1] as this man's fame was becoming always the more extensively diffused throughout different localities, and when it had now penetrated even beyond the river Stranga, the honourable report of his name was carried into the territory of Persia. In this country dwelt a person called Manes, who, when this man's repute had reached him, deliberated largely with himself as to how he might entangle him in the snares of his doctrine, hoping that Marcellus might be made an upholder of his dogma. For he reckoned that he might make himself master of the whole province, if he could only first attach such a man to himself. In this project, however, his mind was agitated with the doubt whether he should at once repair in person to the man, or first attempt to get at him by letter ; for he was afraid lest, by any sudden and unexpected introduction of himself upon the scene, some mischance might possibly befall him. At last, in obedience to a subtler policy, he resolved to write ; and calling to him one of his disciples, by name Turbo,[2] who had been instructed by Addas, he handed to him an epistle, and bade him depart and convey it to Marcellus. This adherent accordingly received the letter, and carried it to the person to whom he had been commissioned by Manes to deliver it, overtaking the whole journey within five days. The above-mentioned Turbo, indeed, used great expedition on this journey, in the course of which he also underwent very considerable exertion and trouble. For whenever he arrived,[3] as[4] a traveller in for-

eign parts, at a hospice, — and these were inns which Marcellus himself had supplied in his large hospitality,[5] — on his being asked by the keepers of these hostels whence he came, and who he was, or by whom he had been sent, he used to reply : " I belong to the district of Mesopotamia, but I come at present from Persis, having been sent by Manichæus, a master among the Christians." But they were by no means ready to welcome a name unknown[6] to them, and were wont sometimes to thrust Turbo out of their inns, refusing him even the means of getting water for drinking purposes. And as he had to bear daily things like these, and things even worse than these, at the hands of those persons in the several localities who had charge of the mansions and hospices, unless he had at last shown that he was conveying letters to Marcellus, Turbo would have met the doom of death in his travels.

5. On receiving the epistle, then, Marcellus opened it, and read it in the presence of Archelaus, the bishop of the place. And the following is a copy of what it contained :[7] —

Manichæus, an apostle of Jesus Christ, and all the saints who are with me, and the virgins, to Marcellus, my beloved son : Grace, mercy, and peace be with you from God the Father, and from our Lord Jesus Christ ; and may the right hand of light preserve you safe from this present evil world, and from its calamities, and from the snares of the wicked one. Amen.

I was exceedingly delighted to observe the love cherished by you, which truly is of the largest measure. But I was distressed at your faith, which is not in accordance with the right standard. Wherefore, deputed as I am to seek the elevation of the race of men, and sparing,[8] as I do, those who have given themselves over to deceit and error, I have considered it needful to despatch this letter to you, with a view, in the first place, to the salvation of your own soul, and in the second place also to that of the souls of those who are with you, so as to secure you against[9] dubious opinions, and specially against notions like those in which the guides of the simpler class of minds indoctrinate their subjects, when they allege that good and evil have the same original subsistence,[10] and when they posit the same beginning for them, without making any distinction or discrimination between light and darkness, and between the good and the

---

[1] At this point begins the portion of the work edited by Valesius from the Codex Bobiensis, which is preserved now in the Ambrosian Library.

[2] The Codex Bobiensis reads, *Adda Turbonem.* This Adda, or Addas, as the Greek gives it below in ch. xi., was one of those disciples of Manes whom he charged with the dissemination of his heretical opinions in the East, as we see from ch. xi.

[3] Codex Bobiensis adds, *ad vesperam,* towards evening.

[4] The text gives *veluti peregrinans.* The Codex Bobiensis has *quippe peregrinans.*

[5] On the attention paid by the primitive Church to the duties of hospitality, see Tertullian, *De Præscriptionibus,* ch. 20 [vol. iii. p. 252, this series]: Gregory Nazianzenus, in his *First Invective against Julian;* also Priorius, *De literis canonicis,* ch. 5, etc.; and Thomassin, *De Tesseris hospitalitatis,* ch. 26.

[6] In the text, *ignotum;* in the Codex Bobiensis, *ignoratum.*

[7] This letter, along with the reply of Marcellus, is given by Epiphanius in his *Hereses,* n. 6, from which the Greek text is taken.

[8] φειδόμενος. The Latin gives *subveniens,* relieving.

[9] The Greek text of Epiphanius gave πρὸς τὸ ἀδιάκριτον. Petavius substituted πρὸς τὸ μὴ ἀδιάκριτον; and that reading is confirmed by the Latin, *uti ne indiscrètos animos geras.*

[10] απο του αυτου φέρεσθαι.

evil or worthless, and between the inner man and the outer, as we have stated before, and without ceasing to mix up and confound together the one with the other. But, O my son, refuse thou thus thoughtlessly to identify these two things in the irrational and foolish fashion common to the mass of men, and ascribe no such confusion to the God of goodness. For these men refer the beginning and the end and the paternity of these ills to God Himself, — "whose end is near a curse." [1] For they do not believe the word spoken by our Saviour and Lord Jesus Christ Himself in the Gospels,[2] namely, that "a good tree cannot bring forth evil fruit, neither can a corrupt tree bring forth good fruit."[3] And how they can be bold enough to call God the maker and contriver of Satan and his wicked deeds, is a matter of great amazement to me. Yea, would that even this had been all the length to which they had gone with their silly efforts, and that they had not declared that the only-begotten Christ, who has descended from the bosom of the Father,[4] is the son of a certain woman, Mary, and born of blood and flesh and the varied impurities proper to women![5] Howbeit, neither to write too much in this epistle, nor to trespass at too great length upon your good nature, — and all the more so that I have no natural gift of eloquence, — I shall content myself with what I have said. But you will have full knowledge of the whole subject when I am present with you, if indeed you still continue to care for[6] your own salvation. For I do not "cast a snare upon any one,"[7] as is done by the less thoughtful among the mass of men. Think of what I say, most honourable son.

6. On reading this epistle, Marcellus, with the kindest consideration, attended hospitably to the needs of the bearer of the letter. Archelaus, on the other hand, did not receive very pleasantly the matters which were read, but "gnashed[8] with his teeth like a chained lion," impatient to have the author of the epistle given over to him. Marcellus, however, counselled him to be at peace; promising that he would himself take care to secure the man's presence? And accordingly Marcellus resolved to send an answer to what had been written to him, and indited an epistle containing the following statements: —

Marcellus, a man of distinction, to Manichæus, who has made himself known to me by his epistle, greeting.

An epistle written by you has come to my hand, and I have received Turbo with my wonted kindness; but the meaning of your letter I have by no means apprehended, and may not do so unless you give us your presence, and explain its contents in detail in the way of conversation, as you have offered to do in the epistle itself. Farewell.

This letter he sealed and handed to Turbo, with instructions to deliver it to the person from whom he had already conveyed a similar document. The messenger, however, was extremely reluctant to return to his master, being mindful of what he had had to endure on the journey, and begged that another person should be despatched in his stead, refusing to go back to Manes, or to have any intercourse whatever with him again. But Marcellus summoned one of his young men,[9] Callistus by name, and directed him to proceed to the place. Without any loss of time this young man set out promptly on his journey thither; and after the lapse of three days he came to Manes, whom he found in a certain fort, that of Arabion [10] to wit, and to whom he presented the epistle. On perusing it, he was glad to see that he had been invited by Marcellus; and without delay he undertook the journey; yet he had a presentiment that Turbo's failure to return boded no good, and proceeded on his way to Marcellus, not, as it were, without serious reflections. Turbo, for his part, was not at all thinking of leaving the house of Marcellus; neither did he omit any opportunity of conversing with Archelaus the bishop. For both these parties were very diligently engaged in investigating the practices of Manichæus, being desirous of knowing who he was and whence he came, and what was his manner of discourse. And he, Turbo, accordingly gave a lucid account of the whole position, narrating and expounding the terms of his faith in the following manner:[11] —

If you are desirous of being instructed in the faith of Manes by me, attend to me for a short space. That man worships two deities, unoriginated, self-existent, eternal, opposed the one to the other. Of these he represents the one as good, and the other as evil, and assigns the name of *Light* to the former, and that of *Darkness* to the latter. He alleges also that the soul in men is a portion of the *light*, but that the body and the formation of matter are parts of the *darkness*. He maintains, further, that a certain commingling or blending [12] has been effected between the two in the manner about to be stated, the following

---

[1] ὧν τὸ τέλος κατάρας ἐγγύς. Cf. Heb. vi. 8.
[2] The text gives ἐν τοῖς εἰρημένοις εὐαγγελίοις, for which τοῖς εἰρημένοις ἐν τοῖς εὐαγγελίοις may be proposed.
[3] Matt. vii. 18.
[4] John i. 18.
[5] τῆς ἄλλης δυσωδίας τῶν γυναικῶν.
[6] φείδη.
[7] 1 Cor. vii. 35.
[8] The text gives *infrendebat;* the Codex Bobiensis has *infringebat*. [It seems to be a proverb, and I have so marked it. We should say, "he *chafed* like a lion," etc.]

[9] *Ex pueris suis.*
[10] Epiphanius, under this *Heresy*, num. 7, says that this was a fort situated on the other side of the river Stranga, between Persia and Mesopotamia.
[11] The section extending from this point on to ch. xii. is found word for word in the Greek of Epiphanius, num. 25.
[12] μιξιν δε ητοι συγκρασιν.

analogy being used as an illustration of the same ; to wit, that their relations may be likened to those of two kings in conflict with each other, who are antagonists from the beginning, and have their own positions, each in his due order. And so he holds that the darkness passed without its own boundaries, and engaged in a similar contention with the light ; but that the good Father then, perceiving that the darkness had come to sojourn on His earth, put forth from Himself a power [1] which is called the Mother of Life ; and that this power thereupon put forth from itself *the first man, and* the five elements.[2] And these five elements are wind,[3] light, water, fire, and matter. Now this primitive man, being endued with these, and thereby equipped, as it were, for war, descended to these lower parts, and made war against the darkness. But the princes of the darkness, waging war in turn against him, consumed that portion of his panoply which is the soul. Then was that *first man* grievously injured there underneath by the darkness ; and had it not been that the Father heard his prayers, and sent a second power, which was also put forth from Himself and was called the *living Spirit*, and came down and gave him the right hand, and brought him up again out of the grasp of the darkness, that *first man* would, in those ancient times, have been in peril of absolute overthrow. From that time, consequently, he left the soul beneath. And for this reason the Manichæans, if they meet each other, give the right hand, in token of their having been saved from darkness ; for he holds that the heresies have their seat all in the darkness. Then the living Spirit created the world ; and bearing in himself three other powers, he came down and brought off the princes, and settled [4] them in the firmament, which is their body, (though it is called) the sphere. Then, again, the living Spirit created the luminaries, which are fragments of the soul, and he made them thus to move round and round the firmament ; and again he created the earth

in its eight species.[5] And the Omophorus [6] sustains the burden thereof beneath ; and when he is wearied with bearing it he trembles, and in that manner becomes the cause of a quaking of the earth in contravention of its determinate times. On account of this the good Father sent His Son forth from His own bosom [7] into the heart of the earth, and into these lowest parts of it, in order to secure for him the correction befitting him.[8] And whenever an earthquake occurs, he is either trembling under his weariness, or is shifting his burden from one shoulder to the other. Thereafter, again, the matter also of itself produced growths ; [9] and when these were carried off as spoil on the part of some of the princes, he summoned together all the foremost of the princes, and took from all of them individually power after power, and made up the man who is after the image of that *first man*, and united [10] the soul (with these powers) in him. This is the account of the manner in which his constitution was planned.

8. But when the living Father perceived that the soul was in tribulation in the body, being full of mercy and compassion, He sent His own beloved Son for the salvation of the soul. For this, together with the matter of Omophorus, was the reason of His sending Him. And the Son came and transformed Himself into the likeness of man, and manifested [11] Himself to men as a man, while yet He was not a man, and men supposed that He was begotten. Thus He came and prepared the work which was to effect the salvation of the souls, and with that object constructed an instrument with twelve urns,[12] which is made to revolve by the sphere, and draws up with it the souls of the dying. And the greater luminary receives these souls, and purifies them with its rays, and then passes them over to the moon ; and in this manner the moon's disc, as it is designated by us, is filled up. For he says that these two luminaries are ships or passage-boats.[13] Then, if the moon becomes full, it ferries its passengers across toward the east wind, and thereby effects its own waning [14] in getting itself delivered of its freight. And in this manner it goes on making the pas-

---

[1] προβάλλειν ἐξ αὐτοῦ δύναμιν. But the Codex Bobiensis gives *produxit ex virtute*, put forth from His power one, etc. The Codex Casinensis has *produxerit et esse virtutem*, etc.

[2] The text is simply καὶ αὐτὴν προβεβληκέναι τὸν πρῶτον ἄνθρωπον, τὰ πέντε στοιχεῖα. The Latin, with emendations from the Codex Bobiensis and Epiphanius, gives *quâ virtute circumdedit primum hominem, quæ sunt quinque elementa*, etc., = with which power He begirt the first man, which is the same as the five elements, etc. With slight differences the Codex Bobiensis reads *quâ circumdedit*, and the Codex Casinensis, *quæ virtute*. Petavius pointed out that there is probably an omission in the text here. And from a passage in Epiphanius, *Hær.*, lxvi. n. 45, it has been proposed to fill out the sentence thus: προβάλλειν ἐξ ἑαυτοῦ δύναμιν μητέρα τῆς ζωῆς, καὶ αὐτὴν προβεβληκέναι τὸν πρῶτον ἄνθρωπον, αὐτὴν δὲ τὴν μητέρα τῆς ζωῆς τόν τε πρῶτον ἄνθρωπον τὰ πέντε στοιχεῖα. The sense might then be, that the good Father put forth from Himself a power called the *Mother of Life*, that this Mother of Life put forth the *first man*, and that the said Mother of Life and the first man put forth (or constituted) the five elements. See the note in Routh's *Reliquiæ Sacræ*, v. p. 49.

[3] The Codex Bobiensis omits the *ventus*, wind.

[4] The Greek gives ἐστερέωσεν ἐν τῷ στερεώματι. The Latin version has, " crucifixit eos in firmamento." And Routh apparently favours the reading ἐσταύρωσεν = crucified them, etc. Valesius and the Codex Bobiensis have, " descendens eduxit principes Jesu, exiens in firmamentum quod est," etc.

[5] εἰς εἴδη ὀκτώ. The Latin, however, gives *et sunt octo*, " and they are eight ; " thus apparently having read εισι δὲ ὀκτώ, instead of εἰς εἴδη ὀκτώ.

[6] i c., one who bears on his shoulders, the upholder.

[7] Reading ἐκ τῶν κόλπων, *de sinibus suis*. But the Codex Bobiensis gives *de finibus*, from His own territories.

[8] The Greek text is, ὅπως αὐτῷ τὴν προσήκουσαν ἐπιτιμίαν δῷ. The Latin gives, " quo illum, ut par erat, coerceret." The Codex Bobiensis reads, " quod illum, ut pareret, coerceret." It is clear also that Petavius read correctly ἐπιτιμίαν for ἐπιθυμίαν in Epiphanius.

[9] τὰ φυτά.

[10] ἔδησεν. The Codex Bobiensis gives, " vexit animam in eo."

[11] But certain codices read *et parebat*, " and was obedient," in stead of *apparebat*.

[12] κάδους.

[13] πορθμεῖα.

[14] ἀπόκρουσιν. The Codex Casinensis has *apocrisin ;* but the Codex Bobiensis gives *apocrusin*.

sage across, and again discharging its freight of souls drawn up by the urns, until it saves its own proper portion of the souls.[1] Moreover, he maintains that every soul, yea, every living creature that moves, partakes of the substance of the good Father. And accordingly, when the moon delivers over its freight of souls to the æons of the Father, they abide there in that pillar of glory, which is called the perfect air.[2] And this air is a pillar of light, for it is filled with the souls that are being purified. Such, moreover, is the agency by which the souls are saved. But the following, again, is the cause of men's dying: A certain virgin, fair in person, and beautiful in attire, and of most persuasive address, aims at making spoil of the princes that have been borne up and crucified on the firmament by the living Spirit; and she appears as a comely female to the princes, but as a handsome and attractive young man to the princesses. And the princes, when they look on her in her splendid figure, are smitten with love's sting; and as they are unable to get possession of her, they burn fiercely with the flame of amorous desire, and lose all power of reason. While they thus pursue the virgin, she disappears from view. Then the great prince sends forth from himself the clouds, with the purpose of bringing darkness on the whole world, in his anger. And then, if he feels grievously oppressed, his exhaustion expresses itself in perspiration, just as a man sweats under toil; and this sweat of his forms the rain. At the same time also the harvest-prince,[3] if he too chances to be captivated by the virgin, scatters pestilence[4] on the whole earth, with the view of putting men to death. Now this body (of man) is also called a *cosmos*, i.e., a microcosm, in relation to the great *cosmos*, i.e., the macrocosm of the universe; and all men have roots which are linked beneath with those above. Accordingly, when this prince is captivated by the virgin's charms, he then begins to cut the roots of men; and when their roots are cut, then pestilence commences to break forth, and in that manner they die. And if he shakes the upper parts of the root mightily,[5] an earthquake bursts, and follows as the consequence of the commotion to which the Omophorus is subjected. This is the explanation of (the phenomenon of) death.

9. I shall explain to you also how it is that the soul is transfused into five bodies.[6] First of all, in this process some small portion of it is purified; and then it is transfused into the body of a dog, or a camel, or some other animal. But if the soul has been guilty of homicide, it is translated into the body of the celephi;[7] and if it has been found to have engaged in cutting,[8] it is made to pass into the *body of the* dumb. Now these are the designations of the soul, — namely, intelligence, reflection, prudence, consideration, reasoning.[9] Moreover, the reapers who reap are likened to the princes who have been in darkness from the beginning,[10] since they consumed somewhat of the panoply of the first man. On this account there is a necessity for these to be translated into hay, or beans, or barley, or corn, or vegetables, in order that in these forms they, in like manner, may be reaped and cut. And again, if any one eats bread, he must needs also become bread and be eaten. If one kills a chicken,[11] he will be a chicken himself. If one kills a mouse, he will also become a mouse himself. If, again, one is wealthy in this world, it is necessary that, on quitting the tabernacle of his body, he should be made to pass into the body of a beggar, so as to go about asking alms, and thereafter he shall depart into everlasting punishment. Moreover, as this body pertains to the princes and to matter, it is necessary that he who plants a persea[12] should pass through many bodies until that persea is prostrated. And if one builds a house for himself, he will be divided and scattered among all the bodies.[13] If one bathes in water, he freezes[14] his soul; and if one refuses to give pious regard[15] to his elect, he will be punished through the generations,[16] and will be translated into the bodies of catechumens, until he render many tributes of piety; and for this reason they offer to the elect whatever is best in their meats. And when they are about to eat

---

[1] The text gives τῆς ψυχῆς. But from the old Latin version, which has *animarum*, we may conjecture that τῶν ψυχῶν was read.

[2] The Latin version has "*vir* perfectus," — a reading which is due apparently to the fact that the author had mistaken the ἀήρ of the Greek for ἀνήρ. [See note 2, p. 176, *supra*.]

[3] ὁ θερισμὸς ἄρχων. The version of Petavius has, "Sic et princeps alter, messor appellatus." Perhaps the reading should be ὁ θερισμοῦ ἄρχων.

[4] λοιμόν. Other codices give *famem*, as reading λιμόν, famine.

[5] ἐὰν δὲ τὰ ἄνω τῆς ῥίζης πόνῳ σαλευθῇ. It may be also = And if the upper parts of the root shake under the exertion.

[6] πῶς μεταγγίζεται ἡ ψυχὴ εἰς πέντε σώματα. But the Codex Bobiensis reads *transferuntur;* and the Latin version gives, "quomodo et animæ in alia quoque corpora transfunduntur" = how the souls are also transfused into other bodies.

[7] The text gives κελεφῶν, which is spoken of in Migne as an unknown animal, though κέλεφος (thus accentuated) occurs in ecclesiastical writers in the sense of a *leper*. It is proposed to read ἐλεφαντιῶν, "of elephants;" and so the Codex Bobiensis gives "elephantorum corpora," and Codex Casinensis has "in elefantia eorum corpora," which is probably an error for "in elephantiacorum corpora." Routh suggests ἐλεφαντείων. [*Reliqu. Sac.*, vol. v. p. 58.]

[8] θερίσασα, reaping.

[9] νοῦς, ἔννοια, φρόνησις, ἐνθύμησις, λογισμός. The Latin version renders, *mens, sensus, prudentia, intellectus, cogitatio.* Petavius gives, *mens, notio, intelligentia, cogitatio, ratiocinatio.*

[10] τοῖς ἀπαρχῆς οὖσιν εἰς σκότος. But the Latin version gives "qui ex materia orti," etc. — who, having sprung from matter, are in darkness.

[11] ὀρνίθιον.

[12] Explained as a species of Egyptian tree, in which the fruit grows from the stem. The Codex Casinensis has the strange reading, *per se ad illam*, for *perseam*, etc. See also Epiphanius, num. 9.

[13] εἰς τὰ ὅλα σώματα.

[14] πήσσει. But the Latin version gives *vulnerat*, "wounds," from the reading πλήσσει. [Note 2, p. 176, *supra*.]

[15] εὐσέβειαν. But the Latin version gives *alimenta*.

[16] εἰς τὰς γενεάς. But the Latin version has "poenis subdetur gehennæ" = will suffer the pains of hell. [Compare p. 185, *infra*, "Gehen "]

bread, they offer up prayer first of all, addressing themselves in these terms to the bread : " I have neither reaped thee, nor ground thee, nor pressed thee, nor cast thee into the baking-vessel ; but another has done these things, and brought thee to me, and I have eaten thee without fault." And when he has uttered these things to himself, he says to the catechumen,[1] " I have prayed for thee ; " and in this manner that person then takes his departure. For, as I remarked to you a little before, if any one reaps, he will be reaped ; and so, too, if one casts grain into the mill, he will be cast in himself in like manner, or if he kneads he will be kneaded, or if he bakes he will be baked ; and for this reason they are interdicted from doing any such work. Moreover, there are certain other worlds on which the luminaries rise when they have set on our world.[2] And if a person walks upon the ground here, he injures the earth ; and if he moves his hand, he injures the air ; for the air is the soul (*life*) of men and living creatures, both fowl, and fish, and creeping thing. And as to every one[3] existing in this world, I have told you that this body of his does not pertain to God, but to matter, and is itself darkness, and consequently it must needs be cast in darkness.

10. Now, with respect to paradise, it is not called *a cosmos*.[4] The trees that are in it are lust and other seductions, which corrupt the rational powers of those men. And that tree in paradise, by which men know the good, is Jesus Himself, *or*[5] the knowledge of Him in the world. He who partakes thereof discerns the good and the evil. The world itself, however, is not God's *work ;* but it was the structure of a portion of matter, and consequently all things perish in it. And what the princes took as spoil from the first man, that is what makes the moon full, and what is being purged day by day of the world. And if the soul makes its exit without having gained the knowledge of the truth, it is given over to the demons, in order that they may subdue it in the Gehennas of fire ; and after that discipline it is made to pass into bodies with the purpose of being brought into subjection, and in this manner it is cast into the mighty fire until the consummation. Again, regarding the prophets amongst you,[6] he speaks thus : Their spirit is one of impiety, or of the lawlessness of the darkness which arose at the beginning. And being deceived by this spirit, they have not spoken *truth ;* for the prince blinded their mind. And if any one follows their words, he dies for ever, bound to the clods of earth, because he has not learned the knowledge of the Paraclete. He also gave injunctions to his elect alone, who are not more than seven in number. And the charge was this : " When ye cease eating, pray, and put upon your head an olive, sworn with the invocation of many names for the confirmation of this faith." The names, however, were not made known to me ; for only these seven make use of them. And again, the name Sabaoth, which is honourable and mighty with you, he declares to be the nature of man, and the parent of desire ; for which reason the simple[7] worship desire, and hold it to be a deity. Furthermore, as regards the manner of the creation of Adam, he tells us that he who said, " Come and let us make man in our image, after our likeness," or " after the form which we have seen," is the prince who addressed the other princes in terms which may be thus interpreted : " Come, give me of the light which we have received, and let us make man after the form of us princes, even after that form which we have seen, that is to say,[8] the first man." And in that manner he[9] created the man. They created Eve also after the like fashion, imparting to her of their own lust, with a view to the deceiving of Adam. And by these means the construction of the world proceeded from the operations of the prince.

11. He holds also that God has no part with the world itself, and finds no pleasure in it, by reason of its having been made a spoil of from the first by the princes, and on account of the ill that rose on it. Wherefore He sends and takes away from them day by day the soul belonging to Him, through the medium of these luminaries, the sun and the moon, by which the whole world and all creation are dominated. Him, again, who spake with Moses, and the Jews, and the priests, he declares to be the prince of the darkness ; so that the Christians, and the Jews, and the Gentiles are one and the same body, worshipping the same God : for He seduces them in His own passions, being no God of truth. For this reason all those who hope in that God who spake with Moses and the prophets have to be bound together with the said deity,[10] because they have not hoped in the God of truth ; for that deity spake with him in accordance with their own passions. Moreover, after

---

[1] But the Latin version gives, " respondet ad eum qui ei detulit" = he makes answer to the person who brought it to him.

[2] The text is, καὶ πάλιν εἰσὶν ἕτεροι κόσμοι τινές, τῶν φωστήρων δυνάντων ἀπὸ τούτου τοῦ κόσμου, ἐξ ὧν ἀνατέλλουσι. Routh suggests οἷς τινές, deleting ἐξ ὧν.

[3] Reading εἰ τις, as in the text. Routh suggests εἰ τι, = As to everything existing in this world, I have told you that the body thereof does, etc.

[4] But the Latin has "qui vocatur," etc. = which is called, etc. And Routh thereof proposes ὃς καλεῖται for · ὑ καλεῖται.

[5] The text gives simply ἡ γνῶσις. The Codex Bobiensis has *et scientia*. Hence Routh would read καὶ ἡ γνῶσις, *and* the knowledge.

[6] Retaining the reading ὑμῖν, though Petavius would substitute ἡμῖν, us. [Routh corrects Petav., *R. S.*, vol. v. pp. 63, 64.]

[7] ἁπλάριοι, in the Latin version *Simpliciores*, a name apparently given to the Catholics by the Manichæans. See Ducangii *Glossarium mediæ et infimæ Græcitatis*. [Routh, v. p. 65, worth noting.]

[8] The text gives ὅ ἐστι πρῶτος ἄνθρωπος. Routh proposes ὃ ἐστί, etc.

[9] Or, they.

[10] μετ' αὐτοῦ ἔχουσι δεθῆναι.

all these things, he speaks in the following terms with regard to the end,[1] as he has also written: When the elder has displayed his image,[2] the Omophorus then lets the earth go from him, and so the mighty fire gets free, and consumes the whole world. Then, again, he lets the soil go with the new æon,[3] in order that all the souls of sinners may be bound for ever. These things will take place at the time when the man's image[4] has come.[5] And all these powers put forth by God,[6] — namely, Jesus, who is in the smaller ship,[7] and the Mother of Life, and the twelve helmsmen,[8] and the virgin of the light, and the third elder, who is in the greater ship, and the living spirit, and the wall[9] of the mighty fire, and the wall of the wind, and the air, and the water, and the interior living fire, — have their seat in the lesser luminary, until the fire shall have consumed the whole world: and that is to happen within so many years, the exact number of which, however, I have not ascertained. And after these things there will be a restitution of the two natures;[10] and the princes will occupy the lower parts proper to them, and the Father the higher parts, receiving again what is His own due possession. — All this doctrine he delivered to his three disciples, and charged each to journey to a separate clime.[11] The Eastern parts fell thus to the lot of Addas; Thomas[12] obtained the Syrian territories as his heritage; and another, to wit, Hermeias, directed his course towards Egypt. And to this day they sojourn there, with the purpose of establishing the propositions contained in this doctrine.[13]

12. When Turbo had made this statement, Archelaus was intensely excited; but Marcellus remained unmoved, for he expected that God would come to the help of His truth. Archelaus, however, had additional cares in his anxiety about the people, like the shepherd who becomes concerned for his sheep when secret perils threaten them from the wolves. Accordingly Marcellus loaded Turbo with the most liberal gifts, and instructed him to remain in the house of Archelaus the bishop.[14] But on that selfsame day Manes arrived, bringing along with him certain chosen youths and virgins to the number of twenty-two.[15] And first of all he sought for Turbo at the door of the house of Marcellus; and on failing to find him there, he went in to salute Marcellus. On seeing him, Marcellus at first was struck with astonishment at the costume in which he presented himself. For he wore a kind of shoe which is usually called in common speech the quadrisole;[16] he had also a party-coloured cloak, of a somewhat airy[17] appearance; in his hand he grasped a very sturdy staff of ebony-wood;[18] he carried a Babylonian book under his left arm; his legs were swathed in trousers of different colours, the one being red, and the other green as a leek; and his whole mien was like that of some old Persian master and commandant.[19] Thereupon Marcellus sent forthwith for Archelaus, who arrived so quickly as almost to outstrip the word, and on entering was greatly tempted at once to break out against him, being provoked to that instantly by the very sight of his costume and his appearance, though more especially also by the fact that he had himself been turning over in his mind in his retirement[20] the various matters which he had learned from the recital of Turbo, and had thus come carefully prepared. But Marcellus, in his great thoughtfulness, repressed all zeal for mere wrangling, and decided to hear both parties. With that view he invited the leading men of the city; and from among them he selected as judges *of the discussion* certain adherents of the Gentile religion, four in number. The names of these umpires were as follows: Manippus, a person deeply versed in the art of grammar and the practice of rhetoric; Ægialeus,[21] a very eminent physician, and a man of the highest reputation for learning; and Claudius and Cleobolus,[22] two brothers famed as rhetoricians.[23] A splendid assemblage was thus convened; so large, indeed, that the house of Marcellus, which was of immense size, was filled with those who had been called to be hearers. And when the parties who proposed to speak in opposition to each other

---

1 ἐπὶ τέλει.

2 The text is κάθως αὐτὸς ἔγραψεν· Ὁ πρεσβύτης, etc. The Codex Bobiensis gives, "Sicut ipse senior scripsit: Cum manifestam feceris," etc., = As the elder himself wrote: When thou hast, etc. The *elder* here is probably the same as the *third elder* farther on.

3 The Greek is, ἀφίησι τὸν βῶλον μετὰ τοῦ νέον αἰῶνος; but the Latin version has the strangely diverse rendering, "dimittunt animam quæ objicitur inter medium novi sæculi" = they let go the soul that is placed in the midst of the new age. [Routh has τὴν βῶλον.]

4 ἀνδριάς.

5 But the Latin gives, "cum statuta venerit dies" = when the appointed day has come.

6 αἱ δὲ προβολαὶ πᾶσαι.

7 πλοίῳ. [See Routh, p. 68, on this *locus mire depravatus*.]

8 κυβερνῆται.

9 τεῖχος.

10 τῶν δύο φύσεων. But the Latin version gives *duorum luminarium*, and the Codex Casinensis has *luminariorum*, the two luminaries.

11 Reading κλίματα, with Petavius, for κλήματα.

12 The Codex Casinensis makes no mention of Thomas.

13 Here ends the Greek of Epiphanius.

14 The words, *the bishop*, are omitted in the Codex Bobiensis.

15 But Codex Bobiensis gives *duodecim*, twelve.

16 But the Codex Bobiensis gives *trisolium*, the trisole. Strabo, book xv., tells us that the Persians wore high shoes.

17 Aёrina, sky-like. [This portrait seems from life.]

18 Ducange in his *Glossary*, under the word Εβεάλλινος, shows from Callisthenes that the prophets or interpreters of sacred things carried an ebony staff. [Ezek. xxvii. 15; Routh, p. 71.]

19 The text is, "vultus vero ut senis Persæ artificis et bellorum ducis videbatur." Philippus Buonarruotius, in the *Osservazioni sopra alcuni frammenti di vasi antichi di Vetro*, Florence, 1716, p. 69, thinks that this rendering has arisen from the Latin translator's having erroneously read ὡς δημιουργοῦ καὶ στρατηγοῦ instead of ὡς δημάρχου καὶ στρατηγοῦ. Taking στρατηγοῦ, therefore, in the civil sense which it bears in various passages, he would interpret the sentence thus: "His whole mien was like that of an old Persian *tribune and magistrate*." See Gallandi's note [in Routh, p. 71].

20 The text is *secretius factum*, etc. Routh suggests *secretius factus*, etc.

21 The Codex Bobiensis reads "Ægidius."

22 Epiphanius gives Κλεοβουλος.

23 Codex Casinensis reads *rectores*, governors. And Epiphanius, num. 10, makes the first a professor of Gentile philosophy, the second a physician, the third a grammarian, and the fourth a rhetorician.

had taken their places in view of all, then those who had been elected as judges took their seats in a position elevated above all others : and the task of commencing the disputation was assigned to Manes. Accordingly, when silence was secured, he began [1] the discussion in the following terms : [2] —

13. My brethren, I indeed am a disciple of Christ, and, moreover, an apostle of Jesus ; and it is owing to the exceeding kindness of Marcellus that I have hastened hither, with the view of showing him clearly in what manner he ought to keep the system of divine religion, so that the said Marcellus verily, who at present has put himself, like one who has surrendered himself prisoner, under the doctrine of Archelaus, may not, like the dumb animals, which are destitute of intellect and understand not what they do, be fatally smitten to the ruin of his soul, in consequence of any failure in the possession of further facilities for setting about the right observance of divine worship. I know, furthermore, and am certain, that if Marcellus is once set right,[3] it will be quite possible that all of you may also have your salvation effected ; for your city hangs suspended upon his judgment. If vain presumption is rejected by every one of you, and if those things which are to be declared by me be heard with a real love for the truth, ye will receive the inheritance of the age to come, and the kingdom of heaven. I, in sooth, am the Paraclete, whose mission was announced of old time by Jesus, and who was to come to "convince the world of sin and unrighteousness." [4] And even as Paul, who was sent before me, said of himself, that "he knew in part, and prophesied in part," [5] so I reserve the perfect for myself, in order that I may do away with that which is in part. Therefore receive ye this third testimony, that I am an elect apostle of Christ ; and if ye choose to accept my words, ye will find salvation ; but if ye refuse them, eternal fire will have you to consume you. For as Hymenæus and Alexander were "delivered unto Satan, that they might learn not to blaspheme," [6] so will all ye also be delivered unto the prince of punishments, because ye have done injury to the Father of Christ, in so far as ye declare Him to be the cause of all evils, and the founder of unrighteousness, and the creator of all iniquity. By such doctrine ye do, indeed, bring forth from the same fountain both sweet water and bitter, — a thing which can in no possible way be either done or apprehended. For who ought to be believed? Should it be those masters of yours whose enjoyment is in the flesh, and who pamper themselves with the richest delights ; or our Saviour Jesus Christ, who says, as it is written in the book of the Gospels, "A good tree cannot bring forth evil fruit, neither can a corrupt tree bring forth good fruit," [7] and who in another place assures us that the "father of the devil [8] is a liar and a murderer from the beginning," [9] and tells us again that men's desire was for the darkness,[10] so that they would not follow that Word that had been sent forth in the beginning from the light,[11] and (once more shows us) the man who is the enemy of the same, the sower of tares,[12] and the god and prince of the age of this world, who blinds the minds of men that they may not be obedient to the truth in the Gospel of Christ? [13] Is that God good who has no wish that the men who are his own should be saved? And, not to go over a multitude of other matters, and waste much time, I may defer [14] till another opportunity the exposition of the true doctrine ; and taking it for granted that I have said enough on this subject for the present, I may revert to the matter immediately before me, and endeavour satisfactorily to demonstrate the absurdity of these men's teaching, and show that none of these things can be attributed to the God and Father of our Lord and Saviour, but that we must take Satan to be the cause of all our ills. To him, certainly, these must be carried back, for all ills of this kind are generated by him. But those things also which are written in the prophets and the law are none the less to be ascribed to him ; for he it is who spake then in the prophets, introducing into their minds very many ignorant notions of God, as well as temptations and passions. They, too, set forth that devourer of blood and flesh ; and to that Satan and to his prophets all these things properly pertain which he wished to transfer [15] to the Father of Christ, prepared as he was to write a few things in the way of truth, that by means of these he might also gain credence for those other statements of his which are false. Hence it is well for us to receive nothing at all of all those things which have been written of old even down to John, and indeed to embrace only the kingdom of heaven, which has been preached in the Gospel since his days ; for they verily but made a

---

[1] For *primum* the Codex Casinensis reads *plurima*, = he began a lengthened statement, etc.
[2] Thus far Valesius edited the piece from the Codex Bobiensis.
[3] Reading *emendato*. Codex Casinensis gives *enim dato*.
[4] John xvi. 8. *Injustitia*. This reading, *de injustitia*, may be due to an error on the part of the scribe, but is more probably to be referred to the practice pursued by Manes in altering and corrupting the sacred text to suit his own tenets. See Epiphanius on this heresy, num. 53, and cap. 53, *infra*. [" He introduced much new matter."]
[5] 1 Cor. xiii. 9.
[6] 1 Tim. i. 20.

[7] Matt. vii. 18.
[8] *Patrem diaboli*.
[9] John viii. 44.
[10] Referring, perhaps, to John i. 5.
[11] The text gives, " ut insequerentur. . . . Verbum, et inimicum," etc. The sense seems to be as above, supposing either that the verb *insequerentur* is used with the meaning of assailing, persecuting, or that the *ut* is put for *ut ne*, as is the case with the *excæcat ut* at the close of the sentence.
[12] Matt. xiii. 25.
[13] Eph. vi. 12: 2 Cor. iv. 4.
[14] Reading *differens*. But Codex Casinensis gives *disserens*.
[15] *Transformare*.

mockery of themselves, introducing as they did things ridiculous and ludicrous, keeping some small words given in obscure outline in the law, but not understanding that, if good things are mixed up with evil, the result is, that by the corruption of these evil things, even those others which are good are destroyed. And if, indeed, there is any one who may prove himself able to demonstrate that the law upholds the right, that law ought to be kept; but if we can show it to be evil, then it ought to be done away with and rejected, inasmuch as it contains the ministration of death, which was graven,[1] which also covered and destroyed the glory on the countenance of Moses.[2] It is a thing not without peril, therefore, for any one of you to teach the New Testament along with the law and the prophets, as if they were of one and the same origin; for the knowledge of our Saviour renews *the one* from day to day, while the other grows old and infirm, and passes almost into utter destruction.[3] And this is a fact manifest to those who are capable of exercising discernment. For just as, when the branches of a tree become aged, or when the trunk ceases to bear fruit any more, they are cut down; and just as, when the members of the body suffer mortification, they are amputated, for the poison of the mortification diffuses itself from these members through the whole body, and unless some remedy be found for the disease by the skill of the physician, the whole body will be vitiated; so, too, if ye receive the law without understanding its origin, ye will ruin your souls, and lose your salvation. For " the law and the prophets were until John; "[4] but since John the law of truth, the law of the promises, the law of heaven, the new law, is made known to the race of man. And, in sooth, as long as there was no one to exhibit to you this most true knowledge of our Lord Jesus, ye had not sin. Now, however, ye both see and hear, and yet ye desire to walk in ignorance,[5] in order that ye may keep[6] that law which has been destroyed and abandoned. And Paul, too, who is held to be the most approved *apostle* with us, expresses himself to the same effect in one of his epistles, when he says: " For if I build again the things which I destroyed, I make myself a prevaricator."[7] And in saying this he pronounces on them as Gentiles, because they were under the elements of the world,[8] before the fulness of faith came, believing then as they did in the law and the prophets.

14. *The judges said:* If you have any clearer statement yet to make, give us some explanation of the nature[9] of your doctrine and the designation[10] of your faith. *Manes replied:* I hold that there are two natures, one good and another evil; and that the one which is good dwells indeed in certain parts proper to it, but that the evil one is this world, as well as all things in it, which are placed there like objects imprisoned[11] in the portion of the wicked one, as John says, that " the whole world lieth in wickedness,"[12] and not in God. Wherefore we have maintained that there are two localities, — one good, and another which lies outside of this,[13] so that, having space therein *in his*, it might be capable of receiving into itself the creature, i.e., *creation*, of the world. For if we say that there is but a monarchy of one nature, and that God fills all things, and that there is no location outside of Him, what will be the sustainer of the creature, i.e., *creation?* where will be the Gehenna of fire? where the outer darkness? where the weeping? Shall I say in Himself? God forbid; else He Himself will also be made to suffer in and with these. Entertain no such fancies, whosoever of you have any care for your salvation; for I shall give you an example, in order that you may have fuller understanding of the truth. The world is one vessel;[14] and if[15] the substance of God has already filled this entire vessel, how is it possible now that anything more can be placed in this same vessel? If it is full, how shall it receive what is placed in it, unless a certain portion of the vessel is emptied? Or whither shall that which is to be emptied out make its way, seeing that there is no locality for it? Where then is the earth? where the heavens? where the abyss? where the stars? where the settlements?[16] where the powers? where the princes? where the outer darkness? Who is he that has laid the foundations of these, and where? No one is able to tell us that without stumbling on blasphemy. And in what way, again, has He been able to make the creatures, if there is no subsistent matter? For if He has made them out of the non-existent, it will follow that these visible creatures should be superior, and full of all virtues. But if in these there are wickedness, and death, and corruption, and whatever is opposed to the good, how say we that they owe their formation to a nature different from themselves? Howbeit if you consider the way in which the sons of men are begotten, you will

[1] *Informatum.*
[2] 1 Cor. iii. 7.
[3] Cf. Heb. viii. 13.
[4] Luke xvi. 16.
[5] In inscitias ire vultis. It is proposed to read *inficias* = and yet ye desire to deny the truth. Routh suggests, *et odistis et in inscitiam ire vultis* = and ye hate it, and choose to take your way into ignorance.
[6] Supplying *observetis* in the clause *ut legem*, etc.
[7] *Prævaricatorem.* Gal. ii. 18 [Vulgate. But see p. 176].
[8] Gal. iv. 3.

[9] Or, standard.
[10] *Titulo.*
[11] *Ergastula.*
[12] Or, in the wicked one. 1 John v. 19.
[13] The text gives " extra *eum*." Routh suggests *Deum*, outside of God.
[14] *Vas.*
[15] The text gives simply " quod Dei substantia," etc. We may perhaps adopt, with Routh, " quod *si* Dei," etc.
[16] *Sedes.* [" Thrones," as in Milton.] Routh suggests *sidera*, luminaries.

find that the creator of man is not the Lord, but another being, who is also himself of an unbegotten[1] nature, who has neither founder, nor creator, nor maker, but who, such as he is, has been produced by his own malice alone. In accordance with this, you men have a commerce with your wives, which comes to you by an occasion of the following nature. When any one of you has satiated himself with carnal meats, and meats of other kinds, then the impulse of concupiscence rises in him, and in this way the enjoyment[2] of begetting a son is increased; and this happens not as if that had its spring in any virtue, or in philosophy, or in any other gift of mind, but in fulness of meats only, and in lust and fornication. And how shall any one tell me that our father Adam was made after the image of God, and in His likeness, and that he is like Him who made him? How can it be said that all of us who have been begotten of him are like him? Yea, rather, on the contrary, have we not a great variety of forms, and do we not bear the impress of different countenances? And how true this is, I shall exhibit to you in parables. Look, for instance, at a person who wishes to seal up a treasure, or some other object, and you will observe how, when he has got a little wax or clay, he seeks to stamp it with an impression of his own countenance from the ring which he wears;[3] but if another countenance also stamps the figure of itself on the object in a similar manner, will the impression seem like? By no means, although you may be reluctant to acknowledge what is true. But if we are not like in the _common_ impression, and if, instead of that, there are differences in us, how can it fail to be proved thereby that we are the workmanship of the princes, and of matter? For in due accordance with their form, and likeness, and image, we also exist as diverse forms. But if you wish to be fully instructed as to that commerce which took place at the beginning, and as to the manner in which it occurred, I shall explain the matter to you.

15. _The judges said_: We need not inquire as to the manner in which that primitive commerce took place until we have first seen it proved that there are two natural principles. For when once it is made clear that there are two unbegotten natures, then others of your averments may also gain our assent, even although something in them may not seem to fit in very readily with what is

credible. For as the power of pronouncing judgment has been committed to us, we shall declare what may make itself clear to our mind. We may, however, also grant to Archelaus the liberty of speaking to these statements of yours, so that, by comparing what is said by each of you, we may be able to give our decision in accordance with the truth. _Archelaus said_: Notwithstanding, the adversary's intent is replete with gross audacity and blasphemy. _Manes said_: Hear, O judges, what he has said _of the adversary_.[4] He admits, then, that there are two objects. _Archelaus said_: It seems to me that this man is full of madness rather than of prudence, who would stir up a controversy with me to-day because I chance to speak of the _adversary_. But this objection of yours may be removed with few words, notwithstanding that you have supposed from this expression of mine that I shall allow that there are these two natures.[5] You have come forward with a most extravagant[6] doctrine; for neither of the assertions made by you holds good. For it is quite possible that one who is an adversary, not by nature, but by determination, may be made a friend, and cease to be an adversary; and thus, when the one of us has come to acquiesce with the other, we twain shall appear to be, as it were, one and the same object. This account also indicates that rational creatures have been entrusted with free-will,[7] in virtue of which they also admit of conversions. And consequently there cannot be _two_ unbegotten natures.[8] What do you say, then? Are these two natures inconvertible? or are they convertible? or is one of them converted? _Manes_, however, held back, because he did not find a suitable reply; for he was pondering the conclusion which might be drawn from either of two answers which he might make, turning the matter over thus in his thoughts: If I say that they are converted, he will meet me with that statement which is recorded in the Gospel about the trees;[9] but if I say that they are not convertible, he will necessarily ask me to explain the condition and cause of their intermingling. In the meantime, after a little delay, _Manes replied_: They are indeed both inconvertible in so far as contraries are concerned; but they are convertible as far as properties[10] are concerned. _Archelaus then said_: You seem to me to be out

---

[1] _Ingenitæ._

[2] _Fructus._

[3] The reference is to the ancient custom of using wax and certain earths and clays for the purpose of affixing, by means of the ring, a seal with an impression on any object which it was desired to secure. Thus Herodotus, ii. 38, tell us how the Egyptians marked the pure victim by wrapping it round the horns with papyrus, and then smearing some sealing earth (γῆν σημαντρίδα) on it, and stamping it with a ring. See also Cicero, _Pro Flacco_, where he speaks of the _laudatio obsignata cretâ illa Asiatica_; and Plautus, _Pseudolus_, Scene i., where he mentions the _expressam in cera ex annulo suam imaginem_, etc. [Compare vol. v. p. 466, note 3, this series.]

[4] The text is "quid dixerit adversarii;" some propose "_quod_" or "_quia_ dixerit," etc.

[5] The manuscript reading is, "tam si quidem ex hoc arbitratus est se affirmaturum." For this it is proposed to read, as in the translation, "tametsi quidem ex hoc arbitratus es me affirmaturum."

[6] The text gives _ingentem_. Routh suggests _inscientem_, stupid.

[7] [Vol. iii. 301-302. See Coleridge (on Donne), _English Divines_, vol. i. p. 87.]

[8] Adopting the proposed reading, "et ideo _duæ_ ingenitæ naturæ esse non possunt." The text omits the _duæ_, however; and in that case the sense would be simply, And consequently there cannot be unbegotten natures; or perhaps, And so they (the creatures) cannot be of an unbegotten nature.

[9] [Matt. vii. 15-20.]

[10] _Propria._

of your mind, and oblivious of your own propositions ; yea, you do not appear even to recognise the powers or qualities of the very words which you have been learning.[1] For you do not understand either what conversion is, or what is meant by *unbegotten*, or what duality implies, or what is past, or what is present, or what is future, as I have gathered from the opinions to which you have just now given expression. For you have affirmed, indeed, that each of these two natures is inconvertible so far as regards contraries, but convertible so far as regards properties. But I maintain that one who moves in properties does not pass out of himself, but subsists in these same properties, in which he is ever inconvertible ; while in the case of one who is susceptible of conversion, the effect is that he is placed outside the pale of properties, and passes within the sphere of accidents.[2]

16. *The judges said:* Convertibility translates the person whom it befalls into another ; as, for example, we might say that if a Jew were to make up his mind to become a Christian, or, on the other hand, if a Christian were to decide to be a Gentile, this would be a species of convertibility, and a cause of the same.[3] But, again, if we suppose a Gentile to keep by all his own *heathen* properties, and to offer sacrifices to his gods, and to do service to the temples as usual, surely you would not be of opinion that he could be said to be converted, while he yet holds by his properties, and goes on in them? What, then, do you say? Do they sustain convertibility or not? *And as Manes hesitated, Archelaus proceeded thus:* If, indeed, he says that both natures are convertible,[4] what is there to prevent our thinking them to be one and the same object? For if they are inconvertible, then surely in natures which are similarly inconvertible and similarly unbegotten there is no distinction, neither can the one of them be recognised as good or as evil. But if they are both convertible, then, forsooth, the possible result may be both that the good is made evil, and that the evil is made good. If, however, this is the possible result, why should we not speak of one only as unbegotten,[5] which would be a conception in worthier accordance with the reckoning of truth? For we have to consider how that evil one became so at first, or against what objects he exercised his wickedness before the formation of the world. When the heavens

had not yet appeared, when the earth did not yet subsist, and when there was neither man nor animal, against whom did he put his wickedness in operation? whom did he oppress unjustly? whom did he rob and kill? But if you say that he first appeared in his evil nature to his own kin,[6] then without doubt you give the proof that he comes of a good nature. And if, again, all these are also evil, how can Satan then cast out Satan?[7] But while thus reduced to a dilemma on this point, you may change your position in the discussion, and say that the good suffered violence from the evil. But none the more is it without peril for you to make such a statement, to the effect of affirming the vanquishing of the light ; for what is vanquished has destruction near it.[8] For what says the divine word? "Who can enter into a strong man's house, and spoil his goods, except he be stronger than he?"[9] But if you allege that he first appeared in his evil nature to men, and only from that time showed openly the marks of his wickedness, then it follows that before this time he was good, and that he took on this quality of conversion because the creation of man[10] was found to have emerged as the cause of his wickedness. But, in fine, let him tell us what he understands by evil, lest perchance he may be defending or setting up a mere name. And if it is not the name but the substance of evil that he speaks of, then let him set before us the fruits of this wickedness and iniquity, since the nature of a tree can never be known but by its fruit.

17. *Manes said:* Let it first be allowed on your side that there is an alien root of wickedness, which God has not planted, and then I shall tell you its fruits. *Archelaus said:* Truth's reckoning does not make any such requirement ; and I shall not admit to you that there is a root of any such evil tree, of the fruit whereof no one has ever tasted. But just as, when a man desires to make any purchase, he does not produce the money unless he first ascertains by tasting the object whether it is of a dry or a moist species, so I shall not admit to you that the tree is evil and utterly corrupt, unless the quality of its fruit is first exhibited ; for it is written, that "the tree is known by its fruits."[11] Tell us, therefore, O Manes, what fruit is yielded by that tree which is called evil, or of what nature it is, and what virtue it is, that we may also believe with you that the root of that same tree

---

[1] Didicisti. But perhaps we ought to read *dixisti*, which you have been uttering.

[2] *Aliena*, of what is alien.

[3] The text runs thus: " ut si dicamus, Judæus, si velit fieri Christianus, aut si Christianus velit esse gentilis, hæc species est convertibilitatis et causa."

[4] The text gives *convertibiles*. Routh suggests *inconvertibiles*, inconvertible.

[5] The text is *unum dicamus ingenitum*. Routh suggests *unum bonum*, etc. = Why should we not speak of only one unbegotten good?

[6] The text is, " quod si suis eum dicas extitisse malum, sine dubio ergo ostenditur illum bonæ esse naturæ." Routh suggests, " quia istis suis adversatur qui mali sunt," etc. = The fact that he is adverse to those who are of his own kin, and who are evil, would be a proof that he comes of a good nature.

[7] Mark iii. 23.

[8] Or, kin to it, *vicinum habet interitum*.

[9] Mark iii. 27.

[10] The text is, " creati hominis causa invenitur exstitisse malitiæ," for which we read " creatio hominis," etc.

[11] Matt. vii. 16.

is of that character which you ascribe to it. *Manes said:* The root indeed is evil, and the tree is most corrupt, but the increase is not from God. Moreover, fornications, adulteries, murders, avarice, and all evil deeds, are the fruits of that evil root. *Archelaus said:* That we may credit you when you say that these are the fruits of that evil root, give us a taste of these things; for you have pronounced the substance of this tree to be ungenerate,[1] the fruits of which are produced after its own likeness. *Manes said:* The very unrighteousness which subsists in men offers the proof itself, and in avarice too you may taste that evil root. *Archelaus said:* Well, then, as you have stated the question, those iniquities which prevail among men are fruits of this tree. *Manes said:* Quite so. *Archelaus proceeded:* If these, then, are the fruits, that is to say, the wicked deeds of men, it will follow that the men themselves will hold the place of the root and of the tree; for you have declared that they produce fruits of this nature. *Manes said:* That is my statement. *Archelaus answered:* Not well say you, *That is my statement:* for surely that cannot be your statement; otherwise, when men cease from sinning, this tree of wickedness will appear to be unfruitful. *Manes said:* What you say is an impossibility; for even though one or another, or several, were to cease sinning, there would yet be others doing evil still. *Archelaus said:* If it is at all possible for one or another, or several, as you admit, not to sin, it is also possible for all to do the same; for they are all of one parent, and are all men of one lump. And, not to follow at my ease those affirmations which you have so confusedly made through all their absurdities, I shall conclude their refutation by certain unmistakeable counter-arguments. Do you allege that the fruits of the evil root and the evil tree are the deeds of men, that is to say, fornications, adulteries, perjuries, murders, and other similar things? *Manes said:* I do. *Archelaus said:* Well, then, if it happened that the race of men was to die off the face of the earth, so that they should not be able to sin any more, the substance of that tree would then perish, and it would bear fruit no more. *Manes said:* And when will that take place of which you speak? *Archelaus said:* What[2] is in the future I know not, for I am but a man; nevertheless I shall not leave these words of yours unexamined. What say you of the race of men? Is it unbegotten, or is it a production? *Manes said:* It is a production. *Archelaus said:* If man is a production, who is the parent of adultery and fornication, and such other things? Whose

fruit is this? Before man was made, who was there to be a fornicator, or an adulterer, or a murderer? *Manes said:* But if the man is fashioned of the evil nature, it is manifest that he is such a fruit,[3] albeit he may sin, albeit he may not sin; whence also the name and race of men are once for all and absolutely of this character, whether they may do what is righteous or what is unrighteous. *Archelaus said:* Well, we may also take notice of that matter. If, as you aver, the wicked one himself made man, why is it that he practises his malignity on him?

18. *The judges said:* We desire to have information from you on this point, Manichæus, to wit, to what effect you have affirmed him to be evil. Do you mean that he has been so from the time when men were made, or before that period? For it is necessary that you should give some proof of his wickedness from the very time from which you declare him to have been evil. Be assured[4] that the quality of a wine cannot be ascertained unless one first tastes it; and understand that, in like manner, every tree is known by its fruit. What say you, then? From what time has this personality been evil? For an explanation of this problem seems to us to be necessary. *Manes said:* He has always been so. *Archelaus said:* Well, then, I shall also show from this, most excellent friends, and most judicious auditors, that his statement is by no means correct. For iron, to take an example, has not been an evil thing always, but only from the period of man's existence, and since his art turned it to evil by applying it to false uses; and every sin has come into existence since the period of man's being. Even that great serpent himself was not evil previous to man, but only after man, in whom he displayed the fruit of his wickedness, because he willed it himself. If, then, the father of wickedness makes his appearance to us after man *has come into being*, according to the Scriptures, how can he be unbegotten who has thus been constituted evil subsequently to man, who is himself a production? But, again, why should he exhibit himself as evil just from the period when, on your supposition, he did himself create man?[5] What did he desire in him? If man's whole body was his own workmanship, what did he ardently affect in him? For one who ardently affects or desires, desires something which is different and better. If, indeed, man takes his origin from him in respect of the evil nature, we see how man was his own, as I have fre-

---

[1] *Ingenitam.*
[2] The text gives "quoniam quod futurum est nescio, homo enim sum, non tamen," etc. Routh suggests "*quonam?* quod futurum," etc. = What has that to do with the matter? The future I know not, etc.
[3] The text is, "sed homo a mala natura plasmatus manifestum est quia ipse sit fructus," etc.
[4] Routh, however, points differently, so that the sense is: Be assured that it is necessary to give some proof, etc. . . . For the quality of a wine, etc.
[5] The text is, "ex hominis tempore a se creati cur malus ostendatur," which is taken to be equivalent to, "ex tempore quo hominem ipse creavit," etc.

quently shown.[1] For if man was his own, he was also evil himself, just as it holds with our illustration of the like tree and the like fruit; for an evil tree, as you say, produces evil fruit. And seeing that all were evil, what did he desiderate, or in what could he show the beginning of his wickedness, if from the time of man's formation man was the cause of his wickedness? Moreover, the law and precept having been given to the man himself, the man had not by any means the power to yield obedience to the serpent, and to the statements which were made by him; and had the man then yielded no obedience to him, what occasion would there have been for him to be evil? But, again, if evil is unbegotten, how does it happen that man is sometimes found to be stronger than it? For, by obeying the law of God, he will often overcome every root of wickedness; and it would be a ridiculous thing if he, who is but the production, should be found to be stronger than the unbegotten. Moreover, whose is that law with its commandment — that commandment, I mean, which has been given to man? Without doubt it will be acknowledged to be God's. And how, then, can the law be given to an alien? or who can give his commandment to an enemy? Or, to speak of him who receives the commandment, how can he contend against the devil? that is to say, on this supposition, how can he contend against his own creator, as if the son, while he is a debtor to him for deeds of kindness, were to choose to inflict injuries on the father? Thus you but mark out the profitlessness[2] of man on this side, if you suppose him to be contradicting by the law and commandment him who has made him, and to be making the effort to get the better of him. Yea, we shall have to fancy the devil himself to have gone to such an excess of folly, as not to have perceived that in making man he made an adversary for himself, and neither to have considered what might be his future, nor to have foreseen the actual consequence of his act; whereas even in ourselves, who are but productions, there are at least some small gifts of knowledge, and a measure of prudence, and a moderate degree of consideration, which is sometimes of a very trustworthy nature. And how, then, can we believe that in the unbegotten there is not some little portion of prudence, or consideration, or intelligence? Or how can we make the contrary supposition, according to your

assertion, namely, that he is discovered to be of the most senseless apprehension, and the dullest heart, and, in short, rather like the brutes in his natural constitution? But if the case stands thus, again, how is it that man, who is possessed of no insignificant power in mental capacity and knowledge, could have received his substance from one who thus is, of all beings, the most ignorant and the bluntest in apprehension? How shall any one be rash enough to profess that man is the workmanship of an author of this character? But, again, if man consists both of soul and of body, and not merely of body without soul, and if the one cannot subsist apart from the other, why will you assert that these two are antagonistic and contrary to each other? For our Lord Jesus Christ, indeed, seems to me to have spoken of these in His parables, when He said: "No man can put new wine into old bottles, else the bottles will break, and the wine run out."[3] But new wine is to be put into new bottles, as there is indeed one and the same Lord for the bottle and for the wine. For although the substance may be different, yet by these two substances, in their due powers, and in the maintenance of their proper mutual relations,[4] the one person of man subsists. We do not say, indeed, that the soul is of one substance with the body, but we aver that they have each their own characteristic qualities; and as the bottle and the wine are applied in the similitude to one race and one species of men, so truth's reckoning requires us to grant that man was produced complete by the one God: for the soul rejoices in the body, and loves and cherishes it; and none the less does the body rejoice that it is quickened by the soul. But if, on the other hand, a person maintains that the body is the work of the wicked one, inasmuch as it is so corruptible, and antiquated, and worthless, it would follow then that it is incapable of sustaining the virtue of the spirit or the movement of the soul, and the most splendid creation of the same. For just as, when a person puts a piece of new cloth into an old garment, the rent is made worse;[5] so also the body would perish if it were to be associated, under such conditions, with that most brilliant production the soul. Or, to use another illustration: just as, when a man carries the light of a lamp into a dark place, the darkness is forthwith put to flight and makes no appearance; so we ought to understand that, on the soul's introduction into the body, the darkness is straightway banished, and one nature at once effected, and one man constituted in one species. And thus, agreeably therewith, it will be allowed that the new wine is

---

[1] The reading adopted by Migne is, "si ergo ex eo homo est, mala natura, demonstratur quomodo suus fuit, ut frequenter ostendi." Others put the sentence interrogatively = If man takes his origin from him, (and) the evil nature is thus demonstrated, in what sense was man his own, etc.? Routh suggests *ex quo* for *ex eo* = If the evil nature is demonstrated just from the time of man's existence, how was man, etc.?

[2] The reading is *inutilitatem*. But Routh points out that this is probably the translation of την εὐτέλειαν, *vilitatem*, meanness.

[3] Matt. ix. 17.
[4] *Dominatione et observantiæ usu.*
[5] Matt. ix. 16.

put into new bottles, and that the piece of new cloth is not put into the old garment. But from this we are able to show that there is a unison of powers in these two substances, that is to say, in that of the body and in that of the soul; of which unison that greatest teacher in the Scriptures, Paul, speaks, when he tells us, that "God hath set the members every one of them in the body as it hath pleased Him."[1]

19. But if it seems difficult for you to understand this, and if you do not acquiesce in these statements, I may at all events try to make them good by adducing illustrations. Contemplate man as a kind of temple, according to the similitude of Scripture:[2] the spirit that is in man may thus be likened to the image that dwells in the temple. Well, then, a temple cannot be constituted unless first an occupant is acknowledged for the temple; and, on the other hand, an occupant cannot be settled in the temple unless the structure has been erected. Now, since these two objects, the occupant and the structure, are both consecrated together, how can any antagonism or contrariety be found between them, and how should it not rather appear that they have both been the products of subjects that are in amity and of one mind? And that you may know that this is the case, and that these subjects are truly at one both in fellowship and in lineage, He who knows and hears[3] all has made this response, "Let us make man," and so forth. For he who constructs[4] the temple interrogates him who fashions the image, and inquires carefully about the measurements of magnitude, and breadth, and bulk, in order that he may mark off the space for the foundations in accordance with these dimensions; and no one sets about the vain task of building a temple without first making himself acquainted with the measurements needed for the placing of the image. In like manner, therefore, the mode and the measure of the body are made the subject of inquiry, in order that the soul may be appropriately lodged in it by God, the Artificer of all things. But if any one say that he who has moulded the body is an enemy to the God who is the Creator of my soul,[5] then how is it that, while regarding each other with a hostile eye, these two parties have not brought disrepute upon the work, by bringing it about either that he who constructs the temple should make it of such narrow dimensions as to render it incapable of accommodating what is placed within it, or that he who fashions the image should come with something so massive and ponderous, that, on its introduction into the temple, the edifice would at once collapse? If such is not the case, then, with these things, let us contemplate them in the light of what we know to be the objects and intents of antagonists. But if it is right for all to be disposed with the same measures and the same equity, and to be displayed with like glory, what doubt should we still entertain on this subject? We add, if it please you, this one illustration more. Man appears to resemble a ship which has been constructed by the builder and launched into the deep, which, however, it is impossible to navigate without the rudder, by which it can be kept under command, and turned in whatsoever direction its steersman may wish to sail. Also, that the rudder and the whole body of the ship require the same artificer, is a matter admitting no doubt; for without the rudder the whole structure of the ship, that huge body, will be an inert mass. And thus, then, we say that the soul is the rudder of the body; that both these, moreover, are ruled by that liberty of judgment and sentiment which we possess, and which corresponds to the steersman; and that when these two are made one by union,[6] and thus possess a unison of function applicable to all kinds of work, whatever may be the products of their own operation, they bear a testimony to the fact that they have both one and the same author and maker.

20. On hearing these argumentations, the multitudes who were present were exceedingly delighted; so much so, indeed, that they were almost laying hands on Manes; and it was with difficulty that Archelaus restrained them, and kept them back, and made them quiet again. *The judges said:* Archelaus has given us proof sufficient of the fact that the body and soul of man are the works of one hand; because an object cannot subsist in any proper consonance and unison as the work of one hand, if there is any want of harmony in the design and plan. But if it is alleged that one could not possibly have sufficed to develop both these objects, *namely, body and soul,* this is simply to exhibit the incapacity of the artificer. For thus, even though one should grant that the soul is the creation of a good deity, it will be found to be but an idle work so far as the man is concerned, unless it also takes to itself the body. And if, again, the body is held to be the formation of an evil deity, the work will also none the less be idle unless it receives the soul; and, in truth, unless the soul be in unison with the body by commixture and due introduction, so

---

[1] 1 Cor. xii. 13.
[2] 1 Cor. iii. 17; 2 Cor. vi. 16.
[3] The reading is *scit et audit.* Routh somewhat needlessly suggests *scite audit* = he who hears intelligently.
[4] The codex gives "hic enim qui exstruis." It is proposed to read "sic enim qui exstruit" = For in this very way he who constructs.
[5] The text gives "quod si dicat quis inimicum esse eum qui plasmaverit corpus; Deus qui Creator," etc. The Codex Casinensis reads *Deum.* We adopt the emendation *Deo* and the altered punctuation, thus: "quod si dicat cuis inimicum esse eum qui plasmaverit corpus Deo qui creator est animæ," etc.

[6] Reading "*per* conjunctionem" for the simple *conjunctionem*

that the two are in mutual connections, the man will not exist, neither can we speak of him. Hence *we are of opinion that* Archelaus has proved by a variety of illustrations that there is but one and the same maker for the whole man. *Archelaus said:* I doubt not, Manes, that you understand this, namely, that one who is born and created[1] is called the son of him who begets or creates. But if the wicked one made man, then he ought to be his father, according to nature. And to whom, then, did the Lord Jesus address Himself, when in these terms He taught men to pray: "When ye pray, say, Our Father which art in heaven;"[2] and again, "Pray to your Father which is in secret?"[3] But it was of Satan that He spake when He said, that He "beheld him as lightning fall from heaven;"[4] so that no one dare say that He taught us to pray to him. And surely Jesus did not come down from heaven with the purpose of bringing men together, and reconciling them to Satan; but, on the contrary, He gave him over to be bruised beneath the feet of His faithful ones. However, for my part, I would say that those Gentiles are the more blessed who do indeed bring in a multitude of deities, but at least hold them all to be of one mind, and in amity with each other; whereas this man, though he brings in but two gods, does not blush to posit enmities and discordant sentiments between them. And, in sooth, if these *Gentiles* were to bring in[5] their counterfeit deities under conditions of that kind, we would verily have it in our power to witness something like a gladiatorial contest proceeding between them, with their innumerable natures and diverse sentiments.

21. But now, what it is necessary for me to say on the subject of the inner and the outer man, may be expressed in the words of the Saviour to those who swallow a camel, and wear the outward garb of the hypocrite, begirt with blandishments and flatteries. It is to them that Jesus addresses Himself when He says: "Woe unto you, scribes and Pharisees, hypocrites! for ye make clean the outside of the cup and of the platter, but within they are full of uncleanness. Or know you not, that He that made that which is without, made that which is within also?"[6] Now why did He speak of the cup and of the platter? Was He who uttered these words a glassworker, or a potter who made vessels of clay? Did He not speak most manifestly of the body and the soul? For the Pharisees truly looked to the "tithing of anise and cummin, and

left undone the weightier matters of the law;"[7] and while devoting great care to the things which were external, they overlooked those which bore upon the salvation of the soul. For they also had respect to "greetings in the market-place,"[8] and "to the uppermost seats at feasts:"[9] and to them the Lord Jesus, knowing their perdition, made this declaration, that they attended to those things only which were without, and despised as strange things those which were within, and understood not that He who made the body made also the soul. And who is so unimpressible and stolid in intellect, as not to see that those sayings *of our Lord* may suffice him for all cases? Moreover, it is in perfect harmony with these sayings that Paul speaks, when he interprets to the following intent certain things written in the law: "Thou shalt not muzzle the mouth of the ox that treadeth out the corn. Doth God take care for oxen? Or saith He it altogether for our sakes?"[10] But why should we waste further time upon this subject? Nevertheless I shall add a few things out of many that might be offered. Suppose now that there are two unbegotten *principles*, and that we determine fixed localities for these: it follows then that God is separated,[11] if He is *supposed to be* within a certain location, and not diffused everywhere; and He will consequently *be represented as* much inferior to the locality in which He is understood to be *for the object which contains is always greater*[12] *than the object which is contained in it:* and thus God is made to be of that magnitude which corresponds with the magnitude of the locality in which He is contained, just as is the case with a man in a house.[13] Then, further, reason asks who it is that has divided between them, or who has appointed for them their determinate limits; and thus both would be made out to be the decided inferiors of man's own power.[14] For Lysimachus and Alexander held the empire of the whole world, and were able to subdue all foreign nations, and the whole race of men; so that throughout that period there was no other in possession of empire besides themselves under heaven. And how will any one be rash enough to say that God, who is the true light that never suffers eclipse, and whose is also the kingdom that is holy and everlasting, is not everywhere present, as[15] is the way with this most depraved man, who, in his impiety,

---

[1] Reading "natus est et creatus." The Codex Casinensis has "natus est creatus"
[2] Matt. vi. 9; Luke xi. 2.
[3] Matt. vi. 6.
[4] Luke x. 18.
[5] Codex Casinensis gives *introduceret;* but, retaining the reference to the Gentiles, we read *introducerent.*
[6] Matt. xxiii. 25; Luke xi. 39.

[7] Luke xi. 42.
[8] Matt. xxiii. 6; Mark xii. 38; Luke xx. 46.
[9] The Codex Casinensis gives a strangely corrupt reading here: "primos discipulos subitos in cœnis, quod scientes Dominus." It is restored thus: "primos discubitus in cœnis, quos sciens Dominus," etc.
[10] 1 Cor. ix. 9.
[11] *Dividitur.*
[12] Reading *majus* for the inept *malus* of the Codex Casinensis.
[13] Routh refers us here to Maximus, *De Natura,* § 2. See *Reliquiæ Sacræ,* ii. 89-91.
[14] The text is "multo inferior virtutis humanæ," which is probably a Græcism.
[15] Reading *ceu* for the *eu* of the Codex Casinensis.

refuses to ascribe to the Omnipotent God even equal power with men?[1]

22. *The judges said:* We know that a light shines through the whole house, and not in some single part of it; as Jesus also intimates when He says, that "no man lighting a candle puts it under a bushel, but on a candlestick, but it may give light unto all that are in the house."[2] If, then, God is a light, it must needs be that that light (if Jesus is to be credited) shall shine on the whole world, and not on any portions of it merely. And if,[3] then, that light holds possession of the whole world, where now can there be any ungenerated darkness? or how can darkness be understood to exist at all, unless it is something simply accidental? *Archelaus said:* Forasmuch, indeed, as the word of the Gospel is understood much better by you than by this person who puts himself forward as the Paraclete, although I could call him rather parasite than paraclete, I shall tell you how it has happened that there is darkness. When the light had been diffused everywhere, God began to constitute the universe, and commenced with the heaven and the earth; in which process this issue appeared, to wit, that the midst,[4] which is the locality of earth covered with shadow, as a consequence of the interposition[5] of the creatures which were called into being, was found to be obscure, in such wise that circumstances required light to be introduced into that place, which was thus situated in the midst. Hence in Genesis, where Moses gives an account of the construction of the world, he makes no mention of the darkness either as made or as not made. But he keeps silence on that subject, and leaves the explanation of it to be discovered by those who may be able to give proper attention to it. Neither, indeed, is that a very arduous and difficult task. For to whom may it not be made plain that this sun of ours is visible, when it has risen in the east, and taken its course toward the west, but that when it has gone beneath the earth, and been carried farther within that formation which among the Greeks is called the *sphere*, it then ceases to appear, being overshadowed in darkness in consequence of the interposition of the bodies?[6] When it is thus covered, and when the body of the earth stands opposite it, a shadow is superinduced, which produces from itself the

darkness; and it continues so until again, after the course of the inferior space has been traversed in the night, it rolls towards the east, and is seen to rise once more in its wonted seats. Thus, then, the cause of the shadow and the night is discovered in the solidity of the body of the earth, — a thing, indeed, which a man may understand from the fact of the shadow cast by his own body.[7] For before the heaven and the earth and all those corporeal creatures appeared, the light remained always constant, without waning or eclipse, as there existed no body which might produce shadow by its opposition or intervention; and consequently one must say that nowhere was there darkness then, and nowhere night. For if, to take an illustration, it should please Him who has the power of all things to do away with the quarter[8] which lies to the west, then, as the sun would not direct its course toward that region, there would nowhere emerge either evening or darkness, but the sun would be on its course always, and would never set, but would almost always hold the centre tract of heaven, and would never cease to appear; and by this the whole world would be illumined with the clearest light, in virtue of which no part of it would suffer obscuration, but the equal power of one light would remain everywhere. But on the other hand, while the western quarter keeps its position, and the sun executes[9] its course in three parts of the world, then those who are under the sun will be seen to be illuminated more brightly; so that I might almost say, that while the people who belong to the diverse tract are still asleep, those former are in possession of the day's beginning. But just[10] as those Orientals have the light rising on them earlier than the people who live in the west, so they have it also more quickly obscured, and they only who are settled in the middle of the globe see always an equality of light. For when the sun occupies the middle of the heavens, there is no place that can appear to be either brighter or darker (than another), but all parts of the world are illuminated equally and impartially by the sun's effulgence.[11] If, then, as we have said above, that portion of the western tract were done away with, the part which is adjacent to it would now no more suffer obscuration. And these things I could indeed set forth somewhat more simply, as I might also describe the zodiacal circle; but I have not thought of looking into these matters at present.[12] I shall therefore say

---

1 The Codex Casinensis gives "nec quæ vellem quidem," for which "nec æqualem quidem," etc., is suggested, as in the translation.

2 Matt. v. 16.

3 The text gives *a quo si*, etc. Routh suggests *atqui si*, etc.

4 *Medietas.*

5 Reading *objectu . . . creaturarum*, instead of *obtectu*, etc., in Codex Casinensis.

6 The text of this sentence stands thus in Migne and Routh: "cui enim non fiat manifestum, solem istum visibilem, cum ab oriente fuerit exortus, et tetenderit iter suum ad occidentem, cum sub terram ierit, et interior effectus fuerit ea quæ apud Græcos *sphæra* vocatur, quod tunc objectu corporum obumbratus non appareat?" The Codex Casinensis reads *quod nunc oblectu*, etc. We should add that it was held by Anaximander and others that there was a species of globe or sphere (σφαῖρα) which surrounded the universe. [Vol. ii. p. 136, n. 2.]

7 Reading *ex suimet ipsius umbra* for *exuet ipsius umbra*, which is given in the Codex Casinensis.

8 *Plagam.*

9 *Ministrante.*

10 The text is "Sicut autem ante," etc. Routh suggests, *Sole adeunte*, etc.

11 Reading "ex æquo et justo, solis fulgore," etc. The Codex Casinensis has "ex ea quo solis fulgure."

12 The text is altogether corrupt — *sed non intui hunc fieri ratus sum;* so that the sense can only be guessed at. Routh suggests *istud* for *intui*.

nothing of these, but shall revert to that capital objection urged by my adversary, in his affirming so strenuously [1] that the darkness is ungenerated; which position, however, has also been confuted already, as far as that could have been done by us.

23. *The judges said:* If we consider that the light existed before the estate of the creatures was introduced, and that there was no object in an opposite position which might generate shadow, it must follow that the light was then diffused everywhere, and that all places were illuminated with its effulgence, as has been shown by what you have stated just now; and as we perceive that the true explanation is given in that, we assign the palm to the affirmations of Archelaus. For if the universe is clearly divided, as if some wall had been drawn through the centre of it, and if on the one side the light dwells, and on the other side the darkness, it is yet to be understood that this darkness has been brought accidentally about through the shadow generated in consequence of the objects which have been set up in the world; and hence again we must ask who it is that has built this wall between the two divisions, provided you indeed admit the existence of such a construction, O Manichæus. But if we have to take account of this matter on the supposition that no such wall has been built, then again it comes to be understood that the universe forms but one locality, without any exception, and is placed under one power; and if so, then the darkness can in no way have an ungenerated nature. *Archelaus said:* Let him also explain the following subject with a view to what has been propounded. If God is seated in His kingdom, and if the wicked one in like manner is seated in his kingdom, who can have constructed the wall between them? For no object can divide two substances except one that is greater than either,[2] even as it is said[3] in the book of Genesis, that "God divided the light from the darkness."[4] Consequently the constructor of this wall must also be some one of a capacity like that: for the wall marks the boundaries of these two parties, just as among people who dwell in the rural parts a stone is usually taken to mark off the portion of each several party; which custom, however, would afford a better apprehension of the case were we to take the division to refer specially to the marking out of an inheritance falling to brothers. But for the present I have not to speak of matters like these, however essential they may appear. For what we are in quest of is an answer to the question, Who can have constructed the wall required for the designation of the limits of the kingdom of each of these twain? No answer has been given. Let not this perfidious fellow hesitate, but let him now acknowlege that the substance of his duality has been reduced again to a unity. Let him mention any one who can have constructed that middle wall. What could the one of these two parties have been engaged in when the other was building? Was he asleep? or was he ignorant of the fact? or was he unable to withstand the attempt? or was he bought over with a price? Tell us what he was about, or tell us who in all the universe was the person that raised the construction. I address my appeal to you, O judges, whom God has sent to us with the fullest plenitude of intelligence; judge ye which of these two could have erected the structure, or what the one could have been doing all the while that the other was engaged in the building.

24. *The judges said:* Tell us, O Manes, who designated the boundaries for the kingdom of each, and who made the middle wall? For Archelaus begs that due importance be attached to the practice of interrogation in this discussion. *Manes said:* The God who is good, and who has nothing in common with evil, placed the firmament in the midst, in order to make it plain [5] that the wicked one is an alien to Him. *Archelaus said:* How fearfully you belie the dignity of that name! You do indeed call Him God, but you do so in name only, and you make His deity resemble man's infirmities. At one time out of the non-existent, and at another time out of underlying matter, which indeed thus existed before Himself, you assert that He did build the structure, as builders among men are wont to do. Sometimes also you speak of Him as apprehensive, and sometimes as variable. It is, however, the part of God to do what is proper to God, and it is the part of man to do what is proper to man. If, then, God, as you say, has constructed a wall, this is a God who marks Himself out as apprehensive, and as possessed of no fortitude. For we know that it is always the case that those who are suspicious of the preparation of secret perils against them by strangers, and who are afraid of the plots of enemies, are accustomed to surround their cities with walls, by which procedure they at once secure themselves in their ignorance, and display their feeble capacity. But here, too, we have something which ought not to be passed over by us in silence, but rather brought prominently forward; so that even by the great abundance of our declarations on the subject our adversary's manifold craftiness may be brought to nought, with the help of the

[1] Codex Casinensis gives " omni nisi," for which we adopt " omni nisu."

[2] Reading *utriusque majus.* The Codex Casinensis has *utrunque majus.*

[3] The text is *dicit,* for which *dicitur* may be adopted.

[4] Gen. i. 4.

[5] Reading "patefaceret" for the "partum faceret" of Codex Casinensis.

truth on our side. We may grant, then, that the structure of the wall has been made with the purpose of serving to distinguish between the two kingdoms; for without this one division [1] it is impossible for either of them to have his own proper kingdom. But granting this, then it follows further that in the same manner it will also be impossible for the wicked one to pass without his own proper limits and invade the territories of the good *King*, inasmuch as the wall stands there as an obstacle, unless it should chance first to be cast down, for we have heard that such things have been done by enemies, and indeed with our own eyes we have quite recently seen an achievement of that nature successfully carried out.[2] And when a king attacks a citadel surrounded by a strong wall, he uses first of all the ballista [3] and projectiles; then he endeavours to cut through the gates with axes, and to demolish the walls by the battering-rams; and when he at last obtains an entrance, and gains possession of the place, he does whatever he listeth, whether it be his pleasure to carry off the citizens into captivity, or to make a complete destruction of the fortress and its contents, or whether, on the other hand, it may be his will to grant indulgence to the captured stronghold on the humble suit of the conquered. What, then, does my opponent here say to this analogy? Did no adversary substantially — which is as much as to say, designedly — overthrow the muniment cast up between the two? [4] For in his former statements he has avouched that the darkness passed without its own limits, and supervened upon the kingdom of the good God. Who, then, overthrew that munition before the one could thus have crossed over to the other? For it was impossible for the evil one to find any entrance while the munition stood fast. Why are you silent? Why do you hesitate, Manichæus? Yet, although you may hold back, I shall proceed with the task of my own accord. For if we suppose you to say that God destroyed it, then I have to ask what moved Him in this way to demolish the very thing which He had Himself previously constructed on account of the importunity of the wicked one, and for the purpose of preserving the separation between them? In what fit of passion, or under what sense of injury, did He thus set about contending against Him-

self? Or was it that He lusted after some of the possessions of the wicked one? But if none of these things formed the real cause that led God to destroy those very things which He had constructed a long time before with the view of estranging and separating the wicked one from Him, then it must needs be considered no matter of surprise if God should also have become delighted with his society; [5] for, on your supposition, the munition which had been set up with the purpose of securing God against trouble from him, will appear to have been removed just because now he is to be regarded no more as an enemy, but as a friend. And, on the other hand, if you aver that the wall was destroyed by the wicked one, tell us then how it can be possible for the works of the good God to be mastered by the wicked one. For if that is possible, then the evil nature will be proved to be stronger than God. Furthermore, how can that being, seeing that he is pure and total darkness, surprise the light and apprehend it, while the evangelist gives us the testimony that "the light shineth in darkness, and the darkness comprehended it not?"[6] How is this blind one armed? How does the darkness fight against the kingdom of light? For even as the creatures of God [7] here cannot take in the rays of the sun with uninjured eye,[8] so neither can that being bear the clear vision of the kingdom of light, but he remains for ever a stranger to it, and an alien.

25. *Manes said:* Not all receive the word of God, but only those to whom it is given to know the mysteries of the kingdom of heaven.[9] And even now [10] I know who are ours; for "my sheep," He says, "hear my voice."[11] For the sake of those who belong to us, and to whom is given the understanding of the truth, I shall speak in similitudes. The wicked one is like a lion that sought to steal upon the flock of the good shepherd; and when the shepherd saw this, he dug a huge pit, and took one kid out of the flock and cast it into the pit. Then the lion, hungering to get at it, and bursting with passion to devour it, ran up to the pit and fell in, and discovered no strength sufficient to bring him out again. And thereupon the shepherd seized him and shut him up carefully in a den, and at the same time secured the safety of the kid which had been with him in the pit. And it is in this way that the wicked one has been enfeebled, — the lion, so to speak, possessing no more capacity for doing aught injurious; and so all

---

[1] The text gives *sine hoc uno*. But perhaps Routh is right in suggesting *muro* for *uno* = without this wall.
[2] Some suppose that Archelaus refers here to the taking of Charræ by the Persians in the time of Valerianus Augustus, or to its recapture and restoration to the Roman power by the Eastern king Odenathus during the empire of Gallienus.
[3] The ballista was a large engine fitted with cords somewhat like a bow, by which large masses of stone and other missiles were hurled to a great distance.
[4] The sense is obscure here. The text gives, "non substantia id est proposito adversarius quis dejecit," etc. Migne edits the sentence without an interrogation. We adopt the interrogative form with Routh. The idea perhaps is, Did no adversary with materials such as the kings of earth use, and that is as much as to say also with a determinate plan, overthrow, etc.?

[5] The Codex Casinensis has "nec mirum putandum est consortio," etc. We read with Routh and others, *si ejus consorti*, or *quod ejus consortio*, etc.
[6] John i. 5.
[7] The text gives simply, *sicut enim hæc*. Routh suggests *hæ*.
[8] Reading *illæsis oculis* for the *illius oculis* of Codex Casinensis.
[9] Matt. xix. 11.
[10] The text gives *et jam quidem* for the *etiam quidem* of the Cod. Casin.
[11] John x. 27.

the race of souls will be saved, and what once perished will yet be restored to its proper flock. *Archelaus said:* If you compare the wicked one to the lion, and God to the true shepherd, tell us, whereunto shall we liken the sheep and the kid? *Manes said:* The sheep and the kid seem to me to be of one nature : and they are taken as figures of souls. *Archelaus said:* Well, then, God gave a soul over to perdition when He set it before the lion in the pit. *Manes said:* By no means ; far from it. But He was moved by a particular disposition,[1] and in the future He will save that other, *the soul.* *Archelaus said:* Now, surely it would be an absurd procedure, my hearers, if a shepherd who dreaded the inroad of a lion were to expose to the beast's devouring fury a lamb that he was wont to carry in his bosom, and if it were then to be said that he meant to save the creature hereafter. Is not this something supremely ridiculous? Yea, there is no kind of sense in this. For *on the supposition implied in your similitude* God thus handed over to Satan a soul that he might seize and ruin. But when did the shepherd ever do anything like that?[2] Did not David deliver a sheep out of the mouth of a lion or of a bear? And we mention this on account of the expression, *out of the mouth of the lion;* for, on your theory, this would imply that the shepherd can bring forth out of the mouth of the lion, or out of the belly of the same, the very object which it has devoured.[3] But you will perhaps make this answer, that it is of God we speak, and that He is able to do all things. Hear, however, what I have to say to that : Why then do you not rather assert His real capacity, and affirm simply His ability to overcome the lion in His own might, or with the pure power of God, and without the help of any sort of cunning devices, or by consigning a kid or a lamb to a pit?[4] Tell me this, too, if the lion were to be supposed to come upon the shepherd at a time when he has no sheep, what would the consequence be? For he who is here called the shepherd is supposed to be unbegotten, and he who is here the lion is also unbegotten. Wherefore, when man did not yet exist — in other words, before the shepherd had a flock — if the lion had then come upon the shepherd, what would have followed, seeing that there could have been nothing for the lion to eat before the kid was in existence? *Manes said:* The lion certainly had nothing to devour, but yet he exercised his wickedness on whatever he was able to light upon as he coursed over the peaks of the mountains ; and if at any time food was a matter of necessity with him, he seized some of the beasts which were under his own kingdom. *Archelaus said:* Are these two objects, then, of one substance — the beasts which are under the kingdom of the wicked one, and the kids which are in the kingdom of the good God?[5] *Manes said:* Far from it ; not at all : they have nothing in common either between themselves or between the properties which pertain to them severally. *Archelaus said:* There is but one and the same use made of the food in the lion's eating. And though he sometimes got that food from the beasts belonging to himself, and sometimes from those belonging to the good God, there is still no difference between them as far as regards the meats furnished ; and from this it is apparent that those are of but one substance. On the other hand, if we say that there is a great difference between the two, we do but ascribe ignorance to the shepherd,[6] in so far as he did not present or set before the lion food adapted to his use, but rather alien meats. Or perchance again, in your desire to dissemble your real position, you will say to me that that lion ate nothing. Well, supposing that to be the case, did God then in this way challenge that being to devour a soul while he knew not how to devour aught? and was the pit not the only thing which God sought to employ with the view of cheating him? — if indeed it is at all worthy of God to do that sort of thing, or to contrive deceitful schemes. And that would be to act like a king who, when war is made upon him, puts no kind of confidence in his own strength, but gets paralyzed with the fears of his own feebleness, and shuts himself up within the walls of his city, and erects around him a rampart and other fortifications, and gets them all equipped, and trusts nothing to his own hand and prowess ; whereas, if he is a brave man, the king so placed will march a great distance from his own territories to meet the enemy there, and will put forth every possible exertion until he conquers and brings his adversary into his power.

26. *The judges said:* If you allege that the shepherd exposed the kid or the lamb to the lion, when the said lion was meditating an assault[7] on the unbegotten, the case is closed. For seeing that the shepherd of the kids and lambs is himself proved to be in fault to them, on what creature can he pronounce judgment, if it happens that the lamb which has been given

---

[1] *Apprehensus est hoc ingenio.* For *hoc* here, Routh suggests *hic* in reference to the *leo ;* so that the sense might be = But by this plan the lion was caught, and hereafter He will save the soul.

[2] The text is, "Quando enim pastor, nonne David de ore leonis," etc. We adopt the amended reading, "Quando enim pastor hoc fecit? Nonne David," etc.

[3] Routh would put this interrogatively = Can he bring out of the mouth or the belly of the lion what it has once devoured?

[4] This seems to be the sense intended. The text in the Codex Casinensis runs thus: "Cur igitur quod possit non illud potius asseris quod poterit propria virtute vincere leonem, si et pura Dei potentia," etc. For *si et pura* we may read *sive pura,* or *si est pura,* etc.

[5] Routh takes it as a direct assertion = It follows, then, that these two objects are of one substance, etc.

[6] The text runs, " sed aliud alio longe differre ignorantiam pastori ascribimus: " for which we adopt the emendation, " sed alium ab alio longe differre si dicamus, ignorantiam pastori ascribimus."

[7] Migne reads *irrueret.* Routh gives *irruerat,* had made an assault.

up [1] through the shepherd's weakness has proved unable to withstand the lion, and if the consequence is that the lamb has had to do whatever has been the lion's pleasure? Or, to take another instance, that would be just as if a master were to drive out of his house, or deliver over in terror to his adversary, one of his slaves, whom he is unable afterwards to recover by his own strength. Or supposing that by any chance it were to come about that the slave was recovered, on what reasonable ground could the master inflict the torture on him, if it should turn out that the man yielded obedience to all that the enemy laid upon him, seeing that it was the master himself [2] who gave him up to the enemy, just as the kid was given up to the lion? You affirm, too, that the shepherd understood the whole case beforehand. Surely, then, the lamb, when under the lash, and interrogated by the shepherd as to the reason why it had submitted to the lion in these matters, would make some such answer as this: "Thou didst thyself deliver me over to the lion, and thou didst offer no resistance to him, although thou didst know and foresee what would be my lot, when it was necessary for me to yield myself to his commandments." And, not to dilate on this at greater length, we may say that *by such an illustration* neither is God exhibited as a perfect shepherd, nor is the lion shown to have tasted alien meats; and consequently, under the instruction of the truth itself, it has been made clear that we ought to give the palm to the reasonings adduced by Archelaus. *Archelaus said:* Considering that, on all the points which we have hitherto discussed, the thoughtfulness of the judges has assigned us the amplest scope, it will be well for us to pass over other subjects in silence, and reserve them for another period. For just as, if [3] a person once crushes the head of a serpent, he will not need to lop off any of the other members of its body; so, if we once dispose [4] of this question of the duality, as we have endeavoured to do to the best of our ability, other matters which have been maintained in connection with it may be held to be exploded along with it. Nevertheless I shall yet address myself, at least in a few sentences, to the assertor of these opinions himself, who is now in our presence; so that it may be thoroughly understood by all who he is, and whence he comes, and what manner of person he proves himself to be. For he has given out that he is that Paraclete whom Jesus on His departure promised to send to the race of man for the salvation of the souls of the faithful; and this profession he makes as if he were somewhat superior even to Paul,[5] who was an elect vessel and a called apostle, and who on that ground, while preaching the true doctrine, said: [6] "Or seek ye a proof of that Christ who speaks in me?" [7] What I have to say, however, may become clearer by such an illustration as the following: [8] — A certain man gathered into his store a very large quantity of corn, so that the place was perfectly full. This place he shut and sealed in a thoroughly satisfactory fashion, and gave directions to keep careful watch over it. And the master himself then departed. However, after a lengthened lapse of time another person came to the store, and affirmed that he had been despatched by the individual who had locked up and sealed the place with a commission also to collect and lay up a quantity of wheat in the same. And when the keepers of the store saw him, they demanded of him his credentials, in the production of the signet, in order that they might assure themselves of their liberty to open the store to him, and to render their obedience to him as to one sent by the person who had sealed the place. And when he could [9] neither exhibit the keys nor produce the credentials of the signet, *for indeed he had no right*, he was thrust out by the keepers, and compelled to flee. For, instead of being what he professed to be, he was detected to be a thief and a robber by them, and was convicted and found out [10] through the circumstance that, although, as it seemed, he had taken it into his head to make his appearance a long time after the period that had been determined on beforehand, he yet could neither produce keys, or signet, or any token whatsoever to the keepers, nor display any knowledge of the quantity of corn that was in store: all which things were so many unmistakeable proofs that he had not been sent across by the proper owner; and accordingly, as was matter of course,[11] he was forbidden admittance by the keepers.

---

[5] This seems to be the general sense of the corrupt text here, *et non longe possit ei Paulus*, etc., in which we must either suppose something to have been lost, or correct it in some such way as this: "ut non longe post sit ei Paulus." Compare what Manes says also of Paul and himself in ch. xiii. above. It should be added, however, that another idea of the passage is thrown out in Routh. According to this, the *ei* refers to *Jesus*, and the text being emended thus, *etsi non longe post sit ei*, the sense would be: although not long after His departure He had Paul as an elect vessel, etc. The allusion thus would be to the circumstance that Manes made such a claim as he did, in spite of the fact that after Christ's departure Paul was gifted with the Spirit in so eminent a measure for the building up of the faithful.

[6] Reading *aiebat* for the *agebat* of Codex Casinensis.

[7] 2 Cor. xiii. 3. The reading here is, "Aut documentum quæritis," etc. The Vulgate also gives *An experimentum*, for the Greek ἔπει, etc.

[8] The text is, "et quidem quod dico tali exemplo sed clarius." For *sed* it is proposed to read *fit*, or *sit*, or *est*.

[9] Codex Casinensis has *quicunque*. We adopt the correction, *qui cum nec.*

[10] Reading *confutatus* for *confugatus.*

[11] The text gives " et ideo ut consequenter erat," etc. Codex Casinensis omits the. *ut.* Routh proposes, " et ideo consequenter thesaurus," etc. = and thus, of course, the treasure was preserved, etc. Comp. ch. xxvii. and xxxiv.

---

[1] The text gives *si causa traditus*, etc. Routh suggests *sive causa. Traditus*, etc.: so that the sense would be, For on what creature can the shepherd of the kids and lambs pronounce judgment, seeing that he is himself proved to be in fault to them, or to be the cause of their position? For the lamb, having been given up, etc.

[2] Reading *eum ipse* for *eum ipsum.*

[3] Reading *si quis* for the simple *quis* of Codex Casinensis.

[4] Reading "quæstione *rejecta*" for the *relecta* of Codex Casinensis.

27. We may give yet another illustration, if it seems good to you. A certain man, the head of a household, and possessed of great riches, was minded to journey abroad for a time, and promised to his sons that he would send them some one who would take his place, and divide among them equally the substance falling to them. And, in truth, not long after that, he did despatch to them a certain trustworthy and right-eous and true man. And on his arrival, this man took charge of the whole substance, and first of all exerted himself to arrange it and ad-minister it, giving himself great labour in journey-ing, and even [1] working diligently with his own hands, and toiling like a servant for the good of the estate. Afterwards feeling that his end was at hand,[2] the man wrote out a will, demitting the inheritance to the relations and all the next of kin ; and he gave them his seals, and called them together one by one by name, and charged them to preserve the inheritance, and to take care of the substance, and to administer it rightly, even as they had received it, and to take their use of its goods and fruits, as they were them-selves left its owners and heirs. If, moreover, any person were to ask to be allowed to benefit by the fruits of this field, they were to show themselves indulgent to such. But if, on the other hand, any one were to declare himself partner in the heirship with them, and were to make his demands on that ground,[3] they were to keep aloof from him, and pronounce him an alien ; and further, *they were to hold* that the in-dividual who desired to be received among them ought all the more on that account to do work.[4] Well, then, granting that all these things have been well and rightly disposed of and settled, and that they have continued in that condition for a very long time, how shall we deal with one who presents himself well-nigh three hundred years after, and sets up his claim to the heirship? Shall we not cast him off from us? Shall we not justly pronounce such a one an alien — one who cannot prove himself to have belonged to those related *to our Master*, who never was with our departed Lord in the hour of His sickness, who never walked in the funeral procession of the Crucified, who never stood by the sepulchre, who has no knowledge whatsoever of the manner or the character of His departure, and who, in fine, is now desirous of getting access to the storehouse of corn without presenting any token

from him who placed it under lock and seal? Shall we not cast him off from us like a robber and a thief, and thrust him out of our number by all possible means? Yet this man is now in our presence, and fails to produce any of the credentials which we have summarized in what we have already said, and declares that he is the Paraclete whose mission was presignified by Jesus. And by this assertion, in his ignorance perchance, he will make out Jesus Himself to be a liar ;[5] for thus He who once said that He would send the Paraclete no long time after, will be proved only to have sent this person, if we accept the testimony which he bears to himself, after an interval of three hundred years and more.[6] In the day of judgment, then, what will those say to Jesus who have departed this life from that time on to the present period? Will they not meet Him with words like these : " Do not punish us rigorously if we have failed to do Thy works. For why, when Thou didst promise to send the Paraclete under Tiberius Cæsar, to convince us of sin and of righteousness,[7] didst Thou send Him only under Probus the Roman emperor, and didst leave us orphaned, notwith-standing that Thou didst say, ' I will not leave you comfortless (orphaned),'[8] and after Thou hadst also assured us that Thou wouldest send the Paraclete presently after Thy departure? What could we orphans do, having no guardian? We have committed no fault ; it is Thou that hast deceived us." But away with such a sup-position in the case of our Lord Jesus Christ, the Saviour of every soul.[9] For He did not con-fine Himself to mere promises ;[10] but when He had once said, " I go to my Father, and I send the Paraclete to you,"[11] straightway He sent (that gift of the Paraclete), dividing and impart-ing the same to His disciples, — bestowing it, however, in greater fulness upon Paul.[12]

28. *Manes said:*[13] You are caught in the

---

[1] The text has, " sedens ipse per se," etc.: for which we adopt, " sed et ipse," etc.

[2] The Codex Casinensis gives, " deinde die moriturus," which may be either a mistake for " deinde moriturus," or a contraction for " deinde die qua moriturus " — then on the day that he was about to die, etc.

[3] The codex has, " Sin autem conderem se dicens, exposceret, devitarent persequi," etc. ; which is corrected to, " Sin autem cohære-dem se dicens exposceret, devitarent atque," etc., which emendation is followed in the translation.

[4] *Opus autem magis facere debere.*

[5] The same sort of argument is employed against the Montanists by Theodorus of Heracleia on John's Gospel, ch. xiv. 17.

[6] It is remarked in Migne, that it is only in the heat of his con-tention that this statement is made by Archelaus as to the date of the appearance of Manes: for from the death of Christ on to the time of this discussion there are only some 249 years. [Is it not probable that here is a token of the spurious character of not a little of this work?]

[7] John xvi. 8.

[8] John xiv. 18.

[9] Reading " sed absit hoc a Domino nostro Jesu Christo Salvatore omnis animæ," instead of the codex's " sed absit hanc a Domino Jesu Christo Salvatore omne animæ."

[10] If the reference, however, is to 2 Pet. iii. 9, as Routh suggests, it may rather be = He was not slack concerning His promises. The text is, " non enim moratus est in promissionibus suis." [A note-worthy reference to the second Epistle of St. Peter. For, if this work be a mere romance, yet its undoubted antiquity makes it useful, not only in this, but in many other critical matters.]

[11] John xiv. 12, xvi. 28.

[12] Reading " abundantius vero conferens Paulo," instead of the corrupt text in the Codex Casinensis, " abundantibus vero confitens Paulo."

[13] The opening sentences of this chapter are given in a very cor-rupt form in our Codex Casinensis. Its text stands thus: " Tuum et ipsius indicio comprehensus es; hæc enim versum te locutus, ignorans, qui dum, me vis probra conjicere majori culpæ se succumbit. Dic age mihi studias qua Tiberio usque ad Probum defuncti sunt, dicent

charge you yourself bring forward. For you have been speaking now against yourself, and have not perceived that, in trying to cast reproaches in my teeth, you lay yourself under the greater fault. Tell me this now, I pray you: if, as you allege, those who have died from the time of Tiberius on to the days of Probus are to say to Jesus, "Do not judge us if we have failed to do Thy works, for Thou didst not send the Paraclete to us, although Thou didst promise to send Him; "[1] will not those much more use such an address who have departed this life from the time of Moses on to the advent of Christ Himself? And will not those with still greater right express themselves in terms like these: "Do not deliver us over to torments,[2] seeing that we had no knowledge of Thee imparted to us?" And will it only be those that have died thus far previously to His advent who may be seen making such a charge with right? Will not those also do the same who have passed away from Adam's time on to Christ's advent? For none of these either obtained any knowledge of the Paraclete, or received instruction in the doctrine of Jesus. But only this latest generation of men, which has run its course from Tiberius onward, as you make it out,[3] is to be saved: for it is Christ Himself that "has redeemed them from the curse of the law; "[4] as Paul, too, has given these further testimonies, that "the letter killeth, and quickeneth no man," [5] and that "the law is the ministration of death," [6] and "the strength of sin." [7] *Archelaus said:* You err, not knowing the Scriptures, neither the power of God.[8] For many have also perished after the period of Christ's advent on to this present period, and many are still perishing,—those, to wit, who have not chosen to devote themselves to works of righteousness; whereas only those who have received Him, and yet receive Him, "have obtained power to become the sons of God." [9] For the evangelist has not said all *have obtained that power;* neither, on the other hand, however, has he put any limit on the time. But this is his expression: "As many as received Him." Moreover, from the creation of the world He has ever been with righteous men, and has never ceased to require their blood *at the hands of the wicked,* from the blood of righteous Abel to the blood

of Zacharias.[10] And whence, then, did righteous Abel and all those succeeding worthies,[11] who are enrolled among the righteous, derive their righteousness, when as yet there was no law of Moses, and when as yet the prophets had not arisen and discharged the functions of prophecy? Were they not constituted righteous in virtue of their fulfilling the law, "every one of them showing the work of the law written in their hearts, their conscience also bearing them witness?" [12] For when a man "who has not the law does naturally the things contained in the law, he, not having the law, is a law unto himself." [13] And consider now the multitude of laws thus existing among the several righteous men who lived a life of uprightness, at one time discovering for themselves the law of God implanted in their hearts, at another learning of it from their parents, and yet again being instructed in it further by the ancients and the elders. But inasmuch as only few were able to rise by this medium [14] to the height of righteousness, that is to say, by means of the traditions of parents, when as yet there was no law embodied in writing, God had compassion on the race of man, and was pleased to give through Moses a written law to men, since verily the equity of the natural law failed to be retained in all its perfection in their hearts. In consonance, therefore, with man's first creation, a written legislation was prepared, which was given through Moses in behoof of the salvation of very many. For if we reckon that man is justified without the works of the law, and if Abraham was counted righteous, how much more shall those obtain righteousness who have fulfilled the law which contains the things that are expedient for men? And seeing that you have made mention only of three several scriptures, in terms of which the apostle has declared that "the law is a ministration of death," [15] and that "Christ has redeemed us from the curse of the law," [16] and that "the law is the strength of sin," [17] you may now advance others of like tenor, and bring forward any passages which may seem to you to be written against the law, to any extent you please.

29. *Manes said:* Is not that word also to the same effect which Jesus spake to the disciples, when He was demonstrating those men to be unbelieving: "Ye are of your father the devil, and the lusts of your father ye will do?" [18] By this He means, in sooth, that whatever the

---

ad Jesum nolite nos judicare," etc. We have adopted these emendations: *tuimet* for *tuum et; adversum* for *versum; ignoras* for *ignorans; in me* for *me; succumbis* for *se succumbit; si, ut ais, qui a,* for *studias qua;* and *noli* for *nolite.*

[1] Supplying *missurum,* which is not in the codex.

[2] Reading "noli nos tradere tormentis," instead of the meaningless "noli nostra de tormentis" of the codex.

[3] Reading *ut ais* instead of *ut eas.*

[4] Gal. iii. 13.

[5] *Nec quemquam vivificat.* 2 Cor. iii. 6.

[6] 2 Cor. iii. 7.

[7] 1 Cor. xv. 56.

[8] Matt. xxii. 29.

[9] John i. 12.

[10] Matt. xiii. 35.

[11] Reading *reliqui per ordinem* for the *qui per ordinem* of the codex.

[12] Rom. ii. 15.

[13] Rom. ii. 14.

[14] Reading "per hunc modum." But the Codex Casinensis gives "per hunc mundum"—through this world.

[15] 2 Cor. iii. 7.

[16] Gal. iii. 13.

[17] 1 Cor. xv. 56.

[18] John viii. 44.

wicked prince of this world desired, and whatever he lusted after, he committed to writing through Moses, and by that medium gave it to men for their doing. For " he was a murderer from the beginning, and abode not in the truth, because there is no truth in him. When he speaketh a lie, he speaketh of his own : for he is a liar, and the father of it." [1] *Archelaus said:* Are you satisfied [2] with what you have already adduced, or have you other statements still to make? *Manes said:* I have, indeed, many things to say, and things of greater weight even than these. But with these I shall content myself. *Archelaus said:* By all means. Now let us select some instance from among those statements which you allege to be on your side ; so that if these be once found to have been properly dealt with, other questions may also be held to rank with them ; and if the case goes otherwise, I shall come under the condemnation of the judges, that is to say, I shall have to bear the shame of defeat.[3] You say, then, that the law is a ministration of death, and you admit that " death, the prince of this world, reigned from Adam even to Moses ; " [4] for the word of Scripture is this : " even over them that did not sin." [4] *Manes said:* Without doubt death did reign thus, for there is a duality, and these two antagonistic powers were nothing else than both unbegotten.[5] *Archelaus said:* Tell me this then, — how can an unbegotten death take a beginning at a certain time? For " from Adam " is the word of Scripture, and not " before Adam." *Manes said:* But tell me, I ask you in turn, how it obtained its kingdom over both the righteous and the sinful. *Archelaus said:* When you have first admitted that it has had that kingdom from a determinate time and not from eternity, I shall tell you that. *Manes said:* It is written, that " death reigned from Adam to Moses." *Archelaus said:* And consequently it has an end, because it has had a beginning in time.[6] And this saying is also true, that " death is swallowed up in victory." [7] It is apparent, then, that death cannot be unbegotten, seeing that it is shown to have both a beginning and an end. *Manes said:* But in that way it would also follow that God was its maker. *Archelaus said:* By no means ; away with such a supposition ! " For God made not death ; neither hath He pleasure in the destruc-

tion of the living." [8] *Manes said:* God made it not ; nevertheless it was made, as you admit. Tell us, therefore, from whom it received its empire, or by whom it was created. *Archelaus said:* If I give the most ample proof of the fact that death cannot have the substance of an unbegotten nature, will you not confess that there is but one God, and that an unbegotten God? *Manes said:* Continue your discourse, for your aim is to speak [9] with subtlety. *Archelaus said:* Nay, but you have put forward those allegations in such a manner, as if they were to serve you for a demonstration of an unbegotten root. Nevertheless the positions which we have discussed above may suffice us, for by these we have shown most fully that it is impossible for the substances of two unbegotten natures to exist together.

30. *The judges said:* Speak to those points, Archelaus, which he has just now propounded. *Archelaus said:* By the prince of the world, and the wicked one, and darkness, and death, he means one and the same thing, and alleges that the law has been given by that being, on the ground of the scriptural statement that it is " the ministration of death," as well as on the ground of other things which he has urged against it. Well, then, I say [10] that since, as we have explained above, the law which was written naturally on men's hearts did not keep carefully by the memory of evil things, and since there was not a sufficiently established tradition among the elders, inasmuch as hostile oblivion always attached itself to the memory,[11] and one man was instructed *in the knowledge of that law* by a master, and another by himself, it easily came about that transgressions of the law engraved by nature did take place, and that through the violation of the commandments death obtained its kingship among men. For the race of men is of such a nature, that it needs to be ruled by God with a rod of iron. And so death triumphed and reigned with all its power on to Moses, even over those who had not sinned, in the way which we have explained : over sinners indeed, as these were its proper objects, and under subjection to it, — men after the type of Cain and Judas ; [12] but also over the righteous, because they refused to consent to it, and rather withstood it, by putting away from themselves the vices and concupiscence of lusts, — men like those who have arisen at times from Abel

---

[1] John viii. 44.
[2] The text is " sufficit tibi hæc sunt an habes et alia." Routh proposes " sufficientia tibi hæc sunt," etc.
[3] Routh would make it = *You* will come under the condemnation . . . *you* will have to bear: he suggests *eris ergo* for *ero ego*, and *feras* for *feram*.
[4] Rom. v. 14.
[5] *Nec aliter nisi essent ingenita.* Routh, however, would read *esset* for *essent*, making it = and that death could be nothing else than unbegotten.
[6] Reading *ex tempore* for the corrupt *exemplo re* of the codex.
[7] 1 Cor. xv. 54.

[8] Wisd. i. 13.
[9] The text gives *discere*, to learn; but *dicere* seems the probable reading.
[10] Reading *inquam* for the *iniquam* of the Codex Casinensis. But Routh suggests *iniquæ*, in reference to what has been said towards the close of ch. xxviii.
[11] The codex gives, " cum eas inimica semper memoriæ ineresis sed oblivio; " which is corrected thus, " cum eis inimica semper memoriæ inhæsisset oblivio."
[12] The text writes it *Juda.*

on to Zacharias;[1] — death thus always passing, up to the time *of Moses*, upon those after that similitude.[2]

But after Moses had made his appearance, and had given the law to the children of Israel, and had brought into their memory all the requirements of the law, and all that it behoved men to observe and do under it, and when he delivered over to death only those who should transgress the law, then death was cut off from reigning over all men; for it reigned then over sinners alone, as the law said to it, "Touch not those that keep my precepts."[3] Moses therefore served the ministration of this word upon death, while he delivered up to destruction[4] all others who were transgressors of the law; for it was not with the intent that death might not reign in any territory at all that Moses came, inasmuch as multitudes were assuredly held under the power of death even after Moses. And the law was called a "ministration of death" from the fact that then only transgressors of the law were punished, and not those who kept it, and who obeyed and observed the things which are in the law, as Abel did, whom Cain, who was made a vessel of the wicked one, slew. However, even after these things death wished to break the covenant which had been made by the instrumentality of Moses, and to reign again over the righteous; and with this object it did indeed assail the prophets, killing and stoning those who had been sent by God, on to Zacharias. But my Lord Jesus, as maintaining the righteousness of the law of Moses, was wroth with death for its transgression of the covenant[5] and of that whole ministration, and condescended to appear in the body of man, with the view ot avenging not Himself, but Moses, and those who in a continuous succession after him had been oppressed by the violence of death. That wicked one, however, in ignorance *of the meaning* of a dispensation of this kind, entered into Judas, thinking to slay Him by that man's means, as before he had put righteous Abel to death. But when he had entered into Judas, he was overcome with penitence, and hanged himself; for which reason also the divine word says: "O death, where is thy victory? O death,[6] where is thy sting?" And again: "Death is swallowed up of victory."[7] It is for this reason, therefore, that the law is called a "ministration of death," because it delivered sinners and transgressors

over to death; but those who observed it, it defended from death; and these it also established in glory, by the help and aid of our Lord Jesus Christ.

31. Listen also to what I have to say on this other expression which has been adduced, viz., "Christ, who redeemed us from the curse of the law."[8] My view of this passage is that Moses, that illustrious servant of God, committed to those who wished to have the right vision,[9] an emblematic[10] law, and also a real law. Thus, to take an example, after God had made the world, and all things that are in it, in the space of six days, He rested on the seventh day from all His works; by which statement I do not mean to affirm that He rested because He was fatigued, but that He did so as having brought to its perfection every creature which He had resolved to introduce. And yet in the sequel it, *the new law*, says: "My Father worketh hitherto, and I work."[11] Does that mean, then, that He is still making heaven, or sun, or man, or animals, or trees, or any such thing? Nay; but the meaning is, that when these visible objects were perfectly finished, He rested from that kind of work; while, however, He still continues to work at objects invisible with an inward mode of action,[12] and saves men. In like manner, then, the legislator desires also that every individual amongst us should be devoted unceasingly to this kind of work, even as God Himself is; and he enjoins us consequently to rest continuously from secular things, and to engage in no worldly sort of work whatsoever; and this is called our Sabbath. This also he added in the law, that nothing senseless[13] should be done, but that we should be careful and direct our life in accordance with what is just and righteous. Now this law was suspended over men, discharging most sharply its curse against those who might transgress it. But because its subjects, too, were but men, and because, as happens also frequently with us, controversies arose and injuries were inflicted, the law likewise at once, and with the severest equity, made any wrong that was done

---

[1] Matt. xxiii. 35.
[2] This would appear to be the meaning of these words, "transfere ns semper usque ad tempus in similes illius," if we suppose the speaker still to be keeping Rom. v. 12-14 in view. Routh suggests *transcins.*
[3] Referring perhaps to Ps. cv. 15.
[4] Reading *interitui tradens* for the *interit ut tradens* of the codex.
[5] Reading *pacti* for the *acti* of the codex.
[6] *Mors.*
[7] 1 Cor. xv. 54, 55.

[8] Gal. iii. 13.
[9] Recte videre. But perhaps we should read "recte *vivere*," to lead a righteous life.
[10] The phrase is *imaginariam legem.* On this expression there is a note in Migne, which is worth quoting, to this effect: Archelaus calls the Old Testament an *emblematic* or *imaginary law*, because it was the type or image of a future new law. So, too, Petrus de Vineis, more than once in his Epistles, calls a messenger or legate a *homo imaginarius*, as Du Cange observes in his *Glossary*, because he represents the person by whom he is sent, and, as it were, reflects his image. This word is also used in a similar manner by the old interpreter of Evagrius the monk, in the *Disputation between Theophilus, bishop of Alexandria, and Simon the Jew*, ch. 13, where the Sabbath is called the *requies imaginaria* of that seventh day on which God rested. Hence Archelaus, in his answer to the presbyter Diodorus, ch. xli. beneath, devotes himself to proving that the Old Testament is not to be rejected, because, like a mirror, it gives us a true image of the new law.
[11] John v. 17.
[12] Reading "invisibilia autem et intrinsecus." The Codex Casinensis has "invisibili autem et trinsecus."
[13] *Absurdum*, standing probably for ἄτοπον, which may also be = flagitious.

return upon the head of the wrong-doer;[1] so that, for instance, if a poor man was minded to gather a bundle of wood upon the Sabbath, he was placed under the curse of the law, and exposed to the penalty of instant death.[2] The men, therefore, who had been brought up with the Egyptians were thus severely pressed by the restrictive power of the law, and they were unable to bear the penalties and the curses of the law. But, again, He who is ever the Saviour, our Lord Jesus Christ, came and delivered those men from these pains and curses of the law, forgiving them their offences. And He indeed did not deal with them as Moses did, putting the severities of the law in force, and granting indulgence to no man for any offence; but He declared that if any man suffered an injury at the hands of his neighbour, he was to forgive him not once only, nor even twice or thrice, nor only seven times, but even unto seventy times seven;[3] but that, on the other hand, if after all this the offender still continued to do such wrong, he ought then, as the last resource, to be brought under the law of Moses, and that no further pardon should be granted to the man who would thus persist in wrong-doing, even after having been forgiven unto seventy times seven. And He bestowed His forgiveness not only on a transgressor of such a character as that, but even on one who did offence to the Son of man. But if a man dealt thus with the Holy Spirit, He made him subject to two curses,—namely, to that of the law of Moses, and to that of His own law; to the law of Moses in truth in this present life, but to His own law at the time of the judgment: for His word is this: "It shall not be forgiven him, neither in this world, neither in the world to come."[4] There is the law of Moses, thus, that in this world gives pardon to no *such* person; and there is the law of Christ that punishes in the future world. From this, therefore, mark how He confirms the law, not only not destroying it, but fulfilling it. Thus, then, He redeemed them from that curse of the law which belongs to the present life; and from this fact has come the appellation "the curse of the law." This is the whole account *which needs be given* of that mode of speech. But, again, why the law is called the "strength of sin," we shall at once explain in brief to the best of our ability. Now it is written that "the law is not made for a righteous man, but for the lawless and disobedient, for the ungodly and for sinners."[5] In these times, then, before Moses, there was no written law for transgressors; whence also

Pharaoh, not knowing the strength of sin, transgressed in the way of afflicting the children of Israel with unrighteous burdens, and despised the Godhead, not only himself, but also all who were with him. But, not to make any roundabout statement, I shall explain the matter briefly as follows. There were certain persons of the Egyptian race mingling with the people of Moses, when that people was under his rule in the desert; and when Moses had taken his position on the mount, with the purpose of receiving the law, the impatient people, I do not mean those who were the true Israel, but those who had been intermixed with the Egyptians,[6] set up a calf as their god, in accordance with their ancient custom of worshipping idols, with the notion that by such means they might secure themselves against ever having to pay the proper penalties for their iniquities.[7] Thus were they altogether ignorant of the strength of their sin. But when Moses returned (from the mount) and found that out, he issued orders that those men should be put to death with the sword. From that occasion a beginning was made in the correct perception of the strength of sin on the part of these persons through the instrumentality of the law of Moses, and for that reason the law has been called the "strength of sin."

32. Moreover, as to this word which is written in the Gospel, "Ye are of your father the devil,"[8] and so forth, we say in brief that there is a devil working in us, whose aim it has been, in the strength of his own will, to make us like himself. For all the creatures that God made, He made very good; and He gave to every individual the sense of free-will, in accordance with which standard He also instituted the law of judgment. To sin is ours, and that we sin not is God's gift, as our will is constituted to choose either to sin or not to sin. And this you doubtless understand well enough yourself, Manes; for you know that, although you were to bring together all your disciples and admonish[9] them not to commit any transgression or do any unrighteousness, every one of them might still pass by the law of judgment. And certainly whosoever will, may keep the commandments; and whosoever shall despise them, and turn aside to what is contrary to them, shall yet without doubt have to face this law of judgment. Hence also certain of the angels, refusing to submit

---

[1] The codex reads, "ultionem fecerat retorquebat." We adopt either "ultionem quam fecerat retorquebat," or "ultionem fecit retorqueri."

[2] Num. xv. 32.

[3] Matt. xviii. 21.

[4] Matt. xii. 32.

[5] 1 Tim. i. 9.

[6] This is one of those passages in which we detect the tendency of many of the early fathers to adopt the peculiar opinions of the Jewish rabbis on difficult points of Scripture. See also the *Disputation between Theophilus of Alexandria and the Jew Simon*, ch. 13. In accordance with the opinion propounded here by Archelaus, we find, for instance, in the *Scemoth Rabba*, p. 157, col. 1, that the making of the golden calf is ascribed to the Egyptian proselytes. See the note in Migne. [The passage is a note of antiquity and in so far of authenticity.]

[7] The text is *in quo nec scelerum pœnas aliquando rependeret.*

[8] John viii. 44.

[9] Reading *commonens* for *communis ne. Communiens* is also suggested.

themselves to the commandment of God, resisted His will; and one of them indeed fell like a flash of lightning [1] upon the earth, while others,[2] harassed by the dragon, sought their felicity in intercourse with the daughters of men,[3] and thus brought on themselves the merited award of the punishment of eternal fire. And that angel who was cast down to earth, finding no further admittance into any of the regions of heaven, now flaunts about among men, deceiving them, and luring them to become transgressors like himself, and even to this day he is an adversary to the commandments of God. The example of his fall and ruin, however, will not be followed by all, inasmuch as to each is given liberty of will. For this reason also has he obtained the name of *devil*, because he has passed over from the heavenly places, and appeared on earth as the disparager of God's commandment.[4] But because it was God who first gave the commandment, the Lord Jesus Himself said to the devil, "Get thee behind me, Satan;"[5] and, without doubt, to go behind God is the sign of being His servant. And again He says, "Thou shalt worship the Lord thy God, and Him only shalt thou serve."[5] Wherefore, as certain men were inclined to yield obedience to his wishes, they were addressed in these terms by the Saviour: "Ye are of your father the devil, and the lusts of your father ye will do."[6] And, in fine, when they are found to be actually doing his will, they are thus addressed: "O generation of vipers, who hath warned you to flee from the wrath to come? Bring forth therefore fruits meet for repentance."[7] From all this, then, you ought to see how weighty a matter it is for man to have freedom of will. However, let my antagonist here say whether there is a judgment for the godly and the ungodly, or not. *Manes said:* There is a judgment. *Archelaus said:* I think that what we [8] have said concerning the devil contains no small measure of reason as well as of piety. For every creature, moreover, has its own order; and there is one order for the human race, and another for animals, and another for angels. Furthermore, there is but one only inconvertible substance, the divine substance, eternal and invisible, as is known to all, and as is also borne out by this scripture: "No man hath seen God at any time, save the only begotten Son, which is in the bosom of the Father."[9] All the other creatures, consequently, are of necessity visible, — such as heaven, earth, sea, men, angels, archangels. But if God has not been seen by any man at any time, what consubstantiality can there be between Him and those creatures? Hence we hold that all things whatsoever have, in their several positions, their own proper substances, according to their proper order. You, on the other hand, allege that every living thing which moves is made of one,[10] and you say that every object has received like substance from God, and that this substance is capable of sinning and of being brought under the judgment; and you are unwilling to accept the word which declares that the devil was an angel, and that he fell in transgression, and that he is not of the same substance with God. Logically, you ought to do away with any allowance of the doctrine of a judgment, and that would make it clear which of us is in error.[11] If, indeed, the angel that has been created by God is incapable of falling in transgression, how can the soul, as a part of God, be capable of sinning? But, again, if you say that there is a judgment for sinning souls, and if you hold also that these are of one substance with God; and if still, even although you maintain that they are of the divine nature, you affirm that, notwithstanding that fact, they do not keep [12] the commandments of God, then, even on such grounds, my argument will pass very well,[13] which avers that the devil fell first, on account of his failure to keep the commandments of God. He was not indeed of the substance of God. And he fell, not so much to do hurt to the race of man, as rather to be set at nought [14] by the same. For He "gave unto us power to tread on serpents and scorpions, and over all the strength of the enemy."[15]

---

[1] Luke x. 18.

[2] We have another instance here of a characteristic opinion of the Jewish rabbis adopted by a Christian father. This notion as to the intercourse of the angels with the daughters of men was a current interpretation among the Jews from the times of Philo and Josephus, and was followed in whole or in part by Tertullian, Justin, Irenæus, Clemens Alexandrinus, Athenagoras, Methodius, Cyprian, Lactantius, etc. Consult the note in Migne; [also p. 131, note 2, *supra*].

[3] We give the above as a *possible* rendering. Routh, however, understands the matter otherwise. The text is, " alii vero in felicitate hominum filiabus admisti a dracone afflicti," etc. Routh takes the phrase *in felicitate* as = " adhuc in statu felici existentes:" so that the sense would be, "others, while they still abide in the blessed estate, had intercourse," etc. [Routh, *R. S.*, vol. v. pp. 118-122.]

[4] Archelaus seems here to assign a twofold etymology for the name *devil*, deriving the Greek διάβολος, accuser, from διαβάλλω, in its two senses of *trajicere* and *traducere*, to cross over and to slander.

[5] Matt. iv. 10.

[6] John viii. 44.

[7] Matt. iii. 7, 8.

[8] Reading *a nobis* for the *a vobis* of the codex.

[9] John i. 18.

[10] *Ex uno.*

[11] The sense is obscure here. The text runs, "Interimere debes judicii ratione ut quis nostrum fallat appareat." Migne proposes to read *rationem*, as if the idea intended was this: That, consistently with his reasonings, Manes ought not to admit the fact of a judgment, because the notions he has propounded on the subject of men and angels are not reconcilable with such a belief. — If this can be accepted as the probable meaning, then it would seem that the use of the verb *interimere* may be due to the fact that the Greek text gave ἀναιρεῖν, between the two senses of which — viz. to kill and to remove — the translator did not correctly distinguish. Routh, however, proposes to read *interimi*, taking it as equivalent to *condemnari*, so that the idea might be = on all principles of sound judgment you ought to be condemned, etc.

[12] The codex reads simply, *Dei servare mandata*. We may adopt either *Dei non servare mandata*, as above, or, *Dei servare vel non servare mandata*, in reference to the freedom of will, and so = they may or may not keep the commandments.

[13] The codex has *præcedit*, for which *procedit* is proposed.

[14] Reading " læderet — illuderetur." But might it not rather be " læderet — *illideretur*," not to bruise, but rather to be bruised, etc.?

[15] Luke x. 19.

33. *The judges said:* He has given demonstration enough of the origin of the devil. And as both sides admit that there will be a judgment, it is necessarily involved in that admission that every individual is shown to have free-will; and since this is brought clearly out, there can be no doubt that every individual, in the exercise of his own proper power of will, may shape his course in whatever direction he pleases.[1] *Manes said:* If (only) the good is from (your) God, as you allege, then you make Jesus Himself a liar.[2] *Archelaus said:* In the first place, admit that the account of what we have adduced is true, and then I will give you proof about the "father of him."[3] *Manes said:* If you prove to me that his father is a liar, and yet show me that for all that you ascribe no such (evil) notion to God, then credit will be given you on all points. *Archelaus said:* Surely when a full account of the devil has once been presented, and the dispensation set forth, any one now, with an ordinarily vigorous understanding, might simply, by turning the matter carefully over in his own mind, get an idea of who this is that is here called the father of the devil. But though you give yourself out to be the Paraclete, you come very far short of the ordinary sagacity of men. Wherefore, as you have betrayed your ignorance, I shall tell you what is meant by this expression, the "father of the devil." *Manes said:* I say so[4] . . . ; *and he added:* Every one who is the founder or maker of anything may be called the father, *parent*, of that which he has made. *Archelaus said:* Well, I am verily astonished that you have made so correct an admission in reply to what I have said, and have not concealed either your intelligent apprehension of the affirmation, or the real nature of the same. Now, from this learn who is this father of the devil. When he fell from the kingdom of heaven, he came to dwell upon earth, and there he remained, ever watching and seeking out some one to whom he might attach himself, and whom, through an alliance with himself, he might also make a partner in his own wickedness. Now as long, indeed, as man was not yet existent, the devil was never called either a murderer or a liar together with his father. But subsequently, when man had once been made, and when further he had been deceived by the devil's lies and craftiness, and when the devil had also introduced himself into the body of the serpent, which was the most sagacious of all the beasts, then from that time the devil was called a liar together with his father, and then[5] also the curse was made to rest not only on himself, but also on his father. Accordingly, when the serpent had received him, and had indeed admitted him wholly into its own being, it was, as it were, rendered pregnant, for it bore the burden of the devil's vast wickedness; and it was like one with child, and under the strain of parturition, as it sought to eject the agitations[6] of his malignant suggestions. For the serpent, grudging the glory of the first man, made its way into paradise; and harbouring these pains of parturition in itself,[7] it began to produce mendacious addresses, and to generate death for the men who had been fashioned by God, and who had received the gift of life. The devil, however, was not able to manifest himself completely through the serpent; but he reserved his perfection for a time, in order that he might demonstrate it through Cain, by whom he was generated completely. And thus through the serpent, on the one hand, he displayed his hypocrisies and deceits to Eve; while through Cain, on the other hand, he effected the beginning of murder, introducing himself into the firstlings of the "fruits," which that man administered so badly. From this the devil has been called a murderer from the beginning, and also a liar, because he deceived the parties to whom he said, "Ye shall be as gods;"[8] for those very persons whom he falsely declared destined to be gods were afterwards cast out of paradise. Wherefore the serpent which conceived him in its womb, and bore him, and brought him forth to the light of day, is constituted the devil's first father; and Cain is made his second father, who through the conception of iniquities produced pains and parricide: for truly the taking of life was the perpetrating of iniquity, unrighteousness, and impiety all together. Furthermore, all who receive him, and do his lusts, are constituted his brothers. Pharaoh is his father in perfection. Every impious man is made his father. Judas became his father, since he conceived him indeed, though he miscarried: for he did not present a perfect parturition there, since it was really a

---

[1] This appears to be the general sense of the very corrupt passage, " Quo videntur ostenso nulli dubium est unusquisque in quamcunque elegerit partem propria usus arbitrii potestate." In Migne it is amended thus: " Quo evidenter ostenso, nulli dubium est, quod unusquisque in quamcunque elegerit partem, propria usus fuerit arbitrii potestate."

[2] Adopting the emendation, " si a Deo bonus, ut asseris, mendacem esse dixisti Jesum." In the Codex Casinensis it stands thus: " sic a Deo bonus ut as mendacem esse dixisti Jesus." But Routh would substitute " si a Deo *diabolus*" = if the devil is from God.

[3] The argumentation throughout this passage seems to rest on the fact that, in support of the dogma of the evil deity, Manes perverted, among other passages, our Lord's words in John viii. 44, as if they were not only " Ye are of your father the devil," but possibly also, " Ye are of the father of the devil;" and again, " He is a liar, and the father of him *is the same*." Thus what Manes urges against Archelaus is this: If only what is good proceeds from the Deity, and if He is the Supreme God Himself, you make out Jesus to have spoken falsely, when in John's Gospel He uses expressions which imply that the devil's father is a liar, and also the Creator of the *lying* devil.

[4] There are some words deficient in this sentence. The text reads, " Manes dixit: . . . dico: et adjecit, Omnis qui conditor est vel Creator aliquorum pater eorum . . . condiderit appellatur." It is proposed to supply *jam* before *dico*, and *quæ* before *condiderit*.

[5] Reading *et effectum* for the *ut effectum* of the codex.

[6] Or it may be " cogitations," reading *cogitata* for *agitata*.

[7] *Conceptis in se doloribus*.

[8] Gen. iii. 5.

greater person who was assailed through Judas; and consequently, as I say, it proved an abortion. For just as the woman receives the man's seed, and thereby also becomes sensible of a daily growth within her, so also did Judas make daily advances in evil, the occasions for that being furnished him like seed by the wicked one. And the first seed of evil in him, indeed, was the lust of money; and its increment was theft, for he purloined the moneys which were deposited in the bag. Its offspring, moreover, consisted of less vexations, and compacts with the Pharisees, and the scandalous bargain for a price; yet it was the abortion, and not the birth, that was witnessed in the horrid noose by which he met his death. And exactly in the same way shall it stand also with you: if you bring the wicked one to light in your own deeds, and do his lusts, you have conceived him, and will be called his father; but, on the other hand, if you cherish penitence, and deliver yourself of your burden, you will be like one that brings to the birth.[1] For, as in school exercises, if one gets the subject-matter from the master, and then creates and produces the whole body of an oration by himself, he is said to be the author of the compositions to which he has thus given birth; so he who has taken in any little leaven of evil from the prime evil, is of necessity called the father and pro-creator of that wicked one, who from the beginning has resisted the truth. The case may be the same, indeed, with those who devote themselves to virtue; for I have heard the most valiant men say to God, "For Thy fear, O Lord, we have conceived in the womb, and we have been in pain, and have brought forth the spirit of salvation."[3] And so those, too, who conceive in respect of the fear of the wicked one, and bring forth the spirit of iniquity, must needs be called the fathers of the same. Thus, on the one hand, they are called sons of that wicked one, so long as they are still yielding obedience to his service; but, on the other hand, they are called fathers if they have attained to the perfec-tion of iniquity. For it is with this view that our Lord says to the Pharisees, "Ye are of your father the devil,"[4] thereby making them his sons, as long as they appeared still to be perturbed[5] by him, and meditated in their hearts evil for good toward the righteous. Accordingly, while they deliberated in such a spirit with their own hearts, and while their wicked devices were made chargeable upon[6] themselves, Judas, as the head of all the evil, and as the person who carried out

their iniquitous counsels to their consummation, was constituted the father of the crime, having received at their hands the recompense of thirty pieces of silver for his impious cruelty. For "after the sop Satan entered into him"[7] com-pletely. But, as we have said, when his womb was enlarged, and the time of his travail came on, he delivered himself only of an abortive bur-den in the conception of unrighteousness, and consequently he could not be called the father in perfection, except only at that very time when the conception was still in the womb; and after-wards, when he betook himself to the hangman's rope, he showed that he had not brought it to a complete birth, because remorse[8] followed.

34. I think that you cannot fail to understand this too, that the word "father" is but a single term indeed, and yet one admitting of being understood in various ways. For one is called father, as being the parent of those children whom he has begotten in a natural way; another is called father, as being the guardian of chil-dren whom he has but brought up; and some, again, are called fathers in respect of the privi-leged standing accruing through time or age. Hence our Lord Jesus Christ Himself is said to have a variety of fathers: for David was called His father, and Joseph was reckoned to be His father, while neither of these two was His father in respect of the actuality of nature. For David is called His father as touching the prerogative of time and age,[9] and Joseph is designated His father as concerning the law of upbringing; but God Himself is His only Father by nature, who was pleased to make all things manifest in short space[10] to us by His word. And our Lord Jesus Christ, making no tarrying,[11] in the space of one year[12] restored multitudes of the sick to health, and gave back the dead to the light of life; and He did indeed embrace all things in the power of His own word.[13] And wherein, forsooth, did He make any tarrying, so that we should have to believe Him to have waited so long, *even to these days*, before He actually sent the Para-clete?[14] Nay, rather, as has been already said above, He gave proof of His presence with us forthwith, and did most abundantly impart Him-self to Paul, whose testimony we also believe when he says, "Unto me only is this grace given."[15] For this is he who formerly was a persecutor of the Church of God, but who

1 The text gives *parturies*. Routh suggests *parturiens*. The sense then might be, But if you repent, you will also deliver yourself of your burden like one who brings to the birth.
2 Reading *Domine* for *Dominum*, which is given in the text.
3 The quotation may refer to Isa. xxvi. 18. [A curious version.]
4 John viii. 44.
5 *Conturbari*.
6 *Translatis in se*.
7 John xiii. 27.
8 *Pœnitentia*. [2 Cor. vii. 10.]
9 *Ætatis ac temporis privilegio*.
10 *Velociter*.
11 *Nec in aliquo remoratus*.
12 The text gives, "inter unius anni spatium," for which *intra*, etc., is proposed. With certain others of the fathers, Archelaus seems to assign but one year to the preaching of Christ and to His working of miracles. See ch. xlix. [Vol. i. p. 391, this series.]
13 Referring probably to Heb i. 3.
14 Migne gives this sentence as a direct statement. We adopt the interrogative form with Routh.
15 Eph. iii 8. *Mihi autem soli*, etc.

afterwards appeared openly before all men as a faithful minister of the Paraclete ; by whose instrumentality His singular clemency was made known to all men, in such wise that even to us who some time were without hope the largess of His gifts has come. For which of us could have hoped that Paul, the persecutor and enemy of the Church, would prove its defender and guardian? Yea, and not that alone, but that he would become also its ruler, the founder and architect of the churches? Wherefore after him, and after those who were with Himself — that is, the disciples — we are not to look for the advent of any other (such), according to the Scriptures ; for our Lord Jesus Christ says of this Paraclete, " He shall receive of mine." [1] Him therefore He selected as an acceptable vessel ; and He sent this Paul to us in the Spirit. Into him the Spirit was poured ; [2] and as that Spirit could not abide upon all men, but only on Him who was born of Mary the mother of God, so 'that Spirit, the Paraclete, could not come into any other, but could only come upon the apostles and the sainted Paul. " For he is a chosen vessel," He says, " unto me, to bear my name before kings and the Gentiles." [3] The apostle himself, too, states the same thing in his first epistle, where he says : " According to the grace that is given to me of God, that I should be the minister of Jesus Christ to the Gentiles, ministering [4] the Gospel of God." [5] " I say the truth in Christ, I lie not, my conscience also bearing me witness in the Holy Ghost." [6] And again : " For I will not dare to speak of any of those things which Christ hath not wrought by me by word and deed." [7] " I am the last of all the apostles, that am not meet to be called an apostle. But by the grace of God I am what I am." [8] And it is his wish to have to deal with [9] those who sought the proof of that Christ who spake in him, for this reason, that the Paraclete was in him : and as having obtained His gift of grace, and as being enriched with magnificent honour, [10] he says : " For this thing I besought the Lord thrice, that it might depart from me. And He said unto me, My grace is sufficient for thee ; for strength is made perfect in weakness." [11]   Again, that it was the Paraclete Him-

self who was in Paul, is indicated by our Lord Jesus Christ in the Gospel, when He says : " If ye love me, keep my commandments. And I will pray my Father, and He shall give you another Comforter." [12]   In these words He points to the Paraclete Himself, for He speaks of " another " Comforter. And hence we have given credit to Paul, and have hearkened to him when he says, " Or [13] seek ye a proof of Christ speaking in me ? " [14] and when he expresses himself in similar terms, of which we have already spoken above. Thus, too, he seals his testament for us as for his faithful heirs, and like a father he addresses us in these words in his Epistle to the Corinthians : " I delivered unto you first of all that which I also received, how that Christ died for our sins according to the Scriptures ; and that He was buried, and that He rose again the third day according to the Scriptures ; and that He was seen of Cephas, then of the eleven apostles : [15] after that He was seen of above five hundred brethren at once ; of whom the greater part remain unto this present, but some are fallen asleep. After that He was seen of James ; then of all the apostles. And last of all He was seen of me also, as of one born out of due time. For I am the last of the apostles." [16]   " Therefore, whether it were I or they, so we preach, and so ye believed." [17] And again, in delivering over to his heirs that inheritance which he gained first himself, he says : " But I fear, lest by any means, as the serpent beguiled Eve through his subtilty, so your minds should be corrupted from the simplicity that is in Christ. For if he that cometh preacheth another Christ, [18] whom we have not preached, or if ye receive another Spirit, which ye have not received, or another gospel, which ye have not accepted, ye might well bear with him. For I suppose that I did nothing less for you than the other apostles." [19]

35. These things, moreover, he has said with the view of showing us that all others who may come after him will be false apostles, deceitful workers, transforming themselves into the apostles of Christ. And no marvel ; for Satan himself is transformed, like an angel of light. What great thing therefore is it, if his ministers also be transformed into the ministers of righteousness? — whose end shall be according to their works. [20]   He indicates, further, what manner of men these were, and points out by whom they

---

[1] John xvi. 14.
[2] The text reads, " quem misit ad nos Paulum in Spiritus influxit Spiritus," etc. We adopt the emendation, " quem misit ad nos Paulum in Spiritu. Influxit Spiritus," etc. Routh suggests, " Paulum cujus in spiritum influxit Spiritus " = this Paul, into whose spirit the Spirit was poured.
[3] *In conspectu regum et gentium.* Acts ix. 15.
[4] *Consecrans.* [Vol. v. p. 290, note 8; also p. 409.]
[5] Rom. xv. 15, 16.
[6] Rom. ix. 1.
[7] Rom. xv. 18.
[8] 1 Cor. xv. 9, 10. Archelaus here gives " *novissimus* omnium apostolorum " for the ἐλάχιστος of the Greek, and the " minimus " of the Vulgate. [" The last" instead of *least.*]
[9] *Vult habere.*
[10] Reading " magnifico *honore*" for the " magnifico *hoc ore*" of the codex.
[11] 2 Cor. xii. 8, 9.

[12] John xiv. 15, 16.
[13] *Aut.*
[14] 2 Cor. xiii. 3.
[15] *Undecim apostolis.*
[16] 1 Cor. xv. 3-9. [Note 8, *supra.*]
[17] 1 Cor. xv. 11.
[18] *Christum.*
[19] *Nihil minus feci vobis a cæteris apostolis.* 2 Cor. xi. 3-5.
[20] 2 Cor. ix. 14, 15. The text gives " *velut* angelum lucis," as if the Greek had read ὡς. So also Cyprian, in the beginning of his book on *The Unity of the Church.* [Vol. v. p. 422, sec. 3.]

were being circumvented. And when the Galatians are minded to turn away from the Gospel, he says to them : " I marvel that ye are so soon removed from Him that called you unto another gospel : which is not another ; but there be some that trouble you, and would turn you away [1] from the Gospel of Christ. But though we, or an angel from heaven, preach any other gospel unto you than that which has been delivered to you, let him be accursed." [2] And again he says : " To me, who am the least of all the apostles,[3] is this grace given ; " [4] and, " I fill up that which was behind of the afflictions of Christ in my flesh." [5] And once more, in another place, he declares of himself that he was a minister of Christ more than all others,[6] as though after him none other was to be looked for at all ; for he enjoins that not even an angel from heaven is thus to be received. And how, then, shall we credit the professions of this Manes, who comes from Persis,[7] and declares himself to be the Paraclete ? By this very thing, indeed, I rather recognise in him one of those men who transform themselves, and of whom the Apostle Paul, that elect vessel, has given us very clear indication when he says : " Now in the last times some shall depart from the faith, giving heed to seducing spirits, and doctrines of devils ; speaking lies in hypocrisy ; having their conscience seared with a hot iron ; forbidding to marry, and *commanding* to abstain from meats, which God hath created to be received [8] with thanksgiving of them which believe and know the truth. For every creature of God is good, and nothing to be refused, if it be received with thanksgiving." [9] The Spirit in the evangelist Matthew is also careful to give note of these words of our Lord Jesus Christ : " Take heed that no man deceive you : for many shall come in my name, saying, I am Christ ; and shall deceive many. But if any man shall say unto you, Lo, here is Christ, or there ; believe it not. For there shall arise false Christs, and false apostles,[10] and false prophets, and shall show great signs and wonders ; insomuch that, if it were possible, they shall deceive the very elect. Behold, I have told you before. If they shall say unto you, Behold, he is in the desert ; go not forth : if they shall say, Behold, he is in the secret chambers ; believe it not." [11] And yet,

after all these directions, this man, who has neither sign nor portent of any kind to show, who has no affinity to exhibit, who never even had a place among the number of the disciples, who never was a follower of our departed Lord, in whose inheritance we rejoice, — this man, I say, although he never stood by our Lord in His weakness, and although he never came forward as a witness of His testament, yea rather, although he never came even within the acquaintance of those who ministered to Him in His sickness, and, in fine, although he obtains the testimony of no person whatsoever, desires us to believe this profession which he makes of being the Paraclete ; whereas, even were you to do signs and wonders, we would still have to reckon you a false Christ, and a false prophet, according to the Scriptures. And therefore it is well for us to act with the greater caution, in accordance with the warning which the sainted apostle gives us, when, in the epistle which he wrote to the Colossians, he speaks in the following terms : " Continue in the faith grounded and rooted,[12] and not to be moved away [13] from the hope of the Gospel, which we have heard,[14] and which was preached to every creature which is under heaven." [15] And again : " As ye have therefore received Christ Jesus the Lord, so walk ye in Him ; rooted and built up in Him, and stablished in the faith, as ye have been taught, abounding therein with thanksgiving. Beware lest any one spoil you through philosophy and vain deceit, after the rudiments of the world, and not after Christ. For in Him dwelleth all the fulness of the Godhead." [16] And after all these matters have been thus carefully set forth, the blessed apostle, like a father speaking to his children, adds the following words, which serve as a sort of seal to his testament : " I have fought a good fight, I have finished my course,[17] I have kept the faith : henceforth there is laid up for me a crown of righteousness, which the Lord, the righteous Judge, shall give me at that day ; and not to me only, but unto all them also that love His appearing." [18]

36. None of your party,[19] O Manes, will you make a Galatian ; neither will you in this fashion divert us [20] from the faith of Christ. Yea, even although you were to work signs and wonders, although you were to raise the dead, although you were to present to us the very image of Paul

---

[1] *Avertere vos.*
[2] Gal. i. 6-8.
[3] *Infimo omnium apostolorum.*
[4] Eph. iii. 8.
[5] Col. i. 24.
[6] 2 Cor. xi. 23.
[7] The Codex Casinensis gives, " de Persida venientem monet ; " for which corrupt reading it is proposed to substitute " de Perside venientem Manem," etc.
[8] Reading *percipiendum* with the Vulgate. But the Codex Casinensis has *perficiendum.*
[9] 1 Tim. iv. 1-4.
[10] These words *falsi apostoli* seem to be added by way of explanation, as they are not found either in the Greek or the Vulgate.
[11] Matt. xxiv. 4, 5, 23-26.

[12] *Radicati.*
[13] *Immobiles.*
[14] *Audivimus.*
[15] Col. i. 23.
[16] Col ii. 6-9.
[17] The text gives " *circum* cucurri," perhaps for " *cursum* cucurri." The Vulgate has " cursum consummavi."
[18] 2 Tim. iv. 7, 8.
[19] The text gives " ex vobis." But perhaps we should read " ex nobis " = none of us.
[20] The Codex Casinensis has " Galatam facies vicit, o nostras feras," for which we adopt the correction, " Galatam facies, nec ita nos."

himself, you would remain accursed still.[1] For we have been instructed beforehand with regard to you : we have been both warned and armed against you by the Holy Scriptures. You are a vessel of Antichrist ; and no vessel of honour, in sooth, but a mean and base one, used by him as any barbarian or tyrant may do, who, in attempting to make an inroad on a people living under the righteousness of the laws,[2] sends some select vessel on beforehand, as it were destined to death, with the view of finding out the exact magnitude and character of the strength possessed by the legitimate king and his nation : for the man is too much afraid to make the inroad himself wholly at unawares, and he also lacks the daring to despatch any person belonging to his own immediate circle on such a task, through fear that he may sustain some harm. And so it is that your king, Antichrist, has despatched you in a similar character, and as it were destined to death, to us who are a people placed under the administration of the good and holy King. And this I do not say inconsiderately or without due inquiry ; but from the fact that I see you perform no miracle, I hold myself entitled to entertain such sentiments concerning you. For we are given to understand beforehand that the devil himself is to be transformed into an angel of light, and that nis servants are to make their appearance in similar guise, and that they are to work signs and wonders, insomuch that, if it were possible, the very elect should be deceived.[3] But who, pray, are you then, to whose lot no such position of kinship has been assigned by your father Satan ?[4] For whom have you raised from the dead ? What issue of blood do you ever staunch ? What[5] eyes of the blind do you ever anoint with clay, and thus cause them to have vision ? When do you ever refresh a hungering multitude with a few loaves ? Where do you ever walk upon the water, or who of those who dwell in Jerusalem has ever seen you ? O Persian barbarian, you have never been able to have a knowledge of the language of the Greeks, or of the Egyptians, or of the Romans, or of any other nation ; but the Chaldean tongue alone has been known to you, which verily is not a language prevalent among any great number of people,[6] and you are not capable of understanding any one of another nationality when he speaks. Not thus is it with the Holy Spirit :

God forbid ; but He divides to all, and knows all kinds of tongues, and has understanding of all things, and is made all things to all men, so that the very thoughts of the heart cannot escape His cognizance. For what says the Scripture ? " That every man heard the apostles speak in his own language through the Spirit, the Paraclete."[7] But why should I say more on this subject ?[8] Barbarian[9] priest and crafty coadjutor of Mithras, you will only be a worshipper of the sun-god Mithras, who is the illuminator of places of mystic import, as you opine, and the self-conscious deity ; "[10] that is, you will sport as his worshippers do, and you will celebrate, though with less elegance as it were, his mysteries.[11] But why should I take all this so indignantly ? Is it not accordant with all that is fitting, that you should multiply yourself like the tares, until that same mighty father of yours comes, raising the dead, *as he will profess to do*, and persecuting almost to hell itself all those who refuse to yield to his bidding, keeping multitudes in check by that terror of arrogance in which he entrenches himself, and employing threatenings against others, and making sport of them by the changing of his countenance and his deceitful dealing ?[12] And yet beyond that he shall proceed no further ; for his folly shall be made manifest to all men, as was the case with Jamnes and Mambres.[13] *The judges said :* As we have heard now from you, as Paul himself also seems to tell us, and, further, as we have learned likewise from the earlier account given in the Gospel, an introduction to preaching, or teaching, or evangelizing, or prophesying, is not, in this life at least, held out on the same terms to any person in times subsequent *to the apostle's :*[14] and if the opposite appears ever to be the case, the person can only be held to be a false prophet or a false Christ. Now, since you have alleged that the Paraclete was in Paul, and that He attested all things in him, how is it that Paul himself said, " We know in part, and we prophesy

---

[1] O Satan! The Codex Casinensis gives " anathema esse *ana*," which may be an error, either for " anathema es, Satana," or for " anathema es et maranatha." [" O Satan " is less probable.]

[2] The text is *legum;* for which *regum*, kings, is also suggested.

[3] Matt. xxiv. 24.

[4] The text gives, " qui neque necessarium aliquem locum sortitus es," etc. Routh proposes " necessarii." The sense seems to be that Manes had nothing to prove any connection between him and Christ.

[5] Reading " *quos* luto," etc., for the " *quod* luto " of the codex.

[6] [Note, against Canon Farrar and moderns, the persuasion of antiquity as to the miraculous gift of tongues; the *charismata* of others, also, besides the Apostles.] The text is, " quæ ne in numerum quidem aliquem ducitur."

[7] Acts ii. 6.

[8] The text gives " Quid dicabo," which may stand for " quid dicam;" or perhaps the translator intends to use " dicare " in the sense of *urge*.

[9] Reading *barbare*, for which the text offers *barba*.

[10] *Conscium*. [For Mithras, see vol. iii. p. 475.]

[11] In this sentence the sense is somewhat obscure, in consequence of the corruptions of the text in the codex. We adopt the emendations " locorum *mysticorum* " for *mysteriorum*, and " apud eos *ludes* " for *ludis*. In the end of the clause Migne gives, as in the translation, " et tanquam *minus* elegans," etc. But Routh reads *minus* = and like an elegant pantomiimist, etc.

[12] The Codex Casinensis gives the sentence thus : " . . . adveniat? suscitans mortuos? pene usque ad gehennam omnes persequens, qui si ut obtemperare noluerit, plurimos deterrens arrogantiæ metu, Quod est ipse circumdatus, aliis adhibet minas vultus sui conversione circumdatio ludificat." The emendations adopted by Migne and Routh consist in removing these two interrogative marks, and in reading *qui sibi* for *q..i si ut*, *noluerint* for *noluerit*, *quo est* for *Quod est*, *adhibens* for *adhibet*, and *et circumductione ludificans* for the last two words.

[13] 2 Tim. iii. 8, 9.

[14] The sense is again obscure throughout this sentence, owing to the state of the text. The codex gives us this clause, " nulli alio atque posterum," etc., for which " nulli alii æque in posterum " is proposed.

in part; but when that which is perfect is come, then that which is in part shall be done away?"[1] What other one did he look for, when he uttered these words? For if he professes himself to be looking for some perfect one, and if some one must needs come, show us who it is of whom he speaks; lest that word of his perchance appear to carry us back to this man, *Manes*, or to him who has sent him, that is to say, Satan, according to your affirmation. But if you admit that that which is perfect is yet to come, then this excludes Satan; and if you look for the coming of Satan, then that excludes the perfect.

37. *Archelaus said:* Those sayings which are put forth by the blessed Paul were not uttered without the direction of God, and therefore it is certain that what he has declared to us is that we are to look for our Lord Jesus Christ as the perfect one, who[2] is the only one that knows the Father, with the sole exception of him to whom He has chosen also to reveal Him,[3] as I am able to demonstrate from His own words. But let it be observed, that it is said that when that which is perfect is come, then that which is in part shall be done away. Now this man (Manes) asserts that he is the perfect one. Let him show us, then, what he has done away with; for what is to be done away with is the ignorance which is in us. Let him therefore tell us what he has done away with, and what he has brought into *the sphere of our* knowledge. If he is able to do anything of this nature, let him do it now, in order that he may be believed. These very words of Paul's, if one can but understand them in the full power of their meaning, will only secure entire credit to the statements made by me. For in that first Epistle to the Corinthians, Paul speaks in the following terms of the perfection that is to come: "Whether there be prophecies, they shall fail; whether there be tongues, they shall cease; whether there be knowledge, it shall be destroyed: for we know in part, and we prophesy in part; but when that which is perfect is come, then that which is in part shall be done away."[4] Observe now what virtue that which is perfect possesses in itself, and of what order that perfection is. And let this man, then, tell us what prophecy of the Jews or Hebrews he has done away with; or what tongues he has caused to cease, whether of the Greeks or of others who worship idols; or what alien dogmas he has destroyed, whether of a Valentinian, or a Marcion, or a Tatian, or a Sabellius, or any others of those who have constructed for themselves their peculiar systems of knowledge. Let him

tell us which of all these he has already done away with, or when he is yet to do away with any one of them, in this character of the perfect one. Perchance he seeks some sort of truce — does he?[5] But not thus inconsiderable, not thus obscure[6] and ignoble, will be the manner of the advent of Him who is the truly perfect one, that is to say, our Lord Jesus Christ. Nay, but as a king, when he draws near to his city, does first of all send on before him his life-guardsmen,[7] his ensigns and standards and banners,[8] his generals and chiefs and prefects, and then forthwith all objects are roused and excited in different fashions, while some become inspired with terror and others with exultation at the prospect of the king's advent; so also my Lord Jesus Christ, who is the truly perfect one, at His coming will first send on before Him His glory, *and* the consecrated heralds of an unstained and untainted kingdom: and then the universal creation will be moved and perturbed, uttering prayers and supplications, until He delivers it from its bondage.[9] And it must needs be that the race of man shall then be in fear and in vehement agitation on account of the many offences it has committed. Then the righteous alone will rejoice, as they look for the things which have been promised them; and the subsistence of the affairs of this world will no longer be maintained, but all things shall be destroyed: and whether they be prophecies or the books of prophets, *they shall fail;* whether they be the tongues of the whole race, they shall cease; for men will no longer need to feel anxiety or to think solicitously about those things which are necessary for life; whether it be knowledge, by what teachers soever it be possessed, it shall also be destroyed: for none of all these things will be able to endure the advent of that mighty King. For just as a little spark, if[10] taken and put up against the splendour of the sun, at once perishes from the view, so the whole creation, all prophecy, all knowledge, all tongues, as we have said above, shall be destroyed. But since the capacities of common human nature are all insufficient to set forth in a few words, and these so weak and so extremely poor, the coming of this heavenly King, — so much so, indeed, that perchance it should be the privilege only of the saintly and the highly worthy to attempt any statement on such a subject, — it may yet be enough for me to *be able to say that I* have advanced what I have now advanced on that theme on the ground of simple necessity, — compelled, as I have been, to do thus much by this person's

---

[1] 1 Cor. xiii. 9, 10.
[2] Reading "*qui* solus," for the *sed*, etc., of the codex. See also Luke x. 22.
[3] Matt. xi. 27.
[4] 1 Cor. xiii. 8-10.

[5] *Inducias fortassis aliquas quærit.*
[6] Reading "non plane, non tam obscure," etc., instead of the "non plane nota," etc., of the Codex Casinensis.
[7] "Protectores," on which term consult Ducangius in his *Glossary.*
[8] *Signa, dracones, labaros.*
[9] Rom. viii. 21, 22.
[10] The text gives simply, *sicut enim parva.* We may adopt, with Routh, "sicut enim *cum* parva," etc.

importunity, and simply with the view of showing you what kind of character he is.

38. And, in good truth, I hold Marcion, and Valentinian, and Basilides, and other heretics, to be sainted men when compared [1] with this person. For they did display a certain kind of intellect, and they did, indeed, think themselves capable of understanding all Scripture, and did thus constitute themselves leaders [2] for those who were willing to listen to them. But notwithstanding this, not one of these dared to proclaim himself to be either God, or Christ, or the Paraclete, as this fellow has done, who is ever disputing, on some occasions about the ages,[3] and on others about the sun, and how these objects were made, as though he were superior to them himself; for every person who offers an exposition of the method in which any object has been made, puts himself forward as superior to and older than the subject of his discussion. But who may venture to speak of the substance of God, unless, it may be, our Lord Jesus Christ alone? And, indeed, I do not make this statement on the bare authority of my own words, but I confirm it by the authority of that Scripture which has been our instructor. For the apostle addresses the following words to us : " That ye may be lights in this world, holding [4] the word of life for my glory against the day of Christ, seeing that I have not run in vain, neither laboured in vain." [5] We ought to understand what is the force and meaning of this saying ; for the word may suit the leader, but the effectual work suits the king.[6] And accordingly, as one who looks for the arrival of his king, strives to be able to present all who are under his charge as obedient, and ready, and estimable, and lovely, and faithful, and not less also as blameless, and abounding in all that is good, so that he may himself get commendation from the king, and be deemed by him to be worthy of greater honours, as having rightly governed the province which was entrusted to his administration ; so also does the blessed Paul give us to understand our position when he uses these words : " That ye may be as lights in this world, holding the word of life for my glory against the day of Christ." For the meaning of this saying is, that our Lord Jesus Christ, when He comes, will see that his doctrine has proved profitable in us, and that, finding that he, *the apostle*, has not run in vain, neither laboured in vain, He will bestow on him the

crown of recompense. And again, in the same epistle, he also warns us not to mind earthly things, and tells us that we ought to have our conversation in heaven ; from which also we look for the Saviour, our Lord Jesus Christ.[7] And as the knowledge of the date of the last day is no secure position for us, he has given us, to that effect, a declaration on the subject in the epistle which he wrote to the Thessalonians, thus : " But of the times and the seasons, brethren, ye have no need that I write unto you ; for yourselves know perfectly that the day of the Lord so cometh as a thief in the night." [8] How, then, does this man stand up and try to persuade us to embrace his opinions, importuning every individual whom he meets to become a Manichæan, and going about and creeping into houses, and endeavouring to deceive minds laden with sins? [9] But we do not hold such sentiments. Nay, rather, we should be disposed to present the things themselves before you all, and bring them into comparison, if it please you, with *what we know of* the perfect Paraclete. For you observe that [10] sometimes he uses the interrogative style, and sometimes the deprecatory. But in the Gospel of our Saviour it is written that those who stand on the left hand of the King will say : " Lord, when saw we Thee an hungered, or athirst, or naked, or a stranger, or in prison, and did not minister unto Thee ? " [11] Thus they will implore Him to be indulgent with them. But what reply is that righteous Judge and King represented as making to them? " Depart from me into everlasting fire, ye workers of iniquity." [12] He casts them into everlasting fire, although they cease not to direct their entreaties to Him. Do you see, then, *O Manes*, what manner of event that advent of the perfect King is destined to be? Do you not perceive that it will not be such a perfection, *or consummation*, as you allege? But if the great day of judgment is to be looked for after that King, surely this man is greatly inferior to Him. But if he is inferior, he cannot be perfect. And if he is not to be perfect, it is not of him that the apostle speaks. But if it is not of him that the apostle speaks, while he still makes the mendacious statement that it is of himself that the said word *of the apostle* was spoken, then surely he is to be judged a false prophet. Much more, too, might be said to the same effect. But if we were to think of going over in detail all that might thus be adduced, time would fail us for the accomplishment of so large a task. Hence I have deemed it abundantly sufficient thus to have brought under your

---

[1] Reading " sic ut istius comparatione," for the " sicut istius paratione " of the codex.
[2] Reading *se ductores*, for the *seductores*, etc., of the codex.
[3] *Seculis.*
[4] *Continentes.*
[5] Phil. ii. 13.
[6] The precise meaning and connection are somewhat obscure here. The text gives, " verbum enim ducis obtinet locum, opera vero regis." And the idea is taken to be, that the actual work of thoroughly doing away with the ignorance of men was something that suited only the perfect King who was expected, and that had not been accomplished by Manes.

[7] Phil. iii. 19.
[8] 1 Thess. v. 1, 2.
[9] Alluding to 2 Tim. iii. 6.
[10] Routh inserts *interdum pœnitet* = sometimes he uses the penitential style, which Migne omits.
[11] Matt. xxv. 44.
[12] Matt. xxv. 40; Luke xiii. 27.

notice only a few things out of many, leaving the yet remaining portions of such a discussion to those who have the inclination to go through with them.

39. On hearing these matters, those who were present gave great glory to God, and ascribed to Him such praise as it is meet for Him to receive. And on Archelaus himself they bestowed many tokens of honour. Then Marcellus rose up ; and casting off his cloak,[1] he threw his arms round Archelaus, and kissed him, and embraced him, and clung to him. Then, too, the children who had chanced to gather about the place began and set the example of pelting Manes and driving him off ;[2] and the rest of the crowd followed them, and moved excitedly about, with the intention of compelling Manes to take to flight. But when Archelaus observed this, he raised his voice like a trumpet above the din, in his anxiety to restrain the multitude, and addressed them thus : "Stop, my beloved brethren, lest mayhap we be found to have the guilt of blood on us at the day of judgment ; for it is written of men like this, that ' there must be also heresies among you, that they which are approved may be made manifest among you.' "[3] And when he had uttered these words, the crowds of people were quieted again.[4] — Now, because it was the pleasure of Marcellus that this disputation should have a place given it,[5] and that it should also be described, I could not gainsay his wish, but trusted to the kind consideration of the readers, believing that they would pardon me if my discourse should sound somewhat inartistic or boorish : for the great thing which we have had in view has been, that the means of knowing what took place on this occasion should not fail to be brought within the reach of all who desired to understand the subject. Thereafter, it must be added, when Manes had once taken to flight, he made his appearance nowhere *there again*. His attendant Turbo, however, was handed over by Marcellus to Archelaus ; and on Archelaus ordaining him as a deacon, he remained in the suite of Marcellus. But Manes in his flight came to a certain village which was at a considerable distance from the city, and bore the name of Diodorus. Now in that place there was also a presbyter whose name likewise was Diodorus,[6] a man of quiet and gentle disposition, and well reputed both for his faith and for the excellence of his general character. Now when, on a certain day, Manes had

gathered a crowd of auditors around him, and was haranguing[7] them, and putting before the people who were present certain outlandish assertions altogether foreign to the tradition of the fathers, and in no way apprehending any opposition that might be made to him on the part of any of these, Diodorus perceived that he was producing some effect by his wickedness, and resolved then to send to Archelaus a letter couched in the following terms : —

Diodorus sends greeting to Bishop Archelaus.[8]

40. I wish you to know, most pious father, that in these days there has arrived in our parts a certain person named Manes, who gives out that he is to complete the doctrine of the New Testament. And in the statements which he has made there have been some things, indeed, which may harmonize with our faith ; but there have been also certain affirmations of his which seem very far removed from what has come down to us by the tradition of our fathers. For he has interpreted some doctrines in a strange fashion, imposing on them certain notions of his own, which have appeared to me to be altogether foreign and opposed to the faith. On the ground of these facts I have now been induced to write this letter to you, knowing the completeness and fulness of your intelligence in doctrine, and being assured that none of these things can escape your cognizance. Accordingly, I have also indulged the confident hope that you cannot be kept back by any grudge[9] from explaining these matters to us. As to myself, indeed, it is not possible that I shall be drawn away into any novel doctrine ; nevertheless, in behalf of all the less instructed, I have been led to ask a word with your authority. For, in truth, the man shows himself to be a person of extraordinary force of character, both in speech and in action ; and indeed his very aspect and attire also bear that out. But I shall here write down for your information some few points which I have been able to retain in my memory out of all the topics which have been expounded by him : for I know that even by these few you will have an idea of the rest. You well understand, no doubt, that those who seek to set up any new dogma have the habit of very readily perverting into a conformity with their own notions any proofs they desire to take from the Scriptures.[10] In anticipation, however, of this, the apostolic word marks out the case thus : " If any one preach any other gospel unto you than that which you have received, let him be accursed."[11] And consequently, in addition to what has been once

---

[1] The text gives the plural form *stolas*, perhaps for *stolam*.
[2] The text gives *fugere*, apparently in the sense of *fugare*.
[3] 1 Cor. xi. 19.
[4] [Note the testimony against the persecution of heretics, — a characteristic of early Christians which too soon began to disappear, notably in Alexandria under Cyril.]
[5] *Excipi.*
[6] This Diodorus appears to be called Trypho by Epiphanius, on this Manichæan heresy, n. 11.

[7] Reading *concionaretur* for *continuaretur*.
[8] This epistle is also mentioned, and its argument noticed, by Epiphanius, *Hæres.*, 11.
[9] *Invidia.*
[10] [Tertullian, vol. iii. p. 251, this series.]
[11] Gal. i. 8.

committed to us by the apostles, a disciple of Christ ought to receive nothing new as doctrine.[1] But not to make what I have got to say too long, I return to the subject directly in view. This man then maintained that the law of Moses, to speak shortly, does not proceed from the good God, but from the prince of evil; and that it has no kinship with the new law of Christ, but is contrary and hostile to it, the one being the direct antagonist of the other. When I heard such a sentiment propounded, I repeated to the people that sentence of the Gospel in which our Lord Jesus Christ said of Himself: "I am not come to destroy the law, but to fulfil it."[2] The man, however, averred that He did not utter this saying at all; for he held that when we find that He did abrogate[3] that same law, we are bound to give heed, above all other considerations, to the thing which He actually did. Then he began to cite a great variety of passages from the law, and also many from the Gospel and from the Apostle Paul, which have the appearance of contradicting each other. All this he gave forth at the same time with perfect confidence, and without any hesitation or fear; so that I verily believe he has that serpent as his helper, who is ever our adversary. Well, he declared that there *in the law* God said, "I make the rich man and the poor man;"[4] while here *in the Gospel* Jesus called the poor blessed,[5] and added, that no man could be His disciple unless he gave up all that he had.[6] Again, he maintained that there Moses took silver and gold from the Egyptians when the people[7] fled out of Egypt;[8] whereas Jesus delivered the precept that we should lust after nothing belonging to our neighbour. Then he affirmed that Moses had provided in the law, that an eye should be given in penalty for an eye, and a tooth for a tooth;[9] but that our Lord bade us offer the other cheek also to him who smote the one.[10] He told us, too, that there Moses commanded the man to be punished and stoned who did any work on the Sabbath, and who failed to continue in all things that were written in the law,[11] as in fact was done to that person who, yet being ignorant, had gathered a bundle of sticks on the Sabbath-day; whereas Jesus cured a cripple on the Sabbath, and ordered him then also to take up his bed.[12] And further,

He did not restrain His disciples from plucking the ears of corn and rubbing them with their hands on the Sabbath-day,[13] which yet was a thing which it was unlawful to do on the Sabbaths. And why should I mention other instances? For with many different assertions of a similar nature these dogmas of his were propounded with the utmost energy and the most fervid zeal. Thus, too, on the authority of an apostle, he endeavoured to establish the position that the law of Moses is the law of death, and that the law of Jesus, on the contrary, is the law of life. For he based that assertion on the passage which runs thus: "In which also may God make us[14] able ministers of the New Testament; not of the letter, but of the spirit: for the letter killeth, but the spirit giveth life. But if the ministration of death, engraven in letters on the stones,[15] was made in glory, so that the children of Israel could not stedfastly behold the face of Moses for the glory of his countenance; which glory was to be done away; how shall not the ministration of the Spirit be rather glorious? For if the ministration of condemnation be glory, much more doth the ministration of righteousness exceed in glory. For even that which was made glorious had no glory in this respect, by reason of the glory that excelleth. For if that which shall be done away is glorious, much more that which remaineth is glorious."[16] And this passage, as you are also well aware, occurs in the second Epistle to the Corinthians. Besides, he added to this another passage out of the first epistle, on which he based his affirmation that the disciples of the Old Testament were earthly and natural; and in accordance with this, that flesh and blood could not possess the kingdom of God.[17] He also maintained that Paul himself spake in his own proper person when he said: "If I build again the things which I destroyed, I make myself a transgressor."[18] Further, he averred that the same apostle made this statement most obviously on the subject of the resurrection of the flesh, when he also said that " he is not a Jew who is one outwardly, neither is that circumcision which is outward in the flesh,"[19] and that according to the letter the law has in it no advantage.[20] And again he adduced the statement, that "Abraham has glory, but not before God;"[21] and that "by the law there comes only the knowledge of sin."[22] And many other things did he introduce, with the view of detracting from the honour of the law, on the ground that

---

[1] [Against Scripture and the torrent of patristic testimony, the men of this generation have seen new dogmas imposed upon a great portion of Christendom by the voice of a single bishop, and without synodical deliberation or consent. The whole claim to "Catholicity" perishes wherever such dogmas are accepted.]
[2] Matt. v. 17.
[3] *Resolvisse.*
[4] Prov. xxii. 2.
[5] Matt. v. 3.
[6] Luke xiv. 33.
[7] Reading *cum populus* for the *cum populo* of the text.
[8] Ex. xii. 35.
[9] Ex. xxi. 24.
[10] Luke vi. 29.
[11] Num. xv. 32.
[12] Mark ii. 11.

[13] Luke vi. 1.
[14] *Faciat Deus.*
[15] *In litteris formatum in lapidibus.*
[16] 2 Cor. iii. 6-11.
[17] 1 Cor. xv. 46-50.
[18] Gal. ii. 18.
[19] Rom. ii. 28.
[20] Rom. iv. 1.
[21] Rom. iv. 2.
[22] Rom. iii. 20.

the law itself is sin ; by which statements the simpler people were somewhat influenced, as he continued to bring them forward ; and in accordance with all this, he also made use of the affirmation, that " the law and the prophets were until John." [1] He declared, however, that John preached the *true* kingdom of heaven ; for verily he held, that by the cutting off of his head it was signified that all who went before him, and who had precedence over him, were to be cut off, and that what was to come after him was alone to be maintained. With reference to all these things, therefore, O most pious Archelaus, send us back a short reply in writing : for I have heard that you have studied such matters in no ordinary degree ; and that *capacity which you possess* is God's gift, inasmuch as God bestows these gifts upon those who are worthy of them, and who are His friends, and who show themselves allied to Him in community of purpose and life. For it is our part to prepare ourselves, and to approach the gracious and liberal mind,[2] and forthwith we receive from it the most bountiful gifts. Accordingly, since the learning which I possess for the discussion of themes like these does not meet the requirements of my desire and purpose, for I confess myself to be an unlearned man, I have sent to you, as I have already said more than once, in the hope of obtaining from your hand the amplest solution to this question. May it be well with you, incomparable and honourable father !

41. On receiving this epistle, Archelaus was astonished at the man's boldness. But in the meantime, as the case called for the transmission of a speedy reply, he immediately sent off a letter with reference to the statements made by Diodorus. That epistle ran in the following terms : [3] —

Archelaus sends greeting to the presbyter Diodorus, his honourable son.

The receipt of your letter has rejoiced me exceedingly, my dearly beloved friend. I have been given to understand, moreover, that this man, who made his way to me before these days, and sought to introduce a novel kind of knowledge here, different from what is apostolic and ecclesiastical, has also come to you. To that person, indeed, I gave no place : for presently, when we held a disputation together, he was confuted. And I could wish now to transcribe for your behoof all the arguments of which I made use on that occasion, so that by means of

these you might get an idea of what that man's faith is. But as that could be done only with leisure at my disposal, I have deemed it requisite, in view of the immediate exigency, to write a short reply to you with reference to what you have written me on the subject of the statements advanced by him. I understand, then, that his chief [4] effort was directed to prove that the law of Moses is not consonant with the law of Christ ; and this position he attempted to found on the authority of our Scriptures. Well, on the other hand, not only did we establish the law of Moses, and all things which are written in it, by the same Scripture ; but we also proved that the whole Old Testament agrees with the New Testament, and is in perfect harmony with the same, and that they form really one texture, just as a person may see one and the same robe made up of weft and warp together.[5] For the truth is simply this, that just as we trace the purple in a robe, so, if we may thus express it, we can discern the New Testament in the texture of the Old Testament ; for we see the glory of the Lord mirrored in the same.[6] We are not therefore to cast aside the mirror,[7] seeing that it shows us the genuine image of the things themselves, faithfully and truly ; but, on the contrary, we ought to honour it all the more. Think you, indeed, that the boy who is brought by his pædagogue to the teachers of learning [8] when he is yet a very little fellow, ought to hold that pædagogue in no honour [9] after he has grown up to manhood, simply because he needs his services [10] no longer, but can make his course without any assistance from that attendant to the schools, and quickly find his way to the lecture-rooms ? Or, to take another instance, would it be right for the child who has been nourished on milk at first, after he has grown to be capable of receiving stronger meats, then injuriously to spurn the breasts of his nurse, and conceive a horror of them ? Nay, rather he should honour and cherish them, and confess himself a debtor to their good services. We may also make use, if it please you, of another illustration. A certain man on one occasion having noticed an infant

---

[1] Luke xvi. 16.

[2] Reading " præparare et proximos fieri benignæ ac diviti menti " for " præparet proximus fieri benignæ hac," etc., as it stands in the Codex Casinensis. Routh suggests " præparare proximos fieri benignæ ac diviti menti et continuo . . . consequemur " = to take care to draw near to the gracious and liberal mind, and then we shall forthwith receive steadily from it, etc.

[3] This epistle is edited not only from the Codex Casinensis, but also by Valesius from the Codex Bobiensis. The most important varieties of reading shall therefore be noted.

[4] Summum studium. But the Codex Bobiensis reads *suum studium*.

[5] Reading " ex subtegmine atque stamine," etc., with the Codex Bobiensis, instead of " subtemine et, quæ stamine," etc., as it is given in the Codex Casinensis. [A beautiful anticipation of Augustine's *dictum*, " The New is *veiled* in the Old, the Old *unveiled* in the New."]

[6] We read here " gloriam enim Domini in eodem speculamur." The Codex Bobiensis is vitiated here, giving *gloriam um Domini*, which was changed by Valesius into *gloriam Jesu*, etc.

[7] Reading, with the Codex Bobiensis, " speculum, cum nobis ipsam imaginem," etc., instead of " speculum nobis per ipsam imaginem," etc.

[8] [Here is the literal use of the word " pædagogue," with which Clement took liberties. Vol. ii. p. 209, note 3, this series.] Adopting " qui ad doctores a pædagogo," instead of " qui a doctore iis a pædagogo."

[9] " Dehonorare," or, as in the Codex Bobiensis, " dehonestare."

[10] Reading " opera ejus non indiget." But the Codex Casinensis gives " ore ejus," etc.

exposed on the ground and already suffering excessively, picked it up, and undertook to rear it in his own house until it should reach the age of youth, and sustained all the toils and anxieties which are wont to fall to the lot of those who have to bring up children. After a time, however, it happened that he who was the child's natural father came seeking the boy, and found him with this person who had brought him up.[1] What ought this boy to do on learning that this is his real father? For I speak, of course, of a boy of the right type. Would he not see to it, that he who had brought him up should be recompensed with liberal gifts; and would he not then follow his natural father, having his proper inheritance in view?[2] Even so, then, I think we must suppose that that distinguished servant of God, Moses, in a manner something like this, found[3] a people afflicted by the Egyptians; and he took this people to himself, and nurtured them in the desert like a father, and instructed them like a teacher, and ruled them as a magistrate. This people he also preserved against the coming of him whose people they were. And after a considerable period the father[4] did come, and did receive his sheep. Now will not that guardian be honoured in all things by him to whom he delivered that flock; and will he not be glorified by those who have been preserved by him? Who, then, can be so senseless, my dearly beloved Diodorus, as to say that those are aliens to each other who have been allied with each other, who have prophesied in turn for each other, and who have shown signs and wonders which are equal and similar, the one to the other, and of like nature with each other;[5] or rather, to speak in truth, which belong wholly to the same stock the one with the other? For, indeed, Moses first said to the people: "A Prophet will the Lord our God raise up unto you, like unto me."[6] And Jesus afterwards said: "For Moses spake of me."[7] You see[8] how these twain give the right hand to each other, although[9] the one was the prophet and the other was the beloved Son,[10] and although in the one we are to recognise the faithful servant, but in the other the Lord Himself. Now, on the other hand, I might refer to the fact, that one who of old was minded to make his way to the schools without the pædagogue was not taken in by the master.

For the master said: "I will not receive him unless he accepts the pædagogue." And who the person is, who is spoken of under that figure, I shall briefly explain. There was a certain rich man,[11] who lived after the manner of the Gentiles, and passed his time in great luxury every day; and there was also another man, a poor man, who was his neighbour, and who was unable to procure even his daily bread. It happened that both these men departed this life, that they both descended into the grave,[12] and that the poor man was conveyed into the place of rest, and so forth, as is known to you. But, furthermore, that rich man had also five brothers, living as he too had lived, and disturbed by no doubt as to lessons which they had learned at home from such a master. The rich man then entreated that these should be instructed in the superior doctrine together and at once.[13] But Abraham, knowing that they still stood in need of the pædagogue, said to him: "They have Moses and the prophets." For if they received not these, so as to have their course directed by him, i.e., *Moses*, as by a pædagogue, they would not be capable of accepting the doctrine of the superior master.

42. But I shall also offer, to the best of my ability, some expositions of the other words referred to; that is to say, I shall show that Jesus neither said nor did aught that was contrary to Moses. And first, as to the word, "An eye for an eye, and a tooth for a tooth,"[14] — that is *the expression of* justice. And as to His injunction, that a man, when struck on the one cheek, should offer the other also, that is *the expression of* goodness. Well, then, are justice and goodness opposed to each other? Far from it! There has only been an advance from simple justice to positive goodness. And again, we have the saying, "The workman is worthy of his hire."[15] But if a person seeks to practise any fraud therein, it is surely most just[16] that what he has got possession of by fraud should be required of him, most especially when the hire is large. Now this I say, that when the Egyptians afflicted the children of Israel by the taskmasters who were set over them in the process of making bricks, Moses required and exacted the whole at once, with penalties, within one moment of time. But is this, then, to be called iniquity? Far from it! Surely it is the absti-

---

[1] The Codex Bobiensis reads here, "accidit vero post tempus ut is qui . . . requireret," etc. The other codex has, "accedit vero post tempus is qui . . . requirere."
[2] Reading *pro respectu* with Codex Bobiensis. The other codex gives *prospectu*.
[3] Reading *invenisse*. The Codex Casinensis gives *venisse*.
[4] Routh suggests *pastor*, the shepherd, for *pater*.
[5] Reading *cognata*, with Codex Bobiensis, instead of *cognita*.
[6] Deut. xviii. 18.
[7] John v. 46.
[8] We adopt the reading *vides*, instead of the faulty *unde* of the Codex Casinensis.
[9] Reading *quamvis* for *quum*.
[10] See Heb. iii. 5, 6.

[11] Luke xvi. 19, etc.
[12] *Infernum.* [*Sheol*, rather, or *Hades*.]
[13] The reading of the Codex Casinensis is, "rogavit dives simul uno tempore ut edisceret majorem doctrinam." But the other codex gives, "uno tempore discere majorem doctrinam ab Abraham" = entreated that he might learn the superior doctrine of Abraham. For *edisceret* we may read with Routh *ediscerent*.
[14] Matt. v. 32.
[15] Matt. x. 10.
[16] The Codex Casinensis gives, "exige ab eo illa quæ fraudem interceperat;" the other codex gives, "et exigi ab eo illa quæ fraude interceperat." The correct reading probably would be, "exigi ab eo illa quæ per fraudem interceperat."

nence [1] of goodness, indeed, when one makes but a moderate use of what is really necessary, and gives up all that goes beyond that. Let us look, again, at the fact that in the Old Testament we find the words, " I make the rich man and the poor man," [2] whereas Jesus calls the poor blessed. [3] Well, in that saying Jesus did not refer to those who are poor simply in worldly substance, but to those who are poor in spirit, that is to say, who are not inflamed [4] with pride, but have the gentle and lowly dispositions of humility, not thinking of themselves more than they ought to think. [5] This question, however, is one which our adversary has not propounded correctly. For here I perceive that Jesus also looks on willingly at the gifts of the rich men, when they are put into the treasury. [6] All too little, at the same time, is it [7] if gifts are cast into [8] the treasury by the rich alone ; and so there are the two mites of the poor widow which are also received with gladness ; and in that offering verily something is exhibited that goes beyond what Moses prescribed on the subject of the receipt of moneys. For he received gifts from those who had ; but Jesus receives them even from those who have not. But this man says, further, that it is written, that " except a man shall forsake all that he hath, he cannot be my disciple." [9] Well, I observe again, that the centurion, a man exceedingly wealthy and well dowered with worldly influence, possessed a faith surpassing that of all Israel ; [10] so that, even if there was any one who had forsaken all, that man was surpassed in faith by this centurion. But some one may now reason with us thus : It is not a good thing, consequently, to give up riches. Well, I reply that it is a good thing for those who are capable of it ; but, at the same time, to employ [11] riches for the work of righteousness and mercy, is a thing as acceptable as though one were to give up the whole at once. Again, as to the assertion that the Sabbath has been abolished, we deny that He has abolished it plainly ; [12] for He was Himself also Lord of the Sabbath. [13] And this, *the law's relation to the Sabbath*, was like the servant who has

charge of the bridegroom's chamber, and who prepares the same with all carefulness, and does not suffer it to be disturbed or touched by any stranger, but keeps it intact against the time of the bridegroom's arrival ; so that when he is come, the same may be used as it pleases himself, or as it is granted to those to use it whom he has bidden enter along with him. And the Lord Jesus Christ Himself gave His testimony to what we affirm, when He said with His heavenly voice, " Can ye make the children of the bride-chamber fast so long as the bridegroom is with them ? " [14] And again, He did not actually reject circumcision ; but we should rather say that He received in Himself and in our stead the cause of circumcision, [15] relieving us by what He Himself endured, and not permitting us to have to suffer any pain to no purpose. [16] For what, indeed, can it profit a man to circumcise himself, if nevertheless he cherishes the worst of thoughts against his neighbour ? He desired, accordingly, rather to open up to us the ways of the fullest life by a brief path, [17] lest perchance, after we had traversed lengthened courses of our own, we should find our day prematurely closing upon us in night, and lest, while outwardly indeed we might appear splendid to men's view, we should inwardly be comparable only to ravening wolves, [18] or be likened to whited sepulchres. [19] For far above any person of that type of character is to be placed the man who, although clad only in squalid and threadbare attire, keeps no evil hidden in his heart against his neighbour. For it is only the circumcision of the heart that brings salvation ; and that merely carnal circumcision can be of no advantage to men, unless they happen also to be fortified with the spiritual circumcision. Listen also to what Scripture has to say on this subject : " Blessed are the pure in heart, for they shall see God." [20] What need, therefore, is there for me to labour *and suffer*, seeing that I have been made acquainted with the compendious way of life, [21] and know that it shall be mine if only I can be pure in heart? And that is quite in accordance with the truth which we have learned now, to wit, that if one prevails in the keeping of the two commandments, he fulfils the whole law and the prophets. [22] Moreover Paul, the chief of the apostles, after all these sayings, gives us yet clearer instruction on the subject, when he says, " Or seek ye a

---

[1] We adopt the conjecture of Valesius, viz., *abstinentia*. The Codex Bobiensis gives *absentia*.
[2] Prov. xxii. 2.
[3] Matt. v. 3.
[4] Reading *inflammantur*. It may perhaps be *inflantur* = puffed up.
[5] Rom. xii. 3.
[6] Mark xii. 41.
[7] Reading *et parum hoc est*, with Codex Bobiensis, instead of the *et pauperum hoc est* of Codex Casinensis. We may also render it as = " but it is far from being the case that gifts are cast," etc.
[8] The Codex Bobiensis reads *inferuntur ;* the other codex gives *offeruntur*, offered.
[9] Luke xiv. 33.
[10] Matt. viii 10.
[11] The text gives *sed abuti*, and the Codex Bobiensis has *sed et abuti*. But the reading ought probably to be *sed et uti*, or *sed etiam uti*. Routh, however, notices that *abutor* is found with the sense of *utor*.
[12] *Plane.*
[13] Matt. xii. 8.

[14] Mark ii. 19. [I have slightly accommodated the translation to this text.]
[15] *In semetipsum causam circumcisionis excepit.*
[16] [From Job (ii. 10) to St. Paul (Heb. iv. 15 and vi. to 8) Scripture abounds in this teaching. Comp. Lam. iii. 33.]
[17] The Codex Bobiensis gives, " viæ compendiosum nobis tramitem demonstrare." We adopt the reading, " viæ spatia compendioso nobis tramite demonstrare."
[18] Matt. vii. 15.
[19] Matt. xxiii. 27.
[20] Matt. v. 8.
[21] *Compendia viæ.*
[22] Matt. vii. 12.

proof of that Christ who speaketh in me?"[1] What have I then to do with circumcision, seeing that I may be justified in uncircumcision? For it is written : " Is any man circumcised? let him not become uncircumcised. Or is any in uncircumcision? let him not be circumcised. For neither of these is anything, but only the keeping of the commandments of God."[2] Consequently, as circumcision is incompetent to save any, it is not greatly to be required, especially when we see that if a man has been called in uncircumcision, and wishes then to be circumcised, he is made forthwith a transgressor[3] of the law. For if I am circumcised, I also fulfil the commandments of the law with the view of being in a position to be saved ; but if I am uncircumcised, and remain in uncircumcision, much more in keeping the commandments shall I have life. For I have received the circumcision of the heart, in the spirit, and not that of the letter in the mere ink,[4] in which former there is praise, not of men, but of God.[5] Wherefore let no charge of this kind be brought against me. For just as the man of wealth, who possesses great treasures of gold and silver, so that he gets everything which is necessary for the uses of his house made of these precious metals, has no need to display any vessel of earthenware in anything belonging to his family, and yet it does not follow from this circumstance that the productions of the potter, or the art of making vessels of pottery,[6] are to be held in abhorrence by him ; so also I, who have been made rich by the grace of God, and who have obtained the circumcision of the heart, cannot by any means[7] stand in need of that most profitless *fleshly* circumcision, and yet, for all that, it does not follow that I should call it evil. Far be it from me to do so ! If, however, any one desires to receive still more exact instruction on these matters, he will find them discussed with the greatest fulness in the apostle's first epistle.[8]

43. I shall speak now with the utmost brevity of the veil of Moses and the ministration of death. For I do not think that these things at least can introduce very much to the disparagement of the law. The text in question,[9] then, proceeds thus : " But if the ministration of death,

engraven[10] in letters on the stones, was made in glory, so that the children of Israel could not stedfastly behold the face of Moses for the glory of his countenance ; which glory was to be done away ; "[11] and so on. Well, this passage at any rate acknowledges the existence of a glory on the countenance of Moses, and that surely is a fact favourable to our position. And even although it is to be done away, and although there is a veil in the reading of the same, that does not annoy me or disturb me, provided there be glory in it still. Neither is it the case, that whatever is to be done away is reduced thereby under all manner of circumstances to a condition of dishonour.[12] For when the Scripture speaks of glory, it shows us also that it had cognizance[13] of differences in glory. Thus it says : " There is one glory of the sun, and another glory of the moon, and another glory of the stars : for one star differeth from another star in glory."[14] Although, then, the sun has a greater glory than the moon, it does not follow that the moon is thereby reduced to a condition of dishonour. And even thus, too, although my Lord Jesus Christ excelleth Moses in glory, as the lord excelleth the servant, it does not follow from this that the glory of Moses is to be scorned. For in this way, too, we are able to satisfy our hearers, as the nature of the word itself carries the conviction[15] with it, in that we affirm what we allege on the authority of the Scriptures themselves, or verily make the proof of our statements all the clearer also by illustrations taken from them. Thus, although a person kindles a lamp in the night-time, after the sun has once risen he has no further need of the paltry light of his lamp, on account of that effulgence of the sun which sends forth its rays all the world over ; and yet, for all that, the man does not throw his lamp contemptuously away, as if it were something absolutely antagonistic to the sun ; but rather, when he has once found out its use, he will keep it with all the greater carefulness. Precisely in this way, then, the law of Moses served as a sort of guardian to the people, like the lamp, until the true Sun, who is our Saviour, should arise, even as the apostle also says to us : " And Christ shall give thee light."[16] We must look, however, to what is said further on : " Their minds were blinded : for until this day remaineth the same veil in the reading of the Old Testament ; it is untaken away, because

---

[1] 2 Cor. xiii. 3.
[2] 1 Cor. vii. 18, 19.
[3] Reading " prævaricator " instead of " prædicator." The sense would seem strictly to require, *a debtor to the law.*
[4] *Atramentum.*
[5] Rom. ii. 29.
[6] The Codex Bobiensis gives, " figuli opus aufers aut fictilium." The Codex Casinensis has, " figuli opus et ars aut fictilium." We adopt " figuli opus aut ars fictilium."
[7] Adopting " nequaquam " for " nec quemquam."
[8] By this he means the Epistle to the Romans, to which the first place among the epistles of Paul was assigned from the most ancient times. In Epiphanius, under heresy 42, it is alleged as an offence against Marcion, that he put the Epistle to the Romans in the fourth place among Paul's epistles. See a note in Migne. [Again, this expression is a note of genuine antiquity.]
[9] Reading " propositus " for " propheticus."

[10] The Codex Casinensis has *formatum ;* the other codex gives *firmatum.*
[11] 2 Cor. iii. 7.
[12] The text gives, " neque vero omnigene in ignobilitatem redigitur," etc. The Codex Bobiensis has, " neque vero omni genere in nobilitate."
[13] Reading " scisse se differentias gloriæ," etc. Codex Bobiensis gives *scis esse,* etc. = *you know that there are differences.*
[14] 1 Cor. xv. 21.
[15] *Sicut et verbi ipsius natura persuadet.* Reading " natura *persuadet.*" But the Codex Bobiensis gives *demonstrat, demonstrates.*
[16] Eph. v. 14.

it is done away in Christ.[1] For even unto this day, when Moses is read, the veil is upon their heart. Nevertheless, when it shall turn to the Lord, the veil shall be taken away. Now the Lord is that Spirit."[2] What, then, is meant by this? Is Moses present with us even unto this day? Is it the case that he has never slept, that he has never gone to his rest, that he has never departed this life? How is it that this phrase "unto this day" is used here? Well, only mark the veil, which is placed, where he says it is placed, on their hearts in their reading. This, therefore, is the word of censure upon the children of Israel, because they read Moses and yet do not understand him, and refuse to turn to the Lord; for it is He that is prophesied of by Moses as about to come. This, then, is the veil which was placed upon the face of Moses,[3] and this also is his testament;[4] for he says in the law:[5] "A prince shall not be wanting from Judah, nor a leader from his thighs,[6] until He come whose he is;[7] and He will be the expectation of the nations: who shall bind[8] His foal unto the vine, and His ass's colt unto the choice vine; He shall wash His garments in wine, and His clothes in the blood of grapes; His eyes shall be suffused[9] with wine, and His teeth white with milk;" and so on. Moreover, he indicated who He was, and whence He was to come. For he said: "The Lord God will raise up unto you a Prophet from among your brethren, like unto me: unto Him hearken ye."[10] Now it is plain that this cannot be understood to have been said of Jesus the son of Nun.[11] For there is nothing of this circumcision[12] found in him. After him, too, there have still been kings from Judah; and consequently this prophecy is far from being applicable to him. And this is the veil which is on Moses; for it was not, as some among the unlearned perhaps fancy, any piece of linen cloth, or any skin that covered his face. But the apostle also takes care to make this plain to us, when he tells us that the veil is put on in the reading of the Old Testament, inasmuch as they who are called Israel from olden time still look for the coming of Christ, and perceive not that the princes have been wanting from Judah, and the leaders from his thighs; as even at present we see them in subjection to kings and princes, and paying tribute to these, without having any power left to them either of judgment or of punishment, such as Judah certainly had, for after he had condemned Thamar, he was able also to justify her.[13] "But you will also see your life hang (in doubt) before your eyes."[14]

44. Now this word also has the veil. For up to the time of Herod they did appear to retain a kingdom in some sort; and it was by Augustus that the first enrolment took place among them, and that they began to pay tribute, and to be rated.[15] Now it was also from the time when our Lord Jesus Christ began to be prophesied of and looked for that there began to be princes from Judah and leaders of the people; and these, again, failed just at the approach of His advent. If, then, the veil is taken away which is put on in that reading of theirs, they will understand the true virtue of the circumcision; and they will also discover that the generation of Him whom we preach, and His cross, and all the things that have happened in the history of our Lord, are those very matters which had been predicted of that Prophet. And I could wish, indeed, to examine every such passage of Scripture by itself, and to point out its import, as it is meet that it should be understood.[16] But as it is another subject that is now urgent, these passages shall be discussed by us at some season of leisure. For at present, what I have already said may be sufficient for the purpose of showing, that it is not without reason that the veil is (said to be) put upon the heart of certain persons in the reading of the Old Testament. But those who turn to the Lordsh all have the veil taken away from them. What precise force all these things, however, may possess, I leave to the apprehension of those who have sound intelligence. Let us come now again to that word of Moses, in which he says: "The Lord your God shall raise up a Prophet unto you, of your brethren, like unto me." In this saying I perceive a great prophecy delivered by the servant Moses, as by one cognizant[17] that He who is to

---

[1] *Non revelatur quia in Christo destruitur.*
[2] 2 Cor. iii. 14–17.
[3] Ex. xxxiv. 33; 2 Cor. iii. 13.
[4] The text is, " hoc est velamen, quod erat positum super faciem Moysi, quod est testamentum ejus," etc.
[5] Gen. xlix. 10–12.
[6] The reading in the text is, " non deficiet princeps ex Juda, neque dux de femoribus ejus usquequo veniat," etc. Codex Bobiensis coincides, only giving " de femore ejus." On the whole quotation, which is given in forms so diverse among the old versions and fathers, see Novatian, *De Trin.*, ch. 9 [vol. v. p. 618], and Cyprian, *Adv. Judæos*, i. 21 [vol. v. p. 513].
[7] The text gives, " veniat, cujus est," etc. Prudentius Maranus on Justin's *Apology*, i. § 32 [vol. i. p. 173, this series], thinks this was originally an error of transcription for *cui jus est*, which reading would correspond very much with the ᾧ ἀπόκειται of some of the most ancient authorities. See Cotelerius on the *Constitut. Apostol.*, i. 1, and the note in Migne.
[8] Qui alligabit. But Codex Casinensis has " quia alligabit," and Codex Bobiensis " qui alligavit."
[9] Suffusi oculi. Codex Bobiensis gives " effusi oculi." See, on the whole, Grabe's Dissert. *De variis vitiis LXX. interpret.*, 19, p. 36.
[10] Deut. xviii. 15.
[11] We adopt the reading " Jesu *Nave*." But the Codex Bobiensis gives " Jesu Mane." See a discussion on this name by Cotelerius on the Epistle of Barnabas, ch. 12. [Vol. i. p. 145, this series.]
[12] For *circumcisionis* Routh suggests *circumstationis*, which might perhaps be taken as = these surroundings do not suit him.

[13] Gen. xxxviii. 26. We read " justificare." But the Codex Casinensis gives " justificari" = *he* (or *she*) *could be justified*.
[14] The text is, " sed et videbitis vitam vestram pendentem ante oculos vestros." The reference is apparently to Deut. xxviii. 66.
[15] *Censum dare.*
[16] Reading " sermonem, et ostendere ut intelligi dignum est." The Codex Bobiensis gives a mutilated version: " sermonem, ut intelligi, dignum est."
[17] Reading " Moysi scientis," which is the emendation of Valesius. But Codex Casinensis gives " scientibus," and Codex Bobiensis has " scientes."

come is indeed to be possessed of greater authority than himself, and nevertheless is to suffer like things with him, and to show like signs and wonders. For there, Moses after his birth was placed by his mother in an ark, and exposed beside the banks of the river;[1] here, our Lord Jesus Christ, after His birth by Mary His mother, was sent off in flight into Egypt through the instrumentality of an angel.[2] There, Moses led forth his people from the midst of the Egyptians, and saved them;[3] and here, Jesus, leading forth His people from the midst of the Pharisees, transferred them to an eternal salvation.[4] There, Moses sought bread by prayer, and received it from heaven, in order that he might feed the people with it in the wilderness;[5] here, my Lord Jesus by His own power satisfied[6] with five loaves five thousand men in the wilderness.[7] There, Moses when he was tried was set upon the mountain and fasted forty days;[8] and here, my Lord Jesus was led by the Spirit into the wilderness when He was tempted of the devil, and fasted in like manner forty days.[9] There, before the sight of Moses, all the first-born of the Egyptians perished on account of the treachery of Pharaoh;[10] and here, at the time of the birth of Jesus, every male among the Jews suddenly perished by reason of the treachery of Herod.[11] There, Moses prayed that Pharaoh and his people might be spared the plagues;[12] and here, our Lord Jesus prayed that the Pharisees might be pardoned, when He said, "Father, forgive them, for they know not what they do."[13] There, the countenance of Moses shone with the glory of the Lord, so that the children of Israel could not stedfastly look upon his face, on account of the glory of his countenance;[14] and here, the Lord Jesus Christ shone like the sun,[15] and His disciples were not able to look upon His face by reason of the glory of His countenance and the intense splendour of the light. There, Moses smote down with the sword those who had set up the calf;[16] and here, the Lord Jesus said, "I came to send a sword upon the earth, and to set a man at variance with his neighbour,"[17] and so on. There, Moses went without fear into the darkness of the clouds that carry water;[18] and here, the Lord Jesus walked

with all power upon the waters.[19] There, Moses gave his commands to the sea;[20] and here, the Lord Jesus, when he was on the sea,[21] rose and gave His commands to the winds and the sea.[22] There, Moses, when he was assailed, stretched forth his hands and fought against Amalek;[23] and here, the Lord Jesus, when we were assailed and were perishing by the violence of that erring spirit who works now in the just,[24] stretched forth His hands upon the cross, and gave us salvation. But there are indeed many other matters of this kind which I must pass by, my dearly beloved Diodorus, as I am in haste to send you this little book with all convenient speed; and these omissions of mine you will be able yourself to supply very easily by your own intelligence. Write me, however, an account of all that this servant of the adversary's cause may do hereafter. May the Omnipotent[25] God preserve you whole in soul and in spirit!

45. On receipt of this letter, Diodorus made himself master of its contents, and then entered the lists against Manes. This he did too with such spirit, that he was commended greatly by all for the careful and satisfactory demonstration which he gave of the fact that there is a mutual relationship between the two testaments, and also between the two laws.[26] Discovering also more arguments for himself, he was able to bring forward many points of great pertinency and power against the man, and in defence of the truth. He also reasoned in a conclusive manner against his opponent on verbal grounds.[27] For example, he argued with him in the following manner: — Did you say that the testaments are two? Well, then, say either that there are two old testaments, or that there are two new testaments. For you assert that there are two unbegottens[28] belonging to the same time, or rather eternity; and if there are in this way two, there should be either two old testaments or two new testaments. If, however, you do not allow this, but affirm, on the contrary, that there is one old testament and that there is also another new testament, that will only prove again that there is but one author for both; and the very sequence will show that the Old Testament belongs to Him to whom also the New Testament pertains. We may illustrate this by the case of a man who

[1] Ex. ii.
[2] Matt. ii. 13.
[3] Ex. xiv.
[4] Mark viii. 15.
[5] Ex. xvi.
[6] Adopting "satiavit." The Codex Bobiensis gives "saturavit."
[7] Matt. xiv.
[8] Ex. xxxiv.
[9] Matt. iv. 2.
[10] Ex. xii.
[11] Matt. ii. 16.
[12] Ex. viii.
[13] Luke xxiii. 34.
[14] Ex. xxxiv. 35.
[15] Matt. xvii. 2.
[16] Ex. xxxii.
[17] Matt. x. 34.
[18] Ex. xxiv. 18.

[19] Matt. xiv. 25.
[20] Ex. xiv.
[21] Reading "in mari." But the Codex Bobiensis has *in navi* = on a ship.
[22] Matt. viii. 26.
[23] Ex. xvii.
[24] The text gives *in justis*. But the Codex Bobiensis has *in istis* = in those men. The true reading may be *in injustis* = in the unrighteous. See Eph ii. 2.
[25] But the Codex Casinensis gives "Deus omnium" = the God of all.
[26] [See p. 215, *supra*.]
[27] Ex nominibus. The Codex Bobiensis offers the extraordinary reading, *ex navibus*.
[28] *Ingenita*.

says to some other individual,[1] Lease me your old house. For by such a mode of address does he not pronounce the man to be also the owner of a new house? Or, on the other hand, if he says to him, Show me[2] your new house; does he not by that very word designate him also as the possessor of an old house? Then, again, this also is to be considered, that since there are two beings, having an unbegotten nature, it is also necessary from that to suppose each of them to have (what must be called) an old testament, and thus there will appear to be two old testaments; if indeed you affirm that both these beings are ancient, and both indeed without a beginning.[3] But I have not learned doctrine like that; neither do the Scriptures contain it. You, however, who allege that the law of Moses comes from the prince of evil, and not from the good God, tell me who those were who withstood Moses to the face — I mean Jamnes and Mambres?[4] For every object that withstands, withstands not itself, but some other one, either better or worse; as Paul also gives us to understand when he writes in the following terms in his second Epistle to Timothy: "As Jamnes and Mambres withstood Moses, so have these also resisted the truth: men of corrupt mind, reprobate concerning the faith. But they shall proceed no further: for their folly is manifest unto all men, as theirs also was."[5] Do you observe how he compares Jamnes and Mambres to men of corrupt mind, and reprobate concerning the faith; while he likens Moses, on the other hand, to the truth? But the holy John, the greatest of the evangelists, also tells us of the giving and diffusing of grace for grace;[6] for he indicates, indeed, that we have received the law of Moses out of the fulness of Christ, and he means that for that one grace this other grace has been made perfect in us through Jesus Christ. It was also to show this to be the case that our Lord Jesus Christ Himself spake in these terms: "Do not think that I will accuse you to the Father: there is one that accuseth you, even Moses, in whom ye hope. For had ye believed Moses, ye would indeed have believed me: for he wrote of me. But if ye believe not his writings, how shall ye believe my words?"[7] And besides all these words, there are still many other passages that might be adduced both from the Apostle Paul and from the Gospels, by which we are able to prove that the old law belongs to no other one than that Lord to whom also the new testament appertains, and which it would suit us very well to set forth, and to make use of in a satisfactory manner.[8] Now, however, the evening prevents us from doing so; for the day is drawing to its close, and it is right that we should now bring our disputation to an end. But an opportunity will be given you to-morrow to put questions to us on any points you are pleased to take up. And after these words they went their way.[9]

46. Next morning, however, Archelaus suddenly made his appearance at this residence[10] in which Diodorus was staying, before any one was yet stirring abroad. Manes accordingly, all unconscious of the fact that Archelaus was now on the spot again, challenged Diodorus publicly to engage in a disputation with him; his intention being to crush him with a verbal display, because he perceived that he was a man of a simple nature, and not very deeply learned in questions concerning the Scriptures. For he had now had a taste of the doctrine of Archelaus. When, therefore, the multitudes had again collected in the place usually set apart for the disputation, and when Manes had just begun to reason, all on a sudden Archelaus appeared among them, and embraced Diodorus, and saluted him with an holy kiss. Then truly were Diodorus, and all those who were present, filled with wonder at the dispensation of divine providence which thus provided that Archelaus should arrive among them at the very time when the question was *just* raised; for in reality, as must be confessed, Diodorus, with all his religiousness, had been somewhat afraid of the conflict. But when Manes caught sight of Archelaus, he at once drew back from his insulting attitude; and with his pride cast down not a little, he made it quite plain that he would gladly flee from the contest. The multitude of hearers, however, looked upon the arrival of Archelaus as something like the advent of an apostle, because he had shown himself so thoroughly furnished, and so prompt and ready for a defence *of the truth* by speech. Accordingly, after demanding silence from the people by a wave of his right hand, — *for no inconsiderable tumult had arisen*, — Archelaus began an address in the following terms: — Although some amongst us have gained the honour of wisdom and the meed of glory, yet this I beg of you, that you retain *in your minds* the testimony of those things which have been said before my arrival.[11]

---

[1] We read, with the Codex Bobiensis, "dicat homini, Loca mihi," etc. The Codex Casinensis has the meaningless reading, "homini diviti," etc.

[2] *Præsta.*

[3] The text of this obscure passage runs thus: "Quia ex quo duo sunt, ingenitam habentes naturam, ex eo necesse est etiam habere unumquemque ipsorum vetus Testamentum. et fient duo vetera Testamenta; si tamen ambos antiquos et sine initio esse dicis." The Codex Bobiensis gives a briefer but evidently corrupt reading: "ex quo duo sunt ingenita habentes naturam ipsorum Testamentum, et fient," etc.

[4] *Jamnem dico et Mambrem.* [So in *Vulg.*, except "Jannes."]

[5] 2 Tim. iii. 8, 9.

[6] *Gratiam gratia præstare et differre.* John i. 16.

[7] John v. 45-47.

[8] The Codex Bobiensis gives, "exponere et a Patre ut convenit." For these meaningless words Valesius proposed to read, "exponere et aperire ut convenit." The Codex Casinensis, however, offers the satisfactory reading, "exponere et aptare convenit."

[9] Here ends the section edited by Valesius.

[10] *Castellum.* [Note, *infra*, the "holy kiss."]

[11] The text runs: "tametsi prudentiam, gloriam etiam, nostrorum nonnulli assecuti sunt, tamen hoc vos deprecor ut eorum quæ ante me dicta sunt, testimonium reservetis." Routh suggests *prudentia* = Although by their prudence some have gained glory, etc.

For I know and am certain, brethren, that I now take the place of Diodorus, not on account of any impossibilities attaching to him,[1] but because I came to know this person here at a previous time, when he made his way with his wicked designs into the parts where I reside, by the favour of Marcellus,[2] that man of illustrious name, whom he endeavoured to turn aside from our doctrine and faith, with the object, to wit, of making him an effective supporter of this impious teaching. Nevertheless, in spite of all his plausible addresses, he failed to move him or turn him aside from the faith in any one particular. For this most devout Marcellus was only found to be like the rock on which the house was built with the most solid foundations; and when the rain descended, and the floods and the winds burst in and beat upon that house, it stood firm: for it had been built on the most solid and immoveable foundations.[3] And the attempt thus made by this person who is now before you, brought dishonour rather than glory upon himself. Moreover, it does not seem to me that he can be very excusable if he proves to be ignorant of what is in the future; for surely he ought to know beforehand those who are on his own side: certainly he should have this measure of knowledge, if it be true indeed that the Spirit of the Paraclete dwells in him. But inasmuch as he is really a person blinded with the darkness of ignorance, he ran in vain when he journeyed to Marcellus, and he did but show himself to be like the stargazer,[4] who busies himself with describing things celestial, while all the time he is ignorant of what is passing in his own home. But lest it should appear as if I were setting aside the question in hand by speaking in this strain, I shall now refrain from such discourse. And I shall also give this man the privilege of taking up any point which may suit him best as a commencement to any treatment of the subject and the question. And to you, as I have said already, I only address the request that ye be impartial judges, so as to give to him who speaks the truth the proper honour and the palm.

47. Then Manes, after silence had been secured among all, thus began his address: Like others, Archelaus, you too smite me with the most injurious words, notwithstanding that my sentiments on the subject of God are correct, and that I hold also a proper conception of Christ; and yet the family of the apostles is rather of the character that bears all things and endures all things, even although a man may assail them with revilings and curses. If it is your intention to persecute me, I am prepared for it; and if you wish to involve me in punishment, I shall not shrink from it; yea, if you mean even to put me to death, I am not afraid: "For we ought to fear Him only who is able to destroy both soul and body in hell."[5] Archelaus said: Far be that from me! Not such is my intention. For what have you ever had to suffer at my hands, or at the hands of those who think with us, even when you were disparaging us and doing us injury, and when you were speaking in detraction of the traditions of our fathers, and when it was your aim to work the death of the souls of men that were well established in the truth, and that were kept with the most conscientious carefulness; for which, in truth, the whole wealth of the world would not serve as a sufficient compensation?[6] Nevertheless, what ground have you for assuming this position? What have you to show? Tell us this, — what signs of salvation have you to bring before us? For the bare bravado of words will not avail to satisfy the multitude here present, neither will it be enough to qualify them for recognising which of us holds the knowledge of the truth the more correctly. Wherefore, as you have got the opportunity of speaking first, tell us first to what particular head of the subject you wish us to direct the disputation. Manes said: If you do not offer a second time an unfair resistance to the positions which shall be stated with all due propriety by us, I shall speak with you; but if you mean to show yourself still in the character which on a former occasion I perceived you to take up, I shall address myself to Diodorus, and shall keep clear of your turbulence. Archelaus said: I have already expressed my opinion that we shall be simply abusing the occasion by the mere bandying of empty words. If any one on our side is found to offer an unfair resistance, leave that to the decision of the judges. But now, tell us what you have got to advance. Manes said: If you do not mean a second time merely to gainsay the positions which are stated with all due correctness by me, I shall begin. Archelaus said: "If not this," and "if not that," are ways of speaking which mark out an ignorant man. You are ignorant, therefore, of what is in the future. But as to this particular thing which you do declare to be still future, to gainsay or not to gainsay is a matter in my own power. How, then, will that argument about the two trees stand, in which you place your trust as in a buckler of the most approved strength? For if I am of the contrary side, how do you require my obedience? And if, on the other hand, there

---

[1] *Pro ipsius impossibilitate.* But Routh suggests that the *impossibilitate* is just an inexact translation of the ἀδυνατία = *impotentia,* incapacity, which may have stood in the Greek text.
[2] Reading "Marcelli viri illustris gratia." The Codex Casinensis has, "viri in legis gratia."
[3] Matt. vii. 24.
[4] The text gives "similis facere astrologo," for which Routh proposes "similis factus est," etc.

[5] Matt. x. 28.
[6] The text is, "quibus utique *repensari* non possunt," etc Routh proposes *repensare.*

is in me the disposition of obedience, how are you so greatly alarmed lest I should gainsay you? For you maintain that evil remains evil always, and that good remains good always, in utter ignorance of the force of your words. *Manes said:* Have I employed you as the advocate of my words, so that you may determine also the intelligence that may suit my knowledge? And how will you be able to explain what belongs to another person, when you cannot make what pertains to yourself clear? But if Diodorus now admits himself to be vanquished, my reasonings will then be addressed to you. If, however, he still stands out, and is prepared to speak, I beg you to give over and cease from interfering with the substantiating of the truth. For you are a strange sheep; nevertheless hereafter you will be introduced into the number of the same flock, as the voice of Jesus[1] also intimates, — that Jesus, namely, who appeared in the form of man indeed, and yet was not a man. *Archelaus said:* Are you not, then, of opinion that He was born of the Virgin Mary? *Manes said:* God forbid that I should admit that our Lord Jesus Christ came down to us through the natural womb of a woman! For He gives us His own testimony that He came down from the Father's bosom;[2] and again He says, "He that receiveth me, receiveth Him that sent me;"[3] and. "I came not to do mine own will, but the will of Him that sent me;"[4] and once more, "I am not sent but unto the lost sheep of the house of Israel."[5] And there are also innumerable other passages of a similar import, which point Him out as one that *came*, and not as one that was *born*. But if you are greater than He, and if you know better than He what is true, how do we yet believe Him? *Archelaus said:* Neither am I greater than He, for I am His servant; nor can I be even the equal of my Lord, for I am His unprofitable servant; I am a disciple of His words, and I believe those things which have been spoken by Him, and I affirm that they are unchangeable. *Manes said:* A certain person somewhat like you once said to Him, "Mary Thy mother, and Thy brethren, stand without;"[6] and He took not the word kindly, but rebuked the person who had uttered it, saying, "Who is my mother, and who are my brethren?" And He showed that those who did His will were both His mothers and His brethren. If you, however, mean to say that Mary was actually His mother, you place yourself in a position of considerable peril. For, without any doubt, it would be proved on the

same principles that He had brethren also by her. Now tell me whether these brethren were begotten by Joseph or by the same Holy Spirit. For if you say that they were begotten by the same Holy Spirit, it will follow that we have had many Christs. And if you say that these were not begotten by the same Holy Spirit, and yet aver that He had brethren, then without doubt we shall be under the necessity of understanding that, in succession to the Spirit and after Gabriel, the most pure and spotless virgin[7] formed an actual marriage connection with Joseph. But if this is also a thing altogether absurd — I mean the supposition that she had any manner of intercourse with Joseph — tell me whether then He had brethren. Are you thus to fix the crime of adultery also on her, most sagacious Marcellus?[8] But if none of these suppositions suits the position of the Virgin undefiled, how will you make it out that He had brothers? And if you are unable to prove clearly to us that He had brethren, will it be any the easier for you to prove Mary to be His mother, in accordance with the saying of him who ventured to write,[9] "Behold, Thy mother and Thy brethren stand without?" Yet, although that man was bold enough to address Him thus, no one can be mightier or greater than this same person Himself who shows us His mother or His brethren. Nay, He does not deign even to hear it said that He is David's son.[10] The Apostle Peter, however, the most eminent of all the disciples, was able to acknowledge Him on that occasion, when all were putting forth the several opinions which they entertained respecting Him: for he said, "Thou art the Christ, the Son of the living God;"[11] and immediately He names him blessed, addressing him thus: "For my heavenly Father hath revealed it unto thee." Observe what a difference there is between these two words which were spoken by Jesus. For to him who had said, "Behold, Thy mother stands without," He replied, "Who is my mother, or who are my brethren?" But to him who said, "Thou art the Christ, the Son of the living God," He makes the return of a beatitude and benediction. Consequently, if you will have it that He was born of Mary, then it follows that no less than Peter, He is Himself thus proved to have spoken falsely. But if, on the other hand, Peter states what is true, then without doubt that former person was in error. And if the former was in error, the matter is to be referred back to the

---

[1] Reading "sicut vox Jesu." The Codex Casinensis gives, "sicut vos Jesu." Routh suggests *servator*.
[2] John i. 18, iii. 13.
[3] Matt. x. 40.
[4] John vi. 38.
[5] Matt. xv. 24.
[6] Matt. xii. 47.

[7] The text gives, "Virgo castissima et immaculata ecclesia," = the most pure virgin and spotless church. But the word "ecclesia" is probably an erroneous addition by the hand of the scribe. Or, as Routh hints, there may be an allusion, in the word *ecclesia*, to the beginning of the twelfth chapter of the Apocalypse. [See Pearson, *On the Creed*, art. iii. p. 290.]
[8] From this it may perhaps be gathered that Marcellus had now come along with Archelaus to the residence of Diodorus.
[9] *Scribere* ausus est. Compare (note 1) p. 224, *infra*.
[10] Matt. xxii. 42. We read *Davidis esse* for *David Jesse*.
[11] Matt. xvi. 16.

writer.[1] We know, therefore, that there is one Christ, according to the Apostle Paul, whose words, as in consonance at least[2] with His advent, we believe.

48. On hearing these statements, the multitudes assembled were greatly moved, as if they felt that these reasonings gave the correct account of the truth, and that Archelaus could have nothing to urge against them ; for this was indicated by the commotion which arose among them. But when the crowd of auditors became quiet again, Archelaus made answer in the following manner : No one, truly, shall ever be able to prove himself mightier than the voice of our Lord Jesus Christ, neither is there found any name equal to His, as it is written : "Wherefore God hath exalted Him, and given Him a name which is above every name."[3] Nor, again, in the matter of testimony can any one ever be equal to Him ; and accordingly I shall simply adduce the testimonies of His own voice in answer to you, — first of all, indeed, with the view of solving those difficulties which have been enunciated by you, so that you may not say, as is your wont to do, that these are matters which are not in harmony with the Person Himself.[4] Now, you maintain that the man who brought the word to Jesus about His mother and His brethren was rebuked by Him as if he was in error, as the writer was in error.[5] Well, I affirm that neither was this person rebuked who brought Him the message about His mother and His brethren, nor was Peter only named blessed above him ; but each of these two parties received from Him the answer that was properly called forth by their several utterances, as the discourse will demonstrate in what follows. When one is a child, he thinks as a child, he speaks as a child ; but when he becomes a mature man, those things are to be done away which are proper for a child :[6] in other words, when one reaches forth unto those things which are before, he will forget those which are behind.[7] Hence, when our Lord Jesus Christ was engaged in teaching and healing the race of men, so that all pertaining to it might not utterly perish together, and when the minds of all those who were listening to Him were intently occupied with these interests, it made an interruption altogether inopportune when this messenger came in and put Him in mind of His mother and His brethren. What then? Ought He, now,[8] yourself being

judge,[9] to have left those whom He was healing and instructing, and gone to speak with His mother and His brethren? Would you not by such a supposition at once lower the character of the Person Himself? When, again, He chose certain men who were laden and burdened with sins for the honour of discipleship,[10] to the number of twelve, whom He also named His apostles, He gave them this injunction, Leave father and mother, that you may be made worthy of me ;[11] intending by this that thenceforward the memory of father or mother should no more impair the stedfastness of their heart. And on another occasion, when a different individual chose to say to Him, "I will go and bury my father," He answered, "Let the dead bury their dead."[12] Behold, then, how my Lord Jesus Christ edifies His disciples unto all things necessary, and delivers His sacred words to every one, in due accordance with what is meet for him. And just in the same way, too, on this other occasion, when a certain person came in with the inconsiderate message about His mother, He did not embrace the occurrence as an opportunity for leaving His Father's commission unattended to even for the sake of having His mother with Him. But in order to show you still more clearly that this is the real account of the matter, let me remind you that Peter, on a certain season, subsequent to the time of his receiving that declaration of blessedness from Him, said to Jesus, "Be it far from Thee, Lord :[13] this shall not be unto Thee."[14] This he said after Jesus had announced to him that the Son of man must go up to Jerusalem, and be killed, and rise again the third day.[15] And in answer then to Peter He said : "Get thee behind me, Satan ; for thou savourest not the things that be of God, but those that be of men."[16] Now, since it is your opinion that the man who brought the message about His mother and His brethren was rebuked by Jesus, and that he who said a little before, "Thou art the Christ, the Son of the living God," obtained the word of blessing, mark you that Jesus (may be said to have) rather preferred that person to whom He condescended to give the more gracious and indulgent answer ; whereas Peter, even after that benediction, now got no appellation expressive of indulgence addressed to him, by reason of his having failed carefully to observe the nature of the announcement that

---

[1] The text gives, "Quod si prior fefellit, causa ad scriptorem rejicienda est." [i.e., to the copyist; in this case the *corrupter.*]
[2] *Consonantibus duntaxat.*
[3] Phil. ii. 9.
[4] *Sibi ipsi.*
[5] *Secundum id quod scriptorem fefellit.* [i.e, on that supposition.]
[6] 1 Cor. xiii. 11.
[7] Phil. iii. 13.
[8] Reading "debuitne etiam" for the bad version of the Codex Casinensis, "debuit et etiam."

[9] The text gives, "*se* ipso judicante," for which "*te* ipso," etc., may be substituted.
[10] In the Codex Casinensis the sentence stands in this evidently corrupt form : "cum enim peccatis bonus et gravatus ad discipulatum diligit." We adopt the emendation given in Migne : "cum enim peccatis onustos et gravatos ad discipulatum delegit."
[11] Matt. x. 37.
[12] Luke ix. 59, 60.
[13] *Propitius esto, Domine.*
[14] Matt. xvi. 22. [Possibly the first words by which Satan fell.]
[15] Matt. xvi. 21.
[16] Matt. xvi. 23. [Satan seems to have rebelled against man's creation.]

was made to him. For the error of that messenger was at once corrected by the tenor of the reply; but the dulness of this apostle's apprehension was condemned with a severer rebuke. And from this you may perceive that the Lord Jesus, observing what was proper and opportune with regard to the interrogations thus addressed to Him, gave to each the reply that was worthy of it, and suited to it. But supposing that, as you say, Peter was pronounced blessed on the ground of his having said what was true, and that that messenger was reproved on account of the error he committed, tell me then why it is, that when the devils confessed Him, and said, "We know Thee, who Thou art, the holy God,"[1] He rebuked them, and commanded them to be silent?[2] Why was it not the case, if He does indeed take pleasure in the testimonies borne to Him by those who confess Him, that He recompensed them also with benedictions, as He did to Peter when he gave utterance to the truth? But if that would be an absurd supposition, it only remains that we must understand the words spoken by Him always in accordance with the place, the time, the persons, the subjects, and the due consideration of the circumstances.[3] For only this method will save us from falling into the error of pronouncing rashly on His sayings, and thus making ourselves liable to merited chastisement: and this will also help me to make it more and more intelligible to you, that the man who brought the tidings of His mother was much rather the person honoured.[4] However, in forgetfulness of the subject which was proposed to us for discussion, you have turned off to a different theme. Nevertheless listen to me for a brief space. For if you choose, indeed, to consider those words somewhat more carefully, we shall find that the Lord Jesus displayed great clemency in the case of the former of these two parties; and this I shall prove to you by illustrations suited to your capacity. A certain king who had taken up arms, and gone forth to meet an enemy, was earnestly considering and planning how he might subdue those hostile and foreign forces. And when his mind was occupied with many cares and anxieties, after he had forced his way among his adversaries, and when, further, as he began afterwards to make captives of them, the anxious thought was now also pressing upon him as to how he might secure the safety and interests of those who had toiled with him, and borne the burden of the war,[5] a

certain messenger broke inopportunely in upon him, and began to remind him of domestic matters. But he was astonished at the man's boldness, and at his unseasonable suggestions, and thought of delivering such a fellow over to death. And had that messenger not been one who was able to appeal to his tenderest affections in bringing the news that it was well with those at home, and that all went on prosperously and successfully there, that punishment might have been his instant and well-merited doom. For what else should be a king's care, so long as the time of war endures, than to provide for the safety of the people of his province, and to look after military matters? And even thus it also was that that messenger came inopportunely in upon my Lord Jesus Christ, and brought the report about His mother and His brethren unseasonably, just when He was fighting against ills which had assailed the very citadel of the heart, and when He was healing those who for a long time had been under the power of diverse infirmities, and when He had now put forth His utmost effort to secure the salvation of all. And truly that man might have met with a sentence like that pronounced on Peter, or even one severer still. But the hearing of the name of His mother and His brethren drew forth His clemency.

49. But in addition to all that has been said already, I wish to adduce still further proof, so that all may understand what impiety is contained in this assertion of yours. For if your allegation is true, that He was not born, then it will follow undoubtedly that He did not suffer; for it is not possible for one to suffer who was not also born. But if He did not suffer, then the name of the cross is done away with. And if the cross was not endured, then Jesus did not rise from the dead. And if Jesus rose not from the dead, then no other person will rise again. And if no one shall rise again, then there will be no judgment. For it is certain that, if I am not to rise again, I cannot be judged. But if there is to be no judgment, then the keeping of God's commandments will be to no purpose, and there will be no occasion for abstinence: nay, we may say, "Let us eat and drink, for to-morrow we shall die."[6] For all these consequences follow when you deny that He was born of Mary. But if you acknowledge that He was born of Mary, then His passion will necessarily follow, and His resurrection will be consequent on His passion, and the judgment on His resurrection: and thus the injunctions of Scripture will have their proper value[7] for us. This is not therefore an idle question, but there are the mightiest issues involved in this word. For just as all the law and the prophets are summed up in two words, so also all our hope

---

[1] Luke iv. 34, reading *sanctus Deus*. [i.e., not the received text.]
[2] Reading *silere*. The Codex Casinensis gives *sinire*, which may be meant for *sinere* = give over.
[3] *Pro accidentium salute.*
[4] We have adopted Migne's arrangement of these clauses. Routh, however, puts them thus: *And that it may be made more intelligible to you*, etc., . . . (*for in forgetfulness*, etc., *you have turned off*, etc.), *listen to me now for a brief space.*
[5] Reading "pondus belli toleraverant," instead of the "pondus bellico tolerarant" of the Codex Casinensis.

[6] 1 Cor. xv. 32.
[7] *Salva.*

is made to depend on the birth by the blessed Mary. Give me therefore an answer to these several questions which I shall address to you. How shall we get rid of these many words of the apostle, so important and so precise, which are expressed in terms like the following : " But when the good pleasure of God was with us, He sent His Son, made of a woman ; "[1] and again, " Christ our passover is sacrificed for us ; "[2] and once more, " God hath both raised up the Lord, and will raise up us together with Him by His own power?"[3] And there are many other passages of a similar import ; as, for example, this which follows : " How say some among you,[4] that there is no resurrection of the dead? For if there be no resurrection of the dead, then is not Christ risen : and if Christ be not risen, then is our preaching vain. Yea, and we shall be found false witnesses of God ; who have testified against God that He raised up Christ : whom He raised not up. For if the dead rise not, then is not Christ risen : and if Christ be not raised, your[5] faith is vain ; ye are yet in your sins : Then they also which are fallen asleep in Christ are perished. If in this life only we have hope in Christ, we are more miserable than all men. But now is Christ risen from the dead, the beginning[6] of them that sleep ; "[7] and so on. Who, then, I ask, can be found so rash and audacious as not to make his faith fit in with these sacred words, in which there is no qualification[8] nor any dubiety? Who, I ask you, O foolish Galatian, has bewitched you, as those were bewitched " before whose eyes Jesus Christ was evidently set forth, crucified?"[9] From all this I think that these testimonies should suffice in proof of the judgment, and the resurrection, and the passion ; and the birth by Mary is also shown to be involved naturally and at once in these facts. And what matters it though you refuse to acquiesce in this, when the Scripture proclaims the fact most unmistakeably? Nevertheless I shall again put a question to you, and let it please you to give me an answer. When Jesus gave His testimony concerning John, and said, " Among them that are born of women there hath not risen a greater than John the Baptist : notwithstanding,

he that is less[10] in the kingdom of heaven is greater than he,"[11] tell me what is meant by there being a greater than he in the kingdom of heaven. Was Jesus less in the kingdom of heaven than John? I say, God forbid ! Tell me, then, how this is to be explained, and you will certainly surpass yourself. Without doubt *the meaning is, that* Jesus was less than John among those that are born of woman ; but in the kingdom of heaven He is greater than he.[12] Wherefore tell me this too, O Manichæus : If you say that Christ was not born of Mary, but that He only appeared like a man, while yet He was not really a man, the appearance being effected and produced by the power that is in Him, tell me, I repeat, on whom then was it that the Spirit descended like a dove? Who is this that was baptized by John? If He was perfect, if He was the Son, if He was the Power, the Spirit could not have entered into Him ;[13] just as a kingdom cannot enter within a kingdom. And whose, too, was that voice which was sent forth out of heaven, and which gave Him this testimony, " This is my beloved Son, in whom I am well pleased?"[14] Come, tell me ; make no delay ; who is this that acquires[15] all these things, that does all these things? Answer me : Will you thus audaciously adduce blasphemy for reason, and will you attempt to find a place for it?[16]

50. *Manes said :* No one, certainly, who may be able to give a reply to what has just been alleged by you, need fear incurring the guilt of blasphemy, but should rather be deemed thoroughly worthy of all commendation. For a true master of his art,[17] when any matters are brought under his notice, ought to prepare his reply with due care, and make all clearly to understand the points that are in question or under doubt ; and most especially ought he to do so to uninstructed persons. Now since the account of our doctrine does not satisfy you, be pleased, like a thorough master of your art, to solve this question also for me in a reasonable manner. For to me it seems but pious to say that the Son of God stood in need of nothing whatsoever in the

---

[1] Gal. iv. 4. The reading is, " cum autem fuit Dei voluntas in nobis." The Vulgate, following the ordinary Greek text, gives, " at ubi venit plenitudo temporis." And so Irenæus, Tertullian, Cyprian, etc. [This should have been in the margin of the Revised Version.]
[2] 1 Cor. v. 7.
[3] 1 Cor. vi. 14. The text here inserts the words *cum illo,* which are found neither in the Greek, nor in the Vulgate, nor in Irenæus, *Adv. Hæres.,* v. 6, 7 [vol. i. pp. 530, 532, this series], nor in Tertullian, *Adv. Marc.,* v. 7, etc. [vol. iii. p. 443, this series]. According to Sabatier, however, they are found in Jerome, *Ep. ad Amand.*
[4] Reading *in vobis.* But the Codex Casinensis seems to give *in nobis,* amongst us.
[5] But the Codex Casinensis seems to make it *fides nostra,* our faith.
[6] *Initium.*
[7] 1 Cor. xv. 12-20.
[8] *Distinctio.*
[9] Gal. iii. 1. The word in the text is *rescriptus est.* The Vulgate gives *præscriptus est.* The Vetus Itala gives *proscriptus est.*

[10] *Minor.*
[11] Matt. xi. 11.
[12] It would seem that Archelaus read the passage in Matthew as meaning, *notwithstanding, he that is less, is, in the kingdom of heaven, greater than he.* Thus, *he that is less* is understood to be *Jesus* in His natural relations. [A very lean and hungry *proculdubio* of the author.]
[13] Routh appends a note here which may be given. It is to this effect: I am afraid that Archelaus has not expressed with sufficient correctness the mystery of the Divine Incarnation, in this passage as well as in what follows; although elsewhere he has taught that the Lord Jesus was conceived by divine power, and in ch. xxxiv. has called the Virgin Mary *Dei genetrix,* Θεοτόκος. For at the time of the Saviour's baptism the Holy Spirit was not given in His first communication with the Word of God (which Word, indeed, had been united with the human nature from the time of the conception itself), but was only received by the Christ ἀνθρωπίνως and οἰκονομικῶς, and for the sake of men. See Cyril of Alexandria, *De Recta Fide,* xxxiv. vol. v. 2, p. 153, *editio Auberti.* [Routh, *R.S.,* vol. v. p. 178.]
[14] Matt. iii. 17.
[15] *Parat.*
[16] *Inferre coneris.*
[17] *Artifex.*

way of making good His advent upon earth; and that He in no sense required either the dove, or baptism, or mother, or brethren, or even may hap a father, — which father, however, according to your view, was Joseph; but that He descended altogether by Himself alone, and transformed Himself, according to His own good pleasure, into *the semblance of* a man, in accordance with that word of Paul which tells us that " He was found in fashion as a man."[1] Show me, therefore, what thing He could possibly need who was able to transform Himself into all manner of appearances. For when He chose to do so, He again transformed this human fashion[2] and mien into the likeness of the sun. But if you gainsay me once more, and decline to acknowledge that I state the faith correctly, listen to my definition of the position in which you stand. For if you say that He was only man *as born* of Mary,[3] and that He received the Spirit at His baptism, it will follow that He will be made out to be Son by increase[4] and not by nature. If, however, I grant you to say that He is Son according to increase,[5] and that He was made as a man, your opinion is that He is really a man, that is to say, one who is flesh and blood.[6] But then it will necessarily follow that the Spirit also who appeared like a dove was nothing else than a natural dove. For the two expressions are the same, — namely, " as a man " and " like[7] a dove ; " and consequently whatever may be the view you take of the one passage which uses the phrase " as a man," you ought to hold that same view[8] also of this other passage in which the expression " like a dove " is used. It is a clear matter of necessity to take these things in the same way, for only thus can we find out the real sense of what is written concerning Him in the Scriptures. *Archelaus said:* As you cannot do so much for yourself, like a thorough master of your art, so neither should I care to put this question right and with all patience to make it clear, and to give the evident solution of the difficulty,[9] were it not for the sake of those who are present with us, and who listen to us. For this reason, therefore, I shall also explain the answer that ought to be given to this question as it may be done most appropriately. It does not seem to you, then, to be a pious thing to say that Jesus had a mother in Mary;

and you hold a similar view on certain other positions which you have now been discussing in terms which I, for my part, altogether shrink from repeating.[10] Now, sometimes a master of any art happens to be compelled by the ignorance of an opponent both to say and to do things which time would *make him* decline;[11] and accordingly, because the necessity is laid upon me, by consideration for the multitude present, I may give a brief answer to those statements which have been made so erroneously by you. Let us suppose, now, your allegation to be, that if we understand Jesus to be a man made of Mary after the course of nature, and regard him consequently as having flesh and blood, it will be necessary also to hold that the Holy Spirit was a real dove, and not a spirit. Well, then, how can a real dove enter into a real man, and abide in him? For flesh cannot enter into flesh. Nay rather, it is only when we acknowledge Jesus to be a true man, and also hold him who is there said to be like a dove to be the Holy Spirit, that we shall give the correct account according to reason on both sides. For, according to right reason, *it may be said that* the Spirit dwells in a man, and descends upon him, and abides in him ; and these, indeed, are things which have happened already in all due competence, and the occurrence of which is always possible still, as even you yourself *admit, inasmuch as you* did aforetime profess to be the Paraclete of God, you flint,[12] as I may call you, and no man, so often forgetful of the very things which you assert. For you declared that the Spirit whom Jesus promised to send has come upon you ; and whence can He come but by descending from Heaven? And if the Spirit descends thus on the man worthy of Him, then verily must we fancy that real doves descended upon you? Then truly should we rather discover in you the thieving dove-merchant,[13] who lays snares and lines for the birds. For surely you well deserve to be made a jest of with words of ridicule. However, I spare you, lest perchance I appear to offend the auditors by such expressions, and also most especially because it is beside my purpose to throw out against you all that you deserve to hear said about you. But let me return to the proper subject. For I am mindful of that transformation of thine,[14] in virtue of which you say that God has transformed

---

1 Phil. ii. 7.
2 *Hominem.*
3 *Hominem eum tantummodo ex Maria.*
4 Or, effect, *per profectum.*
5 Effect. [i.e., progressively.]
6 Routh puts this interrogatively = Is it then your position that He really is a man, that is to say, one who is flesh and blood? Well, but if so, then it will follow, etc.
7 Or, *as.*
8 Reading " sicut homo, hac opinione," for the " sicut homo ac opinione " of the Codex Casinensis.
9 The Codex Casinensis reads, " hanc quæstionem diffigenter aptare tam manifestarem atque manifeste dissolverem." We follow the emendation, " hanc quæstionem diligenter aptatam manifestarem," etc.

10 [A *signum verecundiæ* which rebukes the awful inquisitiveness concerning the conception of Mary which disgraced the late pontiff, Pius IX. To what blasphemous pruriency of thought and expression has not such an invasion of decency given rise! See St. Bernard, *Opp.*, tom. i. p. 392. He rebukes the heresy as profane.]
11 The text gives *tempus recusat.* Routh proposes *tempus requirit* = which the occasion requires.
12 This is a purely conjectural reading, " ut dicam silex," etc. The Codex Casinensis gives, " ut dicam dilere non homo." But Routh, in reference to ch. xv., throws out the idea that we should read *delire* = thou dotard, or, lunatic. [P. 190, *supra*, as if Manes = μανικὸς.]
13 *Columbarium furem.*
14 The text gives *suæ.* Routh suggests *tuæ.*

Himself into *the fashion of* a man or *into that of* the sun, by which position you think to prove that our Jesus was made man only in fashion and in appearance ; which assertion may God save any of the faithful from making. Now, for the rest, that opinion of yours would reduce the whole matter to a dream, so far as we are concerned, and to mere figures ; and not that only,[1] but the very name of an advent would be done away : for He might have done what He desired to do, though still seated in heaven, if He is, as you say, a spirit, and not a true man. But it is not thus that " He humbled Himself, and took the form of a servant ; "[2] and I say this of Him who was made man of Mary. For what? Might not we, too, have set forth things like those with which you have been dealing, and that, too, all the more easily and the more broadly? But far be it from us to swerve one jot or one tittle from the truth. For He who was born of Mary is the Son, who chose of His own accord to sustain this[3] mighty conflict, — namely, Jesus. This is the Christ of God, who descended upon him who is of Mary. If, however, you refuse to believe even the voice that was heard from heaven, all that you can bring forward in place of the same is but some rashness of your own ; and though you were to declare yourself on that, no one would believe you. For forthwith Jesus was led by the Spirit into the wilderness to be tempted by the devil ; and as the devil had no correct knowledge of Him, he said to Him, " If thou be the Son of God."[4]   Besides, he did not understand the reason of this bearing of the Son of God *by Mary*, who preached the kingdom of heaven, whose was also indeed a great tabernacle,[5] and one that could not have been prepared by any other :[6] whence, too, He who was nailed to the cross, on rising again from the dead, was taken up thither where Christ the Son of God reigned ; so that when He begins to conduct His judgment, those who have been ignorant of Him shall look on Him whom they pierced.[7] But in order to secure your credence, I propose this question to you : Why was it, that although His disciples sojourned a whole year with Him, not one of them fell prostrate on his face before Him, as you were saying a little ago, save only in that one hour when His countenance shone

like the sun? Was it not by reason of that tabernacle which had been made *for Him* of Mary? For just as no other had the capacity sufficient for sustaining the burden of the Paraclete except only the disciples and the blessed Paul, so also no other was able to bear the Spirit who descended from heaven, and through whom that voice of the Father gave its testimony in these terms, " This is my beloved Son,"[8] save only He who was born of Mary, and who is above all the saints, — namely, Jesus. But now give us your answer to those matters which I bring forward against you. If you hold that He is man only in mien and form, how could He have been laid hold of and dragged off to judgment by those who were born of man and woman — to wit, the Pharisees — seeing that a spiritual body cannot be grasped by bodies of grosser capacities? But if you, who as yet have made no reply to the arguments brought before you, have now any kind of answer to offer to the word and proposition I have adduced, proceed, I pray you, and fetch me at least a handful or some fair modicum of your sunlight.[9] But that very sun, indeed, inasmuch as it is possessed of a more subtle body, is capable of covering and enveloping you ; while you, on the other hand, can do it no injury, even although you were to trample it under foot. My Lord Jesus, however, if He was laid hold of, was laid hold of as a man by men. If He is not a man, neither was He laid hold of. If He was not laid hold of, neither did He suffer, nor was He baptized. If He was not baptized, neither is any of us baptized. But if there is no baptism, neither will there be any remission of sins, but every man will die in his own sins. *Manes said :* Is baptism, then, given on account of the remission of sins ? *Archelaus said :* Certainly. *Manes said :* Does it not follow, then, that Christ has sinned, seeing that He has been baptized? *Archelaus said :* God forbid ! Nay, rather, He was made sin for us, taking on Him our sins.[10] For this reason He was born of a woman, and for this reason also He approached the rite of baptism, in order that He might receive the purification of this part,[11] and that thus the body which He had taken to Himself might be capable of bearing the Spirit, who had descended in the form of a dove.

51. When Archelaus had finished this speech, the crowds of people marvelled at the truth of his doctrine, and expressed their vehement commendations of the man with loud outcries, so that they exerted themselves most energetically, and would have kept him from his return.[12]   There-

---

[1] The text is, " non solum autem, sed adventus nomen delebitur." It may perhaps be = and not the foundation, but the name, of an advent would be done away.

[2] Phil. ii. 7.

[3] The text gives " *quo* magnum," etc., for which we adopt " *quod* magnum," etc.

[4] Matt. iv. 3.

[5] Or perhaps, = which was also, *quod erat tabernaculum*, etc.

[6] The Codex Casinensis gives, " Ignorabat autem propter qui genuisset Filium Dei prædicabat regnum cœlorum, qui erat," etc. We follow generally the emendations adopted in Migne: " Ignorabat autem propter quid genuisset Filium Dei, qui prædicabat regnum cœlorum, quod erat habitaculum magnum," etc. Routh would read " genitus esset Filius Dei," etc.

[7] John xix. 37.

[8] Matt. iii. 17.

[9] *Pugillum plenum solis mihi affer aut modium plenum.*

[10] 2 Cor. v. 21.

[11] *Partis.*

[12] The text is, " et ultra ei non sinerent ad propria remeare." Routh suggests *ultro* for *ultra*.

after, however, they withdrew. After some time, again, when they were gathered together, Archelaus persuaded them to accede to his desire, and listen quietly to the word. And among his auditors were not only those who were with Diodorus, but also all who were present from his province and from the neighbouring districts. When silence, then, was secured, Archelaus proceeded to speak to them of Manes in the following manner: You have heard, indeed, what is the character of the doctrine which we teach, and you have got some proof of our faith; for I have expounded the Scriptures before you all, precisely in accordance with the views which I myself have been able to reach in studying them. But I entreat you now to listen to me in all silence, while I speak with the utmost possible brevity, with the view of giving you to understand who this person is who has made his appearance among us, and whence he comes, and what character he has, exactly as a certain man of the name of Sisinius, one [1] of his comrades, has indicated the facts to me; which individual [2] I am also prepared, if it please you, to summon in evidence of the statements I am about to make. And, in truth, this person did not decline to affirm the very same facts which we now adduce,[3] even when Manes was present; for the above-mentioned individual became a believer of our doctrine, as did also another person who was with me, named Turbo. Accordingly, all that these parties have conveyed in their testimony to me, and also all that we ourselves have discovered in the man, I shall not suffer to be kept back from your cognizance.

Then, indeed, the multitudes became all the more excited, and crowded together to listen to Archelaus; for, in good sooth, the statements which were made by him offered them the greatest enjoyment. Accordingly, they earnestly urged him to tell them all that he pleased, and all that he had on his mind; and they declared themselves ready to listen to him there and then, and engaged to stay on even to the evening, and until the lights should be lit.

Stimulated therefore by their heartiness, Archelaus began his address with all confidence in the following terms:— My brethren, you have heard, indeed, the primary causes [4] relating to my Lord Jesus,— I mean those which are decided out of the law and the prophets; and of the subsidiary causes also relating to my Lord Jesus Christ, our Saviour, you are not ignorant. And why should I say more? From the loving desire for the Saviour we have been called Christians, as the

whole world itself attests, and as the apostles also plainly declare. Yea, further, that best master-builder of His, Paul himself,[5] has laid our foundation,[6] that is, the foundation of the Church, and has put us in trust of the law, ordaining ministers, and presbyters,[7] and bishops in the same, and describing in the places severally assigned to that purpose, in what manner and with what character the ministers of God ought to conduct themselves, of what repute the presbyters ought to be possessed, and how they should be constituted, and what manner of persons those also ought to be who desire the office of bishop.[8] And all these institutions, which were once settled well and rightly for us, preserve their proper standing and order with us to this day, and the regular administration of these rules abides amongst us still. But as to this fellow, Manes by name, who has at present burst boastfully forth upon us from the province of Persia, and between whom and me a disputation has now for the second time been stirred, I shall tell you about his lineage, and that, too, in all fulness; and I shall also show you most lucidly the source from which his doctrine has descended. This man is neither the first nor the only originator of this type of doctrine. But a certain person belonging to Scythia, bearing the name Scythianus,[9] and living in the time of the apostles, was the founder and leader of this sect, just as many other apostates have constituted themselves founders and leaders, who from time to time, through the ambitious desire of arrogating positions of superior importance to themselves, have given out falsehoods for the truth, and have perverted the simpler class of people to their own lustful appetencies, on whose names and treacheries, however, time does not permit us at present to descant. This Scythianus, then, was the person who introduced this self-contradictory dualism; and for that, too, he was himself indebted to Pythagoras, as also all the other followers of this dogma have been, who all uphold the notion of a dualism, and turn aside from the direct course of Scripture: but they shall not gain any further success therein.

52. No one, however, has ever made such an unblushing advance in the promulgation of these tenets as this Scythianus. For he introduced the notion of a feud between the two unbegottens, and all those other fancies which are the consequences of a position of that kind. This Scythianus himself belonged to the stock of

[1] Reading *unus*, instead of " *vos*, comitibus," etc.
[2] Reading " quem etiam " instead of "quæ etiam."
[3] The Codex Casinensis gives, " ipse quidem me dicere recusavit," etc. We adopt the correction in Migne, " sed ne ipse quidem dicere recusavit," etc.
[4] *Superiores quidem causas Domini*, etc.

[5] Reading " sed et optimus architectus ejus, fundamentum," etc. The Codex Casinensis has the corrupt lection, " sed et optimos architectos ei fundamentum," etc. [Had this been said of Peter?]
[6] Cf. 1 Cor. iii. 10. [Had this been said of Peter, what then?]
[7] Cf. Acts xiv. 23.
[8] Cf. 1 Tim. iii. 1. [Clement, cap. xliv., vol. 1. p. 17, this series.]
[9] Various other forms are found for this name Scythianus. Thus we find Scutianus and Excutianus,—forms which may have arisen through mere clerical errors. The Codex Reg. Alex. Vat. gives Stutianus. [But see Routh, *R.S.*, vol. v. p. 186.]

the Saracens, and took as his wife a certain captive from the Upper Thebaid, who persuaded him to dwell in Egypt rather than in the deserts. And would that he had never been received by that province, in which, as he dwelt in it for a period, he found the opportunity for learning the wisdom of the Egyptians![1] for, to speak truth, he was a person of very decided talent, and also of very liberal means, as those who knew him, have likewise testified in accounts transmitted to us. Moreover, he had a certain disciple named Terebinthus,[2] who wrote four books for him. To the first of these books he gave the title of the *Mysteries*, to the second that of the *Heads*,[3] to the third that of the *Gospel*, and to the last of all that of the *Treasury*.[4] He had these four books, and this one disciple whose name was Terebinthus. As, then, these two persons had determined to reside alone by themselves for a considerable period, Scythianus thought of making an excursion into Judea, with the purpose of meeting with all those who had a reputation there as teachers ; but it came to pass that he suddenly departed this life soon after that, without having been able to accomplish anything. That disciple, moreover, who had sojourned with him had to flee,[5] and made his way toward Babylonia, a province which at present is held[6] by the Persians, and which is distant now a journey of about six days and nights from our parts. On arriving there, Terebinthus succeeded in giving currency to a wonderful account of himself, declaring that he was replete with all the wisdom of the Egyptians, and that he was really named now, not Terebinthus, but another Buddas,[7] and that this designation had been put upon him. He asserted further that he was the son of a certain virgin, and that he had been brought up by an angel[8]

on the mountains. A certain prophet, however, of the name of Parcus, and Labdacus the son of Mithras,[9] charged[10] him with falsehood, and day after day unceasingly they had keen and elevated contentions[11] on this subject. But why should I speak of that at length? Although he was often reproved, he continued, nevertheless, to make declarations to them on matters which were antecedent to the world,[12] and on the sphere, and the two luminaries ; and also on the question whither and in what manner the souls depart, and in what mode they return again into the bodies ; and he made many other assertions of this nature, and others even worse than these, — as, for instance, that war was raised with God among the elements,[13] that the prophet himself might be believed. However, as he was hard pressed for assertions like these, he betook himself to a certain widow, along with his four books : for he had attached to himself no disciple in that same locality, with the single exception of an old woman who became an intimate of his.[14] Then,[15] on a subsequent occasion, at the earliest dawn one morning, he went up to the top[16] of a certain house, and there began to invoke certain names, which Turbo has told us only the seven elect have learned. He ascended to the housetop, then, with the purpose of engaging in some religious ceremony, or some art of his own ; and he went up alone, so as not to be detected by any one :[17] for he considered that, if he was convicted of playing false with, or holding of little account, the religious beliefs of the people, he would be liable to be punished by the real princes of the country. And as he was revolving these things then in his mind, God in His perfect justice decreed that he should be thrust beneath earth by a spirit ;[18] and forthwith he was cast down from the roof of the house ; and his body, being precipitated lifeless to the ground, was taken up in pity by the old woman mentioned above, and was buried in the wonted place of sepulture.

53. After this event all the effects which he had brought with him from Egypt remained in her possession. And she rejoiced greatly over his death, and that for two reasons : first, because she did not regard his arts with satisfaction ; and secondly, because she had obtained such an in-

---

[1] This seems the general idea meant to be conveyed. The text, which is evidently corrupt, runs thus: " in qua cum eum habitaret, cum Ægyptiorum sapientiam didicisset." The Codex Reg. Alex. Vat. reads, " in qua cum habitaret et Ægyptiorum," etc. In Migne it is proposed to fill up the lacunæ thus: " in qua cum diu habitaret, depravatus est, cum Egyptiorum sapientiam didicisset." Routh suggests, " in qua cum ea habitaret," etc.

[2] The Codex Casinensis reads *Terbonem* for *Terebinthum*. But in Cyril of Jerusalem, in his *Catechesis*, 6, as well as in others, we regularly find Τερβύνθον, *Terbinthum*, or *Terebinthum*, given as the name of the disciple of Scythianus. The form *Terebentus* is also given; and the Codex Reg. Alex. Vat. has *Terybeneus*. The statement made here as to these books being written by Terebinthus is not in accordance with statements made by Cyril and others, who seem to recognise Scythianus alone as the author. As to the name Terebinthus itself, C. Ritter, in his *Die Stupa's*, etc., p. 29, thinks that it is a Græcized form of a predicate of Buddha, viz., *Tere-hintu*, Lord of the Hindoos. Others take it simply to be a translation of the Hebrew אֵלָה, the *terebinth*. See a note on this subject in Neander's *Church Hist.*, ii. 166 (Bohn). [Routh, *ut supra*, p. 187.]

[3] *Capitulorum.*

[4] *Thesaurus.*

[5] The Codex Reg. Alex. Vat. inserts here, " omnibus quæcunque ejus fuerant congregatis " = gathering together all that was his.

[6] Reading " habetur." But Codex Reg. Alex. Vat. gives *habitatur*, is inhabited.

[7] The Codex Casinensis gives, " sed aliud cujusdam homine." We adopt " sed alium Buddam nomine," with which the narratives of Cyril, Epiphanius, and others agree. Routh proposes " alio Buddam nomine " = by another name, Buddas. [Buddha is a *title*, not a name.]

[8] The text gives " natum esse, simul et ab angelo." The Codex Reg. Alex. Vat. reads, " natum se esse simulabat et ab angelo."

[9] On these Persian priests, see Epiphanius on this heresy, num. 3.

[10] Reading *arguebant*, with Routh, for *arguebat*.

[11] *Animosa exaggeratio.*

[12] *Ante seculum.*

[13] Or, in the origins of things, *in principiis.*

[14] *Particeps ejus.*

[15] Reading *tunc* for *nunc.*

[16] *Solarium quoddam excelsum.*

[17] The Codex Casinensis gives, " ut inde ab aliquo convinci possit." But the Codex Reg. Alex. Vat. reads, " ut ne ab aliquo," etc. We adopt, therefore, " ne ab aliquo," etc., taking the idea to be, as is suggested in Migne, that Manes went up alone, because he feared that, if observed by Parcus and Labdacus, the priests of Mithras, they might expose himself to punishment at the hands of the Persian rulers for an offence against their religion. [*Manes* here seems put for Terebinthus.]

[18] *Sub terras eum detrudi per spiritum.*

heritance, for it was one of great value.[1] But as she was all alone, she bethought herself of having some one to attend her; and she got for that purpose a boy of about seven years of age, named Corbicius,[2] to whom she at once gave his freedom, and whom she also instructed in letters. When this boy had reached his twelfth year the old woman died, and left to him all her possessions, and among other things those four books which Scythianus had written, each of them consisting of a moderate number of lines.[3] When his mistress was once buried, Corbicius began to make his own use of all the property that had been left him. Abandoning the old locality, he took up his abode in the middle of the city, where the king of Persia had his residence; and there altering his name, he called himself Manes instead of Corbicius, or, to speak more correctly, not Manes, but Mani:[4] for that is the kind of inflection employed in the Persian language. Now, when this boy had grown to be a man of well-nigh sixty years of age,[5] he had acquired great erudition in all the branches of learning taught in those parts, and I might almost say that in these he surpassed all others. Nevertheless he had been a still more diligent student of the doctrines contained in these four books; and he had also gained three disciples, whose names were Thomas, Addas, and Hermas. Then, too, he took these books, and transcribed[6] them in such wise that he introduced into them much new matter which was simply his own, and which can be likened only to old wives' fables. Those three disciples, then, he thus had attached to him as conscious participants in his evil counsels; and he gave, moreover, his own name to the books, and deleted the name of their former owner, as if he had composed them all by himself. Then it seemed good to him to send his disciples, with the doctrines which he had committed to writing in the books, into the upper districts of that province, and through various cities and villages, with the view of securing followers. Thomas accordingly determined to take possession of the regions of Egypt, and Addas those of Scythia, while Hermas alone chose to remain with the man himself. When these, then, had set out on their course, the king's son was seized with a certain sickness; and as the king was very anxious to see him cured, he published a decree offering a large reward, and engaging to bestow it upon any one who should

prove himself capable of restoring the prince.[7] On the report of this, *all at haphazard*, like the men who are accustomed to play the game of cubes, which is another name for the dice,[8] Manes presented himself before the king, declaring that he would cure the boy. And when the king heard that, he received him courteously, and welcomed him heartily. But not utterly to weary my hearers with the recital of the many things which he did, let me simply say that the boy died, or rather was bereft of life, in his hands. Then the king ordered Manes to be thrust into prison, and to be loaded with chains of iron weighing half a hundredweight.[9] Moreover, those two disciples of his who had been sent to inculcate his doctrine among the different cities were also sought for with a view to punishment. But they took to flight, without ever ceasing,[10] however, to introduce into the various localities which they visited that teaching of theirs which is so alien to the faith, and which has been inspired only by Antichrist.

54. But after these events they returned to their master, and reported what had befallen them; and at the same time they got an account of the numerous ills which had overtaken him. When, therefore, they got access to him, as I was saying,[11] they called his attention to all the sufferings they had had to endure in each several region; and as for the rest, they urged it upon him that regard ought now to be had to the question of safety;[12] for they had been in great terror lest any of the miseries which were inflicted on him should fall to their own lot. But he counselled them to fear nothing, and rose to harangue them. And then, while he lay in prison, he ordered them to procure copies of the books of the law of the Christians; for these disciples who had been despatched by him through the different communities were held in execration by all men, and most of all by those with whom the name of Christians was an object of honour. Accordingly, on receiving a small supply of money, they took their departure for those districts in which the books of the Christians were published;[13] and pretending that they were Christian messengers,[14] they requested that the books might be shown them, with a view to their

---

[1] But the Codex Reg. Alex. Vat. reads, "erat enim multum pecuniæ arida"—for she had a great greed for money.

[2] But Cyril, Epiphanius, and others, make the name Cubricus (Κούβρικος).

[3] *Versuum*.

[4] This may express with sufficient nearness the original, "nec Manem sed Manes."

[5] The Codex Casinensis gives *sexaginta* regularly. The Codex Reg. Alex. Vat. reads *septuaginta*, seventy.

[6] *Transfert* eos. It may be also "translated them."

[7] The text gives, "edictum proposuit in vita," etc. For *in vita* it is proposed to read *invitans;* and that is confirmed by the Codex Reg. Alex. Vat.

[8] We adopt the reading, "qui cubum, quod nomen est tali, ludere solent." The text gives, qui cibum quod nomen est tale eludere solent." The Codex Reg. Alex Vat. seems to read, "qui cubum quod nomen est aleæ ludere solent."

[9] *Ferri talento*.

[10] The text gives, "quique fugientes licet nunquam cessarunt," etc. Codex Reg. Alex. Vat. has, "licet nunquam cessarent" etc.

[11] Reading "dicebam." But the Codex Casinensis gives "dicebant," and the Codex Reg. Alex. Vat. has "decebat"—as became them.

[12] Reading "converti ad salutem," for "conventi," etc., as it is given in the Codex Casinensis.

[13] *Conscribebantur*. [Note this concerning the Christian books.]

[14] Nuntios. But Codex Reg. Alex. Vat. gives "novitios," novices.

acquiring copies. And, not to make a lengthened narrative of this, they thus got possession of all the books of our Scriptures, and brought them back with them to their master, who was still in prison. On receiving these copies, that astute personage set himself to seek out all the statements in our books that seemed to favour his notion of a dualism; which, however, was not really his notion, but rather that of Scythianus, who had promulgated it a long time before him. And just as he did in disputing with me, so then too, by rejecting some things and altering others in our Scriptures, he tried to make out that they advanced his own doctrines, only that the name of Christ was attached to them there. That name, therefore, he pretended on this account to assume to himself, in order that the people in the various communities, hearing the holy and divine name of Christ, might have no temptation to execrate and harass[1] those disciples of his. Moreover, when they[2] came upon the word which is given us in our Scriptures touching the Paraclete, he took it into his head that he himself might be that Paraclete; for he had not read with sufficient care to observe that the Paraclete had come already, — namely, at the time when the apostles were still upon earth. Accordingly, when he had made up these impious inventions, he sent his disciples also to proclaim these fictions and errors with all boldness, and to make these false and novel words known in every quarter. But when the king of Persia learned this fact, he prepared to inflict condign punishment upon him. Manes, however, received information of the king's intention, having been warned of it in sleep, and made his escape out of prison, and succeeding in taking to flight, for he had bribed his keepers with a very large sum of money. Afterwards he took up his residence in the castle of Arabion; and from that place he sent by the hand of Turbo the letter which he wrote to our Marcellus, in which letter he intimated his intention of visiting him. On his arrival there, a contest took place between him and me, resembling the disputation which you have observed and listened to here; in which discussion we sought to show, as far as it was in our power, that he was a false prophet. I may add, that the keeper of the prison who had let him escape was punished, and that the king gave orders that the man should be sought for and apprehended wherever he might be found. And as these things have come under my own cognizance, it was needful that I should also make the fact known to you, that search is being made for this fellow even to the present day by the king of Persia.

55. On hearing this, the multitude wished to seize Manes and hand him over to the power of those foreigners who were their neighbours, and who dwelt beyond the river Stranga,[3] especially as also some time before this certain parties had come to seek him out; who, however, had to take their leave again without finding any trace of him, for at that time he was in flight. However, when Archelaus made this declaration, Manes at once took to flight, and succeeded in making his escape good before any one followed in pursuit of him. For the people were detained by the narrative which was given by Archelaus, whom they heard with great pleasure;[4] nevertheless some of them did follow in close pursuit after him. But he made again for the roads by which he had come, and crossed the river, and effected his return to the castle of Arabion.[5] There, however, he was afterwards apprehended and brought before the king, who, being inflamed with the strongest indignation against him, and fired with the desire of avenging two deaths upon him, — namely, the death of his own son, and the death of the keeper of the prison, — gave orders that he should be flayed and hung before the gate of the city, and that his skin should be dipped in certain medicaments and inflated; his flesh, too, he commanded to be given as a prey to the birds.[6] When these things came under the knowledge of Archelaus at a later period, he added *an account of* them to the former discussion, so that all the facts might be made known to all, even as I, who have written[7] the narrative of[8] these matters, have explained the circumstances in what precedes. And all the Christians, therefore, having assembled, resolved that the decision should be given against him, transmitting that as a sort of epilogue to his death which would be in proper consonance with the other circumstances of his life. Besides that, Archelaus added words to the following effect: — My brethren, let none of you be incredulous in regard to the statements made by me: I refer to the assertion that Manes was not himself the first author of this impious dogma, but that it was only made public by him in certain regions of the earth. For assuredly that man is not at once to be reckoned the author of anything who has simply been the bearer of it to some quarter or other, but only he has a right to that credit who has been the discoverer of it. For as the helmsman who receives the

---

[1] The text gives "fatigarent." But Codex Reg. Alex. Vat. gives "fugarent" — expel.
[2] The text gives "invenientes." The Codex Reg. Alex. Vat. more correctly has "inveniens" — when he came upon.

[3] But Codex Reg. Alex. Vat. reads "*Stracum* fluvium."
[4] The text gives, "evadere potuit dum nemo eum insequeretur. Sed populus, cum Archelai quem libenter audiebant relatione tenerentur," etc. The Codex Reg. Alex. Vat. reads, "evadere potuit dum ne eum insequeretur is populus, et Archelai quem libenter audiebant relatione tenerentur." Routh suggests, "dum eum nemo insequeretur, sed populus Archelai," etc.
[5] The same Codex Vat. reads Adrabion here.
[6] The Codex Reg. Alex. Vat. ends with these words.
[7] [See p. 177, *supra*. A fair discussion as to authenticity.]
[8] *Inscripsi.*

ship which another has built, may convey it to any countries he pleases, and yet he remains one who has had nothing to do with the construction of the vessel, so also is this man's position to be understood. For he did not impart its origin to this matter really from the beginning ; but he was only the means of transmitting to men what had been discovered by another, as we know on the evidence of trustworthy testimonies, on the ground of which it has been our purpose to prove to you that the invention of this wickedness did not come from Manes,[1] but that it originated with another, and that other indeed a foreigner, who appeared a long time before him. And further, that the dogma remained unpublished for a time, until at length the doctrines which had thus been lying in obscurity for a certain period were brought forward publicly by him as if they were his own, the title of the writer having been deleted, as I have shown above. Among the Persians there was also a certain promulgator of similar tenets, one Basilides,[2] of more ancient date, who lived no long time after the period of our apostles. This man was of a shrewd disposition himself, and as he observed that at that time all other subjects were preoccupied, he determined to affirm that same dualism which was maintained also by Scythianus. And as, in fine, he had nothing to advance which was properly his own, he brought the sayings of others before his adversaries.[3] And all his books contain some matters at once difficult and extremely harsh. The thirteenth book of his *Tractates*, however, is still extant, which begins in the following manner : " In writing the thirteenth

book of our *Tractates*, the wholesome word furnished us with the necessary and fruitful word."[4] Then he illustrates how it, *the antagonism between good and evil*, is produced under the figures of a rich principle and a poor principle, of which the latter is by nature without root and without place, and only supervenes upon things.[5] This is the only topic[6] which the book contains. Does it not then contain a strange[7] word ;[8] and, as certain parties have been thus minded, will ye not also all be offended with the book itself, which has such a beginning as this? · But Basilides, returning to the subject after an introduction of some five hundred lines,[9] more or less, proceeds thus : " Give up this vain and curious variation,[10] and let us rather find out what inquiries the foreigners[11] have instituted on the subject of good and evil, and what opinions they have been led to adopt on all these subjects. For certain among them have maintained that there are for all things two beginnings,[12] to which they have referred good and evil, holding that these beginnings are without beginning and ungenerate ; that is to say, that in the origins of things there were light and darkness, which existed of themselves, and which were not merely declared to exist.[13] While these subsisted by themselves, they led each its own proper mode of life, such as it was its will to lead, and such as was competent to it ; for in the case of all things, what is proper to any one is also in amity with the same, and nothing seems evil to itself. But after they came to know each other, and after the darkness began to contemplate the light, then, as if fired with a passion for something superior to itself, the darkness pressed on to have intercourse with the light."

[1] Codex Casinensis reads, " non ex Manen originem mali hujus Manes esse." We adopt the conjecture, " non ex Mane originem mali hujus manasse."
[2] The following note on this Basilides may be given from Migne :—Although Eusebius (*Hist. Eccles.*, iv. 7) tells us that the Basilides who taught heresy shortly after the times of the apostles was an Alexandrian, and opened schools of error in Egypt, the Basilides mentioned here by Archelaus may still be one and the same person with that Alexandrian, notwithstanding that it is said that he taught his heresy among the Persians. For it may very well be the case that Basilides left Alexandria, and made an attempt to infect the Persians also with his heretical dogmas. At the same time, there is no mention among ancient authorities, so far as I know, of a Persian Basilides. The Alexandrian Basilides also wrote twenty-four books on the Gospel, as the same Eusebius testifies; and these do not appear to be different from those books of *Tractates* which Archelaus cites, and from the *Exegetics*, from the twenty-third book of which certain passages are given by Clement of Alexandria in the fourth book of his *Stromateis*. It is not clear, however, whether that Gospel on which Basilides wrote was the Gospel of the Apostles, or another which he made up for himself, and of which mention is made in Origen's first Homily on Luke, in Jerome's prologue to his Commentary on Matthew, and in Ambrose's prologue to the Gospel of Luke." We may add that Gieseler (*Studien und Kritiken*, i. 1830, p. 397) denies that the person meant here is Basilides the Gnostic, specially on account of the peculiar designation, *Basilides quidam antiquior*. But his objections are combated by Baur and Neander. See the *Church History* of the latter, ii. p. 50, ed. Bohn.
[3] The text is, " aliis dictis proposuit adversariis." Perhaps we may read, " aliorum dicta," etc.

[4] The text is, " necessarium sermonem uberemque salutaris sermo præstavit." May it be = the word of salvation furnished the word which was requisite, etc.?
[5] The text is, " per parvulam divitis et pauperis naturam sine radice et sine loco rebus supervenientem unde pullulaverit indicat." The reading seems defective. But the general intention of this very obscure and fragmentary sentence appears to be as given above. So Neander understands it as conveying a figurative description of the two principles of light and darkness, expressed in the Zoroastrian doctrine immediately cited, — the rich being the good principle, and the poor the evil. He also supposes the phrase " without root and without place " to indicate the " absoluteness of the principle, that springs up all at once, and mixes itself up with the development of existence." — See *Church History*, ii. 51 (Bohn). Routh confesses his inability to understand what can be meant by the term *parvulam*, and suggests *parabolam*.
[6] *Caput*.
[7] *Alium*.
[8] Routh adopts the interrogative form here, so as to make the connection stand thus: But is this the only topic which the book contains? Does it not also contain another discussion, etc.?
[9] *Versibus*.
[10] *Varietate*.
[11] By the *barbari* here are evidently meant the Persians.
[12] Principles.
[13] The text is, " non quæ esse dicebantur." Routh proposes, " non quæ factæ, or genitæ, esse dicebantur," = which were not declared to have been made.

A FRAGMENT OF THE SAME DISPUTATION.[1]

The fragment is introduced by Cyril in the following terms : — He, i.e., *Manes*, fled from prison and came into Mesopotamia ; but there he was met by that buckler of righteousness,[2] Bishop Archelaus. And in order to bring him to the test in the presence of philosophical judges, this person convened an assembly of Grecian auditors, so as to preclude the possibility of its being alleged that the judges were partial, as might have been the case had they been Christians. *Then the matter proceeded as we shall now indicate :* —

1. Archelaus said to Manes : Give us a statement now of the doctrines you promulgate. — Thereupon the man, whose mouth was like an open sepulchre,[3] began at once with a word of blasphemy against the Maker of all things, saying : The God of the Old Testament is the inventor of evil, who speaks thus of Himself : " I am a consuming fire."[4] — But the sagacious Archelaus completely undid this blasphemy. For he said : If the God of the Old Testament, according to your allegation, calls Himself a fire, whose son is He who says, " I am come to send fire upon the earth ? "[5] If you find fault with one who says, " The Lord killeth and maketh alive," [6] why do you honour Peter, who raised Tabitha to life,[7] but also put Sapphira to death ? [8] And if, again, you find fault with the one because He has prepared a fire,[9] why do you not find fault with the other, who says, " Depart from me into everlasting fire ? "[10] If you find fault with Him who says, " I, God, make peace, and create evil," [11] explain to us how Jesus says, " I came not to send peace, but a sword."[12] Since both persons speak in the same terms, one or other of these two things must follow : namely, either they are both good [13] because they use the same language ; or, if Jesus passes without censure though He speaks in such terms, you must tell us why you reprehend Him who employs a similar mode of address in the Old Testament.

2. Then Manes made the following reply to him : And what manner of God now is it that blinds one ? For it is Paul who uses these words : " In whom the God of this world hath blinded the minds of them which believe not, lest the light of the Gospel should shine in them." [14] But Archelaus broke in and refuted this very well, saying : Read, however, a word or two of what precedes that sentence, namely, " But if our Gospel be hid, it is hid in them that are lost." You see that it is hid in them that are lost. " For it is not meet to give the holy things to dogs." [15] And furthermore, is it only the God of the Old Testament that has blinded the minds of them who believe not ? Nay, has not Jesus Himself also said : " Therefore speak I to them in parables : that seeing, they may not see ? " [16] Is it then because He hated them that He desired them not to see ? Or is it *not* on account of their unworthiness, since they closed their own eyes ? For wherever wickedness is a matter self-chosen, there too there is the absence of grace. " For unto him that hath shall be given, but from him that hath not shall be taken away even that which he seemeth to have." [17]

3. But even although [18] we should be under the necessity of accepting the exegesis advocated by some, — for the subject is not altogether unworthy of notice, — and of saying thus, that He hath actually blinded the minds [19] of them that believe not, we should still have to affirm that He hath blinded them for good, in order that they may recover their sight to behold things that are holy. For it is not said that He hath blinded their soul,[20] but only that He hath blinded the minds of them that believe not. And that mode of expression means something like this : Blind the whorish mind of the whoremonger, and the man is saved ; blind the rapacious and thievish mind of the thief, and the man is saved. But do you decline to understand the sentence thus ? Well, there is still another interpretation. For the sun blinds those who have bad sight ; and those who have watery eyes are also blinded when they are smitten by the light : not, however, because it is of the nature of the sun to blind, but because the eye's own constitution [21] is not one of correct vision. And in like manner, those whose hearts are afflicted with the ailment of unbelief are not capable of looking upon the rays *of the glory*

---

[1] From Cyril of Jerusalem, *Catecheses*, vi. § 27-29. [And see the Introductory Notice, p. 175.]

[2] Reading ὅπλον δικαιοσύνης. Others read ὅπλῳ = Archelaus met him with the buckler of righteousness.

[3] Ps. v. 9.

[4] Deut. iv. 24.

[5] Luke xii. 49.

[6] 1 Sam. ii. 6.

[7] Acts ix. 40.

[8] Acts v. 10.

[9] Deut. xxxii. 22.

[10] Matt. xxv. 41.

[11] Isa. xlv. 7.

[12] Matt. x. 34. Various of the MSS. add, ἐπὶ τὴν γῆν, upon the earth.

[13] The text gives καλοί. Routh seems to prefer κακοί, evil.

[14] 2 Cor. iv. 4.

[15] Matt. vii. 6.

[16] Matt. xiii. 13. The text is, ἵνα βλέποντες μὴ βλέπωσι.

[17] Matt. xxv. 29.

[18] For εἰ δὲ δεῖ καὶ ὡς, etc., various codices read εἰ δὲ δικαίως, etc.

[19] νοήματα, thoughts.

[20] ψυχήν.

[21] ὑπόστασις.

of the Godhead. And again, it is not said, "He hath blinded their minds lest they should hear the Gospel," but rather "lest the light of the glory of the Gospel of our Lord Jesus Christ should shine unto them." For to hear the Gospel is a thing committed [1] to all; but the glory of the Gospel of Christ is imparted only to the sincere and genuine. For this reason the Lord spake in parables to those who were incapable of hearing, but to His disciples He explained these parables in private. For the illumination of the glory is for those who have been enlight-

ened, while the blinding is for them who believe not. These mysteries, which the Church now declares to you who are transferred from the lists of the catechumens, it is not her custom to declare to the Gentiles. For we do not declare the mysteries touching the Father, and the Son, and the Holy Spirit to a Gentile ; neither do we speak of the mysteries plainly in presence of the catechumens ; but many a time we express ourselves in an occult manner, so that the faithful who have intelligence may apprehend the truths referred to, while those who have not that intelligence may receive no hurt.

[1] ἐφίεται.

ELUCIDATIONS.

I.

(Spotless virgin, etc., p. 223 and note 7.)

Oh that "foolish and unlearned questions" had been avoided, as the Scripture [1] bids ! Surely, we should be as decent about the conjugal relations of the Blessed Virgin as we are socially in all such matters. Pearson, as in the note, says all that should be said on such a subject. Photius, in his thirtieth epistle, expounds the text Matt. i. 25. But it did not rest there. Let it rest here.

II.

(Get thee behind me, Satan, p. 224 and note 13.)

I adopt the views of those who reverently suppose that when it was said, "Let us make man," etc., Lucifer conceived rebellion, and said, "This be far from Thee, Lord ; " fearing the creature made in God's own image might outshine himself. Hence our Lord applies the epithet "Satan" to Peter when he ventures to use similar language. Possibly there lurks a reference to this in such language as Job iv. 18. I have previously referred to the *Messias and Anti-Messias* of the Rev. Charles Ingham Black (London, 1854), in which this view is singularly well argued. It is well to halt, however, with a confession, that, while it seems intimated in Holy Scripture, it cannot be proved as revealed. Hence let us reverently say what is said by the Psalmist in Ps. cxxxi. 1, and confess what is written in Deut. xxix. 29. I go so far, only because the words on which this note is a comment seem to authorize inquiry as to the force of "Satan" just there. I state *what seems* the reference, but go no farther. Compare Dan. iv. 35.

III.

(I shrink from repeating, p. 227 and note 10.)

The delicacy of feeling here expressed is most honourable to the sentiment of the Church at this period. Not till St. Bernard's day was it hinted,[3] even in the West, that the Blessed Virgin was conceived without taint of original sin ; and he rebukes the innovators with a holy indignation.[2] It shocks him that questions were thus raised as to her parents, their *amplexus maritales*, etc.

---

[1] 2 Tim. ii. 23; Tit. iii. 9.

[2] St. Bernard, *Opp.*, tom. i. Compare note 10, p. 227, *supra*. See the Abbé Laborde on the *Impossibility*, etc., translated by the editor of this series, ed. Baltimore, 1855.

[3] Save only by Mohammed.

IV.

(In presence of the catechumens, p. 235.)

Here is testimony to the catechumen system of the primitive Church which appears to me not inconsistent with the period to which it is assigned. No doubt this gradual instruction of the disciple is based upon the example of our Lord Himself, who spoke in parables,[1] and taught " as they were able to hear it." But the *disciplina arcani* was designed chiefly to protect the Church from the profaneness of the heathen, and it fell into desuetude after the Council of Nice.

GENERAL NOTE.

As I have not infrequently treated the rise of the great Alexandrian school as an outcrop from the learinng and piety of Apollos, I take this space to record my reasons : 1. Apart from the question in formal shape, I hold that the character and influence of this brilliant Alexandrian *must* have operated upon Alexandrian converts. 2. But the frequent employment by the Alexandrians of the expressions (Acts xviii. 24) used concerning him by St. Luke, almost textually, confirms my suspicion that they had his high example always before them. 3. The catechetical school was certainly established in Alexandria from apostolic times.[2] By whom more probably than by Apollos? 4. St. Mark's connection with Alexandria rests on no scriptural evidence, yet it is credited. 5. That of Apollos is narrated in Scripture, and I can conceive of nothing so probable as that, remembering his own instruction by Aquila and Priscilla (Acts xviii. 26), he should have founded catechetical schools for others. 6. All this is conjectural, indeed, but it agrees with known facts. 7. The silence of Clement and the rest is an objection quite as fatal to the claims of St. Mark. 8. The unanimity of the Alexandrians, from Pantænus downward, in assigning to St. Paul the authorship of the Epistle to the Hebrews, while it was so much debated elsewhere, suggests that they had early evidence on this point. 9. Clement's testimony about St. Luke convinces me that Apollos had no claim to it, but had testified to the Alexandrians that the Apostle was the author, and St. Luke his *inspired* amanuensis, by whom the words were not servilely taken down, but reported in idioms of his own : whether out of St. Paul's " Hebrew " or not, is another question. 10. Apollos disappears from history about A.D. 64, *on his way homeward*,[3] bearing the Epistle to Titus, and (who can doubt?) a copy of that to the Hebrews, written the previous year. All these facts agree with my conjectures that Apollos closed his labours in his native city.

---

[1] Matt. xiii. 34 : Mark iv. 33.
[2] See vol. ii. p. 342, Elucidation II., this series. Note also, in the same volume, what is said, pp. 166–167.
[3] Lewin, *St. Paul*, vol. ii. p. 340.

ALEXANDER

[TRANSLATED BY THE REV. JAMES B. H. HAWKINS, M.A., OXON.]

INTRODUCTORY NOTICE

TO

ALEXANDER, BISHOP OF LYCOPOLIS.[1]

[A.D. 301.] To the following account, translated from Galland, I prefix only the general date of Alexander's episcopate. He was succeeded in the bishopric of Lycopolis by the turbulent Meletius, of whose schism we need not say anything here. But his early relations with the heresy of Manes, and his subsequent orthodoxy (in all which he was a foreshadowing of Augustine), render his treatise on the Manichæan opinions especially valuable.

COMBEFIS conjectured that Alexander was called Λυκοπολίτης, as having been born at Lycus, a city of the Thebaid, and so by race an Egyptian, and to his opinion both Cave and Fabricius are inclined. But this conjecture is plainly uncertain, if we are to trust Photius, in his *Epitome De Manichæis*, which Montfaucon has edited.[2] For in this work Photius, whilst speaking of the authors who wrote against those heretics, makes mention also of Alexander as bishop of the city of Lycus, ὅτε τῆς πόλεως Λύκων Ἀλέξανδρος τοὺς ἀρχιερατικοὺς νόμους ἐγκεχειρισμένος.[3] So that it is no easy matter to state whether our author was called Λυκοπολίτης, because he was born either at Lycopolis in the Thebaid, or at another Lycopolis in Lower Egypt, which Stephanus places close to the sea in the Sebennytic nome, or whether he was not rather called Λυκοπολίτης, as having held the bishopric of Lycopolis. The unwonted manner of speaking employed by Photius need not delay the attention of any one, when he makes Alexander to have been Archbishop of Lycopolis; for it is established that the Bishop of Alexandria alone was Archbishop and Patriarch of the whole Egyptian diocese. Epiphanius[4] certainly says, when speaking of Meletius,[5] the schismatical Bishop of Lycopolis, ἐδόκει δὲ ὁ Μελήτιος τῶν κατὰ τὴν Αἴγυπτον προήκων, καὶ δευτερεύων τῷ Πέτρῳ τῷ τῆς Ἀλεξανδρείας κατὰ τὴν ἀρχιεπισκοπήν. And to the same purpose he says elsewhere, Μελήτιος, ὁ τῆς Αἰγύπτου ἀπὸ Θηβαίδος δοκῶν εἶναι καὶ αὐτὸς ἀρχιεπίσκοπος. But however these matters are understood, it is admitted that Alexander came just before Meletius in the See of Lycopolis, and we know that he occupied the episcopal chair of that city in the beginning of the fourth century, in which order Le Quien places him among the Lycopolitan prelates, on the authority of Photius.

---

[1] Translated from Gallandi, *Vet. Patr. Biblioth.* The reverend translator is styled in the Edinburgh edition, "Curate of Ilminster, Somerset."

[2] *Cf.* Combef., *Auctar. Noviss.*, part ii. p. 2; Cav., *Dissert. de. Script. Eccl.*, incert. ætat. p. 2; Fabricius, *Bibl. Gr.*, tom. v. p. 287; Montfaucon, *Bibl. Coisl.*, p. 349, *seqq.*

[3] Photius, *Epist. de Manich.*, *Bibliotheca Coisliniana*, p. 354.

[4] Epiph., *Hær.*, lxviii. n. 1, lxix. n. 2; Le Quien, *Oriens Christianus*, tom. ii. p. 597.

[5] Meletius of Lycopolis, a schismatical bishop of the third and fourth centuries. Athanasius tells us that Meletius, who was Bishop of Lycopolis in Upper Egypt at the time of the persecution under Diocletian and his successors, yielded to fear and sacrificed to idols: and being subsequently deposed, on this and other charges, in a Synod over which Peter, Bishop of Alexandria, presided, determined to separate from the Church, and to constitute with his followers a separate community. Epiphanius, on the other hand, relates that both Peter and Meletius, being in confinement for the faith, differed concerning the treatment to be used toward those who, after renouncing their Christian profession, became penitent, and wished to be restored to the communion of the Church. The Meletians afterwards co-operated with the Arians in their hostility to Athanasius. — *See* Art. Meletius, in *Smith's Biograph. Dict.* — Tr.

In the time of Constantine, the Eastern and Western Empire were each divided into seven districts, called dioceses,[1] which comprised about one hundred and eighteen provinces;[2] each province contained several cities, each of which had a district[3] attached to it. The ecclesiastical rulers of the dioceses were called patriarchs, exarchs, or archbishops, of whom there were four-teen; the rulers of the provinces were styled metropolitans, i.e., governors of the $\mu\eta\tau\rho\delta\pi o\lambda\iota s$ or mother city, and those of each city and its districts were called bishops. So that the division which we now call a diocese, was in ancient times a union of dioceses, and a parish was a combination of modern parishes.[4]

But however it be, whether Alexander was called $\Lambda\nu\kappa o\pi o\lambda\ell\tau\eta s$ from his birthplace, or from his episcopal See, this is certain and acknowledged, that he of good right claims for himself a place among ecclesiastical writers, for he has given us an elaborate treatise against the Manichæan tenets; and he is therefore styled by Allatius *auctor eruditissimus et* $\phi\iota\lambda o\sigma o\phi\iota\kappa\omega\tau a\tau os$, and his work *libellus aureus*. Allatius wrote out and brought to light two passages from it, while as yet it was lying hid in the libraries. From the inscription of the work, we learn that Alexander was first a pagan; and afterwards, having given up the religion of the Greeks, became an adherent of the Manichæan doctrines, which he says that he learnt from those who were on terms of familiar intercourse with the heresiarch, $\dot{a}\pi\dot{o}\ \tau\hat{\omega}\nu\ \gamma\nu\omega\rho\ell\mu\omega\nu\ \tau o\hat{\nu}\ \dot{a}\nu\delta\rho\delta s$;[5] so that he would seem to be not far wrong in his conjecture who would place our author at no very distant date from the times of Manes himself. From the errors of this sect he was divinely reclaimed, and, taking refuge in the Church, he exposed the scandals attaching to the heresiarch, and solidly refuted his unwholesome dogmas. From having been an adherent of the sect himself, he has given us more information concerning their tenets than it was in the power of others to give, and on that account his treatise seems to be held in much estimation.[6]

---

[1] $\delta\iota o\iota\kappa\dot{\eta}\sigma\epsilon\iota s$.

[2] $\dot{\epsilon}\pi a\rho\chi\ell a\iota$.

[3] $\pi a\rho o\iota\kappa\ell a$.

[4] [More simply, the Church's system naturally kept to the lines of the civil divisions. A *diæcese* was, in fact, a *patriarchate;* a *province* was presided over by a *metropolitan;* a *parish* was what we call a *diocese*. Before Constantine's time these arrangements existed for convenience, but were not invested with worldly consequence. Neale adopts this twofold spelling (*diæcese* and *diocese*) in his *Alexandra*, vol. i. p. xiv.

[5] *Cf.* Alex., *De Manich. placit.*, cap. 2.

[6] This treatise of Alexander was first published by Combefis, with a Latin version, in the *Auctarium novissimum, Bibl. S. S. Patrum*, Ps. ii. p. 3. It is published also by Gallandi, *Bibl. Patrum*, vol. iv. p. 73.

OF THE MANICHÆANS.[1]

CHAP. I. — THE EXCELLENCE OF THE CHRISTIAN PHILOSOPHY; THE ORIGIN OF HERESIES AMONGST CHRISTIANS.

THE philosophy of the Christians is termed simple. But it bestows very great attention to the formation of manners, enigmatically insinuating words of more certain truth respecting God; the principal of which, so far as any earnest serious purpose in those matters is concerned, all will have received when they assume an efficient cause, very noble and very ancient, as the originator of all things that have existence. For Christians leaving to ethical students matters more toilsome and difficult, as, for instance, what is virtue, moral and intellectual; and to those who employ their time in forming hypotheses respecting morals, and the passions and affections, without marking out any element by which each virtue is to be attained, and heaping up, as it were, at random precepts less subtle — the common people, hearing these, even as we learn by experience, make great progress in modesty, and a character of piety is imprinted on their manners, quickening the moral disposition which from such usages is formed, and leading them by degrees to the desire of what is honourable and good.[2]

But this being divided into many questions by the number of those who come after, there arise many, just as is the case with those who are devoted to dialectics,[3] some more skilful than others, and, so to speak, more sagacious in handling nice and subtle questions; so that now they come forward as parents and originators of sects and heresies. And by these the formation of morals is hindered and rendered obscure; for those do not attain unto certain verity of discourse who wish to become the heads of the sects, and the common people is to a greater degree excited to strife and contention. And there being no rule nor law by which a solution may be obtained of the things which are called in question, but, as in other matters, this ambitious rivalry running out into excess, there is nothing to which it does not cause damage and injury.

CHAP. II. — THE AGE OF MANICHÆUS, OR MANES; HIS FIRST DISCIPLES; THE TWO PRINCIPLES; MANICHÆAN MATTER.

So in these matters also, whilst in novelty of opinion each endeavours to show himself first and superior, they brought this philosophy, which is simple, almost to a nullity. Such was he whom they call Manichæus,[4] a Persian by race, my instructor in whose doctrine was one Papus by name, and after him Thomas, and some others followed them. They say that the man lived when Valerian was emperor, and that he served under Sapor, the king of the Persians, and having offended him in some way, was put to death. Some such report of his character and reputation has come to me from those who were intimately acquainted with him. He laid down two principles, God and Matter. God he called good, and matter he affirmed to be evil. But God excelled more in good than matter in evil. But he calls matter not that which Plato calls it,[5] which becomes everything when it has received quality and figure, whence he terms it all-embracing — the mother and nurse of all things; nor what Aristotle[6] calls an element, with which form and privation have to do, but something beside these. For the motion which in individual things is incomposite, this he calls matter. On the side of God are ranged powers, like handmaids, all good; and likewise, on the side of matter are ranged other powers, all evil. Moreover, the bright shining, the light, and the superior, all these are with God; while the

---

[1] A treatise on their tenets by Alexander of Lycopolis, who first turned from paganism to the Manichæan opinions.

[2] [Note the *practical* character of Christian ethics, which he so justly contrasts with the ethical philosophy of the heathen. This has been finely pointed out by the truly illustrious William Wilberforce in his *Practical View*, cap. ii. (Latin note), p. 25, ed. London, 1815.]

[3] ἐν τοῖς ἐριστικοῖς. The philosophers of the Megarean school, who were devoted to dialectics, were nicknamed οἱ Ἐριστικοί. *See* Diog. Laertius.

[4] Manes, or Manichæus, lived about A.D. 240. He was a Persian by birth, and this accounts for the Parseeism which can be detected in his teaching. He was probably ordained a priest, but was afterwards expelled from the Christian community, and put to death by the Persian government. His tenets spread considerably, and were in early youth embraced by St. Augustine. [See *Confess.*, iii. 6.]

[5] Plato, *Timæus*, 51.

[6] In substance, but not in words, Aristotle, *Met.*, Book Λ 4 (1070′ b).

obscure, and the darkness, and the inferior are with matter. God, too, has desires, but they are all good; and matter, likewise, which are all evil.

CHAP. III. — THE FANCIES OF MANICHÆUS CONCERNING MATTER.

It came to pass on a time that matter conceived a desire to attain to the superior region; and when it had arrived there, it admired the brightness and the light which was with God. And, indeed, it wished to seize on for itself the place of pre-eminence, and to remove God from His position. God, moreover, deliberated how to avenge Himself upon matter, but was destitute of the evil necessary to do so, for evil does not exist in the house and abode of God. He sent, therefore, the power which we call the soul into matter, to permeate it entirely. For it will be the death of matter, when at length hereafter this power is separated from it. So, therefore, by the providence of God, the soul was commingled with matter, an unlike thing with an unlike. Now by this commingling the soul has contracted evil, and labours under the same infirmity as matter. For, just as in a corrupted vessel, the contents are oftentimes vitiated in quality, so, also the soul that is in matter suffers some such change, and is deteriorated from its own nature so as to participate in the evil of matter. But God had compassion upon the soul, and sent forth another power, which we call *Demiurge*[1] that is, the Creator of all things; and when this power had arrived, and taken in hand the creation of the world, it separated from matter as much power as from the commingling had contracted no vice and stain, and hence the sun and moon were first formed; but that which had contracted some slight and moderate stain, this became the stars and the expanse of heaven. Of the matter from which the sun and the moon was separated, part was cast entirely out of the world, and is that fire in which, indeed, there is the power of burning, although in itself it is dark and void of light, being closely similar to night. But in the rest of the elements, both animal and vegetable, in those the divine power is unequally mingled. And therefore the world was made, and in it the sun and moon who preside over the birth and death of things, by separating the divine virtue from matter, and transmitting it to God.

CHAP. IV. — THE MOON'S INCREASE AND WANE; THE MANICHÆAN TRIFLING RESPECTING IT; THEIR DREAMS ABOUT MAN AND CHRIST; THEIR FOOLISH SYSTEM OF ABSTINENCE.

He ordained this, forsooth, to supply to the *Demiurge*,[1] or Creator, another power which

---
[1] δημιουργός.

might attract to the splendour of the sun; and the thing is manifest, as one might say, even to a blind person. For the moon in its increase receives the virtue which is separated from matter, and during the time of its augmentation comes forth full of it. But when it is full, in its wanings, it remits it to the sun, and the sun goes back to God. And when it has done this, it waits again to receive from another full moon a migration of the soul to itself, and receiving this in the same way, it suffers it to pass on to God. And this is its work continually, and in every age. And in the sun some such image is seen, as is the form of man. And matter ambitiously strove to make man from itself by mingling together all its virtue, so that it might have some portion of soul. But his form contributed much to man's obtaining a greater share, and one beyond all other animals, in the divine virtue. For he is the image of the divine virtue, but Christ is the intelligence. Who, when He had at length come from the superior region, dismissed a very great part of this virtue to God. And at length being crucified, in this way He furnished knowledge, and fitted the divine virtue to be crucified in matter. Because, therefore, it is the Divine will and decree that matter should perish, they abstain from those things which have life, and feed upon vegetables, and everything which is void of sense. They abstain also from marriage and the rites of Venus, and the procreation of children, that virtue may not strike its root deeper in matter by the succession of race; nor do they go abroad, seeking to purify themselves from the stain which virtue has contracted from its admixture with matter.

CHAP. V. — THE WORSHIP OF THE SUN AND MOON UNDER GOD; SUPPORT SOUGHT FOR THE MANICHÆANS IN THE GRECIAN FABLES; THE AUTHORITY OF THE SCRIPTURES AND FAITH DESPISED BY THE MANICHÆANS.

These things are the principal of what they say and think. And they honour very especially the sun and moon, not as gods, but as the way by which it is possible to attain unto God. But when the divine virtue has been entirely separated off, they say that the exterior fire will fall, and burn up both itself and all else that is left of matter. Those of them who are better educated, and not unacquainted with Greek literature, instruct us from their own resources. From the ceremonies and mysteries, for instance: by Bacchus, who was cut out from the womb, is signified that the divine virtue is divided into matter by the Titans, as they say; from the poet's fable of the battle with the Giants, is indicated that not even they were ignorant of the rebellion of matter against God. I indeed will not deny, that these things are not sufficient to lead away the minds of those who receive words without examining them, since the deception caused by discourse of this sort has drawn over to itself some of those who have pursued the study of philosophy with me ; but in what manner I should approach the thing to examine into it, I am at a loss indeed. For their hypotheses do not proceed by any legitimate method, so that one might institute an examination in accordance with these ; neither are there any principles of demonstrations, so that we may see what follows on these ; but theirs is the rare discovery of those who are simply said to philosophize. These men, taking to themselves the Old and New Scriptures, though they lay it down that these are divinely inspired, draw their own opinions from thence ; and then only think they are refuted, when it happens that anything not in accordance with these is said or done by them. And what to those who philosophize after the manner of the Greeks, as respects principles of demonstration, are intermediate propositions ; this, with them, is the voice of the prophets. But here, all these things being eliminated, and since those matters, which I before mentioned, are put forward without any demonstration, and since it is necessary to give an answer in a rational way, and not to put forward other things more plausible, and which might prove more enticing, my attempt is rather troublesome, and on this account the more arduous, because it is necessary to bring forward arguments of a varied nature. For the more accurate arguments will escape the observation of those who have been convinced beforehand by these men without proof, if, when it comes to persuasion, they fall into the same hands. For they imagine that they proceed from like sources. There is, therefore, need of much and great diligence, and truly of God, to be the guide of our argument.

CHAP. VI. — THE TWO PRINCIPLES OF THE MANI-CHÆANS ; THEMSELVES CONTROVERTED ; THE PYTHAGOREAN OPINION RESPECTING FIRST PRINCIPLES ; GOOD AND EVIL CONTRARY ; THE VICTORY ON THE SIDE OF GOOD.

They lay down two principles, God and Matter. If he (Manes) separates that which comes into being from that which really exists, the supposition is not so faulty in this, that neither does matter create itself, nor does it admit two contrary qualities, in being both active and passive ; nor, again, are other such theories proposed concerning the creative cause as it is not lawful to speak of. And yet God does not stand in need of matter in order to make things, since in His mind all things substantially exist, so far as the possibility of their coming into being is concerned. But if, as he seems rather to mean, the

unordered motion of things really existent under Him is matter, first, then, he unconsciously sets up another creative cause (and yet an evil one), nor does he perceive what follows from this, namely, that if it is necessary that God and matter should be supposed, some other matter must be supposed to God ; so that to each of the creative causes there should be the subject matter. Therefore, instead of two, he will be shown to give us four first principles. Wonderful, too, is the distinction. For if he thinks this to be God, which is good, and wishes to conceive of something opposite to Him, why does he not, as some of the Pythagoreans, set evil over against Him ? It is more tolerable, indeed, that two principles should be spoken of by them, the good and the evil, and that these are continually striving, but the good prevails. For if the evil were to prevail, all things would perish. Wherefore matter, by itself, is neither body, nor is it exactly incorporeal, nor simply any particular thing ; but it is something indefinite, which, by the addition of form, comes to be defined ; as, for instance, fire is a pyramid, air an octahedron, water an eikosahedron, and earth a cube ; how, then, is matter the unordered motion of the elements ? By itself, indeed, it does not subsist, for if it is motion, it is in that which is moved ; but matter does not seem to be of such a nature, but rather the first subject, and unorganized, from which other things proceed. Since, therefore, matter is unordered motion, was it always conjoined with that which is moved, or was it ever separate from it ? For, if it were ever by itself, it would not be in existence ; for there is no motion without something moved. But if it was always in that which is moved, then, again, there will be two principles — that which moves, and that which is moved. To which of these two, then, will it be granted that it subsists as a primary cause along with God ?

CHAP. VII. — MOTION VINDICATED FROM THE CHARGE OF IRREGULARITY ; CIRCULAR ; STRAIGHT ; OF GENERATION AND CORRUPTION ; OF ALTERATION, AND QUALITY AFFECTING SENSE.

There is added to the discourse an appendix quite foreign to it.[1] For you may reasonably speak of motion not existing. And what, also, is the matter of motion ? Is it straight or circular ? Or does it take place by a process of change, or by a process of generation and corruption ? The circular motion, indeed, is so orderly and composite, that it is ascribed to the order of all created things ; nor does this, in the Manichæan system, appear worthy to be impugned, in which move the sun and the moon, whom alone, of the gods, they say that they

---

[1] τὸ ἄτακτον.

venerate. But as regards that which is straight : to this, also, there is a bound when it reaches its own place. For that which is earthly ceases entirely from motion, as soon as it has touched the earth. And every animal and vegetable makes an end of increasing when it has reached its limit. Therefore the stoppage of these things would be more properly the death of matter, than that endless death, which is, as it were, woven for it by them. But the motion which arises by a process of generation and corruption it is impossible to think of as in harmony with this hypothesis, for, according to them, matter is unbegotten. But if they ascribe to it the motion of alteration, as they term it, and that by which we suffer change by a quality affecting the sense, it is worth while to consider how they come to say this. For this seems to be the principal thing that they assert, since by matter it comes to pass, as they say, that manners are changed, and that vice arises in the soul. For in altering, it will always begin from the beginning ; and, proceeding onwards, it will reach the middle, and thus will it attain unto the end. But when it has reached the end, it will not stand still, at least if alteration is its essence. But it will again, by the same route, return to the beginning, and from thence in like manner to the end ; nor will it ever cease from doing this. As, for instance, if a and γ suffer alteration, and the middle is β, a by being changed, will arrive at β, and from thence will go on to γ. Again returning from the extreme γ to β, it will at some time or other arrive at a ; and this goes on continuously. As in the change from black, the middle is dun, and the extreme, white. Again, in the contrary direction, from white to dun, and in like manner to black ; and again from white the change begins, and goes the same round.

CHAP. VIII. — IS MATTER WICKED? OF GOD AND MATTER.

Is matter, in respect of alteration, an evil cause? It is thus proved that it is not more evil than good. For let the beginning of the change be from evil. Thus the change is from this to good through that which is indifferent. But let the alteration be from good. Again the beginning goes on through that which is indifferent. Whether the motion be to one extreme or to the other, the method is the same, and this is abundantly set forth. All motion has to do with quantity ; but quality is the guide in virtue and vice. Now we know that these two are generically distinguished. But are God and matter alone principles, or does there remain anything else which is the mean between these two? For if there is nothing, these things remain unintermingled one with another. And it is well said, that if the extremes are intermingled, there is a

necessity for some thing intermediate to connect them. But if something else exists, it is necessary that that something be either body or incorporeal, and thus a third adventitious principle makes its appearance. First, therefore, if we suppose God and matter to be both entirely incorporeal, so that neither is in the other, except as the science of grammar is in the soul ; to understand this of God and matter is absurd. But if, as in a vacuum, as some say, the vacuum is surrounded by this universe ; the other, again, is without substance, for the substance of a vacuum is nothing. But if as accidents, first, indeed, this is impossible ; for the thing that wants substance cannot be in any place ; for substance is, as it were, the vehicle underlying the accident. But if both are bodies, it is necessary for both to be either heavy or light, or middle ; or one heavy, and another light, or intermediate. If, then, both are heavy, it is plainly necessary that these should be the same, both among light things and those things which are of the middle sort ; or if they alternate, the one will be altogether separate from the other. For that which is heavy has one place, and that which is middle another, and the light another. To one belongs the superior, to the other the inferior, and to the third the middle. Now in every spherical figure the inferior part is the middle ; for from this to all the higher parts, even to the topmost superficies, the distance is every way equal, and, again, all heavy bodies are borne from all sides to it. Wherefore, also, it occurs to me to laugh when I hear that matter moving without order, — for this belongs to it by nature, — came to the region of God, or to light and brightness, and such-like. But if one be body, and the other incorporeal, first, indeed, that which is body is alone capable of motion And then if they are not intermingled, each is separate from the other according to its proper nature. But if one be mixed up with the other, they will be either mind or soul or accident. For so only it happens that things incorporeal are mixed up with bodies.

CHAP. IX. — THE RIDICULOUS FANCIES OF THE MANICHÆANS ABOUT THE MOTION OF MATTER TOWARDS GOD ; GOD THE AUTHOR OF THE REBELLION OF MATTER IN THE MANICHÆAN SENSE ; THE LONGING OF MATTER FOR LIGHT AND BRIGHTNESS GOOD ; DIVINE GOOD NONE THE LESS FOR BEING COMMUNICATED.

But in what manner, and from what cause, was matter brought to the region of God? for to it by nature belong the lower place and darkness, as they say ; and the upper region and light are contrary to its nature. Wherefore there is then attributed to it a supernatural motion ; and something of the same sort happens to it, as if a man were to throw a stone or a lump of earth upwards; in this way, the thing being raised a little by the force of the person throwing, when it has reached the upper regions, falls back again into the same place. Who, then, hath raised matter to the upper region? Of itself, indeed, and from itself, it would not be moved by that motion which belongs to it. It is necessary, then, that some force should be applied to it for it to be borne aloft, as with the stone and the lump of earth. But they leave nothing else to it but God. It is manifest, therefore, what follows from their argument. That God, according to them, by force and necessity, raised matter aloft to Himself. But if matter be evil, its desires are altogether evil. Now the desire of evil is evil, but the desire of good is altogether good. Since, then, matter has desired brightness and light, its desire is not a bad one; just as it is not bad for a man living in vice, afterwards to come to desire virtue. On the contrary, he is not guiltless who, being good, comes to desire what is evil. As if any one should say that God desires the evils which are attaching to matter. For the good things of God are not to be so esteemed as great wealth and large estates, and a large quantity of gold, a lesser portion of which remain with the owner, if one effect a transfer of them to another. But if an image of these things must be formed in the mind, I think one would adduce as examples wisdom and the sciences. As, therefore, neither wisdom suffers diminution nor science, and he who is endowed with these experiences no loss if another be made partaker of them; so, in the same way, it is contrary to reason to think that God grudges matter the desire of what is good; if, indeed, with them we allow that it desires it.

CHAP. X. — THE MYTHOLOGY RESPECTING THE GODS; THE DOGMAS OF THE MANICHÆANS RESEMBLE THIS: THE HOMERIC ALLEGORY OF THE BATTLE OF THE GODS; ENVY AND EMULATION EXISTING IN GOD ACCORDING TO THE MANICHÆAN OPINION; THESE VICES ARE TO BE FOUND IN NO GOOD MAN, AND ARE TO BE ACCOUNTED DISGRACEFUL.

Moreover, they far surpass the mythologists in fables, those, namely, who either make Coelus suffer mutilation, or idly tell of the plots laid for Saturn by his son, in order that that son might attain the sovereignty; or those again who make Saturn devour his sons, and to have been cheated of his purpose by the image of a stone that was presented to him. For how are these things which they put forward dissimilar to those? When they speak openly of the war between God and matter, and say not these things either in a mythological sense, as Homer in the *Iliad;* [1]

when he makes Jupiter to rejoice in the strife and war of the gods with each other, thus obscurely signifying that the world is formed of unequal elements, fitted one into another, and either conquering or submitting to a conqueror. And this has been advanced by me, because I know that people of this sort, when they are at a loss for demonstration, bring together from all sides passages from poems, and seek from them a support for their own opinions. Which would not be the case with them if they had only read what they fell in with with some reflection. But, when all evil is banished from the company of the gods, surely emulation and envy ought especially to have been got rid of. Yet these men leave these things with God, when they say that God formed designs against matter, because it felt a desire for good. But with which of those things which God possessed could He have wished to take vengeance on matter? In truth, I think it to be more accurate doctrine to say that God is of a simple nature, than what they advance. Nor, indeed, as in the other things, is the enunciation of this fancy easy. For neither is it possible to demonstrate it simply and with words merely, but with much instruction and labour. But we all know this, that anger and rage, and the desire of revenge upon matter, are passions in him who is so agitated. And of such a sort, indeed, as it could never happen to a good man to be harassed by them, much less then can it be that they are connected with the Absolute Good.

CHAP. XI. — THE TRANSMITTED VIRTUE OF THE MANICHÆANS; THE VIRTUES OF MATTER MIXED WITH EQUAL OR LESS AMOUNT OF EVIL.

To other things, therefore, our discourse has come round about again. For, because they say that God sent virtue into matter, it is worth our while to consider whether this virtue, so far as it pertains to good, in respect of God is less, or whether it is on equal terms with Him. For if it is less, what is the cause? For the things which are with God admit of no fellowship with matter. But good alone is the characteristic of God, and evil alone of matter. But if it is on equal terms with Him, what is the reason that He, as a king, issues His commands, and it involuntarily undertakes this labour? Moreover, with regard to matter, it shall be inquired whether, with respect to evil, the virtues are alike or less. For if they are less, they are altogether of less evil. By fellowship therefore with the good it is that they become so. For there being two evils, the less has plainly by its fellowship with the good attained to be what it is. But they leave nothing good around matter. Again, therefore, another question arises. For if some other virtue, in respect of evil, excels the matter

---

[1] Hom., *Il.*, xx. 23–54.

which is prevailing, it becomes itself the presiding principle. For that which is more evil will hold the sway in its own dominion.

But that God sent virtue into matter is asserted without any proof, and it altogether wants probability. Yet it is right that this should have its own explanation. The reason of this they assert, indeed, to be that there might be no more evil, but that all things should become good. It was necessary for virtue to be intermingled with evil, after the manner of the athletes, who, clasped in a firm embrace, overcome their adversaries, in order that, by conquering evil, it might make it to cease to exist. But I think it far more dignified and worthy of the excellence of God, at the first conception of things existent, to have abolished matter. But I think they could not allow this, because that something evil is found existing, which they call matter. But it is not any the more possible that things should cease to be such as they are, in order that one should admit that some things are changed into that which is worse. And it is necessary that there should be some perception of this, because these present things have in some manner or other suffered diminution, in order that we might have better hopes for the future. For well has it been answered to the opinion of Zeno of Citium, who thus argued that the world would be destroyed by fire : " Everything which has anything to burn will not cease from burning until it has consumed the whole ; and the sun is a fire, and will it not burn what it has ? " Whence he made out, as he imagined, that the universe would be destroyed by fire. But to him a facetious fellow is reported to have said, " But I indeed yesterday, and the year before, and a long time ago, have seen, and now in like manner do I see, that no injury has been experienced by the sun ; and it is reasonable that this should happen in time and by degrees, so that we may believe that at some time or other the whole will be burnt up. And to the doctrine of Manichæus, although it rests upon no proof, I think that the same answer is apposite, namely, that there has been no diminution in the present condition of things, but what was before in the time of the first man, when brother killed brother, even now continues to be ; the same wars, and more diverse desires. Now it would be reasonable that these things, if they did not altogether cease, should at least be diminished, if we are to imagine that they are at some time to cease. But while the same things come from them, what is our expectation of them for the future?

But what things does he call evil? As for the sun and moon, indeed, there is nothing lacking ; but with respect to the heavens and the stars, whether he says that there is some such thing, and what it is, it is right that we should next in order examine. But irregularity is according to them evil, and unordered motion, but these things are always the same, and in the same manner ; nor will any one have to blame any of the planets for venturing to delay at any time in the zodiac beyond the fixed period ; nor again any of the fixed stars, as if it did not abide in the same seat and position, and did not by circumvolution revolve equally around the world, moving as it were one step backward in a hundred years. But on the earth, if he accuses the roughness of some spots, or if pilots are offended at the storms on the sea ; first, indeed, as they think, these things have a share of good in them. For should nothing germinate upon earth, all the animals must presently perish. But this result will send on much of the virtue which is intermingled with matter to God, and there will be a necessity for many moons, to accommodate the great multitude that suddenly approaches. And the same language they hold with respect to the sea. For it is a piece of unlooked-for luck to perish, in order that those things which perish may pursue the road which leads most quickly to God. And the wars which are upon the earth, and the famines, and everything which tends to the destruction of life, are held in very great honour by them. For everything which is the cause of good is to be had in honour. But these things are the cause of good, because of the destruction which accompanies them, if they transmit to God the virtue which is separated from those who perish.

And, as it seems, we have been ignorant that the Egyptians rightly worship the crocodile and the lion and the wolf, because these animals being stronger than the others devour their prey, and entirely destroy it ; the eagle also and the hawk, because they slaughter the weaker animals both in the air and upon the earth. But perhaps also, according to them, man is for this reason held in especial honour, because most of all, by his subtle inventions and arts, he is wont to subdue most of the animals. And lest he himself should have no portion in this good, he becomes the food of others. Again, therefore, those generations are, in their opinion, absurd, which from a small and common seed produce what is great; and it is much more becoming, as they think, that these should be destroyed by God, in order that the divine virtue may be quickly liberated from the troubles incident to living in this world. But what shall we say with respect to lust, and injustice, and things of this sort, Manichæus will ask. Surely against these things discipline and law come to the rescue. Discipline, indeed, using careful forethought that nothing of this sort may have place amongst men; but law inflicting punishment upon any one who has been caught in the commission of anything unjust. But, then, why should it be imputed to the earth as a fault, if the husbandman has neglected to subdue it? because the sovereignty of God, which is according to right, suffers diminution, when some parts of it are productive of fruits, and others not so; or when it has happened that when the winds are sweeping, according to another cause, some derive benefit therefrom, whilst others against their will have to sustain injuries? Surely they must necessarily be ignorant of the character of the things that are contingent, and of those that are necessary. For they would not else thus account such things as prodigies.

CHAP. XV. — THE LUST AND DESIRE OF SENTIENT THINGS; DEMONS; ANIMALS SENTIENT; SO ALSO THE SUN AND THE MOON AND STARS; THE PLATONIC DOCTRINE, NOT THE CHRISTIAN.

Whence, then, come pleasure and desire? For these are the principal evils that they talk of and hate. Nor *does matter appear* to be anything else. That these things, indeed, only belong to animals which are endowed with sense, and that nothing else but that which has sense perceives desire and pleasure, is manifest. For what perception of pleasure and pain is there in a plant? What in the earth, water, or air? And the demons, if indeed they are living beings endowed with sense, for this reason, perhaps, are delighted with what has been instituted in regard to sacrifices, and take it ill when these are wanting to them; but nothing of this sort can be imagined with respect to God. Therefore those who say, "Why are animals affected by pleasure and pain?" should first make the complaint, "Why are these animals endowed with sense, or why do they stand in need of

food?" For if animals were immortal, they would have been set free from corruption and increase; such as the sun and moon and stars, although they are endowed with sense. They are, however, beyond the power of these, and of such a complaint. But man, being able to perceive and to judge, and being potentially wise, — for he has the power to become so, — when he has received what is peculiar to himself, treads it under foot.

CHAP. XVI. — BECAUSE SOME ARE WISE, NOTHING PREVENTS OTHERS FROM BEING SO; VIRTUE IS TO BE ACQUIRED BY DILIGENCE AND STUDY; BY A SOUNDER PHILOSOPHY MEN ARE TO BE CARRIED ONWARDS TO THE GOOD; THE COMMON STUDY OF VIRTUE HAS BY CHRIST BEEN OPENED UP TO ALL.

In general, it is worth while to inquire of these men, " Is it possible for no man to become good, or is it in the power of any one?" For if no man is wise, what of Manichæus himself? I pass over the fact that he not only calls others good, but he also says that they are able to make others such. But if one individual is entirely good, what prevents all from becoming good? For what is possible for one is possible also for all. And by the means by which one has become virtuous, by the same all may become so, unless they assert that the larger share of this virtue is intercepted by such. Again, therefore, first, What necessity is there for labour in submitting to discipline (for even whilst sleeping we may become virtuous), or what cause is there for these men rousing their hearers to hopes of good? For even though wallowing in the mire with harlots, they can obtain their proper good. But if discipline, and better instruction and diligence in acquiring virtue, make a man to become virtuous, let all become so, and that oft-repeated phrase of theirs, the unordered motion of matter, is made void. But it would be much better for them to say that wisdom is an instrument given by God to man, in order that by bringing round by degrees to good that which arises to them, from the fact of their being endowed with sense, out of desire or pleasure, it might remove from them the absurdities that flow from them. For thus they themselves who profess to be teachers of virtue would be objects of emulation for their purpose, and for their mode of life, and there would be great hopes that one day evils will cease, when all men have become wise. And this it seems to me that Jesus took into consideration; and in order that husbandmen, carpenters, builders, and other artisans, might not be driven away from good, He convened a common council of them altogether, and by simple and easy conversations He both raised them to a sense of God, and brought them to desire what was good.

CHAP. XVII. — THE MANICHÆAN IDEA OF VIRTUE IN MATTER SCOUTED ; IF ONE VIRTUE HAS BEEN CREATED IMMATERIAL, THE REST ARE ALSO IMMATERIAL ; MATERIAL VIRTUE AN EXPLODED NOTION.

Moreover, how do they say, did God send divine virtue into matter? For if it always was, and neither is God to be understood as existing prior to it, nor matter either, then again, according to Manichæus, there are three first principles. Perhaps also, a little further on, there will appear to be many more. But if it be adventitious, and something which has come into existence afterwards, how is it void of matter? And if they make it to be a part of God, first, indeed, by this conception, they assert that God is composite and corporeal. But this is absurd, and impossible. And if He fashioned it, and is without matter, I wonder that they have not considered, neither the man himself, nor his disciples, that if (as the orthodox say, the things that come next in order subsist while God remains) God created this virtue of His own free-will, how is it that He is not the author of all other things that are made without the necessity of any pre-existent matter? The consequences, in truth, of this opinion are evidently absurd ; but what does follow is put down next in order. Was it, then, the nature of this virtue to diffuse itself into matter? If it was contrary to its nature, in what manner is it intermingled with it? But if this was in accordance with its nature, it was altogether surely and always with matter. But if this be so, how is it that they call matter evil, which, from the beginning, was intermingled with the divine virtue? In what manner, too, will it be destroyed, the divine virtue which was mingled with it at some time or other seceding to itself? For that it preserves safely what is good, and likely to be productive of some other good to those to whom it is present, is more reasonable than that it should bring destruction or some other evil upon them.

CHAP. XVIII. — DISSOLUTION AND INHERENCE ACCORDING TO THE MANICHÆANS ; THIS IS WELL PUT, AD HOMINEM, WITH RESPECT TO MANES, WHO IS HIMSELF IN MATTER.

This then is the wise assertion which is made by them — namely, that as we see that the body perishes when the soul is separated from it, so also, when virtue has left matter, that which is left, which is matter, will be dissolved and perish. First, indeed, they do not perceive that nothing existent can be destroyed into a non-existent. For that which is non-existent does not exist. But when bodies are disintegrated, and experience a change, a dissolution of them takes place ; so that a part of them goes to earth, a part to air, and a part to something else.

Besides, they do not remember that their doctrine is, that matter is unordered motion. But that which moves of itself, and of which motion is the essence, and not a thing accidentally belonging to it — how is it reasonable to say that when virtue departs, that which was, even before virtue descended into it, should cease to be? Nor do they see the difference, that every body which is devoid of soul is immoveable. For plants also have a vegetable soul. But motion itself, and yet unordered motion, they assert to be the essence of matter. But it were better, that just as in a lyre which sounds out of tune, by the addition of harmony, everything is brought into concord ; so the divine virtue when intermixed with that unordered motion, which, according to them, is matter, should add a certain order to it in the place of its innate disorder, and should always add it suitably to the divine time. For I ask, how was it that Manichæus himself became fitted to treat of these matters, and when at length did he enunciate them? For they allow that he himself was an admixture of matter, and of the virtue received into it. Whether therefore being so, he said these things in unordered motion, surely the opinion is faulty ; or whether he said them by means of the divine virtue, the dogma is dubious and uncertain ; for on the one side, that of the divine virtue, he participates in the truth ; whilst on the side of unordered motion, he is a partaker in the other part, and changes to falsehood.

CHAP. XIX. — THE SECOND VIRTUE OF THE MANICHÆANS BESET WITH THE FORMER, AND WITH NEW ABSURDITIES ; VIRTUE, ACTIVE AND PASSIVE, THE FASHIONER OF MATTER, AND CONCRETE WITH IT ; BODIES DIVIDED BY MANICHÆUS INTO THREE PARTS.

But if it had been said that divine virtue both hath adorned and does adorn matter, it would have been far more wisely said, and in a manner more conducing to conciliate faith in the doctrine and discourses of Manichæus. But God hath sent down another virtue. What has been already said with respect to the former virtue, may be equally said with respect to this, and all the absurdities which follow on the teaching about their first virtue, the same may be brought forward in the present case. But another, who will tolerate? For why did not God send some one virtue which could effect everything? If the human mind is so various towards all things, so that the same man is endowed with a knowledge of geometry, of astronomy, of the carpenter's art, and the like, is it then impossible for God to find one such virtue which should be sufficient for him in all respects, so as not to stand in need of a first and second? And why has one virtue the force rather of a creator, and another that of the patient and recipient, so as to be well fitted for admixture with matter. For I do not again see here the cause of good order, and of that excess which is contrary to it. If it was evil, it was not in the house of God. For since God is the only good, and matter the only evil, we must necessarily say that the other things are of a middle nature, and placed as it were in the middle. But there is found to be a different framer of those things which are of a middle nature, when they say that one cause is creative, and another admixed with matter? Perhaps, therefore, it is that primary antecedent cause which more recent writers speak of in the book περὶ τῶν διαφορῶν. But when the creative virtue took in hand the making of the world, then they say that there was separated from matter that which, even in the admixture, remained in its own virtue, and from this the sun and the moon had their beginning. But that which to a moderate and slight degree had contracted vice and evil, this formed the heaven and the constellations. Lastly came the rest encompassed within these, just as they might happen, which are admixtures of the divine virtue and of matter.

CHAP. XX. — THE DIVINE VIRTUE IN THE VIEW OF THE SAME MANICHÆUS CORPOREAL AND DIVISIBLE ; THE DIVINE VIRTUE ITSELF MATTER WHICH BECOMES EVERYTHING ; THIS IS NOT FITTING.

I, indeed, besides all these things, wonder that they do not perceive that they are making the divine virtue to be corporeal, and dividing it, as it were, into parts. For why, as in the case of matter, is not the divine virtue also passible and divisible throughout, and from one of its parts the sun made, and from another the moon? For clearly this is what they assert to belong to the divine virtue ; and this is what we said was the property of matter, which by itself is nothing, but when it has received form and qualities, everything is made which is divided and distinct. If, therefore, as from one subject, the divine virtue, only the sun and the moon have their beginning, and these things are different, why was anything else made? But if all things are made, what follows is manifest, that divine virtue is matter, and that, too, such as is made into forms. But if nothing else but the sun and moon are what was created by the divine virtue, then what is intermixed with all things is the sun and moon ; and each of the stars is the sun and moon, and each individual animal of those who live on land, and of fowls, and of creatures amphibious. But this, not even those who exhibit juggling tricks would admit, as, I think, is evident to every one.

CHAP XXI. — SOME PORTIONS OF THE VIRTUE HAVE GOOD IN THEM, OTHERS MORE GOOD ; IN THE SUN AND THE MOON IT IS INCORRUPT, IN OTHER THINGS DEPRAVED ; AN IMPROBABLE OPINION.

But if any one were to apply his mind to what follows, the road would not appear to be plain and straightforward, but more arduous even than that which has been passed. For they say that the sun and moon have contracted no stain from their admixture with matter. And now they cannot say how other things have become deteriorated contrary to their own proper nature. For if, when it was absolute and by itself, the divine virtue was so constituted that one portion of it was good, and another had a greater amount of goodness in it, according to the old tale of the centaurs, who as far as the breast were men, and in the lower part horses, which are both good animals, but the man is the better of the two ; so also, in the divine virtue, it is to be understood that the one portion of it is the better and the more excellent, and the other will occupy the second and inferior place. And in the same way, with respect to matter, the one portion possesses, as it were, an excess of evil ; while others again are different, and about that other the language will be different.[1] For it is possible to conceive that from the beginning the sun and moon, by a more skilful and prudent judgment, chose for themselves the parts of matter that were less evil for the purposes of admixture, that they might remain in their own perfection and virtue ;' but in the lapse of time, when the evils lost their force and became old, they brought out so much of the excess in the good, while the rest of its parts fell away, not, indeed, without foresight, and yet not with the same foresight, did each object share according to its quantity in the evil that was in matter. But since, with respect to this virtue, nothing of a different kind is asserted by them, but it is to be understood throughout to be alike and of the same nature, their argument is improbable ; because in the admixture part remains pure and incorrupt, while the other has contracted some share of evil.

CHAP. XXII. — THE LIGHT OF THE MOON FROM THE SUN ; THE INCONVENIENCE OF THE OPINION THAT SOULS ARE RECEIVED IN IT ; THE TWO DELUGES OF THE GREEKS.

Now, they say that the sun and the moon having by degrees separated the divine virtue from matter, transmit it to God. But if they had only to a slight degree frequented the schools of the astronomers, it would not have happened to them to fall into these fancies, nor would they

---

[1] This passage and the following sentences are corrupt. Possibly something is wanting. — Tr.

have been ignorant that the moon, which, according to the opinion of some, is itself without light, receives its light from the sun, and that its configurations are just in proportion to its distance from the sun, and that it is then full moon when it is distant from the sun one hundred and eighty degrees. It is in conjunction when it is in the same degree with the sun. Then, is it not wonderful how it comes to pass that there should be so many souls, and from such diverse creatures? For there is the soul of the world itself, and of the animals, of plants, of nymphs, and demons, and amongst these are distinguished by appearance those of fowls, of land animals, and animals amphibious; but in the moon one like body is always seen by us. And what of the continuity of this body? When the moon is half-full, it appears a semicircle, and when it is in its third quarter, the same again. How then, and with what figure, are they assumed into the moon? For if it be light as fire, it is probable that they would not only ascend as far as the moon, but even higher, continually; but if it be heavy, it would not be possible for them at all to reach the moon. And what is the reason that that which first arrives at the moon is not immediately transmitted to the sun, but waits for the full moon until the rest of the souls arrive? When then the moon, from having been full, decreases, where does the virtue remain during that time? until the moon, which has been emptied of the former souls, just as a desolated city, shall receive again a fresh colony. For a treasure-house should have been marked out in some part of the earth, or of the clouds, or in some other place, where the congregated souls might stand ready for emigration to the moon. But, again, a second question arises. What then is the cause that it is not full immediately? or why does it again wait fifteen days? Nor is this less to be wondered at than that which has been said, that never within the memory of man has the moon become full after the fifteen days. Nay, not even in the time of the deluge of Deucalion, nor in that of Phoroneus, when all things, so to speak, which were upon the face of the earth perished, and it happened that a great quantity of virtue was separated from matter. And, besides these things, one must consider the productiveness of generations, and their barrenness, and also the destruction of them; and since these things do not happen in order, neither ought the order of the full moon, nor the times of the waning moon, to be so carefully observed.

CHAP. XXIII. — THE IMAGE OF MATTER IN THE SUN, AFTER WHICH MAN IS FORMED; TRIFLING FANCIES; IT IS A MERE FANCY, TOO, THAT MAN IS FORMED FROM MATTER; MAN IS EITHER A COMPOSITE BEING, OR A SOUL, OR MIND AND UNDERSTANDING.

Neither is this to be regarded with slight attention. For if the divine virtue which is in matter be infinite, those things cannot diminish it which the sun and moon fashion. For that which remains from that finite thing which has been assumed is infinite. But if it is finite, it would be perceived by the senses in intervals proportionate to the amount of its virtue that had been subtracted from the world. But all things remain as they were. Now what understanding do these things not transcend in their incredibleness, when they assert that man was created and formed after the image of matter that is seen in the sun? For images are the forms of their archetypes. But if they include man's image in the sun, where is the exemplar after which his image is formed? For, indeed, they are not going to say that man is really man, or divine virtue; for this, indeed, they mix up with matter, and they say that the image is seen in the sun, which, as they think, was formed afterwards from the secretion of matter. Neither can they bring forward the creative cause of all things, for this they say was sent to preserve safety to the divine virtue; so that, in their opinion, this must be altogether ascribed to the sun; for this reason, doubtless, that it happens by his arrival and presence that the sun and moon are separated from matter.

Moreover, they assert that the image is seen in the sun; but they say that matter fashioned man. In what manner, and by what means? For it is not possible that this should fashion him. For besides that, thus according to them, man is the empty form of an empty form, and having no real existence, it has not as yet been possible to conceive how man can be the product of matter. For the use of reason and sense belongs not to that matter which they assume. Now what, according to them, is man? Is he a mixture of soul and body? Or another thing, or that which is superior to the entire soul, the mind? But if he is mind, how can the more perfect and the better part be the product of that which is worse; or if he be soul (for this they say is divine virtue), how can they, when they have taken away from God the divine virtue, subject this to the creating workmanship of matter? But if they leave to him body alone, let them remember again that it is by itself immovable, and that they say that the essence of matter is motion. Neither do they think that anything of itself, and its own genius, is attracted to matter. Nor is it reasonable to lay it down, that what is composed of these things is the product of this. To think, indeed, that that which is fashioned by any one is inferior to its fashioner seems to be beyond controversy. For thus the world is inferior to its Creator or Fashioner, and the works of art inferior to the artificer. If then man be the product of matter, he must surely be inferior to it. Now, men leave nothing inferior to matter; and it is not reasonable that the divine virtue should be commingled with matter, and with that which is inferior to it. But the things which they assert out of indulgence, as it were, and by way of dispensation, these they do not seem to understand. For what is the reason of their thinking that matter has bound the image of God to the substance of man? Or, why is not the image sufficient, as in a mirror, that man should appear? Or, as the sun himself is sufficient for the origination and destruction of all things that are made, hath he imitated an image in the work of their creation? With which of those things which he possessed? Was it with the divine virtue which was mingled with it, so that the divine virtue should have the office of an instrument in respect of matter? Is it by unordered motion that he will thus give matter a form? But all like things, in exquisite and accurate order, by imitating, attain their end. For they do not suppose that a house, or a ship, or any other product of art, is effected by disorder; nor a statue which art has fashioned to imitate man.

CHAP. XXIV. — CHRIST IS MIND, ACCORDING TO THE MANICHÆANS; WHAT IS HE IN THE VIEW OF THE CHURCH? INCONGRUITY IN THEIR IDEA OF CHRIST; THAT HE SUFFERED ONLY IN APPEARANCE, A DREAM OF THE MANICHÆANS; NOTHING IS ATTRIBUTED TO THE WORD BY WAY OF FICTION.

Christ, too, they do not acknowledge; yet they speak of Christ, but they take some other element, and giving to the Word, designating His sacred person, some other signification than that in which it is rightly received, they say that He is mind. But if, when they speak of Him as that which is known, and that which knows, and wisdom as having the same meaning, they are found to agree with those things which the Church doctors say of Him, how comes it then that they reject all that is called ancient history? But let us see whether they make Him to be something adventitious and new, and which has come on from without, and by accident, as the opinion of some is. For they who hold this opinion say, as seems very plausible, that about the seventh year, when the powers of perception became distinct, He made His entrance into the body. But if Christ be mind, as they imagine, then will He be both Christ and not Christ. For before that mind and sense entered, He was not. But if Christ, as they will have it, be mind, then into Him already existing does the mind make its entrance, and thus, again, according to their

opinion, will it be mind. Christ, therefore, is and is not at the same time. But if, according to the more approved sect of them, mind is all things which are, since they assume matter to be not produced, and coeval so to speak with God, this first mind and matter they hold to be Christ; if, indeed, Christ be the mind, which is all things, and matter is one of those things which are, and is itself not produced.

They say it was by way of appearance, and in this manner, that the divine virtue in matter was affixed to the cross; and that He Himself did not undergo this punishment, since it was impossible that He should suffer this; which assertion Manichæus himself has taken in hand to teach in a book written upon the subject, that the divine virtue was enclosed in matter, and again departs from it. The mode of this they invent. That it should be said, indeed, in the doctrine of the Church, that He gave Himself up for the remission of sins, obtains credit from the vulgar, and appears likewise in the Greek histories, which say that some "surrendered themselves to death in order to ensure safety to their countrymen." And of this doctrine the Jewish history has an example, which prepares the son of Abraham as a sacrifice to God.[1] But to subject Christ to His passion merely for the sake of display, betrays great ignorance, for the Word is God's representative, to teach and inform us of actual verities.

CHAP. XXV. — THE MANICHÆAN ABSTINENCE FROM LIVING THINGS RIDICULOUS; THEIR MADNESS IN ABHORRING MARRIAGE; THE MYTHOLOGY OF THE GIANTS; TOO ALLEGORICAL AN EXPOSITION.

They abstain also from living things. If, indeed, the reason of their abstinence were other than it is, it ought not to be too curiously investigated. But if they do so for this reason, that the divine virtue is more or less absent or present to them, this their meaning is ridiculous. For if plants be more material, how is it in accordance with reason to use that which is inferior for food and sustenance? or, if there be more of the divine virtue in them, how are things of this sort useful as food, when the soul's faculty of nourishing and making increase is more corporeal? Now in that they abstain from marriage and the rites of Venus, fearing lest by the succession of the race the divine virtue should dwell more in matter, I wonder how in thinking so they allow of themselves? For if neither the providence of God suffices, both by generations and by those things which are always and in the same manner existent, to separate off the divine virtue from matter, what can the cunning and subtlety of Manichæus effect for that purpose?

[1] Gen. xxii. 1.

For assuredly by no giant's co-operation does assistance come to God, in order by the removal of generations to make the retreat of the divine virtue from matter quick and speedy. But what the poets say about the giants is manifestly a fable. For those who lay it down about these, bring forward such matters in allegories, by a species of fable hiding the majesty of their discourse ; as, for instance, when the Jewish history relates that angels came down to hold[1] intercourse with the daughters of men ; for this saying signifies that the nutritive powers of the soul descended from heaven to earth. But the poets who say that they, when they had emerged in full armour from the earth, perished immediately after they stirred up rebellion against the gods, in order that they might insinuate the frail and quickly-perishing constitution of the body, adorn their poetry in this way for the sake of refreshing the soul by the strangeness of the occurrence. But these, understanding nothing of all this, wheresoever they can get hold of a paralogism from whatsoever quarter it comes, greedily seize on it as a God-send, and strive with all their arts to overturn truth by any means.

CHAP. XXVI. — THE MUCH-TALKED-OF FIRE OF THE MANICHÆANS ; THAT FIRE MATTER ITSELF.

That fire, endowed indeed with the power of burning, yet possessing no light, which is outside the world, in what region has it place? For if it is in the world, why does the world hitherto continue safe? For if at some time or other it is to destroy it, by approaching it, now also it is conjoined with it. But if it be apart from it, as it were on high in its own region, what will hereafter happen to make it descend upon the world? Or in what way will it leave its own place, and by what necessity and violence? And what substance of fire can be conceived without fuel, and how can what is moist serve as fuel to it, unless what is rather physiologically said about this does not fall within the province of our present disquisition? But this

[1] Gen. vi. 2.

is quite manifest from what has been said. For the fire existing outside the world is just that which they call matter, since the sun and the moon, being the purest of the pure, by their divine virtue, are separate and distinct from that fire, no part of them being left in it. This fire is matter itself, absolutely and *per se*, entirely removed from all admixture with the divine virtue. Wherefore when the world has been emptied of all the divine virtue which is opposed to it, and again a fire of this sort shall be left remaining, how then shall the fire either destroy anything, or be consumed by it? For, from that which is like, I do not see in what way corruption is to take place. For what matter will become when the divine virtue has been separated from it, this it was before that the divine virtue was commingled with it. If indeed matter is to perish when it is bereft of the divine virtue, why did it not perish before it came in contact with the divine virtue, or any creative energy? Was it in order that matter might successively perish, and do this *ad infinitum?* And what is the use of this? For that which had not place from the first volition, how shall this have place from one following? or what reason is there for God to put off things which, not even in the case of a man, appears to be well? For as regards those who deliberate about what is impossible, this is said to happen to them, that they do not wish for that which is possible. But if nothing else, they speak of God transcending substance, and bring Him forward as some new material, and that not such as intelligent men always think to be joined with Him, but that which investigation discovers either to be not existing at all, or to be the extreme of all things, and which can with difficulty be conceived of by the human mind. For this fire, devoid of light, is it of more force than matter, which is to be left desolate by divine virtue, or is it of less? And if it is of less, how will it overcome that which is of more? but if it is of more, it will be able to bring it back to itself, being of the same nature ; yet will it not destroy it, as neither does the Nile swallow up the streams that are divided off from it.

ELUCIDATION.

IF anything could be more dreary than the Manichæan heresy itself, it may be questioned whether it be not the various views that have been entertained concerning our author. I have often remarked the condensation of valuable information given by Dr. Murdock in his notes upon Mosheim, but he fails to get in the half that needs to be noted.[1] He tells us that "Alexander of Lycopolis flourished probably about A.D. 350." He adds, "Fabricius supposes that he

[1] Mosheim, *E. H.,* vol. i. p 383, note 5, Murdock's edition, New York, 1844. His references to Lardner in this case do not accord with my copy.

was first a Pagan and a Manichee, and afterwards a Catholic Christian. Cave is of the same opinion. Beausobre thinks he was a *mere pagan*.[1] Lardner thinks he was a Gentile, but well acquainted with the Manichees and other Christians,[2] and that he had *some knowledge* of the Old and New Testaments, to which he occasionally refers. He *speaks with respect of Christ* and the Christian philosophy, and appears to have been "a learned and candid man." Of an eminent Christian bishop, all this seems very puzzling; and I feel it a sort of duty to the youthful student to give the statements of the learned Lardner in an abridged form, with such references to the preceding pages as may serve in place of a series of elucidations.

According to this invaluable critic, the learned are not able to agree concerning Alexander. *Some think* he was a Christian, others believe that he was a heathen. Fabricius, who places him in the *fourth* century, holds to this latter opinion;[3] all which agrees with our Cave.[4] Photius makes him Archbishop of Nicopolis.[5] Tillemont thinks[6] he was a pagan philosopher, who wrote to persuade his friends to prefer "the doctrine of the churches" to that of Manes. Combefis, his editor,[7] thinks him very ancient, because he appears to have learned the principles of this heresy from the immediate disciples of the heretic. Beausobre,[8] the standard authority, is of like opinion, and Mosheim approves his reasoning.

Nothing in his work, according to Lardner, proves that our author wrote near the beginning of the fourth century, and he decides upon the middle of that century as his epoch.

Alexander gives a very honourable character to the genuine Christian philosophy, and asserts its adaptation to the common people, and, indeed, to all sorts of men.[9] He certainly is not mute as to Christ. His tribute to the Saviour is, if not affectionate, yet a just award to Him.[10] By the "council of all together," he intends the College of the Apostles,[11] made up of fishermen and publicans and tent-makers, in which he sees a design of the blessed Jesus to meet this class, and, in short, all classes. It is clear enough that Alexander has some knowledge of Christ, some knowledge of the received doctrine of the churches,[12] or orthodox Christians; and he appears to blame the Manichees for not receiving the Scripture of the Old Testament.[12]

He argues against their absurd opinion that Christ was "Mind;"[12] also that, though crucified, He did not suffer:[12] and he affirms[12] that it would be more reasonable to say, agreeably to the ecclesiastical doctrine, that "He *gave Himself for the remission of sins.*" He refers to the sacrifice of Isaac,[12] and to the story of Cain and Abel;[13] also to the mysterious subject of the angels and the daughters of men.[14] Like an Alexandrian theologian, he expounds this, however, against the literal sense, as an allegory.

My reader will be somewhat amused with the terse summing-up of Lardner: "I am rather inclined to think he was a Gentile. . . . He was evidently a learned and rational man. His observations concerning the Christian philosophy deserve particular notice. To me this work of Alexander appears very curious."

---

[1] *Histoire des Manichéens* (Lardner's reference), pp. 236–237.

[2] *Credib.*, vol. vii. p. 574, ed. London, 1829.

[3] Lardner's reference is: *Bib. G.*, lib. v. c. 1, tom. 5, p. 290.

[4] Long extract from Cave *ubi supra*. He quotes the Latin of Cave's *Diss. on Writers of Uncertain Date.*

[5] Lardner's reference is to Photius, *Contra Manich.*, i. cap. 11.

[6] Lardner quotes from the *Hist. des Manich.*, art. 16., *Mémoires*, etc., tom. iv.

[7] Reference defective. See Lardner, *Credib.*, vol. iii. 269. Here will be found (p. 252) a learned examination of Archelaus, and what amounts to a treatise on these Manichæans.

[8] For Beausobre's summary of Alexander's deficiencies, see condensed statement in Lardner, vol. iii. p. 575.

[9] Cap. i. p. 241, *supra*. A beautiful exordium. A recent writer, speaking of Potamiæna and Herais, virgin martyrs, and catechumens of Origen, remarks, that "the number of young women of high character who appreciated the teachings of this great master, *many of whom were employed as copyists of his works*, is creditable to the state of Christian society at that period" (Mahan, *Church Hist.*, p. 237). It was to avoid scandal as well as temptation in his relations with these that he fell into his heroic mistake.

[10] Cap. xxiv. p. 251, *supra*. Who can imagine that the author of this chapter is not a Christian? Observe what he says of "the Word."

[11] Cap. xvi. p. 247.

[12] Cap xxiv. p. 251.

[13] Note the reference to the Old and New Testaments entire, p. 243, *supra*.

[14] Cap. xxv. p. 252, *supra*.

PETER

[TRANSLATED BY THE REV. JAMES B. H. HAWKINS, M.A.]

INTRODUCTORY NOTICE

TO

PETER, BISHOP OF ALEXANDRIA.

[A.D. 260 [1] –300–311.] Entering upon the fourth century, we may well pause to reflect upon what Alexandria has been to the Church of Christ,— the mother of churches, the mother of saints, maintaining always the intellectual and even the ecclesiastical primacy of Christendom. " Ye are the light of the world," said the great Enlightener to the Galileans of an obscure and despised Roman province. But who could have prophesied that Egypt should again be the pharos of the world, as it was in Moses? Who could have foreseen the " men of Galilee " taking possession of the Alexandrian Library, and demonstrating the ways of Providence in creating the Bible of the Seventy, and in the formation of the Hellenistic Greek, for their ultimate use? Who could have imagined the Evangelist Mark and the eloquent Apollos to be the destined instruments for founding the schools of Christendom, and shaping scientific theology? Who would not have looked for all this in some other way, and preferably in Athens or in Rome? But who would have expected the visit of God Incarnate to Nazareth, and not to Alexandria?

In Peter's day Antioch was coming to be a school under the influence of Malchion's genius and that of the bishops who withstood Paulus of Samosata. Malchion had taught there in the " School of Sciences," and learning was once more to be made the handmaid of true religion. But Alexandria was still the seat of Christian illumination and the fountain of orthodoxy ; its very ferment always clarifying its thought, and leaving " wine well refined," and pure from the lees.

To this subject I shall have occasion to refer again in an elucidation subjoined to the works of Alexander (successor to Peter), in which, for a final view of the great Alexandrian school, I shall gather up some fragments in brief outline. Here it may be enough to remark, that, until the definite development of the school of Antioch (*circa* A.D. 350), I have regarded the whole Orient as dominated and formed by the brain of the grand metropolis of Egypt and the Pentapolis. I have considered the great Dionysius as really presiding in the Synod of Antioch, though absent in the body, and have regarded Malchion as his voice in that council, which we must not forget was presided over by Firmilian, a pupil of Origen, and a true Alexandrian disciple.

Peter's conflict with Meletius shall be noted in an elucidation. We shall see that the heresy of Paulus as well as the Meletian schism are but chapters in one prolonged history, of which the outcrop was Arianism. Now, as to Alexandria we owe the intrepid defenders of truth in all these conflicts, we must not forget that they are to be judged by the *product* of their united testimony, and not by their occasional individualisms and infirmities of mind and speech while they were creating the theological dialect of Christendom and the formulas of orthodoxy.

Peter was able to maintain his canonical authority against the mischievous rebellion of Meletius ; and the history of this schism is forcibly illustrative of those ἀρχαῖα ἔθη which the Nicene Synod recognised, confirming the primacy of Alexandria, and striving to suppress Meletianism by

---

[1] This first date is conjectural.

firm but moderate measures based upon the primitive maxims.   Peter left a pure and holy memory to the Church, and sealed his testimony in martyrdom.

TRANSLATOR'S INTRODUCTORY NOTICE.[1]

EUSEBIUS alone, of the more ancient writers, speaks in terms of the highest praise of Peter, Bishop of Alexandria.   He was, says he, a divine bishop, both for the sanctity of his life, and also for his diligent study and knowledge of the Holy Scriptures ;[2] and in another place he styles him " that excellent doctor of the Christian religion," who, indeed, during the whole period of his episcopate, which he held for twelve years, obtained for himself the highest renown.   He obtained the bishopric of Alexandria next in succession to Theonas.   He governed that church about three years before the persecution broke out :[3] the rest of his time he spent in the exercise of a closer discipline over himself, yet did he not in the meanwhile neglect to provide for the common interests of the Church.   In the ninth year of the persecution he was beheaded, and gained the crown of martyrdom.   So far we have the account of Eusebius, whom Dodwell[4] proves to have accurately distributed the years of Peter's episcopate.   After Peter had spent twelve years as bishop, and in the ninth year of the persecution which broke out under Maximin, he was beheaded ; so that his martyrdom falls in the year of our Lord 311 — as the Egyptians reckon on the 29th day of the month Athyr, which answers to our 25th of November, as Lequien,[5] after Renaudot,[6] has observed.

St. Peter wrote in the fourth year of the persecution, A.D. 306, some Canons Penitential with reference to those who had lapsed.   They are to be met with in every collection of Canons.   In the *Pandecta Canonum* of Bishop Beveridge,[7] they are accompanied by the notes of Joannes Zonaras and Theodorus Balsamon.   Upon these Penitential Canons, however, Tillemont[8] should be consulted.   Moreover, according to Renaudot,[9] Echmimensis, Ebnapalus, Abulfaragius, and other Oriental Christians of every sect, make use of the testimony of these Canons ; and in the anonymous collections of them called *Responsa*, some fragments of other works of Peter are extant.   Some of these are praised by the Jacobites, in the work which they call *Fides patrum*.   In another work, entitled *Unio pretiosus*, occurs a homily of Peter on the baptism of Christ.

The fragments of the other writings of this holy martyr, which have been preserved by the Greeks, are here appended to the Penitential Canons.   For instance : (1) An extract from his book *De Deitate*, which is extant in the *Acta Conciliorum Ephesini et Chalcedonensis ;* (2) Another fragment from the homily *De Adventu Salvatoris*, cited by Leontius Byzantinus in his first book against Nestorius and Eutyches ; (3) An epistle of the same prelate to the Alexandrine Church recently published, together with some other old ecclesiastical monuments by Scipio Maffei.[10]   Peter is said to have written this epistle after one addressed to Meletius, Bishop of Lycopolis.   In it, after interdicting the Alexandrians from communion with Meletius, he says that he will himself come in company with some wise doctors, and will examine into his tenets ; alluding, most probably, to the synod held afterwards at Alexandria, in which Meletius was deposed from his office.   Athanasius says,[11] respecting this synod, " Peter, who was amongst us as bishop before the persecution, and who died a martyr in the persecution, deposed in common council of the bishops, Meletius, an Egyptian bishop, who had been convicted of many crimes."   But with

---

[1] [After Gallandi, by the translator, the Rev. James B. H. Hawkins, M.A.]

[2] θεῖον ἐπισκόπων χρῆμα, βίου τε καὶ ἀρετῆς ἕνεκα καὶ τῆς τῶν ἱερῶν λόγων συνασκήσεως.   Eusebius, *Hist. Eccles.*, lib. ix. cap. 6; lib. viii. cap. 13; lib. vii. cap. 32, towards the end.

[3] πρὸ τοῦ διωγμοῦ τρίσιν οὐδ' ὅλοις ἡγησάμενος τῆς Ἐκκλησίας.

[4] Dodwell, *Dissert. Sing. ad. Pears.*, cap. 6, sec. 21, p. 74.

[5] Lequien, *Oriens Christ*, tom. ii. p. 397.

[6] Renaudot, *Hist. Patriarch. Alex.*, p. 60.

[7] Συνοδικὸν.   Vol. ii. p. 8, fol., Oxon., 1672.

[8] Tillemont, *Mem.*, tom. v. p. 450.

[9] Renaudot, *l.c.*, p. 61, *seqq.*

[10] Maffei, *Osservazione Letterarie*, tom. iii p. 17.

[11] Athanasius, *Apol. contra Arian*, sec. 39, tom. i. p. 177.

respect to the time in which the mournful Meletian schism commenced, Maffei [1] defends the opinions of Baronius,[2] who connects it with the year A.D. 306, against Pagius and Montfaucon, both from this epistle of Petrus Alexandrinus, and also from another of the four bishops, of which Peter makes mention in his own; (4) A passage from the *Sermo in Sanctum Pascha*, or from some other work of Peter's on the same subject, is given in the *Diatriba de Paschate*, prefixed to the *Chronicon Alexandrinum S. Paschale*, and published separately in the *Uranologion* of Petavius, fol. Paris, 1630, p. 396.

[1] Maffei, *l.c.*, p. 24.
[2] Baronius, *Ad Annum*, 306, sec. 44. [Elucidation I.]

THE GENUINE ACTS OF PETER.[1]

WERE all the limbs of my body to be turned into tongues, and all the joints of my limbs to utter articulate sounds, it would noways be sufficient to express who, how great and how good, was our most blessed Father Peter, Archbishop of Alexandria. Especially incongruous do I consider it to commit to paper what perils he underwent by tyrants, what conflicts he endured with Gentiles and heretics, lest I should seem to make these the subjects of my panegyric rather than that passion to which he manfully submitted to make safe the people of God. Nevertheless, because the office of the narrator must fail in narrating his inmost conversation and wonderful deeds, and language is noways sufficient for the task, I have considered it convenient to describe only those exploits of his by which he is known to have attained to the pontificate,[2] and after Arius had been cut off from the unity of the Church,[3] to have been crowned with the martyr's laurel. Yet this do I consider to be a glorious end, and a spectacle of a magnificent contest, sufficient for those who do not doubt of a truthful narration, which is unstained by falsehood. In commencing, therefore, our account of the episcopate of this most holy man, let us call to our aid his own language, in order that we may make it co-operate with our own style.

Alexandria is a city of exceeding magnitude, which holds the first place not only among the Egyptians, but the Thebans also and the Libyans, who are at no great distance from Egypt.[4] A cycle of two hundred and eighty-five years from the incarnation of our Lord and Saviour Jesus Christ had rolled round, when the venerable Theonas, the bishop of this city, by an ethereal flight, mounted upwards to the celestial kingdoms. To him Peter, succeeding at the helm of the Church, was by all the clergy and the whole Christian community appointed bishop, the sixteenth in order from Mark the Evangelist, who was also archbishop of the city. He in truth, like Phosphor rising among the stars, shining forth with the radiance of his sacred virtues, most magnificently governed the citadel of the faith. Inferior to none who had gone before him in his knowledge of Holy Scripture, he nobly applied himself to the advantage and instruction of the Church; being of singular prudence, and in all things perfect, a true priest and victim of God, he watchfully laboured night and day in every sacerdotal care.

But because virtue is the mark of the zealot, "it is the tops of the mountains that are struck by lightning,"[5] he hence endured multifarious conflicts with rivals. Why need I say more? He lived in persecution almost the whole of his life. Meanwhile he ordained fifty-five bishops. Meletius lastly — in mind and name most black — was made the schismatical bishop of the city of Lycopolis, doing many things against the rule of the canons, and surpassing even the bloody soldiery in cruelty who, at the time of the Lord's Passion, feared to rend His coat; he was so hurried on by giving the rein to his madness, that, rending asunder the Catholic Church not only in the cities of Egypt, but even in its villages, he ordained bishops of his own party, nor cared he aught for Peter, nor for Christ, who was in the person of Peter. To him Arius, who was yet a laic, and not marked with the clerical tonsure,[6] adhered, and was to him and his family most dear; and not without reason: every ani-

---

[1] As interpreted by Anastasius Bibliothecarius. Apud Maium, *Spicilegii*, tom. iii. p. 671. That Anastasius Bibliothecarius translated from the Greek the *Passion* of St. Peter, Bishop of Alexandria, is affirmed by Anastasius himself in his prologue, *Ad Passionem Martyrum*, MCCCCLXXX., published by Mabillon in the *Museum Italicum*, tom. i. part ii. p. 80: "Post translatam a me ad petitionem sanctitatis tuæ (he is addressing Peter, Bishop of Gavinum), passionem præcipui doctoris et martyris, Petri Alexandrinæ urbis episcopi." And then an anonymous biographer of John viii., in *Muratori R. I. S.*, tom. iii. p. i. p. 269, confirms the same. Anastasius, the librarian of the Roman church, translated from the Greek into Latin the *Passion* of St. Peter, Archbishop of Alexandria. But it is a matter of conjecture which of the different *Passions* of St. Peter Anastasius translated. Of the Acts of St. Peter, there are three different records: — (1) *Acta Sincera*, which, according to Baronius, are the most genuine. (2) A shorter Latin version, by Surius. (3) A Greek version, by Combefis.

[2] [Significant to find this term applied from Western thought to this great bishopric by such a translator as Anastasius.]

[3] [See p. 257, *supra*, and p. 263, *infra*, note 2. Not his final rejection after the Nicene Council.]

[4] [He is here speaking of its civil importance only.]

[5] Hor., *Od.*, ii. 10, 11.

[6] [Anastasius, *more Romano*, uses the Middle-Age terminology as if it had existed in the Ante-Nicene period. So all the successors of the apostles at Rome, including St. Peter himself, are transformed into "Popes." We owe this abuse to the "False Decretals," of which we treat hereafter. But why is exploded fiction and demonstrated untruth perpetuated by enlightened historians? See vol. v. p. 155.]

261

mal, as says the Scripture, loves its like. But upon this coming to his knowledge, the man of God being affected with grief, said that this persecution was worse than the former. And although he was in hiding, yet, so far as his strength permitted, directing everywhere his exhortations, and preaching up the unity of the Church, he strengthened men to withstand the ignorance and nefarious temerity of Meletius. Whence it came to pass that not a few, being influenced by his salutary admonitions, departed from the Meletian impiety.

Nearly about the same time Arius, armed with a viper's craft, as if deserting the party of Meletius, fled for refuge to Peter, who at the request of the bishops raised him to the honours of the diaconate, being ignorant of his exceeding hypocrisy. For he was even as a snake suffused with deadly poison. Yet neither can the imposition of hands upon this false one be imputed as a crime to this holy man, as the simulated magic arts of Simon is not ascribed to Philip. Meanwhile, the detestable wickedness of the Meletians increased beyond measure ; and the blessed Peter, fearing lest the plague of heresy should spread over the whole flock committed to his care, and knowing that there is no fellowship with light and darkness, and no concord betwixt Christ and Belial, by letter separated the Meletians from the communion of the Church. And because an evil disposition cannot long be concealed, upon that instant the wicked Arius, when he saw his aiders and abettors cast down from the dignity of the Church, gave way to sadness and lamentation. This did not escape the notice of this holy man. For when his hypocrisy was laid bare, immediately using the evangelical sword, "If thy right eye offend thee, pluck it out and cast it from thee," [1] and cutting off Arius from the body of the Church as a putrid limb, he expelled and banished him from the communion of the faithful.

This done, the storm of persecution suddenly abating, peace, although for a short time, smiled. Then this most choice priest of the Lord shone manifestly before the people, and the faithful began to run in crowds to keep the memory of the martyrs, and to assemble in congregations to the praise of Christ. Whom this priest of the divine law quickened with his holy eloquence, and so roused and strengthened that the multitude of believers increased continually in the Church. But the old enemy of salvation of man did not long remain quiet and look on these things with favouring eyes. For on a sudden the storm-cloud of paganism gave forth its hostile thunder, and like a winter shower struck against the serenity of the Church, and chased it away

in flight. But that this may be understood more clearly, we must necessarily turn back to the atrocities of Diocletian, that impious one, and rebel against God, and also to Maximian Galerius, who at that time, with his son Maximin, harassed the regions of the East with his tyrannical sway.

For in the time of this man the fire of Christian persecution so raged, that not only in one region of the universe, but even throughout the whole world, both by land and by sea, the storm of impiety gave forth its thunder. The imperial edicts and most cruel decrees running hither and thither, the worshippers of Christ were put to death now openly, and now by clandestine snares ; no day, no night, passed off free from the effusion of Christian blood. Nor was the type of slaughter of one kind alone ; some were slain with diverse and most bitter tortures ; some again, that they might want the humanity of kinsmen, and burial in their own country, were transported to other climes, and by certain new machinations of punishment, and as yet to the age unknown, were driven to the goal of martyrdom. Oh, the horrible wickedness ! So great was their impiety that they even upturned from their foundations the sanctuaries of divine worship, and burned the sacred books in the fire. Diocletian of execrable memory having died, Constantinus Major was elected to administer the kingdom, and in the western parts began to hold the reins of government.

In these days information was brought to Maximin about the aforesaid archbishop,[2] that he was a leader and holding chief place among the Christians ; and he, inflamed with his accustomed iniquity, on the instant ordered Peter to be apprehended and cast into prison. For which purpose he despatched to Alexandria five tribunes, accompanied with their bands of soldiers, who, coming thither as they had been commanded, suddenly seized the priest of Christ and committed him to the custody of a prison. Wonderful was the devotion of the faithful ! When it was known that this holy man was shut up in the dungeon of the prison, an incredibly large number ran together, principally a band of monks and of virgins, and with no material arms, but with rivers of tears and the affection of pious minds, surrounded the prison's circuit.[3] And as good sons towards a good father, nay, rather as the Christian members of a most Christian head, adhered to him with all their bowels of compassion, and were to him as walls, observing that

---

[1] Matt. v. 29.

[2] [Post-Nicene terminology, condemned even by the Gallicans, as, e.g., Dupin. Alexandria, founded by St. Mark, was virtually an Apostolic See, though commonly called the Evangelic See.]
[3] Thus watched the faithful at Milan around Ambrose, their bishop, against whom the wrath of the Arian Empress Justina was directed, according to the testimony of Augustine, who was an eye-witness. Cf. *Confess.*, lib. ix. cap. 7.

no pagan might get an opportunity of access to him. One indeed was the vow of all, one their voice, and one their compassion and resolve to die rather than see any evil happen to this holy man. Now while the man of God was being kept for a few days in the same stocks, with his body thrust back, the tribunes made a suggestion to the king concerning him, but he, after his ferocious manner, gave his sentence for capitally punishing the most blessed patriarch. And when this got to the ears of the Christians, they all with one mind began to guard the approaches to the prison with groaning and lamentation, and persistently prevented any Gentile from obtaining access to him. And when the tribunes could by no means approach him to put him to death, they held a council, and determined that the soldiers should with drawn swords break in upon the crowd of people, and so draw him forth to behead him ; and if any one opposed, he should be put to death.

Arius, in the meanwhile, having as yet been endowed only with the dignity of a Levite,[1] and fearing lest, after the death of so great a father, he should noways be able to get reconciled to the Church, came to those who held the chief place amongst the clergy, and, hypocrite that he was, by his sorrowful entreaties and plausible discourse, endeavoured to persuade the holy archbishop to extend to him his compassion, and to release him from the ban of excommunication. But what is more deceptive than a feigned heart? What more simple than a holy composure? There was no delay ; those who had been requested went in to the priest of Christ, and, after the customary oration, prostrating themselves on the ground, and with groans and tears kissing his sacred hands, implored him, saying : "Thee, indeed, most blessed father, for the excellence of thy faith, the Lord hath called to receive the martyr's crown, which we noways doubt does quickly await thee. Therefore do we think it right that, with thy accustomed piety, thou shouldest pardon Arius, and extend thy indulgence to his lamentations."

Upon hearing this the man of God, moved with indignation, put them aside, and, raising his hands to heaven, exclaimed : " Do ye dare to supplicate me on behalf of Arius? Arius, both here and in the future world, will always remain banished and separate from the glory of the Son of God, Jesus Christ our Lord."[2] He thus protesting, all who were present, being struck with terror, like men dumb, kept silence.

Moreover they suspected that he, not without some divine notification,[3] gave forth such a sentence against Arius. But when the merciful father beheld them silent and sad from compunction of heart, he would not persist in austerity, or leave them, as if in contempt, without satisfaction ; but taking Achillas and Alexander, who amongst the priests appeared to be the elders and the most holy, having one of them at his right hand, and the other on his left, he separated them a little from the rest, and at the end of his discourse said to them : "Do not, my brethren, take me for a man inhuman and stern ; for indeed I too am living under the law of sin ; but believe my words. The hidden treachery of Arius surpasses all iniquity and impiety, and not asserting this of mine own self, have I sanctioned his excommunication. For in this night, whilst I was solemnly pouring forth my prayers to God, there stood by me a boy of about twelve years, the brightness of whose face I could not endure, for this whole cell in which we stand was radiant with a great light. He was clothed with a linen tunic[4] divided into two parts, from the neck to the feet, and holding in his two hands the rents of the tunic, he applied them to his breast to cover his nudity. At this vision I was stupefied with astonishment. And when boldness of speech was given to me, I exclaimed : Lord, who hath rent thy tunic? Then said he, Arius hath rent it, and by all means beware of receiving him into communion ; behold, to-morrow they will come to entreat you for him. See, therefore, that thou be not persuaded to acquiesce : nay, rather lay thy commands upon Achillas and Alexander the priests, who after thy translation will rule my Church, not by any means to receive him. Thou shalt very quickly fulfil the lot of the martyr. Now there was no other cause of this vision. So now I have satisfied you, and I have declared unto you what I was ordered. But what you will do in consequence of this, must be your own care." Thus much concerning Arius.

He continued: "Ye know too, beloved, and ye know well, what has been the manner of my conversation amongst you, and what conflicts I have endured from the idolatrous Gentiles, who, being ignorant of the Lord and Saviour, do not cease in their madness to spread abroad the fame

---

[1] [i.e., deacon; Isa. lxvi. 21. So Clement of Rome, cap. xl. p 14, vol. i , this series.]

[2] The *Acta Combefisiana* add, " quemadmodum ille Dei Filium a paterna gloria et substantia sequestravit," even as he has separated the Son of God from the glory and substance of His Father. But Arius had not as yet laid bare his heresy, but had been excluded from the Church for joining in the Meletian schism, and a suspicious course of action.

[3] [" The dying are wont to vaticinate; " but the prophetic *charismata* (1 Cor. xiv. 31) were not yet extinct in the Church, in all probability, hence this conjecture was natural.]

[4] κολόβιον — this is the tunicle, tunica, tunicella, dalmatica. It originally had no sleeves; it is said that wide sleeves were added in the West about the fourth century; and the garment was then called dalmatic, and was the deacon's vestment when assisting at the holy communion; while that worn by sub-deacons, called by the Anglo-Saxons " roc," and " tunicle " generally after the 13th century, was of the same form, but smaller and less ornamented (Palmer, *Orig. Liturgicæ*, vol. ii. p. 314). The word. in its classical use, meant an under-garment with its sleeves curtailed (κολοβός) — i.e., reaching only half down to the elbow, or entirely without sleeves. [But the reference here is clearly to St John xix. 23; and the introduction of the mediæval *dalmatic*, to translate κολόβιον, is out of place.]

of a multitude of gods who are no gods. Ye know likewise how, in avoiding the rage of my persecutors, I wandered an exile from place to place. For long time I lay in hiding in Mesopotamia, and also in Syria amongst the Phœnicians; in either Palestine also I had for a long time to wander; and from thence, if I may so say, in another element, that is, in the islands, I tarried no short time. Yet in the midst of all these calamities I did not cease day and night writing to the Lord's flock committed to my poor care, and confirming them in the unity of Christ. For an anxious solicitude for them constantly kept urging my heart, and suffered me not to rest; then only did I think it to be more tolerable to me when I committed them to the Power above.

" Likewise also, on account of those fortunate prelates, Phileus, I mean, Hesychius and Theodorus, who of divine grace have received a worthy vocation, what great tribulation agitated my mind. For these, as ye know, for the faith of Christ were with the rest of the confessors wasted with diverse torments. And because in such a conflict they were not only of the clergy but of the laity also the standard-bearers and preceptors, I on this account greatly feared lest they should be found wanting under their long affliction, and lest their defection, which is terrible to speak of, should be to many an occasion of stumbling and of denying the faith, for there were more than six hundred and sixty confined along with them within the precincts of a dungeon. Hence, although oppressed with great labour and toil, I ceased not to write to them with reference to all those predicted passages,[1] exhorting them to earn the martyr's palm with the power of divine inspiration. But when I heard of their magnificent perseverance, and the glorious end of the passion of them all, falling on the ground I adored the majesty of Christ, who had thought fit to count them amongst the throng of the martyrs.

" Why should I speak to you about Meletius of Lycopolis? What persecutions, what treachery, he directed against me, I doubt not but that ye well know. Oh, the horrible wickedness! he feared not to rend asunder the holy Church, which the Son of God redeemed with His precious blood, and to deliver which from the tyranny of the devil He hesitated not to lay down His life. This Church, as I have begun to say, the wicked Meletius rending asunder, ceased not to imprison in dungeons, and to afflict holy bishops even, who have a little before us by martyrdom penetrated to the heavens. Beware therefore of his insidious devices. For I, as ye see, go bound by divine charity, preferring

above all things the will of God. I know, indeed, that under their breath the tribunes whisper of my death with eager haste; but I will not from this circumstance open any communication with them, nor will I count my life more precious than myself. Nay, rather, I am prepared to finish the course which my Lord Jesus Christ hath deigned to promise to me, and faithfully render up to Him the ministry which from Him I have received. Pray for me, my brothers; you will not see me longer living in this life with you. Wherefore I testify before God and your brotherhood, that before all of you have I preserved a clean conscience. For I have not shunned to declare unto you the injunctions of the Lord, and I have refused not to make known to you the things which will hereafter be necessary.

" Wherefore take heed unto yourselves, and the whole flock over which the Holy Ghost has appointed you as overseers in succession — thee Achillas in the first place, and next to thee Alexander. Behold with living voice I protest to you, that after my death men will arise in the Church speaking perverse things,[2] and will again divide it, like Meletius, drawing away the people after their madness. So I have told you before. But I pray you, mine own bowels, be watchful; for ye must undergo many tribulations. For we are no better than our fathers. Are ye ignorant what things my father endured from the Gentiles, he who brought me up, the most holy bishop Theonas, whose pontifical[3] chair I have undertaken to fill? Would that I had his manners also! Why too should I speak of the great Dionysius his predecessor, who wandering from place to place sustained many calamities from the frantic Sabellius? Nor will I omit to mention you, ye most holy fathers and high priests of the divine law, Heraclius and Demetrius, for whom Origen, that framer of a perverse dogma, laid many temptations, who cast upon the Church a detestable schism, which to this day is throwing it into confusion. But the grace of God which then protected them, will, I believe, protect you also. But why do I delay you longer, my very dear brethren, with the outpouring of my prolix discourse. It remains, that with the last words of the Apostle[4] who thus prayed I address you: ' And now I commend you to God and the word of His grace, which is powerful to direct both you and His flock.' " When he had finished, falling on his knees, he prayed with them. And his speech ended, Achillas and Alexander kissing his hands and feet

---

[1] Of Scripture.

[2] Cf. 1 Tim. iv. 1.
[3] [Another anachronism, but noteworthy as applied to the See of Alexandria. See p. 261, note 2.]
[4] Cf. St. Paul's farewell address to the elders at Miletus, Acts xx 28. [Acts xx. 32 The whole of this affecting address is borrowed from the touching eloquence of St. Paul.]

and bursting into tears sobbed bitterly, specially grieving at those words of his which they heard when he said that they should henceforth see him in this life no more. Then this most gentle teacher going to the rest of the clergy, who, as I have said, had come in to him to speak in behalf of Arius, spake to them his last consoling words, and such as were necessary ; then pouring forth his prayers to God, and bidding them adieu, he dismissed them all in peace.[1]

These things having thus ended, it was everywhere published far and wide that Arius had not been cut off from the Catholic unity without a divine interposition. But that contriver of deceit, and disseminator of all wickedness, ceased not to keep hidden his viper's poison in the labyrinth of his bosom, hoping that he should be reconciled by Achillas and Alexander. This is that Arius the heresiarch, the divider of the consubstantial and indivisible Trinity. This is he who with rash and wicked mouth, was not afraid to blaspheme the Lord and Saviour, beyond all other heretics ; the Lord, I say, and Saviour, who out of pity for our human wanderings, and being sorely grieved that the world should perish in deadly destruction and condemnation, deigned for us all to suffer in the flesh. For it is not to be believed that the Godhead which is impassible was subject to the passion. But because the theologians and fathers have taken care in better style to remove from Catholic ears the blasphemies of this nature, and another task is ours, let us return to our subject.

This most sagacious pontiff[2] then, perceiving the cruel device of the tribunes, who, in order to bring about his death, were willing to put to the sword the whole Christian multitude that was present, was unwilling that they should together with him taste the bitterness of death, but as a faithful servant imitating his Lord and Saviour, whose acts were even as his words, "The good Shepherd giveth His life for the sheep,"[3] prompted by his piety, called to him an elder of those who there waited on his words, and said to him : "Go to the tribunes who seek to kill me, and say to them, Cease ye from all your anxiety, lo ! I am ready and willing of mine own accord to give myself to them." Bid them come this night to the rereward of the house of this prison, and in the spot in which they shall hear a signal given on the wall from within, there let them make an excavation, and take me and do with me as they have been commanded. The

elder, obeying the commands of this most holy man, — for so great a father could not be contradicted, — departed to the tribunes, and made the intimation to them as he had been commanded. They, when they had received it, were exceedingly rejoiced, and taking with them some stonemasons, came about the dawn of the day without their soldiers to the place which had been pointed out to them. The man of God had passed the whole night as a vigil, without sleep, in prayer and watchfulness. But when he heard their approach, whilst all who were with him were rapt in slumber, with a slow and gentle step he descended to the interior part of the prison, and according to the agreement made, made a sound on the wall ; and those outside hearing this, forcing an aperture, received this athlete of Christ armed on all sides with no brazen breastplate, but with the virtue of the cross of the Lord, and fully prepared to carry out the Lord's words who said, " Fear not them which kill the body, but are not able to kill the soul : but rather fear Him which is able to destroy both soul and body in hell."[4] Wonderful was the occurrence ! Such a heavy whirlwind of wind and rain prevailed during that night, that no one of those who kept the door of the prison could hear the sound of the excavation. This martyr most constant too, kept urging on his murderers, saying, Do what ye are about to do, before those are aware who are guarding me.

But they took him up and brought him to the place called Bucolia, where the holy St. Mark underwent martyrdom for Christ. Astonishing is the virtue of the saints ! As they carried him along, and beheld his great constancy and strength of mind when in peril of death, on a sudden a fear and trembling came upon them to such a degree, that none of them could look stedfastly into his face. Moreover, the blessed martyr entreated them to allow him to go to the tomb of St. Mark, for he desired to commend himself to his patronage.[5] But they from confusion, looking down on the ground, said, " Do as you wish, but make haste." Therefore approaching the burial-place of the evangelist, he embraced it, and speaking to him as if he were yet alive in the flesh, and able to hear him, he prayed after this manner : " O father most honourable, thou evangelist of the only-begotten Saviour, thou witness of His passion, thee did Christ choose, who is the Deliverer of us all, to be the first pontiff and pillar of this See ; to thee did He commit the task of proclaiming the faith throughout the whole of Egypt and its boundaries. Thou, I say, hast watchfully fulfilled that ministry of our human salvation which was

---

[1] [Acts xx. 38. The spirit of Ignatius and of Polycarp is here clearly to be recognised in the fourth century.]
[2] [Another anachronism; but, as applied to the Alexandrian primate, it is a concession to truth. The word was already used in the West, but not exclusively with respect to the Apostolic Sees. See vol. v. p. 270, note 1.]
[3] John x. 11.

[4] Matt. x. 28.
[5] [Another anachronism. No such invocation of saints at this period. See note 6, p. 261, *supra*.]

intrusted to thee ; as the reward of this labour thou hast doubtless obtained the martyr's palm. Hence, not without justice, art thou counted worthy to be saluted evangelist and bishop. Thy successor was Anianus, and the rest in descending series down to the most blessed Theonas, who disciplined my infancy, and deigned to educate my heart. To whom I, a sinner and unworthy, have been beyond my deservings appointed as successor by an hereditary descent. And, what is best of all, lo! the largeness of the divine bounty has granted me to become a martyr of His precious cross and joyful resurrection, giving to my devotion the sweet and pleasant odour of His passion, that I should be made meet to pour out unto Him the offering of my blood. And because the time of making this offering is now instant, pray for me that, the divine power assisting me, I may be meet to reach the goal of this agony with a stout heart and ready faith. I commend also to thy glorious patronage the flock of Christ's worshippers which was committed to my pastoral care ; to thee, I say, I with prayers commend it, who are approved as the author and guardian of all preceding and subsequent occupiers of this pontifical chair, and who, holding its first honours, art the successor not of man, but of the God-man, Christ Jesus." Saying these words,[1] he went back to a little distance from the sacred tomb, and, raising his hands to heaven, prayed with a loud voice, saying : " O thou Only-begotten, Jesus Christ, Word of the Eternal Father, hear me invoking Thy clemency. Speak peace, I beseech Thee, to the tempest that shakes Thy Church, and with the effusion of my blood, who am Thy servant, make an end to the persecution of Thy people." Then a certain virgin dedicated to God, who had her cell adjoining to the tomb of the evangelist, as she was spending the night in prayer, heard a voice from heaven, saying : " Peter was the first of the apostles, Peter is the last of the martyred bishops of Alexandria."

Having ended his prayer, he kissed the tomb of the blessed evangelist, and of the other pontiffs who were buried there, and went forth to the tribunes. But they seeing his face as it had been the face of an angel, being terror-stricken, feared to speak to him of his instant agony. Nevertheless, because God does not desert those who trust in Him, He willed not to leave His martyr without consolation in the moment of so great a trial. For lo! an old man and an aged virgin, coming from the smaller towns, were hastening to the city, one of whom was carrying four skins for sale, and the other two sheets of linen. The blessed prelate, when he perceived them, recognised a divine dispensation with reference to himself. He inquired of them on the instant, " Are ye Christians?" And they replied, " Yes." Then said he, " Whither are ye going?" And they replied, " To the market in the city to sell these things that we are carrying." Then the most merciful father answered, " My faithful children, God has marked you out, persevere with me." And they immediately recognising him, said, " Sire, let it be as thou hast commanded." Then turning to the tribunes, he said, " Come, do what ye are about to do, and fulfil the king's command ; for the day is now on the point of breaking."[2] But they, suffering violence as it were on account of the wicked decree of the prince, brought him to a spot opposite to the sanctuary of the evangelist, into a valley near the tombs. Then said the holy man, " Spread out, thou aged man, the skins which thou carriest, and thou too, O aged woman, the linen sheets."[3] And when they had been spread out, this most constant martyr, mounting upon them, extended both his hands to heaven, and bending his knees on the ground, and fixing his mind upon heaven, returned his thanks to the Almighty Judge[4] of the contest, and fortifying himself with the sign of the cross, said, Amen. Then loosening his *omophorion*[5] from his neck, he stretched it forth, saying, " What is commanded you, do speedily."

Meanwhile the hands of the tribunes were paralyzed, and looking upon one another in turn, each urged his fellow to the deed, but they were all held fast with astonishment and fear. At length they agreed that out of their common stock a reward for the execution should be appointed, and that the man who should venture to perpetrate the murder should enjoy the reward. There was no delay, each of them brought forth five solidi.[6] But, as says the heathen poet, —

---

[1] [Wholly apocryphal in all probability, or based on a mere apostrophe. Such " patronage " was yet unknown.]

[2] [Gen. xxxii. 26.]
[3] The Latin reads here: " Spread out, ye aged men, the skins which ye are carrying."
[4] ἀγωνοθέτης — the president of the Grecian games, the judge.
[5] [Probably he wore *ordinarily* what afterwards became an ecclesiastical ornament. So the *casula* and other vestments were retained by the clergy after they ceased to be commonly worn. Marriott, *Vestiar. Christian.*, p. 198.] The *omophorion*, which is worn by every Eastern bishop, resembles the Latin pallium, except that it is broader, and tied round the neck in a knot. *Cf.* following passage from Neale's *Introduction to the Translation of the Eastern Liturgies :* " But while the Gospel is being read, the bishop lays aside his *omophorion*, thereby making profession of his service to the Lord. For since it is the Lord who is represented as speaking by the Gospel, and is, as it were, Himself present, the bishop at that time ventures not to be arrayed with the symbol of His incarnation — I mean the *omophorion*, but taking it off from his shoulders, he gives it to the deacon, who holds it folded in his right hand, himself standing near the bishop, and preceding the holy gifts. When he has finished the liturgy, and comes to the communion, he again assumes the *omophorion*, manifesting that before this he was one of the ministers, and was afraid to put upon himself that holy garment. But when the work is accomplished, and he goes on to elevate the bread, and to divide it into parts, and to receive it himself, and distribute it to others, it is necessary that he should put on all the sacred symbols of his dignity; and since the *omophorion* is the principal vest of a pontiff, he necessarily assumes that, and in that is partaker of the most divine things." [All this unknown to antiquity.]
[6] A *solidus* or *aureus* worth 25 denarii, denarius being 8½d.: it was worth 17s. 8½d.; five solidi, £4, 8s. 6½d. [More than $20.]

"Quid non mortalia pectora cogis,
Auri sacra fames?"[1]

one of them, after the manner of the traitor Judas, emboldened by the desire of money, drew his sword and beheaded the pontiff, on the 25th day of November, after he had held the pontificate twelve years — three of which were before the persecution, but the nine remaining were passed by him under persecutions of diverse kinds. The blood-money being instantly claimed by the executioner, these wicked purchasers, or rather destroyers, of man's life quickly returned, for they feared the multitude of the people, since, as I have said, they were without their military escort. But the body of the blessed martyr, as the fathers affirm who went first to the place of execution, remained erect, as if instant in prayer, until many people, coming together, discovered it standing[2] in the same posture; so that what was his constant practice whilst living, to this his inanimate body testified. They found also the aged man and woman watching with grief and lamentation the most precious relic of the Church. So, honouring him with a triumphal funeral, they covered his body with the linen sheets; but the sacred blood which had been poured forth, they collected reverently in a wallet.

In the meanwhile an innumerable multitude of either sex, flocking together from the populous city, with groans and ejaculations asked each other in turn, being ignorant, in what manner this had happened. In truth, from the least to the greatest, a very great grief was prevalent amongst all. For when the chief men of the city beheld the laudable importunity of the multitude, who were busied in dividing his sacred spoils to keep them as relics, they wrapped him up the tighter in the skins and linen sheets. For the most holy minister of God was always clothed in sacerdotal vestments of a white colour[3] — that is, with the tunic, the *kolobion*, and the *omophorion*. Then there arose among them no small contention; for some were for carrying the most sacred limbs to the church which he had himself built, and where he now rests, but others were endeavouring to carry him to the sanctuary of the evangelist, where he attained the goal of martyrdom; and since neither party would yield to the other, they began to turn their religious observance into a wrangling and a fight.[4] In the meanwhile a spirited body of senators of those who are en-

gaged in the public transport service, seeing what had happened, for they were near the sea, prepared a boat, and suddenly seizing upon the sacred relics, they placed them in it, and scaling the Pharos from behind, by a quarter which has the name of Leucado, they came to the church of the most blessed mother of God, and Ever-Virgin Mary, which, as we began to say, he had constructed in the western quarter, in a suburb, for a cemetery of the martyrs. Thereupon the throng of the people, as if the heavenly treasure had been snatched from them, some by straight roads, and others by a more devious route, followed with hasty steps. And when they at length arrived there, there was no longer any altercation where he was to be placed, but by a common and unimpeachable counsel they agreed first to place him in his episcopal chair, and then to bury him.

And this, most prudent reader, I would not have you regard as a wild fancy and superstition, since, if you learn the cause of this novelty, you will admire and approve of the zeal and deed of the populace. For this blessed priest, when he celebrated the sacrament of the divine mysteries, did not, as is the ecclesiastical custom, sit upon his pontifical throne, but upon its footstool underneath, which, when the people beheld, they disliked, and complainingly exclaimed, "Thou oughtest, O father, to sit upon thy chair;" and when they repeated this frequently, the minister of the Lord rising, calmed their complaints with tranquil voice, and again took his seat upon the same stool. So all this seemed to be done by him from motives of humility. But upon a certain great festival it happened that he was offering the sacrifice of the mass,[5] and wished to do this same thing. Thereupon, not only the people, but the clergy also, exclaimed with one voice, "Take thy seat upon thy chair, bishop." But he, as if conscious of a mystery, feigned not to hear this; and giving the signal for silence, — for no one dared pertinaciously to withstand him, — he made them all quiet, and yet, nevertheless, sat down on the footstool of the chair; and the solemnities of the mass[6] having been celebrated as usual, each one of the faithful returned to his own home.

But the man of God sending for the clergy, with tranquil and serene mind, charged them with rashness, saying, "How is it that ye blush not for having joined the cry of the laity, and reproaching me? Howbeit, since your reproach flows not from the muddy torrent of arrogance, but from the pure fountain of love, I will unfold

---

[1] Virgil, *Æn.*, book iii. 56: —

"O sacred hunger of pernicious gold,
    What bands of faith can impious lucre hold?" — *Dryden.*

[2] [Here "standing" = continuing. He knelt, no doubt, to be beheaded; but the corpse *remained* in this posture. A noble horse, shot on the field of Antietam, remained on the field in an attitude of raising himself from the ground, as I saw it myself.]

[3] [This may be credited. See Cyprian's *Passion.* But the technical names which follow seem an anachronism if *technically* understood. I say this with no spirit of objection to these vestments, however.]

[4] [See Kingsley's *Hypatia.* In Cyril's time this might have happened: one trusts that for Peter's day this, too, is an anachronism.]

[5] [Another anachronism, and Occidental also.]

[6] [See vol. v. p. 256, note 6, and p. 259, Elucidation II. *Missa*, a Latin word, has clearly no place here save by the Roman rule of reading modern rites into antiquity. Thus, in Raphael's picture illustrating the story of 2 Macc. iii. 15, the Jewish high-priest is made a Roman pontiff. Compare note 6, p. 261, *supra.*]

to you the secret of this mystery. Very often when I wish to draw near to that seat, I see a virtue as it were sitting upon it, exceeding radiant with the brightness of its light. Then, being in suspense between joy and fear, I acknowledge that I am altogether unworthy to sit upon such a seat, and if I did not hesitate to cause an occasion of offence to the people, without doubt I should not even venture to sit upon the stool itself. Thus it is, my beloved sons, that I seem to you, in this, to ,transgress the pontifical rule.[1] Nevertheless, many times when I see it vacant, as ye yourselves are witnesses, I refuse not to sit upon the chair after the accustomed manner. Wherefore do ye, now that ye are acquainted with my secret, and being well assured that, if I shall be indulged, I will sit upon the chair, for I hold not in slight esteem the dignity of my order, cease any further from joining in the exclamations of the populace." This explanation the most holy father, whilst he was yet alive, was compelled to give to the clergy. The faithful of Christ, therefore, remembering all this with pious devotion, brought his sacred body, and caused it to sit upon the episcopal throne. As much joy and exultation arose then to heaven from the people, as if they were attending him alive and in the body. Then embalming him with sweet spices, they wrapped him in silken coverings; what each one of them could be the first to bring, this he accounted to himself as greatest gain. Then carrying palms, the tokens of victory, with flaming tapers, with sounding hymns, and with fragrant incense, celebrating the triumph of his heavenly victory, they laid down the sacred relics, and buried them in the cemetery which had been long ago constructed by him, where too from henceforth, and even to this day, miraculous virtues cease not to show themselves. Pious vows, forsooth, are received with a propitious hearing; the health of the impotent is restored; the expulsion of unclean spirits testifies to the martyr's merits. These gifts, O Lord Jesus, are Thine, whose wont it is thus magnificently to honour Thy martyrs after death: Thou who with the Father and the Holy Consubstantial Spirit livest and reignest for evermore. Amen.

After this, how that wolf and framer of treach-ery, that is Arius, covered with a sheep's skin, entered into the Lord's fold to worry and torment it, or in what manner he was enabled to attain to the dignity of the priesthood, let us employ ourselves in relating in brief.[2] And this not to annoy those who ventured to recall to the threshing-floor of the Lord those tares of apostacy and contagion that had been winnowed out of the Church by a heavenly fan; for these are without doubt reckoned eminent for sanctity, but thinking it a light thing to believe so holy a a man, they transgressed the injunctions of the divine command. What then? Do we reprehend them? By no means. For as long as this corruptible body weighs us down, and this earthly habitation depresses the sense of our infirmity, many are easily deceived in their imaginations, and think that which is unjust to be just, that to be holy which is impure. The Gibeonites who, by the divine threatenings, were to be utterly destroyed, having one thing in their wishes and another in their voice and mien, were able quickly to deceive Joshua,[3] that just distributor of the land of promise. David[4] also, full of prophetic inspiration, when he had heard the words of the deceitful youth, although it was by the inscrutable and just judgment of God, yet acted very differently from what the true nature of the case required. What also can be more sublime than the apostles, who have not removed themselves from our infirmity? For one of them writes, "In many things we offend all;"[5] and another, "If we say we have no sin, we deceive ourselves, and the truth is not in us."[6] But when we repent of these, so much the more readily do we obtain pardon, when we have sinned not willingly, but through ignorance or frailty. And certainly offences of this sort come not of prevarication, but of the indulgence of compassion. But I leave to others to write an apology for this; let us pursue what is in hand. After that magnificent defender of the faith, Peter, worthy of his name, had by the triumph of martyrdom, etc.

THE REST IS WANTING.

---

[1] [See note 2, p. 265, *supra*.]

[2] Achillas, the successor of Peter, admitted Arius to the priesthood.
[3] *Cf.* Joshua ix.
[4] Perhaps Absalom, or it may be Ziba, is referred to. (2 Sam. xiv. 33, xvi. 3.)
[5] Jas. iii. 2.
[6] 1 John i. 8.

THE CANONICAL EPISTLE,[1]

COMMENTARIES OF THEODORE BALSAMON AND JOHN ZONARAS.

THE CANONS OF THE BLESSED PETER, ARCHBISHOP OF ALEXANDRIA, AS THEY ARE GIVEN IN HIS SERMON ON PENITENCE.[2]

CANON I.

But since the fourth passover of the persecution has arrived, it is sufficient, in the case of those who have been apprehended and thrown into prison, and who have sustained torments not to be borne,[3] and stripes intolerable, and many other dreadful afflictions, and afterwards have been betrayed by the frailty of the flesh, even though they were not at the first received on account of their grievous fall that followed, yet because they contended sorely and resisted long ; for they did not come to this of their own will, but were betrayed by the frailty of the flesh ; for they show in their bodies the marks of Jesus,[4] and some are now, for the third year, bewailing their fault : it is sufficient, I say, that from the time of their submissive approach, other forty days should be enjoined upon them, to keep them in remembrance of these things ; those forty days during which, though our Lord and Saviour Jesus Christ had fasted, He was yet, after He had been baptized, tempted of the devil. And when they shall have, during these days, exercised themselves much, and constantly fasted, then let them watch in prayer, meditating upon what was spoken by the Lord to him who tempted Him to fall down and worship him : " Get thee behind me, Satan ; for it is written, Thou shalt worship the Lord thy God, and Him only shalt thou serve." [5]

BALSAMON. The present canons treat of those who have in the persecution denied the faith, and are doing penance. And the first canon ordains, that upon those

who after many torments have sacrificed to the gods, not being able by reason of frailty to persevere, and who have passed three years in penitence, other forty days should be enjoined, and that then they should be admitted into the Church. Observe these present canons which lay down various and useful rules in favour of those who have denied their God, and seek for repentance, and concerning those who have of their own accord sought martyrdom, and have lapsed, and then have again confessed the faith, and other things of the like nature. Consult also, for you will profitably do so, many canons of the Council of Ancyra.

ZONARAS. Amongst those who in these turbulent times denied the faith, the holy Peter makes a distinction, and says, that upon those who had been brought before the tyrant, and thrown into prison, and who had endured very grievous torments, and intolerable scourgings, and such as could be cured by no care or medicine (for ἄκος signifies medical care, and ἀνήκεστον is the same as immedicabile), and other dreadful afflictions, and afterwards yielding, sacrificed to the gods, being betrayed as it were by the weakness of the flesh, which could not hold out under the pain unto the end, that for them the time past should suffice for punishment ; since, indeed, says he, the fourth passover has now past since they made this very grievous fall. And although perhaps at first, when they approached in penitence, they were not received, yet because they did not of their own free-will proceed to sacrifice to the gods, and resisted long, and bear about with them the marks of Jesus, that is to say, the scars of the wounds which, in behalf of Christ, they have endured, and the third year has now elapsed since they first bewailed their fall, he decrees that, as an additional punishment, other forty days from the time that they came asking to be admitted to communion should be enjoined on them in the place of any further severity ; during which they should exercise a still greater degree of penance, and should fast more earnestly, that is, with more attentive care, keeping guard over themselves, being watchful in prayer, meditating upon, that is, turning over perpetually in their minds, and saying in words, the text quoted by the Lord against the tempter, " Get thee behind me, Satan ; for it is written, Thou shalt worship the Lord thy God, and Him only shalt thou serve."

CANON II.

But in the case of those who, after that they were thrown into prison, and in the dungeon, as in a place besieged, endured afflictions and

---

[1] [The Canonical Epistles of Basil have been heretofore mentioned. Vol. v. p. 572, elucidation.]
[2] These Canons of Peter of Alexandria are interesting as bearing upon the controversy between Cyprian and the clergy of Carthage, with regard to the treatment of the lapsed. They also bear upon the subject-matter of the Novatian schism.
[3] Another reading is ἀνηκέστους, " which cannot be cured."
[4] The marks of Jesus, στίγματα. Cf. Gal. vi. 17.
[5] Matt. iv. 10.

nauseous odours, but afterwards, without the conflict of torments, were led captive, being broken in spirit by poverty of strength, and a certain blindness of the understanding, a year in addition to the foregoing time will suffice ; for they gave themselves up to be afflicted for the name of Christ, even though in their dungeon they enjoyed much consolation from their brethren ; which, indeed, they shall return many fold, desiring to be set free from that most bitter captivity of the devil, especially remembering Him who said : "The spirit of the Lord is upon me, because He hath anointed me to preach the Gospel to the poor ; He hath sent me to heal the broken-hearted, to preach deliverance to the captives, and recovering of sight to the blind, to set at liberty them that are bruised ; to preach the acceptable year of the Lord, and the day of recompense unto our God." [1]

BALSAMON. This canon enacts that those who have only been evil entreated in prison, and who without torment have lapsed, should be punished after the three years with an additional year. For though they obtained consolation, certain of the faithful ministering to them the necessaries of life, yet they ought to obtain pardon, as being those who have suffered severely for the faith.

ZONARAS. In the second order, he places those who have only been thrown into prison, and evil entreated in the dungeon, and yet, though harassed by no torments, have offended ; upon whom, besides the time past, the three years, namely, of which we have spoken, he proposes to inflict the penalty of an additional year, since they also, says he, have for Christ's name endured hardness, even though it may be that they obtained some consolation from the brethren whilst in prison. For it is probable that the faithful, who were not in custody, ministered to those in bonds the necessaries of life, and brought to them some alleviation of their lot. Which things, indeed, they shall return many fold ; for those consolations which they enjoyed in prison they shall vex themselves with penance, and afflict themselves in diverse ways, if they wish to be set free from the captivity of the devil, having become his captives and slaves by their denial of Christ. He subjoins the words of the prophet, taken from Isaiah, which he says that they ought to keep in remembrance.

CANON III.

But as for those who have suffered none of these things, and have shown no fruit of faith, but of their own accord have gone over to wickedness, being betrayed by fear and cowardice, and now come to repentance, it is necessary and convenient to propose the parable of the unfruitful fig-tree, as the Lord says : "A certain man had a fig-tree planted in his vineyard ; and he came and sought fruit thereon, and found none. Then said he unto the dresser of his vineyard, Behold, these three years I come seeking fruit on this fig-tree, and find none : cut it down ; why cumbereth it the ground? And he answering, said unto him, Lord, let it alone this year also, till I shall dig about it, and dung it. And

if it bear fruit, well ; and if not, then after that thou shalt cut it down." Keeping this before their eyes, and showing forth fruit worthy of repentance, after so long an interval of time, they will be profited.

BALSAMON. Those who from fear only and timidity deserted the faith, and then had an eye towards repentance, the canon punishes with three years' exclusion, according to the parable of the fig-tree in the Gospels. For the Lord said, Three years I come to it seeking fruit, and find none ; but the vine-dresser replies, Lord, let it alone this year also.

ZONARAS. But those, he says, who having suffered no hardness, have deserted from fear only and timidity, in that they of their own accord have approached to wickedness, and then looked towards repentance, their case the parable of the fig-tree in the Gospels will exactly suit. Let them keep this before their eyes, and show forth for an equal period labours worthy of penitence, and they shall be profited ; that is, after the fourth year. For the Lord said, Three years I come to it seeking fruit, and find none ; and the vine-dresser answered, Lord, let it alone this year also.

CANON IV.

To those who are altogether reprobate, and unrepentant, who possess the Ethiopian's unchanging skin,[2] and the leopard's spots, it shall be said, as it was spoken to another fig-tree, "Let no fruit grow on thee henceforward for ever ; and it presently withered away." [3] For in them is fulfilled what was spoken by the Preacher : "That which is crooked cannot be made straight ; and that which is wanting cannot be numbered." [4] For unless that which is crooked shall first be made straight, it is impossible for it to be adorned ; and unless that which is wanting shall first be made up, it cannot be numbered. Hence also, in the end, will happen unto them what is spoken by Esaias the prophet : "They shall look upon the carcases of the men that have transgressed against Me ; for their worm shall not die, neither shall their fire be quenched ; and they shall be an abhorring unto all flesh." [5] Since as by the same also has been predicted, "But the wicked are like the troubled sea, when it cannot rest, whose waters cast up mire and dirt. There is no peace, saith my God, to the wicked." [6]

BALSAMON. What has been previously said of the lapsed, has been said of the repentant. But against those who are unrepentant, he brings forward the cursing of another fig-tree, to which the Lord said, because of its unprofitableness, "No fruit grow on thee henceforward for ever."

ZONARAS. What has been previously said of the lapsed, has been said of the repentant. Against those whom, from desperation or depraved opinion, are impenitent, and carry about with them perpetually the inherent and indelible blackness of sin, as of an Ethiopian's skin, or the leopard's spots, he brings forward the cursing of another fig-tree. To which the Lord said for

[1] Isa. lxi. 1, 2 ; Luke iv. 18, 19.

[2] Jer. iii. 23.
[3] Matt. xxi. 19.
[4] Eccles. i. 15.
[5] Isa. lxvi. 24.
[6] Isa. lvii. 20, 21.

its barrenness, "Let no fruit grow on thee henceforward for ever. And he says that in them must be fulfilled that word of the Preacher: "That which is crooked cannot be made straight; and that which is wanting cannot be numbered." Then having explained these things, he subjoins the words of Isaiah.

CANON V.

But upon those who have used dissimulation like David, who feigned himself to be mad [1] to avoid death, being not mad in reality; and those who have not nakedly written down their denial of the faith, but being in much tribulation, as boys endowed with sagacity and prudence amongst foolish children, have mocked the snares of their enemies, either passing by the altars, or giving a writing, or sending heathen to do sacrifice instead of themselves, even though some of them who have confessed have, as I have heard, pardoned individuals of them, since with the greatest caution they have avoided to touch the fire with their own hands, and to offer incense to the impure demons; yet inasmuch as they escaped the notice of their persecutors by doing this, let a penalty of six months' penance be imposed upon them. For thus will they be the rather profited, meditating upon the prophet's words, and saying, "Unto us a child is born, unto us a Son is given; and the government shall be upon His shoulder: and His name shall be called the Messenger of My mighty counsel." [2] Who, as ye know, when another infant in the sixth month [3] of his conception had preached before His coming repentance for the remission of sins, was himself also conceived to preach repentance. Moreover, we hear both also preaching, in the first place, not only repentance, but the kingdom of heaven, which, as we have learned, is within us; [4] for the word which we believe is near us, in our mouth, and in our heart; which they, being put in remembrance of, will learn to confess with their mouths that Jesus is the Christ; believing in their heart that God hath raised him from the dead, and being as those who hear, that "with the heart man believeth unto righteousness; and with the mouth confession is made unto salvation." [5]

BALSAMON. But if any have pretended to approach the altars, or to write their denial of the faith, and have not done this nakedly and openly, but by feigned arts have illuded those who offered them violence, as David did, who, when he was flying from Saul, and was amongst strangers, feigned himself to be mad, and thus escaped death. So they mocked the snares of their enemies, as children endowed with wisdom and prudence mock foolish children; that they deceived the impious heathen, in that they seemed to sacrifice, although they did not sacrifice, or perhaps they suborned heathens and infidels to take their place, and by these means they thought that they offered sacrifice; for them, he says, a period of six months will suffice for penance. For although they did not sacrifice, yet because they promised to sacrifice, or sent others to do so in their place, they are thought to stand in need of repentance, even though some of those who have given their testimony for the faith have pardoned individuals of them. He compares them to children, as not having manfully withstood the idolaters, but to prudent children, because by artifice they avoided doing sacrifice.

ZONARAS. But if any have pretended to approach the altars, or to write their denial of the faith, but have not nakedly written down their abnegation, that is, not manifestly, not openly; but by a sort of trick have cheated those who offered them violence; as David, who while he was flying from Saul, and had come amongst strange people, feigned himself to be mad, and in this way avoided death. They mocked indeed, he says, the insidious devices of their enemies; as prudent children, endowed with wisdom and sagacity, and those who skilfully take counsel, deceive foolish children. Now he compares those to prudent children by whom the impious heathen were deceived, and those who though they did not sacrifice, yet seemed to sacrifice, prudent indeed, as having thus far avoided sacrificing; but children, in that they did not show forth a mature and manly spirit, and did not nobly resist the worshippers of idols, but covenanted to sacrifice, even though they suborned some in their places, heathens, forsooth, and infidels, and when these sacrificed, they were considered to have sacrificed. For men of this sort, he says, a period of six months will suffice for penance. For although they did not sacrifice, yet because they covenanted to sacrifice, or suborned others to do so, and thus themselves appeared to have sacrificed, they were judged to stand in need of repentance; even though some confessors might have pardoned individuals of them; for some of those who witnessed to the faith and suffered for it, pardoned those who by an artifice, as has been said, escaped offering sacrifice, and admitted them to communion with the faithful, because they studiously avoided offering sacrifice to demons. And on account of the fixing of this term of six months, he calls to remembrance the annunciation made by Gabriel, in the sixth month of the conception of the Forerunner, in which the Lord was conceived. Then he subjoins the words of the apostle.

CANON VI.

In the case of those who have sent Christian slaves to offer sacrifice for them, the slaves indeed as being in their master's hands, and in a manner themselves also in the custody of their masters, and being threatened by them, and from their fear having come to this pass and having lapsed, shall during the year show forth the works of penitence, learning for the future, as the slaves of Christ, to do the will of Christ and to fear Him, listening to this especially, that "whatsoever good thing any man doeth, the same shall he receive of the Lord, whether he be bond or free." [6]

BALSAMON. The slaves who under the commands and threatenings of their masters offered sacrifice, this father punishes with a year's exclusion; yet he pardons them as having acted under the orders of a master, and does not inflict a heavy punishment upon them. But yet since they are much more the servants of Christ, even as they ought to fear Him more, he imposes on

---

[1] Cf. 1 Sam. xxi. 13.
[2] Isa. ix. 6.
[3] Luke i. 76, 77.
[4] Luke xvii. 21.
[5] Rom. x. 8–10.
[6] Eph. vi. 8.

them a moderate punishment; for, as says the great Paul, "whatsoever good thing any man doeth, the same shall he receive of the Lord, whether he be bond or free."

ZONARAS. Some have sent their own Christian servants, even against their will, to offer sacrifice in their stead. These servants, therefore, although not of their own free-will, but being compelled by their masters, they offered sacrifice, this father ordains shall pass a year in penance, and enjoins them to remember that, being of the number of the faithful, they are the servants of Christ, and that Him they ought rather to fear; for "whatsoever any man doeth," says the great apostle, "the same shall he receive, whether he be bond or free."

CANON VII.

But the freemen shall be tried by penance for three years, both for their dissimulation, and for having compelled their fellow-servants to offer sacrifice, inasmuch as they have not obeyed the apostle, who would have the masters do the same things unto the servant, forbearing threatening;[1] knowing, says he, that our and their Master is in heaven; and that there is no respect of persons with Him.[2] Now, if we all have one Master, with whom is no respect of persons, since Christ is all and in all, in barbarian, Scythian, bond or free,[3] they ought to consider what they have done, wishing to preserve their own lives. They have drawn their fellow-servants to idolatry who would have been able to escape, had they given to them that which is just and equal, as again says the apostle.

BALSAMON. But upon the freemen, or the masters of the servant compelled to sacrifice, he enjoins a punishment of three years, both because they pretended to sacrifice, and seemed to assent to it; and also because they compelled their fellow-servants to offer sacrifice, and did not obey the apostle, who ordered them to forbear threatening their servants, inasmuch as they themselves, the masters, are the servants of God, and fellow-servants with their own domestics And then they have made haste to preserve their own lives, and have driven their fellow-servants to idolatry who might have escaped.

ZONARAS. But upon the freemen, that is, the masters of the servants who were compelled to sacrifice, he enjoins a penalty of three years, both because they pretended to sacrifice, and altogether appeared to succumb; and also because they compelled their fellow-servants to offer sacrifice, and did not obey the apostle's injunction to forbear threatening their servants; since they also, the masters, are the servants of God, and the fellow-servants of their own domestics. And they indeed made haste to preserve their own lives, and drove their fellow-servants, who might have escaped, to idolatry.

CANON VIII.

But to those who have been delivered up, and have fallen, who also of their own accord have approached the contest, confessing themselves to be Christians, and have been tormented and thrown into prison, it is right with joy and exultation of heart to add strength, and to com-

municate to them in all things, both in prayer, and in partaking of the body and blood of Christ, and in hortatory discourse; in order that contending the more constantly, they may be counted worthy of "the prize of their high calling."[4] For "seven times," he says, "a just man falleth, and riseth up again,"[5] which, indeed, if all that have lapsed had done, they would have shown forth a most perfect penitence, and one which penetrates the whole heart.

BALSAMON. Some had had information laid against them before the tyrant, and had been delivered up, or themselves had of their own accord given themselves up, and then being overcome by their torments, had failed in their testimony. Afterwards repenting, and acknowledging what was right and good, they confessed themselves to be Christians, so that they were cast into prison, and afflicted with torments. These this holy man thinks it right to receive with joy of heart, and to confirm in the orthodox faith, and to communicate with, both in prayers and in partaking of the sacraments, and to exhort with cheering words, that they may be more constant in the contest, and counted worthy of the heavenly kingdom. And that it might not be thought that they ought not to be received, because they had lapsed, he brings forward the testimony of Scripture to the effect that "seven times," that is, often, "the just man falleth, and riseth up again." And, says he, if all who have failed in their confession had done this, namely, taken up their struggle again, and before the tyrant confessed themselves to be Christians, they would have shown forth a most perfect penitence. The subject, therefore, comprehended in this canon differs from that contained in the first canon, for there indeed those who by reason of their torment had lapsed, were not converted so as to confess the faith before the tyrants; but here those who by reason of their torment have lapsed, with a worthy penitence, confess the Lord before the tyrants, wherefore they are reckoned not to have fallen.

ZONARAS. But, says he, if any have had information laid against them before the tyrants, and have been delivered up, or have of themselves given themselves up, and being overcome by the violence of their torments have failed in their testimony, not being able to endure the distresses and afflictions with which in the dungeon they were afflicted; and afterwards taking up the contest anew, have confessed themselves to be Christians, so that they have been again cast into prison and afflicted with torments: such men this holy martyr judges it reasonable that they should be joyfully received; and that they should be strengthened, that is, have strength, spirit, and confidence added to them, in order that they may confess the faith, and that they should be communicated with in all things, both in prayer, and in partaking of the sacraments, and that they should be exhorted with loving words, to rouse themselves to give testimony to the faith, that they may be more constant in the contest, and counted worthy of the heavenly kingdom. And that it might not be thought by any that they ought not to be received from the fact that they had lapsed, and sacrificed to the idols, he brings forth this testimony from Holy Scripture: "Seven times," that is, often, "the just man falleth, and riseth up again." And, says he, if all who have failed in their confession had done this, that is, after their fall, taken up the contest afresh, and confessed themselves to be Christians before the tyrants, they would have given proof of a most perfect repentance.

---

[1] Eph. vi. 9.
[2] Rom. ii. 11.
[3] Col. iii. 11.

[4] Philipp. iii. 14.
[5] Prov. xxiv. 16.

CANON IX.

With those also who, as it were from sleep, themselves leap forth upon a contest which is travailing long and likely to be protracted, and draw upon themselves the temptations as it were of a sea-fight, and the inundations of many waves, or rather are for the brethren kindling the coals of the sinners, with them also we must communicate, inasmuch as they come to this in the name of Christ, even though they take no heed unto His words, when He teaches us " to pray that we enter not into temptation;"[1] and again in His prayer, He says to His Father, " and lead us not into temptation, but deliver us from evil."[2] And perhaps also they know not that the Master of the House and our Great Teacher often retired from those who would lay snares for Him, and that sometimes He walked not openly because of them ; and even when the time of His passion drew on, He delivered not up Himself, but waited until they came to Him with " swords and staves." He said to them therefore, " Are ye come out, as against a thief, with swords and staves, for to take Me ? "[3] And they " delivered Him," He says, " to Pilate."[4] As it was with Him it happens to those who walk keeping Him before them as an example, recollecting His divine words, in which, confirming us, He speaks of persecution : " Take heed unto yourselves, for they will deliver you up to the councils, and they will scourge you in their synagogues."[5] Now, He says, they will deliver you up, and not, ye shall deliver up yourselves ; and " ye shall be brought before rulers and kings for My sake,"[6] but not, ye shall bring yourselves, for He would have us pass from place to place as long as there are those who persecute us for His name's sake ; even as again we hear Him saying, " But when they persecute you in this city, flee ye into another."[7] For He would not have us go over to the ministers and satellites of the devil, that we might not be the cause to them of a manifold death, inasmuch as thus we should be compelling them both to be harsher, and to carry out their deadly works, but He would have us to wait, and to take heed to ourselves, to watch and to pray, lest we enter into temptation.[1] Thus first Stephen, pressing on His footsteps, suffered martyrdom, being apprehended in Jerusalem by the transgressors, and being brought before the council, he was stoned, and glorified for the name of Christ, praying with the words, " Lord, lay not this sin to their charge."[8] Thus James, in the second place,

being of Herod apprehended, was beheaded with the sword. Thus Peter, the first of the apostles, having been often apprehended, and thrown into prison, and treated with igominy, was last of all crucified at Rome. Likewise also, the renowned Paul having been oftentimes delivered up and brought in peril of death, having endured many evils, and making his boast in his numerous persecutions and afflictions, in the same city was also himself beheaded ; who, in the things in which he gloried, in these also ended his life ; and at Damascus he was let down by night in a basket by the wall, and escaped the hands[9] of him who sought to take him. For what they set before themselves, first and foremost, was to do the work of an evangelist, and to teach the Word of God, in which, confirming the brethren, that they might continue in the faith, they said this also, " that we must out of much tribulation enter into the kingdom of God."[10] For they sought not what was profitable for them, but that which was profitable for the many, that they might be saved, and that they might be enabled to say unto them many things conducing to this, that they might act suitably to the Word of God, " unless," as says the apostle, " the time should fail me in speaking."[11]

BALSAMON. Those who have but just arisen from sleep, and especially if they were weighed down with a heavy and profound sleep, have no constant reason, but one perturbed and unsteady. To such as these this blessed martyr likens those who, not in due order, but rashly and inconsiderately, thrust themselves upon the contest, which is as it were in travail, and delayed and protracted, inasmuch as it has not yet burst forth openly, but meditates and delays, hesitating in truth to bring forth the combatants, who bring temptation upon themselves, or draw it towards them. Now these especially are, for the rest of the faithful, kindling the coals of the sinners, that is to say, the punishment of the tyrants. But although he reprehends those who act so, yet he enjoins the faithful nevertheless to communicate with them, because on account of Christ they have undergone the contest, even though they have ignored His teaching, for He teaches them to pray that they may not be tempted ; and He did not deliver up Himself, but was delivered up; and we are not to go over to the tormentors, that we may not be the cause of bringing upon them the guilt of many murders, as those do who incite them to inflict punishment upon the godly. The canon brings forward different examples from Holy Scripture.

ZONARAS. Those who have recently arisen from sleep, especially if they were oppressed with a heavy sleep, have no steady reason, but one inconstant and perturbed. To men of this sort this holy martyr likens those who rush upon the contest, that is, those who, not in due course, but rashly and inconsiderately, intrude themselves upon it. It is, as it were, in travail, and delayed and protracted, inasmuch as it has not yet burst forth openly, but meditates and delays, and hesitates to bring forth the combatants, who bring temptation upon themselves, that is, draw it towards themselves, or rather, for the rest of the faithful, kindle the coals of the

---

[1] Matt. xxvi. 41.
[2] Matt. vi. 13.
[3] Matt. xxvi. 55.
[4] Matt. xxvii. 2.
[5] Matt. x. 17.
[6] Matt. x. 18.
[7] Matt. x. 23.
[8] Acts vii. 59.

[9] 2 Cor. xi. 32, 33.
[10] Acts xiv. 22.
[11] Heb. xi. 32.

sinners, the torments, namely, which are by the tyrants inflicted. But although he finds fault with those who act in this way, he nevertheless decrees that the faithful must communicate with them, because in the name of Christ they come forward to this, trusting, that is, in Christ, or in His name demanding this trial for themselves, even though, perhaps, they are not obeying His precepts; for He taught them to pray that they might not be tempted; and they are ignoring the fact too that the Lord retired from those who were laying snares for Him, and was wont sometimes to walk not openly; neither did He give up Himself to His passion, but was given up by others; and He commanded His disciples, when their enemies persecuted them, to fly from city to city, and not of their own accord to give themselves up to the tormentors, lest they should be the cause of bringing the guilt of much blood upon their heads, irritating them as it were to inflict punishment upon godly men. And he brings forward the example of the apostles, of Stephen, of James, and the chiefs of the order, Peter and Paul.

CANON X.

Whence it is not right either that those of the clergy who have deserted of their own accord, and have lapsed, and taken up the contest afresh, should remain any longer in their sacred office, inasmuch as they have left destitute the flock of the Lord, and brought blame upon themselves, which thing did not one of the apostles. For when the blessed apostle Paul had undergone many persecutions, and had shown forth the prizes of many contests, though he knew that it was far better to " depart, and to be with Christ," yet he brings this forward, and says, " Nevertheless to abide in the flesh is more needful for you." [1] For considering not his own advantage but the advantage of many, that they might be saved, he judged it more necessary than his own rest to remain with the brethren, and to have a care for them; who also would have him that teacheth to be " in doctrine " [2] an example to the faithful. Whence it follows that those who, contending in prison, have fallen from their ministry, and have again taken up the struggle, are plainly wanting in perception. For how else is it that they seek for that which they have left, when in this present time they can be useful to the brethren? For as long as they remained firm and stable, of that which they had done contrary to reason, of this indulgence was accorded them. But when they lapsed, as having carried themselves with ostentation,[3] and brought reproach upon themselves, they can no longer discharge their sacred ministry; and, therefore, let them the rather take heed to pass their life in humility, ceasing from vainglory. For communion is sufficient for them, which is granted them with diligence and care for two causes; both that they should not seem to be afflicted with sorrow, and hence by violence seize on their departure

from this world; and also lest any of the lapsed should have a pretext for being remiss by occasion of the punishment. And these indeed will reap more shame and ignominy than all others, even as he who laid the foundation and was not able to finish it; for " all that pass by," He says, " will begin to mock him, saying, " This man laid the foundation, and was not able to finish it."

BALSAMON. The father having spoken of those who of their own accord went over to the contest of martyrdom, now also speaks of those of the clergy who are in such a case, and he says, that if any clergyman hath of his own accord sought the contest, and then, not being able to bear the tortures, has fallen, but returning to himself, has recanted his error, and before the tyrants confessed himself a Christian, such a one shall no longer discharge his sacred ministry, because he hath deserted the Lord's flock, and because, having of his own accord sought the contest, through not being able to endure the torment, he hath brought reproach upon himself. For to neglect the teaching of the people, and to prefer their own advantage, this did not the apostles. For the mighty Paul, after that he had endured many torments, though he perceived that it was far better to leave this life, yet chose rather to live and to be tormented for the salvation and instruction of the people. They are therefore altogether devoid of perception who seek the sacred ministry from which they have fallen of their own accord. For how is it that they seek for that which they have left, when they are able in this season of persecution, that is, to be useful to their brethren? If indeed they had not fallen, of that which they had done contrary to reason, their spontaneous flight for instance, or their slackness in teaching and confirming the brethren, of these things indulgence would be extended to them. But if from their own arrogance and conceit they have lapsed, — for of such a nature is it rashly to venture to expose themselves to torture, and not to be able to endure it, and thus a triumph has been gained over them, — they cannot any longer execute their sacred office. Wherefore let them the rather take heed that they perfect their confession by humility, ceasing from the vainglory of seeking for the sacred ministry; for communion with the faithful is sufficient for them, which is granted for two reasons, with diligent caution, and just judgment. For if we say that we will not hold them to be communicants, we shall both afflict them with grief, giving our sentence as it were that they should depart this life with violence; and we shall cause others also, who may have lapsed, and wish to return to what is right, to be negligent and remiss in this respect, having as a pretext, that they will not be admitted to communicate with the faithful, even though after their fall they should confess the faith, who, if they are not converted, will undergo more shame and ignominy than others, even as he who laid the foundation, and did not finish the building. For such a one do those resemble, who, for Christ's sake indeed, have offered themselves to be tormented, and having laid as it were a good foundation, have not been able to perfect that which is good by reason of their fall. Observe, then, that not even confession for Christ's sake restores him who has once lapsed and thus become an alien from his clerical office.

ZONARAS. The father having spoken of those who have of their own accord exposed themselves to the contest of martyrdom, now begins to discourse about those of the clergy who have done the same thing; and says that if any clergyman has of his own accord given himself up, and then, not being able to endure the violence of the torment, has fallen, and again recollecting himself has roused himself afresh to the contest, and has confessed himself a Christian before the tyrants, a

---

[1] Philipp. i. 23, 24.
[2] Tit. ii. 7.
[3] Cf. St. Paul's description of charity, 1 Cor. xiii. 4: " Charity vaunteth not itself," οὐ περπερεύεται.

man of this sort is not any longer to be admitted to the sacred ministry. And the reason of this he subjoins; because he has forsaken the Lord's flock, and because having of his own accord offered himself to the enemy, and not having with constancy endured his torments, he has brought reproach upon himself. But that they should despise the instruction of the people, and prefer their own advantage, this did not the apostles. For the mighty Paul, though he had endured many torments, and felt that it was better for him to leave this life, preferred to live and to be tormented for the salvation and instruction of the people. Wherefore he demonstrates those to be altogether devoid of perception who ask for the sacred ministry from which they have voluntarily fallen. For how is it, says he, that they ask for that which they have left, when in a season of this sort, of raging persecution forsooth, they can be of great assistance to the brethren? As long as they were free from the charge of having lapsed, they would have obtained pardon for their action that was rashly undertaken, that, namely, of voluntarily offering themselves to the adversary, or their negligence in instructing the brethren. But since they have fallen, inasmuch as they have acted ostentatiously, they are not to be permitted any longer to discharge their sacred functions. If, says he, that they had not fallen they would have obtained pardon for their action which was devoid of reason; calling that action devoid of reason, not only because they gave themselves up to the enemy, but rather because they deserted the Lord's flock, and did not remain to guard it, and to confirm the brethren who were harassed in this time of persecution. But if they have fallen, from the fact that they have carried themselves vauntingly, and he here calls pride and arrogance περπερεία, because it is from arrogance that they have put confidence in themselves, and have put an end to the contest, and have brought reproach upon themselves; that is, by reason of their fall, they have contracted a blemish and stain, it is not lawful for them any longer to be occupied in the sacred ministry. Wherefore let them study, says he, to perfect their confession by humility, ceasing forsooth from all vainglory. For in that they seek to be enrolled in the sacred ministry, this proceeds from ambition and self-seeking. For communion is sufficient for them, that the faithful should communicate with them, and pray with them, and that they should participate in the sacred mysteries. And this should be granted with diligent caution and care, both lest they should seem to be afflicted with grief, seizing on a dissolution of this life, lest, that is, as he says, being overcome with grief, they should depart and get free from the body, that is, go out from it, from the violence of the torment and afflictions which they undergo in the prison; and that none should have the pretext of their punishment for carrying themselves dissolutely and cowardly in the contest of confession, and thus fall away. Who will the rather be put to shame, according to the saying in the Gospel, "Who could not finish after that he had laid the foundation." [1]

Moreover, let those apply their minds to what is in this place brought forward by this great father and holy martyr, who say that it is lawful for bishops to give up their Sees, and to retain the dignity of the priesthood. For if to the clergy who voluntarily offered themselves to the contest of confession, and who, when tormented, failed in constancy and yielded, and afterwards returned to the contest, if to them indulgence is scarcely granted, because they deferred to execute their ministerial duties; nor, in the opinion of this divine father, is any thing else objected to them but that they deserted the brethren, when in adverse and turbulent times they might have been useful in confirming them in the faith, and that after that they had been counted worthy to bear testimony to the faith, and carried about in their flesh the marks of Christ; how shall that chief priest and

pastor, who ought to lay down his life for the sheep, when he has deserted the flock that was committed unto him, and repudiated its care and administration, and as far as in him lies given it over to the wolf, be thought worthy to retain the dignity of the sacred ministry, and not rather be judged worthy of the severest punishments for deserting the people entrusted to his care? Nay, but he will demand a reward for this thing, or rather he will himself supply it to himself: refusing that which brings labour to them, namely, the office of teaching and of correcting vice; but embracing that which gains for them honour and glory, making it their own, keeping hold of it with their teeth as it were, and not letting it go in the least. For if in the case of the clergy it be called an action contrary to reason to desert the people, and to go away from them to the contest in the cause of piety; how much more contrary to reason shall it be judged for a bishop to desert his people, not in order that he may contend in a contest, but that he may deliver himself up to ease and indolence, and lay aside and escape entirely from his cares for the salvation of souls? The sixteenth canon also of the Seventh Œcumenical Council [2] gravely accuses those of folly who decree that the dignity of the sacred ministry can be retained by a bishop who has repudiated his bishopric. For if according to the sentence of the aforesaid canon, a bishop who has been absent from his See more than six months, unless some one of the causes there enumerated shall have intervened, has both fallen from the episcopate and the highest dignity of the priesthood, and is deprived of both; how shall he who has repudiated the episcopate, and refuses any longer to feed the flock entrusted to him, and despises the care of it through his desire of an easy life, be held to be of the number of bishops? For if he who has committed the lesser fault, of leaving for more than six months the people placed under him destitute of the care and administration of a pastor, incurs the privation of the episcopate and of his sacred dignity; he who offends in a way greater and much more grievous, namely, in deserting altogether the multitude which the grace of the Holy Spirit has committed to him to be cared for and guarded, shall deservedly be punished with greater severity, and will pay the heavier penalty of losing, as far as he is concerned, the flock of which he was appointed shepherd by the great and chief Shepherd and High Priest. But those who decree the dignity of the priesthood to him as a reward and *honorarium* for declining his office, in my opinion make both themselves and him obnoxious to the judgment of God.

CANON XI.

For those who first, when the persecution waxed warm, leaped forth, standing around the judgment-seat, and beholding the holy martyrs who were hastening to the "prize of their high calling," [3] then, fired with a holy zeal, gave themselves up to this, using much boldness, and especially when they saw those who were drawn aside and lapsed, on their account they were roused mightily within, and, as it were by some inward voice, impelled to war down and subdue the adversary who was exulting; for this they earnestly contended, that he might not seem "to be wise in his own conceit," [4] on account of those things in which by reason of his subtlety they appeared to be inferior to him, even though it

---

[1] A digression which follows is entirely directed against Muzalon.

[2] [Not Œcumenical.]
[3] Philipp. iii. 14.
[4] Rom. xii. 16.

escaped his observation that he was overcome by those who with constancy endured the torments of the lash and scourge, and the sharp edge of the sword, the burning in the fire, and the immersion in the water. To those also who entreat that the prayers and supplications of faith should be made either in behalf of those who have been punished by imprisonment, and have been delivered up by hunger and thirst, or for those who out of prison have by the judges been tortured with whippings and scourgings, and afterwards have been overcome by the infirmity of the flesh, it is right to give our consent. For to sympathize with the sorrow and affliction of those who sorrow and mourn for those who in the contest have been overcome by the great strength of the evil-contriving devil, whether it be for parents, or brethren, or children, hurts no one. For we know that on account of the faith of others some have obtained the goodness of God, both in the remission of sins, and in the health of their bodies, and in the resurrection of the dead. Therefore, being mindful of the many labours and distresses which for the name of Christ they have sustained, since they have themselves also repented, and have bewailed that which was done by them through their being betrayed by the languor and mortification of the body; and since, besides this, they testify that in their life they have as it were been aliens from their city, let us pray together with them and entreat for their reconciliation, together with other things that are befitting, through Him who is "our Advocate with the Father, and makes propitiation for our sins." "And if any man sin," says he, "we have an Advocate with the Father, Jesus Christ the righteous: and He is the propitiation for our sins."[1]

BALSAMON. The saint having said before that those who of their own accord entered upon the contest and lapsed, and did not repent nor recant their error, would be covered with more shame, as being like men who did not go on with the building beyond the foundation, that is, did not perfect that which is good, now brings forward a confirmation of this and other matters, saying, Those who taking their stand in the fervour and vehemence of the persecution, seeing the holy martyrs, and with what divine zeal they contended to receive the celestial crown, gave themselves up to martyrdom with much boldness, and especially when they saw some drawn aside, that is, led astray and deluded by the devil, and lapsing or denying godliness; wherefore being inwardly inflamed, and with hearts enkindled, as hearing that they by this means should war down and subdue the proud adversary the devil, were eager to undergo martyrdom lest the devil should boast and seem "to be wise in his own conceit," as having by his subtlety and malice overcome those who of their own accord sought martyrdom: even though it escaped him that he was rather overcome by those combatants who bravely withstood the torments. Therefore to the faithful who pray for those who are enduring punishment, and afflicted by it, it is right to assent or to concur in this, which is also

decreed; and it can by no means be hurtful to sympathize in their sorrow and affliction with the parents or other relatives in behalf of those who have given their testimony and undergone martyrdom, but have lapsed by the arts and snares of the devil. For we know that many have obtained the goodness and compassion of God by the prayers of others. Therefore we will pray for them that remission of their sins be granted them by God; and with the others who have lapsed, and have afterwards recanted their error, and confessed godliness, we will communicate, being mindful of those contests which before their fall they sustained for God's sake, and also of their subsequent worthy repentance, and that they testify that on account of their sin they have been as it were aliens from their city; and we will not only communicate with them, but pray also for their reconciliation, together with other things that are convenient, either with the good works which ought to be done by them — fasting, for instance, almsgiving, and penance; by which things He who is our Advocate makes the Father propitious towards us. Then he makes use of a passage of Holy Scripture, and this is taken from the first catholic epistle of the holy apostle and evangelist John.

ZONARAS. The meaning of the present canon is as follows: — Those, he says, who set in the fervour of the persecution, that is, in its greatest height and most vehement heat, beheld the martyrdoms of the saints, and how eagerly they hastened to receive the celestial crown, fired with a holy emulation, gave themselves up to martyrdom, leaping as it were into the contest with much boldness, in imitation of the saints who suffered, and offered themselves readily for the confirming of the faith by their testimony; and on that account especially, because they beheld many who were drawn aside, that is, led astray, denying their faith. Whereupon they being inflamed, that is, fired in heart, endeavoured to subdue the adversary that was hostile to them, that he might not, as a victor, exult over the godly. Although it escaped him that he was rather conquered by them, many even unto death showing forth constancy for the faith. They hastened, therefore, says he, to do this, but overcome by the violence of their torments, by reason of the infirmity of the flesh, being some of them evil entreated in prison, and others punished by decree of the judges, and not being able to endure their punishment. It is meet, therefore, to sympathize with those who mourn for their sakes. Now they mourn, says he, some the lapse of parents, others of brethren, and others of children. To mourn, therefore, with those who bewail the lapsed, hurts no one; neither to join in prayer and grief with those who pray for themselves, together with other things that are reasonable, namely, that they who have lapsed may show forth other things that are consistent with penitence; such as are fasting and tears and other humiliations, and observe the punishment inflicted on them, and, if their means allow, bestow money upon the poor; by which means He who is the Advocate in our behalf will render the Father propitious to us. Then he brings forward a passage from Holy Scripture, which is taken from the first epistle of the holy apostle and evangelist John.

CANON XII.

Against those who have given money that they might be entirely undisturbed by evil,[2] an accusation cannot be brought. For they have sustained the loss and sacrifice of their goods that they might not hurt or destroy their soul, which others for the sake of filthy lucre have not done; and yet the Lord says, "What is a man profited, if he shall gain the whole world, and lose his own

---

[1] 1 John ii. 1.

[2] κακία.

soul?"[1] and again, "Ye cannot serve God and mammon."[2] In these things, then, they have shown themselves the servants of God, inasmuch as they have hated, trodden under foot, and despised money, and have thus fulfilled what is written: "The ransom of a man's life are his riches."[3] For we read also in the Acts of the Apostles that those who in the stead of Paul and Silas were dragged before the magistrates at Thessalonica, were dismissed with a heavy fine. For after that they had been very burdensome to them for his name, and had troubled the people and the rulers of the city, "having taken security," he says, "of Jason, and of the others, they let them go. And the brethren immediately sent away Paul and Silas by night unto Berea."[4]

BALSAMON. After that the saint had finished his discourse concerning those who of their own accord had offered themselves to martyrdom, he said that those were not to be reprehended who by a sum of money paid down freed themselves from the affliction of persecution. For they preferred to make a sacrifice of their money rather than of their souls. Then he confirms this, and brings forward different Scripture examples from the Acts of the Apostles concerning the blessed apostle Paul and others.

ZONARAS. But those, he says, are not to be reprehended who have paid money down, and thus escaped, and maintained their piety, nor for this thing may any one bring an accusation against them. For they have preferred to lose their money rather than their souls, and have shown that they wish to serve God and not mammon; that is, riches. And he brings forward the words of Scripture, and the example, as in the Acts of the Apostles, of the blessed apostle Paul and others. Now, when it is said that they have been undisturbed by all evil,[5] it is to be so taken, either that they have been left undisturbed, so far as the denial of the faith is concerned, which overcomes all evil,[5] or he means[6] the afflictions of persecutions.

CANON XIII.

Hence neither is it lawful to accuse those who have left all, and have retired for the safety of their life, as if others had been held back by them. For at Ephesus also they seized Gaius and Aristarchus instead of Paul, and rushed to the theatre, these being Paul's companions in travel,[7] and he wishing himself to enter in unto the people, since it was by reason of his having persuaded them, and drawing away a great multitude to the worship of the true God, that the tumult arose. "The disciples suffered him not," he says. "Nay, moreover, certain of the chief of Asia, who were his friends, sent unto him, desiring him that he would not adventure himself into the theatre." But if any persist in contending with them, let them apply their minds with sincerity to him who says, "Escape for thy life; look not behind thee."[8] Let them recall to their minds also how Peter, the chief of the apostles, "was thrown into prison, and delivered to four quaternions of soldiers to keep him;"[9] of whom, when he had escaped by night, and had been preserved out of the hand of the Jews by the commandment of the angel of the Lord, it is said, "As soon as it was day, there was no small stir among the soldiers, what was become of Peter. And when Herod had sought for him, and found him not, he examined the keepers, and commanded that they should be put to death,"[10] on account of whom no blame is attributed to Peter; for it was in their power, when they saw what was done, to escape, just as also all the infants in Bethlehem,[11] and all the coast thereof, might have escaped, if their parents had known what was going to happen. These were put to death by the murderer Herod, in order to secure the death of one Infant whom he sought, which Infant itself also escaped at the commandment of the angel of the Lord, who now began quickly to spoil, and to hasten the prey, according to the name whereby he was called; as it is written, "Call his name Maher-shalal-hash-baz: for before the child shall have knowledge to cry, My father and my mother, the riches of Damascus and the spoil of Samaria shall be taken away before the king of Assyria."[12] The Magi then as now having been despoiled and divided for a prey, humbly, and in the guise of suppliants, adore the Child, opening their treasures, and offering unto Him gifts most opportune and magnificent — gold, and frankincense, and myrrh — as to a king, to God, and to man; whence they were no longer willing to return to the Assyrian king, being forbidden to do so by Providence. For "being warned of God in a dream," he says, "that they should not return to Herod, they departed into their own country another way."[13] Hence the bloodthirsty "Herod, when he saw that he was mocked of the wise men, was exceeding wroth, and sent forth," he says, "and slew all the children that were in Bethlehem, and in all the coast thereof, from two years old and under, according to the time that he had diligently inquired of the wise men."[14] Together with whom, having sought to kill another infant that had been previously born, and not being able to find him, he slew *the child's* father Zacharias between the temple and the altar, the child having escaped with his mother Elisabeth.[15]

---

[1] Matt. xvi. 26.
[2] Matt. vi. 24.
[3] Prov. xiii. 8.
[4] Acts xvii. 9, 10.
[5] κακία.
[6] By κακίας.
[7] Acts xix. 26–30.

[8] Gen. xix. 17.
[9] Acts xii. 4.
[10] Acts xii. 18, 19.
[11] Matt. ii. 13–16.
[12] Isa. viii. 3, 4. The literal meaning of the name Maher-shalal-hash-baz is, "In speed spoil, booty hastens."
[13] Matt. ii. 11–13.
[14] Matt. ii. 16.
[15] [Matt. xxiii. 35.]

Whence these men that have withdrawn themselves are not at all to be blamed.

BALSAMON. But if any, says he, have left their good and gone away, lest they should be detained and brought into peril, as being those perhaps who might not be able to persist in their confession to the end, on account of the cruelty of their tormentors, they shall not be found fault with, even though others have been detained on their account. And he brings forward as an instance on this score Gaius and Aristarchus, who were detained instead of Paul; the soldiers who kept Peter; the infants who were massacred by Herod on account of Christ; and Zacharias, the father of the revered and blessed forerunner.

ZONARAS. But if any, says he, have left their possessions, and have gone away, lest being detained they should be endangered, and because, perhaps, they would not be able to persist in their confession unto the end, on account of the cruelty of the tormentors, they are not to be accused, even if others are detained and punished on their account. And, again, he brings forward an example from the Acts of the Apostles, saying that at Ephesus also Gaius and Aristarchus were apprehended in the stead of Paul, and that Paul was not blamed for this; nor was Peter, when he was brought forth out of prison by an angel, and escaped the danger, and the soldiers who guarded him were on his account punished. Then he cites another example from the Gospel, namely, the infants who were put to death by Herod; on account of which, says he, our Lord was not blamed. And when Elisabeth had taken to flight with John, and had preserved him, his father Zacharias was put to death, the child being demanded of him; nor was this imputed as a crime to John.

CANON XIV.

But if any have endured much violence and the strong pressure of necessity, receiving into their mouths iron and chains, and for their good affection towards the faith have bravely borne the burning of their hands that against their will had been put to the profane sacrifice, as from their prison the thrice-blessed martyrs have written to me respecting those in Libya, and others their fellow-ministers; such, on the testimony of the rest of their brethren, can be placed in the ministry amongst the confessors, as those who have been mortified by many torments, and were no longer able either to speak, or to give utterance, or to move, so as to resist those who vainly offered them violence. For they did not assent to their impiety; as I have again heard from their fellow-ministers, they will be reckoned amongst the confessors, as also he who hath after the example of Timothy ordered his life, obeying him who says, " Follow after righteousness, godliness, faith, love, patience, meekness. Fight the good fight of faith, lay hold on eternal life, whereunto thou art also called, and hast professed a good profession before many witnesses." [1]

BALSAMON. Those who by the violence of the tyrant seemed to eat meat that had been offered to idols, or to drink wine from the Greek libations,—for it happened sometimes that they were thrown upon the ground, and

hooks or pieces of iron put into their mouths to keep them open, and then the tyrants poured wine down their throats, or threw into them pieces of meat; or putting hot coals into their hands, together with incense, they compelled them to sacrifice,—if they were clergymen, the canon decrees that they should each in his own degree be ranked amongst the confessors; but if laymen, that they should be reckoned as martyrs, because they did not these things of their own free-will, nor did they at all assent to the action. As also amongst the confessors are to be reckoned those who from the extremity of the tortures lost their strength of body, and were not able to resist those who poured into their mouths the wine of the libations. And next in order he speaks of those who give the testimony of a good conscience, and enumerates them amongst the confessors.

ZONARAS. Those who chastised the blessed martyrs, after many torments, in the case of some violently poured into their mouths the wine of the libations, or even crammed into their mouths some of the meat that had been offered to idols, and putting incense into their hands, they dragged them to the altars, and then violently seizing on their hands, they either sprinkled the incense upon the altar, or placed hot coals together with the incense into their hands, that, not being able to bear the pain of the burning, they might drop the incense together with the coals upon the altar; for they were constrained by them. Men of this sort, he affirms, can remain enrolled in the sacred ministry, or rather be placed in the rank of confessors. For they did not by their own choice either taste the libations, or place the incense upon the altar, but being compelled by violence, their reason not consenting to the action; as also those who from the extremity of the suffering lost their bodily vigour, so as neither to be able to speak or move, nor to resist those who were violently pouring into their mouths the wine of libations, these also are to be placed amongst the confessors. And next in order he discourses of those who give the testimony of a good conscience, and places them also in the number of confessors.

CANON XV.

No one shall find fault with us for observing the fourth day of the week, and the preparation,[2] on which it is reasonably enjoined us to fast according to the tradition.[3] On the fourth day, indeed, because on it the Jews took counsel for the betrayal of the Lord; and on the sixth, because on it He himself suffered for us. But the Lord's day we celebrate as a day of joy, because on it He rose again, on which day we have received it for a custom not even to bow the knee.

BALSAMON. Conformably to the sixty-fourth Apostolical canon, which decrees that we are not to fast on the Sabbath, with one exception, the great Sabbath; and to the sixty-ninth canon, which severely punishes those who do not fast in the Holy Lent, and on every fourth day of the week and day of preparation. Thus also does the present canon decree.

ZONARAS. Always, says he, are the fourth and sixth days of every week to be kept as fasts; nor will any one find fault with us for fasting on them; and the reasons he subjoins. But on the Lord's day we ought not to fast, for it is a day of joy for the resurrection of the Lord, and on it, says he, we have received that we ought not even to bow the knee. This word, therefore,

---

[1] 1 Tim. vi. 11, 12.

[2] The sixth day, the day before the Hebrew Sabbath.—TR. [The *Parasceve.*]
[3] [Stationary days. See Vol. ii. p. 33, note 6.]

is to be carefully observed, "we have received," and "it is enjoined upon us according to the tradition." For from hence it is evident that long-established custom was taken for law.[1] Moreover, the great Basil annexes also the causes for which it was forbidden to bend the knee on the Lord's day, and from the Passover to Pentecost. Read also the sixty-sixth and sixty-ninth Apostolical canons.[2]

[1] [Vol. v. pp. 382, 571, the notes.]

[2] [So called. Vol. viii., this series. Elucidation II.]

NOTE BY THE AMERICAN EDITOR.

HERE may be noted the historic fact that this terrible epoch of persecutions had driven many to the deserts, where they dwelt as hermits.[1] It now introduced *monasticism*, in its earliest and least objectionable forms, into Egypt, whence it soon spread into the Church at large. For a favourable view of the character and life of St. Antony, see Neale's history [2] of this period ; but, if he turns it into an indirect plea for the subsequent history of monasticism, we shall find in Canon Kingsley's *Hypatia* a high-wrought testimony of an antagonistic character. Bingham,[3] avoiding the entanglements of primitive with mediæval history, affords a just view of what may be said of the rise of this mighty institution, based upon two texts [4] of Holy Scripture, proceeding from the Incarnate Word Himself, which impressed themselves on the fervid spirit of Antony. Who can wonder that fire and sword and ravening wolves predisposed men and women to avoid the domestic life, and the bringing of hapless families into existence as a prey to the remorseless cruelty of the empire? Far be it from me to forget what the world owes, directly and indirectly, to the nobler and purer orders, — what learning must ever acknowledge as its debt to the Benedictines of the West.[5] But, on the other hand, after the melancholy episcopate of Cyril, we cannot but trace, in the history of Oriental monasticism, not only the causes of the decay of Alexandrian scholarship and influence, but of the ignominious fate of the Byzantine Empire, and of that paltry devotion to images which seemed to invoke the retributions of a "jealous god," and which favoured the rise of an impostor who found in his "abhorrence of idols" an excuse for making himself the "Scourge of God."

[1] Luke i. 80, ix. 10; Gal. i. 17. But compare 1 Kings xix. 9.

[2] *Patriarchate*, etc., vol. i. p. 107. Antony was born *circa* A.D. 251, died A.D. 356.

[3] *Antiqu.*, book vii. cap. i.

[4] Matt. xix. 21 and Matt. vi. 34.

[5] Montalembert's *Monks of the West* is but a fascinating romance, but is well worthy of attention

FRAGMENTS FROM THE WRITINGS OF PETER.

I. — LETTER TO THE CHURCH AT ALEXANDRIA.[1]

PETER, to the brethren beloved and established in the faith of God, peace in the Lord. Since I have found out that Meletius acts in no way for the common good, — for neither is he contented with the letter of the most holy bishops and martyrs, — but, invading my parish,[2] hath assumed so much to himself as to endeavour to separate from my authority the priests,[3] and those who had been entrusted with visiting the needy ; [4] and, giving proof of his desire for pre-eminence, has ordained in the prison several unto himself; now, take ye heed to this, and hold no communion with him, until I meet him in company with some wise and discreet men, and see what the designs are which he has thought upon. Fare ye well.

II. — ON THE GODHEAD.[5]

Since certainly " grace and truth came by Jesus Christ," [6] whence also by grace we are saved, according to that word of the apostle, " and that not of yourselves, nor of works, lest any man should boast ; " [7] by the will of God, " the Word was made flesh," [8] and " was found in fashion as a man." [9] But yet He was not left without His divinity. For neither " though He was rich did He become poor " [10] that He might absolutely be separated from His power and glory, but that He might Himself endure death for us sinners, the just for the unjust, that He might bring us to God, " being put to death in the flesh, but quickened by the Spirit ; " and afterwards other things. Whence the evangelist also asserts the truth when he says, " The Word was made flesh, and dwelt among us ; " then indeed, from the time when the angel had saluted

the virgin, saying, " Hail, thou that art highly favoured, the Lord is with thee." Now when Gabriel said, " The Lord is with thee," he meant God the Word is with thee. For he shows that He was conceived in the womb, and was to become flesh ; as it is written, " The Holy Ghost shall come upon thee, and the power of the Highest shall overshadow thee ; therefore also that holy thing which shall be born of thee shall be called the Son of God ; " [11] and afterwards other things. Now God the Word, in the absence of a man, by the will of God, who easily effects everything, was made flesh in the womb of the virgin, not requiring the operation of the presence of a man. For more efficacious than a man was the power of God overshadowing the virgin, together with the Holy Ghost also who came upon her.

III. — ON THE ADVENT OF OUR SAVIOUR.[12]

And He said unto Judas, " Betrayest thou the Son of God with a kiss ? " [13] These things and the like, and all the signs which He showed, and His miracles, prove that He is God made man. Both things therefore are demonstrated, that He was God by nature, and that He was man by nature.

IV. — ON THE SOJOURNING OF CHRIST WITH US.[14]

Both therefore is proved, that he was God by nature, and was made man by nature.

V. — THAT UP TO THE TIME OF THE DESTRUCTION OF JERUSALEM, THE JEWS RIGHTLY APPOINTED THE FOURTEENTH DAY OF THE FIRST LUNAR MONTH.

I.[15]

1. Since the mercy of God is everywhere great, let us bless Him, and also because He has sent unto us the Spirit of truth to guide us into all truth. For for this cause the month

---

[1] From Gallandius.
[2] [See p. 240, *supra*. But note, the *parish* was greater than the *diocese* In ancient terminology.]
[3] [Presbyters.]
[4] [Deacons.]
[5] A fragment from his book, from the Acts of the Council of Ephesus, i. and vii. 2. — GALLAND.
[6] John i. 17.
[7] Eph. ii. 8, 9.
[8] John i. 14.
[9] Phil. ii. 7.
[10] 2 Cor. viii. 9.

[11] Luke i. 35.
[12] A fragment from the homily. Apud Leontium Byzant., lib. i., contra Nestor. et Eutych., tom. i. Thes. Canis., p. 550.
[13] Luke xxii. 48.
[14] A fragment from the homily. Ex Leontio Hierosolymitano, contra Monophysitas, *Ap. Mai. Script. Vet.*, tom. vii. p. 134.
[15] Apud Galland, *Ex Chronico Paschal.*, p. 1, *seqq.*, edit. Venet., 1729.

Abib was appointed by the law to be the beginning of months, and was made known unto us as the first among the months of the year; both by the ancient writers who lived before, and by the later who lived after the destruction of Jerusalem, it was shown to possess a most clear and evidently definite period, especially because in some places the reaping is early, and sometimes it is late, so as to be sometimes before the time and sometimes after it, as it happened in the very beginning of the giving of the law, before the Passover, according as it is written, "But the wheat and the rye were not smitten, for they were not grown up." [1] Whence it is rightly prescribed by the law, that from the vernal equinox, in whatsoever week the fourteenth day of the first month shall fall, in it the Passover is to be celebrated, becoming and conformable songs of praise having been first taken up for its celebration. For this first month, says he, "shall be unto you the beginning of months," [2] when the sun in the summer-time sends forth a far stronger and clearer light, and the days are lengthened and become longer, whilst the nights are contracted and shortened. Moreover, when the new seeds have sprung up, they are thoroughly purged, and borne into the threshing floor; nor only this, but also all the shrubs blossom, and burst forth into flower. Immediately therefore they are discovered to send forth in alternation various and diverse fruits, so that the grape-clusters are found at that time; as says the lawgiver, "Now, it was the time of spring, of the first ripe grapes;" [3] and when he sent the men to spy out the land, they brought, on bearers, a large cluster of grapes, and pomegranates also, and figs. For then, as they say, our eternal God also, the Maker and Creator of all things, framed all things, and said to them, "Let the earth bring forth grass, the herb yielding seed, and the fruit tree yielding fruit after his kind, whose seed is in itself upon the earth." Then he adds, "And it was so; and God saw that it was good." [4] Moreover, he makes quite clear that the first month amongst the Hebrews was appointed by law, which we know to have been observed by the Jews up to the destruction of Jerusalem, because this has been so handed down by the Hebrew tradition. But after the destruction of the city it was mocked at by some hardening of heart, which we observing, according to the law, with sincerity have received; and in this, according to the Word, when he speaks of the day of our holy festivity, which the election hath attained: but the rest have become hardened, [5] as said the Scripture; and after other things.

2. And He says as follows: "All these things will they do unto you for My name's sake, because they know not Him that sent Me." [6] But if they knew not Him who sent, and Him who was sent, there is no reason to doubt but that they have been ignorant of the Passover as prescribed by the law, so as not merely to err in their choice of the place, but also in reckoning the beginning of the month, which is the first amongst the months of the year, on the fourteenth day of which, being accurately observed, after the equinox, the ancients celebrated the Passover according to the divine command; whereas the men of the present day now celebrate it before the equinox, and that altogether through negligence and error, being ignorant how they celebrated it in its season, as He confesses who in these things was described.

3. Whether therefore the Jews erroneously sometimes celebrate their Passover according to the course of the moon in the month Phamenoth, or according to the intercalary month, every third year in the month Pharmuthi, [7] matters not to us. For we have no other object than to keep the remembrance of His Passion, and that at this very time; as those who were eye-witnesses of it have from the beginning handed down, before the Egyptians believed. For neither by observing the course of the moon do they necessarily celebrate it on the sixteenth day of Phamenoth, but once every three years in the month Pharmuthi; for from the beginning, and before the advent of Christ, they seem to have so done. Hence, when the Lord reproves them by the prophet, He says, "They do always err in their heart; and I have sworn in My wrath that they shall not enter into My rest." [8]

4. Wherefore, as thou seest, even in this thou appearest to be lying greatly, not only against men, but also against God. First, indeed, since in this matter the Jews never erred, as consorting with those who were eye-witnesses and ministers, much less from the beginning before the advent of Christ. For God does not say that they did always err in their heart as regards the precept of the law concerning the Passover, as thou hast written, but on account of all their other disobedience, and on account of their evil and unseemly deeds, when, indeed, He perceived them turning to idolatry and to fornication.

5. And after a few things. So that also in this respect, since thou hast slumbered, rouse thyself much, and very much, with the scourge of the Preacher, being mindful especially of that passage where he speaks of "slipping on the pavement, and with the tongue." [9] For, as thou

---

[1] Exod. ix. 32.
[2] Exod. xii. 2.
[3] Num. xii. 24.
[4] Gen. i. 11, 12. [*As* "in summer-time," probably.]
[5] Rom. xi. 7. ["Our holy festivity" = Easter.]

[6] John xv. 21.
[7] [Vol. ii. p. 333, note 4. Clement is always worth noting, for his influence is thus traceable very widely in the early literature.]
[8] Ps. xcv. 10, 11.
[9] Ecclus. xx. 18.

seest again, the charge cast by thee upon their leaders is reflected back ; nay, and one may suspect a great subsequent danger, inasmuch as we hear that the stone which a man casts up on high falls back upon his head. Much more reckless is he who, in this respect, ventures to bring a charge against Moses, that mighty servant of God, or Joshua, the son of Nun, who succeeded him, or those who in succession rightly followed them and ruled ; the judges, I mean, and the kings who appeared, or the prophets whom the Holy Spirit inspired, and those who amongst the high-priests were blameless, and those who, in following the traditions, changed nothing, but agreed as to the observance of the Passover in its season, as also of the rest of their feasts.

6. And after other things. But thou oughtest rather to have pursued a safer and more auspicious course, and not to have written rashly and slanderously, that they seem from the beginning, and always, to have been in error about the Passover, which you cannot prove, whatever charge you may wish to bring against those who, at the present time, have erred with a grievous wandering, having fallen away from the commandment of the law concerning the Passover and other things. For the ancients seem to have kept it after the vernal equinox, which you can discover if you read ancient books, and those especially which were written by the learned Hebrews.

7. That therefore up to the period of the Lord's Passion, and at the time of the last destruction of Jerusalem, which happened under Vespasian, the Roman emperor, the people of Israel, rightly observing the fourteenth day of the first lunar month, celebrated on it the Passover of the law, has been briefly demonstrated. Therefore, when the holy prophets, and all, as I have said, who righteously and justly walked in the law of the Lord, together with the entire people, celebrated a typical and shadowy Passover, the Creator and Lord of every visible and invisible creature, the only-begotten Son, and the Word co-eternal with the Father and the Holy Spirit, and of the same substance with them, according to His divine nature, our Lord and God, Jesus Christ, being in the end of the world born according to the flesh of our holy and glorious lady, Mother of God, and Ever-Virgin, and, of a truth, of Mary the Mother of God ; and being seen upon earth, and having true and real converse as man with men, who were of the same substance with Him, according to His human nature, Himself also, with the people, in the years before His public ministry and during His public ministry, did celebrate the legal and shadowy Passover, eating the typical lamb. For " I came not to destroy the law, or the prophets,

but to fulfil them," the Saviour Himself said in the Gospel.

But after His public ministry He did not eat of the lamb,[1] but Himself suffered as the true Lamb in the Paschal feast, as John, the divine and evangelist, teaches us in the Gospel written by him, where he thus speaks : "Then led they Jesus from Caiaphas unto the hall of judgment : and it was early ; and they themselves went not into the judgment-hall, lest they should be defiled, but that they might eat the passover."[2] And after a few things more. "When Pilate therefore heard that saying, he brought Jesus forth, and sat down in the judgment-seat, in a place that is called the Pavement, but in the Hebrew, Gabbatha. And it was the preparation of the passover, and about the third hour,"[3] as the correct books render it, and the copy itself that was written by the hand of the evangelist, which, by the divine grace, has been preserved in the most holy church of Ephesus, and is there adored by the faithful. And again the same evangelist says : "The Jews therefore, because it was the preparation, that the bodies should not remain upon the cross on the Sabbath-day (for that Sabbath-day was an high day), besought Pilate that their legs might be broken, and that they might be taken away."[4] On that day, therefore, on which the Jews were about to eat the Passover in the evening, our Lord and Saviour Jesus Christ was crucified, being made the victim to those who were about to partake by faith of the mystery concerning Him, according to what is written by the blessed Paul : " For even Christ our Passover is sacrificed for us ; "[5] and not as some who, carried along by ignorance, confidently affirm that after He had eaten the Passover, He was betrayed ; which we neither learn from the holy evangelists, nor has any of the blessed apostles handed it down to us. At the time, therefore, in which our Lord and God Jesus Christ suffered for us, according to the flesh, He did not eat of the legal Passover ; but, as I have said, He Himself, as the true Lamb, was sacrificed for us in the feast of the typical Passover, on the day of the preparation, the fourteenth of the first lunar month. The typical Passover, therefore, then ceased, the true Passover being present : " For Christ our Passover was sacrificed for us," as has been before said, and as that chosen vessel, the apostle Paul, teaches.[6]

---

1 [But compare Browne, *On the Thirty-nine Articles*, p. 717, note 3, American edition, 1874.]

2 John xviii. 28.

3 John xix. 13, 14. And about the sixth hour is the reading of our English version. According to St. Mark, the crucifixion took place at the third hour (chap. xxv. 25). Eusebius, Theophylact, and Severus (in the Catena, ed. Lücke, ii.) suppose that there has been some very early erratum in our copies. *See* Alford's note on the passage.

4 John xix. 31.

5 1 Cor. v. 7.

6 [Compare Anatolius, p. 151, *supra*.]

II.[1]

Now it was the preparation, about the third hour, as the accurate books have it, and the autograph copy itself of the Evangelist John, which up to this day has by divine grace been preserved in the most holy church of Ephesus, and is there adored[2] by the faithful.

VI.—OF THE SOUL AND BODY.[3]

The things which pertain to the divinity and humanity of the Second Man from heaven, in what has been written above, according to the blessed apostle, we have explained ; and now we have thought it necessary to explain the things which pertain to the first man, who is of earth and earthy, being about, namely, to demonstrate this, that he was created at the same time one and the same, although sometimes he is separately designated as the man external and internal. For if, according to the Word of salvation, He who made what is without, made also that which is within, He certainly, by one operation, and at the same time, made both, on that day, indeed, on which God said, " Let us make man in our image, after our likeness ; "[4] whence it is manifest that man was not formed by a conjunction of the body with a certain pre-existent type. For if the earth, at the bidding of the Creator, brought forth the other animals endowed with life, much rather did the dust which God took from the earth receive a vital energy from the will and operation of God.

VII.— FRAGMENT.[5]

Wretch that I am ! I have not remembered

---

[1] Apud Galland, *Ex Chronico Paschal.*, p. 175, D.
[2] [Adored, i.e., *etymologically,* = kissed.]
[3] Ex Leontii et Joannis *Rer. Sacr.*, lib. ii. Apud Mai, *Script. Vet.*, tom. vii. p. 85. From his demonstration that the soul was not pre-existent to the body.
[4] Gen. i. 26.
[5] Ex Leontio et Joanne *Rer. Sacr.*, lib. ii. Apud Mai, *Script. Vet.*, tom. vii. p. 96.

---

that God observes the mind, and hears the voice of the soul. I turned consciously to sin, saying to myself, God is merciful, and will bear with me ; and when I was not instantly smitten, I ceased not, but rather despised His forbearance, and exhausted the long-suffering of God.

VIII. — ON ST. MATTHEW.[6]

And in the Gospel according to Matthew, the Lord said to him who betrayed Him : " Betrayest thou the Son of Man with a kiss?" which Peter the Martyr and Archbishop of Alexandria expounding, says, this and other things like, " All the signs which He showed, and the miracles that He did, testify of Him that He is God incarnate ; both things therefore are together proved, that He was God by nature, and was made man by nature."

IX.— FROM A SERMON.[7]

In the meanwhile the evangelist says with firmness, "The Word was made flesh, and dwelt among us."[8] From this we learn that the angel, when he saluted the Virgin with the words, " Hail, thou that art highly favoured, the Lord is with thee,"[9] intended to signify God the Word is with thee, and also to show that He would arise from her bosom, and would be made flesh, even as it is written, " The Holy Ghost shall come upon thee, and the power of the Highest shall overshadow thee ; therefore also that holy thing which shall be born of thee shall be called the Son of God."[10]

---

[6] From the Treatise of the Emperor Justinian against the Monophysites. Apud Mai, *Script. Vet.*, vii. 306, 307.
[7] Or, from a treatise on theology.
[8] John i. 14.
[9] Luke i. 28.
[10] Luke i. 35.

ELUCIDATIONS.

I.

(Meletian schism, p. 259.)

THE date of the Meletian schism is very much in need of elucidation. I follow Neale, however, as follows : Athanasius places its origin A.D. 306 (according to Tillemont and Baronius) or A.D. 301 ; the latter more probable, as demonstrated by the Benedictine editors. But the dates are, perhaps, the least of the difficulties which encumber the whole matter. Somewhat distrustfully I have, after several efforts to construct an original elucidation, adopted the theory of Neale, as a diligent and conscientious inquirer whose Oriental studies qualify him to utter almost a decisive voice, albeit he never forgets his Occidentalism, and hence fails to speak with absolute fidelity to the spirit of Catholic antiquity.

We know something of Lycopolis from the blessed Alexander; it seems to have been a sort of centre to the bishoprics of the Thebais. It was just the sort of centre, in a region sufficient for a separate patriarchate, to suggest to an ambitious and unscrupulous prelate an effort at independency. Meletius, who succeeded the good Alexander, was just the man to set up for himself; a man not unlikely to be stimulated by the bad example of Paul of Samosata, and by the ingenuity that triumphed over the first council that called Paul to account. Bearing all this in mind, we may accept Neale's conviction that Meletius had long been a scandal to the churches, and in the time of persecution had lapsed, and sacrificed to idols. Peter summoned him to a council, by which he was convicted and degraded; whereupon he not only refused to submit, but arrogated to himself the *cathedra* of Alexandria, and began to ordain other bishops, and, in short, to reorganize its jurisdiction.[1] Owing, I think probable, to the exceptional and overgrown extent of this enormous "patriarchate," as it was called a little later, the schism gained a considerable following. The distance of Lycopolis from Lower Egypt must have favoured the attempt, and Peter's recent accession made it easy for Meletius to circulate evil stories against him. The schism, as usual, soon developed into heresy, which even the Nicene Synod failed to extinguish. Arius had joined the first outbreak, but conformed for a time, and was ordained a deacon by Achillas. His troublesome spirit, however, soon showed itself again after his ordination to the priesthood; and the remnant of the Meletians made common cause with him after his condemnation at Nicæa. Of Peter's legitimate exercise of authority, and of the impurity and wickedness of Meletius before his invasion of Alexandria, there is no reason to doubt; but for the details, recourse must be had to Neale.[2] The famous Sixth Canon of Nice finds its explanation in this rebellion; but, incidentally, it defines the position of other great centres, which now began to be known as patriarchates. Neale's remarks[3] on the excessive leniency of the council in settling the case of Meletius, are specially to be noted.

II.

(Canonical Epistle, p. 279.)

The judgment of Dupin is so exceptionally eulogistic touching these canons, that I quote it, as follows:[4] —

"Of all the canons of antiquity concerning the discipline of the lapsed, there are none more judicious or more equitable than those we have now described. There appear in them a wisdom and prudence altogether singular in tempering the rigours of punishment by a reasonable moderation, without which justice would be weakened. He examines carefully all the circumstances which might augment or diminish the quality of the crime; and as he does not lengthen out penance by methods too severe, so neither does he deceive the sinner by a facility too remiss."

Like the famous Canonical Epistles of St. Basil, however, these are compilations of canons accepted by the churches of his jurisdiction. Dupin says of those of Basil[5] (*To Amphilochius*), "They are not to be considered as the particular opinions of St. Basil, but as *the laws of the Church in his time;* and therefore they are not written in the form of personal letters, but after the manner of synodical decisions."

---

[1] He reported to the Nicene Council that he had ordained twenty-eight bishops and eight priests or deacons.
[2] *Patriarchate of Alexandria*, vol. i. pp. 91, 146.
[3] *Ibid.*, p. 146.
[4] *Eccl. Hist. Cent. IV.*, sub tit. " Peter of Alexandria."
[5] *Ibid.*, sub tit. " Basil."

THE ROMAN EMPERORS.

IN the study of these volumes a table is useful, such as I find it convenient to place here, showing the Ante-Nicene succession of Cæsars.

	A.D.		A.D.
1. AUGUSTUS	1	23. HELIOGABALUS	218
2. TIBERIUS	14	24. ALEXANDER SEVERUS	222
3. CALIGULA	37	25. MAXIMINUS	235
4. CLAUDIUS	41	26. GORDIAN	235
5. NERO	54	27. PUPIENUS (BALBINUS)	235
6. GALBA	68	28. GORDIAN THE YOUNGER	238
7. OTHO	69	29. PHILIP	244
8. VITELLIUS	69	30. DECIUS	249
9. VESPASIAN	69	31. GALLUS (VOLUSIANUS)	251
10. TITUS	79	32. VALERIAN	254
11. DOMITIAN	81	33. GALLIENUS	260
12. NERVA	96	34. CLAUDIUS II.	268
13. TRAJAN	98	35. AURELIAN	270
14. HADRIAN	117	36. TACITUS (PROBUS)	275
15. ANTONINUS PIUS	138	37. FLORIAN	276
16. MARCUS AURELIUS	161	38. CARUS (CARINUS, NUMERIAN)	282
17. COMMODUS	180	39. DIOCLETIAN	284
18. PERTINAX	192	40. MAXIMIAN (GALERIUS)	286
19. DIDIUS JULIANUS (NIGER)	193	41. CONSTANTIUS CHLORUS	292
20. SEPTIMIUS SEVERUS	193	42. MAXIMIN	306
21. CARACALLA (GETA)	211	43. CONSTANTINE THE GREAT (LICINIUS, etc.)	307
22. MACRINUS	217		

Suetonius includes Julius, and therefore his *Twelve Cæsars* end with Domitian, the last of the Flavian family. With Nerva the "five good emperors" (so called) begin, but the "good Aurelius" was a persecutor. St. John, surviving the cruelty of Domitian, lived and died under Trajan.

The "vision of Constantine" is dated, at Trèves, A.D. 312.

The *Labarum* became the Roman standard thenceforth.

The Dominical ordinance dates from Milan, June 2, A.D. 321.

He founds the city of Constantinople A.D. 324, convokes the Council of Nicæa A.D. 325.

ALEXANDER.

[TRANSLATED BY THE REV. JAMES B. H. HAWKINS, M.A.]

INTRODUCTORY NOTICE

TO

ALEXANDER, BISHOP OF ALEXANDRIA.

[A.D. 273¹–313–326.] The records of the Ante-Nicene period, so far as Alexandria is concerned, are complete in this great primate, the friend and patron of Athanasius, and, with him, the master-spirit of the great Council of Nicæa. I have so arranged the "Fragments" of the Edinburgh series in this volume as to make them a great and important integer in rounding out and fulfilling the portraiture of the school and the See of Alexandria. The student will thus have at hand the materials for a covetable survey of the Alexandrian Fathers, — their history, their influence, and their immense authority in early Christendom. In an elucidation² I venture to condense my thoughts upon some points which it has been the interest of unbelievers to misrepresent, and to colour for their own purposes. But, as the limitations of my editorial duty do not allow me to enter upon a dissertation, I am thankful to refer the reader to the truly valuable though by no means exhaustive work of Dr. Neale on *The Patriarchate of Alexandria*. His statements are not, indeed, to be received with unreserving confidence ; for, in spite of his pure and lofty purposes, his mind had been formed under the strong bias of a transient fashion in divinity, and he always surveyed his subject from an Occidental if not from a Latin (I do not mean a strictly Roman) point of view. To other popular historians I need not refer the student, save, by anticipation, to the list of authorities which will be furnished in the concluding volume of this series.³

Let us reflect, then, upon the epoch to which we have now come. The intense sufferings, labours, and intellectual as well as moral struggles, of the three heroic centuries, are closing, and Alexander of Alexandria is the grand figure of the period. Diocletian is preparing to let loose upon the sheep of Christ the ferocious wolves of the tenth persecution. Lucian is founding the school of Antioch,⁴ revising the New Testament, and, in fact, the whole Bible of the Fathers, for his labours included the version of the Seventy. Unhappily, the ambitious Arius, who calls him master, has begun to trouble the evangelical See of St. Mark ; and Achillas, notwithstanding the warnings of Peter, has laid hands upon him, and made him a presbyter. He aspires to be made a bishop. But anon a boy is playing on the shore at Alexandria in whom a flaming genius for the priesthood already manifests itself. Alexander, looking forth from his windows, sees him " playing church " with his schoolmates, and actually dipping a young pagan in the sea, " in the name of the Father," etc. No doubt something of the kind did occur, and thus was the boy Athanasius brought to the notice of his bishop. But even Dupin rejects the rest of the story,

---

¹ The first date is conjectural.

² Elucidation I.

³ For liberal references, consult Hagenbach, *Text-Book of the History of Doctrine ;* by all means using Professor Smith's edition, New York, 1861.

⁴ For the matters touching the theology of the period, the student should prepare himself by consulting Waterland, *History of the Athanasian Creed* (*Works*, vol. iv., London), and Van Oosterzee, *Christian Dogmatics*, New York, 1874. I wonder that Professor Smith could, so unreservedly, commend Hagenbach.

that Alexander decided the question of the boy-baptism in favour of its validity, as the Latins would have us believe. Anyhow, we have this miracle of precocity attending Alexander as his deacon at the Council of Nicæa, and then soon after succeeding to his episcopal chair. Athanasius is the grandest figure of the primitive ages after the apostles fell asleep. Raised up to complete their testimony to the eternal Logos, and to suffer like them, we soon behold him the noble example of constancy against the new perils of the world's favour and the patronage of the Cæsars. "Athanasius *against* the world" was in two senses his great encomium, and the epitome of his glorious life and warfare. Not less was it "Athanasius *for* the world." Alas! the majestic school of Pantænus and Clement soon after comes to its enigmatical decline. Some plants, when they have borne their superlative flower and fruit, mysteriously decay. It was so, alas! with the great Christian academy that not improbably owes its beginnings to Apollos.

TRANSLATOR'S INTRODUCTORY NOTICE.

ALEXANDER was appointed successor to Achillas,[1] as Bishop of Alexandria, about A.D. 312. The virtues of this prelate, which Eusebius has passed over entirely without mention, other ecclesiastical writers have greatly extolled. For on all sides he is styled "the staunchest upholder of evangelical doctrine," "the patron and protector of apostolic doctrine;" and "that bishop of divine faith, full of wisdom and of zeal enkindled by the Holy Spirit." He was the first to detect and to condemn Arius;[2] and taking his stand upon passages of Holy Scripture, as Theodoret remarks,[3] he taught that the Son of God was of one and the same majesty with the Father, and had the same substance with the Father who begat Him.

At first he sought to bring back Arius from his heresy. But when he perceived that he openly and obstinately taught his false doctrines, he assembled a first and then a second synod of the bishops of Egypt, and degraded him from the order of the priesthood,[4] and cut him off from the communion of the Church. This proving ineffectual, the Council of Nicæa was convened, in which he was finally condemned. In combating the Arian heresy, Alexander endured, although at a great age, many trials, and died shortly after the holding of the council.

---

[1] [Here given *Achilles;* but I preserve unity of usage in this respect, the rather as *Achilles* is the name of a contemporary heretic.]

[2] [i.e., in his great and final heresy. Of his former condemnation, see pp. 262-263, *supra.*]

[3] *H. E.,* i. 2.

[4] [To which Achillas had admitted him. See p. 268, *supra.* In spite of the warnings, pp. 263-265, *supra.*]

EPISTLES[1] ON THE ARIAN HERESY

THE DEPOSITION OF ARIUS.

I.—TO ALEXANDER, BISHOP OF THE CITY OF CONSTANTINOPLE.

To the most reverend and like-minded brother, Alexander, Alexander sends greeting in the Lord:

1. THE ambitious and avaricious will of wicked men is always wont to lay snares against those churches which seem greater, by various pretexts attacking the ecclesiastical piety of such. For incited by the devil who works in them, to the lust of that which is set before them, and throwing away all religious scruples, they trample under foot the fear of the judgment of God. Concerning which things, I who suffer, have thought it necessary to show to your piety, in order that you may be aware of such men, lest any of them presume to set foot in your dioceses, whether by themselves or by others; for these sorcerers know how to use hypocrisy to carry out their fraud; and to employ letters composed and dressed out with lies, which are able to deceive a man who is intent upon a simple and sincere faith. Arius, therefore, and Achilles,[2] having lately entered into a conspiracy, emulating the ambition of Colluthus, have turned out far worse than he. For Colluthus, indeed, who reprehends these very men, found some pretext for his evil purpose; but these, beholding his[3] bartering of Christ, endured no longer to be subject to the Church; but building for themselves dens of thieves, they hold their assemblies in them unceasingly, night and day directing their calumnies against Christ and against us. For since they call in question all pious and apostolical doctrine, after the manner of the Jews, they have constructed a workshop for contending against Christ, denying the Godhead of our Saviour, and preaching that He is only the equal of all others. And having collected all the passages which speak of His plan of salvation and His humiliation for our sakes, they endeavour from these to collect the preaching of their impiety, ignoring altogether the passages in which His eternal Godhead and unutterable glory with the Father is set forth. Since, therefore, they back up the impious opinion concerning Christ, which is held by the Jews and Greeks, in every possible way they strive to gain their approval; busying themselves about all those things which they are wont to deride in us, and daily stirring up against us seditions and persecutions. And now, indeed, they drag us before the tribunals of the judges, by intercourse with silly and disorderly women, whom they have led into error; at another time they cast opprobrium and infamy upon the Christian religion, their young maidens disgracefully wandering about every village and street. Nay, even Christ's indivisible tunic, which His executioners were unwilling to divide, these wretches have dared to rend.[4]

2. And we, indeed, though we discovered rather late, on account of their concealment, their manner of life, and their unholy attempts, by the common suffrage of all have[5] cast them forth from the congregation of the Church which adores the Godhead of Christ. But they, running hither and thither against us, have begun to betake themselves to our colleagues who are of the same mind with us; in appearance, indeed, pretending to seek for peace and concord, but in reality seeking to draw over some of them by fair words to their own diseases, asking long wordy letters from them, in order that reading these to the men whom they have deceived, they

---

[1] [A.D. 321.] Apud. Theodoritum, *Hist. Eccl.*, book i. chap. 4.
[2] [See p. 290, note 1, *supra.*]
[3] Colluthus, being a presbyter of Alexandria, puffed up with arrogance and temerity, had acted as a bishop, and had ordained many priests and deacons. But in the synod that was assembled at Alexandria all his acts of ordination were rescinded; and those who had been ordained by him degraded to the rank of laymen. —TR.

[4] [Perhaps a quotation, and hence a token of verity as to what is narrated of Peter, p. 263, note 4, *supra.*]
[5] It is inferred from these words that this letter of Alexander was written after the Synod of Alexandria in which Arius and his companion were condemned. But Alexander convened two synods of the bishops of Egypt against Arius and his friends. —TR.

may make them impenitent in the errors into which they have fallen, and obdurate in impiety, as if they had bishops thinking the same thing and siding with them. Moreover, the things which amongst us they have wrongly taught and done, and on account of which they have been expelled by us, they do not at all confess to them, but they either pass them over in silence, or throwing a veil over them, by feigned words and writings they deceive them. Concealing, therefore, their pestilent doctrine by their specious and flattering discourse, they circumvent the more simple-minded and such as are open to fraud, nor do they spare in the meanwhile to traduce our piety to all. Hence it comes to pass that some, subscribing their letters, receive them into the Church, although in my opinion the greatest guilt lies upon those ministers who venture to do this ; because not only does the apostolic rule not allow of it, but the working of the devil in these men against Christ is by this means more strongly kindled. Wherefore without delay, brethren beloved, I have stirred myself up to show you the faithlessness of these men who say that there was a time when the Son of God was not ; and that He who was not before, came into existence afterwards, becoming such, when at length He was made, even as every man is wont to be born. For, they say, God made all things from things which are not, comprehending even the Son of God in the creation of all things, rational and irrational. To which things they add as a consequence, that He is of mutable nature, and capable both of virtue and vice. And this hypothesis being once assumed, that He is "from things which are not," they overturn the sacred writings concerning His eternity, which signify the immutability and the Godhead of Wisdom and the Word, which are Christ.

3. We, therefore, say these wicked men, can also be the sons of God even as He. For it is written, "I have nourished and brought up children."[1] But when what follows was objected to them, "and they have rebelled against me," which indeed is not applicable to the nature of the Saviour, who is of an immutable nature ; they, throwing off all religious reverence, say that God, since He foreknew and had foreseen that His Son would not rebel against Him, chose Him from all. For He did not choose Him as having by nature anything specially beyond His other sons, for no one is by nature a son of God, as they say ; neither as having any peculiar property of His own ; but God chose Him who was of a mutable nature, on account of the carefulness of His manners and His practice, which in no way turned to that which is evil ; so that, if Paul and Peter had striven for this, there would

have been no difference between their sonship and His. And to confirm this insane doctrine, playing with Holy Scripture, they bring forward what is said in the Psalms respecting Christ : "Thou lovest righteousness, and hatest wickedness : therefore God, Thy God, hath anointed Thee with the oil of gladness above Thy fellows."[2]

4. But that the Son of God was not made "from things which are not," and that there was no "time when He was not,"[3] the evangelist John sufficiently shows, when he thus writes concerning Him : "The only-begotten Son, who is in the bosom of the Father."[4] For since that divine teacher intended to show that the Father and the Son are two things inseparable the one from the other, he spoke of Him as being in the bosom of the Father. Now that also the Word of God is not comprehended in the number of things that were created "from things which are not," the same John says, "All things were made by Him." For he set forth His proper personality, saying, "In the beginning was the Word, and the Word was with God, and the Word was God. All things were made by Him ; and without Him was not anything made that was made."[5] For if all things were made by Him, how comes it that He who gave to the things which are made their existence, at one time Himself was not. For the Word which makes is not to be defined as being of the same nature with the things which are made ; since He indeed was in the beginning, and all things were made by Him, and fashioned "from things which are not." Moreover, that which *is* seems to be contrary to and far removed from those things which are made "from things which are not." For that indeed shows that there is no interval between the Father and the Son, since not even in thought can the mind imagine any distance between them. But that the world was created "from things which are not," indicates a more recent a and later origin of substance, since the universe receives an essence of this sort from the Father by the Son. When, therefore, the most pious John contemplated the essence of the divine Word at a very great distance, and as placed beyond all conception of those things that are begotten, he thought it not meet to speak of His generation and creation ; not daring to designate the Creator in the same terms as the things that are made. Not that the Word is unbegotten, for the Father alone is unbegotten, but because the inexplicable subsistence of the only-begotten Son transcends the acute comprehension of the evangelists, and perhaps also of angels.

---

[1] Isa. i. 2.

[2] Ps. xlv. 7.
[3] [The two tests, or *criteria*, of Arianism. The Arians affirmed (1) the formula ἐξ οὐκ ὄντων, and (2) the ἦν ποτε ὅτε οὐκ ἦν.]
[4] John i. 18.
[5] John i. 1-3.

5. Wherefore I do not think that he is to be reckoned amongst the pious who presumes to inquire into anything beyond these things, not listening to this saying : " Seek not out the things that are too hard for thee, neither search the things that are above thy strength." [1] For if the knowledge of many other things that are incomparably inferior to this, are hidden from human comprehension, such as in the apostle Paul, " Eye hath not seen, nor ear heard, neither have entered into the heart of man, the things which God hath prepared for them that love Him." [2] As also God said to Abraham, that " he could not number the stars ; " [3] and that passage, " Who can number the sand of the sea, and the drops of rain." [4] How shall any one be able to investigate too curiously the subsistence of the divine Word, unless he be smitten with frenzy ? Concerning which the Spirit of prophecy says, " Who shall declare his generation ? " [5] And our Saviour Himself, who blesses the pillars of all things in the world, sought to unburden them of the knowledge of these things, saying that to comprehend this was quite beyond their nature, and that to the Father alone belonged the knowledge of this most divine mystery. " For no man," says He, " knoweth the Son, but the Father ; neither knoweth any man the Father, save the Son." [6] Of this thing also I think that the Father spoke, in the words, " My secret is to Me and Mine."

6. Now that it is an insane thing to think that the Son was made from things which are not, and was in being in time, the expression, " from things which are not," itself shows, although these stupid men understand not the insanity of their own words. For the expression, " was not," ought either to be reckoned in time, or in some place of an age. But if it be true that "all things were made by Him," it is established that both every age and time and all space, and that "when" in which the " was not " is found, was made by Him. And is it not absurd that He who fashioned the times and the ages and the seasons, in which that "was not" is mixed up, to say of Him, that He at some time was not? For it is devoid of sense, and a mark of great ignorance, to affirm that He who is the cause of everything is posterior to the origin of that thing. For according to them, the space of time in which they say that the Son had not yet been made by the Father, preceded the wisdom of God that fashioned all things, and the Scripture speaks falsely according to them, which calls Him " the First-born of every creature." Conformable to which, that which the majestically-speaking Paul says of Him : " Whom He hath appointed heir of all things. By whom also He made the worlds. But by Him also were all things created that are in heaven, and that are in earth, visible and invisible, whether they be thrones or dominions, or principalities, or powers ; all things were created by Him, and for Him ; and He is before all things." [7]

7. Wherefore, since it appears that this hypothesis of a creation from things which are not is most impious, it is necessary to say that the Father is always the Father. But He is the Father, since the Son is always with Him, on account of whom He is called the Father. Wherefore, since the Son is always with Him, the Father is always perfect, being destitute of nothing as regards good ; who, not in time, nor after an interval, nor from things which are not, hath begotten His only-begotten Son. How, then, is it not impious to say, that the wisdom of God once was not, which speaks thus concerning itself : " I was with Him forming all things ; I was His delight ; " [8] or that the power of God once did not exist ; or that His Word was at any time mutilated ; or that other things were ever wanting from which the Son is known and the Father expressed? For he who denies that the brightness of the glory existed, takes away also the primitive light of which it is the brightness. And if the image of God was not always, it is clear also that He was not always, of which it is the image. Moreover, in saying that the character of the subsistence of God was not, He also is done away with who is perfectly expressed by it. Hence one may see that the Sonship of our Saviour has nothing at all in common with the sonship of the rest. For just as it has been shown that His inexplicable subsistence excels by an incomparable excellence all other things to which He has given existence, so also His Sonship, which is according to the nature of the Godhead of the Father, transcends, by an ineffable excellence, the sonship of those who have been adopted by Him. For He, indeed, is of an immutable nature, every way perfect, and wanting in nothing ; but these, since they are either way subject to change, stand in need of help from Him. For what progress can the wisdom of God make ? What increase can the truth itself and God the Word receive ? In what respect can the life and the true light be made better? And if this be so, how much more unnatural is it that wisdom should ever be capable of folly ; that the power of God should be conjoined with infirmity ; that reason should be obscured by unreason ; or that darkness should be mixed up with the true light? And the apostle says, on this place, " What communion hath light

1 Ecclus. iii. 22. [Compare the canonical equivalent, Ps. cxxxi. 1.]
2 1 Cor. ii. 9.
3 Gen. xv. 5.
4 Ecclus. i. 2.
5 Isa. liii. 8.
6 Matt. xi. 27.
7 Col. i. 16, 17.
8 Prov. viii. 30 (LXX.).

with darkness? and what concord hath Christ with Belial?"[1] And Solomon says, that it is not possible that it should come to pass that a man should comprehend with his understanding "the way of a serpent upon a rock," which is Christ, according to the opinion of Paul. But men and angels, who are His creatures, have received His blessing that they might make progress, exercising themselves in virtues and in the commandments of the law, so as not to sin. Wherefore our Lord, since He is by nature the Son of the Father, is by all adored. But these, laying aside the spirit of bondage, when by brave deeds and by progress they have received the spirit of adoption, being blessed by Him who is the Son by nature, are made sons by adoption.

8. And His proper and peculiar, natural and excellent Sonship, St. Paul has declared, who thus speaks of God: "Who spared not His own Son, but for us," who were not His natural sons, "delivered Him up."[2] For to distinguish Him from those who are not properly sons, He said that He was His own Son. And in the Gospel we read: "This is My beloved Son, in whom I am well pleased."[3] Moreover, in the Psalms the Saviour says: "The Lord hath said unto Me, Thou art my Son."[4] Where, showing that He is the true and genuine Son, He signifies that there are no other genuine sons besides Himself. And what, too, is the meaning of this: "From the womb before the morning I begat thee"?[5] Does He not plainly indicate the natural sonship of paternal bringing forth, which he obtained not by the careful framing of His manners, not by the exercise of and increase in virtue, but by property of nature? Wherefore, the only-begotten Son of the Father, indeed, possesses an indefectible Sonship; but the adoption of rational sons belongs not to them by nature, but is prepared for them by the probity of their life, and by the free gift of God. And *it* is mutable as the Scripture recognises: "For when the sons of God saw the daughters of men, they took them wives,"[6] etc. And in another place: "I have nourished and brought up children, but they have rebelled against Me,"[7] as we find God speaking by the prophet Isaiah.

9. And though I could say much more, brethren beloved, I purposely omit to do so, as deeming it to be burdensome at great length to call these things to the remembrance of teachers who are of the same mind with myself. For ye yourselves are taught of God, nor are ye ignorant that this doctrine, which hath lately raised its head against the piety of the Church,

is that of Ebion and Artemas; nor is it aught else but an imitation of Paul of Samosata, bishop of Antioch, who, by the judgment and counsel of all the bishops, and in every place, was separated from the Church.[8] To whom Lucian succeeding, remained for many years separate from the communion of three bishops.[9] And now lately having drained the dregs of their impiety, there have arisen amongst us those who teach this doctrine of a creation from things which are not,[10] their hidden sprouts, Arius and Achilles, and the gathering of those who join in their wickedness. And three bishops in Syria, having been, in some manner, consecrated on account of their agreement with them, incite them to worse things. But let the judgment concerning these be reserved for your trial. For they, retaining in their memory the words which came to be used with respect to His saving Passion, and abasement, and examination, and what they call His poverty, and in short of all those things to which the Saviour submitted for our sakes, bring them forward to refute His supreme and eternal Godhead. But of those words which signify His natural glory and nobility, and abiding with the Father, they have become unmindful. Such as this: "I and My Father are one,"[11] which indeed the Lord says, not as proclaiming Himself to be the Father, nor to demonstrate that two persons are one; but that the Son of the Father most exactly preserves the expressed likeness of the Father, inasmuch as He has by nature impressed upon Him His similitude in every respect, and is the image of the Father in no way discrepant, and the expressed figure of the primitive exemplar. Whence, also, to Philip, who then was desirous to see Him, the Lord shows this abundantly. For when he said, "Show us the Father,"[12] He answered: "He that hath seen Me, hath seen the Father," since the Father was Himself seen through the spotless and living mirror of the divine image. Similar to which is what the saints say in the Psalms: "In Thy light shall we see light."[13] Wherefore he that honoureth the Son, honoureth the Father also;"[13] and with reason, for every impious word which they dare to speak against the Son, has reference to the Father.

10. But after these things, brethren beloved, what is there wonderful in that which I am about to write, if I shall set forth the false calumnies against me and our most pious laity? For those who have set themselves in array against the Godhead of Christ, do not scruple to utter their ungrateful ravings against us. Who will not

---

[1] 2 Cor. vi. 14, 15.
[2] Rom. viii. 32.
[3] Matt. iii. 17.
[4] Ps. xi. 7.
[5] Ps. cx. 3 (LXX.).
[6] Gen. vi. 2.
[7] Isa. i. 2.

[8] [A.D. 269.]
[9] [By the canons three bishops were necessary to ordain one to the episcopate, nor was communion with fewer than these Catholic.]
[10] [See p. 292, note 3, *supra.*]
[11] John x. 30.
[12] John xiv. 8, 9.
[13] Ps. xxxvi. 9.

either that any of the ancients should be compared with them, or suffer that any of those whom, from our earliest years, we have used as instructors should be placed on a level with them. Nay, and they do not think that any of all those who are now our colleagues, has attained even to a moderate amount of wisdom ; boasting themselves to be the only men who are wise and divested of worldly possessions, the sole discoverers of dogmas, and that to them alone are those things revealed which have never before come into the mind of any other under the sun. Oh, the impious arrogance ! Oh, the immeasurable madness ! Oh, the vainglory befitting those that are crazed ! Oh, the pride of Satan which has taken root in their unholy souls. The religious perspicuity of the ancient Scriptures caused them no shame, nor did the consentient doctrine of our colleagues concerning Christ keep in check their audacity against Him. Their impiety not even the demons will bear, who are ever on the watch for a blasphemous word uttered against the Son.

11. And let these things be now urged according to our power against those who, with respect to matter which they know nothing of, have, as it were, rolled in the dust against Christ, and have taken in hand to calumniate our piety towards Him. For those inventors of stupid fables say, that we who turn away with aversion from the impious and unscriptural blasphemy against Christ, of those who speak of His coming from the things which are not assert, that there are two unbegottens. For they ignorantly affirm that one of two things must necessarily be said, either that He is from things which are not, or that there are two unbegottens ; nor do those ignorant men know how great is the difference between the unbegotten Father, and the things which were by Him created from things which are not, as well the rational as the irrational. Between which two, as holding the middle place, the only begotten nature of God, the Word by which the Father formed all things out of nothing, was begotten of the true Father Himself. As in a certain place the Lord Himself testified, saying, " Every one that loveth Him that begat, loveth Him also that is begotten of Him." [1]

12. Concerning whom we thus believe, even as the Apostolic Church believes. In one Father unbegotten, who has from no one the cause of His being, who is unchangeable and immutable, who is always the same, and admits of no increase or diminution ; who gave to us the Law, the prophets, and the Gospels ; who is Lord of the patriarchs and apostles, and all the saints. And in one Lord Jesus Christ, the only-begotten Son of God ; not begotten of things which are not,

but of Him who is the Father ; not in a corporeal manner, by excision or division as Sabellius and Valentinus thought, but in a certain inexplicable and unspeakable manner, according to the words of the prophet cited above : " Who shall declare His generation?" [2] Since that His subsistence no nature which is begotten can investigate, even as the Father can be investigated by none ; because that the nature of rational beings cannot receive the knowledge of His divine generation by the Father. But men who are moved by the Spirit of truth, have no need to learn these things from me, for in our ears are sounding the words before uttered by Christ on this very thing, " No man knoweth the Father, save the Son ; and no man knoweth who the Son is, save the Father." [3] That He is equally with the Father unchangeable and immutable, wanting in nothing, and the perfect Son, and like to the Father, we have learnt ; in this alone is He inferior to the Father, that He is not unbegotten. For He is the very exact image of the Father, and in nothing differing from Him. For it is clear that He is the image fully containing all things by which the greatest similitude is declared, as the Lord Himself hath taught us, when He says, " My Father is greater than I." [4] And according to this we believe that the Son is of the Father, always existing. " For He is the brightness of His glory, the express image of His *Father's* person." [5] But let no one take that word *always* so as to raise suspicion that He is unbegotten, as they imagine who have their senses blinded. For neither are the words, " He was," or " always," or " before all worlds," equivalent to unbegotten. But neither can the human mind employ any other word to signify unbegotten. And thus I think that you understand it, and I trust to your right purpose in all things, since these words do not at all signify unbegotten. For these words seem to denote simply a lengthening out of time, but the Godhead, and as it were the antiquity of the only-begotten, they cannot worthily signify ; but they have been employed by holy men, whilst each, according to his capacity, seeks to express this mystery, asking indulgence from the hearers, and pleading a reasonable excuse, in saying, Thus far have we attained. But if there be any who are expecting from mortal lips some word which exceeds human capacity, saying that those things have been done away which are known in part, it is manifest that the words, " He was," and " always," and " before all ages," come far short of what they hoped. And whatever word shall be employed is not equivalent to unbegotten. Therefore to the unbegotten

---

[1] John v. 1.

[2] Isa. liii. 8.
[3] Matt. xi. 27.
[4] John xiv. 28.
[5] Heb. i. 3.

Father, indeed, we ought to preserve His proper dignity, in confessing that no one is the cause of His being; but to the Son must be allotted His fitting honour, in assigning to Him, as we have said, a generation from the Father without beginning, and allotting adoration to Him, so as only piously and properly to use the words, " He was," and " always," and " before all worlds," with respect to Him; by no means rejecting His Godhead, but ascribing to Him a similitude which exactly answers in every respect to the Image and Exemplar of the Father. But we must say that to the Father alone belongs the property of being unbegotten, for the Saviour Himself said, " My Father is greater than I." [1] And besides the pious opinion concerning the Father and the Son, we confess to one Holy Spirit, as the divine Scriptures teach us; who hath inaugurated both the holy men of the Old Testament, and the divine teachers of that which is called the New. And besides, also, one only Catholic and Apostolic Church, which can never be destroyed, though all the world should seek to make war with it; but it is victorious over every most impious revolt of the heretics who rise up against it. For her Goodman hath confirmed our minds by saying, " Be of good cheer, I have overcome the world." [2] After this we know of the resurrection of the dead, the first-fruits of which was our Lord Jesus Christ, who in very deed, and not in appearance merely, carried a body, of Mary, Mother of God, who in the end of the world came to the human race to put away sin, was crucified and died, and yet did He not thus perceive any detriment to His divinity, being raised from the dead, taken up into heaven, seated at the right hand of majesty.

13. These things in part have I written in this epistle, thinking it burdensome to write out each accurately, even as I said before, because they escape not your religious diligence. Thus do we teach, thus do we preach. These are the apostolic doctrines of the Church, for which also we die, esteeming those but little who would compel us to forswear them, even if they would force us by tortures, and not casting away our hope in them. To these Arius and Achilles opposing themselves, and those who with them are the enemies of the truth, have been expelled from the Church, as being aliens from our holy doctrine, according to the blessed Paul, who says, '' If any man preach any other gospel unto you than that ye have received, let him be accursed; even though he feign himself an angel from heaven." [3] And also, " If any man teach otherwise, and consent not to the wholesome words of our Lord Jesus Christ, and to the doctrine

which is according to godliness; he is proud, knowing nothing," [4] and so forth. These, therefore, who have been anathematized by the brotherhood, let no one of you receive, nor admit of those things which are either said or written by them. For these seducers do always lie, nor will they ever speak the truth. They go about the cities, attempting nothing else but that under the mark of friendship and the name of peace, by their hypocrisy and blandishments, they may give and receive letters, to deceive by means of these a few " silly women, and laden with sins, who have been led captive by them," [5] and so forth.

14. These men, therefore, who have dared such things against Christ; who have partly in public derided the Christian religion; partly seek to traduce and inform against its professors before the judgment-seats; who in a time of peace, as far as in them lies, have stirred up a persecution against us; who have enervated the ineffable mystery of Christ's generation; from these, I say, beloved and like-minded brethren, turning away in aversion, give your suffrages with us against their mad daring; even as our colleagues have done, who being moved with indignation, have both written to us letters against these men, and have subscribed our letter. Which also I have sent unto you by my son Apion the deacon, being some of them from the whole of Egypt and the Thebaid, some from Libya and Pentapolis. There are others also from Syria, Lycia, Pamphylia, Asia, Cappadocia, and the other neighbouring provinces. After the example of which I trust also that I shall receive letters from you. For though I have prepared many helps towards curing those who have suffered injury, this is the especial remedy that has been devised for healing the multitudes that have been deceived by them, that they may comply with the general consent of our colleagues, and thus hasten to return to repentance. Salute one another, together with the brethren who are with you. I pray that ye may be strong in the Lord, beloved, and that I may profit by your love towards Christ.

II. — EPISTLE CATHOLIC. [6]

To our beloved and most reverend fellow-ministers of the Catholic Church in every place, Alexander sends greeting in the Lord:

1. Since the body of the Catholic Church is one, [7] and it is commanded in Holy Scripture that we should keep the bond of unanimity and peace, it follows that we should write and signify to one another the things which are done by each

---

[1] John xiv. 28.
[2] John xvi. 33.
[3] Gal. i. 8, 9.

[4] 1 Tim. vi. 3, 4.
[5] 2 Tim. iii. 4.
[6] Taken from the Works of St. Athanasius, vol i part 1. p. 397, *seqq.*, edit. Benedic. Paris, 1698.
[7] [Elucidation II.]

of us; that whether one member suffer or rejoice we may all either suffer or rejoice with one another. In our diocese, then, not so long ago, there have gone forth lawless men, and adversaries of Christ, teaching men to apostatize; which thing, with good right, one might suspect and call the precursor of Antichrist. I indeed wished to cover the matter up in silence, that so perhaps the evil might spend itself in the leaders of the heresy alone, and that it might not spread to other places and defile the ears of any of the more simple-minded. But since Eusebius, the present bishop of Nicomedia, imagining that with him rest all ecclesiastical matters,[1] because, having left Berytus and cast his eyes upon the church of the Nicomedians, and no punishment has been inflicted upon him, he is set over these apostates, and has undertaken to write everywhere, commending them, if by any means he may draw aside some who are ignorant to this most disgraceful and Antichristian heresy; it became necessary for me, as knowing what is written in the law, no longer to remain silent, but to announce to you all, that you may know both those who have become apostates, and also the wretched words of their heresy; and if Eusebius write, not to give heed to him.

2. For he, desiring by their assistance to renew that ancient wickedness of his mind, with respect to which he has for a time been silent, pretends that he is writing in their behalf, but he proves by his deed that he is exerting himself to do this on his own account. Now the apostates from the Church are these: Arius, Achilles,[2] Aithales, Carpones, the other Arius, Sarmates, who were formerly priests; Euzoius, Lucius, Julius, Menas, Helladius, and Gaius, formerly deacons; and with them Secundus and Theonas, who were once called bishops. And the words invented by them, and spoken contrary to the mind of Scripture, are as follows:—

"God was not always the Father; but there was a time when God was not the Father. The Word of God was not always, but was made 'from things that are not;' for He who is God fashioned the non-existing from the non-existing; wherefore there was a time when He was not. For the Son is a thing created, and a thing made: nor is He like to the Father in substance; nor is He the true and natural Word of the Father; nor is He His true Wisdom; but He is one of the things fashioned and made. And He is called, by a misapplication of the terms, the Word and Wisdom, since He is Himself made by the proper Word of God, and by that wisdom which is in God, in which, as God made all other things, so also did He make Him. Wherefore,

He is by His very nature changeable and mutable, equally with other rational beings. The Word, too, is alien and separate from the substance of God. The father also is ineffable to the Son; for neither does the Word perfectly and accurately know the Father, neither can He perfectly see Him. For neither does the Son indeed know His own substance as it is. Since He for our sakes was made, that by Him as by an instrument God might create us; nor would He have existed had not God wished to make us. Some one asked of them whether the Son of God could change even as the devil changed; and they feared not to answer that He can; for since He was made and created, He is of mutable nature."

3. Since those about Arius speak these things and shamelessly maintain them, we, coming together with the Bishops of Egypt and the Libyas, nearly a hundred in number, have anathematized them, together with their followers. But those about Eusebius have received them, earnestly endeavouring to mix up falsehood with truth, impiety with piety. But they will not prevail; for the truth prevails, and there is no communion betwixt light and darkness, no concord between Christ and Belial.[3] For who ever heard such things? or who, now hearing them, is not astonished, and does not stop his ears that the pollution of these words should not touch them? Who that hears John saying, "In the beginning was the Word,"[4] does not condemn those who say there was a time when He was not? Who that hears these words of the Gospel, "the only-begotten Son;"[5] and, "by Him were all things made,"[6] will not hate those who declare He is one of the things made? For how can He be one of the things made by Him? or how shall He be the only-begotten who, as they say, is reckoned with all the rest, if indeed He is a thing made and created? And how can He be made of things which are not, when the Father says, "My heart belched forth a good Word;"[7] and, "From the womb, before the morning have I begotten Thee?"[8] Or how is He unlike to the substance of the Father, who is the perfect image and brightness of the Father, and who says, "He that hath seen Me hath seen the Father?"[9] And how, if the Son is the Word or Wisdom and Reason of God, was there a time when He was not? It is all one as if they said, that there was a time when God was without reason and wisdom. How, also, can He be changeable and mutable, who says indeed by Himself: "I am in the Father, and the Father

1 [Imagining. Compare Hippolytus, vol. v. pp. 156 and 158, *supra*. This expression seems to have been a sort of formula.]
2 [See p. 290, note 1, *supra*.]

3 2 Cor. vi. 14.
4 John i. 1.
5 John i. 18.
6 John i. 3.
7 Ps. xlv. 1.
8 Ps. cx. 3; Heb. i. 3.
9 John xiv. 9.

in Me,"[1] and, "I and My Father are one;"[2] and by the prophet, "I am the Lord, I change not?"[3] For even though one saying may refer to the Father Himself, yet it would now be more aptly spoken of the Word, because when He became man, He changed not; but, as says the apostle, "Jesus Christ, the same yesterday, to-day, and for ever."[4] Who hath induced them to say, that for our sakes He was made; although Paul says, "for whom are all things, and by whom are all things?"[5]

4. Now concerning their blasphemous assertion who say that the Son does not perfectly know the Father, we need not wonder: for having once purposed in their mind to wage war against Christ, they impugn also these words of His, "As the Father knoweth Me, even so know I the Father."[6] Wherefore, if the Father only in part knoweth the Son, then it is evident that the Son doth not perfectly know the Father. But if it be wicked thus to speak, and if the Father perfectly knows the Son, it is plain that, even as the Father knoweth His own Word, so also the Word knoweth His own Father, of whom He is the Word.

5. By saying these things, and by unfolding the divine Scriptures, we have often refuted them. But they, chameleon-like, changing their sentiments, endeavour to claim for themselves that saying: "When the wicked cometh, then cometh contempt."[7] Before them, indeed, many heresies existed, which, having dared more than was right, have fallen into madness. But these by all their words have attempted to do away with the Godhead of Christ, have made those seem righteous, since they have come nearer to Antichrist. Wherefore they have been excommunicated and anathematized by the Church.[8] And indeed, although we grieve at the destruction of these men, especially that after having once learned the doctrine of the Church, they have now gone back; yet we do not wonder at it; for this very thing Hymenæus and Philetus suffered,[9] and before them Judas, who, though he followed the Saviour, afterwards became a traitor and an apostate. Moreover, concerning these very men, warnings are not wanting to us, for the Lord foretold: "Take heed that ye be not deceived: for many shall come in My name, saying, I am Christ; and the time draweth near: go ye not therefore after them."[10] Paul, too, having learnt these things from the Saviour, wrote, "In the latter times some shall depart from the faith, giving heed to seducing spirits, and doctrines of devils which turn away from the truth."[11]

6. Since, therefore, our Lord and Saviour Jesus Christ has thus Himself exhorted us, and by His apostle hath signified such things to us; we, who have heard their impiety with our own ears, have consistently anathematized such men, as I have already said, and have declared them to be aliens from the Catholic Church and faith, and we have made known the thing, beloved and most honoured fellow-ministers, to your piety, that you should not receive any of them, should they venture rashly to come unto you, and that you should not trust Eusebius or any one else who writes concerning them. For it becomes us as Christians to turn with aversion from all who speak or think against Christ, as the adversaries of God and the destroyers of souls, and "not even to wish them Godspeed, lest at any time we become partakers of their evil deeds,"[12] as the blessed John enjoins. Salute the brethren who are with you. Those who are with me salute you.

SIGNATORS.

PRESBYTERS OF ALEXANDRIA.

I, Colluthus, presbyter,[13] give my suffrage to the things which are written, and also for the deposition of Arius, and those who are guilty of impiety with him.

Alexander, presbyter, in like manner.	Arpocration, presbyter, in like manner.
Dioscorus, presbyter, in like manner.	Agathus, presbyter.
	Nemesius, presbyter.
Dionysius, presbyter, in like manner.	Longus, presbyter.
	Silvanus, presbyter.
Eusebius, presbyter, in like manner.	Perous, presbyter.
	Apis, presbyter.
Alexander, presbyter, in like manner.	Proterius, presbyter.
	Paulus, presbyter.
Nilaras, presbyter, in like manner.	Cyrus, presbyter, in like manner.

DEACONS.

Ammonius, deacon, in like manner.	Ambytianus, deacon.
Macarius, deacon.	Gaius, deacon, in like manner.
Pistus, deacon, in like manner.	Alexander, deacon.
Athanasius, deacon.	Dionysius, deacon.
Eumenes, deacon.	Agathon, deacon.
Apollonius, deacon.	Polybius, deacon, in like manner.
Olympius, deacon.	Theonas, deacon.
Aphthonius, deacon.	Marcus, deacon.
Athanasius, deacon.[14]	Commodus, deacon.
Macarius, deacon, in like manner.	Serapion, deacon.
Paulus, deacon.	Nilus, deacon.
Petrus, deacon.	Romanus, deacon, in like manner.

---

1 John xiv. 10.
2 John x. 30.
3 Mal. iii. 6.
4 Heb. xiii. 8.
5 Heb. xi. 10.
6 John x. 15.
7 Prov. xviii. 3.
8 [See the signators to this decree in the subjoined fragment.]
9 2 Tim. ii. 17.
10 Luke xxi. 8.

11 1 Tim. iv. 1.
12 2 John x.
13 [See p. 291, note 3, *supra.*]
14 [Note this name.]

I, Apollonius, presbyter, give my suffrage to the things which are written, and also for the deposition of Arius, and of those who are guilty of impiety with him.

Ingenius, presbyter, in like manner.	Dioscorus, presbyter.
	Sostras, presbyter.
Ammonius, presbyter.	Theon, presbyter.
Tyrannus, presbyter.	Boccon, presbyter.
Copres, presbyter.	Agathus, presbyter.
Ammonas, presbyter.	Achilles, presbyter.
Orion, presbyter.	Paulus, presbyter.
Serenus, presbyter.	Thalelæus, presbyter.
Didymus, presbyter.	Dionysius, presbyter, in like manner.
Heracles, presbyter.	

Sarapion, deacon, in like manner.	Didymus, deacon.
	Ptollarion, deacon.
Justus, deacon, in like manner.	Seras, deacon.
	Gaius, deacon.
Didymus, deacon.	Hierax, deacon.
Demetrius, deacon.	Marcus, deacon.
Maurus, deacon.	Theonas, deacon.
Alexander, deacon.	Sarmaton, deacon.
Marcus, deacon.	Carpon, deacon.
Comon, deacon.	Zoilus, deacon, in like manner.
Tryphon, deacon.	
Ammonius, deacon.	

III. — EPISTLE.[1]

Alexander, to the priests and deacons, of Alexandria and Mareotis, being present to them present, brethren beloved in the Lord, sends greeting:

Although you have been forward to subscribe the letters that I sent to those about Arius, urging them to abjure their impiety, and to obey the wholesome and Catholic faith; and in this manner have shown your orthodox purpose, and your agreement in the doctrines of the Catholic Church; yet because I have also sent letters to all our fellow-ministers in every place with respect to the things which concern Arius and his companions; I have thought it necessary to call together you the clergy of the city, and to summon you also of Mareotis; especially since of your number Chares and Pistus, the priests; Sarapion, Parammon, Zosimus, and Irenæus, the deacons, have gone over to the party of Arius, and have preferred to be deposed with them; that you may know what is now written, and that you should declare your consent in these matters, and give your suffrage for the deposition of those about Arius and Pistus. For it is right that you should know what I have written, and that you should each one, as if he had written it himself, retain it in his heart.

IV. — EPISTLE TO ÆGLON, BISHOP OF CYNOPOLIS, AGAINST THE ARIANS.[2]

From a letter of St. Alexander, bishop of Alexandria, to Æglon, bishop of Cynopolis, against the Arians.

1. Natural will is the free faculty of every intelligent nature as having nothing involuntary which is in respect of its essence.

2. Natural operation is the innate motion of all substance. Natural operation is the substantial and notifying reason of every nature. Natural operation is the notifying virtue of every substance.

V. — ON THE SOUL AND BODY AND THE PASSION OF THE LORD.[3]

1. The Word which is ungrudgingly sent down from heaven, is fitted for the irrigation of our hearts, if we have been prepared for His power, not by speaking only, but by listening. For as the rain without the ground does not produce fruit, so neither does the Word fructify without hearing, nor hearing without the Word. Moreover, the Word then becomes fruitful when we pronounce it, and in the same way hearing, when we listen. Therefore since the Word draws forth its power, do you also ungrudgingly lend your ears, and when you come to hear, cleanse yourselves from all ill-will and unbelief. Two very bad things are ill-will and unbelief, both of which are contrary to righteousness; for ill-will is opposed to charity, and unbelief to faith; just in the same way as bitterness is opposed to sweetness, darkness to light, evil to good, death to life, falsehood to truth. Those, therefore, who abound in these vices that are repugnant to virtue, are in a manner dead; for the malignant and the unbelieving hate charity and faith, and they who do this are the enemies of God.

2. Since therefore ye know, brethren beloved, that the malignant and the unbelieving are the enemies of righteousness, beware of these, embrace faith and charity, by which all the holy men who have existed from the beginning of the world to this day have attained unto salvation. And show forth the fruit of charity, not in words only, but also in deeds, that is, in all godly patience for God's sake. For, see! the Lord Himself hath shown His charity towards us, not only in words but also in deeds, since He

---

[1] Athanas., *ibid.*, p. 396. On the deposition of Arius and his followers by Alexander, archbishop of Alexandria.

[2] Two fragments from an epistle. St. Maxim., *Theological and Polemical Works*, vol. ii. pp. 152-155. Edit. Paris, 1675.
[3] Many writings of the ancients, as Cardinal Mai has remarked, may be disinterred from the Oriental manuscripts in the Vatican library, some of which have been brought to light by that eminent scholar. In an Arabic MS. he discovered a large portion of the following discourse by St. Alexander, the patriarch of Alexandria, which he afterwards met with entire in the Syrian Vatican manuscript 368. The Greek version being lost, Mai, with the assistance of the erudite Maronites, Matthæus Sciahuanus, and Franciscus Mehasebus, translated the discourse into Latin, and his version has been chiefly followed in the following translation. Of its genuineness there is no doubt, and it is quite worthy of a place among his other writings.

hath given Himself up as the price of our salvation. Besides, we were not created, like the rest of the world, by word alone, but also by deed. For God made the world to exist by the power of a single word, but us He produced by the efficacy alike of His word and working. For it was not enough for God to say, " Let us make man in our image, after our likeness," [1] but deed followed word ; for, taking the dust from the ground, He formed man out of it, conformable to His image and similitude, and into him He breathed the breath of life, so that Adam became a living soul.

3. But when man afterwards by his fall had inclined to death, it was necessary that that form should be recreated anew to salvation by the same Artificer. For the form indeed lay rotting in the ground ; but that inspiration which had been as the breath of life, was detained separate from the body in a dark place, which is called Hades. There was, therefore, a division of the soul from the body ; it was banished *ad inferos*, whilst the latter was resolved into dust ; and there was a great interval of separation between them ; for the body, by the dissolution of the flesh, becomes corrupt ; the soul being loosened from it, its action ceases. For as when the king is thrown into chains, the city falls to ruin ; or as when the general is taken captive, the army is scattered abroad ; or as when the helmsman is shaken off, the vessel is submerged ; so when the soul is bound in chains, its body goes to pieces ; as the city without its king, so its members are dissolved ; as is the case with an army when its general is lost, they are drowned in death, even as happens to a vessel when deprived of its helmsman. The soul, therefore, governed the man, as long as the body survived ; even as the king governs the city, the general the army, the helmsman the ship. But it was powerless to rule it, from the time when it was immoveably tied to it, and became immersed in error ; therefore it was that it declined from the straight path, and followed tempters, giving heed to fornication, idolatry, and shedding of blood ; by which evil deeds it has destroyed the proper manhood. Nay, but itself also being carried at length to the lower regions, it was there detained by the wicked tempter. Else was it wont, as the king restores the ruined city, the general collects the dispersed army, the sailor repairs the broken ship, even so, I say, the soul used to minister supplies to the body before that the body was dissolved in the dust, being not as yet itself bound fast with fetters. But after that the soul became bound, not with material fetters but with sins, and thus was rendered impotent to act, then it left its body in the ground, and being

cast down to the lower regions, it was made the footstool of death, and despicable to all.

4. Man went forth from paradise to a region which was the sink of unrighteousness, fornication, adultery, and cruel murder. And there he found his destruction ; for all things conspired to his death, and worked the ruin of him who had hardly entered there. Meanwhile man wanted some consolation and assistance and rest. For when was it well with man? In his mother's womb? But when he was shut up there, he differed but little from the dead. When he was nourished with milk from the breast? Not even then, indeed, did he feel any joy. Was it rather whilst he was coming to maturity? But then, especially, dangers impended over him from his youthful lusts. Was it, lastly, when he grew old? Nay, but then does he begin to groan, being pressed down by the weight of old age, and the expectation of death. For what else is old age but the expectation of death? Verily all the inhabitants of earth do die, young men and old, little children and adults, for no age or bodily stature is exempt from death. Why, then, is man tormented by this exceeding grief? Doubtless the very aspect of death begets sadness ; for we behold in a dead man the face changed, the figure dead, the body shrunk up with emaciation, the mouth silent, the skin cold, the carcase prostrate on the ground, the eyes sunken, the limbs immoveable, the flesh wasted away, the veins congealed, the bones whitened, the joints dissolved, all parts of him reduced to dust, and the man no longer existing. What, then, is man? A flower, I say, that is but for a little time, which in his mother's womb is not apparent, in youth flourishes, but which in old age withers and departs in death.

5. But now, after all this bondage to death and corruption of the manhood, God hath visited His creature, which He formed after His own image and similitude ; and this He hath done that it might not for ever be the sport of death. Therefore God sent down from heaven His incorporeal Son to take flesh upon Him in the Virgin's womb ; and thus, equally as thou, was He made man ; to save lost man, and collect all His scattered members. For Christ, when He joined the manhood to His person, united that which death by the separation of the body had dispersed. Christ suffered that we should live for ever.

For else why should Christ have died? Had He committed anything worthy of death? Why did He clothe Himself in flesh who was invested with glory? And since He was God, why did He become man? And since He reigned in heaven, why did He come down to earth, and become incarnate in the virgin's womb? What necessity, I ask, impelled God

---

[1] Gen. i. 26.

to come down to earth, to assume flesh, to be wrapped in swaddling clothes in a manger-cradle, to be nourished with the milk from the breast, to receive baptism from a servant, to be lifted up upon the cross, to be interred in an earthly sepulchre, to rise again the third day from the dead? [1]

What necessity, I say, impelled Him to this? It is sufficiently discovered that He suffered shame for man's sake, to set him free from death; and that He exclaimed, as in the words of the prophet, "I have endured as a travailing woman." [2] In very deed did He endure for our sakes sorrow, ignominy, torment, even death itself, and burial. For thus He says Himself by the prophet: "I went down into the deep." [3] Who made Him thus to go down? The impious people. Behold, ye sons of men, behold what recompense Israel made unto Him! She slew her Benefactor, returning evil for good, affliction for joy, death for life. They slew by nailing to the tree Him who had brought to life their dead, had healed their maimed, had made their lepers clean, had given light to their blind. Behold, ye sons of men! behold, all ye people, these new wonders! They suspended Him on the tree, who stretches out the earth; they transfixed Him with nails who laid firm the foundation of the world; they circumscribed Him who circumscribed the heavens; they bound Him who absolves sinners; they gave Him vinegar to drink who hath made them to drink of righteousness; they fed Him with gall who hath offered to them the Bread of Life; they caused corruption to come upon His hands and feet who healed their hands and feet; they violently closed His eyes who restored sight to them; they gave Him over to the tomb, who raised their dead to life both in the time before His Passion and also whilst He was hanging on the tree.

6. For when our Lord was suffering upon the cross, the tombs were burst open, the infernal region was disclosed, the souls leapt forth, the dead returned to life, and many of them were seen in Jerusalem, whilst the mystery of the cross was being perfected; what time our Lord trampled upon death, dissolved the enmity, bound the strong man, and raised the trophy of the cross, His body being lifted up upon it, that the body might appear on high, and death to be depressed under the foot of flesh. Then the heavenly powers wondered, the angels were astonished, the elements trembled, every creature was shaken whilst they looked on this new mystery, and the terrific spectacle which was being enacted in the universe. Yet the entire people, as unconscious of the mystery, exulted over Christ in derision; although the earth was rocking, the mountains, the valleys, and the sea were shaken, and every creature of God was smitten with confusion. The lights of heaven were afraid, the sun fled away, the moon disappeared, the stars withdrew their shining, the day came to end; [4] the angel in astonishment departed from the temple after the rending of the veil, and darkness covered the earth on which its Lord had closed His eyes. Meanwhile hell [5] was with light resplendent, for thither had the star descended. The Lord, indeed, did not descend into hell in His body but in His Spirit. He forsooth is working everywhere, for whilst He raised the dead by His body, by His spirit was He liberating their souls. For when the body of the Lord was hung upon the cross, the tombs, as we have said, were opened; hell was unbarred, the dead received their life, the souls were sent back again into the world, and that because the Lord had conquered hell, had trodden down death, had covered the enemy with shame; therefore was it that the souls came forth from Hades, and the dead appeared upon the earth.

7. Ye see, therefore, how great was the effect of the death of Christ, for no creature endured His fall with equal mind, nor did the elements His Passion, neither did the earth retain His body, nor hell His Spirit. All things were in the Passion of Christ disturbed and convulsed. The Lord exclaimed, as once before to Lazarus, Come forth, ye dead, from your tombs and your secret places; for I, the Christ, give unto you resurrection. For then the earth could not long hold the body of our Lord that it was buried; but it exclaimed, O my Lord, pardon mine iniquities, save me from Thy wrath, absolve me from the curse, for I have received the blood of the righteous, and yet I have not covered the bodies of men or Thine own body! What is at length this wonderful mystery? Why, O Lord, didst Thou come down to earth, unless it was for man's sake, who has been scattered everywhere: for in every place has Thy fair image been disseminated? Nay! but if thou shouldest give but one little word, at the instant all bodies would stand before Thee. Now, since Thou hast come to earth, and hast sought for the members of Thy fashioning, undertake for man who is Thine own, receive that which is committed to Thee,

---

[1] The passage, as far as to "rise again the third day from the dead," is generally marked with inverted commas, and Mai remarks that it had been already brought to light by him under the name of the same Alexander, in the *Spicileg. Roman.*, vol. iii. p. 699, amongst some extracts of the Fathers from the Arabic Vatican Codex, 101, in which is contained the celebrated Monophysite work entitled *Fides Patrum*. It is established therefore that this discourse was written in Greek by Alexander, and afterwards translated not only into the Syriac, but also into the Arabic language. [I have made this passage into a paragraph distinct from the rest.]

[2] Isa. xlii. 14.

[3] Jonah ii. 4.

[4] [Vol. iii. 58, this series. The patristic testimony is overwhelming and sufficient. See Africanus, p. 136, *supra*, and a full discussion of his statement in Routh, *R. S.*, ii. p. 477.]

[5] Hades.

recover Thine image, Thine Adam. Then the Lord, the third day after His death, rose again, thus bringing man to a knowledge of the Trinity. Then all the nations of the human race were saved by Christ. One submitted to the judgment, and many thousands were absolved. Moreover, He being made like to man whom He had saved, ascended to the height of heaven, to offer before His Father, not gold or silver, or precious stones, but the man whom He had formed after His own image and similitude ; and the Father, raising Him to His right hand, hath seated Him upon a throne on high, and hath made Him to be judge of the peoples, the leader of the angelic host, the charioteer of the cherubim, the Son of the true Jerusalem, the Virgin's spouse, and King for ever and ever. Amen.

VI.—THE ADDITION IN THE CODEX, WITH A VARIOUS READING.

God, therefore, wishing to visit His own form which He had fashioned after His own image and similitude, hath in these last times sent into the world His incorporeal and only Son, who being in the Virgin's womb incarnate, was born perfect man to raise erect lost man, re-collecting His scattered members. For why else should Christ have died? Was He capitally accused? And since He was God, why was He made man? Why did He who was reigning in heaven come down to earth? Who compelled God to come down to earth, to take flesh of the holy Virgin, to be wrapped in swaddling clothes and laid in a manger, to be nourished with milk, to be baptized in the Jordan, to be mocked of the people, to be nailed to the tree, to be buried in the bosom of the earth, and the third day to rise again from the dead ; in the cause of redemption to give life for life, blood for blood, to undergo death for death? For Christ, by dying, hath discharged the debt of death to which man was obnoxious. Oh, the new and ineffable mystery! the Judge was judged. He who absolves from sin was bound ; He was mocked who once framed the world ; He was stretched upon the cross who stretched out the heavens ; He was fed with gall who gave the manna to be bread ; He died who gives life. He was given

up to the tomb who raises the dead. The powers were astonished, the angels wondered, the elements trembled, the whole created universe was shaken, the earth quaked, and its foundations rocked ; the sun fled away, the elements were subverted, the light of day receded ; because they could not bear to look upon their crucified Lord.[1] The creature, in amazement, said, What is this novel mystery? The judge is judged and is silent ; the invisible is seen and is not confounded ; the incomprehensible is grasped and is not indignant at it ; the immeasurable is contained in a measure and makes no opposition ; the impassable suffers and does not avenge its own injury ; the immortal dies and complains not ; the celestial is buried and bears it with an equal mind. What, I say, is this mystery? The creature surely is transfixed with amazement. But when our Lord rose from death and trampled it down, when He bound the strong man and set man free, then every creature wondered at the Judge who for Adam's sake was judged, at the invisible being seen, at the impassable suffering, at the immortal dead, at the celestial buried in the earth. For our Lord was made man ; He was condemned that He might impart compassion ; He was bound that He might set free ; He was apprehended that He might liberate ; He suffered that He might heal our sufferings ; He died to restore life to us ; He was buried to raise us up. For when our Lord suffered, His humanity suffered, that which He had like unto man ; and He dissolves the sufferings of him who is His like, and by dying He hath destroyed death. It was for this cause that He came down upon earth, that by pursuing death He might kill the rebel that slew men. For one underwent the judgment, and myriads were set free ; one was buried, and myriads rose again. He is the Mediator between God and man ; He is the resurrection and the salvation of all ; He is the Guide of the erring, the Shepherd of men who have been set free, the life of the dead, the charioteer of cherubim, the standard-bearer of the angels, and the King of kings, to whom be glory for ever and ever. Amen.

---

[1] Here, again, we have this fact insisted on. See p. 301, note 4.

ELUCIDATIONS.

I.

(Some points, p. 289.)

THAT the theology of the great school of Alexandria had a character of its own, is most apparent; I should be the last to deny it. As its succession of teachers was like that of hereditary descent in a family, a family likeness is naturally to be found in this school, from the great Clement to the great Athanasius. It is a school that hands on the traditions in which Apollos had been reared; it not less reflects the Greek influences always dominant in the capital of the Macedonian hero; but it is a school in which the Gospel of Christ as the Light of the world was always made *predominant:* and, while a most liberal view of human *knowledge* was inculcated in it, yet *the faith* was always exalted as the mother and mistress of the true *gnosis* and of all science. The wise men of this world were summoned with an imperial voice, from this eldest seat and centre of Christian learning, to cast their crowns and their treasures at the feet of Jesus. With a generous patronage Clement conceded all he could to the philosophy of the Greeks, and yet sublimely rose above it to a sphere it never discovered, and looked down upon all merely human intellect and its achievements like Uriel in the sun.

It was the special though unconscious mission of this school to prepare the way, and to shape the thought of Christendom, for the great epoch of the (nominal) conversion of the empire, and for the all-important synodical period, its logical consequence. It was in this school that the technical formulas of the Church were naturally wrought out. The process was like that of the artist who has first to make his own tools. He does many things, and resorts to many contrivances, never afterwards necessary when once the tools are complete and his laboratory furnished with all he wants for his work. To my mind, therefore, it is but a pastime of no practical worth to contrast the idiosyncrasies of Clement with those of Origen, and to set up distinctions between the Logos of this doctor and that.[1] The differences to be descried belong to the personal peculiarities of great minds not yet guided to unity of diction by a scientific theology. The marvel is their harmony of thought. Their ends and their antagonisms are the same. The outcome of their mental efforts and their pious faith is seen in the result. Alexander was their product, and Athanasius (bringing all their sheaves to the Church's garner, winnowed and harvested) is the perpetual *gnomon* of the Alexandrian school. Its testimony, its prescription, its harmony and unity, are all summed up in him.

It is extraordinary that many truly evangelical critics seem to see, in the *subordination* taught by Origen,[2] something not reconcileable with the Nicene orthodoxy. Even Bishop Bull is a *subordinationist*, and so are all the great orthodox divines. When Origen maintains the μοναρχία (the Father as the root and source of the Godhead, as do all the Greeks[3]), and also a subordination of the Son in the divine οὐσία, he is surely consistent with the Athanasian doctrine; [4] and, if he is led to affirm a diversity of essence in connection with this subordination, he does it with such limitations as should convince us that he, too, would have subscribed the ὁμοούσιον, in which Alexandrians no whit inferior to him finally formulated the convictions and testimonies of their predecessors.[5]

---

[1] See, against Petavius and others, Dr. Holmes's learned note, vol. iii. p. 628, Elucidation I.

[2] Vol. iv. p. 343, this series; also Elucidation II. p. 382.

[3] On Tertullian's orthodoxy, see notes, vol. iii. p. 600, etc.

[4] When we consider his refinements about the words *substance, idea, image*, etc., in the dispute with Celsus, while yet these terms were not reduced to precision, we cannot but detect his effort to convey an orthodox notion. Observe Dr. Spencer's short but useful note, vol. iv. p. 603, note 3.

[5] See vol. iv. p. 382, Elucidations I., II., and III.

II.

(Since the body of the Catholic Church is one, etc., p. 296.)

As so shortly preceding the meeting of the Great Council, this letter is most important as a clear testimony to the meaning the first council attached to that article of the Creed which affirms "one holy Catholic and Apostolic Church." We must compare the *Treatises* of Cyprian for the West, with this and the Letter of Firmilian [1] for the East, as clearly elucidating the contemporary mind of the Church, and hence the meaning of those words which reflect their mind in the Creed. To make any reflections of my own would be out of place, save only, negatively, as I compare it with the modern creed of the Council of Trent (Pius IV.), which defines the Catholic Church to be the communion which acknowledges the Church of Rome as "the mother and mistress of churches."

The concluding section of this letter is decisive as to the absolute *autonomy* of the Alexandrian *diœcese*.[2] To all the other churches Alexander merely communicates his sentence, which they are all bound to respect. Whether the Christian Church at this period reflected the Apostolic Institutions is not the question, but merely what its theory was in the fourth century, and how far East and West accorded with the theory of Cyprian.

---

[1] Vol. v. p. 390, this series.   [2] See the force of this spelling, p. 240, *supra.*

METHODIUS

[TRANSLATED BY THE REV. WILLIAM R. CLARK, M.A., VICAR OF ST. MARY MAGDALEN, TAUNTON.]

INTRODUCTORY NOTICE

TO

METHODIUS.

[A.D. 260–312]. Considering the strong language in which Methodius is praised by ancient writers, as well as by the moderns, I feel that our learned translator has too hastily dismissed his name and works in the biographical introduction below. Epiphanius makes great use of him in his refutations of Origen; and Dupin's critical and historical notice of him is prolonged and highly discriminating, furnishing an abridgment of all his writings and of those vulgarly attributed to him heretofore.[1] I have made into an elucidation some references which may be of use to the student. In like manner, I have thrown into the form of notes and elucidations what would be less pertinent and less useful in a preface. There are no facts to be added to what is here given by the translator; and remarks on the several works, which he has too sparingly annotated, will be more conveniently bestowed, perhaps, on the pages to which they immediately refer. The following is the translator's brief but useful

INTRODUCTION.

METHODIUS, who is also called Eubulius,[2] was, first of all bishop, simultaneously of Olympus and Patara, in Lycia, as is testified by several ancient writers.[3] He was afterwards removed, according to St. Jerome, to the episcopal See of Tyre in Phœnicia, and at the end of the latest of the great persecutions of the Church, about the year 312, he suffered martyrdom at Chalcis in Greece. Some consider that it was at Chalcis in Syria, and that St. Jerome's testimony ought to be thus understood, as Syria was more likely to be the scene of his martyrdom than Greece, as being nearer to his diocese. Others affirm that he suffered under Decius and Valerian; but this is incorrect, since he wrote not only against Origen long after the death of Adamantius, but also against Porphyry, whilst he was alive, in the reign of Diocletian.

Methodius is known chiefly as the antagonist of Origen; although, as has been pointed out, he was himself influenced in no small degree by the method of Origen, as may be seen by his tendency to allegorical interpretations of Holy Scripture. The only complete work of this writer which has come down to us is his *Banquet of the Ten Virgins*, a dialogue of considerable power and grace, in praise of the virginal life. His antagonism to Origen, however, comes out less in this than in his works *On the Resurrection*, and *On Things Created*. The treatise *On Free Will* is, according to recent critics, of doubtful authorship, although the internal evidence must be said to confirm the ancient testimonies which assign it to Methodius. His writings against Porphyry, with the exception of some slight fragments, are lost, as are also his exegetical writings.[4]

---

[1] [In Dr. Schaff's *History* (vol. ii. p. 809) is just such a notice and outline as would be appropriate here.]

[2] St. Epiph., *Hæres.*, 64, sec. 63. [But this seems only his *nom de plume*, assumed in his fiction of the *Banquet.*]

[3] St. Hieronymus, *De viris illust.*, c. 83.

[4] For the larger fragments we are indebted to Epiphanius (*Hæres.*, 64) and Photius (*Bibliotheca*, 234–237).

Combefis published an edition of his works in 1644; but only so much of the *Banquet* as was contained in the *Bibliotheca* of Photius. In 1656 Leo Allatius published for the first time a complete edition of this work at Rome from the Vatican MS. Combefis in 1672 published an edition founded chiefly upon this; and his work has become the basis of all subsequent reprints.

The following translation has been made almost entirely from the text of Migne, which is generally accurate, and the arrangement of which has been followed throughout. The edition of Jahn in some places rearranges the more fragmentary works, especially that *On the Resurrection;* but, although his text was occasionally found useful in amending the old readings, and in improving the punctuation, it was thought better to adhere in general to the text which is best known.

A writer who was pronounced by St. Epiphanius [1] to be "a learned man and a most valiant defender of the truth," and by St. Jerome, *disertissimus martyr,* [2] who elsewhere speaks of him as one who *nitidi compositique sermonis libros confecit,* [3] cannot be altogether unworthy the attention of the nineteenth century.

---

[1] Epiph., *Hær.*, 64, sec. 63. ἀνὴρ λόγιος καὶ σφόδρα περὶ τῆς ἀληθείας ἀγωνισάμενος. [Petavius renders this: "vir apprime doetus acerrimusque veritatis patronus."]

[2] Hieron., *Com. in Dan.*, c. 13.

[3] Id., *De vir ill.*, c. 83. Many more such testimonies will be found collected in the various editions of his works in Greek.

THE BANQUET OF THE TEN VIRGINS;[1]

OR,

CONCERNING CHASTITY.

PERSONS OF THE DIALOGUE: EUBOULIOS,[2] GREGORION, ARETE; MARCELLA, THEOPH-ILA, THALEIA, THEOPATRA, THALLOUSA, AGATHE, PROCILLA, THEKLA, TUSIANE, DOMNINA.

INTRODUCTION.

PLAN OF THE WORK; WAY TO PARADISE; DESCRIPTION AND PERSONIFICATION OF VIRTUE; THE AGNOS A SYMBOL OF CHASTITY; MARCELLA, THE ELDEST AND FOREMOST AMONG THE VIRGINS OF CHRIST.

EUBOULIOS. You have arrived most seasonably, Gregorion, for I have just been looking for you, wanting to hear of the meeting of Marcella and Theopatra, and of the other virgins who were present at the banquet, and of the nature of their discourses on the subject of chastity; for it is said that they argued with such ability and power that there was nothing lacking to the full consideration of the subject. If, therefore, you have come here for any other purpose, put that off to another time, and do not delay to give us a complete and connected account of the matter of which we are inquiring.

GREGORION.[3] I seem to be disappointed of my hope, as some one else has given you intelligence beforehand on the subject respecting which you ask me. For I thought that you had heard nothing of what had happened, and I was flattering myself greatly with the idea that I should be the first to tell you of it. And for this reason I made all haste to come here to you, fearing the very thing which has happened, that some one might anticipate me.

EUBOULIOS. Be comforted, my excellent friend, for we have had no precise information respecting anything which happened; since the person who brought us the intelligence had nothing to tell us, except that there had been dialogues; but when he was asked what they were, and to what purpose, he did not know.

GREGORION. Well then, as I came here for this reason, do you want to hear all that was said from the beginning; or shall I pass by parts of it, and recall only those points which I consider worthy of mention?

EUBOULIOS. By no means the latter; but first, Gregorion, relate to us from the very beginning where the meeting was, and about the setting forth of the viands, and about yourself, how you poured out the wine

"They in golden cups
Each other pledged, while towards broad heaven they
looked."[4]

GREGORION. You are always skilful in discussions, and excessively powerful in argument — thoroughly confuting all your adversaries.

EUBOULIOS. It is not worth while, Gregorion, to contend about these things at present; but do oblige us by simply telling us what happened from the beginning.

GREGORION. Well, I will try. But first answer me this: You know, I presume, Arete,[5] the daughter of Philosophia?

EUBOULIOS. Why do you ask?

GREGORION. "We went by invitation to a garden of hers with an eastern aspect, to enjoy the fruits of the season, myself, and Procilla, and Tusiane." I am repeating the words of Theo-

---

[1] [The idea, and some of the ideas borrowed from the *Symposium* of Plato, but designed to furnish a contrast as strong as possible between the swinish sensuality of false " philosophy " in its best estate, and the heavenly chastity of those whom the Gospel renders " pure in heart," and whose life on earth is controlled by the promise, " they shall see God."]
[2] In Migne's ed. *Euboulion*, but apparently with less authority; and probably because the name is connected with that of Gregorion. *Euboulios* is a man, and Gregorion a woman.
[3] [*Gregorion* answers to the *Diotima* of Socrates in Plato's *Banquet*, and talks like a philosopher on these delicate subjects.]

[4] Hom., *Il.*, iv. 3, 4.
[5] A personification of virtue, the daughter of philosophy. [i.e., of philosophy *not* falsely so called]

patra, for it was of her I obtained the information. "We went, Gregorion, by a very rough, steep, and arduous path : when we drew near to the place," said Theopatra, "we were met by a tall and beautiful woman walking along quietly and gracefully, clothed in a shining robe as white as snow. Her beauty was something altogether inconceivable and divine. Modesty, blended with majesty, bloomed on her countenance. It was a face," she said, "such as I know not that I had ever seen, awe-inspiring, yet tempered with gentleness and mirth ; for it was wholly unadorned by art, and had nothing counterfeit. She came up to us, and, like a mother who sees her daughters after a long separation, she embraced and kissed each one of us with great joy, saying, 'O, my daughters, you have come with toil and pain to me who am earnestly longing to conduct you to the pasture of immortality ; toilsomely have you come by a way abounding with many frightful reptiles ; for, as I looked, I saw you often stepping aside, and I was fearing lest you should turn back and slip over the precipices. But thanks to the Bridegroom to whom I have espoused[1] you, my children, for having granted an effectual answer to all our prayers.' And, while she is thus speaking," said Theopatra, "we arrive at the enclosure, the doors not being shut as yet, and as we enter we come upon Thekla and Agathe and Marcella preparing to sup. And Arete immediately said, 'Do you also come hither, and sit down here in your place along with these your fellows.' Now," said she to me, "we who were there as guests were altogether, I think, ten in number ; and the place was marvellously beautiful, and abounding in the means of recreation. The air was diffused in soft and regular currents, mingled with pure beams of light, and a stream flowing as gently as oil through the very middle of the garden, threw up a most delicious drink ; and the water flowing from it, transparent and pure, formed itself into fountains, and these, overflowing like rivers, watered all the garden with their abundant streams ; and there were different kinds of trees there, full of fresh fruits, and the fruits that hung joyfully from their branches were of equal beauty ; and there were ever-blooming meadows strewn with variegated and sweet-scented flowers, from which came a gentle breeze laden with sweetest odour. And the agnos[2] grew near, a lofty tree, under which we reposed, from its being exceedingly widespreading and shady."

EUBOULIOS. You seem to me, my good friend, to be making a revelation of a second paradise.[3]

GREGORION. You speak truly and wisely. "When there," she said, "we had all kinds of food and a variety of festivities, so that no delight was wanting. After this Arete,[4] entering, gave utterance to these words : —

"'Young maidens, the glory of my greatness, beautiful virgins, who tend the undefiled meadows of Christ with unwedded hands, we have now had enough of food and feasting, for all things are abundant and plentiful with us.[5] What is there, then, besides which I wish and expect? That each of you shall pronounce a discourse in praise of virginity. Let Marcella begin, since she sits in the highest place, and is at the same time the eldest. I shall be ashamed of myself if I do not make the successful disputant an object of envy, binding her with the unfading flowers of wisdom.'

"And then," I think she said, "Marcella immediately began to speak as follows."

DISCOURSE I. — MARCELLA.

CHAP. I. — THE DIFFICULTY AND EXCELLENCE OF VIRGINITY ; THE STUDY OF DOCTRINE NECESSARY FOR VIRGINS.

Virginity is something supernaturally great, wonderful, and glorious ; and, to speak plainly and in accordance with the Holy Scriptures, this best and noblest manner of life alone is the root[6] of immortality, and also its flower and first-fruits ; and for this reason the Lord promises that those shall enter into the kingdom of heaven who have made themselves eunuchs, in that passage[7] of the Gospels in which He lays down the various reasons for which men have made themselves eunuchs. Chastity with men is a very rare thing, and difficult of attainment, and in proportion to its supreme excellence and magnificence is the greatness of its dangers.[8]

For this reason, it requires strong and generous natures, such as, vaulting over the stream of pleasure, direct the chariot of the soul upwards from the earth, not turning aside from their aim, until having, by swiftness of thought, lightly bounded above the world, and taken their stand truly upon the vault of heaven, they purely contemplate immortality itself as it springs forth[9] from the undefiled bosom of the Almighty.

Earth could not bring forth this draught ; heaven alone knew the fountain from whence it flows ; for we must think of virginity as walking indeed upon the earth, but as also reaching up

---

[1] 2 Cor. xi. 2.
[2] "A tall tree like the willow, the branches of which were strewn by matrons on their beds at the Thesmophoria, *vitex agnuscastus.* It was associated with the notion of chastity, from the likeness of its name to ἁγνός." — LIDDELL and SCOTT.
[3] [Much of this work suggests a comparison with the *Hermas* of vol ii., and Minucius Felix seems not infrequently reflected.]

[4] [Virtue presides, and "to the pure all things are pure;" but the freedoms of the converse must offend unless we bear in mind that these are allegorical beings, not women in flesh and blood.]
[5] [See the oration on *Simeon and Anna,* cap. 10, *infra.*]
[6] Lit. the udder.
[7] Matt. ix. 12.
[8] [I think evidence abounds, in the course of this allegory, that it was designed to meet the painful discussions excited in the Church by the fanatical conduct of Origen, vol. iv. pp. 225-226.]
[9] Lit. "leaps out."

to heaven. And hence some who have longed for it, and considering only the end of it, have come, by reason of coarseness of mind, ineffectually with unwashed feet, and have gone aside out of the way, from having conceived no worthy idea of the *virginal* manner of life. For it is not enough to keep the body only undefiled, just as we should not show that we think more of the temple than of the image of the god ; but we should care for the souls of men as being the divinities of their bodies, and adorn them with righteousness. And then do they most care for them and tend them when, striving untiringly to hear divine discourses, they do not desist until, wearing the doors of the wise,[1] they attain to the knowledge of the truth.

For as the putrid humours and matter of flesh, and all those things which corrupt it, are driven out by salt, in the same manner all the irrational appetites of a virgin are banished from the body by divine teaching. For it must needs be that the soul which is not sprinkled with the words of Christ, as with salt, should stink and breed worms, as King David, openly confessing with tears in the mountains, cried out, " My wounds stink and are corrupt,"[2] because he had not salted himself with the exercises of self-control, and so subdued his carnal appetites, but self-indulgently had yielded to them, and became corrupted in adultery. And hence, in Leviticus,[3] every gift, unless it be seasoned with salt, is forbidden to be offered as an oblation to the Lord God. Now the whole spiritual meditation of the Scriptures is given to us as salt which stings in order to benefit, and which disinfects, without which it is impossible for a soul, by means of reason, to be brought to the Almighty ; for " ye are the salt of the earth,"[4] said the Lord to the apostles.

It is fitting, then, that a virgin should always love things which are honourable, and be distinguished among the foremost for wisdom, and addicted to nothing slothful or luxurious, but should excel, and set her mind upon things worthy of the state of virginity, always putting away, by the word, the foulness of luxury, lest in any way some slight hidden corruption should breed the worm of incontinence ; for " the unmarried woman careth for the things of the Lord," how she may please the Lord, " that she may be holy both in body and in spirit,"[5] says the blessed Paul. But many of them who consider the hearing of the word quite a secondary matter, think they do great things if they give their attention to it for a little while. But discrimination must be exercised with respect to

these ; for it is not fitting to impart divine instruction to a nature which is careful about trifles, and low, and which counterfeits wisdom. For would it not be laughable to go on talking to those who direct all their energy towards things of little value, in order that they may complete most accurately those things which they want to bring to perfection, but do not think that the greatest pains are to be taken with those necessary things by which most of all the love of chastity would be increased in them?

CHAP. II. — VIRGINITY A PLANT FROM HEAVEN, INTRODUCED LATE ; THE ADVANCEMENT OF MANKIND TO PERFECTION, HOW ARRANGED.

For truly by a great stretch of power the plant of virginity was sent down to men from heaven, and for this reason it was not revealed to the first generations. For the race of mankind was still very small in number ; and it was necessary that it should first be increased in number, and then brought to perfection. Therefore the men of old times thought it nothing unseemly to take their own sisters for wives, until the law coming separated them, and by forbidding that which at first had seemed to be right, declared it to be a sin, calling him cursed who should " uncover the nakedness " of his sister ;[6] God thus mercifully bringing to our race the needful help in due season, as parents do to their children. For they do not at once set masters over them, but allow them, during the period of childhood, to amuse themselves like young animals, and first send them to teachers stammering like themselves, until they cast off the youthful wool of the mind, and go onwards to the practice of greater things, and from thence again to that of greater still. And thus we must consider that the God and Father of all acted towards our forefathers. For the world, while still unfilled with men, was like a child, and it was necessary that it should first be filled with these, and so grow to manhood. But when hereafter it was colonized from end to end, the race of man spreading to a boundless extent, God no longer allowed man to remain in the same ways, considering how they might now proceed from one point to another, and advance nearer to heaven, until, having attained to the very greatest and most exalted lesson of virginity, they should reach to perfection ; that first they should abandon the intermarriage of brothers and sisters, and marry wives from other families ; and then that they should no longer have many wives, like brute beasts, as though born for the mere propagation of the species ; and then that they should not be adulterers ; and then again that they should go on to continence, and from continence to virginity, when, having trained

---

[1] Ecclus. vi. 36.
[2] Ps. xxxvii. 6 (LXX.), xxxviii. 5 (E. V.).
[3] Lev. ii. 13; Mark ix. 40.
[4] Matt. v. 13.
[5] 1 Cor. vii. 34.

[6] Lev. xviii. 19, xx. 17.

themselves to despise the flesh, they sail fearlessly into the peaceful haven of immortality.[1]

CHAP. III. — BY THE CIRCUMCISION OF ABRAHAM, MARRIAGE WITH SISTERS FORBIDDEN ; IN THE TIMES OF THE PROPHETS POLYGAMY PUT A STOP TO ; CONJUGAL PURITY ITSELF BY DEGREES ENFORCED.

If, however, any one should venture to find fault with our argument as destitute of Scripture proof, we will bring forward the writings of the prophets, and more fully demonstrate the truth of the statements already made. Now Abraham, when he first received the covenant of circumcision, seems to signify, by receiving circumcision in a member of his own body, nothing else than this, that one should no longer beget children with one born of the same parent ; showing that every one should abstain from intercourse with his own sister, as his own flesh. And thus, from the time of Abraham, the custom of marrying with sisters has ceased ; and from the times of the prophets the contracting of marriage with several wives has been done away with ; for we read, " Go not after thy lusts, but refrain thyself from thine appetites ; "[2] for " wine and women will make men of understanding to fall away ; "[3] and in another place, " Let thy fountain be blessed ; and rejoice with the wife of thy youth,"[4] manifestly forbidding a plurality of wives. And Jeremiah clearly gives the name of " fed horses "[5] to those who lust after other women ; and we read, " The multiplying brood of the ungodly shall not thrive, nor take deep rooting from bastard slips, nor lay any fast foundation."[6]

Lest, however, we should seem prolix in collecting the testimonies of the prophets, let us again point out how chastity succeeded to marriage with one wife, taking away by degrees the lusts of the flesh, until it removed entirely the inclination for sexual intercourse engendered by habit. For presently one is introduced earnestly deprecating, from henceforth, this seduction, saying, " O Lord, Father, and Governor of my life, leave me not to their counsels ; give me not a proud look ; let not the greediness of the belly, nor lust of the flesh, take hold of me."[7] And in the Book of Wisdom, a book full of all virtue, the Holy Spirit, now openly drawing His hearers to continence and chastity, sings on this

wise, " Better it is to have no children, and to have virtue, for the memorial thereof is immortal ; because it is known with God and with men. When it is present men take example at it ; and when it is gone they desire it : it weareth a crown and triumpheth for ever, having gotten the victory, striving for undefiled rewards."[8]

CHAP. IV. — CHRIST ALONE TAUGHT VIRGINITY, OPENLY PREACHING THE KINGDOM OF HEAVEN ; THE LIKENESS OF GOD TO BE ATTAINED IN THE LIGHT OF THE DIVINE VIRTUES.

We have already spoken of the periods of the human race, and how, beginning with the intermarriage of brothers and sisters, it went on to continence ; and we have now left for us the subject of virginity. Let us then endeavour to speak of this as well as we can. And first let us inquire for what reason it was that no one of the many patriarchs and prophets and righteous men, who taught and did many noble things, either praised or chose the state of virginity. Because it was reserved for the Lord alone to be the first to teach this doctrine, since He alone, coming down to us, taught man to draw near to God ; for it was fitting that He who was first and chief of priests, of prophets, and of angels, should also be saluted as first and chief of virgins.[9] For in old times man was not yet perfect, and for this reason was unable to receive perfection, which is virginity. For, being made in the *Image* of God, he needed to receive that which was according to His *Likeness* ;[10] which the Word being sent down into the world to perfect, He first took upon Him our form, disfigured as it was by many sins, in order that we, for whose sake He bore it, might be able again to receive the divine *form*. For it is then that we are truly fashioned in the likeness of God, when we represent His features in a human life, like skilful painters, stamping them upon ourselves as upon tablets, learning the path which He showed us. And for this reason He, being God, was pleased to put on human flesh, so that we, beholding as on a tablet the divine Pattern of our life, should also be able to imitate Him who painted it. For He was not one who, thinking one thing, did another ; nor, while He considered one thing to be right, taught another. But whatever things were truly useful and right, these He both taught and did.

CHAP. V. — CHRIST, BY PRESERVING HIS FLESH INCORRUPT IN VIRGINITY, DRAWS TO THE EXERCISE OF VIRGINITY ; THE SMALL NUMBER OF

---

[1] [Contending with the worse than bestial sensuality of paganism, and inured to the sorrows of martyr-ages, when Christian families could not be reared in peace, let us not wonder at the high conceptions of these heroic believers, based on the words of Christ Himself, and on the promise, " Blessed are the pure in heart, for they shall see God."]

[2] Ecclus. xviii. 30.

[3] Ecclus. xix. 2.

[4] Prov. v. 18.

[5] Jer. v. 8.

[6] Wisd. iv. 3.

[7] Ecclus. xxiii. 1, 4, 6.

[8] Wisd. iv. 1, 2.

[9] [This seems to me admirable. Our times are too little willing to see all that Scripture teaches in this matter.]

[10] A distinction common among the Fathers.

VIRGINS IN PROPORTION TO THE NUMBER OF SAINTS.

What then did the Lord, who is the Truth and the Light, take in hand when He came down from heaven? He preserved the flesh which He had taken upon Him incorrupt in virginity, so that we also, if we would come to the likeness of God and Christ, should endeavour to honour virginity. For the likeness of God is the avoiding of corruption. And that the Word, when He was incarnate, became chief Virgin, in the same way as He was chief Shepherd and chief Prophet of the Church, the Christ-possessed John shows us, saying, in the Book of the Revelation, "And I looked, and, lo, a Lamb stood on the mount Sion, and with Him an hundred forty and four thousand, having His name and His Father's name written in their foreheads. And I heard a voice from heaven, as the voice of many waters, and as the voice of a great thunder ; and I heard the voice of harpers harping with their harps : And they sung as it were a new song before the throne, and before the four beasts, and the elders : and no man could learn that song but the hundred and forty and four thousand, which were redeemed from the earth. These are they which were not defiled with women ; for they are virgins. These are they who follow the Lamb whithersoever He goeth ; " [1] showing that the Lord is leader of the choir of virgins. And remark, in addition to this, how very great in the sight of God is the dignity of virginity : "These were redeemed from among men, being the first-fruits unto God and to the Lamb. And in their mouth was found no guile : for they are without fault," [2] he says, "and they follow the Lamb whithersoever He goeth." And he clearly intends by this to teach us that the number of virgins was, from the beginning, restricted to so many, namely, a hundred and forty and four thousand, while the multitude of the other saints is innumerable. For let us consider what he means when discoursing of the rest. "I beheld a great multitude, which no man could number, of all nations, and kindreds, and people, and tongues." [3] It is plain, therefore, as I said, that in the case of the other saints he introduces an unspeakable multitude, while in the case of those who are in a state of virginity he mentions only a very small number, so as to make a strong contrast with those who make up the innumerable number. [4]

This, O Arete, is my discourse to you on the subject of virginity. But, if I have omitted anything, let Theophila, who succeeds me, supply the omission.

DISCOURSE II.—THEOPHILA.

CHAP. I. — MARRIAGE NOT ABOLISHED BY THE COMMENDATION OF VIRGINITY.

And then, she said, Theophila spoke : —

Since Marcella has excellently begun this discussion without sufficiently completing it, it is necessary that I should endeavour to put a finish to it. Now, the fact that man has advanced by degrees to virginity, God urging him on from time to time, seems to me to have been admirably proved ; but I cannot say the same *as to the assertion* that from henceforth they should no longer beget children. For I think I have perceived clearly from the Scriptures that, after He had brought in virginity, the Word did not altogether abolish the generation of children ; for although the moon may be greater than the stars, the light of the other stars is not destroyed by the moonlight.

Let us begin with Genesis, that we may give its place of antiquity and supremacy to this scripture. Now the sentence and ordinance of God respecting the begetting of children [5] is confessedly being fulfilled to this day, the Creator still fashioning man. For this is quite manifest, that God, like a painter, is at this very time working at the world, as the Lord also taught, "My Father worketh hitherto." [6] But when the rivers shall cease to flow and fall into the reservoir of the sea, and the light shall be perfectly separated from the darkness, — for the separation is still going on, — and the dry land shall henceforth cease to bring forth its fruits with creeping things and four-footed beasts, and the predestined number of men shall be fulfilled ; then from henceforth shall men abstain from the generation of children. But at present man must co operate in the forming of the image of God, while the world exists and is still being formed ; for it is said, "Increase and multiply." [5] And we must not be offended at the ordinance of the Creator, from which, moreover, we ourselves have our being. For the casting of seed into the furrows of the matrix is the beginning of the generation of men, so that bone taken from bone, and flesh from flesh, by an invisible power, are fashioned into another man. And in this way we must consider that the saying is fulfilled, "This is now bone of my bone, and flesh of my flesh." [7]

CHAP. II. — GENERATION SOMETHING AKIN TO THE FIRST FORMATION OF EVE FROM THE SIDE AND NATURE OF ADAM ; GOD THE CREATOR OF MEN IN ORDINARY GENERATION.

And this perhaps is what was shadowed forth by the sleep and trance of the first man, which

---

[1] Rev. xiv. 1-4.
[2] Rev. xiv. 4, 5.
[3] Rev. vii. 9.
[4] [Compare Cyprian, vol. v. p. 475, this series.]

[5] Gen. i. 28.
[6] ἕως ἄρτι, even until now. John v. 17.
[7] Gen. ii. 23.

prefigured the embraces of connubial love. When thirsting for children a man falls into a kind of trance,[1] softened and subdued by the pleasures of generation as by sleep, so that again something drawn from his flesh and from his bones is, as I said, fashioned into another man. For the harmony of the bodies being disturbed in the embraces of love, as those tell us who have experience of the marriage state, all the marrow-like and generative part of the blood, like a kind of liquid bone, coming together from all the members, worked into foam and curdled, is projected through the organs of generation into the living body of the female. And probably it is for this reason that a man is said to leave his father and his mother, since he is then suddenly unmindful of all things when united to his wife in the embraces of love, he is overcome by the desire of generation, offering his side to the divine Creator to take away from it, so that the father may again appear in the son.

Wherefore, if God still forms man, shall we not be guilty of audacity if we think of the generation of children as something offensive, which the Almighty Himself is not ashamed to make use of in working with His undefiled hands; for He says to Jeremiah, " Before I formed thee in the belly I knew thee ; "[2] and to Job, " Didst thou take clay and form a living creature, and make it speak upon the earth? "[3] and Job draws near to Him in supplication, saying, " Thine hands have made me and fashioned me."[4] Would it not, then, be absurd to forbid marriage unions, seeing that we expect that after us there will be martyrs, and those who shall oppose the evil one, for whose sake also the Word promised that He would shorten those days?[5] For if the generation of children henceforth had seemed evil to God, as you said, for what reason will those who have come into existence in opposition to the divine decree and will be able to appear well-pleasing to God? And must not that which is begotten be something spurious, and not a creature of God, if, like a counterfeit coin, it is moulded apart from the intention and ordinance of the lawful authority? And so we concede to men the power of forming men.

CHAP. III. — AN AMBIGUOUS PASSAGE OF SCRIPTURE ; NOT ONLY THE FAITHFUL BUT EVEN PRELATES SOMETIMES ILLEGITIMATE.

But Marcella, interrupting, said, " O Theophila, there appears here a great mistake, and something contrary to what you have said ; and do you think to escape under cover of the cloud which you have thrown around you? For there comes that argument, which perhaps any one who addresses you as a very wise person will bring forward : What do you say of those who are begotten unlawfully in adultery? For you laid it down that it was inconceivable and impossible for any one to enter into the world unless he was introduced by the will of the divine Ruler, his frame being prepared for him by God. And that you may not take refuge behind a safe wall, bringing forward the Scripture which says, ' As for the children of the adulterers, they shall not come to their perfection,'[6] he will answer you easily, that we often see those who are unlawfully begotten coming to perfection like ripe fruit.

And if, again, you answer sophistically, ' O, my friend, by those who come not to perfection I understand being perfected in Christ-taught righteousness ; ' he will say, ' But, indeed, my worthy friend, very many who are begotten of unrighteous seed are not only numbered among those who are gathered into the flock of the brethren, but are often called even to preside over them.[7] Since, then, it is clear, and all testify, that those who are born of adultery do come to perfection, we must not imagine that the Spirit was teaching respecting conceptions and births, but rather perhaps concerning those who adulterate the truth, who, corrupting the Scriptures by false doctrines, bring forth an imperfect and immature wisdom, mixing their error with piety.' And, therefore, this plea being taken away from you, come now and tell us if those who are born of adultery are begotten by the will of God ; for you said that it was impossible that the offspring of a man should be brought to perfection unless the Lord formed it and gave it life.''

CHAP. IV. — HUMAN GENERATION, AND THE WORK OF GOD THEREIN SET FORTH.

Theophila, as though caught round the middle by a strong antagonist, grew giddy, and with difficulty recovering herself, replied, " You ask a question, my worthy friend, which needs to be solved by an example, that you may still better understand how the creative power of God, pervading all things, is more especially the real cause in the generation of men, making those things to grow which are planted in the productive earth. For that which is sown is not to be blamed, but he who sows in a strange soil by unlawful embraces, as though purchasing a slight pleasure by shamefully selling his own seed. For imagine our birth into the world to be like some such thing as a house having its entrance lying close to lofty mountains ; and that the house ex-

---

[1] Remark the connection, ἔκστασις and ἐξίσταται.
[2] Jer. i. 5.
[3] Job xxxviii. 14 (LXX.).
[4] Job x. 8.
[5] Matt. xxiv. 22.

[6] Wisd. iii. 16.
[7] [Bastardy seems to have been regarded as washed out by baptism, thousands of pagan converts having been born under this stain.]

tends a great way down, far from the entrance, and that it has many holes behind, and that in this part it is circular." "I imagine it," said Marcella. "Well, then, suppose that a modeller seated within is fashioning many statues; imagine, again, that the substance of clay is incessantly brought to him from without, through the holes, by many men who do not any of them see the artist himself. Now suppose the house to be covered with mist and clouds, and nothing visible to those who are outside but only the holes." "Let this also be supposed," she said. "And that each one of those who are labouring together to provide the clay has one hole allotted to himself, into which he alone has to bring and deposit his own clay, not touching any other hole. And if, again, he shall officiously endeavour to open that which is allotted to another, let him be threatened with fire and scourges.

"Well, now, consider further what comes after this: the modeller within going round to the holes and taking privately for his modelling the clay which he finds at each hole, and having in a certain number of months made his model, giving it back through the same hole; having this for his rule, that every lump of clay which is capable of being moulded shall be worked up indifferently, even if it be unlawfully thrown by any one through another's hole, for the clay has done no wrong, and, therefore, as being blameless, should be moulded and formed; but that he who, in opposition to the ordinance and law, deposited it in another's hole, should be punished as a criminal and transgressor. For the clay should not be blamed, but he who did this in violation of what is right; for, through incontinence, having carried it away, he secretly, by violence, deposited it in another's hole." "You say most truly."

And now that these things are completed, it remains for you to apply this picture, my wisest of friends, to the things which have been already spoken of; comparing the house to the invisible nature of our generation, and the entrance adjacent to the mountains to the sending down of our souls from heaven, and their descent into the bodies; the holes to the female sex, and the modeller to the creative power of God, which, under the cover of generation, making use of our nature, invisibly forms us men within, working the garments for the souls. Those who carry the clay represent the male sex in the comparison; when thirsting for children, they bring and cast in seed into the natural channels of the female, as those in the comparison cast clay into the holes. For the seed, which, so to speak, partakes of a divine creative power, is not to be thought guilty of the incentives to incontinence; and art always works up the matter submitted to it; and nothing is to be considered as evil in itself, but becomes so by the act of those who used it in such a way; for when properly and purely made use of, it comes out pure, but if disgracefully and improperly, then it becomes disgraceful. For how did iron, which was discovered for the benefit of agriculture and the arts, injure those who sharpened it for murderous battles? Or how did gold, or silver, or brass, and, to take it collectively, the whole of the workable earth, injure those who, ungratefully towards their Creator, make a wrong use of them by turning parts of them into various kinds of idols? And if any one should supply wool from that which had been stolen to the weaving art, that art, regarding this one thing only, manufactures the material submitted to it, if it will receive the preparation, rejecting nothing of that which is serviceable to itself, since that which is stolen is here not to be blamed, being lifeless. And, therefore, the material itself is to be wrought and adorned, but he who is discovered to have abstracted it unjustly should be punished. So, in like manner, the violators of marriage, and those who break the strings of the harmony of life, as of a harp, raging with lust, and letting loose their desires in adultery, should themselves be tortured and punished, for they do a great wrong stealing from the gardens of others the embraces of generation; but the seed itself, as in the case of the wool, should be formed and endowed with life.

But what need is there to protract the argument by using such examples? for nature could not thus, in a little time, accomplish so great a work without divine help. For who gave to the bones their fixed nature? and who bound the yielding members with nerves, to be extended and relaxed at the joints? or who prepared channels for the blood, and a soft windpipe for the breath? or what god caused the humours to ferment, mixing them with blood and forming the soft flesh out of the earth, but only the Supreme Artist making us to be man, the rational and living image of Himself, and forming it like wax, in the womb, from moist slight seed? or by whose providence was it that the foetus was not suffocated by damp when shut up within, in the connexion of the vessels? or who, after it was brought forth and had come into the light, changed it from weakness and smallness to size, and beauty, and strength, unless God Himself, the Supreme Artist, as I said, making by His creative power copies of Christ, and living pictures? Whence, also, we have received from the inspired writings, that those who are begotten, even though it be in adultery, are committed to guardian angels. But if they came into being in opposition to the will and the decree of the blessed nature of God, how should they be delivered over to angels, to be nourished with much gentleness and indulgence? and how, if they had to accuse their own parents, could they confidently, before the judgment seat of Christ, invoke Him and say, "Thou didst not, O Lord, grudge us this common light; but these appointed us to death, despising Thy command?" "For," He says, "children begotten of unlawful beds are witnesses of wickedness against their parents at their trial."[1]

CHAP. VII. — THE RATIONAL SOUL FROM GOD HIMSELF; CHASTITY NOT THE ONLY GOOD, ALTHOUGH THE BEST AND MOST HONOURED.

And perhaps there will be room for some to argue plausibly among those who are wanting in discrimination and judgment, that this fleshly garment of the soul, being planted by men, is shaped spontaneously apart from the sentence of God. If, however, he should teach that the immortal being of the soul also is sown along with the mortal body, he will not be believed; for the Almighty alone breathes into man the undying and undecaying part, as also it is He alone who is Creator of the invisible and indestructible. For, He says, He "breathed into his nostrils the breath of life; and man became a living soul."[2] And those artificers who, to the destruction of men, make images in human form, not perceiving and knowing their own Maker, are blamed by the Word, which says, in the Book of Wisdom, a book full of all virtue,[3] "his heart is ashes, his hope is more vile than earth, and his life of less value than clay; forasmuch as he knew not his Maker, and Him that inspired into him an active soul, and breathed in a living spirit;"[4] that is, God, the Maker of all men; therefore, also, according to the apostle, He "will have all men to be saved, and to come unto the knowledge of the truth."[5] And now, although this subject be scarcely completed, yet there are others which remain to be discussed. For when one thoroughly examines and understands those things which happen to man according to his nature, he will know not to despise the procreation of children, although he applauds chastity, and prefers it in honour. For although honey be sweeter and more pleasant than other things, we are not for that reason to consider

other things bitter which are mixed up in the natural sweetness of fruits. And, in support of these statements, I will bring forward a trustworthy witness, namely, Paul, who says, "So then he that giveth her[6] in marriage doeth well; but he that giveth her not in marriage doeth better."[7] Now the word, in setting forth that which is better and sweeter, did not intend to take away the inferior, but arranges so as to assign to each its own proper use and advantage. For there are some to whom it is not given to attain virginity; and there are others whom He no longer wills to be excited by procreations to lust, and to be defiled, but henceforth to meditate and to keep the mind upon the transformation of the body to the likeness of angels, when they "neither marry nor are given in marriage,"[8] according to the infallible words of the Lord; since it is not given to all to attain that undefiled state of being a eunuch for the sake of the kingdom of heaven,[9] but manifestly to those only who are able to preserve the ever-blooming and unfading flower of virginity. For it is the custom of the prophetic Word to compare the Church to a flower-covered and variegated meadow, adorned and crowned not only with the flowers of virginity, but also with those of child-bearing and of continence; for it is written, "Upon thy[10] right hand did stand the queen in a vesture of gold, wrought about with divers colours."[11]

These words, O Arete, I bring according to my ability to this discussion in behalf of the truth.

And when Theophila had thus spoken, Theopatra said that applause arose from all the virgins approving of her discourse; and that when they became silent, after a long pause, Thaleia arose, for to her had been assigned the third place in the contest, that which came after Theophila. And she then, as I think, followed, and spoke.

DISCOURSE III. — THALEIA.

CHAP. I. — PASSAGES OF HOLY SCRIPTURE[12] COMPARED.

You seem to me, O Theophila, to excel all in action and in speech, and to be second to none in wisdom. For there is no one who will find fault with your discourse, however contentious and contradictory he may be. Yet, while everything else seems rightly spoken, one thing, my friend, distresses and troubles me, considering that that wise and most spiritual man — I mean

---

[1] Wisd. iv. 6.
[2] Gen. ii. 7.
[3] [This language shows that it is not cited as Holy Scripture. It confirms St. Jerome's testimony, *Prolog. in Libros Salomonis*.]
[4] Wisd. xv. 10, 11.
[5] 1 Tim. ii. 4.

[6] His virgin. [St. Paul was married, and then a widower, in the opinion of many of the ancients. See Euseb., *H. E.*, iii. 30.]
[7] 1 Cor. vii. 38.
[8] Matt. xxii. 30.
[9] Matt. xix. 12.
[10] The bridegroom's.
[11] Ps xlv. 10 (xliv. 10, LXX.).
[12] Gen. ii. 23, 24, and Eph. v. 28-32.

Paul—would not vainly refer to Christ and the Church the union of the first man and woman,[1] if the Scripture meant nothing higher than what is conveyed by the mere words and the history; for if we are to take the Scripture as a bare representation wholly referring to the union of man and woman, for what reason should the apostle, calling these things to remembrance, and guiding us, as I opine, into the way of the Spirit, allegorize the history of Adam and Eve as having a reference to Christ and the Church? For the passage in Genesis reads thus: "And Adam said, This is now bone of my bones, and flesh of my flesh: she shall be called Woman, because she was taken out of man. Therefore shall a man leave his father and his mother, and shall cleave unto his wife: and they shall be one flesh."[2] But the apostle considering this passage, by no means, as I said, intends to take it according to its mere natural sense, as referring to the union of man and woman, as you do; for you, explaining the passage in too natural a sense, laid down that the Spirit is speaking only of conception and births; that the bone taken from the bones was made another man, and that living creatures coming together swell like trees at the time of conception. But he, more spiritually referring the passage to Christ, thus teaches: "He that loveth his wife loveth himself. For no man ever yet hated his own flesh, but nourisheth and cherisheth it, even as the Lord the Church: for we are members of His body, of His flesh, and of His bones. For this cause shall a man leave his father and mother, and shall be joined unto his wife, and they two shall be one flesh. This is a great mystery: but I speak concerning Christ and the Church."[3]

CHAP. II.—THE DIGRESSIONS OF THE APOSTLE PAUL; THE CHARACTER OF HIS DOCTRINE: NOTHING IN IT CONTRADICTORY; CONDEMNATION OF ORIGEN, WHO WRONGLY TURNS EVERYTHING INTO ALLEGORY.

Let it not disturb you, if, in discussing one class of subjects, he, i.e., *Paul*, should pass over into another, so as to appear to mix them up, and to import matters foreign to the subject under consideration, departing from the question, as now for instance. For wishing, as it seems, to strengthen most carefully the argument on behalf of chastity, he prepares the mode of argument beforehand, beginning with the more persuasive mode of speech. For the character of his speech being very various, and arranged for the purpose of progressive proof, begins gently, but flows forward into a style which is loftier and more magnificent. And then, again changing to what is deep, he sometimes finishes with what is simple and easy, and sometimes with what is more difficult and delicate; and yet introducing nothing which is foreign to the subject by these changes, but, bringing them all together according to a certain marvellous relationship, he works into one the question which is set forth as his subject. It is needful, then, that I should more accurately unfold the meaning of the apostle's arguments, yet rejecting nothing of what has been said before. For you seem to me, O Theophila, to have discussed those words of the Scripture amply and clearly, and to have set them forth as they are without mistake. For it is a dangerous thing wholly to despise the literal meaning,[4] as has been said, and especially of Genesis, where the unchangeable decrees of God for the constitution of the universe are set forth, in agreement with which, even until now, the world is perfectly ordered, most beautifully in accordance with a perfect rule, until the Lawgiver Himself having re-arranged it, wishing to order it anew, shall break up the first laws of nature by a fresh disposition. But, since it is not fitting to leave the demonstration of the argument unexamined—and, so to speak, half-lame—come let us, as it were completing our pair, bring forth the analogical sense, looking more deeply into the Scripture; for Paul is not to be despised when he passes over the literal meaning, and shows that the words extend to Christ and the Church.

CHAP. III.—COMPARISON INSTITUTED BETWEEN THE FIRST AND SECOND ADAM.

And, first, we must inquire if Adam can be likened to the Son of God, when he was found in the transgression of the Fall, and heard the sentence, "Dust thou art, and unto dust shalt thou return."[5] For how shall he be considered "the first-born of every creature,"[6] who, after the creation of the earth and the firmament, was formed out of clay? And how shall he be admitted to be "the tree of life" who was cast out for his transgression,[7] lest "he should again stretch forth his hand and eat of it, and live for ever?"[8] For it is necessary that a thing which is likened unto anything else, should in many respects be similar and analogous to that of which it is the similitude, and not have its constitution opposite and dissimilar. For one who should venture to compare the uneven to the even, or harmony to discord, would not be con-

---

[1] Eph. v. 32. [A forcible argument.]
[2] Gen. ii. 23, 24.
[3] Eph. v. 28–32. [Compare the next chapter, note 4.]

[4] This is the obvious English equivalent of the Greek text.—TR. [A singularly cautious testimony against Origen, whom our author follows too closely in allegorizing interpretations of Scripture. Origen, having literalized so sadly in one case, seems to have erred ever afterward in the other extreme. Here is a prudent *caveat*.]
[5] Gen. iii. 19.
[6] Col. i. 15.
[7] Rev. ii. 7.
[8] Gen. iii. 22.

sidered rational. But the even should be compared to that which in its nature is even, although it should be even only in a small measure ; and the white to that which in its nature is white, even although it should be very small, and should show but moderately the whiteness by reason of which it is called white. Now, it is beyond all doubt clear to every one, that that which is sinless and incorrupt is even, and harmonious, and bright as wisdom ; but that that which is mortal and sinful is uneven and discordant, and cast out as guilty and subject to condemnation.

CHAP. IV. — SOME THINGS HERE HARD AND TOO SLIGHTLY TREATED, AND APPARENTLY NOT SUFFICIENTLY BROUGHT OUT ACCORDING TO THE RULE OF THEOLOGY.

Such, then, I consider to be the objections urged by many who, despising, as it seems, the wisdom of Paul, dislike the comparing of the first man to Christ. For come, let us consider how rightly Paul compared Adam to Christ, not only considering him to be the type and image, but also that Christ Himself became the very same thing,[1] because the Eternal Word fell upon Him. For it was fitting that the first-born of God, the first shoot, the only-begotten, even the wisdom of God, should be joined to the first-formed man, and first and first-born of mankind, and should become incarnate. And this was Christ, a man filled with the pure and perfect Godhead, and God received into man. For it was most suitable that the oldest of the Æons and the first of the Archangels, when about to hold communion with men, should dwell in the oldest and the first of men, even Adam. And thus, when renovating those things which were from the beginning, and forming them again of the Virgin by the Spirit, He frames the same[2] just as at the beginning. When the earth was still virgin and untilled, God, taking mould, formed the reasonable creature from it without seed.[3]

CHAP. V. — A PASSAGE OF JEREMIAH EXAMINED.

And here I may adduce the prophet Jeremiah as a trustworthy and lucid witness, who speaks thus : " Then I went down to the potter's house ; and, behold, he wrought a work on the wheels. And the vessel that he made of clay was marred in the hand of the potter : so he made it again another vessel, as seemed good to the potter to make it."[4] For when Adam, having been formed

out of clay, was still soft and moist, and not yet, like a tile, made hard and incorruptible, sin ruined him, flowing and dropping down upon him like water. And therefore God, moistening him afresh and forming anew the same clay to His honour, having first hardened and fixed it in the Virgin's womb, and united and mixed it with the Word, brought it forth into life no longer soft and broken ; lest, being overflowed again by streams of corruption from without, it should become soft, and perish as the Lord in His teaching shows in the parable of the finding of the sheep ; where my Lord says to those standing by, " What man of you, having an hundred sheep, if he lose one of them, doth not leave the ninety and nine in the wilderness, and go after that which is lost until he find it ? and when he hath found it, he layeth it on his shoulders rejoicing ; and when he cometh home, he calleth together his friends and neighbours, saying unto them, Rejoice with me ; for I have found my sheep which was lost."

CHAP. VI. — THE WHOLE NUMBER OF SPIRITUAL SHEEP ; MAN A SECOND CHOIR, AFTER THE ANGELS, TO THE PRAISE OF GOD ; THE PARABLE OF THE LOST SHEEP EXPLAINED.

Now, since He truly was and is, being in the beginning with God, and being God,[5] He is the chief Commander and Shepherd of the heavenly ones, whom all reasonable creatures obey and attend, who tends in order and numbers the multitudes of the blessed angels. For this is the equal and perfect number of immortal creatures, divided according to their races and tribes, man also being here taken into the flock. For he also was created without corruption, that he might honour the king and maker of all things, responding to the shouts of the melodious angels which came from heaven. But when it came to pass that, by transgressing the commandment (of God), he suffered a terrible and destructive fall, being thus reduced to a state of death, for this reason the Lord says that He came from heaven into (a human) life, leaving the ranks and the armies of angels. For the mountains are to be explained by the heavens, and the ninety and nine sheep by the principalities and powers[6] which the Captain and Shepherd left when He went down to seek the lost one. For it remained that man should be included in this catalogue and number, the Lord lifting him up and wrapping him round, that he might not again, as I said, be overflowed and swallowed up by the waves of deceit. For with this purpose the Word assumed the nature of man, that, having overcome the serpent, He might by Himself destroy the

---

[1] Namely, the second Adam.
[2] Second Adam.
[3] The obscurity of this chapter is indicated in the heading placed over it by the old Latin translator. The general meaning, however, will be clear enough to the theological reader. — TR.
[4] Jer. xviii. 3, 4.

[5] St. John i. 1.
[6] Eph. i. 21, iii. 10.

condemnation which had come into being along with man's ruin. For it was fitting that the Evil One should be overcome by no other, but by him whom he had deceived, and whom he was boasting that he held in subjection, because no otherwise was it possible that sin and condemnation should be destroyed, unless that same man on whose account it had been said, " Dust thou art, and unto dust thou shalt return," [1] should be created anew, and undo the sentence which for his sake had gone forth on all, that " as in Adam " at first " all die, even so " again " in Christ," who assumed the *nature and position of* Adam, should " all be made alive." [2]

CHAP. VII. — THE WORKS OF CHRIST, PROPER TO GOD AND TO MAN, THE WORKS OF HIM WHO IS ONE.

And now we seem to have said almost enough on the fact that man has become the organ and clothing of the Only-begotten, and what He was who came to dwell in him. But the fact that there is no *moral* inequality or discord [3] may again be considered briefly from the beginning. For he speaks well who says that that is in its own nature good and righteous and holy, by participation of which other things become good, and that wisdom is in connection with [4] God, and that, on the other hand, sin is unholy and unrighteous and evil. For life and death, corruption and incorruption, are two things in the highest degree opposed to each other. For life is a *moral* equality, but corruption an inequality ; and righteousness and prudence a harmony, but unrighteousness and folly a discord. Now, man being between these is neither righteousness itself, nor unrighteousness ; but being placed midway between incorruption and corruption, to whichever of these he may incline is said to partake of the nature of that which has laid hold of him. Now, when he inclines to corruption, he becomes corrupt and mortal, and when to incorruption, he becomes incorrupt and immortal. For, being placed midway between the tree of life and the tree of the knowledge of good and evil, of the fruit of which he tasted,[5] he was changed into the nature of the latter, himself being neither the tree of life nor that of corruption ; but having been shown forth as mortal, from his participation in and presence with corruption, and, again, as incorrupt and immortal by connection with and participation in life ; as Paul also taught, saying, " Corruption

shall not inherit incorruption, nor death life," [6] rightly defining corruption and death to be that which corrupts and kills, and not that which is corrupted and dies ; and incorruption and life that which gives life and immortality, and not that which receives life and immortality. And thus man is neither a discord and an inequality, nor an equality and a harmony. But when he received discord, which is transgression and sin, he became discordant and unseemly ; but when he received harmony, that is righteousness, he became a harmonious and seemly organ, in order that the Lord, the Incorruption which conquered death, might harmonize the resurrection with the flesh, not suffering it again to be inherited by corruption. And on this point also let these statements suffice.

CHAP. VIII. — THE BONES AND FLESH OF WISDOM ; THE SIDE OUT OF WHICH THE SPIRITUAL EVE IS FORMED, THE HOLY SPIRIT ; THE WOMAN THE HELP-MEET OF ADAM ; VIRGINS BETROTHED TO CHRIST.

For it has been already established by no contemptible arguments from Scripture, that the first man may be properly referred to Christ Himself, and is no longer a type and representation and image of the Only-begotten, but has become actually Wisdom and the Word.

For man, having been composed, like water, of wisdom and life, has become identical with the very same untainted light which poured into him. Whence it was that the apostle directly referred to Christ the words which had been spoken of Adam. For thus will it be most certainly agreed that the Church is formed out of His bones and flesh ; and it was for this cause that the Word, leaving His Father in heaven, came down to be " joined to His wife ; " [7] and slept in the trance of His passion, and willingly suffered death for her, that He might present the Church to Himself glorious and blameless, having cleansed her by the laver,[8] for the receiving of the spiritual and blessed seed, which is sown by Him who with whispers implants it in the depths of the mind ; and is conceived and formed by the Church, as by a woman, so as to give birth and nourishment to virtue. For in this way, too, the command, " Increase and multiply," [9] is duly fulfilled, the Church increasing daily in greatness and beauty and multitude, by the union and communion of the Word, who now still comes down to us and falls into a trance by the memorial of His passion ; for otherwise the Church could not con-

---

[1] Gen. iii. 19.
[2] 1 Cor. xv. 22.
[3] In Him.
[4] Here, as in the previous chapter, and in many other passages, I have preferred the text of *Jahn* to that of *Migne*, as being generally the more accurate. — TR.
[5] Gen. ii. 9.

[6] 1 Cor. xv. 22. The words are, " Neither doth corruption inherit incorruption."
[7] Eph. v. 31.
[8] Eph. v. 26, 27.
[9] Gen. i. 18.

ceive believers, and give them new birth by the laver of regeneration, unless Christ, emptying Himself for their sake, that He might be contained by them, as I said, through the recapitulation of His passion, should die again, coming down from heaven, and being "joined to His wife," the Church, should provide for a certain power being taken from His own side, so that all who are built up in Him should grow up, even those who are born again by the laver, receiving of His bones and of His flesh, that is, of His holiness and of His glory. For he who says that the bones and flesh of Wisdom are understanding and virtue, says most rightly ; and that the side [1] is the Spirit of truth, the Paraclete, of whom the illuminated [2] receiving are fitly born again to incorruption. For it is impossible for any one to be a partaker of the Holy Spirit, and to be chosen a member of Christ, unless the Word first came down upon him and fell into a trance, in order that he, being filled [3] with the Spirit, and rising again from sleep with Him who was laid to sleep for his sake, should be able to receive renewal and restoration. For He may fitly be called the side [1] of the Word, even the sevenfold Spirit of truth, according to the prophet ; [4] of whom God taking, in the trance of Christ, that is, after His incarnation and passion, prepares a help-meet for Him [5] — I mean the souls which are betrothed and given in marriage to Him. For it is frequently the case that the Scriptures thus call the assembly and mass of believers by the name of the Church, the more perfect in their progress being led up to be the one person and body of the Church. For those who are the better, and who embrace the truth more clearly, being delivered from the evils of the flesh, become, on account of their perfect purification and faith, a church and help-meet of Christ, betrothed and given in marriage to Him as a virgin, according to the apostle, [6] so that receiving the pure and genuine seed of His doctrine, they may co-operate with Him, helping in preaching for the salvation of others. And those who are still imperfect and beginning their lessons, are born to salvation, and shaped, as by mothers, by those who are more perfect, until they are brought forth and regenerated unto the greatness and beauty of virtue ; and so these, in their turn making progress, having become a church, assist in labouring for the birth and nurture of other children, accomplishing in the receptacle of the soul, as in a womb, the blameless will of the Word.

CHAP. IX. — THE DISPENSATION OF GRACE IN PAUL THE APOSTLE.

Now we should consider the case of the renowned Paul, that when he was not yet perfect in Christ, he was first born and suckled, Ananias preaching to him, and renewing him in baptism, as the history in the Acts relates. But when he was grown to a man, and was built up, then being moulded to spiritual perfection, he was made the help-meet and bride of the Word ; and receiving and conceiving the seeds of life, he who was before a child, becomes a church and a mother, himself labouring in birth of those who, through him, believed in the Lord, until Christ was formed and born in them also. For he says, " My little children, of whom I travail in birth again until Christ be formed in you ; " [7] and again, " In Christ Jesus I have begotten you through the Gospel." [8]

It is evident, then, that the statement respecting Eve and Adam is to be referred to the Church and Christ. For this is truly a great mystery and a supernatural, of which I, from my weakness and dulness, am unable to speak, according to its worth and greatness. Nevertheless, let us attempt it. It remains that I speak to you on what follows, and of its signification.

CHAP. X. — THE DOCTRINE OF THE SAME APOSTLE CONCERNING PURITY.

Now Paul, when summoning all persons to sanctification and purity, in this way referred that which had been spoken concerning the first man and Eve in a secondary sense to Christ and the Church, in order to silence the ignorant, now deprived of all excuse. For men who are incontinent in consequence of the uncontrolled impulses of sensuality in them, dare to force the Scriptures beyond their true meaning, so as to twist into a defence of their incontinence the saying, " Increase and multiply ; " [9] and the other, " Therefore shall a man leave his father and his mother ; " [10] and they are not ashamed to run counter to the Spirit, but, as though born for this purpose, they kindle up the smouldering and lurking passion, fanning and provoking it ; and therefore he, cutting off very sharply these dishonest follies and invented excuses, and having arrived at the subject of instructing them how men should behave to their wives, showing that it should be as Christ did to the Church, " who gave Himself for it, that He might sanctify and cleanse it by the washing [11] of water by the Word," [12] he referred back to Genesis, men-

---

[1] Rib.
[2] Commonly used by the Greek Fathers for the *Baptized*. [Following Holy Scripture, Heb. x. 32, and Calvin's Commentary, *ad loc.* Also his comment on Tit. iii. 5.]
[3] *Jahn's* reading, ἀναπλησθείς. *Migne* has ἀναπλασθείς, *moulded*.
[4] Isa. xi. 2.
[5] Gen. ii. 18.
[6] 2 Cor. xi. 12.

[7] Gal. iv. 19.
[8] 1 Cor. iv. 15.
[9] Gen. ii. 18.
[10] Gen. ii. 24.
[11] [Laver (Gr. λουτρὸν). Compare Tit. iii. 5 and Calvin's comment, *Opp.*, tom. ii. p. 506, ed. 1667.]
[12] Eph. v. 25, 26. [Baptismus = lavacrum animæ. — CALVIN, *Ib.*, p. 350.]

tioning the things spoken concerning the first man, and explaining these things as bearing on the subject before him, that he might take away occasion for the abuse of these passages from those who taught the sensual gratification of the body, under the pretext of begetting children.

CHAP. XI. — THE SAME ARGUMENT.

For consider, O virgins, how he,[1] desiring with all his might that believers in Christ should be chaste, endeavours by many arguments to show them the dignity of chastity, as when he says,[2] " Now, concerning the things whereof ye wrote unto me : It is good for a man not to touch a woman," thence showing already very clearly that it is good not to touch[3] a woman, laying it down and setting it forth unconditionally. But afterwards, being aware of the weakness of the less continent, and their passion for intercourse, he permitted those who are unable to govern the flesh to use their own wives, rather than, shamefully transgressing, to give themselves up to fornication. Then, after having given this permission, he immediately added these words,[4] " that Satan tempt you not for your incontinency ; " which means, " if you, such as you are, cannot, on account of the incontinence and softness of your bodies, be perfectly continent, I will rather permit you to have intercourse with your own wives, lest, professing perfect continence, ye be constantly tempted by the evil one, and be inflamed with lust after other men's wives."

CHAP. XII. — PAUL AN EXAMPLE TO WIDOWS, AND TO THOSE WHO DO NOT LIVE WITH THEIR WIVES.

Come, now, and let us examine more carefully the very words which are before us, and observe that the apostle did not grant these things unconditionally to all, but first laid down the reason on account of which he was led to this. For, having set forth that " it is good for a man not to touch a woman,"[2] he added immediately, " Nevertheless, to avoid fornication, let every man have his own wife "[5] — that is, " on account of the fornication which would arise from your being unable to restrain your voluptuousness " — and let every woman have her own husband. Let the husband render unto the wife due benevolence : and likewise also the wife unto the husband. The wife hath not power of her own body, but the husband : and likewise also the husband hath not power of his own body, but the wife. Defraud ye not one the other, except it be with consent for a time, that ye may give yourselves

to prayer ;[6] and come together again, that Satan tempt you not for your incontinency. But I speak this by permission, and not of commandment."[7]. And this is very carefully considered. " By permission," he says, showing that he was giving counsel, " not of command ; " for he receives *command* respecting chastity and the not touching of a woman, but *permission* respecting those who are unable, as I said, to chasten their appetites. These things, then, he lays down concerning men and women who are married to one spouse, or who shall hereafter be so ; but we must now examine carefully the apostle's language respecting men who have lost their wives, and women who have lost their husbands, and what he declares on this subject.

" I say therefore," he goes on,[8] " to the unmarried and widows, It is good for them if they abide even as I. But if they cannot contain, let them marry : for it is better to marry than to burn." Here also he persisted in giving the preference to continence. For, taking himself as a notable example, in order to stir them up to emulation, he challenged his hearers to this state of life, teaching that it was better that a man who had been bound to one wife should henceforth remain single, as he also did.[9] But if, on the other hand, this should be a matter of difficulty to any one, on account of the strength of animal passion, he allows that one who is in such a condition may, " by permission," contract a second marriage ; not as though he expressed the opinion that a second marriage was in itself good,[10] but judging it better than burning. Just as though, in the fast which prepares for the Easter celebration, one should offer food to another who was dangerously ill, and say, " In truth, my friend, it were fitting and good that you should bravely hold out like us, and partake of the same things,[11] for it is forbidden even to think of food to-day ; but since you are held down and weakened by disease, and cannot bear it, therefore, ' by permission,' we advise you to eat food, lest, being quite unable, from sickness, to hold up against the desire for food, you perish." Thus also the apostle speaks here, first saying that he wished all were healthy and continent, as he also was, but afterwards allowing a second marriage to those who are burdened with the disease of the passions, lest they should be wholly defiled by fornication, goaded on by the itchings of the organs of generation to promiscuous intercourse, considering such a second marriage far preferable to burning and indecency.

---

[1] Paul.
[2] 1 Cor. vii. 1. [All vulgar familiarity included.]
[3] In the original the two words are different. In the quotation from St. Paul it is ἅπτεσθαι: here it is προσψαύειν. Nothing could be gained by using two words in the translation. — TR.
[4] 1 Cor. vii. 5.
[5] 1 Cor. vii. 2.

[6] E. V. " Fasting and prayer." As in the best MSS., τῇ νηστείᾳ καί is wanting in the text.
[7] 1 Cor. vii. 2–6.
[8] 1 Cor. vii. 8, 9.
[9] [See p. 316, *supra* (note), and also Eusebius, there cited. *Per contra*, see Lewin, vol. i. 382, 386.]
[10] Καλόν. It is the same word which is translated *good* in ver. 1, " It is good for a man."
[11] i.e., participate in the same ordinances, and in their fruits.

CHAP. XIII. — THE DOCTRINE OF PAUL CONCERN-
ING VIRGINITY EXPLAINED.

I have now brought to an end what I have to
say respecting continence and marriage and chastity, and intercourse with men, and in which of
these there is help towards progress in righteousness ; but it still remains to speak concerning
virginity — if, indeed, anything be prescribed on
this subject. Let us then treat this subject also ;
for it stands thus : [1] " Now concerning virgins,
I have no commandment of the Lord : yet I
give my judgment, as one that hath obtained
mercy of the Lord to be faithful. I suppose
therefore that this is good for the present distress ; I say, that it is good for a man so to be.
Art thou bound unto a wife ? seek not to be
loosed. Art thou loosed from a wife ? seek not
a wife. But and if thou marry, thou hast not
sinned ; and if a virgin marry, she has not sinned.
Nevertheless such shall have trouble in the flesh :
but I spare you." Having given his opinion
with great caution respecting virginity, and being
about to advise him who wished it to give his
virgin in marriage, so that none of those things
which conduce to sanctification should be of
necessity and by compulsion, but according to
the free purpose of the soul, for this is acceptable to God, he does not wish these things to
be said as by authority, and as the mind of the
Lord, with reference to the giving of a virgin in
marriage ; for after he had said,[2] " if a virgin
marry, she hath not sinned," directly afterwards,
with the greatest caution, he modified his statement, showing that he had advised these things
by human permission, and not by divine. So,
immediately after he had said, " if a virgin marry, she hath not sinned," he added, " such shall
have trouble in the flesh : but I spare you." [2]
By which he means : " I sparing you, such as
you are, consented to these things, because you
have chosen to think thus of them, that I may
not seem to hurry you on by violence, and compel any one to this.[3] But yet if it shall please
you who find chastity hard to bear, rather to
turn to marriage ; I consider it to be profitable
for you to restrain yourselves in the gratification
of the flesh, not making your marriage an occasion for abusing your own vessels to uncleanness." Then he adds,[4] " But this I say, brethren,
the time is short : it remaineth, that both they
that have wives be as though they had none."
And again, going on and challenging them to
the same things, he confirmed his statement,
powerfully supporting the state of virginity, and

adding expressly the following words to those
which he had spoken before, he exclaimed,[5] " I
would have you without carefulness. He that
is unmarried careth for the things that belong to
the Lord : [6] but he that is married careth for
the things that are of the world, how he may
please his wife. There is a difference also between a wife and a virgin. The unmarried
woman careth for the things of the Lord, that
she may be holy both in body and in spirit : but
she that is married careth for the things of the
world, how she may please her husband." Now
it is clear to all, without any doubt, that to care
for the things of the Lord and to please God, is
much better than to care for the things of the
world and to please one's wife. For who is
there so foolish and blind, as not to perceive in
this statement the higher praise which Paul ac-
cords to chastity ? " And this," he says,[7] " I
speak for your own profit, not that I may cast
a snare upon you, but for that which is comely."

CHAP. XIV. — VIRGINITY A GIFT OF GOD : THE PUR-
POSE OF VIRGINITY NOT RASHLY TO BE ADOPTED
BY ANY ONE.

Consider besides how, in addition to the words
already quoted, he commends the state of virginity as a gift of God. Wherefore he rejects
those of the more incontinent, who, under the
influence of vain-glory, would advance to this
state, advising them to marry, lest in their time
of manly strength, the flesh stirring up the desires and passions, they should be goaded on to
defile the soul. For let us consider what he lays
down : [8] " But if any man think that he behaveth
himself uncomely towards his virgin," he says,
" if she pass the flower of her age, and need so
require, let him do what he will, he sinneth not :
let him marry ; " properly here preferring marriage to " uncomeliness," in the case of those who
had chosen the state of virginity, but afterwards
finding it intolerable and grievous, and in word
boasting of their perseverance before men, out
of shame, but indeed no longer having the power
to persevere in the life of a eunuch. But for him
who of his own free will and purpose decides to
preserve his flesh in virgin purity, " having no
necessity," [9] that is, passion calling forth his loins
to intercourse, for there are, as it seems, differences in men's bodies ; such a one contending
and struggling, and zealously abiding by his profession, and admirably fulfilling it, he exhorts to
abide and to preserve it, according the highest
prize to virginity. For he that is able, he says,
and ambitious to preserve his flesh pure, does

---

[1] 1 Cor. vii. 25–28.
[2] 1 Cor. vii. 28.
[3] Which I recommend.
[4] 1 Cor. vii. 29. [Nobody can feel more deeply than I do the
immeasurable evils of an *enforced* celibacy ; nobody can feel more
deeply the deplorable state of the Church which furnishes only rare and
exceptional examples of *voluntary* celibacy for the sake of Christ.
On *chastity*, see Jer. Taylor's *Holy Living*, *Works*, i. p. 424.]

[5] 1 Cor. vii. 32–34.
[6] A clause is omitted here in the text.
[7] 1 Cor. vii. 35.
[8] 1 Cor. vii. 36. [On *virginity*, see Taylor, i. 426, ed. London,
1844.]
[9] 1 Cor. vii. 37.

better; but he that is unable, and enters into marriage lawfully, and does not indulge in secret corruption, does well. And now enough has been said on these subjects.

Let any one who will, take in his hand the Epistle to the Corinthians, and, examining all its passages one by one, then consider what we have said, comparing them together, as to whether there is not a perfect harmony and agreement between them. These things, according to my power, O Arete, I offer to thee as my contribution on the subject of chastity.

EUBOULIOS. Through many things, O Gregorion, she has scarcely come to the subject, having measured and crossed a mighty sea of words.

GREGORION. So it seems; but come, I must mention the rest of what was said in order, going through it and repeating it, while I seem to have the sound of it dwelling in my ears, before it flies away and escapes; for the remembrance of things lately heard is easily effaced from the aged.

EUBOULIOS. Say on, then; for we have come to have the pleasure of hearing these discourses.

GREGORION. And then after, as you observed, Thaleia had descended from her smooth and unbroken course to the earth, Theopatra, she said, followed her in order, and spoke as follows.

DISCOURSE IV.—THEOPATRA.

CHAP. I. — THE NECESSITY OF PRAISING VIRTUE, FOR THOSE WHO HAVE THE POWER.

If the art of speaking, O virgins, always went by the same ways, and passed along the same path, there would be no way to avoid wearying you for one who persisted in the arguments which had already been urged. But since there are of arguments myriads of currents and ways, God inspiring us "at sundry times and in divers manners,"[1] who can have the choice of holding back or of being afraid? For he would not be free from blame to whom the gift has been given, if he failed to adorn that which is honourable with words of praise. Come then, we also, according to our gifts, will sing the brightest and most glorious star of Christ, which is chastity. For this way of the Spirit is very wide and large. Beginning, therefore, at the point from which we may say those things which are suitable and fitting to the subject before us, let us from thence consider it.

CHAP. II. — THE PROTECTION OF CHASTITY AND VIRGINITY DIVINELY GIVEN TO MEN, THAT THEY MAY EMERGE FROM THE MIRE OF VICES.

Now I at least seem to perceive that nothing has been such a means of restoring men to paradise, and of the change to incorruption, and of

reconciliation to God, and such a means of salvation to men, by guiding us to life, as chastity. And I will now endeavour to show why I think so concerning these things, that having heard distinctly the power of the grace already spoken of, you may know of how great blessings it has become the giver to us. Anciently, then, after the fall of man, when he was cast out by reason of his transgression, the stream of corruption poured forth abundantly, and running along in violent currents, not only fiercely swept along whatever touched it from without, but also rushing within it, overwhelmed the souls of men. And they,[2] continuously exposed to this, were carried along dumb and stupid, neglecting to pilot their vessels,[3] from having nothing firm to lay hold of. For the senses of the soul, as those have said who are learned in these things, when, being overcome by the excitements to passion which fall upon them from without, they receive the sudden bursts of the waves of folly which rush into them, being darkened turn aside from the divine course its whole vessel, which is by nature easily guided. Wherefore God, pitying us who were in such a condition, and were able neither to stand nor to rise, sent down from heaven the best and most glorious help, virginity, that by it we might tie our bodies fast, like ships, and have a calm, coming to an anchorage without damage, as also the Holy Spirit witnesses. For this is said in the hundred and thirty-sixth[4] psalm, where the souls send joyfully up to God a hymn of thanksgiving,[5] as many as have been taken hold of and raised up to walk with Christ in heaven, that they might not be overwhelmed by the streams of the world and the flesh. Whence, also, they say that Pharaoh was a type of the devil in Egypt, since he mercilessly commanded the males to be cast into the river,[6] but the females to be preserved alive. For the devil, ruling[7] from Adam to Moses over this great Egypt, the world, took care to have the male and rational offspring of the soul carried away and destroyed by the streams of passions, but he longs for the carnal and irrational offspring to increase and multiply.

CHAP. III. — THAT PASSAGE OF DAVID EXPLAINED;[8] WHAT THE HARPS HUNG UPON THE WILLOWS SIGNIFY; THE WILLOW A SYMBOL OF CHASTITY; THE WILLOWS WATERED BY STREAMS.

But not to pass away from our subject, come, let us take in our hands and examine this psalm,

---

[1] πολυμερῶς καὶ πολυτρόπως. Heb. i. 1.

[2] i.e., αἱ ψυχαί.
[3] The body.
[4] Ps. cxxxvii. E. V., and in Heb. [Does not our author follow the Hebrew here? I must think his reference here is to the cxxxviith Psalm, as we have it. It is Eucharistic, and verses 10–16 seem to be specially referred to.]
[5] Or, Eucharistic hymn.
[6] Exod. i. 16.
[7] Rom. v. 14.
[8] " By the waters of Babylon," etc. [He passes to the next psalm.]

which the pure and stainless souls sing to God, saying:[1] "By the rivers of Babylon there we sat down; yea, we wept, when we remembered Zion. We hanged our harps upon the willows in the midst thereof," clearly giving the name of harps to their bodies which they hung upon the branches of chastity, fastening them to the wood that they might not be snatched away and dragged along again by the stream of incontinence. For Babylon, which is interpreted "disturbance" or "confusion," signifies this life around which the water flows, while we sit in the midst of which the water flows round us, as long as we are in the world, the rivers of evil always beating upon us. Wherefore, also, we are always fearful, and we groan and cry with weeping to God, that our harps may not be snatched off by the waves of pleasure, and slip down from the tree of chastity. For everywhere the divine writings take the willow as the type of chastity, because, when its flower is steeped in water, if it be drunk, it extinguishes whatever kindles sensual desires and passions within us, until it entirely renders barren, and makes every inclination to the begetting of children without effect, as also Homer indicated, for this reason calling the willows destructive of fruit.[2] And in Isaiah the righteous are said to "spring up as willows by the water courses."[3] Surely, then, the shoot of virginity is raised to a great and glorious height, when the righteous, and he to whom it is given to preserve it and to cultivate it, bedewing it with wisdom, is watered by the gentlest streams of Christ. For as it is the nature of this tree to bud and grow through water, so it is the nature of virginity to blossom and grow to maturity when enriched by words, so that one can hang his body[4] upon it.

CHAP. IV. — THE AUTHOR GOES ON WITH THE INTERPRETATION OF THE SAME PASSAGE.

If, then, the rivers of Babylon are the streams of voluptuousness, as wise men say, which confuse and disturb the soul, then the willows must be chastity, to which we may suspend and draw up the organs of lust which overbalance and weigh down the mind, so that they may not be borne down by the torrents of incontinence, and be drawn like worms to impurity and corruption. For God has bestowed upon us virginity as a most useful and a serviceable help towards incorruption, sending it as an ally to those who are contending for and longing after Zion, as the psalm shows, which is resplendent charity and

the commandment respecting it, for Zion is interpreted "The commandment of the watchtower."[5] Now, let us here enumerate the points which follow. For why do the souls declare that they were asked by those who led them captive to sing the Lord's song in a strange land? Surely because the Gospel teaches a holy and secret song, which sinners and adulterers sing to the Evil One. For they insult the commandments, accomplishing the will of the spirits of evil, and cast holy things to dogs, and pearls before swine,[6] in the same manner as those of whom the prophet says with indignation, "They read the law[7] without;"[8] for the Jews were not to read the law going forth out of the gates of Jerusalem or out of their houses; and for this reason the prophet blames them strongly, and cries that they were liable to condemnation, because, while they were transgressing the commandments, and acting impiously towards God, they were pretentiously reading the law, as if, forsooth, they were piously observing its precepts; but they did not receive it in their souls, holding it firmly with faith, but rejected it, denying it by their works. And hence they sing the Lord's song in a strange land, explaining the law by distorting and degrading it, expecting a sensual kingdom, and setting their hopes on this alien world, which the Word says will pass away,[9] where those who carry them captive entice them with pleasures, lying in wait to deceive them.

CHAP. V. — THE GIFTS OF VIRGINS, ADORNED WITH WHICH THEY ARE PRESENTED TO ONE HUSBAND, CHRIST.

Now, those who sing the Gospel to senseless people seem to sing the Lord's song in a strange land, of which Christ is not the husbandman; but those who have put on and shone in the most pure and bright, and unmingled and pious and becoming, ornament of virginity, and are found barren and unproductive of unsettled and grievous passions, do not sing the song in a strange land; because they are not borne thither by their hopes, nor do they stick fast in the lusts of their mortal bodies, nor do they take a low view of the meaning of the commandments, but well and nobly, with a lofty disposition, they have regard to the promises which are above, thirsting for heaven as a congenial abode, whence God, approving their dispositions, promises with an oath to give them choice honours, appointing and establishing them "above His chief joy;" for He says thus:[10] "If I forget thee, O Jerusa-

---

[1] Ps. cxxxvii 1, 2. [Here is a transition to Psalm cxxxvii., which has been the source of a confusion in the former chapter. This psalm is not Eucharistic, but penitential.]
[2] Odyss. K'. 510.
[3] Isa. xliv. 4.
[4] ὄργανον. The word used for harp above, and here employed with a double meaning. ["Body" here = man's physical system.]

[5] In Hebrew the word means simply "a memorial."
[6] Matt. vii. 6.
[7] i.e., To those without.
[8] Amos iv. 5 (LXX.). The E. V. is, "Offer a sacrifice of thanksgiving in the leaven."
[9] 1 Pet. ii. 10.
[10] Ps. cxxxvii. 5, 6.

lem, let my right hand forget her cunning. If I do not remember thee, let my tongue cleave to the roof of my mouth ; if I prefer not Jerusalem above my chief joy ; " meaning by Jerusalem, as I said, these very undefiled and incorrupt souls, which, having with self-denial drawn in the pure draught of virginity with unpolluted lips, are " espoused to one husband," to be presented " as a chaste virgin to Christ " [1] in heaven, " having gotten the victory, striving for undefiled rewards." [2]   Hence also the prophet Isaiah proclaims, saying,[3] " Arise, shine,[4] for thy light is come, and the glory of the Lord is risen upon thee." Now these promises, it is evident to every one, will be fulfilled after the resurrection.[5] For the Holy Spirit does not speak of that well-known town in Judea ; but truly of that heavenly city, the blessed Jerusalem, which He declares to be the assembly of the souls which God plainly promises to place first, " above His chief joy," in the new dispensation, settling those who are clothed in the most white robe of virginity in the pure dwelling of unapproachable light ; because they had it not in mind to put off their wedding garment — that is, to relax their minds by wandering thoughts.

CHAP. VI. — VIRGINITY TO BE CULTIVATED AND COMMENDED IN EVERY PLACE AND TIME.

Further, the expression in Jeremiah,[6] " That a maid should not forget her ornaments, nor a bride her attire," [7] shows that she should not give up or loosen the band of chastity through wiles and distractions. For by the heart are properly denoted our heart and mind. Now the breastband, the girdle which gathers together and keeps firm the purpose of the soul to chastity, is love to God, which our Captain and Shepherd, Jesus, who is also our Ruler and Bridegroom, O illustrious virgins, commands both you and me to hold fast unbroken and sealed up even to the end ; for one will not easily find anything else a greater help to men than this possession, pleasing and grateful to God. Therefore, I say, that we should all exercise and honour chastity, and always cultivate and commend it.

Let these first-fruits of my discourse suffice for thee, O Arete, in proof of my education and my zeal. " And I receive the gift," she said that

Arete replied, " and bid Thallousa speak after thee ; for I must have a discourse from each one of you." And she said that Thallousa, pausing a little, as though considering somewhat with herself, thus spoke.

DISCOURSE V. — THALLOUSA.

CHAP. I. — THE OFFERING OF CHASTITY A GREAT GIFT.[8]

I pray you, Arete, that you will give your assistance now too, that I may seem to speak something worthy in the first place of yourself, and then of those who are present. For I am persuaded, having thoroughly learnt it from the sacred writings, that the greatest and most glorious offering and gift, to which there is nothing comparable, which men can offer to God, is the life [9] of virginity. For although many accomplished many admirable things, according to their vows, in the law, they alone were said to fulfil a great vow who were willing to offer themselves of their free-will. For the passage runs thus : " And the Lord spake unto Moses, saying, Speak unto the children of Israel, and say unto them, when either man or woman shall separate themselves . . . unto the Lord." [10]   One vows to offer gold and silver vessels for the sanctuary when he comes, another to offer the tithe of his fruits, another of his property, another the best of his flocks, another consecrates his being ; and no one is able to vow a great vow to the Lord, but he who has offered himself entirely to God.

CHAP. II. — ABRAHAM'S SACRIFICE OF A HEIFER THREE YEARS OLD, OF A GOAT, AND OF A RAM ALSO THREE YEARS OLD : ITS MEANING ; EVERY AGE TO BE CONSECRATED TO GOD ; THE THREE-FOLD WATCH AND OUR AGE.

I must endeavour, O virgins, by a true exposition, to explain to you the mind of the Scripture according to its meaning.[11] Now, he who watches over and restrains himself in part, and in part is distracted and wandering, is not wholly given up to God. Hence it is necessary that the perfect man offer up all, both the things of the soul and those of the flesh, so that he may be complete and not lacking. Therefore also God commands Abraham,[12] " Take Me an heifer of three years old, and a she goat of three years old, and a ram of three years old, and a turtle dove, and a young pigeon ; " which is admirably said ; for remark, that concerning those things, He also gives this command, Bring them Me and keep

---

[1] 2 Cor. xi. 2.
[2] Wisd. iv. 2.
[3] Isa. lx. 1.
[4] O Jerusalem.
[5] Commentators have remarked the allusion to Phil. iii. 11. See Migne's note. The thought of the marriage of the heavenly bridegroom, Christ, to His virgin bride, the Church, at the second Advent, when " the dead shall be raised," was obviously present to the mind of the writer.
[6] Jer. ii. 32. The author, in quoting from the LXX., slightly alters the text, so as to make it almost a command, instead of a question. The original has ἐπιλήσεται; in the text it is ἐπιλαθέσθαι.
[7] Literally, breastband.

[8] [Compare vol. v. p. 587, this series.]
[9] Lit. game or toil, ἆθλον.
[10] Lit. shall greatly vow a vow to offer, with sacrifices of purification, chastity to the Lord. Num vi. 1, 2.
[11] There are two readings. The above rendering may fairly embrace them both.
[12] Gen. xv. 9. [Our author has in mind (the triad) 1 Thess. v. 23.]

them free from the yoke, even thy soul uninjured, like a heifer, and your flesh, and your reason ; the last like a goat, since he traverses lofty and precipitous places, and the other like a ram, that he may in nowise skip away, and fall and slip off from the right way. For thus shalt thou be perfect and blameless, O Abraham, when thou hast offered to Me thy soul, and thy sense, and thy mind, which He mentioned under the symbol of the heifer, the goat, and the ram of three years old, as though they represented the pure knowledge of the Trinity.

And perhaps He also symbolizes the beginning, the middle, and the end of our life and of our age, wishing as far as possible that men should spend their boyhood, their manhood, and their more advanced life purely, and offer them up to Him. Just as our Lord Jesus Christ commands in the Gospels, thus directing : " Let not your lights be extinguished, and let not your loins be loosed. Therefore also be ye like men who wait for their lord, when he will return from the wedding ; that, when he cometh and knocketh, they may open unto him immediately. Blessed are ye, when he shall make you sit down, and shall come and serve you. And if he come in the second, or in the third watch, ye are blessed." [1] For consider, O virgins, when He mentions three watches of the night, and His three comings, He shadows forth in symbol our three periods of life, that of the boy, of the full-grown man, and of the old man ; so that if He should come and remove us from the world while spending our first period, that is, while we are boys, He may receive us ready and pure, having nothing amiss ; and the second and the third in like manner. For the evening watch is the time of the budding and youth of man, when the reason begins to be disturbed and to be clouded by the changes of life, his flesh gaining strength and urging him to lust. The second is the time when, afterwards advancing to a full-grown man, he begins to acquire stability, and to make a stand against the turbulence of passion and self-conceit. And the third, when most of the imaginations and desires fade away, the flesh now withering and declining to old age.

CHAP. III. — FAR BEST TO CULTIVATE VIRTUE FROM BOYHOOD.

Therefore, it is becoming that we should kindle the unquenchable light of faith in the heart, and gird our loins with purity, and watch and ever wait for the Lord ; so that, if He should will to come and take any of us away in the first period of life, or in the second, or in the third, and should find us most ready, and working what He appointed, He may make us to lie

down in the bosom of Abraham, of Isaac, and of Jacob. Now Jeremiah says, " It is good for a man that he bear the yoke in his youth ; " [2] and " that his soul should not depart from the Lord." It is good, indeed, from boyhood, to submit the neck to the divine Hand, and not to shake off, even to old age, the Rider who guides with pure mind, when the Evil One is ever dragging down the mind to that which is worse. For who is there that does not receive through the eyes, through the ears, through the taste and smell and touch, pleasures and delights, so as to become impatient of the control of continence as a driver, who checks and vehemently restrains the horse from evil? Another who turns his thoughts to other things will think differently ; but we say that he offers himself perfectly to God who strives to keep the flesh undefiled from childhood, practising virginity ; for it speedily brings great and much-desired gifts of hopes to those who strive for it, drying up the corrupting lusts and passions of the soul. But come, let us explain how we give ourselves up to the Lord.

CHAP. IV. — PERFECT CONSECRATION AND DEVOTION TO GOD : WHAT IT IS.

That which is laid down in the Book of Numbers,[3] " greatly to vow a vow," serves to show, as, with a litle more explanation, I proceed to prove, that chastity is the great vow above all vows. For then am I plainly consecrated altogether to the Lord, when I not only strive to keep the flesh untouched by intercourse, but also unspotted by other kinds of unseemliness. For " the unmarried woman," it is said,[4] " careth for the things of the Lord, how she may please the Lord ; " not merely that she may bear away the glory in part of not being maimed in her virtue, but in both parts, according to the apostle, that she may be sanctified in body and spirit, offering up her members to the Lord. For let us say what it is to offer up oneself perfectly to the Lord. If, for instance, I open my mouth on some subjects, and close it upon others ; thus, if I open it for the explanation of the Scriptures, for the praise of God, according to my power, in a true faith and with all due honour, and if I close it, putting a door and a watch upon it [5] against foolish discourse, my mouth is kept pure, and is offered up to God. " My tongue is a pen," [6] an organ of wisdom ; for the Word of the Spirit writes by it in clearest letters, from the depth and power of the Scriptures, even the Lord, the swift Writer of the ages, that He

---

[1] Luke xii. 35-38. The author apparently quotes from memory.

[2] Lam. iii. 27.
[3] Num. vi. 2 (LXX.).
[4] 1 Cor. vii. 34 ; quoted from memory.
[5] Cf. Ps. cxxxix. 4, and cxli. 3.
[6] Ps. xlv. 2.

quickly and swiftly registers and fulfils the counsel of the Father, hearing the words, "quickly spoil, swiftly plunder."[1] To such a Scribe the words may be applied, "My tongue is a pen;" for a beautiful pen is sanctified and offered to Him, writing things more lovely than the poets and orators who confirm the doctrines of men. If, too, I accustom my eyes not to lust after the charms of the body, nor to take delight in unseemly sights, but to look up to the things which are above, then my eyes are kept pure, and are offered to the Lord. If I shut my ears against detraction and slanders, and open them to the word of God, having intercourse with wise men,[2] then have I offered up my ears to the Lord. If I keep my hands from dishonourable dealing, from acts of covetousness and of licentiousness, then are my hands kept pure to God. If I withhold my steps from going[3] in perverse ways, then have I offered up my feet, not going to the places of public resort and banquets, where wicked men are found, but into the right way, fulfilling something of the[4] commands. What, then, remains to me, if I also keep the heart pure, offering up all its thoughts to God; if I think no evil, if anger and wrath gain no rule over me, if I meditate in the law of the Lord day and night? And this is to preserve a great chastity, and to vow a great vow.

CHAP. V. — THE VOW OF CHASTITY, AND ITS RITES IN THE LAW; VINES, CHRIST, AND THE DEVIL.

I will now endeavour to explain to you, O virgins, the rest of that which is prescribed; for this is attached to your duties, consisting of laws concerning virginity, which are useful as teaching how we should abstain, and how advance to virginity. For it is written thus:[5] "And the Lord spake unto Moses, saying, Speak unto the children of Israel, and say unto them, When either man or woman shall separate themselves to vow a vow of a Nazarite, to separate themselves unto the Lord; he shall separate himself from wine and strong drink, and shall drink no vinegar of wine, or vinegar of strong drink, neither shall he drink any liquor of grapes, nor eat moist grapes, or dried, all the days of his separation." And this means, that he who has devoted and offered himself to the Lord shall not take of the fruits of the plant of evil, because of its natural tendency to produce intoxication and distraction of mind. For we perceive from the Scriptures two kinds of vines which were separate from each other, and were unlike. For the one is productive of immortality and righteousness; but the other of madness and insanity. The sober and joy-producing vine, from whose instructions, as from branches, there joyfully hang down clusters of graces, distilling love, is our Lord Jesus, who says expressly to the apostles,[6] "I am the true vine, ye are the branches; and my Father is the husbandman." But the wild and death-bearing vine is the devil, who drops down fury and poison and wrath, as Moses relates, writing concerning him,[7] "For their vine is of the vine of Sodom, and of the fields of Gomorrah: their grapes are grapes of gall, their clusters are bitter: their wine is the poison of dragons, and the cruel venom of asps." The inhabitants of Sodom having gathered grapes from this, were goaded on to an unnatural and fruitless desire for males. Hence, also, in the time of Noah, men having given themselves up to drunkenness, sank down into unbelief, and, being overwhelmed by the deluge, were drowned. And Cain, too, having drawn from this, stained his fratricidal hands, and defiled the earth with the blood of his own family. Hence, too, the heathen, becoming intoxicated, sharpen their passions for murderous battles; for man is not so much excited, nor goes so far astray through wine, as from anger and wrath. A man does not become intoxicated and go astray through wine, in the same way as he does from sorrow, or from love, or from incontinence. And therefore it is ordered that a virgin shall not taste of this vine, so that she may be sober and watchful from the cares of life, and may kindle the shining torch of the light of righteousness in the Word. "Take heed to yourselves," says the Lord,[8] "lest at any time your hearts be overcharged with surfeiting, and drunkenness, and cares of this life, and so that day come upon you unawares, as a snare."

CHAP. VI. — SIKERA, A MANUFACTURED AND SPURIOUS WINE, YET INTOXICATING; THINGS WHICH ARE AKIN TO SINS ARE TO BE AVOIDED BY A VIRGIN; THE ALTAR OF INCENSE (A SYMBOL OF) VIRGINS.

Moreover, it is not only forbidden to virgins in any way to touch those things which are made from that vine, but even such things as resemble them and are akin to them. For Sikera, which is manufactured, is called a spurious kind of wine, whether made of palms or of other fruit-trees. For in the same way that draughts of wine overthrow man's reason, so do these exceedingly; and to speak the plain truth, the wise are accustomed to call by the name of Sikera all that produces drunkenness and distraction of mind, besides wine. In order, therefore, that

---

[1] Isa. viii. 1. The LXX. is quoted from memory. The meaning, however, is nearer the original than the E. V. Cf. Keil and Delitzsch, Bib. Com., in loc.
[2] Cf. Ecclus. vi. 36.
[3] τὸ πορευτικόν, the power of going.
[4] Divine.
[5] Num. vi. 1-4.

[6] St. John xv. 1, 5.
[7] Deut. xxxii. 32, 33.
[8] Luke xxi. 34.

the virgin may not, when guarding against those sins which are in their own nature evil, be defiled by those which are like them and akin to them, conquering the one and being conquered by the other, that is, decorating herself with textures of different cloths, or with stones and gold, and other decorations of the body, things which intoxicate the soul; on this account it is ordered that she do not give herself up to womanish weaknesses and laughter, exciting herself to wiles and foolish talking, which whirl the mind around and confuse it; as it is indicated in another place,[1] " Ye shall not eat the hyæna and animals like it ; nor the weasel and creatures of that kind." For this is the straight and direct way to heaven, not merely not to avoid any stumbling-block which would trip up and destroy men who are agitated by a desire for luxuries and pleasures, but also from such things as resemble them.

Moreover, it has been handed down that the unbloody altar of God signifies the assembly of the chaste; thus virginity appears to be something great and glorious. Therefore it ought to be preserved undefiled and altogether pure, having no participation in the impurities of the flesh; but it should be set up before the presence of the testimony, gilded with wisdom, for the Holy of holies, sending forth a sweet savour of love to the Lord ; for He says,[2] " Thou shalt make an altar to burn incense upon : of shittim-wood shalt thou make it. And thou shalt make the staves of shittim-wood, and overlay them with gold. And thou shalt put it before the veil that is by the ark of the testimony, before the mercy-seat that is over the testimony, where I will meet with thee. And Aaron shall burn thereon sweet incense every morning : when he dresseth the lamps, he shall burn incense upon it. And when Aaron lighteth the lamps at even, he shall burn incense upon it ; a perpetual incense before the Lord throughout your generations. Ye shall offer no strange incense thereon, nor burnt-sacrifices nor meat-offering ; neither shall ye pour drink-offering thereon."

CHAP. VII. — THE CHURCH INTERMEDIATE BETWEEN THE SHADOWS OF THE LAW AND THE REALITIES OF HEAVEN.

If the law, according to the apostle, is spiritual, containing the images " of future good things,"[3] come then, let us strip off the veil of the letter which is spread over it, and consider its naked and true meaning. The Hebrews were commanded to ornament the Tabernacle as a type of the Church, that they might be able, by means of sensible things, to announce beforehand the image of divine things. For the pattern which was shown to Moses[4] in the mount, to which he was to have regard in fashioning the Tabernacle, was a kind of accurate representation of the heavenly dwelling, which we now perceive more clearly than through types, yet more darkly than if we saw the reality. For not yet, in our present condition, has the truth come unmingled to men, who are here unable to bear the sight of pure immortality, just as we cannot bear to look upon the rays of the sun. And the Jews declared that the shadow of the image (of the heavenly things which was afforded to them), was the third from the reality ; but we clearly behold the image of the heavenly order ; for the truth will be accurately made manifest after the resurrection, when we shall see the heavenly tabernacle (the city in heaven " whose builder and maker is God "[5]) " face to face," and not " darkly " and " in part."[6]

CHAP. VIII. — THE DOUBLE ALTAR, WIDOWS AND VIRGINS ; GOLD THE SYMBOL OF VIRGINITY.

Now the Jews prophesied our state, but we foretell the heavenly ; since the Tabernacle was a symbol of the Church, and the Church of heaven. Therefore, these things being so, and the Tabernacle being taken for a type of the Church, as I said, it is fitting that the altars should signify some of the things in the Church. And we have already compared the brazen altar to the company and circuit of widows ; for they are a living altar of God, to which they bring calves and tithes, and free-will offerings, as a sacrifice to the Lord ; but the golden altar within the [7] Holy of holies, before the presence of the testimony, on which it is forbidden to offer sacrifice and libation, has reference to those in a state of virginity, as those who have their bodies preserved pure, like unalloyed gold, from carnal intercourse. Now gold is commended for two reasons : the first, that it does not rust, and the second, that in its colour it seems in a measure to resemble the rays of the sun ; and thus it is suitably a symbol of virginity, which does not admit any stain or spot, but ever shines forth with the light of the Word. Therefore, also, it stands nearer *to God* within the Holy of holies, and before the veil, with undefiled hands, like incense, offering up prayers to the Lord, acceptable as a sweet savour ; as also John indicated, saying that the incense in the vials of the four-and-twenty elders were the prayers of the saints. This, then, I offer to thee, O Arete, on the spur of the moment, according to my ability, on the subject of chastity.

---

[1] Lev. xi. 29; not an exact quotation.
[2] Exod. xxx. 1-9.
[3] Heb. x. 1. The apostle says, " a shadow," and " not the very image." The difference, however, is verbal only. — TR.

[4] Exod. xxv. 40.
[5] Heb. xi. 10.
[6] 1 Cor. xiii. 12.
[7] An apparent confusion between the altar of incense, to which the author refers, and which stood in the Holy Place, and the Mercy-Seat, which was within the vale in the Holy of holies. — TR.

And when Thallousa had said this, Theopatra said that Arete touched Agathe with her sceptre, and that she, perceiving it, immediately arose and answered.

DISCOURSE VI.—AGATHE.

CHAP. I. — THE EXCELLENCE OF THE ABIDING GLORY OF VIRGINITY ; THE SOUL MADE IN THE IMAGE OF THE IMAGE OF GOD, THAT IS OF HIS SON ; THE DEVIL A SUITOR FOR THE SOUL.

With great confidence of being able to persuade, and to carry on this admirable discourse, O Arete, if thou go with me, will I also endeavour, according to my ability, to contribute something to the discussion of the subject before us ; something commensurate to my own power, and not to be compared with that which has already been spoken. For I should be unable to put forth in philosophizing anything that could compete with those things which have already been so variously and brilliantly worked out. For I shall seem to bear away the reproach of silliness, if I make an effort to match myself with my superiors in wisdom. If, however, you will bear even with those who speak as they can, I will endeavour to speak, not lacking at least in good will. And here let me begin.

We have all come into this world, O virgins, endowed with singular beauty, which has a relationship and affinity to *divine* wisdom. For the souls of men do then most accurately resemble Him who begat and formed them, when, reflecting the unsullied representation of His likeness, and the features of that countenance, to which God looking formed them to have an immortal and indestructible shape, they remain such. For the unbegotten and incorporeal beauty, which neither begins nor is corruptible, but is unchangeable, and grows not old and has need of nothing, He resting in Himself, and in the very light which is in unspeakable and inapproachable places,[1] embracing all things in the circumference of His power, creating and arranging, made the soul after the image of His image. Therefore, also, it is reasonable and immortal. For being made after the image of the Only-begotten, as I said, it has an unsurpassable beauty, and therefore evil spirits[2] love it, and plot and strive to defile its godlike and lovely image, as the prophet Jeremiah shows, reproaching Jerusalem, " Thou hadst a whore's forehead, thou refusedst to be ashamed ; "[3] speaking of her who prostituted herself to the powers which came against her to pollute her. For her lovers are the devil and his angels, who plan to defile and pollute our

reasonable and clear-sighted beauty of mind by intercourse with themselves, and desire to cohabit with every soul which is betrothed to the Lord.

CHAP. II. — THE PARABLE OF THE TEN VIRGINS.[4]

If, then, any one will keep this beauty inviolate and unharmed, and such as He who constructed it formed and fashioned it, imitating the eternal and intelligible nature of which man is the representation and likeness, and will become like a glorious and holy image, he will be transferred thence to heaven, the city of the blessed, and will dwell there as in a sanctuary. Now our beauty is then best preserved undefiled and perfect when, protected by virginity, it is not darkened by the heat of corruption from without ; but, remaining in itself, it is adorned with righteousness, being brought as a bride to the Son of God ; as He also Himself suggests, exhorting that the light of chastity should be kindled in their flesh, as in lamps ; since the number of the ten virgins[5] signifies the souls that have believed in Jesus Christ, symbolizing by the ten the only right way to heaven. Now five of them were prudent and wise ; and five were foolish and unwise, for they had not the forethought to fill their vessels with oil, remaining destitute of righteousness. Now by these He signifies those who strive to come to the boundaries of virginity, and who strain every nerve to fulfil this love, acting virtuously and temperately, and who profess and boast that this is their aim ; but who, making light of it, and being subdued by the changes of the world, come rather to be sketches of the shadowy image of virtue, than workers who represent the living truth itself.

CHAP. III. — THE SAME ENDEAVOUR AND EFFORT AFTER VIRGINITY, WITH A DIFFERENT RESULT.

Now when it is said[5] that " the kingdom of heaven is likened unto ten virgins, which took their lamps and went forth to meet the bridegroom," this means that the same way towards the goal had been entered upon, as is shown by the mark X.[6] By profession they had equally proposed the same end, and therefore they are called ten, since, as I have said, they chose the same profession ; but they did not, for all that, go forth in the same way to meet the bridegroom. For some provided abundant future nourishment for their lamps which were fed with oil, but others were careless, thinking only of the present. And, therefore, they are divided into two

---

[1] Cf. Tim. vi. 16.
[2] πνευματικὰ τῆς πονηρίας (Eph. vi. 12). In E. V. " spiritual wickedness."
[3] Jer. iii. 3.

[4] [Which has suggested the form of this allegorical work.]
[5] Matt. xxv.
[6] In Greek ι = ten. The word employed signifies the index of a sun-dial. — TR. [The lamps found in the Roman catacombs have this mark (X), which is at once a monogram for Christ and a reference to the ten virgins. In the Greek the accented *Iota* might yet be associated with the initial of Jesus.]

equal numbers of five, inasmuch as the one class preserved the five senses, which most people consider the gates of wisdom, pure and undefiled by sins; but the others, on the contrary, corrupted them by multitudes of sins, defiling themselves with evil. For having restrained them, and kept them free from righteousness, they bore a more abundant crop of transgressions, in consequence of which it came to pass that they were forbidden, and shut out from the divine courts. For whether, on the one hand, we do right, or, on the other, do wrong through these senses, our habits of good and evil are confirmed. And as Thallousa said that there is a chastity of the eyes, and of the ears, and of the tongue, and so on of the other senses; so here she who keeps inviolate the faith of the five pathways of virtue — sight, taste, smell, touch, and hearing — is called by the name of the five virgins, because she has kept the five forms of the sense pure to Christ, as a lamp, causing the light of holiness to shine forth clearly from each of them. For the flesh is truly, as it were, our five-lighted lamp, which the soul will bear like a torch, when it stands before Christ the Bridegroom, on the day of the resurrection, showing her faith springing out clear and bright through all the senses, as He Himself taught, saying,[1] "I am come to send fire on the earth; and what will I if it be already kindled?" meaning by the earth our bodies, in which He wished the swift-moving and fiery operation of His doctrine to be kindled. Now the oil represents wisdom and righteousness; for while the soul rains down unsparingly, and pours forth these things upon the body, the light of virtue is kindled unquenchably, making its good actions to shine before men, so that our Father which is in heaven may be glorified.[2]

CHAP. IV. — WHAT THE OIL IN THE LAMPS MEANS.

Now they offered, in Leviticus,[3] oil of this kind, "pure oil olive, beaten for the light, to cause the lamps to burn continually, without the veil . . . before the Lord." But they were commanded to have a feeble light from the evening to the morning. For their light seemed to resemble the prophetic word, which gives encouragement to temperance, being nourished by the acts and the faith of the people. But the temple (in which the light was kept burning) refers to "the lot of their inheritance,"[4] inasmuch as a light can shine in only one house. Therefore it was necessary that it should be lighted before day. For he says,[5] "they shall burn

it until the morning," that is, until the coming of Christ. But the Sun of chastity and of righteousness having arisen, there is no need of other light.

So long, then, as this people treasured up nourishment for the light, supplying oil by their works, the light of continence was not extinguished among them, but was ever shining and giving light in the "lot of their inheritance." But when the oil failed, by their turning away from the faith to incontinence, the light was entirely extinguished, so that the virgins have again to kindle their lamps by light transmitted from one to another, bringing the light of incorruption to the world from above. Let us then supply now the oil of good works abundantly, and of prudence, being purged from all corruption which would weigh us down; lest, while the Bridegroom tarries, our lamps may also in like manner be extinguished. For the delay is the interval which precedes the appearing of Christ. Now the slumbering and sleeping of the virgins signifies the departure from life; and the midnight is the kingdom of Antichrist, during which the destroying angel passes over the houses.[6] But the cry which was made when it was said,[7] "Behold the bridegroom cometh, go ye out to meet him," is the voice which shall be heard from heaven, and the trumpet, when the saints, all their bodies being raised, shall be caught up, and shall go on the clouds to meet the Lord.[8]

For it is to be observed that the word of God says, that after the cry all the virgins arose, that is, that the dead shall be raised after the voice which comes from heaven, as also Paul intimates,[9] that "the Lord Himself shall descend from heaven with a shout, with the voice of the archangel, and with the trump of God: and the dead in Christ shall rise first;" that is the tabernacles,[10] for they died, being put off by their souls. "Then we which are alive shall be caught up together with them," meaning our souls.[11] For we truly who are alive are the souls which, with the bodies, having put them on again, shall go to meet Him in the clouds, bearing our lamps trimmed, not with anything alien and worldly, but like stars radiating the light of prudence and continence, full of ethereal splendour.

CHAP. V. — THE REWARD OF VIRGINITY.

These, O fair virgins, are the orgies of our mysteries; these the mystic rites of those who are initiated in virginity; these the "undefiled rewards"[12] of the conflict of virginity. I am be-

---

[1] Luke xii. 49. The Latin version is certainly more accurate, "Quid volo nisi ut accendatur?" — TR. [A visionary interpretation follows. But has not this text been too much overlooked in its literal significance? "It is the last time." The planet is now on fire.]
[2] Matt. v. 16.
[3] Lev. xxiv. 2, 3.
[4] Ps. cv. 11.
[5] Lev. xxiv. 3.

[6] Exod. xi., xii.
[7] Matt. xxv. 6. [This parable greatly stimulated primitive celibacy.]
[8] 1 Thess. iv. 16, 17.
[9] 1 Thess. iv. 16.
[10] Bodies.
[11] 1 Thess. iv. 17. Commentators have remarked on the peculiarity of the interpretation. We give simply the writer's meaning. — TR.
[12] Wisd. iv. 2.

trothed to the Word, and receive as a reward the eternal crown of immortality and riches from the Father ; and I triumph in eternity, crowned with the bright and unfading flowers of wisdom. I am one in the choir with Christ dispensing His rewards in heaven, around the unbeginning and never-ending King. I have become the torch-bearer of the unapproachable lights,[1] and I join with their company in the new song of the archangels, showing forth the new grace of the Church ; for the Word says that the company of virgins always follow the Lord, and have fellow-ship with Him wherever He is. And this is what John signifies in the commemoration of the hundred and forty-four thousand.[2]

Go then, ye virgin band of the new ages. Go, fill your vessels with righteousness, for the hour is coming when ye must rise and meet the bride-groom. Go, lightly leaving on one side the fas-cinations and the pleasures of life, which confuse and bewitch the soul ; and thus shall ye attain the promises, " This I swear by Him who has shown me the way of life." This crown, woven by the prophets, I have taken from the prophetic meadows, and offer to thee, O Arete.

Agathe having thus admirably brought her discourse to an end, she said, and having been applauded for what she had uttered, Arete again commanded Procilla to speak. And she, rising and passing before the entrance, spoke thus.

DISCOURSE VII.—PROCILLA.

CHAP. I.—WHAT THE TRUE AND SEEMLY MANNER OF PRAISING ; THE FATHER GREATER THAN THE SON, NOT IN SUBSTANCE, BUT IN ORDER ; VIRGINITY THE LILY ; FAITHFUL SOULS AND VIRGINS, THE ONE BRIDE OF THE ONE CHRIST.

It is not lawful for me to delay, O Arete, after such discourses, seeing that I confide undoubt-ingly in the manifold wisdom of God, which gives richly and widely to whomsoever it wills. For sailors who have experience of the sea declare that the same wind blows on all who sail ; and that different persons, managing their course differently, strive to reach different ports. Some have a fair wind ; to others it blows across their course ; and yet both easily accomplish their voyage. Now, in the same way, the " under-standing Spirit,[3] holy, one only,"[4] gently breath-ing down from the treasures of the Father above, giving us all the clear fair wind of knowledge, will suffice to guide the course of our words without offence.

And now it is time for me to speak.

This, O virgins, is the one true and seemly mode of praising, when he who praises brings forward a witness better than all those who are praised. For thence one may learn with cer-tainty that the commendation is given not from favour, nor of necessity, nor from repute, but in accordance with truth and an unflattering judg-ment. And so the prophets and apostles, who spoke more fully concerning the Son of God, and assigned to Him a divinity above other men, did not refer their praises of Him to the teaching of angels, but to Him upon whom all authority and power depend. For it was fitting that He who was greater than all things after the Father, should have the Father, who alone is greater than Himself,[5] as His witness. And so I will not bring forward the praises of virginity from mere human report, but from Him who cares for us, and who has taken up the whole matter, showing that He is the husbandman of this grace, and a lover of its beauty, and a fitting witness. And this is quite clear, in the Song of Songs,[6] to any one who is willing to see it, where Christ Him-self, praising those who are firmly established in virginity, says,[7] " As the lily among thorns, so is my love among the daughters ; " comparing the grace of chastity to the lily, on account of its purity and fragrance, and sweetness and joyous-ness. For chastity is like a spring flower, always softly exhaling immortality from its white petals. Therefore He is not ashamed to confess that He loves the beauty of its prime, in the following words :[8] " Thou hast ravished my heart, my sister, my spouse ; thou hast ravished my heart with one of thine eyes, with one chain of thy neck. How fair is thy love, my sister, my spouse ! how much better is thy love than wine ! and the smell of thine ointments than all spices ! Thy lips, O my spouse, drop as the honeycomb ; honey and milk are under thy tongue ; and the smell of thy garments is like the smell of Leba-non. A garden enclosed is my sister, my spouse ; a spring shut up, a fountain sealed."

These praises does Christ proclaim to those who have come to the boundaries of virginity, describing them all under the one name of His spouse ; for the spouse must be betrothed to the Bridegroom, and called by His name. And, moreover, she must be undefiled and unpolluted, as a garden sealed, in which all the odours of the fragrance of heaven are grown, that Christ alone may come and gather them, blooming with incorporeal seeds. For the Word loves none of the things of the flesh, because He is not of such a nature as to be contented with any of the things which are corruptible, as hands, or face,

---

[1] Although the Greek word is not the same as in 1 Tim. vi. 16, the meaning is probably this rather than *unquenchable*, as it is rendered in the Latin. — Tr. [See Discourse XI. cap. 2, *infra*.]
[2] Rev. vii. 4, xiv. 4.
[3] πνεῦμα here, and for *wind* above.
[4] Literally, only begotten. Wisd. vii. 22.

[5] St. John xiv. 28.
[6] [That the Canticles demand allegorical interpretation, we may admit: nor can I object to our author's ideas here.]
[7] Cant. ii. 2.
[8] Cant. iv. 9-12.

or feet; but He looks upon and delights in the beauty which is immaterial and spiritual, not touching the beauty of the body.

CHAP. II. — THE INTERPRETATION OF THAT PASSAGE OF THE CANTICLES.[1]

Consider now, O virgins, that, in saying to the bride, "Thou hast ravished my heart, my sister, my spouse," He shows the clear eye of the understanding, when the inner man has cleansed it and looks more clearly upon the truth. For it is clear to every one that there is a twofold power of sight, the one of the soul, and the other of the body. But the Word does not profess a love for that of the body, but only that of the understanding, saying, "Thou hast ravished my heart with one of thine eyes, with one chain of thy neck;" which means, By the most lovely sight of thy mind, thou hast urged my heart to love, radiating forth from within the glorious beauty of chastity. Now the chains of the neck are necklaces which are composed of various precious stones; and the souls which take care of the body, place around the outward neck of the flesh this visible ornament to deceive those who behold; but those who live chastely, on the other hand, adorn themselves within with ornaments truly composed of various precious stones, namely, of freedom, of magnanimity, of wisdom, and of love, caring little for those temporal decorations which, like leaves blossoming for an hour, dry up with the changes of the body. For there is seen in man a twofold beauty, of which the Lord accepts that which is within and is immortal, saying, "Thou hast ravished my heart with one chain of thy neck;" meaning to show that He had been drawn to love by the splendour of the inner man shining forth in its glory, even as the Psalmist also testifies, saying, "The King's daughter is all glorious within."[2]

CHAP. III. — VIRGINS BEING MARTYRS FIRST AMONG THE COMPANIONS OF CHRIST.

Let no one suppose that all the remaining company of those who have believed are condemned, thinking that we who are virgins alone shall be led on to attain the promises, not understanding that there shall be tribes and families and orders, according to the analogy of the faith of each. And this Paul, too, sets forth, saying,[3] "There is one glory of the sun, and another glory of the moon, and another glory of the stars: for one star differeth from another star in glory. So also is the resurrection of the dead." And the Lord does not profess to give the same honours to all; but to some He prom-

ises that they shall be numbered in the kingdom of heaven, to others the inheritance of the earth, and to others to see the Father.[4] And here, also, He announces that the order and holy choir of the virgins shall first enter in company with Him into the rest of the new dispensation, as into a bridal chamber. For they were martyrs, not as bearing the pains of the body for a little moment of time, but as enduring them through all their life, not shrinking from truly wrestling in an Olympian contest for the prize of chastity; but resisting the fierce torments of pleasures and fears and griefs, and the other evils of the iniquity of men, they first of all carry off the prize, taking their place in the higher rank of those who receive the promise. Undoubtedly these are the souls whom the Word calls alone His chosen spouse and His sister, but the rest concubines and virgins and daughters, speaking thus:[5] "There are threescore queens and fourscore concubines, and virgins without number. My dove, my undefiled, is but one; she is the only one of her mother, she is the choice one of her that bare her: the daughters saw her and blessed her: yea, the queens and the concubines, and they praised her." For there being plainly many daughters of the Church, one alone is the chosen and most precious in her eyes above all, namely, the order of virgins.

CHAP. IV. — THE PASSAGE[5] EXPLAINED; THE QUEENS, THE HOLY SOULS BEFORE THE DELUGE; THE CONCUBINES, THE SOULS OF THE PROPHETS; THE DIVINE SEED FOR SPIRITUAL OFFSPRING IN THE BOOKS OF THE PROPHETS; THE NUPTIALS OF THE WORD IN THE PROPHETS AS THOUGH CLANDESTINE.

Now if any one should have a doubt about these things, inasmuch as the points are nowhere fully wrought out, and should still wish more fully to perceive their spiritual significance, namely, what the queens and the concubines and the virgins are, we will say that these may have been spoken concerning those who have been conspicuous for their righteousness from the beginning throughout the progress of time; as of those before the flood, and those after the flood, and so on of those after Christ. The Church, then, is the spouse. The queens are those royal souls before the deluge, who became well-pleasing to God, that is, those about Abel and Seth and Enoch. The concubines[6] those after the flood, namely, those of the prophets, in whom, before the Church was betrothed to the Lord, being united to them after the manner

---

[1] Chap. iv. ver. 9–12.
[2] Ps. xlv. 14.
[3] 1 Cor. xv. 41, 42.

[4] Matt. v. 3–16.
[5] Cant. vi. 8, 9.
[6] [Here allegorizing is refuted and perishes in fanciful and overstrained analogies.]

of concubines, He sowed true words in an incorrupt and pure philosophy, so that, conceiving faith, they might bring forth to Him the spirit of salvation. For such fruits do the souls bring forth with whom Christ has had intercourse, fruits which bear an ever-memorable renown. For if you will look at the books of Moses, or David, or Solomon, or Isaiah, or of the prophets who follow, O virgins, you will see what offspring they have left, for the saving of life, from their intercourse with the Son of God. Hence the Word has with deep perception called the souls of the prophets concubines, because He did not espouse them openly, as He did the Church, having killed for her the fatted calf.[1]

CHAP. V. — THE SIXTY QUEENS : WHY SIXTY, AND WHY QUEENS ; THE EXCELLENCE OF THE SAINTS OF THE FIRST AGE.

In addition to these matters, there is this also to be considered, so that nothing may escape us of things which are necessary, why He said that the queens were sixty, and the concubines eighty, and the virgins so numerous as not to be counted from their multitude, but the spouse one. And first let us speak of the sixty. I imagine that He named under the sixty queens, those who had pleased God from the first-made man in succession to Noah, for this reason, since these had no need of precepts and laws for their salvation, the creation of the world in six days being still recent. For they remembered that in six days God formed the creation, and those things which were made in paradise ; and how man, receiving a command not to touch[2] the tree of knowledge, ran aground, the author of evil having led him astray.[3] Thence he gave the symbolical name of sixty queens to those souls who, from the creation of the world, in succession chose God as the object of their love, and were almost, so to speak, the offspring of the first age, and neighbours of the great six days' work, from their having been born, as I said, immediately after the six days. For these had great honour, being associated with the angels, and often seeing God manifested visibly, and not in a dream. For consider what confidence Seth had towards God, and Abel, and Enos, and Enoch, and Methuselah, and Noah, the first lovers of righteousness, and the first of the first-born children who are written in heaven,[4] being thought worthy of the kingdom, as a kind of first-fruits of the plants for salvation, coming out as early fruit to God. And so much may suffice concerning these.

CHAP. VI. — THE EIGHTY CONCUBINES, WHAT ; THE KNOWLEDGE OF THE INCARNATION COMMUNICATED TO THE PROPHETS.

It still remains to speak concerning the concubines. To those who lived after the deluge the knowledge of God was henceforth more remote, and they needed other instruction to ward off the evil, and to be their helper, since idolatry was already creeping in. Therefore God, that the race of man might not be wholly destroyed, through forgetfulness of the things which were good, commanded His own Son to reveal to the prophets His own future appearance in the world by the flesh, in which the joy and knowledge of the spiritual eighth day[5] shall be proclaimed, which would bring the remission of sins and the resurrection, and that thereby the passions and corruptions of men would be circumcised. And, therefore, He called by the name of the eighty virgins the list of the prophets from Abraham, on account of the dignity of circumcision, which embraces the number eight, in accordance with which also the law is framed ; because they first, before the Church was espoused to the Word, received the divine seed, and foretold the circumcision of the spiritual eighth day.

CHAP. VII. — THE VIRGINS,[6] THE RIGHTEOUS ANCIENTS ; THE CHURCH, THE ONE ONLY SPOUSE, MORE EXCELLENT THAN THE OTHERS.

Now he calls by the name of virgins, who belong to a countless assembly, those who, being inferior to the better ones, have practised righteousness, and have striven against sin with youthful and noble energy. But of these, neither the queens, nor the concubines, nor the virgins, are compared to the Church. For she is reckoned the perfect and chosen one beyond all these, consisting and composed of all the apostles, the Bride who surpasses all in the beauty of youth and virginity. Therefore, also, she is blessed and praised by all, because she saw and heard freely what those desired to see, even for a little time, and saw not, and to hear, but heard not. For "blessed," said our Lord to His disciples,[7] "are your eyes, for they see ; and your ears, for they hear. For verily I say unto you, That many prophets have desired to see those things which ye see, and have not seen them ; and to hear those things which ye hear, and have not heard them." For this reason, then, the prophets count them blessed, and admire them, because the Church

---

[1] Luke xv. 23.
[2] This was Eve's testimony to the serpent, not the original command. — Tr. [But I do not see the force of this note. Eve in her innocency is surely a competent witness.]
[3] Gen. iii. 3.
[4] Heb. xi. 23.

[5] Here, and in many other places, the prevalent millenarian belief of the first centuries is expressed by Methodius. — Tr. [See Barnabas, vol. i. p. 147, this series; also Irenæus (same vol.), p. 562, at note 11.]
[6] This word, as being that employed in the E.T. of the Canticles, is adopted throughout. It must be remembered, that, in this connection, it stands for νεάνιδες, and not for παρθένοι. — Tr.
[7] Matt. xiii. 16, 17.

was thought worthy to participate in those things which they did not attain to hear or see. For "there are threescore queens, and fourscore concubines, and virgins without number. My dove, my undefiled, is but one." [1]

CHAP. VIII. — THE HUMAN NATURE OF CHRIST HIS ONE DOVE.

Can any one now say otherwise than that the Bride is the undefiled flesh of the Lord, for the sake of which He left the Father and came down here, and was joined to it, and, being incarnate, dwelt in it? Therefore He called it figuratively a dove, because that creature is tame and domestic, and readily adapts itself to man's mode of life. For she alone, so to speak, was found spotless and undefiled, and excelling all in the glory and beauty of righteousness, so that none of those who had pleased God most perfectly could stand near to her in a comparison of virtue. And for this reason she was thought worthy to become a partaker of the kingdom of the Onlybegotten, being betrothed and united to Him. And in the forty-fourth psalm,[2] the queen who, chosen out of many, stands at the right hand of God, clothed in the golden ornament of virtue, whose beauty the King desired,[3] is, as I said, the undefiled and blessed flesh, which the Word Himself carried into the heavens, and presented at the right hand of God, "wrought about with divers colours," that is, in the pursuits of immortality, which he calls symbolically golden fringes. For since this garment is variegated and woven of various virtues, as chastity, prudence, faith, love, patience, and other good things, which, covering, as they do, the unseemliness of the flesh, adorn man with a golden ornament.

CHAP. IX. — THE VIRGINS IMMEDIATELY AFTER THE QUEEN AND SPOUSE.

Moreover, we must further consider what the Spirit delivers to us in the rest of the psalm, after the enthronization of the manhood assumed by the Word at the right hand of the Father. "The virgins," He says,[4] "that be her fellows shall bear her company, and shall be brought unto thee. With joy and gladness shall they be brought, and shall enter into the King's palace." Now, here the Spirit seems quite plainly to praise virginity, next, as we have explained, to the Bride of the Lord, who promises that the virgins shall approach second to the Almighty with joy and gladness, guarded and escorted by angels. For so lovely and desirable is in truth the glory of virginity, that, next to the Queen, whom the Lord exalts, and presents in sinless glory to the Father, the choir and order of virgins bear her company, assigned to a place second to that of the Bride. Let these efforts of mine to speak to thee, O Arete, concerning chastity, be engraven on a monument.

And Procilla having thus spoken, Thekla said, It is my turn after her to continue the contest; and I rejoice, since I too have the favouring wisdom of words, perceiving that I am, like a harp, inwardly attuned, and prepared to speak with elegance and propriety.

ARETE. I most willingly hail thy readiness, O Thekla, in which I confide to give me fitting discourse, in accordance with thy powers; since thou wilt yield to none in universal philosophy and instruction, instructed by Paul in what is fitting to say of evangelical and divine doctrine.

DISCOURSE VIII. — THEKLA.

CHAP. I. — METHODIUS' DERIVATION OF THE WORD VIRGINITY: [5] WHOLLY DIVINE; VIRTUE, IN GREEK ἀρετή, WHENCE SO CALLED.

Well, then, let us first say, beginning from the origin of the name, for what cause this supreme and blessed pursuit was called παρθενία, what it aims at, what power it has, and afterwards, what fruits it gives forth. For almost all have been ignorant of this virtue as being superior to ten thousand other advantages of virtue which we cultivate for the purification and adornment of the soul. For virginity [5] is divine by the change of one letter,[6] as she alone makes him who has her, and is initiated by her incorruptible rites like unto God, than which it is impossible to find a greater good, removed, as it is, from pleasure and grief; and the wing of the soul sprinkled by it becomes stronger and lighter, accustomed daily to fly from human desires.

For since the children of the wise have said that our life is a festival, and that we have come to exhibit in the theatre the drama of truth, that is, righteousness, the devil and the demons plotting and striving against us, it is necessary for us to look upwards and to take our flight aloft, and to flee from the blandishments of their tongues, and from their forms tinged with the outward appearance of temperance, more than from the Sirens of Homer. For many, bewitched by the pleasures of error, take their flight downwards, and are weighed down when they come into this life, their nerves being relaxed and unstrung, by means of which the power of the wings of temperance is strengthened, lightening the downward tendency of the corruption of the body. Whence, O Arete, whether thou hast thy name, *signifying virtue,*

---

[1] Cant. vi. 8, 9.
[2] The forty-fifth in our arrangement.
[3] Ps. xlv. 2.
[4] Ps. xlv. 15, 16.

[5] παρθενία.
[6] παρθενία . . . παρθεία.

because thou art worthy of being chosen [1] for thyself, or because thou raisest [2] and liftest up to heaven, ever going in the purest minds, come, give me thy help in my discourse, which thou hast thyself appointed me to speak.

CHAP. II. — THE LOFTY MIND AND CONSTANCY OF THE SACRED VIRGINS; THE INTRODUCTION OF VIRGINS INTO THE BLESSED ABODES BEFORE OTHERS.

Those who take a downward flight, and fall into pleasures, do not desist from grief and labours until, through their passionate desires, they fulfil the want of their intemperance, and, being degraded and shut out from the sanctuary, they are removed from the scene of truth, and, instead of procreating children with modesty and temperance, they rave in the wild pleasures of unlawful amours. But those who, on light wing, ascend into the supramundane life, and see from afar what other men do not see, the very pastures of immortality, bearing in abundance flowers of inconceivable beauty, are ever turning themselves again to the spectacles there; and, for this reason, those things are thought small which are here considered noble — such as wealth, and glory, and birth, and marriage; and they think no more of those things.[3] But yet if any of them should choose to give up their bodies to wild beasts or to fire, and be punished, they are ready to have no care for pains, or for the desire of them or the fear of them; so that they seem, while in the world, not to be in the world, but to have already reached, in thought and in the tendency of their desires, the assembly of those who are in heaven.

Now it is not right that the wing of virginity should, by its own nature, be weighed down upon the earth, but that it should soar upwards to heaven, to a pure atmosphere, and to the life which is akin to that of angels. Whence also they, first of all, after their call and departure hence, who have rightly and faithfully contended as virgins for Christ, bear away the prize of victory, being crowned by Him with the flowers of immortality. For, as soon as their souls have left the world, it is said that the angels meet them with much rejoicing, and conduct them to the very pastures already spoken of, to which also they were longing to come, contemplating them in imagination from afar, when, while they were yet dwelling in their bodies, they appeared to them divine.

CHAP. III. — THE LOT AND INHERITANCE OF VIRGINITY.

Furthermore, when they have come hither, they see wonderful and glorious and blessed things of beauty, and such as cannot be spoken to men. They see there righteousness itself and prudence, and love itself, and truth and temperance, and other flowers and plants of wisdom, equally splendid, of which we here behold only the shadows [4] and apparitions, as in dreams, and think that they consist of the actions of men, because there is no clear image of them here, but only dim copies, which themselves we see often when making dark copies of them. For never has any one seen with his eyes the greatness or the form or the beauty of righteousness itself, or of understanding, or of peace; but there, in Him whose name is I AM,[5] they are seen perfect and clear, as they are. For there is a tree of temperance itself, and of love, and of understanding, as there are plants of the fruits which grow here — as of grapes, the pomegranate, and of apples; and so, too, the fruits of those trees are gathered and eaten, and do not perish and wither, but those who gather them grow to immortality and a likeness to God. Just as he from whom all are descended, before the fall and the blinding of his eyes, being in paradise, enjoyed its fruits, God appointing man to dress and to keep the plants of wisdom. For it was entrusted to the first Adam to cultivate those fruits. Now Jeremiah saw that these things exist specially in a certain place, removed to a great distance from our world, where, compassionating those who have fallen from that good state, he says:[6] "Learn where is wisdom, where is strength, where is understanding; that thou mayest know also where is length of days, and life, where is the light of the eyes, and peace. Who hath found out her place? or who hath come into her treasures?" The virgins having entered into the treasures of these things, gather the reasonable fruits of the virtues, sprinkled with manifold and well-ordered lights, which, like a fountain, God throws up over them, irradiating that state with unquenchable lights. And they sing harmoniously, giving glory to God. For a pure atmosphere is shed over them, and one which is not oppressed by the sun.

CHAP. IV. — EXHORTATION TO THE CULTIVATION OF VIRGINITY; A PASSAGE FROM THE APOCALYPSE [7] IS PROPOSED TO BE EXAMINED.

Now, then, O Virgins, daughters of undefiled temperance, let us strive for a life of blessedness and the kingdom of heaven. And do ye unite with those before you in an earnest desire for the same glory of chastity, caring little for the

---

[1] αἱρετή.
[2] αἱρεῖν.
[3] Than of the most ordinary things of life.

[4] The influence of Plato is traceable, here and elsewhere, throughout the works of Methodius. It has been fully examined in the able work of Jahn, *Methodius Platonizans.* — TR. [Elucidation I.]
[5] Exod. iii. 14.
[6] Baruch iii. 14, 15. The apocryphal book of Baruch, as bearing the name of the companion of Jeremiah, was usually quoted, in the second and third centuries, as the work of that great prophet. — TR.
[7] Rev. xii. 1-6.

things of this life. For immortality and chastity do not contribute a little to happiness, raising up the flesh aloft, and drying up its moisture and its clay-like weight, by a greater force of attraction. And let not the uncleanness which you hear creep in and weigh you down to the earth; nor let sorrow transform your joy, melting away your hopes in better things; but shake off incessantly the calamities which come upon you, not defiling your mind with lamentations. Let faith conquer wholly, and let its light drive away the visions of evil which crowd around the heart. For, as when the moon brightly shining fills the heaven with its light, and all the air becomes clear, but suddenly the clouds from the west, enviously rushing in, for a little while overshadow its light, but do not destroy it, since they are immediately driven away by a blast of the wind; so ye also, when causing the light of chastity to shine in the world, although pressed upon by afflictions and labours, do not grow weary and abandon your hopes. For the clouds which come from the Evil One are driven away by the Spirit,[1] if ye, like your Mother, who gives birth to the male Virgin in heaven, fear nothing the serpent that lies in wait and plots against you; concerning whom I intend to discourse to you more plainly; for it is now time.

John, in the course of the Apocalypse, says:[2] "And there appeared a great wonder in heaven; a woman clothed with the sun, and the moon under her feet, and upon her head a crown of twelve stars: and she, being with child, cried, travailing in birth, and pained to be delivered. And there appeared another wonder in heaven; and behold a great red dragon, having seven heads and ten horns, and seven crowns upon his heads. And his tail drew the third part of the stars of heaven, and did cast them to the earth: and the dragon stood before the woman which was ready to be delivered, for to devour her child as soon as it was born. And she brought forth a man-child, who was to rule all nations with a rod of iron: and her child was caught up unto God, and to His throne. And the woman fled into the wilderness, where she hath a place prepared of God, that they should feed her there a thousand two hundred and threescore days." So far we have given, in brief, the history of the woman and the dragon. But to search out and explain the solution of them is beyond my powers. Nevertheless, let me venture, trusting in Him who commanded to search the Scriptures.[3] If, then, you agree with this, it will not be difficult to undertake it; for you will quite pardon me, if I am unable sufficiently to explain the exact meaning of the Scripture.

CHAP. V. — THE WOMAN WHO BRINGS FORTH, TO WHOM THE DRAGON IS OPPOSED, THE CHURCH; HER ADORNMENT AND GRACE.

The woman who appeared in heaven clothed with the sun, and crowned with twelve stars, and having the moon for her footstool, and being with child, and travailing in birth, is certainly, according to the accurate interpretation, our mother,[4] O virgins, being a power by herself distinct from her children; whom the prophets, according to the aspect of their subjects, have called sometimes Jerusalem, sometimes a Bride, sometimes Mount Zion, and sometimes the Temple and Tabernacle of God. For she is the power which is desired to give light in the prophet, the Spirit crying to her:[5] "Arise, shine; for thy light is come, and the glory of the Lord is risen upon thee. For, behold, the darkness shall cover the earth, and gross darkness the people: but the Lord shall arise upon thee, and His glory shall be seen upon thee. And the Gentiles shall come to thy light, and kings to the brightness of thy rising. Lift up thine eyes round about, and see; all they gather themselves together, they come to thee: thy sons shall come from far, and thy daughters shall be nursed at thy side." It is the Church whose children shall come to her with all speed after the resurrection, running to her from all quarters. She rejoices receiving the light which never goes down, and clothed with the brightness of the Word as with a robe. For with what other more precious or honourable ornament was it becoming that the queen should be adorned, to be led as a Bride to the Lord, when she had received a garment of light, and therefore was called by the Father? Come, then, let us go forward in our discourse, and look upon this marvellous woman as upon virgins prepared for a marriage, pure and undefiled, perfect and radiating a permanent beauty, wanting nothing of the brightness of light; and instead of a dress, clothed with light itself; and instead of precious stones, her head adorned with shining stars. For instead of the clothing which we have, she had light; and for gold and brilliant stones, she had stars; but stars not such as those which are set in the invisible heaven, but better and more resplendent, so that these may rather be considered as their images and likenesses.

CHAP. VI. — THE WORKS OF THE CHURCH, THE BRINGING FORTH OF CHILDREN IN BAPTISM; THE MOON IN BAPTISM, THE FULL MOON OF CHRIST'S PASSION.

Now the statement that she stands upon the moon, as I consider, denotes the faith of those who are cleansed from corruption in the laver

---

[1] The same word in the text which is translated wind: πνεῦμα. The play upon the word cannot be preserved in the translation. — TR.
[2] Rev. xii. 1-6.
[3] St. John v. 39.

[4] [i.e., the Church. See p. 337, note 4, infra.]
[5] Isa. lx. 1-4.

of regeneration, because the light of the moon has more resemblance to tepid water, and all moist substance is dependent upon her. The Church, then, stands upon our faith and adoption, under the figure of the moon, until the fulness of the nations come in, labouring and bringing forth natural men as spiritual men ; for which reason too she is a mother. For just as a woman receiving the unformed seed of a man, within a certain time brings forth a perfect man, in the same way, one should say, does the Church conceive those who flee to the Word, and, forming them according to the likeness and form of Christ, after a certain time produce them as citizens of that blessed state. Whence it is necessary that she should stand upon the laver, bringing forth those who are washed in it. And in this way the power which she has in connection with the laver is called the moon,[1] because the regenerate shine being renewed with a new ray,[2] that is, a new light. Whence, also, they are by a descriptive term called newly-enlightened ;[3] the moon ever showing forth anew to them the spiritual full moon, namely, the period and the memorial of the passion, until the glory and the perfect light of the great day arise.

CHAP. VII. — THE CHILD OF THE WOMAN IN THE APOCALYPSE NOT CHRIST, BUT THE FAITHFUL WHO ARE BORN IN THE LAVER.

If any one, for there is no difficulty in speaking distinctly, should be vexed, and reply to what we have said : " But how, O virgins, can this explanation seem to you to be according to the mind of Scripture, when the Apocalypse plainly defines that the Church brings forth a male, while you teach that her labour pains have their fulfilment in those who are washed in the laver?" We will answer, But, O faultfinder, not even to you will it be possible to show that Christ Himself[4] is the one who is born. For long before the Apocalypse, the mystery of the Incarnation of the Word was fulfilled. And John speaks concerning things present and things to come. But Christ, long ago conceived, was not caught up to the throne of God when He was brought forth, from fear of the serpent injuring Him. But for this was He begotten, and Himself came down from the throne of the Father, that He should remain and subdue the dragon who made an assault upon the flesh. So that you also must confess that the Church labours and gives birth to those who are baptized.

As the spirit says somewhere in Isaiah :[5] " Before she travailed, she brought forth ; before her pain came, she was delivered of a man-child. Who hath heard such a thing? who hath seen such things? Shall the earth be made to bring forth in one day? or shall a nation be born at once? for as soon as Zion travailed, she brought forth her children."[6] From whom did he flee? Surely from the dragon, that the spiritual Zion might bear a masculine people, who should come back from the passions and weakness of women to the unity of the Lord, and grow strong in manly virtue.

CHAP. VIII. — THE FAITHFUL IN BAPTISM MALES, CONFIGURED TO CHRIST ; THE SAINTS THEMSELVES CHRISTS.

Let us then go over the ground again from the beginning, until we come in course to the end, explaining what we have said. Consider if the passage seems to you to be explained to your mind. For I think that the Church is here said to give birth to a male ; since the enlightened[7] receive the features, and the image, and the manliness of Christ, the likeness of the form of the Word being stamped upon them, and begotten in them by a true knowledge and faith, so that in each one Christ is spiritually born. And, therefore, the Church swells and travails in birth until Christ is formed in us,[8] so that each of the saints, by partaking of Christ, has been born a Christ. According to which meaning it is said in a certain scripture,[9] " Touch not mine anointed,[10] and do my prophets no harm," as though those who were baptized into Christ had been made Christs[11] by communication of the Spirit, the Church contributing here their clearness and transformation into the image of the Word. And Paul confirms this, teaching it plainly, where he says :[12] " For this cause I bow my knees unto the Father of our Lord Jesus Christ, of whom the whole family in heaven and earth is named, that He would grant you, according to the riches of His glory, to be strengthened with might by His Spirit in the inner man ; that Christ may dwell in your hearts by faith." For it is necessary that the word of truth should be imprinted and stamped upon the souls of the regenerate.

CHAP. IX. — THE SON OF GOD, WHO EVER IS, IS TO-DAY BEGOTTEN IN THE MINDS AND SENSE OF THE FAITHFUL.

Now, in perfect agreement and correspondence with what has been said, seems to be this

---

1 σελήνη.
2 σέλας.
3 νεοφώτιστοι.
4 It is hardly necessary to observe, that amid many interpretations of the passage, this which Methodius condemns is probably the true one, as it is certainly the most natural. — Tr. [It is certainly worth observing, that Methodius has on his side a strong following among the ancients; the interpretation the translator favours having little support save among modern defenders of the late pontiff's bull *Ineffabilis.* Elucidation II.]

5 Isa. lxvi. 7, 8.
6 In the LXX. " a male."
7 The baptized.
8 Gal iv. 19.
9 Ps. cv. 15.
10 χριστῶν.
11 Anointed.
12 Eph. iii. 14–17.

which was spoken by the Father from above to Christ when He came to be baptized in the water of the Jordan, "Thou art my son: this day have I begotten thee;"[1] for it is to be remarked that He was declared to be His Son unconditionally, and without regard to time; for He says "Thou art," and not "Thou hast become," showing that He had neither recently attained to the relation of Son, nor again, having begun before, after this had an end, but having been previously begotten,[2] that He was to be, and was the same. But the expression, "This day have I begotten thee," signifies that He willed that He who existed before the ages in heaven should be begotten on the earth — that is, that He who was before unknown should be made known. Now, certainly, Christ has never yet been born in those men who have never perceived the manifold wisdom of God — that is, has never been known, has never been manifested, has never appeared to them. But if these also should perceive the mystery of grace, then in them too, when they were converted and believed, He would be born in knowledge and understanding. Therefore from hence the Church is fitly said to form and beget the male Word in those who are cleansed.[3] So far I have spoken according to my ability concerning the travail of the Church; and here we must change to the subject of the dragon and the other matters. Let us endeavour, then, to explain it in some measure, not deterred by the greatness of the obscurity of the Scripture; and if anything difficult comes to be considered, I will again help you to cross it like a river.

CHAP. X. — THE DRAGON, THE DEVIL; THE STARS STRUCK FROM HEAVEN BY THE TAIL OF THE DRAGON, HERETICS; THE NUMBERS OF THE TRINITY, THAT IS, THE PERSONS NUMBERED; ERRORS CONCERNING THEM.

The dragon, which is great, and red, and cunning, and manifold, and seven-headed, and horned, and draws down the third part of the stars, and stands ready to devour the child of the woman who is travailing, is the devil, who lies in wait to destroy the Christ-accepted mind of the baptized, and the image and clear features of the Word which had been brought forth in them. But he misses and fails of his prey, the regenerate being caught up on high to the throne of God — that is, the mind of those who are renovated is lifted up around the divine seat and the basis of truth against which there is no stumbling, being taught to look upon and regard

the things which are there, so that it may not be deceived by the dragon weighing them down. For it is not allowed to him to destroy those whose thoughts and looks are upwards. And the stars, which the dragon touched with the end of his tail, and drew them down to earth, are the bodies of heresies; for we must say that the stars, which are dark, obscure, and falling, are the assemblies of the heterodox; since they, too, wish to be acquainted with the heavenly ones, and to have believed in Christ, and to have the seat of their soul in heaven, and to come near to the stars as children of light. But they are dragged down, being shaken out by the folds of the dragon, because they did not remain within the triangular forms of godliness, falling away from it with respect to an orthodox service. Whence also they are called the third part of the stars, as having gone astray with regard to one of the three Persons of the Trinity. As when they say, like Sabellios, that the Almighty Person of the Father Himself suffered;[4] or as when they say, like Artemas, that the Person of the Son was born and manifested only in appearance;[5] or when they contend, like the Ebionites, that the prophets spoke of the Person of the Spirit, of their own motion. For of Marcion and Valentinus, and those about Elkesaios and others, it is better not even to make mention.

CHAP. XI. — THE WOMAN WITH THE MALE CHILD IN THE WILDERNESS THE CHURCH; THE WILDERNESS BELONGS TO VIRGINS AND SAINTS; THE PERFECTION OF NUMBERS AND MYSTERIES; THE EQUALITY AND PERFECTION OF THE NUMBER SIX; THE NUMBER SIX RELATED TO CHRIST; FROM THIS NUMBER, TOO, THE CREATION AND HARMONY OF THE WORLD COMPLETED.

Now she who brings forth, and has brought forth, the masculine Word in the hearts of the faithful, and who passed, undefiled and uninjured by the wrath of the beast, into the wilderness, is, as we have explained, our mother the Church. And the wilderness into which she comes, and is nourished for a thousand two hundred and sixty days, which is truly waste and unfruitful of evils, and barren of corruption, and difficult of access and of transit to the multitude; but fruitful and abounding in pasture, and blooming and easy of access to the holy, and full of wisdom, and productive of life, is this most lovely, and beautifully wooded and well-watered abode of Arete.[6] Here the south wind awakes, and the north wind blows, and the spices flow out,[7] and all things are filled with refreshing dews, and crowned with the unfading plants of immortal

---

[1] Ps. ii. 7.
[2] Certain phrases like this have led to the opinion that Methodius was inclined to Arianism. There is no ground for the supposition. In the writer's mind, as is clear from the previous statements, the previous generation was eternal. — TR.
[3] In the baptismal font.

[4] Patripassianism: nearly the same as Sabellianism. — TR.
[5] Δοκήσει, hence Docetæ. — TR.
[6] Virtue.
[7] Cant. iv. 16.

life; in which we now gather flowers, and weave with sacred fingers the purple and glorious crown of virginity for the queen. For the Bride of the Word is adorned with the fruits of virtue. And the thousand two hundred and sixty days that we are staying here, O virgins, is the accurate and perfect understanding concerning the Father, and the Son, and the Spirit, in which our mother increases, and rejoices, and exults throughout this time, until the restitution of the new dispensation, when, coming into the assembly in the heavens, she will no longer contemplate the I AM through the means of *human* knowledge, but will clearly behold entering in together with Christ. For a thousand,[1] consisting of a hundred multiplied by ten, embraces a full and perfect number, and is a symbol of the Father Himself, who made the universe by Himself, and rules all things for Himself. Two hundred embraces two perfect numbers united together, and is the symbol of the Holy Spirit, since He is the Author of our knowledge of the Son and the Father. But sixty has the number six multiplied by ten, and is a symbol of Christ, because the number six proceeding[2] from unity is composed of its proper parts, so that nothing in it is wanting or redundant, and is complete when resolved into its parts. Thus it is necessary that the number six, when it is divided into even parts by even parts, should again make up the same quantity from its separated segments.[3] For, first, if divided equally, it makes three; then, if divided into three parts, it makes two; and again, if divided by six, it makes one, and is again collected into itself. For when divided into twice three, and three times two, and six times one, when the three and the two and the one are put together, they complete the six again. But everything is of necessity perfect which neither needs anything else in order to its completion, nor has anything over. Of the other numbers, some are more than perfect, as twelve. For the half of it is six, and the third four, and the fourth three, and the sixth two, and the twelfth one. The numbers into which it can be divided, when put together, exceed twelve, this number not having preserved itself equal to its parts, like the number six. And those which are imperfect, are numbers like eight. For the half of it is four, and the fourth two, and the eighth one. Now the numbers into which it is divided, when put together, make seven, and one is wanting to its completion, not being in all points harmonious with itself, like six, which has reference to the Son of God, who came from the fulness of the

Godhead into a human life. For having emptied Himself,[4] and taken upon Him the form of a slave, He was restored again to His former perfection and dignity. For He being humbled, and apparently degraded, was restored again from His humiliation and degradation to His former completeness and greatness, having never been diminished from His essential perfection.

Moreover, it is evident that the creation of the world was accomplished in harmony with this number, God having made heaven and earth, and the things which are in them, in six days; the word of creative power containing the number six, in accordance with which the Trinity is the maker of bodies. For length, and breadth, and depth make up a body. And the number six is composed of triangles. On these subjects, however, there is not sufficient time at present to enlarge with accuracy, for fear of letting the main subject slip, in considering that which is secondary.

CHAP. XII. — VIRGINS ARE CALLED TO THE IMITATION OF THE CHURCH IN THE WILDERNESS OVERCOMING THE DRAGON.

The Church, then, coming hither into this wilderness, a place unproductive of evils, is nourished, flying on the heavenward wings of virginity, which the Word called the "wings of a great eagle,"[5] having conquered the serpent, and driven away from her full moon the wintry clouds. It is for the sake of these things, meanwhile, that all these discourses are held, teaching us, O fair virgins, to imitate according to our strength our mother, and not to be troubled by the pains and changes and afflictions of life, that you may enter in exulting with her into the bride-chamber, showing your lamps. Do not, therefore, lose courage on account of the schemes and slanders of the beast, but bravely prepare for the battle, armed with the helmet of salvation,[6] and the breastplate, and the greaves. For you will bring upon him an immense consternation when you attack him with great advantage and courage; nor will he at all resist, seeing his adversaries set in array by One more powerful; but the many-headed and many-faced beast will immediately allow you to carry off the spoils of the seven contests: —

> " Lion in front, but dragon all behind,
> And in the midst a she-goat breathing forth
> Profuse the violence of flaming fire.
> Her slew Bellerophon in truth. And this
> Slew Christ the King; for many she destroyed,
> Nor could they bear the fetid foam which burst
> From out the fountain of her horrid jaws; "[7]

unless Christ had first weakened and overcome

---

[1] Methodius is not the first or the last who has sought to explore the mystery of numbers. An interesting and profound examination of the subject will be found in Bähr's *Symbolik;* also in Delitzsch's *Bib. Psychology.* — TR. [*On the Six Days' Work,* p. 71, translation, Edinburgh, 1875.]
[2] i.e., in a regular arithmetical progression.
[3] i.e., its divisors or dividends.

[4] " Make Himself of no reputation." — E. T., Phil. ii. 7.
[5] Ezek. xvii. 3.
[6] Eph. vi. 17.
[7] Hom., *Il.,* vi. 181.

her, making her powerless and contemptible before us.

CHAP. XIII. — THE SEVEN CROWNS OF THE BEAST TO BE TAKEN AWAY BY VICTORIOUS CHASTITY; THE TEN CROWNS OF THE DRAGON, THE VICES OPPOSED TO THE DECALOGUE; THE OPINION OF FATE THE GREATEST EVIL.

Therefore, taking to you a masculine and sober mind, oppose your armour to the swelling beast, and do not at all give way, nor be troubled because of his fury. For you will have immense glory if you overcome him, and take away the seven crowns which are upon him, on account of which we have to struggle and wrestle, according to our teacher Paul. For she who having first overcome the devil, and destroyed his seven heads, becomes possessed of the seven crowns of virtue, having gone through the seven great struggles of chastity. For incontinence and luxury is a head of the dragon; and whoever bruises this is wreathed with the crown of temperance. Cowardice and weakness is also a head; and he who treads upon this carries off the crown of martyrdom. Unbelief and folly, and other similar fruits of wickedness, is another head; and he who has overcome these and destroyed them carries off the honours connected with them, the power of the dragon being in many ways rooted up. Moreover, the ten horns and stings which he was said to have upon his heads are the ten opposites, O virgins, to the Decalogue, by which he was accustomed to gore and cast down the souls of many imagining and contriving things in opposition to the law, "Thou shalt love the Lord thy God,"[1] and to the other precepts which follow. Consider now the fiery and bitter horn of fornication, by which he casts down the incontinent; consider adultery, consider falsehood, covetousness, theft, and the other sister and related vices, which flourish by nature around his murderous heads, which if you root out with the aid of Christ, you will receive, as it were, divine heads, and will bloom with the crowns gained from the dragon. For it is our duty to prefer and to set forward the best things, who have received, above the earth-born, a commanding and voluntary mind, and one free from all necessity, so as to make choice like masters of the things which please us, not being in bondage to fate or fortune. And so no man would be master of himself and good, unless selecting the human example of Christ, and bringing himself to the likeness of Him, he should imitate Him in his manner of life. For of all evils the greatest which is implanted in many is that which refers the causes of sins to the motions of the stars, and says that our life is guided by the ne-

cessities of fate, as those say who study the stars, with much insolence. For they, trusting more in guessing than in prudence, that is, in something between truth and falsehood, go far astray from the sight of things as they are. Whence, if you permit me, O Arete, now that I have completed the discourse which you, my mistress, appointed to be spoken, I will endeavour, with your assistance and favour, to examine carefully the position of those who are offended, and deny that we speak the truth, when we say that man is possessed of free-will, and prove that

"They perish self-destroyed,
By their own fault,"[2]

choosing the pleasant in preference to the expedient.

ARETE. I do permit you and assist you; for your discourse will be perfectly adorned when you have added this to it.

CHAP. XIV. — THE DOCTRINE OF MATHEMATICIANS NOT WHOLLY TO BE DESPISED, WHEN THEY ARE CONCERNED ABOUT THE KNOWLEDGE OF THE STARS; THE TWELVE SIGNS OF THE ZODIAC MYTHICAL NAMES.

THEKLA. Resuming then, let us first lay bare, in speaking of those things according to our power, the imposture of those who boast as though they alone had comprehended from what forms the heaven is arranged, in accordance with the hypothesis of the Chaldeans and Egyptians. For they say that the circumference of the world is likened to the turnings of a well-rounded globe, the earth having a central point. For its outline being spherical, it is necessary, they say, since there are the same distances of the parts, that the earth should be the centre of the universe, around which, as being older, the heaven is whirling. For if a circumference is described from the central point, which seems to be a circle, — for it is impossible for a circle to be described without a point, and it is impossible for a circle to be without a point, — surely the earth consisted before all, they say, in a state of chaos and disorganization. Now certainly the wretched ones were overwhelmed in the chaos of error, " because that, when they knew God, they glorified Him not as God, neither were thankful; but became vain in their imaginations, and their foolish heart was darkened;"[3] and their wise men said that nothing earth-born was more honourable or more ancient than the Olympians. Whence they are not mere children who know Christ, like the Greeks, who, burying the truth in fables and fictions, rather than in artistic words, ascribing human calamities to the heavens, are not ashamed to describe the circumfer-

---

[1] Deut. vi. 5.

[2] Hom., *Od.*, i. 7.
[3] Rom. i. 21.

ence of the world by geometrical theorems and figures, and explain that the heaven is adorned with the images of birds and of animals that live in water and on dry land, and that the qualities of the stars were made from the calamities of the men of old, so that the movements of the planets, in their opinion, depended upon the same kind of bodies. And they say that the stars revolve around the nature of the twelve signs of the Zodiac, being drawn along by the passage of the circle of the Zodiac, so that through their intermingling they see the things which happen to many, according to their conjunctions and departures, their rising and setting.

For the whole heaven being spherical, and having the earth for its central point, as they think,[1] because all the straight lines from the circumference falling upon the earth are equal to one another, holds back from the circles which surround it, of which the meridian is the greatest; and the second, which divides it into two equal parts, is the horizon; and the third, which separates these, the equinoctial; and on each side of this the two tropics, the summer and the winter — the one on the north, and the other on the south. Beyond is that which is called the axis, around which are the greater and lesser Bears, and beyond them is the tropic. And the Bears, turning about themselves, and weighing upon the axis, which passes through the poles, produce the motion of the whole world, having their heads against each other's loins, and being untouched by our horizon.

Then they say that the Zodiac touches all the circles, making its movements diagonally, and that there are in it a number of signs, which are called the twelve signs of the Zodiac, beginning with the Ram, and going on to the Fishes, which, they say, were so determined from mythical causes; saying that it was the Ram that conveyed Helle, the daughter of Athamas, and her brother Phryxos into Scythia; and that the head of the Ox is in honour of Zeus, who, in the form of a Bull, carried over Europe into Crete; and they say the circle called the Galaxy, or milky way, which reaches from the Fishes to the Ram, was poured forth for Herakles from the breasts of Hera, by the commands of Zeus. And thus, according to them, there was no natal destiny before Europe or Phryxos, and the Dioscuroi,[2] and the other signs of the Zodiac, which were placed among the constellations, from men and beasts. But our ancestors lived without destiny. Let us endeavour now to crush falsehood, like

physicians, taking its edge off, and quenching it with the healing medicine of words, here considering the truth.

CHAP. XV. — ARGUMENTS FROM THE NOVELTY OF FATE AND GENERATION; THAT GOLDEN AGE, EARLY MEN; SOLID ARGUMENTS AGAINST THE MATHEMATICIANS.

If it were better, O wretched ones, that man should be subject to *the star of* his birth, than that he should not, why was not his generation and birth from the very time when the race of man began to be? And if it was, what is the need of those which had lately been placed among the stars, of the Lion, the Crab, the Twins, the Virgin, the Bull, the Balance, the Scorpion, the Ram, the Archer, the Fishes, the Goat, the Watercarrier, Perseus, Cassiopeia, Cepheus, Pegasus, Hydra, the Raven, the Cup, the Lyre, the Dragon, and others, from which you introduce, by your instructions, many to the knowledge of mathematics, or, rather, to a knowledge which is anathema?[3] Well, then, either there was generation among those before, and the removal of these *creatures above* was absurd; or else there was not, and God changed human life into a better state and government than that of those who before that lived an inferior life. But the ancients were better than those of the present time; whence theirs was called the golden age. There was then no natal destiny.

If the sun, driving through the circles and passing along the signs of the Zodiac in his annual periods, accomplishes the changes and turnings of the seasons, how did those who were born before the signs of the Zodiac were placed among the stars, and the heaven was adorned with them, continue to exist, when summer, autumn, winter, and spring, were not as yet separated from each other, by means of which the body is increased and strengthened? But they did exist, and were longer lived and stronger than those who live now, since God then disposed the seasons in the same manner. The heaven was not then diversified by such shapes.

If the sun and the moon and the other stars were made for the division and protection of the members of the time,[4] and for the adornment of the heaven, and the changes of the seasons, they are divine, and better than men; for these must needs pass a better life, and a blessed and peaceful one, and one which far exceeds our own life in righteousness and virtue, observing a motion which is well-ordered and happy. But if they are the causes of the calamities and mischief of mortals, and busy themselves

---

[1] ["As they think." Had Methodius any leaning to Pythagoras and his school? To "science" the world owes its rejection of the true theory of the universe for two thousand years, till Copernicus, a Christian priest, broke that spell. Could the Christian Fathers know more than science taught them? Methodius hints it.]

[2] Castor and Pollux.

[3] We cannot preserve the play upon words of the original. There it is — μαθηματικήν and καταθεματικήν. — Tr.

[4] Gen. i. 14, etc.

in working the lasciviousness, and the changes and vicissitudes of life, then they are more miserable than men, looking upon the earth, and their weak and lawless actions, and doing nothing better than men, if at least our life depends upon their revolutions and movements.

CHAP. XVI. — SEVERAL OTHER THINGS TURNED AGAINST THE SAME MATHEMATICIANS.

If no action is performed without a previous desire, and there is no desire without a want, yet the Divine Being has no wants, and therefore has no conception of evil. And if the nature of the stars be nearer in order to that of God, being better than the virtue of the best men, then the stars also are neither productive of evil, nor in want.

And besides, every one of those who are persuaded that the sun and moon and stars are divine, will allow that they are far removed from evil, and incapable of human actions which spring from the sense of pleasure and pain; for such abominable desires are unsuitable to heavenly beings. But if they are by nature exempt from these, and in no want of anything, how should they be the causes to men of those things which they do not will themselves, and from which they are exempt?

Now those who decide that man is not possessed of free-will, and affirm that he is governed by the unavoidable necessities of fate, and her unwritten commands, are guilty of impiety towards God Himself, making Him out to be the cause and author of human evils. For if He harmoniously orders the whole circular motion of the stars, with a wisdom which man can neither express nor comprehend, directing the course of the universe; and the stars produce the qualities of virtue and vice in human life, dragging men to these things by the chains of necessity; then they declare God to be the Cause and Giver of evils. But God is the cause of injury to no one; therefore fate [1] is not the cause of all things.

Whoever has the least intelligence will confess that God is good, righteous, wise, true, helpful, not the cause of evils, free from passion, and everything of that kind. And if the righteous be better than the unrighteous, and unrighteousness be abominable to them, God, being righteous, rejoices in righteousness, and unrighteousness is hateful to Him, being opposed and hostile to righteousness. Therefore God is not the author of unrighteousness.

If that which profits is altogether good, and temperance is profitable to one's house and life and friends, then temperance is good. And if

temperance be in its nature good, and licentiousness be opposed to temperance, and that which is opposed to good be evil, then licentiousness is evil. And if licentiousness be in its nature evil, and out of licentiousness come adulteries, thefts, quarrels, and murders, then a licentious life is in its nature evil. But the Divine Being is not by nature implicated in evils. Therefore our birth is not the cause of these things.

If the temperate are better than the incontinent, and incontinence is abominable to them, and God rejoices in temperance, being free from the knowledge of passions, then incontinence is hateful also to God. Moreover, that the action which is in accordance with temperance, being a virtue, is better than that which is in accordance with incontinence, which is a vice, we may learn from kings and rulers, and commanders, and women, and children, and citizens, and masters, and servants, and pedagogues, and teachers; for each of these is useful to himself and to the public when he is temperate; but when he is licentious he is injurious to himself and to the public. And if there be any difference between a filthy man and a noble man, a licentious and a temperate; and if the character of the noble and the temperate be the better, and that of the opposite the worse; and if those of the better character be near to God and His friends, and those of the worse be far from Him and His enemies, those who believe in fate make no distinction between righteousness and unrighteousness, between filthiness and nobility, between licentiousness and temperance, which is a contradiction. For if good be opposed to evil, and unrighteousness be evil, and this be opposed to righteousness and righteousness be good, and good be hostile to evil, and evil be unlike to good, then righteousness is different from unrighteousness. And therefore God is not the cause of evils, nor does He rejoice in evils. Nor does reason commend them, being good. If, then, any are evil, they are evil in accordance with the wants *and desires* of their minds, and not by necessity.

"They perish self-destroyed,
By their own fault." [2]

If destiny [3] leads one on to kill a man, and to stain his hands with murder, and the law forbids this, punishing criminals, and by threats restrains the decrees of destiny, such as committing injustice, adultery, theft, poisoning, then the law is in opposition to destiny; for those things which destiny appointed the law prohibits, and those things which the law prohibits destiny compels men to do. Hence law is hostile to destiny. But if it be hostile, then lawgivers do

---

[1] γένεσις = birth, i.e., our life is not controlled by the star of our nativity. — TR. [See Hippolytus, vol. v. p. 27, this series.]

[2] Hom., *Od.*, i. 7.

[3] γένεσις = birth, h. the star of man's nativity, h. destiny.

not act in accordance with destiny; for by passing decrees in opposition to destiny they destroy destiny. Either, then, there is destiny and there was no need of laws; or there are laws and they are not in accordance with destiny. But it is impossible that anyone should be born or anything done apart from destiny; for they say it is not lawful for anyone even to move a finger apart from fate. And therefore it was in accordance with destiny that Minos and Dracon, and Lycurgus, and Solon, and Zaleukos were lawgivers and appointed laws, prohibiting adulteries, murders, violence, rape, thefts, as things which neither existed nor took place in accordance with destiny. But if these things were in accordance with destiny, then the laws were not in accordance with destiny. For destiny itself would not be destroyed by itself, cancelling itself, and contending against itself; here appointing laws forbidding adultery and murders, and taking vengeance upon and punishing the wicked, and there producing murders and adulteries. But this is impossible: for nothing is alien and abhorrent to itself, and self-destructive, and at variance with itself. And, therefore, there is no destiny.

If everything in the world falls out in accordance with destiny, and nothing without it, then the law must needs be produced by destiny. But the law destroys destiny, teaching that virtue should be learnt, and diligently performed; and that vice should be avoided, and that it is produced by want of discipline. Therefore there is no destiny.

If destiny makes men to injure one another, and to be injured by one another, what need is there of laws? But if laws are made that they may check the sinful, God having a care for those who are injured, it were better that the evil should not act in accordance with Fate, than that they should be set right, after having acted. But God is good and wise, and does what is best. Therefore there is no fixed destiny.

Either education and habit are the cause of sins, or the passions of the soul, and those desires which arise through the body. But whichever of these be the cause, God is not the cause.

If it is better to be righteous than to be unrighteous, why is not man made so at once from his birth? But if afterwards he is tempered by instruction and laws, that he may become better, he is so tempered as possessing free-will, and not by nature evil.

If the evil are evil in accordance with destiny, by the decrees of Providence, they are not blameworthy and deserving of the punishment which is inflicted by the laws, since they live according to their own nature, and are not capable of being changed.

And, again, if the good, living according to their own proper nature, are praiseworthy, their natal destiny being the cause of their goodness; yet the wicked, living according to their own proper nature, are not blamable in the eye of a righteous judge. For, if we must speak plainly, he who lives according to the nature which belongs to him, in no way sins. For he did not make himself thus, but Fate; and he lives according to its motion, being urged on by unavoidable necessity. Then no one is bad. But some men are bad: and vice is blameworthy, and hostile to God, as reason has shown. But virtue is lovable and praiseworthy, God having appointed a law for the punishment of the wicked. Therefore there is no Fate.

CHAP. XVII. — THE LUST OF THE FLESH AND SPIRIT: VICE AND VIRTUE.

But why do I draw out my discourse to such length, spending the time with arguments, having set forth the things which are most necessary for persuasion, and to gain approval for that which is expedient; and having made manifest to all, by a few words, the inconsistency of their trick, so that it is now possible even for a child to see and perceive their error; and that to do good or evil is in our own power, and not decided by the stars. For there are two motions in us, the lust of the flesh and that of the soul, differing from each other,[1] whence they have received two names, that of virtue and that of vice. And we ought to obey the most noble and most useful leading of virtue, choosing the best in preference to the base. But enough on these points. I must come to the end of my discourse; for I fear, and am ashamed, after these discourses on chastity, that I should be obliged to introduce the opinions of men who study the heavens, or rather who study nonsense, who waste their life with mere conceits, passing it in nothing but fabulous figments. And now may these offerings of ours, composed from the words which are spoken by God, be acceptable to thee, O Arete, my mistress.

EUBOULIOS. How bravely and magnificently, O Gregorion, has Thekla debated!

GREGORION. What, then, would you have said, if you had listened to herself, speaking fluently, and with easy expression, with much grace and pleasure? So that she was admired by every one who attended, her language blossoming with words, as she set forth intelligently. and in fact picturesquely, the subjects on which she spoke, her countenance suffused with the blush of modesty; for she is altogether brilliant in body and soul.

EUBOULIOS. Rightly do you say this, Grego-

---

[1] Gal. v. 17.

rion, and none of these things is false; for I knew her wisdom also from other noble actions, and what sort of things she succeeded in speaking, giving proof of supreme love to Christ; and how glorious she often appeared in meeting the chief conflicts of the martyrs, procuring for herself a zeal equal to her courage, and a strength of body equal to the wisdom of her counsels.

GREGORION. Most truly do you also speak. But let us not waste time; for we shall often be able to discuss these and other subjects. But I must now first relate to you the discourses of the other virgins which followed, as I promised; and chiefly those of Tusiane and Domnina; for these still remain. When, then, Thekla ceased speaking these things, Theopatra said that Arete directed Tusiane to speak; and that she, smiling, passed before her and said.

DISCOURSE IX.— TUSIANE.

CHAP. I. — CHASTITY THE CHIEF ORNAMENT OF THE TRUE TABERNACLE; SEVEN DAYS APPOINTED TO THE JEWS FOR CELEBRATING THE FEAST OF TABERNACLES: WHAT THEY SIGNIFY; THE SUM OF THIS SEPTENARY UNCERTAIN; NOT CLEAR TO ANY ONE WHEN THE CONSUMMATION OF THE WORLD WILL BE; EVEN NOW THE FABRIC OF THE WORLD COMPLETED.

O Arete, thou dearest boast to the lovers of virginity, I also implore thee to afford me thine aid, lest I should be wanting in words, the subject having been so largely and variously handled. Wherefore I ask to be excused exordium and introductions, lest, whilst I delay in embellishments suitable to them, I depart from the subject: so glorious, and honourable, and renowned a thing is virginity.

God, when He appointed to the true Israelites the legal rite of the true feast of the tabernacles, directed, in Leviticus, how they should keep and do honour to the feast; above all things, saying that each one should adorn his tabernacle with chastity. I will add the words themselves of Scripture, from which, without any doubt, it will be shown how agreeable to God, and acceptable to Him, is this ordinance of virginity: "In the fifteenth day of the seventh month, when ye have gathered in the fruit of the land, ye shall keep a feast unto the Lord seven days: on the first day shall be a Sabbath, and on the eighth day shall be a Sabbath. And ye shall take you on the first day the boughs of goodly trees, branches of palm-trees, and the boughs of thick trees, and willows [1] of the brook; and ye shall rejoice before the Lord your God seven days. And ye shall keep it a feast unto the Lord seven days in the

year. It shall be a statute for ever in your generations; ye shall celebrate it in the seventh month. Ye shall dwell in booths seven days; all that are Israelites born shall dwell in booths; that your generations may know that I made the children of Israel to dwell in booths, when I brought them out of Egypt: I am the Lord your God." [2]

Here the Jews, fluttering about the bare letter of Scripture, like drones about the leaves of herbs, but not about flowers and fruits as the bee, fully believe that these words and ordinances were spoken concerning such a tabernacle as they erect; as if God delighted in those trivial adornments which they, preparing, fabricate from trees, not perceiving the wealth of good things to come; whereas these things, being like air and phantom shadows, foretell the resurrection and the putting up of our tabernacle that had fallen upon the earth, which at length, in the seventh thousand of years, resuming again immortal, we shall celebrate the great feast of true tabernacles in the new and indissoluble creation, the fruits of the earth having been gathered in, and men no longer begetting and begotten, but God resting from the works of creation.[3]

For since in six days God made the heaven and the earth, and finished the whole world, and rested on the seventh day from all His works which He had made, and blessed the seventh day and sanctified it,[4] so by a figure in the seventh month, when the fruits of the earth have been gathered in, we are commanded to keep the feast to the Lord, which signifies that, when this world shall be terminated at the seventh thousand years, when God shall have completed the world, He shall rejoice in us.[5] For now to this time all things are created by His all-sufficient will and inconceivable power; the earth still yielding its fruits, and the waters being gathered together in their receptacles; and the light still severed from darkness, and the allotted number of men not yet being complete; and the sun arising to rule the day, and the moon the night; and four-footed creatures, and beasts, and creeping things arising from the earth, and winged creatures, and creatures that swim, from the water. Then, when the appointed times shall have been accomplished, and God shall have ceased to form this creation, in the seventh month, the great resurrection-day, it is commanded that the Feast of our Tabernacles shall be celebrated to the Lord, of which the things said in Leviticus are symbols and figures, which things, carefully investigating, we should con-

---

[2] Lev. xxiii. 39–42.
[3] [Methodius did not adopt the errors of the Chiliasts, but he kept up the succession of witnesses to this primitive idea. Coleridge's remarks on Jeremy Taylor, touching this point, may be worth consulting. *Notes on Old English Divines*, vol. i. p. 218.]
[4] Gen. ii. 1.
[5] Ps. civ. 31.

---

[1] The LXX. adds "And of the Agnos." See note on this tree at the beginning of the treatise, p. 310, note 2.]

sider the naked truth itself, for He saith, "A wise man will hear, and will increase learning; and a man of understanding shall attain unto wise counsels : to understand a proverb, and the interpretation ; the words of the wise, and their dark sayings." [1]

Wherefore let it shame the Jews that they do not perceive the deep things of the Scriptures, thinking that nothing else than outward things are contained in the law and the prophets ; for they, intent upon things earthly, have in greater esteem the riches of the world than the wealth which is of the soul. For since the Scriptures are in this way divided that some of them give the likeness of past events, some of them a type of the future, the miserable men, going back, deal with the figures of the future as if they were already things of the past. As in the instance of the immolation of the Lamb, the mystery of which they regard as solely in remembrance of the deliverance of their fathers from Egypt, when, although the first-born of Egypt were smitten, they themselves were preserved by marking the door-posts of their houses with blood. Nor do they understand that by it also the death of Christ is personified, by whose blood souls made safe and sealed shall be preserved from wrath in the burning of the world ; whilst the first-born, the sons of Satan, shall be destroyed with an utter destruction by the avenging angels, who shall reverence the seal of the Blood impressed upon the former.

CHAP. II. — FIGURE, IMAGE, TRUTH : LAW, GRACE, GLORY ; MAN CREATED IMMORTAL : DEATH BROUGHT IN BY DESTRUCTIVE SIN.

And let these things be said for the sake of example, showing that the Jews have wonderfully fallen from the hope of future good, because they consider things present to be only signs of things already accomplished ; whilst they do not perceive that the figures represent images, and images are the representatives of truth. For the law is indeed the figure and the shadow of an image, that is, of the Gospel ; but the image, namely, the Gospel, is the representative of truth itself. For the men of olden time and the law foretold to us the characteristics of the Church, and the Church represents those of the new dispensation which is to come. Whence we, having received Christ, saying, " I am the truth," [2] know that shadows and figures have ceased ; and we hasten on to the truth, proclaiming its glorious images. For now we know " in part," and as it were " through a glass," [3] since that which is perfect has not yet come to us ; namely, the kingdom of heaven and the resurrection, when

" that which is in part shall be done away." [4] For then will all our tabernacles be firmly set up, when again the body shall rise, with bones again joined and compacted with flesh. Then shall we celebrate truly to the Lord a glad festal-day, when we shall receive eternal tabernacles, no more to perish or be dissolved into the dust of the tomb. Now, our tabernacle was at first fixed in an immoveable state, but was moved by transgression and bent to the earth, God putting an end to sin by means of death, lest man immortal, living a sinner, and sin living in him, should be liable to eternal curse. Wherefore he died, although he had not been created liable to death or corruption, and the soul was separated from the flesh, that sin might perish by death, not being able to live longer in one dead. Whence sin being dead and destroyed, again I shall rise immortal ; and I praise God who by means of death frees His sons from death, and I celebrate lawfully to His honour a festal-day, adorning my tabernacle, that is my flesh, with good works, as there did the five virgins with the five-lighted lamps.

CHAP. III. — HOW EACH ONE OUGHT TO PREPARE HIMSELF FOR THE FUTURE RESURRECTION.

In the first day of the resurrection I am examined whether I bring these things which are commanded, whether I am adorned with virtuous works, whether I am overshadowed by the boughs of chastity. For account the resurrection to be the erection of the tabernacle. Account that the things which are taken for the putting together of the tabernacle are the works of righteousness. I take, therefore, on the first day the things which are set down, that is, on the day in which I stand to be judged, whether I have adorned my tabernacle with the things commanded ; if those things are found on that day which here in time we are commanded to prepare, and there to offer to God. But come, let us consider what follows.

" And ye shall take you," He says, " on the first day the boughs of goodly trees, branches of palm-trees, and the boughs of thick trees, and willows (and the tree of chastity) of the brook ; and ye shall rejoice before the Lord your God." [5] The Jews, uncircumcised in heart, think that the most beautiful fruit of wood is the citron wood, on account of its size ; nor are they ashamed to say that God is worshipped with cedar, to whom not all the quadrupeds of the earth would suffice as a burnt-offering or as incense for burning. And moreover, O hard breasts, if the citron appear beautiful to you, why not the pomegranate, and other fruits of trees, and amongst them

---

[1] Prov. i. 5, 6.
[2] St. John xiv. 16.
[3] 1 Cor. xiii. 12.

[4] 1 Cor. xiii. 10.
[5] Lev. xxiii. 40.

apples, which much surpass the citron? Indeed, in the Song of Songs,[1] Solomon having made mention of all these fruits, passes over in silence the citron only. But this deceives the unwary, for they have not understood that the tree of life[2] which Paradise once bore, now again the Church has produced for all, even the ripe and comely fruit of faith.

Such fruit it is necessary that we bring when we come to the judgment-seat of Christ, on the first day of the feast; for if we are without it we shall not be able to feast with God, nor to have part, according to John,[3] in the first resurrection. For the tree of life is wisdom first begotten of all. "She is a tree of life to them that lay hold upon her," says the prophet;[4] "and happy is every one that retaineth her." "A tree planted by the waterside, that will bring forth his fruit in due season;"[5] that is, learning and charity and discretion are imparted in due time to those who come to the waters of redemption.

He that hath not believed in Christ, nor hath understood that He is the first principle and the tree of life, since he cannot show to God his tabernacle adorned with the most goodly of fruits, how shall he celebrate the feast? How shall he rejoice? Desirest thou to know the goodly fruit of the tree? Consider the words of our Lord Jesus Christ, how pleasant they are beyond the children of men. Good fruit came by Moses, that is the Law, but not so goodly as the Gospel. For the Law is a kind of figure and shadow of things to come, but the Gospel is truth and the grace of life. Pleasant was the fruit of the prophets, but not so pleasant as the fruit of immortality which is plucked from the Gospel.

CHAP. IV. — THE MIND CLEARER WHEN CLEANSED FROM SIN; THE ORNAMENTS OF THE MIND AND THE ORDER OF VIRTUE; CHARITY DEEP AND FULL; CHASTITY THE LAST ORNAMENT OF ALL; THE VERY USE OF MATRIMONY TO BE RESTRAINED.

"And ye shall take you on the first day the boughs of goodly trees, branches of palm-trees."[6] This signifies the exercise of divine discipline, by which the mind that subdues the passions is cleansed and adorned by the sweeping out and ejection from it of sins. For it is necessary to come cleansed and adorned to the feast, arrayed, as by a decorator, in the discipline and exercise of virtue. For the mind being cleansed by laborious exercises from the distracting thoughts which darken it, quickly perceives the truth; as

the widow in the Gospels[7] found the piece of money after she had swept the house and cast out the dirt, that is, the passions which obscure and cloud the mind, which increase in us from our luxuriousness and carelessness.

Whoso, therefore, desires to come to that Feast of Tabernacles, to be numbered with the saints, let him first procure the goodly fruit of faith, then palm branches, that is, attentive meditation upon and study of the Scriptures, afterwards the far-spreading and thickly-leaved branches of charity, which He commands us to take after the palm branches; most fitly calling charity dense boughs, because it is all thick and close and very fruitful, not having anything bare or empty, but all full, both branches and trunks. Such is charity, having no part void or unfruitful. For "though I sell all my goods and give to the poor, and though I yield up my body to the fire, and though I have so great faith that I can remove mountains, and have not charity, I am nothing."[8] Charity, therefore, is a tree the thickest and most fruitful of all, full and abounding, copiously abounding in graces.

After this, what else does He will that we should take? Willow branches; by that figure indicating righteousness, because "the just," according to the prophet, shall spring up "as grass in the midst of the waters, as willows by the watercourses,"[9] flourishing in the word. Lastly, to crown all, it is commanded that the bough of the Agnos tree be brought to decorate the Tabernacle, because it is by its very name the tree of chastity, by which those already named are adorned. Let the wanton now be gone, who, through their love of pleasure, reject chastity. How shall they enter into the feast with Christ who have not adorned their tabernacle with boughs of chastity, that God-making and blessed tree with which all who are hastening to that assembly and nuptial banquet ought to be begirt, and to cover their loins? For come, fair virgins, consider the Scripture itself, and its commands, how the Divine word has assumed chastity to be the crown of those virtues and duties that have been mentioned, showing how becoming and desirable it is for the resurrection, and that without it no one will obtain the promises which we who profess viginity supremely cultivate and offer to the Lord. They also possess it who live chastely with their wives, and do, as it were about the trunk, yield its lowly branches bearing chastity, not being able like us to reach its lofty and mighty boughs, or even to touch them; yet they, too, offer no less truly, although in a less degree, the branches of chas-

[1] Cant. iv. 13.
[2] Gen. ii. 9.
[3] Rev. xx. 6.
[4] Prov. iii. 18.
[5] Ps. i. 3.
[6] Lev. xxiii. 40.

[7] Luke xv. 8.
[8] 1 Cor. xiii. 2, 3. Quoted from memory and in meaning, not verbally. — Tr.
[9] Isa. xliv. 4. The reading of the LXX.

tity.[1] But those who are goaded on by their lusts, although they do not commit fornication, yet who, even in the things which are permitted with a lawful wife, through the heat of unsubdued concupiscence are excessive in embraces, how shall they celebrate the feast? how shall they rejoice, who have not adorned their tabernacle, that is their flesh, with the boughs of the Agnos, nor have listened to that which has been said; that "they that have wives be as though they had none?"[2]

CHAP. V. — THE MYSTERY OF THE TABERNACLES.

Wherefore, above all other things, I say to those who love contests, and who are strong-minded, that without delay they should honour chastity, as a thing the most useful and glorious. For in the new and indissoluble creation, whoever shall not be found decorated with the boughs of chastity, shall neither obtain rest, because he has not fulfilled the command of God according to the law, nor shall he enter into the land of promise, because he has not previously celebrated the Feast of Tabernacles. For they only who have celebrated the Feast of Tabernacles come to the Holy Land, setting out from those dwellings which are called tabernacles, until they come to enter into the temple and city of God, advancing to a greater and more glorious joy, as the Jewish types indicate. For like as the Israelites, having left the borders of Egypt, first came to the Tabernacles,[3] and from hence, having again set forth, came into the land of promise, so also do we. For I also, taking my journey, and going forth from the Egypt of this life, came first to the resurrection, which is the true Feast of the Tabernacles, and there having set up my tabernacle, adorned with the fruits of virtue, on the first day of the resurrection, which is the day of judgment, celebrate with Christ the millennium of rest, which is called the seventh day, even the true Sabbath. Then again from thence I, a follower of Jesus, "who hath entered into the heavens,"[4] as they also, after the rest of the Feast of Tabernacles, came into the land of promise, come into the heavens, not continuing to remain in tabernacles — that is, my body not remaining as it was before, but, after the space of a thousand years, changed from a human and corruptible form into angelic size and beauty, where at last we virgins, when the festival of the resurrection is consummated, shall pass from the wonderful place of the tabernacle to greater and better things, ascending into the very house of God above the heavens, as, says the Psalmist, "in the voice of praise and thanksgiving, among such as keep holy day."[5] I, O Arete, my mistress, offer as a gift to thee this robe, adorned according to my ability.

EUBOULIOS. I am much moved, O Gregorion, considering within myself in how great anxiety of mind Domnina must be from the character of the discourses, perplexed in heart as she is, and with good cause, fearing lest she should be at a loss for words, and should speak more feebly than the rest of the virgins, since they have spoken on the subject with such ability and variety. If, therefore, she was evidently moved, come and complete this too; for I wonder if she had anything to say, being the last speaker.

GREGORION. Theopatra told me, Euboulios, that she was greatly moved, but she was not perplexed from want of words. After, therefore, Tusiane had ceased, Arete looked at her and said, Come, my daughter, do thou also deliver a discourse, that our banquet may be quite complete. At this Domnina, blushing, and after a long delay, scarcely looking up, rose to pray, and turning round, invoked Wisdom to be her present helper. And when she had prayed, Theopatra said that suddenly courage came to her, and a certain divine confidence possessed her, and she said:—

DISCOURSE X.—DOMNINA.

CHAP. I. — CHASTITY ALONE AIDS AND EFFECTS THE MOST PRAISEWORTHY GOVERNMENT OF THE SOUL.

O Arete, I also, omitting the long preludes of exordiums, will endeavour according to my ability to enter upon the subject, lest, by delaying upon those matters which are outside the subject in hand, I should speak of them at greater length than their importance would warrant. For I account it a very great part of prudence not to make long speeches, which merely charm the ears, before coming to the main question, but to begin forthwith at the point in debate. So I will begin from thence, for it is time.

Nothing can so much profit a man, O fair virgins, with respect to moral excellence, as chastity; for chastity alone accomplishes and brings it about that the soul should be governed in the noblest and best way, and should be set free, pure from the stains and pollutions of the world. For which reason, when Christ taught us to cultivate it, and showed its unsurpassable beauty, the kingdom of the Evil One was destroyed, who aforetime led captive and enslaved the whole race of men, so that none of the more ancient people pleased the Lord, but all were overcome by errors, since the law was not of itself sufficient to free the human race from

---

[1] [See Jer. Taylor, *Holy Living*, cap. ii. sec. 3, *Works*, vol. i. p. 427, ed. Bohn, 1844. This is a token of antiquity.]
[2] 1 Cor. vii. 29.
[3] In Hebrew, *Succoth*. Num. xxxiii. 5.
[4] Heb. iv. 14.

[5] Ps. xlii. 4.

corruption, until virginity, succeeding the law, governed men by the precepts of Christ. Nor truly had the first men so often run headlong into combats and slaughter, into lust and idolatry, if the righteousness that is by the law had been to them sufficient for salvation. Now truly they were then confused by great and frequent calamities ; but from the time when Christ was incarnate, and armed and adorned His flesh with virginity, the savage tyrant who was master of incontinence was taken away, and peace and faith have dominion, men no longer turning so much as before to idolatry.

CHAP. II.— THE ALLEGORY OF THE TREES DE-
    MANDING A KING, IN THE BOOK OF JUDGES,[1]
    EXPLAINED.

But lest I should appear to some to be sophistical, and to conjecture these things from mere probabilities, and to babble, I will bring forward to you, O virgins, from the Old Testament, written prophecy from the Book of Judges, to show that I speak the truth, where the future reign of chastity was already clearly foretold. For we read : " The trees went forth on a time to anoint a king over them ; and they said unto the olive-tree, Reign thou over us. But the olive-tree said unto them, Should I leave my fatness, wherewith by me they honour God and man, and go to be promoted over the trees? And the trees said to the fig-tree, Come thou, and reign over us. But the fig-tree said unto them, Should I forsake my sweetness, and my good fruit, and go to be promoted over the trees? Then said the trees unto the vine, Come thou, and reign over us. And the vine said unto them, Should I leave my wine, which cheereth God and man, and go to be promoted over the trees? Then said all the trees unto the bramble, Come thou, and reign over us. And the bramble said unto the trees, If in truth ye anoint me king over you, then come and put your trust in my shadow ; and if not, let fire come out of the bramble, and devour the cedars of Lebanon."

Now, that these things are not said of trees growing out of the earth, is clear. For inanimate trees cannot be assembled in council to choose a king, inasmuch as they are firmly fixed by deep roots to the earth. But altogether are these things narrated concerning souls which, before the incarnation of Christ, too deeply luxuriating in transgressions, approach to God as suppliants, and ask His mercy, and that they may be governed by His pity and compassion, which Scripture expresses under the figure of the olive, because oil is of great advantage to our bodies, and takes away our fatigues and ailments, and affords light. For all lamp-light

increases when nourished by oil. So also the mercies of God entirely dissolve death, and assist the human race, and nourish the light of the heart.[2] And consider whether the laws, from the first created man until Christ in succession, were not set forth in these words by the Scripture by figments, in opposition to which the devil has deceived the human race. And it has likened the fig-tree to the command given to man in paradise, because, when he was deceived, he covered his nakedness with the leaves of a fig-tree ;[3] and the vine to the precept given to Noah at the time of the deluge, because, when overpowered by wine, he was mocked.[4] The olive signifies the law given to Moses in the desert, because the prophetic grace, the holy oil, had failed from their inheritance when they broke the law. Lastly, the bramble not inaptly refers to the law which was given to the apostles for the salvation of the world ; because by their instruction we have been taught virginity, of which alone the devil has not been able to make a deceptive image. For which cause, also, four Gospels have been given, because God has four times given the Gospel[5] to the human race, and has instructed them by four laws, the times of which are clearly known by the diversity of the fruits. For the fig-tree, on account of its sweetness and richness, represents the delights of man, which he had in paradise before the fall. Indeed, not rarely, as we shall afterwards show, the Holy Spirit[6] takes the fruit of the fig-tree as an emblem of goodness. But the vine, on account of the gladness produced by wine, and the joy of those who were saved from wrath and from the deluge, signifies the change produced from fear and anxiety into joy.[7] Moreover, the olive, on account of the oil which it produces, indicates the compassion of God, who again, after the deluge, bore patiently when men turned aside to ungodliness, so that He gave them the law and manifested Himself to some, and nourished by oil the light of virtue, now almost extinguished.

CHAP. III.— THE BRAMBLE AND THE AGNOS THE
    SYMBOL OF CHASTITY ; THE FOUR GOSPELS,
    THAT IS, TEACHINGS OR LAWS, INSTRUCTING
    TO SALVATION.

Now the bramble commends chastity, for the bramble and the agnos is the same tree : by some it is called bramble, by others *agnos*.[8]

---

[1] Judg. ix. 8-15.

[2] For this use of heart, *cf.* 2 Cor. iv. 6. — TR. [See Coleridge on Leighton, *Old English Divines*, vol. ii. p. 137.]
[3] Gen. iii. 7.
[4] Gen. ix. 22.
[5] Good news.
[6] Jer. viii. 13.
[7] Joel ii. 22.
[8] Jahn's reading is here followed. [This is a puzzle as well as a parable ; the Seventy give ῥάμνος, which is not = ἄγνος. It spoils the force of Jotham's caustic satire to adopt this conception of our author.]

Perhaps it is because the plant is akin to virginity that it is called bramble and *agnos;* bramble, because of its strength and firmness against pleasures ; agnos, because it always continues chaste. Hence the Scripture relates that Elijah, fleeing from the face of the woman Jezebel,[1] at first came under a bramble, and there, having been heard, received strength and took food ; signifying that to him who flies from the incitements of lust, and from a woman — that is, from pleasure — the tree of chastity is a refuge and a shade, ruling men from the coming of Christ, the chief of virgins. For when the first laws, which were published in the times of Adam and Noah and Moses, were unable to give salvation to man, the evangelical law alone has saved all.

And this is the cause why the fig-tree may be said not to have obtained the kingdom over trees, which, in a spiritual sense, mean men ; and the fig-tree the command, because man desired, even after the fall, again to be subject to the dominion of virtue, and not to be deprived of the immortality of the paradise of pleasure. But, having transgressed, he was rejected and cast far away, as one who could no longer be governed by immortality, nor was capable of receiving it. And the first message to him after the transgression was preached by Noah,[2] to which, if he had applied his mind, he might have been saved from sin ; for in it he promised both happiness and rest from evils, if he gave heed to it with all his might, just as the vine promises to yield wine to those who cultivate it with care and labour. But neither did this law rule mankind, for men did not obey it, although zealously preached by Noah. But, after they began to be surrounded and drowning by the waters, they began to repent, and to promise that they would obey the commandments. Wherefore with scorn they are rejected as subjects ; that is, they are contemptuously told that they cannot be helped by the law ; the Spirit answering them back and reproaching them because they had deserted those men whom God had commanded to help them, and to save them, and make them glad ; such as Noah and those with him. "Even to you, O rebellious," said he, " I come, to bring help to you who are destitute of prudence, and who differ in nothing from dry trees, and who formerly did not believe me when I preached that you ought to flee from present things."

CHAP. IV.—THE LAW USELESS FOR SALVATION ; THE LAST LAW OF CHASTITY UNDER THE FIGURE OF THE BRAMBLE.

And so those men, having been thus rejected from the divine care, and the human race having again given themselves up to error, again God sent forth, by Moses, a law to rule them and recall them to righteousness. But these, thinking fit to bid a long farewell to this law, turned to idolatry. Hence God gave them up to mutual slaughters, to exiles, and captivities, the law itself confessing, as it were, that it could not save them. Therefore, worn out with ills and afflicted, they again promised that they would obey the commandments ; until God, pitying man the fourth time, sent chastity to rule over them, which Scripture consequently called the bramble. And she consuming pleasures threatens besides, that unless all undoubtingly obey her, and truly come to her, she will destroy all with fire, since there will be hereafter no other law or doctrine but judgment and fire. For this reason, man henceforth began to do righteousness, and firmly to believe in God, and to separate himself from the devil. Thus chastity was sent down, as being most useful and helpful to men. For of her alone was the devil unable to forge an imitation to lead men astray, as is the case with the other precepts.

CHAP. V. — THE MALIGNITY OF THE DEVIL AS AN IMITATOR IN ALL THINGS ; TWO KINDS OF FIG-TREES AND VINES.

The fig-tree, as I said, from the sweetness and excellence of its fruit, being taken as a type of the delights of paradise, the devil, having beguiled the man by its imitations, led him captive, persuading him to conceal the nakedness of his body by fig-leaves ; that is, by their friction he excited him to sexual pleasure. Again, those that had been saved from the deluge, he intoxicated with a drink which was an imitation of the vine of spiritual joy ; and again he mocked them, having stripped them of virtue. And what I say will hereafter be more clear.

The enemy, by his power, always imitates[3] the forms of virtue and righteousness, not for the purpose of truly promoting its exercise, but for deception and hypocrisy. For in order that those who fly from death he may entice to death, he is outwardly dyed with the colours of immortality. And hence he wishes to seem a fig-tree or vine, and to produce sweetness and joy, and is " transformed into an angel of light,"[4] ensnaring many by the appearance of piety.

For we find in the Sacred Writings that there are two kinds of fig-trees and vines, " the good figs, very good ; and the evil, very evil ; "[5] " wine that maketh glad the heart of man,"[6] and wine which is the poison of dragons, and the incurable

---

[1] 1 Kings xix. 4.
[2] Gen. v. 29.

[3] [*Diabolus simia Dei*, an idea very common to the Fathers. He is the malignant caricature of the Most High, exulting in the deformity which he gives to his copies. Exod. vii. 11.]
[4] 2 Cor. xi. 14.
[5] Jer. xxiv. 3.
[6] Ps. civ. 15.

venom of asps.[1] But from the time when chastity began to rule over men, the fraud was detected and overcome, Christ, the chief of virgins, overturning it. So both the true fig-tree and the true vine yield fruit after that the power of chastity has laid hold upon all men, as Joel the prophet preaches, saying: "Fear not, O land; be glad and rejoice, for the Lord will do great things. Be not afraid, ye beasts of the field; for the pastures of the wilderness do spring, for the tree beareth her fruit, the fig-tree and the vine do yield their strength. Be glad then, ye children of Zion, and rejoice in the Lord your God, for He hath given you food unto righteousness;"[2] calling the former laws the vine and the fig, trees bearing fruit unto righteousness for the children of the spiritual Zion, which bore fruit after the incarnation of the Word, when chastity ruled over us, when formerly, on account of sin and much error, they had checked and destroyed their buds. For the true vine and the true fig-tree were not able to yield such nourishment to us as would be profitable for life, whilst as yet the false fig-tree, variously adorned for the purpose of fraud, flourished. But when the Lord dried up the false branches, the imitations of the true branches, uttering the sentence against the bitter fig-tree, "Let no fruit grow on thee henceforward for ever,"[3] then those which were truly fruit-bearing trees flourished and yielded food unto righteousness.

The vine, and that not in a few places, refers to the Lord Himself,[4] and the fig-tree to the Holy Spirit, as the Lord "maketh glad the hearts of men," and the Spirit healeth them. And therefore Hezekiah is commanded[5] first to make a plaster with a lump of figs — that is, the fruit of the Spirit — that he may be healed — that is, according to the apostle — by love; for he says, "The fruit of the Spirit is love, joy, peace, longsuffering, gentleness, goodness, faith, meekness, temperance;"[6] which, on account of their great pleasantness, the prophet calls figs. Micah also says, "They shall sit every man under his vine and under his fig-tree; and none shall make them afraid."[7] Now it is certain that those who have taken refuge and rested under the Spirit, and under the shadow of the Word, shall not be alarmed, nor frightened by him who troubles the hearts of men.

CHAP. VI. — THE MYSTERY OF THE VISION OF ZECHARIAH.

Moreover, Zechariah shows that the olive shadows forth the law of Moses, speaking thus:

"And the angel that talked with me came again, and waked me, as a man that is wakened out of his sleep, and said unto me, What seest thou? And I said, I have looked, and behold a candlestick all of gold, with a bowl upon the top of it. . . . And two olive-trees by it, one upon the right side of the bowl, and the other upon the left side thereof."[8] And after a few words, the prophet, asking what are the olives on the right and left of the candlestick, and what the two olive-boughs in the hands of the two pipes, the angel answered and said: "These are the two sons of fruitfulness[9] which stand by the Lord of the whole earth," signifying the two first-born virtues that are waiting upon God, which, in His dwelling, supply around the wick, through the boughs, the spiritual oil of God, that man may have the light of divine knowledge. But the two boughs of the two olives are the law and the prophets, around, as it were, the lot[10] of the inheritance, of which Christ and the Holy Spirit are the authors, we ourselves meanwhile not being able to take the whole fruit and the greatness of these plants, before chastity began to rule the world, but only their boughs — to wit, the law and the prophets — did we formerly cultivate, and those moderately, often letting them slip. For who was ever able to receive Christ or the Spirit, unless he first purified himself? For the exercise which prepares the soul from childhood for desirable and delectable glory, and carries this grace safely thither with ease, and from small toils raises up mighty hopes, is chastity, which gives immortality to our bodies; which it becomes all men willingly to prefer in honour and to praise above all things; some, that by its means they may be betrothed to the Word, practising virginity; and others, that by it they may be freed from the curse, "Dust thou art, and unto dust shalt thou return."[11]

This, O Arete, is the discourse on virginity which you required of me, accomplished according to my ability; which I pray, O mistress, although it is mediocre and short, that thou wilt receive with kindness from me who was chosen to speak last.

DISCOURSE XI. — ARETE.

CHAP. I. — THE TRUE AND CHASTE VIRGINS FEW; CHASTITY A CONTEST; THEKLA CHIEF OF VIRGINS.

I do accept it, Theopatra related that Arete said, and approve of it all. For it is an excellent thing, even although you had not spoken so clearly, to take up and go through with earnestness those things which have been said, not to

---

[1] Deut. xxxii. 33.
[2] Joel ii. 21-23. The last words of the quotation are from the LXX. version. — TR.
[3] Matt. xxi. 19.
[4] John xv. 1.
[5] 2 Kings xx. 7; Isa. xxxviii. 21.
[6] Gal. v. 22, 23.
[7] Micah iv. 4.

[8] Zech. iv. 1-3.
[9] E. V. "Anointed ones," ver. 14.
[10] σχοίνισμα: same word as that translated "wick." — TR.
[11] Gen. iii. 19.

prepare a sweet entertainment for those who listen, but for correction, recollection, and abstinence. For whoever teaches that chastity is to be preferred and embraced first of all among my pursuits, rightly advises ; which many think that they honour and cultivate, but which few, so to speak, really honour. For it is not one who has studied to restrain his flesh from the pleasure of carnal delight that cultivates chastity, if he do not keep in check the rest of the desires ; but rather he dishonours it, and that in no small degree, by base lusts, exchanging pleasures for pleasures. Nor if he have strongly resisted the desires of the senses, but is lifted up with vainglory, and from this cause is able to repress the heats of burning lust, and reckon them all as nothing, can he be thought to honour chastity ; for he dishonours it in that he is lifted up with pride, cleansing the outside of the cup and platter, that is, the flesh and the body, but injuring the heart by conceit and ambition. Nor when any one is conceited of riches is he desirous of honouring chastity ; he dishonours it more than all, preferring a little gain to that to which nothing is comparable of those things that are in this life esteemed. For all riches and gold " in respect of it are as a little sand." [1] And neither does he who loves himself above measure, and eagerly considers that which is expedient for himself alone, regardless of the necessities of his neighbour, honour chastity, but he also dishonours it. For he who has repelled from himself charity, mercy, and humanity, is much inferior to those who honourably exercise chastity. Nor is it right, on the one hand, by the use of chastity to keep virginity, and, on the other hand, to pollute the soul by evil deeds and lust ; nor here to profess purity and continence, and there to pollute it by indulgence in vices. Nor, again, here to declare that the things of this world bring no care to himself ; there to be eager in procuring them, and in concern about them. But all the members are to be preserved intact and free from corruption ; not only those which are sexual, but those members also which minister to the service of lusts. For it would be ridiculous to preserve the organs of generation pure, but not the tongue ; or to preserve the tongue, but neither the eyesight, the ears, nor the hands ; or lastly, to preserve these pure, but not the mind, defiling it with pride and anger.

It is altogether necessary for him who has resolved that he will not err from the practice of chastity, to keep all his members and senses clean and under restraint, as is customary with the planks of ships, whose fastenings the shipmasters diligently join together, lest by any means the way and access may lie open for sin

to pour itself into the mind. For great pursuits are liable to great falls, and evil is more opposed to that which is really good than to that which is not good. For many who thought that to repress vehement lascivious desires constituted chastity, neglecting other duties connected with it, failed also in this, and have brought blame [2] upon those endeavouring after it by the right way, as you have proved who are a model in everything, leading a virgin life in deed and word. And now what that is which becomes a virgin state has been described.

And you all in my hearing having sufficiently contended in speaking, I pronounce victors and crown ; but Thekla with a larger and thicker chaplet, as the chief of you, and as having shone with greater lustre than the rest.

CHAP. II. — THEKLA SINGING DECOROUSLY A HYMN, THE REST OF THE VIRGINS SING WITH HER ; JOHN THE BAPTIST A MARTYR TO CHASTITY ; THE CHURCH THE SPOUSE OF GOD, PURE AND VIRGIN.

Theopatra said that Arete having said these things, commanded them all to rise, and, standing under the Agnos, to send up to the Lord in a becoming manner a hymn of thanksgiving ; and that Thekla should begin and should lead the rest. And when they had stood up, she said that Thekla, standing in the midst of the virgins on the right of Arete, decorously sang ; but the rest, standing together in a circle after the manner of a chorus, responded to her : " I keep myself pure for Thee, O Bridegroom, and holding a lighted torch I go to meet Thee." [3]

THEKLA. 1. From above, O virgins, the sound of a noise that wakes the dead has come, bidding us all to meet the Bridegroom in white robes, and with torches towards the east. Arise, before the King enters within the gates.

CHORUS. I keep myself pure for Thee, O Bridegroom, and holding a lighted torch I go to meet Thee.

THEKLA. 2. Fleeing from the sorrowful happiness of mortals, and having despised the luxuriant delights of life and its love, I desire to be protected under Thy life-giving arms, and to behold Thy beauty for ever, O blessed One.

CHORUS. I keep myself pure for Thee, O Bridegroom, and holding a lighted torch I go to meet Thee.

THEKLA. 3. Leaving marriage and the beds of mortals and my golden home for Thee, O King, I have come in undefiled robes, in order

---

[1] Wisd. vii. 9.

[2] [Compare our Lord's wisdom and mercy, Matt. xix. 11.]
[3] The text of Jahn is here followed. — TR. [I have been obliged to arrange this hymn (so as to bring out the refrain as sung by the chorus of virgins) somewhat differently from the form in the Edinburgh edition. I invite a comparison.]

that I might enter with Thee within Thy happy bridal chamber.

CHORUS. I keep myself pure for Thee, O Bridegroom, and holding a lighted torch I go to meet Thee.

THEKLA. 4. Having escaped, O blessed One, from the innumerable enchanting wiles of the serpent, and, moreover, from the flame of fire, and from the mortal-destroying assaults of wild beasts, I await Thee from heaven.

CHORUS. I keep myself pure for Thee, O Bridegroom, and holding a lighted torch I go to meet Thee.

THEKLA. 5. I forget my own country, O Lord, through desire of Thy grace.[1] I forget, also, the company of virgins, my fellows, the desire even of mother and of kindred, for Thou, O Christ, art all things to me.

CHORUS. I keep myself pure for Thee, O Bridegroom, and holding a lighted torch I go to meet Thee.

THEKLA. 6. Giver of life art Thou, O Christ. Hail, light that never sets, receive this praise. The company of virgins call upon Thee, Perfect Flower, Love, Joy, Prudence, Wisdom, Word.

CHORUS. I keep myself pure for Thee, O Bridegroom, and holding a lighted torch I go to meet Thee.

THEKLA. 7. With open gates, O beauteously adorned Queen, admit us within thy chambers. O spotless, gloriously triumphant Bride, breathing beauty, we stand by Christ, robed as He is, celebrating thy happy nuptials, O youthful maiden.

CHORUS. I keep myself pure for Thee, O Bridegroom, and holding a lighted torch I go to meet Thee.

THEKLA. 8. The virgins standing without the chamber,[2] with bitter tears and deep moans, wail and mournfully lament that their lamps are gone out, having failed to enter in due time the chamber of joy.

CHORUS. I keep myself pure for Thee, O Bridegroom, and holding a lighted torch I go to meet Thee.

THEKLA. 9. For turning from the sacred way of life, unhappy ones, they have neglected to prepare sufficiency of oil for the path of life; bearing lamps whose bright light is dead, they groan from the inward recesses of their mind.

CHORUS. I keep myself pure for Thee, O Bridegroom, and holding a lighted torch I go to meet Thee.

THEKLA. 10. Here are cups full of sweet nectar; let us drink, O virgins, for it is celestial drink, which the Bridegroom hath placed for those duly called to the wedding.

CHORUS. I keep myself pure for Thee, O Bridegroom, and holding a lighted torch I go to meet Thee.

THEKLA. 11. Abel, clearly prefiguring Thy death,[3] O blessed One, with flowing blood, and eyes lifted up to heaven, said, Cruelly slain by a brother's hand, O Word, I pray Thee to receive me.

CHORUS. I keep myself pure for Thee, O Bridegroom, and holding a lighted torch I go to meet Thee.

THEKLA. 12. Thy valiant son Joseph,[4] O Word, won the greatest prize of virginity, when a woman heated with desire forcibly drew him to an unlawful bed; but he giving no heed to her fled stripped, and crying aloud : —

CHORUS. I keep myself pure for Thee, O Bridegroom, and holding a lighted torch I go to meet Thee.

THEKLA. 13. Jephthah offered his fresh slaughtered virgin daughter a sacrifice to God, like a lamb; and she, nobly fulfilling the type of Thy body, O blessed One, bravely cried : —

CHORUS. I keep myself pure for Thee, O Bridegroom, and holding a lighted torch I go to meet Thee.

THEKLA. 14. Daring Judith,[5] by clever wiles having cut off the head of the leader of the foreign hosts, whom previously she had allured by her beautiful form, without polluting the limbs of her body, with a victor's shout said : —

CHORUS. I keep myself pure for Thee, O Bridegroom, and holding a lighted torch I go to meet Thee.

THEKLA. 15. Seeing the great beauty of Susanna, the two Judges, maddened with desire, said, O dear lady, we have come desiring secret intercourse with thee; but she with tremulous cries said : —

CHORUS. I keep myself pure for Thee, O Bridegroom, and holding a lighted torch I go to meet Thee.

THEKLA. 16. It is far better for me to die than to betray my nuptials to you, O mad for women, and so to suffer the eternal justice of God in fiery vengeance. Save me now, O Christ, from these evils.

CHORUS. I keep myself pure for Thee, O Bridegroom, and holding a lighted torch I go to meet Thee.

THEKLA. 17. Thy Precursor, washing multitudes of men in flowing lustral water, unjustly by a wicked man, on account of his chastity, was led to slaughter; but as he stained the dust with his life-blood, he cried to Thee, O blessed One : —

CHORUS. I keep myself pure for Thee, O Bridegroom, and holding a lighted torch I go to meet Thee.

---

[1] Ps. xlv. 10.
[2] Matt. xxv. 11.
[3] Gen. iv. 10.
[4] Gen. xxxix. 12.
[5] Jud. viii.

THEKLA. 18. The parent of Thy life, that unspotted Grace [1] and undefiled Virgin, bearing in her womb without the ministry of man, by an immaculate conception,[2] and who thus became suspected of having betrayed the marriage-bed, she, O blessed One, when pregnant, thus spoke : —

CHORUS. I keep myself pure for Thee, O Bridegroom, and holding a lighted torch I go to meet Thee.

THEKLA. 19. Wishing to see Thy nuptial day, O blessed One, as many angels as Thou, O King, calledst from above, bearing the best gifts to Thee, came in unsullied robes : —

CHORUS. I keep myself pure for Thee, O Bridegroom, and holding a lighted torch I go to meet Thee.

THEKLA. 20. In hymns, O blessed spouse of God, we attendants of the Bride honour Thee, O undefiled virgin Church of snow-white form, dark haired, chaste, spotless, beloved.

CHORUS. I keep myself pure for Thee, O Bridegroom, and holding a lighted torch I go to meet Thee.

THEKLA. 21. Corruption has fled, and the tearful pains of diseases ; death has been taken away, all folly has perished, consuming mental grief is no more ; for again the grace of the God-Christ has suddenly shone upon mortals.

CHORUS. I keep myself pure for Thee, O Bridegroom, and holding a lighted torch I go to meet Thee.

THEKLA. 22. Paradise is no longer bereft of mortals, for by divine decree he no longer dwells there as formerly, thrust out from thence when he was free from corruption, and from fear by the various wiles of the serpents, O blessed One.

CHORUS. I keep myself pure for Thee, O Bridegroom, and holding a lighted torch I go to meet Thee.

THEKLA. 23. Singing the new song, now the company of virgins attends thee towards the heavens, O Queen, all manifestly crowned with white lilies, and bearing in their hands bright lights.

CHORUS. I keep myself pure for Thee, O Bridegroom, and holding a lighted torch I go to meet Thee.

THEKLA. 24. O blessed One, who inhabited the undefiled seats of heaven without beginning, who governed all things by everlasting power, O Father, with Thy Son, we are here, receive us also within the gates of life.

CHORUS. I keep myself pure for Thee, O Bridegroom, and holding a lighted torch I go to meet Thee.

CHAP. III. — WHICH ARE THE BETTER, THE CONTINENT, OR THOSE WHO DELIGHT IN TRANQUILLITY OF LIFE ? CONTESTS THE PERIL OF CHASTITY : THE FELICITY OF TRANQUILLITY ; PURIFIED AND TRANQUIL MINDS GODS : THEY WHO SHALL SEE GOD ; VIRTUE DISCIPLINED BY TEMPTATIONS.

EUBOULIOS. Deservedly, O Gregorion, has Thekla borne off the chief prize.

GREGORION. Deservedly indeed.

EUBOULIOS. But what about the stranger Telmisiake ?[3] Tell me, was she not listening from without ? I wonder if she could keep silence on hearing of this banquet, and would not forthwith, as a bird flies to its food, listen to the things which were spoken.

GREGORION. The report is that she was present with Methodios [4] when he inquired respecting these things of Arete. But it is a good as well as a happy thing to have such a mistress and guide as Arete, that is virtue.

EUBOULIOS. But, Gregorion, which shall we say are the better, those who without lust govern concupiscence, or those who under the assaults of concupiscence continue pure ?

GREGORION. For my part, I think those who are free from lust, for they have their mind undefiled, and are altogether uncorrupted, sinning in no respect.

EUBOULIOS. Well, I swear by chastity, and wisely, O Gregorion. But lest in any wise I hinder you, if I gainsay your words, it is that I may the better learn, and that no one hereafter may refute me.

GREGORION. Gainsay me as you will, you have my permission. For, Euboulios, I think that I know sufficient to teach you that he who is not concupiscent is better than he who is. If I cannot, then there is no one who can convince you.

EUBOULIOS. Bless me ! I am glad that you answer me so magnanimously, and show how wealthy you are as regards wisdom.

GREGORION. A mere chatterer, so you seem to be, O Euboulios.

EUBOULIOS. Why so ?

GREGORION. Because you ask rather for the sake of amusement than of truth.

EUBOULIOS. Speak fair, I pray you, my good friend ; for I greatly admire your wisdom and renown. I say this because, with reference to the things that many wise men often dispute among themselves, you say that you not only understand them, but also vaunt that you can teach another.

GREGORION. Now tell me truly whether it is a difficulty with you to receive the opinion, that they who are not concupiscent excel those who

---

[1] Matt. i. 18.
[2] [The only one. See p. 355, Elucidation II., *infra*.]

[3] In Jahn, Telmesiake. — TR. [Comp. p. 356, n. 2, *infra*.]
[4] [Contrast the shameful close of Plato's *Symposium*.]

are concupiscent, and yet restrain themselves? or are you joking?

EUBOULIOS. How so, when I tell you that I do not know? But, come, tell me, O wisest lady, in what do the non-concupiscent and chaste excel the concupiscent who live chastely?

GREGORION. Because, in the first place, they have the soul itself pure, and the Holy Spirit always dwells in it, seeing that it is not distracted and disturbed by fancies and unrestrained thoughts, so as to pollute the mind. But they are in every way inaccessible to lust, both as to their flesh and to their heart, enjoying tranquillity from passions. But they who are allured from without, through the sense of sight, with fancies, and receiving lust flowing like a stream into the heart, are often not less polluted, even when they think that they contend and fight against pleasures, being vanquished in their mind.

EUBOULIOS. Shall we then say that they who serenely live and are not disturbed by lusts are pure?

GREGORION. Certainly. For these [1] are they whom God makes gods in the beatitudes; they who believe in Him without doubt. And He says that they shall look upon God with confidence, because they bring in nothing that darkens or confuses the eye of the soul for the beholding of God; but all desire of things secular being eliminated, they not only, as I said, preserve the flesh pure from carnal connection, but even the heart, in which, especially, as in a temple, the Holy Spirit rests and dwells, is open to no unclean thoughts.

EUBOULIOS. Stay now; for I think that from hence we shall the better go on to the discovery of what things are truly the best; and, tell me, do you call anyone a good pilot?

GREGORION. I certainly do.

EUBOULIOS. Whether is it he that saves his vessel in great and perplexing storms, or is it he who does so in a breathless calm?

GREGORION. He that does so in a great and perplexing storm.

EUBOULIOS. Shall we not then say that the soul, which is deluged with the surging waves of the passions, and yet does not, on that account, weary or grow faint, but direct her vessel — that is, the flesh — nobly into the port of chastity, is better and more estimable than he that navigates in calm weather?

GREGORION. We will say so.

EUBOULIOS. For to be prepared against the entrance of the gales of the Evil Spirit, and not to be cast away or overcome, but to refer all to Christ, and strongly to contend against pleasures, brings greater praise than he wins who lives a virgin life calmly and with ease.

GREGORION. It appears so.

EUBOULIOS. And what saith the Lord? Does He not seem to show that he who retains continence, though concupiscent, excels him who, having no concupiscence, leads a virgin life?

GREGORION. Where does He say so?

EUBOULIOS. Where, comparing a wise man to a house well founded, He declares him immoveable because he cannot be overthrown by rains, and floods, and winds; likening, as it would seem, these storms to lusts, but the immoveable and unshaken firmness of the soul in chastity to the rock.

GREGORION. You appear to speak what is true.

EUBOULIOS. And what say you of the physician? Do you not call him the best who has been proved in great diseases, and has healed many patients?

GREGORION. I do.

EUBOULIOS. But the one who has never at any time practised, nor ever had the sick in his hands, is he not still in all respects the inferior?

GREGORION. Yes.

EUBOULIOS. Then we may certainly say that a soul which is contained by a concupiscent body, and which appeases with the medicaments of temperance the disorders arising from the heat of lusts, carries off the palm for healing, over one to whose lot it has fallen to govern aright a body which is free from lust.[2]

GREGORION. It must be allowed.

EUBOULIOS. And how is it in wrestling? Whether is the better wrestler he who has many and strong antagonists, and continually is contending without being worsted, or he who has no opponents?

GREGORION. Manifestly he who wrestles.

EUBOULIOS. And, in wrestling, is not the athlete who contends the more experienced?

GREGORION. It must be granted.

EUBOULIOS. Therefore it is clear that he whose soul contends against the impulses of lust, and is not borne down by it, but draws back and sets himself in array against it, appears stronger than he who does not lust.[2]

GREGORION. True.

EUBOULIOS. What then? Does it not appear to you, Gregorion, that there is more courage in being valiant against the assaults of base desires?

GREGORION. Yes, indeed.

EUBOULIOS. Is not this courage the strength of virtue?

GREGORION. Plainly so.

EUBOULIOS. Therefore, if endurance be the strength of virtue, is not the soul, which is troubled by lusts, and yet perseveres against them, stronger than that which is not so troubled?

---

[1] Matt. v. 8.

[2] [Recur to what is said of Origen and his epoch on p. 224, vol. iv. of this series.]

GREGORION.   Yes.

EUBOULIOS.   And if stronger, then better?

GREGORION.   Truly.

EUBOULIOS.   Therefore the soul which is concupiscent, and exercises self-control, as appears from what has been said, is better than that which is not concupiscent, and exercises self-control.[1]

GREGORION.   You speak truly, and I shall desire still more fully to discourse with you concerning these things. If, therefore, it pleases you, to-morrow I will come again to hear respecting them.   Now, however, as you see, it is time to betake ourselves to the care of the outward man.

---

[1] [Here is our author's conclusive condemnation of Origen, whose great mistake, I have supposed, gave occasion to this extraordinary work. Possibly the epoch of Anthony had revived such discussions when this was written.]

ELUCIDATIONS.

I.

(We here behold only shadows, etc., p. 335.)

SCHLEIERMACHER,[1] in commenting on Plato's *Symposium*, remarks : " Even natural birth (i.e., in Plato's system) was nothing but a reproduction of the same *eternal form and idea*. . . . The whole discussion displays the gradation, not only from that pleasure which arises from the contemplation of personal beauty through that which every larger object, whether single or manifold, may occasion, to that immediate pleasure of which the source is in the Eternal Beauty," etc.   Our author ennobles such theorizing by mounting up to the great I AM.

II.

(Christ Himself is the one who is born, p. 337.)

Wordsworth, and many others of the learned, sustain our author's comment on this passage.[2] So Aquinas, *ad loc.*, Bede, and many others.   Methodius is incorrectly represented as *rejecting*[3] the idea that " the woman " is the Blessed Virgin Mary, for no such idea existed for him to reject. He rejects the idea that the man-child is Christ ; but that idea was connected with the supposition that the woman was the Church of the Hebrews bringing forth the Messiah.   Gregory the Great regards the woman as the Christian Church.   So Hippolytus :[4] " By the woman . . . is meant most manifestly the Church, endued with the Father's Word, whose brightness is above the sun," etc.   Bossuet says candidly,[5] " C'est l'Église, tout éclatante de la lumière de J. C.," etc.

Now, note the progress of corruption, one fable engendering another.   The text of Gen. iii. 15, contrary to the Hebrew, the Seventy, the Syriac, and the Vulgate itself, in the best MSS., is made to read, " *She* shall bruise thy head," etc.   The "woman," therefore, becomes the Mother of our Lord, and the " great red dragon " (of verse 3), from which the woman "fled into the wilderness," is next represented as *under her feet* (where the moon appears in the sacred narrative) ; and then the Immaculate Conception of her Holy Seed is transferred back to the mother of Mary, who is indecently discussed, and affirmed to have been blest with an " Immaculate Conception " when, in the ordinary process of nature, she was made the mother of the Virgin.   So, then, the bull *Ineffabilis* comes forth, eighteen hundred years after the event,[6] with the announcement that what thousands of saints and many bishops of Rome have denounced as a fable must be received by all Christians on peril of eternal damnation.[7]   The worst of it all is the fact, that, as the mystery of the Incarnation of the Son of God has heretofore been the only " Immaculate Conception " known to the faith of Christendom, thousands now imagine that *this* is what was only so lately set forth, and what we must therefore renounce as false.

---

[1] *Introduction to the Dialogues*, etc., Dobson's translation, Cambridge, 1836.
[2] See his work *On the Apocalypse*, Lecture IX. p. 198, ed. Philadelphia, 1852.
[3] Speaker's Com , *ad loc.*

[4] Vol. v. p. 217, this series.
[5] *Works*, vol. i. p. 447, ed. Paris, 1845.
[6] Dec. 8, 1854.

[7] See *The Eirenicon* of Dr. Pusey, ed. New York, 1866.

CONCERNING FREE-WILL.[1]

ORTHODOXUS. The old man of Ithaca, according to the legend of the Greeks, when he wished to hear the song of the Sirens, on account of the charm of their voluptuous voice, sailed to Sicily in bonds, and stopped up the ears of his companions ; not that he grudged them the hearing, or desired to load himself with bonds, but because the consequence of those singers' music to those who heard it was death. For such, in the opinion of the Greeks, are the charms of the Sirens. Now I am not within hearing of any such song as this ; nor have I any desire to hear the Sirens who chant men's dirges, and whose silence is more profitable to men than their voice ; but I pray to enjoy the pleasure of a divine voice, which, though it be often heard, I long to hear again ; not that I am overcome with the charm of a voluptuous voice, but I am being taught divine mysteries, and expect as the result, not death but eternal salvation. For the singers are not the deadly Sirens of the Greeks, but a divine choir of prophets, with whom there is no need to stop the ears of one's companions, nor to load one's-self with bonds, in fear of the penalty of hearing. For, in the one case, the hearer, with the entrance of the voice, ceases to live ; in the other, the more he hears, the better life will he enjoy, being led onwards by a divine Spirit. Let every one come, then, and hear the divine song without any fear. There are not with us the Sirens from the shore of Sicily, nor the bonds of Ulysses, nor the wax poured melting into men's ears ; but a loosening of all bonds, and liberty to listen to every one that approaches. For it is worthy of us to hear such a song as this ; and to hear such singers as these, seems to me to be a thing to be prayed for. But if one wishes to hear the choir of the apostles as well, he will find the same harmony of song. For the others sang beforehand the divine plan in a mystical manner ; but these sing an interpretation of what has been mystically announced by the former. Oh, concordant harmony, composed by the Divine Spirit ! Oh, the comeliness of those who sing of the mysteries *of God!* Oh, that I also may join in these songs in my prayer. Let us then also sing the like song, and raise the hymn to the Holy Father, glorifying in the Spirit Jesus, who is in His bosom.[2]

Shun not, man, a spiritual hymn, nor be ill-disposed to listen to it. Death belongs not to it ; a story of salvation is our song. Already I seem to taste better enjoyments, as I discourse on such subjects as these ; and especially when there is before me such a flowering meadow, that is to say, our assembly of those who unite in singing and hearing the divine mysteries. Wherefore I dare to ask you to listen to me with ears free from all envy, without imitating the jealousy of Cain,[3] or persecuting your brother, like Esau,[4] or approving the brethren of Joseph,[5] because they hated their brother on account of his words ; but differing far from all these, insomuch that each of you is used to speak the mind of his neighbour. And, on this account, there is no evil jealousy among you, as ye have undertaken to supply your brother's deficiencies. O noble audience, and venerable company, and spiritual food ! That I may ever have a right to share in such pleasures, be this my prayer !

VALENTINIAN. As I was walking yesterday evening, my friend, along the shore of the sea, and was gazing on it somewhat intently, I saw an extraordinary instance of divine power, and a work of art produced by wise science, if at least such a thing may be called a work of art. For as that verse of Homer[6] says, —

" As when two adverse winds blowing from Thrace,
   Boreas and Zephyrus, the fishy deep
   Vex sudden, all around, the sable flood
   High curled, flings forth the salt weed on the shore ; " —

So it seemed to me to have happened yesterday. For I saw waves very like mountain-tops, and, so to speak, reaching up to heaven itself. Whence I expected nothing else but that the whole land would be deluged, and I began to form in my mind a place of escape, and a Noah's ark. But it was not as I thought ; for, just as the sea rose

---

[1] [This debate between *Orthodoxus* and a Valentinian reminds us of the *Octavius* of Minucius Felix, vol iv.]

[2] John i. 18.
[3] Gen. iv. 5.
[4] Gen. xxvii. 41.
[5] Gen. xxxvii. 4
[6] *Iliad*, ix. 4, H. (Cowper's Tr.).

to a crest, it broke up again into itself, without overstepping its own limits, having, so to speak, a feeling of awe for a divine decree.[1] And as oftentimes a servant, compelled by his master to do something against his will, obeys the command through fear, while he dares not say a word of what he suffers in his unwillingness to do it, but, full of rage, mutters to himself, — somewhat so it appeared to me that the sea, as if enraged and confining its awe within itself, kept itself under, as not willing to let its Master perceive its anger.

On these occurrences I began to gaze in silence, and wished to measure in my mind the heaven and its sphere. I began to inquire whence it rises and where it sets; also what sort of motion it had — whether a progressive one, that is to say, one from place to place, or a revolving one; and, besides, how its movement is continued. And, of a truth, it seemed worth while to inquire also about the sun, — what is the manner of his being set in the heaven; also what is the orbit he traverses; also whither it is that, after a short time, he retires; and why it is that even he does not go out of his proper course: but he, too, as one may say, is observing a commandment of a higher power, and appears with us just when he is allowed to do so, and departs as if he were called away.

So, as I was investigating these things, I saw that the sunshine was departing, and the daylight failing, and that immediately darkness came on; and the sun was succeeded by the moon, who, at her first rising, was not of full size, but after advancing in her course presented a larger appearance. And I did not cease inquiring about her also, but examined the cause of her waning and waxing, and why it is that she, too, observes the revolution of days; and it seemed to me from all this that there is a divine government and power controlling the whole, which we may justly call God.

And thereupon I began to praise the Creator, as I saw the earth fast fixed, and living creatures in such variety, and the blossoms of plants with their many hues. But my mind did not rest upon these things alone; but thereupon I began to inquire whence they have their origin — whether from some source eternally co-existent with God, or from Himself alone, none co-existing with Him; for that He has made nothing out of that which has no existence appeared to me the right view to take, unless my reason were altogether untrustworthy. For it is the nature of things which come into being to derive their origin from what is already existing. And it seemed to me that it might be said with equal truth, that nothing is eternally co-existent with God distinct from Himself, but that whatever exists has its

origin from Him, and I was persuaded of this also by the undeniable disposition of the elements, and by the orderly arrangement of nature about them.

So, with some such thoughts of the fair order of things, I returned home. But on the day following, that is to-day, as I came I saw two beings of the same race — I mean men — striking and abusing one another; and another, again, wishing to strip his neighbour. And now some began to venture upon a more terrible deed; for one stripped a corpse, and exposed again to the light of day a body that had been once hidden in the earth, and treated a form like his own with such insult as to leave the corpse to be food for dogs; while another bared his sword, and attacked a man like himself. And he wanted to procure safety by flight; but the other ceased not from pursuing, nor would control his anger. And why should I say more? It is enough that he attacked him, and at once smote him with his sword. So *the wounded man* became a suppliant to his fellow, and spread out his hands in supplication, and was willing to give up his clothing, and only made a claim for life. But the other did not subdue his anger, nor pity his fellow-man, nor would he see his own image in the being before him; but, like a wild beast, made preparations with his sword for feeding upon him. And now he was even putting his mouth to the body so like his own, such was the extent of his rage. And there was to be seen one man suffering injurious treatment, and another forthwith stripping him, and not even covering with earth the body which he denuded of clothing. But, in addition to these, there was another who, robbing others of their marriage rights, wanted to insult his neighbour's wife, and urged her to turn to unlawful embraces, not wishing her husband to be father to a child of his own.

After that I began to believe the tragedies, and thought that the dinner of Thyestes had really taken place; and believed in the unlawful lust of Oinomaos, nor doubted of the strife in which brother drew the sword on brother.

So, after beholding such things as these, I began to inquire whence they arise, and what is their origin, and who is the author of such devices against men, whence came their discovery, and who is the teacher of them. Now to dare to say that God was the author of these things was impossible; for surely it could not even be said that they have from Him their substance, or their existence. For how were it possible to entertain these thoughts of God? For He is good, and the Creator of what is excellent, and to Him belongs nothing bad. Nay, it is His nature to take no pleasure in such things; but He forbids their production, and rejects those

---

[1] Job xxxviii. 11.

who delight in them, but admits into His presence those who avoid them. And how could it be anything but absurd to call God the maker of these things of which He disapproves? For He would not wish them not to be, if He had first been their creator; and He wishes those who approach Him to be imitators of Him.

Wherefore it seemed to me unreasonable to attribute these things to God, or to speak of them as having sprung from Him; though it must certainly be granted that it is possible for something to come into existence out of what has no existence, in case He made what is evil. For He who brought them into existence out of non-existence would not reduce them to the loss of it. And again, it must be said that there was once a time when God took pleasure in evil things, which now is not the case. Wherefore it seems to me impossible to say this of God. For it is unsuitable to His nature to attach this to Him. Wherefore it seemed to me that there is co-existent with Him somewhat which has the name of matter, from which He formed existing things, distinguishing between them with wise art, and arranging them in a fair order, from which also evil things seem to have come into being. For as this matter was without quality or form, and, besides this, was borne about without order, and was untouched by divine art, God bore no grudge against it, nor left it to be continually thus borne about, but began to work upon it, and wished to separate its best parts from its worst, and thus made all that it was fitting for God to make out of it; but so much of it as was like lees, so to speak, this being unfitted for being made into anything, He left as it was, since it was of no use to Him; and from this it seems to me that what is evil has now streamed down among men. This seemed to me the right view to take of these things. But, my friend, if you think that anything I have said is wrong, mention it, for I exceedingly desire to hear about these things.

ORTHODOXUS. I appreciate your readiness, my friend, and applaud your zeal about the subject; and as for the opinion which you have expressed respecting existing things, to the effect that God made them out of some underlying substance, I do not altogether find fault with it. For, truly, the origin of evil *is a subject that* has called out opinions from many men.[1] Before you and me, no doubt, there have been many able men who have made the most searching inquiry into the matter. And some of them expressed the same opinion as you did, but others

again represented God as the creator of these things, fearing to allow the existence of substance as coeval with Him; while the former, from fear of saying that God was the author of evil, thought fit to represent matter as coeval with Him.[2] And it was the fate of both of these to fail to speak rightly on the subject, in consequence of their fear of God not being in agreement with an accurate knowledge of the truth.

But others declined to inquire about such a question at all, on the ground that such an inquiry is endless. As for me, however, my connection with you in friendship does not allow me to decline the subject of inquiry, especially when you announce your own purpose, that you are not swayed by prejudice, — although you had your opinion about the condition of things derived from your conjectures, — but say that you are confirmed in a desire of knowing the truth.

Wherefore I will willingly turn to the discussion of the question. But I wish this companion of mine here to listen to our conversation.[3] For, indeed, he seems to have much the same opinions about these things as you have, wherefore I wish that you should both have a share in the discussion. For whatever I should say to you, situated as you are, I shall say just as much to him. If, then, you are indulgent enough to think I speak truly on this great subject, give an answer to each question I ask; for the result of this will be that you will gain a knowledge of the truth, and I shall not carry on my discussion with you at random.

VALENTINIAN. I am ready to do as you say; and therefore be quite ready to ask those questions from which you think I may be able to gain an accurate knowledge of this important subject. For the object which I have set before myself is not the base one of gaining a victory, but that of becoming thoroughly acquainted with the truth. Wherefore apply yourself to the rest of the discussion.

ORTHODOXUS. Well, then, I do not suppose you are ignorant that it is impossible for two uncreated things to exist together, although you seem to have expressed nearly as much as this in an earlier part of the conversation. Assuredly we must of necessity say one of two things: either that God is separate from matter, or, on the other hand, that He is inseparable from it. If, then, one would say that they are united, he will say that that which is uncreated is one only, for each of the things spoken of will be a part of the other; and as they are parts of each other, there will not be two uncreated things, but one composed of different elements. For

[1] [See the essay of Archbishop King *On the Origin of Evil*, ed. Cambridge, 1739. Law's annotations in this edition are valuable. See also Dr. Bledsoe, *Theodicy*, and Elucidation VIII. p. 522, vol. ii , this series. Of Leibnitz (refuting Bayle), no need to speak here. Comp. Addison, *Spectator*, Nos. 237 and 519; also Parnell's *Hermit;* also Jer. xii. 1.]

[2] The reader will here naturally think of the great and long-continued Manichæan controversy. — TR.

[3] [See Routh, *R. S.*, tom. ii. p. 98, and note p. 115, and all Routh's notes on Maximus, the original of Methodius, of whom see Eusebius, *H. E.*, book v. cap. 27.]

we do not, because a man has different members, break him up into many beings. But, as the demands of reason require, we say that a single being, man, of many parts, has been created by God. So it is necessary, if God be not separate from matter, to say that that which is uncreated is one only; but if one shall say that He is separate, there must necessarily be something intermediate between the two, which makes their separation evident. For it is impossible to estimate the distance of one thing from another, unless there be something else with which the distance between them may be compared. And this holds good, not only as far as the instance before us, but also to any number of others. For the argument which we advanced in the case of two uncreated things would of necessity be of equal force, were the uncreated things granted to be three in number. For I should ask also respecting them, whether they are separate from each other, or, on the other hand, are united each to its neighbour. For if any one resolve to say that they are united, he will be told the same as before; if, again, that they are separate, he will not escape the necessary existence of that which separates them.

If, then, any one were to say that there is a third account which might fitly be given of uncreated things, namely, that neither is God separate from matter, nor, again, are they united as part of a whole; but that God is locally situate in matter, and matter in God, he must be told as the consequence,[1] that if we say that God is placed in matter, we must of necessity say that He is contained within limits, and circumscribed by matter. But then He must, equally with matter, be carried about without order. And that He rests not, nor remains by Himself, is a necessary result of that in which He is being carried, now this way, and now that. And besides this, we must say that God was in worse case still.

For if matter were once without order, and He, determining to change it for the better, put it into order, there was a time when God was in that which had no order. And I might fairly ask this question also, whether God filled matter completely, or existed in some part of it. For if one resolve to say that God was in some part of matter, how far smaller than matter does he make Him; that is, if a part of it contained God altogether. But if he were to say that He is in all of it, and is extended through the whole of matter, he must tell us how He wrought upon it. For we must say that there was a sort of contraction of God, which being effected, He wrought upon that from which He was withdrawn,

or else that He wrought in union with matter, without having a place of withdrawal. But if any one say that matter is in God, there is equal need of inquiry, namely, whether it is by His being separated from Himself, and as creatures exist in the air, by His being divided and parted for the reception of the beings that are in Him; or whether it is locally situated, that is to say, as water in land; for if we were to say, as in the air, we must say that God is divisible; but if, as water in earth, — since matter was without order and arrangement, and besides, contained what was evil, — we must say that in God were to be found the disorderly and the evil. Now this seems to me an unbecoming conclusion, nay, more, a dangerous one. For you wish for the existence of matter, that you may avoid saying that God is the author of evil; and, determining to avoid this, you say that He is the receptacle of evil.

If, then, under the supposition that matter is separate from created substances, you had said that it is uncreated, I should have said much about it, to prove that it is impossible for it to be uncreated; but since you say that the *question of* the origin of evil is the cause of this supposition, it therefore seems to me right to proceed to inquire into this. For when it is clearly stated how evil exists, and that it is not possible to say that God is the cause of evil, because of matter being subject to Him, it seems to me to destroy such a supposition, to remark, that if God created the qualities which did not exist, He equally created the substances.[2]

Do you say, then, that there co-exists with God matter without qualities out of which He formed the beginning of this world?

VALENTINIAN. So I think.

ORTHODOXUS. If, then, matter had no qualities, and the world were produced by God, and qualities exist in the world, then God is the maker of qualities?

VALENTINIAN. It is so.

ORTHODOXUS. Now, as I heard you say some time ago that it is impossible for anything to come into being out of that which has no existence, answer my question: Do you think that the qualities of the world were not produced out of any existing qualities?

VALENTINIAN. I do.

ORTHODOXUS. And that they are something distinct from substances?

VALENTINIAN. Yes.

ORTHODOXUS. If, then, qualities were neither made by God out of any ready at hand, nor derive their existence from substances, because they are not substances, we must say that they were produced by God out of what had no

---

[1] Jahn's reading is here followed.

[2] The text is here in an uncertain state. *Cf.* Migne and Jahn.

existence. Wherefore I thought you spoke extravagantly in saying that it was impossible to suppose that anything was produced by God out of what did not exist.

But let our discussion of this matter stand thus. For truly we see among ourselves men making things out of what does not exist, although they seem for the most part to be making them with something. As, for instance, we may have an example in the case of architects; for they truly do not make cities out of cities, nor in like manner temples out of temples.[1]

.   .   .   .

But if, because substances underlie these things, you think that the builders make them out of what does exist, you are mistaken in your calculation. For it is not the substance which makes the city or the temples, but art applied to substance. And this art is not produced out of some art which lies in the substances themselves, but from that which is not in them.

But you seem likely to meet me with this argument: that the artificer makes the art which is connected with the substance out of the art which he has. Now I think it is a good reply to this to say, that in man it is not produced from any art lying beneath; for it is not to be granted that substance by itself is art. For art is in the class of accidents, and is one of the things that have an existence only when they are employed about some substance. For man will exist even without the art of building, but it will have no existence unless man be previously in being. Whence we must say that it is in the nature of things for arts to be produced in men out of what has no existence. If, then, we have shown that this is so in the case of men, why was it improper to say that God is able to make not only qualities, but also substances, out of that which has no existence? For as it appears possible for something to be produced out of what exists not, it is evident that this is the case with substances. To return to the question of evil. Do you think evil comes under the head of substances, or of qualities of substances?

VALENTINIAN. Of qualities.

ORTHODOXUS. But matter was found to be without quality or form?

VALENTINIAN. It was.

ORTHODOXUS. Well, then, the connection of these names with substance is owing to its accidents. For murder is not a substance, nor is any other evil; but the substance receives a cognate name from putting it into practice. For a man is not (spoken of as) murder, but by committing it he receives the derived name of murderer, without being himself murder; and, to speak concisely, no other evil is a substance;

but by practising any evil, it can be called evil. Similarly consider, if you imagine anything else to be the cause of evil to men, that it too is evil by reason of its acting by them, and suggesting the committal of evil. For a man is evil in consequence of his actions. For he is said to be evil, because he is the doer of evil. Now what a man does, is not the man himself, but his activity, and it is from his actions that he receives the title of evil. For if we were to say that he is that which he does, and he commits murders, adulteries, and such-like, he will be all these. Now if he is these, then when they are produced he has an existence, but when they are not, he too ceases to be. Now these things are produced by men. Men then will be the authors of them, and the causes of their existing or not existing. But if each man is evil in consequence of what he practises, and what he practises has an origin, he also made a beginning in evil, and evil too had a beginning. Now if this is the case, no one is without a beginning in evil, nor are evil things without an origin.

VALENTINIAN. Well, my friend, you seem to me to have argued sufficiently against the other side. For you appeared to draw right conclusions from the premises which we granted to the discussion. For truly if matter is without qualities, then God is the maker of qualities; and if evils are qualities, God will be the author of evils. But it seems to me false to say that matter is without qualities; for it cannot be said respecting any substance that it is without qualities. But indeed, in the very act of saying that it is without qualities, you declare that it has a quality, by describing the character of matter, which is a kind of quality. Therefore, if you please, begin the discussion from the beginning; for it seems to me that matter never began to have qualities. For such being the case, I assert, my friend, that evil arises from its emanation.

ORTHODOXUS. If matter were possessed of qualities from eternity, of what will God be the creator? For if we say substances, we speak of them as pre-existing; if, again, we say qualities, these too are declared to have an existence. Since, then, both substances and qualities exist, it seems to me superfluous to call God a creator. But answer me a question. In what way do you say that God was a creator? Was it by changing the existence of those substances into non-existence, or by changing the qualities while He preserved the substances?

VALENTINIAN. I think that there was no change of the substances, but only of the qualities; and in respect to these we call God a creator. And just as if one might chance to say that a house was made of stones, it cannot be said of them that they do not still continue stones in substance, because they are called a house;

for I affirm that the house is made by the quality of construction. So I think that God, while substance remained, produced a change of its qualities, by reason of which I say that this world was made by God.

ORTHODOXUS. Do you think, too, that evil is among the qualities of substances?

VALENTINIAN. I do.

ORTHODOXUS. And were these qualities in matter from the first, or had they a beginning?

VALENTINIAN. I say that these qualities were eternally co-existent with matter.

ORTHODOXUS. But do you not say that God has made a change in the qualities?

VALENTINIAN. I do say this.

ORTHODOXUS. For the better?

VALENTINIAN. I think so.

ORTHODOXUS. If, then, evil is among the qualities of matter, and its qualities were changed by God for the better, the inquiry must be made whence evil arose. For either all of them, being evil, underwent a change for the better, or some of them being evil, and some not, the evil ones were not changed for the better; but the rest, as far as they were found superior, were changed by God for the sake of order.

VALENTINIAN. That is the opinion I held from the beginning.

ORTHODOXUS. How, then, do you say it was that He left the qualities of evil as they were? Was it that He was able to do away with them, or that, though He wished to do so, He was unable? For if you say that He was able, but disinclined to do so, He must be the author of these things; because, while He had power to bring evil to an end, He allowed it to remain as it was, especially when He had begun to work upon matter. For if He had had nothing at all to do with matter, He would not have been the author of what He allowed to remain. But since He works upon a part of it, and leaves a part of it to itself, while He has power to change it for the better, I think He is the author of evil, since He left part of matter in its vileness. He wrought then for the ruin of a part; and, in this respect, it seems to me that this part was chiefly injured by His arranging it in matter, so that it became partaker of evil. For before matter was put in order, it was without the perception of evil; but now each of its parts has the capacity of perceiving evil. Now, take an example in the case of man. Previously to becoming a living creature, he was insensible to evil; but from the time when he is fashioned by God into the form of man, he gains the perception of approaching evil. So this act of God, which you say was done for the benefit of matter, is found to have happened to it rather for the worse. But if you say that God was not able to stop evil, does the impossibility result from His being naturally weak, or from His being overcome by fear, and in subjection to some more powerful being? See which of these you would like to attribute to the almighty and good God. But, again, answer me about matter. Is matter simple or compound? For if matter be simple and uniform, and the universe compound, and composed of different substances, it is impossible to say that it is made of matter, because compound things cannot be composed of one pure and simple ingredient. For composition indicates the mixture of several simple things. But if, on the other hand, you say that matter is compound, it has been entirely composed of simple elements, and they were once each separately simple, and by their composition matter was produced; for compound things derive their composition from simple things. So there was once a time when matter did not exist — that is to say, before the combination of the simple elements. But if there was once a time when matter did not exist, and there was never a time when what is uncreated did not exist, then matter is not uncreated. And from this it follows that there are many things which are uncreated. For if God were uncreated, and the simple elements of which matter was composed were uncreated, the number of the uncreated would be more than two. But to omit inquiring what are the simple elements, matter or form — for this would be followed by many absurdities — let me ask, do you think that nothing that exists is contrary to itself?

VALENTINIAN. I do.

ORTHODOXUS. Yet water is contrary to fire, and darkness to light, and heat to cold, and moisture to dryness.

VALENTINIAN. I think it is.

ORTHODOXUS. If, then, nothing that exists is contrary to itself, and these are contrary to one another, they will not be one and the same matter — no, nor formed from one and the same matter. But, again, I wish to ask, do you think that the parts of a thing are not destructive of one another?

VALENTINIAN. I do.

ORTHODOXUS. And that fire and water, and the rest likewise, are parts of matter?

VALENTINIAN. I hold them to be so.

ORTHODOXUS. Why, then, do you not think that water is destructive of fire, and light of darkness, and so on with the rest?

VALENTINIAN. I do.

ORTHODOXUS. Then, if parts of a thing are not destructive of one another, and these are found to be so, they will not be parts of the same thing. But if they are not parts of the same thing, they will not be parts of one and the same matter. And, indeed, they will not be matter either, because nothing that exists is destructive of itself. And this being the case with the contraries, it is shown that they are not matter. This is enough on the subject of matter.

Now we must come to the examination of evils, and must necessarily inquire into the evils among men. As to these, are they forms of the principle of evil, or parts of it? If forms, evil will not have a separate existence distinct from them, because the species are to be sought for in the forms, and underlie them. But if this is the case, evil has an origin. For its forms are shown to have an origin—such as murder, and adultery, and the like. But if you will have them to be parts of some principle of evil, and they have an origin, it also must have an origin. For those things whose parts have an origin, are of necessity originated likewise. For the whole consists of parts. And the whole will not exist if the parts do not, though there may be some parts, even if the whole be not there.

Now there is nothing existing of which one part is originated, and another part not. But if I were even to grant this, then there was a time when evil was not complete, namely, before matter was wrought by God. And it attains completeness when man is produced by God; for man is the maker of the parts of evil. And from this it follows that the cause of evil being complete, is God the Creator, which it is impious to say. But if you say that evil is neither of the things supposed, but is the doing of something evil, you declare that it has an origin. For the doing of a thing makes the beginning of its existence. And besides this, you have nothing further to pronounce evil. For what other action have you to point out as such, except what happens among men? Now, it has been already shown that he who acts is not evil according to his being, but in accordance with his evil doing.

Because there is nothing evil by nature, but it is by use that evil things become such. So I say, says he, that man was made with a free-will, not as if there were already evil in existence, which he had the power of choosing if he wished, but on account of his capacity of obeying or disobeying God.

For this was the meaning of the gift of Free Will. And man after his creation receives a commandment from God; and from this at once rises evil, for he does not obey the divine command; and this alone is evil, namely, disobedience, which had a beginning.

.   .   .   .

For man [1] received power, and enslaved himself, not because he was overpowered by the irresistible tendencies of his nature, nor because

the capacity with which he was gifted deprived him of what was better for him; for it was for the sake of this that I say he was endowed with it (but he received the power above mentioned), in order that he may obtain an addition to what he already possesses, which accrues to him from the Superior Being in consequence of his obedience, and is demanded as a debt from his Maker. For I say that man was made not for destruction, but for better things. For if he were made as any of the elements, or those things which render a similar service to God, he would cease to receive a reward befitting deliberate choice, and would be like an instrument of the maker; and it would be unreasonable for him to suffer blame for his wrong-doings, for the real author of them is the one by whom he is used. But man did not understand better things, since he did not know the author (of his existence), but only the object for which he was made. I say therefore that God, purposing thus to honour man, and to grant him an understanding of better things, has given him the power of being able to do what he wishes, and commends the employment of his power for better things; not that He deprives him again of free-will, but wishes to point out the better way. For the power is present with him, and he receives the commandment; but God exhorts him to turn his power of choice to better things. For as a father exhorts his son, who has power to learn his lessons, to give more attention to them, inasmuch as, while he points out this as the better course, he does not deprive his son of the power which he possessed, even if he be not inclined to learn willingly; so I do not think that God, while He urges on man to obey His commands, deprives him of the power of purposing and withholding obedience. For He points out the cause of His giving this advice, in that He does not deprive him of the power. But He gives commands, in order that man may be able to enjoy better things. For this is the consequence of obeying the commands of God. So that He does not give commands in order to take away the power which He has given, but in order that a better gift may be bestowed, as to one worthy of attaining greater things, in return for his having rendered obedience to God, while he had power to withhold it. I say that man was made with free-will, not as if there were already existing some evil, which he had the power of choosing if he wished, . . . but that the power of obeying and disobeying God is the only cause.[2]

For this was the object to be obtained by free-will. And man after his creation receives a commandment from God, and from this at once rises evil; for he does not obey the divine com-

---

[1] The whole of this work, as preserved, is in a very fragmentary state. We have followed Migne in general, as his edition is most widely known, and but little is gained by adopting Jahn's, which is somewhat more complete. — Tr.

[2] Of the bestowal of free-will.

mand, and this alone is evil, namely, disobedience, which had a beginning. For no one has it in his power to say that it is without an origin, when its author had an origin. But you will be sure to ask whence arose this disobedience. It is clearly recorded in Holy Scripture, by which I am enabled to say that man was not made by God in this condition, but that he has come to it by some teaching. For man did not receive such a nature as this. For if it were the case that his nature was such, this would not have come upon him by teaching. Now one says in Holy Writ, that "man has learnt (evil)."[1] I say, then, that disobedience to God is taught. For this alone is evil which is produced in opposition to the purpose of God, for man would not learn evil by itself. He, then, who teaches evil is the Serpent.

. . . .

For my part, I said that the beginning of evil was envy, and that it arose from man's being distinguished by God with higher honour. Now evil is disobedience to the commandment of God.

---

[1] Jer. xiii. 23.

FROM THE DISCOURSE ON THE RESURRECTION.[1]

PART I.

I. God did not make evil,[2] nor is He at all in any way the author of evil ; but whatever failed to keep the law, which He in all justice ordained, after being made by Him with the faculty of free-will, for the purpose of guarding and keeping it, is called evil. Now it is the gravest fault to dis-obey God, by overstepping the bounds of that righteousness which is consistent with free-will.

II. Now the question has already been raised,[3] and answered,[4] that the " coats of skins "[5] are not bodies. Nevertheless, let us speak of it again, for it is not enough to have mentioned it once. Before the preparation of these coats of skins, the first man himself acknowledges that he has both bones and flesh ; for when he saw the woman brought to him : " This is now," he cried,[6] " bone of my bone, and flesh of my flesh." And again : " She shall be called Woman, because she was taken out of man.[7] For this cause shall a man leave his father and mother, and shall be joined unto his wife, and they two shall be one flesh." For I cannot endure the trifling of some who shamelessly do violence to Scripture, in order that their opinion, that the resurrection is without flesh, may find support ; supposing rational bones and flesh, and in different ways changing it backwards and forwards by allego-rizing. And Christ confirms the taking of these things as they are written, when, to the question of the Pharisees about putting away a wife, He answers : " Have ye not read that He which made them at the beginning made them male and female ; and said, For this cause shall a man leave his father,"[8] and so on.

III. But it is evidently absurd to think that the body will not co-exist with the soul in the eternal state, because it is a bond and fetters ; in order that, according to their view, we who are to live in the kingdom of light may not be for ever con-demned to be bondmen of corruption. For as the question has been sufficiently solved, and the statement refuted in which they defined the flesh to be the soul's chain, the argument also is destroyed, that the flesh will not rise again, lest, if we resume it, we be prisoners in the kingdom of light.

IV. In order, then, that man might not be an undying or ever-living evil, as would have been the case if sin were dominant within him, as it had sprung up in an immortal body, and was provided with immortal sustenance, God for this cause pronounced him mortal, and clothed him with mortality. For this is what was meant by the coats of skins, in order that, by the dissolu-tion of the body, sin might be altogether de-stroyed from the very roots, that there might not be left even the smallest particle of root from which new shoots of sin might again burst forth.

V. For as a fig-tree, which has grown in the splendid buildings [9] of a temple, and has reached a great size, and is spread over all the joints of the stones with thickly-branching roots, ceases not to grow, till, by the loosening of the stones from the place in which it sprung up, it is alto-gether torn away ; for it is possible for the stones to be fitted into their own places, when the fig-tree is taken away, so that the temple may be preserved, having no longer to support what was the cause of its own destruction ; while the fig-tree, torn away by the roots, dies ; in the same way also, God, the builder, checked by the sea-sonable application of death, His own temple, man, when he had fostered sin, like a wild fig-tree, " killing,"[10] in the words of Scripture, " and making alive," in order that the flesh, after sin is withered and dead, may, like a restored temple, be raised up again with the same parts, uninjured and immortal, while sin is utterly and entirely destroyed. For while the body still lives, before it has passed through death, sin must also live with it, as it has its roots concealed within us, even though it be externally checked by the

---

[1] [Compare Athenagoras, vol. ii. p. 149, and other Fathers *passim.*]

[2] [See p. 363, *supra.*]

[3] *Cf.* Anastasius, in *Doctrina Patrum de Verbi Incarnatione,* c. 25. — Jahn.

[4] By Epiphanius, *Hær.*, lxiv. n. 22. — Migne.

[5] Gen. iii. 21.

[6] Gen. ii. 23, 24.

[7] [See vol. iv. p. 38, this series.]

[8] Matt. xix. 4, 5.

[9] [i.e., " in the *courts* of the Lord's house; " *among* the build-ings.]

[10] Deut. xxxii. 39.

wounds inflicted by corrections and warnings; since, otherwise, it would not happen that we do wrong after baptism, as we should be entirely and absolutely free from sin. But now, even after believing, and after the time of being touched by the water of sanctification, we are oftentimes found in sin. For no one can boast of being so free from sin as not even to have an evil thought. So that it is come to pass that sin is now restrained and lulled to sleep by faith, so that it does not produce injurious fruits, but yet is not torn up by the roots. For the present we restrain its sprouts, such as evil imaginations, "lest any root of bitterness springing up trouble"[1] us, not suffering its leaves to unclose and open into shoots; while the Word, like an axe, cuts at its roots which grow below. But hereafter the very thought of evil will disappear.

VI. But come now, since there is need of many examples in matters of this kind, let us examine them particularly from this point of view, without desisting till our argument ends in clearer explanation and proof. It appears, then, as if an eminent craftsman were to cast over again a noble image, wrought by himself of gold or other material, and beautifully proportioned in all its members, upon his suddenly perceiving that it had been mutilated by some infamous man, who, too envious to endure the image being beautiful, spoiled it, and thus enjoyed the empty pleasure of indulged jealousy. For take notice, most wise Aglaophon, that, if the artificer wish that that upon which he has bestowed so much pains and care and labour, shall be quite free from injury, he will be impelled to melt it down, and restore it to its former condition. But if he should not cast it afresh, nor reconstruct it, but allow it to remain as it is, repairing and restoring it, it must be that the image, being passed through the fire and forged, cannot any longer be preserved unchanged, but will be altered and wasted. Wherefore, if he should wish it to be perfectly beautiful and faultless, it must be broken up and recast, in order that all the disfigurements and mutilations inflicted upon it by treachery and envy, may be got rid of by the breaking up and recasting of it, while the image is restored again uninjured and unalloyed to the same form as before, and made as like itself as possible. For it is impossible for an image under the hands of the original artist to be lost, even if it be melted down again, for it may be restored; but it is possible for blemishes and injuries to be put off, for they melt away and cannot be restored; because in every work of art the best craftsman looks not for blemish or failure, but for symmetry and correctness in his work. Now God's plan seems to me to have been the same as that

which prevails among ourselves. For seeing man, His fairest work, corrupted by envious treachery, He could not endure, with His love for man, to leave him in such a condition, lest he should be for ever faulty, and bear the blame to eternity; but dissolved him again into his original materials, in order that, by remodelling, all the blemishes in him might waste away and disappear. For the melting down of the statue in the former case corresponds to the death and dissolution of the body in the latter, and the remoulding of the material in the former, to the resurrection after death in the latter; as also saith the prophet Jeremiah, for he addresses *the Jews* in these words, "And I went down to the potter's house; and, behold, he wrought a work upon the stones. And the vessel which he made in his hands was broken; and again he made another vessel, as it pleased him to make it. And the word of the Lord came to me, saying, Cannot I do to you as this potter, O house of Israel? Behold, as the clay of the potter are ye in my hands."[2]

VII. For I call your attention to this, that, as I said, after man's transgression the Great Hand was not content to leave as a trophy of victory its own work, debased by the Evil One, who wickedly injured it from motives of envy; but moistened and reduced it to clay, as a potter breaks up a vessel, that by the remodelling of it all the blemishes and bruises in it may disappear, and it may be made afresh faultless and pleasing.

VIII. But it is not satisfactory to say that the universe will be utterly destroyed, and sea and air and sky will be no longer. For the whole world will be deluged with fire from heaven, and burnt for the purpose of purification and renewal; it will not, however, come to complete ruin and corruption. For if it were better for the world not to be than to be, why did God, in making the world, take the worse course? But God did not work in vain, or do that which was worst. God therefore ordered the creation with a view to its existence and continuance, as also the *Book of Wisdom* confirms, saying, "For God created all things that they might have their being; and the generations of the world were healthful, and there is no poison of destruction in them."[3] And Paul clearly testifies this, saying, "For the earnest expectation of the creature[4] waiteth for the manifestation of the sons of God. For the creature[4] was made subject to vanity, not willingly, but by reason of him that subjected the same in hope: because the creature[4] itself also shall be delivered from the

---

[1] Heb. xii. 15.

[2] Jer. xviii. 3-6.
[3] Wisd. i. 14.
[4] [Greek, creation, κτίσις. The English version faulty and confusing.]

bondage of corruption into the glorious liberty of the children of God." [1] For the creation was made subject to vanity, he says, and he expects that it will be set free from such servitude, as he intends to call this world by the name of creation. For it is not what is unseen but what is seen that is subject to corruption. The creation, then, after being restored to a better and more seemly state, remains, rejoicing and exulting over the children of God at the resurrection; for whose sake it now groans and travails,[2] waiting itself also for our redemption from the corruption of the body, that, when we have risen and shaken off the mortality of the flesh, according to that which is written, "Shake off the dust, and arise, and sit down, O Jerusalem," [3] and have been set free from sin, it also shall be freed from corruption and be subject no longer to vanity, but to righteousness. Isaiah says, too, "For as the new heaven and the new earth which I make, remaineth before me, saith the Lord, so shall your seed and your name be;" [4] and again, "Thus saith the Lord that created the heaven, it is He who prepared the earth and created it, He determined it; He created it not in vain, but formed it to be inhabited." [5] For in reality God did not establish the universe in vain, or to no purpose but destruction, as those weak-minded men say, but to exist, and be inhabited, and continue. Wherefore the earth and the heaven must exist again after the conflagration and shaking of all things.

IX. But if our opponents say, How then is it, if the universe be not destroyed, that the Lord says that "heaven and earth shall pass away;" [6] and the prophet, that "the heaven shall perish as smoke, and the earth shall grow old as a garment;" [7] we answer, because it is usual for the Scriptures to call the change of the world from its present condition to a better and more glorious one, destruction; as its earlier form is lost in the change of all things to a state of greater splendour; for there is no contradiction nor absurdity in the Holy Scriptures. For not "the world" but the "fashion of this world" passeth away,[8] it is said; so it is usual for the Scriptures to call the change from an earlier form to a better and more comely state, destruction; just as when one calls by the name of destruction the change from a childish form into a perfect man, as the stature of the child is turned into *manly* size and beauty. We may expect that the creation will pass away, as if it were to perish in the burning, in order that it may be

renewed, not however that it will be destroyed, that we who are renewed may dwell in a renewed world without taste of sorrow; according as it is said, "When Thou lettest Thy breath go forth, they shall be made, and Thou shalt renew the face of the earth;" [9] God henceforth providing for the due temperature of that which surrounds it. For as the earth is to exist after the present age,[10] there must be by all means inhabitants for it, who shall no longer be liable to death, nor shall marry, nor beget children, but live in all happiness, like the angels, without change or decay. Wherefore it is silly to discuss in what way of life our bodies will then exist, if there is no longer air, nor earth, nor anything else.

X. But in addition to what has been said, there is this point worth consideration, since it misleads very much, if we may be outspoken about matters of such importance, Aglaophon. For you said that the Lord declared plainly [11] that those who shall obtain the resurrection shall then be as the angels.[12] You brought this objection: The angels, being without flesh, are on this account in the utmost happiness and glory. We must then, as we are to be made equal to the angels, be like them stripped of flesh, and be angels. But you overlooked this, my excellent friend, that He who created and set in order the universe out of nothing, ordained the nature of immortal beings to be distributed not only among angels and ministers, but also among principalities, and thrones, and powers. For the race of angels is one, and that of principalities and powers another; because immortal beings are not all of one order, and constitution, and tribe, and family, but there are differences of race and tribe. And neither do the cherubim, departing from their own nature, assume the form of angels; nor, again, do angels assume the form of the others. For they cannot be anything but what they are and have been made. Moreover, man also having been appointed by the original order of things to inhabit the world, and to rule over all that is in it, when he is immortal, will never be changed from being a man into the form either of angels or any other; for neither do angels undergo a change from their original form to another. For Christ at His coming did not proclaim that the human nature should, when it is immortal, be remoulded or transformed into another nature, but into what it was before the fall. For each one among created things must remain in its own proper place, that none may be wanting to any, but all may be full: heaven of angels, thrones of powers, luminaries of ministers; and the more divine spots, and the undefiled and untainted lumina-

---

[1] Rom. viii. 19–21.
[2] The reading and punctuation of Jahn are here adopted.
[3] Isa. lii. 2.
[4] Isa. lxvi. 22.
[5] Isa. xlv. 18.
[6] Matt. xxiv. 35.
[7] Isa. li. 6.
[8] 1 Cor. vii. 31.

[9] Ps. civ. 30.
[10] Or, "dispensation."
[11] When tempted by the Sadducees.
[12] Matt. xxii. 30.

ries, with seraphim, who attend the Supreme Council, and uphold the universe ; and the world of men. For if we granted that men are changed into angels, it would follow that we say that angels also are changed into powers, and these into one thing and the other, until our argument proceed too far for safety.

XI. Neither did God, as if He had made man badly, or committed a mistake in the formation of him, determine afterwards to make an angel, repenting of His work, as the worst of craftsmen do ; nor did He fashion man, after He had wished originally to make an angel, and failed ; for this would be a sign of weakness, etc. Why even then did He make man and not angels, if He wished men to be angels and not men ? Was it because He was unable ? It is blasphemy to suppose so. Or was He so busy in making the worse as to loiter about the better ? This too is absurd. For He does not fail in making what is good, nor defers it, nor is incapable of it ; but He has the power to act how and when He pleases, inasmuch as He is Himself power. Wherefore it was because He intended man to be man, that He originally made him so. But if He so intended — since He intends what is good — man is good. Now man is said to be composed of soul and body ; he cannot then exist without a body, but with a body, unless there be produced another man besides man. For all the orders of immortal beings must be preserved by God, and among these is man. " For," says *the Book of Wisdom*, " God created man to be immortal, and made him to be an image of His own eternity."[1] The body then perishes not ; for man is composed of soul and body.

XII. Wherefore observe that these are the very things which the Lord wished to teach to the Sadducees, who did not believe in the resurrection of the flesh. For this was the opinion of the Sadducees. Whence it was that, having contrived the parable about the woman and the seven brethren, that they might cast doubt upon the resurrection of the flesh, " There came to Him,"[2] it is said, " the Sadducees also, who say that there is no resurrection." Christ, then, if there had been no resurrection of the flesh, but the soul only were saved, would have agreed with their opinion as a right and excellent one. But as it was, He answered and said, " In the resurrection they neither marry, nor are given in marriage, but are as the angels in heaven,"[2] not on account of having no flesh, but of not marrying nor being married, but being henceforth incorruptible. And He speaks of our being near the angels in this respect, that as the angels in heaven, so we also in paradise, spend our time

no more in marriage-feasts or other festivities. but in seeing God and cultivating life, under the direction of Christ. For He did not say " they shall be angels," but like angels, in being, for instance, crowned, as it is written, with glory and honour ; differing a little from the angels,[3] while near to being angels. Just as if He had said. while observing the fair order of the sky, and the stillness of the night, and everything illumined by the heavenly light of the moon, " the moon shines like the sun." We should not then say that He asserted that the moon was absolutely the sun, but like the sun. As also that which is not gold, but approaching the nature of gold, is said not to be gold, but to be like gold. But if it were gold, it would be said to be, and not to be like, gold. But since it is not gold, but approaching to the nature of it, and has the appearance of it, it is said to be like gold ; so also when He says that the saints shall. in the resurrection, be like the angels, we do not understand Him to assert that they will then be actually angels, but approaching to the condition of angels. So that it is most unreasonable to say, " Since Christ declared that the saints in the resurrection appear as angels, therefore their bodies do not rise," although the very words employed give a clear proof of the real state of the case. For the term " resurrection " is not applied to that which has not fallen, but to that which has fallen and rises again ; as when the prophet says, " I will also raise up again the tabernacle of David which has fallen down."[4] Now the much-desired tabernacle of the soul is fallen, and sunk down into " the dust of the earth."[5] For it is not that which is not dead, but that which is dead, that is laid down. But it is the flesh which dies ; the soul is immortal. So, then, if the soul be immortal, and the body be the corpse, those who say that there is a resurrection, but not of the flesh, deny any resurrection ; because it is not that which remains standing, but that which has fallen[6] and been laid down, that is set up ; according to that which is written, " Does not he who falls rise again, and he who turns aside return ? "[7]

XIII. Since flesh was made to border on incorruption and corruption, being itself neither the one nor the other, and was overcome by corruption for the sake of pleasure, though it was the work and property of incorruption ; therefore it became corruptible, and was laid in the dust of the earth. When, then, it was overcome by corruption, and delivered over to death through disobedience, God did not leave it to corruption, to be triumphed over as an inheritance ; but,

---

[1] Wisd. ii. 23.
[2] Matt. xxii. 23.
[3] Ps. viii. 5.
[4] Amos ix. 11.
[5] Dan. xii. 2.
[6] [A play on the Greek ἀνάστασις, but good exegesis.]
[7] Jer. viii. 4.

after conquering death by the resurrection, delivered it again to incorruption, in order that corruption might not receive the property of incorruption, but·incorruption that of corruption. Therefore the apostle answers thus, " For this corruptible must put on incorruption, and this mortal must put on immortality." [1] Now the corruptible and mortal putting on immortality, what else is it but that which is " sown in corruption and raised in incorruption," [2] — for the soul is not corruptible or mortal ; but this which is mortal and corrupting is of flesh, — in order that, " as we have borne the image of the earthy, we shall also bear the image of the heavenly ? " [3] For the image of the earthy which we have borne is this, " Dust thou art, and unto dust shalt thou return." [4] But the image of the heavenly is the resurrection from the dead, and incorruption, in order that " as Christ was raised up from the dead by the glory of the Father, so we also should walk in newness of life." [5] But if any one were to think that the earthy image is the flesh itself, but the heavenly image some other spiritual body besides the flesh ; let him first consider that Christ, the heavenly man, when He appeared, bore the same form of limbs and the same image of flesh as ours, through which also He, who was not man, became man, that " as in Adam all die, even so in Christ shall all be made alive." [6] For if He bore flesh for any other reason than that of setting the flesh free, and raising it up, why did He bear flesh superfluously, as He purposed neither to save it, nor to raise it up? But the Son of God does nothing superfluously. He did not then take the form of a servant uselessly, but to raise it up and save it. For He truly was made man, and died, and not in mere appearance, but that He might truly be shown to be the first begotten from the dead, changing the earthy into the heavenly, and the mortal into the immortal. When, then, Paul says that " flesh and blood cannot inherit the kingdom of God," [7] he does not give a disparaging opinion of the regeneration of the flesh, but would teach that the kingdom of God, which is eternal life, is not possessed by the body, but the body by the life. For if the kingdom of God, which is life, were possessed by the body, it would happen that the life would be consumed by corruption. But now the life possesses what is dying, in order that " death may be swallowed up in victory " [8] by life, and the corruptible may be seen to be the possession of incorruption and immortality, while it be-

comes unbound and free from death and sin, but the slave and servant of immortality ; so that the body may be the possession of incorruption, and not incorruption that of the body.

xiv. If, then, out of such a drop, small, and previously without any existence, in its actual state of moistness, contractedness, and insignificance, in fact out of nothing, man is brought into being, how much rather shall man spring again into being out of a previously existing man? For it is not so difficult to make anything anew after it has once existed and fallen into decay, as to produce out of nothing that which has never existed. Now, in case we choose to exhibit the seminal fluid discharged from a man, and place by it a corpse, each by itself, which of them, as they both lie exposed to view, will the spectators think most likely to become a man — that drop, which is nothing at all, or that which has already shape, and size, and substance? For if the very thing which is nothing at all, merely because God pleases, becomes a man, how much rather shall that which has existence and is brought to perfection become again a man, if God pleases? For what was the purpose of the theologian Moses, in introducing, under a mystical sense, the Feast of Tabernacles in the Book of Leviticus? Was it that we may keep a feast to God, as the Jews with their low view of the Scriptures interpret it? as if God took pleasure in such tabernacles, decked out with fruits and boughs and leaves, which immediately wither and lose their verdure. We cannot say so. Tell me, then, what was the object of the Feast of Tabernacles? It was introduced to point to this real tabernacle of ours, which, after it was fallen down to corruption through the transgression of the law, and broken up by sin, God promised to put together again, and to raise up in incorruptibility, in order that we may truly celebrate in His honour the great and renowned Feast of Tabernacles at the resurrection ; when our tabernacles are put together in the perfect order of immortality and harmony, and raised up from the dust in incorruption ; when the dry bones, [9] according to the most true prophecy, shall hear a voice, and be brought to their joints by God, the Creator and Perfect Artificer, who will then renew the flesh and bind it on, no more with such ties as those by which it was at first held together, but by such as shall be for ever undecaying and indissoluble. For I once saw [10] on Olympus, which is a mountain of Lycia, fire bursting up from the ground spontaneously on the summit of the mountain ; and by it was standing an Agnos tree, so flourishing, green, and shady, that one might suppose a

---

[1] 1 Cor. xv. 53.
[2] 1 Cor. v. 42.
[3] 1 Cor. xv. 49.
[4] Gen. iii. 19.
[5] Rom. vi. 4.
[6] 1 Cor. xv. 22.
[7] 1 Cor. xv. 50.
[8] 1 Cor. xv. 54.

[9] Ezek. xxxvii. 4.
[10] [See part ii. cap. viii., p. 375, *infra*. What he *testifies* may be accepted, at least, as his genuine conviction.]

never-failing stream of water had nourished its growth, rather than what was really the case. For which cause, therefore, though the natures of things are corruptible, and their bodies consumed by fire, and it is impossible for things which are once of an inflammable nature to remain unaffected by fire ; yet this tree, so far from being burnt, is actually more vigorous and green than usual, though it is naturally inflammable, and that too when the fire is glowing about its very roots. I certainly cast some boughs of trees from the adjoining wood on to the place where the fire burst forth, and they immediately caught fire and were burnt to ashes. Now, then, tell me why it is that that which cannot bear even to feel the heat of the sun, but withers up under it unless it be sprinkled with water, is not consumed when beset by such fiery heat, but both lives and thrives? What is the meaning of this marvel? God appointed this as an example and introduction to the day that is coming, in order that we may know more certainly that, when all things are deluged with fire from heaven, the bodies which are distinguished by chastity and righteousness will be taken up by Him as free from all injury from the fire as from cold water. For truly, O beneficent and bountiful Lord, "the creature that serveth Thee, who art the Maker, increaseth his strength against the unrighteous for their punishment, and abateth his strength for the benefit of such as put their trust in Thee ;"[1] and at Thy pleasure fire cools, and injures nothing that Thou determinest to be preserved ; and again, water burns more fiercely than fire, and nothing opposes Thine unconquerable power and might. For Thou createdst all things out of nothing ; wherefore also Thou changest and transformest all things as Thou wilt, seeing they are Thine, and Thou alone art God.

xv. The apostle certainly, after assigning the planting and watering to art and earth and water, conceded the growth to God alone, where he says, "Neither is he that planteth anything, neither he that watereth ; but God that giveth the increase."[2] For he knew that Wisdom, the first-born of God, the parent and artificer of all things, brings forth everything into the world ; whom the ancients called Nature and Providence, because she, with constant provision and care, gives to all things birth and growth. "For," says the Wisdom of God, "my Father worketh hitherto, and I work."[3] Now it is on this account that Solomon called Wisdom the artificer of all things, since God is in no respect poor, but able richly to create, and make, and vary, and increase all things.

xvi. God, who created all things, and provides and cares for all things, took dust from the ground, and made our outer man.

PART II.

THE SECOND DISCOURSE ON THE RESURRECTION.[4]

For instance, then, the images of our kings here, even though they be not formed of the more precious materials — gold or silver — are honoured by all. For men do not, while they treat with respect those of the far more precious material, slight those of a less valuable, but honour every image in the world, even though it be of chalk or bronze. And one who speaks against either of them, is not acquitted as if he had only spoken against clay, nor condemned for having despised gold, but for having been disrespectful towards the King and Lord Himself. The images of God's angels, which are fashioned of gold, the principalities and powers, we make to His honour and glory.

PART III.

I. FROM THE DISCOURSE ON THE RESURRECTION.[5]

I. Read the Book on the Resurrection by St. Methodius, Bishop and Martyr, of which that which follows is a selection, that the body is not the fetter of the soul, as Origen thought, nor are souls called by the prophet Jeremiah "fettered" on account of their being within bodies. For he lays down the principle that the body does not hinder the energies of the soul, but that rather the body is carried about with it, and co-operates in whatever the soul commits to it. But how are we to understand the opinion of Gregory[6] the theologian, and many others?

II. That Origen said that the body was given to the soul as a fetter after the fall, and that previously it lived without a body ; but that this body which we wear is the cause of our sins ; wherefore also he called it a fetter, as it can hinder the soul from good works.

III. That if the body was given to the soul after the fall as a fetter, it must have been given as a fetter upon the evil or the good. Now it is impossible that it should be upon the good ; for no physician or artificer gives to that which has gone wrong a remedy to cause further error, much less would God do so. It remains, then, that it was a fetter upon evil. But surely we see that, at the beginning, Cain, clad in this body, committed murder ; and it is evident into

---

[1] Wisd. xvi. 24.
[2] 1 Cor. iii. 7.
[3] John v. 17.

[4] From St. John Damascene, Orat. 2, *De Imagin.*, tom. i. p. 389, ed. Paris, 1712.
[5] From Photius, *Bibliotheca*, cod. 234.
[6] Gregory, surnamed Theologus, commonly known as Gregory Nazianzen.

what wickedness those who succeeded him ran. The body is not, then, a fetter upon evil, nor indeed a fetter at all; nor was the soul clothed in it for the first time after the fall.

IV. That man, with respect to his nature, is most truly said to be neither soul without body, nor, on the other hand, body without soul; but a being composed out of the union of soul and body into one form of the beautiful. But Origen said that the soul alone is man, as did Plato.

V. That there is a difference between man and other living creatures; and to them are given varieties of natural form and shape, as many as the tangible and visible forces of nature produced at the command of God; while to him was given the form and image of God, with every part accurately finished, after the very original likeness of the Father and the only-begotten Son. Now we must consider how the saint states this.

VI. He says that Phidias the statuary, after he had made the Pisæan image of ivory, ordered oil to be poured out before it, that, as far as he could secure it, it might be preserved imperishable.

VII. He says, as was said also by Athenagoras,[1] that the devil is a spirit, made by God, in the neighbourhood of matter, as of course the rest of the angels are, and that he was entrusted with the oversight of matter, and the forms of matter. For, according to the original constitution of angels, they were made by God, in His providence, for the care of the universe; in order that, while God exercises a perfect and general supervision over the whole, and keeps the supreme authority and power over all — for upon Him their existence depends — the angels appointed for this purpose take charge of particulars. Now the rest of them remained in the positions for which God made and appointed them; but the devil was insolent, and having conceived envy of us, behaved wickedly in the charge committed to him; as also did those who subsequently were enamoured of fleshly charms, and had illicit intercourse with the daughters of men.[1] For to them also, as was the case with men, God granted the possession of their own choice. And how is this to be taken?

VIII. He says that by the coats of skins is signified death. For he says of Adam, that when the Almighty God saw that by treachery he, an immortal being, had become evil, just as his deceiver the devil was, He prepared the coats of skins on this account; that when he was thus, as it were, clothed in mortality, all that was evil in him might die in the dissolution of the body.

IX. He holds that St. Paul had two revelations. For the apostle, he says, does not suppose paradise to be in the third heaven, in the opinion of those who knew how to observe the niceties of language, when he says, "I know such a man caught up to the third heaven; and I know such a man, whether in the body or out of the body, God knoweth, that was caught up into paradise."[2] Here he signifies that he has seen two revelations, having been evidently taken up twice, once to the third heaven, and once into paradise. For the words, "I know such a man caught up," make it certain that he was personally shown a revelation respecting the third heaven. And the words which follow, "And I know such a man, whether in the body or out of the body, God knoweth, that he was caught up into paradise," show that another revelation was made to him respecting paradise. Now he was led to make this statement by his opponent's having laid it down from the apostle's words that paradise is a mere conception, as it is above the heaven, in order to draw the conclusion that life in paradise is incorporeal.[3]

X. He says that it is in our power to do, or to avoid doing, evil; since otherwise we should not be punished for doing evil, nor be rewarded for doing well; but the presence or absence of evil thoughts does not depend upon ourselves. Wherefore even the sainted Paul says, "For what I would, that do I not, but what I would not, that I do;"[4] that is to say, "My thoughts are not what I would, but what I would not." Now he says that the habit of imagining evil is rooted out by the approach of physical death,[5] — since it was for this reason that death was appointed by God for the sinner, that evil might not remain for ever.

But what is the meaning of this statement? It is to be noted that it has been made by others of our Fathers as well. *What is the meaning, seeing that those who meet death find in it at the time neither increase nor decrease of sins?*

II. A SYNOPSIS OF SOME APOSTOLIC WORDS FROM THE SAME DISCOURSE.[6]

I. Read a compendious interpretation of some apostolic words from the same discourse. Let us see, then, what it is that we have endeavoured to say respecting the apostle. For this saying of his, "I was alive without the law once,"[7] refers to the life which was lived in paradise before the law, not without a body, but with a body, by our first parents, as we have shown above; for we lived without concupiscence, being altogether ignorant of its assaults. For not to have a law according to which we ought to live, nor a power of establishing what manner of life we ought to

1 [Athenagoras, *Plea*, cap. xxiv. vol. ii. p. 142, this series.]

2 2 Cor. xii. 2, 3.
3 [Gregory's opponent, not St. Paul's.]
4 Rom. vii. 15.
5 [Gregory says.]
6 From Photius, *Bibliotheca*, cod. 234.
7 Rom. vii. 9.

adopt, so that we might justly be approved or blamed, is considered to exempt a person from accusation. Because one cannot lust after those things from which he is not restrained, and even if he lusted after them, he would not be blamed. For lust is not directed to things which are before us, and subject to our power, but to those which are before us, and not in our power. For how should one care for a thing which is neither forbidden nor necessary to him? And for this reason it is said, " I had not known lust, except the law had said, Thou shalt not covet." [1] For when (our first parents) heard, " Of the tree of the knowledge of good and evil, thou shalt not eat of it ; for in the day thou eatest thereof thou shalt surely die," [2] then they conceived lust, and gathered it. Therefore was it said, " I had not known lust, except the law had said, Thou shalt not covet ;" nor would they have desired to eat, except it had been said, " Thou shalt not eat of it." For it was thence that sin took occasion to deceive me. For when the law was given, the devil had it in his power to work lust in me ; " for without the law, sin was dead ; " [3] which means, " when the law was not given, sin could not be committed." But I was alive and blameless before the law, having no commandment in accordance with which it was necessary to live ; " but when the commandment came, sin revived, and I died. And the commandment, which was ordained to life, I found to be unto death." [4] For after God had given the law, and had commanded me what I ought to do, and what I ought not to do, the devil wrought lust in me. For the promise of God which was given to me, this was for life and incorruption, so that obeying it I might have ever blooming life and joy unto incorruption ; but to him who disobeyed it, it would issue in death. But the devil, whom he calls sin, because he is the author of sin, taking occasion by the commandment to deceive me to disobedience, deceived and slew me, thus rendering me subject to the condemnation, " In the day that thou eatest thereof thou shalt surely die." [2] " Wherefore the law is holy, and the commandment holy, and just and good ; " [5] because it was given, not for injury, but for safety ; for let us not suppose that God makes anything useless or hurtful. What then? " Was then that which is good made death unto me ? " [6] namely, that which was given as a law, that it might be the cause of the greatest good? " God forbid." For it was not the law of God that became the cause of my being brought into subjection to corruption, but the devil ; that he might be made manifested who, through that which is good, wrought evil ; that the inventor of evil might become and be proved the greatest of all sinners. " For we know that the law is spiritual ; " [7] and therefore it can in no respect be injurious to any one ; for spiritual things are far removed from irrational lust and sin. " But I am carnal, sold under sin ; " [7] which means : But I being carnal, and being placed between good and evil as a voluntary agent, am so that I may have it in my power to choose what I will. For " behold I set before thee life and death ; " [8] meaning that death would result from disobedience of the spiritual law, that is of the commandment ; and from obedience to the carnal law, that is the counsel of the serpent ; for by such a choice " I am sold " to the devil, fallen under sin. Hence evil, as though besieging me, cleaves to me and dwells in me, justice giving me up to be sold to the Evil One, in consequence of having violated the law. Therefore also the expressions : " That which I do, I allow not," and " what I hate, that do I," [9] are not to be understood of doing evil, but of only thinking it. For it is not in our power to think or not to think of improper things, but to act or not to act upon our thoughts. For we cannot hinder thoughts from coming into our minds, since we receive them when they are inspired into us from without ; but we are able to abstain from obeying them and acting upon them. Therefore it is in our power to will not to think these things ; but not to bring it about that they shall pass away, so as not to come into the mind again ; for this does not lie in our power, as I said ; which is the meaning of that statement, " The good that I would, I do not ; " [10] for I do not will to think the things which injure me ; for this good is altogether innocent. But " the good that I would, I do not ; but the evil which I would not, that I do ; " not willing to think, and yet thinking what I do not will. And consider whether it was not for these very things that David entreated God, grieving that he thought of those things which he did not will : " O cleanse Thou me from my secret faults. Keep Thy servant also from presumptuous sins, lest they get the dominion over me ; so shall I be undefiled, and innocent from the great offence." [11] And the apostle too, in another place : " Casting down imaginations, and every high thing that exalteth itself against the knowledge of God, and bringing into captivity every thought to the obedience of Christ." [12]

II. But if any one should venture to oppose this statement, and reply, that the apostle teaches

---

[1] Rom. vii. 7.
[2] Gen. ii. 17.
[3] Rom. vii. 8.
[4] Rom. vii. 9, 10.
[5] Rom. vii. 12.
[6] Rom. vii. 13.

[7] Rom. vii. 14.
[8] Jer. xxi. 8; Ecclus. xv. 8; Deut. xxx. 15.
[9] Rom. vii. 15.
[10] Rom. vii. 19.
[11] Ps. xix. 12, 13.
[12] 2 Cor. x. 5.

that we hate not only the evil which is in thought, but that we do that which we will not, and we hate it even in the very act of doing it, for he says, "The good which I would, I do not; but the evil which I would not, that I do;"[1] if he who says so speaks the truth, let us ask him to explain what was the evil which the apostle hated and willed not to do, but did; and the good which he willed to do, but did not; and conversely, whether as often as he willed to do good, so often he did not do the good which he willed, but did the evil which he willed not? And how he can say, when exhorting us to shake off all manner of sin, "Be ye followers of me, even as I also am of Christ?"[2] Thus he meant the things already mentioned which he willed not to do, not to be done, but only to be thought of. For how otherwise could he be an exact imitation of Christ? It would be excellent then, and most delightful, if we had not those who oppose us, and contend with us; but since this is impossible, we cannot do what we will. For we will not to have those who lead us to passion, for then we could be saved without weariness and effort; but that does not come to pass which we will, but that which we will not. For it is necessary, as I said, that we should be tried. Let us not then, O my soul, let us not give in to the Evil One; but putting on "the whole armour of God," which is our protection, let us have "the breastplate of righteousness, and your feet shod with the preparation of the Gospel (of peace). Above all, taking the shield of faith, wherewith ye shall be able to quench all the fiery darts of the wicked. And take the helmet of salvation, and the sword of the spirit, which is the Word of God,"[3] that ye may be able to stand against the wiles of the devil; "casting down imaginations, and every high thing that exalteth itself against the knowledge of Christ,"[4] "for we wrestle not against flesh and blood;"[5] for that which I do, I allow not; for what I would, that do I not: but what I hate, that do I. If then I do that which I would not, I consent unto the law that it is good. Now then it is no more I that do it, but sin that dwelleth in me. For I know that in me — that is, in my flesh — dwelleth no good thing."[6] And this is rightly said. For remember how it has been already shown that, from the time when man went astray and disobeyed the law, thence sin, receiving its birth from his disobedience, dwelt in him. For thus a commotion was stirred up, and we were filled with agitations and foreign imaginations, being emptied of the divine inspiration and filled with carnal desire, which the cunning serpent infused into us. And, therefore, God invented death for our sakes, that He might destroy sin, lest rising up in us immortals, as I said, it should be immortal. When the apostle says, "for I know that in me — that is, in my flesh — dwelleth no good thing," by which words he means to indicate that sin dwells in us, from the transgression, through lust; out of which, like young shoots, the imaginations of pleasure rise around us. For there are two kinds of thoughts in us; the one which arises from the lust which lies in the body, which, as I said, came from the craft of the Evil Spirit; the other from the law, which is in accordance with the commandment, which we had implanted in us as a natural law, stirring up our thoughts to good, when we delight in the law of God according to our mind, for this is the inner man; but in the law of the devil according to the lust which dwells in the flesh. For he who wars against and opposes the law of God, that is, against the tendency of the mind to good, is the same who stirs up the carnal and sensual impulses to lawlessness.

III. For the apostle here sets forth clearly, as I think, three laws: One in accordance with the good which is implanted in us, which clearly he calls the law of the mind. One the law which arises from the assault of evil, and which often draws on the soul to lustful fancies, which, he says, "wars against the law of the mind."[7] And the third, which is in accordance with sin, settled in the flesh from lust, which he calls the "law of sin which dwells in our members;"[7] which the Evil One, urging on, often stirs up against us, driving us to unrighteousness and evil deeds. For there seems to be in ourselves one thing which is better and another which is worse. And when that which is in its nature better is about to become more powerful than that which is worse, the whole mind is carried on to that which is good; but when that which is worse increases and overbalances, man is on the contrary urged on to evil imaginations. On account of which the apostle prays to be delivered from it, regarding it as death and destruction; as also does the prophet when he says, "Cleanse Thou me from my secret faults."[8] And the same is denoted by the words, "For I delight in the law of God after the inward man; but I see another law in my members, warring against the law of my mind, and bringing me into captivity to the law of sin which is in my members. O wretched man that I am! who shall deliver me from the body of this death?"[9] By which he does not mean that the body is death, but the law of sin which is in his members, lying hidden in us

---

[1] Rom. vii. 19.
[2] 1 Cor. xi. 1.
[3] Eph. vi. 13, 14-17.
[4] 2 Cor. x. 5.
[5] Eph. vi. 12.
[6] Rom. vii. 15-18.

[7] Rom. vii. 23.
[8] Ps. xix. 12.
[9] Rom. vii. 22-24.

through the transgression, and ever deluding the soul to the death of unrighteousness. And he immediately adds, clearly showing from what kind of death he desired to be delivered, and who he was who delivered him, "I thank God, through Jesus Christ."[1] And it should be considered, if he said that this body was death, O Aglaophon, as you supposed, he would not afterwards mention Christ as delivering him from so great an evil. For in that case what a strange thing should we have had from the advent of Christ? And how could the apostle have said this, as being able to be delivered from death by the advent of Christ; when it was the lot of all to die before Christ's coming into the world? And, therefore, O Aglaophon, he says not that this body was death, but the sin which dwells in the body through lust, from which God has delivered him by the coming of Christ. "For the law of the Spirit of life in Christ Jesus hath made me free from the law of sin and death;" so that "He that raised up Jesus from the dead shall also quicken your mortal bodies by His Spirit that dwelleth in you;" having "condemned sin" which is in the body to its destruction; "that the righteousness of the law"[2] of nature which draws us to good, and is in accordance with the commandment, might be kindled and manifested. For the good which "the law" of nature "could not do, in that it was weak," being overcome by the lust which lies in the body, God gave strength to accomplish, "sending His own Son in the likeness of sinful flesh;" so that sin being condemned, to its destruction, so that it should never bear fruit in the flesh, the righteousness of the law of nature might be fulfilled, abounding in the obedience of those who walk not according to the lust of the flesh, but according to the lust and guidance of the Spirit; "for the law of the Spirit of life," which is the Gospel, being different from earlier laws, leading by its preaching to obedience and the remission of sins, delivered us from the law of sin and death, having conquered entirely sin which reigned over our flesh.

IV. He[3] says that plants are neither nourished nor increased from the earth. For he says, let any one consider how the earth can be changed and taken up into the substance of trees. For then the place of the earth which lay around, and was drawn up through the roots into the whole compass of the tree, where the tree grew, must needs be hollowed out; so that such a thing as they hold respecting the flux of bodies is absurd. For how could the earth first enter in through the roots into the trunks of the plants, and then, passing through their channels into all their branches, be turned into leaves and fruit?

Now there are large trees, such as the cedar, pines, firs, which annually bear much leaves and fruit; and one may see that they consume none of the surrounding earth into the bulk and substance of the tree. For it would be necessary, if it were true that the earth went up through the roots, and was turned into wood, that the whole place where the earth lay round about them should be hollowed out; for it is not the nature of a dry substance to flow in, like a moist substance, and fill up the place of that which moves away. Moreover, there are fig-trees, and other similar plants, which frequently grow in the buildings of monuments, and yet they never consume the entire building into themselves. But if any one should choose to collect their fruit and leaves for many years, he would perceive that their bulk had become much larger than the earth upon the monuments. Hence it is absurd to suppose that the earth is consumed into the crop of fruits and leaves; and even if they were all made by it, they would be so only as using it for their seat and place. For bread is not made without a mill, and a place, and time, and fire; and yet bread is not made out of any of these things. And the same may be said of a thousand other things.

v. Now the followers of Origen bring forward this passage, "For we know that if our earthly house of this tabernacle were dissolved,"[4] and so forth, to disprove the resurrection of the body, saying that the "tabernacle" is the body, and the "house not made with hands" "in the heavens" is our spiritual clothing. Therefore, says the holy Methodius, by this earthly house must metaphorically[5] be understood our short-lived existence here, and not this tabernacle; for if you decide to consider the body as being the earthly house which is dissolved, tell us what is the tabernacle whose house is dissolved? For the tabernacle is one thing, and the house of the tabernacle another, and still another we who have the tabernacle. "For," he says, "if our earthly house of this tabernacle be dissolved"—by which he points out that the souls are ourselves, that the body is a tabernacle, and that the house of the tabernacle figuratively represents the enjoyment of the flesh in the present life. If, then, this present life of the body be dissolved like a house, we shall have that which is not made with hands in the heavens. "Not made with hands," he says, to point out the difference; because this life may be said to be made with hands, seeing that all the employments and pursuits of life are carried on by the hands of men. For the body, being the workmanship of God, is not said to be made with hands, inasmuch as

---

[1] Rom. vii. 25.
[2] Rom. viii. 2, 11, 3, 4.
[3] Methodius.

[4] 2 Cor. v. 1.
[5] The word means literally, "by an abuse, or misapplication;" but the author's meaning is very nearly that expressed in the text. — TR.

it is not formed by the arts of men. But if they shall say that it is made with hands, because it was the workmanship of God, then our souls also, and the angels, and the spiritual clothing in the heavens, are made with hands ; for all these things, also, are the workmanship of God. What, then, is the house which is made with hands? It is, as I have said, the short-lived existence which is sustained by human hands. For God said, " In the sweat of thy face shalt thou eat bread ; "[1] and when that life is dissolved, we have the life which is not made with hands. As also the Lord showed, when He said : " Make to yourselves friends of the mammon of unrighteousness ; that, when ye fail, they may receive you into everlasting habitations."[2] For what the Lord then called " habitations,"[3] the apostle here calls " clothing."[4] And what He there calls " friends " " of unrighteousness," the apostle here calls " houses " " dissolved." As then, when the days of our present life shall fail, those good deeds of beneficence to which we have attained in this unrighteous life, and in this " world " which " lieth in wickedness,"[5] will receive our souls ; so when this perishable life shall be dissolved, we shall have the habitation which is before the resurrection — that is, our souls shall be with God, until we shall receive the new house which is prepared for us, and which shall never fall. Whence also " we groan," " not for that we would be unclothed," as to the body, " but clothed upon "[6] by it in the other life. For the " house in heaven," with which we desire to be " clothed," is immortality ; with which, when we are clothed, every weakness and mortality will be entirely " swallowed up " in it, being consumed by endless life. " For we walk by faith, not by sight ; "[7] that is, for we still go forward by faith, viewing the things which are beyond with a darkened understanding, and not clearly, so that we may see these things, and enjoy them, and be in them. " Now this I say, brethren, that flesh and blood cannot inherit the kingdom of God ; neither doth corruption inherit incorruption."[8] By flesh, he did not mean flesh itself, but the irrational impulse towards the lascivious pleasures of the soul. And therefore when he says, " Flesh and blood cannot inherit the kingdom of God," he adds the explanation, " Neither doth corruption inherit incorruption." Now corruption is not the thing which is corrupted, but the thing which corrupts. For when death prevails the body sinks into corruption ; but when life still remains in it, it stands uncor-

rupted. Therefore, since the flesh is the boundary between corruption and incorruption, not being either corruption or incorruption, it was vanquished by corruption on account of pleasure, although it was the work and the possession of incorruption. Therefore it became subject to corruption. When, then, it had been overcome by corruption, and was given over to death for chastisement, He did not leave it to be vanquished and given over as an inheritance to corruption ; but again conquering death by the resurrection, He restored it to incorruption, that corruption might not inherit incorruption, but incorruption that which is corruptible. And therefore the apostle answers, " This corruptible must put on incorruption, and this mortal immortality."[9] But the corruptible and mortal putting on incorruption and immortality, what else is this, but that which is sown in corruption rising in incorruption?[10] For, " as we have borne the image of the earthly, we shall also bear the image of the heavenly."[11] For the " image of the earthly " which we have borne refers to the saying, " Dust thou art, and unto dust thou shalt return."[12] And the " image of the heavenly is the resurrection from the dead and incorruption."

VI. Now Justin of Neapolis,[13] a man not far removed either from the times or from the virtues of the apostles, says that that which is mortal is inherited, but that life inherits ; and that flesh dies, but that the kingdom of heaven lives. When then, Paul says that " flesh and blood cannot inherit the kingdom of heaven,"[14] he does not so speak as seeming to slight the regeneration of the flesh, but as teaching that the kingdom of God, which is eternal life, is not inherited by the body, but the body by life. For if the kingdom of God, which is life, were inherited by the body, it would happen that life was swallowed up by corruption. But now life inherits that which is mortal, that death may be swallowed up of life unto victory, and that which is corruptible appear the possession of incorruption ; being made free from death and sin, and become the slave and subject of immortality, that the body may become the possession of incorruption, and not incorruption of the body.

VII. Now the passage, " The dead in Christ shall rise first : then we which are alive," St. Methodius thus explains : Those are our bodies ; for the souls are we ourselves, who, rising, resume that which is dead from the earth ; so that being caught up with them to meet the Lord, we may gloriously celebrate the splendid festival of

---

1 Gen. iii. 19.
2 Luke xvi. 9.
3 σκηνάς.
4 ἐπενδύσασθαι. 2 Cor. v. 2, 3.
5 1 John v. 19.
6 2 Cor. v. 4.
7 2 Cor. v. 7.
8 1 Cor. xv. 50.

9 1 Cor. xv. 53.
10 1 Cor. xv. 42.
11 1 Cor. xv. 49.
12 Gen. iii. 19.
13 Commonly known as St. Justin Martyr. — Tr. [See his treatise *On the Resurrection*, vol. i. p. 295; also *On Life*, p. 198, this series.]
14 1 Cor. xv. 50.

the resurrection, because we have received our everlasting tabernacles, which shall no longer die nor be dissolved.

VIII. I saw, he says, on Olympus [1] (Olympus is a mountain in Lycia), a fire spontaneously arising on the top of the mountain from the earth, beside which is the plant Puragnos, so flourishing, green, and shady, that it seemed rather as though it grew from a fountain. For what cause, although they are by nature corruptible, and their bodies consumed by fire, was this plant not only not burnt, but rather more flourishing, although in its nature it is easily burnt, and the fire was burning about its roots? Then I cast branches of trees out of the surrounding wood into the place where the fire streamed forth, and, immediately bursting up into flame, they were converted into cinders. What then is the meaning of this contradiction? This God appointed as a sign and prelude of the coming Day, that we may know that, when all things are overwhelmed by fire, the bodies which are endowed with chastity and righteousness shall pass through it as though it were cold water.

IX. Consider, he says, whether too the blessed John, when he says, " And the sea gave up the dead which were in it : and death and hell delivered up the dead which were in them," [2] does not mean the parts which are given up by the elements for the reconstruction of each one? By the sea is meant the moist element ; by hell,[3] the air, derived from ἀειδές, because it is invisible, as was said by Origen ; and by death, the earth, because those who die are laid in it ; whence also it is called in the Psalms the " dust of death," [4] Christ saying that He is brought " into the dust of death."

X. For, he says, whatever is composed and consists of pure air and pure fire, and is of like substance with the angelic beings, cannot have the nature of earth and water ; since it would then be earthy. And of such nature, and consisting of such things, Origen has shown that the body of man shall be which shall rise, which he also said would be spiritual.

XI. And he asks what will be the appearance of the risen body, when this human form, as according to him useless, shall wholly disappear ; since it is the most lovely of all things which are combined in living creatures, as being the form which the Deity Himself employs, as the most wise Paul explains : " For a man indeed ought not to cover his head, forasmuch as he is the image and glory of God ; " [5] in accordance with which the rational bodies of the angels are set in order? will it be circular, or polygonal, or cubical, or pyramidal? For there are very many kinds of forms ; but this is impossible.[6] Well then, what are we to think of the assertion, that the godlike shape is to be rejected as more ignoble, for he himself allows that the soul is like the body, and that man is to rise again without hands or feet?

XII. The transformation, he says, is the restoration into an impassible and glorious state. For now the body is a body of desire and of humiliation,[7] and therefore Daniel was called " a man of desires." [8] But then it will be transfigured into an impassible body, not by the change of the arrangement of the members, but by its not desiring carnal pleasures.

Then he says, refuting Origen, Origen therefore thinks that the same flesh will not be restored to the soul, but that the form of each, according to the appearance by which the flesh is now distinguished, shall arise stamped upon another spiritual body ; so that every one will again appear the same in form ; and that this is the resurrection which is promised. For, he says, the material body being fluid, and in no wise remaining in itself, but wearing out and being replaced around the appearance by which its shape is distinguished, and by which the figure is contained, it is necessary that the resurrection should be only that of the form.

XIII. Then, after a little, he says : If then, O Origen, you maintain that the resurrection of the body changed into a spiritual body is to be expected only in appearance, and put forth the vision of Moses and Elias as a most convincing proof of it ; saying that they appeared after their departure from life, preserving no different appearance from that which they had from the beginning ; in the same way will be the resurrection of all men. But Moses and Elias arose and appeared with this form of which you speak, before Christ suffered and rose. How then could Christ be celebrated by prophets and apostles as " the first begotten of the dead?" [9] For if the Christ is believed to be the first begotten of the dead, He is the first begotten of the dead as having risen before all others. But Moses appeared to the apostles before Christ suffered, having this form in which you say the resurrection is fulfilled. Hence, then, there is no resurrection of the form without the flesh. For either there is a resurrection of the form as you teach, and then Christ is no longer " the first begotten of the dead," from the fact that souls appeared before Him, having this form after death ; or He is truly the first begotten, and it is quite impossible that any should have

---

[1] Cf. p. 368, supra. [Pyragnos = fire-proof agnos.]
[2] Rev. xx. 13.
[3] Hades.
[4] Ps. xxii. 15.
[5] I Cor. xi. 7.

[6] [Justin Martyr, vol. i. p. 295, this series.]
[7] Phil. iii. 21.
[8] Dan. ix. 23, marginal reading.
[9] Rev. i. 5.

been thought meet for a resurrection before Him, so as not to die again. But if no one arose before Him, and Moses and Elias appeared to the apostles not having flesh, but only its appearance, the resurrection in the flesh is clearly manifested. For it is most absurd that the resurrection should be set forth only in form, since the souls, after their departure from the flesh, never appear to lay aside the form which, he says, rises again. But if that remains with them, so that it cannot be taken away, as with the soul of Moses and Elias; and neither perishes, as you think, nor is destroyed, but is everywhere present with them; then surely that form which never fell cannot be said to rise again.

XIV. But if any one, finding this inadmissible, answers, But how then, if no one rose before Christ went down into Hades, are several recorded as having risen before Him? Among whom is the son of the widow of Sarepta, and the son of the Shunammite, and Lazarus. We must say: These rose to die again; but we are speaking of those who shall never die after their rising. And if any one should speak doubtfully concerning the soul of Elias, as that the Scriptures say that he was taken up in the flesh, and we say that he appeared to the apostles divested of the flesh, we must say, that to allow that he appeared to the apostles in the flesh is more in favour of our argument. For it is shown by this case that the body is susceptible of immortality, as was also proved by the translation of Enoch. For if he could not receive immortality, he could not remain in a state of insensibility so long a time. If, then, he appeared with the body, that was truly after he was dead, but certainly not as having arisen from the dead. And this, we may say, if we agree with Origen when he says that the same form is given to the soul after death; when it is separated from the body, which is of all things the most impossible, from the fact that the form of the flesh was destroyed before by its changes, as also the form of the melted statue before its entire dissolution. Because the quality cannot be separated from the material, so as to exist by itself; for the shape which disappears around the brass is separated from the melted statue, and has not longer a substantial existence.

XV. Since the form is said to be separated in death from the flesh, come, let us consider in how many ways that which is separated is said to be separated. Now a thing is said to be separated from another either in act and subsistence, or in thought; or else in act, but not in subsistence. As if, for instance, one should separate from each other wheat and barley which had been mingled together; in as far as they are separated in motion, they are said to be separated in act; in as far as they stand apart

when separated, they are said to be separated in subsistence. They are separated in thought when we separate matter from its qualities, and qualities from matter; in act, but not in subsistence, when a thing separated from another no longer exists, not having a substantive existence. And it may be observed that it is so also in mechanics, when one looks upon a statue or a brazen horse melted. For, when he considers these things, he will see their natural form changing; and they alter into another figure from which the original form disappears. For if any one should melt down the works formed into the semblance of a man or a horse, he will find the appearance of the form disappearing, but the material itself remaining. It is, therefore, untenable to say, that the form shall arise in nowise corrupted, but that the body in which the form was stamped shall be destroyed.

XVI. But he says that it will be so; for it will be changed in a spiritual body. Therefore, it is necessary to confess that the very same form as at first does not arise, from its being changed and corrupted with the flesh. For although it be changed into a spiritual body, that will not be properly the original substance, but a certain resemblance of it, fashioned in an ethereal body. If, however, it is not the same form, nor yet the body which arises, then it is another in the place of the first. For that which is like, being different from that which it resembles, cannot be that very first thing in accordance with which it was made.

XVII. Moreover, he says that that is the appearance or form which shows forth the identity of the members in the distinctive character of the form.

XVIII. And, when Origen allegorises that which is said by the prophet Ezekiel concerning the resurrection of the dead, and perverts it to the return of the Israelites from their captivity in Babylon, the saint in refuting him, after many other remarks, says this also: For neither did they[1] obtain a perfect liberty, nor did they overcome their enemies by a greater power, and dwell again in Jerusalem; and when they frequently intended to build (the temple), they were prevented by other nations. Whence, also, they were scarce able to build that in forty-six years, which Solomon completed from the foundations in seven years. But what need we say on this subject? For from the time of Nebuchadnezzar, and those who after him reigned over Babylon, until the time of the Persian expedition against the Assyrians, and the empire of Alexander, and the war which was stirred up by the Romans against the Jews, Jerusalem was six times overthrown by its enemies. And this

---

[1] The Israelites.

is recorded by Josephus, who says : " Jerusalem was taken in the second year of the reign of Vespasian. It had been taken before five times ; but now for the second time it was destroyed. For Asochæus, king of Egypt, and after him Antiochus, next Pompey, and after these Sosius, with Herod, took the city and burnt it ; but before these, the king of Babylon conquered and destroyed it."

XIX. He says that Origen holds these opinions which he refutes. And there may be a doubt concerning Lazarus and the rich man. The simpler persons think that these things were spoken as though both were receiving their due for the things which they had done in life in their bodies ; but the more accurate think that, since no one is left in life after the resurrection, these things do not happen at the resurrection. For the rich man says : " I have five brethren ; . . . lest they also come into this place of torment, "[1] send Lazarus, that he may tèll them of those things which are here. And, therefore, if we ask respecting the " tongue," and the " finger," and " Abraham's bosom," and the reclining there, it may perhaps be that the soul receives in the change a form similar in appearance to its gross and earthly body. If, then, any one of those who have fallen asleep is recorded as having appeared, in the same way he has been seen in the form which he had when he was in the flesh. Besides, when Samuel appeared, it is clear that, being seen, he was clothed in a body ; and this must especially be admitted, if we are pressed by arguments which prove that the essence of the soul is incorporeal, and is manifested by itself.[3] But the rich man in torment, and the poor man who was comforted in the bosom of Abraham, are said, the one to be punished in Hades, and the other to be comforted in Abraham's bosom, before the appearing of the Saviour, and before the end of the world, and therefore before the resurrection ; teaching that now already, at the change, the soul uses a body. Wherefore, the saint says as follows : Setting forth that the soul, after its removal hence, has a form similar in appearance to this sensitive body ; does Origen represent the soul, after Plato, as being incorporeal? And how should that which, after removal from the world, is said to have need of a vehicle and a clothing, so that it might not be found naked, be in itself other than incorporeal? But if it be incorporeal, must it not also be incapable of passion? For it follows, from its being incorporeal, that it is also impassible and imperturbable. If, then, it was not distracted by any irrational desire, neither was it changed by a pained or suffering body. For neither can that which is incorporeal sympathize with a body, nor a body with that which is incorporeal, if,[4] indeed, the soul should seem to be incorporeal, in accordance with what has been said. But if it sympathize with the body, as is proved by the testimony of those who appear, it cannot be incorporeal. Therefore God alone is celebrated, as the unbegotten, independent, and unwearied nature ; being incorporeal, and therefore invisible ; for " no man hath seen God."[5] But souls, being rational bodies, are arranged by the Maker and Father of all things into members which are visible to reason, having received this impression. Whence, also, in Hades, as in the case of Lazarus and the rich man, they are spoken of as having a tongue, and a finger, and the other members ; not as though they had with them another invisible body, but that the souls themselves, naturally, when entirely stripped of their covering, are such according to their essence.

XX. The saint says at the end : The words, " For to this end Christ both died, and rose, and revived, that He might be Lord both of the dead and living,"[6] must be taken as referring to souls and bodies ; the souls being the *living*, as being immortal, and the bodies being *dead*.

XXI. Since the body of man is more honourable than other living creatures, because it is said to have been formed by the hands of God, and because it has attained to be the vehicle of the reasonable soul ; how is it that it is so short-lived, shorter even than some of the irrational creatures? Is it not clear that its long-lived existence will be after the resurrection?

---

[1] Luke xvi. 28.
[2] 1 Sam. xxviii. 12. [See vol. v. p. 169, note 11, this series.]
[3] The reading of Jahn, " καθ' ἑαυτήν," is here adopted. — TR.
[4] Jahn's reading.
[5] John i. 18.
[6] Rom. xiv. 9.

FRAGMENTS

ON THE HISTORY OF JONAH.

FROM THE BOOK ON THE RESURRECTION.[1]

I. THE history of Jonah [2] contains a great mystery. For it seems that the whale signifies Time, which never stands still, but is always going on, and consumes the things which are made by long and shorter intervals. But Jonah, who fled from the presence of God, is himself the first man who, having transgressed the law, fled from being seen naked of immortality, having lost through sin his confidence in the Deity. And the ship in which he embarked, and which was tempest-tossed, is this brief and hard life in the present time ; just as though we had turned and removed from that blessed and secure life, to that which was most tempestuous and unstable, as from solid land to a ship. For what a ship is to the land, that our present life is to that which is immortal. And the storm and the tempests which beat against us are the temptations of this life, which in the world, as in a tempestuous sea, do not permit us to have a fair voyage free from pain, in a calm sea, and one which is free from evils. And the casting of Jonah from the ship into the sea, signifies the fall of the first man from life to death, who received that sentence because, through having sinned, he fell from righteousness : " Dust thou art, and unto dust shalt thou return." [3] And his being swallowed by the whale signifies our inevitable removal by time. For the belly in which Jonah, when he was swallowed, was concealed, is the all-receiving earth, which receives all things which are consumed by time.

II. As, then, Jonah spent three days and as many nights in the whale's belly, and was delivered up sound again, so shall we all, who have passed through the three stages of our present life on earth — I mean the beginning, the middle, and the end, of which all this present time consists — rise again. For there are altogether three intervals of time, the past, the future, and the present. And for this reason the Lord spent so many days in the earth symbolically, thereby teaching clearly that when the fore-mentioned intervals of time have been fulfilled, then shall come our resurrection, which is the beginning of the future age, and the end of this. For in that age [4] there is neither past nor future, but only the present. Moreover, Jonah having spent three days and three nights in the belly of the whale, was not destroyed by his flesh being dissolved, as is the case with that natural decomposition which takes place in the belly, in the case of those meats which enter into it, on account of the greater heat in the liquids, that it might be shown that these bodies of ours may remain undestroyed. For consider that God had images of Himself made as of gold, that is of a purer spiritual substance, as the angels ; and others of clay or brass, as ourselves. He united the soul which was made in the image of God to that which was earthy. As, then, we must here honour all the images of a king, on account of the form which is in them, so also it is incredible that we who are the images of God should be altogether destroyed as being without honour. Whence also the Word descended into our world, and was incarnate of our body, in order that, having fashioned it to a more divine image, He might raise it incorrupt, although it had been dissolved by time. And, indeed, when we trace out the dispensation which was figuratively set forth by the prophet, we shall find the whole discourse visibly extending to this.

[1] [A fragment given by Combefis, in Latin, in the *Bibliotheca Concionatoria*, t. ii. p. 263, etc. Published in Greek from the Vatican MS. (1611), by Simon de Magistris, in *Acta Martyrum ad ostia Tiberina sub Claudio Gothico*. (Rome, 1792, folio. Append. p. 462.)]
[2] [Matt. xii. 40. This history comes to us virtually from the Son of God, who confirms the testimony of His prophet. See the very curious remarks of Edward King in his *Morsels of Criticism*, vol. i. p. 601, ed. 1788.]
[3] Gen. iii. 19.

[4] Or, dispensation.

EXTRACTS FROM THE WORK ON THINGS CREATED.[1]

I. This selection is made, by way of compendium or synopsis, from the work of the holy martyr and bishop Methodius, concerning things created. The passage, "Give not that which is holy unto the dogs, neither cast ye your pearls before swine,"[2] is explained by Origen as signifying that the pearls are the more mystical teachings of our God-given religion, and the swine those who roll in impiety and in all kinds of pleasures, as swine do in mud; for he said that it was taught by these words of Christ not to cast about the divine teachings, inasmuch as they could not bear them who were held by impiety and brutal pleasures. The great Methodius says: If we must understand by pearls the glorious and divine teachings, and by swine those who are given up to impiety and pleasures, from whom are to be withheld and hidden the apostle's teachings, which stir men up to piety and faith in Christ, see how you say that no Christians can be converted from their impiety by the teachings of the apostles. For they would never cast the mysteries of Christ to those who, through want of faith, are like swine. Either, therefore, these things were cast before all the Greeks and other unbelievers, and were preached by the disciples of Christ, and converted them from impiety to the faith of Christ, as we believers certainly confess, and then the words, "Cast not your pearls before swine," can no longer mean what has been said; or meaning this, we must say that faith in Christ and deliverance from impiety have been accorded to none of the unbelievers, whom we compare to swine, by the apostolic instructions enlightening their souls like pearls. But this is blasphemous. Therefore the pearls in this place are not to be taken to mean the deepest doctrines, and the swine the impious; nor are we to understand the words, "Cast not your pearls before swine," as forbidding us to cast before the impious and unbelieving the deep and sanctifying doctrines of faith in Christ; but we must take the pearls to mean virtues, with which the soul is adorned as with precious pearls; and not to cast them before swine, as meaning that we are not to cast these virtues, such as chastity, temperance, righteousness, and truth, that we are not to cast these to impure pleasures, for these are like swine, lest they, fleeing from the virtues, cause the soul to live a swinish and a vicious life.

II. Origen says that what he calls the Centaur is the universe which is co-eternal with the only wise and independent God. For he says, since there is no workman without some work, or maker without something made, so neither is there an Almighty without an object of His power. For the workman must be so called from his work, and the maker from what he makes, and the Almighty Ruler from that which He rules over. And so it must be, that these things were made by God from the beginning, and that there was no time in which they did not exist. For if there was a time when the things that are made did not exist, then, as there were no things which had been made, so there was no maker; which you see to be an impious conclusion. And it will result that the unchangeable and unaltered God has altered and changed. For if He made the universe later, it is clear that He passed from not making to making. But this is absurd in connection with what has been said. It is impossible, therefore, to say that the universe is not unbeginning and co-eternal with God. To whom the saint replies, in the person of another, asking, "Do you not consider God the beginning and fountain of wisdom and glory, and in short of all virtue in substance and not by acquisition?" "Certainly," he says. "And what besides? Is He not by Himself perfect and independent?" "True; for it is impossible that he who is independent should have his independence from another. For we must say, that all which is full by another is also imperfect. For it is the thing which has its completeness of itself, and in itself alone, which can alone be considered perfect." "You say most truly. For would you pronounce that which is neither by itself complete, nor its own completeness, to be independent?" "By no means. For that which is perfect through anything else must needs be in itself imperfect." "Well, then shall God be considered perfect by Himself, and not by some other?" "Most rightly." "Then God is something different from the world, and the world from God?" "Quite so." "We must not then say that God is perfect, and Creator, and Almighty, through the world?" "No; for He must surely by Himself, and not by the world, and that changeable, be found perfect by Himself." "Quite so." "But you will say that the rich man is called rich on account of his riches? And that the wise man is called wise not as being wisdom itself, but as being a possessor of substantial wisdom?" "Yes." "Well, then, since God is something different from the world, shall He be called on account of the world rich, and beneficent, and Creator?" "By no means.

[1] From Photius, *Bibliotheca*, cod. 235.
[2] Matt. vii. 6.

Away with such a thought!" "Well, then, He is His own riches, and is by Himself rich and powerful." "So it seems." "He was then before the world altogether independent, being Father, and Almighty, and Creator; so that He by Himself, and not by another, was this." "It must be so." "Yes; for if He were acknowledged to be Almighty on account of the world, and not of Himself, being distinct from the world, —may God forgive the words, which the necessity of the argument requires, — He would by Himself be imperfect and have need of these things, through which He is marvellously Almighty and Creator. We must not then admit this pestilent sin of those who say concerning God, that He is Almighty and Creator by the things which He controls and creates, which are changeable, and that He is not so by Himself.

III. Now consider it thus: "If, you say, the world was created later, not existing before, then we must change the passionless and unchangeable God; for it must needs be, that he who did nothing before, but afterwards, passes from not doing to doing, changes and is altered." Then I said, "Did God rest from making the world, or not?" "He rested." "Because otherwise it would not have been completed." "True." "If, then, the act of making, after not making, makes an alteration in God, does not His ceasing to make after making the same?" "Of necessity." "But should you say that He is altered as not doing to-day, from what He was, when He was doing?" "By no means. There is no necessity for His being changed, when He makes the world from what He was when He was not making it; and neither is there any necessity for saying that the universe must have co-existed with Him, on account of our not being forced to say that He has changed, nor that the universe is co-eternal with Him."

IV. But speak to me thus: "Should you call that a thing created which had no beginning of its creation?" "Not at all." "But if there is no beginning of its creation, it is of necessity uncreated. But if it was created, you will grant that it was created by some cause. For it is altogether impossible that it should have a beginning without a cause." "It is impossible." "Shall we say, then, that the world and the things which are in it, having come into existence and formerly not existing, are from any other cause than God?" "It is plain that they are from God." "Yes; for it is impossible that that which is limited by an existence which has a beginning should be co-existent with the infinite." "It is impossible." "But again, O Centaur, let us consider it from the beginning. Do you say that the things which exist were created by Divine knowledge or not?" "Oh, begone, they will say; not at all." "Well, but was it from

the elements, or from matter, or the firmaments, or however you choose to name them, for it makes no difference; these things existing beforehand uncreated and borne along in a state of chaos; did God separate them and reduce them all to order, as a good painter who forms one picture out of many colours?" "No, nor yet this." For they will quite avoid making a concession against themselves, lest agreeing that there was a beginning of the separation and transformation of matter, they should be forced in consistency to say, that in all things God began the ordering and adorning of matter which hitherto had been without form.

V. But come now, since by the favour of God we have arrived at this point in our discourse; let us suppose a beautiful statue standing upon its base; and that those who behold it, admiring its harmonious beauty, differ among themselves, some trying to make out that it had been made, others that it had not. I should ask them: For what reason do you say that it was not made? on account of the artist, because he must be considered as never resting from his work? or on account of the statue itself? If it is on account of the artist, how could it, as not being made, be fashioned by the artist? But if, when it is moulded of brass, it has all that is needed in order that it may receive whatever impression the artist chooses, how can that be said not to be made which submits to and receives his labour? If, again, the statue is declared to be by itself perfect and not made, and to have no need of art, then we must allow, in accordance with that pernicious heresy, that it is self-made. If perhaps they are unwilling to admit this argument, and reply more inconsistently, that they do not say that the figure was not made, but that it was always made, so that there was no beginning of its being made, so that artist might be said to have this subject of his art without any beginning. Well then, my friends, we will say to them, if no time, nor any age before can be found in the past, when the statue was not perfect, will you tell us what the artist contributed to it, or wrought upon it? For if this statue has need of nothing, and has no beginning of existence, for this reason, according to you, a maker never made it, nor will any maker be found. And so the argument seems to come again to the same conclusion, and we must allow that it is self-made. For if an artificer is said to have moved a statue ever so slightly, he will submit to a beginning, when he began to move and adorn that which was before unadorned and unmoved. But the world neither was nor will be for ever the same. Now we must compare the artificer to God, and the statue to the world. But how then, O foolish men, can you imagine the creation to be co-eternal with its Artificer, and to have no need of an artificer? For it is of necessity that the co-eternal should never have had a beginning of being, and should be equally uncreated and powerful with Him. But the uncreated appears to be in itself perfect and unchangeable, and it will have need of nothing, and be free from corruption. And if this be so, the world can no longer be, as you say it is, capable of change.

VI. He says that the Church [1] is so called from being called out [2] with respect to pleasures.

VII. The saint says: We said there are two kinds of formative power in what we have now acknowledged; the one which works by itself what it chooses, not out of things which already exist, by its bare will, without delay, as soon as it wills. This is the power of the Father. The other which adorns and embellishes, by imitation of the former, the things which already exist. This is the power of the Son, the almighty and powerful hand of the Father, by which, after creating matter not out of things which were already in existence, He adorns it.

VIII. The saint says that the Book of Job is by Moses. He says, concerning the words, "In the beginning God created the heaven and the earth," [3] that one will not err who says that the "Beginning" is Wisdom. For Wisdom is said by one of the Divine band to speak in this manner concerning herself: "The Lord created me the beginning of His ways for His works: of old He laid my foundation." [4] It was fitting and more seemly that all things which came into existence, should be more recent than Wisdom, since they existed through her. Now consider whether the saying: "In the beginning was the Word, and the Word was with God, and the Word was God. The same was in the beginning with God;" [5] — whether these statements be not in agreement with those. For we must say that the Beginning, out of which the most upright Word came forth, is the Father and Maker of all things, in whom it was. And the words, "The same was in the beginning with God," seem to indicate the position of authority of the Word, which He had with the Father before the world came into existence; "beginning" signifying His power. And so, after the peculiar unbeginning beginning, who is the Father, He is the beginning of other things, by whom all things are made.

IX. He says that Origen, after having fabled many things concerning the eternity of the universe, adds this also: Nor yet from Adam, as some say, did man, previously not existing, first take his existence and come into the world. Nor again did the world begin to be made six days before the creation of Adam. But if any one should prefer to differ in these points, let him first say, whether a period of time be not easily reckoned from the creation of the world, according to the Book of Moses, to those who so receive it, the voice of prophecy here proclaiming: "Thou art God from everlasting, and world without end. . . . For a thousand years in Thy sight are but as yesterday: seeing that is past as a watch in the night." [6] For when a thousand years are reckoned as one day in the sight of God, and from the creation of the world to His rest is six days, so also to our time, six days are defined, as those say who are clever arithmeticians. Therefore, they say that an age of six thousand years extends from Adam to our time. For they say that the judgment will come on the seventh day, that is in the seventh thousand years. Therefore, all the days from our time to that which was in the beginning, in which God created the heaven and the earth, are computed to be thirteen days; before which God, because he had as yet created nothing according to their folly, is stripped of His name of Father and Almighty. But if there are thirteen days in the sight of God from the creation of the world, how can Wisdom say, in the Book of the Son of Sirach: "Who can number the sand of the sea, and the drops of rain, and the days of eternity?" [7] This is what Origen says seriously, and mark how he trifles.

---

[1] Ἐκκλησία.
[2] ἐκκεκληκέναι.
[3] Gen. i. 1.
[4] Prov. viii. 22.
[5] John i. 1, 2.

[6] Ps. xc. 2, 4.
[7] Ecclus. i. 2.

FROM THE WORKS OF METHODIUS AGAINST PORPHYRY.

I.[1]

This, in truth, must be called most excellent and praiseworthy, which God Himself considers excellent, even if it be despised and scoffed at by all. For things are not what men think them to be.

II.[2]

Then repentance effaces every sin, when there is no delay after the fall of the soul, and the disease is not suffered to go on through a long interval. For then evil will not have power to leave its mark in us, when it is drawn up at the moment of its being set down like a plant newly planted.

III.[3]

In truth, our evil comes out of our want of resemblance to God, and our ignorance of Him; and, on the other hand, our great good consists in our resemblance to Him. And, therefore, our conversion and faith in the Being who is incorruptible and divine, seems to be truly our proper good, and ignorance and disregard of Him our evil; if, at least, those things which are produced in us and of us, being the evil effects of sin, are to be considered ours.

[1] From the *Parallels* of St. John Damascene, *Opera*, tom. ii. p. 778, ed. Lequien.
[2] *Ibid.*, p. 784, B.

[3] *Ibid.*, p. 785, E.

FROM HIS DISCOURSE CONCERNING MARTYRS.[1]

For martyrdom is so admirable and desirable, that the Lord, the Son of God Himself, honouring it, testified, " He thought it not robbery to be equal with God,"[2] that He might honour man to whom He descended with this gift.

[1] From Theodoretus, *Dial.*, 1, 'Ατρεπτ. *Opp.*, ed. Sirmond, tom. iv. p. 37.

[2] Phil. ii. 5.

GENERAL NOTE.

THE *Banquet* appears to me a genuine work, although, like other writings of this Father, it may have been corrupted. Tokens of such corruptions are not wanting, and there can be little doubt that Methodius the monkish artist and missionary of the ninth century has been often copied into the works of his earlier namesake.[1]

In a fragment, for example, found on a preceding page,[2] there is a passage on God's image in angels and men, which appears in its more probable form in another fragment,[3] discovered by Combefis. As quoted by St. John Damascene, it is enough to say of it, with the candid Dupin, " *I very much question whether the passage belongs to Methodius;* or, if it does, it must be taken in another sense [4] than that in which Damascene understood it, . . . as the words which immediately precede seem to intimate." That it is a positive *anachronism* in any other sense, is proved by the history of Images, on which see Epiphanius, quoted by Faber, *Difficulties of Romanism,* p. 488, ed. 1830. He gives St. Jerome, *Opp.*, ii. p. 177. A learned friend suggests that the Rev. J. Endell Tyler's popular work on *Primitive Christian Worship* may supply an accessible reference.[5] It is a very good thought, for the whole book is worth reading, on other points also.

[1] Murdock's Mosheim, *Eccles. Hist.*, ii. 51.
[2] P. 369, note 4, *supra*.
[3] The *Jonah Fragment*, p. 378, *supra*.
[4] The sense, that is, of the golden image of God in angels, and " in clay or brass, *as ourselves*." See p. 378, *supra*.
[5] See pp. 131, 132, edition of the London Society for the Promotion of Christian Knowledge.

ORATION CONCERNING SIMEON AND ANNA

ON THE DAY THAT THEY MET IN THE TEMPLE.[1]

1. ALTHOUGH I have before, as briefly as possible, in my dialogue on chastity, sufficiently laid the foundations, as it were, for a discourse on virginity, yet to-day the season has brought forward the entire subject of the glory of virginity, and its incorruptible crown, for the delightful consideration of the Church's foster-children. For to-day the council chamber of the divine oracles is opened wide, and the signs prefiguring this glorious day, with its effects and issues, are by the sacred preachers read over to the assembled Church. To-day the accomplishment of that ancient and true counsel is, in fact and deed, gloriously manifested to the world. To-day, without any covering,[2] and with unveiled face, we see, as in a mirror, the glory of the Lord, and the majesty of the divine ark itself. To-day, the most holy assembly, bearing upon its shoulders the heavenly joy that was for generations expected, imparts it to the race of man. "Old things are passed away"[3] — things new burst forth into flowers, and such as fade not away. No longer does the stern decree of the law bear sway, but the grace of the Lord reigneth, drawing all men to itself by saving long-suffering. No second time is an Uzziah[4] invisibly punished, for daring to touch what may not be touched; for God Himself invites, and who will stand hesitating with fear? He says: "Come unto Me, all ye that labour and are heavy laden."[5] Who, then, will not run to Him? Let no Jew contradict the truth, looking at the type which went before the house of Obededom.[6] The Lord has "*manifestly come to His own.*"[7] And sitting on a living and not inanimate ark, as upon the mercy-seat, He comes forth in solemn procession upon the earth. The publican, when he touches this ark, comes away just; the harlot, when she approaches this, is remoulded, as it were, and becomes chaste; the leper, when he touches this, is restored whole without pain. It repulses none; it shrinks from none; it imparts the gifts of healing, without itself contracting any disease; for the Lord, who loves and cares for man, in it makes His resting-place. These are the gifts of this new grace. This is that new and strange thing that has happened under the sun[8] — a thing that never had place before, nor will have place again. That which God of His compassion toward us foreordained has come to pass, He hath given it fulfilment because of that love for man which is so becoming to Him. With good right, therefore, has the sacred trumpet sounded, "Old things are passed away, behold all things are become new."[3] And what shall I conceive, what shall I speak worthy of this day? I am struggling to reach the inaccessible, for the remembrance of this holy virgin far transcends all words of mine. Wherefore, since the greatness of the panegyric required completely puts to shame our limited powers, let us betake ourselves to that hymn which is not beyond our faculties, and boasting in our own[9] unalterable defeat, let us join the rejoicing chorus of Christ's flock, who are keeping holyday. And do you, my divine and saintly auditors, keep strict silence, in order that through the narrow channel of ears, as into the harbour of the understanding, the vessel freighted with truth may peacefully sail. We keep festival, not according to the vain customs of the Greek mythology; we keep a feast which brings with it no ridiculous or frenzied banqueting[10] of the gods, but which teaches us the wondrous condescension to us men of the awful glory of Him who is God over all.[11]

---

[1] The oration likewise treats of the Holy *Theotocos*. [Published by Pantinus, 1598, and obviously corrupt. Dupin states that it is "not mentioned by the ancients, nor even by Photius." The style resembles that of Methodius in many places.]

[2] 2 Cor. iii. 18.

[3] 2 Cor. v. 17.

[4] 2 Sam. vi. 7.

[5] Matt. xi. 28.

[6] 2 Sam. vi. 10.

[7] John i. 11; Ps. l. 3. ἦλθεν — ἐμφανῶς. The text plainly requires this connection with evident allusion to Ps. l. "Our God will manifestly come" ἐμφανῶς ἥξει, which passage our author connects with another from John i. — Tr.

[8] Ecclus. i. 10.

[9] τὴν ἀκίνητον ἧτταν ἐγκαυχησάμενοι. It seems better to retain this. Pantinus would substitute ἀνίκητον for ἀκίνητον, and render less happily "invicto hoc certamine victos."

[10] [See p. 309, note 1, *supra*, and the reflection upon even the *Banquet of Philosophers*, the *Symposium* of Plato.]

[11] Rom. ix. 5.

II. Come, therefore, Isaiah, most solemn of preachers and greatest of prophets, wisely unfold to the Church the mysteries of the congregation in glory, and incite our excellent guests abundantly to satiate themselves with enduring dainties, in order that, placing the reality which we possess over against that mirror of thine, truthful prophet as thou art, thou mayest joyfully clap thine hands at the issue of thy predictions. It came to pass, he says, "in the year in which king Uzziah died, I saw the Lord sitting upon a throne, high and lifted up ; and the house was full of His glory. And the seraphim stood round about him : each one had six wings. And one cried unto another, and said, Holy, holy, holy, is the Lord of hosts : the whole earth is full of His glory. And the posts of the door were moved at the voice of him that cried, and the house was filled with smoke. And I said, Woe is me ! I am pricked to the heart, for I am a man of unclean lips, and I dwell in the midst of a people of unclean lips : for mine eyes have seen the King, the Lord of hosts. And one of the seraphim was sent unto me, having a live coal in his hand, which he had taken with the tongs from off the altar. And he touched my mouth, and said, Lo, this hath touched thy lips ; and thine iniquity is taken away, and thy sin is purged. Also I heard the voice of the Lord, saying, Whom shall I send, and who will go unto this people? Then said I, Here am I ; send me. And He said, Go, and tell this people, Hear ye indeed, but understand not ; and see ye indeed, but perceive not." [1] These are the proclamations made beforehand by the prophet through the Spirit. Do thou, dearly beloved, consider the force of these words. So shalt thou understand the issue of these sacramental [2] symbols, and know both what and how great this assembling together of ourselves is. And since the prophet has before spoken of this miracle, come thou, and with the greatest ardour and exultation, and alacrity of heart, together with the keenest sagacity of thine intelligence, and therewith approach Bethlehem the renowned, and place before thy mind an image clear and distinct, comparing the prophecy with the actual issue of events. Thou wilt not stand in need of many words to come to a knowledge of the matter ; only fix thine eyes on the things which are taking place there. "All things truly are plain to them that understand, and right to them that find knowledge." [3] For, behold, as a throne high and lifted up by the glory of Him that fashioned it, the virgin-mother is there made ready, and that most evidently for the King, the Lord of hosts. Upon this, consider the Lord now

coming unto thee in sinful flesh. Upon this virginal throne, I say, worship Him who now comes to thee by this new and ever-adorable way. Look around thee with the eye of faith, and thou wilt find around Him, as by the ordinance of their courses,[4] the royal and priestly company of the seraphim. These, as His body-guard, are ever wont to attend the presence of their king. Whence also in this place they are not only said to hymn with their praises the divine substance of the divine unity, but also the glory to be adored by all of that one of the sacred Trinity, which now, by the appearance of God in the flesh, hath even lighted upon earth. They say : "The whole earth is full of His glory." For we believe that, together with the Son, who was made man for our sakes, according to the good pleasure of His will,[5] was also present the Father, who is inseparable from Him as to His divine nature, and also the Spirit, who is of one and the same essence with Him.[6] For, as says Paul, the interpreter of the divine oracle,[7] "God was in Christ reconciling the world unto Himself, not imputing their trespasses unto them." [8] He thus shows that the Father was in the Son, because that one and the same will worked in them.

III. Do thou, therefore, O lover of this festival, when thou hast considered well the glorious mysteries of Bethlehem, which were brought to pass for thy sake, gladly join thyself to the heavenly host, which is celebrating magnificently thy salvation.[9] As once David did before the ark, so do thou, before this virginal throne, joyfully lead the dance. Hymn with gladsome song the Lord, who is always and everywhere present, and Him who from Teman,[10] as says the prophet, hath thought fit to appear, and that in the flesh, to the race of men. Say, with Moses, "He is my God, and I will glorify Him ; my father's God, and I will exalt Him." [11] Then, after thine hymn of thanksgiving, we shall usefully inquire what cause aroused the King of Glory to appear in Bethlehem. His compassion for us compelled Him, who cannot be compelled, to be born in a human body at Bethlehem. But what necessity was there that He, when a suckling infant,[12] that

---

[1] Isa. vi. 1–9. The quotations are from LXX. version.
[2] μυστήριον is, in the Greek Fathers, equivalent to the Latin *Sacramentum.* — Tr.
[3] Prov. viii. 9.

[4] ἱεράτευμα. Perhaps less definitely priesthood. Acc. Arist. it is ἡ περὶ τοὺς θεοὺς ἐπιμέλεια. The cult and ordinances of religion to be observed especially by the priests, whose business it is to celebrate the excellence of God. — Tr.
[5] κατὰ τὴν εὐδοκίαν. Allusion is made to Eph. i. 5, According to the good pleasure of God, and His decree for the salvation of man. Less aptly Pantinus renders, ob propensam secæm in nos voluntatem. — Tr.
[6] "One and the same essence." This is the famous ὁμοούσιος of the Nicene Council. — Tr.
[7] ἱεροφάντης, teacher of the divine oracles. This, which is the technical term for the presiding priest at Eleusis, and the Greek translation of the Latin "Pontifex Maximus," is by our author applied to St. Paul. — Tr.
[8] 2 Cor. v. 19.
[9] 2 Sam. vi. 14.
[10] Hab. iii. 3.
[11] Exod. xv. 2.
[12] ὑποτίτθιον τυγχάνοντα. It is an aggravation, so to speak, that He not only willed to become an infant, and to take upon Him, of necessity, the infirmities of infancy, but even at that tender age to be

He who, though born in time, was not limited by time, that He, who though wrapped in swaddling clothes, was not by them held fast, what necessity was there that He should be an exile and a stranger from His country? Should you, forsooth, wish to know this, ye congregation most holy, and upon whom the Spirit of God hath breathed, listen to Moses proclaiming plainly to the people, stimulating them, as it were, to the knowledge of this extraordinary nativity, and saying, "Every male that openeth the womb, shall be called holy to the Lord."[1] O wondrous circumstance! "O the depth of the riches both of the wisdom and knowledge of God!"[2] It became indeed the Lord of the law and the prophets to do all things in accordance with His own law, and not to make void the law, but to fulfil it, and rather to connect with the fulfilment of the law the beginning of His grace. Therefore it is that the mother, who was superior to the law, submits to the law. And she, the holy and undefiled one, observes that time of forty days that was appointed for the unclean. And He who makes us free from the law, became subject to the law; and there is offered for Him, who hath sanctified us, a pair of clean birds,[3] in testimony of those who approach clean and blameless. Now that that parturition was unpolluted, and stood not in need of expiatory victims, Isaiah is our witness, who proclaims distinctly to the whole earth under the sun: "Before she travailed," he says, "she brought forth; before her pains came, she escaped, and brought forth a man-child."[4] Who hath heard such a thing? Who hath seen such things? The most holy virgin mother, therefore, escaped entirely the manner of women even before she brought forth: doubtless, in order that the Holy Spirit, betrothing her unto Himself, and sanctifying her, she might conceive without intercourse with man. She hath brought forth her first-born Son, even the only-begotten Son of God, Him, I say, who in the heavens above shone forth as the only-begotten, without mother, from out His Father's substance, and preserved the virginity of His natural unity undivided and inseparable; and who on earth, in the virgin's nuptial chamber, joined to Himself the nature of Adam, like a bridegroom, by an inalienable union, and preserved His mother's purity uncorrupt and un injured — Him, in short, who in heaven was begotten without corruption, and on earth brought

forth in a manner quite unspeakable. But to return to our subject.

IV. Therefore the prophet brought the virgin from Nazareth, in order that she might give birth at Bethlehem to her salvation-bestowing child, and brought her back again to Nazareth, in order to make manifest to the world the hope of life. Hence it was that the ark of God removed from the inn at Bethlehem, for there He paid to the law that debt of the forty days, due not to justice but to grace, and rested upon the mountains of Sion, and receiving into His pure bosom as upon a lofty throne, and one transcending the nature of man, the Monarch of all,[5] she presented Him there to God the Father, as the joint-partner of His throne and inseparable from His nature, together with that pure and undefiled flesh which he had of her substance assumed. The holy mother goes up to the temple to exhibit to the law a new and strange wonder, even that child long expected, who opened the virgin's womb, and yet did not burst the barriers of virginity; that child, superior to the law, who yet fulfilled the law; that child that was at once before the law, and yet after it; that child, in short, who was of her incarnate beyond the law of nature.[6] For in other cases every womb being first opened by connection with a man, and, being impregnated by his seed, receives the beginning of conception, and by the pangs which make perfect parturition, doth at length bring forth to light its offspring endowed with reason, and with its nature consistent, in accordance with the wise provision of God its Creator. For God said, "Be fruitful, and multiply, and replenish the earth." But the womb of this virgin, without being opened before, or being impregnated with seed, gave birth to an offspring that transcended nature, while at the same time it was cognate to it, and that without detriment to the indivisible unity, so that the miracle was the more stupendous, the prerogative of virginity likewise remaining intact. She goes up, therefore, to the temple, she who was more exalted than the temple, clothed with a double glory — the glory, I say, of undefiled virginity, and that of ineffable fecundity, the benediction of the law, and the sanctification of grace. Wherefore he says who saw it: "And the whole house was full of His glory, and the seraphim stood round about him; and one cried unto another, and said, Holy, holy, holy, is the Lord of hosts: the whole earth is full of His glory."[7] As also the blessed prophet Habakkuk has charmingly sung, saying, "In the midst of two living creatures thou shalt be known: as the years draw nigh

---

banished from His country, and to make a forcible change of residence, μέτοικος γενέσθαν. μέτοικοι are those who, at the command of their princes, are transferred, by way of punishment, to another State. Their lands are confiscated. They are sometimes called ἀνάσπαστοι. Like to the condition of these was that of Jesus, who fled into Egypt soon after His birth. For the condition of the μέτοικοι at Athens, see Art. *Smith's Dict. Antiq.* — TR.
[1] Exod. xxxi. 19.
[2] Rom. xi. 33.
[3] Luke xi. 24.
[4] Isa. lxvi. 7.

[5] *Cf.* Luke ii. 22.
[6] [Here seems to me a deep and true insight regarding the scriptural topics and events touched upon.]
[7] Isa. vi. 3.

thou shalt be recognised — when the time is come thou shalt be shown forth." [1]   See, I pray you, the exceeding accuracy of the Spirit. He speaks of knowledge, recognition, showing forth. As to the first of these : " In the midst of two living creatures thou shalt be known," [2] he refers to that overshadowing of the divine glory which, in the time of the law, rested in the Holy of holies upon the covering of the ark, between the typical cherubim, as He says to Moses, " There will I be known to thee." [3]   But He refers likewise to that concourse of angels, which hath now come to meet us, by the divine and ever adorable manifestation of the Saviour Himself in the flesh, although He in His very nature cannot be beheld by us, as Isaiah has even before declared. But when He says, " As the years draw nigh, thou shalt be recognised," He means, as has been said before, that glorious recognition of our Saviour, God in the flesh, who is otherwise invisible to mortal eye ; as somewhere Paul, that great interpreter of sacred mysteries, says : " But when the fulness of the time was come, God sent forth His Son, made of a woman, made under the law, to redeem them that were under the law, that we might receive the adoption of sons." [4] And then, as to that which is subjoined, " When the time is come, Thou shalt be shown forth," what exposition doth this require, if a man diligently direct the eye of his mind to the festival which we are now celebrating ? " For then shalt Thou be shown forth," He says, " as upon a kingly charger, by Thy pure and chaste mother, in the temple, and that in the grace and beauty of the flesh assumed by Thee." All these things the prophet, summing up for the sake of greater clearness, exclaims in brief : " The Lord is in His holy temple ; " [5] " Fear before Him all the earth." [6]

v. Tremendous, verily, is the mystery connected with thee, O virgin mother, thou spiritual throne, glorified and made worthy of God. [7] Thou hast brought forth, before the eyes of those in heaven and earth, a pre-eminent wonder.   And it is a proof of this, and an irrefragable argument, that at the novelty of thy supernatural child-bearing, the angels sang on earth, " Glory to God in the highest, and on earth peace, good-will towards men," [8] by their threefold song bringing in a threefold holiness. [9]

Blessed art thou among the generations of women, O thou of God most blessed, for by thee the earth has been filled with that divine glory of God ; as in the Psalms it is sung : " Blessed be the Lord God of Israel, and the whole earth shall be filled with His glory. Amen. Amen." [10]   And the posts of the door, says the prophet, moved at the voice of him that cried, by which is signified the veil of the temple drawn before the ark of the covenant, which typified thee, that the truth might be laid open to me, and also that I might be taught, by the types and figures which went before, to approach with reverence and trembling to do honour to the sacred mystery which is connected with thee ; and that by means of this prior shadow-painting of the law I might be restrained from boldly and irreverently contemplating with fixed gaze Him who, in His incomprehensibility, is seated far above all. [11]   For if to the ark, which was the image and type of thy sanctity, such honour was paid of God that to no one but to the priestly order only was the access to it open, or ingress allowed to behold it, the veil separating it off, and keeping the vestibule as that of a queen, what, and what sort of veneration is due to thee from us who are of creation the least, to thee who art indeed a queen ; to thee, the living ark of God, the Lawgiver ; to thee, the heaven that contains Him who can be contained of none?   For since thou, O holy virgin, [12] hast dawned as a bright day upon the world, and hast brought forth the Sun of Righteousness, that hateful horror of darkness has been chased away ; the power of the tyrant has been broken, death hath been destroyed, hell swallowed up, and all enmity dissolved before the face of peace ; noxious diseases depart now that salvation looks forth ; and the whole universe has been filled with the pure and clear light of truth. To which things Solomon alludes in the Book of Canticles, and begins thus : " My beloved is mine, and I am his ; he feedeth among the lilies until the day break, and the shadows flee away." [13] Since then, the God of gods hath appeared in Sion, and the splendour of His beauty hath appeared in Jerusalem ; and " a light has sprung up for the righteous, and joy for those who are true of heart." [14]   According to the blessed David, the Perfecter and Lord of the perfected [15] hath, by the Holy Spirit, called the teacher and

---

[1] The quotation from the prophet Habakkuk is from the LXX. version. — Tr.
[2] Hab. iii. 2.
[3] Exod. xxv. 22.
[4] Gal. iv. 4, 5.
[5] Hab. ii. 20.
[6] Ps xcvi. 9.
[7] [Note " *made* worthy ; " so " found grace " and " *my* Saviour," in St. Luke. Hence not immaculate by nature.]
[8] Luke ii. 14.
[9] τὸν τῆιπλασιασμὸν τῆς ἁγιότητος, Pantinus translates *triplicem sanctitatis rationem*, but this is hardly theological. Allusion is made to the song of the seraphim, Isa. vi.; and our author contends that the threefold hymn sung by the angels at Christ's birth answers to that threefold acclamation of theirs in sign of the triune Deity. — Tr.

[10] Ps. lxxii. 18, 19.
[11] τὸν τὰ πάντα ἐν ἀκαταληψίᾳ ὑπεριδρυμένον. *Cf.* 1 Tim. vi. 16, φῶς οἰκῶν ἀπρόσιτον, ὃν εἶδεν οὐδεὶς ἀνθρώπων οὐδὲ ἰδεῖν δύναται. — Tr.
[12] [This *apostrophe* is not prayer nor worship. (See sec. xiv., *infra*.) It may be made by any orator. See Burgon's pertinent references to Legh Richmond and Bishop Horne, *Lett. from Rome*, pp. 237, 238.]
[13] Cant. ii. 16, 17.
[14] Ps. xcvii. 11.
[15] ὁ τῶν τελουμένων τελειωτής, initiator, consummator. διὰ τοῦ Πνεύματος ἁγίου is to be referred to συνεκάλεσεν, rather than to τῶν πραττομένων. — Tr.

minister of the law to minister and testify of those things which were done.

VI. Hence the aged Simeon, putting off the weakness of the flesh, and putting on the strength of hope, in the face of the law hastened to receive the Minister of the law, the Teacher [1] with authority, the God of Abraham, the Protector of Isaac, the Holy One of Israel, the Instructor of Moses; Him, I say, who promised to show him His divine incarnation, as it were His hinder parts; [2] Him who, in the midst of poverty, was rich; Him who in infancy was before the ages; Him who, though seen, was invisible; Him who in comprehension was incomprehensible; Him who, though in littleness, yet surpassed all magnitude — at one and the same time in the temple and in the highest heavens — on a royal throne, and on the chariot of the cherubim; Him who is both above and below continuously; Him who is in the form of a servant, and in the form of God the Father; a subject, and yet King of all. He was entirely given up to desire, to hope, to joy; he was no longer his own, but His who had been looked for. The Holy Spirit had announced to him the joyful tidings, and before he reached the temple, carried aloft by the eyes of his understanding, as if even now he possessed what he had longed for, he exulted with joy. Being thus led on, and in his haste treading the air with his steps, he reaches the shrine hitherto held sacred; but, not heeding the temple, he stretches out his holy arms to the Ruler of the temple, chanting forth in song such strains as become the joyous occasion: I long for Thee, O Lord God of my fathers, and Lord of mercy, who hast deigned, of Thine own glory and goodness, which provides for all, of Thy gracious condescension, with which Thou inclinest towards us, as a Mediator bringing peace, to establish harmony between earth and heaven. I seek Thee, the Great Author of all. With longing I expect Thee who, with Thy word, embracest all things. I wait for Thee, the Lord of life and death. For Thee I look, the Giver of the law, and the Successor of the law. I hunger for Thee, who quickenest the dead; I thirst for Thee, who refreshest the weary; I desire Thee, the Creator and Redeemer of the world.[3] Thou art our God, and Thee we adore; Thou art our holy Temple, and in Thee we pray; Thou art our Lawgiver, and Thee we obey; Thou art God of all things the First. Before Thee was no other god begotten of God the Father; neither after Thee shall there be any other son consubstantial and of one glory with the Father. And to know Thee is perfect righteousness, and to know Thy power is the root of immortality.[4]

Thou art He who, for our salvation, was made the head stone of the corner, precious and honourable, declared before to Sion.[5] For all things are placed under Thee as their Cause and Author, as He who brought all things into being out of nothing, and gave to what was unstable a firm coherence; as the connecting Band and Preserver of that which has been brought into being; as the Framer of things by nature different; as He who, with wise and steady hand, holds the helm of the universe; as the very Principle of all good order; as the irrefragable Bond of concord and peace. For in Thee we live, and move, and have our being.[6] Wherefore, O Lord my God, I will glorify Thee, I will praise Thy name; for Thou hast done wonderful things; Thy counsels of old are faithfulness and truth; Thou art clothed with majesty and honour.[7] For what is more splendid for a king than a purple robe embroidered around with flowers, and a shining diadem? Or what for God, who delights in man, is more magnificent than this merciful assumption of the manhood, illuminating with its resplendent rays those who sit in darkness and the shadow of death?[8] Fitly did that temporal king and Thy servant once sing of Thee as the King Eternal, saying, Thou art fairer than the children of men, who amongst men art very God and man.[9] For Thou hast girt, by Thy incarnation, Thy loins with righteousness, and anointed Thy veins with faithfulness, who Thyself art very righteousness and truth, the joy and exultation of all.[10] Therefore rejoice with me this day, ye heavens, for the Lord hath showed mercy to His people. Yea, let the clouds drop the dew of righteousness upon the world; let the foundations of the earth sound a trumpet-blast to those in Hades, for the resurrection of them that sleep is come.[11] Let the earth also cause compassion to spring up to its inhabitants; for I am filled with comfort; I am exceeding joyful since I have seen Thee, the Saviour of men.[12]

VII. While the old man was thus exultant, and rejoicing with exceeding great and holy joy, that which had before been spoken of in a figure by the prophet Isaiah, the holy mother of God now manifestly fulfilled. For taking, as from a pure and undefiled altar, that coal living and ineffable, with man's flesh invested, in the embrace of her sacred hands, as it were with the tongs, she held Him out to that just one, addressing and exhorting him, as it seems to me, in words to this effect: Receive, O reverend senior, thou of priests

---

[1] τὸν αὐθέντην διδάσκαλον. The allusion is to Mark i. 22.
[2] Exod. iii. 23.
[3] Isa. xliii. 10.
[4] Wisd. xv. 3.

[5] Ps. cxviii. 22; Isa. xxviii. 16; 1 Pet. ii. 6.
[6] Acts xviii. 28.
[7] Exod. xv. 2; Isa. xxv. 1; Ps. civ. 1.
[8] Isa. xlii. 7; Luke i. 79.
[9] 1 Tim. i. 17; Ps. xlv. 2.
[10] Isa. xi. 5.
[11] Isa. xiv. 8.
[12] 2 Cor. vii. 4.

the most excellent, receive the Lord, and reap the full fruition of that hope of thine which is not left widowed and desolate. Receive, thou of men the most illustrious, the unfailing treasure, and those riches which can never be taken away. Take to thine embrace, O thou of men most wise, that unspeakable might, that unsearchable power, which can alone support thee. Embrace, thou minister of the temple, the Greatness infinite, and the Strength incomparable. Fold thyself around Him who is the very life itself, and live, O thou of men most venerable. Cling closely to incorruption and be renewed, O thou of men most righteous. Not too bold is the attempt; shrink not from it then, O thou of men most holy. Satiate thyself with Him thou hast longed for, and take thy delight in Him who has been given, or rather who gives Himself to thee, O thou of men most divine. Joyfully draw thy light, O thou of men most pious, from the Sun of Righteousness, that gleams around thee through the unsullied mirror of the flesh. Fear not His gentleness, nor let His clemency terrify thee, O thou of men most blessed. Be not afraid of His lenity, nor shrink from His kindness, O thou of men most modest. Join thyself to Him with alacrity, and delay not to obey Him. That which is spoken to thee, and held out to thee, savours not of over-boldness. Be not then reluctant, O thou of men the most decorous. The flame of the grace of my Lord does not consume, but illuminates thee, O thou of men most just.[1] Let the bush which set forth me in type, with respect to the verity of that fire which yet had no subsistence, teach thee this, O thou who art in the law the best instructed.[2] Let that furnace which was as it were a breeze distilling dew persuade thee, O master, of the dispensation of this mystery. Then, beside all this, let my womb be a proof to thee, in which He was contained, who in nought else was ever contained, of the substance of which the incarnate Word yet deigned to become incarnate. The blast[3] of the trumpet does not now terrify those who approach, nor a second time does the mountain all on smoke cause terror to those who draw nigh, nor indeed does the law punish relentlessly[4] those who would boldly touch. What is here present speaks of love to man; what is here apparent, of the Divine condescension. Thankfully, then, receive the God who comes to thee, for He shall take away thine iniquities, and thoroughly purge thy sins. In thee, let the cleansing of the world first, as in type, have place. In thee, and by thee, let that justification which is of grace become known beforehand to the Gentiles. Thou art worthy of the quickening first-fruits. Thou hast made good use of the law. Use grace henceforth. With the letter thou hast grown weary; in the spirit be renewed. Put off that which is old, and clothe thyself with that which is new. For of these matters I think not that thou art ignorant.

VIII. Upon all this that righteous man, waxing bold and yielding to the exhortation of the mother of God, who is the handmaid of God in regard to the things which pertain to men, received into his aged arms Him who in infancy was yet the Ancient of days, and blessed God, and said, " Lord, now lettest Thou Thy servant depart in peace, according to Thy word: for mine eyes have seen Thy salvation, which Thou hast prepared before the face of all people; a light to lighten the Gentiles, and the glory of Thy people Israel."[5] I have received from Thee a joy unmixed with pain. Do thou, O Lord, receive me rejoicing, and singing of Thy mercy and compassion. Thou hast given unto me this joy of heart. I render unto Thee with gladness my tribute of thanksgiving. I have known the power of the love of God. Since, for my sake, God of Thee begotten, in a manner ineffable, and without corruption, has become man. I have known the inexplicable greatness of Thy love and care for us, for Thou hast sent forth Thine own bowels to come to our deliverance. Now, at length, I understand what I had from Solomon learned: " Strong as death is love: for by it shall the sting of death be done away, by it shall the dead see life, by it shall even death learn what death is, being made to cease from that dominion which over us he exercised. By it, also, shall the serpent, the author of our evils, be taken captive and overwhelmed."[6] Thou hast made known to us, O Lord, Thy salvation,[7] causing to spring up for us the plant of peace, and we shall no longer wander in error. Thou hast made known to us, O Lord, that Thou hast not unto the end overlooked Thy servants; neither hast Thou, O beneficent One, forgotten entirely the works of Thine hands. For out of Thy compassion for our low estate Thou hast shed forth upon us abundantly that goodness of Thine which is inexhaustible, and with Thy very nature cognate, having redeemed us by Thine only begotten Son, who is unchangeably like to Thee, and of one substance with Thee; judging it unworthy of Thy majesty and goodness to entrust to a servant the work of saving and benefiting Thy servants, or to cause that those who had offended should be reconciled by a minister. But by means of that light, which is of one substance with Thee, Thou hast given light to those that sat in darkness[8] and in the shadow of

[1] Exod. iii. 2.
[2] Dan. iii. 21.
[3] Exod. xix. 16.
[4] Ps. vi. 6.

[5] Luke ii. 29-32.
[6] Cant. viii. 6.
[7] Ps. xcviii. 2.
[8] Isa. ix. 2, xlii. 7; Luke i. 79.

death, in order that in Thy light they might see the light of knowledge; [1] and it has seemed good to Thee, by means of our Lord and Creator, to fashion us again unto immortality; and Thou hast graciously given unto us a return to Paradise by means of Him who separated us from the joys of Paradise; and by means of Him who hath power to forgive sins Thou hast [2] blotted out the handwriting which was against us. [3] Lastly, by means of Him who is a partaker of Thy throne, and who cannot be separated from Thy divine nature, Thou hast given unto us the gift of reconciliation, and access unto Thee with confidence, in order that, by the Lord who recognises the sovereign authority of none, by the true and omnipotent God, the subscribed sanction, as it were, of so many and such great blessings might constitute the justifying gifts of grace to be certain and indubitable rights to those who have obtained mercy. And this very thing the prophet before had announced in the words: No ambassador, nor angel, but the Lord Himself saved them; because He loved them, and spared them, and He took them up, and exalted them. [4] And all this was, not of works of righteousness [5] which we have done, nor because we loved Thee, — for our first earthly forefather, who was honourably entertained in the delightful abode of Paradise, despised Thy divine and saving commandment, and was judged unworthy of that life-giving place, and mingling his seed with the bastard off-shoots of sin, he rendered it very weak; — but Thou, O Lord, of Thine own self, and of Thine ineffable love toward the creature of Thine hands, hast confirmed Thy mercy toward us, and, pitying our estrangement from Thee, hast moved Thyself at the sight of our degradation [6] to take us into compassion. Hence, for the future, a joyous festival is established for us of the race of Adam, because the first Creator of Adam of His own free-will has become the Second Adam. And the brightness of the Lord our God hath come down to sojourn with us, so that we see God face to face, and are saved. Therefore, O Lord, I seek of Thee to be allowed to depart. I have seen Thy salvation; let me be delivered from the bent yoke of the letter. I have seen the King Eternal, to whom no other succeeds; let me be set free from this servile and burdensome chain. I have seen Him who is by nature my Lord and Deliverer; may I obtain, then, His decree for my deliverance. Set me free from the yoke of condemnation, and place me under the yoke of justification. Deliver me from the

yoke of the curse, and of the letter that killeth; [7] and enrol me in the blessed company of those who, by the grace of this Thy true Son, who is of equal glory and power with Thee, have been received into the adoption of sons.

IX. Let then, says he, what I have thus far said in brief, suffice for the present as my offering of thanks to God. But what shall I say to thee, O mother-virgin and virgin-mother? For the praise even of her who is not man's work exceeds the power of man. Wherefore the dimness of my poverty I will make bright with the splendour of the gifts of the spirits that around thee shine, and offering to thee of thine own, from the immortal meadows I will pluck a garland for thy sacred and divinely crowned head. With thine ancestral hymns will I greet thee, O daughter of David, and mother of the Lord and God of David. For it were both base and inauspicious to adorn thee, who in thine own glory excellest with that which belongeth unto another. Receive, therefore, O lady most benignant, gifts precious, and such as are fitted to thee alone, O thou who art exalted above all generations, and who, amongst all created things, both visible and invisible, shinest forth as the most honourable. Blessed is the root of Jesse, and thrice blessed is the house of David, in which thou hast sprung up. [8] God is in the midst of thee, and thou shalt not be moved, for the Most High hath made holy the place of His tabernacle. For in thee the covenants and oaths made of God unto the fathers have received a most glorious fulfilment, since by thee the Lord hath appeared, the God of hosts with us. That bush which could not be touched, [9] which beforehand shadowed forth thy figure endowed with divine majesty, bare God without being consumed, who manifested Himself to the prophet just so far as He willed to be seen. Then, again, that hard and rugged rock, [10] which imaged forth the grace and refreshment which has sprung out from thee for all the world, brought forth abundantly in the desert out of its thirsty sides a healing draught for the fainting people. Yea, moreover, the rod of the priest which, without culture, blossomed forth in fruit, [11] the pledge and earnest of a perpetual priesthood, furnished no contemptible symbol of thy supernatural child-bearing. [12] What, moreover? Hath not the mighty Moses expressly declared, that on account of these types of thee, hard to be understood, [13] he delayed longer on the mountain, in order that he might learn, O holy one, the mysteries that with thee

---

[1] Ps. xxxvi. 9.
[2] Mark ii. 10.
[3] Col. ii. 4.
[4] Isa. lxiii. 9, Sept. version.
[5] Tit. iii. 5.
[6] John iv. 9.

[7] 2 Cor. iii. 6.
[8] Ps. xlvi. 4, 5.
[9] Exod. iii. 2.
[10] Exod. xvii. 6.
[11] Num. xvii. 8.
[12] Heb. ix. 4.
[13] Exod. xxv. 8.

are connected? For being commanded to build the ark as a sign and similitude of this thing, he was not negligent in obeying the command, although a tragic occurrence happened on his descent from the mount; but having made it in size five cubits and a half, he appointed it to be the receptacle of the law, and covered it with the wings of the cherubim, most evidently presignifying thee, the mother of God, who hast conceived Him without corruption, and in an ineffable manner brought forth Him who is Himself, as it were, the very consistence of incorruption, and that within the limits of the five and a half circles of the world. On thy account, and the undefiled Incarnation of God, the Word, which by thee had place for the sake of that flesh which immutably and indivisibly remains with Him for ever.[1] The golden pot also, as a most certain type, preserved the manna contained in it, which in other cases was changed day by day, unchanged, and keeping fresh for ages. The prophet Elijah[2] likewise, as prescient of thy chastity, and being emulous of it through the Spirit, bound around him the crown of that fiery life, being by the divine decree adjudged superior to death. Thee also, prefiguring his successor Elisha,[3] having been instructed by a wise master, and anticipating thy presence who wast not yet born, by certain sure indications of the things that would have place hereafter,[4] ministered help and healing to those who were in need of it, which was of a virtue beyond nature; now with a new cruse, which contained healing salt, curing the deadly waters, to show that the world was to be recreated by the mystery manifested in thee; now with unleavened meal, in type responding to thy child-bearing, without being defiled by the seed of man, banishing from the food the bitterness of death; and then again, by efforts which transcended nature, rising superior to the natural elements in the Jordan, and thus exhibiting, in signs beforehand, the descent of our Lord into Hades, and His wonderful deliverance of those who were held fast in corruption. For all things yielded and succumbed to that divine image which prefigured thee.

x. But why do I digress, and lengthen out my discourse, giving it the rein with these varied illustrations, and that when the truth of thy matter stands like a column before the eye, in which it were better and more profitable to luxuriate and delight in? Wherefore, bidding adieu to the spiritual narrations and wondrous deeds of the saints throughout all ages, I pass on to thee who art always to be had in remembrance, and who holdest the helm, as it were, of this festival.[5]

Blessed art thou, all-blessed, and to be desired of all. Blessed of the Lord is thy name, full of divine grace, and grateful exceedingly to God, mother of God, thou that givest light to the faithful. Thou art the circumscription, so to speak, of Him who cannot be circumscribed; the root[6] of the most beautiful flower; the mother of the Creator; the nurse of the Nourisher; the circumference of Him who embraces all things; the upholder of Him[7] who upholds all things by His word; the gate through which God appears in the flesh;[8] the tongs of that cleansing coal;[9] the bosom in small of that bosom which is all-containing; the fleece of wool,[10] the mystery of which cannot be solved; the well of Bethlehem,[11] that reservoir of life which David longed for, out of which the draught of immortality gushed forth; the mercy-seat[12] from which God in human form was made known unto men; the spotless robe of Him who clothes Himself with light as with a garment.[13] Thou hast lent to God, who stands in need of nothing, that flesh which He had not, in order that the Omnipotent might become that which it was his good pleasure to be. What is more splendid than this? What than this is more sublime? He who fills earth and heaven,[14] whose are all things, has become in need of thee, for thou hast lent to God that flesh which He had not. Thou hast clad the Mighty One with that beauteous panoply of the body by which it has become possible for Him to be seen by mine eyes. And I, in order that I might freely approach to behold Him, have received that by which all the fiery darts of the wicked shall be quenched.[15] Hail! hail! mother and handmaid of God. Hail! hail! thou to whom the great Creditor of all is a debtor. We are all debtors to God, but to thee He is Himself indebted.

For He who said, "Honour thy father and thy mother,"[16] will have most assuredly, as Himself willing to be proved by such proofs, kept inviolate that grace, and His own decree towards her who ministered to Him that nativity to which He voluntarily stooped, and will have glorified with a divine honour her whom He, as being without a father, even as she was without a husband, Himself has written down as mother. Even so must these things be. For the hymns[17]

---

ical beauty. Its language, however, like that of other parts of this Oration, suggests at least interpolation, subsequent to the Nestorian controversy. Previously, there would have been no call for such vehemence of protestation.]

[1] Heb. ix. 4.
[2] 2 Kings ii. 11.
[3] Ecclus. xlviii. 1.
[4] 2 Kings ii. 20, iv. 41, v.
[5] [The feast of the Purification. Here follows an impassioned apostrophe, which apart from its Oriental extravagance is full of poet-

[6] Isa. xl. 1.
[7] Heb. i. 3.
[8] Ezek. xliv. 2.
[9] Isa. vi. 6.
[10] Judg. vi. 37.
[11] 2 Sam. xxiii. 17.
[12] Exod. xxxv. 17.
[13] Ps. civ. 2.
[14] Jer. xxiii. 24.
[15] Ephes. vi. 16.
[16] Exod. xx. 12.
[17] [Apostrophes like the above; panegyrical, not odes of worship.]

which we offer to thee, O thou most holy and admirable habitation of God, are no merely useless and ornamental words. Nor, again, is thy spiritual laudation mere secular trifling, or the shoutings of a false flattery, O thou who of God art praised; thou who to God gavest suck; who by nativity givest unto mortals their beginning of being, but they are of clear and evident truth. But the time would fail us, ages and succeeding generations too, to render unto thee thy fitting salutation as the mother of the King Eternal,[1] even as somewhere the illustrious prophet says, teaching us how incomprehensible thou art.[2] How great is the house of God, and how large is the place of His possession! Great, and hath none end, high and unmeasurable. For verily, verily, this prophetic oracle, and most true saying, is concerning thy majesty; for thou alone hast been thought worthy to share with God the things of God; who hast alone borne in the flesh Him, who of God the Father was the Eternally and Only-Begotten. So do they truly believe who hold fast to the pure faith.[3]

XI. But for the time that remains, my most attentive hearers, let us take up the old man, the receiver of God, and our pious teacher, who hath put in here, as it were, in safety from that virginal sea, and let us refresh him, both satisfied as to his divine longing, and conveying to us this most blessed theology; and let us ourselves follow out the rest of our discourse, directing our course unerringly with reference to our prescribed end, and that under the guidance of God the Almighty, so shall we not be found altogether unfruitful and unprofitable as to what is required of us. When, then, to these sacred rites, prophecy and the priesthood had been jointly called, and that pair of just ones elected of God — Simeon, I mean, and Anna, bearing in themselves most evidently the images of both peoples — had taken their station by the side of that glorious and virginal throne, — for by the old man was represented the people of Israel, and the law now waxing old; whilst the widow represents the Church of the Gentiles, which had been up to this point a widow, — the old man, indeed, as personating the law, seeks dismissal; but the widow, as personating the Church, brought her joyous confession of faith,[4] and spake of Him to all that looked for redemption in Jerusalem, even as the things that were spoken of both have been appositely and excellently recorded, and quite in harmony with the sacred festival. For it was fitting and necessary that the old man who knew so accurately that decree of the law, in which it is said: Hear Him, and

every soul that will not hearken unto Him shall be cut off from His people,[5] should seek a peaceful discharge from the tutorship of the law; for in truth it were insolence and presumption, when the king is present and addressing the people, for one of his attendants to make a speech over against him, and that to this man his subjects should incline their ears. It was necessary, too, that the widow who had been increased with gifts beyond measure, should in festal strains return her thanks to God; and so the things which there took place were agreeable to the law. But, for what remains, it is necessary to inquire how, since the prophetic types and figures bear, as has been shown, a certain analogy and relation to this prominent feast, it is said that the house was filled with smoke. Nor does the prophet say this incidentally, but with significance, speaking of that cry of the Thrice-Holy,[6] uttered by the heavenly seraphs. You will discover the meaning of this, my attentive hearer, if you do but take up and examine what follows upon this narration: For hearing, he says, ye shall hear, and shall not understand; and seeing, ye shall see, and not perceive.[7] When, therefore, the foolish Jewish children had seen the glorious wonders which, as David sang, the Lord had performed in the earth, and had seen the sign from the depth [8] and from the height meeting together, without division or confusion; as also Isaiah had before declared, namely, a mother beyond nature, and an offspring beyond reason; an earthly mother and a heavenly son; a new taking of man's nature, I say, by God, and a child-bearing without marriage; what in creation's circuit could be more glorious and more to be spoken of than this! yet when they had seen this it was all one as if they had not seen it; they closed their eyes, and in respect of praise were supine. Therefore the house in which they boasted was filled with smoke.

XII. And in addition to this, when besides the spectacle, and even beyond the spectacle, they heard an old man, very righteous, very worthy of credit, worthy also of emulation, inspired by the Holy Spirit, a teacher of the law, honoured with the priesthood, illustrious in the gift of prophecy, by the hope which he had conceived of Christ, extending the limits of life, and putting off the debt of death — when they saw him, I say, leaping for joy, speaking words of good omen, quite transformed with gladness of heart, entirely rapt in a divine and holy ecstasy; who from a man had been changed into an angel by a godly change, and, for the immensity of his joy, chant-

---

[1] 1 Tim. i. 17.
[2] Baruch iii. 24, 25.
[3] [This must have been interpolated after the Council of Ephesus, A.D. 431. The whole Oration is probably after that date.]
[4] Luke ii. 38.

[5] Deut. xviii. 15-19.
[6] Isa. vi. 4.
[7] Isa. vi. 9; Acts xxviii. 26.
[8] Ps. xlvi. 8; Isa. vii. 11.

ed his hymn of thanksgiving, and openly proclaimed the " Light to lighten the Gentiles, and the glory of Thy people Israel." [1] Not even then were they willing to hear what was placed within their hearing, and held in veneration by the heavenly beings themselves; wherefore the house in which they boasted was filled with smoke. Now smoke is a sign and sure evidence of wrath; as it is written, " There went up a smoke in His anger, and fire from His countenance devoured;" [2] and in another place, " Amongst the disobedient people shall the fire burn," [3] which plainly, in the revered Gospels, our Lord signified, when He said to the Jews, " Behold your house is left unto you desolate." [4] Also, in another place, " The king sent forth his armies, and destroyed those murderers, and burnt up their city." [5] Of such a nature was the adverse reward of the Jews for their unbelief, which caused them to refuse to pay to the Trinity the tribute of praise. For after that the ends of the earth were sanctified, and the mighty house of the Church was filled, by the proclamation of the Thrice Holy, with the glory of the Lord, as the great waters cover the seas, [6] there happened to them the things which before had been declared, and the beginning of prophecy was confirmed by its issue, the preacher of truth signifying, as has been said, by the Holy Spirit, as it were in an example, the dreadful destruction which was to come upon them, in the words: " In the year in which king Uzziah died, I saw the Lord " — Uzziah, doubtless, as an apostate, being taken as the representative of the whole apostate body — the head of which he certainly was — who also, paying the penalty due to his presumption, carried on his forehead, as upon a brazen statue, the divine vengeance engraved, by the loathsomeness of leprosy, exhibiting to all the retribution of their loathsome impiety. Wherefore with divine wisdom did he, who had foreknowledge of these events, oppose the bringing in of the thankful Anna to the casting out of the ungrateful synagogue. Her very name also presignifies the Church, that by the grace of Christ and God is justified in baptism. For Anna is, by interpretation, grace.

XIII. But here, as in port, putting in the vessel that bears the ensign of the cross, let us reef the sails of our oration, in order that it may be with itself commensurate. Only first, in as few words as possible, let us salute the city of the Great King, [7] together with the whole body of the Church, as being present with them in spirit, and keeping holy-day with the Father, and the breth-

ren most held in honour there. Hail, thou city of the Great King, in which the mysteries of our salvation are consummated. Hail, thou heaven upon earth, Sion, the city that is for ever faithful unto the Lord. Hail, and shine thou Jerusalem, for thy light is come, the Light Eternal, the Light for ever enduring, the Light Supreme, the Light Immaterial, the Light of one substance with God and the Father, the Light which is in the Spirit, and in which is the Father; the Light which illumines the ages; the Light which gives light to mundane and supramundane things, Christ our very God. Hail, city sacred and elect of the Lord. Joyfully keep thy festal days, for they will not multiply so as to wax old and pass away. Hail, thou city most happy, for glorious things are spoken of thee; thy priest shall be clothed with righteousness, and thy saints shall shout for joy, and thy poor shall be satisfied with bread.[8] Hail! rejoice, O Jerusalem, for the Lord reigneth in the midst of thee.[9] That Lord, I say, who in His simple and immaterial Deity, entered our nature, and of the virgin's womb became ineffably incarnate; that Lord, who was partaker of nothing else save the lump of Adam, who was by the serpent tripped up. For the Lord laid not hold of the seed of angels [10] — those, I say, who fell not away from that beauteous order and rank that was assigned to them from the beginning. To us He condescended, that Word who was always with the Father co-existent God. Nor, again, did He come into the world to restore; nor will He restore, as has been imagined by some impious advocates of the devil, those wicked demons who once fell from light; but when the Creator and Framer of all things had, as the most divine Paul says, laid hold of the seed of Abraham, and through him of the whole human race, He was made man for ever, and without change, in order that by His fellowship with us, and our joining on to Him, the ingress of sin into us might be stopped, its strength being broken by degrees, and itself as wax being melted, by that fire which the Lord, when He came, sent upon the earth.[11] Hail to thee, thou Catholic Church,[12] which hast been planted in all the earth, and do thou rejoice with us. Fear not, little flock, the storms of the enemy,[13] for it is your Father's good pleasure to give you the kingdom, and that you should tread upon the necks of your enemies.[14] Hail, and rejoice, thou that wast once barren, and without seed unto godliness, but who

[1] Luke ii. 32.
[2] Ps. xviii. 8.
[3] Ecclus. xxii. 7.
[4] Matt. xxiii. 38.
[5] Matt. xvii. 7.
[6] Isa. vi. 3, 4, i.
[7] Ps. xlviii. 2; Matt. v. 35; Isa. i. 26.

[8] Isa. lx. 1; Ps. lxxxvii. 3; Ps. cxxxii. 16.
[9] Isa. xii. 6.
[10] Heb. ii. 16.
[11] Luke xii. 49.
[12] [Here is an apostrophe to the Church, a hymn to " the Elect Lady." See, illustrating note 17, p. 390, *supra*.]
[13] τρικυμίας, stormy waves. *Latin*, decumani fluctus. Methodius perhaps alludes to Diocletian's persecution, in which he perished as a martyr. — Tr.
[14] Luke xii. 32.

hast now many children of faith.[1] Hail, thou people of the Lord, thou chosen generation, thou royal priesthood, thou holy nation, thou peculiar people — show forth His praises who hath called you out of darkness into His marvellous light ; and for His mercies glorify Him.[2]

XIV. Hail to thee for ever, thou virgin mother of God, our unceasing joy, for unto thee do I again return.[3] Thou art the beginning of our feast ; thou art its middle and end ;[4] the pearl of great price that belongest unto the kingdom ; the fat of every victim, the living altar of the bread of life. Hail, thou treasure of the love of God. Hail, thou fount of the Son's love for man. Hail, thou overshadowing mount[5] of the Holy Ghost. Thou gleamedst, sweet gift-bestowing mother, of the light of the sun ; thou gleamedst with the insupportable fires of a most fervent charity, bringing forth in the end that which was conceived of thee before the beginning, making manifest the mystery hidden and unspeakable, the invisible Son of the Father — the Prince of Peace, who in a marvellous manner showed Himself as less than all littleness. Wherefore, we pray thee, the most excellent among women, who boastest in the confidence of thy maternal honours, that thou wouldest unceasingly keep us in remembrance. O holy mother of God, remember us, I say, who make our boast in thee, and who in hymns august celebrate the memory, which will ever live, and never fade away. And do thou also, O honoured and venerable Simeon, thou earliest host of our holy religion, and teacher of the resurrection of the faithful, be our patron and advocate with that Saviour God, whom thou wast deemed worthy to receive into thine arms. We, together with thee, sing our praises to Christ, who has the power of life and death, saying, Thou art the true Light, proceeding from the true Light ; the true God, begotten of the true God ; the one Lord, before Thine assumption of the humanity ; that One nevertheless, after Thine assumption of it, which is ever to be adored ; God of Thine own self and not by grace, but for our sakes also perfect man ; in Thine own nature the King absolute and sovereign, but for us and for our salvation existing also in the form of a servant, yet immaculately and without defilement. For Thou who art incorruption hast come to set corruption free, that Thou mightest render all things uncorrupt. For Thine is the glory, and the power, and the greatness, and the majesty, with the Father and the Holy Spirit, for ever. Amen.

---

[1] Isa. liv. 1.
[2] 1 Pet. ii. 9.
[3] [He again apostrophizes the Blessed *Theotocos*, but in language hardly appropriate to the period preceding Cyril of Alexandria.]
[4] [Not so, for he *ends* with a noble strain of worship to the Son of God. This expression suggests interpolation.]
[5] Hab. iii. 3.

ORATION ON THE PALMS.[1]

I. BLESSED be God; let us proceed, brethren, from wonders to the miracles of the Lord, and as it were, from strength to strength.[2] For just as in a golden chain the links are so intimately joined and connected together, as that the one holds the other, and is fitted on to it, and so carries on the chain — even so the miracles that have been handed down by the holy Gospels, one after the other, lead on the Church of God, which delights in festivity, and refresh it, not with the meat that perisheth, but with that which ·endureth unto everlasting life.[3] Come then, beloved, and let us, too, with prepared hearts, and with ears intent, listen to what the Lord our God shall say unto us out of the prophets and Gospels concerning this most sacred feast. Verily, He will speak peace unto His people, and to His saints, and to those which turn their hearts unto Him. To-day,[4] the trumpet-blast of the prophets have roused the world, and have made glad and filled with joyfulness the churches of God that are everywhere amongst the nations. And, summoning the faithful from the exercise of holy fasting, and from the palæstra, wherein they struggle against the lusts of the flesh, they have taught them to sing a new hymn of conquest and a new song of peace to Christ who giveth the victory. Come then, every one, and let us rejoice in the Lord; O come, all ye people, and let us clap our hands, and make a joyful noise to God our Saviour, with the voice of melody.[5] Let no one be without portion in this grace; let no one come short of this calling; for the seed of the disobedient is appointed to destruction. — Let no one neglect to meet the King, lest he be shut out from the Bridegroom's chamber. — Let no one amongst us be found to receive Him with a sad countenance, lest he be condemned with those wicked citizens — the citizens, I mean, who refused to receive the Lord as King over them.[6] Let us all come together cheerfully; let us all receive Him gladly, and hold our feast with all honesty. Instead of our garments, let us strew our hearts before Him,[7] In psalms and hymns, let us raise to Him our shouts of thanksgiving; and, without ceasing, let us exclaim, "Blessed is He that cometh in the name of the Lord;"[8] for blessed are they that bless Him, and cursed are they that curse Him.[9] Again I will say it, nor will I cease exhorting you to good, Come, beloved, let us bless Him who is blessed, that we may be ourselves blessed of Him. Every age and condition does this discourse summon to praise the Lord; kings of the earth, and all people; princes, and all judges of the earth; both young men and maidens[10] — and what is new in this miracle, the tender and innocent age of babes and sucklings hath obtained the first place in raising to God with thankful confession the hymn which was of God taught them in the strains in which Moses sang before to the people when they came forth out of Egypt — namely, "Blessed is He that cometh in the name of the Lord."

II. To-day, holy David rejoices with great joy, being by babes despoiled of his lyre, with whom also, in spirit, leading the dance, and rejoicing together, as of old, before the ark of God,[11] he mingles musical harmony, and sweetly lisps out in stammering voice, Blessed is He that cometh in the name of the Lord. Of whom shall we inquire? Tell us, O prophet, who is this that cometh in the name of the Lord? He will say it is not my part to-day to teach you, for He hath consecrated the school to infants, who hath out of the mouth of babes and sucklings perfected praise to destroy the enemy and the avenger,[12] in order that by the miracle of these the hearts of the fathers might be turned to the children, and the disobedient unto the wisdom of the just.[13] Tell us, then, O children, whence is this, your beautiful and graceful contest of song?

---

1 [Dupin hardly credits this oration to Methodius. See elucidation, p. 398.
2 Ps. lxxxiv. 8.
3 John vi. 27.
4 [Evidently a homily for Palm Sunday, the first day of the Paschal week.]
5 Ps. lxxxv. 9, xcv. 1, xlvii. 1.
6 Luke xix. 27.

7 Ps. lxii. 8.
8 Ps. cxviii. 26; Matt. xxi. 9; Mark xi. 9; Luke xix. 38; John xii. 13.
9 Gen. xxvii. 29.
10 Ps. cxlviii. 11, 12.
11 2 Sam. vi. 14.
12 Ps. viii. 2.
13 Mal. iv. 6; Luke i. 17.

Who taught it you? Who instructed you? Who brought you together? What were your tablets? Who were your teachers? Do but you, they say, join us as our companions in this song and festivity, and you will learn the things which were by Moses and the prophet earnestly longed for.[1] Since then the children have invited us, and have given unto us the right hand of fellowship,[2] let us come, beloved, and ourselves emulate that holy chorus, and with the apostles, let us make way for Him who ascends over the heaven of heavens towards the East,[3] and who, of His good pleasure, is upon the earth mounted upon an ass's colt. Let us, with the children, raise the branches aloft, and with the olive branches make glad applaud, that upon us also the Holy Spirit may breathe, and that in due order we may raise the God-taught strain: "Blessed is He that cometh in the name of the Lord; Hosanna in the highest."[4] To-day, also, the patriarch Jacob keeps feast in spirit, seeing his prophecy brought to a fulfilment, and with the faithful adores the Father, seeing Him who bound his foal to the vine,[5] mounted upon an ass's colt. To-day the foal is made ready, the irrational exemplar of the Gentiles, who before were irrational, to signify the subjection of the people of the Gentiles; and the babes declare their former state of childhood, in respect of the knowledge of God, and their after perfecting, by the worship of God and the exercise of the true religion. To-day, according to the prophet,[6] is the King of Glory glorified upon earth, and makes us, the inhabitants of earth, partakers of the heavenly feast, that He may show Himself to be the Lord of both, even as He is hymned with the common praises of both. Therefore it was that the heavenly hosts sang, announcing salvation upon earth, "Holy, holy, holy, is the Lord God of hosts; the whole earth is full of His glory."[7] And those below, joining in harmony with the joyous hymns of heaven, cried: "Hosanna in the highest; Hosanna to the Son of David." In heaven the doxology was raised, "Blessed be the glory of the Lord from His place;"[8] and on earth was this caught up in the words, "Blessed is he that cometh in the name of the Lord."

III. But while these things were doing, and the disciples were rejoicing and praising God with a loud voice for all the mighty works that they had seen, saying, Blessed be the King that cometh in the name of the Lord; peace in heaven, and glory in the highest;[9] the city began to inquire, saying, Who is this?[10] stirring up its hardened and inveterate envy against the glory of the Lord. But when thou hearest me say the city, understand the ancient and disorderly multitude of the synagogue. They ungratefully and malignantly ask, Who is this? as if they had never yet seen their Benefactor, and Him whom divine miracles, beyond the power of man, had made famous and renowned; for the darkness comprehended not[11] that unsetting light which shone in upon it. Hence quite appositely with respect to them hath the prophet Isaiah exclaimed, saying, Hear, ye deaf; and look, ye blind, that ye may see. And who is blind, but my children? and deaf, but they that have the dominion over them?[12] And the servants of the Lord have become blind; ye have often seen, but ye observed not; your ears are opened, yet ye hear not. See, beloved, how accurate are these words; how the Divine Spirit, who Himself sees beforehand into the future, has by His saints foretold of things future as if they were present. For these thankless men saw, and by means of His miracles handled the wonder-working God, and yet remained in unbelief.[13] They saw a man, blind from his birth, proclaiming to them the God who had restored his sight. They saw a paralytic, who had grown up, as it were, and become one with his infirmity, at His bidding loosed from his disease.[14] They saw Lazarus, who was made an exile from the region of death.[15] They heard that He had walked on the sea.[16] They heard of the wine that, without previous culture, was ministered;[17] of the bread that was eaten at that spontaneous banquet;[18] they heard that the demons had been put to flight; the sick restored to health.[19] Their very streets proclaimed His deeds of wonder; their roads declared His healing power to those who journeyed on them. All Judea was filled with His benefit; yet now, when they hear the divine praises, they inquire, Who is this? O the madness of these falsely-named teachers! O incredulous fathers! O foolish seniors! O seed of the shameless Canaan, and not of Judah the devout![20] The children acknowledge their Creator, but their unbelieving parents said, Who is this? The age that was young and inexperienced sang praises to God, while they that had waxen old in wickedness inquired, Who is this? Sucklings praise His Divinity, while seniors utter blasphemies; children piously offer the sacrifice of praise, whilst profane priests are impiously indignant.[21]

[1] Luke x. 24.
[2] Gal. ii. 9.
[3] Ps. lxviii. 4, 34.
[4] Matt. xxi. 5.
[5] Gen. xlix. 10.
[6] Ps. cxlviii. 9.
[7] Isa. vi. 3.
[8] Ezek. iii. 22.
[9] Luke xix. 37, 38.

[10] Matt. xxi. 10.
[11] John i. 5.
[12] Isa. xlii. 18–20.
[13] John ix.
[14] John v. 5.
[15] John xi. 44.
[16] Matt. xiv. 26.
[17] John ii. 7.
[18] John vi. 11.
[19] Luke viii. 29, etc.
[20] Dan. iii. 56 (LXX.).
[21] Matt. xxi. 15.

IV. O ye disobedient as regards the wisdom of the just,[1] turn your hearts to your children. Learn the mysteries of God; the very thing itself which is being done bears witness that it is God that is thus hymned by uninstructed tongues. Search the Scriptures, as ye have heard[2] from the Lord; for they are they which testify of Him, and be not ignorant of this miracle. Hear ye men without grace, and thankless, what good tidings the prophet Zechariah brings to you. He says, Rejoice greatly, O daughter of Zion; behold thy King cometh unto thee: just and having salvation; lowly, and riding upon the foal of an ass.[3] Why do ye repel the joy? Why, when the sun shineth, do ye love darkness? Why do ye against unconquerable peace meditate war? If, therefore, ye be the sons of Zion, join in the dance together with your children. Let the religious service of your children be to you a pretext for joy. Learn from them who was their Teacher; who called them together; whence was the doctrine; what means this new theology and old prophecy. And if no man hath taught them this, but of their own accord they raise the hymn of praise, then recognise the work of God, even as it is written in the law: "Out of the mouth of babes and sucklings hast Thou perfected praise."[4] Redouble, therefore, your joy, that you have been made the fathers of such children who, under the teaching of God, have celebrated with their praises things unknown to their seniors. Turn your hearts to your children,[5] and close not your eyes against the truth. But if you remain the same, and hearing, hear not, and seeing, perceive not,[6] and to no purpose dissent from your children, then shall they be your judges,[7] according to the Saviour's word. Well, therefore, even this thing also, together with others, has the prophet Isaiah spoken before of you, saying, Jacob shall not now be ashamed, neither shall his face now wax pale. But when they see their children doing my works, they shall for me sanctify My name, and sanctify the Holy One of Jacob, and shall fear the God of Israel. They also that err in spirit shall come to understanding, and they that murmured shall learn obedience, and the stammering tongues shall learn to speak peace.[8] Seest thou, O foolish Jew, how from the beginning of his discourse, the prophet declares confusion to you because of your unbelief. Learn even from him how he proclaims the God-inspired hymn of praise that is raised by your children, even as the blessed David hath declared beforehand, saying, Out of the mouth of babes and sucklings hast Thou perfected praise. Either then, — as is right, — claim the piety of your children for your own, or devoutly give your children unto us. We with them will lead the dance, and to the new glory will sing in concert the divinely-inspired hymn.

V. Once, indeed, the aged Simeon met the Saviour,[9] and received in his arms, as an infant, the Creator of the world, and proclaimed Him to be Lord and God; but now, in the place of foolish elders, children meet the Saviour, even as Simeon did, and instead of their arms, strew under Him the branches of trees, and bless the Lord God seated upon a colt, as upon the cherubim, Hosanna to the son of David: Blessed is He that cometh in the name of the Lord; and together with these let us also exclaim, Blessed is He that cometh, God the King of Glory, who, for our sakes, became poor, yet, in His own proper estate, being ignorant of poverty, that with His bounty He might make us rich. Blessed is He who once came in humility, and who will hereafter come again in glory: at the first, lowly, and seated upon an ass's colt, and by infants extolled in order that it might be fulfilled which was written: Thy goings have been seen, O God; even the goings of my God, my King, in the sanctuary; but at the second time seated on the clouds, in terrible majesty, by angels and powers attended. O the mellifluous tongue of the children! O the sincere doctrine of those who are well pleasing to God! David in prophecy hid the spirit under the letter; children, opening their treasures, brought forth riches upon their tongues, and, in language full of grace, invited clearly all men to enjoy them. Therefore let us with them draw forth the unfading riches. In our bosoms insatiate, and in treasure-houses which cannot be filled, let us lay up the divine gifts. Let us exclaim without ceasing, Blessed is He that cometh in the name of the Lord! Very God, in the name of the Very God, the Omnipotent from the Omnipotent, the Son in the name of the Father. The true King from the true King, whose kingdom, even as His who begat Him, is with eternity, coeval and pre-existent to it. For this is common to both; nor does the Scripture attribute this honour to the Son, as if it came from another source, nor as if it had a beginning, or could be added to or diminished — away with the thought! — but as that which is His of right by nature, and by a true and proper possession. For the kingdom of the Father, of the Son, and of the Holy Ghost, is one, even as their substance is one and their dominion one. Whence also, with one and the same adoration, we worship the one

---

[1] Luke i. 17.
[2] John v. 39.
[3] Zech. ix. 9.
[4] Ps. viii. 2.
[5] Luke i. 17.
[6] Isa. vi. 10.
[7] Matt. xii. 27.
[8] Isa. xxix. 22, 24.

9 Luke ii. 29.

Deity in three Persons, subsisting without beginning, uncreate, without end, and to which there is no successor. For neither will the Father ever cease to be the Father, nor again the Son to be the Son and King, nor the Holy Ghost to be what in substance and personality He is. For nothing of the Trinity will suffer diminution, either in respect of eternity, or of communion, or of sovereignty. For not on that account is the Son of God called king, because for our sakes He was made man, and in the flesh cast down the tyrant that was against us, having, by taking this upon Him, obtained the victory over its cruel enemy, but because He is always Lord and God; therefore it is that now, both after His assumption of the flesh and for ever, He remains a king, even as He who begat Him. Speak not, O heretic, against the kingdom of Christ, lest thou dishonour Him who begat Him. If thou art faithful, in faith approach Christ, our very God, and not as using your liberty for a cloak of maliciousness. If thou art a servant, with trembling be subject unto thy Master; for he who fights against the Word is not a well-disposed servant, but a manifest enemy, as it is written: He that honoureth not the Son, honoureth not the Father which hath sent Him.

VI. But let us, beloved, return in our discourse to that point whence we digressed, exclaiming, Blessed is He that cometh in the name of the Lord: that good and kind Shepherd, voluntarily to lay down His life for His sheep. That just as hunters take by a sheep the wolves that devour sheep, even so the Chief Shepherd,[1] offering Himself as man to the spiritual wolves and those who destroy the soul, may make His prey of the destroyers by means of that Adam who was once preyed on by them. Blessed is He that cometh in the name of the Lord: God against the devil; not manifestly in His might, which cannot be looked on, but in the weakness of the flesh, to bind the strong man[2] that is against us. Blessed is He that cometh in the name of the Lord: the King against the tyrant; not with omnipotent power and wisdom, but with that which is accounted the foolishness[3] of the cross, which hath reft his spoils from the serpent who is wise in wickedness. Blessed is He that cometh in the name of the Lord: the True One against the liar; the Saviour against the destroyer; the Prince of Peace[4] against him who stirs up wars; the Lover of mankind against the hater of mankind. Blessed is He that cometh in the name of the Lord: the Lord to have mercy upon the creature of His hands. Blessed is He that cometh in the name of the Lord:

the Lord to save man who had wandered in error; to put away error; to give light to those who are in darkness; to abolish the imposture of idols; in its place to bring in the saving knowledge of God; to sanctify the world; to drive away the abomination and misery of the worship of false gods. Blessed is He that cometh in the name of the Lord: the one for the many; to deliver the poor[5] out of the hands of them that are too strong for him, yea, the poor and needy from him that spoileth him. Blessed is He that cometh in the name of the Lord, to pour wine and oil upon him who had fallen amongst thieves,[6] and had been passed by. Blessed is He that cometh in the name of the Lord: to save us by Himself, as says the prophet; no ambassador, nor angel, but the Lord Himself saved us.[7] Therefore we also bless Thee, O Lord; Thou with the Father and the Holy Spirit art blessed before the worlds and for ever. Before the world, indeed, and until now being devoid of body, but now and for ever henceforth possessed of that divine humanity which cannot be changed, and from which Thou art never divided.

VII. Let us look also at what follows. What says the most divine evangelist? When the Lord had entered into the temple, the blind and the lame came to Him; and He healed them. And when the chief priests and Pharisees saw the wonderful things that He did, and the children crying, and saying, Hosanna to the Son of David: Blessed is He that cometh in the name of the Lord,[8] they brooked not this honour that was paid Him, and therefore they came to Him, and thus spake, Hearest Thou not what these say? As if they said, Art Thou not grieved at hearing from these innocents things which befit God, and God alone? Has not God of old made it manifest by the prophet, "My glory will I not give unto another;"[9] and how dost Thou, being a man, make Thyself God?[10] But what to this answers the long-suffering One, He who is abundant in mercy,[11] and slow to wrath?[12] He bears with these frenzied ones; with an apology He keeps their wrath in check; in His turn He calls the Scriptures to their remembrance; He brings forward testimony to what is done, and shrinks not from inquiry. Wherefore He says, Have ye never heard Me saying by the prophet, Then shall ye know that I am He that doth speak?[13] nor again, Out of the mouth of babes and sucklings hast Thou perfected praise be-

---

[1] 1 Pet. v. 4.
[2] Matt. xii. 29.
[3] 1 Cor. i. 21.
[4] Isa. ix. 6.

[5] Ps. xxxv. 10.
[6] Luke x. 34.
[7] Isa. lxiii. 9.
[8] Matt. xxi. 14–16.
[9] Isa. xlii. 8.
[10] John x. 33.
[11] Joel ii. 13.
[12] Jas. i. 18.
[13] Isa. lii. 6.

cause of Thine enemies, that Thou mightest still the enemy and the avenger? Which without doubt are ye, who give heed unto the law, and read the prophets, while yet ye despise Me who, both by the law and the prophets, have been beforehand proclaimed. Ye think, indeed, under a pretence of piety, to avenge the glory of God, not understanding that he that despiseth Me despiseth My Father also.[1] I came forth from God, and am come into the world,[2] and My glory is the glory of My Father also. Even thus these foolish ones, being convinced by our Saviour-God, ceased to answer Him again, the truth stopping their mouths; but adopting a new and foolish device, they took counsel against Him. But let us sing, Great is our Lord, and great is His power;[3] and of His understanding there is no number. For all this was done that the Lamb and Son of God, that taketh away the sins of the world, might, of His own will, and for us, come to His saving Passion, and might be recognised, as it were, in the market and place of selling; and that those who bought Him might for thirty pieces of silver covenant for Him who, with His life-giving blood, was to redeem the world; and that Christ, our pass-over, might be sacrificed for us, in order that those who were sprinkled with His precious blood, and sealed on their lips, as the posts of the door,[4] might escape from the darts of the destroyer; and that Christ having thus suffered in the flesh, and having risen again the third day, might, with equal honour and glory with the Father and the Holy Ghost, be by all created things equally adored; for to Him every knee shall bow, of things in heaven, and things in earth, and things under the earth,[5] sending up glory to Him, for ever and ever. Amen.

[1] John xv. 23.
[2] John xvi. 28.
[3] Ps. clxvii. 5.

[4] Exod. xi. 7.
[5] Phil. ii. 10.

ELUCIDATION.

The candid Dupin [1] says that we owe this to Père Combefis,[2] on the authority of a ms. in the Royal Library of Paris. It appeared in Sir Henry Savile's edition of Chrysostom ascribed to that Father. Dupin doubts as to parts of this homily, if not as to the whole. He adds, " The style of Methodius is Asiatic, diffuse, swelling, and abounding in epithet. His expressions are figurative, and the turn of his sentences artificial. He is full of similitudes and far-fetched allegories. His thoughts are mysterious, and he uses many words to say a few things." His doctrine, apart from these faults, is sound, and free from some errors common to the ancients : such faults as I have frequently apologized for in Origen, whom Methodius so generally condemns.

[1] *Ecclesiastical Writers*, vol. i. p. 161.   [2] He was a Dominican, and learned in Greek. Died 1679.

THREE FRAGMENTS FROM THE HOMILY ON THE CROSS AND PASSION OF CHRIST.

I.[1]

METHODIUS, Bishop, to those who say : What doth it profit us that the Son of God was crucified upon earth, and made man? And wherefore did He endure to suffer in the manner of the cross, and not by some other punishment? And what was the advantage of the cross?

Christ, the Son of God, by the command of the Father, became conversant with the visible creature, in order that, by overturning the dominion of the tyrants, the demons, that is, He might deliver our souls from their dreadful bondage, by reason of which our whole nature, intoxicated by the draughts of iniquity, had become full of tumult and disorder, and could by no means return to the remembrance of good and useful things. Wherefore, also, it was the more easily carried away to idols, inasmuch as evil had overwhelmed it entirely, and had spread over all generations, on account of the change which had come over our fleshy tabernacles in consequence of disobedience ; until Christ, the Lord, by the flesh in which He lived and appeared, weakened the force of Pleasure's onslaughts, by means of which the infernal powers that were in arms against us reduced our minds to slavery, and freed mankind from all their evils. For with this end the Lord Jesus both wore our flesh, and became man, and by the divine dispensation was nailed to the cross ; in order that by the flesh in which the demons had proudly and falsely feigned themselves gods, having carried our souls captive unto death by deceitful wiles, even by this they might be overturned, and discovered to be no gods. For he prevented their arrogance from raising itself higher, by becoming man ; in order that by the body in which the race possessed of reason had become estranged from the worship of the true God, and had suffered injury, even by the same receiving into itself in an ineffable manner the Word of Wisdom, the enemy might be discovered to be the destroyers and not the benefactors of our souls.

For it had not been wonderful if Christ, by the terror of His divinity, and the greatness of His invincible power, had reduced to weakness the adverse nature of the demons. But since this was to cause them greater grief and torment, for they would have preferred to be overcome by one stronger than themselves, therefore it was that by a man He procured the safety of the race ; in order that men, after that very Life and Truth had entered into them in bodily form, might be able to return to the form and light of the Word, overcoming the power of the enticements of sin ; and that the demons, being conquered by one weaker than they, and thus brought into contempt, might desist from their over-bold confidence, their hellish wrath being repressed. It was for this mainly that the cross was brought in, being erected as a trophy against iniquity, and a deterrent from it, that henceforth man might be no longer subject to wrath, after that he had made up for the defeat which, by his disobedience, he had received, and had lawfully conquered the infernal powers, and by the gift of God had been set free from every debt. Since, therefore, the first-born Word of God thus fortified the manhood in which He tabernacled with the armour of righteousness, He overcame, as has been said, the powers that enslaved us by the figure of the cross, and showed forth man, who had been oppressed by corruption, as by a tyrant power, to be free, with unfettered hands. For the cross, if you wish to define it, is the confirmation of the victory, the way by which God to man descended, the trophy against material spirits, the repulsion of death, the foundation of the ascent to the true day ; and the ladder for those who are hastening to enjoy the light that is there, the engine by which those who are fitted for the edifice of the Church are raised up from below, like a stone four square, to be compacted on to the divine Word. Hence it is that our kings, perceiving that the figure of the cross is used for the dissipating of every evil, have made *vexillas*, as they are called in the Latin language. Hence the sea, yielding to this figure, makes itself navigable to men. For every creature, so to speak, has, for the sake of liberty, been marked with this sign ; for the birds which fly aloft, form the figure of the cross by the expansion of their wings ; and man himself, also, with his hands outstretched, represents the

---

[1] Apud. Gretserum, *De Sancta Cruce*, p. 401, tom. ii. Nov. edit. Ratisb., 1754. [Concerning which I quote from Dupin as follows: " The Père Combefis has collected some other fragments, *attributed to Methodius*, cited by St. John Damascene and by Nicetas as drawn out of his books against Porphyry. But, besides that, we cannot depend upon the authority of these two authors, who are not very exact: these fragments have nothing considerable, and we think it not worth while to say anything more concerning them."]

same. Hence, when the Lord had fashioned him in this form, in which He had from the beginning framed him, He joined on his body to the Deity, in order that it might be henceforth an instrument consecrated to God, freed from all discord and want of harmony. For man cannot, after that he has been formed for the worship of God, and hath sung, as it were, the incorruptible song of truth, and by this hath been made capable of holding the Deity, being fitted to the lyre of life as the chords and strings, he cannot, I say, return to discord and corruption.

II.[1]

THE SAME METHODIUS TO THOSE WHO ARE ASHAMED OF THE CROSS OF CHRIST.

Some think that God also, whom they measure with the measure of their own feelings, judges the same thing that wicked and foolish men judge to be subjects of praise and blame, and that He uses the opinions of men as His rule and measure, not taking into account the fact that, by reason of the ignorance that is in them, every creature falls short of the beauty of God. For He draws all things to life by His Word, from their universal substance and nature. For whether He would have good, He Himself is the Very Good, and remains in Himself; or, whether the beautiful is pleasing to Him, since He Himself is the Only Beautiful, He beholds Himself, holding in no estimation the things which move the admiration of men. That, verily, is to be accounted as in reality the most beautiful and praiseworthy, which God Himself esteems to be beautiful, even though it be contemned and despised by all else — not that which men fancy to be beautiful. Whence it is, that although by this figure He hath willed to deliver the soul from corrupt affections, to the signal putting to shame of the demons, we ought to receive it, and not to speak evil of it, as being that which was given us to deliver us, and set us free from the chains which for our disobedience we incurred. For the Word suffered, being in the flesh affixed to the cross, that He might bring man, who had been deceived by error, to His supreme and godlike majesty, restoring him to that divine life from which he had become alienated. By this figure, in truth, the passions are blunted; the passion of the passions having taken place by the Passion, and the death of death by the death of Christ, He not having been subdued by death, nor overcome by the pains of the Passion. For neither did the Passion cast Him down from His equanimity, nor did death hurt Him, but He was in the passible remaining impassible, and in the mortal remaining immortal, comprehending all that the air,

and this middle state, and the heaven above contained, and attempering the mortal to the immortal divinity. Death was vanquished entirely; the flesh being crucified to draw forth its immortality.

III.[2]

THE SAME METHODIUS : HOW CHRIST THE SON OF GOD, IN A BRIEF AND DEFINITE TIME, BEING ENCLOSED BY THE BODY, AND EXISTING IMPASSIBLE, BECAME OBNOXIOUS TO THE PASSION.

For since this virtue was in Him, now it is of the essence of power to be contracted in a small space, and to be diminished, and again to be expanded in a large space, and to be increased. But if it is possible for Him to be with the larger extended, and to be made equal, and yet not with the smaller to be contracted and diminished, then power is not in Him. For if you say that this is possible to power, and that impossible, you deny it to be power; as being infirm and incapable with regard to the things which it cannot do. Nor again, further, will it ever contain any excellence of divinity with respect to those things which suffer change. For both man and the other animals, with respect to those things which they can effect, energise ; but with respect to those things which they cannot perform, are weak, and fade away. Wherefore for this cause the Son of God was in the manhood enclosed, because this was not impossible to Him. For with power He suffered, remaining impassible; and He died, bestowing the gift of immortality upon mortals. Since the body, when struck or cut by a body, is just so far struck or cut as the striker strikes it, or he that cuts it cut it. For according to the rebound of the thing struck, the blow reflects upon the striker, since it is necessary that the two must suffer equally, both the agent and the sufferer. If, in truth, that which is cut, from its small size, does not correspond to that which cuts it, it will not be able to cut it at all. For if the subject body does not resist the blow of the sword, but rather yields to it, the operation will be void of effect, even as one sees in the thin and subtle bodies of fire and air ; for in such cases the impetus of the more solid bodies is relaxed, and remains without effect. But if fire, or air, or stone, or iron, or anything which men use against themselves for the purposes of mutual destruction — if it is not possible to pierce or divide these, because of the subtle nature which they possess, why should not rather Wisdom remain invulnerable and impassible, in nothing injured by anything, even though it were conjoined to the body which was pierced and transfixed with nails, inasmuch as it is purer and more excellent than any other nature, if you except only that of God who begat Him?

---

[1] Apud. Gretserum, *De Sancta Cruce*, tom. ii. p. 403.

[2] Apud. Allatium, *Diatr. de Methodiorum scriptis*, p. 349.

SOME OTHER FRAGMENTS OF THE SAME METHODIUS.

I.[1]

But, perhaps, since the friends of Job imagined that they understood the reason why he suffered such things, that just man, using a long speech to them, confesses that the wisdom of the divine judgment is incomprehensible, not only to him, but also to every man, and declares that this earthly region is not the fitting place for understanding the knowledge of the divine counsels. One might say, that perfect and absolute piety — a thing plainly divine, and of God alone given to man, is in this place called wisdom. But the sense of the words is as follows: God, he says, hath given great things unto men, sowing, as it were, in their nature the power of discovery, together with wisdom, and the faculty of art. And men having received this, dig metals out of the earth, and cultivate it; but that wisdom which is conjoined with piety, it is not possible in any place to discover. Man cannot obtain it from his own resources, nor can he give it unto others. Hence it was that the wise men of the Greeks, who in their own strength sought to search out piety, and the worship of the Deity, did not attain their end. For it is a thing, as we have said, which exceeds human strength, the gift and the grace of God; and therefore from the beginning, partly by visions, partly by the intervention of angels, partly by the discourses of the divinely-inspired prophets, God instructed man in the principles of true religion. Nay, moreover, that contemplative wisdom by which we are impelled to the arts, and to other pursuits, and with which we are all in common, just and unjust, alike endued, is the gift of God: if we have been made rational creatures, we have received this. Wherefore, also, in a former place it was said, as of a thing that is of God bestowed, "Is it not the Lord who teacheth understanding and knowledge?"[2]

II.[3]

Observe that the Lord was not wont from the begining to speak with man; but after that the soul was prepared, and exercised in many ways, and had ascended into the height by contemplation, so far as it is possible for human nature to ascend, then is it His wont to speak, and to reveal His Word unto those who have attained unto this elevation. But since the whirlwind is the producer of the tempests, and Job, in the tempest of his afflictions, had not made shipwreck of his faith, but his constancy shone forth the rather; therefore it was that He who gave him an answer answered him by the whirlwind, to signify the tempest of calamity which had befallen him; but, because He changed the stormy condition of his affairs into one of serene tranquillity, He spoke to him not only by the whirlwind, but in clouds also.

III.[4]

Many have descended into the deep, not so as to walk on it, but so as to be by its bonds restrained. Jesus alone walked on the deep, where there are no traces of walkers, as a free man. For He chose death, to which He was not subject, that He might deliver those who were the bondslaves of death; saying to the prisoners, "Go forth; and to them that are in darkness, show yourselves."[5] With which, also, the things which follow are consistent.

IV.[6]

Seest thou how, at the end of the contest, with a loud proclamation he declares the praises of the combatant, and discovers that which was in his afflictions hidden, in the words: "Thinkest thou that I had else answered thee, but that thou shouldest appear just?"[7] This is the salve of his wounds, this the reward of his patience. For as to what followed, although he received double his former possessions, these may seem to have been given him by divine providence as small indeed, and for trifling causes, even though to some they may appear great.

---

[1] Ex Nicetæ *Catena on Job*, cap. xix. p 429, edit. Londin., 1637. All the shorter fragments collected in the editions of Migne and Jahn are here appended.
[2] Job xxi. 22, xxii. 2.
[3] Ex Nicetæ *Catena on Job*, cap. xxvi. p. 538.
[4] Ex Nicetæ *Catena on Job*, p. 547.
[5] Isa. xlix. 9.
[6] Ex Nicetæ *Catena on Job*, cap. xxviii. p. 570.
[7] Job xl. 3 (LXX.).

FRAGMENT, UNCERTAIN.

Thou contendest with Me, and settest thyself against Me, and opposest those who combat for Me. But where wert thou when I made the world? What wert thou then? Hadst thou yet, says He, fallen from thy mother? for there was darkness, in the beginning of the world's creation, He says, upon the face of the deep. Now this darkness was no created darkness, but one which of set purpose had place, by reason of the absence of light.

V.[1]

But Methodius : The Holy Spirit, who of God is given to all men, and of whom Solomon said, " For Thine incorruptible Spirit is in all things," [2] He receives for the conscience, which condemns the offending soul.

VI.[3]

THE SAME METHODIUS.

I account it a greater good to be reproved than

to reprove, inasmuch as it is more excellent to free oneself from evil than to free another.

VII.[4]

THE SAME METHODIUS.

Human nature cannot clearly perceive pure justice in the soul, since, as to many of its thoughts, it is but dim-sighted.

VIII.

THE SAME METHODIUS.

Wickedness never could recognise virtue or its own self.

IX.

THE SAME METHODIUS.

Justice, as it seems, is four square, on all sides equal and like.

The just judgment of God is accommodated to our affections ; and such as our estate is, proportionate and similar shall the retribution be which is allotted us.

---

[1] Ex Nicetæ *Catena on Job*, cap xix. p. 418, ex Olympiodoro.
[2] Wisd. xii. 1. [" The Spirit of Christ," given to all; John i. 9.]
[3] Ex Parallelis. Damascen., *Opp.*, tom. ii. p. 331, D.

[4] *Ibid.*, p. 488, B.

TWO FRAGMENTS, UNCERTAIN.

I.

The beginning of every good action has its foundation in our wills, but the conclusion is of God.

II.

Perhaps these three persons of our ancestors, being in an image the consubstantial representatives of humanity, are, as also Methodius thinks, types of the Holy and Consubstantial Trinity,[1]

the innocent and unbegotten Adam being the type and resemblance of God the Father Almighty, who is uncaused, and the cause of all ; his begotten son [2] shadowing forth the image of the begotten Son and Word of God ; whilst Eve, that proceedeth forth from Adam,[3] signifies the person and procession of the Holy Spirit.[4]

---

[1] [Such is the fact, no doubt, as to the ancestors of the Jewish race; the fatherly character of Abraham, the filial character of Isaac, and the missionary offices of Jacob — whose wisdom and organizing faculties are so conspicuous — interpreting, in some degree, " the Holy and Consubstantial Trinity." This seems to be hinted, indeed, in the formula, " I am the God of Abraham, and the God of Isaac, and the

God of Jacob." Isaac's submission to be sacrificed upon Mount Moriah, and Jacob's begetting and sending forth the twelve patriarchs, singularly identify them as types of the Atoning Son and the regenerating Spirit, whose gifts and mission were imparted to the twelve Apostles.]
[2] [Abel.]
[3] [Note the single procession. The formula of the Hebrews, however, above noted, supplies a type of the *Filioque* and the *ab utroque* in the true sense of those terms.]
[4] [Recur to chap. v. of *The Banquet*, p. 333, *supra*.]

GENERAL NOTE.

(*Vexillas*, — as they are called, p. 399.)

It is very curious to note how certain ideas are inherited from the earliest Fathers, and travel down, as here, to find a new expression in a distant age. Here our author reflects Justin Martyr,[1] and the *Labarum* [2] itself is the outcrop of what Justin wrote to Antoninus Pius.

---

[1] See vol. i p. 181, this series.   [2] See p. 285, *supra*, under *the Emperors*.

ARNOBIUS

[TRANSLATED BY ARCHDEACON HAMILTON BRYCE, LL.D., D.C.L., AND HUGH CAMPBELL, M.A.]

INTRODUCTORY NOTICE

TO

ARNOBIUS.

[A.D. 297–303.] Arnobius appears before us, not as did the earlier apologists, but as a token that the great struggle was nearing its triumphant close. He is a witness that Minucius Felix and Tertullian had not preceded him in vain. He is a representative character, and stands forth boldly to avow convictions which were, doubtless, now struggling into light from the hearts of every reflecting pagan in the empire. In all probability it was the alarm occasioned by tokens that could not be suppressed — of a spreading and deepening sense of the nothingness of Polytheism — that stimulated the Œcumenical rage of Diocletian, and his frantic efforts to crush the Church, or, rather, to overwhelm it in a deluge of flame and blood.

In our author rises before us another contributor to Latin Christianity, which was still North-African in its literature, all but exclusively. He had learned of Tertullian and Cyprian what he was to impart to his brilliant pupil Lactantius. Thus the way was prepared for Augustine, by whom and in whom Latin Christianity was made distinctly Occidental, and prepared for the influence it has exerted, to this day, under the mighty *prestiges* of his single name.

And yet Arnobius, like Boethius afterwards, is much discredited, and has even been grudged the name of a Christian. Coleridge is one of the many who have disparaged Arnobius, but he always talked like an inspired madman, and often contradicted himself. Enough to say, that, emerging from gross heathenism in mature life, and forced to learn as he could what is now taught to Christian children, our author is a witness to the diffusion of truth in his day. He shows also such a faculty of assimilation, that, as a practical Christian, Coleridge himself does not shine in comparison ; and if, as is probable, he closed his life in martyrdom, we may well be ashamed to deny him our gratitude and the tribute of our praise. Our author is an interesting painter of many features of paganism in conflict with the Church, which we gain from no one else. Economizing Clement of Alexandria, he advances to an assured position and form of assault. He persistently impeaches Jove himself in a daring confidence that men will feel his terrible charges to be true, and that the victory over heathenism is more than half gained already.[1] I doubt not that, as a heathen, he was influenced by a dream to study Christianity. As a believer, he discarded dreams as vain. Converted late in life, we need not wonder at some tokens of imperfect knowledge ; but, on the whole, he seems a well-informed disciple, and shows how thoroughly the *catechumens* were trained. But what does he prove? In short, he gives us a most fascinating insight into the mental processes by which he, and probably Constantine soon after him, came to the conclusion that heathenism was outworn and must disappear. He proves that the Church was salt that had not "lost its savour." It is true, that, reasoning with pagans, he does not freely cite the Scriptures, which had no force with them ; yet his references to the facts of Scripture show that he had studied them conscientiously, and could present the truths of the Gospel clearly

---

[1] Lardner's *Testimony of Ancient Heathenism*, *Works*, vol. vii. p. 17.

and with power. Lardner has demonstrated[1] this in a fair spirit and with conclusive evidence. Referring the reader to his admirable criticisms, I am glad to say that a full and satisfactory outline of his career is presented in the following : —

TRANSLATOR'S INTRODUCTORY NOTICE.

§ 1. ARNOBIUS has been most unjustly neglected in modern times ; but some excuse for this may be found in the fact that even less attention seems to have been paid to him in the ages immediately succeeding his own. We find no mention of him in any author except Jerome ; and even Jerome has left only a few lines about him, which convey very little information.

In his list of ecclesiastical writers he says,[2] " During the reign of Diocletian, Arnobius taught rhetoric with the greatest success, at Sicca, in Africa, and wrote against the heathen the books extant ; " and again speaks of this work more particularly when he says,[3] " Arnobius published seven books against the heathen." In his *Chronicon*, however, he writes under the year 2342,[4] " Arnobius is considered a distinguished rhetorician in Africa, who, while engaged at Sicca in teaching young men rhetoric, was led by visions to the faith ; and not being received by the bishop as hitherto a persistent enemy to Christ, composed very excellent books against his former belief." It must at once be seen that there is here a mistake, for Arnobius is put some twenty-three years later than in the former passage. Jerome himself shows us that the former date is the one he meant, for elsewhere[5] he speaks of Lactantius as the disciple of Arnobius. Lactantius, in extreme old age,[6] was appointed tutor of Constantine's son Crispus ; and this, we are told in the *Chronicon*,[7] was in the year 317. No one will suppose that if the disciple was a very old man in 317, his master could have been in his prime in 326. It is certain, therefore, that this date is not correct ; and it seems very probable that Oehler's conjecture is true, who supposes that Jerome accidentally transposed his words from the year 303 to the place where we find them, misled by noticing the *vicenalia* of Constantine when he was looking for those of Diocletian.

It is with some difficulty that we can believe that Arnobius was led to embrace Christianity by dreams, as he speaks of these with little respect,[8] — which he could hardly have done if by them the whole course of his life had been changed ; but in our utter ignorance we cannot say that this may not have been to some extent the case. The further statement, that his apology for Christianity was submitted as a proof of his sincerity to the bishop of Sicca, is even less credible, — for these two reasons, that it is evidently the fruit not of a few weeks' but of protracted labour, and that it is hardly likely that any bishop would have allowed some parts of it to pass into circulation. It is just possible that the first or third books may have been so presented ; but it is not credible that any pledge would be required of a man seeking to cast in his lot with the persecuted and terrified Church referred to in the fourth.

§ 2. If we learn but little from external sources as to the life of Arnobius, we are not more fortunate when we turn to his own writings. One or two facts, however, are made clear ; and these are of some importance. " But lately," he says, " O blindness, I worshipped images just brought from the furnaces, gods made on anvils and forged with hammers : now, led by so great a teacher into the ways of truth, I know what all these things are."[9] We have thus his own assurance of his conversion from heathenism. He speaks of himself, however, as actually a Christian, — not as a waverer, not as one purposing to forsake the ancient superstitions and embrace the new religion, but as a firm believer, whose faith is already established, and whose side has

---

[1] *Credib.*, iii. 463.
[2] *Cat. Script. Eccl.*, lxxix. f. 121, Bened. ed. tom. iv.
[3] Ep. lxxiii. f. 656.
[4] i.e., A.D. 326.

[5] *Cat. Script. Eccl.*, lxxx. f. 121, ep. lxxxiii.
[6] *Cat. Script. Eccl.*, lxxx.
[7] Anno 2333.
[8] As " vain." [But see p. 405, *supra*.]

[9] Book i. sec. 39, p. 423, *infra*.

been taken and stedfastly maintained. In a word, he refers to himself as once lost in error, but now a true Christian.

Again, in different passages he marks pretty accurately the time or times at which he wrote. Thus, in the first book [1] he speaks of about three hundred years as the time during which Christianity had existed; and in the second,[2] of a thousand and fifty, or not many less, having elapsed since the foundation of Rome. There has been much discussion as to what era is here referred to; and it has been pretty generally assumed that the Fabian must be intended, — in which case 303 would be the year meant. If it is observed, however, that Arnobius shows an intimate acquaintance with Varro, and great admiration for him, it will probably be admitted that it is most likely that the Varronian, or common, era was adopted by him; and in this case the year referred to will be 297 A.D. This coincides sufficiently with the passage in the first book, and is in harmony with the idea which is there predominant, — the thought, that is, of the accusation so frequently on the lips of the heathen, that Christianity was the cause of the many and terrible afflictions with which the empire was visited. These accusations, ever becoming more bitter and threatening, would naturally be observed with care and attention by thoughtful Christians towards the close of the third century; and accordingly we find that the words with which Arnobius begins his apology, express the feeling of awakening anxiety with which he viewed the growth of this fear and hatred in the minds of the heathen. He declares, in effect, that one great object — indeed the main object — which he had proposed to himself, was to show that it was not because of the Christians that fresh evils and terrible calamities were continually assailing the state. And it must be remembered that we cannot refer such a proposal to a later period than that assigned. It would certainly not have occurred to a Christian in the midst of persecution, with death overhanging him, and danger on every side, to come forward and attempt calmly to show the heathen that there was no reason for their complaints against the Christians. In the later books there is a change in tone, upon which we cannot now dwell, although it is marked. In one passage he asks indignantly,[3] "Why should our writings be given to the flames, our meetings be cruelly broken up, in which prayer is offered to the supreme God, peace and pardon are asked for all in authority, for soldiers, kings, friends, enemies?" In the calm tranquillity of the last half of the third century these words could hardly have been written, but they are a striking testimony to the terms of the imperial edict issued in the year 303 A.D. So, too, the *popular* expression of anger and disgust at the anti-pagan character of some of Cicero's works [4] belongs to the incipient stages of persecution.

Nor must it be supposed that the whole work may be referred to the era which ensued after the abdication of Diocletian, in 305. From this time an apology for Christianity with such a design would have been an anachronism, for it was no longer necessary to disarm the fears of the heathen by showing that the gods could not be enraged at the Christians. It has further to be noticed, that although it is perfectly clear that Arnobius spent much time on his apology, it has never been thoroughly revised, and does not seem to have been ever finished.[5]

We surely have in all this sufficient reason to assign the composition of these books *adversus Gentes* to the end of the third and beginning of the fourth centuries. Beyond this we cannot go, for we have no *data* from which to derive further inferences.

§ 3. We have seen that the facts transmitted to us are very few and scanty indeed; but, few as they are, they suggest an interesting picture. Arnobius comes before us in Sicca; we are made spectators of two scenes of his life there, and the rest — the beginning and the end — are

---

[1] i. 13, p. 417.
[2] ii. 71, p. 461.
[3] iv. 36.
[4] Noticed in iii. 7, *infra.*-
[5] Cf. note on book vii. sec. 36, *infra.* [It is not at all improbable that some sketch of his convictions, written to assure the bishop of his conversion, was the foundation of what afterwards grew into a work.]

shrouded in darkness. Sicca Veneria was an important town, lying on the Numidian border, to the south-west of Carthage. As its name signifies, it was a seat of that vile worship of the goddess of lust, which was dear to the Phœnician race. The same cultus was found there which disgraced Corinth ; and in the temple of the goddess the maidens of the town were wont to procure for themselves, by the sacrifice of their chastity, the dowries which the poverty of their parents could not provide.

In the midst of traditions of such bestial foulness Arnobius found himself, — whether as a native, or as one who had been led to settle there. He has told us himself how true an idolater he was, how thoroughly he complied with the ceremonial demands of superstition ; but the frequency and the vehemence of language with which his abhorrence of the sensuality of heathenism is expressed, tell us as plainly that practices so horrible had much to do in preparing his mind to receive another faith.

In strong contrast to the filthy indulgences with which paganism gratified its adherents, must have appeared the strict purity of life which was enjoined by Christianity and aimed at by its followers ; and perhaps it was in such a place as Sicca that considerations of this nature would have most influence. There, too, the story of Cyprian's martyrdom must have been well known, — may indeed have been told in the nursery of the young Arnobius, — and many traditions must have been handed down about the persistency with which those of the new religion had held fast their faith, in spite of exile, torture, and death. However distorted such tales might be, there would always remain in them the evidence of so exalted nobility of spirit, that every disclosure of the meanness and baseness of the old superstition must have induced an uneasy feeling as to whether that could be impiety which ennobled men, — that piety which degraded them lower than the brutes.

For some time all went well with Arnobius. He was not too pure for the world, and his learning and eloquence won him fame and success in his profession. But in some way, we know not how, a higher learning was communicated to him, and the admired rhetorician became first a suspected, then a persecuted Christian. He has left us in no doubt as to the reason of the change. Upon his darkness, he says, there shone out a heavenly light,[1] a great teacher appeared to him and pointed out the way of truth ; and he who had been an earnest worshipper of images, of stones, of unknown gods, was now as earnest, as zealous in his service of the true God. Of the trials which he must have endured we know nothing. A terrible persecution swept over the world, and many a Christian perished in it. Such a man as Arnobius must have been among the first to be assailed, but we hear of him no more. With his learning and talents he could not have failed to make himself a name in the Church, or outside its pale, if he had lived. The conclusion seems inevitable, that he was one of the victims of that last fiery trial to which Christians under the Roman empire were exposed.

§ 4. The vast range of learning shown in this apology has been admitted on all sides. Even Jerome says that it should at times be read on account of the learning displayed in it.[2] In another passage Jerome says,[3] "Arnobius is unequal and prolix, confused from want of arrangement." This may be admitted to a certain extent ; but although such defects are to be found in his work, they are certainly not characteristic of Arnobius. So, too, many passages may be found strangely involved and mystical, and it is at times hard to understand what is really meant. Solecisms and barbarisms are also met with, as Nourry has objected, so that it cannot be said that Arnobius writes pure Latin. Still we must not be misled into supposing that by enumerating these defects we have a fair idea of his style.

If we remember that no man can wholly escape the influences of his age, and that Arnobius was so warm an admirer of Varro and Lucretius that he imitated their style and adopted their

---

[1] [Conf. Constantine's " vision."]   [2] Ep. lxii. *ad Tranquill.*   [3] Ep. xlix. *ad Paulinum.*

vocabulary, we shall be able to understand in what way he may be fairly spoken of as a good writer, although not free from defects. His style is, in point of fact, clear and lucid, rising at times into genuine eloquence ; and its obscurity and harshness are generally caused by an attempt to express a vague and indefinite idea. Indeed very considerable power of expression is manifested in the philosophical reasonings of the second book, the keen satire of the fourth and fifth, and the vigorous argument of the sixth and seventh.

Jerome's last stricture is scarcely applicable. Arnobius wrote *adversus Gentes ;* he addressed himself to meet the taunts and accusations of the heathen, and in so doing he retorts upon them the charges which they preferred against the Christians. His work must therefore be criticised from this standpoint, not as a systematic exposition or vindication of Christianity. Christianity is indeed defended, but it is by attacking heathenism. We must consider, also, that evidently the work was not revised as a whole, and that the last book would have been considerably altered had Arnobius lived or found opportunity to correct it.[1] If we remember these things, we shall find little to object to in the arrangement.

After making all deductions, it may be said fairly that in Arnobius the African Church found no unfitting champion. Living amidst impurity and corruption, and seeing on every side the effects of a superstitious and sensual faith, he stands forward to proclaim that man has a nobler ideal set before him than the worship of the foul imaginations of his depraved fancy, to call his fellows to a purer life, and to point out that the Leader who claims that men should follow Him is both worthy and able to guide. This he does with enthusiasm, vigour, and effect ; and in doing this he accomplishes his end.

§ 5. Various opinions have been entertained as to the position which Arnobius occupied with regard to the Bible. We cannot here enter into a discussion of these, and shall merely present a brief statement of facts.

It is evident that with regard to the Jews and the Old Testament Arnobius was in a state of perfect ignorance ; for he confounds the Sadducees with the Pharisees,[2] makes no allusion to the history of the Israelites, and shows that he was not acquainted with their forms of sacrifice.[3]

He was evidently well acquainted with the life of Christ and the history of the Church, and alludes at times to well-known Christian sayings ; but how far in so doing he quotes the Gospels and Epistles, is not easily determined. Thus it has been supposed, and with some probability, that in referring to the miracles of Christ he must allude to the Gospels as recording them. But it must be observed that he ascribes to Christ a miracle of which the New Testament makes no mention, — of being understood by men of different nations, as though He spoke in several languages at the same moment.[4] So, too, his account[5] of the passion differs from that of the New Testament. On the other hand, we find that he speaks of Christ as having taught men "not to return evil for evil,"[6] as "the *way* of salvation, the door of life, by whom alone there is access to the light,"[7] and as having been seen by "countless numbers of men" after His resurrection.[8] Still further, he makes frequent references to accounts of Christ written by the apostles and handed down to their followers,[9] and asks why their writings should be burned.[10] In one place,[11] also, he asks, "Have the well-known words never rung in your ears, that the wisdom of man is foolishness with God?" where the reference seems to be very distinct ;[12] but he nowhere says that he is quoting, or mentions any books.

This is, however, less remarkable when we take into account his mode of dealing with Clemens Alexandrinus and Cicero. The fourth, fifth, and sixth books are based on these two

---

[1] Cf. book vii. cap. 36, note, and *Ib.* cap. 51, note, with the Appendix.
[2] Book iii. cap. 12, note.
[3] Cf. book vii., on sacrifices generally. [Proves nothing.]
[4] Book i. cap. 46, note.
[5] Book i. cap. 53, note.
[6] Book i. cap. 6.
[7] Book ii. cap. 65, note.
[8] Book i. cap. 46 ; cf. 1 Cor. xv. 6.
[9] i. 55, 56, 58, 59.
[10] iv. 36.
[11] ii. 6, note.
[12] Cf. 1 Cor. iii. 19.

authors, and from Clement, in particular, whole sentences are taken unchanged.[1] Yet the only reference made to either is the very general allusion in the third and fourth books.[2]

On the other hand, he quotes frequently and refers distinctly to many authors, and is especially careful to show that he has good authority for his statements, as will be seen by observing the number of books to which he refers on the mysteries and temples. If we bear this in mind, the principle which guided him seems to have been, that when he has occasion to quote an author once or twice, he does so by name, but that he takes it for granted that every one knows what are the great sources of information, and that it is therefore unnecessary to specify in each case what is the particular authority.

There are many interesting questions connected with his subject, but these we must for the present leave untouched.

§ 6. No other works by Arnobius have been preserved, and only two MSS. are known to exist. Of these, the one in Brussels is merely a transcript of that preserved in the public library at Paris, on which all editions have been based. This is a MS. of the ninth or tenth century, and contains the *Octavius* of Minucius Felix immediately after the seventh book *adversus Gentes*, in consequence of which that treatise was at first printed as the eighth book of Arnobius. Although it has been collated several times, we are still in doubt as to its true readings, — Hildebrand, who last examined it, having done so with too little care.

The first[3] edition was printed at Rome in 1542, and was followed by that of Gelenius,[4] in which much was done for the emendation of the text; but arbitrary conjectures were too frequently admitted. Next in order follow those of Canterus,[5] who did especial service by pointing out what use Arnobius has made of Clement, Ursinus,[6] Elmenhorst,[7] Stewechius,[8] Heraldus,[9] and the Leyden[10] *variorum* edition, based on a recension of the text by Salmasius.[11] The later editions are those of Oberthür,[12] whose text is adopted by Orelli,[13] Hildebrand,[14] and Oehler.[15] Oberthür's edition is of little importance, and that of Orelli is valuable solely as a collection of notes gathered from many sources into a crude and undigested mass. Hildebrand seems to have taken too little pains with his work; and Oehler, whose critical sagacity and industry might have given us a most satisfactory edition, was unfortunately hampered by want of space.

No edition of Arnobius has been published in England; and the one Englishman who has taken any pains with this author seems to be John Jones, who, under the pseudonym of Leander de St. Martino, prepared summaries, which were added to a reprint of Stewechius at Douay, 1634. As this edition has not come into our hands, we are unable to speak of it more particularly.

§ 7. It will be observed that *adversus Gentes* is the title of this work in all editions except those of Hildebrand and Oehler, in which it is *adversus Nationes*. The difference is very slight, but it may be well to mention that neither can be said with certainty to be correct. The first is the form used by Jerome in two passages of his writings;[16] and as he must have seen earlier MSS.

---

[1] [Compare the *Exhortation* of Clement, vol. ii. p. 171, *passim*; and Tertullian, vol. iii. and *passim*.]

[2] Book iii. cap. 7, and book iv. cap. 13, note.

[3] Arnobii *Disputationum adversus Gentes*, libri octo, nunc primum in lucem editi Romæ, apud Franc. Priscianum Florentinum, 1542.

[4] Basileæ, 1546.

[5] Antverpiæ, 1582.

[6] Romæ, 1583. This is the second Roman edition, and restores the *Octavius* to Minucius Felix.

[7] Hanoviæ, 1603; dedicated to Joseph Scaliger.

[8] Antverpiæ, 1604.

[9] Paris, 1605. This edition, which is of great value, and shows great learning and ability, was completed in two months, as Heraldus himself tells us.

[10] Lugduni Batavorum 1651, containing the notes of Canterus, Elmenhorst, Stewechius, and Heraldus.

[11] Salmasius purposed writing commentaries for this edition, but died without doing more than beginning them.

[12] Wirceburgi, 1783, 8vo, preceded by a rambling introductory epistle.

[13] Lipsiæ, 1816-17, 8vo.

[14] Halis Saxonum, 1844, 8vo.

[15] Lipsiæ, 1846, 8vo.

[16] Cf. § 1, notes 2 and 3.

than that now extant, he is supposed to give the title which he found in them. In the Paris MS., however, at the end of the second book, the subscription is, "The second book of Arnobius *adversus Nationes* ends;" and it has been argued that, as the copyist would hardly have gone so far astray, while it is quite possible that Jerome did not attempt to do more than indicate generally the purpose of the book without quoting its titlepage, this must be the true title. The first page of the existing MS. is torn away, and the question remains therefore undecided: fortunately its decision is not of the slightest importance.

§ 8. This translation of Arnobius was begun in the hope that it would be possible to adhere throughout to the text of Orelli, and that very little attention to the various readings would be found necessary. This was, however, found to be impossible, not merely because Hildebrand's collation of the Paris MS. showed how frequently liberties had been taken with the text, but on account of the corrupt state of the text itself.

It has therefore been thought advisable to lay before the reader a close translation founded on the MS., so far as known. A conjectural reading has in no case been adopted without notice.

Throughout the Work use has been made of four editions, — Oehler's, Orelli's, Hildebrand's, and that of Leyden; other editions being consulted only for special reasons.

It is to be regretted that our knowledge of the single MS. of Arnobius is still incomplete; but it is hoped that this will soon be remedied, by the publication of a revised text, based upon a fresh collation of the MS., with a complete *apparatus* and a carefully digested body of notes.[1]

---

[1] [This section (8) appears as a " Preface " to the Edinburgh edition.]

THE SEVEN BOOKS OF ARNOBIUS AGAINST THE HEATHEN.

(*ADVERSUS GENTES.*)

BOOK I.

1. SINCE I have found some who deem themselves very wise in their opinions, acting as if they were inspired,[1] and announcing with all the authority of an oracle,[2] that from the time when the Christian people began to exist in the world the universe has gone to ruin, that the human race has been visited with ills of many kinds, that even the very gods, abandoning their accustomed charge, in virtue of which they were wont in former days to regard with interest our affairs, have been driven from the regions of earth, — I have resolved, so far as my capacity and my humble power of language will allow, to oppose public prejudice, and to refute calumnious accusations; lest, on the one hand, those persons should imagine that they are declaring some weighty matter, when they are merely retailing vulgar rumours;[3] and on the other, lest, if we refrain from such a contest, they should suppose that they have gained a cause, lost by its own inherent demerits, not abandoned by the silence of its advocates. For I should not deny that that charge is a most serious one, and that we fully deserve the hatred attaching to public enemies,[4] if it should appear that to us are attributable causes by reason of which the universe has deviated from its laws, the gods have been driven far away, and such swarms of miseries have been inflicted on the generations of men.

2. Let us therefore examine carefully the real significance of that opinion, and what is the nature of the allegation; and laying aside all desire for wrangling,[5] by which the calm view of subjects is wont to be dimmed, and *even* intercepted, let us test, by fairly balancing the considerations on both sides, whether that which is alleged be true. For it will assuredly be proved by an array of convincing arguments, not that we are discovered to be more impious, but that they themselves are convicted of that charge who profess to be worshippers of the deities, and devotees of an antiquated superstition. And, in the first place, we ask this of them in friendly and calm language : Since the name of the Christian religion began to be used on the earth, what phenomenon, unseen before,[6] unheard of before, what event contrary to the laws established in the beginning, has the so-called " Nature of Things " felt or suffered? Have these first elements, from which it is agreed that all things were compacted, been altered into elements of an opposite character? Has the fabric of this machine and mass *of the universe*, by which we are all covered, and in which we are held enclosed, relaxed in any part, or broken up? Has the revolution of the globe, to which we are accustomed, departing from the rate of its primal motion, begun either to move too slowly, or to be hurried onward in headlong rotation? Have the stars begun to rise in the west, and the setting of the constellations to take place in the east? Has the sun himself, the chief of the heavenly bodies, with whose light all things are clothed, and by whose heat all things are vivified, blazed forth with increased vehemence? has he become less warm, and has he altered for the worse into opposite conditions that well-regulated temperature by which he is wont to act upon the earth? Has the moon ceased to shape herself

---

[1] The words *insanire, bacchari,* refer to the appearance of the ancient seers when under the influence of the deity. So Virgil says, *Insanam vatem aspicies* (*Æn.*, iii. 443), and, *Bacchatur vates* (*Æn.*, vi. 78). The meaning is, that they make their asseverations with all the confidence of a seer when filled, as he pretended, with the influence of the god.

[2] *Et velut quiddam promptum ex oraculo dicere,* i.e., to declare a matter with boldness and majesty, as if most certain and undoubted.

[3] *Popularia verba,* i.e., rumours arising from the ignorance of the common people.

[4] The Christians were regarded as " public enemies," and were so called.

[5] Or, " all party zeal."

[6] So Meursius, — the MS. reading is *inusitatum,* " extraordinary."

413

anew, and to change into former phases by the constant recurrence of fresh ones? Has the cold of winter, has the heat of summer, has the moderate warmth of spring and autumn, been modified by reason of the intermixture of ill-assorted seasons? Has the winter begun to have long days? has the night begun to recall the very tardy twilights of summer? Have the winds at all exhausted their violence? Is the sky not collected[1] into clouds by reason of the blasts having lost their force, and do the fields when moistened by the showers not prosper? Does the earth refuse to receive the seed committed to it, or will not the trees assume their foliage? Has the flavour of excellent fruits altered, or has the vine changed in its juice? Is foul blood pressed forth from the olive berries, and is *oil* no longer supplied to the lamp, now extinguished? Have animals of the land and of the sea no sexual desires, and do they not conceive young? Do they not guard, according to their own habits and their own instinct, the offspring generated in their wombs? In fine, do men themselves, whom an active energy with its first impulses has scattered over habitable lands, not form marriages with due rites? Do they not beget dear children? do they not attend to public, to individual, and to family concerns? Do they not apply their talents, as each one pleases, to varied occupations, to different kinds of learning? and do they not reap the fruit of diligent application? Do those to whom it has been so allotted, not exercise kingly power or military authority? Are men not every day advanced in posts of honour, in offices of power? Do they not preside in the discussions of the law courts? Do they not explain the code of law? do they not expound the principles of equity? All other things with which the life of man is surrounded, in which it consists, do not all men in their own tribes practise, according to the established order of their country's manners?

3. Since this is so, and since no strange influence has suddenly manifested itself to break the continuous course of events by interrupting their succession, what is the ground of the allegation, that a plague was brought upon the earth after the Christian religion came into the world, and after it revealed the mysteries of hidden truth? But pestilences, say my opponents, and droughts, wars, famines, locusts, mice, and hailstones, and other hurtful things, by which the property of men is assailed, the gods bring upon us, incensed as they are by your wrong-doings and by your transgressions. If it were not a mark of stupidity to linger on matters which are already clear, and which require no defence, I should certainly show, by unfolding the history of past ages, that those ills which you speak of were not unknown, were not sudden in their visitation; and that the plagues did not burst upon us, and the affairs of men begin to be attacked by a variety of dangers, from the time that our sect[2] won the honour[3] of this appellation. For if we are to blame, and if these plagues have been devised against our sin, whence did antiquity know these names for misfortunes? Whence did she give a designation to wars? By what conception could she indicate pestilence and hailstorms, or how could she introduce these terms among her words, by which speech was rendered plain? For if these ills are entirely new, and if they derive their origin from recent transgressions, how could it be that the ancients coined terms for these things, which, on the one hand, they knew that they themselves had never experienced, and which, on the other, they had not heard of as occurring in the time of their ancestors? Scarcity of produce, say my opponents, and short supplies of grain, press more heavily on us. For, *I would ask*, were the former generations, even the most ancient, at any period wholly free from such an inevitable calamity? Do not the very words by which these ills are characterized bear evidence and proclaim loudly that no mortal ever escaped from them with entire immunity? But if the matter were difficult of belief, we might urge, on the testimony of authors, how great nations, and what individual nations, and how often *such nations* experienced dreadful famine, and perished by accumulated devastation. Very many hailstorms fall upon and assail all things. For do we not find it contained and deliberately stated in ancient literature, that even showers of stones[4] often ruined entire districts? Violent rains cause the crops to perish, and proclaim barrenness to countries: — were the ancients, indeed, free from these ills, when we have known of[5] mighty rivers even being dried up, and the mud of their channels parched? The contagious influences of pestilence consume the human race: — ransack the records of history written in various languages, and you will find that all countries have often been desolated and deprived of their inhabitants. Every kind of crop is consumed, and devoured by locusts and by mice: — go through your own annals, and you will be taught by these plagues how often former ages were visited by them, and how often they were brought to the wretchedness of poverty.

---

[1] So Gelenius; MS., *coartatur*, " pressed together."

[2] Or, " race," *gens*, i.e., the Christian people.

[3] The verb *mereri*, used in this passage, has in Roman writers the idea of merit or excellence of some kind in a person, in virtue of which he is deemed worthy of some favour or advantage; but in ecclesiastical Latin it means, as here, to gain something by the mere favour of God, without any merit of one's own.

[4] See Livy, i. 31, etc.; and Pliny, *Nat. Hist.*, ii. 38.

[5] The MS. reads, *flumina* cognoverimus ingentia *lim*-in-*is ingentia siccatis*, " that mighty rivers shrunk up, leaving the mud," etc.

Cities shaken by powerful earthquakes totter to their destruction : — what ! did not bygone days witness cities with their populations engulphed by huge rents of the earth?[1] or did they enjoy a condition exempt from such disasters?

4. When was the human race destroyed by a flood? was it not before us? When was the world set on fire,[2] and reduced to coals and ashes? was it not before us? When were the greatest cities engulphed in the billows of the sea? was it not before us? When were wars waged with wild beasts, and battles fought with lions?[3] was it not before us? When was ruin brought on whole communities by poisonous serpents?[4] was it not before us? For, inasmuch as you are wont to lay to our blame the cause of frequent wars, the devastation of cities, the irruptions of the Germans and the Scythians, allow me, with your leave, to say, — In your eagerness to calumniate us, you do not perceive the real nature of that which is alleged.

5. Did we bring it about, that ten thousand years ago a vast number of men burst forth from the island which is called the Atlantis of Neptune,[5] as Plato tells us, and utterly ruined and blotted out countless tribes? Did this form a prejudice against us, that between the Assyrians and Bactrians, under the leadership of Ninus and Zoroaster of old, a struggle was maintained not only by the sword and by physical power, but also by magicians, and by the mysterious learning of the Chaldeans? Is it to be laid to the charge of our religion, that Helen was carried off under the guidance and at the instigation of the gods, and that she became a direful destiny to her own and to after times? Was it because of our name, that that mad-cap Xerxes let the ocean in upon the land, and that he marched over the sea on foot? Did we produce and stir

into action the causes, by reason of which one youth, starting from Macedonia, subjected the kingdoms and peoples of the East to captivity and to bondage? Did we, forsooth, urge the deities into frenzy, so that the Romans lately, like some swollen torrent, overthrew all nations, and swept them beneath the flood? But if there is no man who would dare to attribute to our times those things which took place long ago, how can we be the causes of the present misfortunes, when nothing new is occurring, but all things are old, and were unknown to none of the ancients?

6. Although you allege that those wars which you speak of were excited through hatred of our religion, it would not be difficult to prove, that after the name of Christ was heard in the world, not only were they not increased, but they were even in great measure diminished by the restraining of furious passions. For since we, a numerous band of men as we are, have learned from His teaching and His laws that evil ought not to be requited with evil,[6] that it is better to suffer wrong than to inflict it, that we should rather shed our own blood than stain our hands and our conscience with that of another, an ungrateful world is now for a long period enjoying a benefit from Christ, inasmuch as by His means the rage of savage ferocity has been softened, and has begun to withhold hostile hands from the blood of a fellow-creature. But if all without exception, who feel that they are men not in form of body but in power of reason, would lend an ear for a little to His salutary and peaceful rules, and would not, in the pride and arrogance of enlightenment, trust to their own senses rather than to His admonitions, the whole world, having turned the use of steel into more peaceful occupations, would now be living in the most placid tranquillity, and would unite in blessed harmony, maintaining inviolate the sanctity of treaties.

7. But if, say my opponents, no damage is done to human affairs by you, whence arise those evils by which wretched mortals are now oppressed and overwhelmed? You ask of me a decided statement,[7] which is by no means necessary to this cause. For no immediate and prepared discussion regarding it has been undertaken by me, for the purpose of showing or proving from what causes and for what reasons each event took place; but in order to demonstrate that the reproaches of so grave a charge are far removed from our door. And if I prove this, if by examples and [8] by powerful arguments the truth of the matter is made clear, I care not

---

[1] So Tertullian, *Apologet.*, 40, says, — "We have read that the islands Hiera, Anaphe, Delos, Rhodes, and Cos were destroyed, together with many human beings."

[2] Arnobius, no doubt, speaks of the story of Phaethon, as told by Ovid; on which, cf. Plato, *Tim.*, st. p. 22.

[3] Nourry thinks that reference is here made to the contests of gladiators and athletes with lions and other beasts in the circus. But it is more likely that the author is thinking of African tribes who were harassed by lions. Thus Ælian (*de Nat Anim.*, xvii. 24) tells of a Libyan people, the Nomæi, who were entirely destroyed by lions.

[4] The city of Amyclæ in Italy is referred to, which was destroyed by serpents.

[5] In the *Timæus* of Plato, c. vi. st. p. 24, an old priest of Saïs, in Egypt, is represented as telling Solon that in times long gone by the Athenians were a very peaceful and very brave people, and that 9,000 years before that time they had overcome a mighty host which came rushing from the Atlantic Sea, and which threatened to subjugate all Europe and Asia. The sea was then navigable, and in front of the pillars of Hercules (Strait of Gibraltar) lay an island larger than Africa and Asia together: from it travellers could pass to other islands, and from these again to the opposite continent. In this island great kings arose, who made themselves masters of the whole island, as well as of other islands, and parts of the continent. Having already possessions in Libya and Europe, which they wished to increase, they gathered an immense host; but it was repelled by the Athenians. Great earthquakes and storms ensued, in which the island of Atlantis was submerged, and the sea ever after rendered impassable by shoals of mud produced by the sunken island. For other forms of this legend, and explanations of it, see Smith's *Dictionary of Geography*, under *Atlantis;* [also *Ancient America*, p. 175, Harpers, 1872. This volume, little known, seems to me "stranger than fiction," and far more interesting].

[6] Cf. Matt. v. 39.

[7] The MS. here inserts a mark of interrogation.

[8] So the MS., *si facto et*, corrected, however, by a later copyist, *si facio ut*, "if I cause that," etc.

whence these evils come, or from what sources and first beginnings they flow.

8. And yet, that I may not seem to have no opinion on subjects of this kind, that I may not appear when asked to have nothing to offer, I may say, What if the primal matter which has been diffused through the four elements of the universe, contains the causes of all miseries inherent in its own constitution? What if the movements of the heavenly bodies produce these evils in certain signs, regions, seasons, and tracts, and impose upon things placed under them the necessity of various dangers? What if, at stated intervals, changes take place in the universe, and, as in the tides of the sea, prosperity at one time flows, at another time ebbs, evils alternating with it? What if those impurities of matter which we tread under our feet have this condition imposed upon them, that they give forth the most noxious exhalations, by means of which this our atmosphere is corrupted, and brings pestilence on our bodies, and weakens the human race? What if — and this seems nearest the truth — whatever appears to us adverse, is in reality not an evil to the world itself? And what if, measuring by our own advantages all things which take place, we blame the results of nature through ill-formed judgments? Plato, that sublime head and pillar of philosophers, has declared in his writings, that those cruel floods and those conflagrations of the world are a purification of the earth; nor did that wise man dread to call the overthrow of the human race, its destruction, ruin, and death, a renewal of things, and to affirm that a youthfulness, as it were, was secured by this renewed strength.[1]

9. It rains not from heaven, my opponent says, and we are in distress from some extraordinary deficiency of grain crops. What then, do you demand that the elements should be the slaves of your wants? and that you may be able to live more softly and more delicately, ought the compliant seasons to minister to your convenience? What if, in this way, one who is intent on voyaging complains, that now for a long time there are no winds, and that the blasts of heaven have for ever lulled? Is it therefore to be said that that peacefulness of the universe is pernicious, because it interferes with the wishes of traders? What if one, accustomed to bask himself in the sun, and thus to acquire dryness of body, similarly complains that by the clouds the pleasure of serene weather is taken away? Should the clouds, therefore, be said to hang over with an injurious veil, because idle lust is not permitted to scorch itself in the burning heat, and to devise excuses for drinking? All these events which are brought to pass, and which happen under

this mass of the universe, are not to be regarded as sent for our petty advantages, but as consistent with the plans and arrangements of Nature herself.

10. And if anything happens which does not foster ourselves or our affairs with joyous success, it is not to be set down forthwith as an evil, and as a pernicious thing. The world rains or does not rain: for itself it rains or does not rain; and, though you perhaps are ignorant of it, it either diminishes excessive moisture by a burning drought, or by the outpouring of rain moderates the dryness extending over a very long period. It raises pestilences, diseases, famines, and other baneful forms of plagues: how can you tell whether it does not thus remove that which is in excess, and whether, through loss to themselves, it does not fix a limit to things prone to luxuriance?

11. Would you venture to say that, in this universe, this thing or the other thing is an evil, whose origin and cause you are unable to explain and to analyze?[2] And because it interferes with your lawful, perhaps even your unlawful pleasures, would you say that it is pernicious and adverse? What, then, because cold is disagreeable to your members, and is wont to chill[3] the warmth of your blood, ought not winter on that account to exist in the world? And because you are unable[4] to endure the hottest rays of the sun, is summer to be removed from the year, and a different course of nature to be instituted under different laws? Hellebore is poison to men; should it therefore not grow? The wolf lies in wait by the sheepfolds; is nature at all in fault, because she has produced a beast most dangerous to sheep? The serpent by his bite takes away life; a reproach, forsooth, to creation, because it has added to animals monsters so cruel.

12. It is rather presumptuous, when you are not your own master, even when you are the property of another, to dictate terms to those more powerful; to wish that that should happen which you desire, not that which you have found fixed in things by their original constitution. Wherefore, if you wish that your complaints should have a basis, you must first inform us whence you are, or who you are; whether the world was created and fashioned for you, or whether you came into it as sojourners from other regions. And since it is not in your power to say or to explain for what purpose you live beneath this vault of heaven, cease to believe that anything belongs to you; since those things which take place are not brought about in favour of a part, but have regard to the interest of the whole.

---

[1] Plato, *Tim.*, st. p. 22.

[2] "To analyze" — *dissolvere* — is in the MS. marked as spurious.
[3] In the MS. we find "to chill and numb" — *congelare, constringere;* but the last word, too, is marked as spurious.
[4] MS. *sustinere* (marked as a gloss), "to sustain;" *perferre,* "to endure."

13. Because of the Christians, my opponents say, the gods inflict upon us all calamities, and ruin is brought on our crops by the heavenly deities. I ask, when you say these things, do you not see that you are accusing us with barefaced effrontery, with palpable and clearly proved falsehoods? It is almost three hundred years [1] — something less or more — since we Christians [2] began to exist, and to be taken account of in the world. During all these years, have wars been incessant, has there been a yearly failure of the crops, has there been no peace on earth, has there been no season of cheapness and abundance of all things? For this must first be proved by him who accuses us, that these calamities have been endless and incessant, that men have never had a breathing time at all, and that without any relaxation [3] they have undergone dangers of many forms.

14. And yet do we not see that, in these years and seasons that have intervened, victories innumerable have been gained from the conquered enemy, — that the boundaries of the empire have been extended, and that nations whose names we had not previously heard, have been brought under our power, — that very often there have been the most plentiful yields of grain, seasons of cheapness, and such abundance of commodities, that all commerce was paralyzed, being prostrated by the standard of prices? For in what manner could affairs be carried on, and how could the human race have existed [4] even to this time, had not the productiveness of nature continued to supply all things which use demanded?

15. Sometimes, however, there were seasons of scarcity; yet they were relieved by times of plenty. Again, certain wars were carried on contrary to our wishes. [5] But they were afterwards compensated by victories and successes. What shall we say, then? — that the gods at one time bore in mind our acts of wrong-doing, at another time again forgot them? If, when there is a famine, the gods are said to be enraged at us, it follows that in time of plenty they are not wroth, and ill-to-be-appeased; and so the matter comes to this, that they both lay aside and resume anger with sportive whim, and always renew their wrath afresh by the recollection of the causes of offence.

16. Yet one cannot discover by any rational process of reasoning, what is the meaning of these statements. If the gods willed that the Alemanni [6] and the Persians should be overcome because Christians dwelt among their tribes, how did they grant victory to the Romans when Christians dwelt among their peoples also? If they willed that mice and locusts should swarm forth in prodigious numbers in Asia and in Syria because Christians dwelt among their tribes too, why was there at the same time no such phenomenon in Spain and in Gaul, although innumerable Christians lived in those provinces also? [7] If among the Gætuli and the Tinguitani [8] they sent dryness and aridity on the crops on account of this circumstance, why did they in that very year give the most bountiful harvest to the Moors and to the Nomads, when a similar religion had its abode in these regions as well? If in any one state whatever they have caused many to die with hunger, through disgust at our name, why have they in the same state made wealthier, ay, very rich, by the high price of corn, not only men not of our body, but even Christians themselves? Accordingly, either all should have had no blessing if we are the cause of the evils, for we are in all nations; or when you see blessings mixed with misfortunes, cease to attribute to us that which damages your interests, when we in no respect interfere with your blessings and prosperity. For if I cause it to be ill with you, why do I not prevent it from being well with you? If my name is the cause of a great dearth, why am I powerless to prevent the greatest productiveness? If I am said to bring the *ill* luck of a wound being received in war, why, when the enemy are slain, am I not an evil augury; and why am I not set forth against good hopes, through the ill luck of a bad omen?

17. And yet, O ye great worshippers and priests of the deities, why, as you assert that those most holy gods are enraged at Christian communities, do you not likewise perceive, do you not see what base feelings, what unseemly frenzies, you attribute to your deities? For, to be angry, what else is it than to be insane, to rave, to be urged to the lust of vengeance, and to revel in the troubles of another's grief, through the madness of a savage disposition? Your great gods, then, know, are subject to and feel that which wild beasts, which monstrous brutes experience, which the deadly plant natrix contains in its poisoned roots. That nature which is superior to others, and which is based on the firm foundation of unwavering virtue, experiences, as you allege, the instability which is in man, the faults which are in the animals of earth. And what therefore follows of necessity,

---

[1] See Introduction.

[2] [Our author thus identifies himself with Christians, and was, doubtless, baptized when he wrote these words.]

[3] *Sine ullis feriis,* a proverbial expression, "without any holidays:" i.e., without any intermixture of good.

[4] For *qui durare* Ursinus would read *quiret durare;* but this seems to have no MS. authority, though giving better sense and an easier construction.

[5] That is, unsuccessfully.

[6] *Alemanni,* i.e., the Germans; hence the French *Allemagne.* The MS. has *Alamanni.*

[7] ["Innumerable Christians:" let this be noted.]

[8] The *Gætuli* and *Tinguitani* were African tribes. For *Tinguitanos,* another reading is *tunc Aquitanos;* but *Tinguitanos* is much to be preferred on every ground.

but that from their eyes flashes dart, flames burst forth, a panting breast emits a hurried breathing from their mouth, and by reason of their burning words their parched lips become pale?

18. But if this that you say is true, — if it has been tested and thoroughly ascertained both that the gods boil with rage, and that an impulse of this kind agitates the divinities with excitement, on the one hand they are not immortal, and on the other they are not to be reckoned as at all partaking of divinity. For wherever, as the philosophers hold, there is any agitation, there of necessity passion must exist. Where passion is situated, it is reasonable that mental excitement follow. Where there is mental excitement, there grief and sorrow exist. Where grief and sorrow exist, there is already room for weakening and decay; and if these two harass them, extinction is at hand, viz. death, which ends all things, and takes away life from every sentient being.

19. Moreover, in this way you represent them as not only unstable and excitable, but, what all agree is far removed from the character of deity, as unfair in their dealings, as wrong-doers, and, in fine, as possessing positively no amount of even moderate fairness. For what is a greater wrong than to be angry with some, and to injure others, to complain of human beings, and to ravage the harmless corn crops, to hate the Christian name, and to ruin the worshippers of Christ with every kind of loss?

20. [1] Do they on this account wreak their wrath on you too, in order that, roused by your own private wounds, you may rise up for their vengeance? It seems, then, that the gods seek the help of mortals; and were they not protected by your strenuous advocacy, they are not able of themselves to repel and to avenge[2] the insults offered them. Nay rather, if it be true that they burn with anger, give them an opportunity of defending themselves, and let them put forth and make trial of their innate powers, to take vengeance for their offended dignity. By heat, by hurtful cold, by noxious winds, by the most occult diseases, they can slay us, they can consume[3] us, and they can drive us entirely from all intercourse with men; or if it is impolitic to assail us by violence, let them give forth some token of their indignation,[4] by which it may be clear to all that we live under heaven subject to their strong displeasure.

21. To you let them give good health, to us bad, ay, the very worst. Let them water your farms with seasonable showers; from our little fields let them drive away all those rains which are gentle. Let them see to it that your sheep are multiplied by a numerous progeny; on our

flocks let them bring luckless barrenness. From your olive-trees and vineyards let them bring the full harvest; but let them see to it that from not one shoot of ours one drop be expressed. Finally, and as their worst, let them give orders that in your mouth the products of the earth retain their natural qualities; but, on the contrary, that in ours the honey become bitter, the flowing oil grow rancid, and that the wine when sipped, be in the very lips suddenly changed into disappointing vinegar.

22. And since facts themselves testify that this result never occurs, and since it is plain that to us no less share of the bounties of life accrues, and to you no greater, what inordinate desire is there to assert that the gods are unfavourable, nay, inimical to the Christians, who, in the greatest adversity, just as in prosperity, differ from you in no respect? If you allow the truth to be told you, and that, too, without reserve, these allegations are but words, — words, I say; nay, matters believed on calumnious reports not proved by any certain evidence.

23. But the true[5] gods, and those who are worthy to have and to wear the dignity of this name, neither conceive anger nor indulge a grudge, nor do they contrive by insidious devices what may be hurtful to another party. For verily it is profane, and surpasses all acts of sacrilege, to believe that that wise and most blessed nature is uplifted in mind if one prostrates himself before it in humble adoration; and if this adoration be not paid, that it deems itself despised, and regards itself as fallen from the pinnacle of its glory. It is childish, weak, and petty, and scarcely becoming for those whom the experience of learned men has for a long time called demigods and heroes,[6] not to be versed in heavenly things, and, divesting themselves of their own proper state, to be busied with the coarser matter of earth.

24. These are your ideas, these are your sentiments, impiously conceived, and more impiously believed. Nay, rather, to speak out more truly, the augurs, the dream interpreters, the soothsayers, the prophets, and the priestlings, ever vain, have devised these fables; for they, fearing that their own arts be brought to nought, and that they may extort but scanty contributions from the devotees, now few and infrequent, whenever they have found you to be willing[7]

---

[1] The MS. reads *at*, "but."
[2] *Defendere* is added in the MS., but marked as a gloss.
[3] *Consumere* is in like manner marked as a gloss.
[4] So Orelli, for the MS. *judicationis*, "judgment."

[5] The carelessness of some copyist makes the MS. read *ve-st-ri*, "your," corrected as above by Ursinus.
[6] So Ursinus, followed by Heraldus, LB., and Orelli, for the MS. *errores*, which Stewechius would change into *errones* — "vagrants" — referring to the spirits wandering over the earth: most other edd., following Gelenius, read, " called demigods, that these indeed " — *dæmonas appellat, et hos*, etc.
[7] So the MS., which is corrected in the first ed. " us to be willing " — *nos velle:* Stewechius reads, " us to be making good progress, are envious, enraged, and cry aloud, etc. — *nos belle provenire compererunt, invident, indignantur, declamitantque*, etc.; to both of which it is sufficient objection that they do not improve the passage by their departure from the MS.

that their craft should come into disrepute, cry aloud, The gods are neglected, and in the temples there is now a very thin attendance. Former ceremonies are exposed to derision, and the time-honoured rites of institutions once sacred have sunk before the superstitions of new religions. Justly is the human race afflicted by so many pressing calamities, justly is it racked by the hardships of so many toils. And men — a senseless race — being unable, from their inborn blindness, to see even that which is placed in open light, dare to assert in their frenzy what you in your sane mind do not blush to believe.

25. And lest any one should suppose that we, through distrust in our reply, invest the gods with the gifts of serenity, that we assign to them minds free from resentment, and far removed from all excitement, let us allow, since it is pleasing to you, that they put forth their passion upon us, that they thirst for our blood, and that now for a long time they are eager to remove us from the generations of men. But if it is not troublesome to you, if it is not offensive, if it is a matter of common duty to discuss the points of this argument not on grounds of partiality, but on those of truth, we demand to hear from you what is the explanation of this, what the cause, why, on the one hand, the gods exercise cruelty on us alone, and why, on the other, men burn against us with exasperation. You follow, our opponents say, profane religious systems, and you practise rites unheard of throughout the entire world. What do you, O men, endowed with reason, dare to assert? What do you dare to prate of? What do you try to bring forward in the recklessness of unguarded speech? To adore God as the highest existence, as the Lord of all things that be, as occupying the highest place among all exalted ones, to pray to Him with respectful submission in our distresses, to cling to Him with all our senses, so to speak, to love Him, to look up to Him with faith, — is this an execrable and unhallowed religion,[1] full of impiety and of sacrilege, polluting by the superstition of its own novelty ceremonies instituted of old?

26. Is this, I pray, that daring and heinous iniquity on account of which the mighty powers of heaven whet against us the stings of passionate indignation, on account of which you yourselves, whenever the savage desire has seized you, spoil us of our goods, drive us from the homes of our fathers, inflict upon us capital punishment, torture, mangle, burn us, and at the last expose us to wild beasts, and give us to be torn by monsters? Whosoever condemns that in us, or considers that it should be laid against us as a charge, is he deserving either to be called

by the name of man, though he seem so to himself? or is he to be believed a god, although he declare himself to be so by the mouth of a thousand[2] prophets? Does Trophonius,[3] or Jupiter of Dodona, pronounce us to be wicked? And will he himself be called god, and be reckoned among the number of the deities, who either fixes the charge of impiety on those who serve the King Supreme, or is racked with envy because His majesty and His worship are preferred to his own?

Is Apollo, whether called Delian or Clarian, Didymean, Philesian, or Pythian, to be reckoned divine, who either knows not the Supreme Ruler, or who is not aware that He is entreated by us in daily prayers? And although he knew not the secrets of our hearts, and though he did not discover what we hold in our inmost thoughts, yet he might either know by his ear, or might perceive by the very tone of voice which we use in prayer, that we invoke God Supreme, and that we beg from Him what we require.

27. This is not the place to examine all our traducers, who they are, or whence they are, what is their power, what their knowledge, why they tremble at the mention of Christ, why they regard his disciples as enemies and as hateful persons; but *with regard to ourselves* to state expressly to those who will exercise common reason, in terms applicable to all of us alike, — We Christians are nothing else than worshippers of the Supreme King and Head, under our Master, Christ. If you examine carefully, you will find that nothing else is implied in that religion. This is the sum of all that we do; this is the proposed end and limit of sacred duties. Before Him we all prostrate ourselves, according to our custom; Him we adore in joint prayers; from Him we beg things just and honourable, and worthy of His ear. Not that He needs our supplications, or loves to see the homage of so many thousands laid at His feet. This is our benefit, and has a regard to our advantage. For since we are prone to err, and to yield to various lusts and appetites through the fault of our innate weakness, He allows Himself at all times to be comprehended in our thoughts, that whilst we entreat Him and strive to merit His bounties, we may receive a desire for purity, and may free ourselves from every stain by the removal of all our shortcomings.[4]

28. What say ye, O interpreters of sacred and of divine law?[5] Are they attached to a better cause who adore the Lares Grundules, the Aii

---

[1] [A beautiful appeal, and one sufficient to show that our author was no longer among catechumens.]

[2] So LB. and Orelli; but the MS. reads, "himself to be like *a god* by *his* prophets," etc. — *se esse similem profiteatur in vatibus.*
[3] So corrected by Pithœus for the MS. *profanus.*
[4] [Evidences of our author's Christian *status* abound in this fine passage.]
[5] So Gelenius, followed by Orelli and others, for the MS., reading *divini interpretes viri* (instead of *juris*) — "O men, interpreters of the sacred and divine," which is retained by the 1st ed., Hildebrand, and Oehler.

Locutii,[1] and the Limentini,[2] than we who worship God the Father of all things, and demand of Him protection in danger and distress? They, too, seem to you wary, wise, most sagacious, and not worthy of any blame, who revere Fauni and Fatuæ, and the genii of states,[3] who worship Pausi and Bellonæ : — we are pronounced dull, doltish, fatuous, stupid, and senseless, who have given ourselves up to God, at whose nod and pleasure everything which exists has its being, and remains immoveable by His eternal decree. Do you put forth this opinion? Have you ordained this law? Do you publish this decree, that he be crowned with the highest honours who shall worship your slaves? that he merit the extreme penalty of the cross who shall offer prayers to you yourselves, his masters? In the greatest states, and in the most powerful nations, sacred rites are performed in the public name to harlots, who in old days earned the wages of impurity, and prostituted themselves to the lust of all ;[4] and yet for this there are no swellings of indignation on the part of the deities. Temples have been erected with lofty roofs to cats, to beetles, and to heifers :[5] — the powers of the deities thus insulted are silent; nor are they affected with any feeling of envy because they see the sacred attributes of vile animals put in rivalry with them. Are the deities inimical to us alone? To us are they most unrelenting, because we worship their Author, by whom, if they do exist, they began to be, and to have the essence of their power and their majesty, from whom, having obtained their very divinity, so to speak, they feel that they exist, and realize that they are reckoned among things that be, at whose will and at whose behest they are able both to perish and be dissolved, and not to be dissolved and not to perish?[6] For if we all grant that there is only one great Being, whom in the long lapse of time nought else precedes, it necessarily follows that after Him all things were generated and put forth, and that they burst into an existence each of its kind. But if this is unchallenged and sure, you[7] will be compelled as a consequence to confess, on the one hand, that the deities are created,[8] and on the other, that they derive the spring of their existence from the great source of things. And if they are created and brought forth, they are also doubtless liable to annihilation and to dangers ; but yet they are believed to be immortal, ever-existent, and subject to no extinction. This is also a gift from God their Author, that they have been privileged to remain the same through countless ages, though by nature they are fleeting, and liable to dissolution.

29. And would that it were allowed me to deliver this argument with the whole world formed, as it were, into one assembly, and to be placed in the hearing of all the human race ! Are we therefore charged before you with an impious religion? and because we approach the Head and Pillar[9] of the universe with worshipful service, are we to be considered — to use the terms employed by you in reproaching us — as persons to be shunned, and as godless ones? And who would more properly bear the odium of these names than he who either knows, or inquires after, or believes any other god rather than this of ours? To Him do we not owe this first, that we exist, that we are said to be men, that, being either sent forth from Him, or having fallen from Him, we are confined in the darkness of this body?[10] Does it not come from Him that we walk, that we breathe and live? and by the very power of living, does He not cause us to exist and to move with the activity of animated being? From this do not causes emanate, through which our health is sustained by the bountiful supply of various pleasures? Whose is that world in which you live? or who hath authorized you to retain its produce and its possession? Who hath given that common light, enabling us to see distinctly all things lying beneath it, to handle them, and to examine them? Who has ordained that the fires of the sun should exist for the growth of things, lest elements pregnant with life should be numbed by settling down in the torpor of inactivity? When you believe that the sun is a deity, do you not ask who is his founder, who has fashioned him? Since the moon is a goddess in your estimation, do you in like manner care to know who is her author and framer?

30. Does it not occur to you to reflect and to examine in whose domain you live? on whose property you are? whose is that earth which you till?[11] whose is that air which you inhale, and

[1] Aii Locutii. Shortly before the Gallic invasion, B.C. 390, a voice was heard at the dead of night announcing the approach of the Gauls, but the warning was unheeded. After the departure of the Gauls, the Romans dedicated an altar and sacred enclosure to Aius Locutius, or Loquens, i.e., "The Announcing Speaker," at a spot on the Via Nova, where the voice was heard. The MS. reads *aiaceos boetios*, which Gelenius emended Aios Locutios.

[2] So emended by Ursinus for the MS. *libentinos*, which is retained in the 1st ed., and by Gelenius, Canterus, and others. Cf. iv. 9, where Libentina is spoken of as presiding over lusts.

[3] As a soul was assigned to each individual at his birth, so a genius was attributed to a state. The genius of the Roman people was often represented on ancient coins.

[4] Thus the Athenians paid honours to Leæna, the Romans to Acca Laurentia and Flora.

[5] The superstitions of the Egyptians are here specially referred to.

[6] That is, by whose pleasure and at whose command they are preserved from annihilation.

[7] So Orelli, adopting a conjecture of Meursius, for the MS. *nobis*.

[8] That is, not self-existent, but sprung from something previously in being.

[9] *Columen* is here regarded by some as equal to *culmen ;* but the term " pillar " makes a good sense likewise.

[10] This is according to the doctrine of Pythagoras, Plato, Origen, and others, who taught that the souls of men first existed in heavenly beings, and that on account of sins of long standing they were transferred to earthly bodies to suffer punishment. Cf. Clem. Alex. *Strom.* iii. p. 433.

[11] The Peripatetics called God the *locus rerum*, τόπος πάντων, the "locality and the area of all things; " that is, the being in whom all else was contained.

return again in breathing? whose fountains do you abundantly enjoy? whose water? who has regulated the blasts of the wind? who has contrived the watery clouds? who has discriminated the productive powers of seeds by special characteristics? Does Apollo give you rain? Does Mercury send you water from heaven? Has Æsculapius, Hercules, or Diana devised the plan of showers and of storms? And how can this be, when you give forth that they were born on earth, and that at a fixed period they received vital perceptions? For if the world preceded them in the long lapse of time, and if before they were born nature already experienced rains and storms, those who were born later have no right of rain-giving, nor can they mix themselves up with those methods which they found to be in operation here, and to be derived from a greater Author.

31. O greatest, O Supreme Creator of things invisible! O Thou who art Thyself unseen, and who art incomprehensible! Thou art worthy, Thou art verily worthy — if only mortal tongue may speak of Thee — that all breathing and intelligent nature should never cease to feel and to return thanks; that it should throughout the whole of life fall on bended knee, and offer supplication with never-ceasing prayers. For Thou art the first cause; in Thee created things exist, and Thou art the space in which rest the foundations of all things, whatever they be. Thou art illimitable, unbegotten, immortal, enduring for aye, God Thyself alone, whom no bodily shape may represent, no outline delineate; of virtues inexpressible, of greatness indefinable; unrestricted as to locality, movement, and condition, concerning whom nothing can be clearly expressed by the significance of man's words. That Thou mayest be understood, we must be silent; and that erring conjecture may track Thee through the shady cloud, no word must be uttered. Grant pardon, O King Supreme, to those who persecute Thy servants; and in virtue of Thy benign nature, forgive those who fly from the worship of Thy name and the observance of Thy religion. It is not to be wondered at if Thou art unknown; it is a cause of greater astonishment if Thou art clearly comprehended.[1]

But perchance some one dares — for this remains for frantic madness to do — to be uncertain, and to express doubt whether that God exists or not; whether He is believed in on the proved truth of reliable evidence, or on the imaginings of empty rumour. For of those who have given themselves to philosophizing, we have heard that some[2] deny the existence of any di-

vine power, that others[3] inquire daily whether there be or not; that others[4] construct the whole fabric of the universe by chance accidents and by random collision, and fashion it by the concourse of atoms of different shapes; with whom we by no means intend to enter at this time on a discussion of such perverse convictions.[5] For those who think wisely say, that to argue against things palpably foolish, is a mark of greater folly.

32. Our discussion deals with those who, acknowledging that there is a divine race of beings, doubt about those of greater rank and power, whilst they admit that there are deities inferior and more humble. What then? Do we strive and toil to obtain such results by arguments? Far hence be such madness; and, as the phrase is, let the folly, say I, be averted from us. For it is as dangerous to attempt to prove by arguments that God is the highest being, as it is to wish to discover by reasoning of this kind that He exists. It is a matter of indifference whether you deny that He exists, or affirm it and admit it; since equally culpable are both the assertion of such a thing, and the denial of an unbelieving opponent.

33. Is there any human being who has not entered on the first day of his life with an idea of that Great Head? In whom has it not been implanted by nature, on whom has it not been impressed, aye, stamped almost in his mother's womb even, in whom is there not a native instinct, that He is King and Lord, the ruler of all things that be? In fine, if the dumb animals even could stammer forth their thoughts, if they were able to use our languages; nay, if trees, if the clods of the earth, if stones animated by vital perceptions were able to produce vocal sounds, and to utter articulate speech, would they not in that case, with nature as their guide and teacher, in the faith of uncorrupted innocence, both feel that there is a God, and proclaim that He alone is Lord of all?

34. But in vain, says one, do you assail us with a groundless and calumnious charge, as if we deny that there is a deity of a higher kind, since Jupiter is by us both called and esteemed the best and the greatest; and since we have dedicated to him the most sacred abodes, and have raised huge Capitols. You are endeavouring to connect together things which are dissimilar, and to force them into one class, *thereby* introducing confusion. For by the unanimous judgment of all, and by the common consent of the human race, the omnipotent God is regarded as having never been born, as having never been brought forth to new light, and as not having

---

[1] [This prayer of Arnobius is surely worthy of admiration.]
[2] Diagoras of Melos and Theodorus of Cyrene, called the Atheists. The former flourished about B.C. 430, the latter about B.C. 310. See Cic., *Nat. Deor.*, i. 2. [Note the *universal* faith, cap. 34, *infra*.]

[3] Protagoras of Abdera, b. B.C. 480, d. 411.
[4] Democritus of Abdera, b. B.C. 460, and Epicurus, b. B.C. 342, d. 270.
[5] *Obstinatione*, literally "stubbornness:" Walker conjectures *opinatione*, "imaginings," which Orelli approves.

begun to exist at any time or century. For He Himself is the source of all things, the Father of ages and of seasons. For they do not exist of themselves, but from His everlasting perpetuity they move on in unbroken and ever endless flow. Yet Jupiter indeed, as you allege, has both father and mother, grandfathers, grandmothers, and brothers: now lately conceived in the womb of his mother, being completely formed and perfected in ten months, he burst with vital sensations into light unknown to him before. If, then, this is so, how can Jupiter be God *supreme*, when it is evident that He is everlasting, and the former is represented by you as having had a natal day, and as having uttered a mournful cry, through terror at the strange scene?

35. But suppose they be one, as you wish, and not different in any power of deity and in majesty, do you therefore persecute us with undeserved hatred? Why do you shudder at the mention of our name as of the worst omen, if we too worship the deity whom you worship? or why do you contend that the gods are friendly to you, but inimical, aye, most hostile to us, though our relations to them are the same? For if one religion is common to us and to you, the anger of the gods is stayed;[1] but if they are hostile to us alone it is plain that both you and they have no knowledge of God. And that that God is not Jove, is evident by the very wrath of the deities.

36. But, says my opponent, the deities are not inimical to you, because you worship the omnipotent God; but because you both allege that one born as men are, and put to death on the cross, which is a disgraceful punishment even for worthless men, was God, and because you believe that He still lives, and because you worship Him in daily supplications. If it is agreeable to you, my friends, state clearly what deities those are who believe that the worship of Christ by us has a tendency to injure them? Is it Janus, the founder of the Janiculum, and Saturn, the author of the Saturnian state? Is it Fauna Fatua,[2] the wife of Faunus, who is called the Good Goddess, but who is better and more deserving of praise in the drinking of wine? Is it those gods *Indigetes* who swim in the river, and live in the channels of the Numicius, in company with frogs and little fishes? Is it Æsculapius and father Bacchus, the former born of Coronis, and the other dashed by lightning from his mother's womb? Is it Mercury, son of Maia, and what is more divine, *Maia* the beautiful? Is it the bow-bearing deities Diana and Apollo, who were com-

panions of their mother's wanderings, and who were scarcely safe in floating islands? Is it Venus, daughter of Dione, paramour of a man of Trojan family, and the prostituter of her secret charms? Is it Ceres, born in Sicilian territory, and Proserpine, surprised while gathering flowers? Is it the Theban or the Phœnician Hercules, — the latter buried in Spanish territory, the other burned by fire on Mount Œta? Is it the brothers Castor and Pollux, sons of Tyndareus, — the one accustomed to tame horses, the other an excellent boxer, and unconquerable with the untanned gauntlet? Is it the Titans and the Bocchores of the Moors, and the Syrian[3] deities, the offspring of eggs? Is it Apis, born in the Peloponnese, and in Egypt called Serapis? Is it Isis, tanned by Ethiopian suns, lamenting her lost son and husband torn limb from limb? Passing on, we omit the royal offspring of Ops, which your writers have in their books set forth for your instruction, telling you both who they are, and of what character. Do these, then, hear with offended ears that Christ is worshipped, and that He is accepted by us and regarded as a divine person? And being forgetful of the grade and state in which they recently were, are they unwilling to share with another that which has been granted to themselves? Is this the justice of the heavenly deities? Is this the righteous judgment of the gods? Is not this a kind of malice and of greed? is it not a species of base envy, to wish their own fortunes only to rise, — those of others to be lowered, and to be trodden down in despised lowliness?

37. We worship one who was born a man. What then? do you worship no one who was born a man? Do you not worship one and another, aye, deities innumerable? Nay, have you not taken from the number of mortals all those whom you now have in your temples; and have you not set them in heaven, and among the constellations? For if, perchance, it has escaped you that they once partook of human destiny, and of the state common to all men, search the most ancient literature, and range through the writings of those who, living nearest to the days of antiquity, set forth all things with undisguised truth and without flattery: you will learn in detail from what fathers, from what mothers they were each sprung, in what district they were born, of what tribe; what they made, what they did, what they endured, how they employed themselves, what fortunes they experienced of

---

[1] So the MS.: for which Meursius would read, *nobis vobisque, communis esset* (for *cessat*) — "is to us and to you, the anger of the gods would be *shared in* common."

[2] So Ursinus, followed by most edd., for the reading of the MS. *Fenta Fatua*, cf. v. 18. A later writer has corrected the MS. *Fanda*, which, Rigaltius says, an old gloss renders "mother."

[3] So restored by Salmasius for *Dioscuri*, and understood by him as meaning Dea Syria, i e., Venus, because it is said that a large egg having been found by the fish in the Euphrates, was pushed up by them to the dry land, when a dove came down, and sat upon it until the goddess came forth. Such was the form of the legend according to Nigidius; but Eratosthenes spoke of both Venus and Cupid as being produced in this manner. The Syrian deities were therefore Venus, Cupid, and perhaps Adonis. It should be remembered, however, that the Syrians paid reverence to pigeons and fish as gods (Xen., *Anab.*, i. 4, 9), and that these may therefore be meant.

an adverse or of a favourable kind in discharging their functions. But if, while you know that they were born in the womb, and that they lived on the produce of the earth, you nevertheless upbraid us with the worship of one born like ourselves, you act with great injustice, in regarding that as worthy of condemnation in us which you yourselves habitually do ; or what you allow to be lawful for you, you are unwilling to be in like manner lawful for others.

38. But in the meantime let us grant, in submission to your ideas, that Christ was one of us — similar in mind, soul, body, weakness, and condition ; is He not worthy to be called and to be esteemed God by us, in consideration of His bounties, so numerous as they are ? For if you have placed in the assembly[1] of the gods Liber, because he discovered the use of wine ; Ceres, because she discovered the use of bread ; Æsculapius, because he discovered the use of herbs ; Minerva, because she produced the olive ; Triptolemus, because he invented the plough ; Hercules, because he overpowered and restrained wild beasts and robbers, and water-serpents of many heads, — with how great distinctions is He to be honoured by us, who, by instilling His truth into our hearts, has freed us from great errors ; who, when we were straying everywhere, as if blind and without a guide, withdrew us from precipitous and devious paths, and set our feet on more smooth places ; who has pointed out what is especially profitable and salutary for the human race ; who has shown us what God is,[2] who He is, how great and how good ; who has permitted and taught us to conceive and to understand, as far as our limited capacity can, His profound and inexpressible depths ; who, in in His great kindness, has caused it to be known by what founder, by what Creator, this world was established and made ; who has explained the nature of its origin[3] and essential substance, never before imagined in the conceptions of any ; whence generative warmth is added to the rays of the sun ; why the moon, always uninjured[4] in her motions, is believed to alternate her light and her obscurity from intelligent causes ;[5] what is the origin of animals, what rules regulate seeds ; who designed man himself, who fashioned

him, or from what kind of material did He compact the very build of bodies ; what the perceptions are ; what the soul, and whether it flew to us of its own accord, or whether it was generated and brought into existence with our bodies themselves ; whether it sojourns with us, partaking of death, or whether it is gifted with an endless immortality ; what condition awaits us when we shall have separated from our bodies relaxed in death ; whether we shall retain our perceptions,[6] or have no recollection of our former sensations or of past memories ;[7] who has restrained[8] our arrogance, and has caused our necks, uplifted with pride, to acknowledge the measure of their weakness ; who hath shown that we are creatures imperfectly formed, that we trust in vain expectations, that we understand nothing thoroughly, that we know nothing, and that we do not see those things which are placed before our eyes ; who has guided us from false superstitions to the true religion, — a blessing which exceeds and transcends all His other gifts ; who has raised our thoughts to heaven from brutish statues formed of the vilest clay, and has caused us to hold converse in thanksgiving and prayer with the Lord of the universe.

39. But lately, O blindness, I worshipped images produced from the furnace, gods made on anvils and by hammers, the bones of elephants, paintings, wreaths on aged trees ;[9] whenever I espied an anointed stone and one bedaubed with olive oil, as if some power resided in it I worshipped it, I addressed myself to it and begged blessings from a senseless stock.[10] And these very gods of whose existence I had convinced myself, I treated with gross insults, when I believed them to be wood, stone, and bones, or imagined that they dwelt in the substance of such objects. Now, having been led into the paths of truth by so great a teacher, I know what all these things are, I entertain honourable thoughts concerning those which are worthy, I offer no insult to any divine name ; and what is due to each, whether inferior[11] or superior, I assign with clearly-defined gradations, and on distinct authority. Is Christ, then, not to be regarded by us as God ? and is He, who in other respects may be deemed the very greatest, not

---

[1] So all edd., except those of Hildebrand and Oehler, for the MS. *censum* — "list."

[2] That is, that God is a Spirit. [Note our author's spirit of faith in Christ.]

[3] Orelli would refer these words to God : he thinks that with those immediately following they may be understood of God's spiritual nature, — an idea which he therefore supposes Arnobius to assert had never been grasped by the heathen.

[4] So Gelenius, followed by Orelli and others, for the corrupt reading of the MS., *idem ne quis;* but possibly both this and the preceding clause have crept into the text from the margin, as in construction they differ from the rest of the sentence, both that which precedes, and that which follows.

[5] The phrase *animalibus causis* is regarded by commentators as equal to *animatis causis*, and refers to the doctrine of the Stoics, that in the sun, moon, stars, etc., there was an intelligent nature, or a certain impulse of mind, which directed their movements.

[6] Lit. "shall see" — *visuri*, the reading of the MS.; changed in the first ed. and others to *victuri* — "shall live."

[7] Some have suggested a different construction of these words — *memoriam nullam nostri sensus et recordationis habituri*, thus — "have no memory of ourselves and senses of recollection;" but that adopted above is simpler, and does not force the words as this seems to do.

[8] The MS. and 1st and 2d Roman edd. read, *qui constringit* — "who restrains."

[9] It was a common practice with the Romans to hang the spoils of an enemy on a tree, which was thus consecrated to some deity. Hence such trees were sacred, and remained unhurt even to old age. Some have supposed that the epithet "old" is applied from the fact that the heathen used to offer to their gods objects no longer of use to themselves; thus it was only old trees, past bearing fruit, which were generally selected to hang the *spolia* upon.

[10] [This interesting personal confession deserves especial note.]

[11] *Vel personæ vel capiti.*

to be honoured with divine worship, from whom we have already received while alive so great gifts, and from whom, when the day comes, we expect greater ones?

40. But He died nailed to the cross. What is that to the argument? For neither does the kind and disgrace of the death change His words or deeds, nor will the weight of His teaching appear less; because He freed Himself from the shackles of the body, not by a natural separation, but departed by reason of violence offered to Him. Pythagoras of Samos was burned to death in a temple, under an unjust suspicion of aiming at sovereign power. Did his doctrines lose their peculiar influence, because he breathed forth his life not willingly, but in consequence of a savage assault? In like manner Socrates, condemned by the decision of his fellow-citizens, suffered capital punishment: have his discussions on morals, on virtues, and on duties been rendered vain, because he was unjustly hurried from life? Others without number, conspicuous by their renown, their merit, and their public character, have experienced the most cruel forms of death, as Aquilius, Trebonius, and Regulus: were they on that account adjudged base after death, because they perished not by the common law of the fates, but after being mangled and tortured in the most cruel kind of death? No innocent person foully slain is ever disgraced thereby; nor is he stained by the mark of any baseness, who suffers severe punishment, not from his own deserts, but by reason of the savage nature of his persecutor.[1]

41. And yet, O ye who laugh because we worship one who died an ignominious death, do not ye too, by consecrating shrines to him, honour father Liber, who was torn limb from limb by the Titans? Have you not, after his punishment and his death by lightning, named Æsculapius, the discoverer of medicines, as the guardian and protector of health, of strength, and of safety? Do you not invoke the great Hercules himself by offerings, by victims, and by kindled frankincense, whom you yourselves allege to have been burned alive after his punishment,[2] and to have been consumed on the fatal pyres? Do you not, with the unanimous approbation of the Gauls, invoke as a propitious[3] and as a holy god, in the temples of the Great Mother,[4] that Phrygian Atys[5] who was mangled

and deprived of his virility? Father Romulus himself, who was torn in pieces by the hands of a hundred senators, do you not call Quirinus Martius, and do you not honour him with priests and with gorgeous couches,[6] and do you not worship him in most spacious temples; and in addition to all this, do you not affirm that he has ascended into heaven? Either, therefore, you too are to be laughed at, who regard as gods men slain by the most cruel tortures; or if there is a sure ground for your thinking that you should do so, allow us too to feel assured for what causes and on what grounds we do this.

42. You worship, *says my opponent*, one who was born a *mere* human being. Even if that were true, as has been already said in former passages, yet, in consideration of the many liberal gifts which He has bestowed on us, He ought to be called and be addressed as God. *But* since He is God in reality and without any shadow of doubt, do you think that we will deny that He is worshipped by us with all the fervour we are capable of, and assumed as the guardian of our body? Is that Christ of yours a god, then? some raving, wrathful, and excited man will say. A god, we will reply, and *the* god of the inner powers;[7] and — what may still further torture unbelievers with the most bitter pains — He was sent to us by the King Supreme for a purpose of the very highest moment. My opponent, becoming more mad and more frantic, will perhaps ask whether the matter can be proved, as we allege. There is no greater proof than the credibility of the acts done by Him, than the unwonted excellence of the virtues *He exhibited*, than the conquest and the abrogation of all those deadly ordinances which peoples and tribes saw executed in the light of day,[8] with no objecting voice; and even they whose ancient laws or whose country's laws He shows to be full of vanity and of the most senseless superstition, (even they) dare not allege these things to be false.

---

[1] So all the later edd.: but in the MS., 1st and 2d Roman edd., and in those of Gelenius and Canterus, this clause reads, *cruciatoris perpetitur saevitatem* —" but suffers the cruelty of his persecutor."

[2] The words *post pœnas* in the text are regarded as spurious by Orelli, who supposes them to have crept in from the preceding sentence: but they may be defended as sufficiently expressing the agonies which Hercules suffered through the fatal shirt of Nessus.

[3] The words *deum propitium* are indeed found in the MS., but according to Rigaltius are not in the same handwriting as the rest of the work.

[4] Cybele, whose worship was conjoined with that of Atys.

[5] So Orelli, but the MS. *Attis.*

---

[6] This refers to the practice of placing the images of the gods on pillows at feasts. In the temples there were *pulvinaria*, or couches, specially for the purpose.

[7] The phrase *potentiarum interiorum* is not easily understood. Orelli is of opinion that it means those powers which in the Bible are called the "powers of heaven," the "army of heaven," i.e., the angels. The Jews and the early Fathers of the Church divided the heaven into circles or zones, each inhabited by its peculiar powers or intelligent natures, differing in dignity and in might. The central place was assigned to God Himself, and to Christ, who sat on His right hand, and who is called by the Fathers of the Church the "Angel of the Church," and the "Angel of the New Covenant." Next in order came "Thrones," "Archangels," "Cherubim and Seraphim," and most remote from God's throne, the "Chorus of Angels," the tutelar genii of men. The system of zones and powers seems to have been derived from the Chaldeans, who made a similar division of the heavens. According to this idea, Arnobius speaks of Christ as nearest to the Father, and God of the "inner powers," who enjoyed God's immediate presence. Reference is perhaps made to some recondite doctrine of the Gnostics. It may mean, however, the more subtile powers of nature, as affecting both the souls of men and the physical universe.

[8] So Orelli with most edd., following Ursinus, for the MS. *suo gene-ri-s sub limine*, which might, however, be retained, as if the sense were that these ordinances were coeval with man's origin, and translated, "tribes saw at the beginning of their race."

43. My opponent will perhaps meet me with many other slanderous and childish charges which are commonly urged. Jesus was a Magian;[1] He effected all these things by secret arts. From the shrines of the Egyptians He stole the names of angels of might,[2] and the religious system of a remote country. Why, O witlings, do you speak of things which you have not examined, and which are unknown to you, prating with the garrulity of a rash tongue? Were, then, those things which were done, the freaks of demons, and the tricks of magical arts? Can you specify and point out to me any one of all those magicians who have ever existed in past ages, that did anything similar, in the thousandth degree, to Christ? Who has done this without any power of incantations, without the juice of herbs and of grasses, without any anxious watching of sacrifices, of libations, or of seasons? For we do not press it, and inquire what they profess to do, nor in what kind of acts all their learning and experience are wont to be comprised. For who is not aware that these men either study to know beforehand things impending, which, whether they will or not, come of necessity as they have been ordained? or to inflict a deadly and wasting disease on whom they choose ; or to sever the affections of relatives ; or to open without keys places which are locked ; or to seal the mouth in silence ; or in the chariot race to weaken, urge on, or retard horses ; or to inspire in wives, and in the children of strangers, whether they be males or females, the flames and mad desires of illicit love?[3] Or if they seem to attempt anything useful, to be able to do it not by their own power, but by the might of those deities whom they invoke.

44. And yet it is agreed on that Christ performed all those miracles which[4] He wrought without any aid from external things, without the observance of any ceremonial, without any definite mode of procedure, *but solely* by the inherent might of His authority ; and as was the proper duty of *the* true God, as was consistent with His nature, as was worthy of Him, in the generosity of His bounteous power He bestowed nothing hurtful or injurious, but *only that which is* helpful, beneficial, and full of blessings good[4] for men.

45. What do you say again, oh you[5] —— ? Is He then a man, is He one of us, at whose command, at whose voice, raised in the utterance of audible and intelligible words,[6] infirmities, diseases, fevers, and other ailments of the body fled away? Was He one of us, whose presence, whose very sight, that race of demons which took possession of men was unable to bear, and terrified by the strange power, fled away? Was He one of us, to whose order the foul leprosy, at once checked, was obedient, and left sameness of colour to bodies formerly spotted? Was He one of us, at whose light touch the issues of blood were stanched, and stopped their excessive flow?[7] Was He one of us, whose hands the waters of the lethargic dropsy fled from, and that searching[8] fluid avoided ; and did the swelling body, assuming a healthy dryness, find relief? Was He one of us, who bade the lame run? Was it His work, too, that the maimed stretched forth their hands, and the joints relaxed the rigidity[9] acquired even at birth ; that the paralytic rose to their feet, and persons now carried home their beds who a little before were borne on the shoulders of others ; the blind were restored to sight, and men born without eyes now looked on the heaven and the day?

46. Was He one of us, I say, who by one act of intervention at once healed a hundred or more afflicted with various infirmities and diseases ; at whose word only the raging and maddened seas were still, the whirlwinds and tempests were lulled ; who walked over the deepest pools with unwet foot ; who trod the ridges of the deep, the very waves being astonished, and nature coming under bondage ; who with five loaves satisfied five thousand of His followers ; and who, lest it might appear to the unbelieving and hard of heart to be an illusion, filled twelve capacious baskets with the fragments that remained? Was He one of us, who ordered the breath that had departed to return to the body, persons buried to come forth from the tomb, and after three days to be loosed from the swathings of the undertaker? Was He one of us, who saw clearly in the hearts of the silent what each was pondering,[10] what each had in his secret thoughts? Was He one of us, who, when He uttered a single word, was thought by nations far removed from one another and of different speech to be using well-known sounds, and the peculiar language of each?[11] Was He one of us, who, when He was

---

[1] *Magus*, almost equivalent to sorcerer.

[2] Arnobius uses *nomina*, "names," with special significance, because the Magi in their incantations used barbarous and fearful names of angels and of powers, by whose influence they thought strange and unusual things were brought to pass.

[3] All these different effects the magicians of old attempted to produce: to break family ties by bringing plagues into houses, or by poisons; open doors and unbind chains by charms (Orig., *contra Cels.*, ii.); affect horses in the race — of which Hieronymus in his *Life of Hilarion* gives an example; and use philters and love potions to kindle excessive and unlawful desires.

[4] So Orelli and most edd., following a marginal reading of Ursinus, *auxiliaribus plenum bonis* (for the ms. *nobis*).

[5] In the height of his indignation and contempt, the writer stops short and does not apply to his opponents any new epithet.

[6] This is contrasted with the mutterings and strange words used by the magicians.

[7] So the ms. according to Oehler, and seemingly Heraldus; but according to Orelli, the ms. reads *immoderati* (instead of —*os*) *cohibebant fluores*, which Meursius received as equivalent to "the excessive flow stayed itself."

[8] *Penetrabilis*, "searching," i.e., finding its way to all parts of the body.

[9] So Orelli, LB., Elmenhorst, and Stewechius, adopting a marginal reading of Ursinus, which prefixes *im—* to the ms. *mobilitates* — "looseness" — retained by the other edd.

[10] Cf. John ii. 25. [He often replies to *thoughts* not uttered.]

[11] No such miracle is recorded of Christ, and Oehler suggests with some probability that Arnobius may have here fallen into confusion as to what is recorded of the apostles on the day of Pentecost.

teaching His followers the duties of a religion that could not be gainsaid, suddenly filled the whole world, and showed how great He was and who He was, by unveiling the boundlessness of His authority? Was He one of us, who, after His body had been laid in the tomb, manifested Himself in open day to countless numbers of men; who spoke to them, and listened to them; who taught them, reproved and admonished them; who, lest they should imagine that they were deceived by unsubstantial fancies, showed Himself once, a second time, aye frequently, in familiar conversation; who appears even now to righteous men of unpolluted mind who love Him, not in airy dreams, but in a form of pure simplicity;[1] whose name, when heard, puts to flight evil spirits, imposes silence on soothsayers, prevents men from consulting the augurs, causes the efforts of arrogant magicians to be frustrated, not by the dread of His name, as you allege, but by the free exercise of a greater power?

47. These facts set forth in summary we have put forward, not on the supposition that the greatness of the agent was to be seen in these virtues alone.[2] For however great these things be, how excessively petty and trifling will they be found to be, if it shall be revealed from what realms He has come, of what God He is the minister! But with regard to the acts which were done by Him, they were performed, indeed, not that He might boast Himself into empty ostentation, but that hardened and unbelieving men might be assured that what was professed was not deceptive, and that they might now learn to imagine, from the beneficence of His works, what a true god was. At the same time we wish this also to be known,[3] when, as was said, an enumeration of His acts has been given in summary, that Christ was able to do not only those things which He did, but that He could even overcome the decrees of fate. For if, as is evident, and as is agreed by all, infirmities and bodily sufferings, if deafness, deformity, and dumbness, if shrivelling of the sinews and the loss of sight happen to us, and are brought on us by the decrees of fate, and if Christ alone has corrected this, has restored and cured man, it is clearer than the sun himself that He was more powerful than the fates are when He has loosened and overpowered those things which were bound with everlasting knots, and fixed by unalterable necessity.

48. But, says some one, you in vain claim so much for Christ, when we now know, and have in past times known, of other gods both giving remedies to many who were sick, and healing the diseases and the infirmities of many men. I do not inquire, I do not demand, what god did so, or at what time; whom he relieved, or what shattered frame he restored to sound health: this only I long to hear, whether, without the addition of any substance — that is, of any medical application — he ordered diseases to fly away from men at a touch; whether he commanded and compelled the cause of ill health to be eradicated, and the bodies of the weak to return to their natural strength. For it is known that Christ, either by applying His hand to the parts affected, or by the command of His voice only, opened the ears of the deaf, drove away blindness from the eyes, gave speech to the dumb, loosened the rigidity of the joints, gave the power of walking to the shrivelled, — was wont to heal by a word and by an order, leprosies, agues, dropsies, and all other kinds of ailments, which some fell power[4] has willed that the bodies of men should endure. What act like these have all these gods done, by whom you allege that help has been brought to the sick and the imperilled? for if they have at any time ordered, as is reported, either that medicine or a special diet be given to some,[5] or that a draught be drunk off, or that the juices of plants and of blades be placed[6] on that which causes uneasiness or *have ordered* that persons should walk, remain at rest, or abstain from something hurtful, — and that this is no great matter, and deserves no great admiration, is evident, if you will attentively examine it — a similar mode of treatment is followed by physicians also, a creature earth-born and not relying on true science, but founding on a system of conjecture, and wavering in estimating probabilities. Now there is no *special* merit in removing by remedies those ailments which affect men: the healing qualities belong to the drugs — not virtues inherent in him who applies them; and though it is praiseworthy to know by what medicine or by what method it may be suitable for persons to be treated, there is room for this credit being assigned to man, but not to the deity. For it is, *at least*, no discredit that he[7] should have improved the health of man by things taken from without: it is a disgrace to a god that he is not able to effect it of himself, but that he gives soundness and safety *only* by the aid of external objects.

49. And since you compare Christ and the other deities as to the blessings of health bestowed, how many thousands of infirm persons

---

[1] The Latin is, *per puræ speciem simplicitatis*, which is not easily understood, and is less easily expressed.
[2] [I have already directed attention to Dominic Diodati's essay, *De Christo Græce loquente*. ed. London, 1843.]
[3] So almost all edd.: but the MS. and 1st and 2d Roman edd. read *scire* — " to know," etc.

[4] See book ii. chap. 36, *infra*.
[5] The gods in whose temples the sick lay ordered remedies through the priests.
[6] So all edd. except LB., which reads with the MS. *superponere* — " that (one) place the juices," etc.
[7] That is, the physician.

do you wish to be shown to you by us; how many persons affected with wasting diseases, whom no appliances whatever restored, although they went as suppliants through all the temples, although they prostrated themselves before the gods, and swept the very thresholds with their lips — though, as long as life remained, they wearied with prayers, and importuned with most piteous vows Æsculapius himself, the health-giver, as they call him? Do we not know that some died of their ailments? that others grew old by the torturing pain of their diseases? that others began to live a more abandoned life after they had wasted their days[1] and nights in incessant prayers, and in expectation of mercy?[2] Of what avail is it, then, to point to one or another who may have been healed, when so many thousands have been left unaided, and the shrines are full of all the wretched and the unfortunate? Unless, perchance, you say that the gods help the good, but that the miseries of the wicked are overlooked. And yet Christ assisted the good and the bad alike; nor was there any one rejected by Him, who in adversity sought help against violence and the ills of fortune. For this is the mark of a true god and of kingly power, to deny his bounty to none, and not to consider who merits it or who does not; since natural infirmity and not the choice of his desire, or of his sober judgment, makes a sinner. To say, moreover, that aid is given by the gods to the deserving when in distress, is to leave undecided and render doubtful what you assert: so that both he who has been made whole may seem to have been preserved by chance, and he who is not may appear to have been unable to banish infirmity, not because of his demerit, but by reason of a heaven-sent weakness.[3]

50. Moreover, by His own power He not only performed those miraculous deeds which have been detailed by us in summary, and not as the importance of the matter demanded; but, what was more sublime, He has permitted many others to attempt them, and to perform them by the use of His name. For when He foresaw that you were to be the detractors of His deeds and of His divine work, in order that no lurking suspicion might remain of His having lavished these gifts and bounties by magic arts, from the immense multitude of people, which with admiring wonder strove to gain His favour, He chose fishermen, artisans, rustics, and unskilled persons of a similar kind, that they being sent through various nations should perform all those miracles without any deceit and without any material aids. By a

word He assuaged the racking pains of the aching members; and by a word they checked the writhings of maddening sufferings. By one command He drove demons from the body, and restored their senses to the lifeless; they, too, by no different command, restored to health and to soundness of mind those labouring under the inflictions of these *demons*.[4] By the application of His hand He removed the marks of leprosy; they, too, restored to the body its natural skin by a touch not dissimilar. He ordered the dropsical and swollen flesh to recover its natural dryness; and His servants in the same manner stayed the wandering waters, and ordered them to glide through their own channels, avoiding injury to the frame. Sores of immense size, refusing to admit of healing, He restrained from further feeding on the flesh, by the interposition of one word; and they in like manner, by restricting its ravages, compelled the obstinate and merciless cancer to confine itself to a scar. To the lame He gave the power of walking, to the dark eyes sight, the dead He recalled to life; and not less surely did they, too, relax the tightened nerves, fill the eyes with light already lost, and order the dead to return from the tombs, reversing the ceremonies of the funeral rites. Nor was anything calling forth the bewildered admiration of all done by Him, which He did not freely allow to be performed by those humble and rustic men, and which He did not put in their power.

51. What say ye, O minds incredulous, stubborn, hardened? Did that great Jupiter Capitolinus of yours give to any human being power of this kind? Did he endow with this right any priest of a curia, the Pontifex Maximus, nay, even the Dialis, in whose name he is *revealed as the god of life*?[5] I shall not say, *did he impart power* to raise the dead, to give light to the blind, restore the normal condition of their members to the weakened and the paralyzed, but *did he even enable any one* to check a pustule, a hang-nail, a pimple, either by the word of his mouth or the touch of his hand? Was this, then, a power natural to man, or could such a right be granted, could such a licence be given by the mouth of one reared on the vulgar produce of earth; and was it not a divine and sacred gift? or if the matter admits of any hyperbole, was it

---

[1] So the edd., reading *tri-v-erunt*, for the MS. *tri-bu-erunt* — "given up," which is retained in the first ed.

[2] *Pietatis*, "of mercy," in which sense the word is often used in late writers. Thus it was from his clemency that Antoninus, the Roman emperor, received the title of *Pius*.

[3] So most edd., following a marginal reading of Ursinus, which prefixes *in*— to the MS. *firmitate*.

[4] "They, too, . . . those labouring under the inflictions of these:" so LB., with the warm approval of Orelli (who, however, with previous edd., retains the MS. reading in his text) and others, reading *sub eorum t-ortantes* (for MS. *ƒ*—) *et illi se casibus;* Heraldus having suggested *rotantes*. This simple and elegant emendation makes it unnecessary to notice the harsh and forced readings of earlier edd.

[5] So understood by Orelli, who reads *quo Dius est*, adopting the explanation of Dialis given by Festus. The MS., however, according to Crusius, reads, *Dialem, quod ejus est, flaminem isto jure donavit;* in which case, from the position of the *quod*, the meaning might be, "which *term* is his," or possibly, "because he (i.e., the priest) is his," only that in the latter case a pronoun would be expected: the commentators generally refer it to the succeeding *jure*, with this "right," which is his. Canterus reads, *quod majus est*, i.e., than the Pontifex Maximus. [Compare vol. iv. p. 74, note 7.]

not more than divine and sacred? For if you do that which you are able to do, and what is compatible with your strength and your ability, there is no ground for the expression of astonishment; for you will have done that which you were able, and which your power was bound to accomplish, in order that there should be a perfect correspondence [1] between the deed and the doer. To be able to transfer to a man your own power, share with the frailest being the ability to perform that which you alone are able to do, is a proof of power supreme over all, and holding in subjection the causes of all things, and the natural laws of methods and of means.

52. Come, then, let some Magian Zoroaster [2] arrive from a remote part of the globe, crossing over the fiery zone,[3] if we believe Hermippus as an authority. Let these join him too — that Bactrian, whose deeds Ctesias sets forth in the first book of his History; the Armenian, grandson of Hosthanes; [4] and Pamphilus, the intimate friend of Cyrus; Apollonius, Damigero, and Dardanus; Velus, Julianus, and Bæbulus; and if there be any other one who is supposed to have especial powers and reputation in such magic arts. Let them grant to one of the people to adapt the mouths of the dumb for the purposes of speech, to unseal the ears of the deaf, to give the natural powers of the eye to those born without sight, and to restore feeling and life to bodies long cold in death. Or if that is *too* difficult, and if they cannot impart to others the power to do such acts, let themselves perform them, and with their own rites. Whatever noxious herbs the earth brings forth from its bosom, whatever powers those muttered words and accompanying spells contain — these let them add, we envy them not; *those* let them collect, we forbid them not. We wish to make trial and to discover whether they can effect, with the aid of their gods, what has often been accomplished by unlearned Christians with a word only.

53. Cease in your ignorance to receive such great deeds with abusive language, which will in no wise injure him who did them, but which will bring danger to yourselves — danger, I say, by no means small, but one dealing with matters of great,[5] aye, even the greatest importance, since beyond a doubt the soul is a precious thing, and nothing can be found dearer to a man than himself. There was nothing magical, as you suppose, nothing human, delusive, or crafty in Christ; no deceit lurked in Him,[6] although you smile in derision, as your wont is, and though you split with roars of laughter. He was God on high, God in His inmost nature, God from unknown realms, and was sent by the Ruler of all as a Saviour God; whom neither the sun himself, nor any stars, if they have powers of perception, not the rulers and princes of the world, nor, in fine, the great gods, or those who, feigning themselves so, terrify the whole human race, were able to know or to guess whence and who He was — and naturally so. But [7] when, freed from the body, which He carried about as but a very small part of Himself, He allowed Himself to be seen, and *let it be known* how great He was, all the elements of the universe bewildered by the strange events were thrown into confusion. An earthquake shook the world, the sea was heaved up from its depths, the heaven was shrouded in darkness, the sun's fiery blaze was checked, and his heat became moderate; [8] for what else could occur when He was discovered to be God who heretofore was reckoned one of us?

54. But you do not believe these things; yet those who witnessed their occurrence, and who saw them done before their eyes — the very best vouchers and the most trustworthy authorities — both believed them themselves, and transmitted them to us who follow them, to be believed with no scanty measure of confidence. Who are these? you perhaps ask. Tribes, peoples, nations, and that incredulous human race; but [9] if the matter were not plain, and, as the saying is, clearer than day itself, they would never grant their assent with so ready belief to events of such a kind. But shall we say that the men of that time were untrustworthy, false, stupid, and brutish to such a degree that they pretended to have seen what they never had seen, and that they put forth un-

---

[1] So the MS. reading *æqualitas*, which is retained by Hild. and Oehler; all other editions drop *æ* — " that the quality of deed and doer might be one."

[2] This passage has furnished occasion for much discussion as to text and interpretation. In the text Orelli's punctuation has been followed, who regards Arnobius as mentioning four Zoroasters — the Assyrian or Chaldean, the Bactrian (cf. c. 5 of this book), the Armenian, and finally the Pamphylian, or Pamphilos, who, according to Clem. Alex. (*Strom.* [vol. ii. p. 469]), is referred to in Plato's *Republic*, book x., under the name Er; Meursius and Salmasius, however, regarding the whole as one sentence, consider that only three persons are so referred to, the first being either Libyan or Bactrian, and the others as with Orelli. To seek to determine which view is most plausible even, would be a fruitless task, as will be evident on considering what is said in the index under Zoroaster. [Jowett's Plato, ii. 121.]

[3] So Orelli, reading *veniat qu-is su-per igneam zonam*. LB. reads for the second and third words, *quæ-so per* — " let there come, I pray you, through," etc., from the MS. *quæ super;* while Heraldus would change the last three words into Azonaces, the name of the supposed teacher of Zoroaster. By the "fiery zone" Salmasius would understand Libya; but the legends must be borne in mind which spoke of Zoroaster as having shown himself to a wondering multitude from a hill blazing with fire, that he might teach them new ceremonies of worship, or as being otherwise distinguished in connection with fire. [Plato, *Rep.*, p. 446, Jowett's trans.]

[4] So Stewechius, Orelli, and others, for the MS. *Zostriani* — " grandson of Zostrianus," retained in the 1st ed. and LB.

---

[5] So the edd., reading *in rebus eximiis* for the MS. *exi-gu-is*, which would, of course, give an opposite and wholly unsuitable meaning.

[6] So generally, Heraldus having restored *delitu-it in Christo* from the MS., which had omitted *-it*, for the reading of Gelenius, Canterus, and Ursinus, *delicti* — " no deceit, no sin *was*," etc.

[7] So emended by Salmasius, followed by most later edd. In the earlier edd. the reading is *et merito exutus a corpore* (Salm. reading *at* instead of *a*, and inserting a period after *mer.*) — " and when rightly freed from the body," etc.

[8] It may be instructive to notice how the simpler narrative of the Gospels is amplified. Matthew (xxvii. 51) says that the earth trembled, and Luke (xxiii. 45) that the sun was darkened; but they go no further. [See p. 301, note 4, *supra*.]

[9] Or, "which if . . . itself, would never," etc. [Note the confidence of this appeal to general assent.]

der false evidence, or alleged with childish asseveration things which never took place, and that when they were able to live in harmony and to maintain friendly relations with you, they wantonly incurred hatred, and were held in execration?

55. But if this record of events is false, as you say, how comes it that in so short a time the whole world has been filled with such a religion? or how could nations dwelling widely apart, and separated by climate and by the convexities of heaven,[1] unite in one conclusion? They have been prevailed upon, *say my opponents*, by mere assertions, been led into vain hopes; and in their reckless madness have chosen to incur voluntarily the risks of death, although they had hitherto seen nothing of such a kind as could by its wonderful and strange character induce them to adopt this manner of worship. Nay, because they saw all these things to be done by *Christ* Himself and by His apostles, who being sent throughout the whole world carried with them the blessings of the Father, which they dispensed in benefiting[2] as well the minds as the bodies of men; overcome by the force of the very truth itself they both devoted themselves to God, and reckoned it as but a small sacrifice to surrender their bodies to you and to give their flesh to be mangled.

56. But our writers, *we shall be told*, have put forth these statements with false effrontery; they have extolled[3] small matters to an inordinate degree, and have magnified trivial affairs with most pretentious boastfulness. And[4] would that all things could have been reduced to writing, — both those which were done by Himself, and those which were accomplished by His apostles with equal authority and power. Such an assemblage of miracles, however, would make you more incredulous; and perhaps you might be able to discover a passage from which[5] it would seem very probable, both that additions were made to facts, and that falsehoods were inserted in writings and commentaries. But in nations which were unknown to the writers, and which themselves knew not the use of letters, all that was done could not have been embraced in the records or even have reached the ears of all men; or, if any were committed to written and connected narrative, some insertions and additions would have been made by the malevolence

of the demons and of men like to them, whose care and study it is to obstruct[6] the progress of this truth: there would have been some changes and mutilations of words and of syllables, at once to mar the faith of the cautious and to impair the moral effect of the deeds. But it will never avail them that it be gathered from written testimony *only* who and what Christ was; for His cause has been put on such a basis, that if what we say be admitted to be true, He is by the confession of all proved to have been God.

57. You do not believe our writings, and we do not believe yours. We devise falsehoods concerning Christ, *you say;* and you put forth baseless and false statements concerning your gods: for no god has descended from heaven, or in his own person and life has sketched out your system, or in a similar way thrown discredit on our system and our ceremonies. These were written by men; those, too, were written by men — set forth in human speech; and whatever you seek to say concerning our writers, remember that about yours, too, you will find these things said with equal force. What is contained in your writings you wish to be treated as true; those things, also, which are attested in our books, you must of necessity confess to be true. You accuse our system of falsehood; we, too, accuse yours of falsehood. But ours is more ancient, say you, therefore most credible and trustworthy; as if, indeed, antiquity were not the most fertile source of errors, and did not herself put forth those things which in discreditable fables have attached the utmost infamy to the gods. For could not falsehoods have been both spoken and believed ten thousand years ago, or is it not most probable that that which is near to our own time should be more credible than that which is separated by a long term of years? For these of ours are brought forward on the faith of witnesses, those of yours on the ground of opinions; and it is much more natural that there should be less invention in matters of recent occurrence, than in those far removed in the darkness of antiquity.

58. But they were written by unlearned and ignorant men, and should not therefore be readily believed. See that this be not rather a stronger reason for believing that they have not been adulterated by any false statements, but were put forth by men of simple mind, who knew not how to trick out their tales with meretricious ornaments. But the language is mean and vulgar. For truth never seeks deceitful polish, nor in that which is well ascertained and certain does it allow itself to be led away into excessive prolixity. Syllogisms, enthymemes, definitions, and all those ornaments by which

---

[1] That is, by the climate and the inclination of the earth's surface.

[2] So the 1st ed., Ursinus, Elmenhorst, Orelli, and Hildebrand, reading *munerandis*, which is found in the MS. in a later handwriting, for the original reading of the MS. *munera dis.*

[3] According to Rigaltius the MS. reads *ista promiserunt in immensum* — "have put forth (i.e., exaggerated) these things to an immense degree falsely, small matters and trivial affairs have magnified, etc; while by a later hand has been superscribed over *in immensum,* in ink of a different colour, *extulere* — "have extolled."

[4] So the MS., 1st ed., and Hildebrand, while all others read *atqu-i* — "but."

[5] So LB., reading *quo* for the MS. *quod.*

[6] So most edd., reading *intercip-ere* for the MS. *intercipi* — "it is that the progress be obstructed," etc.

men seek to establish their statements, aid those groping for the truth, but do not clearly mark its great features. But he who really knows the subject under discussion, neither defines, nor deduces, nor seeks the other tricks of words by which an audience is wont to be taken in, and to be beguiled into a forced assent to a proposition.

59. Your narratives, my opponent says, are overrun with barbarisms and solecisms, and disfigured by monstrous blunders. A censure, truly, which shows a childish and petty spirit; for if we allow that it is reasonable, let us cease to use certain kinds of fruit because they grow with prickles on them, and other growths useless for food, which on the one hand cannot support us, and yet do not on the other hinder us from enjoying that which specially excels, and which nature has designed to be most wholesome for us. For how, I pray you, does it interfere with or retard the comprehension *of a statement*, whether anything be pronounced smoothly[1] or with uncouth roughness? whether that have the grave accent which ought to have the acute, or that have the acute which ought to have the grave? Or how is the truth of a statement diminished, if an error is made in number or case, in preposition, participle, or conjunction? Let that pomposity of style and strictly regulated diction be reserved for public assemblies, for lawsuits, for the forum and the courts of justice, and by all means be handed over to those who, striving after the soothing influences of pleasant sensations, bestow all their care upon splendour of language. *But* when we are discussing matters far removed from mere display, we should consider what is said, not with what charm it is said nor how it tickles the ears, but what benefits it confers on the hearers, especially since we know that some even who devoted themselves to philosophy, not only disregarded refinement of style, but also purposely adopted a vulgar meanness when they might have spoken with greater elegance and richness, lest forsooth they might impair the stern gravity of speech and revel rather in the pretentious show of the Sophists. For indeed it evidences a worthless heart to seek enjoyment in matters of importance; and when you have to deal with those who are sick and diseased, to pour into their ears dulcet sounds, not to apply a remedy to their wounds. Yet, if you consider the true state of the case, no language is naturally perfect, and in like manner none is faulty. For what natural reason is there, or what law written in the constitution of the world, that *paries* should be called *hic*,[2] and *sella hæc?* — since neither have they sex

distinguished by male and female, nor can the most learned man tell me what *hic* and *hæc* are, or why one of them denotes the male sex while the other is applied to the female. These conventionalities are man's, and certainly are not indispensable to all persons for the use of forming their language; for *paries* might perhaps have been called *hæc*, and *sella hic*, without any fault being found, if it had been agreed upon at first that they should be so called, and if this practice had been maintained by following generations in their daily conversation. And yet, O you who charge our writings with disgraceful blemishes, have you not these solecisms in those most perfect and wonderful books of yours? Does not one of you make the plur of *uter, utria?* another *utres?*[3] Do you not also say *cælus* and *cælum, filus* and *filum, crocus* and *crocum, fretus* and *fretum?* Also *hoc pane* and *hic panis, hic sanguis* and *hoc sanguen?* Are not *candelabrum* and *jugulum* in like manner written *jugulus* and *candelaber?* For if each noun cannot have more than one gender, and if the same word cannot be of this gender and of that, for one gender cannot pass into the other, he commits as great a blunder who utters masculine genders under the laws of feminines, as he who applies masculine articles to feminine genders. And yet we see you using masculines as feminines, and feminines as masculines, and those which you call neuter both in this way and in that, without any distinction. Either, therefore, it is no blunder to employ them indifferently, and *in that case* it is vain for you to say that our works are disfigured with monstrous solecisms; or if the way in which each ought to be employed is unalterably fixed, you also are involved in similar errors, although you have on your side all the Epicadi, Cæsellii, Verrii, Scauri, and Nisi.

60. But, say my opponents, if Christ was God, why did He appear in human shape, and why was He cut off by death after the manner of men? Could that power which is invisible, and which has no bodily substance, have come upon earth and adapted itself to the world and mixed in human society, otherwise than by taking to itself some covering of a more solid substance, which might bear the gaze of the eyes, and on which the look of the least observant might fix itself? For what mortal is there who could have seen Him, who could have distinguished Him, if He had decreed to come upon the earth such as He is in His own primitive nature, and such as He has chosen to be in His own proper character and divinity? He took upon Him, therefore, the form of man; and under the guise of our race He imprisoned His power, so that He could be seen and carefully

---

[1] So Orelli and Hildebrand, reading *glabre* from a conjecture of Grotius, for the MS. *grave*.

[2] i.e., that the one should be masculine, the other feminine.

[3] i e., does not one of you make the plural of *uter* masc., another neut.? [Note the opponent's witness to the text of the Gospels.]

regarded, might speak and teach, and without encroaching on the sovereignty and government of the King Supreme, might carry out all those objects for the accomplishment of which He had come into the world.

61. What, then, says *my opponent*, could not the Supreme Ruler have brought about those things which He had ordained to be done in the world, without feigning Himself a man? If it were necessary to do as you say, He perhaps would have done so; because it was not necessary, He acted otherwise. The reasons why He chose to do it in this way, and did not choose to do it in that, are unknown, being involved in so great obscurity, and comprehensible by scarcely any; but these you might perhaps have understood if you were not already prepared not to understand, and were not shaping your course to brave unbelief, before that was explained to you which you sought to know and to hear.

62. But, *you will say*, He was cut off by death as men are. Not *Christ* Himself; for it is impossible either that death should befall what is divine, or that that should waste away and disappear in death which is one *in its substance*, and not compounded, nor formed by bringing together any parts. Who, then, *you ask*, was seen hanging on the cross? Who dead? The human form,[1] *I reply*, which He had put on,[2] and which He bore about with Him. It is a tale passing belief, *you say*, and wrapt in dark obscurity; if you will, it is not dark, and *is* established by a very close analogy.[3] If the Sibyl, when she was uttering and pouring forth her prophecies and oracular responses, was filled, as you say, with Apollo's power, had been cut down and slain by impious robbers,[4] would Apollo be said to have been slain in her? If Bacis,[5] if Helenus, Marcius,[6] and other soothsayers, had been in like manner robbed of life and light when raving as inspired, would any one say that those who, speaking by their mouths, declared to inquirers what should be done,[7] had perished according to the conditions of human life? The death of which you speak was *that* of the human body which He had assumed,[8] not His own — of that which was borne,

not of the bearer; and not even this *death* would He[9] have stooped to suffer, were it not that a matter of such importance was to be dealt with, and the inscrutable plan of fate[10] brought to light in hidden mysteries.

63. What are these hidden and unseen mysteries, you will say, which neither men can know, nor those even who are called gods of the world can in any wise reach by fancy and conjecture; *which* none *can discover*,[11] except those whom *Christ* Himself has thought fit to bestow the blessing of so great knowledge upon, and to lead into the secret recesses of the inner treasury *of wisdom?* Do you then see that if He had determined that none should do Him violence, He should have striven to the utmost to keep off from Him His enemies, even by directing His power against them?[12] Could not He, *then*, who had restored their sight to the blind, make *His* enemies blind if it were necessary? Was it hard or troublesome for Him to make them weak, who *had given* strength to the feeble? Did He who bade[13] the lame walk, not know how to take from them all power to move their limbs,[14] by making their sinews stiff?[15] Would it have been difficult for Him who drew the dead from their tombs to inflict death on whom He would? But because reason required that those things which had been resolved on should be done here also in the world itself, and in no other fashion than was done, He, with gentleness passing understanding and belief, regarding as but childish trifles the wrongs which men did Him, submitted to the violence of savage and most hardened robbers;[16] nor did He think it worth while to take account of what their daring had aimed at, if He only showed to His *disciples* what they were in duty bound to look for from Him. For when many things about the perils of souls, many evils about their . . . ; on the other hand, the Introducer,[17] the

---

[1] So the MS., followed by Hildebrand and Oehler, reads and punctuates *quis mortuus? homo*, for which all edd. read *mortuus est?* "Who died?"

[2] Here, as in the whole discussion in the second book on the origin and nature of the soul, the opinions expressed are Gnostic, Cerinthus saying more precisely that Christ having descended from heaven in the form of a dove, dwelt in the body of Jesus during His life, but removed from it before the crucifixion.

[3] So the MS. by changing a single letter, with LB. and others, *similitudine proxim-a* (MS. *o*) *constitutum*; while the first ed., Gelenius, Canterus, Ursinus, Orelli, and others, read -*dini proxime* — "settled very closely to analogy."

[4] In the original *latronibus*; here, as in the next chapter, used loosely to denote lawless men.

[5] So emended by Mercerus for the MS. *vatis*.

[6] So read in the MS. — not -*tius*, as in LB. and Orelli.

[7] Lit., "the ways of things" — *vias rerum*.

[8] The MS. reads unintelligibly *assumpti-o hominis fuit*, which was, however, retained in both Roman edd., although Ursinus suggested the dropping of the *o*, which has been done by all later edd.

[9] The MS. reads, *quam nec ipsam perpeti succubuisset vis* — "would his might," i.e., "would He with His great power have stooped." Orelli simply omits *vis* as Canterus, and seemingly the other later edd. do.

[10] The MS. and 1st ed. read *sati-s*, which has clearly arisen from *f* being confounded with the old form of *s*.

[11] The construction is a little involved, *quæ nulli nec homines scire nec ipsi qui appellantur dii mundi queunt* — "which none, neither men can know, nor those . . . of the world can reach, except those whom," etc.

[12] In the Latin, *vel potestate inversa*, which according to Oehler is the MS. reading, while Orelli speaks of it as an emendation of LB. (where it is certainly found, but without any indication of its source), and with most edd. reads *universa* — "by His universal power."

[13] So the MS. according to Hildebrand, reading *præcipi-bat*. Most edd., however, following Gelenius, read *faciebat* — "made them lame."

[14] Lit., "to bind fast the motions of the members," adopting the reading of most edd., *motus alligare membrorum* (MS. *c-al-igare*).

[15] The MS. reads *nervorum duritia-m*, for which Ursinus, with most edd., reads as above, merely dropping *m*; Hildebrand and Oehler insert *in*, and read, from a conjecture of Ursinus adopted by Elmenhorst, *c-ol-ligare* — "to bind into stiffness."

[16] Ursinus suggested *di-*, "most terrible," for the MS. *durissimis*.

[17] So the MS. reading, *multa mala de illarum contra insinuator* (*mala* is perhaps in the abl., agreeing with a lost word), which has been regarded by Heraldus and Stewechius, followed by Orelli, as mutilated, and is so read in the first ed., and by Ursinus and LB. The passage is in all cases left obscure and doubtful, and we may therefore be excused discussing its meaning here.

Master and Teacher directed His laws and ordinances, that they might find their end in fitting duties;[1] did He not destroy the arrogance of the proud? Did He not quench the fires of lust? Did He not check the craving of greed? Did He not wrest the weapons from their hands, and rend from them all the sources[2] of every *form of* corruption? To conclude, was He not Himself gentle, peaceful, easily approached, friendly when addressed?[3] Did He not, grieving at men's miseries, pitying with His unexampled benevolence all in any wise afflicted with troubles and bodily ills,[4] bring them back and restore them to soundness?

64. What, then, constrains you, what excites you to revile, to rail at, to hate implacably Him whom no man[5] can accuse of any crime?[6] Tyrants and your kings, who, putting away *all* fear of the gods, plunder and pillage the treasuries of temples; who by proscription, banishment,[7] and slaughter, strip the state of its nobles? who, with licentious violence, undermine and wrest away the chastity of matrons and maidens, — *these men* you name *indigites* and *divi;* and you worship with couches, altars, temples, and other service, and by celebrating their games and birthdays, those whom it was fitting that you should assail with keenest[8] hatred. And all those, too, who by writing books assail in many forms with biting reproaches public manners; who censure, brand, and tear in pieces your luxurious habits and lives; who carry down to posterity evil reports of their own times[9] in their enduring writings; who *seek to* persuade *men* that the rights of marriage should be held in common;[10] who lie with boys, beautiful, lustful, naked; who declare that you are beasts, runaways, exiles, and mad and frantic slaves of the most worthless character, — *all these* with wonder and applause you exalt to the stars of heaven, you place in the shrines of your libraries, you present with chariots and statues, and as much as in you lies, gift with a kind of immortality,

as it were, by the witness which immortal titles bear to them. Christ alone you would tear in pieces,[11] you would rend asunder, if you could *do so to* a god; nay, *Him alone* you would, were it allowed, gnaw with bloody mouths, and break His bones in pieces, and devour Him like beasts of the field. For what that He has done, tell, I pray you, for what crime?[12] What has He done to turn aside the course of justice, and rouse you to hatred made fierce by maddening torments? *Is it* because He declared that He was sent by the only *true* King *to be* your soul's guardian, and to bring to you the immortality which you believe that you *already* possess, relying on the assertions of a few men? But *even* if you were assured that He spoke falsely, that He even held out hopes without the slightest foundation, not even in this case do I see *any* reason that you should hate *and* condemn Him with bitter reproaches. Nay, if you were kind and gentle in spirit, you ought to esteem Him even for this alone, that He promised to you things which you might well wish and hope for; that He was the bearer of good news; that His message was such as to trouble no one's mind, nay, rather to fill *all* with less anxious expectation.[13]

65. Oh ungrateful and impious age, prepared[14] for its own destruction by its extraordinary obstinacy! If there had come to you a physician from lands far distant and unknown to you before, offering some medicine to keep off from you altogether every kind of disease and sickness, would you not all eagerly hasten to *him?* Would you not with every kind of flattery and honour receive him into your houses, and treat him kindly? Would you not wish that that kind of medicine should be quite *sure, and* should be genuine, which promised that even to the utmost limits of life you should be free from such countless bodily distresses? And though it were a doubtful matter, you would yet entrust yourselves *to him;* nor would you hesitate to drink the unknown draught, incited by the hope of health set before you and by the love of safety.[15] Christ shone out and appeared to tell us news of the utmost importance, bringing an omen of prosperity, and a message of safety to those who

---

[1] Lit., "to the ends of fitting duties."

[2] In the original, *seminaria abscidit,* — the former word used of nurseries for plants, while the latter may be either as above (from *abscindo*), or may mean "cut off" (from *abscido*); but in both cases the general meaning is the same, and the metaphor is in either slightly confused.

[3] Lit., "familiar to be accosted," — the supine, as in the preceding clause.

[4] So the edd., reading *corporalibus affectos malis,* but the MS. inserts after *malis* the word *morbis* ("with evil bodily diseases") ; but according to Hildebrand this word is marked as spurious.

[5] So the edd., reading *nemo h-om-i-n-um,* except Hildebrand and Oehler, who retain the MS. *om-n-i-um* — "no one of all."

[6] John viii. 46: "Which of you convinceth me of sin?"

[7] So Heraldus and LB., followed by later edd., reading *exiliis* for the MS. *ex-uis,* for which Gelenius, Canterus, and Ursinus read *et suis* — "and by their slaughters."

[8] Here, as frequently in Arnobius, the comparative is used instead of the superlative.

[9] "To posterity evil reports of their own time" — *sui temporis posteris notas* — so emended by Ursinus, followed by Orelli and Hildebrand, for the MS. *in temporis posteri-s,* retained by LB., and with the omission of *s* in the 1st ed.; but this requires our looking on the passage as defective.

[10] The reference is clearly to the well-known passage in Plato's *Republic.* [See the sickening details, book v. p. 282, Jowett's trans.]

[11] So Gelenius, LB., and Orelli, reading *con-v-ell-e-re* for the MS. *con-p-ell-a-re,* "to accost" or "abuse," which is out of place here. Canterus suggested *com-p-il-are,* "to plunder," which also occurs in the sense "to cudgel."

[12] Supply, "do you pursue Him so fiercely?"

[13] These words are followed in the edition of Gelenius by ch. 2–5 of the second book, seemingly without any mark to denote transposition; while Ursinus inserted the same chapters — beginning, however, with the last sentence of the first chapter (read as mentioned in the note on it) — but prefixed an asterisk, to mark a departure from the order of the MS. The later editors have not adopted either change.

[14] So Ursinus suggested in the margin, followed by LB. and Orelli, reading *in privatam perniciem p-a-r-atum* for the MS. *p-r-iv-a-tum,* which is clearly derived from the preceding *privatam,* but is, though unintelligible also, retained in the two Roman edd. The conclusion of the sentence is, literally, "obstinacy of spirit."

[15] In the original, *spe salutis proposita atque amore incolumitatis.*

believe. What, I pray you, means[1] this cruelty, what such barbarity, nay rather, to speak more truly, scornful[2] pride, not only to harass the messenger and bearer of so great a gift with taunting words ; but even to assail Him with fierce hostility, and with all the weapons which can be showered upon Him, and *with all modes of* destruction? Are His words displeasing, and are you offended when you hear them? Count them as *but* a soothsayer's empty tales. Does He speak very stupidly, and promise foolish gifts? Laugh with scorn as wise men, and leave *Him in* His folly[3] to be tossed about among His errors. What means this fierceness, to repeat what has been said more than once ; what a passion, so murderous? to declare implacable hostility towards one who has done nothing to deserve it at your hands ; to wish, if it were allowed you, to tear Him limb from limb, who not only did no man any harm, but with uniform kindness[4] told

His enemies what salvation was being brought to them from God Supreme, what must be done that they might escape destruction and obtain an immortality which they knew not of? And when the strange and unheard-of things which were held out staggered the minds of those who heard Him, and made them hesitate to believe, *though* master of every power and destroyer of death itself He suffered His human form to be slain, that from the result[5] they might know that the hopes were safe which they had long entertained about the soul's salvation, and that in no other way could they avoid the danger of death.

---

[1] Lit., "is"—*est*.
[2] So all the edd., reading *fastidi-os-um supercilium*, which Crusius says the MS. reads with *os* omitted, i.e., "pride, scorn."
[3] So the edd., reading *fatuita-tem*, for the MS. *fatuita-n-tem*, which may, however, point to a verb not found elsewhere.
[4] i.e., to friends and foes alike. The MS. reads *æqualiter benig-*

nus hostibus dicere, which is retained by Orelli, supposing an ellipsis of *fuerit*, i.e., "*He was* kind to say," which might be received ; but it is more natural to suppose that *-t* has dropped off, and read *diceret* as above, with the two Roman editions and LB. Gelenius, followed by Ursinus, emended *omnibus docuerit*—"with uniform kindness taught to all." It may be well to give here an instance of the very insufficient grounds on which supposed references to Scripture are sometimes based. Orelli considers that Arnobius here refers (*videtur respexisse*, he says) to Col. i. 21, 22, "You, that were sometimes alienated and enemies in mind by wicked works, yet now hath He reconciled in the body of His flesh through death," to which, though the words which follow might indeed be thought to have a very distant resemblance, they can in no way be shown to refer.
[5] i.e., from His resurrection, which showed that death's power was broken by Him.

BOOK II.[1]

1. Here, if any means could be found, I should wish to converse thus with all those who hate the name of Christ, turning aside for a little from the defence primarily set up : — If you think it no dishonour to answer when asked a question, explain to us and say what is the cause, what the reason, that you pursue Christ with so bitter hostility? or what offences you remember which He did, that at the mention of His name you are roused to bursts of mad and savage fury?[2] Did He ever, in claiming for Himself

power as king, fill the whole world with bands of the fiercest soldiers ; and of nations at peace from the beginning, did He destroy and put an end to some, *and* compel others to submit to His yoke and serve Him? Did He ever, excited by grasping[3] avarice, claim as His own by right all that wealth to have abundance of which men strive eagerly? Did He ever, transported with lustful passions, break down by force the barriers of purity, or stealthily lie in wait for other men's wives? Did He ever, puffed up with haughty arrogance, inflict at random injuries and insults, without any distinction of persons? (B) And if He was not worthy that you should listen to and believe *Him, yet* He should not have been despised by you even on this account, that He showed to you things concerning your salvation, that He prepared for you a path[4] to heaven, and the immortality for which you long ; although[5]

---

[1] There has been much confusion in dealing with the first seven chapters of this book, owing to the leaves of the MS. having been arranged in wrong order, as was pointed out at an early period by some one who noted on the margin that there was some *transposition*. To this circumstance, however, Oehler alone seems to have called attention ; but the corruption was so manifest, that the various editors gave themselves full liberty to re-arrange and dispose the text more correctly. The first leaf of the MS. concludes with the words *sine ullius personæ discriminibus inrogavit*, "without any distinction of person," and is followed by one which begins with the words (A, end of c. 5) *et non omnium virtutum*, "and (not) by an eager longing," and ends *tanta experiatur examina*, "undergoes such countless ills" (middle of c. 7). The third and fourth leaves begin with the words (B, end of c. 1) *utrum in cunctos . . . amoverit? qui si dignos*, "Now if He was not worthy" (see notes), and run on to end of c. 5, *quadam dulcedine*, "by some charm ;" while the fifth (C, middle of c. 7) begins *atque ne* (or *utrumne*) *illum*, "whether the earth," and there is no further difficulty. This order is retained in the first ed., and also by Hildebrand, who supposes three lacunæ at A, B, and C, to account for the abruptness and want of connection ; but it is at once seen that, on changing the order of the leaves, so that they shall run B A C, the argument and sense are perfectly restored. This arrangement seems to have been first adopted in LB., and is followed by the later editors, with the exception of Hildebrand.
[2] Lit., "boil up with the ardours of furious spirits."

[3] Lit., "by the heats of."
[4] So Meursius, reading *a-* for the MS. *o-ptaret*, which is retained by LB., Orelli, and others. The MS. reading is explained, along with the next words *vota immortalitatis*, by Orelli as meaning "sought by His prayers," with reference to John xvii. 24, in which he is clearly mistaken. Heraldus conjectures *p-o-r-ta-s a-p-er-taret*, "opened paths . . . and the gates of immortality."
[5] The words which follow, *ut non in cunctos*, etc., have been thus transposed by Heraldus, followed by later editors ; but formerly they preceded the rest of the sentence, and, according to Oehler, the MS. gives *utrum*, thus : "(You ask) whether He has both extended to all . . . ignorance? who, if He was not," etc. Cf. book i. (this page) note 3, *supra*.

He neither extended the light of life to all, nor delivered *all* from the danger which threatens them through their ignorance.[1]

2. But indeed, *some one will say*, He deserved our hatred because He has driven religion[2] from the world, because He has kept men back from seeking to honour the gods.[3] Is He then denounced as the destroyer of religion and promoter of impiety, who brought true religion into the world, who opened the gates of piety to men blind and verily living in impiety, and pointed out to whom they should bow themselves? Or is there any truer religion — *one* more serviceable,[4] powerful, *and* right — than to have learned to know the supreme God, to know *how* to pray to God Supreme, who alone is the source and fountain of all good, the creator,[5] founder, and framer of all that endures, by whom all things on earth and all in heaven are quickened, and filled with the stir of life, and without whom there would assuredly be nothing to bear any name, and *have any* substance? But perhaps you doubt whether there is that ruler of whom we speak, and rather *incline to* believe in the existence of Apollo, Diana, Mercury, Mars. Give a true judgment;[6] and, looking round on all these things which we see, *any one* will rather doubt whether *all* the other gods exist, than hesitate with regard to the God whom we all know by nature, whether when we cry out, O God, or when we make God the witness of wicked *deeds*,[7] and raise our face to heaven as though He saw us.

3. But He did not permit men to make supplication to the lesser gods. Do you, then, know who are, or where are the lesser gods? Has

mistrust of them, or the way in which they were mentioned, ever touched you, so that you are justly indignant that their worship has been done away with and deprived of all honour?[8] But if haughtiness of mind and arrogance,[9] as it is called by the Greeks, did not stand in your way and hinder you, you might long ago have been able to understand what He forbade to be done, or wherefore; within what limits He would have true religion lie;[10] what danger arose to you from that which you thought obedience? or from what evils you would escape if you broke away from your dangerous delusion.

4. But all these things will be more clearly and distinctly noticed when we have proceeded further. For we shall show that Christ did not teach the nations impiety, but delivered ignorant and wretched men from those who most wickedly wronged them.[11] We do not believe, you say, that what He says is true. What, then? Have you no doubt as to the things which[12] you say are not true, while, as they are *only* at hand, and not yet disclosed,[13] they can by no means be disproved? But He, too, does not prove what He promises. It is so; for, as I said, there can be no proof of *things still in* the future. Since, then, the nature of the future is such that it cannot be grasped and comprehended by any anticipation,[14] is it not more rational,[15] of two things uncertain and hanging in doubtful suspense, rather to believe that which carries *with it* some hopes, than that which *brings* none at all? For in the one case there is no danger, if that which is said to be at hand should prove vain and groundless; in the other there is the greatest loss, even[16] the loss of salvation, if, when the time has come, it be shown that there was nothing false *in what was declared.*[17]

5. What say you, O ignorant ones, for whom we might well weep and be sad?[18] Are you so void of fear that these things may be true which are despised by you and turned to ridicule? and do you not consider with yourselves at least, in your secret thoughts, lest that which to-day with perverse obstinacy you refuse to believe, time

---

[1] So the MS., reading *periculum i-g-n-ora-tionis*, for which Meursius suggests *i-n-teri-tionis* — "danger of destruction."

[2] Pl.

[3] This seems the true rationale of the sentence, viewed in relation to the context. Immediately before, Arnobius suggests that the hatred of Christ by the heathen is unjustifiable, because they had suffered nothing at His hands; now an opponent is supposed to rejoin, "But He has deserved our hatred by assailing our religion." The introductory particles *at enim* fully bear this out, from their being regularly used to introduce a rejoinder. Still, by Orelli and other editors the sentence is regarded as interrogative, and in that case would be, "Has He indeed merited our hatred by driving out," etc., which, however, not merely breaks away from what precedes, but also makes the next sentence somewhat lame. The older editors, too, read it without any mark of interrogation.

[4] i.e., according to Orelli, to the wants of men; but possibly it may here have the subjunctive meaning of "more full of service," i.e., to God.

[5] So the MS., reading *perpetuarum pater, fundator conditor rerum*, but all the editions *pa-ri-ter*, "alike," which has helped to lead Orelli astray. He suggests *et fons est perpetu us pariter*, etc., "perpetual fountain, . . . of all things alike the founder and framer." It has been also proposed by Oehler (to get rid of the difficulty felt here) to transfer *per metathesin*, the idea of "enduring," to God; but the reference is surely quite clear, viewed as a distinction between the results of God's working and that of all other beings.

[6] So the MS. and almost all edd , reading *da verum judicium*, for which Heraldus suggested *da naturæ*, or *verum animæ judicium*, "give the judgment of nature," or "the true judgment of the soul," as if appeal were made to the inner sense; but in his later observations he proposed *da puerum judicem*, "give a boy as judge," which is adopted by Orelli. Meursius, merely transposing *d-a*, reads much more naturally *ad —* "at a true judgment."

[7] The MS. reading is *illum testem d-e-um constituimus improbarum*, retained in the edd. with the change of *-arum* into *-orum* Perhaps for *deum* should be read *r-e-r-um*, "make him witness of wicked things." With this passage compare iii. 31–33.

[8] It seems necessary for the sake of the argument to read this interrogatively, but in all the edd. the sentence ends without any mark of interrogation.

[9] Typhus — τύφος.

[10] Lit., "He chose . . . to stand."

[11] Lit., "the ignorance of wretched men from the worst robbers," i.e., the false prophets and teachers, who made a prey of the ignorant and credulous. John viii. 46.

[12] Lit., "Are *the things* clear with you which," etc.

[13] So the MS., followed by both Roman edd., Hildebrand and Oehler, reading *passa*, which Cujacius (referring it to *patior*, as the editors seem to have done generally) would explain as meaning "past," while in all other editions *cassa*, "vain," is read.

[14] Lit., "the touching of no anticipation."

[15] Lit., "purer reasoning."

[16] Lit., "that is." This clause Meursius rejects as a gloss.

[17] i.e., If you believe Christ's promises, your belief makes you lose nothing should it prove groundless; but if you disbelieve them, then the consequences to you will be terrible if they are sure. This would seem too clear to need remark, were it not for the confusion of Orelli in particular as to the meaning of the passage.

[18] Lit., "most worthy even of weeping and pity."

may too late show to be true,[1] and ceaseless remorse punish *you?* Do not even these proofs at least give you faith to believe,[2] viz., that already, in so short and brief a time, the oaths of this vast army have spread abroad over all the earth? that already there is no nation so rude and fierce that it has not, changed by His love, subdued its fierceness, and with tranquillity hitherto unknown, become mild in disposition?[3] that *men* endowed with so great abilities, orators, critics, rhetoricians, lawyers, and physicians, those, too, who pry into the mysteries of philosophy, seek to learn these things, despising those in which but now they trusted? that slaves choose to be tortured by their masters as they please, wives to be divorced, children to be disinherited by their parents, rather than be unfaithful to Christ and cast off the oaths of the warfare of salvation? that although so terrible punishments have been denounced by you against those who follow the precepts of this religion, it[4] increases *even* more, and a great host strives more boldly against all threats and the terrors which would keep it back, and is roused to zealous faith by the very attempt to hinder it? Do you indeed believe that these things happen idly and at random? that these feelings are adopted on being met with by chance?[5] Is not this, then, sacred and divine? Or *do you believe* that, without God's *grace*, their minds are so changed, that although murderous hooks and other tortures without number threaten, as we said, those who shall believe, they receive the grounds of faith with which they have become acquainted,[6] as if carried away (A) by some charm, and by an eager longing for all the virtues,[7] and prefer the friendship of Christ to all that is in the world?[8]

6. But perhaps those seem to you weak-minded and silly, who even now are uniting all over the world, and joining together to assent with that readiness of belief *at which you mock.*[9] What then? Do you alone, imbued[10] with the true power of wisdom and understanding, see something wholly different[11] and profound? Do you alone perceive that all these things are trifles? you alone, that those things are mere words and childish absurdities which we declare *are* about to come to us from the supreme Ruler? Whence, pray, has so much wisdom been given to you? whence so much subtlety and wit? Or from what scientific training have you been able to gain so much wisdom, to derive so much foresight? Because you are skilled in declining verbs and nouns by cases and tenses, *and*[12] in avoiding barbarous words and expressions; because you have learned either to express yourselves in[13] harmonious, and orderly, and fitly-disposed language, or to know when it is rude and unpolished;[14] because you have stamped on your memory the Fornix of Lucilius,[15] and Marsyas of Pomponius; because *you know* what the issues to be proposed in lawsuits are, how many kinds of cases there are, how many ways of pleading, what the genus is, what the species, by what methods an opposite is distinguished from a contrary, — do you therefore think that you know what is false, what true, what can or cannot be done, what is the nature of the lowest and highest? Have the well-known words never rung in[16] your ears, that the wisdom of man is foolishness with God?

7. In the first place, you yourselves, too,[17] see clearly that, if you ever discuss obscure subjects, and seek to lay bare the mysteries of nature, on the one hand you do not know the very things

---

[1] *Redarguat.* This sense is not recognised by Riddle and White, and would therefore seem to be, if not unique, at least extremely rare. The derivative *redargutio*, however, is in late Latin used for "demonstration," and this is evidently the meaning here.

[2] *Fidem vobis faciunt argumenta credendi.* Heraldus, joining the two last words, naturally regards them as a gloss from the margin: but read as above, joining the first and last, there is nothing out of place.

[3] Lit., "tranquillity being assumed, passed to placid feelings."

[4] *Res*, "the thing."

[5] Lit., "on chance encounters."

[6] *Rationes cognitas.* There is some difficulty as to the meaning of these words, but it seems best to refer them to the *argumenta credendi* (beginning of chapter, "do not even these proofs"), and render as above. Hildebrand, however, reads *tortiones*, "they accept the tortures which they know will befall them."

[7] The MS. reads *et non omnium*, "and by a love *not* of all the virtues," changed in most edd. as above into *atque omnium*, while Oehler proposes *et novo omnium*, "and by fresh love of all," etc. It will be remembered that the transposition of leaves in the MS. (note on ii. 1) occurs here, and this seems to account for the arbitrary reading of Gelenius, which has no MS. authority whatever, but was added by himself when transposing these chapters to the first book (cf. p. 432, n. 14), *atque nectare ebrii cuncta contemnant*—"As if intoxicated with a certain sweetness and nectar, they despise all things." The same circumstance has made the restoration of the passage by Canterus a connecting of fragments of widely separated sentences and arguments.

[8] Lit., "all the things of the world." Here the argument breaks off, and passes into a new phase, but Orelli includes the next sentence also in the fifth chapter.

[9] Lit., "to the account of that credulity."

[10] So the MS., reading *conditi vi mera*, for which Orelli would read with Oudendorp, *conditæ*—"by the pure force of *recondite* wisdom." The MS., however, is supported by the similar phrase in the beginning of chap. 8, where *tincti* is used.

[11] So the MS., reading *aliud*, for which Stewechius, adopting a suggestion of Canterus, conjectures, *altius et profundius*—"something deeper and more profound." Others propose readings further removed from the text; while Obbarius, retaining the MS. reading, explains it as "not common."

[12] Lit., "because *you are*," etc.

[13] Lit., "either yourselves to utter," etc.

[14] *Incomptus*, for which Heraldus would read *inconditus*, as in opposition to "harmonious." This is, however, unnecessary, as the clause is evidently opposed to the *whole* of the preceding one.

[15] No trace of either of these works has come down to us, and therefore, though there has been abundance of conjecture, we can reach no satisfactory conclusion about them. It seems most natural to suppose the former to be probably part of the lost satires of Lucilius, which had dealt with obscene matters, and the author of the latter to be the Atellane poet of Bononia. As to this there has been some discussion; but, in our utter ignorance of the work itself, it is as well to allow that we must remain ignorant of its author also. The scope of both works is suggested clearly enough by their titles — the statue of Marsyas in the forum overlooking nightly licentious orgies; and their mention seems intended to suggest a covert argument against the heathen, in the implied indecency of the knowledge on which they prided themselves. For *Fornicem Lucilianum* (MS. *Lucialinum*) Meursius reads *Cæcilianum*.

[16] Lit., "Has that *thing* published never struck," etc. There is clearly a reference to 1 Cor. iii. 19, "the wisdom of this world." The argument breaks off here, and is taken up from a different point in the next sentence, which is included, however, in this chapter by Orelli.

[17] So Gelenius, followed by Canterus and Orelli, reading *primum et ipsi*, by rejecting one word of the MS. (*et quæ*). Canterus plausibly combines both words into *itaque*—"therefore." LB. reads *ecquid*—"do you at all," etc., with which Orelli so far agrees, that he makes the whole sentence interrogative.

which you speak of, which you affirm, which you uphold very often with especial zeal, and that each one defends with obstinate resistance his own suppositions as though they were proved and ascertained *truths.* For how can we of ourselves know whether we[1] perceive the truth, even if all ages be employed in seeking out knowledge — *we* whom some envious power[2] brought forth, and formed so ignorant and proud, that, although we know nothing at all, we yet deceive ourselves, and are uplifted by pride and arrogance so as to suppose ourselves possessed of knowledge? For, to pass by divine things, and those plunged in natural obscurity, can any man explain that which in the Phædrus[3] the well-known Socrates cannot comprehend — what man is, or whence he is, uncertain, changeable, deceitful, manifold, of many kinds? for what purposes he was produced? by whose ingenuity he was devised? what he does in the world? (C) why he undergoes such countless ills? whether the earth gave life to him as to worms and mice, being affected with decay through the action of some moisture;[4] or whether he received[5] these outlines of body, and *this* cast of face, from the hand of some maker and framer? Can he, I say, know these things, which lie open to all, and are recognisable by[6] the senses common *to all,* — by what causes we are plunged into sleep, by what we awake? in what ways dreams are produced, in what they are seen? nay rather — as to which Plato in the *Theætetus*[7] is in doubt — whether we are ever awake, or whether that very state which is called waking is part of an unbroken slumber? and what we seem to do when we say that we see a dream? whether we see by means of rays of light proceeding towards the object,[8] or images of the objects fly to and alight on the pupils of our eyes? whether the flavour is in the things *tasted,* or arises from their touching

the palate? from what causes hairs lay aside their natural darkness, and do not become gray all at once, but by adding little by little? why it is that all fluids, on mingling, form one whole; *that* oil, *on the contrary,* does not suffer the others to be poured into it,[9] but is ever brought together clearly into its own impenetrable[10] substance? finally, why the soul also, which is said by you to be immortal and divine,[11] is sick in *men who are* sick, senseless in children, worn out in doting, silly,[12] and crazy old age? Now the weakness and wretched ignorance of these *theories* is greater on this account, that while it may happen that we at times say something which is true,[13] we cannot be sure even of this very thing, whether we have spoken the truth at all.

8. And since you have been wont to laugh at our faith, and with droll jests to pull to pieces *our* readiness of belief too, say, O wits, soaked and filled with wisdom's pure draught, is there in life any kind of business demanding diligence and activity, which the doers[14] undertake, engage in, and essay, without believing *that it can be done?* Do you travel about, do you sail on the sea without believing that you will return home when your business is done? Do you break up the earth with the plough, and fill it with different kinds of seeds without believing that you will gather in the fruit with the changes of the seasons? Do you unite with partners in marriage,[15] without believing that it will be pure, and a union serviceable to the husband? Do you beget children without believing that they will pass[16] safely through the *different* stages of life to the goal of age? Do you commit your sick bodies to the hands of physicians, without believing that diseases can be relieved by their severity being lessened? Do you wage wars with your enemies, without believing that you will carry off the victory by success in battles?[17] Do you worship and serve the gods without believing that they are, and that they listen graciously to your prayers?

9. What, have you seen with your eyes, and handled[18] with your hands, those things which you write yourselves, which you read from time

---

[1] So restored by Stewechius; in the first ed. *perspiciam* (instead of *am-us*) "if I perceive the truth," etc.

[2] So the MS. very intelligibly and forcibly, *res . . . invida,* but the common reading is *invid-i-a* — "whom something . . . with envy." The train of thought which is merely started here is pursued at some length a little later.

[3] The MS. gives *fedro,* but all editions, except the first, Hildebrand, and Oehler, read *Phædone,* referring, however, to a passage in the first Alcibiades (st. p. 129), which is manifestly absurd, as in it, while Alcibiades "cannot tell what man is," Socrates at once proceeds to lead him to the required knowledge by the usual dialectic. Nourry thinks that there is a general reference to *Phædr.,* st. p. 230, — a passage in which Socrates says that he disregards mythological questions that he may study himself. [P. 447, note 2, *infra.*]

[4] Lit., "changed with the rottenness of some moisture." The reference is probably to the statement by Socrates (*Phædo,* st. p. 96) of the questions with regard to the origin of life, its progress and development, which interested him as a young man.

[5] So the MS., LB., and Oehler, but the other edd. make the verb plural, and thus break the connection.

[6] Lit., "established in the common senses."

[7] Arnobius overstates the fact here. In the passage referred to (*Th.,* st. p. 158), Socrates is represented as developing the Protagorean theory from its author's standpoint, not as stating his own opinions.

[8] Lit., "by the stretching out of rays and of light." This, the doctrine of the Stoics, is naturally contrasted in the next clause with that of Epicurus.

[9] Lit., "oil refuses to suffer immersion into itself," i.e., of other fluids.

[10] So LB., followed by Orelli, reading *impenetrabil-em* for the MS. *impenetrabil-is,* which is corrected in both Roman edd. by Gelenius, Canterus, and Elmenhorst *-e,* to agree with the subject *oleum* — "being impenetrable is ever," etc.

[11] Lit., "a god."

[12] So the edd., generally reading *fatua* for the MS. *futura,* which is clearly corrupt. Hildebrand turns the three adjectives into corresponding verbs, and Heinsius emends *deliret* (MS. *-ra*) *et fatue et insane* — "dotes both sillily and crazily." Arnobius here follows Lucr., iii. 445 sqq.

[13] Lit., "something of truth."

[14] The MS. has *a t-tor-o-s,* corrected by a later writer *a-c-tor-e-s,* which is received in LB. and by Meursius and Orelli.

[15] Lit., "unite marriage partnerships."

[16] Lit., "be safe and come."

[17] Or, "in successive battles" — *præliorum successionibus.*

[18] Lit., "with ocular inspection, and held touched."

to time on subjects placed beyond human knowledge? Does not each one trust this author or that? That which any one has persuaded himself is said with truth by another, does he not defend with a kind of assent, as it were, *like that* of faith? Does not he who says that fire [1] or water is the origin of all things, pin his faith to Thales or Heraclitus? he who places the cause *of all* in numbers, to Pythagoras of Samos, *and* to Archytas? he who divides the soul, and sets up bodiless forms, to Plato, the disciple of Socrates? he who adds a fifth element [2] to the primary causes, to Aristotle, the father of the Peripatetics? he who threatens the world with *destruction by* fire, and says that when the time comes it will be *set* on fire, to Panætius, Chrysippus, Zeno? he who is always fashioning worlds from atoms,[3] and destroying *them*, to Epicurus, Democritus, Metrodorus? he who *says* that nothing is comprehended by man, and that all things are wrapt in dark obscurity,[4] to Archesilas,[5] to Carneades?— to some teacher, in fine, of the old and later Academy?

10. Finally, do not even the leaders and founders of the schools [6] already mentioned, say those very things [7] which they do say through belief in their own ideas? For, did Heraclitus see things produced by the changes of fires? Thales, by the condensing of water? [8] *Did* Pythagoras *see them* spring from number? [9] *Did* Plato *see* the bodiless forms? Democritus, the meeting together of the atoms? Or do those who assert that nothing at all can be comprehended by man, know whether what they say is true, so as to [10] understand that the very proposition which they lay down is a declaration of truth? [11] Since, then, you have discovered and learned nothing, and are led by credulity to assert all those things which you write, and comprise in thousands of books; what kind of judgment, pray, is this, so unjust that you mock at faith in us, while you see that you have it in common with our readiness of belief? [12] But *you say* you believe wise men, well versed in all kinds of learning! — those, forsooth, who know nothing, and agree in nothing which they say; who join battle with their opponents on behalf of their own opinions, and are always contending fiercely with obstinate hostility; who, overthrowing, refuting, and bringing to nought the one the other's doctrines, have made all things doubtful, and have shown from their very want of agreement that nothing can be known.

11. But, *supposing that* these things do not at all hinder or prevent your being bound to believe and hearken to them in great measure; [13] and what *reason* is there either that you should have more *liberty* in this respect, or that we *should have* less? You believe Plato,[14] Cronius,[15] Numenius, or any one you please; we believe and confide in Christ.[16] How unreasonable it is, that when we both abide [17] by teachers, and have one and the same thing, belief, in common, you should wish it to be granted to you to receive what is so [18] said by them, *but* should be unwilling to hear and see what is brought forward by Christ! And yet, if we chose to compare cause with cause, we are better able to point out what we have followed in Christ, than *you to point out* what you *have followed* in the philosophers. And we, indeed, have followed in him these things — those glorious works and most potent virtues which he manifested and displayed in diverse miracles, by which any one might be led to *feel* the necessity of believing, and *might* decide with confidence that they were not such as might be regarded as man's, but *such as showed* some divine and unknown power. What virtues

---

1 " Fire " is wanting in the MS.

2 Arnobius here allows himself to be misled by Cicero (*Tusc.*, i. 10), who explains ἐντελέχεια as a kind of perpetual motion, evidently confusing it with ἐνδελέχεια (cf. Donaldson, *New Crat.*, § 339 sqq.), and represents Aristotle as making it a fifth primary cause. The word has no such meaning, and Aristotle invariably enumerates only four primary causes: the material from which, the form in which, the power by which, and the end for which anything exists (*Physics*, ii. 3; *Metaph.*, iv. 2, etc.).

3 Lit., " with indivisible bodies."

4 Pl.

5 So the MS., LB., and Hildebrand, reading *Archesilæ*, while the others read *Archesilao*, forgetting that Arcesilas is the regular Latin form, although Archesilaus is found.

6 *Sententiarum* is read in the first ed. by Gelenius, Canterus, and Ursinus, and seems from Crusius to be the MS. reading. The other edd., however, have received from the margin of Ursinus the reading of the text, *sectarum*.

7 In the first ed., and that of Ursinus, the reading is, *nonne apud ea*, " in those things which they say, do they not say," etc., which Gelenius emended as in the text, *nonne ipsa ea.*

8 Cf. Diog. Laert. ix. 9, where Heraclitus is said to have taught that fire — the first principle — condensing becomes water, water earth, and conversely; and on Thales, Arist., *Met.*, A, 3, where, however, as in other places, Thales is merely said to have referred the generation and maintenance of all things to moisture, although by others he is represented as teaching the doctrine ascribed to him above. Cf. Cic., *de Nat. Deor.*, i. 10, and Heraclides, *Alleg. Hom.*, c. 22, where water evaporating is said to become air, and settling, to become mud.

9 There is some difficulty as to the reading: the MS., first ed., and Ursinus give *numero s-c-ire*, explained by Canterus as meaning " that numbers have understanding," i.e., so as to be the cause of all. Gelenius, followed by Canterus, reads *-os scit* — " does Pyth. know numbers," which is absurdly out of place. Heraldus approved of a reading in the margin of Ursinus (merely inserting *o* after *c*), " that numbers unite," which seems very plausible. The text follows an emendation of Gronovius adopted by Orelli, *-o ex-ire.*

10 So the MS., reading *ut;* but Orelli, and all edd. before him, *aut* —" or do they."

11 i e., that truth knowable by man exists.

12 So the MS. reading *nostra in-credulitate*, for which Ursinus, followed by Stewechius, reads *nostra cum.* Heraldus conjectured *vestra*, i.e., " in your readiness of belief," you are just as much exposed to such ridicule.

13 Heraldus has well suggested that *plurimum* is a gloss arising out of its being met with in the next clause.

14 So the MS. and edd., reading *Platoni;* but Ursinus suggested *Plotino*, which Heraldus thinks most probably correct. There is, indeed, an evident suitableness in introducing here the later rather than the earlier philosopher, which has great weight in dealing with the next name, and should therefore, perhaps, have some in this case also.

15 The MS. and both Roman edd. give *Crotonio*, rejected by the others because no Crotonius is known (it has been referred, however, to Pythagoras, on the ground of his having taught in Croton). In the margin of Ursinus *Cronius* was suggested, received by LB. and Orelli, who is mentioned by Eusebius (*Hist. Eccl.*, vi. 19, 3) with Numenius and others as an eminent Pythagorean, and by Porphyry (*de Ant. Nymph.*, xxi.), as a friend of Numenius, and one of those who treated the Homeric poems as allegories. Gelenius substitutes Plotinus, followed by most edd.

16 [Thus everywhere he writes as a Christian.]

17 *Stemus*, the admirable correction of Gelenius for the MS. *tempus.*

18 Orelli, following Stewechius, would omit *ita.*

did you follow in the philosophers, that it was more reasonable for you *to believe* them than for us to believe Christ? Was any one of them ever able by one word, or by a single command, I will not say to restrain, to check[1] the madness of the sea or the fury of the storm; to restore their sight to the blind, or give it to men blind from their birth; to call the dead back to life; to put an end to the sufferings of years; but — and this is much easier[2] — to heal by one rebuke a boil, a scab, or a thorn fixed in the skin? Not that we deny either that they are worthy of praise for the soundness of their morals, or that they are skilled in all kinds of studies and learning; for we know that they both speak in the most elegant language, and *that their words* flow in polished periods; that they reason in syllogisms with the utmost acuteness; that they arrange their inferences in due order;[3] that they express, divide, distinguish principles by definitions; that they say many things about the *different* kinds of numbers, many things about music; that by their maxims and precepts[4] they settle the problems of geometry also. But what *has* that to *do with* the case? Do enthymemes, syllogisms, and other such things, assure us that these *men* know what is true? or are they therefore such that credence should necessarily be given to them with regard to very obscure subjects? A comparison of persons must be decided, not by vigour of eloquence, but by the excellence of the works *which they have* done. He must not[5] be called a good teacher who has expressed himself clearly,[6] but he who accompanies his promises with the guarantee of divine works.

12. You bring forward arguments against us, and speculative quibblings,[7] which — may I say this without displeasing Him — if Christ Himself were to use in the gatherings of the nations, who would assent? who would listen? who would say that He decided[8] anything clearly? or who, though he were rash and utterly[9] credulous, would follow Him when pouring forth vain and baseless statements? His virtues *have been* made

manifest to you, and that unheard-of power over things, whether that which was openly exercised by Him, or that which was used[10] over the whole world by those who proclaimed Him: it has subdued the fires of passion, and caused races, and peoples, and nations most diverse in character to hasten with one accord to accept the same faith. For the *deeds* can be reckoned up and numbered which have been done in India,[11] among the Seres, Persians, and Medes; in Arabia, Egypt, in Asia, Syria; among the Galatians, Parthians, Phrygians; in Achaia, Macedonia, Epirus; in all islands and provinces on which the rising and setting sun shines; in Rome herself, finally, the mistress *of the world*, in which, although men are[12] busied with the practices introduced by king[13] Numa, and the superstitious observances of antiquity, they have nevertheless hastened to give up their fathers' mode of life,[14] and attach themselves to Christian truth. For they had seen the chariot[15] of Simon Magus, and his fiery car, blown into pieces by the mouth of Peter, and vanish when Christ was named. They had seen *him*, I say, trusting in false gods, and abandoned by them in their terror, borne down headlong by his own weight, lie prostrate with his legs broken; *and* then, when he had been carried to Brunda,[16] worn out with anguish and shame, again cast himself down from the roof of a very lofty house. But all these deeds you neither know nor have wished to know, nor did you ever consider that they were of the utmost importance to you; and while you trust your own judgments, and term *that* wisdom which is overweening conceit, you have given to deceivers — to those guilty *ones*, I say, whose interest it is that the Christian name be degraded — an opportunity of raising clouds of darkness, and concealing truths of so much importance; of robbing you of faith, and putting scorn in its place, in order that, as they already feel that an end such as they deserve threatens them, they might excite in you also a feeling through which you should

---

[1] Hildebrand thinks *compescere* here a gloss, but it must be remembered that redundancy is a characteristic of Arnobius.

[2] The superlative is here, as elsewhere, used by Arnobius instead of the comparative.

[3] i.e., so as to show the relations existing between them.

[4] Perhaps "axioms and postulates."

[5] According to Crusius, *non* is not found in the MS.

[6] White and Riddle translate *candidule*, "sincerely," but give no other instance of its use, and here the reference is plainly to the previous statement of the literary excellence of the philosophers. Heraldus suggests *callidule*, "cunningly," of which Orelli approves; but by referring the adv. to this well-known meaning of its primitive, all necessity for emendation is obviated.

[7] Lit., "subtleties of suspicions." This passage is certainly doubtful. The reading translated, *et suspicionum argutias profertis*, is that of LB., Orelli, and the later edd. generally; while the MS. reads *-atis* — "Bring forward arguments to us, and" (for which Heraldus conjectures very plausibly, *nec*, "and not") "subtleties," etc., which, by changing a single letter, reads in the earlier edd. *proferetis* — "Will you," or, "You will bring forward," etc.

[8] Meursius conjectures *in-* (for MS. *ju-*) *dicare* — "pointed out," of which Orelli approves.

[9] So the MS. and both Roman edd., supported by Heraldus, reading *solidæ facilitatis*, changed by the edd. into *stolidæ* — "stupid."

[10] So all the edd. except Oehler; but as the first verb is plural in the MS., while the second is singular, it is at least as probable that the second was plural originally also, and that therefore the relative should be made to refer both to "virtues" and "power."

[11] Orelli notes that by India is here meant Ethiopia. If so, it may be well to remember that Lucan (x. 29 sq.) makes the Seres neighbours of the Ethiopians, and dwellers at the sources of the Nile.

[12] Instead of *sint*, Stewechius would read *essent* — "were."

[13] Instead of the MS. reading, *Numæ regis artibus et antiquis superstitionibus*, Stewechius, followed by Heraldus, would read *ritibus* — "with the rites of Numa," etc.

[14] So the MS., reading *res patrias*, for which Heraldus, *ritus patrios* — "rites."

[15] So the MS., although the first five edd., by changing *r* into *s*, read *cur-s-um* — "course." This story is of frequent occurrence in the later Fathers, but is never referred to by the earlier, or by any except Christian writers, and is derived solely from the Apostolic Constitutions. In the Greek version of the Apost. Const. the sixth book opens with a dissertation on schisms and heresies, in which the story of Simon and others is told; but that this was interpolated by some compiler seems clear from the arguments brought forward by Bunsen (*Hippolytus and his Age*, more particularly vol. ii. pt. 2, § 2, and the second appendix).

[16] Brunda or Brenda, i.e., Brundisium.

run into danger, and be deprived of the divine mercy.

13. Meantime, however, O you who wonder and are astonished at the doctrines of the learned, and of philosophy, do you not then think it most unjust to scoff, to jeer at us as though we say foolish and senseless things, when you too are found to say either these or just such things which you laugh at when said and uttered by us? Nor do I address those who, scattered through various bypaths of the schools, have formed this and that *insignificant* party through diversity of opinion. You, you I address, who zealously follow Mercury,[1] Plato, and Pythagoras, and the rest of you who are of one mind, and walk in unity in the same paths of doctrine. Do you dare to laugh at us because we[2] revere and worship the Creator and Lord[3] of the universe, and because we commit and entrust our hopes to Him? What *does* your Plato *say* in the *Theæte-tus*, to mention him especially? Does he not exhort the soul to flee from the earth, and, as much as in it lies, to be continually engaged in thought and meditation about Him?[4] Do you dare to laugh at us, because we say that there will be a resurrection of the dead? And this indeed we confess that we say, but *maintain* that it is understood by you otherwise than we hold it. What *says* the same Plato in the *Politicus?* Does he not say that, when the world has begun to rise out of the west and tend towards the east,[5] men will again burst forth from the bosom of the earth, aged, grey-haired, bowed down with years; and that when the remoter[6] years begin to draw near, they will gradually sink down[7] to the cradles of their infancy, through the same steps by which they now grow to manhood?[8]

Do you dare to laugh at us because we see to the salvation of our souls?—that is, ourselves *care* for ourselves: for what are we men, but souls shut up in bodies?—You, indeed, do not take every pains for their safety,[9] in that you do not refrain from all vice and passion; about this you are anxious, that you may cleave to *your* bodies as though inseparably bound to them.[10]—What mean those mystic rites,[11] in which you beseech some *unknown* powers to be favourable to you, and not put any hindrance in your way to impede you when returning to your native seats?

14. Do you dare to laugh at us when we speak of hell,[12] and fires[13] which cannot be quenched, into which we have learned that souls are cast by their foes and enemies? What, does not your Plato also, in the book which he wrote on the immortality of the soul, name the rivers Acheron, Styx,[14] Cocytus, and Pyriphlegethon, and assert that in them souls are rolled along, engulphed, and burned up? But *though* a man of no little wisdom,[15] and of accurate judgment and discernment, he essays a problem which cannot be solved; so that, while he says that the soul is immortal, everlasting, and without bodily substance, he yet says that they are punished, and makes them suffer pain.[16] But what man does not see that that which is immortal, which *is* simple,[17] cannot be subject to any pain; that that, on the contrary, cannot be immortal which does suffer pain? And yet his opinion is not very far from the truth. For although the gentle and kindly disposed man thought it inhuman cruelty to condemn souls to death, he yet not unreasonably[18] supposed that they are cast into rivers blazing with masses of flame, and loathsome from their foul abysses. For they are cast in, and being annihilated, pass away vainly in[19] everlasting destruction. For theirs is an intermediate[20] state, as has been learned from Christ's teaching; and *they are* such that they may on the one hand perish if they have not known God, and on the other be delivered from death if they

---

[1] Hermes Trismegistus. See index.

[2] So the MS., Elmenh., LB., Hildebrand, and Oehler, reading *quod*, for which the other edd. read *qui* — "who."

[3] This seems to be the reading intended by the MS., which according to Hild. gives *dom*, i.e., probably *dominum*, which Oehler adopts, but all other edd. read *deum* — "god."

[4] Arnobius rather exaggerates the force of the passage referred to (st. p. 173), which occurs in the beautiful digression on philosophers. Plato there says that only the philosopher's body is here on earth, while his mind, holding politics and the ordinary business and amusements of life unworthy of attention, is occupied with what is above and beneath the earth, just as Thales, when he fell into a ditch, was looking at the stars, and not at his steps.

[5] *In cardinem vergere qui orientis est solis* seems to be the reading of all edd.; but according to Crusius the MS. reads *vertere* — "to turn." Hildebrand, on the contrary, affirms that instead of *t*, the MS. gives *c*.

[6] i.e., originally earlier.

[7] So most edd., reading *desituros*, for which Stewechius suggests *desulturos* "leap down;" LB. *exituros* — "go out."

[8] Reference is here made to one of the most extraordinary of the Platonic myths (*Pol.*, 269-274), in which the world is represented as not merely material, but as being further possessed of intelligence. It is ever in motion, but not always in the same way. For at one time its motion is directed by a divine governor (τοῦ παντὸς ὁ μὲν κυβερνήτης); but this does not continue, for he withdraws from his task, and thereupon the world loses, or rather gives up its previous bias, and begins to revolve in the opposite direction, causing among other results a reverse development of the phenomena which Arnobius describes. Arnobius, however, gives too much weight to the myth, as in the introduction it is more than hinted that it may be addressed to the young Socrates, as boys like such stories, and he is not much more than a boy. With it should be contrasted the "great year" of the Stoics, in which the universe fulfilled its course, and then began afresh to pass through the same experience as before (Nemesius, *de Nat. Hom.*, c. 38).

[9] LB. makes these words interrogative, but the above arrangement is clearly vindicated by the tenor of the argument: You laugh at our care for our souls' salvation; and truly you do not see to their safety by such precautions as a virtuous life, but do you not seek that which you think salvation by mystic rites?

[10] Lit., "fastened with beam" (i.e., large and strong) "nails."

[11] Cf. on the intercessory prayers of the Magi, c. 62, *infra*.

[12] Pl. Cf. Milman's note on Gibbon, vol. 2, c. xi. p. 7.

[13] Lit., "certain fires."

[14] Plato, in the passage referred to (*Phædo*, st. p. 113, § 61), speaks of the Styx not as a river, but as the lake into which the Cocytus falls. The fourth river which he mentions in addition to the Acheron, Pyriphlegethon, and Cocytus, which he calls Stygian, is the Ocean stream.

[15] So the MS., according to Hild., reading *parvæ*; but acc. to Rigaltius and Crusius, it gives *pravæ* — "of no mean."

[16] So LB., Hild., and Oehler, reading *doloris afficiat sensu*, by merely dropping *m* from the MS. *sensu-m*; while all the other edd. read *doloribus sensuum* — "affects with the pains of the senses."

[17] i.e., not compounded of soul and body.

[18] Or, "not unsuitably," *absone*.

[19] Lit., "in the failure (or ' disappointment') of," etc.

[20] i.e., neither immortal nor necessarily mortal.

have given heed to His threats[1] and *proffered* favours. And to make manifest[2] what is unknown, this is man's real death, this which leaves nothing behind. For that which is seen by the eyes is *only* a separation of soul from body, not the last end—annihilation:[3] this, I say, is man's real death, when souls which know not God shall[4] be consumed in long-protracted torment with raging fire, into which certain fiercely cruel *beings* shall[4] cast them, *who were* unknown[5] before Christ, and brought to light only by His wisdom.

15. Wherefore there is no reason that that[6] should mislead us, should hold out vain hopes to us, which is said by some men till now unheard of,[7] and carried away by an extravagant opinion of themselves, that souls are immortal, next in point of rank to the God and ruler of the world, descended from that parent and sire, divine, wise, learned, and not within reach of the body by contact.[8] Now, because this is true and certain, and because we have been produced by Him who is perfect without flaw, we live unblameably, *I suppose*, and therefore without blame; *are* good, just, and upright, in nothing depraved; no passion overpowers, no lust degrades us; we maintain vigorously the unremitting practice of all the virtues. And because all our souls have one origin, we therefore think exactly alike; we do not differ in manners, we do not differ in beliefs; we all know God; and there are not as many opinions as there are men in the world, nor *are these* divided in infinite variety.[9]

16. But, *they say*, while we are moving swiftly down towards our mortal bodies,[10] causes pursue us from the world's circles,[11] through the working of which we become bad, ay, most wicked; burn with lust and anger, spend our life in shameful deeds, and are given over to the lust of all by the prostitution of our bodies for hire. And how can the material unite with the immaterial? or how can that which God has made, be led by weaker causes to degrade itself through the practice of vice? Will you lay aside your habitual arrogance,[12] O men, who claim God as your Father, and maintain that you are immortal, just as He is? Will you inquire, examine, search what you are yourselves, whose you are, of what parentage you are supposed *to be*, what you do in the world, in what way you are born, how you leap to life? Will you, laying aside *all* partiality, consider in the silence of your thoughts that we are creatures either quite like the rest, or separated by no great difference? For what is there to show that we do not resemble them? or what excellence is in us, such that we scorn to be ranked as creatures? Their bodies are built up on bones, and bound closely together by sinews; and our bodies are in like manner built up on bones, and bound closely together by sinews. They inspire the air through nostrils, and in breathing expire it again; and we in like manner drew in the air, and breathed it out with frequent respirations. They have been arranged in classes, female and male; we, too, have been fashioned by our Creator into the same sexes.[13] Their young are born from the womb, and are begotten through union of the sexes; and we are born from sexual embraces, and are brought forth and sent into life from our mothers' wombs. They are supported by eating and drinking, and get rid of the filth which remains by the lower parts; and we are supported by eating and drinking, and that which nature refuses we deal with in the same way. Their care is to ward off death-bringing famine, and of necessity to be on the watch for food. What else is our aim in the business of life, which presses so much upon us,[14] but to seek the means by which the danger of starvation may be avoided, and carking anxiety put away? They are exposed to disease and hunger, and at last lose their strength by reason of age. What, then? are we not exposed to these evils, and are we not in like manner weakened by noxious diseases, destroyed by wasting age? But if that, too, which is said in the more hidden mysteries is true, that the souls of wicked men, on leaving their human bodies, pass into cattle and other creatures,[15] it is *even* more clearly shown that we are allied to them, and not separated by any great interval, since it is on the same ground that both we and they are said to be living creatures, and to act as such.

---

[1] So Gelenius emended the unintelligible MS. reading *se-mina* by merely adding *s*, followed by all edd., although Ursinus in the margin suggests *se miam*, i.e., *mi-sericordiam*—"pity;" and Heraldus conjectures *munia*—"gifts."

[2] So almost all edd., from a conjecture of Gelenius, supplying *ut*, which is wanting in the MS., first ed., and Oehler.

[3] It is worth while to contrast Augustine's words: "The death which men fear is the separation of the soul from the body. The true death, which men do not fear, is the separation of the soul from God" (Aug. in Ps. xlviii., quoted by Elmenhorst).

[4] In the first ed., Gelenius, Canterus, Ursinus, and Orelli, both verbs are made present, but all other edd. follow the MS. as above.

[5] Lit., "and unknown." Here Arnobius shows himself ignorant of Jewish teaching, as in iii. 12.

[6] So the MS. and LB., followed by Oehler; in the edd. *id* is omitted.

[7] The MS. reading is *a no-b-is quibusdam*, for which LB. reads *nobis a qu.*—"to us," and Hild. *a notis*—"by certain known;" but all others, as above, from a conjecture of Gelenius, *a no-v-is*, although Orelli shows his critical sagacity by preferring an emendation in the margin of Ursinus, *a bonis*—"by certain good men," in which he sees a happy irony!

[8] Lit., "not touchable by any contact of body," *neque ulla corporis attrectatione contiguas.*

[9] Arnobius considers the *reductio ad absurdum* so very plain, that he does not trouble himself to state his argument more directly.

[10] There has been much confusion as to the meaning of Arnobius throughout this discussion, which would have been obviated if it had been remembered that his main purpose in it is to show how unsatisfactory and unstable are the theories of the philosophers, and that he is not therefore to be identified with the views brought forward, but rather with the objections raised to them.

[11] Cf. c. 28, p. 440, note 2.

[12] So the MS., followed by Orelli and others, reading *institutum superciliumque*—"habit and arrogance," for the first word of which LB. reads *istum typhum*—"that pride of yours;" Meursius, *isti typhum*—"Lay aside pride, O ye."

[13] So the edd., reading *in totidem sexus* for the MS. *sexu*—"into so many kinds in sex."

[14] Lit., "in so great occupations of life."

[15] Cf. Plato, *Phædo*, st. p. 81.

17. But we have reason, *one will say*, and excel the whole race of dumb animals in understanding. I might believe that this was quite true, if all men lived rationally and wisely, never swerved aside from their duty, abstained from what is forbidden, and withheld themselves from baseness, and *if* no one through folly and the blindness of ignorance demanded what is injurious and dangerous to himself. I should wish, however, to know what this reason is, through which we are more excellent than all the tribes of animals. *Is it* because we have made for ourselves houses, by which we can avoid the cold of winter and heat of summer? What! do not the other animals show forethought in this respect? Do we not see some build nests as dwellings for themselves in the most convenient situations; others shelter and secure *themselves* in rocks and lofty crags; others burrow in the ground, and prepare for themselves strongholds and lairs in the pits which they have dug out? But if nature, which gave them life, had chosen to give to them also hands to help them, they too would, without doubt, raise lofty buildings and strike out new works of art.[1] Yet, even in those things which they make with beaks and claws, we see that there are many appearances of reason and wisdom which we men are unable to copy, however much we ponder them, although we have hands to serve us dexterously in every kind of work.

18. They have not learned, *I will be told*, to make clothing, seats, ships, and ploughs, nor, in fine, the other furniture which family life requires. These are not the gifts of science, but the suggestions of most pressing necessity; nor did the arts descend with *men's* souls from the inmost heavens, but here on earth have they all been painfully sought out and brought to light,[2] and gradually acquired in process of time by careful thought. But if the soul[3] had *in itself* the knowledge which it is fitting that a race should have indeed *which is* divine and immortal, all men would from the first know everything; nor would there be an age unacquainted with any art, or not furnished with practical knowledge. But now a life of want and in need of many things, noticing some things happen accidentally to its advantage, while it imitates, experiments, and tries, while it fails, remoulds, changes, from continual failure has procured for itself[4] and

wrought out some slight acquaintance with the arts, and brought to one issue the advances of many ages.

19. But if men either knew themselves thoroughly, or had the slightest knowledge of God,[5] they would never claim as their own a divine and immortal nature; nor would they think themselves something great because they have made for themselves gridirons, basins, and bowls,[6] because *they have made* under-shirts, outer-shirts, cloaks, plaids, robes of state, knives, cuirasses and swords, mattocks, hatchets, ploughs. Never, I say, carried away by pride and arrogance, would they believe themselves to be deities of the first rank, and fellows of the highest in his exaltation,[7] because they[8] had devised the arts of grammar, music, oratory, and geometry. For we do not see what is *so* wonderful in these arts, that because of their discovery the soul should be believed to be above the sun as well as all the stars, to surpass both in grandeur and essence the whole universe, of which these are parts. For what else do these assert that they can either declare or teach, than that we may learn to know the rules and differences of nouns, the intervals in the sounds of *different* tones, that we may speak persuasively in lawsuits, that we may measure the confines of the earth? Now, if the soul had brought these arts with it from the celestial regions, and it were impossible not to know them, all men would long before this be busied with them over all the earth, nor would any race of men be found which would not be equally and similarly instructed in them all. But now how few musicians, logicians, and geometricians are there in the world! how few orators, poets, critics! From which it is clear, as has been said pretty frequently, that these things were discovered under the pressure of time and circumstances, and that the soul did not fly hither divinely[9] taught, because neither are all learned, nor can all learn; and[10] there are very many among them somewhat deficient in shrewdness, and stupid, and they are constrained to apply themselves to learning *only* by fear of stripes. But if it were a fact that the things which we learn are but reminiscences[11] — as has been maintained in the systems of the ancients — as we start from the same truth, we should all have learned alike, and remember alike — not have diverse, very numerous, and inconsistent opinions.

---

[1] So, by a later writer in the margin of the MS., who gives *artificiosa-s novitates*, adopted by Stewechius and Oehler, the *s* being omitted in the text of the MS. itself, as in the edd., which drop the final *s* in the next word also — "would raise and with unknown art strike out lofty buildings."

[2] Lit., "born."

[3] Throughout this discussion, Arnobius generally uses the plural, animæ — "souls."

[4] So Elmenhorst, Oberthür, and Orelli, reading *par-a-v-it sibi et* for the MS. *parv-as et*, "from continual failure has wrought out indeed slight smattering of the arts," etc., which is retained in both Roman edd., LB., and Hild.; while Gelenius and Canterus merely substitute *sibi* for *et*, "wrought out for itself slight," etc.

[5] Lit., "or received understanding of God by the breath of any suspicion."

[6] The MS. gives *c-etera-que*, "and the rest," which is retained in both Roman edd., and by Gelenius and Canterus, though rather out of place, as the enumeration goes on.

[7] Lit., "equal to the highness (*summitati*) of the prince."

[8] So LB. and Orelli, reading *qui-a;* the rest, *qui* — "who."

[9] So Gelenius, reading *divinitus* for the MS. *divinas*, i.e., "with a divine nature and origin," which is retained in the first ed. and Orelli.

[10] The MS., both Roman edd., Hild., and Oehler, read *ut*, "so that there are."

[11] Cf. on this Platonic doctrine, ch. 24, p. 443, *infra*.

Now, however, seeing that we each assert different things, it is clear and manifest that we have brought nothing from heaven, but become acquainted with what has arisen here, and maintain what has taken firm root in our thoughts.

20. And, that we may show you more clearly and distinctly what is the worth of man, whom you believe to be very like the higher power, conceive this idea; and because it can be done if we come into direct contact with it, let us conceive it just as if we came into contact. Let us then imagine a place dug out in the earth, fit for dwelling in, formed into a chamber, enclosed by a roof and walls, not cold in winter, not too warm in summer, but so regulated and equable that we suffer neither cold[1] nor the violent heat of summer. To this let there not come any sound or cry whatever,[2] of bird, of beast, of storm, of man — of any noise, in fine, or of the thunder's[3] terrible crash. Let us next devise a way in which it may be lighted not by the introduction of fire, nor by the sight of the sun, but let there be some counterfeit[4] to imitate sunlight, darkness being interposed.[5] Let there not be one door, nor a direct entrance, *but* let it be approached by tortuous windings, and let it never be thrown open unless when it is absolutely necessary.

21. Now, as we have prepared a place for our idea, let us next receive some one born to dwell there, where there is nothing but an empty void,[6] — one of the race of Plato, namely, or Pythagoras, or some one of those who are regarded as of superhuman wit, or have been declared most wise by the oracles of the gods. And when this has been done, he must then be nourished and brought up on suitable food. Let us therefore provide a nurse also, who shall come to him always naked, ever silent, uttering not a word, and shall not open her mouth and lips to speak at all, but after suckling him, and doing what else is necessary, shall leave him fast asleep, and remain day and night before the closed doors; for it is usually necessary that the nurse's care should be near at hand, and that *she* should watch his varying motions. But when the child begins to need to be supported by more substantial food, let it be borne in by the same nurse, still undressed, and maintaining the same unbroken silence. Let the food, too, which is carried in be always precisely the same, with no difference in the material, and without being re-cooked by

means of different flavours; but let it be either pottage of millet, or bread of spelt, or, in imitation of the ancients, chestnuts roasted in the hot ashes, or berries plucked from forest trees. Let him, moreover, never learn to drink wine, and let nothing else be used to quench his thirst than pure cold water from the spring, and *that* if possible raised to his lips in the hollow of his hands. For habit, growing into *second* nature, will become familiar from custom; nor will his desire extend[7] further, not knowing that there is *anything* more to be sought after.

22. To what, then, *you ask*, do these things tend? *We have brought them forward* in order that — as it has been believed that the souls *of men* are divine, and therefore immortal, and that they come to their human bodies with all knowledge — we may make trial from this *child*, whom we have supposed to be brought up in this way, whether this is credible, or has been rashly believed and taken for granted, in consequence of deceitful anticipation. Let us suppose, then, that he grows up, reared in a secluded, lonely spot, spending as many years as you choose, twenty or thirty, — nay, let him be brought into the assemblies of men when he has lived through forty years; and if it is true that he is a part of the divine essence, and[8] lives here sprung from the fountains of life, before he makes acquaintance with anything, or is made familiar with human speech, let him be questioned and answer who he is, or from what father; in what regions he was born, how or in what way brought up; with what work or business he has been engaged during the former part of his life. Will he not, then, stand *speechless*, with less wit and sense than any beast, block, stone? Will he not, when brought into contact with[9] strange and previously unknown things, be above all ignorant of himself? If you ask, will he be able to say what the sun is, the earth, seas, stars, clouds, mist, showers, thunder, snow, hail? Will he be able to know what trees are, herbs, or grasses, a bull, a horse, or ram, a camel, elephant, or kite?[10]

23. If you give a grape to him when hungry, a must-cake, an onion, a thistle,[11] a cucumber, a fig, will he know that his hunger can be appeased by all these, or of what kind each should be *to be fit* for eating?[12] If you made a very great fire, or surrounded him with venomous creatures, will he not go through the midst of flames, vipers,

---

[1] Lit., "a feeling of cold."
[2] Lit., "sound of voice at all."
[3] Lit., "of heaven terribly crashing."
[4] So the later edd., adopting the emendation of Scaliger, *nothum* — "spurious," which here seems to approach in meaning to its use by Lucretius (v. 574 sq.), of the moon's light as borrowed from the sun. The MS. and first four edd. read *notum*, "known."
[5] According to Huet (quoted by Oehler), "between that spurious and the true light;" but perhaps the idea is that of darkness interposed at intervals to resemble the recurrence of night.
[6] Lit., "born, and that, too (*et* wanting in almost all edd.), into the hospice of that place which has nothing, and is inane and empty."

[7] So most edd., reading *porrigetur* for the MS. *corrigetur* — "be corrected," i.e., need to be corrected, which is retained in the first ed.
[8] So Gelenius, followed by Canterus, Elmenh., and Oberthür, reading *portione-m et*, while the words *tam lætam*, "that he is so joyous a part," are inserted before *et* by Stewechius and the rest, except both Roman edd., which retain the MS. *portione jam læta*.
[9] Lit., "sent to."
[10] So the MS., reading *milvus*, for which all edd. (except Oberthür) since Stewechius read *mulus*, "a mule."
[11] *Carduus*, no doubt the esculent thistle, a kind of artichoke.
[12] So, according to an emendation in LB., *esui*, adopted by Orelli and others, instead of the MS. reading *et sui*.

tarantulæ,[1] without knowing that they are dangerous, and ignorant even of fear? But again, if you set before him garments and furniture, both for city and country life, will he indeed be able to distinguish[2] for what each is fitted? to discharge what service they are adapted? Will he declare for what purposes of dress the stragula[3] was made, the coif,[4] zone,[5] fillet, cushion, handkerchief, cloak, veil, napkin, furs,[6] shoe, sandal, boot? What, if you go on to ask what a wheel is, or a sledge,[7] a winnowing-fan, jar, tub, an oil-mill, ploughshare, or sieve, a mill-stone, plough-tail, or light hoe; a curved seat, a needle, a strigil, a laver, an open seat, a ladle, a platter, a candlestick, a goblet, a broom, a cup, a bag; a lyre, pipe, silver, brass, gold,[8] a book, a rod, a roll,[9] and the rest of the equipment by which the life of man is surrounded and maintained? Will he not in such circumstances, as we said, like an ox[10] or an ass, a pig, or any beast more senseless, look[11] at these indeed, observing their various shapes, but[12] not knowing what they all are, and ignorant of the purpose for which they are kept? If he were in any way compelled to utter a sound, would he not with gaping mouth shout something indistinctly, as the dumb usually do?

24. Why, O Plato, do you in the *Meno*[13] put to a young slave certain questions relating to the doctrines of number, and strive to prove by his answers that what we learn we do not learn, but that we *merely* call back to memory those things which we knew in former times? Now, if he answers you correctly, — for it would not be becoming that we should refuse credit to what you say, — he is led *to do so* not by his real knowledge,[14] but by his intelligence; and it results from his having some acquaintance with numbers, through using them every day, that when questioned he follows *your meaning*, and that the very process of multiplication always prompts him. But if you are really assured that the souls *of men are* immortal and endowed with knowledge *when they* fly hither, cease to question that youth whom you see to be ignorant[15] and accustomed to the ways of men:[16] call to you that man of forty years, and ask of him, not anything out of the way or obscure about triangles, about squares, *not* what a cube is, or a second power,[17] the ratio of nine to eight, or finally, of four to three; but ask him that with which all are acquainted — what twice two are, or twice three. We wish to see, we wish to know, what answer he gives when questioned — whether he solves the desired problem. In such a case will he perceive, although his ears are open, whether you are saying anything, or asking anything, or requiring some answer from him? and will he not stand like a stock, or the Marpesian rock,[18] as the saying is, dumb and speechless, not understanding or knowing even this — whether you are talking with him or with another, conversing with another or with him;[19] whether that is intelligible speech which you utter, or *merely* a cry having no meaning, but drawn out and protracted to no purpose?

25. What say you, O men, who assign to yourselves too much of an excellence not your own? Is this the learned soul which you describe, immortal, perfect, divine, holding the fourth place under God the Lord of the universe, and under the kindred spirits,[20] and proceeding from the fountains of life?[21] This is that precious *being* man, endowed[22] with the loftiest powers of reason, who is said *to be* a microcosm, and *to be* made and formed after the fashion of the whole *universe*, superior, as has been seen, to no brute, more senseless than stock *or* stone; for he is unacquainted with men, and always lives, loiters idly in the still deserts although he were rich,[23] lived years without number, and never escaped from the bonds of the body. But when he goes to school, *you say*, and is instructed by the teaching of masters, he is made wise, learned, and lays aside the ignorance which till now clung to him. And an ass, and an ox as well, if com-

---

[1] There has been much discussion as to whether the *solifuga* or *solipuga* here spoken of is an ant or spider.
[2] The MS. reads *discriminare, discernere*, with the latter word, however, marked as spurious.
[3] A kind of rug.
[4] *Mitra*.
[5] *Strophium*, passing round the breast, by some regarded as a kind of corset.
[6] *Mastruca*, a garment made of the skins of the *muflone*, a Sardinian wild sheep.
[7] *Tribula*, for rubbing out the corn.
[8] *Aurum* is omitted in all edd., except those of LB., Hild., and Oehler.
[9] *Liber*, a roll of parchment or papyrus, as opposed to the preceding *codex*, a book of pages.
[10] The MS. reads *vobis* unintelligibly, corrected by Meursius *bovis*.
[11] So Orelli and modern edd.; but Crusius gives as the MS. reading *conspici-etur* (not *-et*), as given by Ursinus, and commonly received — "Will he not . . . be seen?"
[12] The MS. and first five edd. read *et* — "and," changed in LB. to *sed*.
[13] In this dialogue (st. p. 81) Socrates brings forward the doctrine of reminiscence as giving a reasonable ground for the pursuit of knowledge, and then proceeds to give a practical illustration of it by leading an uneducated slave to solve a mathematical problem by means of question and answer.
[14] Lit., "his knowledge of things."

[15] So the MS. and edd., reading *i-gnarum rerum*, except LB., which by merely omitting the *i* gives the more natural meaning, "acquainted with the things," etc.
[16] Lit., "established in the limits of humanity."
[17] i.e., a square numerically or algebraically. The MS., both Roman edd., and Canterus read *di-bus aut dynam-us*, the former word being defended by Meursius as equivalent to *binio*, "a doubling," — a sense, however, in which it does not occur. In the other edd., *cubus aut dynamis* has been received from the margin of Ursinus.
[18] *Æneid*, vi. 472.
[19] This clause is with reason rejected by Meursius as a gloss.
[20] Founded on Plato's words (*Phædrus*, st. p. 247), τῷ δ' (i.e. Zeus) ἔπεται στρατιὰ θεῶν τε καὶ δαιμόνων, the doctrine became prevalent that under the supreme God were lesser gods made by Him, beneath whom again were dæmons, while men stood next. To this Orelli supposes that Arnobius here refers.
[21] The vessels in which, according to Plato (*Timæus*, st. p. 41), the Supreme Being mixed the vital essence of all being. Cf. c. 52.
[22] Lit., "and endowed."
[23] The text and meaning are both rather doubtful, and the edd. vary exceedingly. The reading of Orelli, *demoretur iners, valeat in ære quamvis*, has been translated as most akin to the MS., with which, according to Oehler, it agrees, although Orelli himself gives the MS. reading as *aer-io*.

pelled by constant practice, learn to plough and grind ; a horse, to submit to the yoke, and obey the reins in running ;[1] a camel, to kneel down when being either loaded or unloaded ; a dove, when set free, to fly back to its master's house ; a dog, on finding game, to check and repress its barking ; a parrot, too, to articulate words ; and a crow to utter names.

26. But when I hear the soul spoken of as something extraordinary, as akin and very nigh to God, *and* as coming hither knowing all about past times, I would have it teach, not learn ; and not go back to the rudiments, as the saying is, after being advanced in knowledge, but hold fast the truths it has learned when it enters its earthly body.[2] For unless it were so, how could it be discerned whether *the soul* recalls to memory or learns *for the first time* that which it hears ; seeing that it is much easier to believe that it learns what it is unacquainted with, than that it has forgot what it knew *but* a little before, and that its power of recalling former things is lost through the interposition of the body? And what becomes of the doctrine that souls, *being* bodiless, do not have substance? For that which is not connected with[3] any bodily form is not hampered by the opposition of another, nor can anything be led[4] to destroy that which cannot be touched by what is set against it. For as a proportion established in bodies remains unaffected and secure, though it be lost to sight in a thousand cases ; so must souls, if they are not material, as is asserted, retain their knowledge[5] of the past, however thoroughly they may have been enclosed in bodies.[6] Moreover, the same reasoning not only shows that they are not incorporeal, but deprives them of all[7] immortality even, and refers them to the limits within which life is usually closed. For whatever is led by some inducement to change and alter itself, so that it cannot retain its natural state, must of necessity be considered essentially passive. But that which is liable and exposed to suffering, is declared to be corruptible by that very capacity of suffering.

27. So then, if souls lose all their knowledge on being fettered with the body, they must experience something of such a nature that it makes them become blindly forgetful.[8] For they cannot, without becoming subject to anything whatever, either lay aside their knowledge while they maintain their natural state, or without change in themselves pass into a different state. Nay, we rather think that what is one, immortal, simple, in whatever it may be, must always retain its own nature, and that it neither should nor could be subject to anything, if indeed it purposes to endure and abide within the limits of true immortality. For all suffering is a passage for death and destruction, a way leading to the grave, and bringing an end of life which may not be escaped from ; and if souls are liable to it, and yield to its influence and assaults, they indeed have life given to them only for present use, not as a secured possession,[9] although some come to other conclusions, and put faith in their own arguments with regard to so important a matter.

28. And yet, that we may not be as ignorant when we leave you *as before*, let us hear from you[10] how you say that the soul, on being enwrapt in an earthly body, has no recollection of the past ; while, after being actually placed in the body itself, and rendered almost senseless by union with it, it holds tenaciously and faithfully the things which many years before, eighty if you choose to say *so*, or even more, it either did, or suffered, or said, or heard. For if, through being hampered by the body, it does not remember those things which it knew long ago, and before it came into this world,[11] there is more reason that it should forget those things which it has done from time to time since being shut up in the body, than those which *it did* before entering it,[12] while not yet connected with men. For the same body which[13] deprives of memory the soul which enters it,[14] should cause what is done within itself also to be wholly forgotten ; for one cause cannot bring about two results, and *these* opposed to each other, so as to make some things to be forgotten, *and* allow others to be remembered by him who did them. But if souls, as you call them, are prevented and hindered by their *fleshly* members from recalling their former knowledge,[15] how do they remember what has been arranged[16] in *these* very bodies,

---

[1] Lit., " acknowledge turnings in the course."
[2] Lit., " but retaining its own things, bind itself in earthly bodies."
[3] Lit., " of."
[4] So the MS. and edd., reading *sua-de-ri*, for which Oehler reads very neatly *sua de vi* — " can anything of its own power destroy," etc.
[5] Lit., " not suffer forgetfulness."
[6] Lit., " however the most solid unions of bodies may have bound them round."
[7] So the edd., reading *privat immortalitate has omni*, for which, according to Hildebrand, the MS. reads -*tatem has omnis* — " all these of immortality."
[8] Lit., " put on the blindness of oblivion."

[9] Cf. Lucretius, iii. 969, where life is thus spoken of.
[10] The MS. reads *ne videamu-s*, changed in both Roman edd. into -*amur* — " that we may not be seen by you (as ignorant), how say you," etc. Gelenius proposed the reading of the text, *audiamus*, which has been received by Canterus and Orelli. It is clear from the next words — *quemadmodum dicitis* — that in this case the verb must be treated as a kind of interjection, " How say you, let us hear." LB. reads, to much the same purpose, *scire avemus*, " we desire to know."
[11] Lit., " before man."
[12] Lit., " placed outside."
[13] *Quod enim.*
[14] *Rebus ingressis.*
[15] So read by Orelli, *artes suas antiquas*, omitting *atque*, which, he says, follows in the MS. It is read after *suas*, however, in the first ed., and those of Gelenius, Canterus, Hildebrand ; and according to Oehler, it is so given in the MS., " its own and ancient." Oberthür would supply *res* — " its own arts and ancient things."
[16] So the MS, reading *constitut-a*, followed by all edd. except those of Ursinus, Hildebrand, and Oehler, who read -*æ*, " how do they remember when established in the bodies," which is certainly more in accordance with the context.

and know that they are spirits, and have no bodily substance, being exalted by their condition as immortal beings?[1] *how do they know* what rank they hold in the universe, in what order they have been set apart *from other beings?* how they have come to these, the lowest parts of the universe? what properties they acquired, and from what circles,[2] in gliding along towards these regions? How, I say, do they know that they were very learned, and have lost their knowledge by the hindrance which their bodies afford them? For of this very thing also they should have been ignorant, whether their union with the body had brought any stain upon them; for to know what you were, and what to-day you are not, is no sign that you have lost your memory,[3] but a proof and evidence that it is quite sound.[4]

29. Now, since it is so, cease, I pray you, cease to rate trifling and unimportant things at immense values. Cease to place man in the upper ranks, since he is of the lowest; and in the highest orders, seeing that his person only is taken account of,[5] that he is needy, poverty-stricken in his house and dwelling,[6] and *was* never entitled to be declared of illustrious descent. For while, as just men and upholders of righteousness, you should have subdued pride and arrogance, by the evils[7] of which we are all uplifted and puffed up with empty vanity; you not only hold that these evils arise naturally, but — and this is much worse — you have also added causes by which vice should increase, and wickedness remain incorrigible. For what man is there, although of a disposition which ever shuns what is of bad repute and shameful, who, when he hears it said by very wise men that the soul is immortal, and not subject to the decrees of the fates,[8] would not throw himself headlong into all kinds of vice, *and* fearlessly[9] engage in and set about unlawful things? *who* would not, in short, gratify his desires in all things demanded by his unbridled lust, strengthened even further by its security and freedom from punishment?[10] For what will hinder him from doing so? The fear of a power above and divine judgment? And how shall he be overcome by any fear or dread who has been persuaded that he is immortal, just as the supreme God Himself, and that no sentence can be pronounced upon him by God, seeing that there is the same immortality in both, and that

the one immortal being cannot be troubled by the other, which is *only* its equal?[11]

30. But *will he not be terrified by*[12] the punishments in Hades, of which we have heard, assuming also, *as they do*, many forms of torture? And who[13] will be so senseless and ignorant of consequences,[14] as to believe that to imperishable spirits either the darkness of Tartarus, or rivers of fire, or marshes with miry abysses, or wheels sent whirling through the air,[15] can in any wise do harm? For that which is beyond reach, and not subject to the laws of destruction, though it be surrounded by all the flames of the raging streams, be rolled in the mire, overwhelmed by the fall of overhanging rocks and by the overthrow of huge mountains, must remain safe and untouched without suffering any deadly harm.

Moreover, that conviction not only leads on to wickedness, from the very freedom to sin *which it suggests*, but even takes away the ground of philosophy itself, and asserts that it is vain to undertake its study, because of the difficulty of the work, which leads to no result. For if it is true that souls know no end, and are ever[16] advancing with all generations, what danger is there in giving themselves up to the pleasures of sense — despising and neglecting the virtues by *regard to* which life is more stinted *in its pleasures*, and *becomes* less attractive — and in letting loose their boundless lust to range eagerly and unchecked through[17] all kinds of debauchery? *Is it the danger* of being worn out by such pleasures, and corrupted by vicious effeminacy? And how can that be corrupted which is immortal, which always exists, and *is* subject to no suffering? *Is it the danger* of being polluted by foul and base deeds? And how can that be defiled which has no corporeal substance; or where can corruption seat itself, where there is no place on which the mark of this very corruption should fasten?

But again, if souls draw near to the gates of death,[18] as is laid down in the doctrine of Epicu-

---

[1] Lit., "of immortality."
[2] Cf. ch. 16, p. 440.
[3] Lit., "of a lost memory."
[4] Lit., "of (a memory) preserved."
[5] *Capite cum censeatur.*
[6] Lit., "poor in hearth, and of a poor hut."
[7] So the ms., reading *malis*, for which Ursinus suggested *alis*, "on the wings of which."
[8] i.e., to death.
[9] The ms. reads *securus, intrepidus* — "heedless, fearless;" the former word, however, being marked as a gloss. It is rejected in all edd., except LB.
[10] Lit., "by the freedom of impunity."

[11] Lit., "the one (immortality) . . . in respect of the equality of condition of the other" — *nec in alterius (immortalitatis) altera (immortalitatis) possit æqualitate conditionis vexari;* the reference being clearly to the immediately preceding clause, with which it is so closely connected logically and grammatically. Orelli, however, would supply *anima*, ἀπὸ τοῦ κοινοῦ, as he puts it, of which nothing need be said. Meursius, with customary boldness, emends *nec vi alterius altera*, " nor by the power of one can the other," etc.
[12] So the ellipse is usually supplied, but it seems simpler and is more natural thus: " But punishments (have been) spoken of" (*memoratæ*), etc.
[13] So ms. and Oehler, for which the edd. read *ec quis*, "will any one."
[14] Lit., " the consequences of things."
[15] Lit., " the moving of wheels whirling."
[16] Lit., " in the unbroken course of ages" — *perpetuitate ævorum.*
[17] Lit., " and to scatter the unbridled eagerness of boundless lust through," etc.
[18] Lucretius (iii. 417 sqq.) teaches at great length that the soul and mind are mortal, on the ground that they consist of atoms smaller than those of vapour, so that, like it, on the breaking of their case, they will be scattered abroad; next, on the ground of the analogy between them and the body in regard to disease, suffering, etc.; of their ignorance of the past, and want of developed qualities; and finally, on the ground of the adaptation of the soul to the body, as of a fish to the sea, so that life under other conditions would be impossible.

rus, in this case, too, there is no sufficient reason why philosophy should be sought out, even if it is true that by it[1] souls are cleansed and made pure from all uncleanness.[2] For if they all[3] die, and even in the body[4] the feeling characteristic of life perishes, and is lost ;[5] it is not only a very great mistake, but *shows* stupid blindness, to curb innate desires, to restrict your mode of life within narrow limits, not yield to your inclinations, and do what our passions have demanded and urged, since no rewards await you for so great toil when the day of death comes, and you shall be freed from the bonds of the body.

31. A certain neutral character, then, and undecided and doubtful nature of the soul, has made room for philosophy, and found out a reason for its being sought after : while, that is, that fellow[6] is full of dread because of evil deeds of which he is guilty ; another conceives great hopes if he shall do no evil, and pass his life in obedience to[7] duty and justice. Thence it is that among learned men, and *men* endowed with excellent abilities, there is strife as to the nature of the soul, and some say that it is subject to death, and cannot take upon itself the divine substance ; while others *maintain* that it is immortal, and cannot sink under the power of death.[8] But this is brought about by the law of *the soul's* neutral character :[9] because, on the one hand, arguments present themselves to the one party by which it is found that the soul[10] is capable of suffering, and perishable ; and, on the other hand, are not wanting to their opponents, by which it is shown that the soul is divine and immortal.

32. Since these things are so, and we have been taught by the greatest teacher that souls are set not far from the gaping[11] jaws of death ; that they can, nevertheless, have their lives prolonged by the favour and kindness of the Supreme Ruler if only they try and study to know Him, — for the knowledge of Him is a kind of vital

leaven[12] and cement to bind together that which would otherwise fly apart, — let them,[13] then, laying aside their savage and barbarous nature, return to gentler ways, that they may be able to be ready for that which shall be given.[14] What reason is there that we should be considered by you brutish, as it were, and stupid, if we have yielded and given ourselves up to God our deliverer, because of these fears ? We often seek out remedies for wounds and the poisoned bites of serpents, and defend ourselves by means of thin plates[15] sold by Psylli[16] or Marsi, and other hucksters[17] and impostors ; and that we may not be inconvenienced by cold or intense heat,[18] we provide with anxious and careful diligence coverings in[19] houses and clothing.

33. Seeing that the fear of death, that is, the ruin of our souls, menaces[20] us, in what are we not acting, as we all are wont, from a sense of what will be to our advantage,[21] in that we hold Him fast who assures us that He will be our deliverer from such danger, embrace *Him*, and entrust our souls to His care,[22] if only that[23] interchange is right ? You rest the salvation of your souls on yourselves, and are assured that by your own exertions alone[24] you become gods ; but we, on the contrary, hold out no hope to ourselves from our own weakness, for we see that our nature has no strength, and is overcome by its own passions in every strife for anything.[25] You think that, as soon as you pass away, freed from the bonds of your fleshly members, you will find wings[26] with which you may rise to heaven and soar to the stars. We shun such presumption, and do not think[27] that it is in our power to reach the abodes[28] above, since we have no certainty as to this even, whether we deserve to receive

---

1 The MS. and first four edd. read *has*, " that these souls," etc.; in the other edd., *hac* is received as above from the margin of Ursinus.

2 Cf. Plato, *Phædo* (st. p. 64 sq.), where death is spoken of as only a carrying further of that separation of the soul from the pleasures and imperfections of the body which the philosopher strives to effect in this life.

3 Lit., " in common."

4 Pl.

5 This refers to the second argument of Lucretius noticed above.

6 i.e., the abandoned and dissolute immortal spoken of in last chapter.

7 Lit., " with."

8 Lit., " degenerate into mortal nature."

9 Arnobius seems in this chapter to refer to the doctrine of the Stoics, that the soul must be material, because, unless body and soul were of one substance, there could be no common feeling or mutual affection (so Cleanthes in *Nemes. de Nat. Hom.*, ii. p 33) ; and to that held by some of them, that only the souls of the wise remained after death, and these only till the conflagration (Stob., *Ecl. Phys.*, p. 372) which awaits the world, and ends the Stoic great year or cycle. Others, however, held that the souls of the wise became dæmons and demigods (Diog., *Laert.*, vii. 157 and 151).

10 Lit., " they " — *eas*.

11 Lit., " from the gapings and," etc.

12 There may be here some echo of the words (John xvii. 3), " This is eternal life, that they may know Thee, the only true God," etc.: but there is certainly not sufficient similarity to found a direct reference on, as has been done by Orelli and others.

13 i.e., souls.

14 This passage presents no difficulty in itself, its sense being obviously that, as by God's grace life is given to those who serve Him, we must strive to fit ourselves to receive His blessing. The last words, however, have seemed to some fraught with mystery, and have been explained by Heraldus at some length as a veiled or confused reference to the Lord's Supper, as following upon baptism and baptismal regeneration, which, he supposes, are referred to in the preceding words, " laying aside," etc. [It is not, however, the language of a mere catechumen.]

15 These " thin plates," *laminæ*, Orelli has suggested, were amulets worn as a charm against serpents.

16 MS. *Phyllis*.

17 So the edd., reading *instit-oribus* for the MS. *instit-ut-oribus*, " makers."

18 Lit., " that colds and violent suns may not," etc.

19 Lit., " of."

20 Lit., " is set before."

21 So the MS., first ed., Gelenius, Canterus, Hildebrand, reading *ex commodi sensu*, for which all the other edd., following Ursinus and Meursius, read *ex communi* — " from common sense," i.e., wisely.

22 Perhaps, as Orelli evidently understands it, " prefer Him to our own souls " — *animis præponimus.*

23 So Oehler, reading *ea* for the MS. *ut*, omitted in all edd.

24 Lit., " by your own and internal exertion."

25 Lit., " of things."

26 Lit., " wings will be at hand."

27 The MS. reads *di-*cimus, " say ; " corrected *du*, as above.

28 The first four edd. read *res*, " things above," for which Stewechius reads, as above, *sedes*.

life and be freed from the law of death. You suppose that without the aid of others[1] you will return to the master's palace as if to your own home, no one hindering *you;* but we, on the contrary, neither have any expectation that this can be unless by *the will of* the Lord of all, nor think that so much power and licence are given to any man.

34. Since this is the case, what, pray, is so unfair as that we should be looked on by you as silly in that readiness of belief *at which you scoff,* while we see that you both have like beliefs, and entertain the same hopes? If we are thought deserving of ridicule because we hold out to ourselves such a hope, the same ridicule awaits you too, who claim for yourselves the hope of immortality. If you hold and follow a rational course, grant to us also a share in it. If Plato in the *Phædrus,*[2] or another of this band *of philosophers,* had promised these joys to us — that is, a way to escape death, or were able to provide it and bring *us* to the end which he had promised,[3] it would have been fitting that we should seek to honour him from whom we look for so great a gift and favour. Now, since Christ has not only promised it, but also shown by His virtues, *which were* so great, that it can be made good, what strange thing do we do, and on what grounds are we charged with folly, if we bow down and worship His name[4] and majesty from whom we expect *to receive* both *these blessings,* that we may at once escape a death of suffering, and be enriched with eternal life?[5]

35. But, say *my opponents,* if souls are mortal and[6] of neutral character, how can they from their neutral properties become immortal? If we should say that we do not know this, and only believe it because said by[7] *One* mightier *than we,* when will our readiness of belief seem mistaken if we believe[8] that to the almighty King nothing is hard, nothing difficult, and that[9] what is impossible to us is possible to Him and at His command?[10] For is there *anything* which may withstand His will, or does

it not follow[11] of necessity that what He has willed *must* be done? Are we to infer from our distinctions what either can or cannot be done; and are we not to consider that our reason is as mortal as we ourselves are, and is of no importance with the Supreme? And yet, O ye who do not believe that the soul is of a neutral character, and that it is held on the line midway between life and death, are not all whatever whom fancy supposes to exist, gods, angels, dæmons, or whatever else is their name, themselves too of a neutral character, and liable to change[12] in the uncertainty of their future?[13] For if we all agree that there is one Father of all, *who* alone *is* immortal and unbegotten, and *if* nothing at all is found before Him which could be named,[14] it follows as a consequence that all these whom the imagination of men believes to be gods, have been either begotten by Him or produced at His bidding. Are they[15] produced and begotten? they are also later in order and time; if later in order and time, they must have an origin, and beginning of birth and life; but that which has an entrance *into* and beginning of life in its first stages, it of necessity follows, should have an end also.

36. But the gods are said to be immortal. Not by nature, then, but by the good-will and favour of God their Father. In the same way, then, in which the boon[16] of immortality is God's gift to *these who were* assuredly produced,[17] will He deign to confer eternal life upon souls also, although fell death seems able to cut them off and blot them out of existence in utter annihilation.[18] The divine Plato, many of whose thoughts are worthy of God, and not such as the vulgar hold, in that discussion and treatise entitled the *Timæus,* says that the gods and the world are corruptible by nature, and in no wise beyond the reach of death, but that their being is ever maintained[19] by the will of God, *their* King and Prince:[20] for that that *even* which has been duly clasped and bound together by the surest bands is preserved *only* by God's good-

---

[1] *Sponte.*

[2] Here, as in c. 7, p. 436, n. 3, the edd. read *Phædone,* with the exception of the first ed., LB., Hildebrand, and Oehler, who follow the MS. as above.

[3] Lit., " to the end of promising."

[4] Meursius suggests *numini,* " deity," on which it may be well to remark once for all, that *nomen* and *numen* are in innumerable places interchanged in one or other of the edd. The change, however, is usually of so little moment, that no further notice will be taken of it.

[5] So the MS., according to Rigaltius and Hildebrand, reading *vitæ æternitate,* while Crusius asserts that the MS. gives *vita et* — " with life and eternity."

[6] The MS. reading is, *mortalis est qualitatis.* The first five edd. merely drop *est* — " of mortal, of neutral," etc.; LB. and the others read, *es et,* as above.

[7] Lit., " heard from."

[8] So the MS., according to Crusius, the edd. reading *cred-id-imus* — " have believed."

[9] Lit., " if *we believe* that."

[10] So the MS., reading *ad modum obsecutionis paratum* — " prepared to the mode of compliance; " for which the edd. read *adm. exe-cutioni* — " quite prepared for performing," except Hildebrand, who gives *adm. obsecutioni* — " for obedience."

[11] So the MS., according to Crusius, but all edd. read *sequa-tur* (for *i*) — " Is there anything which He has willed which it does not follow," etc.

[12] So all edd., reading *mutabiles,* except the two Roman edd. and Oehler, who gives, as the reading of the MS., *nu.* — " tottering."

[13] Lit., " in the doubtful condition of their lot."

[14] Lit., " which may have been of a name."

[15] LB., followed by the later edd., inserted *si,* " if they are," which is certainly more consistent with the rest of the sentence.

[16] The MS. reading is utterly corrupt and meaningless — *immortalitatis largiter est donum dei certa prolatis.* Gelenius, followed by Canterus, Oberthür, and Orelli, emended *largi-tio . . . certe,* as above. The two Roman edd. read, *-tatem largitus . . . certam* — " bestowed, assured immortality as God's gift on," etc.

[17] i.e., who must therefore have received it if they have it at all.

[18] Lit., " out, reduced to nothing with annihilation, not to be returned from."

[19] Lit., " they are held in a lasting bond," i.e., of being.

[20] Plato makes the supreme God, creator of the inferior deities, assure these lesser gods that their created nature being in itself subject to dissolution, His will is a surer ground on which to rely for immortality, than the substance or mode of their own being (*Timæus,* st. p. 41; translated by Cicero, *de Univ.,* xi., and criticised *de Nat. Deor.,* i. 8 and iii. 12).

ness; and that by no other than[1] by Him who bound *their elements* together can they both be dissolved if necessary, and have the command given which preserves their being.[2] If this is the case, then, and it is not fitting to think or believe otherwise, why do you wonder that we speak of the soul as neutral in its character, when Plato says that it is so even with the deities,[3] but that their life is kept up by God's[4] grace, without break or end? For if by chance you knew it not, and because of its novelty it was unknown to you before, *now, though* late, receive and learn from Him who knows and has made it known, Christ, that souls are not the children of the Supreme Ruler, and did not begin to be self-conscious, and to be spoken of in their own special character after being created by Him;[5] but that some other is their parent, far enough removed from the chief in rank and power, of His court, however, and distinguished by His high and exalted birthright.

37. But if souls were, as is said, the Lord's children, and begotten by[6] the Supreme Power, nothing would have been wanting to make them perfect, *as they would have been* born with the most perfect excellence: they would all have had one mind, and *been of* one accord; they would always dwell in the royal palace; and would not, passing by the seats of bliss in which they had learned and kept in mind the noblest teachings, rashly seek these regions of earth, that[7] they might live enclosed in gloomy bodies amid phlegm and blood, among these bags of filth and most disgusting[8] vessels of urine. But, *an opponent will say*, it was necessary that these parts too should be peopled, and therefore Almighty God sent souls hither to *form* some colonies, as it were. And of what use are men to the world, and on account of what are they necessary,[9] so that they may not be believed to have been destined to live here and be the

tenants of an earthly body for no purpose? They have a share, *my opponent says*, in perfecting the completeness of this immense mass, and without their addition this whole universe is incomplete and imperfect. What then? If there were not men, would the world cease to discharge its functions? would the stars not go through their changes? would there not be summers and winters? would the blasts of the winds be lulled? and from the clouds gathered and hanging *overhead* would not the showers come down upon the earth to temper droughts? But now[10] all things must go on in their own courses, and not give up following the arrangement established by nature, even if there should be no name of man heard in the world, and this earth should be still with the silence of an unpeopled desert. How then is it alleged that it was necessary that an inhabitant should be given to these regions, since it is clear that by man comes nothing to *aid in* perfecting the world, and that all his exertions regard his private convenience always, and never cease to aim at his own advantage?

38. For, to begin with what is important, what advantage is it to the world that the mightiest kings are here? What, that there are tyrants, lords, *and* other innumerable and very illustrious powers? What, that there are generals of the greatest experience in war, skilled in taking cities; soldiers steady and utterly invincible in battles of cavalry, or in fighting hand to hand on foot? What, that there are orators, grammarians, poets, writers, logicians, musicians, ballet-dancers, mimics, actors, singers, trumpeters, flute and reed players? What, that there are runners, boxers, charioteers, vaulters,[11] walkers on stilts, rope-dancers, jugglers? What, that there are dealers in salt fish, salters, fishmongers, perfumers, goldsmiths, bird-catchers, weavers of winnowing fans and baskets of rushes? What, that there are fullers, workers in wool, embroiderers, cooks, confectioners, dealers in mules, pimps, butchers, harlots? What, that there are other kinds of dealers? What do *the other kinds* of professors and arts, for the enumeration of which all life would be *too* short, contribute to the plan and constitution[12] of the world, that we should believe[13] that it could not have been founded without men, and would not attain its completeness without the addition of[14] a wretched and useless being's exertion?[15]

---

1 The MS. and both Roman edd. read *neque ullo ab-olitio-nis* unintelligibly, for which Gelenius proposed *nexusque abolitione* —"and by the destruction of the bond;" but the much more suitable reading in the margin of Ursinus, translated above, *ullo ab alio nis-i*, has been adopted by later edd.

2 Lit., "be gifted with a saving order." So the MS., reading *salutari iussione*, followed by both Rom. edd.; LB. and Orelli read *vinctione* — "bond;" Gelenius, Canterus, Elmenh., and Oberthür, *m-issione* — "dismissal."

3 Lit., "that to the gods themselves the natures are intermediate."

4 Lit., "supreme" —*principali*.

5 Cf. i. 48. On this passage Orelli quotes Irenæus, i. 21, where are enumerated several gnostic theories of the creation of the world and men by angels, who are themselves created by the "one unknown Father." Arnobius is thought, both by Orelli and others, to share in these opinions, and in this discussion to hint at them, but obscurely, lest his cosmology should be confounded by the Gentiles with their own polytheistic system. It seems much more natural to suppose that we have here the indefinite statement of opinions not thoroughly digested.

6 Lit., "a generation of."

7 Canterus, Elmenhorst, Oberthür, and Orelli omit *ut*, which is retained as above by the rest.

8 Lit., "obscene."

9 Elmenhorst endeavours to show that Arnobius coincides in this argument with the Epicureans, by quoting Lucr. v. 165 sqq. and Lact. vii. 5, where the Epicurean argument is brought forward, What profit has God in man, that He should have created him? In doing this, it

seems not to have been observed that the question asked by Arnobius is a very different one: What place has man in the *world*, that God should be supposed to have sent him to fill it?

10 i.e., so far from this being the case.

11 i e., from one horse to another — *desultores*.

12 *Rationibus et constitutionibus*.

13 Lit., "it should be believed."

14 Lit., "unless there were joined."

15 So the MS., reading *contentio*, which Orelli would understand as meaning "contents," which may be correct. LB. reads *conditio* — "condition," ineptly; and Ursinus in the margin, *completio* — "the filling up."

39. But perhaps, *some one will urge*, the Ruler of the world sent hither souls sprung from Himself for this purpose — a very rash thing for a man to say [1] — that they which had been divine [2] with Him, not coming into contact with the body and earthly limits, [3] should be buried in the germs of men, spring from the womb, burst into and keep up the silliest wailings, draw the breasts in sucking, besmear and bedaub themselves with their own filth, then be hushed by the swaying [4] of the frightened nurse and by the sound of rattles. [5] Did He send souls *hither* for this reason, that they which had been but now sincere and of blameless virtue should learn as [6] men to feign, to dissemble, to lie, to cheat, [7] to deceive, to entrap with a flatterer's abjectness; to conceal one thing in the heart, [8] express another in the countenance; to ensnare, to beguile [9] the ignorant with crafty devices, to seek out poisons by means of numberless arts *suggested* by bad feelings, and to be fashioned [10] with deceitful changeableness to suit circumstances? Was it for this He sent souls, that, living *till then* in calm and undisturbed tranquillity, they might find in [11] their bodies causes by which to become fierce and savage, cherish hatred and enmity, make war upon each other, subdue and overthrow states; load themselves with, and give themselves up to the yoke of slavery; and finally, be put the one in the other's power, having changed the condition [12] in which they were born? Was it for this He sent souls, that, being made unmindful of the truth, and forgetful of what God was, they should make supplication to images which cannot move; address as superhuman deities pieces of wood, brass, and stones; ask aid of them [13] with the blood of slain animals; make no mention of Himself: nay more, that some of them should doubt their own existence, or deny altogether that anything exists? Was it for this He sent souls, that they which in their own abodes had been of one mind, equals in intellect and knowledge, after that they put on

mortal forms, should be divided by differences of opinion; should have different views as to what is just, useful, and right; should contend about the objects of desire and aversion; should define the highest good and greatest evil differently; that, in seeking to know the truth of things, they should be hindered by their obscurity; and, as if bereft of eyesight, should see nothing clearly, [14] and, wandering from the truth, [15] should be led through uncertain bypaths of fancy?

40. Was it for this He sent souls *hither*, that while the other creatures are fed by what springs up spontaneously, and is produced without being sown, and do not seek for themselves the protection or covering of houses or garments, they should be under the sad necessity [16] of building houses for themselves at very great expense and with never-ending toils, preparing coverings for their limbs, making different *kinds of* furniture for the wants [17] of daily life, borrowing help for [18] their weakness from the dumb creatures; using violence to the earth that it might not give forth its own herbs, but might send up the fruits required; and when they had put forth all their strength [19] in subduing the earth, should be compelled to lose the hope with which they had laboured [20] through blight, hail, drought; and at last forced by [21] hunger to throw themselves on human bodies; and when set free, to be parted from their human forms by a wasting sickness? Was it for this that they which, while they abode with Him, had never had any longing for property, should have become exceedingly covetous, and with insatiable craving be inflamed to an eager desire of possessing; that they should dig up lofty mountains, and turn the unknown bowels of the earth into materials, and *to* purposes of a different kind; should force their way to remote nations at the risk of life, and, in exchanging goods, always catch at a high price *for what they sell*, and a low one [22] *for what they buy*, take interest at greedy and excessive rates, and add to the number of their sleepless nights *spent* in reckoning up thousands [23] wrung from the life-blood of wretched men; should be ever extending the limits of their possessions, and, though

---

[1] So the later edd., from the margin of Ursinus, reading *quod temeritatis est maximæ* for the ms. *quem* — "whom it shows the greatest rashness to speak of."
[2] Lit., "goddesses."
[3] So Gelenius (acc. to Orelli), reading as in the margin of Ursinus, *terrenæ circumscriptionis*, for the unintelligible reading of the ms., *temerariæ*, retained in both Roman edd., Canterus, and (acc. to Oehler) Gelenius. LB. reads *metariæ* — "a limiting by boundaries."
[4] Lit., "motions."
[5] Cf. Lucr., v. 229 sq. The same idea comes up again in iv. 21.
[6] Lit., "in."
[7] According to Hildebrand, the ms. reads *dissimular-ent circumscribere*, so that, by merely dropping *nt*, he reads, "to dissemble and cheat;" but according to Crusius, *iri* is found in the ms. between these two words, so that by prefixing *m* Sabæus in the first ed. read *m-ent-iri* as above, followed by all other edd.
[8] Lit., "to roll . . . in the mind."
[9] Rigaltius and Hildebrand regard *decipere* as a gloss.
[10] So the ms., reading *formari*, followed by Hildebrand and Oehler; but all the other edd. give the active form, *-are*.
[11] Lit., "from."
[12] The condition, i.e., of freedom.
[13] LB., seemingly received by Orelli, though not inserted into his text, reads *poscerent eos* for the ms. *-entur*, which Hildebrand modifies *-ent ea* as above.

[14] Lit., "certain."
[15] Lit., "by error."
[16] Lit., "the sad necessity should be laid upon them, that," etc.
[17] Lit., "for the want of daily things," *diurnorum egestati*, for which Stewechius would read *diurna egestate* — "from daily necessity."
[18] Lit., "of."
[19] Lit., "poured forth all their blood."
[20] Lit., "of their labour."
[21] Lit., "at last by force of."
[22] So the ms. and edd., reading *vilitatem*, for which Meursius proposed very needlessly *utilitatem* — "and at an advantage."
[23] So, adhering very closely to the ms., which gives *e-t sanguine supputandis augere-t insomnia milibus*, the *t* of *e-t* being omitted and *n* inserted by all. The first five edd. read, *-tandi se augerent insania: millibus* — "harass themselves with the madness of reckoning; by miles should extend," etc., — the only change in Heraldus and Orelli being a return to *insomnia* — "harass with sleeplessness," etc.

they were to make whole provinces one estate, should weary the forum with suits for one tree, for *one* furrow; should hate rancorously their friends and brethren?

41. Was it for this He sent souls, that they which shortly before had been gentle and ignorant *of what it is* to be moved by fierce passions, should build for themselves markets and amphitheatres, places of blood and open wickedness, in the one of which they should see men devoured and torn in pieces by wild beasts, *and* themselves slay others for no demerit but to please and gratify the spectators,[1] and should spend those very days on which such wicked deeds were done in general enjoyment, and keep holiday with festive gaiety; while in the other, again, they should tear asunder the flesh of wretched animals, some snatch one part, others another, as dogs and vultures do, should grind *them* with their teeth, and give to their utterly insatiable[2] maw, and that, surrounded by[3] faces so fierce and savage, those should bewail their lot whom the straits of poverty withheld from such repasts;[4] that their life should be[5] happy and prosperous while such barbarous doings defiled their mouths and face? Was it for this He sent souls, that, forgetting their importance and dignity *as* divine, they should acquire gems, precious stones, pearls, at the expense of their purity; should entwine their necks with these, pierce the tips of their ears, bind[6] their foreheads with fillets, seek for cosmetics[7] to deck their bodies,[8] darken their eyes with henna; nor, though in the forms of men, blush to curl their hair with crisping-pins, to make the skin of the body smooth, to walk with bare knees, and with every other *kind of* wantonness, both to lay aside the strength of their manhood, and to grow in effeminacy to a woman's habits and luxury?

42. Was it for this He sent souls, that some should infest the highways and roads,[9] others ensnare the unwary, forge[10] false wills, prepare poisoned draughts; that they should break open houses by night, tamper *with slaves*, steal and

drive away, not act uprightly, and betray *their trust* perfidiously; that they should strike out delicate dainties for the palate; that in cooking fowls they should know how to catch the fat as it drips; that they should make cracknels and sausages,[11] force-meats, tit-bits, Lucanian sausages, with these[12] a sow's udder and iced[13] puddings? Was it for this He sent souls, that beings[14] of a sacred and august race should here practise singing and piping; that they should swell out their cheeks in blowing the flute; that they should take the lead in singing impure songs, and raising the loud din of the castanets,[15] by which another crowd of souls should be led in their wantonness to abandon themselves to clumsy motions, to dance and sing, form rings of dancers, and finally, raising their haunches and hips, float along with a tremulous motion of the loins?

Was it for this He sent souls, that in men they should become impure, in women harlots, players on the triangle[16] and psaltery; that they should prostitute their bodies for hire, should abandon themselves to the lust of all,[17] ready in the brothels, to be met with in the stews,[18] ready to submit to anything, prepared to do violence to their mouth even?[19]

43. What say you, O offspring and descendants of the Supreme Deity? Did these souls, then, wise, and sprung from the first causes, become acquainted with such forms of baseness, crime, and bad feeling? and were they ordered to dwell here,[20] and be clothed with the garment of the human body, in order that they might engage in, might practise these evil *deeds*, and that very frequently? And is there a man with any sense of reason who thinks that the world was established because of them, and not rather that it

---

[1] So restored by Cujacius, followed by LB. and Orelli, reading *in grat-i-am* (MS. wants *i*) *voluptatemque*, while the first five edd. merely drop -*que* — " to the gratelul pleasure," etc.

[2] Lit., " most cruel."

[3] Lit., " among," *in oris*, the MS. reading, and that of the first four edd., for which the others have received from the margin of Ursinus *moribus* — " (indulging) in so fierce and savage customs."

[4] Lit., " tables."

[5] Lit., " they should live."

[6] Lit., " lessen."

[7] In the MS. this clause follows the words " loss of their purity," where it is very much in the way. Orelli has followed Heraldus in disposing of it as above, while LB. inserts it after " tips of their ears." The rest adhere to the arrangement of the MS., Ursinus suggesting instead of *his* — " with these," *catenis* — " with chains;" Heraldus, *linis* — " with strings (of pearls);" Stewechius, *tæniis* — " with fillets."

[8] So LB. and Orelli, reading *con-fic-iendis corporibus* for the MS. *con-sp-iendis*, for which the others read -*spic*-, " to win attention." A conjecture by Oudendorp, brought forward by Orelli, is worthy of notice — *con-spu-endis*, " to cover," i.e., so as to hide defects.

[9] Lit., " passages of ways."

[10] Lit., " substitute."

[11] So the later edd., reading *botulos;* the MS. and early edd. give *boletos* — " mushrooms."

[12] For *his*, Heinsius proposes *hiris* — " with the intestines."

[13] Lit., " in a frozen condition." As to the meaning of this there is difference of opinion: some supposing that it means, as above, preserved by means of ice, or at least frozen; while others interpret figuratively, " as hard as ice." [Our Scottish translators have used their local word, " iced *haggises:*" I have put *puddings* instead, which gives us, at least, an idea of something edible. To an American, what is *iced* conveys the idea of a drink. The *budinarius*, heretofore noted, probably made these iced *saucisses*.]

[14] Lit., " things " — *res*.

[15] *Scabilla* were a kind of rattles or castanets moved by the feet.

[16] *Sambuca*, not corresponding to the modern triangle, but a stringed instrument of that shape. Its notes were shrill and disagreeable, and those who played on it of indifferent character.

[17] So the MS. and first four edd., reading *virilitatem sui populo publicarent*. Meursius emended *utilitatem* — " made common the use," etc.; and Orelli, from the margin of Ursinus, *vilitatem* — " their vileness."

[18] The MS. reads *in fornicibus obvi-t-æ*, which, dropping *t*, is the reading translated, and was received by Elmenhorst, LB., and Hildebrand, from the margin of Ursinus. The other edd. insert *nc* before *t* — " bound."

[19] The translation does not attempt to bring out the force of the words *ad oris stuprum paratæ*, which are read by Orelli after Ursinus and Gelenius. The text is so corrupt, and the subject so obscene, that a bare reference to the practice may be sufficient.

[20] The MS. reads, *habitare atque habitare juss-e-r-unt*. All edd. omit the first two words, the first ed. without further change; but the active verb is clearly out of place, and therefore all other edd. read *jussæ sunt*, as above. Oehler, however, from *habitare* omitted by the others, would emend *aditare*, " to approach," — a conjecture with very little to recommend it.

was set up as a seat and home, in which every *kind of* wickedness should be committed daily, all evil deeds be done, plots, impostures, frauds, covetousness, robberies, violence, impiety, *all that is* presumptuous, indecent, base, disgraceful,[1] *and* all the other evil deeds which men devise over all the earth with guilty purpose, and contrive for each other's ruin?

44. But, you say, they came of their own accord, not sent[2] by their lord. And[3] where was the Almighty Creator, where the authority of His royal and exalted place,[4] to prevent their departure, and not suffer them to fall into dangerous pleasures? For if He knew that by change of place they would become base — and, as the arranger of all things,[5] He must have known — or that anything would reach them from without which would make them forget their greatness and moral dignity, — a thousand times would I beg of Him to pardon *my words*, — the cause of all is no other than Himself, since He allowed them to have freedom to wander[6] who He foresaw would not abide by their state of innocence; and thus it is brought about that it does not matter whether they came of their own accord, or obeyed His command, since in not preventing what should have been prevented, by His inaction He made the guilt His own, and permitted it before *it was done* by neglecting to withhold them *from action.*

45. But let this monstrous and impious fancy be put[7] far *from us*, that Almighty God, the creator and framer, the author[8] of things great and invisible, should be believed to have begotten souls so fickle, with no seriousness, firmness, and steadiness, prone to vice, inclining to all kinds of sins; and while He knew that they were such and of this character, to have bid[9] them enter into bodies, imprisoned in which,[10] they should live exposed to the storms and tempests of fortune every day, and now do mean things, now submit to lewd treatment; that they might perish by shipwreck, accidents, destructive conflagrations; that poverty might oppress some, beggary, others; that some might be torn in pieces by wild beasts, others perish by the venom of flies;[11]

that some might limp in walking, others lose their sight, others be stiff with cramped[12] joints; in fine, that they should be exposed to all the diseases which the wretched and pitiable human race endures with agony caused by[13] different sufferings; then that, forgetting that they have one origin, one father and head, they should shake to their foundations and violate the rights of kinship, should overthrow their cities, lay waste their lands as enemies, enslave the free, do violence to maidens and to other men's wives, hate each other, envy the joys and good fortune of others; and further, all malign, carp at, and tear each other to pieces with fiercely biting teeth.

46. But, to say the same things again and again,[14] let this belief, so monstrous and impious, be put far *from us*, that God, who preserves[15] all things, the origin of the virtues and chief in[16] benevolence, and, to exalt Him with human praise, most wise, just, making all things perfect, and that permanently,[17] either made anything which was imperfect and not quite correct,[18] or was the cause of misery or danger to any being, or arranged, commanded, and enjoined the very acts in which man's life is passed and employed to flow from His arrangement. These things are unworthy of[19] Him, and weaken the force of His greatness; and so far from His being believed to be their author, whoever imagines that man is sprung from Him is guilty of blasphemous impiety, *man*, a being miserable and wretched, who is sorry that he exists, hates and laments his state, and understands that he was produced for no other reason than lest evils should not have something[20] through which to spread themselves, and that there might always be wretched ones by whose agonies some unseen and cruel power,[21] adverse to men, should be gratified.

47. But, you say, if God is not the parent and father of souls, by what sire have they been begotten, and how have they been produced? If you wish to hear unvarnished statements not spun out with vain ostentation of words, we, too,[22] admit that we are ignorant of this, do not

---

[1] These are all substantives in the original.
[2] So the MS., reading *non missione* — "not by the sending;" but, unaccountably enough, all edd. except Hildebrand and Oehler read *jussione* — "not by the command."
[3] So the MS.
[4] Lit., "royal sublimity."
[5] Lit., "causes."
[6] The MS. and both Roman edd. read *abscondere* — "to hide," for which the other edd. read, as above, *abscedere*, from the margin of Ursinus.
[7] Lit., "go."
[8] By Hildebrand and Oehler, *procreator* is with reason regarded as a gloss.
[9] The MS., both Roman edd., and Hildebrand read *jussisset;* but this would throw the sentence into confusion, and the other edd. therefore drop *t*.
[10] LB., Hildebrand, and Oehler read *quorum indu-c-tæ corceribus* — "led into the prisons of which," all other edd. omitting *c* as above. According to Oehler, the MS. has the former reading.
[11] The MS. and both Roman edd. read *in-f-ernarum paterentut aliæ laniatus muscularum*, which has no meaning, and is little

improved by Galenius changing *ut* into *ur*, as no one knows what "infernal flies" are. LB. and Orelli, adopting a reading in the margin of Ursinus, change *intern.* into *ferarum*, and join *musc.* with the words which follow as above. Another reading, also suggested by Ursinus, seems preferable, however, *internorum . . . musculorum* — "suffer rendings (i.e., spasms) of the inner muscles."
[12] Lit., "bound."
[13] Lit., "dilaceration of."
[14] Lit., "again and more frequently."
[15] Lit., "the salvation of."
[16] Lit., "height of."
[17] Lit., "things perfect, and preserving the measure of their completeness;" i.e., continuing so.
[18] So the MS., LB., Oberthür, and Oehler, reading *claudum et quod minus esset a recto.* All other edd. read *eminus* — "at a distance from the right."
[19] Lit., "less than."
[20] Lit., "material."
[21] Lit., "some power latent and cruelty."
[22] So the MS. and all edd.; but Orelli would change *item* into *iterum*, not seeing that the reference is to the indicated preference of his opponents for the simple truth.

know it;[1] and we hold that, to know so great a matter, is not only beyond the reach of our weakness and frailty, but *beyond that* also of all the powers which are in the world, and which have usurped the place of deities in men's belief. But are we bound to show whose they are, because we deny that they are God's? That by no means[2] follows necessarily; for if we were to deny that flies, beetles, and bugs, dormice, weevils, and moths,[3] are made by the Almighty King, we should not be required in consequence to say who made and formed them; for without *incurring* any censure, we may not know who, indeed, gave them being, and *yet* assert that not by the Supreme[4] Deity were *creatures* produced so useless, so needless, so purposeless,[5] nay more, at times even hurtful, and causing unavoidable injuries.

48. Here, too, in like manner, when we deny that souls are the offspring of God Supreme, it does not necessarily follow that we are bound to declare from what parent they have sprung, and by what causes they have been produced. For who prevents us from being either ignorant of the source from which they issued and came, or aware that they are not God's descendants? By what method, you say, in what way? Because it is most true and certain[6] that, as has been pretty frequently said, nothing is effected, made, determined by the Supreme, except that which it is right and fitting should be done; except that which is complete and entire, and wholly perfect in its[7] integrity. But further, we see that men, that is, these very souls — for what are men but souls bound to bodies? — themselves show by perversely falling into[8] vice, times without number, that they belong to no patrician race, but have sprung from insignificant families. For we see some harsh, vicious, presumptuous, rash, reckless, blinded, false, dissemblers, liars, proud, overbearing, covetous, greedy, lustful, fickle, weak, and unable to observe their own precepts; but they would assuredly not be *so*, if their original goodness defended[9] them, and they traced their honourable descent from the head of the universe.

49. But, you will say, there are good men also in the world, — wise, upright, of faultless and purest morals. We raise no question as to whether there ever were any such, in whom this

very integrity which is spoken of was in nothing imperfect. Even if they are very honourable *men*, and have been worthy of praise, have reached the utmost height of perfection, and their life has never wavered and sunk into sin, yet we would have you tell us how many there are, or have been, that we may judge from their number whether a comparison[10] has been made *which is* just and evenly balanced.[11] One, two, three, four, ten, twenty, a hundred, yet *are they* at least limited in number, and it may be within the reach of names.[12] But it is fitting that the human race should be rated and weighed, not by a very few good men, but by all the rest *as well.* For the part is in the whole, not the whole in a part; and that which is the whole should draw to it its parts, not the whole be brought to its parts. For what if you were to say that a man, robbed of the use of all his limbs, and shrieking in bitter agony,[13] was quite well, because in[14] one little nail he suffered no pain? or that the earth is made of gold, because in one hillock there are a few small grains from which, when dissolved, gold is produced, and wonder excited at it when formed into a lump?[15] The whole mass shows the nature of an element, not particles fine as air; nor does the sea become forthwith sweet, if you cast or throw into *it* a few drops of less bitter water, for that small quantity is swallowed up in its immense mass; and it must be esteemed, not merely of little importance, but *even* of none, because, being scattered throughout all, it is lost and cut off in the immensity of the vast body *of water.*

50. You say that there are good men in the human race; and perhaps, if we compare them with the very wicked, we may be led[16] to believe that there are. Who are they, pray? Tell *us.* The philosophers, I suppose, who[17] assert that they alone are most wise, and who have been uplifted with pride from the meaning attached to this name,[18] — those, forsooth, who are striving with their passions every day, and struggling to drive out, to expel deeply-rooted passions from their minds by the persistent[19] opposition of their better qualities; who, that it may be impossible for them to be led into wickedness at the suggestion of some opportunity, shun riches

---

[1] *Nescire* Hildebrand, with good reason, considers a gloss.
[2] *Nihil* for the MS. *mihi,* which makes nonsense of the sentence.
[3] This somewhat wide-spread opinion found an amusing counterpart in the doctrines of Rorarius (mentioned by Bayle, *Dict. Phil.*), who affirmed that the lower animals are gifted with reason and speech, as we are.
[4] Lit., "superior."
[5] Lit., "tending to no reasons."
[6] *Omni vero verissimum est certoque certissimum* — the superlative for the comparative.
[7] Lit., "finished with the perfection of."
[8] Lit., "by perversity" — *s-c-œvitate,* the reading of the MS., LB., Orelli, Hild., and Oehler, all others omitting *c* — "by the rage;" except Stewechius, who reads *servitute* — "slavery."
[9] Or, perhaps, "the goodness of the Supreme planted" — *generositas eos adsereret principalis.*

[10] Lit., "opposition;" i.e., "the setting of one party against the other."
[11] Lit., "weighed with balancing of equality."
[12] Lit., "bounded by the comprehensions of names;" i.e., possibly, "the good are certainly few enough to be numbered, perhaps even to be named."
[13] So LB., reading *ex cruciatibus* for the MS. *scruc.*
[14] Lit., "of."
[15] Lit., "admiration is sought for by the putting together" — *congregatione.*
[16] Lit., "a comparison of the worst may effect that we," etc.
[17] So all edd. except Hildebrand, who gives as the reading of the MS., *qui-d* — "what! do they assert."
[18] Lit., "by the force of," *vi,* — an emendation of Heraldus for the MS. *in.*
[19] So most edd., reading *pertinaci* for the MS. *-ium* — "by the opposition of persistent virtues," which is retained in both Roman edd., Gelenius, Canterus, Hildebrand, and Oehler.

and inheritances, that they may remove[1] from themselves occasions of stumbling; but in doing this, and being solicitous about it, they show very clearly that *their* souls are, through their weakness, ready and prone to fall into vice. In our opinion, however, that which is good naturally, does not require to be either corrected or reproved;[2] nay more, it should not know what evil is, if the nature of each kind would abide in its own integrity, for neither can two contraries be implanted in each other, nor can equality be contained in inequality, nor sweetness in bitterness. He, then, who struggles to amend the inborn depravity of his inclinations, shows most clearly that he is imperfect,[3] blameable, although he may strive with all zeal and stedfastness.

51. But you laugh at our reply, because, while we deny that souls are of royal descent, we do not, on the other hand, say in turn from what causes and beginnings they have sprung. But what kind of crime is it either to be ignorant of anything, or to confess quite openly that you do not know that of which you are ignorant? or whether does he rather seem to you most deserving of ridicule who assumes to himself no knowledge of some dark subject; or he who thinks that he[4] knows most clearly that which transcends human knowledge, and which has been involved in dark obscurity? If the nature of everything were thoroughly considered, you too are in a position like that which you censure in our case. For you do not say anything *which has been* ascertained and set most clearly in the light of truth, because you say that souls descend from the Supreme Ruler Himself, and enter into the forms of men. For you conjecture, do not perceive[5] *this;* surmise, do not actually know *it;* for if to know is to retain in the mind that which you have yourself seen or known, not one of those things which you affirm can you say that you have ever seen — that is, that souls descend from the abodes and regions above. You are therefore making use of conjecture, not trusting clear information. But what is conjecture, except a doubtful imagining of things, and directing of the mind upon nothing accessible? He, then, who conjectures, does not comprehend,[5] nor does he walk in the[6] light of knowledge. But if this is true and certain in the opinion of proper and very wise judges, your conjectures, too, in which you trust, must be regarded as *showing your* ignorance.

52. And yet, lest you should suppose that none but yourselves can make use of conjectures and surmises, we too are able to bring them forward as well,[7] as your question is appropriate to either side.[8] Whence, you say, are men; and what or whence are the souls of these men? Whence, *we will ask*, are elephants, bulls, stags, mules,[9] asses? Whence lions, horses, dogs, wolves, panthers; and what or whence are the souls of these creatures? For it is not credible that from that Platonic cup,[10] which Timæus prepares and mixes, either their souls came, or *that* the locust,[11] mouse, shrew, cockroach, frog, centipede, should be believed to have been quickened and to live, because[12] they have a cause and origin of birth in[13] the elements themselves, if there are *in these* secret and very little known means[14] for producing the creatures which live in each of them. For we see that some of the wise say that the earth is mother of men, that others join with it water,[15] that others add to these breath of air, but that some *say* that the sun is their framer, and that, having been quickened by his rays, they are filled with the stir of life.[16] What if it is not these, and is something else, another cause, another method, another power, in fine, unheard of and unknown to us by name, which may have fashioned the human race, and connected it with things as established;[17] may it not be that men sprang up in this way, and that the cause of their birth does not go back to the Supreme God? For what reason do we suppose that the great Plato had — *a man* reverent and scrupulous in his wisdom — when he withdrew the fashioning of man from the highest God, and transferred it to some lesser *deities*, and when he would not have the souls of men formed[18] of that pure mixture of which he

---

[1] So Stewechius and later edd., reading *ut . . . auferant*, except Hildebrand, who gives as the MS. reading, *et . . . -unt* — "shun . . . and remove," etc. The first four edd. read *ne . . . afferant* — "that they may not bring upon themselves," etc.

[2] So the MS. and first four edd., Orelli (who, however, seems to have meant to give the other reading), and Oehler, reading *corri-p-i*, for which the others read *-igi* — "corrected," except Hildebrand, who without due reason gives *-rumpi* — "corrupted."

[3] In the MS. *imperfectum* is marked as a gloss, but is retained in all edd., while *improbabilem* is omitted, except in LB., when *im* is omitted, and *probabilem* joined to the next clause — "however he may strive to be acceptable," in order to provide an object for "strive;" and with a similar purpose Orelli thrusts in *contrarium*, although it is quite clear that the verb refers to the preceding clause, "struggles to amend."

[4] The MS. reads *se esse*, without meaning, from which LB., followed by Hildebrand, and Oehler derived *se ex se* — "himself of himself." The rest simply omit *esse* as above.

[5] Lit., "hold."

[6] Lit., "set in the."

[7] Lit., "utter the same (conjectures)," *easdem*, the reading of LB. and Hildebrand, who says that it is so in the MS.; while Crusius asserts that the MS. has *idem*, which, with Orelli's punctuation, gives — "we have the same power; since it is common (i.e., a general right) to bring forth what you ask," i.e., to put similar questions.

[8] i.e., may be retorted upon you.

[9] Here, as elsewhere, instead of *muli*, the MS. reads *milvi* — "kites."

[10] Cf. Plato, *Timæus*, st. p. 41, already referred to.

[11] Or, perhaps, "cray-fish," *locusta*.

[12] The MS. reads *quidem* — "indeed," retained by the first four edd., but changed into *quia* — "because," by Elmenhorst, LB., and Orelli, while Oehler suggests very happily *si quidem* — "if indeed," i.e., because.

[13] Lit., "from."

[14] *Rationes.*

[15] Cf. chs. 9 and 10 [p 416, *supra*].

[16] Orelli, retaining this as a distinct sentence, would yet enclose it in brackets, for what purpose does not appear; more especially as the next sentence follows directly from this in logical sequence.

[17] Lit., "the constitutions of things."

[18] Lit., "did not choose the souls of the human race to be mixtures of the same purity," *noluit*, received from the margin of Ursinus by

had made the soul of the universe, except that he thought the forming of man unworthy of God, and the fashioning of a feeble being not beseeming His greatness and excellence?

53. Since this, then, is the case, we do nothing out of place or foolish in believing that the souls of men are of a neutral character, inasmuch as they have been produced by secondary beings,[1] made subject to the law of death, *and are* of little strength, *and that* perishable ; and that they are gifted with immortality, if[2] they rest their hope of so great a gift on God Supreme, who alone has power to grant such *blessings*, by putting away corruption. But this, *you say*, we are stupid in believing. What *is that* to you? *In so believing, we act* most absurdly, sillily. In what do we injure you, or what wrong do we do or inflict upon you, if we trust that Almighty God will take care of us when we leave[3] our bodies, and from the jaws of hell, as is said, deliver us?

54. Can, then, anything be made, some one will say, without God's will? We[4] must consider carefully, and examine with no little pains, lest, while we think that we are honouring God[5] by such a question, we fall into the opposite sin, doing despite to His supreme majesty. In what way, *you ask*, on what ground? Because, if all things are brought about by His will, and nothing in the world can either succeed or fail contrary to His pleasure, it follows of necessity that it should be understood that[6] all evils, too, arise by His will. But if, on the contrary, we chose to say that He is privy to and produces no evil, not referring to Him the causes of very wicked deeds, the worst things will begin to seem to be done either against His will, or, a monstrous thing to say, while He knows it not, *but* is ignorant and unaware of them. But, again, if we choose to say that there are no evils, as we find some have believed and held, all races will cry out against *us* and all nations together, showing us their sufferings, and the various kinds of dangers with which the human race is every moment[7] distressed and afflicted. Then they will ask of us, Why, if there are no evils, do you refrain from certain deeds and actions? Why do you not do all that eager lust has required or demanded? Why, finally, do you establish punishments by terrible laws for the guilty? For what more monstrous[8] act of folly can be found than to assert that there are no evils, and *at the same time* to kill and condemn the erring as though they were evil?[9]

55. But when, overcome, we agree that there are these things,[10] and expressly allow that all human affairs are full of them, they will next ask, Why, then, the Almighty God does not take away these evils, but suffers them to exist and to go on without ceasing through all the ages?[11] If we have learned of God the Supreme Ruler, and have resolved not to wander in a maze of impious and mad conjectures, we must answer that we do not know these things, and have never sought and striven to know things which could be grasped by no powers *which we have*, and that we, even thinking it[12] preferable, rather remain in ignorance and want of knowledge than say that without God nothing is made, so that it should be understood that by His will[13] He is at once both the source of evil[14] and the occasion of countless miseries. Whence then, you will say, are all these evils? From the elements, say the wise, and from their dissimilarity ; but how it is possible that things which have not feeling and judgment should be held to be wicked or criminal ; or that he should not rather be wicked and criminal, who, to bring about some result, took what was afterwards to become very bad and hurtful,[15] — is for them to consider, who make the assertion. What, then, do we say? whence? There is no necessity that we should answer, for whether we are able to say *whence evil springs*, or our power fails us, and we are unable, in either case it is a small matter in our opinion ; nor do we hold it of much importance either to know or to be ignorant of it, being content to have laid down but one thing, — that

---

all except the first four edd., which retain the MS. *voluit* — "did choose," which is absurd. Arnobius here refers again to the passage in the *Timæus*, p. 41 sq., but to a different part, with a different purpose. He now refers to the conclusion of the speech of the Supreme God, the first part of which is noticed in ch. 36 (cf. p. 447, n. 20). There the Creator assures the gods He has made of immortality through His grace ; now His further invitation that they in turn should form men is alluded to. That they might accomplish this task, the dregs still left in the cup, in which had been mixed the elements of the world's soul, are diluted and given to form the souls of men, to which they attach mortal bodies.

[1] Lit., "things not principal." Orelli here quotes from Tertullian, *de Anim.*, xxiii., a brief summary of Gnostic doctrines on these points, which he considers Arnobius to have followed throughout this discussion.

[2] *Si* was first inserted in LB., not being found in the MS., though demanded by the context.

[3] Lit., "have begun to leave."

[4] The MS. and first three edd. read *vobis* — "you," corrected *nobis*, as above, by Ursinus.

[5] So the MS.; but most edd., following the Brussels transcript, read *dominum* — "Lord."

[6] *Ut* is omitted in the MS., first four edd., and Hild.

[7] So LB., reading *p-uncta* for the MS. *c-uncta.*

[8] So the MS., Hild., and Oehler, reading *imman-ior ;* LB., from the margin of Ursinus, *major* — "greater; " the rest, *inanior* — "more foolish."

[9] The difficulty felt by Arnobius as to the origin of evil perplexed others also; and, as Elmenhorst has observed, some of the Fathers attempted to get rid of it by a distinction between the evil of guilt and of punishment, — God being author of the latter, the devil of the former (Tertullian, *adv. Marcionem*, ii. 14). It would have been simpler and truer to have distinguished deeds, which can be done only if God will, from wickedness, which is in the sinful purpose of man's heart.

[10] i.e , ills.

[11] Lit., "with all the ages, in steady continuance."

[12] The MS., followed by Oehler alone, reads *ducetis* — "and you will think ;" while all the other edd. read, as above, *ducentes*.

[13] Here, too, there has been much unnecessary labour. These words — *per voluntatem* — as they immediately follow *sine deo dicere nihil fieri* — "to say that without God nothing is made" — were connected with the preceding clause. To get rid of the nonsense thus created, LB. emended *dei . . . voluntate* — "without God's will;" while Heraldus regards them as an explanation of *sine deo*, and therefore interprets the sentence much as LB. Orelli gets rid of the difficulty by calling them a gloss, and bracketing them. They are, however, perfectly in place, as will be seen above.

[14] Pl.

[15] It would not be easy to understand why Orelli omitted these words, if we did not know that they had been accidentally omitted by Oberthür also.

nothing proceeds from God Supreme which is hurtful and pernicious. This we are assured of, this we know, on this one truth of knowledge and science we take our stand, — that nothing is made by Him except that which is for the well-being of all, which is agreeable, which is very full of love and joy and gladness, which has unbounded and imperishable pleasures, which every one may ask in all his prayers to befall him, and think that otherwise [1] life is pernicious and fatal.

56. As for all the other things which are usually dwelt upon in inquiries and discussions — from what parents they have sprung, or by whom they are produced — we neither strive to know,[2] nor care to inquire or examine : we leave all things to their own causes, and do not consider that they have been connected and associated with that which we desire should befall us.[3] For what is there which men of ability do not dare to overthrow, to destroy,[4] from love of contradiction, although that which they attempt to invalidate is unobjectionable [5] and manifest, and evidently bears the stamp of truth? Or what, again, can they not maintain with plausible arguments, although it may be very manifestly untrue, although it may be a plain and evident falsehood? For when a man has persuaded himself that there is or is not something, he likes to affirm what he thinks, and to show greater subtlety than others, especially if the subject discussed is out of the ordinary track, and by nature abstruse and obscure.[6] Some of the wise think that the world was not created, and will never perish ; [7] some that it is immortal, although they say that it was created and made ; [8] while a third party have chosen to say that it both was created and made, and will perish as other things must.[9] And while of these three opinions one only must be true, they nevertheless all find arguments by which at once to uphold their own doctrines, and undermine and overthrow the dogmas of others. Some teach and declare that this same *world* is composed of four elements, others of two,[10] a third party of one ; some say that *it is composed of* none of these, and that atoms are that from which it is formed,[11] and its primary origin. And since of these opinions only one is true, but [12] not one of them certain, here too, in like manner, arguments present themselves to all with which they may both establish the truth of what they say, and show that there are some things false [13] in the others' opinions. So, too, some utterly deny the existence of the gods ; others say that they are lost in doubt as to whether they exist anywhere ; others, however, *say* that they do exist, but do not trouble themselves about human things ; nay, others maintain that they both take part in the affairs of men, and guide the course of earthly events.[14]

57. While, then, this is the case, and it cannot but be that only one of all these opinions is true, they all nevertheless make use of arguments in striving with each other, — and not one of them is without something plausible to say, whether in affirming his own views, or objecting to the opinions of others. In exactly the same way is the condition of souls discussed. For this one thinks that they both are immortal, and survive the end of our earthly life ; that one believes that they do not survive, but perish with the bodies themselves : the opinion of another, however, is that they suffer nothing immediately, but that, after the *form of* man has been laid aside, they are allowed to live a little longer,[15] *and* then come under the power of death. And while all these opinions cannot be alike true, yet all *who hold them* so support their case by strong and very weighty arguments, that you cannot find out anything which seems false to you, although on every side you see that things are being said altogether at variance with each other, and inconsistent from their opposition to each other ; [16] which assuredly would not happen, if man's curiosity could reach any certainty, or if that which seemed *to one* to have been really

---

[1] Lit., "that apart from these it is pernicious."

[2] It must be observed that this sentence is very closely connected with the last words of the preceding chapter, or the meaning may be obscured. The connection may be shown thus: This one thing — that God is author of no evil — we are assured of; but as for all other questions, we neither know, nor care to know, about them.

[3] This seems the most natural arrangement: but the edd. punctuate thus: "have been connected and associated with us for that which we desire." The last part of the sentence is decidedly obscure; but the meaning may perhaps be, that the circumstances of man's life which absorb so much attention and cause such strife, have no bearing, after all, upon his salvation.

[4] So the ms., reading *labefactare dissolvere;* the latter word, however, being marked as spurious.

[5] Lit., "pure."

[6] Lit., "hidden and enwrapt in darkness of nature," *abdita et caligine involuta naturæ,* — the reading of all edd. except Hild. and Oehler, who follow the ms. *abditæ cal.* — "enwrapt in darkness of hidden nature."

[7] This has been supposed to refer to Heraclitus, as quoted by Clem. Alex., *Stromata,* v. p. 469 B., where his words are, "Neither God nor man made the world; but there was always, and is, and will be, an undying flame laying hold of its limits, and destroying them;" on which cf. p. 437. n. 8, *supra.* Here, of course, fire does not mean that perceived by the senses, but a subtle, all-penetrating energy.

[8] Cf. ch. 52, p. 453.

[9] Lit., "by ordinary necessity." The Stoics (Diog. Laert., vii. 134) said that the world was made by God working on uncreated matter, and that it was perishable (§ 141), because made through that of which perception could take cognizance. Cf. ch. 31, n. 9, p. 446.

[10] Orelli thinks that there is here a confusion of the parts of the world with its elements, because he can nowhere find that any philosopher has fixed the number of the elements either above or below four. The Stoics, however (Diog. Laert., vii. 134), said "that the elements (ἀρχάς) of the world are two — the active and passive;" while, of course, the cosmic theories of the early philosophers affirm that the world sprang from one, and it seems clear enough that Arnobius here uses the word "element" in this sense.

[11] Lit., "its material."

[12] A conjecture of Meursius adopted by Oehler, merely dropping *u* from *aut* — "or," which is read in the ms. and edd.

[13] Lit., "refute falsities placed."

[14] Cf. Cicero, *de Nat. Deor.,* i. 1, 12, 19, 23, etc.

[15] Lit., "something is given to them to life." So the Stoics taught, although Chrysippus (cf. n. 9, ch. 31, p. 446) held that only the souls of the wise remained at all after death.

[16] The ms., first four edd., and Oehler read *et rerum contrarietatibus dissonare* — "and that they disagree from the oppositions of things." Hild. reads *dissonora,* a word not met with elsewhere, while the other edd. merely drop the last two letters, -*ra,* as above; a reading suggested in the margin of Ursinus.

discovered, was attested by the approval of all the others. It is therefore wholly [1] vain, a useless task, to bring forward something as though you knew it, or to wish to assert that you know that which, although it should be true, you see can be refuted ; or to receive that as true which it may be is not, and is brought forward as if by men raving. And it is rightly so, for we do not weigh and guess at [2] divine things by divine, but by human methods ; and just as we think that anything should have been made, so we assert that it must be.

58. What, then, are we alone ignorant? do we alone not know who is the creator, who the former of souls, what cause fashioned man, whence ills have broken forth, or why the Supreme Ruler allows them both to exist and be perpetrated, and does not drive them from the world? have you, indeed, ascertained and learned any of these things with certainty? If you chose to lay aside audacious [3] conjectures, can you unfold and disclose whether this world in which we dwell [4] was created or founded at some time? if it was founded and made, by what kind of work, pray, or for what purpose? Can you bring forward and disclose the reason why it does not remain fixed and immoveable, but is ever being carried round in a circular motion? whether it revolves of its own will and choice, or is turned by the influence of some power? what the place, too, and space is in which it is set and revolves, boundless, bounded, hollow, or [5] solid? whether it is supported by an axis resting on sockets at its extremities, or rather itself sustains by its own power, and by the spirit within it upholds itself? Can you, if asked, make it clear, and show most skilfully,[6] what opens out the snow into feathery flakes? what was the reason and cause that day did not, in dawning, arise in the west, and veil its light in the east? how the sun, too, by one and the same influence,[7] produces results so different, nay, even so opposite? what the moon is, what the stars? why, on the one hand, it does not remain of the same shape, or why it was right and necessary that these particles of fire should be set all over the world? why some [8] of them are small, others large and greater, — these have a dim light, those a more vivid and shining brightness?

59. If that which it has pleased us to know is within reach, and if such knowledge is open to all, declare to us,[9] and say how and by what means showers of rain are produced, so that water is held suspended in the regions above and in mid-air, although by nature it is apt to glide away, and so ready to flow and run downwards. Explain, I say, and tell what it is which sends the hail whirling *through the air*, which makes the rain fall drop by drop, which has spread out rain and feathery flakes of snow and sheets of lightning ; [10] whence the wind rises, and what it is ; why the changes of the seasons were established, when it might have been ordained that there should be only one, and one kind of climate, so that there should be nothing wanting to the world's completeness. What is the cause, what the reason, that the waters of the sea are salt ; [11] or that, of those on land, some are sweet, others bitter or cold? From what kind of material have the inner parts of men's bodies been formed and built up into firmness? From what have their bones been made solid? what made the intestines and veins shaped like pipes, and easily passed through? Why, when it would be better to give us light by several eyes, to *guard against* the risk of blindness, are we restricted to two? For what purpose have so infinite and innumerable kinds of monsters and serpents been either formed or brought forth? what purpose do owls serve in the world, — falcons, hawks? what other birds [12] and winged creatures? what the *different* kinds of ants and worms springing up to be a bane and pest in various ways? what fleas, obtrusive flies, spiders, shrew, and other mice, leeches, water-spinners? what thorns, briers, wild-oats, tares? what the seeds of herbs or shrubs, either sweet to the nostrils, or disagreeable in smell? Nay more, if you think that anything can be known or comprehended, say what wheat is, — spelt, barley, millet, the chick-pea, bean, lentil, melon, cumin, scallion, leek, onion? For *even* if they are useful to you, and are ranked among the different kinds of food, it is not a light or easy thing to know what each is, — why they have been formed with such shapes ; *whether* there was any necessity that they should not have had other tastes, smells, and colours than those which each has, or whether they could have taken others also ; further, what these very things are, — taste, I mean,[13] and the rest ; *and* from what relations they derive their differences of quality. From the elements, you say, and from the first beginnings of things. Are the elements, then,

---

[1] Lit., "a most vain thing," etc.

[2] So the MS., LB., Elmenh., Hild., and Oehler, reading *conjectamus*, the other edd. reading *commetamur* or *-imur* — "measure," except Gelenius and Canterus, who read *commentamur* — "muse upon."

[3] Lit., "audacity of."

[4] Lit., "world which holds us."

[5] The first five edd. insert the mark of interrogation after "hollow:" "Whether does a solid axis," etc.

[6] So the edd. except. Hild., who retains the MS. reading *in scientissime* — "most unskilfully" (the others omitting *in-*), and Oehler, who changes *e* into *i* — "and being most witless show," etc.

[7] Lit., "touch."

[8] So the later edd., reading from the margin of Ursinus *figi ?* *cur alia*, for the MS. *figuralia*, except LB., which reads *figurari* — "be formed."

[9] So the MS.; but all edd. except Hild. and Oehler omit *nobis*.

[10] So the MS., reading *folgora dilatarit*, followed by LB.

[11] *Salsa*, corrected from the MS. *sola*.

[12] *Alites et volucres ;* i.e., according to Orelli, the birds from whose flight auguries were drawn, as opposed to the others.

[13] So Heraldus, whose punctuation also is here followed, omitting *id est sapor* — "that is, taste," which Meursius and LB., followed by Orelli, amend, *ut est* — "as taste is" *in each thing*.

bitter or sweet? have they any odour or [1] stench, that we should believe that, from their uniting, qualities were implanted in their products by which sweetness is produced, or something prepared offensive to the senses?

60. Seeing, then, that the origin, the cause, the reason of so many and so important things, escapes you yourselves also, and that you can neither say nor explain what has been made, nor why and wherefore it should not have been *otherwise*, do you assail and attack our timidity, who confess that we do not know that which cannot be known, and who do not care to seek out and inquire into those things which it is quite clear cannot be understood, although human conjecture should extend and spread itself through a thousand hearts? And therefore Christ the divine, — although you are unwilling to allow it, — Christ the divine, I repeat, for this must be said often, that the ears of unbelievers may burst and be rent asunder, speaking in the form of man by command of the Supreme God, because He knew that men are naturally [2] blind, and cannot grasp the truth at all, or regard as sure and certain what they might have persuaded themselves as to things set before their eyes, and do not hesitate, for the sake of their [3] conjectures, to raise and bring up questions that cause much strife, — bade us abandon and disregard all these things of which you speak, and not waste our thoughts upon things which have been removed far from our knowledge, but, as much as possible, seek the Lord of the universe with the whole mind and spirit; be raised above these subjects, and give over to Him our hearts, as yet hesitating whither to turn; [4] be ever mindful of Him; and although no imagination can set Him forth as He is,[5] yet form some faint conception of Him. For *Christ said* that, of all who are comprehended in the vague notion of what is sacred and divine,[6] He alone is beyond the reach of doubt, alone true, and one about whom only a raving and reckless madman can be in doubt; to know whom is enough, although you have learned nothing besides; and if by knowledge you have indeed been related to [7] God, the head of the world, you have gained the true and most important knowledge.

61. What business of yours is it, He [8] says, to examine, to inquire who made man; what is the origin of souls; who devised the causes of ills; whether the sun is larger than the earth, or measures only a foot in breadth: [9] whether the moon shines with borrowed light, or from her own brightness, — things which there is neither profit in knowing, nor loss in not knowing? Leave these things to God, and allow Him to know what is, wherefore, or whence; whether it must have been or not; whether something always existed,[10] or whether it was produced at the first; whether it should be annihilated or preserved, consumed, destroyed, or restored in fresh vigour. Your reason is not permitted to involve you in such questions, and to be busied to no purpose about things so much out of reach. Your interests are in jeopardy, — the salvation, I mean,[11] of your souls; and unless you give yourselves to seek to know the Supreme God, a cruel death awaits you when freed from the bonds of body, not bringing sudden annihilation, but destroying by the bitterness of its grievous and long-protracted punishment.

62. And be not deceived or deluded with vain hopes by that which is said by some ignorant and most presumptuous pretenders,[12] that they are born of God, and are not subject to the decrees of fate; that His palace lies open to them if they lead a life of temperance, and that after death as men, they are restored without hindrance, as if to their father's abode; nor *by that* which the Magi [13] assert, that they have intercessory prayers, won over by which some powers make the way easy to those who are striving to mount to heaven; nor *by that* which Etruria holds out in the Acherontic books,[14] that souls become divine, and are freed from the law [15] of death, if the blood of certain animals is offered to certain deities. These are empty delusions, and excite vain desires. None but the Almighty God can preserve souls; nor is there any one besides who can give them length of days, and grant to them also a spirit which shall never die,[16] except He who alone is immortal and ever-

---

[1] *Vel* is here inserted in all edd., most of which read, as above, *oloris*, which is found in the MS., in later writing, for the original, *coloris* — "colour," retained by Ursinus, LB., and Oehler.

[2] Lit., "that the nature of man is."

[3] So the MS., according to Crusius, reading *nec pro suis*; while, according to Hild., the reading is *prorsus* — "and are utterly without hesitation," adopted in the edd. with the substitution of *et* for *nec* — "and that they altogether hesitate," which, besides departing from the MS., runs counter to the sense.

[4] Lit., "transfer to Him the undecided conversions of the breast."

[5] Lit., "He can be formed by no imagination."

[6] Lit., "which the obscurity of sacred divinity contains;" which Orelli interprets, "the most exalted being holds concealed from mortals."

[7] Lit., "and being fixed on."

[8] i.e., Christ.

[9] As Heraclitus is reported to have said.

[10] The MS., first five edd., and Oehler read *supernatum*, for which the other edd. read, as above, *semper natum*, from the margin of Ursinus. The soul is referred to.

[11] So the later edd., following Elmenhorst, who emended *dico* for the MS. *dici*, omitted by the first four edd.

[12] So most edd., reading *sciolis*, from the emendation of Gelenius; but the MS., first five edd., Hild., and Oehler read *scholis* — "by some schools, and (these) arrogating very much to themselves."

[13] Cf. ch. 13, p. 439; Plato, *Rep.*, ii. st. p. 364, where Glaucon speaks of certain fortune-telling vagrant seers, who persuade the rich that they have power with the gods, by means of charms and sacrifices, to cleanse from guilt; and also Origen, *contra Cels.*, i. 69, where the Magi are spoken of as being on familiar terms with evil powers, and thus able to accomplish whatever is within these spirits' power.

[14] Mentioned by Servius (on *Æn.*, viii. 399) as composed by Tages, cap. 69 [p. 460, *supra*], and seemingly containing directions as to expiatory sacrifices.

[15] Pl.

[16] Lit., "a spirit of perpetuity."

lasting, and restricted by no limit of time. For since all the gods, whether those who are real, or those who are merely said to be from hearsay and conjecture, are immortal and everlasting by His good-will and free gift, how can it be that others [1] are able to give that which they themselves have,[2] while they have it as the gift of another, bestowed by a greater power? Let Etruria sacrifice what victims it may, let the wise deny themselves all the pleasures of life,[3] let the Magi soften and soothe all *lesser* powers, *yet*, unless souls have received from the Lord of all things that which reason demands, and *does so by His* command, it [4] will hereafter deeply repent having made itself a laughing-stock,[5] when it begins to feel the approach [6] of death.

63. But if, my opponents say, Christ was sent by God for this end, that He might deliver unhappy souls from ruin and destruction, of what crime were former ages guilty which were cut off in their mortal state before He came? Can you, then, know what has become of these souls [7] of men who lived long ago? [8] whether they, too, have *not* been aided, provided, and cared for in some way? Can you, I say, know that which could have been learned through Christ's teaching; whether the ages are unlimited in number or not since the human race began to be on the earth; when souls were first bound to bodies; who contrived that binding,[9] nay, rather, who formed man himself; whither the souls of men who lived before us have gone; in what parts or regions of the world they were; whether they were corruptible or not; whether they could have encountered the danger of death, if Christ had not come forward as their preserver at their time of need? Lay aside these cares, and abandon questions to which you can find no answer.[10] The Lord's compassion has been shown to them, too, and the divine kindness [11] has been extended to [12] all alike; they have been preserved, have been delivered, and have laid aside the lot and condition of mortality. Of what kind, *my opponents ask*, what, when? If you were free from presumption, arrogance, and conceit, you might have learned long ago from this teacher.

64. But, *my opponents ask*, if Christ came as

the Saviour of men, as [13] you say, why [14] does He not, with uniform benevolence, free all without exception? *I reply*, does not He free all alike who invites all alike? or does He thrust back or repel any one from the kindness of the Supreme who gives to all alike the power of coming to Him, — to men of high rank, to the meanest slaves, to women, to boys? To all, He says, the fountain of life is open,[15] and no one is hindered or kept back from drinking.[16] If you are so fastidious as to spurn the kindly [17] offered gift, nay, more, if your wisdom is so great that you term those things which are offered by Christ ridiculous and absurd, why should He keep on inviting [18] *you*, while His only duty is to make the enjoyment of His bounty depend upon your own free choice? [19] God, Plato says, does not cause any one to choose his lot in life; [20] nor can another's choice be rightly attributed to any one, since freedom of choice was put in His power who made it. Must you be even implored to deign to accept the gift of salvation from God; and must God's gracious mercy be poured into your bosom while you reject it with disdain, and flee very far from it? Do you choose to take what is offered, and turn it to your own advantage? You will *in that case* have consulted your own interests. Do you reject with disdain, lightly esteem, and despise it? You will *in this case* have robbed yourself of the benefit of the gift.[21] God compels no one, terrifies no one with overpowering fear. For our salvation is not necessary to Him, so that He would gain anything or suffer any loss, if He either made us divine,[22] or allowed us to be annihilated and destroyed by corruption.

65. Nay, *my opponent* says, if God is powerful, merciful, willing to save us, let Him change our dispositions, and compel us to trust in His promises. This, then, is violence, not kindness nor the bounty of the Supreme God, but a childish

---

[1] i.e., than the Supreme God.
[2] Lit., " are."
[3] Lit., " all human things."
[4] i.e., reason.
[5] The MS. reads *fuisse me risui*, which has no meaning; corrected, *fuisse irrisui* in most edd., and *derisui* by Meursius, Hild., and Oehler, — the sense being in either case as above.
[6] Lit., " when it begins to approach to the feeling," *cum ad sensum;* so read by Gelenius for the unintelligible MS. *cum absens cum.*
[7] So the edd., reading *quid sit cum eis animis actum* for the MS. *cum ejus nimis.*
[8] Lit., " of ancient and very old men."
[9] So the MS., LB., Hild., and Oehler, reading *vinctionis;* the other edd. *junctionis* — " union."
[10] Lit., " unknown questions."
[11] Pl.
[12] Lit., " has run over."

[13] So the MS. and Oehler, reading *ut*, which is omitted in all other edd.; in this case, the words in italics are unnecessary.
[14] So Orelli, reading *cur* (*quur* in most edd.) for the MS. *quos.* Instead of *non* — " not," which follows, the MS., according to Oehler, reads *nos*, and he therefore changes *quos* into *quæso* — " I ask, does He free all of us altogether?"
[15] There is clearly no reference here to a particular passage of Scripture, but to the general tone of Christ's teaching: " Him that cometh unto me, I will in nowise cast out." Orelli, however, with his usual infelicity, wishes to see a direct reference, either to Christ's words to the woman of Samaria (John iv. 13-15), or, which is rather extraordinary, to John vi. 35-37: " I am the bread of life," etc. Cf. n. 9, p. 459.
[16] Lit., " the right of drinking."
[17] Lit., " the kindness of."
[18] Lit., " what waits He for, inviting," *quid invitans expectat;* the reading of the MS., both Roman edd., and Oehler. Gelenius, followed by Canterus and Elmenhorst, changed the last word into *peccat* — " in what does He sin," adopted by the other edd., with the addition of *in te* — "against you."
[19] Lit., " exposes under decision of your own right."
[20] Cf. Plato, *Rep.*, ii. st. p. 379: " of a few things God would be the cause, but of many He would not; " and x. st. p. 617 fin.
[21] So LB., Orelli, Oehler, adopting the emendation of Ursinus, *tu te muneris commoditate privaveris*, for the unintelligible reading of the MS., *tuti m. c. probaveris.*
[22] i.e., immortal, *deos*, so corrected by Gelenius for the MS. *deus* — " if either God made us."

and vain [1] strife in seeking to get the mastery. For what is so unjust as to force men who are reluctant and unwilling, to reverse their inclinations; to impress forcibly on their minds what they are unwilling *to receive*, and shrink from; to injure before benefiting, and to bring to another way of thinking and feeling, by taking away the former? You who wish yourself to be changed,[2] and to suffer violence, that you may do and may be compelled to take to yourself that which you do not wish, why do you refuse of your own accord to select that which you wish to do, when changed and transformed? I am unwilling, He says, and have no wish. What, then, do you blame God as though He failed you? do you wish *Him* to bring you help,[3] whose gifts and bounties you not only reject and shun, but term empty [4] words, and assail with jocose witticisms? Unless, then, *my opponent says*, I shall be a Christian, I cannot hope for salvation. It is just as you yourself say. For, to bring salvation and impart to souls what should be bestowed and must be added, *Christ* alone has had given into His charge and entrusted [5] to Him by God the Father, the remote and more secret causes being so disposed. For, as with you, certain gods have fixed offices, privileges, powers, and you do not ask from any of them what is not in his power and permitted to him, so it is the right of [6] Christ alone to give salvation to souls, and assign them everlasting life. For if you believe that father Bacchus can give a good vintage, *but* cannot give relief from sickness; if *you believe* that Ceres *can give* good crops, Æsculapius health, Neptune one thing, Juno [7] another, that Fortune, Mercury, Vulcan, are each the giver of a fixed and particular thing, — this, too, you must needs receive from us,[8] that souls can receive from no one life and salvation, except from Him to whom the Supreme Ruler gave this charge and duty. The Almighty Master of the world has determined that this should be the way of salvation, — this the door, so to say, of life; by Him [9] alone is there access to the light: nor may men either creep in or enter elsewhere, all other *ways* being shut up and secured by an impenetrable barrier.

66. So, then, even if you are pure, and have been cleansed from every stain of vice, have won over and charmed [10] those powers not to shut the ways against you and bar your passage when returning to heaven, by no efforts will you be able to reach the prize of immortality, unless by Christ's gift you have perceived what constitutes this very immortality, and have been allowed to enter on the true life. For as to that with which you have been in the habit of taunting us, that our religion is new,[11] and arose a few days ago, almost, and that you could not abandon the ancient faith which you had inherited from your fathers, and pass over to barbarous and foreign rites, this is urged wholly without reason. For what if in this way we chose to blame the preceding, even the most ancient ages, because when they discovered how to raise crops,[12] they despised acorns, and rejected with scorn the wild strawberry; because they ceased to be covered with the bark of trees and clad in the hides of wild beasts, after that garments of cloth were devised, more useful and convenient in wearing; or because, when houses were built, and more comfortable dwellings erected, they did not cling to their ancient huts, and did not prefer to remain under rocks and caves like the beasts of the field? It is a disposition possessed by all, and impressed on us almost from our cradles even, to prefer good things to bad, useful to useless things, and to pursue and seek that with more pleasure which has been generally regarded [13] as more *than usually* precious, and to set on that our hopes for prosperity and favourable circumstances.

67. Therefore, when you urge against us that we turn away from the religion [14] of past *ages*, it is fitting that you should examine why it is done, not what is done, and not set before you what we have left, but observe especially what we have followed. For if it is a fault or crime to change an opinion, and pass from ancient customs to new conditions and desires, this accusation holds against you too, who have so often changed your habits and mode of life, who have gone over to other customs and ceremonies, so that you are condemned by [15] past ages *as well as we*. Do you indeed have the people distributed into five [16] classes, as your ancestors once had? Do you ever elect magistrates by vote of the people? Do you know what military, urban,

---

[1] So most edd., reading *inanis* for the MS. *animi;* retained, though not very intelligible, in LB., while Hild. reads *anilis* — "foolish."
[2] So the MS. now reads *verti;* but this word, according to Pithœus, is in a later handwriting, and some letters have been erased.
[3] So the edd., reading *tibi desit? opem desideras tibi,* except Hild. and Oehler, who retain the MS. reading, *t. d. o. desideranti* — "as though He failed you desiring *Him* to bring help."
[4] So Ursinus, reading *in ania cognomines* for the MS. *in alia,* which Orelli would interpret, "call the reverse of the truth."
[5] Lit., "For the parts of bringing . . . has enjoined and given over," *partes . . . injunctum habet et traditum,* where it will be important to notice that Arnobius, writing rapidly, had carried with him only the general idea, and forgotten the mode in which this was expressed.
[6] *Pontificium.*
[7] Here, too, according to Pithœus, there are signs of erasure.
[8] i.e., admit.
[9] This passage at once suggests John x. 9 and xiv. 6, and it is therefore the more necessary to notice the way in which Arnobius speaks ("so to say"), which is certainly not the tone of one quoting a passage with which he is well acquainted. [Elucidation I.]

[10] Lit., "bent."
[11] Cf. i. 13 and 58.
[12] Lit., "crops being invented."
[13] So the later edd., reading *constiterit* from the margin of Ursinus; but in the MS. and first four edd. the reading is *constituerit* — "has established," for which there is no subject.
[14] So the later edd., reading *aversionem ex* (LB., and preceding edd. *a*) *religione* for the MS. *et religionem* — "against us the hatred and religion of past ages."
[15] Lit., "with the condemnation of."
[16] This shows that the division of the people into classes was obsolete in the time of Arnobius.

and common [1] comitia are? Do you watch the sky, or put an end to public business because evil omens are announced? When you are preparing for war,[2] do you hang out a flag from the citadel, or practise the forms of the Fetiales, solemnly[3] demanding the return of what has been carried off? or, when encountering the dangers of war, do you begin to hope also, because of favourable omens from the points of the spears?[4] In entering on office, do you still observe the laws fixing the proper times? with regard to gifts and presents *to advocates, do you observe* the Cincian and the sumptuary laws in restricting your expenses? Do you maintain fires, ever burning, in gloomy sanctuaries?[5] Do you consecrate tables by putting on them salt-cellars and images of the gods? When you marry, do you spread the couch with a toga, and invoke the *genii* of husbands? do you arrange the hair of brides with the *hasta cælibaris?* do you bear the maidens' garments to the temple of Fortuna Virginalis? Do your matrons work in the halls of your houses, showing their industry openly? do they refrain from drinking wine? are their friends and relations allowed to kiss them, in order to show that they are sober and temperate?

68. On the Alban hill, it was not allowed in ancient times to sacrifice any but snow-white bulls: have you not changed that custom and religious observance, and *has it not been* enacted by decree of the senate, that reddish ones may be offered? While during the reigns of Romulus and Pompilius the inner parts, having been quite thoroughly cooked and softened, were burnt up *in sacrificing* to the gods, did you not begin, under king Tullius,[6] to hold them out half-raw and slightly warm, paying no regard to the former usage? While before the arrival of Hercules in Italy supplication was made to father Dis and Saturn with the heads of men by Apollo's advice; have you not, in like manner, changed this custom too, by means of cunning deceit and ambiguous names?[7] Since, then, yourselves also have followed at one time these customs, at another different laws, and have repudiated and rejected many things on either perceiving your mistakes or seeing something better, what have we done contrary to com-

mon sense and the discretion all men have, if we have chosen what is greater and more certain, and have not suffered ourselves to be held back by unreasoning respect for impostures?

69. But our name is new, *we are told*, and the religion which we follow arose but a few days ago. Granting for the present that what you urge against us is not untrue, what is there, *I would ask*, among the affairs of men that is either done by bodily exertion and manual labour, or attained by the mind's learning and knowledge, which did not begin at some time, and pass into general use and practice since then? Medicine,[8] philosophy, music, and all the other arts by which social life has been built up and refined, — were these born with men, and did they not rather begin to be pursued, understood, and practised lately, nay, rather, but a short time since? Before the Etruscan Tages saw the [9] light, did any one know or trouble himself to know and learn what meaning there was in the fall of thunderbolts, or in the veins of the victims sacrificed? [10] When did the motion of the stars or the art of calculating nativities begin to be known? Was it not after Theutis [11] the Egyptian; or after Atlas, as some say, the bearer, supporter, stay, *and* prop of the skies?

70. But why do I *speak of* these trivial things? The immortal gods themselves, whose temples you now enter *with reverence*, whose deity you suppliantly adore, did they not at certain times, as is handed down by your writings and traditions, begin to be, to be known and to be invoked by names and titles which were given to them? For if it is true that Jupiter with his brothers was born of Saturn and his wife, before Ops was married and bore children Jupiter had not existed both the Supreme and the Stygian,[12] no, nor the lord of the sea, nor Juno, nay more, no one inhabited the heavenly seats except the two parents; but from their union *the other gods* were conceived and born, and breathed the breath of life. So, then, at a certain time the god Jupiter began to be, at a certain time to merit worship and sacrifices, at a certain time to be set above his brothers in power.[13] But, again, if Liber, Venus, Diana, Mercury, Apollo, Hercules, the Muses, the Tyndarian brothers,[14] and Vulcan the lord of fire, were begotten by father Jupiter, and born of a parent sprung from Saturn, before that Memory, Alcmena, Maia, Juno, Latona, Leda, Dione, and Semele also bore children to Dies-

---

[1] Turnebus has explained this as merely another way of saying the *comitia centuriata, curiata* and *tributa.*

[2] So the edd., reading *cum paratis bella* (Oehler reads *reparantes*) for the MS. *reparatis.*

[3] i.e., *per clarigationem,* the solemn declaration of war, if restitution was not made within thirty-three days.

[4] This seems the most natural way to deal with the clause *et ex acuminibus auspicatis,* looking on the last word as an adjective, not a verb, as most edd. seem to hold it. There is great diversity of opinion as to what this omen was.

[5] The MS. reads *in penetralibus et coliginis.* LB., followed by Orelli, merely omits *et,* as above, while the first five edd. read *in pen. Vestæ ignis.* — "do you maintain the hearths of Vesta's fire." Many other readings and many explanations of the passage are also proposed.

[6] i.e., Servius Tullius. The first four edd. read *Tullo,* i.e., Tullus Hostilius.

[7] Cf. v. c. 1.

[8] The MS. reads *edi in filosophia;* the first four edd., *Philos.;* Elmenh. and Orelli, *Etenim phil.* — "For were phil.;" LB., *Ede an phil.* — "say whether phil.," which is, however, faulty in construction, as the indicative follows. Rigaltius, followed by Oehler, emended as above, *Medicina phil.*

[9] Lit., "reached the coasts of."

[10] Lit., "of the intestines" — *extorum.*

[11] In both Roman edd., *Theutatem,* i.e., Theutas. Cf. Plato, *Phædrus,* st. p. 274.

[12] i.e., Pluto.

[13] Pl.

[14] Lit., "Castors," i.e., Castor and Pollux.

piter; these *deities*, too, were nowhere in the world, nor in any part of the universe, but by Jupiter's embraces they were begotten and born, and began to have some sense of their own existence. So then, these, too, began to be at a certain time, and to be summoned among the gods to the sacred rites. This we say, in like manner, of Minerva. For if, as you assert, she burst forth from Jupiter's head ungenerated,[1] before Jupiter was begotten, and received in his mother's womb the shape and outline of his body,[2] it is quite certain that Minerva did not exist, and was not reckoned among things or as existing at all; but from Jove's head she was born, and began to have a real existence. She therefore has an origin at the first, and began to be called a goddess at a certain time, to be set up in temples, and to be consecrated by the inviolable obligations of religion. Now as this is the case, when you talk of the novelty of our religion, does your own not come into your thoughts, and do you not take care to examine when your gods sprung up, —what origins, what causes they have, or from what stocks they have burst forth and sprung? But how shameful, how shameless it is to censure that in another which you see that you do yourself, — to take occasion to revile and accuse *others* for things which can be retorted upon you in turn!

71. But our rites are[3] new; yours are ancient, and of excessive antiquity, *we are told*. And what help does that give you, or how does it damage our cause and argument? The belief[4] which we hold is new; some day even it, too, will become old: yours is old; but when it arose, it was new and unheard of. The credibility of a religion, however, must not be determined by its age, but by its divinity; and you should consider not when, but what you began to worship. Four hundred years ago, my opponent says, your religion did not exist. And two thousand years ago, *I reply*, your gods did not exist. By what reckoning, *you ask*, or by what calculations, can that be inferred? They are not difficult, not intricate, but can be seen by any one who will take them in hand even, as the saying is. Who begot Jupiter and his brothers? Saturn with Ops, as you relate, sprung from Cœlus and Hecate. Who begot Picus, the father of Faunus and grandfather of Latinus? Saturn, as you again hand down by your books and teachers? Therefore, if this is the case, Picus and Jupiter are in consequence united by the bond of kinship, inasmuch as they are sprung from one stock and race. It is clear, then, that what we say is true. How many steps are there in com-

ing down[5] from Jupiter and Picus to Latinus? Three, as the line of succession shows. Will you suppose Faunus, Latinus, and Picus to have each lived a hundred and twenty years, for beyond this it is affirmed that man's life cannot be prolonged? The estimation is well grounded and clear. There are, then, three hundred and sixty years after these?[6] It is just as the calculation shows. Whose father-in-law was Latinus? Æneas'. Whose father *was* he?[7] *He was father* of the founder of the town Alba. How many years did kings reign in Alba? Four hundred and twenty almost. Of what age is the city Rome shown to be in the annals? It reckons ten[8] hundred and fifty years, or not much less. So, then, from Jupiter, who is the brother of Picus and father of the other and lesser gods, down to the present time, there are nearly, or to add a little to the time, altogether, two thousand years. Now since this cannot be contradicted, not only is the religion to which you adhere shown to have sprung up lately; but *it is also shown* that the gods themselves, to whom you heap up bulls and other victims at the risk of bringing on disease, are young and little children, who should still be fed with their mothers' milk.[9]

72. But your religion precedes ours by many years, and is therefore, *you say*, truer, because it has been supported by the authority of antiquity. And of what avail is it that it should precede *ours* as many years as you please, since it began at a certain time? or what[10] are two thousand years, compared with so many thousands of ages? And yet, lest we should seem to betray *our* cause by so long neglect, say, if it does not annoy you, does the Almighty and Supreme God seem to you to be something new; and do those who adore and worship Him *seem to you* to support and introduce an unheard-of, unknown, and upstart religion? Is there anything older than Him? or can anything be found preceding Him in being,[11] time, name? Is not He alone uncreated, immortal, and everlasting? Who is the head[12] and fountain of things? is not He? To whom does eternity owe its name? is it not to Him? Is it not because He is everlasting, that the ages go on without end? This is beyond doubt, and true: *the religion* which we follow is not new, then, but we have been late in learning what we should follow and revere, or where we should

---

[1] i.e., *sine ullius seminis jactu.*
[2] Lit., "forms of bodily circumscription."
[3] Lit., "what we do is."
[4] Lit., "thing."

[5] Lit., "how many steps are there of race."
[6] i.e., Jupiter and Picus.
[7] The MS. reads *genitor . . . Latinus cujus,* some letters having been erased. The reading followed above — *genitor is cujus* — was suggested to Canterus by his friend Gifanius, and is found in the margin of Ursinus and Orelli.
[8] Cf. above, "four hundred years ago," etc., and i. ch. 13. It is of importance to note that Arnobius is inconsistent in these statements. [In the Edinburgh edition we have here "fifteen hundred years;" but it was changed, in the *Errata*, to ten hundred and fifty.]
[9] Lit., "be nursed with the breasts and dropt milk."
[10] Lit., "of what space."
[11] i.e., *re.*
[12] So the MS., according to Crusius and Livineius, reading *ac;* all edd. except Oehler read *aut* — "head (i.e., source) or fountain."

both fix our hope of salvation, and employ the aid *given* to save us. For He had not yet shone forth who was to point out the way to those wandering *from it,* and give the light of knowledge to those who were lying in the deepest darkness, and dispel the blindness of their ignorance.

73. But are we alone in this position?[1] What! have you not introduced into the number of your gods the Egyptian deities named Serapis and Isis, since the consulship of Piso and Gabinius?[2] What! did you not begin both to know and be acquainted with, and to worship with remarkable honours, the Phrygian mother — who, it is said, was first set up as a goddess by Midas or Dardanus — when Hannibal, the Carthaginian, was plundering Italy and aiming at the empire of the world?[3] Are not the sacred rites of mother Ceres, which were adopted but a little while ago, called Græca because they were unknown to you, their name bearing witness to their novelty? Is it not said[4] in the writings of the learned, that the rituals of Numa Pompilius do not contain the name of Apollo? Now it is clear and manifest from this, that he, too, was unknown to you, but that at some time afterwards he began to be known also. If any one, therefore, should ask you why you have so lately begun to worship those deities whom we mentioned just now, it is certain that you will reply, either because we were *till* lately not aware that they were gods, or because we have now been warned by the seers, or because, in very trying circumstances, we have been preserved by their favour and help. But if you think that this is well said by you, you must consider that, on our part, a similar reply has been made. Our religion has sprung up just now; for now He has arrived who was sent to declare it to us, to bring *us* to its truth; to show what God is; to summon us from mere conjectures, to His worship.

74. And why, *my opponent* says, did God, the Ruler and Lord *of the universe,* determine that a Saviour, Christ, should be sent to you from the heights of heaven a few hours ago, as it is said? We ask you too, on the other hand, what cause, what reason is there that the seasons sometimes do not recur at their own months, but that winter, summer, and autumn come too late? why, after the crops have been dried up and the corn[5] has perished, showers sometimes fall which should

have dropped on them while yet uninjured, and made provision for the wants of the time? Nay, this we rather ask, why, if it were fitting that Hercules should be born, Æsculapius, Mercury, Liber, and some others, that they might be both added to the assemblies of the gods, and might do men some service, — why they were produced so late by Jupiter, that only later ages should know them, while the past ages[6] of those who went before knew them not? You will say that there was some reason. There was then some reason here also that the Saviour of our race came not lately, but to-day. What, then, *you ask,* is the reason? We do not deny that we do not know. For it is not within the power of any one to see the mind of God, or the way in which He has arranged His plans.[7] Man, a blind creature, and not knowing himself even, can[8] in no way learn what should happen, when, or what its nature is: the Father Himself, the Governor and Lord of all, alone knows. Nor, if I have been unable to disclose to you the causes why something is done in this way or that, does it straightway follow, that what has been done becomes not done, and that a thing becomes incredible, which has been shown to be beyond doubt by such[9] virtues and[10] powers.

75. You may object and rejoin, Why was the Saviour sent forth so late? In unbounded, eternal ages, *we reply,* nothing whatever should be spoken of as late. For where there is no end and no beginning, nothing is too soon,[11] nothing too late. For time is perceived from its beginnings and endings, which an unbroken line and endless[12] succession of ages cannot have. For what if the things themselves to which it was necessary to bring help, required that as a fitting time? For what if the condition of antiquity was different from that of later times? What if it was necessary to give help to the men of old in one way, to provide for their descendants in another? Do ye not hear your own writings read, telling that there were once men *who were* demi-gods, heroes with immense and huge bodies? Do you not read that infants on their mothers' breasts shrieked like Stentors,[13] whose bones, when dug up in different parts of the

---

[1] The ms. reads unintelligibly *vertitur solæ;* for which LB., followed by the later edd., reads, as above, *vertimur soli.*

[2] Dr. Schmitz (Smith's *Dict., s. v.* Isis) speaks of these consuls as heading the revolt against the decree of the senate, that the statues of Isis and Serapis should be removed from the Capitol. The words of Tertullian (quoting Varro as his authority) are very distinct: " The consul Gabinius . . . gave more weight to the decision of the senate than the popular impulse, and forbade their altars (i.e., those of Serapis, Isis, Arpocrates, and Anubis) to be set up" (*ad Nationes,* i. 10, cf. *Apol.,* 6).

[3] Cf. vii. 49.

[4] Lit., " contained."

[5] Pl.

[6] Lit., " antiquity."

[7] Lit., " things."

[8] So Gelenius emended the ms., reading *potens* — " being able," which he changed into *potest,* as above, followed by later edd.

[9] Lit., " by such kinds of."

[10] The ms. and first edd. read *et potestatibus potestatum* — " and by powers of powers;" the other edd. merely omit *potestatibus,* as above, except Oehler, who, retaining it, changes *potestatum* into *protestata* — " being witnessed to by," etc.; but there is no instance adduced in which the participle of this verb is used passively.

[11] These words having been omitted by Oberthür, are omitted by Orelli also, as in previous instances.

[12] The ms. and first ed. read *etiam moderata continuatio;* corrected, *et immod. con.* by Gelenius.

[13] So the edd., reading *infantes stentoreos,* except Oehler, who retains the ms. reading *centenarios,* which he explains as " having a hundred " heads or hands, as the case might be, e.g., Typhon, Briareus, etc.

earth, have made the discoverers almost doubt that they were the remains of human limbs? So, then, it may be that Almighty God, the only God, sent forth Christ then indeed, after that the human race, *becoming* feebler, weaker, began to be such as we are. If that which has been done now could have been done thousands of years ago, the Supreme Ruler would have done it ; or if it had been proper, that what has been done now should be accomplished as many thousands after this, nothing compelled God to anticipate the necessary lapse[1] of time. His plans[2] are executed in fixed ways ; and that which has been once decided on, can in no wise be changed again.[3]

76. Inasmuch then, you say, as you serve the Almighty God, and trust that He cares for your safety and salvation, why does He suffer you to be exposed to such storms of persecution, and to undergo all kinds of punishments and tortures? Let us, too, ask in reply, why, seeing that you worship so great and so innumerable gods, and build temples to them, fashion images of gold, sacrifice herds of animals, *and* all heap up[4] boxfuls of incense on the already loaded altars, why you live subject to so many dangers and storms *of calamity*, with which many fatal misfortunes vex you every day? Why, I say, do your gods neglect to avert from you so many kinds of disease and sickness, shipwrecks, downfalls, conflagrations, pestilences, barrenness, loss of children, and confiscation of goods, discords, wars, enmities, captures of cities, and the slavery of those who are robbed of their rights of free birth?[5] But, *my opponent says*, in such mischances we, too, are in no wise helped by God. The cause is plain and manifest. For no hope has been held out to us with respect to this life, nor has any help been promised or[6] aid decreed us for what belongs to the husk of this flesh, — nay, more, we have been taught to esteem and value lightly all the threats of fortune, whatever they be ; and if ever any very grievous calamity has assailed *us*, to count as pleasant in *that* misfortune[7] the end which must follow, and not to fear or flee from it, that we may be the more

easily released from the bonds of the body, and escape from our darkness and[8] blindness.

77. Therefore that bitterness of persecution of which you speak is our deliverance and not persecution, and our ill-treatment will not bring evil upon us, but will lead us to the light of liberty. As if some senseless and stupid fellow were to think that he never punished a man who had been put into prison[9] with severity and cruelty, unless he were to rage against the very prison, break its stones in pieces, and burn its roof, its wall, its doors ; and strip, overthrow, and dash to the ground its other parts, not knowing that thus he was giving light to him whom he seemed to be injuring, and was taking from him the accursed darkness : in like manner, you too, by the flames, banishments, tortures, and monsters with which you tear in pieces and rend asunder our bodies, do not rob us of life, but relieve us of our skins, not knowing that, as far as you assault and seek to rage against these our shadows and forms, so far you free us from pressing and heavy chains, and cutting our bonds, make us fly up to the light.

78. Wherefore, O men, refrain from obstructing what you hope for by vain questions ; nor should you, if anything is otherwise than you think, trust your own opinions rather than that which should be reverenced.[10] The times, full of dangers, urge us, and fatal penalties threaten us ; let us flee for safety to God our Saviour, without demanding the reason of the offered gift. When that at stake is our souls' salvation and our own interests, something must be done even without reason, as Arrhianus approves of Epictetus having said.[11] We doubt, we hesitate, and suspect the credibility of what is said ; let us commit ourselves to God, and let not our incredulity prevail more with us than the greatness of His name and power, lest, while we are seeking out arguments for ourselves, through which that may seem false which we do not wish and deny to be true, the last day steal upon us, and we be found in the jaws of our enemy, death.

---

1 Lit., " measure."
2 Lit., " things."
3 Lit., " can be changed with no novelty."
4 Lit., " provide," *conficiatis*, which, however, some would understand " consume."
5 Lit., " slaveries, their free births being taken away."
6 Lit., " and."
7 So the MS., first five edd., Hild., and Oehler, reading *adscribere infortunio voluptatem*, which is omitted in the other edd. as a gloss which may have crept in from the margin.

8 Lit., " our dark."
9 The MS. and both Roman edd. read *in carcerem natum ingressum ;* LB. and later edd. have received from the margin of Ursinus the reading translated above, *datum*, omitting the last word altogether, which Oehler, however, would retain as equivalent to " not to be passed from."
10 Lit., " than an august thing."
11 Orelli refers to Arrh., i. 12; but the doctrine there insisted on is the necessity of submission to what is unavoidable. Oehler, in addition, refers to Epict., xxxii. 3, where, however, it is merely attempted to show that when anything is withheld from us, it is just as goods are unless paid for, and that we have therefore no reason to complain. Neither passage can be referred to here, and it seems as though Arnobius has made a very loose reference which cannot be specially identified.

BOOK III.

1. All these charges, then, which might truly be better termed abuse, have been long answered with sufficient fulness and accuracy by men of distinction in this respect, and worthy to have learned the truth ; and not one point of any inquiry has been passed over, without being determined in a thousand ways, and on the strongest grounds. We need not, therefore, linger further on this part of the case. For neither is the Christian religion unable to stand though it found no advocates, nor will it be therefore proved true if it found many to agree with it, and gained weight through its adherents.[1] Its own strength is sufficient for it, and it rests on the foundations of its own truth, without losing its power, though there were none to defend it, nay, though all voices assailed and opposed it, and united with common rancour to destroy all faith[2] in it.

2. Let us now return to the order from which we were a little ago compelled to diverge, that our defence may not, through its being too long broken off, be said to have given our detractors cause to triumph in the establishing of their charge. For they propose these questions : If you are in earnest about religion, why do you not serve and worship the other gods with us, or share your sacred rites with your fellows, and put the ceremonies of the *different* religions on an equality? We may say for the present : In essaying to approach the divine, the Supreme Deity[3] suffices us, — the Deity, I say, who is supreme, the Creator and Lord of the universe, who orders and rules all things : in Him we serve all that requires our service ; *in Him* we worship all that should be adored, — venerate[4] that which demands the homage of our reverence. For as we lay hold of the source of the divine itself, from which the very divinity of all gods whatever is derived,[5] we think it an idle task to approach each personally, since we neither know who they are, nor the names by which they are called ; and are further unable to learn, and discover, and establish their number.

3. And as in the kingdoms of earth we are in no wise constrained expressly to do reverence to those who form the royal family as well as to the sovereigns, but whatever honour belongs to them is found to be tacitly[6] implied in the homage offered to the kings themselves ; in just the same way, these gods, whoever they be, for whose existence you vouch, if they are a royal race, and spring from the Supreme Ruler, even though we do not expressly do them reverence, yet feel that they are honoured in common with their Lord, and share in the reverence shown to Him. Now *it must be remembered that* we have made this statement, on the hypothesis only that it is clear and undeniable, that besides the Ruler and Lord Himself, there are still other beings,[7] who, when arranged and disposed in order, form, as it were, a kind of plebeian mass. But do not seek to point out to us pictures instead of gods in your temples, and the images *which you set up*, for you too know, but are unwilling and refuse to admit, that these are formed of most worthless clay, and are childish figures made by mechanics. And when we converse with you on religion, we ask you to prove this, that there are other gods *than the one Supreme Deity* in nature, power, name, not as we see them manifested in images, but in such a substance as it might fittingly be supposed that perfection of so great dignity should reside.

4. But we do not purpose delaying further on this part of the subject, lest we seem desirous to stir up most violent strife, and engage in agitating contests.

Let there be, as you affirm, that crowd of deities, let there be numberless families of gods ; we assent, agree, *and* do not examine *too* closely, nor in any part of the subject do we assail the doubtful and uncertain positions you hold. This, however, we demand, and ask you to tell us, whence you have discovered, or how you have learned, whether there are these gods,[8] whom you believe to be in heaven and serve, or some others unknown by reputation and name? For it may be that beings exist whom you do not believe to do so ; and that those of whose existence you feel assured, are found nowhere in the universe. For you have at no time been borne aloft to the stars of heaven, *at no time*

---

[1] The MS., followed by Oehler, reads *neque enim res stare . . . non potest, Christiana religio aut* — "for neither can a thing not stand, . . . nor will the Christian religion," etc., while L.B. merely changes *aut* into *et* — "for neither can a thing, i e., the Christian religion, . . . nor will it," etc. All other edd. read as above, omitting *at.*

[2] According to Crusius and others, the MS. reads *finem ;* but, according to Hild., *fidem*, as above.

[3] *Deus primus*, according to Nourry, in relation to Christ; but manifestly from the scope of the chapter, God as the fountain and source of all things.

[4] Lit., " propitiate with venerations."

[5] So the MS., reading *ducitur ;* for which Oberthür, followed by Orelli, reads *dicitur* — " is said."

[6] Lit., " whatever belongs to them feels itself to be comprehended with a tacit rendering also of honour in," etc., *tacita et se sentit honorificentia*, read by later edd. for the MS. *ut se sentit* — " but as whatever," retained by Hild. and Oehler; while the first four edd. read *vi* — " feels itself with a silent force comprehended in the honour in," etc.

[7] So LB. and Orelli, reading *alia etiamnum capita* for the MS. *alienum capita*, read in the first five edd., *alia non capita* — " are others not chiefs; " Hild., followed by Oehler, proposes *alia deûm capita* — " other gods."

[8] According to Orelli's punctuation, " whether there are these gods in heaven whom," etc.

have seen the face and countenance of each; and *then* established here the worship of the same gods, whom you remembered to be there, as having been known and seen *by you*. But this, too, we again would learn from you, whether they have received these names by which you call them, or assumed them themselves on the days of purification.[1] If these are divine and celestial names, who reported them to you? But if, on the other hand, these names have been applied to them by you, how could you give names to those whom you never saw, and whose character or circumstances you in no wise[2] knew?

5. But *let it be assumed* that there are these gods, as you wish and believe, and are persuaded; let them be called also by those names by which the common people suppose that those meaner *gods*[3] are known.[4] Whence, however, have you learned who make up the list *of gods* under these names?[5] have any ever become familiar and known *to others* with whose names you were not acquainted?[6] For it cannot be easily known whether their numerous body is settled and fixed *in number;* or whether their multitude cannot be summed up and limited by the numbers of any computation. For let us suppose that you do reverence to a thousand, or rather five thousand gods; but in the universe it may perhaps be that there are a hundred thousand; there may be even more than this,—nay, as we said a little before, it may not be possible to compute the number of the gods, or limit them by a definite number. Either, then, you are yourselves impious who serve a few gods, but disregard the duties which you owe to the rest;[7] or if you claim that your ignorance of the rest should be pardoned, you will procure for us also a similar pardon, if in just the same way[8] we refuse to worship those of whose existence we are wholly ignorant.

6. And yet let no one think that we are perversely determined not to submit to[9] the other deities, whoever they are! For we *lift up* pious minds, and stretch forth our hands in prayer,[10] and do not refuse to draw near whithersoever you may have summoned us; if only we learn who those divine beings are whom you press upon us, and with whom it may be right to share the reverence which we show to the king and prince who is over all. It is Saturn, *my opponent* says, and Janus, Minerva, Juno, Apollo, Venus, Triptolemus, Hercules, Æsculapius, and all the others, to whom the reverence of antiquity dedicated magnificent temples in almost every city. You might, perhaps, have been able to attract us to the worship of these deities you mention, had you not been yourselves the first, with foul and unseemly fancies, to devise such tales about them as not merely to stain their honour, but, by the natures assigned to them, to prove that they did not exist at all. For, in the first place, we cannot be led to believe this,—that that immortal and supreme nature has been divided by sexes, and that there are some male, others female. But this point, indeed, has been long ago fully treated of by men of ardent genius, both in Latin and Greek; and Tullius, the most eloquent among the Romans, without dreading the vexatiousness of a charge of impiety, has above all, with greater piety,[11] declared—boldly, firmly, and frankly—what he thought of such a fancy; and if you would proceed to receive from him opinions written with true discernment, instead of *merely* brilliant sentences, this case would have been concluded; nor would it require at our weak hands[12] a second pleading,[13] as it is termed.

7. But why should I say that men seek from him subtleties of expression and splendour of diction, when I know that there are many who avoid and flee from his books on this subject, and will not hear his opinions read,[14] overthrowing their prejudices; and when I hear others muttering angrily, and saying that the senate should decree the destruction[15] of these writings by which the Christian religion is maintained, and the weight of antiquity overborne? But, indeed, if you are convinced that anything you say regarding your gods is beyond doubt, point out Cicero's error, refute, rebut his rash and impious words,[16] *and* show *that they are so.* For when you would carry off writings, and suppress a book given forth to the public, you are not

---

[1] So LB. and later edd., from a conj. of Meursius, reading *diebus lustricis* for the ms. *ludibriis;* read by some, and understood by others, as *ludicris,* i.e., festal days.

[2] The ms., followed by Hild. and Oehler, reads *neque . . . in ulla cognatione*—"in no relationship," for which the other edd. give *cognitione,* as above.

[3] So all edd., reading *populares,* except Hild. and Oehler, who receive the conj. of Rigaltius, *populatim*—"among all nations;" the ms. reading *popularem.*

[4] *Censeri,* i.e., "written in the list of gods.'

[5] Otherwise, "how many make up the list of this name."

[6] So Orelli, receiving the emendation of Barth, *incogniti nomine,* for the ms. *in cognitione, -one* being an abbreviation for *nomine.* Examples of such deities are the Novensiles, Consentes, etc., cc. 38–41.

[7] Lit., "who, except a few gods, do not engage in the services of the rest."

[8] Orelli would explain *pro parte consimili* as equivalent to *pro uno vero Deo*—"for the one true God."

[9] Lit., "take the oaths of allegiance," or military oaths, using a very common metaphor applied to Christians in the preceding book, c. 5.

[10] Lit., "suppliant hands." It has been thought that the word *supplices* is a gloss, and that the idea originally was that of a band

of soldiers holding out their hands as they swore to be true to their country and leaders; but there is no want of simplicity and congruity in the sentence as it stands, to warrant us in rejecting the word.

[11] i.e., than the inventors of such fables had shown.

[12] Lit., "from us infants;" i.e., as compared with such a man as Cicero.

[13] *Secundas actiones.* The reference is evidently to a second speaker, who makes good his predecessor's defects.

[14] Lit., "are unwilling to admit into their ear the reading of opinions," etc.

[15] Both Christians and heathen, it is probable, were concerned in the mutilation of *de Nat. Deorum.*

[16] So Gelenius, reading *dicta* for the ms. *dictitare.* The last verb is *comprobate,* read *reprobate*—"condemn," by all edd. except Hild. and Oehler.

defending the gods, but dreading the evidence of the truth.

8. And yet, that no thoughtless person may raise a false accusation against us, as though we believed God whom we worship to be male, — for this reason, that is, that when we speak of Him we use a masculine word, — let him understand that it is not sex which is expressed, but His name, and its meaning according to custom, and the way in which we are in the habit of using words.[1] For the Deity is not male, but His name is of the masculine gender: but in your ceremonies you cannot say the same; for in your prayers you have been wont to say *whether thou art god or goddess*,[2] and this uncertain description shows, even by their opposition, that you attribute sex to the gods. We cannot, then, be prevailed on to believe that the divine is embodied; for bodies must needs be distinguished by difference of sex, if they are male and female. For who, however mean his capacity,[3] does not know that the sexes of different gender have been ordained and formed by the Creator of the creatures of earth, only that, by intercourse and union of bodies, that which is fleeting and transient may endure being ever renewed and maintained?[4]

9. What, then, shall we say? That gods beget and are begotten?[5] and that therefore they have received organs of generation, that they might be able to raise up offspring, and that, as each new race springs up, a substitution, regularly occurring,[6] should make up for all which had been swept away by the preceding age? If, then, it is so, — that is, if the gods above beget *other gods*, and are subject to these conditions of sex,[7] and are immortal, and are not worn out by the chills of age, — it follows, as a consequence, that the world[8] should be full of gods, and that countless heavens could not contain their multitude, inasmuch as they are both themselves ever begetting, and the countless multitude of their descendants, always being increased, is augmented by means of their offspring; or if, as is fitting, the gods are not degraded by being subjected to sexual impulses,[9] what cause or reason will be pointed out for their being distinguished by those members by which the sexes are wont to recognise each other at the suggestion of their own desires? For it is not likely that they have these *members* without a purpose,

or that nature had wished in them to make sport of its own improvidence,[10] in providing them with members for which there would be no use. For as the hands, feet, eyes, and other members which form our body,[11] have been arranged for certain uses, each for its own end, so we may well[12] believe that these members have been provided to discharge their office; or it must be confessed that there is something without a purpose in the bodies of the gods, which has been made uselessly and in vain.

10. What say you, ye holy and pure guardians of religion? Have the gods, then, sexes; and are they disfigured by those parts, the very mention of whose names by modest lips is disgraceful? What, then, now remains, but to believe that they, as unclean beasts, are transported with violent passions, rush with maddened desires into mutual embraces, and at last, with shattered and ruined bodies, are enfeebled by their sensuality? And since some things are peculiar to the female sex, we must believe that the goddesses, too, submit to these conditions at the proper time, conceive and become pregnant with loathing, miscarry, carry the full time, and sometimes are prematurely delivered. O divinity, pure, holy, free from and unstained by any dishonourable blot! The mind longs[13] and burns to see, in the great halls and palaces of heaven, gods and goddesses, with bodies uncovered and bare, the full-breasted Ceres nursing Iacchus,[14] as the muse of Lucretius sings, the Hellespontian Priapus bearing about among the goddesses, virgin and matron, those parts[15] ever prepared for encounter. It longs, I say, to see goddesses pregnant, goddesses with child, and, as they daily increase in size, faltering in their steps, through the irksomeness of the burden they bear about with them; others, after long delay, bringing to birth, and seeking the midwife's aid; others, shrieking as they are attacked by keen pangs and grievous pains, tormented,[16] and, under all these influences, imploring the aid of Juno Lucina. Is it not much better to abuse, revile, and otherwise insult the gods, than, with pious pretence, unworthily to entertain such monstrous beliefs about them?

11. And you dare to charge us with offending the gods, although, on examination, it is found that the ground of offence is most clearly in yourselves, and that it is not occasioned by the

---

[1] Lit., " with familiarity of speech."
[2] A formula used when they sought to propitiate the author of some event which could not be traced to a particular deity; referring also to the cases in which there were different opinions as to the sex of a deity.
[3] Lit., " even of mean understanding."
[4] Lit., " by the renewing of perpetual succession."
[5] Lit., " that gods are born."
[6] Lit, " recurring." " arising again."
[7] Lit., " make trial of themselves by these laws of sex."
[8] Lit., " all things," etc.
[9] Lit., " if the impurity of sexual union is wanting to the gods."

[10] So the first five edd.
[11] Lit., " the other arrangement of members."
[12] Lit., " it is fitting to believe."
[13] The MS., followed by Hild., reads *habet et animum* — "has it a mind to, and does it," etc.; for which Gelenius, followed by later edd., reads, as above, *avet animus*.
[14] *Cererem ab Iaccho*, either as above, or "loved by Iacchus." Cf. Lucret. iv. 1160: *At tumida et mammosa Ceres est ipsa ab Iaccho*.
[15] *Sensu obscœno*.
[16] The first five edd. read *hortari* — "exhorted," for which LB., followed by later edd., received *tortari*, as above, — a conjecture of Canterus.

insult which you think [1] *we offer them.* For if the gods are, as you say, moved by anger, and burn with rage in their minds, why should we not suppose that they take it amiss, even in the highest degree, that you attribute to them sexes, as dogs and swine have been created, and that, since this is your belief, they are so represented, and openly exposed in a disgraceful manner? This, then, being the case, you are the cause of all troubles — you lead the gods, you rouse them to harass the earth with every ill, and every day to devise all kinds of fresh misfortunes, that so they may avenge themselves, being irritated at suffering so many wrongs and insults from you. By your insults and affronts, I say, partly in the vile stories, partly in the shameful beliefs which your theologians, your poets, you yourselves too, celebrate in disgraceful ceremonies, you will find that the affairs of men have been ruined, and that the gods have thrown away the helm, if indeed it is by their care that the fortunes of men are guided and arranged. For with us, indeed, they have no reason to be angry, whom they see and perceive neither to mock, as it is said, nor worship them, and to think,[2] to believe much more worthily than you with regard to the dignity of their name.

12. Thus far of sex. Now let us come to the appearance and shapes by which you believe that the gods above have been represented, with which, indeed, you fashion, and set them up in their most splendid abodes, your temples. And let no one here bring up against us Jewish fables and those of the sect of the Sadducees,[3] as though we, too, attribute to the Deity forms;[4] for this is supposed to be taught in their writings, and asserted as if with assurance and authority. For these stories either do not concern us, and have nothing at all in common with us, or if they are shared in *by us,* as you believe, you must seek out teachers of greater wisdom, through whom you may be able to learn how best to overcome the dark and recondite sayings of those writings. Our opinion on the subject is as follows : — that the whole divine nature, since it neither came into existence at any time, nor will ever come to an end of life, is devoid of bodily features, and does not have anything like the forms with which the termination of the several members usually completes the union of parts.[5] For whatever is of this character, we think mortal and perish-

able ; nor do we believe that that can endure for ever which an inevitable end shuts in, though the boundaries enclosing it be the remotest.

13. But it is not enough that you limit the gods by forms : — you even confine them to the human figure, and with even less decency enclose them in earthly bodies. What shall we say then? that the gods have a head modelled with perfect symmetry,[6] bound fast by sinews to the back and breast, and that, to allow the necessary bending of the neck, it is supported by combinations of *vertebræ,* and by an osseous foundation? But if we believe this to be true, it follows that they have ears also, pierced by crooked windings ; rolling eyeballs, overshadowed by the edges of the eyebrows ; a nose, placed as a channel,[7] through which waste fluids and a current of air might easily pass ; teeth to masticate food, of three kinds, and adapted to three services ; hands to do their work, moving easily by means of joints, fingers, and flexible elbows ; feet to support their bodies, regulate their steps, and prompt the first motions in walking. But if *the gods bear* these things which are seen, it is fitting that they should bear those also which the skin conceals under the framework of the ribs, and the membranes enclosing the viscera ; windpipes, stomachs, spleens, lungs, bladders, livers, the long-entwined intestines, and the veins of purple blood, joined with the air-passages,[8] coursing through the whole viscera.

14. Are, then, the divine bodies free from these deformities? and since they do not eat the food of men, are we to believe that, like children, they are toothless, and, having no internal parts, as if they were inflated bladders, are without strength, owing to the hollowness of their swollen bodies? Further, if this is the case, you must see whether the gods are all alike, or are marked by a difference in the contour of their forms. For if each and all have one and the same likeness of shape, there is nothing ridiculous in believing that they err, and are deceived in recognising each other.[9] But if, on the other hand, they are distinguished by their countenances, we should, consequently, understand that these differences have been implanted for no other reason than that they might individually be able to recognise themselves by the peculiarites of the different marks. We should therefore say that some have big heads, prominent brows, broad brows, thick lips ; that others of them have long chins, moles, and high noses ; that these have dilated nostrils, those are snub-

---

[1] So Orelli, reading *nec in contumelia quam opinamini stare* for the MS. *et,* which is retained by all other edd.; Oehler, however, inserts *alia* before *quam* — "and that it is found in an insult other than you think."

[2] So later edd., omitting *quam,* which is read in the MS., both Roman edd., Hild., and Oehler, "to think much more . . . than you believe."

[3] It is evident that Arnobius here confuses the sceptical Sadducees with their opponents the Pharisees, and the Talmudists.

[4] The MS. reads *tribuant et nos* unintelligibly, for which LB. and Hild. read *et os* — "as though they attribute form and face;" the other edd., as above, *tribuamus et nos.*

[5] Lit., "the joinings of the members."

[6] Lit., "with smooth roundness." [Cf. Xenoph., *Mem.,* i. cap. 4.]

[7] Lit., "the raised gutter of the nose, easily passed by," etc.

[8] The veins were supposed to be for the most part filled with blood, mixed with a little air ; while in the arteries air was supposed to be in excess. Cf. Cicero, *de Nat. Deor.* ii. 55: "Through the veins blood is poured forth to the whole body, and air through the arteries."

[9] Lit., "in the apprehension of mutual knowledge."

nosed; some chubby from a swelling of their jaws or growth of their cheeks, dwarfed, tall, of middle size, lean, sleek, fat; some with crisped and curled hair, others shaven, with bald and smooth heads. Now your workshops show and point out that our opinions are not false, inasmuch as, when you form and fashion gods, you represent some with long hair, others smooth and bare, as old, as youths, as boys, swarthy, grey-eyed, yellow, half-naked, bare; or, that cold may not annoy them, covered with flowing garments thrown over them.

15. Does any man at all possessed of judgment, believe that hairs and down grow on the bodies of the gods? that among them age is distinguished? and that they go about clad in dresses and garments of various shapes, and shield themselves from heat and cold? But if any one believes that, he must receive this also as true, that *some* gods are fullers, some barbers; the former to cleanse the sacred garments, the latter to thin their locks when matted with a thick growth of hair. Is not this really degrading, most impious, and insulting, to attribute to the gods the features of a frail and perishing animal? to furnish them with those members which no modest person would dare to recount, and describe, or represent in his own imagination, without shuddering at the excessive indecency? Is this the contempt you entertain, — this the proud wisdom with which you spurn us as ignorant, and think that all knowledge of religion is yours? You mock the mysteries of the Egyptians, because they ingrafted the forms of dumb animals upon their divine causes, and because they worship these very images with much incense, and whatever else is used in such rites: you yourselves adore images of men, as though they were powerful gods, and are not ashamed to give to these the countenance of an earthly creature, to blame others for their mistaken folly, and to be detected in a similarly vicious error.

16. But you will, perhaps, say that the gods have indeed other forms, and that you have given the appearance of men to them *merely* by way of honour, and for form's sake;[1] which is much more insulting than to have fallen into any error through ignorance. For if you confessed that you had ascribed to the divine forms that which you had supposed and believed, your error, originating in prejudice, would not be so blameable. But now, when you believe one thing and fashion another, you both dishonour those to whom you ascribe that which you confess does not belong to them, and show your impiety in adoring that which you fashion, not that which you think really is, and which is in

very truth. If asses, dogs, pigs,[2] had any human wisdom and skill in contrivance, and wished to do us honour also by some kind of worship, and to show respect by dedicating statues *to us*, with what rage would they inflame us, what a tempest of passion would they excite, if they determined that our images should bear and assume the fashion of their own bodies? How would they, I repeat, fill us with rage, and rouse our passions, if the founder of Rome, Romulus, were to be set up with an ass's face, the revered Pompilius with that of a dog, if under the image of a pig were written Cato's or Marcus Cicero's name? So, then, do you think that your stupidity is not laughed at by your deities, if they laugh *at all?* or, since you believe that they may be enraged, *do you think* that they are not roused, maddened to fury, and that they do not wish to be revenged for so great wrongs and insults, and to hurl on you the punishments usually dictated by chagrin, and devised by bitter hatred? How much better it had been to give to them the forms of elephants, panthers, or tigers, bulls, and horses! For what is there beautiful in man, — what, I pray you, worthy of admiration, or comely, — unless that which, some poet[3] has maintained, he possesses in common with the ape?

17. But, they say, if you are not satisfied with our opinion, do you point out, tell us yourselves, what is the Deity's form. If you wish to hear the truth, either the Deity has no form; or if He is embodied in one, we indeed know not what it is. Moreover, we think it no disgrace to be ignorant of that which we never saw; nor are we therefore prevented from disproving the opinions of others, because on this we have no opinion of our own to bring forward. For as, if the earth be said to be of glass, silver, iron, or gathered together and made from brittle clay, we cannot hesitate to maintain that this is untrue, although we do not know of what it is made; so, when the form of God is discussed, we show that it is not what you maintain, even if we are *still* less able to explain what it is.

18. What, then, some one will say, does the Deity not hear? does He not speak? does He not see what is put before Him? has He not sight? He may in His own, but not in our way. But in so great a matter we cannot know the truth at all, or reach it by speculations; for these are, it is clear, in our case, baseless, deceitful, and like vain dreams. For if we said that He sees in the same way as ourselves, it follows that it should be understood that He has

---

[2] This argument seems to have been suggested by the saying of Xenophanes, that the ox or lion, if possessed of man's power, would have represented, after the fashion of their own bodies, the gods they would worship. ["The fair *humanities* of old religion." — COLERIDGE (Schiller).]
[3] Ennius (CIC., *de Nat. Deor.*, i. 35): *Simia quam similis, turpissima bestia, nobis.*

eyelids placed as coverings on the pupils of the eyes, that He closes them, winks, sees by rays or images, or, as is the case in all eyes, can see nothing at all without the presence of other light. So we must in like manner say of hearing, and form of speech, and utterance of words. If He hears by means of ears, these, too, *we must say*, He has, penetrated by winding paths, through which the sound may steal, bearing the meaning of the discourse ; or if His words are poured forth from a mouth, that He has lips and teeth, by the contact and various movement of which His tongue utters sounds distinctly, and forms His voice to words.

19. If you are willing to hear our conclusions, *then learn that* we are so far from attributing bodily shape to the Deity, that we fear to ascribe to so great a being even mental graces, and the very excellences by which a few have been allowed with difficulty to distinguish themselves. For who will say that God is brave, firm, good, wise ? who *will say* that He has integrity, is temperate, even that He has knowledge, understanding, forethought ? that He directs towards fixed moral ends the actions on which He determines ? These things are good in man ; and being opposed to vices, have deserved the great reputation which they have gained. But who is so foolish, so senseless, as to say that God is great by *merely* human excellences ? or that He is above all in the greatness of His name, because He is not disgraced by vice ? Whatever you say, whatever in unspoken thought you imagine concerning God, passes and is corrupted into a human sense, and does not carry its own meaning, because it is spoken in the words which we use, and which are suited *only* to human affairs. There is but one thing man can be assured of regarding God's nature, to know and perceive that nothing can be revealed in human language concerning God.

20. This, then, this matter of forms and sexes, is the first affront which you, noble advocates in sooth, and pious writers, offer to your deities. But what is the next, that you represent to us [1] the gods, some as artificers, some physicians, others working in wool, as sailors, [2] players on the harp and flute, hunters, shepherds, and, as there was nothing more, rustics ? And that god, he says, is a musician, and this other can divine ; for the other gods cannot, [3] and do not know how to foretell what will come to pass, owing to their want of skill and ignorance of the future. One is instructed in obstetric arts, another trained up in the science of medicine. Is each, then, powerful in his own department ; and can they give no assistance, if their aid is asked, in what belongs to another ? This one is eloquent in speech, and ready in linking words together ; for the others are stupid, and can say nothing skilfully, if they must speak.

21. And, I ask, what reason is there, what unavoidable necessity, what occasion for the gods knowing and being acquainted with these handicrafts as though they were worthless mechanics ? For, are songs sung and music played in heaven, that the nine sisters may gracefully combine and harmonize pauses and rhythms of tones ? Are there on the mountains [4] of the stars, forests, woods, groves, that [5] Diana may be esteemed very mighty in hunting expeditions ? Are the gods ignorant of the immediate future ; and do they live and pass the time according to the lots assigned them by fate, that the inspired son of Latona may explain and declare what the morrow or the next hour bears to each ? Is he himself inspired by another god, and is he urged and roused by the power of a greater divinity, so that he may be rightly said and esteemed to be divinely inspired ? Are the gods liable to be seized by diseases ; and is there anything by which they may be wounded and hurt, so that, when there is occasion, he [6] of Epidaurus may come to their assistance ? Do they labour, do they bring forth, that Juno may soothe, and Lucina abridge the terrible pangs of childbirth ? Do they engage in agriculture, or are they concerned with the duties of war, that Vulcan, the lord of fire, may form for them swords, or forge their rustic implements ? Do they need to be covered with garments, that the Tritonian [7] maid may, with nice skill, [8] spin, weave cloth for them, and make [9] them tunics to suit the season, either triple-twilled, or of silken fabric ? Do they make accusations and refute them, that the descendant [10] of Atlas may carry off the prize for eloquence, attained by assiduous practice ?

22. You err, my opponent says, and are deceived ; for the gods are not themselves artificers, but suggest these arts to ingenious men, and teach mortals what they should know, that their mode of life may be more civilized. But he who gives any instruction to the ignorant and unwilling, and strives to make him intelligently expert

---

[1] So the MS., followed by Oehler, reading *nobis*, for which all other edd. give *vobis* — " to you."
[2] Meursius would read *naccas* — " fullers," for *nautas ;* but the latter term may, properly enough, be applied to the gods who watch over seamen.
[3] Or, " for the others are not gods," i.e., cannot be gods, as they do not possess the power of divination. Cf. Lact., i. 11: *Sin autem divinus non sit, ne deus quidem sit.*

[4] The MS., followed by LB. and Hild., reads *sidereis motibus* — " in the motions of the stars; " i.e., can these be in the stars, owing to their motion? Oehler conjectures *molibus* — " in the masses of the stars; " the other edd. read *montibus*, as above.
[5] The MS., both Roman edd., and Oehler read *habetur Diana* — " is Diana esteemed; " the other edd., *ut habeatur*, as above.
[6] i.e., Æsculapius.
[7] i.e., Minerva. [Elucidation II. Conf. n. 4, p. 467, *supra.*]
[8] " With nice skill . . . for them," *curiose iis ;* for which the MS. and first five edd. read *curiosius* — " rather skilfully."
[9] The MS. reads unintelligibly *et imponere*, for which Meursius emended *componat*, as above.
[10] Mercury, grandson of Atlas by Maia.

in some kind of work, must himself first know that which he sets the other to practise. For no one can be capable of teaching a science without knowing the rules of that which he teaches, and having grasped its method most thoroughly. The gods are, then, the first artificers; whether because they inform the minds *of men* with knowledge, as you say yourselves, or because, being immortal and unbegotten, they surpass the whole race of earth by their length of life.[1] This, then, is the question; there being no occasion for these arts among the gods, neither their necessities nor nature requiring in them any ingenuity or mechanical skill, why you should say that they are skilled,[2] one in one craft, another in another, and that individuals are pre-eminently expert[3] in particular departments in which they are distinguished by acquaintance with the several branches of science?

23. But you will, perhaps, say that the gods are not artificers, but that they preside over these arts, *and* have their oversight; nay, that under their care all things have been placed, which we manage and conduct, and that their providence sees to the happy and fortunate issue of these. Now this would certainly appear to be said justly, and with some probability, if all we engage in, all we do, or all we attempt in human affairs, sped as we wished and purposed. But since every day the reverse is the case, and the results of actions do not correspond to the purpose of the will, it is trifling to say that we have, set as guardians over us, gods invented by our superstitious fancy, not grasped with assured certainty. Portunus[4] gives to the sailor perfect safety in traversing the seas; but why has the raging sea cast up so many cruelly-shattered wrecks? Consus suggests to our minds courses safe and serviceable; and why does an unexpected change perpetually issue in results other than were looked for? Pales and Inuus[5] are set as guardians over the flocks and herds; why do they, with hurtful laziness,[6] not take care to avert from the herds in their summer pastures, cruel, infectious, and destructive diseases? The harlot Flora,[7] venerated in lewd sports, sees well to it that the fields blossom; and why are buds and tender plants daily nipt and destroyed by most hurtful frost? Juno presides over childbirth, and aids travailing

mothers; and why are a thousand mothers every day cut off in murderous throes? Fire is under Vulcan's care, and its source is placed under his control; and why does he, very often, suffer temples and parts of cities to fall into ashes devoured by flames? The soothsayers receive the knowledge of their art from the Pythian god; and why does he so often give and afford answers equivocal, doubtful, steeped in darkness and obscurity? Æsculapius presides over the duties and arts of medicine; and why cannot *men in* more kinds of disease and sickness be restored to health and soundness of body? while, on the contrary, they become worse under the hands of the physician. Mercury is occupied with[8] combats, and presides over boxing and wrestling matches; and why does he not make all invincible who are in his charge? why, when appointed to one office, does he enable some to win the victory, while he suffers others to be ridiculed for their disgraceful weakness?

24. No one, says my opponent, makes supplication to the tutelar deities, and they therefore withhold their usual favours and help. Cannot the gods, then, do good, except they receive incense and consecrated offerings?[9] and do they quit and renounce their posts, unless they see their altars anointed with the blood of cattle? And yet I thought but now that the kindness of the gods was of their own free will, and that the unlooked-for gifts of benevolence flowed unsought from them. Is, then, the King of the universe solicited by any libation or sacrifice to grant to the races of men all the comforts of life? Does the Deity not impart the sun's fertilizing warmth, and the season of night, the winds, the rains, the fruits, to all alike, — the good and the bad, the unjust and the just,[10] the free-born and the slave, the poor and the rich? For this belongs to the true and mighty God, to show kindness, unasked, to that which is weary and feeble, and always encompassed by misery of many kinds. For to grant your prayers on the offering of sacrifices, is not to bring help to those who ask it, but to sell the riches of their beneficence. We men trifle, and are foolish in so great a matter; and, forgetting what[11] God is, and the majesty of His name, associate with the tutelar deities whatever meanness or baseness our morbid credulity can invent.

25. Unxia, my opponent says, presides over the anointing *of door-posts;* Cinxia over the loosening of the zone; the most venerable Victa[12] and Potua attend to eating and drinking. O

---

[1] Lit., "by the long duration of time."
[2] Lit., "skilled in notions"—*perceptionibus;* for which *præceptionibus,* i.e., "the precepts of the different arts," has been suggested in the margin of Ursinus.
[3] Lit., "and have skill (*sollertias*) in which individuals excel."
[4] According to Oehler, Portunus (Portumnus or Palæmon — "the god who protects harbours") does not occur in the ms., which, he says, reads *per maria præstant* — "through the seas they afford;" emended as above by Ursinus, *præstat Portunus.* Oehler himself proposes *permarini* — "the sea gods afford."
[5] Pales, i.e., the feeding one; Inuus, otherwise Faunus and Pan.
[6] Otherwise, "from the absence of rain."
[7] So the margin of Ursinus, reading *meretrix;* but in the first four edd., LB., and Oberthür, *genetrix* — "mother," is retained from the ms.

[8] So LB., reading *cura-t,* the ms. omitting the last letter.
[9] Lit., "salted fruits," the grits mixed with salt, strewed on the victim.
[10] Supplied by Ursinus.
[11] So the edd. reading *quid,* except Hild. and Oehler, who retain the ms. *qui* — "who."
[12] The ms. reads *Vita.*

rare and admirable interpretation of the divine powers ! would gods not have names [1] if brides did not besmear their husbands' door-posts with greasy ointment; were it not that husbands, when now eagerly drawing near, unbind the maiden-girdle; if men did not eat and drink? Moreover, not satisfied to have subjected and involved the gods in cares so unseemly, you also ascribe to them dispositions fierce, cruel, savage, ever rejoicing in the ills and destruction of mankind.

26. We shall not here mention Laverna, goddess of thieves, the Bellonæ, Discordiæ, Furiæ; and we pass by in utter silence the unpropitious deities whom you have set up. We shall bring forward Mars himself, and the fair mother of the Desires; to one of whom you commit wars, to the other love and passionate desire. My opponent says that Mars has power over wars; whether to quell those which are raging, or to revive them when interrupted, and kindle them in time of peace? For if he calms the madness of war, why do wars rage every day? but if he is their author, we shall then say that the god, to satisfy his own inclination, involves the whole world in strife; sows the seeds of discord and variance between far-distant peoples; gathers so many thousand men from different quarters, and speedily heaps up the field with dead bodies; makes the streams flow with blood, sweeps away the most firmly-founded empires, lays cities in the dust, robs the free of their liberty, and makes them slaves; rejoices in civil strife, in the bloody death of brothers who die in conflict, and, in fine, in the dire, murderous contest of children with their fathers.

27. Now we may apply this very argument to Venus in exactly the same way. For if, as you maintain and believe, she fills men's minds with lustful thoughts, it must be held in consequence that any disgrace and misdeed arising from such madness should be ascribed to the instigation of Venus. Is it, then, under compulsion of the goddess that even the noble too often betray their own reputation into the hands of worthless harlots; that the firm bonds of marriage are broken; that near relations burn with incestuous lust; that mothers have their passions madly kindled towards their children; that fathers turn to themselves their daughters' desires; that old men, bringing shame upon their grey hairs, sigh with the ardour of youth for the gratification of filthy desires; that wise and brave [2] men, losing in effeminacy the strength of their manhood, disregard the biddings of constancy; that the noose is twisted about their necks; that blazing pyres

are ascended; [3] and that in different places men, leaping voluntarily, cast themselves headlong over very high and huge precipices? [4]

28. Can any man, who has accepted the first principles even of reason, be found to mar or dishonour the unchanging nature of Deity with morals so vile? to credit the gods with natures such as human kindness has often charmed away and moderated in the beasts of the field? How, [5] I ask, can it be said that the gods are far removed from any feeling of passion? that they are gentle, lovers of peace, mild? that in the completeness of their excellence they reach [6] the height of perfection, and the highest wisdom also? or, why should we pray them to avert from us misfortunes and calamities, if we find that they are themselves the authors of all the ills by which we are daily harassed? Call us impious as much as you please, contemners of religion, or atheists, you will never make us believe in gods of love and war, that there are gods to sow strife, and to disturb the mind by the stings of the furies. For either they are gods in very truth, and do not do what you have related; or if [7] they do the things which you say, they are doubtless no gods *at all*.

29. We might, however, even yet be able to receive from you these thoughts, most full of wicked falsehoods, if it were not that you yourselves, in bringing forward many things about the gods so inconsistent and mutually destructive, compel us to withhold our minds from assenting. For when you strive individually to excel each other in reputation for more recondite knowledge, you both overthrow the very gods in whom you believe, and replace them by others who have clearly no existence; and different men give different opinions on the same subjects, [8] and you write that those whom general consent has ever received as single persons are infinite in number. Let us, too, begin duly, then, with father Janus, whom certain of you have declared to be the world, others the year, some the sun. But if we are to believe that this is true, it follows as a consequence, that it should be understood that there never was any Janus, who, they say, being sprung from Cœlus and Hecate, reigned first in Italy, founded the town Janiculum, was the father of Fons, [9] the son-in-law of Vulturnus, the husband of Juturna; and thus you erase the name of the god to whom in all prayers you give the first place, and whom you believe to procure for you a hearing from the

---

[1] [i.e., these names are derived from their offices to men. Have they no names apart from these services?]

[2] i.e., those who subdue their own spirits. "Constancy" is the εὐπάθεια of the Stoics.

[3] Referring to Dido.

[4] As despairing lovers are said to have sought relief in death, by leaping from the Leucadian rock into the sea.

[5] Lit., "where, I ask, is the (assertion) that," etc.

[6] Lit., "hold."

[7] In the MS. these words, *aut si*, are wanting.

[8] Stewechius and Orelli would omit *rebus*, and interpret "about the same gods." Instead of *de* — "about," the MS. has *deos*.

[9] The MS. reads *fonti*, corrected by Meursius *Fontis*, as above.

gods. But, again, if Janus be the year, neither thus can he be a god. For who does not know that the year is a fixed space[1] of time, and that there is nothing divine in that which is formed[2] by the duration of months and lapse of days? Now this very *argument* may, in like manner, be applied to Saturn. For if time is meant under this title, as the expounders of Grecian ideas think, so that that is regarded as Kronos,[3] which is chronos,[4] there is no such deity as Saturn. For who is so senseless as to say that time is a god, when it is but a certain space measured off[5] in the unending succession of eternity? And thus will be removed from the rank of the immortals that deity too, whom the men of old declared, and handed down to their posterity, to be born of father Cœlus, the progenitor of the *dii magni*, the planter of the vine, the bearer of the pruning-knife.[6]

30. But what shall we say of Jove himself, whom the wise have repeatedly asserted to be the sun, driving a winged chariot, followed by a crowd of deities;[7] some, the ether, blazing with mighty flames, and wasting fire which cannot be extinguished? Now if this is clear and certain, there is, then, according to you, no Jupiter at all; who, born of Saturn his father and Ops his mother, is reported to have been concealed in the Cretan territory, that he might escape his father's rage. But now, does not a similar mode of thought remove Juno from the list of gods? For if she is the air, as you have been wont to jest and say, repeating in reversed order the *syllables* of the Greek name,[8] there will be found no sister and spouse of almighty Jupiter, no Fluonia,[9] no Pomona, no Ossipagina, no Februtis, Populonia, Cinxia, Caprotina; and thus the invention of that name, spread abroad with a frequent but vain[10] belief, will be found to be wholly[11] useless.

31. Aristotle, a man of most powerful intellect, and distinguished for learning, as Granius tells, shows by plausible arguments that Minerva is the moon, and proves it by the authority of learned men. Others have said that this very goddess is the depth of ether, and utmost height; some *have maintained* that she is memory, whence her name even, Minerva, has arisen, as if she were some goddess of memory. But if this is credited, it follows that there is no daughter of Mens, no daughter of Victory, no dis-

coverer of the Olive, born from the head of Jupiter, no *goddess* skilled in the knowledge of the arts, and in different branches of learning. Neptune, they say, has received his name and title because he covers the earth with water. If, then, by the use of this name is meant the outspread water, there is no god Neptune at all; and thus is put away, and removed *from us*, the full brother of Pluto and Jupiter, armed with the iron trident, lord of the fish, great and small, king of the depths of the sea, and shaker of the trembling earth.[12]

32. Mercury, also, has been named as though he were a kind of go-between; and because conversation passes between two speakers, and is exchanged by them, that which is expressed by this name has been produced.[13] If this, then, is the case, Mercury is not the name of a god, but of speech and words exchanged *by two persons;* and in this way is blotted out and annihilated the noted Cyllenian bearer of the caduceus, born on the cold mountain top,[14] contriver of words and names, *the god* who presides over markets, and over the exchange of goods and commercial intercourse. Some of you have said that the earth is the Great Mother,[15] because it provides all things living with food; others declare that the same *earth* is Ceres, because it brings forth crops of useful fruits;[16] while some maintain that it is Vesta, because it alone in the universe is at rest, its other members being, by their constitution, ever in motion. Now if this is propounded and maintained on sure grounds, in like manner, on your interpretation, three deities have no existence: neither Ceres nor Vesta are to be reckoned in the number[17] of the gods; nor, in fine, can the mother of the gods herself, whom Nigidius thinks to have been married to Saturn, be rightly declared a goddess, if indeed these are all names of the one earth, and it alone is signified by these titles.

33. We here leave Vulcan unnoticed, to avoid prolixity; whom you all declare to be fire, with one consenting voice. *We pass by* Venus, named because *lust* assails all, and Proserpina, named because plants steal gradually forth into the light, — where, again, you do away with three deities; if indeed the first is the name of an element, and does not signify a living power; the second, of a desire common to all living creatures; while the third refers to seeds rising above ground, and the upward movements[18] of growing crops. What! when you maintain that Bacchus, Apollo, the Sun, are one deity, increased in number by

---

[1] Lit., " circuit."
[2] Lit., " finished."
[3] i.e., the god.
[4] i.e., time.
[5] Lit., " the measuring of a certain space included in," etc.
[6] Cf. vi. 12.
[7] Cf. Plato, *Phædr.*, st. p. 246.
[8] Lit., " the reversed order of the Greek name being repeated," i.e., instead of ἤ-ρα, ἀ-ήρ.
[9] The ms. gives Fluvionia.
[10] Lit., " with the frequency (or fame) of vain," etc.
[11] Lit., " very."

[12] So Meursius emended the ms. *sali* — " sea."
[13] Lit., " the quality of this name has been adjusted."
[14] So Orelli, reading *monte vertice;* the last word, according to Oehler, not being found in the ms.
[15] i.e., Cybele. Cf. Lucr., ii. 991 sqq.
[16] Lit., " seeds."
[17] *Fasti* — " list," " register."
[18] Lit., " motions."

the use of three names, is not the number of the gods lessened, and their vaunted reputation overthrown, by your opinions? For if it is true that the sun is also Bacchus and Apollo, there can consequently be in the universe no Apollo or Bacchus; and thus, by yourselves, the son of Semele *and* the Pythian god are blotted out *and* set aside, — one the giver of drunken merriment, the other the destroyer of Sminthian mice.

34. Some of your learned men [1] — men, too, who do not chatter *merely* because their humour leads them — maintain that Diana, Ceres, Luna, are but one deity in triple union; [2] and that there are not three distinct persons, as there are three different names; that in all these Luna is invoked, and that the others are a series of surnames added to her name. But if this is sure, if this is certain, and the facts of the case show it to be so, again is Ceres but an empty name, and Diana: and thus the discussion is brought to this issue, that you lead and advise us to believe that she whom you maintain to be the discoverer of the earth's fruits has no existence, and Apollo is robbed of his sister, whom once the horned hunter [3] gazed upon as she washed her limbs from impurity in a pool, and paid the penalty of his curiosity.

35. Men worthy to be remembered in the study of philosophy, who have been raised by your praises to its highest place, declare, with commendable earnestness, as their conclusion, that the whole mass of the world, by whose folds we all are encompassed, covered, and upheld, is one animal [4] possessed of wisdom and reason; yet if this is a true, sure, and certain opinion, [5] they also will forthwith cease to be gods whom you set up a little ago in its parts without change of name. [6] For as one man cannot, while his body remains entire, be divided into many men; nor can many men, while they continue to be distinct and separate from each other, [7] be fused into one sentient individual: so, if the world is a single animal, and moves from the impulse of one mind, neither can it be dispersed in several deities; nor, if the gods are parts of it, can they be brought together and changed into one living creature, with unity of feeling throughout all its parts. The moon, the sun, the earth, the ether, the stars, are members and parts of the world; but if they are parts and members, they are

certainly not themselves [8] living creatures; for in no thing can parts be the very thing which the whole is, or think and feel for themselves, for this cannot be effected by their own actions, without the whole creature's joining in; and this being established and settled, the whole matter comes back to this, that neither Sol, nor Luna, nor Æther, Tellus, and the rest, are gods. For they are parts of the world, not the proper names of deities; and thus it is brought about that, by your disturbing and confusing all divine things, the world is set up as the sole god in the universe, while all the rest are cast aside, and that *as* having been set up vainly, uselessly, and without any reality.

36. If we sought to subvert the belief in your gods in so many ways, by so many arguments, no one would doubt that, mad with rage and fury, you would demand for us the stake, the beasts, and swords, with the other kinds of torture by which you usually appease your thirst in its intense craving for our blood. But while you yourselves put away almost the whole race of deities with a pretence of cleverness and wisdom, you do not hesitate to assert that, because of us, men suffer ill at the hands of the gods; [9] although, indeed, if it is true that they anywhere exist, and burn with anger and [10] rage, there can be no better reason for their showing anger against you, [11] than that you deny their existence, and *say* that they are not *found* in any part of the universe.

37. We are told by Mnaseas that the Muses are the daughters of Tellus and Cœlus; others declare *that they are* Jove's by his wife Memory, or Mens; some relate that they were virgins, others that they were matrons. For now we wish to touch briefly on the points where you are shown, from the difference of your opinions, to make different statements about the same thing. Ephorus, then, says that they are three [12] in number; Mnaseas, whom we mentioned, *that they are* four; [13] Myrtilus [14] brings forward seven; Crates asserts that there are eight; finally Hesiod, enriching heaven and the stars with gods, comes forward with nine names. [15]

If we are not mistaken, such want of agreement marks those who are wholly ignorant of the truth, and does not spring from the real

---

[1] Cf. Servius ad Virg., *Georg.*, i. 5: "The Stoics say that Luna, Diana, Ceres, Juno, and Proserpina are one; following whom, Virgil invoked Liber and Ceres for Sol and Luna."
[2] *Triviali* — "common," "vulgar," seems to be here used for *triplici.*
[3] Actæon.
[4] Plato, *Timæus*, st. p. 30.
[5] Lit., " of which things, however, if the opinion," etc.
[6] i.e., deifying parts of the universe, and giving them, as deities, the same names as before.
[7] Lit., "the difference of their disjunction being preserved" — *multi disjunctionis differentia conservata*, suggested in the margin of Ursinus for the MS. *multitudinis junctionis d. c.*, retained in the first five edd.

[8] Lit., " of their own name."
[9] Lit., " for the sake of our name, men's affairs are made harassing."
[10] Lit., " with flames of," etc.
[11] The MS., according to Crusius, reads *nos* — " us."
[12] Three was the most ancient number; and the names preserved by Pausanias, are Μελέτη, Ἀοιδή, Μνήμη.
[13] Cicero (*de Nat. Deor.*, iii. 21, a passage where there is some doubt as to the reading) enumerates as the four Muses, Thelxiope, Aœde, Arche, Melete.
[14] The MS. reads *Murtylus.* Seven are said to have been mentioned by Epicharmus, — Neilous, Tritone, Asopous, Heptapolis, Achelois, Tiyoplous, and Rhodia.
[15] The nine are Clio, Euterpe, Thalia, Melpomene, Terpsichore, Erato, Polymnia, Ourania, and Calliope (*Theog.*, 77-79).

state of the case. For if their number were clearly known, the voice of all would be the same, and the agreement of all would tend to and find issue in the same conclusion.[1]

38. How, then, can you give to religion its whole power, when you fall into error about the gods themselves? or summon us to their solemn worship, while you give us no definite information how to conceive of the deities themselves? For, to take no notice of the other[2] authors, either the first[3] makes away with and destroys six divine Muses, if they are certainly nine; or the last[4] adds six who have no existence to the three who alone really are; so that it cannot be known or understood what should be added, what taken away; and in the performance of religious rites we are in danger[5] of either worshipping that which does not exist, or passing that by which, it may be, does exist. Piso believes that the Novensiles are nine gods, set up among the Sabines at Trebia.[6] Granius thinks that they are the Muses, agreeing with Ælius; Varro teaches that they are nine,[7] because, in doing anything, that number is always reputed most powerful and greatest; Cornificius,[8] that they watch over the renewing of things,[9] because, by their care, all things are afresh renewed in strength, and endure; Manilius, that they are the nine gods to whom alone Jupiter gave power to wield his thunder.[10] Cincius declares them to be deities brought from abroad, named from their very newness, because the Romans were in the habit of sometimes individually introducing into their families the rites[11] of conquered cities, while some they publicly consecrated; and lest, from their great number, or in ignorance, any god should be passed by, all alike were briefly and compendiously invoked under one name — Novensiles.

39. There are some, besides, who assert that those who from being men became gods, are denoted by this name, — as Hercules, Romulus, Æsculapius, Liber, Æneas. These are all, as is clear, different opinions; and it cannot be, in the nature of things, that those who differ in opinion can be regarded as teachers of one truth. For if Piso's opinion is true, Ælius and Granius say what is false; if what they say is certain, Varro,

with all his skill,[12] is mistaken, who substitutes things most frivolous and vain for those which really exist. If they are named Novensiles because their number is nine,[13] Cornificius is shown to stumble, who, giving them might and power not their own, makes them the divine overseers of renovation.[14] But if Cornificius is right in his belief, Cincius is found to be not wise, who connects with the power of the dii Novensiles the gods of conquered cities. But if they are those whom Cincius asserts them to be, Manilius will be found to speak falsely, who comprehends those who wield another's thunder under this name.[15] But if that which Manilius holds is true and certain, they are utterly mistaken who suppose that those raised to divine honours, and deified mortals, are thus named because of the novelty of their rank. But if the Novensiles are those who have deserved to be raised to the stars after passing through the life of men,[16] there are no dii Novensiles at all. For as slaves, soldiers, masters, are not names of persons comprehended under them,[17] but of officers, ranks, and duties, so, when we say that Novensiles is the name[18] of gods who by their virtues have become[19] gods from being men, it is clear and evident that no individual persons are marked out particularly, but that newness itself is named by the title Novensiles.

40. Nigidius taught that the dii Penates were Neptune and Apollo, who once, on fixed terms, girt Ilium[20] with walls. He himself again, in his sixteenth book, following Etruscan teaching, shows that there are four kinds of Penates; and that one of these pertains to Jupiter, another to Neptune, the third to the shades below, the fourth to mortal men, making some unintelligible assertion. Cæsius himself, also, following this teaching, thinks that they are Fortune, and Ceres, the genius Jovialis,[21] and Pales, but not the female deity commonly received,[22] but some male attendant and steward of Jupiter. Varro thinks that they are the gods of whom we speak who are within, and in the inmost recesses of heaven, and that neither their number nor names are known. The Etruscans say that these are the Consentes and Complices,[23] and name them be-

---

[1] Lit., "into the end of the same opinion."
[2] Lit., "in the middle," "intermediate."
[3] i.e., Ephorus.
[4] i.e., Hesiod.
[5] Lit., "the undertaking of religion itself is brought into the danger," etc.
[6] An Umbrian village.
[7] Lit., "that the number is nine." [i.e., a triad of triads; the base a triad, regarded, even by heathen, as of mystical power.]
[8] A grammarian who lived in the time of Augustus, not to be confounded with Cicero's correspondent.
[9] Novitatum.
[10] The Etruscans held (Pliny, H. N., ii. 52) that nine gods could thunder, the bolts being of different kinds: the Romans so far maintained this distinction as to regard thunder during the day as sent by Jupiter, at night by Summanus.
[11] So LB., reading relig- for the MS. reg-iones.

[12] Lit., "the very skilful."
[13] Lit., "if the number nine bring on the name of," etc.
[14] Lit., "gives another's might and power to gods presiding."
[15] Lit., "the title of this name."
[16] Lit., "after they have finished the mortality of life," i.e., either as above, or "having endured its perishableness."
[17] Lit., "lying under."
[18] So most edd., following Gelenius, who reads esse nomen for the MS. si omnes istud.
[19] Lit., "who have deserved to," etc.
[20] The MS. reads immortalium, corrected in the edd. urbem Ilium.
[21] Supposed to be either the genius attending Jupiter; the family god as sent by him; or the chief among the genii, sometimes mentioned simply as Genius.
[22] Lit., "whom the commonalty receives."
[23] Consentes (those who are together, or agree together, i.e., councillors) and Complices (confederate, or agreeing) are said by some to be the twelve gods who composed the great council of heaven; and, in

cause they rise and fall together, six of them being male, and as many female, with unknown names and pitiless dispositions,[1] but they are considered the counsellors and princes of Jove supreme. There were some, too, who said that Jupiter, Juno, and Minerva were the *dii Penates*, without whom we cannot live and be wise, and by whom we are ruled within in reason, passion, and thought. As you see, even here, too, nothing is said harmoniously, nothing is settled with the consent of all, nor is there anything reliable on which the mind can take its stand, drawing by conjecture very near to the truth. For their opinions are so doubtful, and one supposition so discredited[2] by another, that there is either no truth in them all, or if it is uttered by any, it is not recognised amid so many different statements.

41. We can, if it is thought proper, speak briefly of the Lares also, whom the mass think to be the gods of streets and ways, because the Greeks name streets *lauræ*. In different parts of his writings, Nigidius *speaks of them* now as the guardians of houses and dwellings; now as the Curetes, who are said to have once concealed, by the clashing of cymbals,[3] the infantile cries of Jupiter; now the five Digiti Samothracii, who, the Greeks tell *us*, were named *Idæi Dactyli*. Varro, with like hesitation, says at one time that they are the Manes,[4] and therefore the mother of the Lares was named Mania; at another time, again, he maintains that they are gods of the air, and are termed heroes; at another, following the opinion of the ancients, he says that the Lares are ghosts, as it were a kind of tutelary demon, spirits of dead[5] men.

42. It is a vast and endless task to examine each kind separately, and make it evident even from your religious books that you neither hold nor believe that there is any god concerning whom you have not[6] brought forward doubtful and inconsistent statements, expressing a thousand different beliefs. But, to be brief, and avoid prolixity,[7] it is enough to have said what has been said; it is, further, too troublesome to

gather together many things into one mass, since it is made manifest and evident in different ways that you waver, and say nothing with certainty of these things which you assert. But you will perhaps say, Even if we have no personal knowledge of the Lares, Novensiles, Penates, still the very agreement of our authors proves their existence, and that such a race[8] takes rank among the celestial gods. And how can it be known whether there *is* any god, if what he is shall be wholly unknown?[9] or how can it avail even to ask for benefits, if it is not settled and determined who should be invoked at each inquiry?[10] For every one who seeks to obtain an answer from any deity, should of necessity know to whom he makes supplication, on whom he calls, from whom he asks help for the affairs and occasions of human life; especially as you yourselves declare that all the gods do not have all power, and[11] that the wrath and anger of each are appeased by different rites.

43. For if this *deity*[12] requires a black, that[13] a white skin; *if* sacrifice must be made to this one with veiled, to that with uncovered head;[14] this one is consulted about marriages,[15] the other relieves distresses, — may it not be of some importance whether the one or the other is Novensilis, since ignorance of the facts and confusion of persons displeases the gods, and leads necessarily to the contraction of guilt? For suppose that I myself, to avoid some inconvenience and peril, make supplication to any one of these deities, saying, Be present, be near, divine Penates, thou Apollo, and thou, O Neptune, and in your divine clemency turn away all these evils, by which I am annoyed,[16] troubled, and tormented: will there be any hope that I shall receive help from them, if Ceres, Pales, Fortune, or the *genius Jovialis*,[17] not Neptune and Apollo, shall be the *dii Penates?* Or if I invoked the Curetes instead of the Lares, whom some of your writers maintain to be the *Digiti Samothracii*, how shall I enjoy their help and favour, when I have not given them their own names, and *have* given to the others names not their own? Thus does our interest demand that we should rightly know the gods, and not hesitate or doubt about the power, the name of each;

---

accordance with this, the words *una oriantur et occidant una* might be translated " rise and sit down together," i.e., at the council table. But then, the names and number of these are known; while Arnobius says, immediately after, that the names of the dii Consentes are not known, and has already quoted Varro, to the effect that neither names nor number are known. Schelling (*über die Gotth. v. Samothr.*, quoted by Orelli) adopts the reading (see following note), " of whom very little mention is made," i.e., in prayers or rites, because they are merely Jove's councillors, and exercise no power over men, and identifies them with the Samothracian Cabiri — Κάβειροι and Consentes being merely Greek and Latin renderings of the name.

[1] So the MS. and all edd. reading *miserationis parcissimæ*, except Gelenius, who reads *nationis barbarissimæ* — " of a most barbarous nation; " while Ursinus suggested *memorationis parc.* — " of whom very little mention is made," — the reading approved by Schelling."

[2] Lit., " shaken to its foundations."

[3] *Æribus.* Cf. Lucretius, ii. 633–636.

[4] The MS. reads *manas*, corrected as above by all edd. except Hild., who reads *Manias.*

[5] The MS. reads *effunctorum;* LB. *et funct.*, from the correction of Stewechius; Gelenius, with most of the other edd., *def.*

[6] The MS. and first ed. omit *non.*

[7] Lit., " because of aversion."

[8] Lit., " the form of their race."

[9] i.e., *ignorabitur et nescietur.*

[10] The MS. reads *consolationem* — " for each consolation," i.e., to comfort in every distress.

[11] The MS. omits *et.*

[12] The *dii inferi.*

[13] The *dii superi.*

[14] Saturn and Hercules were so worshipped.

[15] Apollo.

[16] The MS., first five edd., and Oehler read *terreor* — " terrified; " the others *tor.*, as above, from the conjecture of Gifanius.

[17] Cf. ch. 40, note 21. It may further be observed that the Etruscans held that the superior and inferior gods and men were linked together by a kind of intermediate beings, through whom the gods took cognizance of human affairs, without themselves descending to earth. These were divided into four classes, assigned to Tina (Jupiter), Neptune, the gods of the nether world, and men respectively.

lest,[1] if they be invoked with rites and titles not their own, they have at once their ears stopped *against our prayers*, and hold us involved in guilt which may not be forgiven.

44. Wherefore, if you are assured that in the lofty palaces of heaven there dwells, there is, that multitude of deities whom you specify, you should make your stand on one proposition,[2] and not, divided by different and inconsistent opinions, destroy belief in the very things which you seek to establish.   If there is a Janus, let

Janus be ; if a Bacchus, let Bacchus be ; if a Summanus,[3] let Summanus be : for this is to confide, this to hold, to be settled in the knowledge of something ascertained, not to say after the manner of the blind and erring, The Novensiles are the Muses, in truth they are the Trebian gods, nay, their number is nine, or rather, they are the protectors of cities which have been overthrown ; and bring so important matters into this danger, that while you remove some, and put others in their place, it may well be doubted of them all if they anywhere exist.

---

[1] So LB., Hild., and Oehler, reading *nomine ne ;* all others *ut,* the MS. having no conjunction.
[2] Lit., "it is fitting that you stand in the limits of," etc.

[3] i.e., Summus Manium, Pluto.

BOOK IV.

1. We would ask you, and you above all, O Romans, lords and princes of the world, whether you think that Piety, Concord, Safety, Honour, Virtue, Happiness, and other such names, to which we see you rear[1] altars and splendid temples, have divine power, and live in heaven?[2] or, as is usual, have you classed them with the deities merely for form's sake, because we desire and wish these blessings to fall to our lot?   For if, while you think them empty names without any substance, you yet deify them with divine honours,[3] you will have to consider whether that is a childish frolic, or tends to bring your deities into contempt,[4] when you make equal, and add to their number vain and feigned names.   But if you have loaded them with temples and couches, holding with more assurance that these, too, are deities, we pray you to teach *us in* our ignorance, by what course, in what way, Victory, Peace, Equity, and the others mentioned among the gods, can be understood to be gods, to belong to the assembly of the immortals?

2. For we — but, perhaps, you *would* rob and deprive us of common-sense — feel and perceive that none of these has divine power, or possesses a form of its own ;[5] but that, *on the contrary*, they are the excellence of manhood,[6] the safety of the safe, the honour of the respected, the victory of the conqueror, the harmony of the allied, the piety of the pious, the recollection of the observant, the good fortune, indeed, of him who lives happily and without exciting any ill-feeling. Now it is easy to perceive that, in speaking thus,

we speak most reasonably when we observe[7] the contrary qualities opposed *to them*, misfortune, discord, forgetfulness, injustice, impiety, baseness of spirit, and unfortunate[8] weakness of body. For as these things happen accidentally, and[9] depend on human acts *and* chance moods, so their contraries, named[10] after more agreeable qualities, must be found in others ; and from these, originating in this wise, have arisen those invented names.

3. With regard, indeed, to your bringing forward to us other bands of unknown[11] gods, we cannot determine whether you do that seriously, and from a belief in its certainty ; or, *merely* playing with empty fictions, abandon yourselves to an unbridled imagination.   The goddess Luperca, you tell us on the authority of Varro, was named because the fierce wolf spared the exposed children.   Was that goddess, then, disclosed, not by her own power, *but* by the course of events? and was it *only* after the wild beast restrained its cruel teeth, that she both began to be herself and was marked by[12] her name? or if she was already a goddess long before the birth of Romulus and his brother, show us what was her name and title.   Præstana was named, according to you, because, in throwing the javelin, Quirinus excelled all in strength ;[13] and the goddess Panda, or Pantica, was named because Titus Tatius was allowed to open up and make passable a

---

[7] Lit., "which it is easy to perceive to be said by us with the greatest truth from," etc., — so most edd. reading *nobis ;* but the MS., according to Crusius, gives *vobis* — "you," as in Orelli and Oberthür.
[8] Lit., "less auspicious."
[9] The MS., first four edd., and Elmenhorst, read *quæ* — "which ;" the rest, as above, *que.*
[10] Lit., "what is opposed to them named." *nominatum ;* a correction by Oehler for the MS. *nominatur* — "is named."
[11] The MS. and both Roman edd. read *signatorum* — "sealed ;" the others, except Hild., *ignotorum,* as above.
[12] Lit., "drew the meaning of her name."
[13] Lit., "excelled the might of all."

---

[1] Lit., "see altars built."
[2] Lit., "in the regions of heaven."
[3] The MS. reads *tam* (corrected by the first four edd. *tamen*) *in regionibus* — "in the divine seats ;" corrected, *religionibus,* as above, by Ursinus.
[4] Lit., "to the deluding of your deities."
[5] Lit., "is contained in a form of its own kind."
[6] i.e., manliness.

road, that he might take the Capitoline. Before these events, then, had the deities never existed? and if Romulus had not held the first place in casting the javelin, and if the Sabine king had been unable to take the Tarpeian rock, would there be no Pantica, no Præstana? And if you say that they[1] existed before that which gave rise to their name, a question which has been discussed in a preceding section,[2] tell us also what they were called.

4. Pellonia is a goddess mighty to drive back enemies. Whose enemies, say, if it is convenient? Opposing armies meet, and fighting together, hand to hand, decide the battle; and to one this side, to another that, is hostile. Whom, then, will Pellonia turn to flight, since on both sides there will be fighting? or in favour of whom will she incline, seeing that she should afford to both sides the might and services of her name? But if she indeed[3] did so, that is, if she gave her good-will and favour to both sides, she would destroy the meaning of her name, which was formed with regard to the beating back of one side. But you will perhaps say, She is goddess of the Romans only, and, being on the side of the Quirites alone, is ever ready graciously to help them.[4] We wish, indeed, that it were so, for we like the name; but it is a very doubtful matter. What! do the Romans have gods to themselves, who do not help[5] other nations? and how can they be gods, if they do not exercise their divine power impartially towards all nations everywhere? and where, I pray you, was this goddess Pellonia long ago, when the national honour was brought under the yoke at the Caudine Forks? when at the Trasimene lake the streams ran with blood? when the plains of Diomede[6] were heaped up with dead Romans? when a thousand other blows were sustained in countless disastrous battles? Was she snoring and sleeping;[7] or, as the base often do, had she deserted to the enemies' camp?

5. The sinister deities preside over the regions on the left hand only, and are opposed to those[8] on the right. But with what reason this is said, or with what meaning, we do not understand ourselves; and we are sure that you cannot in any degree cause it to be clearly and generally understood.[9] For in the first place, indeed, the world itself has in itself neither right nor left, neither upper nor under regions, neither fore nor

after *parts*. For whatever is round, and bounded on every side by the circumference[10] of a solid sphere, has no beginning, no end; where there is no end and beginning, no part can have[11] its own name and form the beginning. Therefore, when we say, This is the right, and that the left side, we do not refer to anything[12] in the world, which is everywhere very much the same, but to our own place and position, we being[13] so formed that we speak of some things as on our right hand, of others as on our left; and yet these very things which we name left, and the others *which we name* right, have in us no continuance, no fixedness, but take their forms from our sides, just as chance, and the accident of the moment, may have placed us. If I look towards the rising sun, the north pole and the north are on my left hand; and if I turn my face thither, the west will be on my left, for it will be regarded as behind the sun's back. But, again, if I turn my eyes to the region of the west, the wind and country of the south are now said to be on[14] my left. And if I am turned to this side by the necessary business of the moment, the result is, that the east is said *to be* on the left, owing to a further change of position,[15] — from which it can be very easily seen that nothing is either on our right or on our left by nature, but from position, time,[16] and according as our bodily position with regard to surrounding objects has been taken up. But in this case, by what means, in what way, will there be gods of the regions of the left, when it is clear that the same regions are at one time on the right, at another on the left? or what have the regions of the right done to the immortal gods, to deserve that they should be without any to care for them, while they have ordained that these should be fortunate, and ever *accompanied* by lucky omens?

6. Lateranus,[17] as you say, is the god and genius of hearths, and received this name because men build that kind of fireplace of unbaked bricks. What then? if hearths were made of baked clay, or any other material whatever, will they have no genii? and will Lateranus, whoever he is, abandon his duty as guardian, because the kingdom which he possesses has not been formed of bricks of clay? And for what purpose,[18] I ask, has that god received the charge of hearths? He runs about the kitchens of men, examin-

---

[1] MS., "that these, too," i.e., as well as Luperca.
[2] No such discussion occurs in the preceding part of the work, but the subject is brought forward in the end of chap. 8, p. 478, *infra*.
[3] In the first sentence the MS. reads *utrique*, and in the second *utique*, which is reversed in most edd., as above.
[4] Lit., "ever at hand with gracious assistances."
[5] Lit., "are not of"
[6] i.e., the field of Cannæ.
[7] [1 Kings xviii. 27.]
[8] Lit., "the parts."
[9] Lit., "it cannot be brought into any light of general understanding by you."

[10] Lit., "convexity."
[11] Lit., "be of."
[12] Lit., "to the state of the world."
[13] Lit., "who have been so formed, that some things are said by us," *nobis*, the reading of Oberthür and Orelli for the MS. *in nos* — "with regard to us," which is retained by the first four edd., Elm., Hild., and Oehler.
[14] i.e., *transit in vocabulum sinistri; in* being omitted in the MS. and both Roman edd.
[15] Lit., "the turning round of the body being changed."
[16] So Oehler, reading *positione, sed tempore sed*, for the MS. *positionis et temporis et*.
[17] No mention is made of this deity by any other author.
[18] Lit., "that he may do what."

ing and discovering with what kinds of wood
the heat in their fires is produced; he gives
strength[1] to earthen vessels, that they may not
fly in pieces, overcome by the violence of the
flames; he sees that the flavour of unspoilt
dainties reaches the taste of the palate with their
own pleasantness, and acts the part of a taster,
and tries whether the sauces have been rightly
prepared. Is not this unseemly, nay — to speak
with more truth — disgraceful, impious, to introduce some pretended deities for this only, not
to do them reverence with fitting honours, but to
appoint them over base things, and disreputable
actions?[2]

7. Does Venus Militaris, also, preside over the
evil-doing[3] of camps, and the debaucheries of
young men? Is there one Perfica,[4] also, of the
crowd of deities, who causes those base and
filthy delights to reach their end with uninterrupted pleasure? Is there also Pertunda, who
presides over the marriage[5] couch? Is there
also Tutunus, on whose huge members[6] and
horrent *fascinum* you think it auspicious, and
desire, that your matrons should be borne? But
if facts themselves have very little effect in suggesting to you a right understanding of the truth,
are you not able, even from the very names, to
understand that these are the inventions of a
most meaningless superstition, and the false gods
of fancy?[7] Puta, you say, presides over the
pruning of trees, Peta over prayers; Nemes-
trinus[8] is the god of groves; Patellana is a deity,
and Patella, of whom the one has been set over
things brought to light, the other over those yet
to be disclosed. Nodutis is spoken of as a god,
because he[9] brings that which has been sown to
the knots; and she who presides over the treading out of grain, Noduterensis;[10] the goddess
Upibilia[11] delivers from straying from the *right*
paths; parents bereaved of their children are
under the care of Orbona, — those very near

to death, under that of Nænia. Again,[12] Ossi-
lago herself is mentioned *as she* who gives firmness and solidity to the bones of young children.
Mellonia is a goddess, strong and powerful in
regard to bees, caring for and guarding the sweetness of their honey.

8. Say, I pray you, — that Peta, Puta, Patella
may graciously favour you, — if there were no[13]
bees at all on the earth then, or if we men were
born without bones, like some worms, would
there be no goddess Mellonia;[14] or would Ossi-
lago, who gives bones their solidity, be without
a name of her own? I ask truly, and eagerly
inquire whether you think that gods, or men, or
bees, fruits, twigs, and the rest, are the more
ancient in nature, time, long duration? No man
will doubt that you say that the gods precede all
things whatever by countless ages and generations. But if it is so, how, in the nature of
things, can it be that, from things produced
afterwards, they received those names which are
earlier in point of time? or that the gods were
charged with the care[15] of those things which
were not yet produced, and assigned to be of
use to men? Or were the gods long without
names; and was it only after things began to
spring up, and be on the earth, that you thought
it right that they should be called by these
names[16] and titles? And whence could you
have known what name to give to each, since
you were wholly ignorant of their existence;
or that they possessed *any* fixed powers, seeing
that you were equally unaware which of them
had any power, and over what he should be
placed to suit his divine might?

9. What then? you say; do you declare that
these gods exist nowhere in the world, and have
been created by unreal fancies? Not we alone,
but truth itself, and reason, say so, and that
common-sense in which all men share. For who
is there who believes that there are gods of gain,
and that they preside over the getting of it, seeing that it springs very often from the basest
employments, and is always at the expense of
others? Who believes that Libentina, who that
Burnus,[17] is set over *those* lusts which wisdom
bids us avoid, and which, in a thousand ways,
vile and filthy wretches[18] attempt and practise?
Who that Limentinus and Lima have the care
of thresholds, and do the duties of their keepers,
when every day we see *the thresholds* of temples

1 Lit., "*good* condition," *habitudinem.*
2 Lit., "a disreputable act."
3 So the MS., reading *flagitiis,* followed by all edd. except LB. and Orelli, who read *plagiis* — "kidnapping."
4 Of this goddess, also, no other author makes mention but the germ may be perhaps found in Lucretius (ii. 1116-7), where nature is termed *perfica,* i.e., "perfecting," or making all things complete. [The learned translator forgets Tertullian, who introduces us to this name in the work Arnobius imitates throughout. See vol. iii. p. 140.]
5 I.e., *in cubiculis præsto est virginalem scrobem effodienti-bus maritis.*
6 The first five edd. read *Mutunus.* Cf. ch. 11. [I think it a mistake to make Mutunus = Priapus. Their horrible deformities are *diverse,* as I have noted in European collections of antiquities. The *specialty* of Mutunus is noted by our author, and is unspeakably abominable. All this illustrates, therefore, the Christian scruples about marriage-feasts, of which see vol. v. note 1, p. 435.]
7 Lit., the "fancies" or "imaginations" of false gods. Meursius proposed to transpose the whole of this sentence to the end of the chapter, which would give a more strictly logical arrangement; but it must be remembered that Arnobius allows himself much liberty in this respect.
8 Of these three deities no other mention is made.
9 The MS., LB., Hild., and Oehler read *qui* — "who brings;" the other edd., as above, *quia.*
10 So the MS. (cf. ch. 11), first five edd., Oberth., Hild., and Oehler; the other edd. read *Nodutim Ter.*
11 So the MS., both Roman edd., and Oehler; the other edd reading *Vibilia,* except Hild., *Viabilia.*

12 The MS. reads *nam* — "for," followed by all edd. except Orelli, who reads *jam* as above, and Oehler, who reads *etiam* — "also."
13 Orelli omits *non,* following Oberthür.
14 Both in this and the preceding chapter the MS. reads *Melonia.*
15 Lit., "obtained by lot the wardships."
16 Lit., "signs."
17 So the MS., both Roman edd., Hild., and Oehler; the others reading *Liburnum,* except Elm, who reads *-am,* while Meursius conjectured *Liberum* — "Bacchus."
18 Lit., "shameful impurity seeks after;" *expetit* read by Gelenius, Canterus, and Oberthür, for the unintelligible MS. reading *expe-ditur,* retained in both Roman edd.; the others reading *experitur* — "tries."

and private houses destroyed and overthrown, and that the infamous approaches to stews are not without them? Who believes that the Limi [1] watch over obliquities? who that Saturnus presides over the sown crops? who that Montinus is the guardian of mountains; Murcia,[2] of the slothful? Who, finally, would believe that Money is a goddess, whom your writings declare, as though *she were* the greatest deity, to give golden rings,[3] the front seats at games and shows, honours in the greatest number, the dignity of the magistracy, and that which the indolent love most of all, — an undisturbed ease, by means of riches.

10. But if you urge that bones, *different kinds of* honey, thresholds, and all the other things which we have either run over rapidly, or, to avoid prolixity, passed by altogether, have [4] their own peculiar guardians, we may in like manner introduce a thousand other gods, who should care for and guard innumerable things. For why should a god have charge of honey only, and not of gourds, rape, cunila, cress, figs, beets, cabbages? Why should the bones alone have found protection, and not the nails, hair, and all the other things which are placed in the hidden parts and members of which we feel ashamed, and are exposed to very many accidents, and stand more in need of the care and attention of the gods? Or if you say that these parts, too, act under the care of their own tutelar deities, there will begin to be as many gods as there are things; nor will the cause be stated why the divine care does not protect all things, if you say that there are certain things over which the deities preside, and for which they care.

11. What say you, O fathers of new religions, and powers?[5] Do you cry out, and complain that these gods are dishonoured by us, and neglected with profane contempt, viz., Lateranus, the genius of hearths; Limentinus, who presides over thresholds; Pertunda,[6] Perfica, Noduterensis:[7] and do you say that things have sunk into ruin, and that the world itself has changed its laws and constitution, because we do not bow

humbly in supplication to Mutunus[8] and Tutunus? But now look and see, lest while you imagine such monstrous things, and form such conceptions, you may have offended the gods who most assuredly exist, if only there are any who are worthy to bear and hold that most exalted title; and it be for no other reason that those evils, of which you speak, rage, and increase by accessions every day.[9] Why, then, some one of you will perhaps say, do you maintain [10] that it is not true that these gods exist? And, when invoked by the diviners, do they obey the call, and come when summoned by their own names, and give answers which may be relied on, to those who consult them? We can show that what is said is false, either because in the whole matter there is the greatest room for distrust, or because we, every day, see many of their predictions either prove untrue, or wrested with baffled expectation *to suit* the opposite issues.

12. But let them [11] be true, as you maintain, yet will you have us also believe [12] that Mellonia, for example, introduces herself into the entrails, or Limentinus, and that they set themselves to make known [13] what you seek to learn? Did you ever see their face, their deportment, their countenance? or can even these be seen in lungs or livers? May it not happen, may it not come to pass, although you craftily conceal it, that the one should take the other's place, deluding, mocking, deceiving, and presenting the appearance of the *deity* invoked? If the magi, *who are* so much akin to [14] soothsayers, relate that, in their incantations, pretended gods [15] steal in frequently instead of those invoked; that some of these, moreover, are spirits of grosser substance,[16] who pretend that they are gods, and delude the ignorant by their lies and deceit, — why [17] should we not similarly believe that here, too, others substitute themselves for those who are not, that they may both strengthen your superstitious beliefs, and rejoice that victims are slain in sacrifice to them under names not their own?

13. Or, if you refuse to believe this on account of its novelty,[18] how can you know whether there is not some one, who comes in place of all whom you invoke, and substituting himself in all parts

[1] The MS. reads *Lemons;* Hild. and Oehler, *Limones;* the others, *Limos,* as above.

[2] The MS., LB., Hild., and Oehler read *Murcidam;* the others, *Murciam,* as above.

[3] i.e., equestrian rank.

[4] The MS. reading is *quid si haberet in sedibus suos,* retained by the first five edd., with the change of *-ret* into *-rent* — "what if in their seats the bones had their own peculiar guardians;" Ursinus in the margin, followed by Hild. and Oehler, reads *in se divos suos* — "if for themselves the bones had gods as their own peculiar," etc.; the other edd. reading, as above, *si habere insistitis suos.*

[5] i.e., deities. So LB. and Orelli, reading *quid potestatum?* — what, *O fathers* of powers." The MS. gives *qui* — "what say you, O fathers of new religions, who cry out, and complain that gods of powers are indecently dishonoured by us, and neglected with impious contempt," etc. Heraldus emends thus: " . . . fathers of great religions and powers? Do you, then, cry out," etc. "Fathers," i.e., those who discovered, and introduced, unknown deities and forms of worship.

[6] The MS. reads *pertus quæ-* (marked as spurious) *dam;* and, according to Hild., *naeniam* is written over the latter word.

[7] So the MS. Cf. ch. 7 [note 10, p. 478, *supra*].

[8] The MS. is here very corrupt and imperfect, — *supplices hoc est uno procumbimus atque est utuno* (Orelli omits *ut-*), emended by Gelenius, with most edd., *supp. Mut-uno proc. atque Tutuno,* as above; Elm. and LB. merely insert *humi* — "on the ground," after *supp.* [See p. 478, note 6, *supra*.]

[9] Meursius is of opinion that some words have slipped out of the text here, and that some arguments had been introduced about augury and divination.

[10] *Contendis,* not found in the MS.

[11] i.e., the predictions.

[12] Lit., "will you make the same belief."

[13] Lit., "adapt themselves to the significations of the things which."

[14] Lit., "brothers of."

[15] i.e., demons.

[16] Perhaps "abilities" — *materiis.*

[17] The MS. reads *cum* — "with similar reason we may believe," instead of *cur,* as above.

[18] Lit., "novelty of the thing."

of the world,[1] shows to you what appear to be[2] many gods and powers? Who is that one? some one will ask. We may perhaps, being instructed by truthful authors, be able to say; but, lest you should be unwilling to believe us, let my opponent ask the Egyptians, Persians, Indians, Chaldeans, Armenians, and all the others who have seen and become acquainted with these things in the more recondite arts. Then, indeed, you will learn who is the one God, or who the very many under Him are, who pretend to be gods, and make sport of men's ignorance.

Even now we are ashamed to come to the point at which not only boys, young and pert, but grave men also, cannot restrain their laughter, and *men who have been* hardened into a strict and stern humour.[3] For while we have all heard it inculcated and taught by our teachers, that in declining *the names* of the gods there was no plural number, because the gods were individuals, and the ownership of each name could not be common to a great many;[4] you in forgetfulness, and putting away the memory of your early lessons, both give to several gods the same names, and, although you are elsewhere more moderate as to their number, have multiplied them, again, by community of names; which subject, indeed, men of keen discernment and acute intellect have before now treated both in Latin and Greek.[5] And that might have lessened *our labour*,[6] if it were not that at the same time we see that some know nothing of these books; and, also, that the discussion which we have begun, compels us to bring forward something on these subjects, although *it has been already* laid hold of, and related by those *writers*.

14. Your theologians, then, and authors on unknown antiquity, say that in the universe there are three Joves, one of whom has Æther for his father; another, Cœlus; the third, Saturn, born and buried[7] in the island of Crete. *They speak of* five Suns and five Mercuries, — of whom, as they relate, the first Sun is called the son of Jupiter, and is regarded as grandson of Æther; the second *is* also Jupiter's son, and the mother who bore him Hyperiona;[8] the third the son of

Vulcan, not *Vulcan* of Lemnos, but the son of the Nile; the fourth, whom Acantho bore at Rhodes in the heroic age, *was* the father of Ialysus; *while* the fifth is regarded as the son of a Scythian king and subtle Circe. Again, the first Mercury, who is said to have lusted after Proserpina,[9] is son of Cœlus, *who is* above all. Under the earth is the second, who boasts that he is Trophonius. The third *was* born of Maia, his mother, and the third Jove;[10] the fourth is the offspring of the Nile, whose name the people of Egypt dread and fear to utter. The fifth is the slayer of Argus, a fugitive and exile, and the inventor of letters in Egypt. But there are five Minervas also, they say, just as *there are five* Suns and Mercuries; the first of whom is no virgin, but the mother of Apollo by Vulcan; the second, the offspring of the Nile, who is asserted to be the Egyptian Sais; the third is descended from Saturn, and is the one who devised the use of arms; the fourth is sprung from Jove, and the Messenians name her Coryphasia; and the fifth is she who slew her lustful[11] father, Pallas.

15. And lest it should seem tedious and prolix to wish to consider each person singly, the same theologians say that there are four Vulcans and three Dianas, as many Æsculapii and five Dionysi, six Hercules and four Venuses, three sets of Castors and the same number of Muses, three winged Cupids, and four named Apollo;[12] whose fathers they mention in like manner, in like manner their mothers, *and* the places where they were born, and point out the origin and family of each. But if it is true and certain, and is told in earnest as a *well*-known matter, either they are not all gods, inasmuch as there cannot be several under the same name, as we have been taught; or if there is one of them, he will not be known and recognised, because he is obscured by the confusion of very similar names. And thus it results from your own action, however unwilling you may be that it should be so, that religion is brought into difficulty and confusion, and has no fixed end to which it can turn itself, without being made the sport of equivocal illusions.

16. For suppose that it had occurred to us,

---

[1] Lit., " of places and divisions," i.e., places separated from each other.

[2] Lit., " affords to you the appearance of."

[3] Lit., " a severity of stern manner " — *moris* for the MS. *mares*.

[4] Orelli here introduces the sentence, " For it cannot be," etc., with which this book is concluded in the MS. Cf. ch. 37, n. 4, *infra*.

[5] There can be no doubt that Arnobius here refers to Clemens Alexandrinus (λόγος Προτρεπτικὸς πρὸς Ἑλλῆνυς), and Cicero (*de Nat. Deor.*), from whom he borrows most freely in the following chapters, quoting them at times very closely. We shall not indicate particular references without some special reason, as it must be understood these references would be required with every statement. [Compare Clement, vol. ii. pp. 305-13, and Tertullian, vol. iii. p. 34.]

[6] Lit., " given to us an abridging," i.e., an opportunity of abridging.

[7] Lit., " committed to sepulture and born in," etc.

[8] Arnobius repeats this statement in ch. 22, or the name would have been regarded as corrupt, no other author making mention of such a goddess; while Cicero speaks of one Sun as born of Hyperion.

It would appear, therefore, to be very probable that Arnobius, in writing from memory or otherwise, has been here in some confusion as to what Cicero did say, and thus wrote the name as we have it. It has also been proposed to read " born of Regina " (or, with Gelenius, Rhea), " and his father Hyperion," because Cybele is termed βασιλεια; for which reading there seems no good reason. — Immediately below, Ialysus is made the son, instead of, as in Cicero, the grandson of the fourth; and again, Circe is said to be mother, while Cicero speaks of her as the daughter of the fifth Sun. These variations, viewed along with the general adherence to Cicero's statements (*de N. D.*, iii. 21 sqq.), seem to give good grounds for adopting the explanation given above.

[9] i.e., *in Proserpinam genitalibus adhinnivisse subrectis*.

[10] Lit., " of Jupiter, but the third."

[11] i.e., *incestorum appetitorem*.

[12] So Cicero (iii. 23); but Clemens [vol. ii. p. 179] speaks of five, and notes that a sixth had been mentioned.

moved either by suitable influence or violent fear of you,[1] to worship Minerva, for example, with the rights you deem sacred, and the usual ceremony: if, when we prepare sacrifices, and approach to make *the offerings* appointed for her on the flaming altars, all the Minervas shall fly thither, and striving for the right to that name, each demand that the offerings prepared be given to herself; what drawn-out animal shall we place among them, or to whom shall we direct the sacred offices which are our duty?[2] For the first one of whom we spoke will perhaps say: "The name Minerva is mine, mine[3] the divine majesty, who bore Apollo and Diana, and by the fruit of my womb enriched heaven with deities, and multiplied the number of the gods." "Nay, Minerva," the fifth will say, "are you speaking,[4] who, being a wife, and so often a mother, have lost the sanctity of spotless purity? Do you not see that in all temples[5] the images of Minervas are those of virgins, and that all artists refrain from giving to them the figures of matrons?[6] Cease, therefore, to appropriate to yourself a name not rightfully[7] yours. For that I am Minerva, begotten of father Pallas, the whole band of poets bear witness, who call me Pallas, the surname being derived from my father." The second will cry on hearing this: "What say you? Do you, then, bear the name of Minerva, an impudent parricide, and one defiled by the pollution of lewd lust, who, decking yourself with rouge and a harlot's arts, roused upon yourself even your father's passions, full of maddening desires? Go further, then, seek for yourself another name; for this belongs to me, whom the Nile, greatest of rivers, begot from among his flowing waters, and brought to a maiden's estate from the condensing of moisture.[8] But if you inquire into the credibility of the matter, I too will bring as witnesses the Egyptians, in whose language I am called Neith, as Plato's *Timæus*[9] attests." What, then, do we suppose will be the result? Will she indeed cease to say that she is Minerva,

who is named Coryphasia, either to mark her mother, or because she sprung forth from the top of Jove's head, bearing a shield, and girt with the terror of arms? Or *are we to suppose* that she who is third will quietly surrender the name? and not argue[10] and resist the assumption of the first *two* with such words as these: "Do you thus dare to assume the honour of my name, O Sais,[11] sprung from the mud and eddies of a stream, and formed in miry places? Or do you usurp[12] another's rank, who falsely say that you were born a goddess from the head of Jupiter, and persuade very silly men that you are reason? Does he conceive and bring forth children from his head? That the arms you bear might be forged and formed, was there even in the hollow of his head a smith's workshop? *were there* anvils, hammers, furnaces, bellows, coals, and pincers? Or if, as you maintain, it is true that you are reason, cease to claim for yourself the name which is mine; for reason, of which you speak, is not a certain form of deity, but the understanding of difficult questions." If, then, as we have said, five Minervas should meet us when we essay to sacrifice,[13] and contending as to whose this name is, each demand that either fumigations of incense be offered to her, or sacrificial wines poured out from golden cups; by what arbiter, by what judge, shall we dispose of so great a dispute? or what examiner will there be, what umpire of so great boldness as to attempt, with such personages, either to give a just decision, or to declare their causes not founded on right? Will he not rather go home, and, keeping himself apart from such matters, think it safer to have nothing to do with them, lest he should either make enemies of the rest, by giving to one what belongs to all, or be charged with folly for yielding[14] to all what should be the property of one?

17. We may say the very same things of the Mercuries, the Suns,—indeed of all the others whose numbers you increase and multiply. But it is sufficient to know from one case that the same principle applies to the rest; and, lest our prolixity should chance to weary our audience, we shall cease to deal with individuals, lest, while we accuse you of excess, we also should ourselves be exposed to the charge of excessive loquacity. What do you say, you who, by *the fear of* bodily tortures, urge us to worship the gods, and constrain us to undertake the service of your deities? We can be easily won, if only something befitting the conception of so great a race be shown to us. Show us Mercury, but *only* one; give us

---

[1] Lit., "by the violence of your terror." The preceding words are read in the MS. *ideo motos*—"so moved by authority," and were emended *idonea*, as in the text, by Gelenius.
[2] Lit., "to what parts shall we transfer the duties of pious service."
[3] The MS. reads *cum numen;* Rigaltius, followed by Oehler, emending, as above, *meum;* the first four edd., with Oberthür, *tum*—"then the deity *is mine;*" while the rest read *cum numine*—"with the deity."
[4] So LB., Orelli, and Oehler, reading *tu tinnis* for the MS. *tutunis.*
[5] *Capitoliis.* In the Capitol were three shrines,—to Jove, Juno, and Minerva; and Roman colonies followed the mother-state's example. Hence the present general application of the term, which is found elsewhere in ecclesiastical Latin.
[6] Lit., "Nor are the forms of married persons given to these by all artists;" *nec* read in all edd. for the MS. *et*—"and of married," etc., which is opposed to the context.
[7] Lit., "not of your own right."
[8] *Concretione roris*—a strange phrase. Cf. Her., iv. 180: "They say that Minerva is the daughter of Poseidon and the Tritonian lake."
[9] St. p. 21. The MS. reads *quorum Nili lingua latonis;* the two Roman edd. merely insert *p., Plat.;* Gelenius and Canterus adding *dicor*—"in whose language I am called the Nile's," *Nili* being changed into *Neith* by Elmenhorst and later edd.

[10] Lit., "take account of herself."
[11] So Ursinus suggested in the margin for the MS. *si verum.*
[12] The third Minerva now addresses the fourth.
[13] Lit., "approaching the duties of religion."
[14] According to the MS. *sic*—"for so (i.e., as you do) yielding," etc.

Bacchus, but *only* one; one Venus, and in like manner one Diana. For you will never make us believe that there are four Apollos, or three Jupiters, not even if you were to call Jove himself as witness, or make the Pythian *god* your authority.

18. But some one on the opposite side says, How do we know whether the theologians have written what is certain and well known, or set forth a wanton fiction,[1] as they thought and judged? That has nothing to do with the matter; nor does the reasonableness of your argument depend upon this, — whether the facts are as the writings of the theologians state, or are otherwise and markedly different. For to us it is enough to speak of things which come before the public; and *we need* not inquire what is true, but *only* confute and disprove that which lies open to all, and *which* men's thoughts have generally received. But if they are liars, declare yourselves what is the truth, and disclose the unassailable mystery. And how can it be done when the services of men of letters are set aside? For what is there which can be said about the immortal gods that has not reached men's thoughts from what has been written by men on these subjects?[2] Or can you relate anything yourselves about their rights and ceremonies, which has not been recorded in books, and made known by what authors have written? Or if you think these of no importance, let all the books be destroyed which have been composed about the gods for you by theologians, pontiffs, *and* even some devoted to the study of philosophy; nay, let us rather suppose that from the foundation of the world no man ever wrote[3] anything about the gods: we wish to find out, and desire to know, whether you can mutter or murmur in mentioning the gods,[4] or conceive those in thought to whom no idea[5] from any book gave shape in your minds. But when it is clear that you have been informed of their names and powers by the suggestions of books,[6] it is unjust to deny the reliableness of these books by whose testimony and authority you establish what you say.

19. But perhaps these things will turn out to be false, and what you say to be true. By what proof, by what evidence, *will it be shown?* For since both parties are men, both those who have said the one thing and those who have said the other, and on both sides the discussion was of doubtful matters, it is arrogant to say that that is true which seems so to you, but that that which offends your feelings manifests wantonness and falsehood. By the laws of the human race, and the associations of mortality itself, when you read and hear, That god was born of this *father* and of that mother, do you not feel in your mind[7] that something is said which belongs to man, and relates to the meanness of our earthly race? Or, while you think that it is so,[8] do you conceive no anxiety lest you should in something offend the gods themselves, whoever they are, because you believe that it is owing to filthy intercourse . . .[9] that they have reached the light they knew not of, thanks to lewdness? For we, lest any one should chance to think that we are ignorant of, do not know, what befits the majesty of that name, assuredly[10] think that the gods should not know birth; or if they are born at all, we hold and esteem that the Lord and Prince of the universe, by ways which He knew Himself, sent them forth spotless, most pure, undefiled, ignorant of sexual pollution,[11] and brought to the full perfection of their natures as soon as they were begotten?[12]

20. But you, on the contrary, forgetting how great[13] their dignity and grandeur are, associate with them a birth,[14] and impute *to them* a descent,[14] which men of at all refined feelings regard as at once execrable and terrible. From Ops, you say, his mother, and from his father Saturn, Diespiter was born with his brothers. Do the gods, then, have wives; and, the matches having been previously planned, do they become subject to the bonds of marriage? Do they take upon themselves[15] the engagements of the bridal couch by prescription, by the cake of spelt, and by a pretended sale?[16] Have they their mistresses,[17] their promised wives, their betrothed brides, on settled conditions? And what do we say about their marriages, too, when indeed you say that some celebrated their nuptials, and entertained joyous throngs. and that the goddesses sported at these; and that *some* threw all things into utter confusion with dissensions because they had no share in *singing* the Fescennine verses, and occasioned danger and destruction[18] to the next generation of men?[19]

---

[7] Lit., "does it not touch the feeling of your mind."
[8] Ursinus would supply *eos* — "that they are so."
[9] *Atque ex seminis, actu,* or *jactu,* as the edd. except Hild. read it.
[10] The ms. reads *dignitati-s aut;* corrected, as above, *d. sane,* in the first five edd., Oberthür, and Orelli. [John x. 35.]
[11] *Quæsit fœditas ista coeundi.*
[12] Lit., "as far as to themselves, their first generation being completed."
[13] Lit., "forgetting the so great majesty and sublimity."
[14] Both plural.
[15] The ms., first four edd., and Oberthür read *conducunt* — "unite;" for which the rest read *condic-unt,* as above.
[16] i.e., *usu, farre, coemptione.*
[17] The word here translated mistresses, *speratas,* is used of maidens loved, but not yet asked in marriage.
[18] Lit., "dangers of destructions."
[19] Instead of "occasioned," *sevisse,* which the later editions give, the ms. and first four edd. read *sævisse* — "that danger and destruction raged against," etc.

---

[1] So all the edd., though Orelli approves of *fictione* (edd. *-em*), which is, he says, the ms. reading, "set forth with wanton fiction."
[2] The ms. and earlier edd., with Hild. and Oehler, read *ex hominum de scriptis;* LB. and Orelli inserting *his* after *de,* as above.
[3] The ms. and both Roman edd. read *esse,* which is clearly corrupt; for which LB. gives *scripsisse* (misprinted *scripse*), as above.
[4] i.e., "speak of them at all."
[5] Lit., "an idea of no writing."
[6] Lit., "been informed by books suggesting to you," etc.

21. But perhaps this foul pollution may be less apparent in the rest. Did, then, the ruler of the heavens, the father of gods and men, who, by the motion of his eyebrow, and by his nod, shakes the whole heavens and makes them tremble, — did he find his origin in man and woman? And unless both sexes abandoned *themselves* to degrading pleasures in sensual embraces,[1] would there be no Jupiter, greatest of all; and even to this time would the divinities have no king, and heaven stand without its lord? And why do we marvel that you say Jove sprang from a woman's womb, seeing that your authors relate that he both had a nurse, and in the next place maintained the life given to him by nourishment *drawn from* a foreign[2] breast? What say you, O men? Did, then, shall I repeat, *the god* who makes the thunder crash, lightens and hurls the thunderbolt, and draws together terrible clouds, drink in the streams of the breast, wail as an infant, creep about, and, that he might *be persuaded to* cease his crying most foolishly protracted, was he made silent by the noise of rattles,[3] and put to sleep lying in a very soft cradle, and lulled with broken words? O devout assertion *of the existence* of gods, pointing out and declaring the venerable majesty of their awful grandeur! Is it thus in your opinion, I ask, that the exalted powers[4] of heaven are produced? do your gods come forth to the light by modes of birth such as these, by which asses, pigs, dogs, by which the whole of this unclean herd[5] of earthly beasts is conceived and begotten?

22. And, not content to have ascribed these carnal unions to the venerable Saturn,[6] you affirm that the king of the world himself begot children even more shamefully than he was himself born and begotten. Of Hyperiona,[7] as his mother, you say, and Jupiter, who wields the thunderbolt, was born the golden and blazing Sun; of Latona and the same, the Delian archer, and Diana,[8] who rouses the woods; of Leda and the same,[9] those named in Greek Dioscori; of Alcmena and the same, the Theban Hercules, whom his club and hide defended; of him and Semele, Liber, who is named Bromius, and was born a second time from his father's thigh; of him, again, and Maia, Mercury, eloquent in speech, and bearer of the harmless snakes. Can any greater insult be put upon your Jupiter, or is there anything else which will destroy and ruin the reputation of the chief of the gods, further than that you believe him to have been at times overcome by vicious pleasures, and to have glowed with the passion of a heart roused to lust after women? And what had the Saturnian king to do with strange nuptials? Did Juno not suffice him; and could he not stay the force of his desires on the queen of the deities, although so great excellence graced her, *such* beauty, majesty of countenance, and snowy and marble whiteness of arms? Or did he, not content with one wife, taking pleasure in concubines, mistresses, and courtezans, a lustful god, show[10] his incontinence in all directions, as is the custom with dissolute[11] youths; and in old age, after intercourse with numberless persons, did he renew his eagerness for pleasures *now* losing their zest? What say you, profane ones; or what vile thoughts do you fashion about your Jove? Do you not, then, observe, do you not see with what disgrace you brand him? of what wrong-doing you make him the author? or what stains of vice, how great infamy you heap upon him?

23. Men, though prone to lust, and inclined, through weakness of character, to *yield to* the allurements of sensual pleasures, still punish adultery by the laws, and visit with the penalty of death those whom they find to have possessed themselves of others' rights by forcing the marriage-bed. The greatest of kings, *however, you tell us*, did not know how vile, how infamous the person of the seducer and adulterer was; and he who, as is said, examines our merits and demerits, did not, owing to the reasonings of his abandoned heart, see what was the fitting course *for him* to resolve on. But this misconduct might perhaps be endured, if you were to conjoin him with persons at least his equals, and *if* he were made by you the paramour of the immortal goddesses. But what beauty, what grace was there, I ask you, in human bodies, which could move, which could turn to it[12] the eyes of Jupiter? Skin, entrails, phlegm, and all that filthy mass placed under the coverings of the intestines, which not Lynceus only with his searching gaze can shudder at, but any other also can *be made to* turn from even by merely thinking. O wonderful reward of guilt, O fitting and precious joy, for which Jupiter, the greatest, should become a swan, and a bull, and beget white eggs!

---

1 *Copulatis corporibus.*
2 i.e., not his mother's, but the dug of the goat Amalthea.
3 Lit., "rattles heard."
4 Lit., "the eminence of the powers."
5 Lit., "inundation."
6 Lit., "Saturnian gravity."
7 Cf. ch. 14, note 8, *supra.*
8 It is worth while to compare this passage with ch. 16. Here Arnobius makes Latona the mother of Apollo and Diana, in accordance with the common legend; but there he represents the first Minerva as claiming them as her children.
9 In the MS. there is here an evident blunder on the part of the copyist, who has inserted the preceding line (" the archer Apollo, and of the woods ") after " the same." Omitting these words, the MS. reading is literally, " the name in Greek is to the Dioscori." Before " the name " some word is pretty generally supposed to have been lost, some conjecturing "to whom;" others (among them Orelli, following Salmasius) " Castores." But it is evidently not really necessary to supplement the text.
10 Lit., "scatter."
11 Orelli reads, with the MS., LB., and Hild., *babecali,* which he interprets *belli,* i.e., "handsome."
12 MS. and first five edd. read *inde* — " thence; " the others *in se,* as above. [Elucidation III.]

24. If you will open your minds' eyes, and see the real [1] truth without gratifying any private end, you will find that the causes of all the miseries by which, as you say, the human race has long been afflicted, flow from such beliefs which you held in former times about your gods; and which you have refused to amend, although the truth was placed before your eyes. For what about them, pray, have we indeed ever either imagined which was unbecoming, or put forth in shameful writings that the troubles which assail men and the loss of the blessings of life [2] should be used to excite a prejudice against us? Do we say that certain gods were produced from eggs,[3] like storks and pigeons? *Do we say* that the radiant Cytherean Venus grew up, having taken form from the sea's foam and the severed genitals of Cœlus? that Saturn was thrown into chains for parricide, and relieved from their weight only on his own days?[4] that Jupiter was saved from death [5] by the services of the Curetes? that he drove his father from the seat of power, and by force and fraud possessed a sovereignty not his own? Do we say that his aged sire, when driven out, concealed himself in the territories of the Itali, and gave his name as a gift to Latium,[6] because he had been *there* protected from his son? Do we say that Jupiter himself incestuously married his sister? or, instead of pork, breakfasted in ignorance upon the son of Lycaon, when invited to his table? that Vulcan, limping on one foot, wrought as a smith in the island of Lemnos? that Æsculapius was transfixed by a thunderbolt because of his greed and avarice, as the Bœotian Pindar [7] sings? that Apollo, having become rich, by his ambiguous responses, deceived the very kings by whose treasures and gifts he had been enriched? Did we declare that Mercury was a thief? that Laverna is *so* also, and along with him presides over secret frauds? Is the writer Myrtilus one of us, who declares that the Muses were the handmaids of Megalcon,[8] daughter of Macarus?[9]

25. Did we say [10] that Venus was a courtezan, deified by a Cyprian king named Cinyras? Who

reported that the palladium was formed from the remains of Pelops? Was it not you? Who that Mars was Spartanus? was it not your writer Epicharmus? Who that he was born within the confines of Thrace? was it not Sophocles the Athenian, with the assent of all his spectators? Who *that he was born* in Arcadia? was it not you? Who that he was kept a prisoner for thirteen months?[11] was it not the son of the river Meles? Who *said* that dogs were sacrificed to him by the Carians, asses by the Scythians? was it not Apollodorus especially, along with the rest? Who that in wronging another's marriage couch, he was caught entangled in snares? was it not your writings, your tragedies? Did we ever write that the gods for hire endured slavery, as Hercules at Sardis [12] for lust and wantonness; as the Delian Apollo, *who served* Admetus, as Jove's brother, *who served* the Trojan Laomedon, whom the Pythian also *served*, but with his uncle; as Minerva, who gives light, and trims the lamps to secret lovers? Is not he one of your poets, who represented Mars and Venus as wounded by men's hands? Is not Panyassis one of you, who relates that father Dis and queenly Juno were wounded by Hercules? Do not the writings of your Polemo say that Pallas [13] was slain,[14] covered with her own blood, overwhelmed by Ornytus? Does not Sosibius declare that Hercules himself was afflicted by the wound and pain he suffered at the hands of Hipocoon's children? Is it related at our instance that Jupiter was committed to the grave in the island of Crete? Do we say that the brothers,[15] who were united in their cradle, were buried in the territories of Sparta and Lacedæmon? Is the author of our number, who is termed Patrocles the Thurian in the titles of his writings, who relates that the tomb and remains of Saturn are found [16] in Sicily? Is Plutarch of Chæronea [17] esteemed one of us, who said that Hercules was reduced to ashes on the top of Mount Œta, after his loss of strength through epilepsy?

26. But what shall I say of the desires with which it is written in your books, and contained in your writers, that the holy immortals lusted after women? For is it by us that the king of

---

[1] Orelli, without receiving into the text, approves of the reading of Stewechius, *promptam*, "evident," for the MS., *propriam*.

[2] Lit., "the benefits diminished by which it is lived."

[3] The MS. reads *ex Jovis;* the first five edd. *Jove* — "from Jove," which is altogether out of place; the others, as above, *ex ovis.* Cf. i. 36.

[4] The MS. reads *et ablui diebus tantis . . . elevari;* LB., Hild., and Oehler, *statis* or *statutis . . . et levari* — "and was loosed and released on fixed days;" Elm., Oberthür, and Orelli receive the conjecture of Ursinus, *et suis diebus tantum . . . rel.*, as above.

[5] Cf. iii. [cap. 41, p. 475, and cap. 30, p. 472].

[6] i.e., hiding-place. Virg., Æn., viii. 322: *Quoniam latuisset tutus in oris.*

[7] *Pyth.*, iii. 102 sq.

[8] MS. *Meglac.*

[9] The MS. and most edd. give *filias*, making the Muses daughters of Macarus; but Orelli, Hild., and Oehler adopt, as above, the reading of Canterus, *filiæ*, in accordance with Clem. Alex.

[10] So the MS. reading *numquid dictatum*, which would refer this sentence to the end of the last chapter. Gelenius, with Canth., Oberth., and Orelli, reads *quis ditatum*, and joins with the following sentence thus: "Who related that Venus, a courtezan, enriched by C., was deified . . . ? who that the palladium," etc. Cf. v. 19.

[11] The MS. reads *quis mensibus in Arcadia tribus et decem vinctum* — "Who that he was bound thirteen months in Arcadia? was it not the son," etc. To which there are these two objections, — that Homer never says so; and that Clemens Alexandrinus [vol. ii. p. 179, this series], from whom Arnobius here seems to draw, speaks of Homer as saying only that Mars was so bound, without referring to Arcadia. The MS. reading may have arisen from carelessness on the part of Arnobius in quoting (cf. ch. 14, n. 2), or may be a corruption of the copyists. The reading translated is an emendation by Jortin, adopted by Orelli.

[12] *Sardibus*, — a conjecture of Ursinus, adopted by LB., Hild., and Oehler for the MS. *sordibus;* for which the others read *sordidi* — "for the sake of base lust."

[13] Lit., "the masculine one."

[14] As this seems rather extravagant when said of one of the immortals, *læsam*, "hurt," has been proposed by Meursius.

[15] Castor and Pollux.

[16] Lit., "contained."

[17] The MS. reads *Hieronymus Pl* — "is Hier., is Pl.," while Clem. Alex. mentions only "Hieronymus the philosopher."

the sea is asserted in the heat of maddened passion to have robbed of their virgin purity Amphitrite,[1] Hippothoe, Amymone, Menalippe, Alope?[2] that the spotless Apollo, Latona's son, most chaste and pure, with the passions of a breast not governed by reason, desired Arsinoe, Æthusa, Hypsipyle, Marpessa, Zeuxippe, and Prothoe, Daphne, and Sterope?[1] Is it shown in our poems that the aged Saturn, already long covered with grey hair, and now cooled by weight of years, being taken by his wife in adultery, put on the form of one of the lower animals, and neighing *loudly*, escaped in the shape of a beast? Do you not accuse Jupiter himself of having assumed countless forms, and concealed by mean deceptions the ardour of his wanton lust? Have we ever written that he obtained his desires by deceit, at one time changing into gold, at another into a sportive satyr; into a serpent, a bird, a bull; and, to pass beyond all limits of disgrace, into a little ant, that he might, forsooth, make Clitor's daughter the mother of Myrmidon, in Thessaly? Who represented him as having watched over Alcmena for nine nights without ceasing? was it not you? — that he indolently abandoned himself to his lusts, forsaking his post in heaven? was it not you? And, indeed, you ascribe[3] *to him* no mean favours; since, in your opinion, the god Hercules was born to exceed and surpass in such matters his father's powers. He in nine nights begot[4] with difficulty one son; but Hercules, a holy god, in one night taught the fifty daughters of Thestius at once to lay aside their virginal title, and to bear a mother's burden. Moreover, not content to have ascribed to the gods love of women, do you also say that they lusted after men? Some one loves Hylas; another is engaged with Hyacinthus; that one burns with desire for Pelops; this one sighs more ardently for Chrysippus; Catamitus is carried off to be a favourite and cup-bearer; and Fabius, that he may be called Jove's darling, is branded on the soft parts, and marked in the hinder.

27. But among you, is it only the males who lust; and has the female sex preserved its purity?[5] Is it not proved in your books that Tithonus was loved by Aurora; that Luna lusted after Endymion; the Nereid after Æacus; Thetis after Achilles' father; Proserpina after Adonis; her mother, Ceres, after some rustic Jasion, and afterwards Vulcan, Phaeton,[6] Mars; Venus herself, the mother of Æneas, and founder of the

Roman power, to marry Anchises? While, therefore, you accuse, without making *any* exception, not one only by name, but the whole of the gods alike, in whose existence you believe, of such acts of extraordinary shamefulness and baseness, do you dare, without violation of modesty, to say either that we are impious, or that you are pious, although they receive from you much greater occasion for offence on account of all the shameful acts which you heap up to their reproach, than in connection with the service and duties required by their majesty, honour, and worship? For either all these things are false which you bring forward about them individually, lessening their credit and reputation; and it is *in that case* a matter quite deserving, that the gods should utterly destroy the race of men; or if they are true and certain, and perceived without any reasons for doubt, it comes to this issue, that, however unwilling you may be, we believe them to be not of heavenly, but of earthly birth.

28. For where there are weddings, marriages, births, nurses, arts,[7] and weaknesses; where there are liberty and slavery; where there are wounds, slaughter, and *shedding of* blood; where there are lusts, desires, sensual pleasures; where there is every mental passion arising from disgusting emotions, — there must of necessity be nothing godlike there; nor can that cleave to a superior nature which belongs to a fleeting race, and to the frailty of earth. For who, if only he recognises and perceives what the nature of that power is, can believe either that a deity had the generative members, and was deprived of them by a very base operation; or that he at one time cut off the children sprung from himself, and was punished by suffering imprisonment; or that he, in a way, made civil war upon his father, and deprived him of the right of governing; or that he, filled with fear of one younger when overcome, turned to flight, and hid in remote solitudes, like a fugitive and exile? Who, I say, can believe that the deity reclined at men's tables, was troubled on account of his avarice, deceived his suppliants by an ambiguous reply, excelled in the tricks of thieves, committed adultery, acted as a slave, was wounded, and in love, and submitted to the seduction of impure desires in all the forms of lust? But yet you declare all these things both were, and are, in your gods; and you pass by no form of vice, wickedness, error, without bringing it forward, in the wantonness of your fancies, to the reproach of the gods. You must, therefore, either seek out other gods, to whom all these *reproaches* shall not apply, for they are a human and earthly race to whom they

---

[1] These names are all in the plural in the original.
[2] So LB. and Orelli, reading *Alopas*, from Clem. Alex., for the MS. *Alcyonas*.
[3] Lit., "you add."
[4] In the original, somewhat at large — *unam potuit prolem extundere, concinnare, compingere.*
[5] All edd. read this without mark of interrogation.
[6] The MS. reads *Phætontem:* for which, both here and in Clem., Potter proposed *Phaonem*, because no such amour is mentioned elsewhere.

[7] i.e., either the arts which belong to each god (cf. the words in ii. 18: "these (arts) are not the gifts of science, but the discoveries of necessity"), or, referring to the words immediately preceding, obstetric arts.

apply; or if there are only these whose names and character you have declared, by your beliefs you do away with them: for all the things of which you speak relate to men.

29. And here, indeed, we can show that all those whom you represent to us as and call gods, were *but* men, by quoting either Euhemerus of Acragas,[1] whose books were translated by Ennius into Latin that all might be thoroughly acquainted *with them;* or Nicanor[2] the Cyprian; or the Pellaean Leon; or Theodorus of Cyrene; or Hippo and Diagoras of Melos; or a thousand other writers, who have minutely, industriously, and carefully[3] brought secret things to light with noble candour. We may, I repeat, at pleasure, declare both the acts of Jupiter, and the wars of Minerva and the virgin[4] Diana; by what stratagems Liber strove to make himself master of the Indian empire; what was the condition, the duty, the gain[5] of Venus; to whom the great mother was bound in marriage; what hope, what joy was aroused in her by the comely Attis; whence *came* the Egyptian Serapis and Isis, or for what reasons their very names[6] were formed.

30. But in the discussion which we at present maintain, we do not undertake this trouble or service, to show and declare who all these were. *But* this is what we proposed to ourselves, that as you call us impious and irreligious, *and*, on the other hand, maintain that you are pious and serve the gods, we should prove and make manifest that by no men are they treated with less respect than by you. But if it is proved by the very insults that it is so, it must, as a consequence, be understood that it is you who rouse the gods to fierce and terrible rage, because you either listen to or believe, or yourselves invent about them, stories so degrading. For it is not he who is anxiously thinking of religious rites,[7] and slays spotless victims, who gives piles of incense to be burned with fire, not he must be thought to worship the deities, or alone discharge the duties of religion. True worship is in the heart, and a belief worthy of the gods; nor does it at all avail to bring blood and gore, if you believe about them things which are not only far remote from and unlike their nature, but even to some extent stain and disgrace both their dignity and virtue.

31. We wish, then, to question you, and invite you to answer a short question, Whether you think it a greater offence to sacrifice to them

no victims, because you think that so great a being neither wishes nor desires these; or, with foul beliefs, to hold opinions about them so degrading, that they might rouse any one's spirit to a mad desire for revenge? If the relative importance of the matters be weighed, you will find no judge so prejudiced as not to believe it a greater crime to defame by manifest insults any one's reputation, than to treat it with silent neglect. For this, perhaps, may be held and believed from deference to reason; *but* the other course manifests an impious spirit, and a blindness despaired of in fiction. If in your ceremonies and rites neglected sacrifices and expiatory offerings may be demanded, guilt is said to have been contracted; if by a momentary forgetfulness[8] any one has erred either in speaking or in pouring wine;[9] or again,[10] if at the solemn games and sacred races the dancer has halted, or the musician suddenly become silent, — you all cry out immediately that something has been done contrary to the sacredness of the ceremonies; or if the boy termed patrimus let go the thong in ignorance,[11] or could not hold *to* the earth:[12] and *yet* do you dare to deny that the gods are ever being wronged by you in sins so grievous, while you confess yourselves that, in less matters, they are often angry, to the national ruin?

32. But all these things, they say, are the fictions of poets, and games arranged for pleasure. It is not credible, indeed, that men by no means thoughtless, who sought to trace out the character of the remotest antiquity, either did not[13] insert in their poems the fables which survived in men's minds[14] and common conversation;[15] or that they would have assumed to themselves so great licence as to foolishly feign what was almost sheer madness, and might give them reason to be afraid of the gods, and bring them into danger with men. But let us grant that the poets are, as you say, the inventors and authors of tales so disgraceful; you are not, however, even thus free from the guilt of dishonouring the gods, who either are remiss in punishing such offences, or have not, by passing laws, and by severity of punishments, opposed

---

[1] Lit., "Euhemerus being opened."
[2] So Elm. and Orelli, reading *Nicanore* for the MS. *Nicagora,* retained by all other edd.
[3] Lit., "with the care of scrupulous diligence."
[4] Meursius would join *virginis* to Minerva, thinking it an allusion to her title Παρθένος.
[5] These terms are employed of hetæræ.
[6] Lit., "the title itself of their names was."
[7] *Qui sollicite relegit. Relegit* is here used by Arnobius to denote the root of *religio,* and has therefore some such meaning as that given above. Cf. Cicero, *de Nat. Deorum,* ii. 28.

[8] Lit., "an error of inadvertence."
[9] Lit., "with the sacrificial bowl."
[10] So the MS., both Roman edd., Elm., Hild., and Oehler, reading *rursus;* the others *in cursu* — "in the course."
[11] *Patrimus,* i.e., one whose father is alive, is probably used loosely for *patrimus et matrimus,*'to denote one both of whose parents were alive, who was therefore eligible for certain religious services.
[12] So the MS. reading *terram tenere,* for which Hild would read *tensam,* denoting the car on which were borne the images of the gods, the thongs or reins of which were held by the *patrimus et matrimus;* Lipsius, *sisérram,* the sacrificial victim. The reading of the text has been explained as meaning to touch the ground with one's hands; but the general meaning is clear enough, — that it was unlucky if the boy made a slip, either with hands or feet.
[13] Oberthür and Orelli omit *non.*
[14] Lit., "notions."
[15] Lit., "placed in their ears."

such indiscretion, and determined[1] that no man should henceforth say that which tended to the dishonour,[2] or was unworthy of the glory of the gods.[3] For whoever allows the wrongdoer to sin, strengthens his audacity; and it is more insulting to brand and mark any one with false accusations, than to bring forward and upbraid their real offences. For to be called what you are, and what you feel yourself to be, is less offensive, because *your resentment* is checked by the evidence supplied against you on privately reviewing your life;[4] but that wounds very keenly which brands the innocent, and defames a man's honourable name and reputation.

33. Your gods, it is recorded, dine on celestial couches, and in golden chambers, drink, and are at last soothed by the music of the lyre, and singing. You fit them with ears not easily wearied;[5] and do not think it unseemly to assign to the gods the pleasures by which earthly bodies are supported, and which are sought after by ears enervated by the frivolity of an unmanly spirit. Some of them are brought forward in the character of lovers, destroyers of purity, to commit shameful and degrading deeds not only with women, but with men also. You take no care as to what is said about matters of so much importance, nor do you check, by any fear of chastisement at least, the recklessness of your wanton literature; others, through madness and frenzy, bereave themselves, and by the slaughter of their own relatives cover themselves with blood, just as though it were that of an enemy. You wonder at these loftily expressed impieties; and that which it was fitting should be subjected to all punishments, you extol with praise that spurs them on, so as to rouse their recklessness to greater vehemence. They mourn over the wounds of their bereavement, and with unseemly wailings accuse the cruel fates; you are astonished at the force of their eloquence, carefully study *and* commit to memory that which should have been wholly put away from human society,[6] and are solicitous that it should not perish through any forgetfulness. They are spoken of as being wounded, maltreated, making war upon each other with hot and furious contests; you enjoy the description; and, to enable you to defend so great daring in the writers, pretend that these things are allegories, and contain the principles of natural science.

34. But why do I complain that you have disregarded the insults[7] offered to the other deities? That very Jupiter, whose name you should not have spoken without fear and trembling over your whole body, is described as confessing his faults when overcome by lust[8] of his wife, and, hardened in shamelessness, making known, as if he were mad and ignorant,[9] the mistresses he preferred to his spouse, the concubines he preferred to his wife; you say that those who have uttered so marvellous things are chiefs and kings among poets endowed with godlike genius, that they are persons most holy; and so utterly have you lost sight of your duty in the matters of religion which you bring forward, that words are of more importance, in your opinion, than the profaned majesty of the immortals. So then, if only you felt any fear of the gods, or believed with confident and unhesitating assurance that they existed at all, should you not, by bills, by popular votes, by fear of the senate's decrees, have hindered, prevented, *and* forbidden any one to speak at random of the gods otherwise than in a pious manner?[10] Nor have they obtained this honour even at your hands, that you should repel insults offered to them by the same laws by which you ward them off from yourselves. They are accused of treason among you who have whispered any evil about your kings. To degrade a magistrate, or use insulting language to a senator, you have made by decree *a crime*, followed by the severest punishment. To write a satirical poem, by which a slur is cast upon the reputation and character of another, you determined, by the decrees of the decemvirs, should not go unpunished; and that no one might assail your ears with too wanton abuse, you established formulæ[11] for severe affronts. With you only the gods are unhonoured, contemptible, vile; against whom you allow any one liberty to say what he will, to accuse them of the deeds of baseness which his lust has invented and devised. And *yet* you do not blush to raise against us the charge of want of regard for deities so infamous, although it is much better to disbelieve the existence of the gods than to think they are such, and of such repute.

35. But is it only poets whom you have thought proper[12] to allow to invent unseemly tales about the gods, and to turn them shamefully into sport? What do your pantomimists, the actors, that crowd of mimics and adulterers?[13] Do they[14] not abuse your gods to make to themselves

---

[1] Lit., "and it has *not* been established by you,"—a very abrupt transition in the structure of the sentence.
[2] Lit., "which was very near to disgrace."
[3] So the margin of Ursinus, followed by later edd., prefixing *d* before the ms. *-eorum*.
[4] Lit., "has less bite, being weakened by the testimony of silent reviewing," *recognitionis*.
[5] Lit., "most enduring."
[6] *Coetu.* The ms. and most edd. read *coalitu*,—a word not occurring elsewhere; which Gesner would explain, "put away that it may not be established among men," the sense being the same in either case.

[7] Lit., "complain of the neglected insults of the other gods."
[8] Lit., "as a lover by." Cf. Homer, *Il.*, 14, 312.
[9] i.e., of himself.
[10] Lit., "except that which was full of religion."
[11] i.e., according to which such offences should be punished.
[12] Lit., "have willed."
[13] Lit., "full-grown race," *exoleti*, a word frequently used, as here, *sensu obscœno*.
[14] i.e., the actors, etc.

gain, and *do not the others* [1] find enticing pleasures in [2] the wrongs and insults offered to the gods? At the public games, too, the colleges of all the priests and magistrates take their places, the chief Pontiffs, and the chief priests of the curiæ; the Quindecemviri take their places, *crowned* with wreaths of laurel, and the flamines diales with their mitres; the augurs take their places, who disclose the divine mind and will; and the chaste maidens also, who cherish and guard the ever-burning fire; the whole people and the senate take their places; the fathers who have done service as consuls, princes next to the gods, and most worthy of reverence; and, shameful to say, Venus, the mother of the race of Mars, and parent of the imperial people, is represented by gestures as in love,[3] and is delineated with shameless mimicry as raving like a Bacchanal, with all the passions of a vile harlot.[4] The Great Mother, too, adorned with her sacred fillets, is represented by dancing; and that Pessinuntic Dindymene [5] is, to the dishonour of her age, represented as with shameful desire using passionate gestures in the embrace of a herdsman; and also in the Trachiniæ of Sophocles,[6] that son of Jupiter, Hercules, entangled in the toils of a death-fraught garment, is exhibited uttering piteous cries, overcome by his violent suffering, and at last wasting away and being consumed, as his intestines soften and are dissolved.[7] But in *these* tales even the Supreme Ruler of the heavens Himself is brought forward, without any reverence for His name and majesty, as acting the part of an adulterer, and changing His countenance for purposes of seduction, in order that He might by guile rob of their chastity matrons, who were the wives of others, and putting on the appearance of their husbands, by assuming the form of another.

36. But this crime is not enough: the persons of the most sacred gods are mixed up with farces also, and scurrilous plays. And that the idle onlookers may be excited to laughter and jollity, the deities are hit at in jocular quips, the spectators shout and rise up, the whole pit resounds with the clapping of hands and applause. And to the debauched scoffers [8] at the gods gifts and presents are ordained, ease, freedom from public burdens, exemption and relief, together with triumphal garlands, — a crime for which no amends can be made by any apologies. And after this do you dare to wonder whence these ills come with which the human race is deluged and overwhelmed without any interval, while you daily both repeat and learn by heart all these things, with which are mixed up libels upon the gods and slanderous sayings; and when [9] you wish your inactive minds to be occupied with useless dreamings, demand that days be given to you, and exhibition made without any interval? But if you felt any real indignation on behalf of your religious beliefs, you should rather long ago have burned these writings, destroyed those books of yours, and overthrown these theatres, in which evil reports of your deities are daily made public in shameful tales. For why, indeed, have our writings deserved to be given to the flames? our meetings to be cruelly broken up,[10] in which prayer is made to the Supreme God, peace and pardon are asked for all in authority, for soldiers, kings, friends, enemies, for those still in life, and those freed from the bondage of the flesh; [11] in which all that is said is such as to make *men* humane,[12] gentle, modest, virtuous, chaste, generous in dealing with their substance, and inseparably united to all embraced in our brotherhood? [13]

37. But this is the state of the case, that as you are exceedingly strong in war and in military power, you think you excel in knowledge of the truth also, and are pious before the gods,[14] whose might you have been the first to besmirch with foul imaginings. Here, if your fierceness allows, and madness suffers, we ask you to answer us this: Whether you think that anger finds a place in the divine nature, or that the divine blessedness is far removed from such passions? For if they are subject to passions so furious,[15] and are excited by feelings of rage as your imaginings suggest, — for you say that they have often shaken the earth with their roaring,[16] and bringing woful misery on men, corrupted with pestilential

---

[1] i.e., the crowd of adulterers, as Orelli suggests.
[2] Lit., "draw enticements of pleasures from."
[3] Or, "Venus, the mother . . . and loving parent," etc.
[4] Lit., "of meretricious vileness."
[5] i.e., Cybele, to whom Mount Dindymus in Mysia was sacred, whose rites, however, were celebrated at Pessinus also, a very ancient city of Galatia.
[6] MS. *Sofocles*, corrected in LB. *Sophocles*. Cf. Trach. 1022 sqq.
[7] Lit., "towards (*in*) the last *of the* wasting consumed by the softening of his bowels flowing apart."
[8] Lit., "debauched and scoffers."

[9] So Orelli, reading *et quando;* MS. and other edd. *et si* — " and if ever."
[10] Arnobius is generally thought to refer here to the persecution under Diocletian mentioned by Eusebius, *Hist. Eccl.*, viii. 2.
[11] The service in which these prayers were offered was presided over by the bishop, to whom the dead body was brought: hymns were then sung of thanksgiving to God, the giver of victory, by whose help and grace the departed brother had been victorious. The priest next gave thanks to God, and some chapters of the Scriptures were read; afterwards the catechumens were dismissed; the names of those at rest were then read in a clear voice, to remind the survivors of the success with which others had combated the temptations of the world. The priest again prayed for the departed, at the close beseeching God to grant him pardon, and admission among the undying. Thereafter the body was kissed, anointed, and buried. — DIONYSIUS, *Eccl. Hier.*, last chapter quoted by Heraldus. Cf. *Const. Apost.*, viii. 41. With the Church's advance in power there was an accession of pomp to these rites. [Elucidation IV.]
[12] Cf. the younger Pliny, *Epist.*, x. 97: "They affirmed that they bound themselves by oath not for any wicked purpose, but to pledge themselves not to commit theft, robbery, or adultery, nor break faith, or prove false to a trust."
[13] Lit., "whom *our* society joins together," *quos solidet germanitas.* [Lardner justly argues that this passage proves our author's familiarity with rites to which catechumens were not admitted. *Credibil.*, vol. iii. p. 458.]
[14] i.e., in their sight or estimation.
[15] Lit., "conceive these torches."
[16] Lit., "have roared with tremblings of the earth."

contagion the character of the times,[1] both because their games had been celebrated with too little care, and because their priests were not received with favour, and because some small spaces were desecrated, and because their rites were not duly performed, — it must consequently be understood that they feel no little wrath on account of the opinions which have been mentioned. But if, as follows of necessity, it is admitted that all these miseries with which men have long been overwhelmed flow from such fictions, if the anger of the deities is excited by these causes, you are the occasion of so terrible misfortunes, because you never cease to jar upon the feelings of the gods, and excite them to a fierce desire for vengeance. But if, on the other hand, the gods are not subject to such passions,

and do not know at all what it is to be enraged, then indeed there is no ground for saying that they who know not what anger is are angry with us, * and they are free from its presence,[2] and the disorder [3] *it causes.* For it cannot be, in the nature of things, that what is one should become two ; and that unity, which is naturally uncompounded, should divide and go apart into separate things.[4]

---

[1] The MS reads *conru-isse auras temporum*, all except the first four edd. inserting *p* as above Meursius would also change *temp.* into *ventorum* — "the breezes of the winds."

[2] So the MS., reading *comptu* — tie, according to Hild., followed by LB. and Orelli.
[3] Lit., "mixture."
[4] The words following the asterisk (*) are marked in LB. as spurious or corrupt, or at least as here out of place. Orelli transposes them to ch. 13, as was noticed there, although he regards them as an interpolation. The clause is certainly a very strange one, and has a kind of affected abstractness, which makes it seem out of place; but it must be remembered that similarly confused and perplexing sentences are by no means rare in Arnobius. If the clause is to be retained, as good sense can be made from it here as anywhere else. The general meaning would be: The gods, if angry, are angry with the pagans; but if they are not subject to passion, it would be idle to speak of them as angry with the Christians, seeing that they cannot possibly at once be incapable of feeling anger, and yet at the same time be angry with them. [See cap. 13, note 4, p. 480, *supra*.]

BOOK V.

1. Admitting that all these things which do the immortal gods dishonour, have been put forth by poets merely in sport, what *of* those found in grave, serious, and careful histories, and handed down by you in hidden mysteries? have they been invented by the licentious fancy of the poets? Now if they seemed [1] to you stories of such absurdity, some of them you would neither retain in their constant use, nor celebrate as solemn festivals from year to year, nor would you maintain them among your sacred rites as shadows of real events. With strict moderation, I shall adduce only one of these stories which are so numerous ; that in which Jupiter himself is brought on the stage as stupid and inconsiderate, being tricked by the ambiguity of words. In the second book of Antias — lest any one should think, perchance, that we are fabricating charges calumniously — the following story is written : —

The famous king Numa, not knowing how to avert evil portended by thunder, and being eager to learn, by advice of Egeria concealed beside a fountain twelve chaste youths provided with chains ; so that when Faunus and Martius [2] Picus came to this place [3] to drink, — for hither they were wont to come [4] to draw water, — they might

rush on them, seize and bind them. But, that this might be done more speedily, the king filled many [5] cups with wine and with mead,[6] and placed them about the approaches to the fountain, where they would be seen — a crafty snare for those who should come. They, as was their usual custom, when overcome by thirst, came to their well-known haunts. But when they had perceived cups with sweetly smelling liquors, they preferred the new to the old ; rushed eagerly upon them ; charmed with the sweetness of the draught, drank too much ; and becoming drunk, fell fast asleep. Then the twelve *youths* threw themselves upon the sleepers, *and* cast chains round them, lying soaked with wine ; and they,[7] when roused, immediately taught the king by what methods and sacrifices Jupiter could be called down to earth. With this knowledge the king performed the sacred ceremony on the Aventine, drew down Jupiter to the earth, and asked from him the due form of expiation. Jupiter having long hesitated, said, " Thou shalt avert what is portended by thunder with a head." [8] The king answered, " With an onion." [9] Jupiter again, " With a man's." The king returned, " But with hair." [10]

---

[1] So most edd., inserting *er ;* in MS. and Oehler, *vid-entur.*
[2] So named either because he was said to have made use of the bird of Mars, i.e., a woodpecker (*picus*), in augury, or because according to the legend he was changed into one by Circe.
[3] i.e., the Aventine. The story is told by Plutarch in his Life of Numa, c. 15, and by Ovid, *Fasti*, iii 291 sqq.
[4] The MS. reads, *sollemniter hæc*, corrected, as above, *solenne iter huc* by all edd. except Hild.

[5] So the MS. and most edd., reading *pocula non parvi numeri*, for which Elmh. and Orelli have received from the margin of Ursinus, *poc non parva mero* — "cups of great size, with pure wine."
[6] i.e., *mulsum.*
[7] i.e., Faunus and Picus.
[8] *Capite.*
[9] *Cæpitio.*
[10] Jupiter is supposed to say *humano*, meaning *capite*, to be understood, i.e., "with a man's head," while the king supplies *capillo* — "with a man's hair."

The deity in turn, "With the life.[1] With a fish,"[2] rejoined Pompilius. Then Jupiter, being ensnared by the ambiguous terms used, uttered these words: "Thou hast overreached me, Numa; for I had determined that evils portended by thunder should be averted with *sacrifices of* human heads, not[3] with hair *and* an onion. Since, however, your craft has outwitted me, have the mode which you wished; and always undertake the expiation of thunder-portents with those things which you have bargained for."

2. What the mind should take up first, what last, or what it should pass by silently, it is not easy to say, nor is it made clear by any amount of reflection; for all have been so devised and fitted to be laughed at, that you should strive that they may be believed to be false — even if they are true — rather than pass current as true, and suggest as it were something extraordinary, and bring contempt upon deity itself. What, then, do you say, O you —? Are we to believe[4] that that Faunus and Martius Picus — if they are of the number of the gods, and of that everlasting and immortal substance — were once parched with thirst, and sought the gushing fountains, that they might be able to cool with water their heated veins? Are we to believe that, ensnared by wine, and beguiled by the sweetness of mead, they dipped so long into the treacherous cups, that they even got into danger of becoming drunk? Are we to believe that, being fast asleep, and plunged in the forgetfulness of most profound slumbers, they gave to creatures of earth an opportunity to bind them? On what parts, then, were those bonds and chains flung? Did they have any solid substance, or had their hands been formed of hard bones, so that it might be possible to bind them with halters and hold them fast by tightly drawn knots? For I do not ask, I do not inquire whether they could have said anything when swaying to and fro in their drunken maunderings; or whether, while Jupiter was unwilling, or rather unwitting, any one could have made known the way to bring him down to earth. This only do I wish to hear, why, if Faunus and Picus are of divine origin and power, they did not rather themselves declare to Numa, as he questioned them, that which he desired to learn from Jove himself at a greater risk? Or[5] did Jupiter alone have knowledge of this — for from him the thunderbolts fall — how training in some

kind of knowledge should avert impending dangers? Or, while he himself hurls these fiery bolts, is it the business of others to know in what way it is fitting to allay his wrath and indignation? For truly it would be most absurd to suppose that he himself appoints[6] the means by which may be averted that which he has determined should befall men through the hurling of his thunderbolts. For this is to say, By such ceremonies you will turn aside my wrath; and if I shall at any time have foreshown by flashes of lightning that some evil is close at hand, do this and that, so that[7] what I have determined should be done may be done altogether in vain, and may pass away idly through the force[8] of these rites.

3. But let us admit that, as is said, Jupiter has himself appointed against himself ways and means by which his own declared purposes might fittingly be opposed: are we also to believe that a deity of so great majesty was dragged down to earth, and, standing on a petty hillock with a mannikin, entered into a wrangling dispute? And what, I ask, was the charm which forced Jupiter to leave the all-important[9] direction of the universe, and appear at the bidding of mortals? the sacrificial meal, incense, blood, the scent of burning laurel-boughs,[10] and muttering of spells? And were all these more powerful than Jupiter, so that they compelled him to do unwillingly what was enjoined, or to give himself up of his own accord to their crafty tricks? What! will what follows be believed, that the son of Saturn had so little foresight, that he either proposed terms by the ambiguity of which he was himself ensnared, or did not know what was going to happen, how the craft and cunning of a mortal would overreach him? You shall make expiation, he says, with a head when thunderbolts have fallen. The phrase is still incomplete, and the meaning is not fully expressed and defined; for it was necessarily right to know whether Diespiter ordains that this expiation be effected with the head of a wether, a sow, an ox, or any other animal. Now, as he had not yet fixed this specifically, and his decision was still uncertain and not yet determined, how could Numa know that Jupiter would say the head of a man, so as to[7] anticipate *and* prevent *him*, and turn his uncertain and ambiguous words[11] into "an onion's head?"

4. But you will perhaps say that the king was a diviner. Could he be more so than Jupiter

---

[1] *Anima* (MS. *lia*).

[2] *Mæna.* There is here a lacuna in the text; but there can be no difficulty in filling it up as above, with Heraldus from Plutarch, or with Gelenius from Ovid, *piscis* — "*with the life* of a fish."

[3] The MS. and both Roman edd. read *Numa*, corrected by Gelenius, as above, *non.*

[4] The MS. and edd. read *cred-i-musne* — "do we believe," for which Meursius suggests -*e*- as above.

[5] Lit., "or whether." Below the MS. reads corruptly *ad ipsum* — "to him."

[6] The MS. reads *scire*, but "knows" would hardly suit the context. Instead of adopting any conjecture, however, it is sufficient to observe, with Oehler, that *scire* is elsewhere used as a contraction for *sciscere.*

[7] The MS. omits *ut.*

[8] So Cujacius, inserting *vi*, omitted by the MS.

[9] Lit., "so great."

[10] Lit., "the fumigation of *verbenæ*," i.e., of boughs of the laurel, olive, or myrtle.

[11] Lit., "the uncertain *things* of that ambiguity."

himself? But for a mortal's anticipating[1] what Jupiter — whom[2] he overreached — was going to say, could the god not know in what ways a man was preparing to overreach him? Is it not, then, clear and manifest that these are puerile and fanciful inventions, by which, while a lively wit is assigned[3] to Numa, the greatest want of foresight is imputed to Jupiter? For what shows so little foresight as to confess that you have been ensnared by the subtlety of a man's intellect, and while you are vexed at being deceived, to give way to the wishes of him who has overcome you, and to lay aside the means which you had proposed? For if there was reason and some natural fitness that[4] expiatory sacrifice for that which was struck with lightning should have been made with a man's head, I do not see why the proposal of an onion's was made by the king; but if it could be performed with an onion also, there was a greedy lust for human blood. And both parts are made to contradict themselves: so that, on the one hand, Numa is shown not to have wished to know what he did wish; and, on the other, Jupiter is shown to have been merciless, because he said that he wished expiation to be made with the heads of men, which could have been done by Numa with an onion's head.

5. In Timotheus, who was no mean mythologist, and also in others equally well informed, the birth of the Great Mother of the gods, and the origin of her rites, are thus detailed, being derived — as he himself writes and suggests — from learned books of antiquities, and from *his acquaintance with* the most secret mysteries: — Within the confines of Phrygia, he says, there is a rock of unheard-of wildness in every respect, the name of which is Agdus, so named by the natives of that district. Stones taken from it, as Themis by her oracle[5] had enjoined, Deucalion and Pyrrha threw upon the earth, at that time emptied of men; from which this Great Mother, too, as she is called, was fashioned along with the others, and animated by the deity. Her, given over to rest and sleep on the very summit of the rock, Jupiter assailed with lewdest[6] desires. But when, after long strife, he could not accomplish what he had proposed to himself, he, baffled, spent his lust on the stone. This the rock received, and with many groanings Acdestis[7] is born in the tenth month, being named from his mother rock. In him there had been resist-

less might, and a fierceness of disposition beyond control, a lust made furious, and *derived* from both sexes.[8] He violently plundered and laid waste; he scattered destruction wherever the ferocity of his disposition had led him; he regarded not gods nor men, nor did he think anything more powerful than himself; he contemned earth, heaven, and the stars.

6. Now, when it had been often considered in the councils of the gods, by what means it might be possible either to weaken or to curb his audacity, Liber, the rest hanging back, takes upon himself this task. With the strongest wine he drugs a spring much resorted to by Acdestis[9] where he had been wont to assuage the heat and burning thirst[10] roused *in him* by sport and hunting. Hither runs Acdestis to drink when he felt the need;[11] he gulps down the draught too greedily into his gaping veins. Overcome by what he is quite unaccustomed to, he is in consequence sent fast asleep. Liber is near the snare *which he had set;* over his foot he throws one end of a halter[12] formed of hairs, woven together very skilfully; with the other end he lays hold of his privy members. When the fumes of the wine passed off, Acdestis starts up furiously, and his foot dragging the noose, by his own strength he robs himself of his[13] sex; with the tearing asunder of *these* parts there is an immense flow of blood; both[14] are carried off and swallowed up by the earth; from them there suddenly springs up, covered with fruit, a pomegranate tree, seeing the beauty of which, with admiration, Nana,[15] daughter of the king or river Sangarius, gathers and places in her bosom *some of the fruit.* By this she becomes pregnant; her father shuts her up, supposing that she had been[16] debauched, and seeks to have her starved to death; she is kept alive by the mother of the gods with apples, and other food,[17] *and* brings forth a child, but Sangarius[18] orders it to be exposed. One Phorbas having found the child, takes it home,[19] brings it up on goats' milk; and

---

[1] Lit., "unless a mortal anticipated" — *præsumeret*, the MS. reading.
[2] So Oehler, supplying *quem.*
[3] Lit., "liveliness of heart is procured."
[4] Lit., "why."
[5] So Ovid also (*Metam.*, i. 321), and others, speak of Themis as the first to give oracular responses.
[6] So the MS. and edd., reading *quam incestis*, except Orelli, who adopts the conjecture of Barthius, *nequam* — "lustful Jupiter with lewd desires."
[7] So the MS. and edd., except Hildebrand and Oehler, who throughout spell *Agdestis*, following the Greek writers, and the derivation of the word from *Agdus.*

[8] So Ursinus suggested, followed by later edd., *ex utroque* (MS. *utra*.) *sexu;* for which Meursius would read *ex utroque sexus* — "and a sex of both," i.e., that he was a hermaphrodite, which is related by other writers.
[9] Lit., "him."
[10] Lit., "of thirsting."
[11] Lit., "in time of need."
[12] So the reading of the MS. and edd., *unum laqueum*, may be rendered; for which Canterus conjectured *imum* — "the lowest part of the noose."
[13] So the edd., reading *eo quo* (MS. *quod*) *fuerat privat sexu;* for which Hild. and Oehler read *fu-tu-erat* — "of the sex with which he had been a fornicator."
[14] Lit., "these (i.e., the parts and the blood) are," etc.
[15] The MS. here reads *Nata*, but in c. 13 the spelling is Nana, as in other writers.
[16] Lit., "as if."
[17] The MS. reads *t-abulis*, corrected as above *p-* by Jos. Scaliger, followed by Hild. and Oehler. The other edd. read *bacculis* — "berries."
[18] So all the edd., except Hild. and Oehler, who retain the MS. reading *sanguinarius* — "bloodthirsty."
[19] So Salmasius, Orelli, and Hild., reading *repertum nescio quis sumit Phorbas, lacte;* but no mention of any Phorbas is made elsewhere in connection with this story, and Oehler has therefore proposed *forma ac lacte* — "some one takes *the child* found, nourishes it with sweet pottage of millet (*forma*) and milk," etc.

as handsome fellows are so named in Lydia, or because the Phrygians in their own way of speaking call their goats *attagi*, it happened in consequence that *the boy* obtained the name Attis.[1] Him the mother of the gods loved exceedingly, because he was of most surpassing beauty ; and Acdestis, *who was* his companion, as he grew up fondling him, and bound *to him* by wicked compliance with his lust in the only way now possible, leading him through the wooded glades, and presenting him with the spoils of many wild beasts, which the boy Attis at first said boastfully were won by his own toil and labour. Afterwards, under the influence of wine, he admits that he is both loved by Acdestis, and honoured by him with the gifts brought from the forest ; whence it is unlawful for those polluted by *drinking* wine to enter into his sanctuary, because it discovered his secret.[2]

7. Then Midas, king of Pessinus, wishing to withdraw the youth from so disgraceful an intimacy, resolves to give him his own daughter in marriage, and caused the *gates of the* town to be closed, that no one of evil omen might disturb their marriage joys. But the mother of the gods, knowing the fate of the youth, and that he would live among men in safety *only* so long as he was free from the ties of marriage, that no disaster might occur, enters the closed city, raising its walls with her head, which began to be crowned with towers in consequence. Acdestis, bursting with rage because of the boy's being torn from himself, and brought to seek a wife, fills all the guests with frenzied madness :[3] the Phrygians shriek aloud, panic-stricken at the appearance of the gods ;[4] a daughter of adulterous[5] Gallus cuts off her breasts ; Attis snatches the pipe borne by him who was goading them to frenzy ; and he, too, now filled with furious passion, raving frantically *and* tossed about, throws himself down at last, and under a pine tree mutilates himself, saying, " Take these,[6] Acdestis, for which you have stirred up so great and terribly perilous commotions."[7] With the streaming blood his life flies ; but the Great Mother of the gods gathers the parts which had been cut off, and throws earth on them, having first covered them, and wrapped[8]

them in the garment of the dead. From the blood which had flowed springs a flower, the violet, and with[9] this the tree[10] is girt. Thence the custom began and arose, whereby you even now veil and wreath with flowers the sacred pine. The virgin who had been the bride, whose name, as Valerius[11] the pontifex relates, was Ia, veils the breast of the lifeless *youth* with soft wool, sheds tears with Acdestis, and slays herself. After her death her blood is changed into purple violets. The mother of the gods sheds tears also,[12] from which springs an almond tree, signifying the bitterness of death.[13] Then she bears away to her cave the pine tree, beneath which Attis had unmanned himself ; and Acdestis joining in her wailings, she beats and wounds her breast, *pacing* round the trunk of the tree now at rest.[14] Jupiter is begged by Acdestis that Attis may be restored to life : he does not permit it. What, however, fate allowed,[15] he readily grants, that his body should not decay, that his hairs should always grow, that the least of his fingers should live, and should be kept ever in motion ; content with which favours, *it is said* that Acdestis consecrated the body in Pessinus, *and* honoured it with yearly rites and priestly services.[16]

8. If some one, despising the deities, and furious with a savagely sacrilegious spirit, had set himself to blaspheme your gods, would he dare to say against them anything more severe than this tale relates, which you have reduced to form, as though *it were* some wonderful narrative, and have honoured without ceasing,[17] lest the power of time and the remoteness[18] of antiquity should cause it to be forgotten? For what is there asserted in it, or what written about the gods, which, if said with regard to a man brought up with bad habits and a pretty rough training, would not make you liable to be accused of wronging and insulting him, and expose you to hatred and dislike, accompanied by implacable resentment? From the stones, you say, which Deucalion and Pyrrha threw, was produced the

---

[1] [See vol. ii. p. 175.]
[2] Lit., " his silence."
[3] Lit., " fury and madness."
[4] The MS., first five edd., and Oberthür, read *exterriti adorandorum Phryges ;* for which Ursinus suggested *ad ora deorum* — " at the faces of gods," adopted by Hild. and Oehler: the other edd. reading *ad horam* — " at the hour, i.e., thereupon."
[5] It seems probable that part of this chapter has been lost, as we have no explanation of this epithet ; and, moreover (as Oehler has well remarked), in c. 13 this Gallus is spoken of as though it had been previously mentioned that he too had mutilated himself, of which we have not the slightest hint.
[6] i.e., *genitalia.*
[7] Lit., " so great motions of furious hazards."
[8] So most edd., reading *veste prius tectis atque involutis* for the MS. reading, retained by Hild. and Oehler, *tecta atque involuta* — " his vest being first drawn over and wrapt about them ; " the former verb being found with this meaning in no other passage, and the second very rarely.

[9] Lit., " from."
[10] i.e., the pine.
[11] Nourry supposes that this may refer to M. Valerius Messala, a fragment from whom on auspices has been preserved by Gellius (xiii. 15) ; while Hild. thinks that Antias is meant, who is mentioned in c. 1.
[12] So Orelli punctuates and explains ; but it is doubtful whether, even if this reading be retained, it should not be translated, " bedewed these (violets)." The MS. reads, *suffodit et as* (probably *has*) — " digs under these," emended as above in LB., *suffudit et has.*
[13] Lit., " burial."
[14] So it has been attempted to render the MS., reading *pausatæ circum arboris robur,* which has perplexed the different edd. Heraldus proposed *pausate* — " at intervals round the trunk of the tree ; " LB. reads *-ata* — " round . . . tree having rested." Reading as above, the reference might be either to the rest from motion after being set up in the cave, or to the absence of wind there.
[15] Lit., " could be done through (i.e , as far as concerns) fate."
[16] So Oehler, reading *sacerdotum antistitiis* for the MS. *antistibus,* changed in both Roman edd. and Hild. to *-stitibus* — " with priests (or overseers) of priests." Salmasius proposed *intestibus* — " with castrated priests."
[17] i e , in the ever-recurring festival of Cybele.
[18] Lit., " length."

mother of the gods. What do you say, O theologians? what, ye priests of the heavenly powers? Did the mother of the gods, then, not exist at all for the sake of the deluge? and would there be no cause or beginning of her birth, had not violent storms of rain swept away the whole race of men? It is through man, then, that she feels herself to exist, and she owes it to Pyrrha's kindness that she sees herself addressed as a real being; [1] but if that is indeed true, this too will of necessity not be false, that she was human, not divine. For if it is certain that men are sprung originally from the casting of stones, it must be believed that she too was one of us, since she was produced by means of the same causes. For it cannot be, for nature would not suffer it, [2] that from one kind of stones, and from the same mode of throwing *them*, some should be formed to rank among the immortals, others with the condition of men. Varro, that famous Roman, distinguished by the diversity of his learning, and unwearied in his researches into ancient times, in the first of four books which he has left in writing on the race of the Roman people, shows by careful calculations, that from the time of the deluge, which we mentioned before, down to the consulship of Hirtius and Pansa,[3] there are not quite two thousand years; and if he is to be believed, the Great Mother, too, must be said to have her whole life bounded by the limits of this number. And thus the matter is brought to this issue, that she who is said to be parent of all the deities is not their mother, but their daughter; nay, rather a *mere* child, a little girl, since we admit that in the never-ending series of ages neither beginning nor end has been ascribed to the gods.

9. But why do we speak of your having bemired the Great Mother of the gods with the filth of earth, when you have not been able for but a little time even to keep from speaking evil of Jupiter himself? While the mother of the gods was then sleeping on the highest peak of Agdus, her son, you say, tried stealthily to surprise her chastity while she slept. After robbing of their chastity virgins and matrons without number, did Jupiter hope to gratify his detestable passion upon his mother? and could he not be turned from his fierce desire by the horror which nature itself has excited not only in men, but in some *other* animals also, and by common [4] feeling? Was he then regardless of piety [5] and honour, who is chief in the temples?

and could he neither reconsider nor perceive how wicked was his desire, his mind being madly agitated? But, as it is, forgetting his majesty and dignity, he crept forward to steal those vile pleasures, trembling and quaking with fear, holding his breath, walking in terror on tiptoe, and, between hope and fear, touched her secret parts, trying how soundly his mother slept, and what she would suffer.[6] Oh, shameful representation! oh, disgraceful plight of Jupiter, prepared to attempt a filthy contest! Did the ruler of the world, then, turn to force, when, in his heedlessness and haste, he was prevented from stealing on by surprise; [7] and when he was unable to snatch his pleasure by cunning craft, did he assail his mother with violence, and begin without any concealment to destroy the chastity which he should have revered? Then, having striven for a very long time when she is unwilling, did he go off conquered, vanquished, and overcome? and did his spent lust part him whom piety was unable to hold back from execrable lust after his mother?

10. But you will perhaps say the human race shuns and execrates such unions; [8] among the gods there is no incest. And why, *then*, did his mother resist with the greatest vehemence her son when he offered her violence? Why did she flee from his embraces, as if she were avoiding unlawful approaches? For if there was nothing wrong in so doing, she should have gratified him without any reluctance, just as he eagerly wished to satisfy the cravings of his lust. And here, indeed, very thrifty men, and frugal even about shameful works, that that sacred seed may not seem to have been poured forth in vain — the rock, one says, drank up Jupiter's foul incontinence. What followed next, I ask? Tell. In the very heart of the rock, and in that flinty hardness, a child was formed and quickened to be the offspring of great Jupiter. It is not easy to object to conceptions so unnatural and so wonderful. For as the human race is said by you to have sprung and proceeded from stones, it must be believed that the stones both had genital parts, and drank in the seed cast on them, and when their time was full were pregnant,[9] and at last brought forth, travailing in distress as women do. That impels our curiosity to inquire, since you say that the birth occurred after ten months, in what womb of the rock was he enclosed at that time? with what food, with what juices, was he supplied? or what could he have drawn to support him from the hard stone, as unborn

---

[1] So the edd., reading *orari in alicujus substantiæ qualitate* for the MS. *erari* restored by Oehler, *num-erari* — "numbered in the quality of some substance," from the reading of an old copy adopted by Livineius.
[2] Lit., "through the resistance of nature."
[3] B.C. 43.
[4] Lit., "the feeling commonly implanted."
[5] Lit., "was regard of piety wanting" — *defuit*, an emendation of Salmasius (according to Orelli) for the MS. *depuit*.

[6] Lit., "the depth and patience of his sleeping mother."
[7] Lit., "from the theft of taking by surprise" — *obreptionis*, for which the MS., first four edd., Oberth., Hild., and Oehler read *object.* — "of what he proposed."
[8] So Heraldus, reading *conventionis hujusmodi cœtum* for the MS. *cœptum.*
[9] *Sustulisse alvos graves.*

infants usually *receive* from their mothers ! He had not yet reached the light, *my informant* says ; and already bellowing and imitating his father's thunderings, he reproduced *their sound*.[1] And after it was given him to see the sky and the light of day, attacking all things which lay in his way, he made havoc of them, and assured himself that he was able to thrust down from heaven the gods themselves. O cautious and foreseeing mother of the gods, who, that she might not undergo the ill-will of so[2] arrogant a son, or that his bellowing while still unborn might not disturb her slumbers or break her repose, withdrew herself, and sent far from her that most hurtful seed, and gave it to the rough rock.

11. There was doubt in the councils of the gods how that unyielding and fierce violence was to be subdued ; and when there was no other way, they had recourse to one means, that he should be soaked with much wine, and bereft of his members, by their being cut off. As if, indeed, those who have suffered the loss of these parts become less arrogant, and *as if* we do not daily see those who have cut them away from themselves become more wanton, and, neglecting all the restraints of chastity and modesty, throw themselves headlong into filthy vileness, making known abroad their shameful deeds. I should like, however, to see — were it granted me to be born at those times — father Liber, who overcame the fierceness of Acdestis, having glided down from the peaks of heaven after the very venerable meetings of the gods, cropping the tails of horses,[3] plaiting pliant halters, drugging the waters harmless while pure with much strong wine, and after that drunkenness sprung from drinking, to have carefully introduced his hands, handled the members of the sleeper, and directed his care skilfully[4] to the parts which were to perish, so that the hold of the nooses placed round *them* might surround them all.

12. Would any one say this about the gods who had even a very low opinion of them ? or, if they were taken up with such affairs, considerations, cares, would any man of wisdom either believe that they are gods, or reckon them among men even? Was that Acdestis, pray, the lopping off of whose lewd members was to give a sense of security to the immortals, *was he* one of the creatures of earth, or one of the gods, and possessed of[5] immortality? For if he was thought *to be* of our lot and in the condi-

tion of men, why did he cause the deities so much terror? But if he was a god, how could he be deceived, or *how* could anything be cut off from a divine body?[6] But we raise no issue on this point : he may have been of divine birth, or one of us, if you think it more correct to say so. Did a pomegranate tree, also, spring from the blood which flowed and from the parts which were cut off? or at the time when[7] that member was concealed in the bosom of the earth, did it lay hold of the ground with a root, and spring up into a mighty tree, put forth branches loaded with blossoms,[8] and in a moment bare mellow fruit perfectly and completely ripe? And because these sprang from red blood, is their colour therefore bright purple, with a dash of yellow? Say further that they are juicy also, that they have the taste of wine, because they spring from the blood of one filled with it, and you have finished your story consistently. O Abdera, Abdera, what occasions for mocking *you would give*[9] to men, if such a tale had been devised by you ! All fathers relate it, and haughty states peruse it ; and you are considered foolish, and utterly dull and stupid.[10]

13. Through her bosom, we are told,[11] Nana conceived a son by an apple. The opinion is self-consistent ; for where rocks and hard stones bring forth, there apples must have their time of generating.[12] The Berecyntian goddess fed the imprisoned maiden with nuts[13] and figs, fitly and rightly ; for it was right that she should live on apples who had been made a mother by an apple. After her offspring was born, it was ordered by Sangarius to be cast far away : that which he believed to be divinely conceived long before, he would not have[14] called the offspring of his child. The infant was brought up on he-goats' milk. O story ever opposed and most inimical to the male sex, in which not only do men lay aside their virile powers, but beasts even which were males become mothers ![15] He was famous for his beauty, and distinguished by his remarkable[16] comeliness. It is wonderful enough that the noisome stench of goats did not cause him to be avoided and fled from. The Great Mother loved him — if as a grandmother her grandson, there is nothing wrong ;, but if as the

---

[6] The MS. here inserts *de* — "from the body from a divine (being)."
[7] So the edd. (except Oehler), reading *tum cum* for the MS. *tum quæ quod.*
[8] *Balaustiis*, the flowers of the wild pomegranate.
[9] *Dares* supplied by Salmasius.
[10] [The Abderitans were proverbially such. "Hinc *Abdera*, non tacente me." — CICERO, *Ep. ad Attic.*, iv. 16.]
[11] Lit., "he says."
[12] Lit., "must rut" — *suriant*, as deer. The MS., first four edd., and Elm. read *surgant* — "rise," corrected as above in the margin of Ursinus.
[13] Lit., "acorns" — *glandibus.*
[14] The MS. reads *des-*, emended as above *ded-ignatus* by Stewe- chius, followed by Heraldus and Orelli.
[15] i e., he-goats are made to yield milk.
[16] Lit., "praiseworthy."

---

[1] Most edd. read as an interrogation.
[2] Perhaps, "that she might not be subject to ill-will, for having borne so."
[3] i.e., to form nooses with. The reading translated is an emendation of Jos. Scaliger, adopted by Orelli, *peniculamenta decurtantem cantheriorum*, for the MS. *peniculantem decurtam tam cantherios*, emended by each ed. as he has thought fit.
[4] Lit., "the cares of art."
[5] Lit., "endowed with the honour of."

theatres tell, her love is infamous and disgraceful. Acdestis, too, loved him above all, enriching him with a hunter's gifts. There could be no danger to his purity from one emasculated, *you say;* but it is not easy to guess what Midas dreaded? The Mother entered bearing[1] the very walls. Here we wondered, indeed, at the might and strength of the deity; but again[2] we blame her carelessness, because when she remembered the decree of fate,[3] she heedlessly laid open the city to its enemies. Acdestis excites to fury and madness those celebrating the nuptial vows. If King Midas had displeased *him* who was binding the youth to a wife, of what had Gallus been guilty, and his concubine's daughter, that he should rob himself of his manhood, she herself of her breasts? "Take and keep these," says he,[4] "because of which you have excited such commotions to the overwhelming of *our* minds with fear." We should none of us yet know what the frenzied Acdestis had desired in his paramour's body, had not the boy thrown to him, to appease his wrath,[5] the parts cut off.

14. What say you, O races and nations, given up to such beliefs? When these things are brought forward, are you not ashamed and confounded to say things so indecent? We wish to hear or learn from you something befitting the gods; but you, on the contrary, bring forward to us the cutting off of breasts, the lopping off of men's members, ragings, blood, frenzies, the self-destruction of maidens, and flowers and trees begotten from the blood of the dead. Say, again, did the mother of the gods, then, with careful diligence herself gather in her grief the scattered genitals with the shed blood?[6] With her own sacred, her own divine[7] hands, did she touch and lift up the instruments of a disgraceful and indecent office? Did she also commit them to the earth to be hid from sight; and lest in this case they should, being uncovered, be dispersed in the bosom of the earth, did she indeed wash and anoint them with fragrant gums before wrapping and covering them with his dress? For whence could the violet's sweet scent have come had not the addition of those ointments modified the putrefying smell of the member? Pray, when you read such tales, do you not seem to yourselves to hear either girls at the loom wiling away their tedious working

hours, or old women seeking diversions for credulous children,[8] and to be declaring manifold fictions under the guise of truth? Acdestis appealed to[9] Jupiter to restore life to his paramour: Jupiter would not consent, because he was hindered by the fates more powerful *than himself;* and that he might not be in every respect very hard-hearted, he granted one favour — that the body should not decay through any corruption; that the hair should always grow; that the least of his fingers alone in his body should live, alone keep always in motion. Would any one grant this, or support it with an unhesitating assent, that hair grows on a dead body, — that part[10] perished, and that the *rest of his* mortal body, free from the law of corruption, remains even still?

15. We might long ago have urged you to ponder this, were it not foolish to ask proofs of such things, as well as to say[11] them. But this story is false, and is wholly untrue. It is no matter to us, indeed, because of whom you maintain that the gods have been driven from the earth, whether it is consistent and rests on a sure foundation,[12] or is, on the contrary, framed and devised in utter falsehood. For to us it is enough — who have proposed this day to make it plain — that those deities whom you bring forward, if they are anywhere on earth, and glow with the fires of anger, are not more excited to furious hatred by us than by you; and that that *story* has been classed as an event and committed to writing by you, and is willingly read over by you every day, and handed down in order for the edifying of later times. Now, if this *story* is indeed true, we see that there is no reason in it why the celestial gods should be asserted to be angry with us, since we have neither declared things so much to their disgrace, nor committed them to writing at all, nor brought them publicly to light[13] by the celebration of sacred rites; but if, as you think, it is untrue, and made up of delusive falsehoods, no man can doubt that you are the cause of offence, who have either allowed certain persons to write such stories, or have suffered *them,* when written, to abide in the memory of ages.

16. And yet how can you assert the falsehood of this story, when the very rites which you celebrate throughout the year testify that you believe *these things* to be true, and consider them perfectly trustworthy? For what is the meaning of

---

[1] Lit., "with."
[2] So the MS., both Roman edd., LB., Hild., and Oehler, reading *rursus,* for which the others receive the emendation of Gelenius, *regis* — "the king's carelessness."
[3] Lit., "the law and fate."
[4] i.e., Attis.
[5] The MS. reads *satietati-s objecisset offensi,* corrected as above by Hild. (omitting *s*), followed by Oehler. The conjectures of previous edd. are very harsh and forced.
[6] Lit., "flows."
[7] Lit., "herself with sacred, herself with divine."

[8] [γραώδεις μύθους, 1. Tim. iv. 7. Compare Ignatius, vol. i. p. 62, note 3. But even the old wives' tales among Hebrews were clean in contrast with the horrible amusements here imputed even to the girls at the loom, and *children,* among the Gentiles.]
[9] Lit., "spoke with."
[10] i.e., the part cut off and buried separately.
[11] So the MS., according to Crusius, the edd. inserting *s, di-s-cere* — "to learn."
[12] Lit., "on firmness of faith."
[13] Lit., "sent to public testifying."

that pine[1] which on fixed days you always bring into the sanctuary of the mother of the gods? Is it not in imitation of that tree, beneath which the raging and ill-fated youth laid hands upon himself, and *which* the parent of the gods consecrated to relieve her sorrow?[2] What mean the fleeces of wool with which you bind and surround the trunk of the tree? Is it not to recall the wools with which Ia[3] covered the dying *youth*, and thought that she could procure some warmth for his limbs *fast* stiffening with cold? What *mean* the branches of the tree girt round and decked with wreaths of violets? Do they not mark this, how the Mother adorned with early flowers the pine which indicates and bears witness to the sad mishap? What *mean* the *Galli*[4] with dishevelled hair beating their breasts with their palms? Do they not recall to memory those lamentations with which the tower-bearing Mother, along with the weeping Acdestis, wailing aloud,[5] followed the boy? What *means* the abstinence from eating bread which you have named *castus?* Is it not in imitation of the time when the goddess abstained from Ceres' fruit in her vehement sorrow?

17. Or if the things which we say are not so, declare, say yourselves — those effeminate and delicate *men* whom we see among you in the sacred rites of this deity — what business, *what* care, *what* concern have they there; and why do they like mourners wound their arms and[6] breasts, and act as those dolefully circumstanced? What *mean* the wreaths, what the violets, what the swathings, the coverings of soft wools? Why, finally, is the very pine, but a little before swaying to and fro among the shrubs, an utterly inert log, set up in the temple of the Mother of the gods next, like some propitious and very venerable deity? For either this is the cause which we have found in your writings and treatises, and *in that case* it is clear that you do not celebrate divine rites, but give a representation of sad events; or if there is any other reason which the darkness of the mystery has withheld from us, even it also must be involved in the infamy of some shameful deed. For who would believe that there is any honour in that which the worth-

less *Galli* begin, effeminate debauchees complete?

18. The greatness of the subject, and our duty to those on their defence also,[7] demand that we should in like manner hunt up the other forms of baseness, whether those which the histories of antiquity record, or those contained in the sacred mysteries named *initia*,[8] and not divulged[9] openly to all, but to the silence of a few; but your innumerable sacred rites, and the loathsomeness of them all,[10] will not allow us to go through them all bodily: nay, more, to tell the truth, we turn aside ourselves from some purposely and intentionally, lest, in striving to unfold all things, we should be defiled by contamination in the very exposition. Let us pass by Fauna[11] Fatua, therefore, who is called Bona Dea, whom Sextus Clodius, in his sixth book in Greek on the gods, declares to have been scourged to death with rods of myrtle, because she drank a whole jar of wine without her husband's knowledge; and this is a proof, that when women show her divine honour a jar of wine is placed *there*, *but* covered from sight, and that it is not lawful to bring in twigs of myrtle, as Butas[12] mentions in his Causalia. But let us pass by with similar neglect[13] the *dii conserentes*, whom Flaccus and others relate to have buried themselves, changed *in humani penis similitudinem* in the cinders under a pot of *exta*.[14] And when Tanaquil, skilled in the arts of Etruria,[15] disturbed these, the gods erected themselves, and became rigid. She then commanded a captive woman from Corniculum to learn and understand what was the meaning of this: Ocrisia, a woman of the greatest wisdom *divos inseruisse genitali, explicuisse motus certos*. Then the holy and burning deities poured forth the power of Lucilius,[16] and *thus* Servius king of Rome was born.

19. We shall pass by the wild Bacchanalia also, which are named in Greek Omophagia, in which with seeming frenzy and the loss of your senses you twine snakes about you; and, to show yourselves full of the divinity and majesty of the god, tear in pieces with gory mouths the flesh of loudly-bleating goats. Those hidden mysteries of Cyprian Venus we pass by also, whose founder is said to have been King Cinyras,[17] in which being initiated, they bring stated fees as to a harlot, and carry away *phalli*, given as signs of

---

[1] The festival of Cybele began on the 22d of March, when a pine tree was introduced into the mysteries, and continued until the 27th, which was marked by a general purification (*lavatio*), as Salmasius observed from a calendar of Constantine the Great. [An equinoctial feast, which the Church deposed by the Paschal observances. March 22 is the *prima sedes Paschæ*.]
[2] Lit., "for solace of so great a wound."
[3] So Stewechius, followed by Orelli and Oehler, reading *quibus Ia* for the MS. *jam*, which would refer the action to Cybele, whereas Arnobius expressly says (c. 7) that it was the newly wedded wife who covered the breast of Attis with wools. *Jam* is, however, received from the MS. by the other edd., except Hild., who asserts that the MS. reads *Iam*, and Elmenh., who reads *Ion*.
[4] i.e., priests of Cybele, their names being derived from the Phrygian river Gallus, whose waters were supposed to bring on frenzy ending in self-mutilation.
[5] Lit., "with wailing."
[6] Lit., "with."

[7] Lit., "and the duty of defence itself."
[8] i.e., secret rites, to which only the initiated were admitted.
[9] Lit., "which you deliver" — *traditis;* so Elmenh., LB., and later edd., for the unintelligible MS. *tradidisse*, retained in both Roman edd.
[10] Lit., "deformity affixed to all."
[11] MS. *fetam f*. Cf. i. 36, n. 2, p. 422, *supra*.
[12] So Heraldus, from Plutarch, *Rom.*, 21, where Butas is said to have written on this subject (αἰτίαι) in elegiacs, for the MS. Putas.
[13] Lit., "in like manner and with dissimulation."
[14] i e., heart, lungs, and liver, probably of a sacrifice.
[15] i e., "divination, augury," etc.
[16] *I'is Lucilii*, i.e., *semen*. [He retails Pliny xxxvi. 27.]
[17] Cf. iv. 24.

the propitious deity. Let the rites of the Corybantes also be consigned to oblivion, in which is revealed that sacred mystery, a brother slain by his brothers, parsley sprung from the blood of the murdered one, that vegetable forbidden to be placed on tables, lest the *manes* of the dead should be unappeasably offended. But those other Bacchanalia also we refuse to proclaim, in which there is revealed and taught to the initiated a secret not to be spoken; how Liber, when taken up with boyish sports, was torn asunder by the Titans; how he was cut up limb by limb by them also, and thrown into pots that he might be cooked; how Jupiter, allured by the sweet savour, rushed unbidden to the meal, and discovering what had been done, overwhelmed the revellers with his terrible thunder, and hurled them to the lowest part of Tartarus. As evidence and proof of which, the Thracian *bard* handed down in his poems the dice, mirror, tops, hoops, and smooth balls, and golden apples taken from the virgin Hesperides.

20. It was our purpose to leave unnoticed those mysteries also into which Phrygia is initiated, and all that [1] race, were it not that the name of Jupiter, *which has been* introduced by them, would not suffer us to pass cursorily by the wrongs and insults offered to him; not that we feel any pleasure in discussing [2] mysteries so filthy, but that it may be made clear to you again and again what wrong you heap upon those whose guardians, champions, worshippers, you profess to be. Once upon a time, they say, Diespiter, burning after his mother Ceres with evil passions and forbidden desires, for she is said by the natives of that district *to be* Jupiter's mother, and yet not daring to seek by open [3] force that for which he had conceived a shameless longing, hits upon a clever trick by which to rob of her chastity his mother, who feared nothing of the sort. Instead of a god, he becomes a bull; and concealing his purpose and daring under the appearance of a beast lying in wait,[4] he rushes madly with sudden violence upon her, thoughtless and unwitting, obtains his incestuous desires; and the fraud being disclosed by his lust, flies off known and discovered. His mother burns, foams, gasps, boils with fury and indignation; and being unable to repress the storm [5] and tempest of her wrath, received the name Brimo [6] thereafter from her ever-raging passion: nor has she any other wish than to punish as she may her son's audacity.

21. Jupiter is troubled enough, being over-whelmed with fear, and cannot find means to soothe the rage of his violated *mother*. He pours forth prayers, and makes supplication; her ears are closed by grief. The whole order of the gods is sent *to seek his pardon;* no one has weight enough to win a hearing. At last, the son seeking how to make satisfaction, devises this means: *Arietem nobilem bene grandibus cum testiculis deligit, exsecat hos ipse et lanato exuit ex folliculi tegmine.* Approaching his mother sadly and with downcast looks, and as if by his own decision he had condemned himself, he casts and throws these [7] into her bosom. When she saw what his pledge was,[8] she is somewhat softened, and allows herself to be recalled to the care of the offspring which she had conceived.[9] After the tenth month she bears a daughter, of beautiful form, whom later ages have called now Libera, now Proserpine; whom when Jupiter Verveceus [10] saw to be strong, plump, and blooming, forgetting what evils and what wickedness, and how great recklessness, he had a little before fallen into,[11] he returns to his former practices; and because it seemed too [12] wicked that a father openly be joined as in marriage with his daughter, he passes into the terrible form of a dragon: he winds his huge coils round the terrified maiden, and under a fierce appearance sports and caresses *her* in softest embraces. She, too, is in consequence filled with the seed of the most powerful Jupiter, but not as her mother *was*, for she [13] bore a daughter like herself; but from the maiden was born something like a bull, to testify to her seduction by Jupiter. If any one asks [14] who narrates this, then we shall quote the well-known senarian verse of a Tarentine poet which antiquity sings,[15] saying: "The bull begot a dragon, and the dragon a bull." Lastly, the sacred rites themselves, and the ceremony of initiation even, named Sebadia,[16] might attest the truth; for in them a golden snake is let down into the bosom of the initiated, and taken away again from the lower parts.

22. I do not think it necessary here also with many words to go through each part, and show how many base and unseemly things there are

---

[1] So the MS. and edd., reading *gens illa*, for which Memmius proposed *Ilia* — "and all the Trojan race."
[2] Lit., "riding upon" — *inequitare*.
[3] Lit., "most open."
[4] *Subsessoris.*
[5] Lit., "growling" — *fremitum*.
[6] The MS. reads *primo*, emended as above by the brother of Canterus, followed by later edd.

[7] i.e., *testiculi.*
[8] *Virilitate pignoris visa.*
[9] So Ursinus suggested, followed by Stewechius and later edd., *concepti fœtus revocatur ad curam;* the MS. reads *concepit —* "is softened and conceived,' etc.
[10] Jupiter may be here called *Verveceus*, either as an epithet of Jupiter Ammon — "like a wether," or (and this seems most probable from the context), "dealing with wethers," referring to the mode in which he had extricated himself from his former difficulty, or "stupid." The MS. reads *virviriceus.*
[11] Lit., "encountered" — *aggressus.*
[12] Lit., "sufficiently."
[13] i.e., Ceres.
[14] Lit., "will any one want."
[15] i.e., handed down by antiquity. [Vol. ii. p. 176, this series.]
[16] These seem to have been celebrated in honour of Dionysius as well as Zeus, though, in so far as they are described by Arnobius, they refer to the intrigue of the latter only. Macrobius, however (*Saturn.*, i. 18), mentions that in Thrace, Liber and Sol were identified and worshipped as Sebadius; and this suggests that we have to take but one more step to explain the use of the title to Jupiter also.

in each particular. For what mortal is there, with but little sense even of what becomes a man, who does not himself see clearly the character of all these things, how wicked *they are*, how vile, and what disgrace is brought upon the gods by the very ceremonies of their mysteries, and by the unseemly origin of their rites? Jupiter, it is said, lusted after Ceres. Why, I ask, has Jupiter deserved so ill of you, that there is no kind of disgrace, no infamous adultery, which you do not heap upon his head, as if on some vile and worthless person? Leda was unfaithful to her nuptial vow; Jupiter is said to be the cause of the fault. Danae could not keep her virginity; the theft is said *to have been* Jupiter's. Europa hastened to the name of woman; he is again declared *to have been* the assailant of her chastity. Alcmena, Electra, Latona, Laodamia, a thousand other virgins, and a thousand matrons, and with them the boy Catamitus, were robbed of their honour and [1] chastity. It is the same story everywhere — Jupiter. Nor is there any kind of baseness in which you do not join and associate his name with passionate lusts; so that the wretched being seems to have been born for no other reason at all except that he might be a field fertile in [2] crimes, an occasion of evil-speaking, a kind of open place into which should gather all filthiness from the impurities of the stage.[3] And yet if you were to say that he had intercourse with strange women, it would indeed be impious, but the wrong done in slandering him might be bearable. Did he lust[4] after his mother also, after his daughter too, with furious desires; and could no sacredness in his parent, no reverence for her, *no* shrinking even from the child which had sprung from himself, withhold him from conceiving so detestable a plan?

23. I should wish, therefore, to see Jupiter, the father of the gods, who ever controls the world and men,[5] adorned with the horns of an ox, shaking his hairy ears, with his feet contracted into hoofs, chewing green grass, and *having* behind him[6] a tail, hams,[7] and ankles smeared over with soft excrement,[8] and bedaubed with the filth cast forth. I should wish, I say, — for it must be said over and over again, — to see him who turns the stars *in their courses*, and who terrifies and overthrows nations pale with fear, pursuing the flocks of wethers, *inspicientem testiculos are-*

tinos, snatching these away with that severe[9] and divine hand with which he was wont to launch the gleaming lightnings and to hurl in his rage the thunderbolt.[10] Then, indeed, *I should like to see him* ransacking their inmost parts with glowing knife;[11] and all witnesses being removed, tearing away the membranes *circumjectas prolibus*, and bringing them to his mother, still hot with rage, as a kind of fillet[12] to draw forth her pity, with downcast countenance, pale, wounded,[13] pretending to be in agony; and to make this believed, defiled with the blood of the ram, and covering his pretended wound with bands of wool and linen. *Is it possible* that this can be heard and read in this world,[14] and that those who discuss these things wish themselves to be thought pious, holy, and defenders of religion? Is there any greater sacrilege than this, or can any mind[15] be found so imbued with impious ideas as to believe such stories, or receive them, or hand them down in the most secret mysteries of the sacred rites? If that Jupiter *of whom you speak*, whoever he is, really[16] existed, or was affected by any sense of wrong, would it not be fitting that,[17] roused to anger, he should remove the earth from under our feet, extinguish the light of the sun and moon; nay more, that he should throw all things into one mass, as of old?[18]

24. But, *my opponent* says, these are not the rites of our state. Who, pray, says this, or who repeats it? *Is he* Roman, Gaul, Spaniard, African, German, or Sicilian? And what does it avail your cause if these stories are not yours, while those who compose them are on your side? Or of what importance is it whether you approve of them or not, since what you yourselves say[19] are found to be either just as foul, or of even greater baseness? For do you wish that we should consider the mysteries and those ceremonies which are named by the Greeks Thesmophoria,[20] in which those holy vigils and,

---

[1] Lit., "of."

[2] Lit., "that he might be a crop of" — *seges*, a correction in the margin of Ursinus for the MS. *sedes* — "a seat."

[3] So all edd., reading *scenarum* (MS. *scr-*, but *r* marked as spurious), except LB., followed by Orelli, who gives *sentinarum* — "of the dregs." Oehler supplies *e*, which the sense seems to require. [Note our author's persistent scorn of Jove *Opt. Max.*]

[4] Lit., "neigh with appetites of an enraged beast."

[5] This clearly refers to the *Æneid*, x. 18.

[6] Lit., "on the rear part."

[7] *Suffragines.*

[8] So the margin of Ursinus, Elmenh., L.B., Oberth., Orelli, and Oehler, reading *molli fimo* for the MS. *molissimo.*

[9] Lit., "censorial."

[10] Lit., "rage with thunders."

[11] So Gelenius, followed by Stewechius and Orelli, reading *smiiia* for the corrupt and unintelligible MS. *nullas.*

[12] *Infulæ*, besides being worn by the priest, adorned the victim, and were borne by the suppliant. Perhaps a combination of the two last ideas is meant to be suggested here.

[13] i e , seemingly so.

[14] Lit , "under this axis of the world."

[15] So the MS., followed by Hild. and Oehler; the other edd. reading *gens* for *mens.*

[16] Lit., "felt himself to be."

[17] Lit., "would the thing not be worthy that angry and roused."

[18] i.e., reduce to chaos, in which one thing would not be distinguished from another, but all be mixed up confusedly.

[19] Lit., "what are your proper things."

[20] Every one since Salmasius (*ad Solinum*, p. 750) has supposed Arnobius to have here fallen into a gross error, by confounding the Eleusinian mysteries with the Thesmophoria; an error the less accountable, because they are carefully distinguished by Clemens Alexandrinus, whom Arnobius evidently had before him, as usual. There seems to be no sufficient reason, however, for charging Arnobius with such a blunder, although in the end of ch. 26 he refers to the story just related, as showing the base character of the Eleusinia (*Eleusiniorum vestrorum notas*); as he here speaks of *mysteria* (i.e., Eleusinia, cf. Nepos, *Alc.*, 3, 16) *et illa divina quæ Thesmophoria nominantur a Græcis.* It should be remembered also that there was much in common between these mysteries: the story of Ceres' wanderings was the subject of both; in both there was a sea-

solemn watchings were consecrated *to the goddess* by the Athenians? Do you wish us, I say, to see what beginnings they have, what causes, that we may prove that Athens itself also, distinguished in the arts and pursuits of civilization, says things as insulting to the gods as others, and that stories are there publicly related under the mask of religion just as disgraceful as are thrown in *our* way by the rest of you? Once, they say, when Proserpine, not yet a woman and still a maiden, was gathering purple flowers in the meadows of Sicily, and when her eagerness to gather them was leading her hither and thither in all directions, the king of the shades, springing forth through an opening of unknown depth, seizes and bears away with him the maiden, and conceals himself again in the bowels[1] of the earth. Now when Ceres did not know what had happened, and had no idea where in the world her daughter was, she set herself to seek the lost one all over the[2] world. She snatches up two torches lit at the fires of Ætna;[3] and giving herself light by means of these, goes on her quest in all parts of the earth.

25. In her wanderings on that quest, she reaches the confines of Eleusis as well as other countries[4] — that is the name of a canton in Attica. At that time these parts were inhabited by aborigines[5] named Baubo, Triptolemus, Eubuleus, Eumolpus,[6] Dysaules: Triptolemus, who yoked oxen; Dysaules, a keeper of goats; Eubuleus, of swine; Eumolpus, of sheep,[7] from whom also flows the race of Eumolpidæ, and *from whom* is derived that name famous among the Athenians,[8] and those who afterwards flourished as *caduceatores*,[9] hierophants, and criers. So, then, that Baubo who, we have said, dwelt in the canton of Eleusis, receives hospitably Ceres, worn out with ills of many kinds, hangs about her with pleasing attentions, beseeches her not to neglect to refresh her body, brings to quench her thirst wine thickened with spelt,[10] which the Greeks term *cyceon*. The goddess in her sorrow turns away from the kindly offered

services,[11] and rejects *them;* nor does her misfortune suffer her to remember what the body always requires.[12] Baubo, on the other hand, begs and exhorts her — as is usual in such calamities — not to despise her humanity; Ceres remains utterly immoveable, and tenaciously maintains an invincible austerity. But when this was done several times, and her fixed purpose could not be worn out by any attentions, Baubo changes her plans, and determines to make merry by strange jests her whom she could not win by earnestness. That part of the body by which women both bear children and obtain the name of mothers,[13] this she frees from longer neglect: she makes it assume a purer appearance, and become smooth like a child, not yet hard and rough with hair. In this wise she returns[14] to the sorrowing goddess; and while trying the common expedients by which it is usual to break the force of grief, and moderate it, she uncovers herself, and baring her groins, displays all the parts which decency hides;[15] and then the goddess fixes her eyes upon these,[16] and is pleased with the strange form of consolation. Then becoming more cheerful after laughing, she takes and drinks off the draught spurned *before*, and the indecency of a shameless action forced that which Baubo's modest conduct was long unable to win.

26. If any one perchance thinks that we are speaking wicked calumnies, let him take the books of the Thracian soothsayer,[17] which you speak of as of divine antiquity; and he will find that we are neither cunningly inventing anything, nor seeking means to bring the holiness of the gods into ridicule, and doing so: for we shall bring forward the very verses which the son of Calliope uttered in Greek,[18] and published abroad in his songs to the human race throughout all ages: —

" With these words she at the same time drew up her
    garments from the lowest *hem*,
And exposed to view *formatas inguinibus res*,
Which Baubo grasping[19] with hollow hand, for
Their appearance was infantile, strikes, touches gently.
Then the goddess, fixing her orbs of august light,
Being softened, lays aside for a little the sadness of her
    mind;
Thereafter she takes the cup in her hand, and laughing,
Drinks off the whole draught of cyceon with gladness."[20]

---

son of fasting to recall her sadness; both had indecent allusions to the way in which that sadness was dispelled; and both celebrated with some freedom the recovery of cheerfulness by the goddess, the great distinguishing feature of the Thesmophoria being that only women could take part in its rites. Now, as it is to the points in which the two sets of mysteries were at one that allusion is made in the passage which follows, it was only natural that Arnobius should not be very careful to distinguish the one from the other, seeing that he was concerned not with their differences, but with their coincidence. It seems difficult, therefore, to maintain that Arnobius has here convicted himself of so utter ignorance and so gross carelessness as his critics have imagined. [Vol. ii. p. 176.]

1 Lit., " caverns."
2 Lit., " in the whole."
3 The MS. is utterly corrupt —*flammis onere pressas etneis*, corrected as above by Gelenius from c. 35., f. *comprehensas.* — ÆL.
4 Lit., " also."
5 Lit., " (they were) earth-born who inhabited."
6 The MS. wants this name; but it has evidently been omitted by accident, as it occurs in the next line.
7 Lit., " of woolly flock."
8 *Cecropios et qui.*
9 i.e., staff-bearers.
10 *Cinnus*, the chief ingredients, according to Hesychius (quoted by Oehler), being wine, honey, water, and spelt or barley. [P. 503, *inf.*]

11 Lit., " offices of humanity."
12 Lit., " common health." Arnobius is here utterly forgetful of Ceres' divinity, and subjects her to the invariable requirements of nature, from which the divine might be supposed to be exempt.
13 So the conjecture of Livineius, adopted by Oehler, *gene-t-ricum* for the MS. *genericum.*
14 So Stewechius, followed by Oehler, reading *redit ita* for the MS. *redita;* the other edd. merely drop *a.*
15 *Omnia illa pudoris loca.*
16 *Pubi.*
17 Orpheus, under whose name there was current in the time of Arnobius an immense mass of literature freely used, and it is probable sometimes supplemented, by Christian writers. Cf. c. 19.
18 Lit., " put forth with Greek mouth."
19 Lit., " tossing."
20 It may be well to observe that Arnobius differs from the Greek versions of these lines found in Clem. Alex. (vol. ii. p. 177) and

What say you, O wise sons of Erectheus?[1] what, you citizens of Minerva?[2] The mind is eager to know with what words you will defend what it is so dangerous to maintain, or what arts you have by which to give safety to personages and causes wounded so mortally. This[3] is no false mistrust, nor are you assailed with lying accusations :[4] the infamy of your Eleusinia is declared both by their base beginnings and by the records of ancient literature, by the very signs, in fine, which you use when questioned in receiving the sacred things, — "I have fasted, and drunk the draught ;[5] I have taken out of the *mystic* cist,[6] and put into the wicker-basket ; I have received again, and transferred to the little chest."[7]

27. Are then your deities carried off by force, and do they seize by violence, as their holy and hidden mysteries relate? do they enter into marriages sought stealthily and by fraud?[8] is their honour snatched from virgins[9] resisting and unwilling? have they no knowledge of impending injury, no acquaintance with what has happened to those carried off by force? Are they, when lost, sought for as men are? and do they traverse the earth's vast extent with lamps and torches when the sun is shining most brightly? Are they afflicted? are they troubled? do they assume the squalid garments of mourners, and the signs of misery? and that they may be able to turn their mind to victuals and the taking of food, is use made not of reason, not of the right time, not of some weighty words or pressing courtesy, but is a display made of the shameful and indecent parts of the body? and are those members exposed which the shame felt by all, and the natural law of modesty, bid us conceal, which it is not permissible to name among pure ears without permission, and saying, "by your leave?"[10] What, I ask you, was there in such a sight,[11] what in the privy parts of Baubo, to move to wonder and laughter a goddess of the same sex, and formed with similar parts? what was there such that, when presented to the divine

eyes[12] and sight, it should at the same time enable her to forget her miseries, and bring her with sudden cheerfulness to a happier state of mind? Oh, what have we had it in our power to bring forward with scoffing and jeering, were it not for respect for the reader,[13] and the dignity of literature!

28. I confess that I have long been hesitating, looking on every side, shuffling, doubling Tellene perplexities ;[14] while I am ashamed to mention those Alimontian[15] mysteries in which Greece erects *phalli* in honour of father Bacchus, and the whole district is covered with images of men's *fascina*. The meaning of this is obscure perhaps, and it is asked why it is done. Whoever is ignorant of this, let him learn, and, wondering at what is so important, ever keep it with reverent care in a pure heart.[16] While Liber, born at Nysa,[17] and son of Semele, was still among men, the story goes, he wished to become acquainted with the shades below, and to inquire into what went on in Tartarus ; but this wish was hindered by some difficulties, because, from ignorance of the route, he did not know by what way to go and proceed. One Prosumnus starts up, a base lover of the god, and *a fellow* too prone to wicked lusts, who promises to point out the gate of Dis, and the approaches to Acheron, if the god will gratify him, and suffer *uxorias voluptates ex se carpi*. The god, without reluctance, swears to put himself[18] in his power and at his disposal, but *only* immediately on his return from the lower regions, having obtained his wish and desire.[19] Prosumnus politely tells him the way, and sets him on the very threshold of the lower regions. In the meantime, while Liber is inspecting[20] and examining carefully Styx, Cerberus, the Furies, and all other things, the informer passed from the number of the living, and was buried according to the manner of men. Evius[21] comes up from the lower regions, and learns that his guide is dead. But that he might fulfil his promise, and free himself from the obligation of his oath, he goes to the place of the funeral, and

Eusebius (*Præpar. Evang.*, ii. 3), omitting all mention of Iacchus, who is made very prominent by them; and that he does not adhere strictly to metrical rules, probably, as Heraldus pointed out, because, like the poets of that age, he paid little heed to questions of quantity. Whether Arnobius had merely paraphrased the original as found in Clement and Eusebius, or had a different version of them before him, is a question which can only be discussed by means of a careful comparison between the Greek and Latin forms of the verses with the context in both cases.

[1] So LB., Hild., and Oehler, reading *Erechthidæ O* (inserted by Hild.) for the ms. *erithideo*.
[2] i.e., Athenians.
[3] The ms., 1st ed., Hild., and Oehler read *ita* — "It is thus not," etc.; the others as above, *ista*.
[4] *Delatione calumniosa.* [Conf. vol. ii. p. 175, col. 2.]
[5] *Cyceon.* [P. 499, *supra*, and 503, *infra*.]
[6] The ms. reads *exci-ta*, corrected as above, *ex cista*, in the margin of Ursinus.
[7] [It is a pity that all this must be retailed anew after Clement, vol. ii. pp. 175, 177, notes.]
[8] Lit., "by stealthy frauds."
[9] Lit., "is the honour of virginity snatched from them?"
[10] *Sine veniâ ac sine honoribus præfatis.*
[11] So Stewechius, LB., and Orelli, reading *spec-t-u in t-ali* for the ms *in specu ali*.

[12] Lit., "light." [Note Clement, vol. ii. p. 175, col. 2, line 12.]
[13] So the ms., Hild., and Oehler, reading *noscentis*.
[14] This allusion is somewhat obscure. Heraldus regards *tricas Tellenas* as akin in sense to *t. Atellanas*, i.e., "comic trifles;" in which case the sense would be, that Arnobius had been heaping up any trifles which would keep him back from the disagreeable subject. Ausonius Popma (quoted by Orelli) explains the phrase with reference to the capture of Tellenæ by Ancus Martius as meaning "something hard to get through."
[15] The ms. reads *alimoniæ*, corrected from Clem. Alex. by Salmasius, *Alimontia*, i.e., celebrated at Halimus in Attica.
[16] Lit., "in pure senses." [Ironically said.]
[17] Cicero (*de Nat. Deor.*, iii. 23) speaks of five Dionysi, the father of the fifth being Nisus. Arnobius had this passage before him in writing the fourth book (cf. c. 15, and n. 2), so that he may here mean to speak of Liber similarly.
[18] Lit., "that he will be."
[19] So the ms., acc. to Hild., reading *expe-titionis;* acc. to Crusius, the ms. gives *-ditionis* — "(having accomplished) his expedition."
[20] Lit., "is surveying with all careful examination."
[21] ms. *cuius.* [Retailed from Clement, vol. ii. p. 180. As to the arguments the Fathers were compelled to use with heathen, see note 5, same volume, p. 206.]

— " ficorum ex arbore ramum validissimum præsecans dolat, runcinat, levigat et humani speciem fabricatur in penis, figit super aggerem tumuli, et posticâ ex parte nudatus accedit, subsidit, insidit. Lascivia deinde surientis assumptâ, huc atque illuc clunes torquet et meditatur ab ligno pati quod jamdudum in veritate promiserat."

29. Now, to prevent any one from thinking that we have devised what is so impious, we do not call upon him to believe Heraclitus as a witness, nor to receive from his account what he felt about such mysteries. Let him [1] ask the whole of Greece what is the meaning of these *phalli* which ancient custom erects and worships throughout the country, throughout the towns : he will find that the causes are those which we say ; or if they are ashamed to declare the truth honestly, of what avail will it be to obscure, to conceal the cause and origin of the rite, while [2] the accusation holds good against the very act of worship? What say you, O peoples? what, ye nations busied with the services of the temples, and given up *to them?* Is it to these rites you drive us by flames, banishment, slaughter, and any other kind of punishments, and by fear of cruel torture? Are these the gods whom you bring to us, whom you thrust and impose upon us, like whom you would neither wish yourselves to be, nor any one related to you by blood and friendship? [3] Can you declare to your beardless sons, still wearing the dress of boys, the agreements which Liber formed with his lovers? Can you urge your daughters-in-law, nay, even your own wives, to *show* the modesty of Baubo, and *enjoy* the chaste pleasures of Ceres? Do you wish your young men to know, hear, *and* learn what even Jupiter showed himself to more matrons than one? Would you wish your grown up maidens and still lusty fathers to learn how the same deity sported with his daughter? Do you wish full brothers, already hot with passion, and sisters sprung from the same parents, to hear that he again did not spurn the embraces, the couch of his sister? Should we not then flee far from such gods ; and should not our ears be stopped altogether, that the filthiness of so impure a religion may not creep into the mind? For what man is there who has been reared with morals so pure, that the example of the gods does not excite him to similar madness? or who can keep back his desires from his kinsfolk, and those of whom he should stand in awe, when he sees that among the gods above nothing is held sacred in the confusion caused by [4] their lusts? For when it is certain that the first and perfect nature has not been able to restrain its passion within right limits, why should not man give

himself up to his desires without distinction, being both borne on headlong by his innate frailty, and aided by the teaching of the holy deities? [5]

30. I confess that, in reflecting on such monstrous stories in my own mind, I have long been accustomed to wonder that you dare to speak of those as atheists,[6] impious, sacrilegious, who either deny that there are *any* gods at all, or doubt *their existence*, or assert that they were men, and have been numbered among the gods for the sake of some power and good desert ; since, if a true examination be made, it is fitting that none should be called by such names, more than yourselves, who, under the pretence of showing them reverence, heap up in so doing[7] more abuse and accusation, than if you had conceived the idea of doing this openly with avowed abuse. He who doubts the existence of the gods, or denies it altogether, although he may seem to adopt monstrous opinions from the audacity of his conjectures, yet refuses to credit what is obscure without insulting any one ; and he who asserts that they were mortals, although he brings them down from the exalted place of inhabitants of heaven, yet heaps upon them other[8] honours, since he supposes that they have been raised to the rank of the gods[9] for their services, and from admiration of their virtues.

31. But you who assert that you are the defenders and propagators of their immortality, have you passed by, have you left untouched, any one of them, without assailing him[10] with your abuse? or is there any kind of insult so damnable in the eyes of all, that you have been afraid to use it upon them, even though hindered[11] by the dignity of their name? Who declared that the gods loved frail and mortal bodies? *was it* not you? Who that they perpetrated those most charming thefts on the couches of others? *was it* not you? Who that children had intercourse with their mothers ; *and* on the other hand, fathers with their virgin daughters? *was it* not you? Who that pretty boys, and even grown-up *men* of very fine appearance, were wrongfully lusted after? *was it* not you? Who *declared that they*[12] *were* mutilated, debauched,[13] skilled in dissimulation, thieves, held in bonds and chains, finally assailed with thunderbolts, *and* wounded, that they died,

---

[1] i.e., the sceptic.
[2] *Cum* wanting in the MS.
[3] Lit., " by right of friendship."
[4] Lit., " of."

[5] Lit., "of holy divinity." Orelli thinks, and with reason, that Arnobius refers to the words which Terence puts into the mouth of Chaerea (*Eun.*, iii. 5, vv. 36-43), who encourages himself to give way to lust by asking, " Shall I, a man, not do this? " when Jove had done as much. [Elucidation III.]
[6] Lit., " to speak of any one as atheist . . . of those who," etc.
[7] So the MS. and edd., reading *in eo*, for which we should perhaps read *in eos* — " heap upon them."
[8] *Subsicivis laudibus.*
[9] Lit., " to the reward (*meritum*) of divinity."
[10] Lit., " unwounded."
[11] So the edd , reading *tardati* for the MS. *tradatis*, except Hild., who reads *tardatis*.
[12] i.e., the gods.
[13] *Exoletos.* Cf. iv. c. 35, note 13, p. 487, *supra*.

and even found graves on earth? *was it* not you? While, then, so many and grievous charges have been raised by you to the injury of the gods, do you dare to assert that the gods have been displeased because of us, while it has long been clear that you are the guilty causes of such anger, and the occasion of the divine wrath?

32. But you err, says *my opponent,* and are mistaken, and show, even in criticising *these* things, that you are rather ignorant, unlearned, and boorish. For all those stories which seem to you disgraceful, and tending to the discredit of the gods, contain in them holy mysteries, theories wonderful and profound, and not such as any one can easily become acquainted with by force of understanding. For that is not meant and said which has been written and placed on the surface of the story; but all these things are understood in allegorical senses, and by means of secret explanations privately supplied.[1] Therefore he who says[2] Jupiter lay with his mother, does not mean the incestuous or shameful embraces of Venus, but names Jupiter instead of rain, and Ceres instead of the earth. And he, again, who says that he[3] dealt lasciviously with his daughter, speaks of no filthy pleasures, but puts Jupiter for the name of a shower, and by his daughter means[4] the crop sown. So, too, he who says that Proserpina was carried off by father Dis, does not say, as you suppose,[5] that the maiden was carried off to *gratify* the basest desires; but because we cover the seed with clods, he signifies that the goddess has sunk under the earth, and unites with Orcus to bring forth fruit. In like manner in the other stories also one thing indeed is said, but something else is understood; and under a commonplace openness of expression there lurks a secret doctrine, and a dark profundity of mystery.

33. These are all quirks, as is evident, and quibbles with which they are wont to bolster up weak cases before a jury; nay, rather, to speak more truly, they are pretences, such as are used in[6] sophistical reasonings, by which not the truth is sought after, but always the image, and appearance, and shadow of the truth. For because it is shameful and unbecoming to receive as true the correct accounts, you have had recourse[7] to this expedient, that one thing should be substituted for another, and that what was in itself shameful should, in being explained, be forced into the semblance of decency. But what is it to

us whether other senses and other meanings underlie *these* vain stories? For we who assert that the gods are treated by you wickedly and impiously, need only[8] receive what is written, what is said,[9] and need not care as to what is kept secret, since the insult to the deities consists not in the idea hidden in its meanings,[10] but in what is signified by the words as they stand out. And yet, that we may not seem unwilling to examine what you say, we ask this first of you, if only you will bear with us, from whom have you learned, or by whom has it been made known, either that these things were written allegorically, or that they should be understood in the same way? Did the writers summon you to *take counsel with them?* or did you lie hid in their bosoms at the time[11] when they put one thing for another, without regard to truth? Then, if they chose, from religious awe[12] and fear on any account, to wrap those mysteries in dark obscurity, what audacity it shows in you to wish to understand what they did not wish, to know yourselves and make all acquainted with that which they vainly attempted to conceal by words which did not suggest the truth!

34. But, agreeing with you that in all these stories stags are spoken of instead of Iphigenias, yet, how are you sure, when you either explain or unfold these allegories, that you give the same explanations or have the same ideas which were entertained by the writers themselves in the silence of their thoughts, but expressed by words not adapted[13] to what was meant, but to something else? You say that the falling of rain into the bosom of the earth was spoken of as the union of Jupiter and Ceres; another may both devise with greater subtlety, and conjecture with some probability, something else; a third, a fourth may *do the same;* and as the characteristics of the minds of the thinkers show themselves, so each thing may be explained in an infinite number of ways. For since all that allegory, as it is called, is taken from narratives expressly made obscure,[14] and has no certain limit within which the meaning of the story,[15] as it is called, should be firmly fixed and unchangeable, it is open to every one to put the meaning into it which he pleases, and to assert that that has been adopted[16] to which his thoughts and surmises[17] led him. But this being the case, how can you obtain certainty from what is doubt-

---

[1] *Subditivis secretis.*
[2] Both Roman edd. and MS. read *dicet* — "shall say;" all others as above — *dicit.*
[3] i.e., Jupiter.
[4] Lit., "in the signification of his daughter."
[5] So the margin of Ursinus — *ut reris* for the MS. *ut ce-reris.*
[6] Lit., "colours of."
[7] The MS. and both Roman edd. read *indecorum est,* which leaves the sentence incomplete. LB., followed by later edd., proposed *decursum est,* as above (Oehler, *inde d.* — "from these recourse has been had"), the other conjectures tending to the same meaning.

[8] "We need only:" lit., "it is enough for us to."
[9] Lit., "heard."
[10] Lit., "in the obscure mind of senses."
[11] "Or at the time," *aut tum,* the correction of LB. for the MS. *sutum.*
[12] Lit., "fear of any reason and of religion."
[13] Lit., "proper."
[14] Lit., "from shut-up things."
[15] *Rei.*
[16] Lit., "placed."
[17] Lit., "his suspicion and conjectural (perhaps "probable") inference."

ful, and attach one sense only to an expression which you see to be explained in innumerable different ways?[1]

35. Finally, if you think it right, returning to our inquiry, we ask this of you, whether you think that all stories about the gods,[2] that is, without any exception,[3] have been written throughout with a double meaning and sense, and in a way[4] admitting of several interpretations ; or that some parts of them are not ambiguous at all, *while*, on the contrary, others have many meanings, and are enveloped in the veil of allegory which has been thrown round them? For if the whole structure and arrangement of the narrative have been surrounded with a veil of allegory from beginning to end, explain *to us*, tell *us*, what we should put and substitute for each thing which every story says, and to what other things and meanings we should refer[5] each. For as, to take an example, you wish Jupiter to be said instead of the rain, Ceres for the earth, and for Libera[6] and father Dis the sinking and casting of seed *into the earth*, so you ought to say what we should understand for the bull, what for the wrath and anger of Ceres ; what the word Brimo[7] means ; what the anxious prayer of Jupiter ; what the gods sent to make intercession for him, but not listened to ; what the castrated ram ; what the parts[8] of the castrated ram ; what the satisfaction made with these ; what the further dealings with his daughter, still more unseemly in their lustfulness ; so, in the other story also, what the grove and flowers of Henna are ; what the fire taken from Ætna, and the torches lit with it ; what the travelling through the world with these ; what the Attic country, the canton of Eleusin, the hut of Baubo, and her rustic hospitality ; what the draught of *cyceon*[9] means, the refusal of it, the shaving and disclosure of the privy parts, the shameful charm of the sight, and the forgetfulness of her bereavement produced by such means. Now, if you point out what should be put in the place of all these, changing the one for the other,[10] we shall admit your assertion ; but if you can neither present another supposition in each case, nor appeal to[11] the context as a whole, why do you make that obscure,[12] by means of fair-seeming allegories, which has been spoken plainly, and disclosed to the understanding of all?

36. But you will perhaps say that these allegories are not *found* in the whole body of the story, but that some parts are written so as to be understood by all, while others have a double meaning, and are veiled in ambiguity. That is refined subtlety, and can be seen through by the dullest. For because it is very difficult for you to transpose, reverse, and divert *to other meanings* all that has been said, you choose out some things which suit your purpose, and by means of these you strive to maintain that false and spurious versions were thrown about the truth which is under them.[13] But yet, supposing that we should grant to you that it is just as you say, how do you know, or whence do you learn, which part of the story is written without any double meaning,[14] which, on the other hand, has been covered with jarring and alien senses? For it may be that what you believe to be so[15] is otherwise, that what you believe to be otherwise[16] has been produced with different, and *even* opposite modes of expression. For where, in a consistent whole, one part is said to be written allegorically, the other in plain and trustworthy language, while there is no sign in the thing itself to point out the difference between what is said ambiguously and what is said simply, that which is simple may as well be thought to have a double meaning, as what has been written ambiguously be believed to be wrapt in obscurity.[17] But, indeed, we confess that we do not understand at all by whom this[18] is either done, or can be believed to be possible.

37. Let us examine, then, what is said in this way. In the grove of Henna, my opponent says, the maiden Proserpine was once gathering flowers : this is as yet uncorrupted, and has been told in a straightforward manner, for all know without any doubt what a grove and flowers are, what Proserpine is, and a maiden. Summanus sprung forth from the earth, borne along in a four-horse chariot : this, too, is just as simple, for a team of four horses, a chariot, and Summanus need no interpreter. Suddenly he carried off Proserpine, and bore her with himself under the earth : the burying of the seed, my opponent says, is meant by the rape of Proserpine. What has happened, pray, that the story should be suddenly turned to something else? that Proserpine should be called the seed? that she who was for

---

[1] Lit., " to be deduced with variety of expositions through numberless ways."

[2] The MS., first four edd., and Hild. read *de his* — " about these," corrected in the others *dis* or *diis*, as above.

[3] Lit., " each."

[4] Pl.

[5] Lit., " call."

[6] i.e., Proserpine. The readiness with which Arnobius breaks the form of the sentence should be noted. At first the gods represent physical phenomena, but immediately after natural events are put for the gods. In the MS. two copyists have been at work, the earlier giving *Libero*, which is rather out of place, and is accordingly corrected by the later, *Libera*, followed by LB., Oberthür, Orelli, Hild., and Oehler.

[7] The MS. reads *primo*. Cf. c. 20.

[8] *Proles.*

[9] [κυκεων, a draught resembling caudle. See p. 499, note 10.]

[10] Lit., " by change of things."

[11] The MS. omits *ad*, supplied by Ursinus.

[12] So all edd., except Hild. and Oehler, reading *obscur-atis* for the MS. *-itatibus.*

[13] Lit., " were placed above the interior truth."

[14] Lit., " with simple senses."

[15] i.e., involved in obscurity.

[16] i.e., free from ambiguity.

[17] Lit., " of shut-off obscurities."

[18] The reference is to the words in the middle of the chapter, " how do you know which part is simple? " etc.; Arnobius now saying that he does not see how this can be known.

a long time held to be a maiden gathering flowers, after that she was taken away and carried off by violence, should begin to signify the seed sown? Jupiter, my opponent says, having turned himself into a bull, longed to have intercourse with his mother Ceres: as was explained before, under these names the earth and falling rain are spoken of. I see the law of allegory expressed in the dark and ambiguous terms. Ceres was enraged and angry, and received the parts [1] of a ram as the penalty demanded by [2] vengeance: this again I see to be expressed in common language, for both anger and (*testes and*) satisfaction are spoken of in their usual circumstances.[3] What, then, happened here,—that from Jupiter, who was named *for* the rain, and Ceres, who was named *for* the earth, the story passed to the true Jove, and to a most straightforward account of events?

38. Either, then, they must all have been written and put forward allegorically, and the whole should be pointed out to us; or nothing has been so written, since what is supposed to be *allegorical* does not seem as if it were part of the narrative.[4] These are all written allegorically, *you say*. This seems by no means certain. Do you ask for what reason, for what cause? Because, *I answer*, all that has taken place and has been set down distinctly in any book cannot be turned into an allegory, for neither can that be undone which has been done, nor can the character of an event change into one which is utterly different. Can the Trojan war be turned into the condemnation of Socrates? or the battle of Cannæ become the cruel proscription of Sulla? A proscription may indeed, as Tullius says [5] in jest, be spoken of as a battle, and be called that of Cannæ; but what has already taken place, cannot be at the same time a battle and a proscription; for neither, as I have said, can that which has taken place be anything else than what has taken place; nor can that pass over into a substance foreign to it which has been fixed down firmly in its own nature and peculiar condition.

39. Whence, then, do we prove that all these narratives are records of events? From the solemn rites and mysteries of initiation, it is clear, whether those which are celebrated at fixed times and on set days, or those which are taught secretly by the heathen without allowing the observance of their usages to be interrupted. For it is not to be believed that these have no origin, are practised without reason or meaning, and have no causes connected with their first beginnings. That pine which is regularly borne into the sanctuary of the Great Mother,[6] is it not in imitation of that tree beneath which Attis mutilated and unmanned himself, which also, they relate, the goddess consecrated to relieve her grief? That erecting of *phalli* and *fascina*, which Greece worships and celebrates in rites every year, does it not recall the deed by which Liber [7] paid his debt? Of what do those Eleusinian mysteries and secret rites contain a narrative? Is it not of that wandering in which Ceres, worn out in seeking for her daughter, when she came to the confines of Attica, brought wheat *with her*, graced with a hind's skin the family of the Nebridæ,[8] and laughed at that most wonderful sight in Baubo's groins? Or if there is another cause, that is nothing to us, so long as they are all produced by *some* cause. For it is not credible that these things were set on foot without being preceded by any causes, or the inhabitants of Attica must be considered mad to have received [9] a religious ceremony got up without any reason. But if this is clear and certain, that is, if the causes and origins of the mysteries are traceable to past events, by no change can they be turned into the figures of allegory; for that which has been done, *which* has taken place, cannot, in the nature of things, be undone.[10]

40. And yet, even if we grant you that this is the case, that is, even if the narratives give utterance to one thing in words, *but* mean [11] something else, after the manner of raving seers, do you not observe in this case, do you not see how dishonouring, how insulting to the gods, this is which is said to be done? [12] or can any greater wrong be devised than to term and call the earth and rain, or anything else,—for it does not matter what change is made in the interpretation,—the intercourse of Jupiter and Ceres? and to signify the descent of rain from the sky, and the moistening of the earth, by charges against the gods? Can anything be either thought or believed more impious than that the rape of Proserpine speaks of seeds buried in the earth, or anything else,—for in like manner it is of no importance,—and that it speaks of the pursuit of agriculture to [13] the dishonour of father Dis?

---

[1] *Proles.*
[2] Lit., "for penalty and."
[3] Lit., "in their customs and conditions."
[4] i.e., if historical, the whole must be so, as bits of allegory would not fit in.
[5] Cicero, *pro Rosc. Am.*, c. 32.

[6] The MS. and edd. read *matris deæ* — " of the mother goddess; " for which Meursius proposed *deûm* —" mother of the gods," the usual form of the title. Cf. cc. 7 and 16. [See Elucidation V.; also note the reference to St. Augustine.]
[7] The name is wanting in the MS Cf. c. 28.
[8] No Attic family of this name is mentioned anywhere: but in Cos the Nebridæ were famous as descendants of Æsculapius through Nebros. In Attica, on the other hand, the initiated were robed in fawn-skins (νεβρίδες), and were on this account spoken of as νεβροζοντες. Salmasius has therefore suggested (*ad Solinum*, p. 864, E) that Arnobius, or the author on whom he relied, transferred the family to Attica on account of the similarity of sound.
[9] Lit., "who have attached to themselves."
[10] Arnobius would seem to have been partial to this phrase, which occurs in the middle of c. 38.
[11] Lit., "say."
[12] Lit., "with what shame and insult of the gods this is said to be done."
[13] Lit., "with."

Is it not a thousand times more desirable to become mute and speechless, and to lose that flow of words and noisy and[1] unseemly loquacity, than to call the basest things by the names of the gods ; nay, more, to signify commonplace things by the base actions of the gods?

41. It was once usual, in speaking allegorically, to conceal under perfectly decent ideas, and clothe[2] with the respectability of decency, what was base and horrible to speak of openly ; but now venerable things are at your instance vilely spoken of, and what is quite pure[3] is related[4] in filthy language, so that that which vice[5] formerly concealed from shame, is now meanly and basely spoken of, the mode of speech which was fitting[6] being changed. In speaking of Mars and Venus as having been taken in adultery by Vulcan's art, we speak of lust, says *my opponent*, and anger, as restrained by the force and purpose of reason. What, then, hindered, what prevented you from expressing each thing by the words and terms proper to it? nay, more, what necessity was there, when you had resolved[7] to declare something or other, by means of treatises and writings, to resolve that that should not be the meaning to which you point, and in one narrative to take up at the same time opposite positions — the eagerness of one wishing to teach, the niggardliness of one reluctant to make public?[8] Was there no risk in speaking of the gods as unchaste? The mention of lust and anger, *my opponent says*, was likely to defile the tongue and mouth with foul contagion.[9] But, assuredly, if this were done,[10] and the veil of allegorical obscurity were removed, the matter would be easily understood, and by the same the dignity of the gods would be maintained unimpaired. But now, indeed, when the restraining of vices is said to be signified by the binding of Mars and Venus, two most inconsistent[11] things are done at the very same time ; so that, on the one hand, a description of something vile suggests an honourable meaning, and on the other, the baseness occupies the mind before any regard for religion can do so.

42. But you will perhaps say, for this only is left which you may think[12] can be brought for-

ward by you, that the gods do not wish their mysteries to be known by men, and that the narratives were therefore written with allegorical ambiguity. And whence have you learned[13] that the gods above do not wish their mysteries to be made public? whence have you become acquainted with these? or why are you anxious to unravel them by explaining them as allegories? Lastly, and finally, what do the gods mean, that while they do not wish honourable, they allow unseemly, even the basest things, to be said about them? When we name Attis, says *my opponent*, we mean and speak of the sun ; but if Attis is the sun, as you reckon *him* and say, who will that Attis be whom your books record and declare to have been born in Phrygia, to have suffered certain things, to have done certain things also, whom all the theatres know in the scenic shows, to whom every year we see divine honours paid expressly by name amongst the *other* religious ceremonies? Whether was this name made to pass from the sun to a man, or from a man to the sun? For if that name is derived in the first instance from the sun, what, pray, has the golden sun done to you, that you should make that name to belong to him in common with an emasculated person? But if it is *derived* from a goat, and is Phrygian, of what has the sire of Phaethon, the father of this light and brightness, been guilty, that he should seem worthy to be named from a mutilated man, and should become more venerable when designated by the name of an emasculated body?

43. But what the meaning of this is, is already clear to all. For because you are ashamed of such writers and histories, and do not see that these things can be got rid of which have once been committed to writing in filthy language, you strive to make base things honourable, and by every kind of subtlety you pervert and corrupt the real senses[14] of words for the sake of spurious interpretations ;[15] and, as ofttimes happens to the sick, whose senses and understanding have been put to flight by the distempered force of disease, you toss about confused and uncertain *conjectures*, and rave in empty fictions.

Let it be *granted* that the irrigation of the earth was meant by the union of Jupiter and Ceres, the burying of the seed[16] by the ravishing *of Proserpine* by father Dis, wines scattered over the earth by the limbs of Liber torn asunder *by the Titans*, that the restraining[17] of lust and rashness has been spoken of as the binding of the adulterous Venus and Mars.

---

1 Lit., " din of."
2 *Passive*.
3 Lit., " strong in chastity."
4 The MS., first three edd., Elm., and Oehler read *commorantur* — " lingers," i.e., " continues to be spoken of ;" the other edd. receive *commemorantur*, as above, from the *errata* in the 1st ed.
5 The MS., first four edd., and Oehler read *gravitas* — seriousness; corrected *pr.* as above, in all edd. after Stewechius.
6 So, perhaps, the unintelligible MS. *dignorum* should be emended *digna rerum*.
7 So all edd. since Stewechius, adding *s* to the MS. *voluisse*.
8 i.e., the mere fact that the stories were published, showed a wish to teach; but their being allegories, showed a reluctance to allow them to be understood.
9 The edd. read this sentence interrogatively.
10 i.e., " if you said exactly what you mean." The reference is not to the immediately preceding words, but to the question on which the chapter is based — " what prevented you from expressing," etc.
11 Lit., " perverse."
12 *Passive*.

13 Lit., " is it clear to you."
14 Lit., " natures."
15 Lit., " things."
16 So most edd., reading *occultatio* for the MS. *occupatio*.
17 So all edd., reading *com-*, except Hild. and Oehler, who retain the MS. reading, *im-pressio* — " the assault of," i.e., " on."

44. But if you come to the conclusion that these fables have been written allegorically, what is to be done with the rest, which we see cannot be forced into such changes *of sense?* For what are we to substitute for the wrigglings[1] into which the lustful heat[2] of Semele's offspring forced him upon the sepulchral mound? and what for those Ganymedes who were carried off[3] and set to preside over lustful practices? what for that conversion of an ant into which Jupiter, the greatest *of the gods,* contracted the outlines of his huge body?[4] what for swans and satyrs? what for golden showers, which the same seductive *god* put on with perfidious guile, amusing himself by changes of form? And, that we may not seem to speak of Jupiter only, what allegories can there be in the loves of the other deities? what in their circumstances as hired servants and slaves? what in their bonds, bereavements, lamentations? what in their agonies, wounds, sepulchres? Now, while in this you might be held guilty in one respect for writing in such wise about the gods, you have added to your guilt beyond measure[5] in calling base things by the names of deities, and again in defaming the gods by *giving to them* the names of infamous things.

But if you believed without any doubt[6] that they were here close at hand, or anywhere at all, fear would check you in making mention of them, and your beliefs and unchanged thoughts should have been exactly[7] as if they were listening to you and heard your words. For among men devoted to the services of religion, not only the gods themselves, but even the names of the gods, should be reverenced, and there should be quite as much grandeur in their names as there is in those even who are thought of under these names.

45. Judge fairly, and you are deserving of censure in this,[8] that in your common conversation you name Mars when you mean[9] fighting, Neptune when you mean the seas, Cerès when you mean bread, Minerva when you mean weaving,[10] Venus when you mean filthy lusts. For what reason is there, that, when things can be classed under their own names, they should be called by the names of the gods, and that such an insult should be offered to the deities as not even we men endure, if any one applies and turns our names to trifling objects? But language, *you say,* is contemptible, if defiled with such words.[11] O modesty,[12] worthy of praise! you blush to name bread and wine, and are not afraid to speak of Venus instead of carnal intercourse!

---

[1] Lit., "waves"—*fluctibus*, the reading of the MS., LB., Hild., and Oehler; the other edd. reading *fustibus*—"stakes."
[2] So Meursius, changing the MS. *o-* into *u-rigo.*
[3] The first four edd. retain the MS., reading *partis*—"brought forth;" the others adopt a suggestion of Canterus, *raptis,* as above.
[4] Lit., "vastness."
[5] *Addere garo gerrem,* a proverb ridiculing a worthless addition, which nullifies something in itself precious, *garum* being a highly esteemed sauce (or perhaps soup), which would be thrown away upon *gerres,* a worthless kind of salt fish. Arnobius merely means, however, that while such stories are wrong, what follows is unspeakably worse.

[6] Lit., "with undubitable knowledge."
[7] Lit., "it ought to have been so believed, and to be held fixed in thought just," etc.
[8] Lit., "are in this part of censure."
[9] Lit., "for."
[10] Lit., "the warp," *stamine.*
[11] i.e., if things are spoken of under their proper names.
[12] The MS. reads *ac* unintelligibly.

BOOK VI.

1. Having shown briefly how impious and infamous *are the* opinions *which* you have formed about your gods, we have now to[1] speak of their temples, their images also, and sacrifices, and of the other things which are[2] united and closely related to them. For you are here in the habit of fastening upon us a very serious charge of impiety because we do not rear temples for the ceremonies of worship, do not set up statues and images[3] of any god, do not build altars,[4] do not offer the blood of creatures slain *in sacrifices,* incense,[5] nor sacrificial meal, and finally, do not bring wine flowing in libations from sacred bowls;

which, indeed, we neglect to build and do, not as though we cherish impious and wicked dispositions, or have conceived any madly desperate feeling of contempt for the gods, but because we think and believe that they[6] — if only they are true gods, and are called by this exalted name[7] — either scorn such honours, if they give way to scorn, or endure *them* with anger, if they are roused by feelings of rage.

2. For — that you may learn what are our sentiments and opinions about that race — we think that they — if only they are true gods, that the same things may be said again till you are wearied hearing them[8] — should have all the virtues in perfection, should be wise, upright, venerable, — if only our heaping upon them

---

[1] Lit., "it remains that we."
[2] Lit., "series which is," etc.
[3] Singular. [But costly churches were built about this time.]
[4] *Non altaria, non aras,* i.e., neither to the superior nor inferior deities. Cf. Virgil, *Ecl.,* v 66.
[5] [It is not with any aversion to incense that I note its absence, so frequently attested, from primitive rites of the Church.]

[6] The earlier edd. prefix *d* to the MS. *eos*—"that the gods," etc.
[7] Lit., "endowed with the eminence of this name."
[8] Lit., "and to satiety."

human honours is not a crime, — strong in excellences within themselves, and should not give themselves [1] up to external props, because the completeness of their unbroken bliss is made perfect ; *should be* free from all agitating and disturbing passions ; should not burn with anger, should not be excited by any desires ; should send misfortune to none, should not find a cruel pleasure in the ills of men ; should not terrify by portents, should not show prodigies to cause fear ; should not hold *men* responsible and liable to be punished for the vows which they owe, nor demand expiatory sacrifices by threatening omens ; should not bring on pestilences *and* diseases by corrupting the air, should not burn up the fruits with droughts ; should take no part in the slaughter of war and devastation of cities ; should not wish ill to one party, and be favourable to the success of another ; but, as becomes great minds, should weigh all in a just balance, and show kindness impartially to all. For it belongs to a mortal race and human weakness to act otherwise ; [2] and the maxims and declarations of wise men state distinctly, that those who are touched by passion live a life of suffering,[3] *and* are weakened by grief,[4] and that it cannot be but that those who have been given over to disquieting feelings, have been bound by the laws of mortality. Now, since this is the case, how can we be supposed to hold the gods in contempt, who we say are not gods, and cannot be connected with the powers of heaven, unless they are just and worthy of the admiration which great minds excite ?

3. But, *we are told*, we rear no temples to them, and do not worship their images ; we do not slay victims in sacrifice, we do not offer incense [5] and libations of wine. And what greater honour or dignity can we ascribe to them, than that we put them in the same position as the Head and Lord of the universe, to whom the gods owe it in common with us,[6] that they are conscious that they exist, and have a living being ? [7] For do we honour Him with shrines, and by building temples ? [8] Do we even slay victims

to Him ? Do we give *Him* the other things, to take which and pour them forth in libation shows not a careful regard to reason, but heed to a practice maintained [9] *merely* by usage ? For it is perfect folly to measure greater powers by your necessities, and to give the things useful to yourself to the gods who give *all things*, and to think this an honour, not an insult. We ask, therefore, to do what service to the gods, or to meet what want, do you say that temples have been reared,[10] and think that they should be again built ? Do they feel the cold of [11] winter, or are they scorched by summer suns ? Do storms of rain flow over them, or whirlwinds shake them ? Are they in danger of being exposed to the onset of enemies, or the furious attacks of wild beasts, so that it is right and becoming to shut them up in places of security,[12] or guard them by throwing up a rampart of stones ? For what are these temples ? If you ask human weakness [13] — something vast and spacious ; if you consider the power of the gods — small caves, as it were,[14] and even, to speak more truly, the narrowest kind of caverns formed and contrived with sorry judgment.[15] Now, if you ask to be told who was their first founder [16] and builder, either Phoroneus or the Egyptian Merops [17] will be mentioned to you, or, as Varro relates in his *treatise " de Admirandis,"* Æacus the offspring of Jupiter. Though these, then, should be built of heaps of marble, or shine resplendent with ceilings fretted with gold, *though* precious stones sparkle here, and gleam like stars set at varying intervals, all these things are made up of earth, and of the lowest dregs of *even* baser matter. For not even, if you value these more highly, is it to be believed that the gods take pleasure in them, or that they do not refuse and scorn to shut themselves up, and be confined within these barriers. This, *my opponent* says, is the temple of Mars, this *that* of Juno and of Venus, this *that* of Hercules, of Apollo, of Dis. What is this but to say this is the house of Mars, this of Juno and Venus,[18] Apollo dwells here, in this abides Hercules, in that Summanus ? Is it not, then, the very [19] greatest affront to hold the

---

[1] The MS. wants *se*, which was supplied by Stewechius.

[2] i.e., not act impartially and benevolently, which may possibly be the meaning of *contrariis agere*, or, as Oehler suggests, " to assail *men* with contrary, i.e., injurious things." All edd. read *egere*, except Oehler, who can see no meaning in it ; but if translated, " to wish for contrary things," it suits the next clause very well.

[3] Lit., " whom passion touches, suffer."

[4] So the MS., Stewechius, Hild., and Oehler, while the first four edd. and Oberthür merely add *m* to *dolore*, and join with the preceding *pati* — " suffer pain, are weakened."

[5] [See note 5, book. vi. p. 506.]

[6] The MS. and most edd. read *di-vina nobiscum* — " the divine things along with us ; " Heraldus rejects *div.* as a gloss, while Meursius, followed by Orelli, corrects *dii una*, and Oehler *divi una*, as above.

[7] Lit., " are contained in vital substance."

[8] Arnobius here expressly denies that the Christians had any temples. There has been some controversy on the subject (Mosheim, book i. cent. 1, ch. 4, sec. 5, Soames' ed.), surely as needless as controversy could be ; for as the Christians must at all times have had stated places of meeting (although in time of persecution these might be changed frequently), it is clear that, in speaking thus, the meaning must be only, that their buildings had no architectural pretensions,

and their service no splendour of ritual. [Diocletian's mild beginning suffered Christians to build costly temples in many places. These he subsequently destroyed with great severity.]

[9] Lit., " drawn out."

[10] So the edd., reading *constructa* for the corrupt MS. *conscripta* — " written."

[11] i.e., to suppose that temples are necessary to the gods, is to make them subject to human weakness.

[12] Lit., " with fortifications of roofs."

[13] i.e., if you have regard merely to the weakness of men, a temple may be something wonderful.

[14] Lit., " some."

[15] Lit., " formed by contrivance of a poor heart."

[16] *Institutor*, wanting in all edd., except Hild. and Oehler.

[17] Arnobius here agrees with Clemens Alexandrinus, but Jos. Scaliger has pointed out that the name should be Cecrops. It is possible that Arnobius may have been misled by what was merely a slip of Clement's pen. [See the passage here referred to, vol. ii. p. 184, this series.]

[18] The preceding words, from " this of Hercules," are omitted by the first four edd. and Elmenh., and were first restored from the MS. by Stewechius.

[19] Lit., " first and."

gods kept fast[1] in habitations, to give to them little huts, to build lockfast places and cells, and to think that the things are[2] necessary to them which are needed by men, cats, emmets, and lizards, by quaking, timorous, and little mice?

4. But, says *my opponent*, it is not for this reason that we assign temples to the gods as though we *wished to* ward off from them drenching storms of rain, winds, showers, or the rays of the sun; but in order that we may be able to see them in person and close at hand, to come near and address them, and impart to them, when in a measure present, the expressions of our reverent feelings. For if they are invoked under the open heaven, and the canopy of ether, they hear nothing, *I suppose;* and unless prayers are addressed to them near at hand, they will stand deaf and immoveable as if nothing were said. And yet we think that every god whatever — if only he has the power of this name — should hear what every one said from every part of the world, just as if he were present; nay, more, should foresee, without waiting to be told,[3] what every one conceived in his secret and silent[4] thoughts. And as the stars, the sun, the moon, while they wander above the earth, are steadily and everywhere in sight of all those who gaze at them without any exception; so, too,[5] it is fitting that the ears of the gods should be closed against no tongue, and should be ever within reach, although voices should flow together to them from widely separated regions. For this *it is that* belongs specially to the gods, — to fill all things with their power, to be not partly at any place, but all everywhere, not to go to dine with the Æthiopians, and return after twelve days to their own dwellings.[6]

5. Now, if this be not the case, all hope of help is taken away, and it will be doubtful whether you are heard[7] by the gods or not, if ever you perform the sacred rites with due ceremonies. For, to make it clear,[8] let us suppose that there is a temple of some deity in the Canary Islands, *another* of the same *deity* in remotest Thyle, also among the Seres, among the tawny Garamantes, and any others[9] who are debarred from knowing each other by seas, mountains, forests, and the four quarters of the world.· If they all at one time beg of the deity with sacrifices what their

wants compel each one to think about,[10] what hope, pray, will there be to all of obtaining the benefit, if the god does not hear the cry sent up to him everywhere, and *if* there shall be any distance to which the words of the suppliant for help cannot penetrate? For either he will be nowhere present, if he may at times not be anywhere,[11] or he will be at one place only, since he cannot give his attention generally, and without making any distinction. And thus it is brought about, that either the god helps none at all, if being busy with something he has been unable to hasten to give ear to their cries, or one only goes away with his prayers heard, *while* the rest have effected nothing.

6. What *can you say* as to this, that it is attested by the writings of authors, that many of these temples which have been raised with golden domes and lofty roofs cover bones and ashes, and are sepulchres of the dead? Is it not plain and manifest, either that you worship dead men for immortal gods, or that an inexpiable affront is cast upon the deities, whose shrines and temples have been built over the tombs of the dead? Antiochus,[12] in the ninth *book* of his *Histories*, relates that Cecrops was buried in the temple of Minerva,[13] at Athens; again, in the temple of the same goddess, which is in the citadel of Larissa,[14] it is related and declared that Acrisius was laid, *and* in the sanctuary of Polias,[15] Erichthonius; *while* the brothers Dairas and Immarnachus *were buried* in the enclosure of Eleusin, which lies near the city. What say you as to the virgin daughters of Celeus? are they not said to be buried[16] in the temple of Ceres at Eleusin? *and* in the shrine of Diana, which was set up in the temple of the Delian Apollo, are not Hyperoche and Laodice buried, who are said to have been brought thither from the country of the Hyperboreans? In the Milesian Didymæon,[17] Leandrius says that Cleochus had the last honours of burial paid to him. Zeno of Myndus openly relates that the monument of Leucophryne is in the sanctuary of Diana at Magnesia. Under the altar of Apollo, which is seen in the city of Tel-

---

[1] So the edd., reading *habere districtos* for the MS. *destructos.*
[2] Lit., "that the things are thought to be."
[3] Lit., "knowledge being anticipated."
[4] These words, *et tacitis*, omitted by Oberthür, are similarly omitted by Orelli without remark.
[5] So the edd., inserting *quo-* into the MS. reading *ita-que* — "it is therefore fitting," which is absurd, as making the connection between the members of the sentence one not of analogy, but of logical sequence.
[6] Cf. the speech of Thetis, *Iliad*, i. 423-425.
[7] So the margin of Ursinus, Elm., LB., and Orelli, with Meursius, reading *audiamini* for the MS. *audiamur* — "we are heard," which does not harmonize with the next clause.
[8] Lit., "for the purpose of coming to know the thing."
[9] Lit., "if there are any others."

[10] So the MS., reading *c-ogitare*, corrected *r-* — "to beg," in the margin of Ursinus and Elm. For the preceding words the MS reads, *poscantque de numine.* The edd. omit *que* as above, except Oehler, who reads *quæ* — "what hope will there be, what, pray, to all," etc.
[11] So the MS., reading *si uspiam poterit aliquando non esse,* which may be understood in two senses, either not limited by space, or not in space, i.e., not existing; but the reading and meaning must be regarded as alike doubtful.
[12] A Syracusan historian. The rest of the chapter is almost literally translated from Clement, who is followed by Eusebius also (*Præp. Evang.*, ii. 6). [See vol. ii. p. 184, this series.]
[13] i.e, the Acropolis.
[14] In Thessaly, whither (acc. to Pausanias) he had fled in vain, to avoid the fulfilment of the oracle that he should be killed by his daughter's son.
[15] i.e., Athena Polias, or guardian of cities. Immediately below, the MS. reads *Immarnachus*, corrected in LB. and Orelli *Immarus* from Clem., who speaks of "Immarus, son of Eumolpus and Daeira."
[16] So the unintelligible reading of the MS., *humation-ibus officia,* was emended by Heraldus, followed by LB. and Orelli, *is habuisse.*
[17] i.e., the temple near Didyma, sacred to Apollo, who was worshipped then under the name Didymus.

messus, is it not invariably declared by writings that the prophet Telmessus lies buried? Ptolemæus, the son of Agesarchus, in the first book of the *History of Philopator* [1] which he published, affirms, on the authority of literature, that Cinyras, king of Paphos, was interred in the temple of Venus with all his family, nay, more, with all his stock. It would be [2] an endless and boundless task to describe in what sanctuaries they all are throughout the world; nor is anxious care required, although [3] the Egyptians fixed a penalty for any one who should have revealed the places in which Apis lay hid, as to those *Polyandria* [4] of Varro, [5] by what temples they are covered, and what heavy masses they have laid upon them.

7. But why *do* I *speak* of these trifles? What man is there who is ignorant that in the Capitol of the imperial people is the sepulchre of Tolus [6] Vulcentanus? Who is there, I say, who does not know that from beneath [7] its foundations there was rolled a man's head, buried for no very long time before, either by itself without the other parts *of the body*, — for some relate this, — or with all its members? Now, if you require this to be made clear by the testimonies of authors, Sammonicus, Granius, Valerianus, [8] and Fabius will declare to you whose son Aulus [9] was, of what race and nation, how [10] he was bereft of life and light by the slave of his brother, of what crime he was guilty against his fellow-citizens, that he was denied burial in his father [11] land. You will learn also — although they pretend to be unwilling to make this public — what was done with his head when cut off, or in what place it was shut up, and the whole affair carefully concealed, in order that the omen which the gods had attested might stand without interruption, [12] unalterable, and sure. Now, while it was proper that this *story* should be suppressed, and concealed, and forgotten in the lapse of time, the

composition of the name published it, and, by a testimony which could not be got rid of, caused it to remain *in men's minds*, together with its causes, so long as it endured itself; [13] and the state *which is* greatest *of all*, and worships all deities, did not blush in giving a name to the temple, to name it from the head of Olus [14] Capitolium rather than from the name of Jupiter.

8. We have therefore — as I suppose — shown sufficiently, that to the immortal gods temples have been either reared in vain, or built in consequence of insulting opinions *held* to their dishonour and to the belittling [15] of the power believed *to be in their hands*. We have next to say something about statues and images, which you form with much skill, and tend with religious care, — wherein if there is any credibility, we can by no amount of consideration settle in our own minds whether you do this in earnest and with a serious purpose, or amuse yourselves in childish dreams by mocking at these very things. [16] For if you are assured that the gods exist whom you suppose, and that they live in the highest regions of heaven, what cause, what reason, is there that those images should be fashioned by you, when you have true beings to whom you may pour forth prayers, and *from whom you may* ask help in trying circumstances? But if, on the contrary, you do not believe, or, to speak with moderation, are in doubt, in this case, also, what reason is there, pray, to fashion and set up images of doubtful *beings*, and to form [17] with vain imitation what you do not believe to exist? Do you perchance say, that under these images of deities there is displayed to you their presence, as it were, and that, because it has not been given you to see the gods, they are worshipped in this fashion, [18] and the duties owed *to them* paid? He who says and asserts this, does not believe that the gods exist; and he is proved not to put faith in his own religion, to whom it is necessary to see what he may hold, lest that which *being* obscure is not seen, may happen to be vain.

9. We worship the gods, you say, by means of images. [19] What then? Without these, do the gods not know that they are worshipped, and will they not think that any honour is shown to them by you? Through by-paths, as it were, then, and by assignments to a third party, [20] as they are called, they receive and accept your

---

[1] i.e., "lover of his father," the name given ironically to the fourth Ptolemy, because he murdered his father.

[2] Lit., "is."

[3] So the ms., both Rom. edd., Hild., and Oehler, reading *quamvis pœnam;* Gelenius, Canterus, Elm., and Oberthür omit *vis,* and the other edd. *v,* i.e., "as to what punishment the Egyptian," etc. This must refer to the cases in which the sacred bull, having outlived the term of twenty-five years, was secretly killed by the priests, while the people were taught that it had thrown itself into the water.

[4] i.e., "burial-places." By this Oehler has attempted to show is meant the *Hebdomades vel de Imaginibus* of Varro, a series of biographical sketches illustrated with portraits, executed in some way which cannot be clearly ascertained.

[5] ms. *Barronis.*

[6] So the ms., first four edd., and Oberthür, reading *Toli,* corrected *Oli* in the others, from Servius (*ad. Æn.,* viii. 345). Arnobius himself gives the form *Aulus,* i.e. *Olus,* immediately below, so that it is probably correct.

[7] Lit., "the seats of."

[8] Ursinus suggested *Valerius Antias,* mentioned in the first chapter of the fifth book; a conjecture adopted by Hild.

[9] The ms., LB., Hild., and Oehler read Aulus, and, acc. to Oehler, all other edd. *Tolus.* Orelli, however, reads *Olus,* as above.

[10] The ms. and both Roman edd. read *germani servuli vita* without meaning, corrected as above by Gelenius, Canterus, Elm., and Oberthür, *ut a g. servulo,* and *ut a g. servulis* — "by the slaves," in the others, except Oehler who reads as above, *g. servulo ut.*

[11] The ms. and both Roman edd. read unintelligibly *patientiæ,* corrected *paternæ* in Hild. and Oehler, *patriæ* in the rest.

[12] Lit., "the perpetuity of the omen sealed might stand."

[13] Lit., "through the times given to itself."

[14] The ms. reads *s-oli,* — changed into *Toli* by the first four edd., Elm., and Oberthür. The others omit *s.*

[15] ["Belittle." This word here is noteworthy. President Jefferson is said to have coined it, and I have never before seen it in a transatlantic book.]

[16] i.e., "which you pretend to worship."

[17] So the edd., reading *formar-e,* except Hild. and Oehler, who retain the ms. reading *i* — "that images be formed."

[18] The ms. and both Roman edd. read corruptly *insolidi,* corrected *ita* or *sic coli,* as above, in all except the last two edd.

[19] [It is manifest that nothing of the kind was said by Christians. See p. 506, note 3, *supra.*]

[20] i e., you do not seek access to the gods directly, and seek to do them honour by giving that honour to the idols instead.

services ; and before those to whom that service is owed experience it, you first sacrifice to images, and transmit, as it were, some remnants to them at the pleasure of others.[1] And what greater wrong, disgrace, hardship, can be inflicted than to acknowledge one god, and yet make supplication to something else — to hope for help from a deity, and pray to an image without feeling? Is not this, I pray you, that which is said in the common proverbs : " to cut down the smith when you strike at the fuller ; "[2] "and when you seek a man's advice, to require of asses and pigs their opinions as to what should be done ?"

10. And whence, finally, do you know whether all these images which you form and put in the place of[3] the immortal gods reproduce and bear a resemblance to the gods? For it may happen that in heaven one has a beard who by you is represented[4] with smooth cheeks ; that *another* is rather advanced in years to whom you give the appearance of a youth ;[5] that here he is fair, *with blue eyes,*[6] who really has grey ones ; that he has distended nostrils whom you make and form with a high nose. For it is not right to call or name that an image which does not derive from the face of the original features like *it;* which[7] can be recognised to be clear and certain from things which are manifest. For while all we men see that the sun is perfectly round by our eyesight, which cannot be doubted, you have given[8] to him the features of a man, and of mortal bodies. The moon is always in motion, and in its restoration every month puts on thirty faces :[9] with you, as leaders and designers, that is *represented as* a woman, and has one countenance, which passes through a thousand different states, changing each day.[10] We understand that all the winds are *only* a flow of air driven and impelled in mundane ways : in your hands they take[11] the forms of men filling with breath twisted

trumpets by blasts from out their breasts.[12] Among *the representations of* your gods we see *that there is* the very stern face of a lion[13] smeared with pure vermilion, and that it is named *Frugifer.* If all these images are likenesses of the gods above, there must then be said to dwell in heaven also a god such as the image which has been made to represent his form and appearance ;[14] and, of course, as here that *figure* of yours, so there the deity himself[15] is a mere mask and face, without the rest of the body, growling with fiercely gaping jaws, terrible, red as blood,[16] holding an apple fast with his teeth, and at times, as dogs *do* when wearied, putting his tongue out of his gaping mouth.[17] But if,[18] indeed, this is not the case, as we all think that it is not, what, pray, is the meaning of so great audacity to fashion to yourself whatever form you please, and to say[19] that it is an image of a god whom you cannot prove to exist at all?

11. You laugh because in ancient times the Persians worshipped rivers, as is told in the writings which hand down *these things* to memory ; the Arabians an unshapen stone ;[20] the Scythian nations a sabre ; the Thespians a branch instead of Cinxia ;[21] the Icarians[22] an unhewn log instead of Diana ; the people of Pessinus a flint instead of the mother of the gods ; the Romans a spear instead of Mars, as the muses of Varro point out ; and, before they were acquainted with the statuary's art, the Samians a plank[23] in-

---

[1] i.e., the transmission of the sacrifice to the gods is made dependent on idols.

[2] This corresponds exactly to the English, "to shoot at the pigeon and hit the crow."

[3] Lit., "with vicarious substitution for." [A very pertinent question as to the images worshipped in Rome to this day. There is one *Madonna* of African hue and features. See also *Murray's Handbook, Italy,* p. 72.]

[4] The MS. reads *effi-gitur,* corrected as above, *effin.,* in all edd. except Hild., who reads *efficitur* — "is made," and Stewechius, *effigiatur* — "is formed."

[5] Lit., "boy's age."

[6] *Flavus,* so invariably associated with blue eyes, that though these are the feature brought into contrast, they are only suggested in this way, and not directly mentioned — a mode of speech very characteristic of Arnobius.

[7] i.e., a fact which can be seen to be true by appealing to analogy.

[8] So the MS., LB., Hild., and Oehler, reading *donastis,* the others *donatis* — "you give."

[9] As the appearance of the moon is the same in some of its phases as in others, it is clear that Arnobius cannot mean that it has thirty distinct forms. We must therefore suppose that he is either speaking very loosely of change upon change day after day, or that he is referring to some of the lunar theories of the ancients, such as that a new moon is created each day, and that its form is thus ever new (*Lucr.,* v. 729-748).

[10] Lit., "is changed through a thousand states with daily instability."

[11] Lit., "are."

[12] Lit., "intestine and domestic."

[13] The MS. reads *leon-e-s torvissimam faciem,* emended, as above, *leonis t. f.,* in LB., Orelli, Hild., and Oehler, and *l. torvissima facie* — "lions of very stern face," in the others. Nourry supposes that the reference is to the use of lions, or lion-headed figures, as architectural ornaments on temples (cf. the two lions rampant surmounting the gate of Mycenæ), but partially coincides in the view of Elm., that mixed figures are meant, such as are described by Tertullian and Minucius Felix (ch. 28: "You deify gods made up of a goat and a lion, and with the faces of lions and of dogs "). The epithet *frugifer,* however, which was applied to the Egyptian Osiris, the Persian Mithras, and Bacchus, who were also represented as lions, makes it probable that the reference is to symbolic statues of the sun.

[14] Lit., "such a god to whose form and appearance the likeness of this image has been directed."

[15] Lit., "that."

[16] The MS. and both Roman edd. read unintelligibly *sanguineo decotoro,* for which *s. de colore,* as above, has been suggested by Canterus, with the approval of Heraldus.

[17] The MS. here inserts *puetuitate,* for which no satisfactory emendation has been proposed. The early edd. read *pituitate,* a word for which there is no authority, while LB. gives *potus aviditate* — "drunk with avidity" — both being equally hopeless.

[18] MS. *sic,* corrected by Gelenius *si.*

[19] So Meursius, *ac dicere,* for MS. *-cidere.*

[20] It is worthy of notice that although in this passage, as often elsewhere, Arnobius adheres pretty closely to the argument proposed by Clemens Alexandrinus, he even in such passages sometimes differs from it, and not at random. Thus Clement speaks merely of a "stone," and Arnobius of an "unshaped stone." The former expression harmonizes with the words of Maximus Tyrius (*Serm.,* xxxviii. p. 225, Steph.), "The Arabians worship I know not whom, but the image which I saw was a square stone;" while Suidas (Küster's ed., s. v. θεὺς Ἀρης) agrees with Arnobius in calling it a "stone, black, square, unfashioned" (ἀτύπωτος). This is the more noteworthy, as at times Arnobius would almost seem to be following Clement blindly. [See Clement, cap. iv. vol. ii. p. 184, this series.]

[21] So Arnobius renders Clement's *Cithæronian Hera.*

[22] So corrected in the notes of Canterus from Clem. for the MS. reading *Carios,* retained by the first four edd. and Elmenh. In Icaria there was a temple of Diana called Ταυροπόλιον.

[23] The MS. and first four edd. read *p-uteum* — "a well," corrected *plut.,* as above, by Gifanius, and in the notes of Canterus.

stead of Juno, as Aëthlius[1] relates: and you do not laugh when, instead of the immortal gods, you make supplication to little images of men and human forms — nay, you even suppose that these very little images are gods, and besides these you do not believe that anything has divine power. What say you, O ye ——— ! Do the gods of heaven have ears, then, and temples, an occiput, spine, loins, sides, hams, buttocks, houghs,[2] ankles, and the rest of the other members with which we have been formed, which were also mentioned in the first part *of this book*[3] a little more fully, and cited with greater copiousness of language? Would that it were possible[4] to look into the sentiments and very recesses of your mind, in which you revolve various and enter into the most obscure considerations: we should find that you yourselves even feel as we do, and have no other opinions as to the form of the deities. But what can we do with obstinate prejudices? what with those who are menacing *us* with swords, and devising new punishments *against us?* In your rage[5] you maintain a bad cause, *and that although you are* perfectly aware *of it;* and that which you have once done without reason, you defend lest you should seem to have ever been in ignorance; and you think it better not to be conquered, than to yield and bow to acknowledge truth.

12. From such causes as these this also has followed, with your connivance, that the wanton fancy of artists has found full scope in *representing* the bodies of the gods, and giving forms to them, at which even the sternest might laugh. And so Hammon is even now formed and represented with a ram's horns; Saturn with his crooked sickle, like some guardian of the fields, *and* pruner of too luxuriant branches; the son of Maia with a broad-brimmed travelling cap, as if he were preparing to take the road, and avoiding the sun's rays and the dust; Liber with tender limbs, and with a woman's perfectly free and easily flowing lines of body;[6] Venus, naked and unclothed, just as if you said that she exposed publicly, and sold to all comers,[7] the beauty of her prostituted body; Vulcan with his cap and hammer, but with his right hand free, and with his dress girt up as a workman prepares[8] for his work; the Delian god with a plectrum and lyre, gesticulating like a player on the cithern and an actor about to sing; the king of the sea with his trident, just as if he had to fight in the gladiatorial contest: nor can any

figure of any deity be found[9] which does not have certain characteristics[10] bestowed *on it* by the generosity of its makers. Lo, if some witty and cunning king were to remove the Sun from *his place before* the gate[11] and transfer him to that of Mercury, *and* again were to carry off Mercury and make him migrate to the shrine of the Sun, — for both are made beardless by you, and with smooth faces, — and to give to this one rays *of light,* to place a little cap[12] on the Sun's head, how will you be able to distinguish between them, whether this is the Sun, or that Mercury, since dress, not the peculiar appearance of the face, usually points out the gods to you? Again, if, having transported them in like manner, he were to take away his horns from the unclad Jupiter, and fix them upon the temples of Mars, and to strip Mars of his arms, and, on the other hand, invest Hammon with them, what distinction can there be between them, since he who had been Jupiter can be also supposed to be Mars, and he who had been Mavors can assume the appearance of Jupiter Hammon? To such an extent is there wantonness in fashioning those images and consecrating names, as if *they were* peculiar to them; since, if you take away their dress, the *means of* recognising each is put an end to, god may be believed to be god, one may seem to be the other, nay, more, both may be considered both!

13. But why do I laugh at the sickles and tridents which have been given to the gods? why at the horns, hammers, and caps, when I know that certain images have[13] the forms of certain men, and the features of notorious courtesans? For who is there that does not know that the Athenians formed the *Hermæ* in the likeness of Alcibiades? Who does not know — if he read Posidippus over again — that Praxiteles, putting forth his utmost skill,[14] fashioned the face of the Cnidian Venus on the model of the courtesan Gratina, whom the unhappy man loved desperately? But is this the only Venus to whom there has been given beauty taken from a harlot's face? Phryne,[15] the well-known native of Thespia — as those who have written *on* Thespian affairs relate — when she was at the height of her beauty, comeliness, and youthful vigour, is said to have been the model of all the Venuses which are *held* in esteem, whether throughout the cities of Greece or here,[16] whither has flowed the longing and eager desire for such figures. All the artists,

---

[1] The MS. reads *ethedius*, corrected in the notes of Canterus.
[2] So all edd., except both Roman edd., which retain the MS. reading in the singular, *suffraginem.*
[3] i.e., iii, 13, p. 467.
[4] Lit., "it was allowed."
[5] So Meursius suggested *amentes* for the MS. reading *animantis,* for which Heraldus proposed *argumentis* — "by arguments."
[6] Lit., "and most dissolved with the laxity of feminine liquidity."
[7] *Divendere.*
[8] Lit., "with a workman's preparing."

[9] Lit., "is there any figure to find."
[10] *Habitus.*
[11] *Ex foribus.* Cf. Tertull., *de Idol.,* ch. 15: "In Greek writers we also read that Apollo Θυραῖος and the *dæmones Antelii* watch over doors."
[12] So the edd, reading *petas-un-culum* for the MS. -*io*-.
[13] Lit., "are."
[14] Lit., "with strife of skills."
[15] MS. *Phyrna,* but below *Phryna,* which is read in both instances by Hild. and Oehler.
[16] So Meursius, followed by Orelli, reading *istic* for the MS. *iste.*

therefore, who lived at that time, and to whom truth gave the greatest ability to portray likenesses, vied in transferring with all painstaking and zeal the outline of a prostitute to the images of the Cytherean. The beautiful *thoughts*[1] of the artists were full of fire; and they strove each to excel the other with emulous rivalry, not that Venus might become more august, but that Phryne[2] might stand for Venus. And so it was brought to this, that sacred honours were offered to courtesans instead of the immortal gods, and an unhappy system of worship was led astray by the making of statues.[3] That well-known and[4] most distinguished statuary, Phidias, when he had raised the form of Olympian Jupiter with immense labour and exertion,[5] inscribed on the finger of the god PANTARCES[6] *is* BEAUTIFUL, — *this*, moreover, was the name of a boy loved by him, and that with lewd desire, — and was not moved by any fear or religious dread to call the god by the name of a prostitute; nay, rather, to consecrate the divinity and image of Jupiter to a debauchee. To such an extent is there wantonness and childish feeling in forming those little images, adoring them as gods, heaping upon them the divine virtues, when we see that the artists themselves find amusement in fashioning them, and set them up as monuments of their own lusts! For what *reason* is there, if you should inquire, why Phidias should hesitate to amuse himself, and be wanton when he knew that, but a little before, the very Jupiter which he had made was gold, stones, and ivory,[7] formless, separated, confused, and that it was he himself who brought all these together and bound them fast, that their appearance[8] had been given to them by himself in the imitation[9] of limbs *which he had* carved; and, which is more than[10] all, that it was his own free gift, that *Jupiter* had been produced and was adored among men?[11]

14. We would here, as if all nations on the earth were present, make one speech, and pour into the ears of them all, words which should be heard in common:[12] Why, pray, is this, O men! that of your own accord you cheat and deceive yourselves by voluntary blindness? Dis-

pel the darkness now, and, returning to the light of the mind, look more closely and see what that is which is going on, if only you retain your right,[13] and are not beyond the reach[14] of the reason and prudence given to you.[15] Those images which fill you with terror, and which you adore prostrate upon the ground[16] in all the temples, are bones, stones, brass, silver, gold, clay, wood taken from a tree, or glue mixed with gypsum. Having been heaped together, it may be, from a harlot's gauds or from a woman's[17] ornaments, from camels' bones or from the tooth of the Indian beast,[18] from cooking-pots *and* little jars, from candlesticks and lamps, or from other less cleanly vessels, *and* having been melted down, they were cast into these shapes and came out into the forms which you see, baked in potters' furnaces, produced by anvils and hammers, scraped with the silversmith's, and filed down with *ordinary* files, cleft *and* hewn with saws, with augers,[19] with axes, dug *and* hollowed out by the turning of borers, *and* smoothed with planes. Is not this, then, an error? Is it not, to speak accurately, folly to believe *that* a god which you yourself made with care, to kneel down trembling in supplication to that which has been formed by you, and while you know, and are assured that it is the product[20] of the labour of your hands,[21] — to cast *yourself* down upon your face, beg aid suppliantly, and, in adversity and time of distress, *ask it* to succour[22] *you* with gracious and divine favour?

15. Lo, if some one were to place before you copper in the lump, and not formed[23] into any works *of art*, masses of unwrought silver, and gold not fashioned into shape, wood, stones, and bones, with all the other materials of which statues and images of deities usually consist, — nay, more, if some one were to place before you the faces of battered gods, images melted down[24] and broken, and were also to bid you slay victims to the bits and fragments, and give sacred and divine honours to masses without form, — we ask you to say to us, whether you would do this, or refuse to obey. Perhaps you will say, why? Because there is no man so stupidly blind that he will class among the gods silver,

---

[1] i.e., either the conceptions in their minds, or realized in their works. Orelli, followed by the German translator Besnard, adopting the former view, translates "the ideas of the artists (die Ideale der Künstler) were full of fire and life."
[2] [See note 15, p. 511.]
[3] [True, alas! to this day; notorious courtesans furnishing the models for the pictures and statues worshipped as saints, angels, etc.]
[4] So Gelenius and Canterus, reading *et* for MS. *est*.
[5] Lit., "with exertion of immense strength."
[6] MS. Pantarches. This was a very common mode of expressing love among the ancients, the name of the loved one being carved on the bark of trees (as if the Loves or the mountain nymphs had done it), on walls, doors, or, as in this case, on statues, with the addition "beautiful" (Suidas, s. v. Καλοί and 'Ραμνουσία Νέμεσις, with Küster's notes). [Vol. ii. p. 187, note 1, this series.]
[7] Lit., "bones."
[8] Lit., "conditions," *habitus*.
[9] Lit., "similitude."
[10] Lit., "first among."
[11] Lit., "human things."
[12] [Isa. xl 18-20, xliv. 9-20, xlvi. 5-8.]

[13] i.e., the faculty of discernment, which is properly man's.
[14] Lit., "are in the limits of."
[15] The MS. reads *his* — "these," emended, as above, *vobis* in the margin of Ursinus, Elm., and LB.
[16] Lit., "and humble."
[17] i.e., a respectable woman.
[18] i.e., the elephant's tusk.
[19] So Salmasius, followed by Orelli, Hild., and Oehler, reading *furfuraculis*, and LB., reading *perforaculis* for the MS. *furfure aculeis*.
[20] So the margin of Ursinus, Meursius (according to Orelli), Hild., and Oehler, reading *part-u-m* for the MS. -e- — "is a part of your labour," etc.
[21] Lit., "of thy work and fingers."
[22] So the MS., both Roman edd., Elm., and Orelli, reading *numinis favore*, for which LB. reads *favorem* — "the favour of the propitious deity to succour." [Isaiah's argument reproduced.]
[23] Lit., "thrown together."
[24] Rigaltius suggested *confracta* — "shattered," for MS. *flata*.

copper, gold, gypsum, ivory, potter's clay, and say that these very things have, and possess in themselves, divine power. What reason is there, then, that all these bodies should want the power of deity and the rank of celestials if they remain untouched and unwrought, *but* should forthwith become gods, and be classed and numbered among the inhabitants of heaven if they receive the forms of men, ears, noses, cheeks, lips, eyes, and eyebrows? Does the fashioning add any newness to these bodies, so that from this addition you are compelled [1] to believe that something divine and majestic has been united to them? Does it change copper into gold, or compel worthless earthenware to become silver? Does it cause things which but a little before were without feeling, to live and breathe? [2] If they had any natural properties previously, [3] all these they retain [4] when built up in the bodily forms of statues. What stupidity it is — for I refuse to call it blindness — to suppose that the natures of things are changed by the kind of form *into which they are forced*, and that that receives divinity from the appearance given to it, which in its original body has been inert, and unreasoning, and unmoved by feeling! [5]

16. And so unmindful and forgetful of what the substance and origin of the images are, you, men, rational beings [6] and endowed with the gift of wisdom and discretion, sink down before pieces of baked earthenware, adore plates of copper, beg from the teeth of elephants good health, magistracies, sovereignties, power, victories, acquisitions, gains, very good harvests, and very rich vintages; and while it is plain *and* clear that you are speaking to senseless things, you think that you are heard, and bring yourselves into disgrace of your own accord, by vainly and credulously deceiving yourselves. [7] Oh, would that you might enter into some statue! rather, would that you might separate [8] and break up into parts [9] those Olympian and Capitoline Jupiters, and behold all those parts alone and by themselves which make up the whole of their bodies! You would at once see that these gods of yours, to whom the smoothness *of their* exterior gives a majestic appearance by its alluring [10] brightness, are *only* a framework

of flexible [11] plates, particles without shape joined together; that they are kept from falling into ruin and fear of destruction, by dove-tails and clamps and brace-irons; and that lead is run into the midst of all the hollows and where the joints meet, and causes delay [12] useful in preserving them. You would see, I say, at once *that they have* faces only without the rest of the head, [13] imperfect hands without arms, bellies and sides in halves, incomplete feet, [14] and, which is most ridiculous, *that they* have been put together without uniformity in the construction of their bodies, being in one part made of wood, but in the other of stone. Now, indeed, if these things could not be seen through the skill with which they were kept out of sight, [15] even those at least which lie open to all should have taught and instructed you that you are effecting nothing, and giving your services in vain to dead things. For, in this case, [16] do you not see that these images, which seem to breathe, [17] whose feet and knees you touch and handle when praying, at times fall into ruins from the constant dropping of rain, at other times lose the firm union of their parts from their decaying and becoming rotten, [18] — how they grow black, being fumigated and discoloured by the steam *of sacrifices*, and by smoke, — how with continued neglect they lose their position [19] *and* appearance, and are eaten away with rust? In this case, I say, do you not see that newts, shrews, mice, and cockroaches, which shun the light, build their nests and live under the hollow parts of these statues? that they gather carefully into these all kinds of filth, and other things suited to their wants, hard and half-gnawed bread, bones dragged *thither* in view of *probable* scarcity, [20] rags, down, *and* pieces of paper to make their nests soft, and keep their young warm? Do you not see sometimes over the face of an image cobwebs and treacherous nets spun by spiders, that they may be able to entangle in them buzzing and imprudent flies while on the wing? Do you not see, finally, that swallows full of filth, flying within the very domes of the temples, toss *themselves* about, and bedaub now the very faces, now the mouths of

---

[1] So the edd, reading *cog-* for the MS. *cogit-amini.*

[2] Lit., "be moved with agitation of breathing."

[3] Lit., "outside," i.e., before being in bodily forms.

[4] So Ursinus and LB., reading *retin-e-nt* for the MS. *-ea-,* which can hardly be correct. There may possibly be an ellipsis of *si* before this clause, so that the sentence would run: "If they had any natural properties, (if) they retain all these, what stupidity," etc.

[5] Lit., "deprived of moveableness of feeling."

[6] Lit., "a rational animal."

[7] Lit., "with deceit of vain credulity." The edd. read this as an interrogation: "Do you, therefore, sink down, adore, and bring yourselves into disgrace?"

[8] So Orelli, Hild., and Oehler, adopting a conjecture of Grævius, *di-,* for the MS. *de-ducere* — "to lead down."

[9] Lit., "resolved into members."

[10] Lit., "by the charm of."

[11] The MS. reads *flev-itium,* for which Hild. suggests *flex-,* as above, previous edd. reading *flat-* — "of cast plates;" which cannot, however, be correct, as Arnobius has just said that the images were in part made of ivory.

[12] Lit., "delays salutary for lastingnesses." The sense is, that the lead prevents the joints from giving way, and so gives permanence to the statue.

[13] *Occipitiis.*

[14] *Plantarum vestigia.*

[15] Lit., "from the art of obscurity."

[16] i.e., if the nature of the images is really concealed by the skill displayed in their construction.

[17] Lit., "breathing." [Ps. cxv. 4-8.]

[18] Lit., "are relaxed from decay of rottenness."

[19] i.e., fall from their pedestals. For the MS. reading *situs* (retained in LB., as above), the margin of Ursinus, followed by the other edd. except the first four, and Oberthür, read *situ-* — "lose their appearance from mould."

[20] So LB. and Oehler, reading *famis in spem* for the MS. *pannis,* omitted in other edd. All prefix *p,* as above, to the next word, *annos.*

the deities, the beard, eyes, noses, and all the other parts on which their excrements[1] fall? Blush, then, even *though it is* late, and accept true methods and views from dumb creatures, and let these teach you that there is nothing divine in images, into which they do not fear or scruple to cast unclean things in obedience to the laws of their being, and led by their unerring instincts.[2]

17. But you err, *says my opponent*, and are mistaken, for we do not consider either copper, or gold and silver, or those other materials of which statues are made, to be in themselves gods and sacred deities; but in them we worship and venerate those whom their[3] dedication as sacred introduces and causes to dwell in statues made by workmen. The reasoning *is* not vicious nor despicable by which any one — the dull, and also the most intelligent — can believe that the gods, forsaking their proper seats — that is, heaven — do not shrink back and avoid entering earthly habitations; nay, more, that impelled by the rite of dedication, they are joined to images! Do your gods, then, dwell in gypsum and in figures of earthenware? Nay, rather, are the gods the minds, spirits, and souls of figures of earthenware and of gypsum? and, that the meanest things may be able to become of greater importance, do they suffer themselves to be shut up and concealed and confined in[4] an obscure abode? Here, then, in the first place, we wish and ask to be told this by you: do they do this against their will — that is, do they enter the images as dwellings, dragged to *them* by the rite of dedication — or are they ready and willing? and do you not summon them by any considerations of necessity? Do they do this unwillingly?[5] and how can it be possible that they should be compelled *to submit* to any necessity without their dignity being impaired? With ready assent?[6] And what do the gods seek for in figures of earthenware that they should prefer these prisons[7] to their starry seats, — that, having been all but fastened to them, they should ennoble[8] earthenware and the other substances of which images are made?

18. What then? Do the gods remain always in such substances, and do they not go away to any place, even though summoned by the most momentous affairs? or do they have free passage, when they please to go any whither, and to leave their own seats and images? If they are under the necessity of remaining, what can be more wretched than they, what more unfortunate than if hooks and leaden bonds hold them fast in this wise on their pedestals? but *if* we allow that they prefer *these images* to heaven and the starry seats, they have lost their divine power.[9] But if, on the contrary, when they choose, they fly forth, and are perfectly free to leave the statues empty, the images will then at some time cease to be gods, and it will be doubtful when sacrifices should be offered, — when it is right and fitting to withhold them. Oftentimes we see that by artists these images are at one time made small, and reduced to the size of the hand, at another raised to an immense height, and built up to a wonderful size. In this way, then, it follows that we should understand that the gods contract themselves in[10] little statuettes, and are compressed till they become like[11] a strange body; or, again, *that they* stretch themselves out to a great length, and extend to immensity in images of vast bulk. So, then, if this is the case, in sitting statues also the gods should be said to be seated, and in standing ones to stand, to be running in those stretching forward to run, to be hurling javelins in those *represented as* casting *them*, to fit and fashion themselves to their countenances, and to make themselves like[12] the other characteristics of the body formed by the *artist.*

19. The gods dwell in images — each wholly in one, or divided into parts, and into members? For neither is it possible that there can be at one time one god in several images, nor, again, divided into parts by his being cut up.[13] For let us suppose that there are ten thousand images of Vulcan in the whole world: is it possible at all, as I said, that at one time one *deity* can be in all the ten thousand? I do not think *so. Do you ask* wherefore? Because things which are naturally single and unique, cannot become many while the integrity of their simplicity[14] is maintained. And this they are further unable

---

[1] *Deonerati proluvies podicis.* [So Clement, vol. ii. p. 186, at note 1, this series.]

[2] Lit., "incited by the truth of nature." The MS. and both Roman edd. read *d-*, all others *instincta*, as above.

[3] Lit., "the sacred dedication."

[4] Lit., "concealed in the restraint of."

[5] The MS. reads *inrogati* (the next letter being erased, having probably been *s* redundant) *si inviti*, corrected in the margin of Ursinus and Oehler, as above, *-tis in.*

[6] Lit., "with the assent of voluntary compliance." "Do you say," or some such expression, must be understood, as Arnobius is asking his opponent to choose on which horn of the dilemma he wishes to be impaled.

[7] Lit., "bindings."

[8] So Gelenius, Canterus, Elm., Oberth., and Orelli, reading *nobilitent.* No satisfactory emendation has been proposed, and contradictory accounts are given as to the reading of the MS. Immediately after this sentence, LB., followed by Orelli, inserts a clause from the next chapter. Cf. the following note.

[9] It will be seen that these words fit into the indirect argument of Arnobius very well, although transposed in LB. to the end of last chapter, and considered a gloss by Orelli and Hildebrand. "See the consequences," Arnobius says, "of supposing that the gods do not quit these images: not merely are they in a wretched case, but they must further lose their power as divinities." Meursius, with, more reason, transposes the clause to the end of the next sentence, which would be justifiable if necessary.

[10] Perhaps "into," as Arnobius sometimes uses the abl. after *in* instead of the acc.

[11] Lit., "compressed to the similitude of."

[12] Lit., "to adapt their similitude to."

[13] Lit., "a cutting taking place."

[14] i.e., of their character as independent and not compounded. This is precisely such an expression as that which closes the fourth book, and its occurrence is therefore an additional ground for regarding the earlier passage as genuine.

to become if the gods have the forms of men, as your belief declares; for either a hand separated from the head, or a foot divided from the body, cannot manifest the perfection of the whole, or it must be said that parts can be the same as the whole, while the whole cannot exist unless it has been made by gathering together its parts. Moreover, if the same *deity* shall be said to be in all *the statues*, all reasonableness and soundness is lost to the truth, if this is assumed that at one time one can remain in *them* all; or each of the gods must be said to divide himself from himself, so that he is both himself and another, not separated by any distinction, but himself the same as another. But as nature rejects and spurns and scorns this, it must either be said and confessed that there are Vulcans without number, if we decide that he exists and is in all the images; or he will be in none, because he is prevented by nature from being divided among several.

20. And yet, O you — if it is plain and clear to you that the gods live, and that the inhabitants of heaven dwell in the inner parts of the images, why do you guard, protect, and keep them shut up under the strongest keys, and under fastenings of immense size, under iron bars, bolts,[1] and other such things, and defend them with a thousand men and a thousand women to keep guard, lest by chance some thief or nocturnal robber should creep in? Why do you feed dogs in the capitols?[2] Why do you give food and nourishment to geese? Rather, if you are assured that the gods are there, and that they do not depart to any place from their figures and images, leave to them the care of themselves, let their shrines be always unlocked and open; and if anything is secretly carried off by any one with reckless fraud, let them show the might of divinity, and subject the sacrilegious robbers to fitting punishments at the moment[3] of their theft and *wicked* deed. For it is unseemly, and subversive of their power and majesty, to entrust the guardianship of the highest deities to the care of dogs, and when you are seeking for some means of frightening thieves so as to keep them away, not to beg it from *the gods* themselves, but to set and place it in the cackling of geese.

21. They say that Antiochus of Cyzicum took from its shrine a statue of Jupiter made of gold ten[4] cubits *high*, and set up in its place one made of copper covered with thin plates of gold. If the gods are present, and dwell in their own images, with what business, with what cares, had Jupiter been entangled that he could not punish the wrong done to himself, and avenge his being substituted in baser metal? When the famous Dionysius — but *it was* the younger[5] — despoiled Jupiter of his golden vestment, and put instead of it one of wool, *and,* when mocking *him* with pleasantries also, he said that that *which he was taking away* was cold in the frosts of winter, this warm, that that one was cumbrous in summer, that this, again, was airy in hot weather, — where was the king of the world that he did not show his presence by some terrible deed, and recall the jocose buffoon to soberness by bitter torments? For why should I mention that the dignity of Æsculapius was mocked by him? For when Dionysius was spoiling him of his very ample beard, *which was* of great weight and philosophic thickness,[6] he said that it was not right that a son sprung from Apollo, a father smooth and beardless, and very like a mere boy,[7] should be formed with such a beard that it was left uncertain which of them was father, which son, or rather whether they were of the same[8] race and family. Now, when all these things were being done, and the robber was speaking with impious mockery, if the deity was concealed in the statue consecrated to his name and majesty, why did he not punish with just and merited vengeance the affront of stripping his face of its beard and disfiguring his countenance, and show by this, both that he was himself present, and that he kept watch over his temples and images without ceasing?

22. But you will perhaps say that the gods do not trouble themselves about these losses, and do not think that there is sufficient cause for them to come forth and inflict punishment upon the offenders for their impious sacrilege.[9] Neither, then, if this is the case, do they wish to have these images, which they allow to be plucked up and torn away with impunity; nay, on the contrary, they tell *us* plainly that they despise these *statues*, in which they do not care to show that they were contemned, by taking any revenge. Philostephanus relates in his *Cypriaca*, that Pygmalion, king[10] of Cyprus, loved as a woman an image of Venus, which was held

---

[1] *Claustris repagulis pessulis.*

[2] Cf. p. 481, n. 5. Geese as well as dogs guarded the Capitol, having been once, as the well-known legend tells, its only guards against the Gauls.

[3] The MS. first four edd., and Elm. read *nomine* — "under the name of," corrected *momine* by Meursius and the rest.

[4] So the MS., reading *decem;* but as Clement says πεντεκαίδεκα πηχῶν, we must either suppose that Arnobius mistook the Greek, or transcribed it carelessly, oi, with the margin of Ursinus, read *quindecim* — "fifteen."

[5] Stewechius and Heraldus regard these words as spurious, and as having originated in a gloss on the margin, *scz. junior* — "to wit, the younger." Heraldus, however, changed his opinion, because Clement, too, says, "Dionysius the younger." The words mean more than this, however, referring probably to the fact that Cicero (*de Nat. Deor.*, iii. 33, 34, 35) tells these and other stories of the elder Dionysius. To this Arnobius calls attention as an error, by adding to Clement's phrase "but."

[6] Only rustics, old-fashioned people, and philosophers wore the beard untrimmed; the last class wearing it as a kind of distinctive mark, just as Juvenal (iii. 15) speaks of a thick woollen cloak as marking a philosopher. [Compare vol. i. p. 160; also ii. p. 321, n. 9.]

[7] *Impuberi.*

[8] Lit., "one."

[9] Lit., "punishment of violated religion."

[10] Clemens says merely "the Cyprian Pygmalion."

by the Cyprians holy,and venerable from ancient times,[1] his mind, spirit, the light of his reason, and his judgment being darkened ; and that he was wont in his madness, just as if he were dealing with his wife, having raised the deity to his couch, to be joined with it in embraces and *face to* face, and to do other vain things, *carried away* by a foolishly lustful imagination.[2] Similarly, Posidippus,[3] in the book which he mentions *to have been* written about Gnidus and about its affairs,[4] relates that a young man, of noble birth, — but he conceals his name, — carried away with love of the Venus because of which Gnidus is famous, joined himself also in amorous lewdness to the image of the same deity, stretched on the genial couch, and enjoying [5] the pleasures which ensue. To ask, again, in like manner: If the powers of the gods above lurk in copper and the other substances of which images have been formed, where in the world was the one Venus and the other to drive far away from them the lewd wantonness of the youths, and punish their impious touch with terrible suffering?[6] Or, as the goddesses are gentle and of calmer dispositions, what would it have been for them to assuage the furious joys of[7] the wretched men, and to bring back their insane minds again to their senses?

23. But perhaps, as you say, the goddesses took the greatest pleasure in these lewd and lustful insults, and did not think that an action requiring vengeance to be taken, which soothed their minds, and which they knew was suggested to human desires by themselves. But if the goddesses, the Venuses, being endowed with rather calm dispositions, considered that favour should be shown to the misfortunes of the blinded *youths;* when the greedy flames so often consumed the Capitol, and had destroyed the Capitoline Jupiter himself with his wife and his daughter,[8] where was the Thunderer at that time to avert that calamitous fire, and preserve from destruction his property, and himself, and all his family? Where was the queenly Juno when a violent fire destroyed her famous shrine, and her priestess[9] Chrysis in Argos? Where the Egyptian Serapis, when by a similar disaster *his temple* fell, burned to ashes, with all the mysteries, and Isis? Where Liber Eleutherius, when *his temple fell* at Athens? Where Diana, when *hers fell* at Ephesus? Where Jupiter of Dodona,

when *his fell* at Dodona? Where, finally, the prophetic Apollo, when by pirates and sea robbers he was both plundered and set on fire,[10] so that out of so many pounds of gold, which ages without number had heaped up, he did not have one scruple even to show to the swallows which built under his eaves,[11] as Varro says in his *Saturæ Menippeæ ?*[12] It would be an endless task to write down what shrines have been destroyed throughout the whole world by earth quakesand tempests — what have been set on fire by enemies, and by kings and tyrants — what have been stript bare by the overseers and priests themselves, even though they have turned suspicion away from them[13] — finally, what *have been robbed* by thieves and Canacheni,[14] opening *them* up, though barred by unknown means ;[15] which, indeed, would remain safe and exposed to no mischances, if the gods were present to defend them, or had any care for their temples, as is said. But now because they are empty, and protected by no indwellers, Fortune has power over them, and they are exposed to all accidents just as much as are all other things which have not life.[16]

24. Here also the advocates of images are wont to say this also, that the ancients knew well that images have no divine nature, and that there is no sense in them, but that they formed them profitably and wisely, for the sake of the unmanageable and ignorant mob, which is the majority in nations and in states, in order that a kind of appearance, as it were, of deities being presented to them, from fear they might shake off their rude natures, and, supposing that they were acting in the presence of the gods, put[17] away their impious deeds, and, changing their manners, learn to act as men ;[18] and that august forms of gold and silver were sought for them, for no other reason than that some power was believed to reside in their splendour, such as not only to dazzle the eyes, but even to strike terror into the mind itself at the majestic beaming lustre. Now this might perhaps seem to be

---

[1] Lit., " of ancient sanctity and religion."
[2] Lit., " imagination of empty lust."
[3] Cf. ch. 13.
[4] So Gelenius, reading *rebus* for the MS. and first ed. *re a* (MS. *ab*) *se.*
[5] Lit., " in the limits of."
[6] Lit., " agonizing restraint."
[7] Lit., " to."
[8] Cf. p. 315, n. 2, *supra.*
[9] So Clemens narrates; but Thucydides (iv. 133) says that "straightway Chrysis flees by night for refuge to Phlious, fearing the Argives;" while Pausanius (ii. 59) says that she fled to Tegea, taking refuge there at the altar of Minerva Alea.

[10] From Varro's being mentioned, Oehler thinks that Arnobius must refer to various marauding expeditions against the temples of Apollo on the coasts and islands of the Ægean, made at the time of the piratical war. Clemens, however, speaks distinctly of the destruction of the temple at Delphi, and it is therefore probable that this is referred to, if not solely, at least along with those which Varro mentions. Clement, vol. ii. p. 187.
[11] Lit., " his visitors," *hospitis.*
[12] *Varro Menippeus,* an emendation of Carrio, adopted in LB. and Orelli for the MS. *se theripeus.*
[13] Lit., " suspicion being averted."
[14] It has been generally supposed that reference is thus made to some kind of thieves, which is probable enough, as Arnobius (end of next chapter) classes all these plunderers as " tyrants, kings, robbers, and nocturnal thieves;" but it is impossible to say precisely what is meant. Heraldus would read *Saraceni* — " Saracens."
[15] Lit., " with obscurity of means." The phrase may refer either to the defence or to the assault of temples by means of magic arts.
[16] Lit., " interior motion."
[17] Lit., " lop away," *deputarent,* the reading of the MS., Hild., and Oehler; the rest reading *deponerent* — " lay aside." [The same plausible defences are used to this day by professed Christians. See *Jesuits at Rome,* by Hobart Seymour, p. 38, ed. New York, 1849.]
[18] Lit., " pass to human offices."

said with some reason, if, after the temples of the gods were founded, and their images set up, there were no wicked man in the world, no villany at all, *if* justice, peace, good faith, possessed the hearts of men, and no one on earth were called guilty and guiltless, all being ignorant of wicked deeds. But now when, on the contrary, all things are full of wicked *men*, the name of innocence has almost perished, *and* every moment, every second, evil deeds, till now unheard of, spring to light in myriads from the wickedness of wrongdoers, how is it right to say that images have been set up for the purpose of striking terror into the mob, while, besides innumerable forms of crime and wickedness,[1] we see that even the temples themselves are attacked by tyrants, by kings, by robbers, and by nocturnal thieves, and that these very gods whom antiquity fashioned and consecrated to cause terror, are carried away[2] into the caves of robbers, in spite even of the terrible splendour of the gold?[3]

25. For what grandeur — if you look at the truth without any prejudice[4] — is there in these images[5] of which they speak, that the men of old should have had reason to hope and think that, by beholding them, the vices of men could be subdued, and their morals and wicked ways brought under restraint?[6] The reaping-hook, for example, which was assigned to Saturn,[7] was it to inspire mortals with fear, that they should be willing to live peacefully, and to abandon their malicious inclinations? Janus, with double face, or that spiked key by which he has been distinguished; Jupiter, cloaked and bearded, and holding in his right hand a piece of wood shaped like a thunderbolt; the cestus of Juno,[8] or the maiden lurking under a soldier's helmet; the mother of the gods, with her timbrel; the Muses, with their pipes and psalteries; Mercury, the winged slayer of Argus; Æsculapius, with his staff; Ceres, with huge breasts, or the drinking cup swinging in Liber's right hand; Mulciber, with his workman's dress; or Fortune, with her horn full of apples, figs, or autumnal fruits; Diana, with half-covered thighs, or Venus naked, exciting to lustful desire; Anubis, with his dog's face; or Priapus, of less importance[9] than his own genitals: *were these expected to make men afraid?*

26. O dreadful forms of terror and [10] frightful bugbears[11] on account of which the human race was to be benumbed for ever, to attempt nothing in its utter amazement, and to restrain itself from every wicked and shameful act — little sickles, keys, caps, pieces of wood, winged sandals, staves, little timbrels, pipes, psalteries, breasts protruding and of great size, little drinking cups, pincers, and horns filled with fruit, the naked bodies of women, and huge *veretra* openly exposed! Would it not have been better to dance *and* to sing, than calling it gravity and pretending to be serious, to relate what is so insipid and so silly, that images[12] were formed by the ancients to check wrongdoing, and to *arouse* the fears of the wicked and impious? Were the men of that age and time, in understanding, so void of reason and good sense, that they were kept back from wicked actions, just as if they were little boys, by the preternatural[13] savageness of masks, by grimaces also, and bugbears?[14] And how has this been so entirely changed, that though there are so many temples in your states filled with images of all the gods, the multitude of criminals cannot be resisted *even* with so many laws and so terrible punishments, and their audacity cannot be overcome[15] by any means, and wicked deeds, repeated again and again, multiply the more it is striven by laws and *severe* judgments to lessen the number of cruel deeds, and to quell them by the check *given by means* of punishments? But if images caused any fear to men, the passing of laws would cease, nor would so many kinds of tortures be established against the daring of the guilty: now, however, because it has been proved and established that the supposed[16] terror which is said to flow out from the images is in reality vain, recourse has been had to the ordinances of laws, by which there might be a dread *of punishment which should be* most certain fixed in men's minds also, and a condemnation settled; to which these very images also owe it that they yet stand safe, and secured by some respect being yielded to them.

---

[1] Lit., "crimes and wickednesses."
[2] Lit., "go," *vadere.*
[3] Lit., "with their golden and to-be-feared splendours themselves."
[4] Lit., "and without any favour," *gratificatione.*
[5] Lit., "what great *thing* have these images in them."
[6] So the MS., first four edd., Elm., Hild., and Oehler, reading *mores et maleficia,* corrected in the others *a maleficio* — "morals withheld from wickedness."
[7] Cf. ch. 12, p. 511.
[8] The reference is probably to some statue or picture of Juno represented as girt with the girdle of Venus (*Il.,* xiv. 214).
[9] Lit., "inferior."

[10] *Formidinum.*
[11] *Terrores.*
[12] Or, perhaps, "relate that images so frigid and so awkward."
[13] The MS. and both Roman edd. read *monstruosissima-s torvitate-s annis;* corrected by Gelenius and later edd. *monstruosissimâ torvitate animos,* and by Salmasius, Orelli, Hild., and Oehler, as above, *m. t. sannis.*
[14] The MS., first four edd., Elm., and Oberthür read *manus,* which, with *animos* read in most (cf. preceding note), would run, "that they were even kept back, as to (i.e., in) minds and hands, from wicked actions by the preternatural savageness of masks." The other edd. read with Salmasius, as above, *maniis.*
[15] Lit., "cut away."
[16] Lit., "opinion of."

BOOK VII.

1. Since it has been sufficiently shown, as far as there has been opportunity, how vain it is to form images, the course of our argument requires that we should next speak as briefly as possible, and without any periphrasis, about sacrifices, about the slaughter and immolation of victims, about pure wine, about incense, and about all the other things which are provided on such occasions.[1] For with respect to this you have been in the habit of exciting against us the most violent ill-will, of calling us atheists, and inflicting upon us the punishment of death, even by savagely tearing us to pieces with wild beasts, on the ground that we pay very little respect[2] to the gods; which, indeed, we admit that we do, not from contempt or scorn of the divine,[3] but because we think that such powers require nothing of the kind, and are not possessed by desires for such things.[4]

What, then,[5] some one will say, do you think that no sacrifices at all should be offered? To answer you not with our own, but with your Varro's opinion — none. Why so? Because, he says, the true gods neither wish nor demand these; while those[6] which are made of copper, earthenware, gypsum, or marble, care much less for these things, for they have no feeling; and you are not blamed[7] if you do not offer them, nor do you win favour if you do. No sounder opinion can be found, *none* truer, and *one* which any one may adopt, although he may be stupid and very hard *to convince*. For who is so obtuse as either to slay victims in sacrifice to those who have no sense, or to think that they should be given to those who are removed far from them in their nature and blessed state?

2. Who are the true gods? you say. To answer you in common and simple language, we do not know;[8] for how can we know who those are whom we have never seen? We have been accustomed to hear from you that an infinite number[9] are gods, and are reckoned among[10] the deities; but if these exist[11] anywhere, and *are* true gods, as Terentius[12] believes, it follows as a consequence, that they correspond to their name; that is, that they are such as we all see that they should be, *and that they are* worthy to be called by this name; nay, more, — to make an end without many words, — *that they are such* as is the Lord of the universe, and *the King* omnipotent Himself, whom we have knowledge and understanding *enough* to speak of as the true God when we are led to mention His name. For one god differs from another in nothing as respects his divinity;[13] nor can that which is one in kind be less or more in its parts while its own qualities remain unchanged.[14] Now, as this is certain, it follows that they should never have been begotten, but should be immortal, seeking nothing from without, and not drawing any earthly pleasures from the resources of matter.

3. So, then, if these things are so, we desire to learn this, first, from you — what is the cause, what the reason, that you offer them sacrifices; *and* then, what gain comes to the gods themselves from this, and remains to their advantage. For whatever is done should have a cause, and should not be disjoined from reason, so as to be lost[15] among useless works, and tossed about among vain and idle uncertainties.[16] Do the gods of heaven[17] live on these sacrifices, and must materials be supplied to maintain the union of their parts? And what man is there so ignorant of what a god is, certainly, as to think that they are maintained by any kind of nourishment, and that it is the food given to them[18] which causes them to live and endure throughout their endless immortality? For whatever is upheld by causes and things external to itself, must be mortal and on the way to destruction, when anything on which it lives begins to be wanting. Again, *it is impossible to suppose that any one believes this*, because we see that of these things

---

[1] Lit., "in that part of years."
[2] Lit., "attribute least."
[3] Lit., "divine spurning."
[4] [When good old Dutch Boyens came to the pontificate as Hadrian VI., he was accounted a "barbarian" because he so little appreciated the art-treasures in the Vatican, on which Leo X. had lavished so much money and so much devotion. His pious spirit seemed oppressed to see so many heathen images in the Vatican: *sunt idola ethnicorum* was all he could say of them, — a most creditable anecdote of such a man in such times. See p. 504, n. 6, *supra*.]
[5] [In the Edin. edition this is the opening sentence, but the editor remarks]: " By some accident the introduction to the seventh book has been tacked on as a last chapter to the sixth, where it is just as out of place as here it is in keeping. [I have restored it to its place accordingly.]
[6] Lit., "those, moreover."
[7] Lit., " nor is any blame contracted."
[8] On this Heraldus [most ignorantly] remarks, that it shows conclusively how slight was the acquaintance with Christianity possessed by Arnobius, when he could not say who were the true gods. [The Edin. editor clears up the cases as follows:] This, however, is to forget that Arnobius is not declaring his own opinions here, but meeting his adversaries on their own ground. He knows who the true God is — the source and fountain of all being, and framer of the uni-

verse (ii. 2), and if there are any lesser powers called gods, what their relation to Him must be (iii. 2, 3); but he does not know any such gods himself, and is continually reminding the heathen that they know these gods just as little. (Cf the very next sentence.)
[9] Lit., " as many as possible."
[10] Lit., " in the series of."
[11] Lit., " are."
[12] i e., M. Terentius Varro, mentioned in the last chapter.
[13] Lit., "in that in which he is a god."
[14] Lit., " uniformity of quality being preserved."
[15] The MS. and edd. read *ut in operibus feratur cassis* — "so as to be borne among," emended by Hild. and Oehler *teratur* — " worn away among."
[16] Lit., "in vain errors of inanity."
[17] The MS. and edd. have here *forte* — " perchance."
[18] Lit., "gift of food."

which are brought to their altars, nothing is added to and reaches the substance of the deities; for either incense is given, and is lost melting on the coals,[1] or the life only of the victim is offered to the gods,[2] and its blood is licked up by dogs; or if any flesh is placed upon the altars, it is set on fire in like manner, and *is* destroyed, *and* falls into ashes, — unless perchance the god seizes upon the souls of the victims, or snuffs up eagerly the fumes and smoke *which rise* from the blazing altars, and feeds upon the odours which the burning flesh gives forth, still wet with blood, and damp with its former juices.[3] But if a god, as is said, has no body, and cannot be touched at all, how is it possible that that which has no body should be nourished by things pertaining to the body, — that what is mortal should support what is immortal, and assist and give vitality to that which it cannot touch? This reason for sacrifices is not valid, therefore, as it seems; nor can it be said by any one that sacrifices are kept up for this reason, that the deities are nourished by them, and supported by feeding on them.

4. If perchance it is not this,[4] are victims not slain in sacrifice to the gods, and cast upon their flaming altars to give them [5] some pleasure and delight? And can any man persuade himself that the gods become mild as they are exhilarated by pleasures, that they long for sensual enjoyment, and, like some base creatures, are affected by agreeable sensations, and charmed and tickled for the moment by[6] a pleasantness which soon passes away? For that which is overcome by pleasure must be harassed by its opposite, sorrow; nor *can that be* free from the anxiety of grief, which trembles with joy, and is elated capriciously with gladness.[7] But the gods should be free from both passions, if we would have them to be everlasting, and freed from the weakness of mortals. Moreover, every pleasure is, as it were, a kind of flattery of the body, and is addressed to the five well-known senses; but if the gods above feel it,[8] they must partake also

of those bodies through which there is a way to the senses, and a door *by which* to receive pleasures. Lastly, what pleasure is it to take delight in the slaughter of harmless creatures, to have the ears ringing often with their piteous bellowings, to see rivers of blood, the life fleeing away with the blood, and the secret parts having been laid open, not only the intestines to protrude with the excrements, but also the heart still bounding with the life left in it, and the trembling, palpitating veins in the viscera? We half-savage men, nay rather, — to say with more candour what it is truer and more candid to say, — we savages, whom unhappy necessity and bad habit have trained to take these as food, are sometimes moved with pity for them; we ourselves accuse and condemn ourselves when the thing is seen and looked into thoroughly, because, neglecting the law which is binding on men, we have broken through the bonds which naturally united us at the beginning.[9] Will [10] any one believe that the gods, *who are* kind, beneficent, gentle, are delighted and filled with joy by the slaughter of cattle, if ever they fall and expire pitiably before their altars?[11] And there is no cause, then, for pleasure in sacrifices, as we see, nor is there a reason why they should be offered, since there is no pleasure *afforded by them;* and if perchance there is some,[12] it has been shown that it cannot in any way belong to the gods.

5. We have next to examine the argument which we hear continually coming from the lips of the common people, and *find* embedded in popular conviction, that sacrifices are offered to the gods of heaven for this purpose, that they may lay aside their anger and passions, and may be restored to a calm and placid tranquillity, the indignation of their fiery spirits being assuaged. And if we remember the definition which we should always bear steadily in mind, that all agitating feelings are unknown to the gods, the consequence is, a belief[13] that the gods are never angry; nay, rather, that no passion is further from them than that which, approaching most nearly to *the spirit of* wild beasts and savage creatures, agitates those who suffer it with tempestuous feelings, and brings them into danger of destruction. For whatever is harassed by any kind of disturbance,[14] is, it is clear, capable of suffering, and frail; that which has been subjected to suffering and frailty must be mortal; but anger harasses and destroys [15] those who are

---

1 [It must have taken much time to overcome this distaste for the use of incense in Christian minds. Let us wait for the testimony of Lactantius.]

2 Or perhaps, simply, " the sacrifice is a living one," *animalis est hostia.* Macrobius, however (*Sat.,* iii. 5), quotes Trebatius as saying that there were two kinds of sacrifices, in one of which the entrails were examined that they might disclose the divine will, while in the other the life only was consecrated to the deity. This is more precisely stated by Servius (*Æn.,* iii. 231), who says that the *hostia animalis* was only slain, that in other cases the blood was poured on the altars, that in others part of the victim, and in others the whole animal, was burned. It is probable, therefore, that Arnobius uses the words here in their technical meaning, as the next clause shows that none of the flesh was offered, while the blood was allowed to fall to the ground. [I am convinced that classical antiquities must be more largely studied in the Fathers of the first five centuries.]

3 i e., the juices which formerly flowed through the living body.

4 The heathen opponent is supposed to give up his first reason, that the sacrifices provided food for the gods, and to advance this new suggestion, that they were intended for their gratification merely.

5 Lit., " for the sake of."

6 Lit., " with the fleeting tickling of."

7 Lit., " with the levities of gladnesses."

8 i.e., pleasure.

9 *Naturalis initii consortia.*

10 So the ms. and first ed , according to Oehler, reading *cred-e-t,* the others -*i-* — " does."

11 Lit., " these."

12 Arnobius says that the sacrifices give no pleasure to any being, or at least, if that is not strictly true, that they give none to the gods. [See Elucidation VI., *infra.*]

13 So the ms., LB., Oberthür, Orelli, Hild., and Oehler, reading *consec-,* for which the rest read *consen-taneum est credere* — " it is fitting to believe."

14 Lit., " motion of anything."

15 Cf. i. 18.

subject to it: therefore that should be called mortal which has been made subject to the emotions of anger. But yet we know that the gods should be never-dying, and should possess an immortal nature ; and if this is clear and certain, anger has been separated far from them and from their state. On no ground, then, is it fitting to wish to appease that in the gods above which you see cannot suit their blessed state.

6. But let us allow, as you wish, that the gods are accustomed to such disturbance, and that sacrifices are offered and sacred solemnities performed to calm it, when, then, is it fitting that these offices should be made use of, or at what time should they be given? — before they are angry and roused, or when they have been moved and displeased even?[1] If we must meet them *with sacrifices* before *their anger is roused*, lest they become enraged, you are bringing forward wild beasts to us, not gods, to which it is customary to toss food, upon which they may rage madly, and turn their desire to do harm, lest, having been roused, they should rage and burst the barriers of their dens. But if these sacrifices are offered to satisfy[2] the gods when already fired and burning with rage, I do not inquire, I do not consider, whether that happy[3] and sublime greatness of spirit which belongs to the deities is disturbed by the offences of little men, and wounded if a creature, blind and ever treading among clouds of ignorance, has committed any blunder, — said *anything* by which their dignity is impaired.

7. But neither do I demand that this should be said, or that I should be told what causes the gods have for their anger against men, that having taken offence they must be soothed. *I do ask, however*, Did they ever ordain any laws for mortals? and was it ever settled by them what it was fitting for them to do, or what it was not? what they should pursue, what avoid ; or even by what means they wished themselves to be worshipped, so that they might pursue with the vengeance of their wrath what was done otherwise than they had commanded, and might be disposed, if treated contemptuously, to avenge themselves on the presumptuous and transgressors? As I think, nothing was ever either settled or ordained by them, since neither have they been seen, nor has it been possible for it to be discerned very clearly whether there are any.[4] What justice is there, then, in the gods of heaven being angry for any reason with those to whom

they have neither deigned at any time to show that they existed, nor given nor imposed any laws which they wished to be honoured by them and perfectly observed?[5]

8. But this, as I said, I do not mention, but allow it to pass away in silence. This one thing I ask, above all, What reason is there if I kill a pig, that a god changes his state of mind, and lays aside his angry feelings and frenzy ; that if I consume a pullet, a calf under his eyes and on his altars, he forgets the wrong *which I did to him*, and abandons completely all sense of displeasure? What passes from this act[6] to *modify* his resentment? Or of what service[7] is a goose, a goat, or a peacock, that from its blood relief is brought to the angry *god?* Do the gods, then, make insulting them a matter of payment? and as little boys, to *induce them to* give up their fits of passion[8] and desist from their wailings, get little sparrows, dolls, ponies, puppets,[8] with which they may be able to divert themselves, do the immortal gods in such wise receive these gifts from you, that for them they may lay aside their resentment, and be reconciled to those who offended them? And yet I thought that the gods — if only it is right to believe that they are really moved by anger — lay aside their anger and resentment, and forgive the sins of the guilty, without any price or reward. For this belongs specially to deities, to be generous in forgiving, and to seek no return for their gifts.[9] But if this cannot be, it would be much wiser that they should continue obstinately offended, than that they should be softened by being corrupted with bribes. For the multitude increases of those who sin, when there is hope given of paying for their sin ; and there is little hesitation to do wrong, when the favour of those who pardon *offences* may be bought.

9. So, if some ox, or any animal you please, which is slain to mitigate and appease the fury of the deities, were to take a man's voice and speak these[10] words : " Is this, then, O Jupiter, or whatever god thou art, humane or right, or should it be considered at all just, that when another has sinned I should be killed, and that you should allow satisfaction to be made to you with my blood, although I never did you wrong, never wittingly or unwittingly did violence to your divinity and majesty, being, as thou knowest, a dumb creature, not departing from[11] the simplicity of my nature, nor inclined to be fickle in my[12] manners? Did I ever celebrate your

---

[1] Lit., " set in indignations."

[2] Lit., " if this satisfaction of sacrifices is offered to."

[3] So the MS. and most edd., reading *lacta*, for which Ursinus suggested *lauta* — " splendid," and Heraldus *elata* — " exalted."

[4] It is perhaps possible so to translate the MS. *neque si sunt ulli apertissima potuit cognitione dignosci*, retained by Orelli, Hild., and Oehler, in which case *si sunt ulli* must be taken as the subject of the clause. The other edd., from regard to the construction, read *visi* — " nor, if they have been seen, has it been possible."

[5] Lit., " kept with inviolable observance."

[6] Lit., " work."

[7] Lit., " remedy."

[8] So *Panes* seems to be generally understood, i.e., images of Pan used as playthings by boys, and very much the same thing as the puppets — *pupuli* — already mentioned.

[9] Lit., " to have liberal pardons and free concessions."

[10] Lit., " in these."

[11] Lit., " following."

[12] Lit., " to varieties of manifold."

games with too little reverence and care? did I drag forward a dancer so that thy deity was offended? did I swear falsely by thee? did I sacrilegiously steal your property and plunder your temples? did I uproot the most sacred groves, or pollute and profane some hallowed places by founding private houses? What, then, is the reason that the crime of another is atoned for with my blood, and that my life and innocence are made to pay for wickedness with which I have nothing to do? Is it because I am a base creature, and am not possessed of reason and wisdom, as these declare who call themselves men, and by their ferocity make themselves beasts?[1] Did not the same nature both beget and form me from the same beginnings? Is it not one breath of life which sways both them and me? Do I not respire and see, and am I not affected by the other senses just as they are? They have livers, lungs, hearts, intestines, bellies; and do not I have as many members? They love their young, and come together to beget children; and do not I both take care to procure offspring, and delight in it when it has been begotten? But they have reason, and utter articulate sounds; and how do they know whether I do what I do for my own reasons, and whether that sound which I give forth is my kind of words, and is understood by us alone? Ask piety whether it is more just that I should be slain, that I should be killed, or that man should be pardoned and be safe from punishment for what he has done? Who formed iron into a sword? was it not man? Who *brought* disaster upon races; who imposed slavery upon nations? was it not man? Who mixed deadly draughts, and gave them to his parents, brothers, wives, friends? was it not man? Who found out or devised so many forms of wickedness, that they can hardly be related in ten thousand chronicles of years, or *even* of days? was it not man? Is not this, then, cruel, monstrous, and savage? Does it not seem to you, O Jupiter, unjust and barbarous that I should be killed, that I should be slain, that you may be soothed, and the guilty find impunity?"

It has been established that sacrifices are offered in vain for this purpose then, viz., that the angry deities may be soothed; since reason has taught us that the gods are not angry at any time, and that they do not wish one thing to be destroyed, to be slain for another, or offences against themselves to be annulled by the blood of an innocent creature.[2]

10. But perhaps some one will say, We give to the gods sacrifices and other gifts, that, being made willing in a measure to grant our prayers, they may give us prosperity and avert from us evil, cause us to live always happily, drive away grief truly, *and any evils* which threaten us from accidental circumstances. This point demands great care; nor is it usual either to hear or to believe what is so easily said. For the whole company of the learned will straightway swoop upon *us*, who, asserting and proving that whatever happens, happens according to *the decrees of* fate, snatch out of our[3] hands that opinion, and assert that we are putting our trust in vain beliefs. Whatever, they will say, has been done in the world, is being done, and shall be done, has been settled and fixed in time past, and has causes which cannot be moved, by means of which events have been linked together, and form an unassailable chain of unalterable necessity between the past and the future. If it has been determined and fixed what evil or good should befall each person, it is already certain; but if this is certain and fixed, there is no room for all the help given by the gods, their hatred, *and* favours. For they are just as unable to do for you that which cannot be done, as to prevent that from being done which must happen, except that they will be able, if they choose, to depreciate somewhat powerfully that belief which you entertain, so that they[4] say that even the gods themselves are worshipped by you in vain, and that the supplications with which you address them are superfluous. For as they are unable to turn aside the course *of events*, and change what has been appointed by fate, what reason, what cause, is there to wish to weary and deafen the ears of those in whose help you cannot trust at your utmost need?

11. Lastly, if the gods drive away sorrow and grief, if they bestow joy and pleasure, how[5] are there in the world so many[6] and so wretched men, whence *come* so many unhappy ones, who lead a life of tears in the meanest condition? Why are not those free from calamity who every moment, every instant, load and heap up the altars with sacrifices? Do we not see that some of them, say *the learned*, are the seats of diseases, the light of their eyes quenched, and their ears stopped, that they cannot move with their feet, that they live *mere* trunks without *the use of* their hands, that they are swallowed up, overwhelmed, *and* destroyed by conflagrations, shipwrecks, and disasters;[7] that, having been stripped of immense fortunes, they support themselves by labouring for hire, *and* beg for alms at last; that they are exiled, proscribed, always in the midst of sorrow, overcome by the loss of children, *and* harassed

---

[1] Lit., "leap into."
[2] [This very striking passage should lead us to compare the widely different purpose of Judaic sacrifices. See Elucidation VI., *infra*.]

[3] Lit., "from the hands to us," *nobis*, the reading of the MS., both Roman edd., Gelenius, LB., and Oehler; for which the rest give *vobis* — "out of your hands."
[4] i.e., the learned men referred to above.
[5] Lit., "whence."
[6] Lit., "so innumerable."
[7] Lit., "ruins."

by other misfortunes, the kinds and forms of which no enumeration can comprehend? But assuredly this would not occur if the gods, who had been laid under obligation, were able to ward off, to turn aside, those evils from those who merited *this favour*. But now, because in these mishaps there is no room *for the interference of the gods*, but all things are brought about [1] by inevitable necessity, the appointed course of events goes on and accomplishes that which has been once determined.

12. Or the gods of heaven should be said to be ungrateful if, while they have power to prevent it, they suffer an unhappy race to be involved in so many hardships and disasters. But perhaps they may say something of importance *in answer to this*, and not such as should be received by deceitful, fickle, and scornful ears. This point, however, because it would require too tedious and prolix discussion,[2] we hurry past unexplained and untouched, content to have stated this alone, that you give to your gods dishonourable reputations if you assert that on no other condition do they bestow blessings and turn away what is injurious, except they have been first bought over with the blood of she-goats and sheep, and with the other things which are put upon their altars. For it is not fitting, in the first place, that the power of the deities and the surpassing eminence of the celestials should be believed to keep their favours on sale, first to receive *a price*, and then to bestow *them; and* then, which is much more unseemly, that they aid no one unless they receive *their demands*, and that they suffer the most wretched to undergo whatever perils may befall them,[3] while they could ward *these* off, and come to their aid. If of two who are sacrificing, one is a scoundrel,[4] and rich, the other of small fortune, but worthy of praise for his integrity and goodness, — if the former should slay a hundred oxen, and as many ewes with their lambkins, the poor man burn a little incense, and a small piece of some odorous substance, — will it not follow that it should be believed that, if only the deities bestow nothing except when rewards are first offered, they will give their favour [5] to the rich man, turn their eyes away from the poor, whose gifts were restricted not by his spirit, but by the scantiness of his means?[6] For where the giver is venal and mercenary, there it must needs be

that favour is granted according to the greatness of the gift *by which it is purchased,* and that a favourable decision is given to him from whom [7] far the greater reward and bribe, *though this be* shameful, flows to him who gives it.[8] What if two nations, on the other hand, arrayed against each other in war, enriched the altars of the gods with equal sacrifices, and were to demand that their power and help should be given to them, the one against the other: must it not, again, be believed that, if they are persuaded to be of service by rewards, they are at a loss between both sides, are struck motionless, and do not perceive what to do, since they understand that their favour has been pledged by the acceptance of the sacrifices? For either they will give assistance to this side and to that, which is impossible, for *in that case* they will fight themselves against themselves, strive against their own favour and wishes; or they will do nothing to aid either nation [9] after the price *of their aid* has been paid and received, which is very wicked. All this infamy, therefore, should be removed far from the gods; nor should it be said at all that they are won over by rewards and payments to confer blessings, and remove what is disagreeable, if only they are true gods, and worthy to be ranked under this name. For either whatever happens, happens inevitably, and there is no place in the gods for ambition and favour; or if fate is excluded and got rid of, it does not belong to the celestial dignity to sell the boon of its services,[10] and the conferring of its bounties.

13. We have shown sufficiently, as I suppose, that victims, and the things which go along with them, are offered in vain to the immortal gods, because they are neither nourished by them, nor feel any pleasure, nor lay aside their anger and resentment, so as either to give good fortune, or to drive away and avert the opposite. We have now to examine that point also which has been usually asserted by some, and applied to forms of ceremony. For they say that these sacred rites were instituted to do honour to the gods of heaven, and that these things which they do, they do to show *them* honour, and to magnify the powers of the deities by them. What if they were to say, in like manner, that they keep awake and sleep, walk about, stand still, write something, and read, to give honour to the gods, and make them more glorious in majesty? For what substance is there added to them from the blood of cattle, and from the other things which are prepared in sacrificing? what power is given and added to them? For all honour, which is

---

[1] So Canterus suggests *conf-iunt* for the ms. *confic-* — "bring about."

[2] Lit., "it is a thing of long and much speech."

[3] Lit., "the fortunes of perils."

[4] The ms. reading is *hoc est unus*, corrected *honestus* — "honourable" (which makes the comparison pointless, because there is no reason why a rich man, if good, should not be succoured as well as a poor), in all edd., except Oehler, who reads *scelestus*, which departs too far from the ms. Perhaps we should read, as above, *inhonestus.*

[5] So the ms., LB., Hild., and Oehler, and the other edd., adding *et auxilium* — "and help."

[6] Lit., "whom not his mind, but the necessity of his property, made restricted."

[7] Lit., "inclines thither whence."

[8] i.e., the decision.

[9] Lit., "both nations."

[10] Lit., "the favours of good work," *boni operis favor-es et,* the reading of Hild. and Oehler (other edd. *-em* — "the favour of its service") for ms. *fabore sed.*

said to be offered by any one, and to be yielded to reverence for a greater being, is of a kind having reference to the other; and consists of two parts, of the concession of the giver, and the increase of honour of the receiver. As, if any one, on seeing a man famed for his very great power [1] and authority, were to make way for him, to stand up, to uncover his head, and leap down from his carriage, then, bending forward to salute him with slavish servility and [2] trembling agitation, I see what is aimed at in showing such respect: by the bowing down of the one, very great *honour* is given to the other, and he is made to appear great whom the respect of an inferior exalts and places above his own rank.[3]

14. But all this conceding and ascribing of honour about which we are speaking are met with among men alone, whom their natural weakness and love of standing above their fellows [4] teach to delight in arrogance, and in being preferred above others. But, I ask, where is there room for honour among the gods, or what greater exaltation is found to be given [5] to them by piling up [6] sacrifices? Do they become more venerable, more powerful, when cattle are sacrificed *to them?* is there anything added to them from this? or do they begin to be more *truly* gods, their divinity being increased? And yet I consider it almost an insult, nay, an insult altogether, when it is said that a god is honoured by a man, and exalted by the offering of some gift. For if honour increases and augments the grandeur of him to whom it is given, it follows that a deity becomes greater by means of the man from whom he has received the gift, and the honour conferred on him; and thus the matter is brought to this issue, that the god who is exalted by human honours is the inferior, while, on the other hand, the man who increases the power of a deity *is* his superior.[7]

15. What then! some one will say, do you think that no honour should be given to the gods at all? If you propose to us gods such as they should be if they do exist, and such as [8] we feel that we all mean when we mention [9] that name, how can we but give them even the greatest honour, since we have been taught by the commands which have especial power over us,[10]

to pay honour to all men even, of whatever rank, of whatever condition they may be? What, pray, *you ask*, is this very great honour? One much more in accordance with duty than is paid by you, and directed to [11] a more powerful race, *we reply*. Tell, us, you say, in the first place, what is an opinion worthy of the gods, right and honourable, and not blameworthy from its being made unseemly by something infamous? *We reply, one such* that you believe that they neither have any likeness to man, nor look for anything which is outside of them and comes from without; then — and this has been said pretty frequently — that they do not burn with the fires of anger, that they do not give themselves up passionately to sensual pleasure, that they are not bribed to be of service, that they are not tempted to injure *our enemies*, that they do not sell their kindness and favour, that they do not rejoice in having honour heaped on them, that they are not indignant and vexed if it is not given; but — and this belongs to the divine — that by their own power they know themselves, and that they do not rate themselves by the obsequiousness of others. And yet, that we may see the nature of what is said, what kind of honour is this, to bind a wether, a ram, a bull before the face of a god, and slay them in his sight? What kind of honour is it to invite a god to *a banquet of* blood, which you see him take and share in with dogs? What kind of honour is it, having set on fire piles of wood, to hide the heavens with smoke, and darken with gloomy blackness the images of the gods? But if it seems good to you that these actions should be considered in themselves,[12] not judged of according to your prejudices, *you will find that* those altars of which you speak, and even those beautiful ones which you dedicate to the superior gods,[13] are places for burning the unhappy race of animals, funeral pyres, and mounds built for a most unseemly office, and formed to be filled with corruption.

16. What say you, O you ——! is that foul smell, then, which is given forth and emitted by burning hides, by bones, by bristles, by the fleeces of lambs, and the feathers of fowls, — *is that* a favour and an honour to the deity? and are the deities honoured by this, to whose temples, when you arrange to go, you come [14] cleansed from all pollution, washed, and perfectly [15] pure? And what can be more polluted

---

[1] Lit., "of most powerful name."
[2] Lit., "imitating a slave's servility" — *ancillatum*, the emendation of Hemsterhuis, adopted by Orelli, Hild., and Oehler for the unintelligible MS. *ancillarum*.
[3] Lit., "things."
[4] Lit., "in higher *places*."
[5] Lit., "what eminences is it found to be added," *addier*. So Hild. and Oehler for the reading of MS., first four edd., and Oberthür *addere* — "to add," emended in rest from margin of Ursinus *accedere*, much as above.
[6] So the MS., reading *conjectionibus*, which is retained in no edd., although its primary meaning is exactly what the sense here requires.
[7] The last clause was omitted in first four edd. and Elmh., and was inserted from the MS. by Meursius.
[8] Lit., "whom."
[9] Lit., "say in the proclamation of."
[10] Lit , "more powerful commands," i.e., by Christ's injunctions. It seems hardly possible that any one should suppose that there is

here any reference to Christ's command to His disciples not to exercise lordship over each other, yet Orelli thinks that there is perhaps a reference to Mark x. 42, 43. If a particular reference were intended, we might with more reason find it in 1 Pet. ii. 17, "Honour all men."
[11] Lit., "established in."
[12] Lit, "weighed by their own force," *vi*.
[13] i.e., *altariaque hæc pulchra*.
[14] Lit., "you show yourselves," *præstatis*.
[15] Lit , "most." So Tibullus (*Eleg.*, ii. 1, 13): "Pure things please the gods. Come (i.e., to the sacrifice) with clean garments, and with clean hands take water from the fountain," — perfect cleanliness being scrupulously insisted on.

than these, more unhappy,[1] more debased, than if their senses are naturally such that they are fond of what is so cruel, and take delight in foul smells which, when inhaled with the breath, even those who sacrifice cannot bear, and *certainly* not a delicate[2] nose? But if you think that the gods of heaven are honoured by the blood of living creatures *being offered to them*, why do you not[3] sacrifice to them both mules, and elephants, and asses? why not dogs also, bears, and foxes, camels, and hyænas, and lions? And as birds also are counted victims by you, why do you not *sacrifice* vultures, eagles, storks, falcons, hawks, ravens, sparrow-hawks, owls, and, along with them, salamanders, water-snakes, vipers, tarantulæ? For indeed there is both blood in these, and they are in like manner moved by the breath of life. What is there more artistic in the former kind *of sacrifices*, or less ingenious in the latter, that these do not add to and increase the grandeur of the gods? Because, says my opponent, it is right to honour the gods of heaven with those things by which we are ourselves nourished and sustained, and live ; which also they have, in their divine benevolence, deigned to give to us for food. But the same gods have given to you both cumin, cress, turnips, onions, parsley, esculent thistles, radishes, gourds, rue, mint, basil, flea-bane, and chives, and commanded them to be used by you as part of your food ; why, then, do you not put these too upon the altars, and scatter wild-marjoram, with which oxen are fed, over them all, and mix amongst *them* onions with their pungent flavour?

17. Lo, if dogs — for a case must be imagined, in order that things may be seen more clearly — if dogs, I say, and asses, and along with them water-wagtails, if the twittering swallows, and pigs also, having acquired some of the feelings of men, were to think and suppose that you were gods, and to propose to offer sacrifices in your honour, not of other things and substances, but *of those* with which they are wont to be nourished and supported, according to their natural inclination, — we ask you to say whether you would consider this an honour, or rather a most outrageous affront, when the swallows slew and consecrated flies to you, the water-wagtails ants ; when the asses put hay upon your altars, and poured out libations of chaff ; when the dogs placed bones, and burned human excrements[4] *at your shrines ;* when, lastly, the pigs poured out before you a horrid mess, taken from

their frightful hog-pools and filthy maws? Would you not in this case, then, be inflamed with rage that your greatness was treated with contumely, and account it an atrocious wrong that you were greeted with filth? But, *you reply*, you honour the gods with the carcasses of bulls, and by slaying[5] other living creatures. And in what respect does this differ from that, since these *sacrifices*, also, if they are not yet, will nevertheless soon be, dung, and will become rotten after a very short time has passed? Finally, cease to place fire upon[6] your altars, then indeed you will[7] see that consecrated flesh of bulls, with which you magnify the honour of the gods, swelling and heaving with worms, tainting and corrupting the atmosphere, and infecting the neighbouring districts with unwholesome smells. Now, if the gods were to enjoin you to turn these things[8] to your own account, to make your meals from them[9] in the usual way; you would flee to a distance, and, execrating the smell, would beg pardon from the gods, and bind yourselves by oath never *again* to offer such sacrifices to them. Is not this conduct of yours mockery, then? is it not to confess, to make known that you do not know what a deity is, nor to what power the meaning and title of this name should be given and applied? Do you give new dignity to the gods by new kinds of food? do you honour them with savours and juices, and because those things which nourish you are pleasing and grateful to you? do you believe that the gods also flock up to *enjoy* their pleasant taste, and, just as barking dogs, lay aside their fierceness for mouthfuls, and pretty often fawn upon those who hold *these* out?

18. And as we are now speaking of the animals sacrificed, what cause, what reason is there, that while the immortal gods — for, so far as we are concerned, they may all be *gods* who are believed to be so — are of one mind, or should be of one nature, kind, and character, all are not appeased with all the victims, but certain *deities* with certain *animals*, according to the sacrificial laws? For what cause is there, to repeat the same question, that that deity should be honoured with bulls, another with kids or sheep, this one with sucking pigs, the other with unshorn lambs, this one with virgin heifers, that one with horned goats, this with barren cows, but that with teeming[10] swine, this with white, that with dusky[11]

---

[1] This Heraldus explains as "of worse omen," and Oehler as "more unclean."

[2] *Ingenuæ*, i.e., such as any respectable person has.

[3] To this the commentators have replied, that mules, asses, and dogs were sacrificed to certain deities. We must either admit that Arnobius has here fallen into error, or suppose that he refers merely to the animals which were usually slain, or find a reason for his neglecting it in the circumstances of each sacrifice.

[4] [The wit of Arnobius must be acknowledged in this scorching satire. Compare the divine ordinances, Exod. xxix. 13, 14.]

[5] Lit., "by slaughters of," *cædibus*.

[6] Lit., "under," i.e., under the sacrifices on your altars.

[7] So all edd., reading *cerne-*, except both Roman edd., Hild., and Oehler, who retain the MS. *cerni-tis* — "you see."

[8] In translating thus, it has been attempted to adhere as closely as possible to the MS. reading (according to Crusius) *qua si* — corrected, as above, *quæ* in LB.; but it is by no means certain that further changes should not be made.

[9] Lit., "prepare luncheons and dinners thence," i.e., from the putrefying carcasses.

[10] The MS. and first four edd. read *ingentibus scrofis* — "with huge breeding swine," changed by rest, as above, *incient-*, from the margin of Ursinus.

[11] Or "gloomy," *tetris*, the reading of MS. and all edd. since LB., for which earlier edd. give *atris* — "black."

victims, one with female, the other, on the contrary, with male animals? For if victims are slain in sacrifice to the gods, to do them honour and show reverence for them, what does it matter, or what difference is there with the life of what animal this debt is paid, their anger and resentment put away? Or is the blood of one victim less grateful and pleasing to one god, while the other's fills him with pleasure and joy? or, as is usually done, does that *deity* abstain from the flesh of goats because of some reverential and religious scruple, another turn with disgust from pork, while to this mutton stinks? and does this one avoid tough ox-beef that he may not overtax his weak stomach, and choose tender[1] sucklings that he may digest them more speedily?[2]

19. But you err, says *my opponent*, and fall into mistakes; for in sacrificing female victims to the female deities, males to the male *deities*, there is a hidden and very[3] secret reason, and one beyond the reach of the mass. I do not inquire, I do not demand, what the sacrificial laws teach or contain; but if reason has demonstrated,[4] and truth declared, that among the gods there is no difference of species, and that they are not distinguished by any sexes, must not all these reasonings be set at nought, and be proved, be found to have been believed under the most foolish hallucinations? I will not bring forward the opinions of wise men, who cannot restrain their laughter when they hear distinctions of sex attributed to the immortal gods: I ask of each man whether he himself believes in his own mind, and persuades himself that the race of the gods is *so* distinguished that they are male and female, and have been formed with members arranged suitably for the begetting of young?

But if the laws of the sacrifices enjoin that like sexes should be sacrificed to like, that is, female *victims* to the female *gods*, male victims, on the contrary, to the male gods, what relation is there in the colours, so that it is right and fitting that to these white, to those dark, even the blackest victims are slain? Because, says *my opponent*, to the gods above, and *those* who have power to give favourable omens,[5] the cheerful colour is acceptable and propitious from the pleasant appearance of pure white; while, on the contrary, to the sinister deities, and those who inhabit the infernal seats, a dusky colour is more pleasing, and *one* tinged with gloomy hues. But if, again, the reasoning holds good, that the infernal regions are an utterly vain and empty name,[6] and that underneath the earth there are no Plutonian realms and abodes, this, too, must nullify your ideas about black cattle and gods under the ground. Because, if there are no infernal regions, of necessity there are no *dii Manium* also. For how is it possible that, while there are no regions, there should be said to be any who inhabit them?

20. But let us agree, as you wish, that there are both infernal regions and *Manes*, and that some gods or other dwell in these by no means favourable to men, and presiding over misfortunes; and what cause, what reason is there, that black victims, even[7] of the darkest hue, should be brought to their altars? Because dark things suit dark, and gloomy things are pleasing to similar beings. What then? Do you not see — that we, too, may joke with you stupidly, and just as you do yourselves[8] — that the flesh of the victims is not black,[9] *nor* their bones, teeth, fat, the bowels, with[10] the brains, and the soft marrow in the bones? But the fleeces are jet-black, and the bristles of the creatures are jet-black. Do you, then, sacrifice to the gods only wool and little bristles torn from the victims? Do you leave the wretched creatures, despoiled it may be, and shorn, to draw the breath of heaven, and rest in perfect innocence upon their feeding-grounds? But if you think that those things are pleasing to the infernal gods which are black and of a gloomy colour, why do you not take care that all the other things which it is customary to place upon their sacrifices should be black, and smoked, and horrible in colour? Dye the incense if it is offered, the salted grits, and all the libations without exception. Into the milk, oil, blood, pour soot and ashes, that this may lose its purple hue, that the others may become ghastly. But if you have no scruple in introducing some things which are white and retain their brightness, you yourselves do away with your own religious scruples and reasonings, while you do not maintain any single and universal rule in performing the sacred rites.

21. But this, too, it is fitting that we should here learn from you: If a goat be slain to Jupiter, which is usually sacrificed to father Liber and Mercury,[11] or if the barren heifer be sacrificed to Unxia, which you give to Proserpine, by what usage and rule is it determined what crime there is in this, what wickedness or guilt has been con-

---

1 Lit., " the tenderness of."
2 [The law of clean and unclean reflects the instincts of man, as here appealed to; but compare and *patiently study* these texts: Lev. x. 10 and Ezek. xxii. 26; Lev. xi. and Acts x. 15; Rom. xiv. 14 and Luke xi. 41.]
3 Lit., " more."
4 So the ms., Elm., LB., Orelli, Hild., and Oehler, reading *vicerit*, for which the others read *jusserit* — " has bidden."
5 Lit., " prevailing with favourableness of omens," *ominum*, for which the ms. and first four edd. read *h-* — " of men."

6 That Arnobius had good reason to appeal to this scepticism as a fact, is evident from the lines of Juvenal (ii. 149–152): " Not even children believe that there are any Manes and subterranean realms."
7 Lit., " and." Immediately after, the ms. is corrected in later writing *color-es* (for *-is*) — " and the darkest colours."
8 *Similiter.* This is certainly a suspicious reading, but Arnobius indulges occasionally in similar vague expressions.
9 Lit., " is white."
10 Or, very probably, " the membranes with (i.e., enclosing) the brains," *omenta cum cerebris.*
11 Goats were sacrificed to Bacchus, but not, so far as is known, to Mercury. Cf. c. 16, p. 524, n. 3.

tracted, since it makes no difference to the worship *offered to the deity* what animal it is with whose head the honour is paid which you owe? It is not lawful, says *my opponent*, that these things should be confounded, and it is no small crime to throw the ceremonies of the rites and the mode of expiation into confusion. Explain the reason, I beg. Because it is right to consecrate victims of a certain kind to certain deities, and that certain forms of supplication should be also adopted. And what, again, is the reason that it is right to consecrate victims of a certain kind to certain deities, and that certain forms of supplication should be also adopted, for this very rightfulness should have its own cause, and spring, be derived from certain reasons? Are you going to speak about antiquity and custom? *If so,* you relate to me merely the opinions of men, and the inventions of a blind creature : but I, when I request a reason to be brought forward to me, wish to hear either that something has fallen from heaven, or, which the subject rather requires, what relation Jupiter has to a bull's blood that it should be offered in sacrifice to him, not to Mercury *or* Liber. Or what are the natural properties of a goat, that they again should be suited to these gods, should not be adapted to the sacrifices of Jupiter? Has a partition of the animals been made amongst the gods? Has some contract been made and agreed to, so that[1] it is fitting that this one should hold himself back from the victim which belongs to that, that the other should cease[2] to claim as his own the blood which belongs to another? Or, as envious boys, are they unwilling to allow others to have a share in enjoying the cattle presented to them? or, as is reported to be done by races which differ greatly in manners, are the same things which by one party are considered fit for eating, rejected as food by others?

22. If, then, these things are vain, and are not supported by any reason, the very offering[3] of sacrifices also is idle. For how can that which follows have a suitable cause, when that very first *statement* from which the second flows is found to be utterly idle and vain, and established on no solid basis? To mother Earth, they say, is sacrificed a teeming[4] and pregnant sow ; but to the virgin Minerva is slain a virgin calf, never forced[5] by the goad to attempt any labour. But yet we think that neither should a virgin have been sacrificed to a virgin, that the virginity might not be violated in the brute, for which the goddess is especially esteemed ; nor *should* gravid and pregnant *victims have been sacrificed* to the Earth from respect for its fruitfulness, which[6] we all desire and wish to go on always in irrepressible fertility.[7] For if because the Tritonian *goddess* is a virgin it is therefore fitting that virgin victims be sacrificed to her, and *if* because the Earth is a mother she is in like manner to be entertained with gravid swine, then also Apollo *should be honoured* by the sacrifice of musicians because he is a musician; Æsculapius, because he is a physician, by the sacrifice of physicians ; and because he is an artificer, Vulcan by the sacrifice of artificers ; and because Mercury is eloquent, sacrifice should be made to him with the eloquent and most fluent. But if it is madness to say this, or, to speak with moderation, nonsense, that shows much greater madness to slaughter pregnant *swine* to the Earth because she is even more prolific ; pure and virgin *heifers* to Minerva because she is pure, of unviolated virginity.

23. For as to that which we hear said by you, that some of the gods are good, that others, on the contrary, are bad, and rather inclined to indulge in wanton mischief,[8] and that the usual rites are paid to the one party that they may show favour, but to the others that they may not do you harm, — with what reason this is said, we confess that we cannot understand. For to say that the gods are most benevolent, and have gentle dispositions, is not only pious and religious, but also true ; but that they are evil and sinister, should by no means be listened to, inasmuch as that divine power has been far removed and separated from the disposition which does harm.[9] But whatever can occasion calamity, it must first be seen what it is, and *then* it should be removed very far from the name of deity.

Then, *supposing* that we should agree with you that the gods promote good fortune and calamity, not even in this case is there any reason why you should allure some of them to grant you prosperity, and, on the other hand, coax others with sacrifices and rewards not to do you harm. First, because the good gods cannot act badly, even if they have been worshipped with no honour, — for whatever is mild and placid by nature, is separated widely from the practice and devising of mischief ; while the bad knows not to restrain his ferocity, although he should be enticed *to do so* with a thousand flocks and a thousand altars. For neither can bitterness change itself into sweetness, dryness into moisture, the heat of

---

[1] Lit., " by the paction of some transaction is it," etc.
[2] So all except both Roman edd., which retain the MS. reading *desi-d-er-t* (corrected *-n-* by Gelenius) — " wish."
[3] So the MS., Hild., and Oehler, reading *d-atio,* approved of by Stewechius also. The others read *r-* — " reasoning on behalf."
[4] *Inci-ens,* so corrected in the margin of Ursinus for MS. *ing-* — " huge." Cf. ch. 18, p. 524, n. 10.
[5] The MS. reads *excitata conatus* (according to Hild.) ; corrected, as above, by the insertion of *ad.*

[6] *Quam,* i.e., the earth.
[7] Singularly enough, for *fecunditate* Oberthür reads *virginitate* — " inextinguishable virginity," which is by no means universally desired in the earth. Orelli, as usual, copies without remark the mistake of his predecessor.
[8] Lit., " more prompt to lust of hurting."
[9] Lit., " nature of hurting."

fire into cold, or what is contrary to anything take and change into its own nature that which is its opposite. So that, if you should stroke a viper with your hand, or caress a poisonous scorpion, the former will attack you with its fangs, the latter, drawing itself together, will fix its sting *in you;* and your caressing will be of no avail, since both creatures are excited to do mischief, not by the stings of rage, but by a certain peculiarity of their nature. It is thus of no avail to wish to deserve well of the sinister deities by means of sacrifices, since, whether you do this, or on the contrary do not, they follow their own nature, and by inborn laws and a kind of necessity are led to those things, *to do* which [1] they were made. Moreover, in this way [2] both *kinds of* gods cease to possess their own powers, and to retain their own characters. For if the good are worshipped that they may be favourable, and supplication is made in the same way to the others, on the contrary, that they may not be injurious, it follows that it should be understood that the propitious *deities* will show no favour if they receive no gifts, and become bad instead of good ; [3] while, on the contrary, the bad, if they receive *offerings,* will lay aside their mischievous disposition, and become thereafter good : and thus it is brought to this issue, that neither are these propitious, nor are those sinister ; or, which is impossible, both are propitious, and both again sinister.

24. Be it so ; let it be conceded that *these* most unfortunate cattle are not sacrificed in the temples of the gods without some religious obligation, and that what has been done in accordance with usage and custom possesses some rational ground : but if it seems a great and grand thing to slay bulls to the gods, and to burn in *sacrifice* the flesh of animals whole and entire, what is the meaning of these relics connected with the arts of the *Magi* which the pontifical mysteries have restored to a place among the secret laws of the sacred rites, and have mixed up with religious affairs? What, I say, is the meaning of these things, *apexaones, hirciæ, silicernia, longavi,* which are names and kinds of sausages,[4] some stuffed with goats' blood,[5] others with minced liver? What *is the meaning of tædæ, uæniæ, offæ,* not those used by the common people, but those named and called *offæ penitæ?*

— of which the first [6] is fat cut into very small pieces, as dainties [7] are ; that which has been placed second is the extension of the gut by which the excrements are given off after being drained of all their nourishing juices ; while the *offa penita* is a beast's tail cut off with a morsel of flesh. What *is the meaning of polimina, omenta, palasea,* or, as some call it, *plasea?* — of which that named *omentum* is a certain part enclosed by the reservoirs of the belly are kept within bounds ; the *plasea* is an ox's tail [8] besmeared with flour and blood ; the *polimina,* again, are those parts which we with more decency call *proles,* — by the vulgar, however, they are usually termed *testes.* What *is the meaning of fitilla, frumen, africia, gratilla, catumeum, cumspolium, cubula?* — of which the first two are names of species of pottage, but differing in kind and quality ; while the series *of names* which follows denotes consecrated cakes, for they are not shaped in one and the same way. For we do not choose to mention the *caro strebula* which is taken from the haunches of bulls, the roasted pieces of meat which are spitted, the intestines first heated, and baked on glowing coals, nor, finally, the pickles,[9] which are made by mixing four kinds of fruit. In like manner, *we do not choose to mention* the *fendicæ,* which also are the *hiræ,*[10] which the language of the mob, when it speaks, usually terms *ilia;*[11] nor, in the same way, the *ærumnæ,*[12] which are the first part of the gullet,[13] where ruminating animals are accustomed to send down their food and bring it back again ; nor the *magmenta,*[14] *augmina,* and thousand other kinds of sausages or pottages which you have given unintelligible names to, and have caused to be more revered by common people.

25. For if whatever is done by men, and especially in religion, should have its causes, — and nothing should be done without a reason in all that men do and perform, — tell us and say what is the cause, what the reason, that these things also are given to the gods and burned upon their sacred altars? For here we delay, *constrained* most urgently *to wait* for this cause, we pause, we stand fast, desiring to learn what a god has to do with pottage, with cakes, with different *kinds of* stuffing prepared in manifold ways, and with different ingredients? Are the

---

[1] The MS. reads *ad ea quæ facti sunt,* understood seemingly as above by the edd., by supplying *ad* before *quæ.* Oehler, however, proposes *quia* — " because they were made *for them.*" The reading must be regarded as doubtful.

[2] i.e., if sacrifices avail to counteract the malevolent dispositions of the gods.

[3] Lit., " these." This clause, omitted by Oberthür, is also omitted without remark by Orelli.

[4] So the edd., reading *farciminum* for the MS. *facinorum,* corrected by Hild. *fartorum* — " of stuffings." Throughout this passage hardly one of the names of these sacrificial dainties is generally agreed upon; as many are met with nowhere else, the MS. has been adhered to strictly.

[5] i.e., probably the *hirciæ:* of the others, *silicernia* seem to have been put on the table at funerals.

[6] i.e., *tæda.*

[7] So Salmasius and Meursius corrected the MS. *catillaminu-a-m* by omitting *a.*

[8] i.e., tail-piece.

[9] *Salsamina,* by which is perhaps meant the grits and salt cast on the victim; but if so, Arnobius is at variance with Servius (Virgil, *Ecl.,* viii. 81), who expressly states that these were of spelt mixed only with salt; while there is no trace elsewhere of a different usage.

[10] The first four edd. retain the unintelligible MS. *diræ.*

[11] i.e., the entrails. The MS., first four edd., and Elm. read *illa.*

[12] So the MS., LB., Oberthür, Orelli, Hild., and Oehler; but *ærumnæ* is found in no other passage with this meaning.

[13] Lit., " first heads in gullets."

[14] By this, and the word which follows, we know from the etymology that " offerings " to the gods must be meant, but we know nothing more.

deities affected by splendid dinners or luncheons, so that it is fitting to devise for them feasts without number? Are they troubled by the loathings of their stomachs, and is variety of flavours sought for to get rid of their aversion, so that there is set before them meat at one time roasted, at another raw, and at another half cooked and half raw? But if the gods like to receive all these parts which you term *præsiciæ*,[1] and if these gratify them with any sense of pleasure or delight, what prevents, what hinders you from laying all these upon *their altars* at once with the whole animals? What cause, what reason is there that the haunch-piece[2] by itself, the gullet, the tail, and the tail-piece[3] separately, the entrails only, and the membrane[4] alone, should be brought to do them honour? Are the gods of heaven moved by various condiments? After stuffing themselves with sumptuous and ample dinners, do they, as is usually done, take these little bits as sweet dainties, not to appease their hunger, but to rouse their wearied palates,[5] and excite in themselves a perfectly voracious appetite? O wonderful greatness of the gods, comprehended by no men, understood by no creatures! if indeed their favours are bought with the testicles and gullets of beasts, and if they do not lay aside their anger and resentment, unless they see the entrails[6] prepared and *offæ* bought and burned upon their altars.

26. We have now to say a few words about incense and wine, for these, too, are connected and mixed up with your ceremonies,[7] and are used largely in your religious acts. And, first, with respect to that very incense which you use, we ask this of you particularly, whence or at what time you have been able to become acquainted with it, and to know it, so that you have just reason to think that it is either worthy to be given to the gods, or most agreeable to their desires. For it is almost a novelty; and there is no endless succession of years since it began to be known in these parts, and won its way into the shrines of the gods. For neither in the heroic ages, as it is believed and declared, was it known what incense was, as is proved by the ancient writers, in whose books is found no mention[8] of it; nor was Etruria, the parent and mother of superstition, acquainted with its fame and renown, as the rites of the chapels prove;

nor was it used by any one in offering sacrifice during the four hundred years in which Alba flourished; nor did even Romulus or Numa, *who was* skilful in devising new ceremonies, know either of its existence or growth, as the sacred grits[9] show with which it was customary that the usual sacrifices should be performed. Whence, therefore, did its use begin to be adopted? or what *desire of* novelty assailed the old and ancient custom, so that that which was not needed for so many ages took the first place in the ceremonies? For if without incense the performance of a religious service is imperfect, and if a quantity of it is necessary to make the celestials gentle and propitious to men, the ancients fell into sin, nay rather, their whole life was full of guilt, for they carelessly neglected to offer that which was most fitted to give pleasure to the gods. But if in ancient times neither men nor gods sought for this incense, it is proved that to-day also that is offered uselessly and in vain which antiquity did not believe necessary, but modern times desired without any reason.[10]

27. Finally, that we may always abide by the rule and definition by which it has been shown and determined that whatever is done by man must have its causes, we will hold it fast here also, so as to demand of you what is the cause, what the reason, that incense is put on the altars before the very images of the deities, and that, from its being burned, they are supposed to become friendly and gentle. What do they acquire from this being done, or what reaches their minds, so that we should be right in judging that these things are well expended, and are not consumed uselessly and in vain? For as you should show why you give incense to the gods, so, too, it follows that you should manifest that the gods have some reason for not rejecting it with disdain, nay more, for desiring it so fondly. We honour the gods with this, some one will perhaps say. But we are not inquiring what your feeling is, but the gods'; nor do we ask what is done by you, but how much they value what is done to purchase their favour. But yet, O piety, what or how great is this honour which is caused by the odour of a fire, and produced from the gum of a tree? For, lest you should happen not to know what this incense is, or what is its origin, it is a gum flowing from the bark of trees, *just* as from the almond-tree, the cherry-tree, solidifying as it exudes in drops. Does this, then, honour and magnify the celestial dignities? or, if their displeasure has been at any time excited, is it melted away before the smoke of incense, and lulled to sleep, their anger being moderated? Why, then, do you not burn indiscriminately the juice of any tree whatever, without making any

---

1 i.e., cut off for sacrifice.
2 *Caro strebula.*
3 *Plasea.*
4 The MS. reads unintelligibly *nomen quæ,* corrected by Gelenius *omentum*, as above.
5 Lit., "admonish the ease of the palate;" a correction of Salmasius, by omitting *a* from the MS. *palati-a admoneant.*
6 *Næniæ.*
7 Lit., "these kinds of ceremonies, too, were coupled and mixed," etc.
8 On this Oehler remarks, that the books of Moses show that it was certainly used in the East in the most ancient times. But Arnobius has expressly restricted his statement to the use of incense "in these parts."

9 *Pium far.*
10 [See p. 519, note 1, *supra.*]

distinction? For if the deities are honoured by this, and are not displeased that Panchæan gums are burned to them, what does it matter from what the smoke proceeds on your sacred altars, or from what kind of gum the clouds of fumigation arise?

28. Will any one say that incense is given to the celestials, for this reason, that it has a sweet smell, and imparts a pleasant sensation to the nose, while the rest are disagreeable, and have been set aside because of their offensiveness? Do the gods, then, have nostrils with which to breathe? do they inhale and respire currents of air so that the qualities of different smells can penetrate them? But if we allow that this is the case, we make them subject to the conditions of humanity, and shut them out from the limits of deity; for whatever breathes and draws in draughts of air, to be sent back in the same way, must be mortal, because it is sustained by feeding on the atmosphere. But whatever is sustained by feeding on the atmosphere, if you take away the means by which communication is kept up,[1] its life must be crushed out, and its vital principle must be destroyed and lost. So then, if the gods also breathe and inhale odours enwrapt in the air that accompanies them, it is not untrue to say that they live upon what is received from others,[2] and that they might perish if their air-holes were blocked up. And whence, lastly, do you know whether, if they are charmed by the sweetness of smells, the same things are pleasant to them which *are pleasant* to you, and charm and affect your *different* natures with a similar feeling? May it not be possible that the things which give pleasure to you, seem, on the contrary, harsh and disagreeable to them? For since the opinions of the gods are not the same, and their substance not one, by what methods can it be brought about that that which is unlike in quality should have the same feeling and perception as to that which touches it.[3] Do we not every day see that, even among the creatures sprung from the earth, the same things are either bitter or sweet to different species, that to some things are fatal which are not pernicious to others, so that the same things which charm some with their delightful odours, give forth exhalations deadly to the bodies of others? But the cause of this is not in the things which cannot be at one and the same time deadly and wholesome, sweet and bitter; but just as each one has been formed to receive impressions from what is external,[4] so he is affected:[5] his condi-

tion is not caused by the influences of the things, but springs from the nature of his own senses, and connection with the external. But all this is set far from the gods, and is separated from them by no small interval. For if it is true, as is believed by the wise, that they are incorporeal, and not supported by any excellence of *bodily* strength, an odour is of no effect upon them, nor can reeking fumes move them by their senses, not *even* if you were to set on fire a thousand pounds of the finest incense, and the whole sky were clouded with the darkness of the abundant vapours. For that which does not have *bodily* strength and corporeal substance, cannot be touched by corporeal substance; but an odour is corporeal, as is shown by the nose when touched *by one:* therefore it cannot, according to reason, be felt by a deity, who has no body, and is without any feeling and thought.[6]

29. Wine is used along with incense; and of this, in like manner, we ask an explanation why it is poured upon it when burning. For if a reason is not[7] shown for doing this, and its cause is not[8] set forth, this action of yours must not now be attributed to a ridiculous error, but, to speak more plainly, to madness, foolishness, blindness. For, as has been already said pretty frequently, everything which is done should have its cause manifest, and not involved in any dark obscurity. If, therefore, you have confidence in what is done, disclose, point out why that liquor is offered; that is, *why* wine is poured on the altars. For do the bodies of the deities feel parching thirst, and is it necessary that their dryness be tempered by some moisture? Are they accustomed, as men are, to combine eating and drinking? In like manner, also, after the solid[9] food of cakes and pottages, and victims slain *in honour of them*, do they drench themselves, and make themselves merry with very frequent *cups of* wine, that their food may be more easily softened, and thoroughly digested? Give, I beg, to the immortal gods to drink; bring forth goblets, bowls,[10] ladles, and cups; and as they stuff themselves with bulls, and luxurious feasts, and rich food, — lest some piece of flesh hastily[11] gulped down should stick in passing through the stomach, run up, hasten, give pure wine to Jupiter, the most excellent, the supreme, lest he be choked. He desires to break wind, and is un-

---

1 Lit., "the returns by which the vital alternation is restored and withdrawn."

2 So the MS., Hild., and Oehler, reading *suffec-tionibus alienis*, for which the rest read *suffi-* — "the fumigations of others."

3 Lit., "feel and receive one contact."

4 Lit., "as each has been made for the touching of a thing coming from without."

5 So Gelenius and later edd., reading *afficitur* for the unintelligible reading of MS. and Roman edd., *efficit* — "effects."

6 So all edd., without remark, reading *cog-it-atione*, although "meditation" has nothing to do with the sense of smell, and has not been previously mentioned. We should probably read *cog-n-atione* — "relation," i.e., to such objects.

7 So LB. and Oehler, reading *ni-si*.(MS. *si*), and other edd. inserting *non*, the negative being absolutely necessary to the sense, and supplied in the next clause.

8 Lit., "nor will it have its cause."

9 Although this is clearly the meaning, Stewechius explained *solidos* by referring to the ancient belief that such offerings should be wholly consumed, and no fragment left.

10 *Briæ*, drinking-cups, but of their peculiar shape or purpose we know nothing.

11 Lit., "badly."

able; and unless that hindrance passes away and is dissolved, there is very great danger that his breathing will be stopped and [1] interrupted, and heaven be left desolate without its rulers.

30. But, says *my opponent*, you are insulting us without reason, for we do not pour forth wine to the gods of heaven for these reasons, as if we supposed that they either thirsted, or drank, or were made glad by tasting its sweetness. It is given to them to do them honour; that their eminence may become more exalted, more illustrious, we pour libations on their altars, and with the *half*-extinguished embers we raise sweet smells,[2] which show our reverence. And what greater insult can be inflicted upon the gods than if you believe that they become propitious on receiving wine, or, if you suppose that great honour is done to them, if you only throw and drop on the live coals a few drops of wine? We are not speaking to men void of reason, or not possessed of common understanding: in you, too, there is wisdom, there is perception, and in your hearts you know, by your own [3] judgment, that we are speaking truly. But what can we do with those who are utterly unwilling to consider things as they are, to converse themselves with themselves? For you do what you see to be done, not that which you are assured should be done, inasmuch [4] as with you a custom without reason prevails, more than a perception of the nature of circumstances based on a careful examination of the truth. For what has a god to do with wine? or what or how great is the power in it, that, on its being poured out, his eminence becomes greater, and his dignity is supposed *to be* honoured? What, I say, has a god to do with wine, which is most closely connected with the pursuits of Venus, which weakens the strength of all virtues, *and* is hostile to the decency of modesty and chastity, — which has often excited *men's* minds, and urged them to madness and frenzy, and compelled the gods to destroy their own authority by raving *and* foul language? Is not this, then, impious, and perfectly sacrilegious, to give that as an honour which, if you take too eagerly, you know not what you are doing, you are ignorant of what you are saying, *and* at last are reviled, and become infamous as a drunkard, a luxurious and abandoned fellow?

31. It is worth while to bring forward the words themselves also, which, when wine is offered, it is customary to use and make supplication with: "Let *the deity* be worshipped with this wine which we bring." [5] The words "which we bring," says Trebatius, are added for this purpose, and put forth for this reason, that all the wine whatever which has been laid up in closets and storerooms, from which was taken that which is poured out, may not begin to be sacred, and be reft from the use of men. This word, then, being added, that alone will be sacred which is brought to *the place*, and the rest will not be consecrated.[6] What kind of honour, then, is this, in which there is imposed on the deity a condition,[7] as it were, not to ask more than has been given? or what is the greed of the god, who, if he were not verbally interdicted, would extend his desires too far, and rob his suppliant of his stores? "Let *the deity* be worshipped with this wine which we bring:" this is a wrong, not an honour. For what if the deity shall wish for more, and shall not be content with what is brought! Must he not be said to be signally wronged who is compelled to receive honour conditionally? For if all wine in cellars whatever must become consecrated were a limitation not added, it is manifest both that the god is insulted to whom a limit is prescribed against his wishes, and that in sacrificing you yourselves violate the obligations of the sacred rites, who do not give as much wine as you see the god wishes to be given to himself. "Let *the deity* be worshipped with this wine which we bring:" what is this but saying, "Be worshipped as much as I choose; receive as much dignity as I prescribe, as much honour as I decide and determine by a strict engagement [8] that you should have?" O sublimity of the gods, excelling in power, which thou shouldst venerate and worship with all ceremonial observances, but on which the worshipper imposes conditions, which he adores with stipulations and contracts, which, through fear of one word, is kept from excessive desire of wine!

32. But let there be, as you wish, honour in wine and in incense, let the anger and displeasure of the deities be appeased by the immolation and slaughter of victims: are the gods moved by garlands also, wreaths and flowers, by the jingling of brass also, and the shaking of cymbals, by timbrels also, *and* also by symphonious *pipes?* [9] What effect has the clattering of castanets, that when the deities have heard them, they think that honour has been shown to them, and lay aside their fiery spirit of resentment in forgetfulness? Or, as little boys are frightened into giving over their silly wailings by hearing

---

[1] Lit., "being strangled, may be."
[2] So LB., Orelli, and Oehler, reading with Salmasius *m-u-scos* (MS. -*i*-). Gelenius proposed *cnissas*, which would refer to the steam of the sacrifices.
[3] Lit., "interior."
[4] So most edd., reading *nimirum quia plus valet*, for which the MS., followed by both Roman edd, Hild., and Oehler, read *primum q. v.*, which Hild. would explain, "because it prevails above all *rather* than;" but this is at least very doubtful.

[5] *Vino inferio.*
[6] Lit., "bound by religion."
[7] This is admirably illustrated in an inscription quoted by Heraldus: "Jupiter most excellent, supreme, when this day I give and dedicate to thee this altar, I give and dedicate it with these conditions and limits which I say openly to-day."
[8] *Circumscriptione verborum.*
[9] *Symphoniæ.* Evidently musical instruments; but while Isidore speaks of them as a kind of drum, other writers call them trumpets and pipes.

the sound of rattles, are the almighty deities also soothed in the same way by the whistling of pipes? and do they become mild, *is* their indignation softened, at the musical sound of cymbals? What is the meaning of those calls[1] which you sing in the morning, joining *your* voices to the *music of the* pipe? Do the gods of heaven fall asleep, so that they should return to their posts? What *is the meaning of* those slumbers[1] to which you commend them with auspicious salutations that they may be in good health? Are they awakened from sleep; and that they may be able to be overcome by it, must soothing lullabies be heard? The purification, says *my opponent*, of the mother of the gods is to-day.[2] Do the gods, then, become dirty; and to get rid of the filth, do those who wash *them* need water, and even some cinders to rub them with?[3] The feast of Jupiter is to-morrow. Jupiter, I suppose, dines, and must be satiated with great banquets, and long filled with eager cravings *for food* by fasting, and hungry after the usual[4] interval. The vintage festival of Æsculapius is being celebrated. The gods, then, cultivate vineyards, and, having collected gatherers, press the wine for their own uses.[5] The *lectisternium* of Ceres[6] will be on the next Ides, for the gods have couches; and that they may be able to lie on softer cushions, the pillows are shaken up when they have been pressed down.[7] It is the birthday of *Tellus;*[8] for the gods are born, and have festal days on which it has been settled that they began to breathe.

33. But the games which you celebrate, called *Floralia* and *Megalensia*,[9] and all the rest which you wish to be sacred, and to be considered religious duties, what reason have they, what cause, that it was necessary that they should be instituted and founded and designated by the names[10] of deities? The gods are honoured by these, says *my opponent;* and if they have any recollection of offences committed[11] by men, they lay

it aside, get rid of it, and show themselves gracious to us again, their friendship being renewed. And what is the cause, again, that they are made quite calm and gentle, if absurd things are done, and idle fellows sport before the eyes of the multitude? Does Jupiter lay aside his resentment if the *Amphitryon* of Plautus is acted and declaimed? or if Europa, Leda, Ganymede, or Danæ is represented by dancing, does he restrain his passionate impulses? Is the Great Mother rendered more calm, more gentle, if she beholds the old story of Attis furbished up by the players? Will Venus forget her displeasure if she sees mimics act the part of Adonis also in a ballet?[12] Does the anger of Alcides die away if the tragedy of Sophocles named *Trachiniæ*, or the *Hercules* of Euripides, is acted? or does Flora think[13] that honour is shown to her if at her games she sees that shameful actions are done, and the stews abandoned for the theatres? Is not this, then, to lessen the dignity of the gods, to dedicate and consecrate to them the basest things which a rigidly virtuous mind will turn from with disgust, the performers of which your law has decided to be dishonoured and to be considered infamous? The gods, forsooth, delight in mimics; and that surpassing excellence which has not been comprehended by any human faculty, opens[14] its ears most willingly to hear these *plays*, with most of which they know they are mixed up to be turned to derision; they are delighted, as it is, with the shaved heads of the fools, by the sound of flaps, and by the *noise of* applause, by shameful actions and words, by huge red *fascina*. But further, if they see men weakening themselves to the effeminacy of women, some vociferating uselessly, others running about without cause,[15] others, while their friendship is unbroken, bruising and maiming each with the bloody *cestus*, these contending in *speaking without drawing* breath,[16] swelling out their cheeks with wind, and shouting out noisily empty vows, do they lift up their hands to heaven *in their admiration*, start up moved by *such* wonders, burst into exclamations, again become gracious to men? If these things cause the gods to forget their resentment, if they derive the highest pleasure from comedies, Atellane farces, *and* pantomimes, why do you delay, why do you hesitate, to say that the gods themselves also play, act lasciviously, dance, compose obscene songs, and undulate with trembling haunches?

---

[1] At daybreak on opening, and at night on closing the temple, the priests of Isis sang hymns in praise of the goddess (cf. Jos. Scaliger, *Castigationes ad Cat.*, etc., p. 132); and to these Arnobius refers sarcastically, as though they had been calls to awake, and lullabies to sing her asleep.

[2] i.e., March 27th, marked *Lavatio* in a calendar prepared during the reign of Constantius.

[3] Lit., "and some rubbing of cinders added," *aliqua frictione cineris;* an emendation of Ursinus for the possibly correct MS. *antiqua f. c.* — "the ancient rubbing," i.e., that practised in early times.

[4] Lit., "anniversary."

[5] So the later edd., adopting the emendation of *ad suas usiones* for the corrupt MS. *ad* (or *ab*) *suasionibus.*

[6] i.e., feast at which the image of Ceres was placed on a couch, probably the *Cerealia*, celebrated in April. This passage flatly contradicts Prof. Ramsay's assertion (*Ant.*, p. 345) that *lectisternium* is not applied to a banquet offered to a goddess; while it corroborates his statement that such feasts were ordinary events, not extraordinary solemnities, as Mr. Yates says (Smith's *Ant.*, s. v.). See p. 519, n. 2.

[7] Lit., "the impression of the cushions is lifted up and raised," i e., smoothed.

[8] Thus the 25th of January is marked as the birthday of the Graces, the 1st of February as that of Hercules, the 1st of March as that of Mars, in the calendar already mentioned.

[9] The former dedicated to Flora (cf. iii. 25), the latter to Cybele.

[10] Singular.

[11] So the margin of Ursinus, Elm., LB., Orelli, Hild., and Oehler; the MS. reading not being known.

[12] Lit., "in dancing motions."

[13] So Meursius, Orelli, and Oehler, reading *existimat-ve*, all the others retaining the MS. *-ur-* — "Is Flora thought to be treated," etc.

[14] Lit., "adapts."

[15] Here also there is doubt as to what the reading of the MS. is. The 1st ed. reads *sine culpa* — "without blame," which is hardly in keeping with the context, emended *causa*, as above, by Gelenius.

[16] So Orelli explains *certare hos spiritu* as referring to a contest in which each strove to speak or sing with one breath longer than the rest.

For what difference is there, or what does it matter, whether they do these things themselves, or are pleased and delighted to see them done by others?

34. Whence, therefore, have these vicious opinions flowed, or from what causes have they sprung? From this it is clear, in great measure, that men *are* unable to know what God is, what is His essence, nature, substance, quality; whether He has a form, or is limited by no bodily outline, does anything or not, is ever watchful, or is at times sunk in slumbers, runs, sits, walks, or is free from such motions and inactivity. Being, as I have said, unable to know all these things, or to discern them by any power of reason, they fell into these fanciful beliefs, so that they fashioned gods after themselves, and gave to these such a nature as they have themselves, in actions, circumstances, and desires. But if they were to perceive that they are worthless creatures,[1] and that there is no great difference between themselves and a little ant, they would cease, indeed, to think that they have anything in common with the gods of heaven, and would confine their unassuming insignificance[2] within its proper limits. But now, because they see that they themselves have faces, eyes, heads, cheeks, ears, noses, and all the other parts of *our* limbs and muscles, they think that the gods also have been formed in the same way, that the divine nature is embodied in a human frame;[3] and because they perceive that they themselves rejoice *and* are glad, and *again* are made sad by what is too disagreeable, they think that the deities also on joyous occasions are glad, and on less pleasant ones become dejected. *They see* that they are affected by the games, and think that the minds of the celestials are soothed by enjoying games; and because they have pleasure in refreshing themselves with warm baths, they think that the cleanness produced by[4] bathing is pleasing to the gods above. We men gather our vintages, and they think and believe that the gods gather and bring in their grapes; we have birthdays, and they affirm that the powers of heaven have birthdays.[5] But if they could ascribe to the gods ill-health, sickness, and bodily disease, they would not hesitate to say that they were splenetic, blear-eyed, and ruptured, because they are themselves both splenetic, and often blear-eyed, and weighed down by huge *herniæ*.

35. Come now: as the discussion has been prolonged and led to these points, let us, bringing forward what each has to say,[6] decide by a brief comparison whether your ideas of the gods above are the better, or our thoughts preferable, and much more honourable and just, and such as to give and assign its own dignity to the divine nature. And, first, you declare that the gods, whom you either think or believe to exist, of whom you have set up images and statues in all the temples, were born and produced from the germs of males and females, under the necessary condition of sexual embraces. But we, on the contrary, if they are indeed true gods. and have the authority, power, dignity of this name, consider that they must either be unbegotten, for it is pious to believe this, or, if they have a beginning in[7] birth, it belongs to the supreme God to know by what methods He made them, or how many ages there are since He granted to them to enter upon the eternal being of His own divine nature. You consider that the deities have sexes, and that some of them are male, others female; we utterly deny that the powers of heaven have been distinguished by sexes, since this distinction has been given to the creatures of earth which the Author of the universe willed should embrace and generate, to provide, by their carnal desires, one generation of offspring after another. You think that they are like men, and have been fashioned with the countenances of mortals; we think that the images of them are wide of the mark,[8] as form belongs to a mortal body; and if they have any, we swear with the utmost earnestness and confidence that no man can comprehend it. By you they are said to have each his trade, like artisans; we laugh when we hear you say such things, as we hold and think that professions are not necessary to gods, and it is certain and evident that these have been provided to assist poverty.

36.[9] You say that some of them *cause* dissensions, that there are others who inflict pestilences, others who *excite* love *and* madness, others, even, who preside over wars, and are delighted by the shedding of blood; but we, indeed, on the contrary, judge that *these things* are remote[10] from the dispositions of the deities;

---

[1] Lit., "an animal of no value."
[2] Lit., "the modesty of their humility."
[3] Lit , "they contain their nature in a corporeal form."
[4] Lit., "of."
[5] Cf. p. 531, n. 8.
[6] Lit., "by opposition of the parts of each." Considerable difficulty has been felt as to the abrupt way in which the book ends as it is arranged in the MS. Orelli has therefore adopted the suggestion of

an anonymous critic, and transposed cc. 35, 36, 37 to the end. This does not, however, meet the difficulty; for the same objection still holds good, that there is a want of connection and harmony in these concluding chapters, and that, even when thus arranged, they do not form a fitting conclusion to the whole work.

[7] Lit., "of."
[8] Lit., "that effigies have been far removed from them." This may be understood, either as meaning that the gods had not visible form at all, or, as above, that their likenesses made by men showed no resemblance.
[9] 50 in Orelli.
[10] It is important to notice the evidence in this one sentence of haste and want of revision. In the first line we find a genitive (*discordiarum* — "dissensions"), but not the noun on which it depends; and in the apodosis a verb (*disjunctas esse* — "have been removed," i.e., "are remote") has no subject, although its gender imperatively requires that *has res*, or some such words, be supplied. One omission might have been easily ascribed to a slip on the part of the copyist; but two omissions such as these occurring so closely, must, it would seem, be assigned to the impetuous disregard of *minutiæ* with which Arnobius blocked out a conclusion which was never carefully revised. (Cf. Appendix, note 1, and p. 539, n. 8.) The importance of such indications is manifest in forming an opinion on the controversy as to this part of the work.

or if there are any who inflict and bring these ills on miserable mortals, we maintain that they are far from the nature of the gods, and should not be spoken of under this name. You judge that the deities are angry and perturbed, and given over and subject to the other mental affections; we think that such emotions are alien from them, for *these* suit savage beings, and those who die as mortals.[1] You think that they rejoice, are made glad, and are reconciled to men, their offended feelings being soothed by the blood of beasts and the slaughter of victims; we hold that there is in the celestials no love of blood, and that they are not so stern as to lay aside their resentment only when glutted with the slaughter of animals. You think that, by wine and incense, honour is given to the gods, and their dignity increased; we judge it marvellous and monstrous that any man thinks that the deity either becomes more venerable by reason of smoke,[2] or thinks himself supplicated by men with sufficient awe and respect when they offer[3] a few drops of wine. You are persuaded that, by the crash of cymbals and the sound of pipes, by horse-races and theatrical plays, the gods are both delighted and affected, and that their resentful feelings conceived before[4] are mollified by the satisfaction which these things give; we hold it *to be* out of place, nay more, we judge it incredible, that those who have surpassed by a thousand degrees every kind of excellence in the height of their perfection, should be pleased and delighted with those things which a wise man laughs at, and which do not seem to have any charm except to little children, coarsely and vulgarly educated.

37. Since these things are so, and since there is so great difference between[3] our opinions and yours, where are we, on the one hand, impious, or you pious, since the decision as to[3] piety and impiety must be founded on the opinions of the *two* parties? For he who makes himself an image which he may worship for a god, or slaughters an innocent beast, and burns it on consecrated altars, must not be held to be devoted to religion.[5] Opinion constitutes religion, and a right way of thinking about the gods, so that you do not think that they desire anything contrary to what becomes their exalted position, *which is* manifest.[6] For since we see all the things which are offered to them consumed here under our eyes, what else can be said to reach

them from us than opinions worthy of the gods, and most appropriate to their name? These are the surest gifts, these true sacrifices; for gruel, incense, and flesh feed the devouring flames, and agree very well with the *parentalia*[7] of the dead.

38.[8] If the immortal gods cannot be angry, says *my opponent*, and their nature is not agitated or troubled by any passions, what do the histories, the annals mean, in which we find it written[9] that the gods, moved by some annoyances, occasioned pestilences, sterility,[10] failure of crops, and other dangers, to states and nations; and that they again, being appeased and satisfied by means of[11] sacrifices, laid aside their burning anger, and changed the state of the atmosphere and times into a happier one? What *is the meaning of* the earth's roarings, the earthquakes, which we have been told occurred because the games had been celebrated carelessly, and their nature and circumstances *had* not been attended to, and yet, on their being celebrated afresh, and repeated with assiduous care, the terrors of the gods were stilled, and *they* were recalled to care and friendship for men? How often, after that — in obedience to the commands of the seers and the responses of the diviners — sacrifice has been offered, and certain gods have been summoned from nations dwelling beyond the sea, and shrines erected to them, and certain images and statues set on loftier pillars, have fears of impending dangers been diverted, and the most troublesome enemies beaten, and the republic extended both by repeated joyous victories, and by gaining possession of several provinces! Now, certainly this would not happen if the gods despised sacrifices, games, and other acts of worship, and did not consider themselves honoured by expiatory offerings. If, then, all the rage and indignation of the deities are cooled when these things are offered, and *if* those things become favourable which seemed fraught with terrors, it is clear that all these things are not done without the gods wishing them, and that it is vain, and shows utter ignorance, to blame us for giving them.

39.[12] We have come, then, in speaking, to the very point of the case, to that on which the question hinges, to the real and most intimate *part of the* discussion, which it is fitting that, laying aside superstitious dread, and putting away partiality, we should examine whether these are gods whom you assert to be furious when offended, and to be rendered mild by sacrifices;

---

[1] Lit., "are of . . . those meeting the functions of mortality," *obeunti-um*, corrected by Gelenius (according to Orelli) for the MS. *-bus*, retained, though unintelligible, by Canterus, Oberth., and Hild.
[2] [See p. 519, note 1, and p. 528, cap. 26, *supra*.]
[3] Lit., "of." [Cap. 29, p. 529, *supra*.]
[4] Lit., "some time."
[5] Lit., "divine things."
[6] So the MS., both Roman edd., Hild., and Oehler, reading *promptæ*; corrected *præsumptæ* — "taken for granted," in the rest.

[7] i.e., offerings to parents, as the name implies, and other relatives who were dead.
[8] 35 in Orelli.
[9] Lit., "in the writings of which we read."
[10] Pl.
[11] Lit., "by satisfaction of."
[12] 36 in Orelli. [See note 1, Appendix, p. 539, *infra*.]

or whether they are something far different, and should be separated from the notion of this name and power. For we do not deny that all these things are to be found in the writings of the annalists which have been brought forward by you in opposition; for we ourselves also, according to the measure and capacity of our abilities, have read, and know, that it has been recorded that once at the *ludi circenses*, celebrated in honour of Jupiter the supreme, a master dragged across the middle of the arena, and afterwards, according to custom, punished with the cross, a very worthless slave *whom he had* beaten with rods. Then, when the games were ended, and the races not long finished, a pestilence began to distress the state; and when each day brought fresh ill worse than what was before,[1] and the people were perishing in crowds, in a dream Jupiter said to a certain rustic, obscure from the lowliness of his lot, that he should go[2] to the consuls, point out that the dancer[3] had displeased him, that it might be better for the state if the respect due to the games were paid to them, and they were again celebrated afresh with assiduous care. And when he had utterly neglected to do this, either because he supposed it was an empty dream, and would find no credence with those to whom he should tell it, or because, remembering his natural insignificance, he avoided and dreaded approaching those who were so powerful,[4] Jupiter was rendered hostile to the lingerer, and imposed as punishment *on him* the death of his sons. Afterwards, when he[5] threatened the man himself with death unless he went to announce his disapproval of the dancer,—overcome by fear of dying, since he was already himself also burning with the fever of the plague, having been infected, he was carried to the senate-house, as his neighbours wished, and, when his vision had been declared, the contagious fever passed away. The repetition of the games being then decreed, great care was, on the one hand, given to the shows, and its former good health was restored to the people.

40.[6] But neither shall we deny that we know this as well, that once on a time, when the state and republic were in difficulties, caused either by[7] a terrible plague continually infecting the people and carrying them off, or by enemies powerful, and at that time almost threatening to rob it of its liberty[8] because of their success in battle,—by order and advice of the seers, cer-

tain gods[9] were summoned from among nations dwelling beyond the sea, and honoured with magnificent temples; and that the violence of the plague abated, and very frequent triumphs were gained, the power of the enemy being broken, and the territory of the empire was increased, and provinces without number fell under our sway. But neither does this escape our knowledge, that we have seen it asserted that, when the Capitol was struck by a thunderbolt, and many other things in it, the image of Jupiter also, which stood on a lofty pillar, was hurled from its place. Thereafter a response was given by the soothsayers, that cruel and very sad mischances were portended from fire and slaughter, from the destruction of the laws, and the overthrow of justice, especially, however, from enemies themselves belonging to the nation, and from an impious band of conspirators; but that these things could not be averted, nay, that these accursed designs could not be revealed, unless Jupiter were again set up firmly on a higher pillar, turned towards the east, and facing the rays of the *rising* sun. Their words were trustworthy, for, when the pillar was raised, and the statue turned towards the sun, the secrets were revealed, and the offences made known were punished.

41.[10] All these things which have been mentioned, have indeed a miraculous appearance,—rather, they are believed to have it,—if they come to men's ears just as they have been brought forward; and we do not deny that there is in them something which, being placed in the fore front, as the saying is, may stun the ears, and deceive by its resemblance to truth. But if you will look closely at what was done, the personages and their pleasures,[11] you will find that there is nothing worthy of the gods, and, as has already been said often, *nothing worthy* to be referred to the splendour and majesty of this race. For, first, who is there who will believe that he was a god who was pleased with horses running to no purpose,[12] and considered it most delightful that he should be summoned[13] by such sports? Rather, who is there who will agree that that was Jupiter—whom you call the supreme god, and the creator of all things which are—who set out from heaven to behold geldings vieing *with each other* in speed, and running[14] the seven rounds of the course; and that, although he had himself determined that they should not be equally nimble, he nevertheless rejoiced to see them pass

---

[1] Lit., "added evil heavier than evil."
[2] So later edd., reading *vaderet* from the margin of Ursinus, while the first three retain the MS. reading *suaderet*—"persuade."
[3] i.e., the slave writhing under the scourge.
[4] Lit., "of so great power."
[5] i.e., Jupiter.
[6] 37 in Orelli.
[7] Lit., "which either a . . . made," etc.
[8] Lit., "very near to danger of carrying off liberty."

[9] Cf. ii. 73.
[10] 38 in Orelli.
[11] So the MS., LB., Hild., and Oehler, reading *volu-p-tates*, i.e., the games and feasts spoken of previously; the other edd. read *-n-*—"wishes."
[12] Oehler explains *frustra* by *otiose*—"who was leisurely delighted;" but there is no reason why it should not have its usual meaning, as above. [See note 1, Appendix, p. 539.]
[13] i.e., from heaven. Instead of *e-vocari*, however, Heraldus has proposed *a-*—"be diverted."
[14] Lit., "unfolding."

each other, and be passed, some in their haste falling forward upon their heads, *and* overturned upon their backs along with their chariots, others dragged along and lamed, their legs being broken ; and that he considered as the highest pleasures fooleries mixed with trifles and cruelties, which any man, *even though* fond of pleasure, and not trained to strive after seriousness and dignity, would consider childish, and spurn as ridiculous ? Who is there, I say, who will believe — to repeat this word assiduously — that he was divine who, being irritated because *a slave* was led across the circus, about to suffer and be punished as he deserved, was inflamed with anger, and prepared himself to take vengeance ? For if the slave was guilty, and deserved to be punished with that chastisement, why should Jupiter have been moved with any indignation when nothing was being done unjustly, nay, when a guilty fellow was being punished, as was right? But if he was free from guilt, and not worthy of punishment at all, *Jupiter* himself was the cause of the dancer's vitiating the games,[1] for when he might have helped him, he did him no service — nay, sought both to allow what he disapproved, and to exact from others the penalty for what he had permitted. And why, then, did he complain and declare that he was wronged in the case of that dancer because he was led through the midst of the circus to suffer the cross, with his back torn by rods and scourges?

42.[2] And what pollution or abomination could have flowed from this, either to make the circus less pure, or to defile Jupiter, seeing that in a few moments, in *a few* seconds, he beheld so many thousands throughout the world perish by different kinds of death, and with various forms of torture? He was led across, says *my opponent,* before the games began to be celebrated. If from a sacrilegious spirit and contempt[3] for religion, we have reason to excuse Jupiter for being indignant that he was contemned, and that more anxious care was not given to his games. But if from mistake or accident that secret fault was not observed and known, would it not have been right and befitting Jupiter to pardon human failings, and grant forgiveness to the blindness of ignorance? But it was necessary that it should be punished. And after this, will any one believe that he was a god who avenged and punished neglect of a childish show by the destruction of a state? that he had any seriousness and dignity, or any steady constancy, who, that he might speedily enjoy pleasure afresh, turned the air men breathed[4] into a baneful poison, and ordered the destruction of mortals by plague

and pestilence? If the magistrate who presided over the games was too careless in learning who on that day had been led across the circus, and blame was therefore contracted, what had the unhappy people done that they should in their own persons suffer the penalty of another's offences, and should be forced to hurry out of life by contagious pestilences? Nay, what had the women, whose weakness did not allow them to take part in public business, the grown-up[5] maidens, the little boys, finally the young children, yet dependent for food on their nurses, — what had these done that they should be assailed with equal, with the same severity, and that before *they tasted* the joy of life[6] they should feel the bitterness of death?

43.[7] If Jupiter sought to have his games celebrated, and that afresh,[8] with greater care ; if he honestly *sought* to restore[9] the people to health, and that the evil which he had caused should go no further and not be increased, would it not have been better that he should come to the consul himself, to some one of the public priests, the *pontifex maximus,* or to his own *flamen Dialis,* and in a vision reveal to him the defect *in the games* occasioned by the dancer, and the cause of the sadness of the times? What reason had there been that he should choose, to announce his wishes and procure the satisfaction desired, a man accustomed to *live in* the country, unknown from the obscurity of his name, not acquainted with city matters, *and* perhaps not knowing what a dancer is? And if he indeed knew, *as he must have known* if he was a diviner,[10] that this fellow would refuse to obey, would it not have been more natural and befitting a god, to change the man's mind, and constrain him to be willing to obey, than to try more cruel methods, and vent his rage indiscriminately, without any reason, as robbers do? For if the old rustic, not being quick in entering upon anything, delayed in *doing* what was commanded, being kept back by stronger motives, of what had his unhappy children been guilty, that *Jupiter's* anger and indignation should be turned upon them, and that they should pay for another's offences by being robbed of their lives? And can any man believe that he *is* a god *who is* so unjust, so impious, and who does not observe even the laws of men, among whom it would be held a great crime to punish one for another, and to avenge one man's offences upon others?[11] But, *I am told,* he caused the

---

[1] Lit., "was in the cause of the vicious dancer."
[2] 39 in Orelli.
[3] So all edd., rejecting *s* from MS. *contemptu-s.*
[4] Lit., "draughts of air."

[5] So, by omitting two letters, all edd except 1st and Ursinus, which retain MS. *adult-er-æ* — " adulterous."
[6] Lit., " light."
[7] 40 in Orelli. The MS., 1st edd., and Ursinus want *si.*
[8] Lit., " and restored." [Conf. *Pont. Max.* here named, with vol. iv. p. 74.]
[9] The MS. and Ursinus read *reddere-t* — " if he was to restore; " corrected, as above, by omission of *t.*
[10] i.e., if he is a god. Cf. iii. 20 ; [specially, note 3, p. 469].
[11] Lit., " the necks of."

man himself to be seized by the cruel pestilence. Would it not then have been better, nay rather, juster, if it seemed that this should be done, that dread of punishment should be first excited by the father, who[1] had been the cause of such passion by[2] his disobedient delay, than to do violence to the children, and to consume and destroy innocent persons to make him sorrowful?[3] What, pray, was *the meaning of* this fierceness, this cruelty, which *was* so great that, his offspring being dead, it afterwards terrified the father by his own danger! But if he had chosen to do this long before, that is, in the first place, not only would not the innocent brothers have been cut off, but the indignant purpose of the deity also would have been known. But certainly, *it will be said*, when he had done his duty by announcing the vision, the disease immediately left him, and the man was forthwith restored to health. And what is there to admire in this if he removed[4] the evil which he had himself breathed *into the man*, and vaunted himself with false pretence? But if you weigh the circumstances thoroughly, there was greater cruelty than kindness in his deliverance, for *Jupiter* did not preserve him to the joys of life *who was* miserable and wishing to perish after his children, but to learn his solitariness and the agonies of bereavement.

44.[5] In like manner we might go through the other narratives, and show that in these also, and in expositions of these, *something* far different from what the gods should be is said and declared about them, as in this very *story* which I shall next relate, one or two *only* being added to it, that disgust may not be produced by excess.[6] After certain gods were brought from among nations dwelling beyond the sea, you say, and after temples were built to them, after their altars were heaped with sacrifices, the plaguestricken people grew strong *and* recovered, and the pestilence fled before the soundness of health which arose. What gods, say, I beseech? Æsculapius, you say, the god of health, from Epidaurus, and *now* settled in the island in the middle of the Tiber. If we were disposed to be very scrupulous in dealing with your assertions, we might prove by your own authority that he was by no means divine who had been conceived and born from a woman's womb, who had by yearly stages reached that term of life at

which, as is related in your books, a thunderbolt drove him at once from life and light. But we leave this question : let the son of Coronis be, as you wish, one of the immortals, and possessed of the everlasting blessedness[7] of heaven. From Epidaurus, however, what was brought except an enormous serpent? If we trust the annals, and ascribe to them well-ascertained truth, nothing else, as it has been recorded. What shall we say then? That Æsculapius, whom you extol, an excellent, a venerable god, the giver of health, the averter, preventer, destroyer of sickness, is contained within the form and outline of a serpent, crawling along the earth as worms are wont to do, which spring from mud ; he rubs the ground with his chin and breast, dragging himself in sinuous coils ; and that he may be able to go forward, he draws on the last part of his body by the efforts of the first.

45.[8] And as we read that he used food also, by which bodily existence is kept up, he has a large gullet, that he may gulp down the food sought for with gaping mouth ; he has a belly to receive it, and[9] a place where he may digest the flesh which he has eaten and devoured, that blood may be given to his body, and his strength recruited ;[10] he has also a draught, by which the filth is got rid of, freeing his body from a disagreeable burden. Whenever he changes his place, and prepares to pass from one region to another, he does not as a god fly secretly through the stars of heaven, and stand in a moment where something requires his presence, but, just as a dull animal *of earth*, he seeks a conveyance on which he may be borne ; he avoids the waves of the sea ; and that he may be safe and sound, he goes on board ship along with men ; and that god of the common safety trusts himself to weak planks and to sheets of wood joined together. We do not think that you can prove and show that that serpent was Æsculapius, unless you choose to bring forward this pretext, that you should say that the god changed himself into a snake, in order that he might be able[11] to deceive *men as to* himself, who he was, or to see what men were. But if you say this, the inconsistency of your own statements will show how weak and feeble such a defence is.[12] For if the god shunned being seen by men, he should not have chosen to be seen in the form of a serpent, since in any form whatever he was not to be other than himself, but *always* himself. But if, on the other hand, he had been intent on allowing himself to be seen — he should not have

---

[1] Lit., " the terror of coercion should begin from the father with whom."
[2] Lit., " even," *et.*
[3] Lit., " to his grief "
[4] The MS. reads *rett-ulit*, emended *ret-* — " gave back," i.e., got rid of, by 1st ed. and Ursinus; and *rep-*, as above, by Gelenius and others.
[5] 41 in Orelli. [See Appendix, note 1, p. 539.]
[6] In the MS. and both Roman edd. the section translated on p. 539 is inserted here. Ursinus, however (pp. 210–211), followed by Heraldus (312–313), enclosed it in brackets, and marked it with asterisks. In all other edd. it is either given as an appendix, or wholly rejected.

[7] Lit., " sublimity."
[8] 42 in Orelli.
[9] So the edd., reading *et* for MS. *ut* (according to Crusius).
[10] Lit., " restoration be supplied to his strength."
[11] So Gelenius, merely adding *t* to the MS. *posse*. The passage is, however, very doubtful.
[12] Lit., " how weakly and feeble it is said."

refused to allow men's eyes to look on him [1] — why did he not show himself such as he knew that he was in his own divine power? [2] For this was preferable, and much better, and more befitting his august majesty, than to become a beast, and be changed into the likeness of a terrible animal, and afford room for objections, which cannot be decided, [3] as to whether he was a true god, or something different and far removed from the exalted nature of deity.

46. [4] But, says *my opponent*, if he was not a god, why, after he left the ship, *and* crawled to the island in the Tiber, did he immediately become invisible, and cease to be seen as before? Can we indeed know whether there was anything in the way under cover of which he hid himself, or any opening *in the earth?* Do you declare, say yourselves, what that was, or to what race of beings it should be referred, if your service of certain personages is *in itself* certain. [5] Since the case is thus, and the discussion deals with your deity, and your religion also, it is your part to teach, and yours to show what that was, rather than to wish to hear our opinions and to await our decisions. For we, indeed, what else can we say than that which took place and was seen, which has been handed down in all the narratives, and has been observed by means of the eyes? This, however, undoubtedly we say *was* a *colubra* [6] of very powerful frame and immense length, or, if the name is despicable, *we say it was* a snake, [7] we call it a serpent, [8] or any other name which usage has afforded to us, or the development of language devised. For if it crawled as a serpent, not supporting itself and walking on feet, [9] but resting upon its belly and breast; it, being made of fleshly substance, it *lay* stretched out in [10] slippery length; if it had a head and tail, a back covered with scales, diversified by spots of various colours; if it had a mouth bristling with fangs, and ready to bite, what else can we say than that it was of earthly origin, although of immense and excessive size, although it exceeded in length of body and *greatness* of might that which was slain by Regulus by the assault of his army? But *if* we think otherwise, we subvert [11] and overthrow the truth. It is yours, then, to explain what that

was, or what was its origin, its name, and nature. For how could it have been a god, seeing that it had those things which we have mentioned, which gods should not have if they intend to be gods, and to possess this exalted title? After it crawled to the island in the Tiber, forthwith it was nowhere to be seen, by which it is shown that it was a deity. Can we, then, know whether there was there anything in the way under cover of which it hid itself, [12] or some opening *in the earth*, or some caverns and vaults, caused by huge masses being heaped up irregularly, into which it hurried, evading the gaze of the beholders? For what if it leaped across the river? what if it swam across it? what if it hid itself in the dense forests? It is weak reasoning from this, [13] to suppose that that serpent was a god because with all speed it withdrew itself from the eyes *of the beholders*, since, by the same reasoning, it can be proved, on the other hand, that it was not a god.

47. [14] But if that snake was not a present deity, *says my opponent*, why, after its arrival, was the violence of the plague overcome, and health restored to the Roman people? We, too, on the other hand, bring forward *the question*, If, according to the books of the fates and the responses of the seers, the god Æsculapius was ordered to be invited to the city, that he might cause it to be safe and sound from the contagion of the plague and of pestilential diseases, and came without spurning *the proposal* contemptuously, as you say, changed into the form of serpents, — why has the Roman state been so often afflicted with such disasters, so often at one time and another torn, harassed, and diminished by thousands, through the destruction of its citizens times without number? For since the god is said to have been summoned for this purpose, that he might drive away utterly all the causes by which pestilence was excited, it followed that the state should be safe, and should be always maintained free from pestilential blasts, and unharmed. But yet we see, as was said before, that it has over and over again had seasons made mournful by these diseases, and that the manly vigour of its people has been shattered and weakened by no slight losses. Where, then, was Æsculapius? where that *deliverer* promised by venerable oracles? Why, after temples were built, and shrines reared to him, did he allow a state deserving his favour to be any longer plague-stricken, when he had been summoned for this purpose, that he should cure the diseases which were raging, and not allow anything of the

---

[1] These words, *non debuit oculorum negare conspectui*, should, Orelli thinks, be omitted; and certainly their connection with the rest of the sentence is not very apparent.

[2] Lit., "he was, and such as he had learned that he was, contained in the power of his divinity."

[3] Lit., "to ambiguous contradictions."

[4] 43 in Orelli.

[5] Lit., "if your services of certain persons are certain," i.e., if these facts on which your worship is built are well ascertained.

[6] What species of snake this was, is not known; the Latin is therefore retained, as the sentence insists on the distinction.

[7] *Anguem.*

[8] *Serpentem.*

[9] Lit., "bearing himself on feet, nor unfolding below his own goings."

[10] Lit., "to a."

[11] So Hild. and Oehler, reading *labefac-t-amus* for the MS. *-i-*.

[12] This sentence alone is sufficient to prove that these chapters were never carefully revised by their author, as otherwise so glaring repetitions would certainly have been avoided.

[13] Here the MS. and both Roman edd. insert the last clause, "what . . . forests."

[14] 44 in Orelli.

sort which might be dreaded to steal on *them afterwards?*

48.[1] But some one will perhaps say that the care of such a god has been denied[2] to later and following ages, because the ways in which men now live are impious and objectionable ; that it brought help to our ancestors, on the contrary, because they were blameless and guiltless. Now this might perhaps have been listened to, and said with some reasonableness, either if in ancient times all were good without exception, or if later times produced[3] only wicked people, and no others.[4] But since this is the case that in great peoples, in nations, nay, in all cities even, men have been of mixed[5] natures, wishes, manners, and the good and bad have been able to exist at the same time in former ages, as well as in modern times, it is rather stupid to say that mortals of a later day have not obtained the aid of the deities on account of their wickedness. For if on account of the wicked of later generations the good men of modern times have not been protected, on account of the ancient evil-doers also the good of former times should in like manner not have gained the favour of the deities. But if on account of the good of ancient times the wicked of ancient times were preserved also, the following age, too, should have been protected, although it was faulty, on account of the good of later times. So, then, either that snake gained the reputation of *being* a deliverer while he had been of no service at all, through his being brought *to the city* when the violence of the disease[6] was already weakened and impaired, or the hymns of the fates must be said to have been far from giving[7] true indications, since the remedy given by them is found to have been useful, not to all in succession, but to one age only.

49.[8] But the Great Mother, also, says *my opponent*, being summoned from Phrygian Pessinus in precisely the same way by command of the seers, was a cause of safety and great joy to the people. For, on the one hand, a long-powerful enemy was thrust out from the position he had gained in[9] Italy ; and, on the other, its ancient glory was restored to the city by glorious and illustrious victories, and the boundaries of the empire were extended far and wide, and their rights as freemen were torn from races, states, peoples without number, and the yoke of slavery

imposed on them, and many other things accomplished at home and abroad established the renown and dignity of the race with irresistible power. If the histories tell the truth, and do not insert what is false in their accounts of events, nothing else truly[10] is said to have been brought from Phrygia, sent by King Attalus, than a stone, not large, which could be carried in a man's hand without any pressure — of a dusky and black colour — not smooth, but having little corners standing out, and which to-day we all see put in that image instead of a face, rough and unhewn, giving to the figure a countenance by no means lifelike.[11]

50.[12] What shall we say then? Was Hannibal, that famous Carthaginian, an enemy strong and powerful, before whom the fortunes of Rome trembled in doubt and uncertainty, and its greatness shook — was he driven from Italy by a stone?[13] was he subdued by a stone? was he made fearful, and timid, and unlike himself by a stone? And with regard to Rome's again springing to the height of power and royal supremacy, was nothing done by wisdom, nothing by the strength of men ; and, in returning to its former eminence, was no assistance given by so many and so great leaders by their military skill, or by their acquaintance with affairs? Did the stone give strength to some, feebleness to others? Did it hurl these down from success, raise the fortunes of others *which seemed* hopelessly overthrown? And what man will believe that a stone taken from the earth, having[14] no feeling, of sooty colour and dark[15] body, was the mother of the gods? or who, again, would listen to this, — for this is the only alternative, — that the power[16] of any deity dwelt in pieces of flint, within[17] its mass,[18] and hidden in its veins? And how was the victory procured if there was no deity in the Pessinuntine stone? We may say, by the zeal and valour of the soldiers, by practice, time, wisdom, reason ; we may *say*, by fate also, and the alternating fickleness of fortune. But if the state of affairs was improved, and success and victory were regained, by the stone's assistance, where was the Phrygian mother at the time when the commonwealth was bowed down by the slaughter of so many and so great armies, and was in danger of utter ruin? Why did she not thrust herself before the threatening, the strong *enemy?* Why did she not crush and re-

1 45 in Orelli.
2 Lit., " wanting."
3 The ms., 1st ed., Hild., and Oehler read *gener-ent*, corrected in the rest, as above, *-arent*.
4 Lit., " all wicked and distinguished by no diversity."
5 Lit., " the human race has been mixed in," etc.
6 So all edd., reading *vi morbi*, except Hild., who retains the ms. *vi urbi*, in which case the italics should denote " of the disease," instead of " to the city." The construction, however, seems to make it impossible to adhere to the ms.
7 Lit., " to have erred much from."
8 46 in Orelli.
9 Lit., " from the possession of Italy."

10 So all edd. to Orelli, adding *-em* to the ms. *quid*. [See, concerning Pessinus, p. 492, *supra*.]
11 Lit., " a face too little expressed with imitation."
12 47 in Orelli.
13 Lit., " did a stone drive," etc.
14 Lit., " moved by."
15 So the ms. and edd.; but, on account of the unnecessary repetition, Ursinus proposed to delete *atri*. Unger (*Anal. Propert.*, p. 87) has suggested very happily *arti* — " of confined, i e., small body."
16 *Vim*, suggested by Orelli, and adopted by Hild. and Oehler.
17 Lit., " subjected to."
18 So Hild. and Oehler, reading *moli* for the unintelligible ms. *more*.

pel assaults [1] so terrible before these awful blows fell, by which all the blood was shed, and the life even failed, the vitals being almost exhausted? She had not been brought yet, *says my opponent*, nor asked to show favour. Be it so; [2] but a kind helper never requires to be asked, always offering assistance of his own accord. She was not able, *you say*, to expel the enemy and put him to flight, while still separated from Italy [3] by much sea and land. But to a deity, if really one, [4] nothing whatever is remote, to whom the earth is a point, and by whose nod all things have been established.

51. [5] But suppose that the deity was present in that very stone, as you demand should be believed: and what mortal is there, although he may be credulous and very ready to listen to any fictions you please, who would consider that she either was a goddess at that time, or should be now so spoken of and named, who at one time desires these things, at another requires those, abandons and despises her worshippers, leaves the humbler provinces, and allies herself with more powerful and richer peoples, truly [6]

loves warfare, and wishes to be in the midst of battles, slaughter, death, and blood? If it is characteristic of the gods — if only they are true gods, and those who it is fitting should be named according to the meaning of this word and the power of divinity — to do [7] nothing wickedly, nothing unjustly, to show [7] themselves equally gracious to all men without any partiality, *would* any man *believe* that she was of divine origin, or showed [8] kindness worthy of the gods, who, mixing herself up with the dissensions of men, destroyed the power of some, gave and showed favour to others, bereft some of their liberty, raised others to the height of power, — who, that one state might be pre-eminent, having been born to be the bane of the human race, subjugated the guiltless world?

---

[1] Lit., " so great assaults of war."

[2] So Oehler, adding *-o* to the MS. *est.* The word immediately preceding is in the MS. *pavorem* — " panic," which is of course utterly out of place, and is therefore corrected, as above, *f-* in all edd., except 1st, Ursinus, and Hild.

[3] So — *ab Italia* — Oehler has admirably emended the MS. *habitabilia*.

[4] Lit., " if he is."

[5] 48 in Orelli.

[6] All edd., except Hild. and Oehler, begin a new sentence here, and change the construction, seemingly following the mistake of the 1st ed.

[7] " To do . . . to show; " so the edd., dropping *-nt* from the MS. *facere-nt . . . præbere-nt.*

[8] Lit., " showed." Ursinus and Heraldus supposed that some paragraphs are now wanting which were originally found here. It should be noticed that in the MS. the usual subscription is found denoting the end of a book. " The seventh book of Arnovius (*sic*) ends, the eighth (i.e., *Octavius* of Minucius Felix) begins," so that the present arrangement is not due to the binder, nor clearly to the copyist who wrote these words. Nothing can be more certain than that we do not have these chapters as Arnobius intended to leave them; but there is not the slighest reason to suppose that he actually left them otherwise than as they have come down to us. Remembering this, we may well suppose that we have only the first draught of them. If so, the difficulties vanish, for nothing would be more natural than that, when Arnobius was drawing near the close of his work, the ideas of the conclusion in which the discussion was to be fairly summed up should force themselves upon his attention, and that he should therefore turn aside at once to give them expression roughly, without seeking completeness and elaboration, and should then hastily resume his argument, of course with the intention of afterwards revising and rearranging the whole. We may infer that the re-arrangement was never effected, as there are sufficient proofs that the revision was never accomplished, whatever may have been the reason.

APPENDIX. [1]

WE do not deny that all these things which have been brought forward by you in opposition are contained in the writings of the annalists. For we have ourselves also, according to the measure and capacity of our powers, read these same things, and know that they have been alleged; but the whole discussion hinges upon this: whether these are gods who you assert are furious when displeased, and are soothed by games and sacrifices, or are something far different, and should be separated from the notion even of this, and from its power.

For who, in the first place, thinks or believes that those are gods who are lost in joyful pleasure at theatrical shows [2] and ballets, at horses running to no purpose; who set out from heaven to behold silly and insipid acting, and grieve that they are injured, and that the honours due to them are withheld if the pantomimist halts for a little, or the player, being wearied, rests a little; who declare that the dancer has displeased them if some guilty *fellow* passes through the middle of the circus to suffer the penalty and punishment of his deeds? All which things, if they be sifted thoroughly and without any partiality, will be found to be alien not only to the gods, but to any man of refinement, even if he has not been trained to the utmost gravity and self-control. [3]

---

[1] This section, which is found in the MS. after the first sentence of ch. 44, was retained in the text of both Roman editions, marked off, however, by asterisks in that of Ursinus, but was rejected by Gelenius and later editors as the useless addition of some copyist. Oehler alone has seen that it is not " a collection of words gathered carelessly and thoughtlessly " (Hildebrand), and maintained that we have in it the corrections of Arnobius himself. If the three paragraphs are read carefully, it will be observed that the first is a transposition and reconstruction of the first two sentences of ch. 39; the second a revision of the interrogations in ch. 41, but with the sentence which there precedes placed after them here, whilst the third is made up of the same sentences in a revised and enlarged form. Now this must be regarded as conclusive evidence against the hypothesis that these sentences were originally scribbled carelessly on the margin, and afterwards accidentally incorporated in the text. Cf. p. 532, n. 10.

[2] Lit., " motions."

[3] Lit., " to the heights (*apices*) of gravity and weight," i.e., of that constancy of mind which is not moved by trifles.

For, in the first place, who is there who would suppose that those had been, or believe that they are, gods, who have a nature which tends to[1] mischief and fury, and lay these[2] aside again, being moved by a cup of blood and fumigation with incense; who spend days of festivity, and *find* the liveliest pleasure in theatrical shows[3] and ballets; who set out from heaven to see geldings running in vain, and without any reason, and rejoice that some of them pass *the rest*, that others are passed,[4] rush on, leaning forward, and, with their heads towards the ground, are overturned on their backs with the chariots *to which they are yoked*, are dragged along crip-pled, and limp with broken legs; who declare that the dancer has displeased them if some wicked fellow passes through the middle of the circus to suffer the punishment and penalty of his deeds; who grieve that they are injured, and that the honours due to them are withheld if the pantomimist halts for a little, the player, being wearied, rests a little, that *puer matrimus* happens to fall, stumbling through some[5] unsteadiness? Now, if all these things are considered thoroughly and without any partiality, they are found to be perfectly[6] alien not only to the *character of the* gods, but to that of any man of common sense, even although he has not been trained to zealous pursuit of truth by becoming acquainted with what is rational.[7]

---

[1] Lit., "of hurting and raging."
[2] i.e., evil dispositions.
[3] Lit., "motions."
[4] So the MS., according to Crusius, inserting *transiri*, which is omitted by Hild., either because it is not in the MS., or because he neglected to notice that Orelli's text was deficient. If omitted, we should translate, "that some pass, leaning forward, and rush with their heads towards the ground."

[5] Lit., "of something."
[6] Lit., "far and far."
[7] [For *puer matrimus* (one whose mother is yet living), see p. 486, note 11, *supra*. And for the argument, here recast, turn to cap. 41, p. 534.]

ELUCIDATIONS.

I.

(Note 9, p. 459.)

THIS is a most extraordinary note. The author uses "so to say" (= "as it were") merely to qualify the *figure*, which a pagan might think extravagant. "This is, *as it were*, the door of life:" the expression qualifies the rhetoric, not the Scripture, as such. On the contrary, I should adduce this very passage as an instance of our author's familiarity alike with the spirit and the letter of two most important texts of the Gospel, which he expounds and enforces with an earnest intelligence, and with a spirit truly evangelical.

II.

(Covered with garments, note 7, p. 469.)

A heathen might have retorted, had he known the Scriptures, by asking about the "white robes" of angels, and the raiment of the risen Redeemer; e.g., Rev. i. 13. "Curious and unlearned questions" concerning these matters have been stirred by a certain class of Christians. (See Stier[1] and Olshausen.[2]) But let us not reason from things *terrestrial* as regards things *celestial*: our coarse material fabrics are "shadows of the true." The robes of light are realities, and are conformed to spiritual bodies, as even here a mist may envelop a tree. Because of men's stupid and carnally gross ideas, let it be said of "harps" and "phials," and all like phraseology as to things heavenly, once for all, "it doth not yet appear" what it means; but they intimate *realities* unknown to sense, and "full of glory."

---

[1] *Words of Jesus*, vol. viii. p. 63, trans., ed. Edinburgh, 1858.
[2] *New-Testament Commentary*, Kendrick's trans., vol. iii. p. 120, ed. 1858.

III.

(The eyes of Jupiter, p. 483.)

Arnobius with remorseless vigour smites Jove himself, — the Optimus Maximus of polytheism, — and, as I have said, with the assurance of one who feels that the Church's triumph over "lords many and gods many" is not far distant. The scholar will recall the language of Terence,[1] where the youth, gazing on the obscene picture of Jupiter and Danäe, exclaims, —

> "What! he who shakes high heaven with his thunder
> Act thus, and I, a mannikin, not do the same?
> Yes, do I, and right merrily, forsooth!"

On which the great African Father[2] remarks pithily, "Omnes enim cultores talium deorum, mox ut eos libido perpulerit, magis intuentur *quid Jupiter fecerit,* quam quid docuerit Plato, vel censuerit Cato." And here is not only the secret of the impotence of heathen ethics, but the vindication of the Divine Wisdom in sending the God-Man. Men will resemble that which they worship: law itself is incapable of supplying a sufficient motive. Hence,[3] "what the law could not do, in that it was weak, . . . *God sending His own Son,*" etc. Thus "the foolishness of God is wiser than men," and "the love of Christ constraineth us."

> "Talk they of morals? O Thou bleeding Lamb!
> The grand morality is love of Thee."

The world may sneer at faith, but only they who *believe* can *love;* and who ever loved Christ without copying into his life the *Sermon on the Mount,* and, in some blest degree, the holy example of his Master?

IV.

(For those freed from the bondage of the flesh, p. 488 and note 11.)

The early Christians prayed for the departed, that they might have their consummation in body and spirit *at the last day.* Thus, these prayers for the faithful dead supply the strongest argument against the purgatorial system, which supposes the dead in Christ (1) *not to be in repose* at first, but (2) capable of being delivered out of "purgatory" into heaven, sooner or later, by masses, etc. Thus, their situation in the intermediate state is not that of Scripture (Rev. xiv. 13), nor do they wait for glory, according to Scripture, until that day (2 Tim. iv. 8). Archbishop Usher, therefore, bases a powerful argument against the Romish dogma, on these primitive prayers for the departed. Compare vol. iii. p. 706, and vol. v. p. 222, this series.

He divides it into five heads, as follows : [4] —

"(1) Of the persons for whom, after death, prayers were offered ;

"(2) Of the primary intention of these prayers ;

"(3) Of the place and condition of souls departed ;

"(4) Of the opinion of Aerius, the heretic, touching these prayers ; and

"(5) Of the profit, to the persons prayed for, of these prayers."

And his conclusion is, after a rich collation of testimonies, that "the commemoration and prayers for the dead used by the ancient Church had not any relation with *purgatory,* and therefore, whatsoever they were, Popish prayers we are sure they were not."

---

[1] *Eunuch.*, iii. 5.

[2] August., *De Civitate*, book ii. cap. 7.

[3] Rom. viii. 3-39.

[4] Quoted in *Tracts for the Times* (p. 30), vol. iii., ed. New York, 1840.

V.

(The pine . . . sanctuary of the Great Mother, p. 504.)

I RECALL with interest the pine-cone of Dante's comparison (*Inferno*, canto xxxi. 59) as I saw it in the gardens of the Vatican. Valuable notes may be found in Longfellow's translation, vol. i. p. 328. It is eleven feet high, and once adorned the summit of Hadrian's mausoleum, so they say; but that was open, and had no apex on which it could be placed. It is made of bronze, and, I think, belonged to the mysteries satirized by our author. It is less pardonable to find the vilest relics of mythology on the very doors of St. Peter's, where I have seen them with astonishment. They were put there, according to M. Valery,[1] under Paul V.; "and among the small mythological groups," he adds, "may be distinguished *Jupiter and Leda*, the *Rape of Ganymede*, some nymphs and satyrs, with other very singular devices for the entrance of the most imposing of *Christian* temples." It is painful to think of it; but the heathenism to which the age of Leo X. had reduced the court of Rome must be contrasted with the ideas of a Clement, an Athenagoras, and even of an Arnobius, in order to give us a due sense of the *crisis* which, after so many appeals for a reformation "in the head and the members" of the Latin communion, brought on the irrepressible revolt of Northern Europe against the papacy.

VI.

(Sacrifices, p. 519.)

It must be felt that Arnobius here lays himself open to a severe retort. The God of Christians is the author of sacrifice, and accepts the unspeakable sufferings of the innocent Lamb for the sins of the whole world.

The answer, indeed, suggests itself, that the sacrifices of the heathen had no apparent relation whatever *to faith* in this Atoning Lamb; none in the mysterious will of God that this faith should be nurtured before the Advent by an institution *in which He had no pleasure*, but which was *profoundly harmonious with human thought* and the self-consciousness of human guilt.

Arnobius would have written better had he been a better-instructed Christian. He demolishes pagan rites, but he should have called up the Gentile mind to the truths covered under its corruptions and superstitions. On this subject the reader will do well to consult the work of a modern Arnobius, the eccentric Soame Jenyns, who called out such a controversy in the last century about the truths and errors of his *View of the Internal Evidence of the Christian Religion*,[2] to which he had become a convert from previous scepticism. This essay attracted the attention of the Count. (Joseph) de Maistre, who read it in the French translations of MM. le Tourneur and de Feller both, reflected it in his *Considérations sur la France*,[3] and reproduced some of its admirable thoughts in the *Soirées de St. Pétersbourg*.[4] From these two striking writers, the one an Anglican and the other a rabid Ultramontane, I must permit myself to condense an outline of their views of sacrifice.

So long as we know nothing of the origin of evil, we are not competent judges of what is or is not a suitable remedy. Nobody can assure us that the sufferings of one may not be in some way *necessary* to the good of the many. A tax may thus be laid upon innocence in behalf of the guilty, and a *voluntary* sacrifice may be accepted from the Innocent (the Holy One) for the payment of the debts of others. In spite of something illogical which seems to cling to this idea, the fact of *its universal adoption in all ages* among men must be accounted for, — the fact

[1] He was royal librarian at Versailles under Charles X. See his *Travels in Italy* (Clifton's trans.), p. 501, ed. Paris, 1842.
[2] It appeared in Paris 1764. A more literal translation (by the Abbé de Feller) was published, Liege, 1779.
[3] Published in 1794.
[4] *Works*, vol. vi. p. 140, ed. Paris, 1850.

that all nations have always accepted this principle of expiatory sacrifice, innocent men and innocent beasts suffering for the unjust. Never could this principle have been thus universalized by human wisdom, for it seems to contradict reason ; nor by human stupidity, for ignorance never could have proposed such a paradox ; nor could priestcraft and kingcraft have obtained for it, among divers races and forms of society, with barbarians and philosophers, freemen and slaves, alike, a common acceptance. It must therefore proceed (1) from a natural instinct of humanity, or (2) from a divine revelation : both alike must be recognised as the work of our Creator. Now, Christianity unveils the secret, presenting the Son of God, made man, a voluntary sacrifice for the sins of the whole world. If it be a mystery, still we do not wonder at the idea when we see one man paying the debts of another, and so ransoming the debtor.[1] Christianity states this as God's plan for the ransom of sinners. Such is the fact : as to the *why*, it says nothing.[2] As to the philosophy of these mysteries, we reason in vain ; and, happily, the Gospel does not require us to reason. The Nicene Creed formulates the truth : " For us men and for our salvation He came down," etc. But we are called to profess no more than " I believe ; help Thou mine unbelief."

De Maistre responds as follows : This dogma is universal, and as old as creation ; viz., *the reversibility of the sufferings of innocence* for *the benefit of the guilty*. As to the fall of man, " earth felt the wound ; "[3] " the whole creation groaneth and travaileth[4] in pain together." In this condition of things the human heart and mind have universally acquiesced in the idea of expiation.[5] . . . And as well the Gentile sacrifices (corrupted from Noah's pure original) as those which were perpetuated in their purity by the Hebrews *on one spot,* and looking to their only explanation in the coming of *one* Redeemer, bear witness to the Wisdom which framed the human mind and adapted its ordinances thereto with profound and divine comprehension of all human wants and all human capabilities. When the infinite Victim exclaimed upon the cross, " IT IS FINISHED," the veil was rent, the grand secret was unfolded. For this event, God had prepared all mankind by the system of sacrifice which, even in its corruption, had made preparation for the true elucidation.

In a word, then, Arnobius should have said this, as the Church was always saying it in the perpetual commemoration of Calvary, in her Holy Eucharist, and in her annual Paschal celebration. It was all summed up by the prophet a thousand years before " the Lamb of God " was slain. By the prophet, the Lamb Himself expounds it all : [6] —

" Sacrifice and meat-offering *Thou wouldest not,* but mine ears hast Thou opened : burnt-offerings and sacrifice for sin *hast Thou not required.* Then said I, Lo, I COME : in the volume of the Book *it is written* of ME, that I should fulfil Thy will, O my God. I *am content to do it;* yea, Thy law is within my heart."

The expiatory sacrifice, the voluntary Victim, the profound design of God the Father, are all here. But the infinite value of the sacrifice was unfolded when the Son of man was identified by the poor Gentile centurion : " Truly this was the Son of God."

---

[1] De Maistre quotes, " Potest unus ita pro alio pœnam compensare vel debitum solvere ut ille *satisfacere* merito dici possit." Bellarmin, *Opp.*, tom. iii. col. 1493, ed. Ingolstadt, 1601.

[2] See Jenyns, p. 67 (ed. eighth), Philadelphia, 1780.

[3] Milton, *Paradise Lost,* ix. 785.

[4] Rom. viii. 19.

[5] Plato, *Repub., Opp.,* tom. vi. pp. 225–226, ed. Bipont.

[6] De Maistre cites the example of Decius from Livy, vol. i. p. 477, *Piaculum deorum iræ,* etc.; and I commend the inquiring reader to his very curious and entertaining *Éclaircissement sur les Sacrifices,* pp. 321–425, *ubi supra,* appended to the same work. Let me also add a reference to the other Decius, vol. i. p. 607. See lib. viii. cap. 9, and lib. x. cap. 28. My edition is the valuable (Parisian) Frousheim & Crevier, A.D. 1735.

GREGORY THAUMATURGUS, DIONYSIUS OF ALEXANDRIA, AND JULIUS AFRICANUS.

INDEX OF SUBJECTS

GREGORY THAUMATURGUS, DIONYSIUS OF ALEXANDRIA, AND JULIUS AFRICANUS.

INDEX OF TEXTS.

ANATOLIUS AND MINOR WRITERS, ARCHELAUS, ALEXANDER OF LYCOPOLIS, PETER OF ALEXANDRIA, ALEXANDER OF ALEXANDRIA.

INDEX OF SUBJECTS

ANATOLIUS AND MINOR WRITERS, ARCHELAUS, ALEXANDER OF LYCOPOLIS, PETER OF ALEXANDRIA, ALEXANDER OF ALEXANDRIA.

INDEX OF TEXTS

METHODIUS

INDEX OF SUBJECTS

METHODIUS

INDEX OF TEXTS

ARNOBIUS

ANALYSIS OF CONTENTS

BOOK I. . . . . . . pp. 413-432

ARGUMENT.— The enemies of Christianity were wont to say that, since its appearance on earth, the gods had shown their hatred of it by sending upon men all manner of calamities, and that, owing to the neglect of sacred rites, the divine care no longer guarded the world. Arnobius begins by showing how baseless this opinion is (1), for the laws and course of nature remain unchanged (2); and though the heathen said that since Christianity came into the world there had been wars, famines, pestilences, and many other similar calamities, these were not new evils, for history tells of terrible misery and destruction resulting from such causes in past ages (3-5); while it should also be noticed, that through the gentle and peaceful spirit of Christianity, the world is already relieved in part, and that war would be unknown, and men live peacefully together, if it prevailed universally (6). If asked, What *are*, then, the causes of human misery? Arnobius answers that this is no part of his subject (7), but suggests that all evil results necessarily from the very nature of things, — is, indeed, perhaps not evil at all, but, however opposed to the pleasures or even interests of individuals, tends to general good (8-11); and that it is therefore somewhat presumptuous in man, a creature so ignorant of himself, to seek to impose conditions on the superior powers (12). He further shows the futility of blaming the Christians for all these ills, by reminding his opponents that there had been no unvarying series of calamities since Christianity came to earth, but that success had counterbalanced defeat, and abundance scarcity; so that arguments such as these would prove that the gods were angry at times, at times forgot their anger (13-16). But, Arnobius asks, if the gods can be enraged, does not this argue mortality and imperfection in them (17, 18), and even injustice (19), or weakness, if they need the aid of men in punishing their enemies (20)? As, however, all alike suffer, it is absurd to say that Christians are specially aimed at; and, indeed, this is a cry raised by those interested in upholding the superstitious rites of antiquity (21-24). But assuming that the gods could be enraged, why should they be angry at Christians more than others? Because, the heathen said, Christianity introduced new and impious forms of religion. In reply to this, Arnobius points out that Christians are nothing but worshippers of the Supreme God, under Christ's teaching and guidance (25-27); and shows how absurd it is to accuse those of impiety who worship the Creator and Supreme Ruler, while those who serve the lesser gods — even foul and loathsome deities — are called religious (28-30); and then turns to God Himself, beseeching pardon for these ignorant worshippers of His creatures, who had neglected Himself (31). He merely notices but refuses to discuss the position of those who deny that God exists, holding it impious even to reason about this, as though it were questionable, while there is an instinctive belief and reverence implanted in our breasts (31-33). But, his opponents said, we worship Jupiter as the supreme God. Jupiter, however, Arnobius points out, cannot claim this rank, for he is admittedly not self-existent (34); or if, as some said, Jupiter is only another name for the Supreme Being, then, as all alike worship Him, all must be regarded by Him alike (35). But, his opponents urged, you are guilty not in worshipping God, but in worshipping a mere man who died on the cross; to which Arnobius replies, in the first place, by retorting the charge as bearing much more forcibly on the heathen themselves (36, 37); and then argues that Christ has sufficiently vindicated His claims to divinity by leading the blind and erring and lost into the ways of truth and salvation, and by His revelation of things previously unknown (38, 39); while, again, His death on the cross does not affect His teaching and miracles, any more than the loss of life deprived of fame Pythagoras, Socrates, Aquilius, Trebonius, or Regulus (40), and contrasts favourably with the stories told about Bacchus, Æsculapius, Hercules, Attis, and Romulus (41); and, finally, asserts Christ's divinity as proved by His miracles (42), which are compared with those of the Magi both as to their end and the manner in which they were wrought (43, 44); and the chief features of the miracles of His life on earth and His resurrection, of the power of His name, and the spread of His Church are summarily noticed (45-47). Arnobius next remarks that the heathen did not even pretend that their gods had healed the sick without using medicines, merely by a word or touch, as Christ did (48); and, recalling the thousands who had in vain sought divine aid at temple or shrine, says that Christ sent none away unhelped (49), and that He gave this same power to His followers also (50), which neither priest nor magician is found to possess (51, 52). His divinity was shown also by the wonders which attended His death (53). Eye-witnesses — and these most trustworthy — testified to Christ's miracles (54); and the acceptance by the whole world, in so short a time, of His religion, attests its truth (55). It might be said, however, that the Christian writers were not trustworthy, and exaggerated the number and importance of Christ's miracles (56): in reply to which, Arnobius shows that their writings rest on as good authority as those

556

of the heathen (57), and that their greater novelty and literary rudeness are in their favour rather than otherwise, and are certainly of no weight against them (57–59). But, said the heathen, if Christ was God, why did He live and die as a man ? Because, it is replied, God's own nature could not be made manifest to men (60), and His reasons for choosing so to manifest Himself, and not otherwise, though they may be within our reach, are certainly concealed in much obscurity (61) ; while as to Christ's death, that was but the dissolution of His human frame (62). Hurrying, it would seem, to conclude this part of the discussion, Arnobius hastily points out the great powers which Christ might have wielded in His own defence, if He had refused to submit to the violence offered Him, which however were unused, because He rather chose to do for His disciples all that He had led them to look for (63). If, then, kings and tyrants and others who lived most wickedly, are honoured and deified, why should Christ, even if He asserted falsely that He was a heaven-sent Saviour, be so hated and assailed (64) ? If one came from distant and unknown regions, promising to deliver all from bodily sickness, how gladly would men flock to do him honour, and strive for his favour ! How extraordinary, then, is the conduct of those who revile and abuse, and would destroy, if they could, Him who has come to deliver us from spiritual evils, and work out our salvation (65) !

BOOK II. . . . . . . pp. 433–463

ARGUMENT.— The question is again asked, Why is Christ so bitterly hated, while it cannot be said that He ever injured any one (1) ? Because, an opponent is supposed to reply, He drove religion from the earth by withholding men from worshipping the gods. In this, however, it is shown that He did not assail, but built up religion, as He taught men to worship the creator and source of all things, God Supreme, the worship of whom is surely the truest religion (2, 3). It is declared to be mere folly in the heathen to disbelieve Christ's message, for the future alone can prove or disprove the truth of what is foretold ; but when there are the two prospects, that if Christ's words are false, His followers lose nothing more than others, but that, on the other hand, if He spoke truly, those who refuse to believe in Him suffer an infinite loss, it is more rational to choose the course which tends to no evil and may lead to blessing, rather than that which it is certain leads to no good, and may bring us to terrible woe (4, 5). Is the truth of Christianity not manifested, he goes on to ask, in the readiness with which it has been received by men of every class in all parts of the world, and by the noble constancy with which so many have endured suffering even to death, rather than abandon or dishonour it (5) ? And if, as was often the case, any one should say that there were indeed many who received Christ's Gospel, but that these were silly and stupid people, Arnobius reminds him that learning and grammatical knowledge alone do not fit a man to decide between truth and falsehood, to say what may and what cannot take place (6) ; and this is shown by the uncertainty and confusion which surround even those matters which force themselves on our notice every day, such as the nature and origin of man, the end of his being, the mode in which he was quickened into life, and many other similar questions (7). Moreover, the heathen laughed at the faith of the Christians ; but in doing so, Arnobius asks, did they not expose themselves to ridicule ? For does not the whole conduct of life depend on

the belief that the end will correspond to our aims and actions (8) ? Again, most men put faith in one or other of the leading philosophers (9) ; and these, in turn, trust their own fancies, and put faith in their own theories, so that faith is common to all men alike (10). And if the heathen put faith in the philosophers, the Christians have no less reason to put faith in Christ ; while, if a comparison be entered into, no other can point to such wonderful powers and such marvellous deeds as are recorded of Him (11). Not by such subtle quibbling as men brought against it did the new religion make its way, but by the marvellous and unheard-of miracles which attested its truth, so that it won followers among all tribes on the face of the earth ; and if any man was ignorant of these facts, it was because he had not chosen to know them, and had suffered the truth to be obscured by those interested in upholding error (12). Arnobius goes on to show that many Christian doctrines which were ridiculed as such by the heathen, were held by the philosophers also ; referring more particularly to the worship of one God, the resurrection of the dead (13), and the quenchless fires of punishment, from which he takes occasion to point out that man's true death comes not at, but after the soul's separation from the body, and to discuss the nature of the soul (14). The soul is not, he maintains, immortal in itself, or of divine origin — if it were born of God, men would be pure and holy, and of one opinion (15) — but has been made vicious and sinful by causes to be found in the world ; while, if it had been made by the Supreme God, how could His work have been marred by that which was less powerful (16) ? Arnobius next endeavours to show that we are in nothing distinguished from the brutes : so far as body, the maintenance of life, and the reproduction of the race are concerned, we are found to be alike, while the heathen are reminded of the doctrine of the transmigration of souls (16) ; and if stress is laid on man's reason and intelligence as a distinctive characteristic, it is first suggested that all men do not act rationally, and the question is then asked, What is the reason which man possesses, and not the beasts (17) ? Man's practical skill is no proof of superior reason, for its exercise is necessitated by his excessive poverty ; and it is, moreover, not a faculty native in the soul, but one acquired only after long years under the pressure of necessity (18). The arts, grammar, music, oratory, and geometry are similarly noticed, and the doctrine of reminiscence rejected (19). Arnobius next supposes a boy to be brought up wholly apart from human society, and seeks to establish his position by the supposed results of imaginary questions put to this hypothetical being (20–23) ; and then goes on to attack the contrary opinions which Plato had sought to establish in a somewhat similar way, by challenging him to question the boy just imagined, who is, of course, found to be exactly what was intended (24) ; and thus gives his creator a triumph, by showing *conclusively* that man untaught is ignorant as a stock or stone, while on being taught other creatures can learn also — the ox and ass to grind and plough, the horse to run in harness, and the like (25). Pursuing the same subject, it is argued that if the soul loses its former knowledge on uniting with the body, it cannot be incorporeal, and cannot therefore be immortal (26, 27) ; and further, that if the soul's former knowledge were lost through the influence of the body, the knowledge acquired in this life should in like manner be lost (28). Those who assert the soul's immortality are accused of teaching that which will add to the wickedness of men : for how shall any one be restrained even by the fear of a higher power, who is persuaded that his life cannot be cut short by any power (29)? while if he is threatened with the punishments of the infernal regions, he will laugh them to scorn, knowing that what is incorruptible cannot be affected by mere bodily ills. If the soul is immortal, Arnobius affirms there is no need or ground for philosophy, that is, ethics, whose purpose is to raise man above the brutish pleasures of sense to a virtuous life: for why should not a soul which cannot perish give itself up to any pleasures? while if the soul is mortal, philosophy is in precisely the same position, aiming to do for man what will not profit him if done (30). The soul, he concludes, is neither mortal nor immortal (31); and there is therefore good reason that those who have no confidence in their power to help themselves, should welcome a saviour in one more powerful (32, 33). Christians and heathen alike, then, look for the deliverance of their souls from death; and neither party, therefore, has any reason to mock the other in this (33, 34). Such, too, is the condition of all spirits which are supposed to exist (35); and it is only through God's goodness that any spirit becomes immortal (36). It is next argued at great length, and with some prolixity, that the soul is not sprung from God, on the ground of its vicious and imperfect nature (37–46); and it is then shown that, in denying the soul's divine origin on this ground, we are acting most reasonably, although we cannot say what its real origin is (47, 48); while if any one attempts to show that the soul is not imperfect and polluted by sin by pointing to good and upright men, he is reminded that the whole race cannot take its character from a few individual members, and that these men were not so naturally (49, 50). There is nothing ridiculous, Arnobius goes on to say, in confessing ignorance of such matters; and the preceding statements are to a certain extent supported by Plato's authority, in so far as he separates the formation of man's soul from the divine acts (51, 52). But if this belief be mistaken, what harm does it do to others (53)? From this there naturally follows a discussion of the origin of evil, the existence of which cannot be denied, though its cause is beyond our knowledge; it is enough to know that all God does is good (54, 55). How idle a task it would be to attempt the solution of such problems, is seen when we consider how diverse are the results already arrived at, and that each is supported on plausible grounds (56, 57); which clearly shows that man's curiosity cannot be certainly satisfied, and that one man cannot hope to win general assent to his opinions (57). Arnobius now proposes to his opponents a series of questions as to men and things, after answering which they may with more reason taunt him with his ignorance of the soul's origin (58, 59); and says that, because of the vanity of all these inquiries, Christ had commanded them to be laid aside, and men to strive after the knowledge of God (60), and the deliverance of their souls from the evils which otherwise await them (61), — a task to be accomplished only through the aid of Him who is all-powerful (62). The condition of those who lived before Christ came to earth is to be learned from His teaching (63); and His bounty extends to all, though all do not accept it (64); for to compel those who turn to Him who *will* not come, would be to use violence, not to show mercy (65). No purity therefore, or holiness, can save the man who refuses to accept Christ as his Saviour (66). Arnobius next deals with the objection that Christianity is a thing of yesterday, for which it would be absurd to give up the more ancient religions, by asking if it is thus that we look upon the various improvements which have been suggested from time to time by the increase of

knowledge and wisdom (66–68). All things, moreover, have had a beginning — philosophy, medicine, music, and the rest (69), even the gods themselves (70); but all this is wholly beside the mark, for the truth of a religion depends not on its age, but on its divine origin. And if, a few hundred years before, there was no Christianity, the gods were in like manner unknown at a still earlier period (71). But Christianity worships that which was before all, the eternal God, although late in its worship, because there was not the needed revelation sooner (72). Arnobius again asserts that Christianity does not stand alone, for it was at a comparatively late time that the worship of Serapis and Isis, and of others, was introduced; and so Christianity too had sprung up but lately, because it was only then that its teacher had appeared (73): and having considered why Christ was so late in appearing among men (74, 75), and why Christians are allowed to undergo such suffering and trial on earth (76, 77), he earnestly exhorts all to see to the safety of their souls, and flee for salvation to God, seeing that such terrible dangers threaten us, lest the last day come upon us, and we be found in the jaws of death (78).

BOOK III. . . . . . . pp. 464–475

ARGUMENT. — In the two preceding books, Arnobius endeavoured to repel the objections raised against Christianity; but already, he says, it had found able defenders, though strong enough in its own might to need none (1); and therefore, having replied to the charge of neglecting the worship of the gods, by asserting that in worshipping the Supreme God, the Creator of the universe, any other gods, if there are such, receive honour, inasmuch as they are sprung from Him (2, 3), he goes on to attack heathenism itself, pointing out that the other gods cannot be proved to exist, their names and number being alike unknown (4, 5). These gods, moreover, are spoken of as male and female, but the divine cannot be liable to such distinctions, as Cicero showed (6); whom it would be well, therefore, for the heathen to refute, instead of merely raising an unreasoning clamour against his writings (7). The use by Christians of a masculine term to denote the Deity, is merely a necessity of speech; but the heathen expressly attributed sex to their deities (8), who would therefore, being immortal, be innumerable; or if the gods did not beget children, why had they sex (9)? Arnobius then inveighs against this opinion as degrading and dishonouring the gods (10), and says that it is far more likely that they would afflict men to punish such insults, than to take vengeance on Christians, who did them no dishonour (11). He then goes on to speak of bodily form, denying that it is attributed to the Deity by Christians (12), while the heathen boldly asserted that their gods had *human* bodies, which, Arnobius shows, makes it necessary to ascribe to some gods the basest offices (13–15). It might, however, be said that the gods were not really supposed to have such bodies, but were so spoken of out of respect. This, Arnobius shows, is not honouring, but insulting, them as much as possible (16). If the Deity has any mortal shape, we do not know it (17); He may hear, see, and speak in His own, but not in our way (18); and it is unbecoming to ascribe even our virtues to God, — we can only say that His nature cannot be declared by man (19).

The offices ascribed to the gods are next derisively commented on (20, 21); and as to the suggestion that the gods impart a knowledge of the arts over which they preside, without being practically acquainted with them, it is asked why the gods should seek this knowledge, when they had no opportunity of turning it to account (22). It might, however, be said that it belonged to the gods to secure a prosperous issue to human undertakings. Why, then, failure, ruin, and destruction (23)? Because, it would be answered, of neglected rites, and sacrifices withheld. Is, then, Arnobius asks, the favour of the gods to be purchased? is it not theirs to give to those utterly destitute (24)? Unxia, Cinxia, Vita, and Potua are held up as foul parodies on Deity (25). Mars and Venus being taken as fair examples (26, 27), the conclusion is reached, that such gods, presiding over lust, discord, and war, cannot be believed in (28). The inconsistent and mutually destructive opinions entertained with regard to Janus, Saturn (29), Jupiter, Juno (30), and other gods, render belief in them impossible (31–34); while if, as some believe, the world is a living being, the deities cannot exist which are said to be parts of it, as the sun, moon, etc., for the whole will have life, not its members (35). Thus the heathen plainly subvert all faith in their religion, however zealous against Christian innovations (36). They do so still further, by the ridiculous inconsistency of their opinions as to the origin and numbers of their gods, in particular of the Muses (37, 38); the Novensiles (38, 39); the Penates (40); and the Lares (41).

Arnobius, having thus shown that the heathen are in doubt and ignorance as to all their gods, a circumstance giving rise to confusion in seeking to celebrate their rites (42, 43), calls upon them to decide on their creed, and abide by it (44).

BOOK IV. . . . . . . pp. 476–488

ARGUMENT. — Arnobius now attacks the heathen mythology, pointing out that such deities as Piety, Concord, Safety, and the like, could only be mere abstractions (1, 2); while, as to many others, it would be difficult to suppose — especially when facts are compared with theories — that they were seriously spoken of as deities, e.g., Luperca, Præstana, Pantica (3), and Pellonia (4); the sinister deities (5); Laterranus, a god degraded to the kitchen (6); and others to whom were assigned obscene and trifling offices (7); and asking whether the existence of these deities depended on the things for which they cared, or the performance of the offices over which they were set, and how, if they were first in the order of existence, they could be named from things which did not then exist, and how their names were known (8). Common-sense will not allow us to believe in gods of Gain, Lust, Money, and the rest (9); and besides, we could not stop here, for if there were gods to preside over bones, honey, thresholds, we should find it impossible to deny that everywhere and for everything there are special gods (10). What proof, it is asked, do the gods give of their existence? do they appear when invoked (11)? do they give true oracles (11)? how were they made known to men, and how could it be certain that some one did not take the place of all those supposed to be present at different rites (12)? Arnobius next goes on to point out that several deities were spoken of under one name, while, on the contrary, several names were sometimes applied to one deity (13); e.g., there were three Jupiters, five Suns and Mercuries, five Minervas (14), four Vulcans, three Dianas and Æsculapii, six called Hercules, and four called Venus, and others, in like manner, from which would arise much confusion (15); for if Minerva were invoked, the five might be supposed to appear, each claiming the honour of deity as her own, in which case the position of

the worshipper would be one of danger and perplexity (16). The others might be similarly referred to, and this alone would make it impossible to believe in these deities (17). And if it should be said that these writings are false, it might be answered that it is only of such published statements that notice could be taken; and that, if they were discredited, this fact should be made evident; and, finally, that from them all the religious ideas of the heathen were drawn(18). In saying that a god was sprung from such a father and mother, the thought might have suggested itself, that in this there was something human, something not befitting deity (19); but, so far from this, they had added everything degrading and horrible (20). Jupiter had such an origin, they said, and the Thunderer was once a helpless infant tended by his nurse (21); and — which was even more degrading and unseemly — in turn he, too, was subject to lust and passion, even descending to intercourse with mortals (22, 23). Here, Arnobius says, would be found the cause of all the miseries of which they complained, and these, therefore, were to be laid to the account, not of the Christians, but of the heathen, for it was they who devised such hideous, absurd, and blasphemous tales about the deities, which are either utterly false, or conclusively disprove the existence of such gods (24–28). Here it might have been shown that all the gods were originally men, by referring to various historians (29); but this is not done, because the purpose of Arnobius was merely to show that it was the heathen, not the Christians, who did the gods dishonour. True worship is not ritual observance, but right thoughts; and therefore the resentment of the gods would be excited rather by the infamous tales of the heathen, than by the neglect of the Christians (30, 31); and whoever might have invented them, the great body of the people were to blame, in that they allowed it to be done, and even took pleasure in reading or hearing such stories, although they had secured not merely the great, but even private persons from libels and calumnies by the strictest laws (32–34). But not merely did they suffer things to be written with impunity which dishonoured the gods, similar plays were also acted on the stage (35); and in these the gods were even made a laughing-stock, to the great delight of crowded audiences (35, 36). And yet, though they were so open and unblushing in the insults which they offered the gods, they did not hesitate to accuse the Christians of impiety, who were not guilty in this respect at all (37). If, therefore, the gods are angry, it is not because of the Christians, but because of their own worshippers (38).

BOOK V. . . . . . . pp. 489–505

ARGUMENT. — It might be said that these charges were founded by Arnobius on the writings of poets and actions of stage-players, and that the heathen generally could not therefore be held guilty. Such a defence, however, would not avail those who in their histories and religious rites were not less impious and insulting to the deities. Arnobius proceeds, therefore, to narrate the story, told by Antias, of Jupiter's being tricked by Numa (1), and criticises it minutely, showing the manifest absurdity and impiety of representing man as overcoming and deluding the gods (2–4). He next relates from Timotheus the origin of Acdestis (5); the base and degrading expedients which the gods were compelled to adopt in order that they might rid themselves of his audacity; and the extraordinary birth (6) and death of Attis, and institution of the rites of the Great Mother in memory of him (7). This story also is criticised at great length, its absurdity, indecency, and silliness being brought prominently forward (8-14); while it is pointed out that the truth or falsehood of the story is of no consequence to the argument, as all that Arnobius wishes to prove is, that any deities which exist are more grossly insulted by their own worshippers than by Christians (15). But, he says, how can you maintain that this story is false, when the ceremonies you are ever observing always refer to the events of which it speaks (16, 17)?

Neglecting many similar stories as too numerous to be related, he merely mentions Fenta Fauna, the birth of Servius Tullius (18), the Omophagia, rites of Venus, Corybantia, and the Bacchanalia which relate the dismembering of Bacchus (19). The story is next related of Jupiter's amours with Ceres as a bull, and with Proserpine as a serpent (20, 21), in which, Arnobius says, it might be thought that it was wished to make Jupiter an embodiment of all the vices (22); and then notes, with bitter irony, how the Supreme Ruler is belittled by their trivial and degrading tales (23). Passing now to the other deities, Arnobius narrates the wanderings of Ceres, and the origin, in consequence, of the Thesmophoria and Eleusinia (24-27). So, too, the obscene Alimontia are shown to have an origin as shameful (28); and Arnobius indignantly asks, whether such a tale does not strike at the foundation of all morality? and whether Christians are to be forced, by fear of torment and death, to worship such deities (29), for disbelief in whom he cannot but wonder that men are called atheists (30)? Since, then, it is the heathen who so insult their own deities, the wrath of the gods must be against their worshippers, not against Christians (31).

The suggestion that these stories are allegories (32) he scouts as utterly absurd, pointing out the impossibilty of finding any meaning in some parts of the fables, insisting that as every detail is not allegorical, no part can be, and supposing that he thus shows that these must be accounts of actual events (33-39). If, however, these tales are allegories, do they not, Arnobius asks, do the gods wrong by imputing to them as crimes what are merely natural phenomena (40)? that is, do they not turn into obscenity that which is pure and honourable in itself, while allegory is rather used to hide under a cloak of decency what is indecent (41)? There is but one other pretext, that the gods themselves would have their mysteries made allegories, not choosing that they should be generally understood. But how was this ascertained? and why would they not allow the truth to be told, against which no objection could be taken, preferring indecent and shameful allegory (42)? These explanations, then, are merely attempts to get rid of difficulties (43); attempts, too, which could not be very successful, for many shameful tales do not admit of explanation as allegories (44). What remarkable modesty is this, to blush at the mention of bread and wine, and fearlessly to say "Venus" for a shameful act! (45.)

BOOK VI. . . . . . pp. 506-517

ARGUMENT. — Having shown how impious were the opinions entertained by the heathen about their own gods, Arnobius next meets the charge of impiety made against Christians because they neither built temples, nor set up statues, nor offered sacrifices. This, however, he asserts was not the fruit of impiety, but of nobler beliefs (1). For, admitting that they are gods, they must be free from all im-

perfection, and therefore self-sufficient, not dependent on aid from without, nor afflicted with the desires and passions of mortals. To think thus, he adds, is not to hold the gods in contempt (2). But if they are such, of what use would temples be to them? Is it not sheer madness to think that you honour your superiors when you judge of them by your own necessities? Do the gods need shelter from cold and heat, from rain or storm? And although to men temples may seem magnificent, to the gods of heaven they can be only mean cells (3). But, it might be said, temples are built not to shelter the gods, but that we may address them face to face, as it were. Then, if prayers were offered to the gods under the open heaven, they would not be heard. But the true God must hear prayers wherever offered, nay, must be present even in the silent recesses of the heart, to know what is thought, what is desired, even though it be not expressed, for it is His to fill all things with His power, and not to be present in one place only (4). Otherwise there could be no hope of help; for if prayers were made to one deity from different parts of the earth, while he could be present only in one, then either all would be alike neglected, or one only would be heard and answered (5).

These temples, however, which were said to have been built in honour of the gods, were in reality places of sepulture. Thus Cecrops was buried in the temple of Minerva at Athens, and others, both men and women, in various well-known shrines (6), even the Capitol being only the sepulchre of Olus; and thus the heathens are shown to have been guilty either of worshipping the dead as gods, or of dishonouring the gods by making tombs their temples (7).

As to images, if there are really gods in heaven to whom supplication can be made, why, Arnobius asks, should figures of them be made on earth? and if they are not believed to be in heaven, it is still more difficult to say of what use these images are (8). We worship the gods, the heathen said, by means of their images. Can the gods, therefore, Arnobius asks, receive homage only when offered to statues? What can be more insulting than to believe in a god, and pray to a statue, to hope for aid from a deity, but to ask it from his image (9)? Moreover, how could it be known that those figures were indeed images of the gods? The moon is ever in motion; how could the figure of a woman which never stirred be her likeness? But if the gods were not such as their statues — which no one supposed — what audacity was shown in giving to them whatever figures men pleased (10)! Little occasion had they to laugh at the superstitious worship of rivers, stones, sabres, and pieces of wood by ancient and barbarous peoples, while they themselves prayed to little figures of men. Did they, then, believe that the gods were like men? No, Arnobius says; only they found themselves committed to a false position, and would rather maintain it with violence and cruelty than admit that they were in error (11). Hence it was that such extraordinary forms and equipments were given to the gods. But if the images were secretly removed from their proper places, and the insignia of one given to another, it would be impossible to say which was Jupiter, which Mars. How absurd to form images of the gods, which depend for their individuality on the dresses put upon them (12)! It was a small thing, however, to distinguish the gods by means of reaping-hooks, tridents, horns, or hammers; but it was no light matter that the gods should be fashioned like lewd men and women, and that thus divine honours should be paid to harlots (13). Arnobius next insists that images are but dead matter, moulded, cut, filed, and hewn into form by men; and that it is therefore absurd for a man to worship what he has himself made (14). No one would worship, he says, a mass of metal or a heap of stones, or even fragments of images; but why, while the parts are thus regarded as merely dead matter, should they, when formed into an image, become divine (15). Still men asked blessings from earthenware, copper, and ivory, and supposed that their prayers were heard by senseless figures, forgetting how and from what they were formed; that it was man's skill which gave them all their grandeur, for within them there was only hideous emptiness; and that they were destroyed by time, used as coverts by mean and loathsome creatures, and bemired by birds, the dumb animals thus teaching their master, man, that the images which he worshipped were beneath his notice (16). But, was the reply of the heathen, we worship not the images, but the deities, which are brought into them by their consecration. Do the gods, then, quit heaven to give dignity to what is base? And if so, do they enter these images willingly or unwillingly? If unwillingly, is their majesty not lessened? If willingly, what can they find there to entice them from their starry seats (17)? It is further asked, Do the gods always remain in these images, or come and go at will? If the former, how wretched is their case! If the latter, how is it to be known when the god is in the image so that he should be worshipped, and when he has quitted it so that it may be safely neglected? Moreover, in small figures, do the gods become small? in those represented as sitting, do they sit? and do they thus conform in all respects to their images (18)? But there are either as many gods as statues, or no statue can be tenanted by a god, because one god cannot occupy different images (19). But if the gods dwell in their own images, why do they not themselves defend these, instead of leaving it to dogs and geese and watchers to protect their effigies from fire or thieves (20)? Nay, more, why do they allow themselves to be robbed and insulted by the stripping from their images of what is valuable (21)? It might be said that the gods despised such trifles; but if so, that showed that they despised the images as well. Arnobius then relates the stories of men falling in love with statues of Venus, and asks, where was the goddess, that she did not repel and punish such insulting wantonness, or at least recall the frenzied youths to their senses (22)? If any explanation could be found for this, there was none, however, for the fact that so many temples had been destroyed by fire and spoiled by robbers, without the interference of their presiding deities (23). Finally, if it were said that images had been devised in ancient times to terrify men from their wickedness by the belief that gods were at hand to see and punish their crimes, Arnobius admits that there would be some reason in this, if temples and images caused peace, justice, and purity to prevail on the earth; but points out that this had not been the result, for crime and wickedness abound everywhere; and temples, and even the images which were to force men to be just, are plundered without fear (24). He then asks what power Saturn's sickle, the winged shoes of Mercury, or any of the other insignia of the gods possess, to move men's minds to fear (25); and whether it had ever been thought that men could be frightened by a hideous face, as children by some bugbear. The enactment of laws, however, shows clearly that images or temples have no such power (26).

BOOK VII.   .   .   .   .   pp. 518–540

ARGUMENT. — He proceeds to meet the charge, that Christians are atheists because they offer none

of the usual divine honours to God. The fact he admits, but asserts that in so doing Christians really comply with God's will. To vindicate the Christians from any charge of impiety because they offered no sacrifices, Arnobius quotes Varro's opinion, that the true gods could not wish for these, whilst the images could care for nothing (1). The true gods, though unknown because unseen, must be, so far as their divinity is concerned, exactly alike, so as never to have been begotten, or be dependent on anything external to themselves (2). But if this is the case, on what ground ought sacrifices to be offered — as food for the gods? but whatever needs help from without, must be liable to perish if this is withheld. Moreover, unless the gods feed on the steam and vapour of the sacrifices, it is plain that they receive nothing, as the fire on the altar destroys what is placed on it; whilst, finally, if the gods are incorporeal, it is difficult to see how they can be supported by corporeal substances (3). It might indeed be supposed that the gods took some pleasure in having victims slain to them; but this is exposed to two objections, — that to feel pleasure necessitates the capacity of feeling pain, whilst these two states are becoming only in the weakness of mortals, and require the possession of the senses, which can only accompany a bodily form, from which the gods are supposed to be free; and that, secondly, to feel pleasure in the sufferings of animals, is hardly consistent with the divine character (4). It was commonly held that sacrifices propitiated the deities, and appeased their wrath. Against this Arnobius protests as utterly inconsistent with the view of the divine nature, which he conceives it necessary to maintain so persistently (5). But conceding this point, for the sake of argument, two alternatives are proposed: such sacrifices should be offered either before or after the divine wrath is excited. If the former is chosen, this is to represent the gods as wild beasts to be won from their savageness by throwing to them sops, or that on which to vent their rage; if the latter, without waiting to discuss whether the divine greatness would be offended by a creature so ignorant and unimportant as man (6), or what laws the gods have established on earth by the violation of which they might be enraged (7), it is asked why the death of a pig, a chicken, or an ox should change the disposition of a god, and whether the gods can be bribed into a gracious mood. Moreover, if the divine pardon is not given freely, it would be better to withhold it, as men sin more readily when they believe that they can purchase pardon for themselves (8). A protest is put into the mouth of an ox against the injustice of compelling cattle to pay the penalty of men's offences (9). Arnobius then points out that the doctrine of fate, that all things proceed from causes, and that therefore the course of events cannot be changed, does away with all need to appeal to the gods to render services which are not in their power (10). Finally, the miseries of men are a conclusive proof that the gods cannot avert evil (11), otherwise they are ungrateful in allowing misfortunes to overwhelm their worshippers. A brief *résumé* is given of the preceding arguments, illustrated by the cases of two men, of whom one has but little to give, whilst the other loads the altars with his offerings; and of two nations at war with each other whose gifts are equal, — which show how untenable the hypothesis is, that sacrifices purchase the favour of the gods (12).

Another pretext urged was, that the gods were honoured by the offering of sacrifices. How could this be? Honour consists in something yielded and something received (13). But what could the gods receive from men? how could their greatness be increased by men's actions (14)? The true deities should indeed be honoured by entertaining thoughts worthy of them; but what kind of honour is it to slay animals before them, to offer them blood, and send up wreaths of smoke into the air (15)? Still, if such horrid sights and smells were thought pleasing to the gods, why were certain animals and certain things chosen to be sacrificed, and not others (16)? The absurdity of offering to the gods the food used by us, is shown by supposing that pigs, dogs, asses, swallows, and other birds and beasts, were to sacrifice to men, in like manner, ants, hay, bones, and the filth even which some of them eat (17). It is then asked why to one god bulls were sacrificed, to another kids, to a third sheep; to some white, to others black, to some male, to others female animals (18). The usual answer was, that to the gods male victims, to the goddesses females, were sacrificed, which brings up again the question as to sex amongst the deities. But passing this by, what is there in difference of colour to make the gods pleased or displeased as the victim might be white or black? The gods of heaven, it might be said, delight in cheerful colours, those of Hades in gloomy ones. In the time of Arnobius, however, few believed that there was any such place as Hades; and if this were so, there could be no gods there (19). But conceding this point also, and admitting that to their savage dispositions gloomy colours might be pleasing, Arnobius suggests that only the skins of animals are black, and that therefore the flesh, bones, etc., should not be offered, nor the wine, milk, oil, and other things used in sacrifices which are not black (20). It is next asked why certain animals were sacrificed to certain gods, and not to others; to which the only answer is, that it had been so determined by the men of former times (21). Or if it be suggested that a reason is seen in the sacrificing of fruitful and barren victims to mother earth and the virgin Minerva, such reasoning requires that musicians should be sacrificed to Apollo, physicians to Æsculapius, and orators to Mercury (22). Returning to the argument, that sacrifices should be offered to the gods to win favours from the good, to avert the malice of the bad, Arnobius points out, first, that it is impossible that there should be evil deities; and, secondly, that to suppose that the sacrifices were effectual, is to suppose that by them an evil deity could be changed into a good, and that, through their being withheld, a beneficent deity might become malevolent; which is as absurd as if one were to expect, on caressing a viper or scorpion, that he would escape being stung (23). He proceeds to call attention to various kinds of puddings, cakes, pottages, and other delicacies used in ceremonies, asking with scorn for what end they were employed (24, 25). It is next pointed out, that no reason can be offered for the use of incense, which was certainly unknown in the heroic ages, and unused even in Etruria, the mother of superstition, and could not have been burned on the altar until after the time of Numa. If, therefore, the ancients were not guilty in neglecting to burn incense, it could not be necessary to do so (26). Moreover, of what service was incense to the gods? If they were honoured by its being burned, why should not any gum be so used (27)? If incense is preferred because of its sweet smell, the gods must have noses, and share man's nature. Further, they may not be affected as we are by odours, and what is pleasant to us may be disagreeable to them; and vice versa. But such considerations are inadmissible with regard to the gods, for reason demands

that they should be immaterial, and that therefore they should not be affected by odours (28). Arnobius next shows that the use of wine in ceremonies was as little based on reason as that of incense, for deities cannot be affected by thirst (29); and how could they be honoured with that which excites to vice and impairs man's reason (30)? The formula with which libations were made is ridiculed as niggardly and stingy (31); and the wreaths and garlands worn by the celebrants, and the noise and clangour of their musical instruments, are also turned into mockery (32); whilst it is shown that, to speak of the gods being honoured by the games dedicated to them, is to say that they were honoured by being publicly insulted in the ribald plays which were acted at these times, and by licentious and lustful conduct (33). All these detestable opinions originated in man's inability to understand what the deity really is, and in his therefore attributing to the divine nature what belongs to himself alone (34). In the three chapters which follow, he contrasts the opinions of heathen and Christians as to the divine nature, showing that to the former nothing seemed too bad to be attributed to their gods; while the latter, not professing to worship the gods, insulted them less by not holding such opinions (35-37).

The pestilences and other calamities are next discussed, which were supposed to have been sent by the gods as punishments for sacrifices or other honours withheld from them (38). Thus it was related that, the ludi Circenses having been violated, a pestilence ensued until they were once more celebrated in due form (39). Other pestilences also were got rid of, and enemies overcome, when gods had been brought across the seas and established at Rome; while, on the Capitol's being struck by lightning, evil was averted only by rearing towards the east an image of Jupiter in a higher place (40). But how can the story of the ludi Circenses be believed, which represents Jupiter as delighting in childish amusements, angry without cause, and punishing those who had done no wrong (41, 42), and going so far astray in making choice of a man to declare the cause of his anger (43)? In like manner Arnobius discusses the transportation of Æsculapius, in the form of a serpent, from Epidaurus to the island in the Tiber, after which it was said the people were restored to health (44-46). In reply to the question how it was that the plague ceased if the god did not really come to Rome, Arnobius asks how it was that, if the god did come to Rome, he did not preserve the city from all disease and pestilence thereafter (47); and as to the argument, that this did not happen because in later ages wickedness and impiety prevailed, reminds his opponent that at no epoch was Rome a city of the good and pious (48). So, too, the Great Mother was said to have been brought from Phrygia to enable the Romans to overcome Hannibal. But all that was brought was a stone (49); and are we to suppose that Hannibal was overcome by a stone, and not by the energy, resolution, and courage of the Romans? But if the Great Mother really drove Hannibal from Italy, why did she delay doing so until carried over the seas to Rome (50)? But without insisting on these objections, who will call her a goddess who is perfectly capricious, abandons her worshippers to settle amongst those who are more powerful, and loves to be in the midst of slaughter and bloodshed, whilst the true gods must be perfectly just and equally well disposed to all men (51)?

ARNOBIUS

INDEX OF SUBJECTS

[It has been thought best to include, in this Index to ARNOBIUS, the very full mythological and historical references of the Edinburgh edition, as valuable to students in antiquarian and classical subjects, though less practically necessary as an aid to Christian inquiry.]

Abdera, proverbial for stupidity, 494.

Abusive language, punished by law, 487.

Acantho, mother of the fourth Sun, 480.

Acdestis, birth of, 491; a hermaphrodite, 491; self-mutilated by the craft of Bacchus, 491; love of Attis, 492; fatal consequences of his fury, 492.

Achaia, Christianity attested by miracles in, 438.

Acheron, 439, 500.

Achilles, 485.

Acorns and chestnuts, the food of primitive men, 442, 459.

Acrisius, buried in temple of Minerva at Larissa, 508.

Actæon, the horned hunter, 473.

Actors, freed from taxes, 488.

Admetus, served by Apollo, 484.

Adonis, loved by Proserpine, 485.

Adulterers, punished with death, 483.

Æacus, son of Jupiter, first builder of temples, 507; loved by the Nereid, 485.

Ælius, held that the Novensiles were the Muses, 474.

Æneas, son-in-law of Latinus, 461; son of Venus, 485; deified, 474.

Æsculapius, son of Coronis, 422; killed by lightning, 424, 484; deified because he discovered use of herbs, 423, 424, 474; giver of health, 459, 470; distinguished by his staff, 517; golden beard torn from a statue of, 515; three gods named, 480; vintage festival of, 531; brought to Rome in form of a serpent, 536.

Æther, father of Jupiter, 480; shown not to be a god, 473.

Æthusa, loved by Apollo, 485.

Ætna, torches of Ceres lit at, 499, 503.

Agdus, Mount, 491.

Agesarchus, 509.

Aii Locutii, 420.

Alba, founded by Ascanius, 461; flourished for 400 years, 528; incense unknown in, 528.

Alban Hill, white bulls sacrificed on, 460.

Alcibiades, the Hermæ modelled after, 511.

Alcmena, seduced by Jupiter, 460, 498; mother of the Theban Hercules, 483.

Alcyone, 485 (note).

Alemanni, said to have been overcome because Christians were to be found amongst them, 417.

Alimontian mysteries, 500.

Allegorical explanation of myths, 464, 475; rejected by Arnobius, 475, 476.

Alope, loved by Neptune, 485.

Ambiguity of words, Jupiter ensnared by, 489.

Amphitheatres, places of bloodshed and wickedness, 488.

Amphitrite, loved by Neptune, 485.

Amymone, loved by Neptune, 485.

Anchises, loved by Venus, 422, 485.

Ancient customs, not adhered to by heathens as well as by Christians, 459, 460.

Angels' names, used as incantations, 425 (note).

Animals, man closely allied to the other, 440, 441, 443, 444; man not morally superior to the other, 520, 521; deified and worshipped, 420.

Ant, Jupiter's conversion into an, 485.

Antiochus of Cyzicum, sacrilege of, 515.

Antiquity, the most fertile source of errors, 429.

Anubis, dog-faced, 517.

Apis, born in the Peloponnese, 422; called Serapis by the Egyptians, 422; those punished who revealed the abode of, 509.

Apollo, son of Jupiter and Latona, 460, 483 (note), 485; son of Mi-

nerva and Vulcan, 480, 481; accompanied his mother in her wanderings, 422; found refuge on a floating island, 422; called Clarian, Delian, Didymean, Philesian, Pythian, 419; bow-bearing, 422, 483; Sminthian, 473; deceived those who enriched his temples, 484; served Admetus and Laomedon, 484; pirates plundered and burned temples of, 516 (note); identified with Bacchus and the sun, 473; Rituals of Numa did not contain name of, 462; four gods named, 480; human heads offered to Dis and Saturn by advice of, 460, and Neptune, the Penates, 475; Hyperoche and Laodice buried in temple of Delian, 508; Telmessus buried under the altar of, 508, 509; god of music, 526; mistresses of, 485; represented with lyre and plectrum, 511.

Apollonius, the Magian, 428.

Aquilius, 424.

Arabia, Christianity tested by miracles in, 438.

Arabians, worshipped an unshaped stone, 510.

Arcadia, Mars born in, 484.

Archesilas, affirms that man knows nothing, 437.

Archytas, assigns all things to numbers, 437.

Argos, destruction by fire of temple of Juno at, 516.

Argus, slain by Mercury, 480, 517.

Aristotle, adds a fifth element to the primary causes, 437; affirmed that Minerva was the moon, 472.

Armenian, Zoroaster an, 428 (note).

Armenians, believed that one god was cause of all divine manifestations, 480.

Arnobius, life, character, and writings of, 403–411; editions of his works, 410; his own account of his conversion, 423.

ARNOBIUS

INDEX OF TEXTS

230-13 RoB

X